# 5th Edition

# Psychology and the Legal System

LAWRENCE S. WRIGHTSMAN
*University of Kansas*

EDIE GREENE
*University of Colorado–Colorado Springs*

MICHAEL T. NIETZEL
*University of Kentucky*

WILLIAM H. FORTUNE
*University of Kentucky*

**WADSWORTH**
™
**THOMSON LEARNING**

Australia • Canada • Mexico • Singapore • Spain • United Kingdom • United States

**WADSWORTH**

**THOMSON LEARNING** ™

Sponsoring Editor: *Marianne Taflinger*
Marketing Team: *Marc Linsenman, Megan Hansen, and Joy Westberg*
Editorial Assistant: *Stacy Green*
Project Editor: *Mary Anne Shahidi*
Production Service: *Martha Emry*
Manuscript Editor: *Laura Larson*
Permissions Editor: *Karyn Morrison*
Interior Design: *Terri Wright*

Cover Design: *Denise Davidson*
Cover Photo/Illustration: *PhotoDisc*
Interior Illustration: *Atherton Customs*
Photo Researcher: *Myrna Engler*
Print Buyer: *Vena Dyer*
Compositor: *Thomspon Type*
Printing and Binding: *R. R. Donnelley–Crawfordsville*

*For more information about our products, contact us:*
WADSWORTH
10 Davis Drive
Belmont, CA 94002-3098 USA
1-800-423-0563 (Thomson Learning Academic Resource Center)
www.wadsworth.com

Printed in the United States of America

10   9   8   7   6   5   4   3

**Library of Congress Cataloging-in-Publication Data**

Psychology & the legal system/Lawrence S. Wrightsman . . . [et al.].—5th ed.
    p. cm.
    Rev. ed. of: Psychology & the legal system/Lawrence S. Wrightsman. 4th ed. 1998.
    Includes bibliographical references and index.
    ISBN 0-534-36544-2 (hard)
    1. Justice, Administration of—United States—Psychology aspects. 2. Practice of Law—United States—Psychology aspects. 3. Psychology, Forensic. I. Title: Psychology and the legal system. II. Wrightsman, Lawrence S. Psychology & the legal system.

KF8700.W75 2002                                              2001026526
347.73'001'9—dc21

*Dedicated to Franz Joseph Haydn, who wrote:*
*"Since God gave me a joyful heart, He will forgive*
*me for having served him joyfully"*

# About the Authors

Photo: Jack W. Brehm

**Lawrence S. Wrightsman** (Ph.D., University of Minnesota, 1959) is a social psychologist and Professor of Psychology at the University of Kansas, Lawrence. Wrightsman is an author or editor of 10 other books relevant to the legal system, including *Forensic Psychology, The American Jury on Trial* (co-authored with Saul M. Kassin), and *Judicial Decision Making: Is Psychology Relevant?* He was invited to contribute the entry on the law and psychology for the recently published *Encyclopedia of Psychology,* sponsored by the American Psychological Association and published by Oxford University Press. His research topics include jury selection procedures, reactions to police interrogations, and the impact of judicial instructions. He has also served as a trial consultant and testified as an expert witness. Wrightsman is a former president of both the Society for the Psychological Study of Social Issues and the Society of Personality and Social Psychology. In 1998 he was the recipient of a Distinguished Contribution Award from the American Psychology-Law Society. This award has been made on only seven occasions in the 30-year history of the organization; the preceding awardee was U.S. Supreme Court Justice Harry Blackmun.

Photo: Barry Kaplan

**Edie Greene** earned her Ph.D. in cognitive psychology and law at the University of Washington in 1983. She served as postdoctoral research associate at the University of Washington from 1983 until 1986, when she joined the faculty at the University of Colorado, Colorado Springs. She is currently Professor of Psychology. From 1994 to 1995, Greene was a fellow in Law and Psychology at Harvard Law School. In 2001 she received her college's award for Outstanding Research and Creative Works. She has been invited to lecture at the National Judicial College and at continuing legal education programs nationwide. Greene has received several federally funded grants to support her research on jury decision making and eyewitness memory. She has acted as a trial consultant on jury selection, trial strategies, and jury decisions and has, on numerous occasions, testified as an expert witness on jury behavior and eyewitness memory. She is the author of more than 70 articles and book chapters and has written a book on jury damage awards for the American Psychological Association series *Law and Public Policy: Psychology and the Social Sciences.*

**Michael T. Nietzel** earned his Ph.D. in clinical psychology at the University of Illinois at Urbana–Champaign in 1973 and joined the faculty at the University of Kentucky, Lexington, that same year. During most of the 1980s, Nietzel served as Director of the Clinical Psychology Program at the University of Kentucky, and is currently Professor of Psychology (and Law) and Dean of the Graduate School at the University of Kentucky. Nietzel's research and teaching interests are focused on forensic psychology, jury behavior, the origin of criminal behavior, abnormal psychology, and psychotherapy. He is a frequent consultant to attorneys, law enforcement agencies, and correctional facilities. Nietzel has assisted in jury selection for more than 50 death-penalty trials and regularly trains police officers on various topics involving mental illness. In addition to more than 75 articles, books, and book chapters, he is the co-author of various textbooks on clinical psychology and abnormal psychology.

**William H. Fortune** (J.D., University of Kentucky, 1964) is Alumni Professor of Law at the University of Kentucky, Lexington, where he currently serves as the Chair of the University Senate. He formerly served as Academic Ombud for the University of Kentucky and Associate Dean of the College of Law. He is the author of five books and numerous journal articles. His most recent publications include *Kentucky Criminal Law* (with co-author Robert Lawson), published in 1998, and the second edition of the *Modern Litigation and Professional Responsibility Handbook* (with co-authors Richard Underwood and Edward Imwinkelried), published in 2001. Fortune has taught a number of law school courses, including criminal law, criminal procedure, evidence, and professional responsibility. Fortune served as one of the drafters of the state of Kentucky's rules of evidence and rules of professional responsibility. He currently chairs the Kentucky Justice Council committee, which is charged with rewriting the Kentucky criminal laws. On three occasions he has taken academic leave to serve as a public defender in state and federal court. With Michael Nietzel, Fortune regularly teaches a course in law and psychology to undergraduate and graduate law students.

# Brief Contents

# Contents

**3** *Legality, Morality, and Justice* 49

**4** *The Legal System and Its Players* 74

## 5  *Theories of Crime   104*

## 6  *The Police and the Criminal Justice System   138*

7

## *Crime Investigation: Witnesses*   168

# Preface

The publication of the fifth edition of *Psychology and the Legal System* has brought together a new set of authors, and with this change has come what we hope is an enlarged and enlightening book that will continue to help students learn about the accomplishments and challenges of legal psychology. Edie Greene, well known for her research on the psychology of jury decision making, has joined the team. Her expertise in a variety of areas has expanded our ability to cover several new topics and has added fresh perspectives on much of the content that has been retained, but updated, from prior editions.

The current team includes three psychologists (one trained in cognitive psychology, one in clinical psychology, and the third in social psychology), who have largely devoted their professional careers to studying and participating in the legal system. They are joined by one law professor, who is an expert on criminal law and a former public defender. We continue to strive for the right mix of psychology and legal analysis in the text. The book's emphasis remains on psychological science and practice, but we also summarize the legal history of many key topics and present the current status of relevant legal theories and court decisions.

For centuries the legal system has exerted an immense influence on people's everyday activities. But as we enter the 21st century, the legal system has become a focus of special interest for the general public and scholars alike. From the Supreme Court's school desegregation decision of 1954 to its recent ones concerning the acceptability of practices as diverse as physician-assisted suicide and "cyberporn" on the Internet, the courts have had an impact on individual lives. Matters of law and psychology have become standard fare in the media. Whether they involve allegations of police corruption, criminal trials of the rich and famous, multi-billion-dollar civil litigation, charges of racism in the criminal justice system, or debates about the utility and morality of capital punishment, headlines and lead stories seem increasingly to focus on some aspect of legal psychology. Although this attention appears to cater to an almost insatiable curiosity about crime and other types of legal disputes, it also engenders a growing ambivalence about the law. Many citizens are suspicious of the police, but the police are still the first officials most of us turn to in a serious emergency or crisis. Attorneys are often held up to ridicule, but the number of people entering the legal professions is still growing. Juries are frequently criticized for their decisions, but, if given a choice, most litigants want their cases decided by juries rather than judges.

This pervasiveness of the law demands analysis and, in the last three decades, scholars from a wealth of disciplines have studied the legal system. As one of these perspectives, psychology has much to offer. The purpose of this book is to examine the legal system through the use of psychological concepts, methods, and research results. The primary audience for *Psychology and the Legal System* is those students taking a course in psychology and the law or the criminal justice system, as well as others who seek to know more about the discoveries and practices of legal psychology. This book may also be used as a supplement in those psychology courses that emphasize applied social psychology, social issues, or policy analysis. In addition, it covers a number of topics relevant to law school courses that introduce law students to social science findings and applications.

## Organization

We have continued to organize the book around four basic conflicts that pervade a psychological analysis of the law: the rights of individuals versus the common good, equality versus discretion as ideals that can guide the legal system, discovering the truth or resolving conflicts as goals that the legal systems strives to accomplish, and science versus the law as a source of legal decisions. These conflicts generate dilemmas that persist and recur, whether the topic is the behavior of the police, rights of persons with mental illness, the training of lawyers, or the decisions rendered by juries. Society demands responses to these conflicts, and psychology provides methods and empirical results that bear on their resolution.

## Improved Pedagogy

The text offers several devices to aid student learning. Each chapter begins with a chapter outline and a set of orienting questions. Answers to these questions serve as a detailed summary at the end of each chapter. Key terms are boldfaced in the text and listed at the end of each chapter; they are then defined in a glossary. Frequently used concepts are cross-referenced. Relevant Web sites are listed so that students can pursue topics of special interest to them in more depth. This fifth edition contains updated coverage of the scholarship occurring in the major areas of legal psychology, and more than 500 new references have been added.

## New Features and Revisions

Several new features, which highlight individual cases, court decisions, and resources, have been introduced.

- *The Science of* boxes present a research topic, a specific experiment, or a methodological procedure that demonstrates how the scientific method can and should be used to analyze psycho-legal questions and resolve controversies in the field.
- *The Case of* boxes summarize real cases or trials in order to illustrate or explain an important legal concept or psychological principle covered in the chapter.
- Internet resources are featured within the chapter content (see *The Case of Billy Burgess: Entrapment on the Internet,* for example) as well as on page xxii.

Overall, this is a moderate revision, with the following major changes:

- Chapter 3, on legality, morality, and justice, has been substantially rewritten and now includes such topics as commonsense justice, good Samaritan and duty to assist laws, more on attribution theory, and a discussion of the just world hypothesis.

◆ Chapter 7, on crime investigation and witnesses, has been broadened to include material on children in the courtroom (formerly found in Chapter 17) and more on lineups. In addition, there is discussion of the National Institute of Justice study, titled *Eyewitness Evidence: A Guide for Law Enforcement,* on mistaken IDs and DNA identification.

◆ Chapter 16, on the psychology of victims, now covers sexual harassment, battering, violent crime victims, physical and sexual abuse of children, posttraumatic stress disorder, and rape. The chapter discussion includes Wiener's research on decision making.

## *The Fifth Edition*

Specific topics that receive special or expanded attention for the first time in this edition include hate crimes, alternative dispute resolution, racial profiling, duty to assist laws, commonsense justice, school and workplace violence, the current status of *Miranda* rights, battered women and battered women syndrome, adjudicative competence, crime victimization and posttraumatic stress disorder, sexual harassment, risk assessment, and the special provisions for the sentencing of sex offenders.

We continue to increase our attention to the psychological dimensions of several of the topics in the text. This emphasis should be especially apparent in our treatment of such topics as jury decision making in civil cases, the psychology of victimization, new guidelines for conducting lineups, the impact of expert testimony, and jury reform.

As the main drama in both criminal and civil litigation, the jury trial has always had a special hold on psychologists' interests. Studying the behavior of jurors and the decisions of juries affords researchers an opportunity to bring many areas of psychology to bear on the questions of how and why juries return their verdicts. Research on attention, perception, and memory; the study of attitude formation and change; the analysis of social influence; and the examination of how individual juror characteristics relate to decision tendencies are all topics that have flourished during a century of psychological scholarship on the jury. We include three chapters on the jury, examining both criminal and civil litigation from the perspectives of trial processes (Chapter 13), jury composition and jury selection (Chapter 14), and jury decision making and competence (Chapter 15).

*This edition includes a thorough, authoritative revision of every chapter.*

◆ Chapter 2, on psychologists and the legal system, greatly expands the discussion of the *Daubert* case, which will help students to understand the role of social scientific evidence and how this evidence is evaluated.

◆ Chapter 4, on the legal system and its players, has been rewritten regarding courts, judges, and alternative dispute resolutions, and now includes the material on juvenile courts formerly found in Chapter 17.

◆ Chapter 5, on the theories of crime, includes updates of crime statistics, reflecting the decrease in crime rates in recent years. Featured boxes discuss hate crimes and juvenile crime. There is new material on biological factors in crime, specifically serotonin levels and subcortical abnormalities, and a brief discussion of female crime—its relative frequency and possible unique dynamics.

◆ Chapter 6, on the police and the criminal justice system, includes new material on assessment and selection of police officers, police-community relations, jail diversion of the mentally ill, hostage taking and negotiation, bioterrorism, and partner violence—with specific discussion of how differences in research designs affect the answers to questions regarding partner violence.

◆ Chapter 8, on identification and evaluation of criminal suspects, features the new Internet case of entrapment and the new *Scheffer* case on the admissibility of polygraphs. The section on criminal profiling and the use of drug couriers has been revised, and the discussion on confessions has been updated.

◆ Chapter 9, on the rights of victims and the rights of the accused, updates the status of *Miranda* rights, in light of the *Dickerson v. United States* decision by the Supreme Court in 2000.

◆ Chapter 10, on what happens between arrest and trial, now includes a discussion of why safeguards fail as a lead-in to the change of venue. The section on bail has been revised.

◆ Chapter 11, on forensic assessment of competence and insanity in criminal cases, now includes discussion of the concept of adjudicative competence and the MacArthur instruments on competence. Juvenile competence is also covered. The relevance of the Ted Kaczynski case as well as other competencies are discussed.

◆ Chapter 12, on forensic assessment in civil cases, now contains all of the material on civil commitment and dangerousness that was formerly in Chapter 17 as well as new material on the *Daubert* and *Kumho* decisions regarding partisanship by experts, risk assessment, child custody standards and assessments, and civil competence.

◆ Chapter 13, on the trial process, updates the consideration of race and jury nullification.

◆ Chapter 14, on representativeness and selection in jury trials, includes new material on peremptory challenges, scientific jury selection, some of the conflicts between different goals of jury selection, and an expanded introduction to the O. J. Simpson case.

◆ Chapter 15, on the concerns and reforms of jury trials, now includes more on civil juries, complex cases, jury reforms, competence of juries, group dynamics as explanations for interesting or unexpected jury outcomes, and expanded discussion of decision making and the story model. The chapter update incorporates relevant psychological theories and research studies that affect juries.

◆ Chapter 17, on punishment and sentencing, now includes the rights of prisoners, plus discussion of what works in corrections and how juries understand mitigating factors. The section on capital punishment has been updated.

## More Instructor Support

An instructor's manual, ISBN 0-534-25040-8, prepared with the assistance of Wendy Heath, is available from the publisher. It includes test questions, suggested activities, and additional Web sites and other sources of information for each chapter.

## InfoTrac

*InfoTrac*® *College Edition* is available (free of charge) to students who purchase this book. InfoTrac is a fully searchable online university library that contains complete articles and images from over 700 scholarly and popular publications. Such access can help students with their independent research on topics relevant to psychology and law. Journals relevant to the study of psychology and law include (among others) *American Behavioral Scientist, American Criminal Law Journal, Annual Review of Psychology, Argumentation and Advocacy, British Journal of Criminology, British Journal of Psychology, Brown University Child and Adolescent Behavior, Canadian Journal of Criminology, Corrections Today, Criminal Justice Ethics, FBI Law Enforcement Bulletin, Journal of Social Psychology,* and the *Psychological Record.*

## *Acknowledgments*

This edition was reviewed by a team of law and psychology scholars commissioned by the publisher. We owe our thanks to the following people who took the time to provide a set of reviews that challenged us to improve our manuscript in important ways: Jennifer Devenport, California State, Fullerton; Ebbe B. Ebbesen, University of California, San Diego; Katherine Ellison, Montclair State University; R. Edward Geiselman, UCLA; Evan Harrington, CUNY, John Jay; Linda Heath, Loyola University; Donn Kaiser, Southwest Missouri State; Roger Levesque, Indiana State University; Dan Linz, University of California, Santa Barbara; Jean Searcy, University of Texas at Dallas; Paul Skolnick, California State, Northridge; Veronica Stinson, St. Mary's University; Christina Studebaker, Federal Judicial Center.

For their assistance in reviewing previous editions, we thank the following people: Dorothea Braginsky, Fairfield University; Michelle D. Leichtman, Harvard University; Steve Penrod, CUNY, John Jay; John S. Shaw, Lafayette College; Gerald Tolchin, Southern Connecticut State University; and Janet K. Wilson, University of Central Arkansas.

Our editor at Wadsworth, Marianne Taflinger, was extremely helpful in obtaining manuscript reviews and helping us focus on the goals of this revision. She provided her usual effective balance of support and concern. Mary Anne Shahidi and Martha Emry coordinated the production with sensitivity and good humor. Karyn Morrison coordinated the job of obtaining permissions, and Jennifer Wilkinson oversaw the production of the instructor's manual. To all of them go our sincere thanks.

The tasks of solving word processing problems, preparing the final manuscript, and coordinating the communication of four authors in separate locations fell to Becky Fister, in Lexington, Debby Black-Tanski, in Colorado Springs, and Bea Gray, in Lawrence. Their assistance in seeing this project through to completion involved a strong, abiding dedication that was absolutely crucial to our success. We can never thank them enough.

*Lawrence S. Wrightsman*
*Edie Greene*
*Michael T. Nietzel*
*William H. Fortune*

# Information on the Internet

A wealth of resources relevant to psychology and the law can be found on the Internet. Of most importance to readers are online discussion groups and Web sites.

## Online Discussion Groups

A listserv list is a discussion group organized around a certain topic; one is basic to the topics in this book:

◆ A forensic psychology list: **forensic-psych@maelstrom.stjohns.edu**

## Web Sites

The number of organizations with Web sites that have information related to psychology and the law is increasing. Here is a partial list:

◆ The organization of psychologists, lawyers, and students interested in the interface of psychology and the law, the American Psychology-Law Society (Division 41 of the American Psychological Association): **http://www.unl.edu/ap-ls/**
◆ The organization of professional trial consultants, the American Society of Trial Consultants: **http://www.astcweb.org**
◆ An organization on criminal profiling, including a journal, *Journal of Behavior Profiling*: **http://www.profiling.org**
◆ U.S. circuit court opinions: **http://www.law.emory.edu/FEDCTS/**
◆ A variety of legal resources: **http://www.findlaw.com**
◆ U.S. Department of Justice, Office of Justice Programs: **http://www.ojp.usdoj.gov**
◆ National Institute of Justice: **http://www.ojp.usdoj.gov/nij**
◆ Current ABA Journal articles: **http://www.abanet.org**
◆ American Psychological Association linking psychology and law: **http://www.psyclaw.org**
◆ American Academy of Forensic Psychology: **http://www.abfp.com**
◆ United States Supreme Court, including the court's schedule and transcripts of oral arguments: **http://www.supremecourtus.gov**

# Psychology and the Law: Impossible Choices

## ORIENTING QUESTIONS

1. *Why do we have laws?*
2. *What are some of the ways of studying the law?*
3. *What dilemmas are reflected in the psychological approach to the law?*
4. *How do recent laws reflect the contrast between the due-process model and the crime-control model of the criminal justice system?*
5. *How does the phenomenon of sentencing disparity reflect a dilemma?*

*A scene from the inside of Columbine High School during the nation's deadliest school shooting*

Consider the following stories, all prominently featured in newspaper headlines in the same one-month span:

♦ Six students were shot by a classmate at a high school in a Conyers, Georgia, school at approximately the same time that President Clinton was meeting with survivors of the previous month's shooting at Columbine High School in Littleton, Colorado, that took the lives of 12 students and a popular teacher.

♦ Acknowledging concerns that the death penalty had been applied unfairly, the Nebraska legislature voted to impose a two-year moratorium on executions, allowing time for a study of the role of race and economic factors in the death sentencing process.

♦ Despondent and paralyzed, Georgette Smith asked to be disconnected from life support systems and allowed to die. Her request was delayed for a day, however, as police questioned her about the circumstances that put her on life support. She had been shot by her blind and ailing

mother after a heated discussion about placing her mother in a nursing home. Smith's mother, 68-year-old Shirley Egan, was charged with attempted murder but was acquitted by a Florida jury.

♦ A Texas appeals court overturned the conviction of a girl who was 11 when she was sentenced in the beating death of a 2-year-old. The infant died of massive injuries while being cared for by the girl's grandparents. The court ruled that the conviction was tainted by a confession in which police did not tell the girl that she could leave or talk to an adult.

♦ New York City police officer Justin Volpe pled guilty to sexually brutalizing a Haitian immigrant in a precinct bathroom. The officer allegedly beat Abner Louima in a patrol car and then rammed a stick into his rectum and down his throat.

♦ During a sentencing hearing in a Colorado death penalty case, a defense-hired psychologist testified that convicted murderer Lucas Salmon suffered from pervasive developmental disorder, a mild form of autism characterized by an inability to form reciprocal relationships with other people. The defense tried to persuade a three-judge panel to spare Salmon's life.

◆ The United States Supreme Court ruled that a school district can be held financially responsible for failing to stop students from sexually harassing other students. (LaShonda Davis had allegedly been subjected to a barrage of sexual harassment and abuse by a fellow fifth grader in Monroe County, Georgia. Davis and her mother claimed that school officials were informed of each incident but did nothing to discipline the boy or stop the abuse.) Soon thereafter, the Canada Supreme Court decided that schools, clubs, and treatment centers can be found liable for sexual attacks on children in their care.

These stories illustrate a few of the psycholegal issues that we consider in this book: the nature of trial procedures, the selection and conduct of police officers, the nature and consequences of victimization, the role of children in the criminal justice system, and discretion and discrepancies in sentencing decisions. They show the real flesh and blood of the major dilemmas we focus on throughout the book.

# The Importance of Laws

To outsiders, the incidents just described may seem commonplace, but they are urgently important to the people involved. Taken together, they illustrate the pervasiveness of the law in our society. But just how does the law work? The purpose of this book is to help you understand how the legal system operates, by applying psychological concepts, findings, and methods to its study.

## The Extensiveness of Laws

Laws are everywhere. They entwine us; they bear on—often intrude on—everything from birth to death. Laws regulate our private lives and our public actions. Laws dictate how long we must stay in school, how fast we can drive, when (and,

to some extent, whom) we can marry, and whether we are allowed to enjoy many individualistic pleasures, such as playing our car stereos at full blast or letting our boisterous dog romp through the neighbors' yards and gardens. As ◆ Box 1-1 argues, some say our society has too many laws, but almost all people agree that some system of laws is necessary. Social life without law as a means of social control would result in anarchy and anarchy—for most of us—carries costs that far outweigh its freedoms.

## Laws as Human Creations

Given that the body of laws is so wide in its impact, we might expect that the law is a part of nature, that it was originally discovered by a set of archaeologists or explorers. Perhaps we summon the image of Moses carrying the Ten Commandments down from the mountain. But our laws are not chiseled in stone. Rather, laws are human creations that evolve out of the need to resolve human conflicts. Any complex society generates differences in what is considered acceptable behavior and hence disagreements among people. When these disagreements occur, society must have mechanisms to resolve them. Thus, societies develop laws and other regulations as conflict resolution mechanisms. The no-smoking policy in California (◆ Box 1-2) is an example.

## Laws and the Resolution of Conflict

Conflict—that is, disagreement, argument, and dispute—is not necessarily bad; nor is it always good. Mainly, conflict is inevitable. It cannot be avoided, any more than you can avoid sneezing when the urge to sneeze begins. But society can establish procedures to control your behavior when your sneezing intrudes on another's rights. We recognize the need for mechanisms—laws, rules, and habits—to discourage a person from sneezing in people's faces or on their food. Customs and rules of etiquette evolve partly to deal with the conflict between one person's impulses and others' rights; hence, we cover our face with a handkerchief when a sneeze is coming on, or we

## THE CASE OF

**BOX 1-1**

### The foul-mouthed canoeist: Too many laws? Too little common sense?

Timothy Boomer had never canoed before. During his inaugural trip on Michigan's Rifle River, he hit a rock and fell into the river. Drenched and angry, Boomer launched into a tirade of curse words that lasted several minutes, according to witnesses. Boomer's foul language tested Michigan's obscure law against swearing in front of women and children because paddling by at the time of his outburst were Tammy Smith, her husband, a 5-year-old son, and a 3-year-old daughter. "I covered her ears," said Mrs. Smith in an interview. "I didn't want her to repeat what he was saying" (Bradsher, 1999).

According to the prosecutor, the case was a matter of civility. The American Civil Liberties Union, which provided free legal advice to Boomer, saw things differently. It claimed that the law criminalizes speech that is heard every day on television and in the streets and that such speech is protected by the First Amendment. The part-time mayor of Standish, Michigan—site of the trial—also had some well-chosen words about the incident. He said that people should always speak as if in church, but then he acknowledged that his own speech falls short of that high standard. "I swear, but I kind of watch where I do it," he said. Apparently canoeist Boomer should have been more careful about where *he* swore. Jurors deliberated for less than an hour before convicting him of violating the 102-year-old law. His sentence consisted of four days of community service and a $75 fine.

Do we have too many laws? Or, put another way, are our laws often applied in a bureaucratic and inhumane manner? That is the thesis of a book by Philip K. Howard (1994), himself a lawyer in New York City. He notes that the Occupational Safety and Health Administration has more than 4000 detailed regulations; of these, 140 pertain to the requirements for wood ladders. The original goal of laws was to provide people with rights and protect them from wrongs, but, in Howard's view, the net effect of so many laws is the opposite, especially when this multitude of laws is administered without flexibility.

---

apologize if the act can't be constrained. Similarly, laws are developed to try to untangle and resolve those conflicts that cannot be prevented.

## The Changing of Laws

Because our society is so technologically developed, it also is constantly changing. As society changes, so does our day-to-day existence. The basic raw material for the construction and the revision of laws is human experience. Laws need to be developed, interpreted, reinterpreted, and modified to keep up with the rapid changes in our lives. As George Will (1984) expressed it, "Fitting the law to a technologically dynamic society often is like fitting trousers to a 10-year-old: Adjustments are constantly needed" (p. 6).

Certainly the framers of the U.S. Constitution, and even the lawmakers of 25 years ago, never anticipated the possibility that frozen embryos and in vitro fertilization procedures would lead a man to sue a fertility clinic for wrongfully impregnating his ex-wife with a frozen embryo created years before. Although Richard Gladu consented to in vitro fertilization while still married, he claims that he should have had a choice about what would happen to the embryos when his marriage was dissolved and that his ex-wife used the frozen embryos without his consent. Gladu has been forced to make child support payments and contends that he has suffered "severe and continuing emotional distress."

Also, no one could have anticipated the ways that DNA testing would change the scope of

## BOX 1-2   The case against smoking

California is serious about smoking. In addition to banning smoking in restaurants, the state legislature, concerned about the effects of secondhand smoke on bar patrons and employees, has also banned smoking in bars. Some local ordinances have gone even further. In San Ramon, because of fire danger, it is illegal to smoke on unirrigated trails and in open spaces. Smoking is banned in 29 San Francisco parks. In Davis, one cannot smoke in public gardens, in open courtyards, or near play areas. And in Palo Alto, smokers cannot light up within 20 feet of building entrances or while standing in line for tickets for movies or buses.

Initially, to comply with the smoking ban in bars and restaurants, proprietors had to simply tell patrons that they couldn't light up. Recently, fines for people caught smoking in bars have increased. Has the ban affected business? Bar owners claim that they are beginning to see a drop in profits. And smokers are plainly contemptuous of the new law. Quipped Liesel Schweizer, a 23-year-old executive assistant, "If you're in a bar, you're not in a bar for your health. If you don't want something that's bad for your health, don't go to a bar. Go to a juice bar and drink a juice. No one is smoking in juice bars."

*Smoking is prohibited in many public settings.*

criminal investigations. (We describe the role of DNA analysis in the exoneration of convicted criminals in Chapters 7 and 17.) In 1995, the Pennsylvania legislature responded to technological advances in this area by approving the DNA Detection of Sexual and Violent Offenders Act, which mandates that offenders convicted of felony sex offenses, murder, harassment, stalking, and indecent assault have to submit DNA samples as a condition of their parole. In 1999, a Pennsylvania appeals court ruled that the law was constitutional, reasoning that the state's need to maintain an identification system to deter recidivism outweighed an inmate's right to privacy.

Recently, the rapidly growing popularity of the Internet has caused legislators to consider what, if any, restrictions should be placed on its use (Cate, 1996). The Communications Decency Act, passed by Congress in 1995, imposed a $250,000 fine and up to two years in prison for transmitting "cyberporn" on the Internet in such a way that it might become available to children. But in 1997, the United States Supreme Court struck down this law as an unconstitutional violation of the First Amendment right to free speech (*Reno et al. v. American Civil Liberties Union,* 1997).

Consider again the examples at the beginning of this chapter. Each reveals how, in our complex and advanced society, basic values come into conflict. As another example, should a woman have the legal right to have her own pregnancy aborted? Although that question has been controversial for centuries, only recently have legally tolerated and medically safe abortions become frequent in the United States. The U.S. Supreme Court, in its 1973 *Roe v. Wade* decision, gave virtual sanction to abortion on demand during the first trimester of pregnancy. Almost two decades later, in the case of *Rust v. Sullivan* (1991), this same court ruled that federally funded family planning clinics could be barred from even discussing abortion as an option with their clients.

These controversial rulings force us to re-examine our basic values and beliefs about the foundations of morality. Citizens of the United States are divided on the abortion issue: On one side are women who have availed themselves of legal abortion, various organizations that advocate for its availability, and many citizens who believe that the right to an abortion is part of a fundamental right to privacy. On the other side are protesters who urge the overthrow of the *Roe v. Wade* decision, legislators attempting to change the ruling, and people who believe that abortion is the killing of an unborn child and is morally justified only in the rarest of circumstances. Which do we value more: an ethic that endorses freedom, especially the right of individual women to control their own bodies, or a principle of interdependence that emphasizes the state's obligations to others, including the unborn (Steffen, 1996)? The 1992 Supreme Court decision of *Planned Parenthood v. Casey* in which the Court upheld its basic ruling of *Roe v. Wade* but allowed the states to place some restrictions on the availability of abortion shows that the Court itself is balanced (perhaps unsteadily) between the conflicting sides of this issue. That same uneasy balance is apparent in Supreme Court decisions related to abortion clinic protests. In *Schenck v. Pro Choice Network of Western New York* (1997), the Supreme Court held that a ban on protests in floating buffer zones (the area around a person or vehicle seeking access to a clinic) violated the First Amendment rights of protestors. But then, in *Hill v. Colorado* (2000), the Court ruled that a Colorado law barring protestors from "knowingly approach[ing] another person within 8 feet for the purpose of passing out literature or engaging in oral protest, education, or counseling" on a public sidewalk was constitutional.

Car accidents—even minor ones—also cause conflicts over basic rights. The technological development of the automobile produced several new adversaries, including pedestrians versus car drivers, and hence new laws. Consider a driver whose car strikes and injures a pedestrian. Does this driver bear a legal requirement to report the incident to the police? Yes, of course. But look again. Doesn't this requirement violate the U.S. Constitution's Fifth Amendment, which safeguards each of us against self-incrimination, against bearing witness in conflict with our own best interests?

Shortly after automobiles became popular in the first two decades of the 20th century, a certain Edward Rosenheimer was charged with violating the newly necessary hit-and-run regulation. He did not contest the charge that he had caused an accident that injured another person, but he claimed that the law requiring him to report it to the police was unconstitutional because it forced him to incriminate himself. Therefore, he argued, that law should be removed from the books, and he should be freed of the charge of leaving the scene of an accident. Surprisingly, the Court of General Sessions in New York State agreed with him and released him from custody.

Authorities in New York were, of course, unhappy with a court decision that permitted a person who had caused an injury to avoid being apprehended, and so they appealed the decision to a higher court, the New York Court of Appeals. This court, recognizing that the Constitution and the recent law clashed with each other, ruled in favor of the state and overturned the previous decision. This appeals court concluded that rights to "constitutional privilege"—that is, to avoid self-incrimination—must give way to the competing principle of the right of injured persons to seek redress for their sufferings (Post, 1963). The U.S. Supreme Court, in its *California v. Byers* (1971) decision, reaffirmed this principle, holding that a California statute requiring motorists involved in accidents to stop and identify themselves did not violate the self-incrimination clause of the Constitution.

This example illustrates once more that the law is an evolving human creation, designed to arbitrate between values in opposition to each other. Before the advent of automobiles, hit-and-run accidents seldom occurred. However, once cars became a part of society, many new laws had to be established, and the courts obliged by holding the new laws to be constitutional.

Most of us learned at an early age that it is illegal for a driver to leave the scene of an accident before information has been exchanged and authorities have been contacted. But other conflicts remain between the rights of individual drivers and society's need to be protected from dangerous forces. For example, if the police stop an automobile and charge the driver with drunk driving, does the driver have a right to have an attorney present before submitting to a Breathalyzer test? We know that, when police read suspects their "*Miranda* rights," the suspects are told they may have a lawyer present before answering any questions. (See Chapter 9 for a description of *Miranda* rights.) Does this right extend to a decision about participating in a chemical breath test that measures one's blood alcohol content? The answer may depend on where you live. In 1984, the Supreme Court of Kansas resolved this question by concluding that people arrested for drunk driving have no right to talk to a lawyer before deciding whether to take a breath test (Toplikar, 1984). In Alaska, on the other hand, people required to take a Breathalyzer test must be "afforded a reasonable opportunity to contact an attorney" before taking the test (*Copelin v. State*, 1983).

But even these decisions do not close the matter. Persons who refuse a Breathalyzer test risk having their driver's license suspended (usually from three months to a year). In addition, the fact that they declined can be used as evidence against them if the authorities decide to prosecute them. The Supreme Court (in *South Dakota v. Neville*, 1983) held that these requirements did not violate defendants' Fifth Amendment privilege against incriminating themselves. So the decision not to take the Breathalyzer test can be a potent one, and it would seem appropriate that the driver's attorney be consulted. Although the Constitution does not require states to allow those stopped for driving under the influence to call their lawyers, states could pass laws establishing such a requirement. A state passing such a law (e.g., Alaska) would be resolving the conflict in

favor of the motorist; a state refusing to pass such a law (e.g., Kansas) would be treating the safety of the public as paramount.

# Different Approaches to the Study of the Law

A system as necessary and pervasive as the law demands study. Scholars from different perspectives have applied their disciplines' concepts and methods to understand the legal system. These different approaches may, at first glance, seem at odds, but they are simply different kinds of explanations, different ways to account for the facts (Black, 1976).

Consider an arrest. Why did it occur? Do we explain a particular arrest as a decision by an individual police officer (i.e., a psychological approach) or as a fulfillment of the officer's role expectations (a sociological approach)? The law also can be studied from a historical perspective; for example, at what points in time and for what historical reasons were children given some of the protections accorded adults under the law? Or economists may study the impact of antitrust legislation on the growth of industry. Some scholars draw on several different disciplines to study the law; their use of a multidisciplinary framework is known as **sociolegal studies.** Likewise, criminal justice departments use a number of approaches in their courses.

Since the 1970s, a number of multidisciplinary approaches to legal scholarship have developed in which one of several different perspectives is emphasized as an overall framework for understanding the law and legal system. Scholars operating within one of these frameworks have usually been trained in a traditional discipline such as sociology or psychology, but their current approach to the law is based on concepts that cut across several disciplines. For example, **critical legal studies,** a movement that received great attention in the 1970s, analyzed most laws and legal procedures as tools of oppression used by a ruling class to maintain control over the poor, ethnic minorities, and other presumably unfavored groups (Fox, 1993). Partially an outgrowth of this perspective, **feminist jurisprudence** studies the law as a form of social control used to enforce masculine-based values often at the expense of, or with a bias against, women (e.g., MacKinnon, 1993). **Therapeutic jurisprudence** is a framework championed by different types of mental health scholars that suggests that the law should be studied at least partly in terms of the therapeutic and antitherapeutic consequences it has on the parties involved (e.g., Winick, 1998). Finally, the **law and economics** school follows the doctrine that the ultimate goal of law and the legal system is to maximize efficiency and prosperity by putting a premium on capital market considerations (e.g., Posner, 1992).

We will return to these perspectives—particularly therapeutic jurisprudence, which has special significance for this book—in later chapters. For now, several other traditional approaches to the study of the law are summarized in the following sections.

## The Anthropological Approach

Anthropologists compare laws (and mechanisms for instituting and altering laws) in different societies and relate them to other characteristics of these societies. They may be interested in how frequently women are raped in different types of societies and the relationship of the incidence of rape to other factors, such as the amount of violence in each society, the extent of separation of the sexes during childhood, or the degree to which males dominate females (Sanday, 1997). An anthropological approach also questions why certain crimes are more frequent in certain societies.

## The Sociological Approach

Sociologists, in contrast, usually study a specific society and examine its institutions (e.g., the family, the church, or the subculture) to determine their role in developing adherence to the law. The sociologist might ask questions such as, What role does social class play in criminal behavior in the United States today? Is the development of a gang the product of racial hostility? Sociologists use concepts such as subculture, social control, and norms to explain deviant behavior and measure its seriousness. In fact, some sociologists define law as governmental social control (Black, 1972). Their approach tries to predict and explain social behavior without regard to the individual as such; the focus of study is on groups of people rather than individuals. Sociological theories of crime are reviewed in Chapter 5.

## The Philosophical Approach

Philosophers seek to understand the nature of justice. They question whether differences exist between what is legal and what is moral. In doing so, they examine the purpose, the value, and the impact of law. For instance, is it just for a wealthy injury victim to receive more compensation than a poor injury victim? Should a man who rapes a 7-year-old child receive more severe punishment than a man who rapes a prostitute? Does a person suffering a painful terminal illness have the right to take her own life? Is it desirable or proper for states to legally recognize same-sex marriages? Chapter 3 evaluates conceptions of justice and distinctions between morality and legality; analyses by philosophers are helpful in understanding these distinctions.

## The Psychological Approach

A psychological approach to the law emphasizes its human determinants. Sociology and anthropology do as well, but the focus in the psychological approach is on the individual as the unit of analysis. Individuals are seen as responsible for their own conduct and as contributing to its causation. Psychology looks at the impact of the police officer, the victim, the juror, the expert witness, the lawyer, the judge, the defendant, the prison guard, and the parole officer on the legal system. Psychology assumes that characteristics of participants in the legal system affect how the system operates, and it also recognizes that the law can affect individuals' characteristics and behavior (Ogloff & Finkelman, 1999). By *characteristics,* we mean these persons' abilities, their perspectives, their values, their experience—all the factors that influence their behavior. Will a police officer arrest a traffic violator or let her go with a reprimand? Will a defendant and his attorney accept a plea bargain, or will they go to trial? Will a Hispanic juror be more sympathetic toward a Hispanic person on trial than toward a non-Hispanic defendant? Will one type of prison inmate respond better than another to rehabilitative efforts?

The behavior of participants in the legal system is a result not only of their personal, internal qualities but also of the setting in which they operate. Kurt Lewin, a founder of social psychology, proposed the equation $B = f(p, e)$; that is, behavior is a function of the person and the environment. Qualities of the external environment and pressures from the situation affect an individual's behavior. A prosecuting attorney may recommend a harsher sentence for a convicted felon if the case has been highly publicized, the community is outraged over the crime, and the prosecutor happens to be waging a reelection campaign. A juror holding out for a guilty verdict may yield if all the other jurors passionately proclaim the defendant's innocence.

This book concentrates on the behavior of participants in the legal system. As the examples at the beginning of this chapter indicate, we are all active participants in the system even if we do not work in occupations directly tied to the administration of justice. We all face daily choices that are colored by the law—whether to speed through a school zone because we are late to class or whether to report the person who removes someone else's book bag from a table at the library. Hence, this book will devote some coverage to the determinants of our conceptions of justice and the moral dilemmas we all face.

But we will pay more concentrated attention to the central participants in the legal system: de-

fendants and witnesses, civil and criminal lawyers, judges and juries, convicts and parole boards. In addition, we will also focus on the activities of **forensic psychologists** who generate and communicate information to answer specific legal questions or to help resolve legal disputes (Grisso, 1987; Nicholson, 1999). Most forensic psychologists are trained as clinical psychologists, whose specialty involves the psychological evaluation and treatment of persons under court jurisdiction. Forensic psychologists are often asked to evaluate a person and then provide expert testimony in court. For example, they may evaluate adult criminal defendants or children involved in the juvenile justice system and offer the court information relevant to determining whether the defendant has a mental disorder that prevents him from going to trial, what the defendant's mental state was at the time of the offense, or what treatment might be appropriate for a particular defendant. Finally, we frequently discuss the activities of **trial consultants** who are social scientists specializing in the application of psychological knowledge to jury selection and to litigation strategies in order to affect trial outcomes (Strier, 1999).

# Basic Choices in the Psychological Study of the Law

Just as each of us has to make decisions, society must decide which values it wants its laws to reflect. Choices lead to conflict, and often the resulting dilemmas are unresolvable. Should the laws uphold the rights of specific individuals or protect society in general? For example, which should take precedence—your right to run a loud floor waxer at 3:00 A.M. or the right of everyone else in your apartment building to get a decent night's sleep? Is it better for ten guilty persons to go free than for one innocent person to be sentenced to death? The law incessantly changes as it struggles to provide and ensure rights that, individually, are desirable but that, in combination, are incompatible.

What kind of a society do we want? What laws will best achieve our society's goals? What functions should the legal system serve in our society? How do we learn how well the system is working? These questions highlight four basic choices that pervade the law in the United States and Canada, as it applies to each of us. Each choice creates a dilemma. No decision about these choices will be completely satisfactory because no decision can simultaneously attain two incompatible goals, both of which our society values. Nevertheless, most modifications of the law represent efforts to be fair and responsive to whichever of these values has been recently neglected. These four dilemmas are so basic that they surface time and again throughout this book.

A dialectic analysis may help us to understand how these dilemmas evolve and change. **Dialectic analysis** is an approach that studies the state of tension existing between competing values. Each value exerts a pull toward it, and society yields to the pull by creating mechanisms to achieve goals consistent with that value. But these changes may create a new tension, or imbalance, so that society shifts its efforts more to the advocacy of a second value that is equally desirable but is in competition with the first.

For example, our society champions both freedom and equality, but it is hard to achieve both at the same time. A small-town civic organization that has always had a "males-only" policy at its Friday night dinners also is a vehicle by which prominent citizens transact their business. The men enjoy the "freedom" to act like "good ol' boys" in the company of their own gender. But what if a woman starts a new insurance agency in the town? Doesn't she have the right to "equality"—to full and equal participation in the civic organization that is influential in the success of any business in this community? It is hard to see how a resolution of this conflict could fully meet each of the goals. So the balance in such cases often shifts from one value to another, emphasizing the fulfillment of first one and then the other.

## The First Dilemma: Rights of Individuals versus the Common Good

Consider the following:

◆  In 2000, 99% of the nation's population lived in states with seat belt laws. (New Hampshire is the only state without a safety belt law for adults.) Twelve states permit the police to ticket any motorists they see unbelted, not just those stopped for another offense, and 37 states permit the police to ticket motorists stopped for other reasons. Despite these laws, only 68% of U.S. drivers buckle up. What if you do not want to be confined by a seat belt, even if you acknowledge that you are running a risk by going without one? What right does society have to tell you that you must wear a seat belt for your own protection? Do some protections enforced by and for society predominate over the right to control your own behavior, even in situations that seemingly affect only you and no one else?

◆  In New York City, police officers can seize the cars of first-time drunk drivers. Librarian Pavel Grinberg, a Polish immigrant who had never before been arrested for drunken driving, was one of the first to lose his car when his blood alcohol level measured 0.11. Federal and state laws have long permitted seizure of property, but typically only from hardened criminals and repeat offenders. Why should the government be able to confiscate property even before people have been convicted? Why should an entire family be made to suffer because one family member violated the law? On the other hand, will this zero-tolerance policy deter drunken driving and ultimately benefit us all?

◆  In California, a federal court held that Vincent Chalk, a teacher of students with disabilities in the public schools who had recently been diagnosed with AIDS, had a right to remain in the classroom over the objections of the school board and some of the parents. What if a majority of parents, concerned over the risk of AIDS transmission to their children, wanted Mr. Chalk out of the classroom? Why shouldn't the parents' rights trump Mr. Chalk's right? (It is worth noting, however, that not all parents felt this way; the mothers of five students greeted him with hugs and homemade gifts on his return to the classroom.)

◆   In 2000, Vermont adopted the most sweeping set of rights for same-sex couples in the country when a bill creating "civil unions" was signed into law by Governor Howard Dean. The bill gives gay and lesbian couples virtually the same rights and privileges as heterosexual couples in widely ranging areas of child custody, probate, worker's compensation, and family leave benefits. It stopped short of calling these same-sex unions "marriages," but many citizens opposed to the new law were unconvinced. Complaining that these unions were marriages in all but name, they distributed small yellow plastic ducks to legislators before the vote, proclaiming that "if it looks, talks, and swims like a duck, then it must be a duck." This legislation raises complex questions about individual rights versus traditional societal definitions of the family.

## Values in Conflict

The preceding vignettes share a common theme. On the one hand, individuals possess rights, and one function of the law is to ensure that these rights are protected. The United States is perhaps the most individualistic society in the world. People can deviate from the norm, or "do their own thing," to a greater degree here than virtually anywhere else. Freedom and personal autonomy are two of our most deeply desired values; "the right to liberty" is a key phrase in the U.S. Constitution.

On the other hand, society has expectations, too. People need to feel secure. They need to believe that potential lawbreakers are discouraged from breaking laws because they know they will be punished. All of us have rights to a peaceful, safe existence. Likewise, society claims a vested interest in restricting those who take risks that may injure themselves or others because these actions can create burdens on society.

What is the justification for requiring the use of seat belts when failure to buckle up might

cause death or injury only to the driver and no one else? "No man is an island," wrote John Donne, and all of us bear some cost when others lose their lives or are permanently injured through an accident. According to figures compiled by the National Highway Traffic Safety Administration, about 42,000 people die in auto accidents in the United States each year (115 people per day), and another 3.4 million are injured (more than 9,000 per day). Use of seat belts reduces rates of injury and death. Without them, costs to society are increased, including lost wages and taxes, higher medical insurance premiums, and welfare payments to dependents of the deceased. A 1996 report to Congress found that the average hospital cost for unbelted motorists who are injured in a crash is 55% higher than the cost for someone wearing a seat belt. It is estimated that if 85% of Americans buckled up, 4200 lives would be saved and 102,000 injuries averted each year and that taxpayers would be spared $6.7 billion per year (www.saferoads.org/reports/deficit/buckle.html).

It is clear that two sets of rights and two goals for the law are often in conflict. The tension between what rights each individual possesses and what constraints society may place on the individual for its collective welfare will always be with us. Sometimes, in trying to address a grievance, new statutes go too far in one direction or the other.

For example, as part of a get-tough policy on gang-related crime, Chicago enacted a Gang Congregation Ordinance in 1992 that allowed police officers to break up a group of people who were loitering in a public place if they believed anyone was a gang member and to arrest those who disobeyed an order to disperse. However, the law was struck down by the Supreme Court in 1999 (*Chicago v. Morales,* 1999) because it was vague and arbitrarily restricted personal liberties protected by the First Amendment. Dissenting justices claimed that the majority focused exclusively on the "rights" of gang members and ignored the desires of many residents of crime-ridden neighborhoods who welcomed the law as a necessary step to control crime and intimidation near their homes.

## The Warren Court versus the Burger/Rehnquist Court

The tension between these two values is clearly reflected in the back-and-forth Supreme Court decisions since the 1960s with respect to the rights of criminal suspects and defendants versus the rights of crime victims and the power of the police. As will be detailed in Chapter 9, the Supreme Court in the 1960s, headed by Chief Justice Earl Warren, established a number of principles that provided or expanded explicit rights for those suspected of breaking the law. The *Miranda* rule was established in 1966. About the same time, the courts required that criminal defendants, in all cases in which incarceration is possible, have the right to an attorney, even if they can't pay for one themselves. These and other rights were established in an effort to redress a perceived imbalance in responding to basic values.

The Supreme Court under Chief Justice Warren Burger, from 1969 to 1986, and Chief Justice William Rehnquist, since 1986, has trimmed the rights established by the Warren Court by frequently ruling in favor of the police. For example, in the 1996 case of *Whren v. United States,* the Supreme Court ruled that the police can properly stop a motorist whom they believe has violated traffic laws even if their ulterior motive is to investigate the possibility of illegal drug dealing. (Because most motorists break the speed limit, most motorists are subject to being pulled over and questioned about drug trafficking.) This shift toward expanding the powers of the government while reducing individual rights accelerated because of the appointments of some politically conservative justices (e.g., Antonin Scalia, Clarence Thomas) to the Supreme Court. However, this shift may be less dramatic than first envisioned because some appointees (e.g., Anthony Kennedy, David Souter) have turned out to be less conservative than many forecast and because of the appointment by President Clinton of more moderate justices Ruth Bader Ginsburg and Stephen Breyer.

## Two Models of the Criminal Justice System

The conflict between the rights of individuals and the rights of society is related to a distinction between two models of the criminal justice system. This distinction is between the **due process model** and the **crime control model** (Packer, 1964).

The due process model places primary value on the protection of citizens—even if they are criminal suspects—from possible abuses by the police and the law enforcement system generally. It assumes the innocence of suspects and requires that they be treated fairly (receive "due process") by the criminal justice system. It subscribes to the maxim that "it is better that ten guilty persons shall go free than one innocent person should suffer." So the due process model emphasizes the rights of individuals, especially those suspected of crimes, over the temptation by society to assume suspects are guilty even before a trial.

In contrast, the crime control model seeks the punishment of lawbreakers. It emphasizes the efficient detection of suspects and effective prosecution of defendants, so that society can be assured that criminal activity is being contained or reduced. The crime control model is exemplified by a statement by the then-attorney general of the United States, William P. Barr, that with regard to career criminals the goal is "incapacitation through incarceration" (Barr, 1992)—that is, to get them out of circulation permanently. When the crime control model is dominant in society, laws may be passed that in other times would be seen as unacceptable violations of individual rights. The Racketeer Influenced and Corrupt Organizations laws (called RICO), passed by Congress in 1970, are an example. Although the original purpose of the RICO laws was to combat the growing influence of organized crime on legitimate business (Vise, 1989), they have been used to prosecute Wall Street executives for stock fraud and tax evasion charges, going beyond the usual definition of "racketeer." Furthermore, one RICO statute permits the federal government to freeze large sums of defendants' assets before trial, thus preventing defendants from hiring the attorneys they want.

The crime control model is clearly in ascendancy in the United States, more so than in Canada, Europe, and Australia. Currently, the United States incarcerates 645 of every 100,000 of its citizens, second only to Russia (Herbert, 1998). Recent anticrime legislation passed by Congress reflects this model; it includes expanding the use of the death penalty, giving life sentences to repeat rapists or sexual offenders, prosecuting juveniles who commit violent crimes as adults, building new federal prisons, and cracking down on drugs and gang-related activity.

Beginning with the state of Washington in 1993, several states and the federal government have begun to adopt statutes that reflect the goal of the crime control model of keeping lawbreakers off the streets. California's 1994 **three-strikes law** is the most stringent. Under this law, criminals convicted of a third felony, no matter how minor, must be sentenced to either 25 years to life in prison or triple the regular sentence, whichever is greater, if their first and second offenses had been serious or violent. Persons convicted a second time of a serious or violent felony have their sentences doubled. Although such laws have the intent of increasing the punishments for habitual criminals, they sometimes lead to results that make it doubtful whether the punishment fits the specific crime. For example, a California man with multiple convictions was sentenced in 1995 to 25 years to life in prison for stealing a slice of pizza; another received the same sentence for impersonating his dead brother in a routine traffic stop.

In fact, one study found that the vast majority of those receiving the stiff sentences had committed, as their third-and-out crime, a nonviolent offense. Almost 200 were sentenced for marijuana possession, compared to 40 who were convicted of murder, 25 of rape, and 24 of kidnapping. "We're worried about Willie Horton [a convicted sex offender], and we lock up the Three Stooges,"

said Professor Franklin Zimring of the University of California at Berkeley (quoted by Butterfield, 1996, p. A8).

Using monthly data from the ten largest cities in California, other researchers found no evidence that the three-strikes law decreased serious crime or petty theft rates below the levels expected from existing trends (Stolzenberg & D'Alessio, 1997). By the end of the 1990s, California courts had begun slowly to back away from mandatory life sentences after the third strike. In *People v. Garcia* (1999), the California Supreme Court ruled that judges may consider the potential length of the defendant's sentence as well as the nature and circumstances of the prior felony cases when deciding whether to disregard one or more of those prior convictions.

In 1998, California voters instituted another tough crime law known as "10-20-Life" that also reflects a crime control orientation. Under this law, criminals who use guns during the commission of a crime could have 10 years, 20 years, or a life sentence added to their terms. Some observers claim that the 10-20-Life, rather than the three-strikes law, is responsible for a drop in the crime rate in California.

Psychology, as an approach to the law, provides methods for assessing public opinion about the desirability of these two models. In one survey, 72% approved of a three-strikes law. In another nationwide telephone survey of about 1000 U.S. adults, 50% responded "true" to the following: "In a criminal trial, it is up to the person who is accused of the crime to prove his innocence." This is a false statement—the accused doesn't even have to offer a defense, other than to plead "not guilty"—but half the respondents answered incorrectly, implicitly advocating the crime control view.

Their error does not mean that the crime control model is wrong. The values underlying each of the contrasting models are legitimate ones, and the goal of our society is to achieve a balance between them. As you will see throughout this book, our government constantly struggles to offer a mix

# THE CASE OF

**BOX 1-3**     **Leroy Hendricks: Lock 'em up and throw away the key?**

Leroy Hendricks had done his time—or so he thought. By August 1994, he had served ten years for taking indecent liberties with two 13-year-old boys. Unfortunately for Hendricks, his reputation preceded him. In fact, he had a long history of sexually abusing children, beginning in 1955 and including five convictions for sex crimes involving children. Hendricks readily admitted to a difficulty controlling his urges. In fact, he told a Kansas state court judge that only his death would guarantee that he would never commit another sexual offense on a child. In 1994, shortly before Hendricks was to be released, the state invoked the Sexually Violent Predator Act and sought his involuntary commitment.

Hendricks challenged the constitutionality of the act, claiming, among other things, that it violated the double jeopardy and ex post facto clauses of the Constitution. (The **double jeopardy** clause prevents the government from punishing people twice for the same crime, and the **ex post facto** clause forbids the enactment of new laws that extend punishment for past crimes.) Resolution of the issue turned on whether Hendricks's continued confinement was considered "punishment."

Writing for the 5–4 majority of the Supreme Court, Justice Clarence Thomas concluded that it was not (*Kansas v. Hendricks,* 1997). Thomas reasoned that Hendricks's confinement could not be considered "punishment" because, in constitutional terms, punishment derives from criminal proceedings, not civil ones. He also pointed to the indefinite duration of the confinement (theoretically, individuals can be released when their "abnormality" is no longer threatening) as proof of its nonpunitive nature. In a bit of irony, Thomas dismissed the fact that the state failed to provide treatment for Hendricks. By analogy to cases upholding quarantine of persons with communicable diseases, Thomas

*Leroy Hendricks*

held that the state could lock up those for whom no treatment was available but who posed a danger to others. Professor Stephen Morse has raised concerns about the role of the *Hendricks* case in striking a balance between the due process and crime control models of criminal justice (Morse, 1998). He asserts that in its quest for public safety, society will now be willing to punish people who are merely *at risk for* reoffending, in essence punishing them more severely than they deserve.

---

of laws that reasonably honors each set of values. For example, President Clinton advocated a national registry of sex offenders. In fact, all states—as well as the U.S. Congress—have passed laws that require convicted sex offenders to register with police where they live, and nearly all states have laws that instruct law enforcement officials to notify neighbors when those sex offenders move into their neighborhoods. In addition to direct notification, some states have opened their

sex offender registries to the general public, and others publish their listings on the Internet.

New Jersey was the first state to pass a **notification law,** named "Megan's Law" after the 1994 kidnapping, rape, and murder of 7-year-old Megan Kanka. Her assailant, Jesse Timmendequas, was a sex offender who had moved into a house across the street from hers. The New Jersey law calls for notification to schools, day care centers, and youth groups about the presence of a moderate-risk offender in the neighborhood and requires that police go door to door to notify neighbors when a high-risk offender moves into their midst. In 1998, the Supreme Court rejected a challenge by sex offenders who argued that the notification law subjected them to double jeopardy because such notice, and the public's reaction to it, amounts to punishment.

Several states have gone even further than New Jersey in their efforts to protect society from dangerous sex offenders. In Wisconsin, for example, a life sentence is mandated for persistent, repeat child sex offenders. Other states have passed so-called **sexual predator laws.** Under these statutes, the state can, in a civil proceeding, commit a person to a mental hospital indefinitely upon that person's release from prison if he or she is found to be a sexually violent predator. Sexually violent predators are individuals who, due to an "abnormality" or "personality disorder," are likely to engage in predatory acts of sexual violence. Leroy Hendricks was the first person to be detained by this law in Kansas (◆ **Box 1-3**).

## The Second Dilemma: Equality versus Discretion

Kenneth Peacock was a long-distance trucker who was caught in an ice storm and came home at the wrong time. He walked in the door to find his wife Sandra in bed with another man. Peacock chased the man away and some four hours later, in the heat of an argument, shot his wife in the head with a hunting rifle. Peacock pled guilty to voluntary manslaughter and was sentenced to 18 months in prison. At the sentencing, Baltimore County Circuit Court Judge Robert E. Cahill said he wished he did not have to send Peacock to prison at all but knew that he must to "keep the system honest" (Lewin, 1994). He continued, "I seriously wonder how many men . . . would have the strength to walk away without inflicting some corporal punishment."

Move the clock ahead one day. A female defendant pleads guilty to voluntary manslaughter in a different Baltimore courtroom. She killed her husband after 11 years of abuse and was given a 3-year sentence, three times longer than what the prosecutors had sought (Lewin, 1994). Some people find no inconsistency in the severity of these punishments, believing that each case should be judged on its own merits. However, psychology analyzes these decisions as examples of a dilemma between the goals of equality and discretion.

What should be the underlying principle in response to persons accused of violating the law? Again, we discover that two equally desirable values are often incompatible and hence create conflict. And again, psychology provides concepts through which this conflict can be studied and better understood.

The principle of **equality** means the same consequences for all people who commit the same crime. Fundamental to our legal system is the assumption advanced by the founders of the American republic that "all men are created equal." This statement is frequently interpreted to mean that no one should receive special treatment by the courts simply because he or she is rich, influential, or otherwise advantaged. We cherish the belief that, in the United States, politically powerful or affluent people are brought before the courts and, if guilty, convicted and punished just like anyone else who commits similar offenses. For example, former Illinois congressman Dan Rostenkowski, a chief architect of congressional tax policy, pled guilty in 1996 to two counts of misuse of federal funds and spent 15 months in prison. But this value of equality before the law is not always implemented.

The late 1990s saw a spate of incidents that—at least on the surface—seemed to indicate unequal treatment of citizens by the legal system. A common practice among police and state patrol in the United States is *profiling*—viewing certain characteristics as indicators of criminal behavior. Black and Hispanic motorists have filed numerous lawsuits over the practice of profiling, alleging that police, in an effort to seize illegal drugs and weapons, apply a "race-based profile" and stop and search them more frequently than white drivers. The plaintiffs in a Maryland case assembled an impressive set of statistics: although 75% of drivers on Interstate 95 are white, only 23% of people stopped and searched between 1995 and 1997 were white. Conversely, although only 17% of drivers are black, 70% of those pulled over were black. Says Representative John Conyers Jr., "There are virtually no African-American males—including Congressmen, actors, athletes and office workers—who have not been stopped at one time or another for . . . driving while black" (Barovick, 1998). (Indeed, State Senator Kevin Murray of California was pulled over and questioned by police as he drove through Beverly Hills on the very night he won his Senate primary in 1998.) Echoing Conyers's concerns, in 1999, President Clinton ordered all federal police agencies to gather statistics on the racial makeup of people targeted for traffic stops, border inspections, and other routine searches. The concerns of minority drivers were confirmed by New Jersey governor Christine Todd Whitman's concession that some state troopers had singled out black and Hispanic drivers and that once they were pulled over, these drivers were three times more likely than white drivers to be subjected to searches.

In keeping with the laudable goal of equality in the law, the Supreme Court has, on occasion, applied a **principle of proportionality;** that is, the punishment should be consistently related to the magnitude of the offense. More serious crimes should earn more severe penalties. If a relatively minor crime leads to a harsh punishment, then the fundamental value of equality has been violated.

In 1983, the Supreme Court agreed to hear the appeal of Jerry Helm, who had been convicted of writing a check for $100 when he had no bank account. A judge in South Dakota had sentenced Helm to life in prison without parole. That sentence sounds severe for just writing a "hot check." But South Dakota had a "recidivist's law" (similar to the three-strikes legislation described earlier) that permitted giving a sentence of life imprisonment without parole to any offender who had three previous felony convictions. Helm had six prior convictions: three for burglary, one for obtaining money under false pretenses, one for driving while

intoxicated, and one for grand larceny. The U.S. Supreme Court decided, by a 5–4 vote, that the sentence given Helm by the South Dakota judge violated the Eighth Amendment of the U.S. Constitution because it constituted a "cruel and unusual punishment." However, less than a decade later, the Supreme Court's requirement of proportional sentencing was modified by the decision of *Harmelin v. Michigan* (1991), which endorsed a state's right to impose mandatory, disproportionate sentences for some crimes. (In this case, Ronald Harmelin, a first-time offender, was convicted of possession of cocaine and sentenced to life without parole after police found 673 grams of cocaine and $2900 cash in a gym bag in the trunk of his car.) The *Harmelin* case illustrates a decisive swing in sentencing values toward longer, mandatory punishments, a position consistent with the crime control orientation of the beginning of the 21st century.

Although equality often remains an overriding principle, society also believes that **discretion** is appropriate. Rigid application of the law can lead to injustices. By discretion, we mean the use of judgments about the circumstances of certain offenses that lead to appropriate *variations* in how the system responds to these offenses. A police officer may decide not to arrest a juvenile who has been caught speeding because the legally prescribed punishment would result in the loss of the juvenile's license. In judging guilt and punishment, according to the principle of discretion, a judge or jury weighs the specific circumstances that surround a crime.

In California, one of the criticisms of the previously described three-strikes law was that it removed discretion from judges while other participants in the criminal justice system gained in discretion. In general, mandatory sentencing regulations shift the power from judges to prosecutors (Tonry, 1996). As Susan Estrich (1996) has written, "Discretion in the criminal justice system is like toothpaste in the tube. Squeeze it at one end and you end up with more somewhere else. Take away judges' discretion and prosecutors get more. Take it away from judges and prosecutors, as the [California] governor has pledged, and police get more power" (p. 13A).

Recently, the three-strikes statute has been reinterpreted to give the sentencing judge more leeway. The case of Johnny Houston Holman is an example. In June 1996, Holman pled guilty to crack cocaine possession; he had a number of previous convictions, mostly for drugs, but two of these were for violent and serious crimes: one robbery in 1980 and another in 1985. Thus, he qualified for the three-strikes rule (recall that the third crime does not have to be violent), and so the prosecutor asked for a sentence of from 29 years to life. But following the reinterpretation of the law, Judge Gregory O'Brien Jr. reasoned differently. He noted that Holman's most recent violent offense was 11 years earlier, he was arrested for possession of only 0.13 gram of cocaine, his crime did not pose a threat to others, and a life sentence would mean at least 20 years in prison. He sentenced Holman to ten years, which means he must serve at least eight (Estrich, 1996).

As we have seen, many players in the legal system have the opportunity to exercise discretion and most do so on a regular basis. Police officers show discretion when they decide not to arrest someone who technically has broken the law. Prosecutors exercise discretion when they decide which of many arrestees to charge and for what particular crime. Juries exercise discretion in not convicting defendants who have killed others but who did so under circumstances that may have justified their actions (e.g., self-defense, heat of passion). On occasion, juries acquit female defendants who have killed their abusive partners, reasoning that the defendants may have been suffering from battered woman syndrome, a controversial theory that explains why a battered woman would act in self-defense (Browne, 1987; Gordon & Dutton, 1996).

Although not usually considered formal participants in the justice system, state governors also have the opportunity to exercise discretion when they decide whether to commute a death sentence to life imprisonment (a process called "granting clemency") or whether to allow an execution to proceed as planned. Governor George W. Bush of Texas faced that stark choice in early 1998. He had to decide whether Karla Faye Tucker, an attractive, seemingly reformed, well-behaved death row inmate, should be executed by lethal injection or allowed to live. This case raises interesting questions about both discretion and the role of gender in the criminal justice system (◆ Box 1-4).

Discretion may be most obvious in the sentences administered by judges to convicted criminals. Community standards differ from one part of the country to another; hence, exactly the same crime will carry a stiffer sentence in one jurisdiction than in another. During the height of protest against the war in Vietnam in the late 1960s and early 1970s, young men who resisted the draft were brought to trial and, if found guilty, were given either a prison sentence or probation. In Oregon, of 33 convicted draft evaders, 18 were put on probation and 15 were sent to prison, but none of those 15 were given a term over three years. Compare those punishments with the outcomes in the southern district of Texas, a region that bristled with strong patriotic sentiments: of 16 violators, none were put on probation, and 14 of the 16 were given the five-year maximum prison sentence allowable by law. In the southern district of Mississippi, every defendant was convicted, and each one was given the maximum of five years.

Because draft resistance is a federal crime, we would assume that it would be judged by the same standards throughout the country (Gaylin, 1974). Yet the United States has a strong tradition that criminal justice is administered by the local jurisdiction; consequently, many people understand and accept that judges in different areas give harsher penalties for the same crime. From what we know about the similarity of the cases, all these men were not treated fairly by the law. This is an example of **sentencing disparity,** or the tendency of different judges to administer a variety of penalties for the same crime (see Chapter 17).

Sentencing disparity also is manifest in the penalties given to African Americans and other minorities. A thorough survey of the sentences

## THE CASE OF

**BOX 1-4**   **Karla Faye Tucker: Is gender relevant?**

In 1983, Karla Faye Tucker was a drug addict and a prostitute. On June 13, she and her boyfriend, Daniel Ryan Garrett, took a pickax and hacked Tucker's former boyfriend and his female companion to death. Police investigating the murder scene found the pickax still embedded in the woman's chest. At her trial, Tucker even boasted of experiencing an orgasm with each plunge of the ax down upon her victims. Both perpetrators were convicted and sentenced to death. (Garrett subsequently died while in prison.)

In the months preceding her scheduled 1998 execution, Karla Faye Tucker became something of a cause célèbre. Her supporters included the Reverend Pat Robertson; Dana Brown, a prison chaplain she married in 1996 during her imprisonment; a homicide detective who recommended the death penalty in the first place; thousands of citizens; and siblings

of one of the victims. In various pleas to save her life, they argued that she was not the same person she had been 15 years earlier. Pointing out Tucker's conversion to Christianity, apparent rehabilitation, and spotless disciplinary record while in prison, her supporters argued that Tucker's life should be spared.

One wonders about the role of Tucker's gender in this dispute and whether a male death row inmate could generate the same loud cries of protest. Tucker was slated to be the first woman executed in the United States since 1984 and only the second to be executed since the death penalty was reinstated in this country in 1976. (Since that time, more than 600 men have been put to death.) Surely some of the gender disparity in executions can be explained by the kinds of crimes that men and women commit (men tend to commit more violent crimes) and by the likeli-

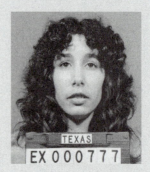

*Karla Faye Tucker*

hood of receiving a death sentence for those crimes. But there have undoubtedly been male death row inmates who exhibited the same clean record and apparent atonement as did Karla Faye Tucker. We typically hear little about their pleas for clemency. In the end, Governor Bush and the Texas Board of Pardons and Paroles refused to intervene in Tucker's case. She was executed by lethal injection on February 3, 1998.

given to convicted murderers in Philadelphia (Baldus, Woodworth, Zuckerman, Weiner, & Broffitt, 1998) found that blacks were significantly more likely than those of other races to receive the death penalty, even controlling for the severity of the crime (see Chapter 17). But inequality in punishment is not limited to the most serious crimes. A study of persons convicted of minor felonies or misdemeanors in New York State between 1990 and 1992 found that a third of the minority defendants given time in local jails would have received more lenient sentences if they had been white (Levy, 1996).

To counteract sentencing disparity, in the last 25 years many states have implemented what is known as **determinate sentencing;** the offense determines the sentence, and courts and parole commissions have little discretion. Furthermore, the U.S. Sentencing Commission has established strict guidelines for the sentences to be meted out for federal crimes. In federal courts, sentences are determined by the Federal Sentencing Guidelines, which went into effect in November 1987. For every crime, the guidelines assign a "Base Offense Level," which is adjusted up or down (usually up) on the basis of certain factors in the case

## THE CASE OF

### BOX 1-5  Alexander Leviner: Caught driving while black

Alexander Leviner had been in trouble before. In 1997, he received an 18-month sentence for possession with intent to sell drugs. But it was not this incident that caught Judge Nancy Gertner's attention. In preparing to sentence Leviner for illegal gun possession in December 1998, Gertner was struck by the number of minor traffic offenses on his arrest record. Indeed, Leviner had been stopped in three largely white Boston suburbs and, each time, charged with driving after his license had been suspended. Noting that none of these motor vehicle charges involved erratic driving or other behavior likely to attract police scrutiny, Judge Gertner deviated from rigid federal sentencing guidelines and reduced Leviner's sentence on the gun charge. She stated that the preponderance of minor traffic violations raises "deep concerns about racial disparity" and reflect the tendency of police to stop black motorists more often than white drivers.

(e.g., serious injury to the victim, the defendant's prior criminal history). Historically, the guidelines have not taken into account all the circumstances of cases, because to do so would prove unworkable and seriously compromise the certainty of punishment and its deterrent effect.

Federal judges have been frustrated by the severe limitation in their discretion, however. One federal judge resigned his appointment in protest over mandatory sentencing rules. In resigning from the federal bench, Judge J. Lawrence Irving of San Diego said, "It's an unfair system that has been dehumanized. There are rarely two cases that are identical. Judges should always have discretion. That's why we're judges. But now we're being made to be robots. I cannot in good conscience play this game any longer."

Judge Nancy Gertner was also unwilling to play the game and opted, instead, to exercise discretion in sentencing. Her judgment in the case of a black defendant represents the first time that a judge has departed from federal sentencing guidelines because the offender's record may have been inflated by racial inequalities (◆ Box 1-5).

The pendulum may now have begun to swing away from determinate sentencing and toward allowing judges some discretion. Permitting judges to consider factors such as the defendant's background, motivations for committing the crime, and any psychological disorders may strike a balance between sentencing uniformity that the guidelines intended and judicial discretion that some judges prefer.

The tension between equality and discretion is also apparent when community standards are used to decide punishments. Mitigating circumstances in specific cases may cry out for mercy as well as justice. Community preferences for discretion are revealed in trials in which juries refuse to convict defendants even though the evidence for the defendants' factual guilt is clear. This preference to acquit legally guilty, but morally blameless, defendants is known as **jury nullification;** it is discussed more fully in Chapter 13. Psychology can play a role not only in identifying what the community standards are but also in determining the degree of public discontent (if any) over sentencing and verdict disparities.

## The Third Dilemma: To Discover the Truth or to Resolve Conflicts

*Time* magazine called the verdict "stunning" (McCarthy, 1997). In the fall of 1997, British au pair Louise Woodward was convicted of second-degree murder in the death of 8-month-old Matthew Eappen. Boston attorney Alex McDonald said, "I don't know any lawyer in the Greater Boston area who has any reaction other than shock." The conviction carried a mandatory sentence of life imprisonment.

Why were people stunned by the verdict? After all, a jury of nine women and three men had listened concertedly to the testimony at trial, deliberated for several hours, and apparently followed the judge's instructions carefully.

What is the purpose of a trial? Your first reaction may be "To find out the truth, of course!" Determining the truth means learning the facts of the case, including events, intentions, actions, and outcomes. All this assumes that "what really happened" between two parties can be ascertained. Finding out the truth is a desirable goal, but it may be a lofty, unattainable one.

In February 1997, Woodward dialed 911 from the Eappens' home and said to the dispatcher, "Help, there's a baby. He's barely breathing." Police investigators who questioned Woodward after the baby was taken to the hospital claimed that she told them she may have been a "little rough" with the baby, tossing him on a bed, and "dropping" him on some towels on the bathroom floor. (During the trial, Woodward denied making these remarks, however.) Woodward was arrested the next day, and, after the baby's life support system was disconnected, she was charged with murder. At first, the evidence looked very bad for Louise Woodward.

Some of that changed as the investigation progressed, however. Defense attorneys did extensive testing on blood and tissue samples from Matthew Eappen and reevaluated X rays and photographs of his skull. In the process, they and their medical experts came to believe that the baby had suffered a fractured skull weeks before his death and that the jolt from Woodward may have triggered internal bleeding that eventually killed him. The defense team presented this theory at the trial.

In the fall of 1997, a Cambridge, Massachusetts, jury was presented with two versions of the facts: The prosecution relied heavily on Woodward's own acknowledgment that she had treated Matthew roughly; the defense contended that it was the previous fracture, and not Woodward's actions, that resulted in Matthew's death. Experts

*Louise Woodward*

suspected that the medical testimony for the two sides effectively canceled each other out, so jurors were left to their own devices to reach a verdict. Could they fathom the truth from the facts that were presented during the trial?

Woodward obviously had to reconstruct the events of that February day in her mind. As we suggest in Chapter 7, memory for short-lived and emotionally charged events from the past may be highly unreliable. Most experimental psychologists doubt that the brain acts like a camera to record brief and sudden events. In some cases, careful analysis of the crime scene can later lead to an accurate reconstruction of the events. And through the use of psychological procedures, including hypnosis, witnesses can sometimes recall more at a later date than they recall right after the crime. Jurors in this case had to rely on Louise Woodward's memory about what happened to Matthew Eappen shortly before he died.

The defense team made a bad bet at the end of the trial. Feeling confident about their case, they asked the judge to present an all-or-nothing verdict option to the jury: second-degree murder or acquittal. The jury's choice? Murder. Reaction to the verdict? Shock.

Even at the conclusion of this trial (and many others), it was not clear whether the truth reigned. Simply because jurors pronounce one verdict as their preference does not mean that they have ascertained the truth about the dispute. Jurors in the Woodward case felt bound by the judge's instructions but uncomfortable with their verdict and, presumably, with whether their deliberations had uncovered the truth. Said juror Jodie Garber, "Nobody thought Louise intended to kill the baby. . . .This was the verdict we had to reach. . . . We'd rather have had a chance to consider a manslaughter option. Nobody liked the finding we felt compelled to reach" (McCarthy, 1997). In the end, Judge Hiller Zobel reduced the verdict to manslaughter and sentenced Woodward to time she had already served.

## The Jury's Task: Providing Stability?

In a trial, jurors are often presented with two versions of the truth—two sets of facts or at least two interpretations of the same event. Was O. J. Simpson involved in the murder of Nicole Brown and Ron Goldman, or was he not? Was the "Unabomber," Theodore Kaczynski, legally insane or simply evil? Our adversarial system of justice forces jurors to choose or sometimes to compromise by finding that the truth lies between the competing versions of the event (as, e.g., in the Woodward case in which "manslaughter" served as a compromise verdict between "murder" and "acquittal"). In a criminal case, the judge tells jurors that their task is to determine whether the government has met its burden of proving every element of the crime beyond a reasonable doubt. In civil cases, the jury must believe that a "preponderance of the evidence" favors the plaintiff's version of the facts for the plaintiff to win; otherwise, the jury should find for the defendant. But, by a jury's verdict, one version of the "truth" assumes the appearance of "correctness"; the other, therefore, must inevitably be wrong.

Given that it is difficult for even well-meaning people to ascertain the true facts in certain cases, some observers have proposed that a trial's real purpose is to provide social stability by resolving conflict. Supreme Court Justice Louis Brandeis once wrote that "it is more important that the applicable rule of law be settled than it be settled right" (in *Burnet v. Coronado Oil and Gas Co.,* 1932). And Kenneth Boulding (1975) has written that "legal and political procedures, such as trials and elections, are essentially social rituals designed to minimize the costs and conflicts" (p. 423). In other words, there is a shift from viewing the trial's purpose as doing justice toward a goal of "creating a sense that justice is being done" (Miller & Boster, 1977, p. 34). Supporters of this viewpoint emphasize the importance of rituals in our society. These rituals provide continuity and stability, as well as, in this instance, maintenance of "the shared perception that our legal system provides an efficient means for resolving conflict peacefully" (Miller & Boster, 1977, p. 34). Moreover, these peaceful means replace earlier methods of resolving conflicts that used force and violence, such as shootouts or duels. But some of these peaceful procedures may have lost their original truth-seeking purpose. For example, in Chapter 10 we will examine whether the grand jury has become a vehicle for "rubber-stamping" prosecutors' recommendations, rather than serving as an independent fact-finding body.

## Attorneys' Opinions about the Purpose of a Trial

Truth is elusive, some advocates say, and so the most important priority of a trial is to provide a setting in which all interested parties have their "day in court." Justice for all parties replaces truth as the predominant goal. The attorneys representing the opposing parties in the case do not necessarily seek "the truth." Nor do they represent themselves as "objective." They reflect a different value—the importance of giving their side the best representation possible, within the limits of the law. The Code of Ethics of the American Bar Association even instructs attorneys to defend their clients "zealously." So lawyers believe the purpose of a trial is to win disputes; they present arguments supporting their client's perspective and support their arguments with the best available evidence.

Some psychologists note that an argument in favor of the adversary system, in which a different attorney represents each party, is that it encourages the attorneys to discover and introduce every bit of evidence that might encourage the jury to react favorably to their client's case. When both sides believe that they have had the chance to voice their case fully and their representatives have revealed all the relevant facts, participants in the trial are more likely to feel they have been treated fairly by the system, and the system is considered to be an effective one.

"Conflict resolution" and "truth," as goals, are not always incompatible. When each participant sees to it that his or her concerns and supporting documentation are presented in court, the goal of knowing the truth often becomes more attainable. Although truth may be too elusive ever to be known fully in all cases, it is dangerous to give up its quest. Jurors take an oath to pursue the truth, and they need to search for it even if it is not completely knowable.

Even though attainment of both values is not incompatible, a tension between the two usually exists. When conflict resolution is sought at the sacrifice of truth, the outcome can often be unsatisfactory. However, in other instances, such as the issue discussed in ◆ Box 1-6, the satisfactory resolution of a conflict may be socially and morally preferable to discovering an objectively established truth.

## Truth versus Conflict Resolution in Plea Bargaining and Settlement Negotiation

The quest for truth is threatened at other points during the criminal justice process. Shortly after the bombing that disrupted the 1996 Summer Olympics in Atlanta, the FBI began to question the security guard, Richard Jewell, who discovered the bomb. Although at first the FBI denied that he was a suspect, they treated him like one, and his name and photograph were circulated to the entire world. The pressure to find the person who caused this terrifying act—the desire to give people a sense that no more bombings would occur because the perpetrator had been caught—doubtless drove the focus on Richard Jewell. Eventually, despite relentless FBI investigation, no charges were brought against Jewell, but it took the FBI three months to acknowledge that they had discovered no evidence linking him to the bombing and that he was no longer a "target" of their inquiry.

The legal system is a massive bureaucracy, and in every bureaucracy, a temptation exists to value pragmatic efficiency rather than correct or just outcomes. The huge reliance on plea bargaining is often criticized because it appears to give priority to conflict resolution over truth seeking. From 80% to 95% of defendants never go to trial; they accept the offer of the prosecutor to plead guilty to a lesser charge. Even some innocent persons plea-bargain after being convinced that the evidence against them is overwhelming. However, plea bargaining remains an integral part of the criminal justice system. The state benefits by avoiding the expense and trouble of trial, by eliminating the possibility of an acquittal, and often by obtaining the testimony of the accused against others involved in the crime. The defendant benefits by receiving some kind of reduction in the penalty imposed. Many would argue that, in addition to these pragmatic benefits, justice is furthered by a system that rewards a show of contrition (which usually accompanies a guilty plea) and enables the prosecutor and defense counsel, often in concert with the judge, to negotiate a resolution appropriate to the degree of wrongdoing (Kamisar, LaFave, & Israel, 1999). Nonetheless, the process illustrates how the goal of maintaining stability and efficiency in the system is achieved at some sacrifice of the public's opportunity to determine the complete truth.

## THE CASE OF

**BOX 1-6**

### The Agent Orange controversy: Search for truth or resolution of a social problem?

Agent Orange (a potent herbicide that contains dioxin) was widely used by the American military during the early stages of the Vietnam War to defoliate the hiding places of the Vietcong. Following a report on the adverse effects of dioxin on laboratory animals, Agent Orange spraying was discontinued in 1970. By that time, thousands of soldiers and civilians had been exposed to it.

In 1977, Paul Rutershan contracted abdominal cancer. As a helicopter pilot in Vietnam, he had flown through clouds of Agent Orange, and he believed his cancer was caused by exposure to dioxin. Rutershan (who was soon to die of the cancer) persuaded an attorney to sue the chemical companies that produced Agent Orange, and Rutershan's case eventually became a class action to litigate the claims of all military personnel suffering from illnesses they believed were caused by Agent Orange. Included in the class action were the claims of wives who miscarried and children born with birth defects because of the alleged

effect of dioxin on the sperm of their husbands and fathers.

This huge lawsuit, potentially involving hundreds of thousands of claims, wound up in the court of United States District Judge Jack Weinstein, who ultimately concluded that Agent Orange did not cause the deaths, illnesses, and birth defects complained of. He cited studies showing that soldiers who handled Agent Orange in Vietnam were as healthy as the general population of the United States, and he believed that the veterans lacked reliable evidence on the crucial question of causation.

Judge Weinstein did not, however, throw the claims of the veterans out of court. Instead, he pressured both sides to produce a settlement that would provide a fund for sick veterans and their families whatever the "true" cause of their illnesses—in part to make up for the nation's failure to discharge its obligation to those who served.

On May 6, 1984, the day before trial, the parties settled for $180 million. Judge Weinstein did

not believe the plaintiffs could prove Agent Orange caused death and illness. He saw the class action as an opportunity, however, to fashion a just end to a national controversy, putting money (though not too much—the award for total disability was about $12,500 per claimant) in the hands of those suffering the most, while penalizing the chemical companies for producing an agent that could cause death and illness. Significantly, the money was to be distributed to anyone exposed, without proof that death or illness was caused by Agent Orange. A veteran dying of a heart attack (never associated with Agent Orange) would be paid from the fund established by the chemical companies.

The Agent Orange case is one in which the judge candidly sacrificed the quest for truth (did Agent Orange cause the plaintiffs' death and illness?) for a partial resolution of a national problem. The nation had betrayed its Vietnam veterans, and the settlement was a step toward making things right.

---

In civil cases, a procedure that parallels plea bargaining resolves about 90% of the conflicts between a plaintiff and a defendant. **Settlement negotiation** involves a sometimes lengthy pretrial process of give-and-take, offer-and-demand that ultimately ends with a plaintiff agreeing to accept what a defendant is willing to offer to end their legal disagreement.

## The Fourth Dilemma: Science versus the Law as a Source of Decisions

When one discipline (in our case, psychology) seeks to understand another (the law), a dilemma is likely because each approaches knowledge in a different way. When asked, "How do you know whether that decision is the right one?" each relies on different methods, even though both share a general goal of understanding human experience. As you will see on several occasions in this book, in its recent decisions, the U.S. Supreme Court has often considered data and conclusions presented by psychologists and other social scientists. Such decisions reflect how the justices use different procedures and concepts from those of social science in forming their judicial opinions (Grisso & Saks, 1991). In several cases in the last 15 years, the American Psychological Association has prepared a supporting brief, called an **amicus curiae** (or "friend of the court") brief, for an appellant whose appeal was considered by the Court. In many of these decisions, the Court has disregarded the social science data, but in others, it has incorporated the findings into its decision.

Beyond the use of different procedures, each profession may use idiosyncratic, or unique, concepts to describe the same phenomenon. An attorney and a social scientist will see the same event through different perspectives. Neither is necessarily more accurate than the other; the differences are the results of exposure to and training in different points of view. The following subsections illustrate the differences in more detail (see also Ogloff & Finkleman, 1999).

## Law Is Doctrinal; Psychology Is Empirical

Psychology, in contrast to the law, is generally committed to the idea that there is an objectifiable world of experience that can best be understood by unwavering adherence to the rules of science—systematic testing of hypotheses by observation and experimental methodology. As a scientist, the psychologist should be committed to a public, impersonal, objective pursuit of truth, using methods that can be repeated by others and faithfully interpreting results by predetermined standards. Although this traditional view of psychology's approach to truth is often challenged as naive and simplistic (Bevan, 1991; Gergen, 1994; Toulmin, 1990) because it ignores the importance of the

personal, political, and historical filters that are used just as much by scientists as by nonscientists, it still represents the values and methods in which most psychologists are trained. It also represents our belief as authors that the scientific method and the research skills of psychologists are the most essential and reliable tools available for examining the many important legal questions we address throughout the book.

Legal experts rely heavily on precedents in establishing new laws. When confronted with a case, judges and attorneys examine rulings in previous cases (as well as the Constitution and the statutes) for guidance. **Case law,** the law made by rulings in individual cases, is very influential; statutes and constitutional safeguards do not apply to every new situation, and so past cases often serve as precedents for deciding current ones. The principle of **stare decisis** ("let the decision stand") is important in this process. Judges typically are reluctant to make decisions that contradict earlier ones, as the history of the Supreme Court's school desegregation decision indicates. When the U.S. Supreme Court voted unanimously in May 1954, in *Brown v. Board of Education,* that public school segregation was contrary to the law, many reports claimed that it "supplanted" or even "overturned" a previous ruling in the 1896 case of *Plessy v. Ferguson.* But when it comes to court decisions, things are not that simple or straightforward. A brief history of rulings that led up to the *Brown v. Board of Education* (1954) decision illustrates this phenomenon.

During a train trip in Louisiana in the 1890s, Homer Plessy sat down in a railroad car labeled "Whites Only." Plessy's ancestry was mostly Caucasian, but he had one Negro great-grandparent. Therefore, according to the laws of Louisiana at that time, Plessy was considered a black (or "colored," in the prevalent term at that time). Plessy refused to move to a car designated for "colored" passengers, as a recently passed state law required. He took his claim to court, but a New Orleans judge ruled that, contrary to Plessy's argument, the statute that segregated railroad cars by race did not violate the Fourteenth Amendment to the

Constitution; that is, it did not fail to give Plessy "equal protection under the law."

Plessy persisted in his appeal, and eventually, in 1896, the Supreme Court acted on his claim. By a 7–1 vote, it affirmed the decision of the judge and the lower courts. Judge Henry Billings Brown, speaking for the majority, declared that laws that had established separate facilities for the races did not necessarily imply that one race was inferior to the other. Part of the judge's decision reflects the predominant view of those times, more than a century ago: "We consider the underlying fallacy of the plaintiff's [i.e., Plessy's] argument to consist in the assumption that the enforced separation of the two races stamps the colored race with a badge of inferiority. If this be so, it is not by reason of anything found in the act, but solely because the colored race chooses to put that construction on it."

Although this opinion was a far cry from the 1954 decision, which highlighted the detrimental effects of segregation on the personality development of black children, intermediate decisions by the Court permitted this seemingly abrupt change to evolve more predictably. One of these was the case of *Sweatt v. Painter,* decided by the Supreme Court in 1950. Heman Sweatt was a black man who wanted to enroll in the University of Texas Law School in Austin. The university was at that time (the late 1940s) racially segregated, and so the board of regents' response was to build a separate law school (in Houston, not in Austin) for Sweatt and any other blacks who chose to apply. Sweatt took the decision to court.

The U.S. Supreme Court ruled in favor of Sweatt, but not on the grounds that separate but equal facilities were unconstitutional. Rather, its decision was based on the conclusion that the separate facilities could not be equal to the law school at the University of Texas at Austin. The new school would not have the established law library or an experienced faculty or other qualities of the established school. It was not equal to the University of Texas, in the words of the Court, "in those qualities which are incapable of objective measurement but which make for greatness in a

law school." Note that even though this decision preceded *Brown v. Board of Education* by only four years, the Court refused to conclude explicitly that all separate facilities are inherently unequal. It merely decided about a very limited type of public facility.

About the same time, the University of Oklahoma took a different strategy to deal with the first black person admitted to its graduate school of education. George McLaurin was allowed to enroll, but he was segregated from all his classmates. His desk was separated from all the others by a rail, to which the sign "Reserved for Colored" was attached. He was given a separate desk at the library, and he was required to eat by himself in the cafeteria. Everything else was "equal." In the case of *McLaurin v. Oklahoma State Regents,* also in 1950, the U.S. Supreme Court ruled unanimously that this procedure denied his right to equal protection of the law; it concluded that such restrictions would "impair and inhibit his ability to study, to engage in discussion and exchange of views with other students." But again, the Court did not strike down *Plessy v. Ferguson.*

It was not until Earl Warren was appointed chief justice in 1953 that enough momentum built to reverse *Plessy v. Ferguson.* Justice Warren was not a precise legal scholar; he was less concerned with the fine points of the law than with whether the law was just. He liked to ask, "What is fair?" It was Warren who spearheaded the unanimous decision that finally overturned the idea that separate facilities can be "equal." He wrote that to separate black children "from others of similar age and qualifications solely because of their race generates a feeling of inferiority as to their status in the community that may affect their hearts and minds in a way unlikely to ever be undone."

## Law Functions by the Case Method; Psychology, by the Experimental Method

Lawyers reason from case to case. They locate cases that are similar to the one at hand and then find ways to distinguish among apparently similar cases. An argument based on the rulings from these other cases (legal precedent) is likely to carry the day. Psychologists, on the other hand, value the experimental method and prefer to gather data that are descriptive of large numbers of people. Just as psychologists are leery of findings based on very small samples, lawyers are hesitant to decide a person's fate based on aggregate data drawn from other people (Ellsworth & Mauro, 1998).

## Law Deals with Absolutes; Psychology Deals with Probabilities

Lawyers think in terms of "either-or": a person was either insane or not insane when he committed a particular act; a person is either fit or unfit to be a parent (Ellsworth & Mauro, 1998). Psychologists are not comfortable reasoning in absolutes; they prefer to think in terms of probabilities (e.g., that a white eyewitness to a crime is more likely to misidentify an African American perpetrator than a white perpetrator). When the law looks to psychologists for either-or answers to questions ("Was this person sane when he committed the crime?"), psychologists usually prefer to answer in terms of likelihoods or quantified "maybes." Lawyers have difficulty with such inconclusive responses because they need a final resolution to a dispute.

## Law Supports Contrasting Views of Reality; Psychology Seeks to Clarify One Muddled View of Reality

As indicated earlier, jurors must decide which of two conceptions of the truth is more acceptable in light of a mixed set of facts. Attorneys representing clients marshal all the facts that support their side. Although this procedure is similar to some scientific activities (a psychologist may do

a study that pits predictions from two theories against each other), the psychologist is trained to be objective and open to all perspectives and types of data. The ultimate goal is to integrate or assimilate conflicting findings into one refined view of the truth, not to choose between alternative views. Once again, this portrayal of the psychologist's goals may sometimes be too idealistic when compared to a candid picture of his or her actual behavior. Social scientists can become personally invested in their favorite explanations for events and may show considerable selectivity and partisanship when defending these positions against critics, but they are still expected to consider the data objectively.

The foregoing distinctions only scratch the surface of the differences between law and psychology. We will encounter their implications many times in subsequent chapters. As with the previous choices, selecting one option here over the other one is not a satisfactory response. The use of both approaches moves us closer to the goal of an adequate understanding than does reliance on one. We must remain aware of the limits of our own perspective and realize that other viewpoints are essential for a full understanding.

However, the contrast in knowledge-generating procedures does raise serious procedural questions. For example, given the differences in approach, how should a psychologist respond to the challenge of studying the law? What kind of role or roles should the psychologist play in understanding the legal system? The fact that science is empirical does not mean that the scientist's choices are free of values. The scientist decides both what to study and how to study it; these matters are examined in Chapter 2.

## SUMMARY

**1.** *Why do we have laws?*  Laws are everywhere. They are human creations that have as their major purpose the resolution of human conflict. As society changes,

new conflicts surface, leading to expansion and revision of the legal system.

**2.** *What are some of the ways of studying the law?*  Many possible approaches exist for the study of the law. Anthropologists compare the legal procedures in different societies and relate these differences to other characteristics of those societies. Sociologists examine the impact of social institutions (the family, the social class, and the neighborhood) on adherence to the law or on social deviation. Philosophers examine how law reflects concepts of morality and justice. A psychological approach focuses on individuals as agents within a legal system, asking how their internal qualities (personality, values, abilities, and experiences) and their environments, including the law itself, affect their behavior.

**3. *What dilemmas are reflected in the psychological approach to the law?*** Several basic choices must be made between pairs of options in the psychological study of the law. These options are often irreconcilable because each is attractive, but both usually cannot be attained at the same time. Society often devotes its efforts first to one and then to the other. The choices are (1) whether the goal of law is achieving personal freedom or ensuring the common good, (2) whether equality or discretion should be the standard for our legal policies, (3) whether the purpose of a

legal inquiry is to discover the truth or to provide a means of conflict resolution, and (4) whether the methods of law or science are the best for making decisions.

**4. *How do recent laws reflect the contrast between the due process model and the crime control model of the criminal justice system?*** Recent laws in several states, including the "three-strikes-and-out" laws and those requiring notification of neighbors when a sex offender is released from prison, reflect the increased salience of a crime control model, which seeks to contain or reduce criminal activity.

**5. *How does the phenomenon of sentencing disparity reflect a dilemma?*** Our society assumes equal treatment by the law. It also recognizes that not all violations deserve the same punishment. Sentencing disparity reflects the tendency to give differing punishments for what appear to be the same crimes. On occasion, this disparity recognizes mitigating or aggravating circumstances, but on other occasions, sentencing disparity reflects the expression of prejudice against minorities.

## KEY TERMS

| | | | |
|---|---|---|---|
| *amicus curiae* | double jeopardy* | jury nullification* | sexual predator laws |
| case law* | due process model | law and economics | sociolegal studies |
| crime control model | equality | notification law | *stare decisis* |
| critical legal studies* | *ex post facto* | principle of | therapeutic |
| determinate sentencing | feminist | proportionality | jurisprudence |
| dialectic analysis | jurisprudence* | sentencing disparity | "three-strikes" law |
| discretion* | forensic psychologists | settlement negotiation | trial consultants |

**InfoTrac**
**College**
**Edition**

For additional readings go to **http://www.infotrac-college.com/wadsworth** and enter a search term related to your interest. The key terms that have been asterisked above will pull up several related articles. *See also*: AMICUS CURIAE: BRIEFS; DUE-PROCESS OF LAW; EQUALITY BEFORE THE LAW; and EX POST FACTO LAWS.

# Psychologists and the Legal System

## ORIENTING QUESTIONS

1. *What are four roles that psychologists may play in the legal system?*
2. *What are the motivations of basic researchers; how are their findings relevant?*
3. *What is the relationship of the psychologist as applied scientist to the legal system?*
4. *How does being an expert witness reflect the consultant role?*
5. *What does a policy evaluator do?*
6. *The role of advocate is the most controversial. Why?*

Chapter 1 described the psychologist's approach to the law as an empirical one. The empirical approach collects data from the real world in order to answer questions. Does the value of a stolen item affect whether a victim will report a crime to the police? Do judges rely on a defendant's past record more than on the severity of the crime in setting the amount of bail? Does going through law school change a person's values? In attempting to answer such questions, the psychologist collects data from the world of experience and offers answers only after such empirical activities are completed.

## The Place of Values

The procedures that researchers use for collecting and analyzing data are not always straightforward. The psychologist must first make two basic decisions: What questions are to be asked? And what should be done with the answers? In responding to these inescapable choices, psychologists reveal their values. Conflicts often exist between contrasting but equally desirable values, leading to dilemmas as thorny as those posed in Chapter 1.

For example, consider the case of *Plessy v. Ferguson* (1896), described in Chapter 1. More than 100 years ago, when black people were required to ride in separate railroad cars in Louisiana and other southern states, the Supreme Court concluded that forced separation of different races did not necessarily imply inferiority of status. Suppose a group of psychologists at that time had evaluated that claim empirically. Their conclusions would doubtless have been influenced by what questions they chose to ask. For example, if they compared the physical layout of the "white" cars and what were then called the "colored" cars, the number of windows, the presence of rest rooms, the padding of the seats, or even the passengers' subjective feelings of comfort, they might conclude—on the basis of empirical data—that

separation meant no inferiority. But suppose they had asked the black passengers other questions, such as, Would you prefer to sit in the "white" car? How does it feel to be seated in a car "for colored only"? What does a separate car mean to you? They might have reached different conclusions, again based on empirical data, that were more in keeping with Homer Plessy's preference for being seated in the "white" car. Sometimes science is called "value-free" because it tries to look objectively at the data collected. But it can never be value-free as long as the scientist has some choice in what questions are asked and what data are collected.

Psychologists must make other choices about the uses of their data. Many psychologists publish their findings in scientific journals that are read by their peers; others write articles for popular magazines or testify before legislative committees. Some psychologists generate research findings to assist underprivileged groups in our society. Decisions about where to publish or how to disseminate data and conclusions also reflect scholars' values, especially about the proper purposes of science. Psychologists sometimes do not agree about how their data should be used (see, e.g., an exchange about the usefulness to the legal system of studies on repressed memory: Wasby & Brody, 1997; Golding, Warren, & Ross, 1997). In this chapter, we explore four possible roles for the psychologist in society. Next we examine how these roles apply to psychologists who study the law and participate in the legal system, and then we evaluate the possible ethical dilemmas resulting from each of these roles.

## The Psychologist's Relationship to Society

What are appropriate activities for a psychologist in society? Most courses in psychology portray only two roles for psychologists: either that of the scientist who conducts basic research about the causes and development of behavior or that of the applied psychologist (usually the clinical psychologist) who tries to understand and assist individuals or groups confronting their problems. The possibilities are more elaborate, however. Four contrasting roles can be ordered on a continuum from isolated academic research, on one end, to collaboration with persons from other disciplines to provide services to the public at large, on the other end.

## The Psychologist as a Basic Scientist

A **basic scientist** pursues knowledge for its own sake. Basic researchers study a phenomenon simply for the joy of understanding it. They do not seek to apply their findings; many have no concern whether the knowledge they generate is ever put to any practical, problem-solving use. Some may even be hostile when, for example, a newspaper reporter takes their conclusions and applies them to a commonplace problem.

As an example of basic research, an investigator may study the relative importance of heredity and environment on intelligence. She may collect data on the similarity of IQ scores of identical twins compared with fraternal twins or with siblings born at different times. She may study identical twins who were put in separate foster homes at an early age in order to tease out the effect of their differing environments. Her predominant motivation is to understand the phenomenon of intelligence or to develop a theory about how psychological characteristics are transmitted from one generation to the next.

Basic research studies, although not conducted for application to real-world problems, are sometimes relevant to concerns outside the laboratory. Social psychologists interested in why members of majority groups process persuasive messages from stigmatized sources more than messages from other sources (Petty, Fleming, & White, 1999) may not have intended or even care that their results can be used in a courtroom. Although the findings certainly have relevance to

that setting, application of the research was not the intention of the basic scientists.

## The Psychologist as an Applied Scientist

Other psychologists—**applied scientists**—are dedicated to applying knowledge to solve real-life problems. Most of the public's awareness of the psychologist's work reflects this role, whether this awareness comes from viewing TV's portrayal of therapist Frasier Crane or reading about psychologists who testify as expert witnesses in trials involving insanity pleas.

Clinical, counseling, and school psychologists apply scientific findings to the betterment of individuals who are having personal difficulties. Industrial/organizational psychologists study and try to enhance the efficiency of organizations and improve the functioning of individuals in various kinds of work settings.

Other psychologists seek to understand and alleviate social problems. Their underlying values reflect social service to a greater degree than do those of the "basic" researcher, whose primary goal is understanding. The Society for the Psychological Study of Social Issues (SPSSI), an organization of some 3000 psychologists and other professionals, concerns itself with matters that affect the well-being of substantial numbers of our compatriots, such as poverty, racism, pollution, and criminal behavior. Members of SPSSI believe that psychological facts ought to be brought to bear on policy dilemmas. For example, in 1999, SPSSI sponsored a conference on immigrants and immigration. Topics included determinants of immigration policy, intergroup attitudes and relations, multiculturalism, ethnic identity, and acculturation.

The applied scientist often acts as a consultant. The director of a government organization or the principal of a school may approach the psychologist with a practical problem. Does exposure to pornography increase men's violence against women? How can we make our schools safer? What is the best way to treat people with severe mental illness? Psychologists may carry out new empirical studies to answer these questions, or they may study existing research to draw conclusions.

When the psychologist in the role of consultant provides a report, policymakers have the right to select what they consider the most relevant findings and base their policies or actions on these conclusions to the extent they desire. Thus, the policymakers retain the control and the power. But the psychologist has contributed, by presenting alternative positions and the empirical support for each, before the policymakers formulate a decision.

## The Psychologist as a Policy Evaluator

In addition to their knowledge of substantive problems, psychologists have methodological skills that they use in assessing how well an intervention has worked. Psychologists and other social scientists have been asked so frequently in the last several decades to conduct evaluation studies that a separate subfield called *policy evaluation,* or *evaluation research,* has emerged. The **policy evaluator** provides data to answer questions such as, I have instituted a change; how do I know whether it was effective? Or, more ideally, I want to make a change in our organization's procedures, but before I do, how do I design it so I will be able to determine later whether it worked?

The role of psychologist as policy evaluator blossomed in the late 1960s, partly as a manifestation of President Lyndon Johnson's goal of transforming American society. The late social psychologist Donald Campbell (1969) envisioned an "experimenting society," in which psychologists would contribute their research expertise to help policymakers determine the effectiveness of Johnson's Great Society attacks on the social problems of unemployment, poverty, racism, and poor health. The underlying value is that public policy will be more intelligently formed if decision makers have input from psychologists (Monahan, 1977).

Psychologists have been asked to evaluate whether programs such as the New Chance Demonstration Project achieved their goals. New

Chance, a program to help welfare recipients get and keep jobs, provides educational and vocational services, parenting instruction, health and social services, and child care to teen mothers on welfare. Psychologists evaluated the parent-training component of the program by comparing women who received these services with a control group of similar welfare mothers who didn't go through the New Chance Program. What they found was surprising: despite improved parenting skills among the mothers who went through training, their children showed no signs of enhanced social or cognitive development. The results may mean that the New Chance training module was too brief and that prolonged poverty, transient housing, and other adverse life circumstances overwhelm whatever positive gains were made by the mothers (Sleek, 1998a).

## The Psychologist as an Advocate

The final role for psychologists, the **advocate,** is often omitted from textbooks. It is the most controversial role because it is the most "activist." Its goal is to change society. One early advocacy effort by social scientists was to challenge the "separate but equal" doctrine that undergirded the racial segregation of public schools that characterized many states in the first half of the 20th century. A group of prominent social scientists in the early 1950s prepared a statement titled "The Effect of Segregation and the Consequences of Desegregation: A Social Science Statement," which became part of the legal brief submitted to the U.S. Supreme Court before its 1954 *Brown v. Board of Education* decision.

The statement began with a review of the detrimental effects of segregation, prejudice, and discrimination on black children. The statement asserted that these children learned from their environment that they were members of what American society considered to be an inferior group. As Stuart Cook (1984), one of the authors of the report, noted, "They react to this knowledge with a sense of humiliation and feelings of inferiority, and come to entertain the possibility that they are, in fact, worthy of second-class treatment" (p. 3). These feelings typically led to self-hatred and self-rejection for being black.

It is uncertain whether the Supreme Court, in its decision overturning school segregation, was strongly influenced by the social science statement. (Several of the empirical findings and the social scientists' statement itself were cited in footnote 11 in the *Brown v. Board of Education* decision.) Seeking evidence of the social scientists' impact, some commentators have noted a resemblance between parts of the statement and one famous passage in the Supreme Court's *Brown* opinion:

> Segregation of white and colored children in public schools has a detrimental effect upon the colored children. The impact is greater when it has the sanction of the law; for the policy of separating the races is usually interpreted as denoting the inferiority of the Negro group. A sense of inferiority affects the motivation of a child to learn. Segregation with the sanction of law, therefore, has a tendency to retard the educational and mental development of Negro children and to deprive them of some of the benefits they would receive in a racially integrated school system. Whatever may have been the extent of psychological knowledge at the time of *Plessy v. Ferguson,* this finding is amply supported by modern authority.

The social protest and unrest of the late 1960s also contributed to the emergence of an advocacy role for psychologists. George Miller, a distinguished experimental psychologist previously known for his basic research on memory, gave a very uncharacteristic message as his presidential address to the American Psychological Association in 1969. He urged his colleagues to "give psychology away"—that is, to help others use psychological knowledge to solve the social problems encountered in everyday society. This may sound like the consultant's role, described previously, but Miller extended it. He noted that powerless groups in our society might better their conditions if they had the benefit of the skills and knowledge

of psychologists. They could improve living conditions by effectively lobbying for better crime control, job-training programs, neighborhood schools, and community health and recreation services. Thus, the goal for the advocate is to fight injustice and oppression (Fox, 1999) and increase the empowerment of citizens (Rappaport, 1981, 1987); **empowerment** refers to the goal of helping disenfranchised groups gain greater control over their lives and increase their personal or collective power to influence social policy and community change.

At about the same time, other psychologists began to urge colleagues to take a partisan role in assisting underprivileged groups. Kenneth Ring (1971) called on his colleagues to take sides and to engage in research and other professional activities that challenged the entrenched establishment. In choosing sides, he stated, "one can, unthinkingly or through choice, ally oneself with the institutional forces which support professional psychology. Or, one may choose to side not with the powerful but with the weak" (p. 5). Some of us may not realize that psychologists take sides when they accept employment by a particular organization. An industrial/organizational psychologist who performs personnel assessment and selection for a large company is paid to help the company select the "best" job candidates; the psychologist is not paid to show concern for those who fail the selection test, nor does he or she ordinarily assist applicants to pass the test.

One psychologist who has taken up the call to advocate for social change is Arthur McDonald, chief executive officer of the Morning Star Memorial Foundation in Lame Deer, Montana. He has spoken out in Congress about the need for more behavioral medicine and prevention services for Native Americans. Four of the leading causes of death among Native Americans—alcohol and drug use, heart disease, accidents, and diabetes—have a behavioral component, and studies show that psychological intervention (e.g., diet modification, smoking cessation, treatment for alcoholism) can reduce or eliminate the risks. McDonald has urged Congress to bolster funding for the Indian Health

Services so that more psychologists can be trained to meet the unique prevention needs of Native Americans (Rabasca, 1998).

The four roles just presented vary in several respects. Each of them is fraught with dangers and ethical dilemmas. What is right? What is proper for a psychologist to do? Before considering such questions, we'll discuss how each role contributes to the study of the law.

# The Psychologist's Relationship to the Law

The fact that the four roles differ on a dimension of "ivory tower" isolation versus involvement with the community is highlighted when we apply the four roles to psychologists' study of and work in the legal system.

## The Psychologist as a Basic Scientist of the Law

Even though "basic scientists" choose topics without regard for their application, and even though they prefer to work alone or collaborate with just a few like-minded souls in their laboratories, the basic knowledge they generate can promote a better understanding of the law.

For example, laboratory research on visual perception helps us understand just how accurate an eyewitness is about a crime or an accident. Psychologists who test different theories of memory promote a better understanding of whether repression can cause long-term forgetting of traumatic events. Basic research on the relationship of one's social attitudes to one's behavior can help us realize why people obey or disobey the law. The study of decision making in the laboratory is useful in understanding how judges conclude to uphold or overturn previous judicial decisions. Likewise, clinical psychologists' professional evaluations of criminal defendants have been found to be affected by the psychologists' basic attitude about the causes of crime (Deitchman, Kennedy, & Beckham, 1991).

The study of conformity has been a popular basic research topic for social psychologists. Conformity is an important dynamic in jury decisions, and an analysis of the responses to conformity pressures by groups of subjects in the laboratory can provide clues for understanding the power of pressure from the majority to affect jury decisions. In summary, opportunities to apply "basic" research findings to understanding the legal system are numerous.

## The Psychologist as an Applied Scientist/ Expert Witness in the Law

Psychologists who are interested in applying the findings of their profession to real-world questions can act as expert witnesses in legislative hearings or in a court of law. For example, as ◆ Box 2-1 illustrates, psychologist Greg Herek has studied the impact of victimization on gays and lesbians and testified about his work in a congressional briefing on hate crimes.

Psychologists often testify as expert witnesses during a trial. Either side, as part of its presentation of the evidence, may ask the judge to allow expert witnesses to testify. Juries—and judges, too, for that matter—cannot be expected to be well versed in every topic from abscesses to zinfandel wine. An expert witness is someone who possesses special knowledge about a subject, knowledge that the average juror does not have. Although people need not always have had formal training before they qualify as expert witnesses (e.g., an antique dealer or a gold prospector might have become an expert as a result of his or her experience on the job), most expert witnesses have had advanced, formal training. At any rate, the judge must be convinced that the testimony any expert will present is of a kind that requires special knowledge, skill, or experience and that the testimony will help resolve the dispute and lead jurors toward the truth. Experts are usually paid for the time they spend testifying in court, as much as $500 or more per hour for some specialties.

For example, if the trial is to determine the responsibility for injuries that a person suffered

## THE CASE OF

**BOX 2-1**

### Matthew Shepard: Psychologists as expert witnesses on hate crimes

On a chilly October evening in 1998, two bicyclists riding on Snowy Mountain View Road outside of Laramie, Wyoming, saw what they thought was a scarecrow tied to a rough-hewn deer fence. Only after coming closer did the horror set in. This was no scarecrow. This was—or had been—a man. His head had been bashed to the brain stem, his face was cut and covered with blood and tears, and his limbs had been scorched with burn marks. Police believe that Matthew Shepard, a slightly built freshman at the University of Wyoming who was comfortable with although not flaunting of his homosexuality, was lured into a pickup truck by two tall, muscular men who pretended that they, too, were gay. All pretense vanished as the pair began pounding Shepard on the head with a .357 Magnum revolver, then tied him

*A memorial to Matthew Shepard*

to the post, beat him relentlessly, and left him to die. He was found 18 hours later, barely alive, and he died within days of the beating.

Even before the Shepard case riveted the nation, state and federal legislators had been concerned about the proliferation of **hate crimes**—criminal acts intended to harm or intimidate people because of their race, ethnicity, sexual orientation, religion, or other minority group status, discussed further in Chapter 5. (According to FBI data, sexual orientation was

the motivation for 14% of reported hate crimes in 1997.) Research psychologist Greg Herek has testified about the impact of anti–gay/lesbian victimization at a congressional briefing. Herek recounted the results of his studies showing that victims of hate crimes experience higher levels of depression, anger, and posttraumatic stress disorder than victims of other crimes (we discuss victimization issues in Chapter 16) and come to view the world and other people as malevolent. In his role as applied scientist/expert witness, Herek has urged the adoption of special policies for hate crimes. To date, nearly 40 states and the District of Columbia have enacted laws that allow stiffer sentencing for defendants who choose their victims based on perceptions of the victim's race, religion, ethnicity, or sexual orientation.

when a bridge collapsed, it is not likely that the jurors possess the technical knowledge to assess the adequacy of the bridge construction. (Were the steel girders thick enough? Was the right mix of concrete used?) Jurors in a medical malpractice trial probably have not had the medical training necessary to form accurate judgments about the justifiability of an injured plaintiff's complaint. The psychological topics calling for expertise are almost limitless. And psychologists, as expert witnesses, have been called on to testify in many types of cases. Here are a few examples:

- The mental state of a defendant at the time of an alleged offense and the mental competence of the defendant to stand trial
- The degree of emotional or brain damage suffered by a victim in an accident
- The extent of mental retardation and the appropriateness of certain treatments for mental retardation
- Employee discrimination through selection and promotion procedures
- The effects of bilingualism on children
- Community standards regarding obscenity

- The battered woman syndrome
- The accuracy of identifications by eye-witnesses
- Trademark infringement and false advertising
- The impact on juries of sensationalistic pre-trial publicity
- The effects of alternative child custody arrangements after divorce
- The effects of warning signs or safety instructions on potentially dangerous equipment
- The prospects for a convicted defendant's rehabilitation in prison or on probation
- The factors that may cause a suspect to make a false confession

Expert witnesses are usually proposed by one side in a trial, and the judge decides whether they will be allowed to testify. Many judges fear that an expert witness's testimony will be so powerful that it will usurp the jury as the fact finder in the case, and so judges sometimes refuse to let experts testify, especially if they are convinced that the topic of expertise is one that most laypeople are familiar with. Thus, in matters of the accuracy of eyewitnesses, psychologists have sometimes been denied the opportunity to testify. We return to this issue in Chapter 7.

On other occasions, judges have disallowed expert testimony as irrelevant or immaterial. Consider the case of unlucky Pedro Gil. On a night of wild abandon in the fall of 1993, Gil hoisted a bucket of plaster over the wall of a Manhattan rooftop. It dropped seven stories to the ground and hit and killed a police officer standing on the street below. Gil claimed that he expected the bucket to drop unceremoniously onto an unoccupied street directly below him, rather than continuing forward as it fell and land on the street where the police officer was positioned. To support his naive belief that objects drop straight down, Gil's attorneys attempted to introduce the testimony of cognitive psychologist Michael McCloskey, an expert in intuitive physics, who was prepared to testify that people commonly misunderstand physical laws. The trial judge did not let McClosky take the stand, claiming that intuitive physics was ir-

relevant to the issues under contention. The jury convicted Gil of second-degree manslaughter.

Judges have tremendous discretion about many kinds of decisions in their courtrooms, and whether to allow a jury to hear expert testimony on a given topic is one of the most important, and often controversial, examples of this discretion. We will discuss this topic at more length in other chapters, but for now it is important to understand that the Supreme Court has indicated (*Daubert v. Merrell Dow Pharmaceuticals, Inc.*, 1993) that judges' decisions about the admissibility of expert testimony based on "scientific" knowledge must turn on the validity of the science in question. In essence, judges now function as "gatekeepers" who must evaluate potential expert testimony by the standards of science. Although the *Daubert* decision did not create an exclusive or rigid set of scientific standards, it did list four factors that should be considered in assessing the validity—and subsequent admissibility—of the expert's testimony: (1) whether the expert's theory or technique can and has been tested, (2) whether it has been evaluated by peer review, (3) the reliability and error rate of the claims, and (4) the extent to which the expert's techniques and claims have been generally accepted by the relevant scientific community.

Technically, *Daubert* applies only in federal courts, but many states have now adopted its standards as well. A few states still follow what is known as the "*Frye* test," based on the 1923 case of *Frye v. United States*, which held that the admissibility of scientific evidence depended on it being "sufficiently established to have gained general acceptance in the particular field to which it belongs." The main problem with *Frye* was that it was both too generous with testimony that was "generally accepted" even if its validity had not been scientifically demonstrated and too restrictive of novel evidence that nonetheless was the result of excellent scientific verification (Melton, Petrila, Poythress, & Slobogin, 1997).

*Daubert,* by contrast, requires that judges' decisions about the admissibility of expert testimony should be made in accord with the Federal Rules of Evidence (FRE), which state, "If scientific, technical, or other specialized knowledge will assist the trier of fact to understand the evidence or to determine a fact in issue, a witness qualified as an expert by knowledge, skill, experience, training, or education may testify thereto in the form of an opinion or otherwise" (FRE Rule 702). Of course, the judge must first decide whether the testimony qualifies as "scientific, technical, or other specialized knowledge," and that is where much of the controversy is found.

During its 1998–1999 term, the Supreme Court also heard the case of *Kumho Tire Co. v. Carmichael*. This case stemmed from a 1988 minivan accident in Alabama that resulted in the death of one member of the Carmichael family and injuries to seven others. At trial, the Carmichael family, as plaintiffs, offered the testimony of a tire failure expert who would have testified that a tire on the minivan was defective (see Figure 2.1). The expert testimony was excluded. The question that was ultimately presented to the Supreme Court was whether *Daubert* also applies to testimony based on technical or nonscientific knowledge that an expert possesses as a result of specialized experience. The Court concluded that it did and insisted that all expert witnesses in federal cases had to meet the criterion of providing opinions based on scientific principles or some generally accepted test of reliability.

What do the *Daubert* and *Kumho* rulings mean for psychologists who are asked to provide expert testimony? Although psychologists have already faced challenges to their testimony under *Daubert,* the impact of the new standards on psychology may not be known for some time (Goodman-Delahunty, 1997). There are already conflicting sentiments about its implications for the field. Are the *Daubert* criteria a more rigorous standard for admissibility or a less stringent test? Will *Daubert* prohibit juries from hearing about important new scientific discoveries, or will it expose them to what some have called "junk science"—unreliable, invalidated opinions masquerading as scientific facts? Some commentators (e.g., Faigman, 1995) believe that as a young science with an uncertain and tentative methodology, psychol-

Radial-Ply Tire Construction

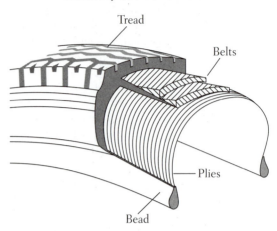

**FIGURE 2.1** *Radial-ply tire construction was the topic of expert testimony in the case of* Kumho Tire Co. v. Carmichael.

ogy experts will be significantly constrained by *Daubert*. Others have expressed concern that clinical psychologists in particular, who provide testimony based as much on clinical expertise as empirical data, may be turned away at the courthouse door by *Kumho's* requirements. Still others (e.g., Rotgers & Barrett, 1996; Bersoff quoted in Sleek, 1998b) see these decisions as an opportunity for psychology to firmly embrace the mantle of science and to adhere to strict scientific standards of data gathering and interpretation, a methodology that some clinicians, in particular, do not follow. These authors maintain that unless these strict standards are satisfied, psychologists should not claim that their opinions are scientific (see also Melton et al., 1997).

One clear ramification of the *Daubert* decision is that if judges must decide what opinions qualify as "scientific," they must become savvy consumers of science. Various groups of psychologists have provided resources for judges to use when faced with cases involving psychological issues, and others have sponsored workshops and training about psychological questions that arise in legal proceedings. The intent of these overtures is to educate judges about the methods of science so that they can make better-informed decisions about which psychological experts will be allowed to testify and which will be excluded. This education requires that judges become familiar with the basic assumptions and procedures of the scientific method. Although it is not likely that many judges will acquire an in-depth understanding of scientific methodology, it is reasonable to expect that most will become acquainted with the general logic of the scientific method (see ◆ Box 2-2).

## The Psychologist as a Policy Evaluator in the Law

The legal system is no different from other elements of our society in its frequent implementation of changes that have not been properly evaluated. As noted in Chapter 1, new laws are constantly being created and old ones revised and reinterpreted as a result of changes in society. These legal modifications cry out for evaluation. What are the effects of changing the legal drinking age from 18 to 21? Does a police crackdown on speeders reduce traffic accidents? Does the chemical castration of released rapists reduce the rate of sexual violence? Such questions encourage evaluation research on legal issues.

Likewise, the law enforcement and criminal justice systems frequently alter their operating procedures. For example, police departments may change from automobile patrols to foot patrols to increase surveillance and to improve police/community relations. Often these innovations are introduced without adequate planning about how they can be evaluated; hence, their outcomes, whether good or bad, cannot be determined (Reppucci & Haugaard, 1989). The methodological skills of the psychologist as policy evaluator are essential in designing an innovation so that its effects can be tested to eliminate other possible explanations for any changes.

For example, a judge in New Philadelphia, Ohio, in an effort to reduce drunk driving, routinely ordered first offenders to spend 15 days in jail plus pay a $750 fine. His practice was well known in that county, and you might expect that it would thus deter drunk driving. But researchers did anonymous spot checks of drivers, includ-

ing Breathalyzer tests, in New Philadelphia and also in Cambridge, Ohio, a neighboring city where sentences were less severe. Similar numbers of drunk drivers were found in both localities, implying that these extreme punishments weren't effective deterrents.

Claims of employment discrimination provide an opportunity for using statistical analyses conducted by a policy evaluator. Tomkins (1988) identifies several Supreme Court cases in which plaintiffs used statistical data and social science evidence to bolster their contentions of having been unfavorably treated by employers because of their race or gender. In one of these, the plaintiff, Ann Hopkins, claimed that she had been rejected for an appointment as a partner in Price Waterhouse, a nationwide accounting firm, because her behaviors had been evaluated as too "unladylike" and aggressive by the current partners. (Hopkins's record and productivity at the firm surpassed those of the men who had been promoted to partner.) In the spring of 1989, the Supreme Court ruled in Hopkins's favor. In reaching its decision, the Court cited the work of social psychologist Susan Fiske and her colleagues on the indications and effects of gender-based stereotyping and how such stereotyping was revealed in Hopkins's employment experiences (Fiske, Bersoff, Borgida, Deaux, & Heilman, 1991).

Sometimes, legal policy is formulated with nary a look toward psychology. More than 25 years ago, several psychologically healthy college students spent six days in a prisonlike environment in the basement of the psychology department at Stanford University. At the time, results of the Stanford Prison Experiment (Haney, Banks, & Zimbardo, 1973) shocked psychologists and the public and even today merit discussion in college classrooms around the world. Over the course of the six days, the behavior of men randomly assigned to be mock prisoners or mock guards bore striking resemblance to patterns found in actual prisons: several of the prisoners suffered acute psychological trauma and breakdowns, and several of the guards became belligerent, cruel, and sadistic. (More details on the Stanford Prison Experiment are described in Chapter 17.)

## BOX 2-2    Scientific methods for law and psychology

When psychologists want to understand the cause of behavior, they employ the **scientific method,** a set of research principles and methods that help them reach valid conclusions. The process usually starts when a researcher states a **hypothesis,** a proposition describing how two or more variables are related (e.g., children younger than 4 will be perceived by adults as less credible witnesses than children who are older than 10). Hypotheses are usually based on prior research and theory that guide a researcher toward such educated hunches. As evidence accumulates in support of a hypothesis, researchers organize their ideas into a **theory,** which is a set of propositions and related hypotheses used to predict and explain a phenomenon, in this case why the age of witnesses affects how others evaluate their credibility.

Researchers then use empirical methods to test their hypotheses. They begin by being certain that the hypothesis is stated clearly in operational definitions. An **operational definition** is a statement that equates a concept with the specific methods used to measure it. An operational definition of credibility might be scores on a rating form used to measure the believability of a witness's statements. Two of the most important

methods for testing operationally defined hypotheses are correlational research and experiments.

**Correlation** measures the degree to which one variable is related to another. Height and weight are positively correlated; they tend to change together in the same direction. The amount of snow on the highway and the speed at which people drive are negatively correlated; as snowfall increases, speed of driving decreases. If the correlation between two variables is large, knowing about one variable allows a researcher to make more accurate predictions about the second variable. However, correlations cannot inform researchers about *why* two variable are related, and they cannot prove that one variable *caused* another to change.

To draw cause-effect conclusions about the relationship between variables and to offer the best explanations about these relationships, researchers perform experiments. In an **experiment,** the researcher manipulates one variable (the independent variable) and measures the effects of this manipulation on a second variable (the dependent variable) while trying to hold all other influences constant. The researcher manipulates the independent variable by randomly assigning subjects to different ex-

perimental groups. Random assignment is vital because it reduces the chances that variables other than the independent variable have influenced the experiment's results. For our example about the effects of witness age on perceived credibility, subjects would be randomly assigned to listen to the "testimony" of either a 3-year-old child or a 12-year-old juvenile. The dependent variable of perceived credibility of these two witnesses would then be measured for the subjects in the two groups.

Even if the results of this experiment were consistent with the hypothesis that younger children are perceived as less credible, it still might be possible that another variable besides age was actually responsible for the results. Suppose the older witness did not wear glasses but the younger one did. Perhaps subjects thought the visual acuity of the older witness was superior, and this was the real reason—not age—they rated her as more credible. Variables that distort the results or compete with the independent variable as explanations are known as **confounding variables;** they make it difficult for researchers to be sure that their explanation for an experiment's results are valid. To rule out the influence of confounding vari-

Have these dramatic findings had any influence on prison policy in the intervening years? That question was addressed recently by two of the authors of the original study (Haney & Zimbardo, 1998). Sadly, the answer they reach is no:

Correctional administrators, politicians, policymakers, and judicial decision makers not only ignored most of the lessons that emerged from the Stanford Prison Experiment but also disregarded the insights of a number of psycholo-

ables, researchers often design experiments that include several experimental groups or conduct a series of experiments about the phenomenon they are studying.

In some cases, researchers cannot conduct true experiments because of ethical requirements or legal constraints. For example, if a researcher were interested in evaluating the effects that lawyer experience had on trial outcomes, it would be both unethical and illegal to assign criminal defendants randomly to lawyers who either had years of trial experience or were complete trial novices. The alternative in this situation, and one that is used often in psycholegal studies, is the **quasi-experiment,** a study that "comes close" to being a true experiment but lacks one or more of the crucial elements of an experiment—usually the random assignment of subjects to manipulated experimental groups. A quasi-experimental test of the hypothesis that experienced lawyers obtain better verdicts than novices would be to measure (not manipulate) years of experience for the lawyers involved in any given case and then observe the outcomes of hundreds of trials. The researcher could then assess whether there was a correlation between attorney experience and verdicts.

The conclusions that can be drawn from quasi-experiments are not as strong as those from true experiments because quasi-experiments are less able to rule out the effects of confounding variables. However, if the results are subject to **replication,** meaning that they are duplicated several times with new groups of subjects, the researcher gains confidence that the observed association between variables represents a cause-effect relationship.

Replication is important for another reason as well. Researchers need to know how well their results apply to people in general, not just their immediate research sample. Are men and women affected differently by the age of a witness? Does a person's educational background modify the effect of witness age on perceived credibility? To study the effects of human diversity on scientific conclusions, researchers pay special attention to the issue of **sampling,** the methods used to select research participants. A common technique is representative sampling, in which participants are selected to represent all levels of important subject variables such as age, gender, and ethnicity. Another strategy is to focus on one subject characteristic at a time and select

people as randomly as possible from that group alone. One other option is to study human diversity by sampling in a way that allows its effects to be analyzed. For example, suppose researchers were interested in the effects of a subject's ethnicity on the relationship between witness age and perceived credibility. They could explore this question by selecting subjects in a way that ensures roughly equal numbers of people from several ethnic backgrounds are included in the study. They can then measure whether the correlation between witness age and perceived credibility is stronger for people in a particular ethnic group.

Scientists are convinced that the scientific method is the best—albeit not a perfect—means for discovering trustworthy knowledge and for resolving the major controversies that face their fields of study. To the extent that psychological experts rely on scientific methods for their testimony, the courts should be generally well served by their testimony. By the same token, the quality of expert testimony should be improved if judges take the gatekeeping role mandated by *Daubert* seriously and insist that experts must measure up to basic scientific standards before they are allowed in court.

gists who preceded us and the scores of others who wrote about, extended, and elaborated on the same lessons in empirical studies and theoretical pieces published over the past several decades. Indeed, there is now a vast social science literature that underscores, in various ways, the critical importance of situation and context in influencing social behavior, especially in psychologically powerful situations like prisons. (p. 718)

Haney and Zimbardo develop a number of reform-minded proposals that they hope will bring correctional policy more in line with psychological research findings. They suggest, for example, that if prison life can cause a person's deterioration, then before release, prisoners should be exposed to a transitional or "decompression" program that would gradually reverse the effects of the confining environment of a prison.

## The Psychologist as an Advocate in the Law

One major difference between an expert witness and an advocate is the fact that the latter identifies strongly with one side. Even if an expert witness (or other kind of consultant) is paid by one side in a trial, he or she is under oath to tell "the truth, the whole truth, and nothing but the truth." Advocates, although using psychological methods and trying to render an objective analysis of data, commit their skills to one side; they become partisans. The contrast with the expert witness role can be best illustrated by the actions of a group of social scientists who aided the defense team in the trial of the Harrisburg Seven (◄► Box 2-3). This trial, by the way, was the first highly publicized application of so-called scientific jury selection procedures, further described in Chapter 14.

The techniques first developed by the social scientists in the Harrisburg Seven trial have been expanded and refined. Today, the field of trial consulting (sometimes called *jury consulting* or *litigation consulting*) is a booming business (see Chapter 1). A national organization, the American Society of Trial Consultants, is composed of more than 300 individual members and 150 firms. Members do more than jury selection; they also conduct community attitude surveys, prepare witnesses to testify, advise lawyers on their presentation strategies, and conduct mock trials (Strier, 1999).

Although most members of this organization remain "advocates" in the sense that they take sides, their employers are no longer the disenfranchised elements of society; instead, they are large corporations or wealthy defendants who can af-

JO-ELLAN DIMITRIUS
*After her successful jury consulting work in the case of Rodney King, Jo-Ellan Dimitrius gained additional fame for her jury selection strategy on behalf of O. J. Simpson, who was acquitted of charges that he murdered his ex-wife Nicole and her friend Ron Goldman.*

ford to pay the consultants for their services. For example, Litigation Sciences, a firm established by Donald E. Vinson in 1979, employs more than 100 Ph.D.-level social scientists as field researchers and consultants; within its first ten years, the firm assisted attorneys in more than 900 cases and interviewed 20,000 jurors (Cox, 1989). In contrast to the Harrisburg Seven defendants, most clients of Litigation Sciences are large corporations involved in huge civil trials dealing with claims of antitrust, product liability, or toxic waste violations.

Occasionally, these trial consultants offer their services *pro bono* (for free), as the social scientists did in the Harrisburg Seven case. In a trial dramatized in the film *Ghosts of Mississippi,* trial consultants assisted the prosecution on a *pro bono*

## The Science of

### "Scientific jury selection"

In 1971, Philip Berrigan and six other defendants were arrested and charged with conspiracy to plan a number of antiwar activities, such as raiding draft boards, blowing up heating tunnels in Washington, D.C., and kidnapping Henry Kissinger, then secretary of state. The federal government chose to hold the trial in Harrisburg, Pennsylvania, considered to be the most conservative, progovernment locality in the district. For the first time, a team of social scientists joined defense attorneys in an effort to select a favorable jury from a largely unfavorable community. A "recipe for a jury" was formulated (Schulman, Shaver, Colman, Emrich, & Christie, 1973). As their first step, the team of social scientists sought to determine whether the pool of prospective jurors was representative of the local population. They compared the demographic characteristics of the pool to a random sample of registered voters in the community and found that the average member of the venire was somewhat older. Partly because of these findings, the presiding judge ordered the drawing of a second, more rep-

resentative, jury pool. Score a minor triumph for the social scientists!

The defense team next sought to discover what background characteristics were related to potential jurors' biases toward the conviction or acquittal of the defendants. They interviewed 252 people from the Harrisburg area to find out whether such qualities as age, religion, gender, and level of education were related to attitudes such as trust in the government and tolerance for protest by dissidents. Counter to their expectations, the social scientists found that people with more education and exposure to metropolitan news media were more conservative politically and more sympathetic to the prosecution. But as expected, members of the Democratic party tended to side with the defense. In summary, the social scientists concluded that their ideal juror would be a female Democrat with no religious preferences who held a white-collar job or a skilled laborer position. Guided by these survey results, the defense sought such jurors.

The task was not easy. There were few such people in the jury panel. But in a sense, the defense

team was successful. The trial ended with a hung jury, split 10–2 with the majority favoring a verdict of not guilty. The U.S. government decided not to hold a second trial. All the charges were dropped. Yet, at another level, the social scientists were completely off base in their selection of two of the jurors—the two who became holdouts for the guilt of the defendants. One of these jurors, a Lutheran man in his 50s who owned two grocery stores, had expressed vaguely antiwar attitudes during jury selection. But as soon as the deliberations began, it became clear that his true feelings were far from peace loving. The other, a 68-year-old woman, belonged to a pacifist church; four of her sons were conscientious objectors to wars on religious grounds. The defense team accepted her immediately on hearing that. But in the deliberations, she showed that she did not share her sons' feelings. In their ratings of prospective jurors, the defense had given rather positive evaluations to both of these people—more positive than for some of the other jurors they had to take.

basis in the successful murder conviction of Byron de la Beckwith, who had killed civil rights leader Medgar Evers 30 years earlier.

The national media devoted extensive coverage to the use of jury consultants in the celebrity-status trials involving O. J. Simpson, the Exxon *Valdez,* and the Menendez brothers. Critics have

labeled these techniques "jury rigging" and jury manipulation (Etzioni, 1974a, 1974b), have pondered whether forecasting jury behavior is really a "science" (Abramson, 1994), and have argued that there are few, if any, convincing demonstrations that scientific jury selection is more effective than routine jury selection (e.g., Fulero & Penrod, 1990;

Saks, 1987). Public concern about jury consulting services has led to legislative proposals in some states that would, if adopted, restrict the use of such consultants by trial attorneys.

For their part, jury consultants usually offer two justifications for these methods. First, they suggest that they are simply borrowing techniques commonly used in the world of politics and bringing them into the courtroom. Politicians hire people to help them project a better image so why shouldn't a lawyer do the same thing? They also argue that because litigation is a complex and traumatic experience (even for seasoned trial lawyers), attorneys should be able to use every tool available to them. Consultants argue that they serve as one of the tools.

A footnote on psychologists' relationship to the law: Students often wonder how they can become involved in this field as basic scientists, applied scientists, policy evaluators, or advocates. What career paths should one pursue, and what professional opportunities exist at the ends of those trails? To address these questions, the American Psychology-Law Society has published a manual entitled *Careers and Training in Psychology and Law*. It can be accessed from the society's Web page (www.unl.edu/ap-ls/).

# Ethical Considerations in Each Role

Whatever role a psychologist chooses, it carries standards about what is acceptable and unacceptable behavior. Indeed, every day we all face choices about what is right and wrong. (Chapter 3 reviews some of the factors we consider in these decisions.) Professional people often develop explicit statements of ethical standards of behavior for their professions. For psychologists in general, the American Psychological Association (APA) (1992) has published a statement entitled "Ethical Principles of Psychologists and Code of Conduct." Members who violate any of these ethical principles are subject to censure and may be expelled from the organization. The ethics code is subject

to constant review, and a new draft is anticipated to be ready for discussion and approval in 2002.

But making the right choice is complicated by the fact that the principles specified by the ethics code may conflict with the psychologist's legal responsibilities. The most explicit illustration of this dilemma is the ethical obligation of confidentiality versus the legal duty to warn potential victims of clients' threats. This conflict was most apparent in the *Tarasoff* decision by the Supreme Court of California, described in ◆ Box 2-4.

Furthermore, each of the psychological roles that serve as the framework for this chapter carries somewhat different ethical obligations, as described in the following sections. In keeping with this diversification, Division 41 (American Psychology-Law Society) of APA developed a set of guidelines for forensic psychologists. These "Specialty Guidelines for Forensic Psychologists," published and approved by the division's membership in 1991, provide "specific guidance to forensic psychologists in monitoring their professional conduct when acting in assistance to courts, parties to legal proceedings, correctional and forensic mental health facilities, and legislative agencies" (Committee on Ethical Guidelines for Forensic Psychologists, 1991). The guidelines amplify the "Ethical Principles of Psychologists" in several areas of forensic practice such as confidentiality, methods of evaluations and reports, and relationships between the psychologist and the contending parties in litigation.

## The Ethics of the Basic Scientist

The APA's "Ethical Principles of Psychologists" provides only an overview of the responsibilities of the basic researcher. Procedures for experimentation with human subjects dictate that the subjects be informed of the risks in participating and that their consent be obtained. When using animals as subjects, experimenters are expected to abide by strict ethical standards; for example, they are to avoid inducing pain or injury unless there is no other way for the research question to be studied. But this prohibition is not sufficient for some supporters of animal rights, who have ques-

## THE CASE OF

### Tanya Tarasoff: The duty to protect

Few legal decisions have had as much impact on the practice of psychotherapy as the now-famous case of *Tarasoff v. Regents of the University of California*. Although there has been much speculation about the personalities of the case's two central figures—Prosenjit Poddar and Tatiana Tarasoff—the decision focuses on the duties required of psychotherapists.

Here are the facts of the case. Prosenjit Poddar was a graduate student in naval engineering at the University of California who became infatuated with Tatiana Tarasoff. Poddar was inexperienced in romantic relationships and was confused about Tatiana's on-and-off again behavior—she was friendly toward him one day but avoided him completely the next night. After Poddar went to the university counseling center and became a client of psychologist Lawrence Moore, he confided to Moore that he intended to kill a girl who had rebuffed him. Moore told his supervisor Dr. Harvey Powelson of this threat and then called the campus police, requesting that they detain Poddar. They did so but soon released him after believing his promise that he would stay away from Tatiana, who was out of the country at the time. Poddar didn't keep his promise; two months later, he went to Tatiana's home and stabbed her to death. He was eventually convicted of murder.

Tatiana's parents sued the university, the psychologists, and the campus police. After a lower court found for the university, the parents appealed to the California Supreme Court, which ruled in the parents' favor by deciding that the university had been negligent. The court established a standard that therapists have a duty to use "reasonable care" to protect identifiable, potential victims from clients in psychotherapy who threaten violence. After the *Tarasoff* decision in 1976, courts in several other states extended this duty to the protection of property and the protection of all foreseeable victims, not just identifiable ones.

---

tioned the use of animals by experimental psychologists (Beauchamp, 1997).

Basic researchers also must follow standards of objectivity in collecting and analyzing data and in writing up their results for publication. Their procedures need to be described thoroughly in their publications so that other scholars can repeat their procedures and check the findings. Any material they publish should be their own work, of course. However, despite these rules, examples of plagiarism and falsification of data still periodically appear in psychology, as well as in other sciences (Hostetler, 1988).

### The Ethics of the Applied Scientist/ Expert Witness

The psychologist as expert witness represents a profession that stands for objectivity and accuracy in its procedures. Even though expert witnesses are usually hired (and paid) by one side, they are responsible for reporting all their conclusions, whether these favor the side paying them or not. Furthermore, it violates the ethical standards of both psychologists and lawyers for expert witnesses to accept payment that is contingent on the outcome of the case.

But achieving objectivity is by no means easy. From the jury's perspective, the psychologist is often perceived as an advocate rather than as an unbiased scientist (Horgan, 1988). Regardless of this perception, a psychologist, when asked to testify, has an ethical requirement to be candid and explicit with the court about his or her opinions. Still, psychologists may be tempted to sympathize with the side that has employed them. This sympathy may not even be conscious; instead, the psychologist may simply filter the facts

## THE CASE OF

**BOX 2-5    Thomas Barefoot: Ethical expert testimony?**

The jury that convicted Thomas Barefoot and imposed the death penalty had heard testimony from a Dallas psychiatrist, Dr. James Grigson, that the defendant had a "100 percent and absolute" chance of committing future violent acts and that he would be a continuing threat to society (Work, 1985, p. 65). The psychiatrist had never examined Thomas Barefoot; in fact, he testified in response to a set of questions about a hypothetical per-son who shared Barefoot's attributes and criminal history (Ewing, 1991).

By 1989, Grigson had testified in more than 120 capital murder cases in Texas (Rosenbaum, 1990). In this state—unlike most others that permit the death penalty—the jury may recommend capital punishment only if it concludes that it is probable that the defendant will commit further acts of violence and will be a continuing threat to society. Grigson characteristically testified that the offender is dangerous, regardless of whether he actually has examined the person; in all but nine of the trials in which he has testified, the defendant was sentenced to death (Belkin, 1988).

When the decision to sentence Barefoot to death was appealed, the American Psychiatric Association strenuously objected to the admissibility of testimony by a psychiatrist who had not personally examined the defendant, especially to the prediction about his future dangerousness. But the U.S. Supreme Court upheld both the decision and the admissibility of the psychiatrist's testimony—though not without dissent from Justice Harry Blackmun, who wrote, "The specious testimony of a psychiatrist, colored in the eyes of an impressionable jury by the inevitable untouchability of a medical specialist's words, equates with death itself" (minority opinion in *Barefoot v. Estelle*, quoted in Work, 1985, p. 65). Echoing Blackmun's sentiments, the American Psychiatric Association has since expelled Grigson.

of the case through perceptions motivated by a spirit of helpfulness to his or her client.

Some experts provide testimony that is ethically questionable because of the methods they use in arriving at their conclusions. One example (described in ◆ Box 2-5) stems from the case of Thomas Andy Barefoot, a convicted murderer of a police officer, who was ultimately executed by lethal injection in a Texas prison (*Barefoot v. Estelle*, 1983).

Another ethical dilemma arises whenever the adversary system forces an expert to make absolute "either-or" judgments. Has the pretrial publicity caused potential jurors to be biased against the defendant? Which parent would be better for the child in a custody case stemming from a divorce? Is a warning label on a product or device understandable and effective? Does the evaluation of a defendant indicate she is insane? In all of these situations, the law requires the psychologist to reach a firm conclusion on the witness stand, regardless of ambiguity in the evidence (Sales & Shuman, 1993).

When psychologists are allowed to testify about the accuracy of eyewitnesses, yet another ethical question arises. Do they really have anything to say that is accurate, precise, and relevant to that particular witness? Is their testimony really beyond the common understanding and experience of the average juror? Psychologists differ in their responses to such questions. The vast majority of research psychologists who possess expertise about the relative accuracy of eyewitnesses believe that jurors' decisions can be aided by access to this information and consider the topic a legitimate one for their testimony (Kassin, Ellsworth, & Smith, 1989, 1994). But a few psychologists (e.g., Egeth, 1995; Elliott, 1993) have argued that the scientific basis for expert testimony on eyewitness memory is generally inadequate and that psychologists should not be "giving testimony that has a high likelihood of being blown away by the next empirical breeze" (Elliott, 1993, p. 432).

Margaret Hagen (1997) has captured many of these concerns in her provocative book *Whores of the Court: The Fraud of Psychiatric Testimony and the Rape of American Justice.* The "whores" to whom Hagen refers are clinical forensic psychologists who, in the process of testifying as experts, "shoot off their mouths" and fill courtrooms with "psychobabble" about the insanity defense, battered woman syndrome, the effects of trauma on memory, and other mental health issues that arise in the law. Hagen's chief complaint is that clinical experts rely too heavily on intuition and too loosely on science. For example, she lashes out at arrogant "hired guns" who testify in child custody battles between warring parents. Asserting that there are no scientific standards by which to determine the attributes of the better parent, Hagen writes, "Tests useful for determining which parent should have custody of a child are not worth a hill of beans" (p. 217). Although Hagen occasionally—perhaps even frequently—overstates her case (Kassin, 1998a), her caustic remarks should cause psychologists to scrutinize more carefully the scientific underpinnings of their testimony. In the end, such professional self-scrutiny should improve forensic psychologists' courtroom contributions.

## The Ethics of the Policy Evaluator

The psychologist who evaluates court reforms and other changes in the law enforcement system faces ethical responsibilities similar to those of the expert witness. The standard canons of scientific procedure apply, but again, because of the source of payment, pressures exist to interpret results in a certain way.

Consider, for example, a large state prison that wants to improve its parole system. Prison officials have identified a problem with convicts eligible for parole who are heavy drug users. If released into society, they are likely to commit further

crimes to maintain their drug habit. Hence, they will soon return to prison. So the prison seeks to introduce and evaluate an innovative halfway house program for those parolees with a history of narcotics addiction. It hires a policy evaluator to design a study and evaluate the effects of this innovation. The prison provides money to carry out the study, and prison officials are sincerely committed to its goals. Assume the psychologist concludes that the halfway house does not significantly reduce drug use by parolees. The authorities are disappointed; they may even attack the integrity of the policy evaluator. Yet, as scientists, program evaluators must "call 'em like they see 'em," regardless of the desirability of the outcome.

Even if the program is successful, the policy evaluator faces other ethical dilemmas. To assess such an innovative program, the researcher might have to deny some parolees access to the program and place them in a "status quo" control group. The ethical dilemma becomes more critical when some potentially lifesaving innovation is being evaluated. But often it is only through such research methods that a potentially helpful new program can be convincingly proven to be effective.

Policy evaluators who study the criminal justice system also need to be aware of the potential narrowness of their viewpoint and its effect on their conclusions. Faced with the fact that almost two-thirds of ex-prisoners are rearrested within three years of their prison release (Lacayo, 1989), the psychologist is tempted to blame the individual ex-convict as the cause of the problem, even though variables more appropriate to sociological or economic perspectives—community orientation, unemployment rates, "secondary deviance" (see Chapter 5)—are equally applicable.

## The Ethics of the Advocate

As we noted earlier, when the psychologist becomes an advocate for one side in the selection of jurors, ethical problems emerge. Just how far should the selection procedures go? Should jurors have to answer consultants' intrusive questions

## The Science of

**BOX 2-6**    **Focus group research: Changing the game by changing the odds**

Marty Cohen, an Allentown, Pennsylvania, personal injury lawyer, was representing a teenage boy who had been hit by a car; the boy's injuries were extensive—he had suffered brain damage and lost control over his emotions (Adler, 1994). His medical bills amounted to almost $150,000, and appropriate treatment and care for the rest of his life would add more than $3 million. But the driver of the car had insurance that would pay only $100,000 in damages. Furthermore, it was a weak case for the plaintiff: The accident occurred 20 minutes after sunset; it was a dangerous intersection; and the boy didn't have a light on his bicycle, a violation of the law.

Marty Cohen decided to contact a trial consultant he had used in several previous cases. Arthur Patterson, a psychologist and formerly a professor at Pennsylvania State University, had established a rapidly expanding trial consulting business.

Patterson arranged for a focus group to listen to a presentation of the case and act as a jury. These mock jurors' reactions would have no bearing on a trial outcome, of course, but they might influence the attorney and the psychologist on how to proceed. Of relevance here was that the driver was drunk, but where had she been drinking? Cohen claimed that she had been drinking at a local Pizza Hut, but

"there wasn't a single witness who could even place the woman at the Pizza Hut that day, let alone prove she'd been drinking there" (Adler, 1994, p. 85). (Immediately after the accident, the defendant said she was drinking with someone at the restaurant, but she couldn't or wouldn't identify who it was, leading the lawyer to suspect that she was shielding someone's identity.)

After the focus group heard the presentation, each participant gave his or her assessment of liability. The majority felt that the driver was negligent, but only 1 of the 12 felt that Pizza Hut was partially liable. In fact, these mock jurors "were angry at the suggestion that

about their private lives? Should their private lives be investigated? Should consultants be able to sculpt the jury to their client's advantage? Do these techniques simply constitute the latest tools in the attorney's arsenal of trial tactics? Or, instead, do they bias the proceedings and jeopardize the willingness of citizens to participate in the process?

All of these questions deal with fairness. Can there be fairness and impartiality in an adversarial system? Systematic jury selection may illustrate a situation in which social scientists and lawyers, in concert, are in conflict with the way most people interpret the intent of the law.

The American Society of Trial Consultants is in the process of defining ethical guidelines for its members. Among the recommendations are these (Gordon, 1995):

◆   A trial consultant must possess both a thorough knowledge of the legal system and expertise in the research methodologies used in behavioral sciences.

◆   Trial consultants must respect the courts, their procedures, and their mandates.

◆   The privacy and sensibilities of jurors and prospective jurors must be respected.

◆   Trial consultants must strive to ensure that the testimony of witnesses is truthful and accurate.

◆   Trial consultants shall accurately and truthfully present their credentials to the bar and the judiciary.

When psychologists become advocates as trial consultants, they also subscribe to the ethi-

Pizza Hut and [its conglomerate entity] PepsiCo might be saddled with liability just because they had deep pockets" (Adler, 1994, p. 96). It seemed likely that, at best, Cohen's client would be awarded $100,000 by the actual jury.

But the trial consultant devised an alternative opening statement for the plaintiff, attempting to shift the blame to the restaurant. The proposed alternative suggested that "Pizza Hut had done wrong by not teaching its servers how to detect drunkenness, and it had done wrong out of greed" (Adler, 1994, p. 98). It noted that a set of manuals for Pizza Hut employees covered almost every topic except discouraging heavy drinkers.

Furthermore, on the advice of Patterson, the young man's attorney changed the portrayal of the defendant from someone whose recklessness was due to her drinking to "a nice woman who had been having some temporary marital difficulties and may have been talking out her problems with a friend over a very long lunch" (Adler, 1994, p. 100).

At the actual jury trial, a mistrial was declared because of an error made by an attorney in the opening statements. Before a second trial could begin, Pizza Hut offered a settlement of $350,000, along with the defendant's insurance of $100,000. The $450,000 total was, in the view of the plain-

tiff's attorneys, more than what the case was worth, so they settled.

In the words of Stephen J. Adler (1994), a journalist to whom Patterson and Cohen granted access to their preparations, "Art Patterson's behind-the-scenes advice to Cohen had proved crucial in forcing Pizza Hut's hand. Thanks to Patterson's work, the plaintiff's lawyers had discovered that their original approach to the case had bombed before a focus group" (p. 113).

---

cal code of the attorneys, who, after all, are in charge of the trial preparation. The "Ethics Code of the American Bar Association" admonishes its members to defend their clients to the best of their abilities, short of lying or encouraging lying. Every litigant—whether a defendant or a plaintiff—regardless of the heinousness of the crime or the mass of evidence presented, is entitled to the best legal representation possible, including the use of psychological techniques to assess the relative favorability of prospective jurors. (The prosecution is entitled to the same opportunities to employ psychological knowledge, but prosecutors rarely use psychologists to assist them in selecting juries.) But how far can and should a psychologist go in structuring the nature of the case? The case against Pizza Hut,

summarized in ◆ Box 2-6, provides a dramatic example.

Are psychologists who work for an advertising agency unethical when they use professional knowledge to encourage consumers to buy one brand of dog food rather than another? Many of us would say no; the free enterprise system permits any such procedures that do not falsify claims. Is this example analogous to jury selection? Probably, especially given that rival attorneys—whether they employ jury consultants or not—always try to select jurors who will sympathize with their version of the facts. The adversarial system rests on the expectation that each side will eliminate those jurors most favorable to the other side, thus resulting in an unbiased jury. As long as the adversarial system permits attorneys from each side to eliminate some prospective jurors without giving reasons, it does not seem unethical for psychologists to assist them, as long as their advocacy is consistent with the law and the administration of justice.

## SUMMARY

**1. What are four roles that psychologists may play in the legal system?** Although empirical in their orientation, psychologists face choices when deciding what role they will play in studying the law or working in the legal system. Four possible roles are identified in this chapter: the psychologist as (1) basic scientist, (2) applied scientist, (3) policy evaluator, and (4) advocate.

**2. What are the motivations of basic scientists; how are their findings relevant?** Basic scientists are interested in knowledge for its own sake; they do not seek to apply their findings to the solution of practical problems. Yet many basic research findings are relevant to practical problems—for example, findings on how memory works, on why eyewitnesses to crimes may be inaccurate, or on how attitudes relate to behavior.

**3. What is the relationship of the psychologist as applied scientist to the legal system?** In the applied scientist role, the psychologist may apply basic research knowledge to a particular problem in response to requests from personnel working in the legal system.

**4. How does being an expert witness reflect the consultant role?** Psychologists who serve as expert witnesses—for example, in child custody disputes or trials involving the insanity plea—exemplify the consultant role. They supply needed information and opinions; their contact with the legal system is initiated by others such as judges, law enforcement officials, prison wardens, and defense attorneys.

**5. What does a policy evaluator do?** As a policy evaluator, the psychologist capitalizes on methodological skills. Policy evaluators design and conduct surveys and experiments so that innovators can learn what effects their innovations have had.

**6. The role of advocate is the most controversial. Why?** The fourth role, the advocate, is the most controversial because the advocate supports and represents segments of the community that seek greater power and influence. This role contains both a research function and a political function. Within the field of law, a psychologist who helps a team of defense attorneys select a jury sympathetic to the defendant is acting as an advocate. Similar problems of ethics are associated with each role, but to some extent, the ethical dilemmas for each are different.

## KEY TERMS

| | | | |
|---|---|---|---|
| advocate | correlation | hypothesis | replication |
| applied scientist | empowerment | operational definition | sampling |
| basic scientist | experiment | policy evaluator | scientific method |
| confounding variables | hate crimes* | quasi-experiment | theory |

---

**InfoTrac COLLEGE EDITION** • For additional readings go to **http://www.infotrac-college.com/wadsworth** and enter a search term related to your interest. The key term that has been asterisked above will pull up several related articles.

## ORIENTING QUESTIONS

1. *Is what society considers moral always the same as what it considers legal?*
2. *What are some theories that explain differing standards for what is right and wrong?*
3. *How does Kohlberg's theory of moral judgment differ from Gilligan's?*
4. *What is the relationship of justice to equity and equality?*
5. *What is commonsense justice?*
6. *Why does the "just world" develop as an explanation for events?*

What would you have done if you had been a juror deciding the fate of Lester Zygmanik? Here's the dilemma: Lester was charged with murdering his own brother, George, but only because George had demanded that he do it. A motorcycle accident a few days earlier had left George, age 26, paralyzed from the neck down. He saw a future with nothing but pain, suffering, and invalidism; as he lay in agony, he insisted that his younger brother Lester, age 23, swear he would not let him continue in such a desperate state. "I want you to promise to kill me; I want you to swear to God," George said. (Other family members later verified that this had, in truth, been George's wish.) So, on the night of June 20, 1973, Lester slipped into his brother's hospital room and shot him in the head with a 20-gauge shotgun. Dropping the gun by the bed, he turned himself in moments later. There was no question about the cause of death; later, on the witness stand during his murder trial, Lester told the jury that he had done it as an act of love for his brother. (The book recounting this case, by Paige Mitchell [1976], is also titled *Act of Love*.) Because New Jersey had no laws regarding mercy killing, the prosecution thought a case could be made for charging Lester with first-degree murder. And in New Jersey at that time, such a conviction would require that Lester be sentenced to life in prison.

The state believed it had a good case against Lester. His actions met every one of the elements that the law required for his guilt to be proved. There was, first of all, premeditation, or a plan to kill; there was deliberation (as defined in the New Jersey criminal code, "the weighing of the 'pros' and 'cons' of that plan, which weighing only need take a few seconds"); and there was willfulness ("the intentional carrying out of that plan"). Lester had even sawed off the shotgun before hiding it under his coat, and he had packed the bullets with candle wax, which compacted the explosion and made it more deadly. Lester forthrightly admitted to his lawyer:

I gave it a lot of thought. You don't know how much thinking I did on it. I had to do something

I knew that would definitely put him away. And the only thing I knew that would definitely do that would be a gun. . . . I wanted to make sure this was done fast and quick. I knew, I felt . . . I'd have one chance to do this. I gave it a lot of thought. You understand? I wanted to make sure he would definitely die. (Mitchell, 1976, p. vii)

At his trial, Lester took the stand and described his motivations. He did not fall back on the insanity plea; he simply explained that he did what his brother wanted.

If you had been a juror in this trial, how would you have voted? College students usually split just about evenly between verdicts of "guilty of first-degree murder" and "not guilty." Those who vote guilty often hope that the sentence will be seen as a humanitarian one, but they believe it is their duty to consider the evidence and apply the law. Certainly, this was an act of murder, they say, regardless of Lester's good intentions. But those who vote not guilty often feel that it is appropriate, on occasion, to disregard the law when mitigating circumstances are present or when community standards argue for forgiveness. Both reactions are reasonable, and they illustrate the dilemma between treating similar defendants equally and showing discretion if circumstances warrant. Jurors in such cases are also faced with another of the conflicts we posed in Chapter 1—responding to society's needs for protection against offenders while at the same time preserving the rights of individuals. A similar challenge faces jurors in trials of physicians such as Dr. Jack Kevorkian who have assisted patients seeking to die (see ◆ Box 3-1).

As Lester Zygmanik's trial began, the prosecutor was confident that he would be found guilty. The jury, composed of seven men and five women, was tough, conservative, blue-collar; all jurors were over age 30. And the judge had even ruled that the term *mercy killing* could not be used in the trial.

But after deliberating for fewer than three hours, the jury found Lester Zygmanik not guilty. The jurors focused, apparently, on the relationship between Lester and his brother, and they con-

## THE CASE OF

### BOX 3-1  Jack Kevorkian: Physician-assisted suicide

Dr. Jack Kevorkian has assisted more than 100 persons to commit suicide, many through the use of the Thanatron, a machine he invented to dispense lethal drugs to his "patients." Although 35 states have laws banning assisted suicide, a 1997 Gallup poll showed that 75% of Americans favor allowing doctors to end the lives of the terminally ill. Perhaps this is why on several different occasions when Kevorkian had been charged with aiding a suicide, a jury refused to convict him. Ultimately, however, public tolerance for his campaign ran out, and in April 1999, he was convicted of second-degree murder in connection with the assisted death of Thomas Youk. A Michigan judge then sentenced Kevor-

kian to 10 to 25 years in prison. Obviously, consensus on this issue is far from clear: voters in Oregon passed a referendum approving doctor-assisted suicide in 1994 (and reaffirmed that position in 1997), but California and Washington voters have rejected similar proposals. In addition, although the Supreme Court issued dual, unanimous decisions in 1997 denying the right to physician-assisted suicide, the court rulings did not preclude states from voting to allow assisted suicide. In fact, Chief Justice William Rehnquist, who wrote the majority opinion in both cases (*Vacco v. Quill*, 1997; *Washington v. Glucksberg*, 1997), urged the debate to continue, "as it should in a democratic society."

JACK KEVORKIAN
*When an individual faces a painful and terminal illness, does he or she have the right to choose suicide over continued suffering? The case of Dr. Jack Kevorkian and his "suicide machine" has forced the public to debate such questions.*

cluded that Lester had been overcome by grief, love, and selflessness. Their decision implicitly acknowledged that moral considerations such as the commitment to care for others were more important to their decision than following the strict guidelines of the law. Perhaps, too, they felt that a prerequisite of a crime, not mentioned in the law, is the lack of consent by the victim. Lester testified that on the night of the killing, "I asked him if he was in pain. At this time he couldn't speak at all. He just nodded that he was. He nodded yes. So, I says, 'I am here to end your pain—is that all right with you?' And he nodded yes. And the next thing I knew, I shot him" (Mitchell, 1976, p. 195).

The criminal justice system of the United States contains no provision for such mitigating

circumstances. In contrast, Belgium, France, Germany, and the Netherlands have laws that recognize "compassionate" or "altruistic" motives as mitigation for **mercy killings.** In several other countries, a request to be put to death by a victim also constitutes an extenuating circumstance, and often no penalty is provided. Since the case was in the United States, however, Lester technically broke the law.

The Lester Zygmanik trial is not the only one in which the defendant claimed his act was a mercy killing, as Box 3-1 indicates. Other cases involving mercy killings and assisted suicides illustrate the often-tragic differences between what an individual feels is the morally right thing to do and what the law dictates is the legally proscribed act to avoid. Another dramatic demonstration of these differences is the case of Richard and Elaine McIlroy.

From the exterior, the Delray Beach, Florida, home of Elaine and Richard McIlroy looked anything but somber. It was the day before Christmas 1997, and the holiday lights were sparkling brightly. Inside, it was a different story. Richard McIlroy, 75, who was terminally ill with leukemia, had been planning his suicide with the assistance of his wife and a controversial book entitled *Final Exit,* a step-by-step guide to painless suicide. That morning, Elaine McIlroy opened about 50 capsules of the barbituate Seconal and sprinkled it over her husband's ice cream. They climbed into bed together and waited for the fatal dose to take effect. Within two hours, Richard McIlroy was dead.

With this act, the McIlroys thrust the Palm Beach County District Attorney's Office into the forefront of a national debate over assisted suicide. ("Assisting in self-murder," defined as the act of helping someone end their life, has been banned in Florida since 1863). Assisted suicide and **euthanasia** (defined as an act of killing an individual for reasons that are considered merciful) have generated passionate ethical, legal, and moral debate. At the heart of the controversy are questions about whether we have a right to die and whether doctors and loved ones should be able to take part in our deaths.

In most states, helping someone commit suicide is a crime. Yet many are loath to call the perpetrators of these acts "criminals," and proponents of assisted suicide often hail them as heroes. Should someone who voluntarily, willfully, and with premeditation assists in killing another human being *always* be punished, or should that person, in some circumstances, be treated with compassion and forgiveness?

Obviously, the circumstances of individual cases dictate our answer. Many people can imagine exceptional circumstances in which people who have technically broken the law should be exonerated. (Consider the McIlroys, for example. By legal standards, the actions of Elaine McIlroy constituted first-degree murder: she acted with premeditation and deliberation. Yet her actions can also be viewed as those of a loving and devoted wife, desiring to help her terminally ill husband end his pain and suffering.) The topic of assisted suicide highlights the inconsistency between legality and people's perceptions of what is moral, ethical, and just.

# Legality versus Morality

Legality and morality are not always the same. On first thought, we might assume that what is defined as "legal" and what is judged to be "morally right" would be synonymous with each other. But in the Zygmanik and Kevorkian examples, the jury concluded that what they considered as a morally right action and what the system required as the proper legal resolution were inconsistent. Legislatures and scholars have argued for centuries whether the law should be consistent with morality. For example, prostitution is universally condemned as immoral, yet it is legal in parts of Nevada and in some European countries. Acts of civil disobedience, whether in racially segregated buses in Montgomery, Alabama, four decades ago or on college campuses today, are applauded by those who consider some laws to be ethically indefensible. Further examples in the following paragraphs illustrate how the legal system struggles over this issue.

# Good Samaritan and Duty to Assist Laws

You are sitting on the edge of a pier, eating a sandwich and watching the sunset, when the fisherman next to you leans forward and tumbles into the ocean. As he thrashes around, he shouts to you, "Help me—I can't swim! Throw me a life preserver!" Although there is a life preserver only five feet away, you make no effort to throw it to him, even though you could do so with absolutely no danger to yourself and only the most minimal ef-

*Princess Diana's death in a fatal car crash in a Parisian tunnel led to much debate about whether the paparazzi on the scene should have been criminally charged for not offering aid to her and the other victims.*

fort. Instead, you sit placidly watching the sun go down, while you munch on your sandwich.

Have you committed any crime by failing to respond? No, wrote the late John Kaplan (1972), a law professor at Stanford University: "Under the law of essentially every Anglo-American jurisdiction you are guilty of no tort (that is, a wrongful act) making you civilly liable to the family of the fisherman you permitted to drown, nor would you be criminally liable in any way for his death" (p. 219).

However, in any number of European countries, this kind of indifference to a victim could result in prosecution. In these countries, the failure to take steps to help an innocent victim can be treated as a criminal act. This tradition was revealed most dramatically in the debate over whether to prosecute the paparazzi who, instead of aiding Princess Diana and others in their fatal car crash in a Parisian tunnel, did nothing but snap photos

of the victims inside the car. In the United States, so-called **good Samaritan laws** have been passed by all states in one form or the other (California was the first to do so in 1959). These laws encourage altruism indirectly by providing immunity from civil lawsuits to passersby who render assistance to victims. For example, Virginia has a fairly broad law that gives immunity to any person who, in good faith and without compensation, renders emergency care or assistance to injured persons at an accident, fire, or other life-threatening emergency. Other states concentrate their good Samaritan immunity on physicians and other health care personnel, but the fundamental goal still applies: to encourage help by private citizens who might be reluctant to volunteer assistance to someone in need because of a concern that they will be sued if their intervention fails to rescue the victim.

A few states, led by Minnesota and Wisconsin, have passed **duty to assist laws,** which are more in line with the European tradition of criminalizing failure to assist victims who are in obvious peril. These laws impose criminal penalties on individuals who see a crime being committed and fail to report it, call for help, or give some type of assistance to the victim (see ◆ **Box 3-2**). They are based on the principle that reckless indifference or willful blindness to the plight of victims is a serious enough threat to society that it deserves to be punished.

Why has the civil and criminal law in the United States not been very concerned about those good acts that we fail to do? Kaplan offers several answers.

The first is the principle of individualism, or the right to be left alone. The law, at least in the United States, does not require you to be "your brother's keeper." As noted in Chapter 1's discussion of the conflict between personal rights and society's needs, a predominant value in our society is individualism, or the right to "do your own thing." Kaplan (1972) concludes that the law "regards the fisherman's falling into the water as an imposition upon the freedom of those around him and asks why should the law permit the fisherman, merely by being careless, to impose legal du-

## THE CASE OF

**BOX 3-2**    **David Cash: Can we legislate the obligation to help?**

In Nevada, duty to assist legislation was introduced after a much-publicized case, including coverage on *60 Minutes,* led to disgust and outrage over the lack of assistance that a college student showed during a young girl's murder. The incident occurred in a casino in Primm, Nevada. Taking time out from a night of gambling, a 19-year-old college student, named Jeremy Strohmeyer, spotted a 7-year-old girl, whom he abducted, sexually molested, and then strangled in a casino rest room. It was later learned that another college student, David Cash, who was Strohmeyer's companion for the evening, knew what was taking place in the rest room but did absolutely nothing to stop the murder or even report it to officials. As a result, a Nevada legislator introduced a bill that would have re-quired bystanders to come to the aid of crime victims. However, the Nevada legislature was unwilling to go that far. Instead, it passed a reporting statute that requires an individual who knows about a sexual offense against a child age 12 or under to report the matter to law enforcement officials within 24 hours. A willful violation of this duty to report is a misdemeanor.

ties on others and to interfere with their freedom to behave as they wish as long as they do not harm anyone?" (p. 220). The European tradition is different; it places greater emphasis on the social obligations individuals have to one another and therefore takes the more direct approach of requiring persons to give assistance. The same interest in social solidarity that permits altruistic motives to mitigate guilt in mercy killings in many European countries makes the failure to behave altruistically in emergencies a possible criminal offense.

The second issue is the principle of "Why me?" Imagine that, instead of sitting on the pier alone, you were one of 200 other people perched there and no one helped. If there were a legal duty to aid, all the bystanders would be liable. Who, then, would be prosecuted? The district attorney could not possibly prosecute all 200, so he or she would pick a few. "Why me?" those few might ask, and a jury would probably be inclined to agree. Although the government occasionally picks a few violators to prosecute in order to bring public attention to a matter, no standard exists in this situation for just which bystanders the prosecutor should pick.

What if the fisherman had been your son, who is a minor in the eyes of the law? Or what if the fisherman had been on a boat for which you were the captain? Now we have a different case. In both these examples, you would have been legally liable because you had a special relationship to the victim that imposed a duty on you to look out for the victim's well-being.

And what if you had tried to save the fisherman but had thrown the life preserver so clumsily that it landed far away from him and he drowned struggling to reach it? The courts usually impose some liability when an argument can be made that a bungled attempt to help ended up putting a victim in a worse predicament than before you made the attempt. This is especially true if your act prevented others from providing competent help—if, for example, you squandered the only life preserver available. Hence, the legal system gives another justification for the ethically questionable position of doing nothing.

### The Hiker in Danger

Consider another example: You are sitting beside the road, and you see a car recklessly bearing down on a hiker. It is too noisy for a shout to be heard, so all you can do is push the hiker out of the path of the car. But in doing so, you are struck by the car and injured. Is the driver liable? Can you sue successfully? In earlier times, the legal system said no, you can't sue, inasmuch as you risked your life without being required to do so. The rescue attempt was solely your responsibility, and you therefore could not collect for your injury from the driver.

Of course, this interpretation of the law does not encourage moral behavior. Hence, modern law has changed so as to promote the helper's rights. In fact, such a shift appears to be one of those rare ones that, in terms of the conflict posed in Chapter 1, aids society's needs for protection while also substantiating individual rights. What has emerged is a principle that "danger invites rescue": thus, "the driver's act of endangering the hiker was also a threat to those around him who might attempt to rescue the hiker" (Kaplan, 1972, p. 225).

## The Concept of Intention in Law and Psychology

A fundamental question of criminal law is, When are people responsible for the consequences of their own actions? Is a person who gets drunk in an apartment, passes out with a lighted cigarette in hand, and sets the building on fire responsible for killing residents in another apartment who perish in the resulting conflagration? For a jury to conclude that a defendant is guilty of certain crimes, the element of **intention** has to be proved. But the law and psychology differ in how they define intention; here we see a manifestation of the fourth dilemma posed in Chapter 1: science versus the law as a source of decisions.

The law sees intention as committing an act deliberately, willfully, and knowingly, as distinguished from committing an act by mistake, by accident, by negligence, or by carelessness. Intentional acts must be voluntary; an act committed under external compulsion is not considered to be intentional.

However, certain qualifications in this definition can confuse the interpretations of "intention." For example, if you yank another person in front of you to act as a human shield when someone is shooting at you, and the "shield" dies, you can be charged with murder. But it is not a crime to duck behind the other person, even if doing so causes the shooter to fire in that person's direction (Katz, 1996). On the other hand, if an armed robber intends only to rob a liquor store but his gun goes off accidentally and he kills the clerk, he can be charged with felony murder in some states, even though he did not intend to kill the victim. In fact, in some states, the robber could be sentenced to death if convicted of the murder. Furthermore, the law does not relieve law violators of responsibility if their behavior is psychologically compulsive or results from a self-induced state, such as intoxication.

Jurors have difficulty, at times, applying these concepts to specific cases. Joel B. Steinberg was tried in New York City for the second-degree murder of his adopted daughter, Lisa. But instead, the jury found him guilty only of first-degree manslaughter. Even though he had beaten Lisa repeatedly, several jurors—aware that he had used cocaine for days—were not convinced that his drug-dulled mind could reflect the "reckless indifference" for another person's life that is an element of second-degree murder in New York State (Glaberson, 1989). Was Steinberg so intoxicated as to partially excuse his conduct? Apparently the jury thought so, even though under the law being drunk does not excuse reckless behavior.

The relative importance of a person's intention versus the ultimate outcome of his or her behavior creates problems for the law. Psychologist Norman Finkel and his colleagues have carefully studied situations in which a person's evil intentions become disconnected from a harmful outcome. In these **impossible act** cases, an individual *intends* to commit a criminal act, but through an accident of fate, no objectively harmful act occurs (Finkel & Groscup, 1997; Finkel, Maloney, Valbuena, & Groscup, 1995). Here is an example: An inveterate pickpocket reaches into a man's pocket, only to find it empty; what's more, the intended victim grasps his hand and tugs him to a police officer. Can he be arrested and convicted for attempting to pick an empty pocket? Clearly a guilty mind (**mens rea**) was present, but—thanks to a simple mistake—a criminal outcome was not. The law has been inconsistent in such cases. In England in the early 1800s, such an act was a crime; then in 1864, a court decision ruled it was not a crime, but a subsequent ruling in 1892 reestablished it as a crime (Finkel et al., 1995). If you ask the opinion of average citizens, their answer is clear. The subjective intent of the pickpocket is enough to convince them that he is guilty of a crime; "they do not let these defendants off the culpability hook because their inept mistakes made the harmful outcome impossible" (Finkel & Groscup, 1997, p. 71).

Another case, *State v. Damms* (1960), dealt with a man who took his wife for a car ride, stopped the car, and brandished a gun. His wife ran away, but Damms caught her. He raised the pistol to her head. Slowly, deliberately, he pulled the trigger. The gun did not fire. He had forgotten to load it! Two police officers witnessed the event and heard Damms exclaim, after he pulled the trigger of the unloaded gun, "It won't fire. It won't fire." (It was not clear whether the exclamation was made in a tone of assurance, disappointment, surprise, or desperation.) Damms was found guilty of attempted murder, but he appealed his conviction on the ground that it was impossible to kill his wife with an unloaded gun. The court upheld his conviction, concluding that just because the gun was unloaded when Damms pulled the trigger did not absolve him of attempted murder if he actually believed that the gun was loaded at the time. Intention is the central issue here; at least for the charge of attempted murder, it is more important than the consequences of the act. The judges concluded that Damms assumed he had put bullets in the gun. And if he had, his wife would have been dead.

What if someone shoots another person, thinking he is already dead, but as it turns out he was still alive at the time? The law has had even greater trouble clarifying its position on such perplexing matters, as the following case reveals.

One night a number of years ago, Melvin Dlugash went drinking with two friends, Mike Geller and Joe Bush. Mike had a basement apartment, and Joe had been staying with him for several months. Joe was supposed to share the rent, but he hadn't been doing so. Mike asked Joe about this several times during the evening, and Joe responded angrily that he didn't owe anything and that, if Mike persisted, he was "going to get hurt."

About midnight, the three returned to Mike's apartment and continued to drink. After two or three hours, the argument grew more intense. Mike demanded the rent money, and Joe threatened to hurt him if he didn't lay off. But Mike repeated the demand. Suddenly, Joe pulled a .38 revolver from his pocket and fired it point-blank at Mike's heart, three times. Joe then turned to Mel Dlugash, pointed the gun at him, and said, "If you don't shoot him, I'll shoot you." Joe wanted it to appear that they were in it together so that Mel would not be able to point an accusing finger at Joe. After some hesitation, Mel walked over to Mike's prone and motionless body and fired five bullets from his .22 pistol into Mike's head.

Mel was arrested by the police. (Joe had run away.) Mel told the police what had happened; he reported that there had been three to five minutes between Joe's shooting and his. Why did he do it? Mel said he feared for his life, and besides, Mike was already dead when he fired at the body. But Mel was arrested and charged with murder.

Joe Bush was caught and charged with murder, too. But he plea-bargained (see Chapter 10), and his murder charge was dropped in exchange for his plea of guilty to manslaughter. He was sentenced to five to ten years in prison.

Mel, in contrast, refused to plead guilty to manslaughter because Mike was dead when he shot him. Mel went to trial, and the judge instructed the jurors that they could convict him of murder only if they were convinced that Mike was alive when Mel shot him and that Mel assumed him to be alive and intended to kill him. The jury deliberated for several days and returned a unanimous verdict: Mel was found guilty of murder and was sentenced to a term of 15 years to life imprisonment for murder, a much longer term than Joe received.

Alan Dershowitz (the source of the information reported here) assisted in Melvin Dlugash's appeal, and much of his legal brief dealt with the issue of impossible acts. The appeals court ultimately overturned Dlugash's conviction, concluding that the prosecution had "failed to prove beyond a reasonable doubt that Geller had been alive at the time he was shot by the defendant." But the state appealed this decision, and a higher-level appeals court ruled that Mel was guilty of attempted murder, since there was sufficient evidence that he believed Mike was alive when he shot him.

Several states, including New York, have now passed laws covering impossible act situations. In New York, actual impossibility does not constitute a defense as long as the crime that was attempted "could have been committed had the attendant circumstances been as the defendant believed them to be." The purpose of the New York law, which squares with the commonsense notions of the public, is that people who act out their bad intentions should be punished.

Dershowitz requested a new trial for Melvin Dlugash. The request was granted, but Mel was willing to plea-bargain to a lesser crime if he would be released from prison (he had already served some prison time by then). The district attorney wanted Mel to plead guilty to manslaughter, but he refused because that would still constitute an acknowledgment that he had killed Mike. Dershowitz countered with an offer that Mel plead guilty to unlawful possession of a gun. Not surprisingly, the prosecutor said no. So they decided to create a new crime category. Mel pleaded guilty to "attempted manslaughter," the judge accepted the plea, and Mel was sentenced to five years' probation.

Psychology's approach to intentions reflects more differentiations and less clear-cut distinctions than those of the legal system. Psychology considers a range of behavior, motivated by at least

eight categories of intention—from unconscious to conscious—along the continuum (Marshall, 1968, p. 72):

1. Pure accidents
2. Reflex actions
3. Actions motivated by unconscious factors
4. Actions taken under stress
5. Actions following hypnotic suggestion
6. Actions growing out of social transactions (peer pressure and social suggestion)
7. Actions in which the consequence is foreseeable
8. Actions directed by conscious intent

Even this continuum may oversimplify variations in intention because it minimizes the importance of the environmental situations and cultural expectations that different persons face. The overall social context in which behavior occurs can strongly influence a person's intention to behave in different ways. Different contexts may make it all but impossible for an individual to conceive of certain behavioral options; therefore, one person's ability to intend a given behavior might be much more limited than that of another person who operates in a context in which more behavioral alternatives are possible.

Psychology has studied how people assign causes, including intentions, to the behavior of others and themselves. The well-established field of **attribution theory** has led to a number of discoveries, including these:

1. Attributions tend to vary along three dimensions: *internality*—whether we explain the cause of an event as due to something within ourselves or something that exists in the environment; *stability*—whether we see the cause of a behavior as enduring or merely temporary; and *globalness*—whether we see the cause as specific to a limited situation or applicable to all situations.

2. An individual who makes internal, stable, global attributions about an act of misconduct ("He is so evil that he doesn't care what anyone thinks or feels about him") will see an offender as more culpable and deserving of punishment than

a person who offers external, unstable, specific explanations for the same act ("As a result of hanging out with a rough crowd, she was in the wrong place at the wrong time").

3. When making inferences about what caused another person's behavior—especially behavior that has negative consequences—we tend to attribute the cause to stable factors that are internal to the person; that is, we are inclined to believe that others are disposed to act the way they do.

4. But when our own actions lead to negative outcomes, we are more likely to blame the external environment for the outcome, suggesting an unstable cause for our behavior that will likely change in the future.

# The Development of Conceptions of Morality

The foregoing examples make clear that what people believe is morally right is not always what is legally proscribed. But individuals also differ in the standards they use to determine right and wrong. Some people rely on the law entirely; others use internalized principles of morality as beacons for action, whether they agree with the law or not. A better understanding of these differences can be gained by examining psychological theories of how our beliefs about right and wrong develop.

## Lawrence Kohlberg's Theory of Moral Development

Why do we obey traffic signals? Why do some of us return a missing wallet to its owner, even if it contains hundreds of dollars? Most psychological explanations of morality (e.g., those by Sigmund Freud and Jean Piaget) take a developmental perspective and emphasize that people's thoughts about moral behavior become more sophisticated as they mature. Whereas the infant knows no other way than to promote self-interest by "looking out for Number One," older children and adolescents

move through different stages that reflect more well-reasoned perspectives on morality.

The most thorough example of the developmental perspective is the theory of moral judgment advanced by the late Harvard psychologist Lawrence Kohlberg (1958, 1963, 1981; Colby, Kohlberg, et al., 1987), who proposed that humans go through six stages of moral development as they move from infancy to childhood to adolescence and adulthood. Although the sequence is the same, said Kohlberg, not all persons attain all stages. Some remain stuck at one stage and continue to use that as a filter through which they view moral dilemmas for the rest of their lives. **Moral dilemmas** are central in Kohlberg's approach; they are choices that we all face, and our choices reflect how we think about what is right and wrong. The determination of what is correct is qualitatively different at each stage. (An example of one of Kohlberg's moral dilemmas is presented in ◆ Box 3-3.) As people progress through the six stages, they move from one level of moral reasoning to the next, changing and refining the ability to make choices in their behavior.

Kohlberg's three levels and the two stages within each level are as follows:

*1. Preconventional level.* Young children respond to labels of behavior such as "good" and "bad" or "right" and "wrong" primarily on the basis of the physical consequences of their actions (i.e., whether the action is punished or rewarded). Young children at this level also interpret good or bad in light of the physical power of those who make the rules. At this level, "might makes right."

The first stage reflects a *punishment and obedience* orientation. If the child does something and gets caught and punished for it, the child concludes that the act must have been wrong. The second stage involves a *hedonistic* orientation. At this stage, the child considers "right actions" to be those that satisfy his or her own immediate needs and personal interests and occasionally the needs and interests of others. Children at this stage are "preconventional" because their actions are still motivated by selfishness. Human relations

## *The Science of*

| BOX 3-3 | **Measuring moral reasoning: Kohlberg's moral dilemmas** |

To determine a person's stage of moral development, Kohlberg used a set of moral dilemmas as the basis for interviewing individuals about their rationale and responses to each of these dilemmas. Kohlberg proposed that the reasons a person gave for his or her decision in this semistructured interview were just as important as the decision itself. A modification of the procedure, called the Defining Issues test (Rest, 1988; Rest, Cooper, Coder, Masanz, & Anderson, 1974), permitted administration of the dilemmas and scoring of the responses by more than one person at a time.

A typical Kohlberg dilemma is the case of Heinz. In Europe, a woman was near death from a special kind of cancer. There was one drug that the doctors thought might save her. It was a form of radium that a druggist in the same town had recently discovered. The drug was expensive to make, but the druggist was charging ten times what the drug cost him to make. He paid $200 for the radium and charged $2000 for a small dose of the drug. The sick woman's husband, Heinz, went to everyone he knew to borrow the money, but he could only get together about $1000, which was half the cost. He told the druggist that his wife was dying and asked him to sell it cheaper or let him pay later. But the druggist said, "No, I discov-

ered the drug, and I'm going to make money from it." So Heinz got desperate and broke into the man's store to steal the drug for his wife. Should the husband have done that? Why?

In Kohlberg's system, a preconventional answer would be that Heinz should not steal the drug because, if he did, he would probably be caught and put in jail. One conventional answer might be that Heinz should steal the drug because he loves his wife and should care for her; another would be that he should not steal the drug because it is wrong to steal. Several postconventional answers to this dilemma are possible; can you think of what some of them might be?

are viewed in the language of the marketplace. Something that is a "good deal" for both parties is considered morally right at this stage. Parents sometimes encourage desirable behavior in their children by appealing to the children's selfish interests: "You should help your grandmother across the street because then she'll remember you in her will."

*2. Conventional level.* According to Kohlberg, morality for most Americans means either obeying the rules or behaving the way people expect you to. At this conventional level, a person shifts from the self-centeredness of the preconventional stages to a greater awareness of the rights, feelings, and concerns of others. Fulfilling the expectations of one's family, religious group, or country becomes valuable in its own right, regardless of the immediate consequences. The attitude reflects

not only conformity to the social order but also loyalty to it.

The *interpersonal concordance,* or *good-boy/nice-girl,* orientation is the third stage in Kohlberg's theory. Moral behavior, as defined by the person at stage 3, is that which pleases, helps, or is expected by others. Intentions become important in defining morality; the notion that someone "means well" becomes salient for the first time, and one earns approval for being "nice."

The next stage at the conventional level is the *law-and-order* orientation. Moral behavior at this fourth stage consists of doing one's duty, showing that one respects authority, and perpetuating the social order because that is what is expected.

*3. Postconventional, or principled, level.* At Kohlberg's highest level of morality, a person further internalizes individual standards of morality.

Moral values and codes of conduct are defined independently from the authoritativeness of the groups or persons who advocate these principles and apart from an individual's identification with these groups.

The *social contract* or *legalistic* orientation is the fifth stage of moral development, according to Kohlberg. At this stage, the person operates from internalized principles but realizes that these principles may be at odds with the norms and laws of society or with the viewpoint of the majority. Thus, a person at stage 5, although objecting to the death penalty on the grounds that it violates the principle of maintaining human life, still recognizes that, for some crimes, the death penalty remains the law of the land. A stage 5 orientation leads the person to say, in effect, "I believe the death penalty is wrong in principle, but I accept that it is the law, and the law represents a consensus view. I may lobby to change the law, I may write letters to newspapers, I may circulate petitions, and I may campaign for political candidates who promise to abolish the death penalty." The person at stage 5 may disagree with society's consensus on some issues but realizes that he or she must exist in society and work within it to change it. This fifth stage represents the official morality of democratic governments and the U.S. Constitution.

The *application of universal ethical principles* is the sixth stage in Kohlberg's scheme. At this highest stage, what is morally right is defined not by the laws of the social order but by one's own conscience and self-determined ethical principles. These principles include universal notions of justice, norms of reciprocity and equality of human rights, and respect for the dignity of human beings as individuals. For example, people with opposing beliefs about abortion may still share a commitment to universal human principles, even though prolife people emphasize a commitment to principles about the sanctity of human life, whereas prochoice people focus on principles about the rights of individuals to control their own bodies. Likewise, one's attitude about the morality of assisting a terminally ill person to commit suicide might reflect a principle that human be-

ings should be able to control their ultimate destinies, or it might embody a belief that all human life is sacred and cannot be sacrificed for personal preference. Kohlberg (1973) suggested that postconventional morality (stages 5 and 6) "is probably attainable only in adulthood and requires some experience in moral responsibility and independent choice" (p. 500). Stage 6 is the most controversial of Kohlberg's stages; thus, it receives extended review in ◆ **Box 3-4.**

A central assumption of Kohlberg's theory is that a person advances from a lower to a higher stage of morality only as a result of being confronted by examples of higher-level moral reasoning by another person or group. Perhaps each of you has experienced an incident in which someone else's conduct led you to reexamine the values on which you have based your own behavior.

A developmental perspective can also be applied to a person's conception of the law. In fact, June Tapp and Felice Levine (1970, 1974; Levine & Tapp, 1977) have applied a similar approach to explain how individuals come to understand and react to the requirements of the law. At Tapp and Levine's *preconventional* level, people obey the law out of fear of punishment or deference to authority. At the *conventional* level, people follow laws to maintain the social order of the community. Group norms become more important than individual rights. At the *postconventional* level, people follow only those laws that coincide with independently derived ethical categories. A subsequent analysis (Cohn & White, 1990) assumes that these beliefs interact with responses we learn from our social environment. Obviously, the development of an appreciation for the law and reasons for abiding by it have major implications for the age at which children should be held legally responsible for their actions, a topic that is considered in Chapter 4.

Empirical studies of moral development and legal socialization among children, adolescents, and adults provide general support for the conceptions of Kohlberg and of Tapp and Levine, as do the infrequent studies that assess children's moral judgment levels and then retest the subjects 5, 10, or 20 years later (Colby, Kohlberg, et al.,

## BOX 3-4    How do you know a stage-6 person when you see one?

Kohlberg considered a person who relied on universal ethical principles to manifest the highest level of moral development. But certain actions can be attributed to different levels of moral development. During the late 1960s and early 1970s, did antiwar activists protest out of principles of nonviolence or out of fear that they could go into the army and lose their lives? Individuals at stage 6 in Kohlberg's scheme—Jesus Christ, Gandhi, Martin Luther King—were willing to sacrifice for their actions and, in fact, did so. Acceptance of the potentiality of punishment for one's principles separates the stage-6 act from a similarly appearing protest that is done for selfish reasons.

Other examples of stage-6 behavior include the following:

◆  Dorothy Eber was an antiwar, antinuclear activist and protester. She and several companions broke through a fence at a nuclear missile site in Missouri.

They planted some flowers, then plopped down on the concrete lid and prayed. Eber, a 64-year-old widowed grandmother, was arrested for trespassing on government property and was sentenced to a two-year term in a federal penitentiary (Royko, 1989).

◆  John Ryan was an FBI agent who was fired in 1987, after more than 20 years of service. He was scheduled to retire at full pension ten months later, at the age of 50. The reason for the firing: he refused to investigate peace groups because of his "personal, religious, and human beliefs." Ryan, a devout Roman Catholic and committed pacifist, had been instructed to investigate two peace-oriented organizations suspected of vandalizing military recruiting activities in Chicago.

◆  Captain Lawrence Rockwood was stationed in Haiti during the United States' intervention there in 1994. He conducted an unauthorized inspection of the national penitentiary because of frequent

reports of mistreatment of inmates; for disobeying his superiors and uncovering examples of abuse, he had his pay forfeited and was summarily dismissed from the army.

◆  When the brother and mother of Theodore Kaczynski read the Unabomber's 30,000-word manifesto in the newspaper, they noted that its themes resembled the contents of their brother's/son's letters and essays. They contacted the authorities, an action that led to the arrest of Kaczynski; they had decided that preventing future killings took precedence over their family allegiance.

Not everyone would agree that these actions reflect the highest stages of morality. Some would argue that, if everyone operated out of universal ethical principles, the result could be anarchy. Furthermore, there is some indication that persons operating out of principled morality are disliked by their peers (Wygant & Williams, 1995).

1987; Kohlberg, 1958, 1963, 1981; Snarey, 1985; Walker, 1984b).

## A Different View of Morality: A Feminine View

Although Kohlberg based his theory on the responses of boys and men, he did little to discourage others from assuming that his ideas also applied to girls' and women's development. Kohlberg believed that fewer women than men achieve higher

stages of moral development because their long-term allegiance to their children precludes their developing the abstract moral principles requisite for stage 6. As a result, some degree of developmental inferiority is attributed to women in Kohlberg's theory (Walker, 1984b).

Carol Gilligan (1977, 1982), a former student of Kohlberg's and later a colleague of his at Harvard University, objected to the male-oriented nature of his theory and its failure to consider the socialization and experiences of women. She asks, for example, why men who say that a person should not steal the drug because it's against the law should occupy an advanced stage of morality beyond that of women who say a person should steal because it is the compassionate thing to do. Through her articles and particularly her book *In a Different Voice* (1982), Gilligan has forced scholars to rethink existing theories of moral development.

Gilligan's theory of women's moral development differs radically from Kohlberg's in content, even though it resembles Kohlberg's in structure. It proposes that young children of both genders are unable to distinguish the perspective of others from their own perspective. Gilligan also proposes that women pass through three levels and that, like the men in Kohlberg's theory, they move from self-centeredness to other-directedness and then to an autonomous conception of morality.

But although Kohlberg's approach follows a rules orientation, with emphasis on abstract concepts and especially the concept of justice, Gilligan finds that women possess a responsibility orientation, with emphasis on sensitivity to others and the concepts of compassion and care. Women's moral development is best understood within a context of complex relationships and connections to other people. In contrast to boys and men, whose identities are defined through their separation from others, identities for girls and women are defined by attachments to others and an "ethic of care" (Gilligan, 1982, p. 8).

For women, moral dilemmas result not from competing rights, as they do for men, but from competing responsibilities. In Gilligan's (1982) words, for women the moral dilemma "requires for resolution a mode of thinking that is contextual and narrative rather than formal and abstract" (p. 19). Acts of caring are designed to sustain "the web of connection so no one is left alone" (1982, p. 62). In fact, abstract thinking brings an unwanted impersonality to a woman's exercise of her responsibility for the care of others as individuals.

Like Kohlberg, Gilligan based her theory on responses to moral dilemmas. But Kohlberg has been criticized for the unfamiliarity and possible irrelevance of his dilemmas, which involve fictitious persons. To overcome this limitation, Gilligan interviewed 29 women who were facing a personal decision about whether to abort a pregnancy. Gilligan's use of personal decisions about everyday problems reflects her belief that the feminine conception of morality is embedded in relationships with actual people. Some of Gilligan's subjects were unmarried and still in high school; others were married but for one reason or another were unsure that they wanted to have the baby.

On the basis of these interviews and follow-up interviews a year later, Gilligan concludes that women move through three levels of moral development, each of which presents a conflict between obligations to oneself and responsibilities to others. The first level is termed *selfishness;* the primary orientation is toward individual survival. When asked what one *should* do, the only thought is what one *would* do for oneself. If there is any sense of obligation, it is only an obligation to one's own survival. No awareness of conflict exists at this level.

But some women move from selfishness to a sense of responsibility and a different interpretation of obligation. For example, a woman values her independence, yet she wants to establish connection with another person; marriage and motherhood have attractions but also limitations. *Should* and *would* begin to conflict. What one wants isn't always right.

Awareness of this conflict leads to level 2, the conventional level of morality, which Gilligan calls *goodness as self-sacrifice.* Morality here is defined as meeting other's expectations and submitting to the norms of society. The primary concern is over meeting others' needs and not hurting them (Gilligan, Ward, & Taylor, 1988).

For example, in considering whether to abort a fetus, a woman must make a choice between potential victims. If she is an unmarried high school student who decides to have the baby, the victim may be expelled from school, subjected to ridicule by her peers, abandoned by her boyfriend, and ostracized by her parents. Or if she is a working woman with little income, having the baby may make the infant a victim of limited funds, little maternal support, and an impoverished future. For the woman at level 2, the concerns of others are salient. Will the child suffer? What will my parents think? Will another child place a financial burden on our family resources? The "right" way to resolve the dilemma at level 2 is to decide in a way that hurts others the least. But the stakes are high for the woman herself; her own needs are sacrificed in the decision, and she may soon struggle to free herself from the powerlessness of her own dependence.

As some women move beyond level 2, they scrutinize the logic of self-sacrifice; an orientation toward oneself returns, but at a higher level of analysis. The woman begins to ask whether it is "selfish or responsible—moral or immoral—to include her own needs within the compass of her care and concern" (Gilligan, 1977, p. 498). She becomes aware of her own inner judgment as well as what other people think (Davis, 1985). The new goal is to be honest with oneself. Gilligan calls this third level the *morality of nonviolence*. The basic injunction is one against hurting, and it becomes a principle governing all moral judgment and action. At level 3, the determinants of the decision whether to have an abortion center on the woman's responsibilities to herself—to her own moral code, to her own development and maturity—as well as to others.

In summary, for Kohlberg and for men, the moral imperative is to use abstract rules to guide the choice between competing rights. By contrast, in Gilligan's view, the moral imperative for women is to alleviate the troubles of the world. The choice is between competing responsibilities, and the operating principle is care.

At this point, a clarification is in order: Throughout this discussion, the morality of men and women has been contrasted. But this distinction does not spring from an inborn gender difference as much as a difference in the childhood socialization experiences of males and females in our society. In addition, not all men and women respond on moral dilemma tests with the values typical of their gender. For these reasons, it is more appropriate to refer to two differing conceptions of morality, masculine and feminine, than to speak simply of male/female differences (Kohlberg, Levine, & Hewer, 1983; Walker, 1984b; Wilson, 1995). In fact, some evidence (see Berk, 1991, p. 499, for a review) suggests that sex differences do not occur on the supposedly more masculine justice-oriented measures of moral reasoning. Even if conceptions of morality are not strongly linked to gender, Gilligan's work has expanded our notions of how moral persons (of either gender) might think and behave. In addition to being committed to abstract principles of fairness, the highly moral person remains concerned about caring for the welfare of individuals.

# What Is Justice?

The foregoing comparison of Kohlberg's and Gilligan's theories suggests that justice can be seen from two different vantage points. It can be based on abstract ideals, or it can be derived from the nature of the relationship between interested parties. We can apply these contrasting perspectives to real-world dilemmas. For example, should the parents of a teenager charged with murder comply with the court's order to testify against him?

A Houston, Texas, couple spent several months in jail after refusing to testify before a grand jury. Their son was a suspect in the abduction and shooting death of a mail carrier. Mrs. Odette Port, stepmother of the suspect, said, "I was faced with a choice, a choice between the law of the land and the law of my conscience." She refused to provide information about the crime scene, the murder weapon, and other facts that might implicate her stepson. As a consequence, she served four and a half months in a Houston jail. Her husband and the father of the suspect, Bernard Port, spent two months in jail before he testified and was released. Before being sent to jail, he had argued that a right of privileged communication exists between parents and children, just as it does between attorneys and clients or between spouses. But the courts rejected the claim.

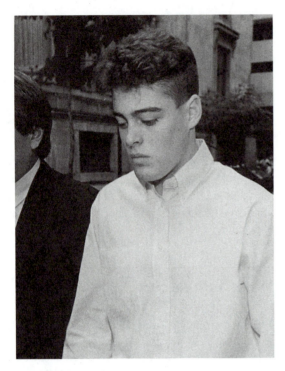

**MICHAEL FAY**
*In 1994, when 18-year-old Michael Fay received a "caning" from Singapore officials as punishment for his vandalism of several cars, people in the United States were divided over whether the caning was excessive, barbaric punishment or a tough, but appropriate disciplinary measure.*

His son, David Port, 17, was later found guilty of murder and sentenced to 75 years in prison. (A book by Rosellen Brown [1992], and later a movie, *Before and After,* were loosely based on this case.)

What is justice? At the beginning of Plato's *Republic,* Socrates posed that question more than 2000 years ago, and we continue to ponder it today. Definitions of justice have changed throughout history; in the Old Testament and in Homer's *The Iliad,* justice meant something like revenge. By the time of the Golden Age of Athens in the fifth century B.C., the concept of justice became less preoccupied with vengeance and more concerned with the achievement of the well-being of individuals (Solomon, 1990). The development of Christianity and Islam accentuated a conception of justice within religious traditions of morality.

As a result, matters of social injustice (e.g., the suffering of the poor and the oppressed) became issues of concern, rather than just offenses against one's person or one's family (Solomon, 1990).

The philosopher Elizabeth Wolgast (1987) has proposed that questions of justice often emerge from the facts of a particular situation, so that the key concept is *injustice,* not justice. In a contested divorce, who has been wronged? In a dispute with an insurance company over an accident claim, was the injured party treated unfairly? In a case of vandalism by juveniles, is it cruel to use physical punishment, or is it justified to teach youngsters a lesson?

Such an orientation leads us to think of **justice** as an outcome of the process in which people receive what they deserve or are due. Several guidelines can help us identify whether justice has been done, and some of the more prominent of these approaches have been studied extensively by psychologists. They are discussed in the next section.

## Equity Theory: An Attempt to Understand Justice

Equity is one of several concepts that has been used to understand perceptions of justice (Folger, Sheppard, & Buttram, 1995). Usually, **equity** refers to the distribution of rewards in society according to some criterion of merit. This is a demonstrable value throughout the world. Almost all societies attempt to apportion rewards and costs equitably among participants.

It should be noted that the goal of fairness can be applied both to the process and the outcome of resolving disputes or allocating consequences. Psychologists use the term **procedural justice** to refer to the way an outcome is decided (Folger & Greenberg, 1985; Lind & Tyler, 1988). Generally, individuals perceive a decision-making process to be fair to the extent that they believe they have a voice in how the process unfolds, are treated with dignity and respect during the process, and trust the authorities in charge of the process to be motivated by concerns about fairness (Folger, Cropanzano, Timmerman, Howes, & Mitchell, 1996; Sydeman, Cascardi, Poythress, & Ritterband, 1997). A full opportunity to state one's viewpoint and to participate actively and personally in the decision makes a strong contribution to an assessment of fairness probably because it allows people to feel as if they retain some control over their affairs (Ebreo, Linn, & Vining, 1996).

Furthermore, in those situations in which authorities—rather than the involved parties—make the decisions, people derive a positive sense of identity when the procedure for allocating rewards is seen as a fair one (Degoey & Tyler, 1994). They evaluate the government policies more favorably (Tyler, 1990; Tyler & Caine, 1981; Tyler, Rasinski, & McGraw, 1985), and they perceive the authority figure or supervisor more favorably in terms of procedural fairness (Cobb & Frey, 1996).

## Definitions of Equitable Relationships

Psychologists define equitable relationships as those in which all participants in a group receive outcomes that accurately reflect their relative contributions to the group's activity (Lerner, 1974, 1977; Leventhal, 1976; Walster, Walster, & Berscheid, 1978). That is, the outcomes (or payoffs) for person A divided by the inputs of person A equal the outcomes for person B divided by the inputs of person B.

For example, consider the case in which persons A and B cut person C's lawn. A works two hours and B works one hour. C has told them he will pay them a total of $15 for the job. How should they divide the $15? Your first reaction probably is that A should get $10 and B $5, since A worked twice as long as B. And that is eminently reasonable; when we are measuring inputs, length of work time is a very plausible choice.

But it is not the only one. Suppose that person A works two hours and person B only one hour, but it happens that A is in excellent physical condition, whereas B has a broken leg. Furthermore, his cast is heavy and awkward, so an hour's yard work has caused him great pain and fatigue. Given those facts, what would be equitable payoffs? Should B receive a greater reward than one-third because his effort entailed more pain and suffering? His work certainly required more effort per hour than A's work did. Maybe his inputs are even greater than A's, even though he worked half as long.

The standards for determining relative inputs reflect value judgments, and there are no easy answers (Sampson, 1975). Different systems for allocating rewards have, of course, different effects. The research literature proposes a trade-off between the use of equity and equality (Tyler & Belliveau, 1995); equity encourages productivity but may harm social harmony and cohesiveness. The use of equality can have the opposite effects. Remember the conflict in Chapter 1 between equality and discretion; it can be argued that each is, in a different sense, fair and just. But of necessity, laws must develop agreed-on definitions or measures of inputs.

Inequity in pay between the genders remains a concern. When all the women in the United States labor force are considered, women's earnings are about 70% of men's (Rothenberg, 1995). For women of color, the gap is even wider. Nor does education close the gap; college-educated women earn $13,000 per year less than college-educated men. Even within a specific occupation, a wage gap exists. Data from the Census Bureau and the National Committee on Pay Equity indicate that female nurses are paid 10% less than male nurses, and female elementary school teachers make 14% less than their male counterparts (cited by Lichtman, 1993).

In response to Title VII of the U.S. Civil Rights Act of 1964, which made it illegal to pay one person less than another because of the person's gender, some states and cities tried to achieve the principle of "equal pay for work of comparable worth" by passing laws and regulations that define comparable worth. For example, is the work of a teacher of comparable worth to that of a newspaper reporter? A practical nurse's work to that of a gardener? During the 1980s, several states instituted salary adjustments for state employees based on such a principle (Lowe & Wittig, 1989). Despite criticism that different jobs were not objectively comparable, the state of Washington, as one example, made comparisons based on four criteria: (1) knowledge and skills, (2) mental demands, (3) accountability, and (4) working conditions. This comparable worth study found that the jobs of warehouse worker and clerk/typist were both rated at a 94-point level, but warehouse workers, typically men, were paid 25% more than were clerk/typists, who were typically women.

Shortly after Washington initiated plans to eliminate such pay discrepancies, the Ninth U.S. Circuit Court of Appeals refused to authorize the procedure, and the state was forced to accept prevailing marketplace rates as the determinants of state employees' salaries. Marketplace rates reflect different criteria from those used by the state of Washington. They are more in keeping with the beliefs found in a cross-sectional public opinion sample of employees, which indicated that the prestige of the occupation and the physical demands of the job should be the major determinants of its pay (Dornstein, 1988).

### Reactions to Inequity

Despite the difficulty in obtaining agreed-on measures of equity, each of us has subjective feelings about what is fair. According to equity theory, people become resentful when they participate in inequitable relationships. Those who receive less than they deserve usually feel anger, whether the payoff is pay for work, tangible goods, or even appreciation and recognition.

Those who receive more than they deserve often feel guilt. Although they want to maximize their outcomes, they also feel embarrassed and guilt ridden about gaining too much (Miller, 1999). The greater the inequity, the greater the distress and the stronger the efforts (by some, at least) to restore equity.

### How Is Equity Restored?

How do you react when you have been overcompensated for some action? You may have received a higher grade than you deserved or been paid more than you consider fair. Or you may have inadvertently caused someone else to suffer an unfair outcome. How do you restore equity?

First, if feasible, we may seek to compensate those who have been undercompensated. We may say, "Here, take part of my pay; you deserve it." Or we may, on future occasions, overreward the other person to make up for the past slight. We may also engage in self-deprivation and reduce our own outcomes to the other person's level.

Others, however, may ridicule people who were undercompensated, either to their faces or, more likely, behind their backs. Your being overcompensated may be so threatening that you cannot acknowledge it. Instead, your reaction may be to make jokes about those who have suffered for your benefit.

### Equity versus Equality: Which Is Justice?

Equity is reflected in the allocation of rewards based on relative contributions. But some have questioned whether this is the best way to define justice (see, e.g., Sampson, 1975). Other rules for allocating rewards include the norms of equality, reciprocity, or individual need (Deutsch, 1975; Elliott & Meeker, 1986; Rusbult, Lowery, Hubbard, Maravankin, & Neises, 1988). For example, some people believe justice is best achieved by the practice of **equality,** giving the same reward to all, regardless of their contributions. For example, in determining salary raises for professors, some colleges prefer "across the board" raises (i.e., equality), whereas others base each raise on each professor's "merit" (i.e., equity).

Psychologists have conducted experiments to identify the conditions under which equity or equality is preferred (Walster et al., 1978). A typical procedure is to have subjects act as a set of workers who simultaneously complete similar tasks but whose outcomes depend on their combined performances. After working on their task, subjects receive feedback about their relative performance. Subjects might be told, for example, "You earned 75 points and the other person earned

## The Science of

**BOX 3-5    Equity versus equality: Are there gender differences?**

In one well-known study of equity (Leventhal & Lane, 1970), pairs of males and pairs of females worked individually on multiplication problems and then were told that one member of the pair had performed much better than the other. Then they were informed that one of them would be chosen at random to allocate the payoffs to their team. Members of the pair were isolated from each other, and each was told that he or she was the member designated to divide the money.

Men, on the average, took about 60% of the outcome when their performance was higher than their co-worker's; they typically took 40% for themselves when their performance was lower. But women took only 50% when theirs was the higher performance level and 34% when theirs was lower. So apparently, women tend to downgrade their own achievement, and apparently rely less than men do on performance differences in making their allocations (Harvey & Smith, 1977).

50 points." Then they are asked to suggest a division of the rewards.

Is equity endorsed in such situations? Sometimes it is. Yet some studies have found a tendency for subjects to accept higher, not lower, outcomes for themselves when there had been a difference in performance that ordinarily would prescribe an unequal division of rewards (Benton, 1971; Lane & Messe, 1971).

### Gender Differences in the Allocation of Rewards

Do men and women use the same standards in assigning payoffs? Some early studies (see ◆ Box 3-5) found that females opted for equality rather than equity, regardless of relative inputs.

Further evidence that women underestimate the worth of their own work appears in the findings of Major, McFarlin, and Gagnon (1984). They found that, when women were asked to do as much work as they thought fair for a fixed amount of money, they worked 25% longer than men did under conditions of no supervision. When told that someone was monitoring them, women worked 52% longer than men did. The women did more work and produced more correct work than the men.

We need to make several qualifications to the conclusion that there are gender differences in the preference for equity versus equality (Kahn, Nelson, & Gaeddert, 1980). First, in the early studies, subjects were led to believe that they would have no contact between themselves in the future. But when the two persons anticipated future contact with each other, they increased their use of equality as a standard for allocating rewards. Perhaps even if we think we have performed better than a partner, we do not want the discomfort of appearing "grabby" to someone we might spend additional time with. For example, roommates tend to distribute rewards equally rather than on the basis of relative merit (Austin, 1980). And in general, within groups of people who must work closely together, a preference for equality occurs because the norm of equity can produce antagonism and competition.

Second, in a different set of studies in which a man decided the allocations of payoffs and a woman was his partner—and the man had done better—he typically assigned himself a smaller amount than if his partner had been a man (Kahn et al., 1980).

Third, the overall context of these studies might also affect their interpretation. Most of the studies employed an industrial simulation or similar work setting in which men might still be more experienced and comfortable than women. Perhaps most important is the fact that the tasks used in these early studies (e.g., solving mathematical problems) are ones at which men are expected to excel.

Subsequent studies have addressed these limitations. Reis and Jackson (1981) had male and female subjects work on one of two tasks. In both tasks, objects were flashed on a screen, and subjects were asked to describe their functions. But in the first task, the objects were ones men were more familiar with, whereas in the second, the objects were more typical of women's experience. Men used equity to divide rewards on both tasks. When the task was male oriented, the females did not divide the reward equitably, but they did use the norm of equity when they worked on a female-oriented task.

If women prefer equality—and men prefer equity—as the norm for payoffs, their preferences might be related to differences along an even more fundamental dimension of behavior. Bakan (1966) makes a distinction between the states of agency and communion. **Agency** refers to a striving for achievement, prominence, and success, whereas **communion** reflects a concern with intimacy, interpersonal relationships, and attachment. There are indications that females base their allocations more on communion than on agency; they are more accommodating than males and more concerned with interpersonal harmony and intimacy (Crano & Meese, 1982; Vinacke, 1959; Watts, Messe, & Vallacher, 1982).

# Commonsense Justice: Everyday Intuitions about Fairness

Another approach to the study of justice is to learn about the untutored intuitions that average people hold about culpability, fairness, and justice. Over the past dozen years, psychologist Norman Finkel has examined the relationship between the "law on the books" as set out in statutes and judicial opinions and what he calls "**commonsense justice**": ordinary citizens' basic notions of what is just and fair. This work has much to say about inconsistencies between the law and public sentiment in the types of cases we have examined in this chapter—cases involving assisted suicide, self-defense, impossible acts, euthanasia, the insanity defense, the death penalty, and felony-murder (Finkel, 1995). Commonsense justice also is reflected in cases in which a jury refuses to convict a defendant who is legally guilty of the crime charged; this phenomenon, known as "jury nullification," is discussed fully in Chapter 13.

According to Finkel and others who have examined the contours of commonsense justice (e.g., Haney, 1997a; Olsen-Fulero & Fulero, 1997), there is mounting evidence that the "black letter" law on the books may be at odds with community sentiment. Jurors depart from legal concepts and procedures in three identifiable ways.

*1. The commonsense context is typically wider than the law's.* Ordinary people tend to consider the bigger picture: their assessment of the event in question extends backward and forward in time (e.g., including the defendant's conduct prior to the incident and behavior after the crime), whereas the law allows consideration of a more limited set of circumstances. For example, in a date rape case or other case in which the victim and defendant knew each other, jurors would likely consider the history of the individuals, both together and apart. Is the incident one in a series of troublesome encounters in a tumultuous relationship? Have these events been alleged by other partners? Does the couple have a history of battering?

Whereas jurors contemplate the wider context of the story, the law freezes the frame at the time of the act and then zooms in on that relatively finite moment. Reasoning that this narrower perspective will result in a cleaner and more precise judgment, the law then asks jurors to determine culpability based on the defendant's actions and intentions within this narrow window. But jurors would often rather learn about the big picture; for many, viewing only the last act does little to reveal the entire drama (Finkel & Groscup, 1997).

**2. Jurors' perspectives on the actions of the defendant and the victim are more subjective than the law allows.** In cases that involve two people with a prior history, jurors construct a story about what happened and why by stepping into the shoes of the defendant and viewing the events through that person's eyes. The stories they construct typically describe the hidden motives of the defendant—considerations that can be discerned only by a "plunge into the subjective waters" (Finkel, 1995, p. 325). But, as Finkel further notes, "such a subjective, discretionary enterprise grounds the law not on terra firma but on the unstable and invisible, where all we have are constructions, interpretations and stories constructed by jurors and judges" (p. 327).

The concern, of course, is that too much subjectivity will result in lawlessness, that jurors' judgments will be rooted in illusion rather than in the more objective premises of the law. But jurors do not yield indiscriminately to their imaginations. In fact, when the individuals in a case are strangers to each other (as is often the situation) jurors tend to judge the circumstances and actors' intentions objectively rather than subjectively.

**3. Jurors take a proportional approach to punishment, whereas the law asks them to consider the defendant in isolation.** Imagine a situation in which an armed robber enters a convenience store while his female accomplice watches guard outside the store. Further imagine that things go awry—the robber ends up shooting the cashier, and the cashier dies. The robber has certainly committed a crime, but what about the accomplice?

As you learned at the beginning of this chapter, according to the felony-murder doctrine (which applies in about half the states), the accomplice is as culpable as the triggerman. Yet, as Finkel points out, this egalitarian approach seems to contradict the notion of proportional justice in which a defendant's actions and intentions are assessed in comparison to others and the more culpable defendants are dealt with more severely. Jurors make distinctions among types of crimes and criminals, and they usually want to punish most those criminals they find most blameworthy. The three ways in which jurors' judgments deviate from the law's expectations come to light in a study of community sentiment concerning the right to die, the subject of ◆▶ Box 3-6.

# Belief in a "Just World"

People have a strong need to believe that justice exists in the world, and most of us assume that people get what they deserve in life (Lerner, 1980). This need reflects more than just believing in a predictable world. The need to believe in a "just world" occurs so that people can go about their daily lives with a sense of trust, hope, and confidence in the future.

Furthermore, people structure the world to fit their beliefs. If something bad happens to someone we know, we may sympathize, but we also may be tempted to believe that the person must have deserved, or even provoked, it. Otherwise, it would not have happened. As the Roman philosopher Seneca observed, people are trained to believe that if we act honorably, we will be rewarded; but if we behave badly, we will be punished:

> In cases where one acts correctly but still suffers disaster, one is left bewildered and unable to fit the event into a scheme of justice. The world seems absurd. One alternates between a feeling that one may after all have been bad and this is why one was punished, and the feeling that one truly was not bad and therefore must have fallen victim to a catastrophic failure in the administration of justice. The continuing belief that the world is fundamentally just is implied in the very complaint that there has been an injustice. (de Botton, 2000, p. 93)

## The Science of

BOX 3-6 Complementary measures: Closed-ended and open-ended questions

Norman Finkel and his colleagues (Finkel, Hurabiell, & Hughes, 1993) examined community sentiment about the right to die by presenting detailed written accounts of cases (including the facts, testimony of key witnesses, and jury instructions admonishing participants to apply the law as given to them by the judge). Participants in the study rendered a verdict on the defendant's guilt. This was a "closed-ended question" in which jurors were given various response options (e.g., first-degree murder, second-degree murder, voluntary manslaughter, involuntary manslaughter, or not guilty) and instructed to choose one of those options. The researchers also employed an "open-ended question" in which participants were asked to write out their reason or reasons for reaching the verdict they did.

The study involved four cases, differing in the extent to which a

patient was competent to make her own end-of-life decisions: the most competent of the patients (all 58-year-old women) had amyotrophic lateral sclerosis (Lou Gehrig's disease) that affected her motor abilities but not her mind, the next most competent had lymph cancer that was exacerbated by emotional and mental symptoms, the third most competent was an Alzheimer's patient, and the least competent was a comatose patient. In all cases, the patient's doctor and hospital had challenged her competence to make a right-to-die decision. Finkel and his colleagues surmised that if jurors were willing to support the right-to-die request only when they were sure the patient was competent, then support for that request should diminish as competence decreases.

A second variable of importance in these cases—the extent to which the patient had expressed

her wish to die—was also examined. The expressed intent of each of the patients was described in one of three ways: at the intermediate level of intent, the patient had expressed her wishes to two people; at the highest level of intent, she had also made a living will; and at the lowest level, she had not expressed this desire aloud, although her husband claimed that she wanted to die. Are jurors' commonsense sentiments influenced by the patient's stated desires or lack thereof? Or do jurors want more than mere words—perhaps the written expression of these sentiments legally documented in a living will?

The defendant in these cases was the patient's husband who entered the hospital and shot and killed his wife. (In some of the case descriptions, the husband had also attempted to seek hospital and court approval to disconnect life support machines and had

---

If an apparently innocent person suffers, this inconsistency threatens our own **belief in a just world.** So we end up derogating the victim rather than accepting the absurdity of an unjust world. The need to believe in a just world might sometimes tempt jurors to explain particularly tragic events that befall some victims as being somehow deserved. Otherwise, it would be too threatening to conclude that innocent people would be victims of heinous acts such as partner or child abuse. Furthermore, it is possible that preserving a belief in a just world is one reason why defendants

convicted of partner abuse are sometimes given rather lenient sentences. In such trials, it might be particularly important to try to counter just-world sentiments; for example, expert testimony about reactions of battered women (Schuller & Vidmar, 1992) or rape victims (Frazier & Borgida, 1992) is often used by attorneys to dispel some just-world assumptions jurors might hold about the behavior of a woman in violent encounters.

This blaming of an innocent victim often happens when observers are unable to intervene on behalf of the victim. In such circumstances, peo-

been turned down. These actions turned out not to matter much to jurors.) So the question is this: Do jurors strictly apply the law to these facts and convict the husband/defendant of first-degree murder—the legally sanctioned verdict—or instead, do they introject their sentiments, beliefs, and some shades of gray into the process? And how do we know this—from the answers to the closed-ended question (the verdicts), the open-ended question (explanation of the verdicts), or both?

The results were clearly not what the law would have predicted. Recall that as verdict options, mock jurors had been offered "lesser offenses" (including second-degree murder, voluntary manslaughter, and involuntary manslaughter) in addition to first-degree murder. Given those choices, only 36% convicted the defendant of first-degree murder, 39% opted for a lesser offense,

and 25% acquitted the defendant completely!

Participants also paid attention to the patient's intent: When the patient had legally documented her intentions in a living will (but not when she had simply announced her desires to others), her husband was more likely to be acquitted. Surprisingly, the patient's level of competence did not influence the verdicts rendered.

This apparent disregard of the law—clearly apparent from the closed-ended data on verdicts—was convincingly confirmed by data from the open-ended question. After coding and categorizing these responses, Finkel and his colleagues determined that many participants simply viewed the law's position in this case as wrong. Some of them, citing their public role as jurors, nonetheless convicted the defendant of first-degree murder (and urged the judge to show mercy), but many others

refused to do so. They considered the death a private rather than a legal matter, endorsing a "zone of privacy" into which the law should not intrude.

Finally, many jurors expressed the view that the husband was not an actor in his own right but, rather, an extension of his wife, essentially functioning as her arms and legs and enabling her to commit suicide. This sentiment helps us to understand why many people voted to acquit the defendant and others chose to convict him on a lesser offense. Had these researchers opted simply to analyze the data on verdicts, we likely would not know what factors motivated jurors' judgments. Indeed, this study shines as an excellent example of the complementarity of data gathered via closed-ended and open-ended questioning.

ple seem to work backward in their reactions. They assess what is happening and then calculate what it would take for someone to deserve that fate. Reactions to injustice include an initial state of upset and then an effort to restore justice. But if justice cannot be restored, observers will be motivated to find evidence that the victim actually deserved his or her fate (Lerner, 1980).

Martyred victims (those who choose to suffer so that others will not) receive even more derogation than innocent victims. The less deserved a person's suffering has been, or the less compensa-

tion the person has received for having suffered, the greater the likelihood that the person will be devalued (Lerner & Simmons, 1966).

Although the foregoing statements imply that the need to believe in a just world is a prevalent orientation among us, there are individual differences in the strength of this response (Wrightsman, Nario, Posey, & Bothwell, 1993). Some people are so threatened by the possibility that negative outcomes can occur without reason that they always grasp at opportunities to blame the victim. Others are more able to tolerate the irrationality of everyday unpleasant occurrences and bad fortune. Rubin and Peplau (1975) have developed an attitude scale, called Beliefs in the Just World Scale, to measure these individual differences. People who have strong beliefs in a just world tend to be conventional people who subscribe to traditional religious beliefs. They justify the status quo, are more likely to give harsh sentences to defendants, and yet are generally optimistic people.

# SUMMARY

**1.** *Is what society considers moral the same as what it considers legal?* What is considered moral is not always what is ruled legal, and vice versa. Sometimes what most of us would consider an immoral failure to act in an emergency is not against the law.

**2.** *What are some theories that explain differing standards for what is right and wrong?* When determining right and wrong, some people rely on the law almost entirely; others have internalized principles of morality that may be inconsistent with the laws. Various theories seek to explain the development of moral judgment. Lawrence Kohlberg proposes six stages of moral development that may be experienced by persons in all cultures; the way a person decides what is correct behavior is qualitatively different at each stage. Although extensive empirical evidence supports Kohlberg's theory, Carol Gilligan has criticized it, proposing that women's development may be described better by a different kind of morality.

**3.** *How does Kohlberg's theory of moral judgment differ from Gilligan's?* Whereas Kohlberg's theory has an orientation toward rules, with an emphasis on abstract concepts and especially the concept of justice, Gilligan argues that women possess a responsibility orientation, with an emphasis on sensitivity to others and the concept of care.

**4.** *What is the relationship of justice to equity and equality?* Justice can be defined as fairness.

Psychologists use equity theory to identify standards for determining whether justice has been done. Equity is defined as a state in which each person's rewards are in keeping with his or her relative contributions. As a standard for allocating resources, equity can be contrasted with equality, in which the same levels of resources are assigned to every participant, regardless of how much he or she contributed. Men characteristically use equity as a norm; women sometimes use equity, sometimes equality.

**5.** *What is commonsense justice?* Commonsense justice reflects the basic notions of everyday citizens about what is just and fair. In contrast to the codified law, commonsense justice emphasizes the overall context in which an act occurs, the subjective intent of the person committing the act, and the desirability of making the legal consequences of the fact proportionate to the perceived culpability of the actor.

**6.** *Why does the "just world" develop as an explanation for events?* The need to believe in justice can be so strong that people will adopt the just-world explanation for events that really are only chance happenings. For example, if a friend is a victim of a rape or serious accident, some people will blame the victim for the tragedy. This reaction is a response to the threat that such terrible occurrences could happen, without reason, to innocent people.

## KEY TERMS

| | | | |
|---|---|---|---|
| agency | duty to assist laws* | impossible acts | moral dilemmas* |
| attribution theory | equality | intention | procedural justice* |
| belief in a just world | equity | justice* | |
| commonsense justice* | euthanasia* | *mens rea* | |
| communion | good Samaritan laws | mercy killing | |

---

**InfoTrac**
**COLLEGE**
**EDITION**

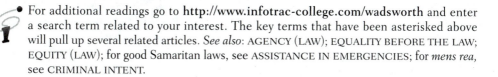

• For additional readings go to **http://www.infotrac-college.com/wadsworth** and enter a search term related to your interest. The key terms that have been asterisked above will pull up several related articles. *See also*: AGENCY (LAW); EQUALITY BEFORE THE LAW; EQUITY (LAW); for good Samaritan laws, see ASSISTANCE IN EMERGENCIES; for *mens rea*, see CRIMINAL INTENT.

# The Legal System and Its Players

## ORIENTING QUESTIONS

1. *What is the difference between the adversarial and inquisitorial models of trials?*
2. *What is a federal court? What is a state court?*
3. *How are judges selected?*
4. *What are juvenile courts? How are juvenile courts changing?*
5. *What is alternate dispute resolution? What are the types of ADR?*
6. *What are the ethical standards applied to lawyers?*
7. *What are some common criticisms of lawyers?*

In this chapter, we describe the legal system and its players. We discuss courts and judges, including juvenile courts, alternative dispute resolution (arbitration and mediation), and conclude with some thoughts about law school, lawyers, and the legal profession.

# The Adversarial System

American trial procedure—whether in criminal or civil cases—involves an **adversarial system** of justice. Exhibits, evidence, and witnesses are introduced by both sides for the purpose of convincing the fact finder that their side's viewpoint is the truthful one. The choice of what evidence to present is left, within broad limits, to the discretion of the parties in dispute and their attorneys (Lind, 1982). Judges rarely call witnesses or introduce evidence on their own. Judges may ask questions of witnesses, but they seldom do, and they usually do not encourage jurors to ask questions, despite evidence that (1) allowing jurors to ask questions increases their satisfaction that witnesses have been thoroughly examined and (2) questioning by jurors is not impractical or disruptive of the trial process (Heuer & Penrod, 1988).

The adversarial system is derived from English common law. This approach contrasts with the **inquisitorial approach,** which is used on the continent of Europe (but not in Great Britain). Lind (1982) describes the procedure in France, for example, as follows:

> The questioning of witnesses is conducted almost exclusively by the presiding judge. The judge interrogates the disputing parties and witnesses, referring frequently to a dossier that has been prepared by a court official who investigated the case. Although the parties probably have partisan attorneys present at the trial, it is evident that control over the presentation of evidence and arguments is firmly in the hands of the judge. (p. 14)

In the inquisitorial system, the two sides do not have separate witnesses; the witnesses testify for the court, and the opposing parties are not allowed to prepare the witnesses before the trial (Sheppard & Vidmar, 1980).

The adversarial model has been criticized on the ground that it promotes a competitive atmosphere that can distort the truth surrounding a dispute (Lind, 1982). Jurors have to choose between two versions of the truth, both of which are probably inaccurate in some ways and are certainly incomplete at best. But the effects of the adversarial system intrude before the jury's decision-making step. Sheppard and Vidmar (1980) found that witnesses who were interviewed by a lawyer with an adversarial orientation biased their reports in favor of the lawyer's client. Chapter 2 described the dilemma that even expert witnesses face in this regard.

However, research on these contrasting approaches reveals several benefits of the adversarial model. A research team led by a social psychologist, John Thibaut, and a law professor, Laurens Walker (Thibaut & Walker, 1975; Thibaut, Walker, & Lind, 1972; Walker, La Tour, Lind, & Thibaut, 1974), carried out a program of research whose conclusion was that the adversarial system led to less biased decisions and to decisions that were more likely to be seen as fair by the parties in dispute. One possible explanation for this more favorable evaluation of the adversarial system is that it is the system that American subjects are accustomed to. But a study by Lind, Erickson, Friedland, and Dickenberger (1978) found that subjects who lived in countries with nonadversarial systems (France and West Germany) also rated the adversarial procedure as fairer. Why? Perhaps because the adversarial system motivates attorneys to try harder to identify all the evidence favorable to their side. Especially when law students (serving as experimental subjects) believed that the weight of the information and evidence favored the other side rather than their client, they conducted more thorough investigations of the case. Thus, when the case was presented to the judge, the arguments appeared less unbalanced than the original distribution of facts would warrant (Lind, 1975; Lind, Thibaut, & Walker, 1973).

A primary advantage of the adversarial system is that it gives participants a full opportunity to present their version of the facts so that they feel as if they have been treated fairly (Lind & Tyler, 1988). Sheppard and Vidmar (1983) point out that any method of dispute resolution that produces this belief is more likely to be viewed favorably than alternatives that do not.

# Courts

Federal courts have subject matter jurisdiction (i.e., authority) over cases arising under the Constitution or laws of the United States. Federal courts do not have subject matter jurisdiction over cases arising under state law, unless there is diversity of citizenship (i.e., the plaintiff and defendant are from different states). When Congress passes a law, for example, making carjacking a federal crime, the effect is to increase the caseload of the federal courts.

Federal trial courts are called *United States District Courts*. There is at least one district in every state; some states (e.g., California) have several districts. The number of judges per district varies according to the district's case load.

The federal appellate courts are called the *United States Courts of Appeals*. There are 13 federal courts of appeal, divided into geographic circuits; there is a circuit for appeals from federal agencies (the Federal Circuit), a circuit for the District of Columbia, and 11 circuits for the rest of the country. In population, the largest circuit is the Ninth Circuit, which includes California, and the smallest is the First Circuit, which includes only a few New England states. The number of judges on each of the appellate courts depends on the caseload of the particular court. Thus, there are 21 active judges on the Ninth Circuit and only 11 on the First Circuit.

Appeals are assigned to three-judge panels; the three judges assigned to a particular case read the record (i.e., the papers, transcripts, and documents that the lawyers feel the judges need to read in order to decide the case), read the briefs (the lawyers' written arguments), and listen to the oral argument (the lawyers' debate about the case), before voting. The panel decides the case by majority vote (either 3–0 or 2–1), and one of the judges writes an opinion explaining why the court decided as it did. The opinion is sent to the parties and is published in bound volumes (the *Reporters*) if the judges think the opinion is significant. All opinions, both published and unpublished, can be accessed through Westlaw and Lexis, computer-assisted legal research services. Very important cases are sometimes heard *en banc*—meaning that all the judges on the particular Court of Appeals will sit on the case. Decisions of a federal appellate court sitting *en banc* are almost always published.

Nine justices make up the United States Supreme Court, which has the authority to review all cases decided by the federal appellate courts. The Supreme Court also has authority to review state court decisions based on the Constitution or laws of the United States. When a state court decision rests on the Constitution or laws of the United States, lawyers and judges refer to the decision as "raising a federal question." The Supreme Court reviews only those cases that the justices think are important. When the Court decides to review a case, the order granting review is called a **writ of certiorari.** The Court reviews only a small percentage of the cases that it is asked to consider.

Justices of the Supreme Court, like other federal judges, are appointed by the president and confirmed by the Senate. Federal judges are appointed for life and, like other federal officers, can be removed by the Congress for "treason, high crimes and misdemeanors." To remove a federal judge, the House impeaches the judge, and the Senate holds a trial on the articles of impeachment, with a two-thirds vote required for removal. Chief Justice William Rehnquist, who presided over the 1999 impeachment trial of President Clinton, has written a fascinating book titled *Grand Inquest* in which he describes the 1805 impeachment and trial of Justice Samuel Chase, whose primary "sin" was to be a Federalist (a member of John Adams's party) at a time when Jeffersonian Republicans controlled the presidency and Congress. Chase was acquitted by the Senate (though a majority of the Senators voted for two of the four impeachment articles). In Rehnquist's opinion, Chase's acquittal established the principle that disagreement with a judge's decisions or judicial philosophy is not grounds for impeachment.

> The acquittal of Samuel Chase by the Senate had a profound effect on the American judiciary. First, it assured the independence of federal judges from congressional oversight of the decisions they made in cases that came before them. Second, by assuring that impeachment would not be used in the future as a method to remove federal judges for their judicial opinions, it helped to safeguard the independence of that body. (Rehnquist, 1992, p. 114)

State court systems are typically divided as follows: (1) "lower" courts, which have jurisdiction only over specific matters—for example, probate of wills (proving that a will was properly signed) and administration of estates (supervising the payment of the deceased's debts and distribution of his or her assets); and (2) courts of general jurisdiction, which might be called the superior court (California), the circuit court (Kentucky), or even the supreme court (New York). A court of general jurisdiction may hear any case, unless denied that authority by the legislative body that created the cause of action. Thus, a state court of general jurisdiction may hear a case arising under the Federal Civil Rights Act (42 U.S.C. 1983), because Congress did not limit the trial of Federal Civil Rights cases to the federal courts, but a state court may not try a person for a federal crime, because Congress authorized only federal courts to try those accused of committing federal crimes.

In addition to lower courts and trial courts of general jurisdiction, state court systems typically include one or more courts of appeal, similar to the federal appellate courts, and a state supreme court. Like the United States Supreme Court, state supreme courts review only those cases that are deemed to be important, and they authorize publication only of significant opinions. Published opinions are found in state reporters, and all opinions are accessible through Westlaw and Lexis.

# Judges

While judges are still predominately white and male, signs indicate that the times are changing. Before 1961, only two women and one African American male had been appointed to lifetime positions on federal courts. Although President Carter moved beyond tokenism by appointing a number of women and African Americans, it was not until the presidency of Bill Clinton that judicial appointments began to mirror the country in an "emerging triumph of affirmative action" (Goldman & Saronson, 1994, p. 73). In President Clinton's first term, more than half the judges he appointed to the federal bench were African American or women. As a result of Clinton's appointments, the number of female judges in the federal courts jumped between 1992 and 1997 from 91 to 143; the number of African American judges increased during the same period from 44 to 70 (Goldman & Slotnick, 1997).

State courts also are increasingly diverse. As of 1995, only six states had no women or African Americans on their supreme courts; 13 of 25 black justices were in the states of the old Confederacy (Curriden, 1995b). In Minnesota, by 1993 women had come to comprise a majority of the state supreme court (Allen & Wall, 1993).

Do male and female judges view cases differently? Davis, Haire, and Songer (1993) analyzed federal court of appeals cases decided between 1981 and 1990 in three areas: employment discrimination, criminal procedural rights, and obscenity. When controlled for political party affiliation, there was no difference in the attitudes of male and female judges toward criminal procedural

## The Science of

**BOX 4-1**   **Judging judges**

The Hearst Corporation funded a national survey in 1999 for the National Center for State Courts (available at www.ncsconline.org). Although the survey indicates that most Americans think judges are fair and honest and attempt to make sure both sides are heard, the survey's conclusions are generally negative. Some of the most significant findings:

◆ Only one-third of the respondents agreed with the statement "It is affordable to bring a case to court."

◆ Eighty percent agreed with the statement "Cases are not resolved in a timely manner."

◆ Whites, Hispanics, and African Americans all thought that African Americans received worse treatment from the courts than that received by other groups.

◆ Eighty-one percent of respondents agreed with the statement that judges' decisions are influenced by political considerations.

◆ Three-fourths of the respondents agreed that elected judges are influenced by campaign contributions.

The survey was discussed at a blue ribbon meeting of 500 court, bar, and civic leaders held in Washing-

ton, D.C., in May 1999—the National Conference on Public Trust and Confidence in the Justice System. The attendees agreed that the judicial system should be more responsive to the public—that is, the litigants, witnesses, and jurors for whose benefit the system exists. The conference summary reported a consensus on what needs to be done: "better communication and outreach to the public, better internal management and use of technology, more diversity, stricter enforcement of court procedures and supervision of lawyers, and a stronger commitment to handling cases fairly, swiftly, and economically" (Podgers, 1999, p. 87).

---

rights and obscenity. In employment discrimination cases, however, female judges were more liberal than their male counterparts—they favored the plaintiff employee to a greater extent than did the male judges. For example, female southern Democratic judges favored the plaintiff 82% of the time, while male southern Democrats favored the plaintiff 52% of the time. The authors cautiously concluded that female judges see employment cases differently than do their male counterparts. The reason? Female judges have likely experienced discrimination and have an affinity for victims of discrimination.

What are judges like? Judge John Kennedy (1998) administered the Myers-Briggs Type Inventory (MBTI) to more than 1300 judges in California and other states. On the Introvert/Extrovert scale, 60% of the males and 43% of the females were introverts. On the Sensing/Intuition scale, 60% of the males and 43% of the females expressed

a sensing preference. On the Thinking/Feeling scale, 84% of the males and 72% of the females were thinkers (in society at large, 60% of males and 35% of females are thinkers). On the Judging/Perceptive scale, 72% of both male and female judges were judgers (not a big surprise) (Kennedy, 1998, p. 8).

What do people think of judges and the judicial system? ◆ Box 4-1 summarizes one set of answers to that question.

As noted at the May 1999 conference mentioned in Box 4-1, public trust is diminished by the belief that judges are influenced by campaign contributions. Concerns about influence raise the question of judicial independence. While there is some legitimacy to the argument that judges should be sensitive to the popular will, judges should not decide cases out of fear that they will be turned out of office for an unpopular decision (see ◆ Box 4-2).

### BOX 4-2    Political pressure and judges

In 1996, Judge Harold Baer, a Clinton appointee to the federal bench, suppressed evidence (80 pounds of cocaine) found as a result of what Judge Baer felt was an illegal search by New York City police officers. Judge Baer's ruling was criticized by the media. The U.S. attorney asked Judge Baer to reconsider. While the motion to reconsider was pending, 200 members of the House of Representatives signed a letter to President Clinton asking him to demand Judge Baer's resignation. Rather than support Judge Baer and the principle of judicial independence, the president implied he would seek the judge's resignation if Judge Baer did not reverse his ruling and allow the cocaine to be admitted into evidence. Presidential candidate Bob Dole, who perhaps had not read Chief Justice Rehnquist's book on impeachment and judicial independence, hopped into the controversy to assert that Judge Baer should be impeached. The judges of the Second Circuit Court of Appeals rallied to Judge Baer's defense, with letters to the president and Senator Dole pointing

out that calling for the resignation or impeachment of a judge because of disagreement over a ruling undermines the independence of the federal judiciary. Senator Dole responded by letter, which asserted that impeachment is appropriate "when a judge makes ridiculous and prejudicial statements demonstrating a deeply held disdain for the police." As the controversy festered, Judge Baer reversed himself and allowed the cocaine to be introduced into evidence. By so doing, he gave the appearance of caving in to the political pressures brought to bear by President Clinton's adversaries (Newman, 1997, p. 163).

Other judges have felt the wrath of the public. The most notable example is that of Penny White, formerly a justice of the Tennessee Supreme Court. Justice White was targeted in a retention election by the Republican party and others ostensibly because she had voted—along with other members of the Tennessee Supreme Court— to set aside a death penalty. Typical of the mailings sent to Tennessee voters was a letter that opened

as follows: "78-year-old Ethel Johnson lay dying in a pool of blood. Stabbed in the heart, lungs, and liver, she fought back as best she could. Her hands were sliced to ribbons as she tried to push the knife away. And then she was raped. Savagely. . . . But her murderer won't be getting the punishment he deserves. Thanks to Penny White." Justice White was voted off the bench and then-governor Don Sundquist was quoted as saying, "Should a judge look over his shoulder [when making decisions] about whether they're going to be thrown out of office? I hope so" (Bright, 1997, pp. 166, 168).

In Alabama, Governor Fob James recently asked United States District Judge Ira DeMent to defy the United States Supreme Court and uphold school-sponsored religious activity. When DeMent ignored the request and forbade the activities (Bible devotions and vocal prayer), Governor James sought to have the judge impeached. However, Governor James couldn't find a representative to sponsor an impeachment resolution (American Judicature Society, 1999).

## How Are Judges Selected?

Federal judges are appointed by the president and confirmed by the Senate. They serve for life, subject to impeachment for "high crimes and misdemeanors." There are many different methods for selection of state judges. The most common are as follows:

◆ *Partisan election.* In Texas, judges run for elective office under party label. Because voters typically know very little about the judicial candidates, the effect of top-of-the-ticket candidates is very strong. "Since Texas provides no voter information pamphlets to voters about judicial candidates, since judges are ethically bound to avoid discussing issues that may come before the court, since the ballot structure encourages party voting, and since Texas has developed two-party competition, the top of the ticket has now clearly emerged as a powerful force affecting the outcomes of contested trial court races" (Kiel, Funk, & Champagne, 1994, p. 293).

◆ *Nonpartisan election.* In Kentucky, judges do not run under party labels and do not publicly identify themselves as Democrats or Republicans. Since judges are ethically bound not to comment on issues that might come before them, voters are forced to rely on the candidates' reputations and endorsements by the media and bar associations. Incumbents, who often were appointed to fill a vacancy, have the advantage in such a system.

◆ *Appointment with retention election.* In a number of states, the governor appoints judges from names submitted by a merit selection commission. After a period on the bench, the judges run for retention. The electorate votes the judge up or down on the basis of the judge's record (Penny White was defeated in such an election). If retained, the judge serves a term of years, after which he or she again runs for retention. With notable exceptions (Penny White, Chief Justice Rose Bird in California), most judges are retained in these elections (Sheldon, 1994).

The balance between public accountability and judicial independence can perhaps best be struck by a system that combines merit appointments with retention elections in which voters are provided with an evaluation of the judge's entire tenure in office by a nonpartisan judicial qualifications commission. Such a system is in place in Alaska and Colorado. Retention elections are generally thought to be a good way of balancing accountability and independence. In a study of ten states, for example, 86% of judges surveyed favored retention elections. The judges said their behavior was improved by knowing that they would have to face the electorate; they were less likely to be arrogant to jurors and litigants and more likely to explain their decisions (Aspin & Hall, 1994, pp. 307, 313).

# The Special Role of Juvenile Courts

As the criminal law developed in England and the American colonies, children under 7 were treated in the same way as were insane persons—that is, as not being criminally responsible for their actions. If the child was between 7 and 14, the state was required to prove that the child understood what he or she was doing and knew the difference between right and wrong. Children 14 or older were treated as adults (Lou, 1927).

**Juvenile courts** grew out of the Progressive movement of the late 19th century. (The Progressive movement also is credited with the creation of "women's courts" in several cities; see ◆ Box 4-3.) Social reformers believed that misbehaving children should be corrected but not subjected to adult punishment (Schwartz, Weiner, & Enosh, 1998). In 1899, the Illinois legislature created for the city of Chicago the first juvenile court in the United States. The premise of the court was that it should treat law-breaking children in the same way as a kind but stern parent would treat a child—with corrective measures rather than punishment. Consider a 1909 description:

> Why is it not just and proper to treat these juvenile offenders as we deal with the neglected children, as a wise and merciful father handles his own child whose errors are not discovered by the authorities? Why is it not the duty of the state, instead of asking merely whether a boy or girl has committed a specific offense, to find out what he is, physically, mentally, morally, and then if it learns that he is treading the path that leads to criminality, to take him in charge, not so much to punish as to reform, not to degrade but to uplift, not to crush but to develop, not to make him a criminal but a worthy citizen. (Mack, 1909, p. 107)

During the first three decades of the 20th century, all but three states established juvenile courts, in which criminal offenses became acts of juvenile delinquency, punishment became reha-

## BOX 4-3   The Los Angeles Women's Court

The Progressive movement spawned "women's courts" in a number of American cities in the early part of the 20th century. The first such court was created in Los Angeles in 1914 as a branch of Los Angeles Municipal Court, with the express purpose of protecting members of the "weaker sex" charged with minor crimes. Women, like juveniles, were thought to need protection and guidance, and the philosophy of the Los Angeles Women's Court was to help wayward women who ran afoul of the law. Like juvenile court, Women's Court was closed to the public, "to exclude the male degenerates that cluster about our police courts, as they do in any large city, to prey upon the girls and women" (Cook, 1993, p. 144).

Georgia Bullock, a formidable person who later became a judge of the Los Angeles Superior Court, was the first judge of Los Angeles Women's Court. Rehabilitation was her sentencing philosophy. She placed "good girls" on probation and worked closely with the social agencies of the time to find resources for women who came to her court. In 1927, she and her staff arranged to find jobs or send home about 150 girls "infected with the movie virus" who were out of money and committing petit larceny or worse.

Men came to Judge Bullock's courtroom on "failure to provide" petitions filed by their wives or girlfriends. She showed no mercy to men who didn't support their children. She gave first offenders

60 days and repeat offenders a year in jail. She lambasted child deserters and urged the legislature to increase the penalties for nonsupport.

Judge Bullock went on to be the first woman on the Los Angeles Superior Court, where she served with distinction until she retired in 1955 at the age of 70. Meanwhile, in the early 1930s, Los Angeles gave up its separate Women's Court. In retrospect, a separate court for women seemed condescending, serving to reinforce the belief that women, like children, needed protection from the evils of the industrial age (Cook, 1993).

bilitation, and "reform school" (for the most incorrigible) replaced the prisons and jails to which children had previously been sent. The movement was based on the belief that wayward youths could be reclaimed and go on to lead orderly and productive lives (Ryerson, 1978). Another premise of the juvenile court movement suggested that juvenile misbehavior resulted as much from the environment as from the child; therefore, the child should not be treated as a criminal (Lou, 1927).

The distinction between neglected and delinquent children became blurred; probation, rather than institutionalizing, became the preferred disposition for child offenders; courtroom procedures were informal and lacked the adversarial nature of adult courts. The public selected juvenile court judges who, it was hoped, were imbued

with humanistic and sympathetic skills that would inspire trust from youthful offenders (Olson-Raymer, 1984). It was assumed that these offenders wanted to be good and had the potential and desire to be productive citizens (Ryerson, 1978).

As we enter the 21st century, the public's attitude toward juvenile offenders is far different than was the public's attitude in the early years of the 20th century. Now the public, believing that juvenile courts are "kiddie courts," clamors for "adult treatment for adult crimes." As a result, 40 states and the District of Columbia have passed laws in recent years making it easier for juveniles to be tried as adults. All states have provisions that allow juvenile courts to transfer certain serious cases to adult courts. In addition, as of 1996 there were 35 states with provisions that essentially excluded certain cases from juvenile court, thus mandating transfer from juvenile to adult court (Office of Juvenile Justice and Delinquency Prevention, 1999).

The public's get-tough attitude results in part from a significant increase in juvenile crimes of violence between 1980 and 1993. Arrests of juveniles for aggravated assault and homicide doubled in that period before starting to decline in 1994. Gun-related homicides, often highly publicized, showed the biggest increase—up almost 300% by 1993 (Zimring, 1998). Though relatively small in numbers (2800 homicides out of a total caseload of 1.7 million cases in 1995), murders committed by juveniles captured headlines and sparked demands to be tough on crime (Office of Juvenile Justice and Delinquency Prevention, 1999).

In 1999, 100 years after the first juvenile offender statute, Illinois made sweeping changes in its juvenile laws in order to emphasize punishment and accountability over rehabilitation. These new statutes often include "purpose provisions"—that is, a statement of what the legislation is intended to accomplish. The purpose provision of the pre-1999 juvenile statute spoke to the "safety and moral, emotional, mental and physical welfare of the minor," but the purpose provision of the 1999 statute speaks to the need to "protect the community, impose accountability for violations of law, and equip juvenile offenders with the competencies to live responsibly and productively." The law was changed to reflect this shift in purpose. For example, in deciding whether to transfer a child to adult court, Illinois judges are now to be guided primarily by the seriousness of the offense rather than the best interests of the child (Geraghty & Rhee, 1998). Recently passed transfer statutes in other states focus on the circumstances of the offense rather than the child's amenability to treatment, a focus that is consistent with a goal of punishment ("just desserts") rather than rehabilitation (Feld, 1997, p. 80).

Most states set a minimum age for transfer to adult court. In Jonesboro, Arkansas, in 1998, Mitchell Johnson, age 13, and Andrew Golden, age 12, lay in ambush and opened fire on their schoolmates with stolen rifles, killing four students and a teacher. They were tried in juvenile court because they were too young to be transferred to adult court (Johnson turned 14, the age for transfer, after the shootings). Judge Ralph Wilson sentenced the pair to confinement until they turn 21, at which time the juvenile court will lose jurisdiction and the boys will go free. In sentencing Johnson and Golden, Judge Wilson expressed frustration because he could not impose a more severe sentence (Moehringer, 1998). Some states set the minimum age for transfer as young as 10, and a few states have no minimum age (Sickmund, 1996). In one of those states, Johnson and Golden could have been tried as adults and subjected to adult penalties.

While states have made it easier to transfer juveniles to adult courts, the vast majority of juveniles stay in juvenile court. From 1986 to 1995, the percentage of cases transferred to adult court has remained both small and stable, falling between 0.6% and 0.7% of the total number each year. In 1995, cases were resolved as follows:

- 0.57% were transferred to adult court,
- 9.69% were placed in some kind of juvenile facility,
- 35.54% were probated,
- 36.62% were released, and
- 17.59% received other disposition (Schwartz, Weiner, & Enosh, 1998).

Crimes against the person (assaults, homicides, robbery, and rape) made up almost half of the cases transferred, which is consistent with the emphasis on incarcerating those who commit crimes of violence. The Office of Juvenile Justice and Delinquency Prevention of the Department of Justice published an extensive report in 1998 on *Serious and Violent Juvenile [SVJ] Offenders*. The study concludes that SVJ offenders are a distinct group with many known predictors that could be incorporated into screening devices and subjected to intervention. Among the strongest, early predictors identified by the study were impulsive behavior, poor school work, substance use, and antisocial parents (Loeber & Farrington, 1998).

## THE CASE OF

**BOX 4-4  Gerald Gault**

When arrested on June 8, 1964, 15-year-old Gerald and another boy were charged with making an obscene call to a neighbor. The hearing was informal, and Gerald did not have a lawyer. Gerald testified that he had only dialed the number, and the other boy had made the call. The neighbor did not testify. The judge found Gerald to be a delinquent and committed him to the State Industrial School until he turned 21. If committed by an adult, the maximum penalty for an obscene call would have been two months in custody.

Gerald objected to the procedures that led to his conviction and confinement. The case eventually went to the United States Supreme Court, which described the Gila

County Arizona juvenile court as a "kangaroo court." The Supreme Court held that the Due Process Clause of the Fourteenth Amendment applies to juvenile court proceedings and that Gerald had been denied due process. The Court held that Gerald had the following rights, which had been denied him by the Arizona court:

- ◆ notice of the charges,
- ◆ the right to an attorney,
- ◆ the right to confront and cross-examine the witnesses against him, and
- ◆ the privilege against self-incrimination (*In re Gault*, 1967).

*Gault* changed the way juvenile courts operated. Prior to *Gault*,

it was unusual for an attorney to represent the child; after *Gault*, lawyers, most appointed, began to appear on behalf of the child, turning juvenile hearings into adversarial affairs. *In re Winship*, decided in 1970, held that the Due Process Clause requires the state to prove every element of the case against the child beyond a reasonable doubt. Professor Feld asserts that *Gault* and *Winship* "unintentionally, but inevitably, transformed the juvenile court system from its original Progressive conception as a social welfare agency into a wholly-owned subsidiary of the criminal justice system" (Feld, 1997, p. 73).

## Juveniles' Constitutional Rights

The idealized juvenile court of the Progressive Era made a virtue of informality. Consider this 1909 description:

> The child who must be brought into court should, of course, be made to know that he is face to face with the power of the state, but he should feel at the same time, and more emphatically, be made to feel that he is the object of its care and solicitude. The ordinary trappings of the court-room are out of place in such a hearings. The judge on a bench, looking down upon the boy standing at the bar, can never evoke a proper sympathetic spirit. Seated at a desk, with the child at his side, where he can on occasion put his arm around his shoulder and draw the lad to him, the judge, while losing none of his judicial dignity, will gain immensely

in the effectiveness of his work. (Mack, 1909, pp. 119–120)

Unlike adult courts, juvenile courts of the early 20th century were not adversarial. Children were not represented by counsel, hearings were informal, and evidence rules were nonexistent. "By separating children from adults and providing a rehabilitative alternative to punishment, juvenile courts rejected both the criminal law's jurisprudence and its procedural safeguards such as juries and lawyers" (Feld, 1997, p. 71). Unfettered discretion, however, led to unequal and unfair treatment. The case of Gerald Gault (see ◆ Box 4-4) is one such case.

After *Gault*, it appeared that the Supreme Court would hold that juveniles were entitled to the same constitutional protections as adults. One year after *Gault,* however, the Court held that the Due Process Clause did not require states to provide jury trials for juveniles. The Court had held that an adult facing a serious charge is entitled to trial by jury (*Duncan v. Louisiana,* 1968), but in *McKeiver v. Pennsylvania* (1971), the Court held that it was not unconstitutional for a state to deny jury trials to juveniles.

Since the age of responsibility at common law was 7, it is not surprising to find accounts of young children sentenced to death in 18th- and 19th-century America. However, death sentences were rarely carried out on children who were under 14 at the time of the crime. Only 16 children under 14 at the time of the offense were executed in the period 1642–1899, and only two children under 14 were executed after 1900. However, there was little reluctance to execute those who were 16 or 17 when the crime was committed. Of 287 juveniles executed in the United States from 1642 to 1982, 196 were 17 at the time of the offense, and 52 were 16 at the time of the offense (Streib, 1983).

In light of the American experience, it is not surprising that the United States Supreme Court drew the line at age 16. In *Thompson v. Oklahoma* (1988), the Court held that contemporary standards of decency bar the execution of a person who was under the age of 16 at the time of the offense. The next year, the Court upheld the execution of persons 16 and over in the companion cases of *Stanford v. Kentucky* and *Wilkins v. Missouri* (1989). Stanford, then 17, and Wilkins, then 16, had committed "adult-type" crimes: robbery and murder of store clerks (Stanford had also raped and sodomized the clerk). Their crimes were brutal and planned. In upholding the death penalties, Justice Scalia rejected the argument that "evolving standards of decency" forbid the execution of one under 18 at the time of the offense. He pointed out that a majority of states authorizing capital punishment fix 16 as the minimum age, adding that there is no consensus that persons of 16 or 17 lack sufficient moral culpability to warrant the imposition of the death penalty.

Other than the death penalty for those under 16, juveniles transferred to adult court face the same penalties as do adults convicted of the same crimes. Juveniles thus might face very lengthy terms of imprisonment, first in a juvenile facility, then in an adult prison on reaching 18. Washington state, for example, sentenced a 13-year old to life without parole. In upholding the sentence, the Washington court said, "The test is whether in view of contemporary standards of elemental decency, the punishment is of such disproportionate character to the offense as to shock the general conscience and violate principles of fundamental fairness. That test does not embody an element or consideration of the defendant's age, only a balance between the crime and the sentence imposed" (*State v. Massey,* 1990).

Such sentences overlook the obvious—a 13-year-old is an adolescent, with the mood swings and lack of judgment that comes with adolescence. As suggested in Chapter 3, some young adolescents might not have yet attained a level of moral development that is sufficient for resisting illegal opportunities. As a matter of policy, youth should operate as a mitigating factor: a 13-year-old should not be sentenced as severely as a 16-year-old and a 16-year-old should not be sentenced as severely as a 21-year-old (Feld, 1997). Scott and Grisso (1997) use the following example to illustrate three factors that influence adolescents' decisions: (1) conformity and compliance in relation to peers, (2) the youth's attitude toward and perception of risk, and (3) a short-sighted perspective:

> A youth hangs out with his buddies on the street. Someone suggests holding up a nearby convenience store. The boy's decision to go along with the plan may proceed in the following way. He has mixed feelings about the proposal but doesn't think of ways to extricate himself—although perhaps a more mature person might develop a strategy, the possibility that one of his friends has a gun and the consequences of that doesn't occur to him. He goes along, mostly because he fears rejection by his friends, a consequence that he attaches to a decision not to

participate—and that carries substantial negative weight. Also the excitement of the hold-up and the possibility of getting some money are attractive. These weigh more heavily in his decision than the cost of possible apprehension by the police, or the long-term costs to his future life of conviction of a serious crime. (p. 166)

Is there is a constitutionally required minimum age for criminal responsibility? Some states have no minimum age for transfer to adult court. Would it be constitutional to try a 7-year-old in adult court and subject the child to adult penalties? At common law it was conclusively presumed that a child younger than 7 was not criminally responsible—that is, did not know the difference between right and wrong or the nature and quality of his or her acts. Perhaps the Supreme Court will fall back on the common law and hold that 7 is the minimum age at which a person may be subjected to criminal penalties. In the get-tough atmosphere of the 21st century ("adult crime, adult time"), it is probable that the Court will have the opportunity to decide this question.

# Alternative Dispute Resolution

From watching television news and entertainment, one might assume that most lawsuits wind up in trial by jury. In fact, however, most cases are resolved through negotiation or by alternate dispute resolution (ADR). **Alternative dispute resolution** refers to the use of a third person, or persons, to help resolve the controversy. Generally, cases are settled, not tried. For example, in Fulton County, Georgia (Atlanta), of 543 cases referred to nonbinding arbitration during a five-year period, only 39 were eventually tried; all the others settled (Boersema, Hanson, & Keilitz, 1991, p. 29).

Many cases are settled by negotiation, without the assistance of a third party. Negotiation might be formal, as happens when management and union representatives negotiate a labor contract, or informal, as happens when attorneys jockey back and forth in a series of phone calls to settle a personal injury claim.

## Arbitration

One form of ADR—binding arbitration—bears the closest resemblance to a trial. When the parties agree to binding arbitration, they agree to be bound by the decision of an arbitrator. Binding arbitration settles the controversy, unless a procedural error of some kind has occurred. Salary arbitration in major league baseball is a good example of binding arbitration. The contract between the owners and the players' union provides that players' salary disputes are to be settled by binding arbitration and that the arbitrator must accept either the owner's offer or the player's offer—that the arbitrator cannot split the difference. Much like the TV show *The Price is Right,* the parties have incentive to make an offer as close to the player's "value" (their estimate of the arbitrator's valuation of the player's worth) as possible.

Contracts often include arbitration clauses. For example, a construction contract might provide that all disputes between the builder and owner be decided by an arbitrator selected by the parties. The owner and builder thus build into the contract a nonlitigation means to settle controversies. Arbitration provides a speedy, flexible, and informal alternative to litigation, and arbitration clauses are often made part of contracts (Cox, 1999).

While contracts generally provide for binding arbitration, court-ordered arbitration is nonbinding. If one of the parties is dissatisfied with the arbitrator's decision, that person may ask that the case be tried before a judge or jury. **Arbitration,** whether binding or nonbinding, is triallike. The parties present evidence and argue the case, and the arbitrator (or arbitrators) makes an award. Court-ordered arbitration in Atlanta is described as follows:

> The arbitrators hear cases in panels of three attorneys (volunteers paid $100 a day). The hearing, which is presided over by the chairperson,

begins with short presentations by each of the respective panel members. They explain the nature and purpose of the hearing, the legal effect of the hearing, and the hearing's ground rules. Additionally, they indicate where, when, and how the panel's decision will be made public. The hearing consists of case summaries by counsel for the plaintiff and the defense, the introduction of exhibits and witnesses, cross-examination, and closing statements by each side. Hearings last for two hours, followed by a half-hour deliberation by the panel. In their discussions, the arbitrators consider the facts and law presented to them and do not speculate on what a judge or jury might do if more evidence had been presented or better arguments had been made. (Boersema et al., 1991, p. 30)

A litigant dissatisfied with an arbitration decision may ask for a trial. Relatively few do. In the Georgia survey, 90% of the attorneys said that the arbitrators on their cases were fair. Though many attorneys did not agree with the outcome (45% believed the award was at least somewhat unfair), attorneys were inclined to accept (not appeal) the arbitrators' decisions, because the hearings were perceived as fair. Litigants usually want to resolve their disputes, not protract them, and the arbitrator's decision serves that function. The litigants usually will be inclined to accept the decision, even though not totally satisfied, rather than prolong the controversy through appeal.

## Summary Jury Trial

The **summary jury trial** (SJT) is an interesting variation on court-ordered arbitration. Developed by Judge Thomas Lambros, the summary jury trial is much like a conventional jury trial. A jury is empaneled, and the lawyers tell the jurors what the witnesses would say if they were present. The lawyers argue the case and try to answer the jurors' questions about the facts. The judge tells the jury what the law is and tries to answer the jurors' questions about the law. The jurors then deliberate and decide the case. While the "verdict" does not bind the parties, the process educates the lawyers and clients as to how a conventional jury might view

the facts and the law. Now educated, the lawyers and their clients are more amenable to settling the case (Lambros, 1993). Commenting favorably on the summary jury trial, federal judge William Bertelsman said:

> I believe that a summary jury trial is a useful device . . . to settle a complex case with one or two key issues, where the problem with settlement is that the parties differ in their views of how the jury will react to the key issues. I believe that substantial amounts of time can be saved by using summary jury trial in a few select cases.
>
> Also . . . the summary jury trial gives the parties a taste of the courtroom and satisfies their psychological need for a confrontation with each other. Any judge or attorney can tell you that emotional issues play a large part in some cases. When emotions are high, whether between attorneys or parties, cases may not settle even when a cost-benefit analysis says they should. A summary jury trial can provide a therapeutic release of this emotion at the expenditure of three days of the court's time instead of three weeks. After the emotions have been released the parties are more likely rationally to do the cost-benefit analysis, and the case may then settle. (*McKay v. Ashland Oil Inc.*, 1988, p. 49)

## Mediation

**Mediation** is the use of a neutral person (the mediator) to work with the litigants and their lawyers to achieve a settlement of the controversy. The mediator does not have authority to decide the controversy but, rather, acts as a facilitator. Mediation often involves "shuttle diplomacy," a term associated with former secretary of state Henry Kissinger. Much as Kissinger would "shuttle" between the two sides in international diplomacy, the mediator goes back and forth between the parties, caucusing first with one side, then with the other, in an attempt to broker an agreement that both sides can live with.

Mediation can be either evaluative or nonevaluative. In an *evaluative* mediation, the mediator is most interested in the substance of the dispute; the mediator questions the litigants and their lawyers about the facts of the controversy and then evaluates the case. In the evaluation, the mediator summarizes the strengths and weaknesses on each side and might even predict how a judge or jury would decide the case. The evaluative mediator tries to lead the parties to a fair settlement—that is, a settlement that closely approximates what the mediator thinks the case is "worth."

A *nonevaluative* mediator is primarily concerned with the process. The mediator strives to open lines of communication and to assist the litigants in reaching an acceptable settlement. The mediator is less concerned with the end than with the means by which the end is achieved. Thus, the mediator will be reluctant to state what the case is "worth," because such an evaluation would impose the mediator's judgment on the process.

After observing judge-mediated settlement conferences in New Jersey, Hyman and Heumann (1996) described the two evaluative styles as the "minitrial" style and the "matchmaker" style. "Judge Jay" (a pseudonym) epitomized the minitrial style in one of the cases described by Hyman and Heumann. The plaintiff claimed he had been permanently injured in an auto accident. Pointing to pictures that showed no damage to plaintiff's car, the defendant denied that the injuries were serious or permanent. In response to Judge Jay's question, the plaintiff admitted he had gone to see his lawyer before going to the doctor. After pointing out the negative implications of seeing a lawyer first, Judge Jay said that $2500 to $3000 would be a good settlement because verdicts were getting lower and lower as juries saw a connection between verdicts and the cost of insurance. This evaluation must have shocked the parties because the defense counsel had already made a tentative offer of $9000. Obviously believing that defense counsel had been very generous (stupidly so), Judge Jay told the plaintiff to take the $9000 or risk the imposition of "reverse interest" if the jury verdict was less than $9000. It took the plaintiff all of 12 minutes to settle for $9000.

"Judge Ellsworth" epitomized the matchmaker style. After obtaining a brief description of the auto accident, he asked the attorneys whether they had attempted to settle the case. The plaintiff had demanded $12,500; the defendant had offered $2500. Judge Ellsworth then began to work back and forth between the attorneys, nudging one up and the other down in a series of separate meetings (caucuses). When the plaintiff's lawyer said his bottom line was $6000, Judge Ellsworth asked the defense counsel whether he could get $5000 to $6000 for the plaintiff. The defense counsel replied that he thought he could get authority to settle for $3500 to $4000. Judge Ellsworth asked the defense lawyer to confer with the adjuster. The lawyer did so and reported that he had authority to settle at $3500 but thought he could get the adjuster up to $4000. Judge Ellsworth then went back to the plaintiff and said he couldn't get $6000. After some discussion, the plaintiff's counsel told Judge Ellsworth he would settle for $4000, but authorized Judge Ellsworth only to tell defense counsel he would settle at $5000. Judge Ellsworth attempted to induce defense counsel to offer more than $4000. When this effort was unsuccessful, plaintiff's counsel accepted the $4000 offer (Hyman & Heumann, 1996).

Hyman and Heumann noted that most judges they observed combined the minitrial and matchmaker styles. Attorneys surveyed liked elements of both styles. They liked caucusing, a necessary element of the matchmaker style, and evaluation, the key element of the minitrial style.

One thinks of lawyers as eager to do battle—to slay their opponents with rhetorical swords. The facts, however, indicate otherwise: lawyers prefer mediation over arbitration and trial by court or jury (Reuben, 1996). Why is this so? One of the authors of this book has mediated more than 50 cases since 1992. In his experience, most lawyers are "risk-averse." They prefer that controversies be *settled* rather than *decided*. In a settlement, there is no winner and no loser. The parties reach an agreement and, having done so, are not in a position to criticize their lawyers' performances. However, if there is a decision (by arbitration or trial), a winner and a loser emerge. The loser might well blame the lawyer for the loss. In general lawyers would rather have the certainty of a settlement than the uncertainty of arbitration or trial.

Mediation facilitates settlement. Lawyers use the mediator to provide a "reality check" on the client's expectations. A client, after hearing the mediator's somewhat negative assessment of the claim, is more likely to accept a reasonable settlement offer. A skillful mediator can make both parties feel they've gotten a good deal and that the lawyers for the parties have done an excellent job.

Should courts force litigants to try ADR (mediation, nonbinding arbitration, summary jury trial, etc.) before setting a case for trial? The reports from courts that mandate ADR are generally positive. Atlanta's mandatory nonbinding arbitration program is very successful, as measured by the percentage of cases settled and attorney satisfaction. The vast majority of cases are settled, either by acceptance of the arbitration award or by subsequent agreement between the parties. Attorneys like the process, believing the process is fair and saves clients time and money (Boersema et al., 1991). A survey of 600 attorneys whose cases in Pennsylvania federal court were referred to nonbinding arbitration produced the same results: 93% approved of the program, and 61% said they preferred arbitration over trial (Broderick, 1991).

The counterargument is that litigants have a right to trial by judge or jury, judges are paid to effectuate that right, and mandating ADR undermines that right. Arkansas federal judge Thomas Eisele put it this way:

> Let us face the truth: from the court's point of view, coerced settlement is the primary objective of these compulsory ADRs, despite protests to the contrary. The many rules requiring parties or persons with settlement authority to be present at ADR sessions should make this obvious—particularly when one realizes that in many cases the presence of such persons would not be required at the actual trial before a judge or jury. (Eisele, 1991, p. 36)

According to Judge Eisele, mandatory ADR leads to an unintended effect—lawyers ("piranhas," he calls them) file meritless claims, knowing that their claims will have "settlement value" in mediation. Recall Judge Ellsworth, the "matchmaker" mediator. He was primarily concerned with the process—ascertaining the litigants' bottom lines and pushing them to offer more and accept less. It's easy to see that a matchmaker mediator, by emphasizing the "transaction costs" (the cost of defending a meritless case), might push a blameless defendant to pay something to settle a case that substantively has no merit.

## Lawyers

Lawyers are plentiful in the United States; over 70% of the world's lawyers live in the United States, three times as many per capita as Great Britain and more than 25 times as many per capita as Japan. Estimates indicate that there are as many as 1 million lawyers in the United States—enough lawyers to populate a fair-sized city. With law school enrollments stabilized at about 125,000, approximately 40,000 new lawyers are sworn in annually, more than replacing those who leave the practice (American Bar Association [ABA], 1997). While he was vice president, Dan Quayle ended a well-publicized speech to the ABA in 1991 with the following rhetorical questions: "Does America really need 70% of the world's lawyers? Is it healthy for our economy to have 18 million new lawsuits coursing through the economy annually?" (Johnson & Kamlani, 1991, p. 55). Lawyer bashing is the mission of Nolo Press and its Web site, nolo.com. A typical joke on Nolo's "Lawyer Joke Emporium":

> A lawyer was filling out a job application when he came to the question: "Have you ever been arrested?"
>
> He answered "no."
>
> The next question, intended for those who answered the preceding question yes, was "why?" Nevertheless, the lawyer answered it "Never got caught." (www.nolo.com/jokes/bashing, last checked July 26, 1999)

With some justification, Nolo believes that lawyers gouge the public and frustrate justice. Indeed, there are many handsomely paid lawyers. The

*National Law Journal*'s 1999 salary survey reported the following annual incomes (www.nlj.com):

- ◆ $615,000: partner in Hale & Dorr, a Boston firm
- ◆ $142,500: California attorney general
- ◆ $770,000: Pepsico general counsel
- ◆ $126,500: professor of law, Boston College
- ◆ $95,000: first-year associate, Heller Ehrman, a San Francisco firm
- ◆ $49,000: law clerk to federal district judge

While some lawyers are modestly paid (staff attorneys at Napa County [California] Legal Assistance started at $25,000 in 1999), figures like those listed here go a long way toward convincing the public that there are too many lawyers paid too much money. Sophisticated clients are increasingly wary of firms that generate large profits and start lawyers fresh out of law school at salaries over $100,000 (Carter, 1998).

## Law Schools and Legal Education

What are the psychological implications of the huge numbers of lawyers currently in the United States? To answer this question, we need to examine the process of becoming a lawyer and its impact on the thinking and behavior of those in the legal profession.

American lawyers of the 18th and 19th centuries typically learned to be lawyers through the apprentice method. An enterprising young man (the first female lawyer graduated in 1869) would attach himself to an attorney for a period of time, until both he and the lawyer were satisfied that he was ready to be "admitted to the bar." He would then be questioned—often superficially—by a judge or lawyer and pronounced fit to practice (Stevens, 1983). In his prize-winning biography of Abraham Lincoln, Carl Sandburg (1926) describes Lincoln as bar examiner:

> When Jonathon Birch came to the hotel in Bloomington to be examined by Lincoln for admission to the bar, Lincoln asked three or four questions about contracts and other law branches. And then, as Birch told it: "He asked nothing more. Sitting on the edge of the bed he began to entertain me with recollections, many of them vivid and racy, of his start in the profession." Birch couldn't figure out whether it was a real examination or a joke. But Lincoln gave him a note to Judge Logan, another member of the examining committee, and he took the note to Logan, and without any more questions was given a certificate to practice law. The note from Lincoln read:

> *My Dear Judge:*

> *The bearer of this is a young man who thinks he can be a lawyer. Examine him if you want to. I have done so and am satisfied. He's a good deal smarter than he looks to be. Yours, Lincoln*

Powerful forces have shaped legal education as we know it today. States began to require those aspiring to be lawyers to pass meaningful examinations. Influenced by the ABA, the states also gradually increased the educational requirements for admission to these exams, first requiring some college, then some law school, and finally graduation from an accredited law school. (Apprenticing still exists as an alternative—albeit seldom used—in a few states, notably California.) Because most states require graduation from an ABA-accredited law school as a condition of admission to the bar, a degree from an unaccredited school is almost worthless. In 1995, 179 schools were listed as ABA approved and only 37 as unaccredited. The 37 unaccredited schools were located in eight states, 24 in California alone (ABA, 1995).

The ABA and the Association of American Law Schools (AALS), which coordinates legal education standards with the ABA, require schools applying for accreditation to demonstrate compliance with the ABA "Standards for Approval," a set of rules covering everything from admissions to placement, from library holdings to curricular content, from faculty-student ratio to teaching loads. Reaccreditation occurs every seven years, and it requires extensive reports and a site visit by a specially appointed evaluation team.

## Going to Law School

Law students come from diverse backgrounds and have varied academic and employment records.

Undergraduate students are advised to take challenging and broadening courses because, they are told, "Law schools prefer students who can think, read, and write well, and who have some understanding of what shapes human experience" (ABA, 1997). Based on one study that compared the dropout rate for students of different personality types at four law schools (Miller, 1967), some evidence indicates that "thinkers" are happier in law school than "feelers." Students who had finished their first year in good standing but did not finish their second year were considered dropouts. Of those studied, 13.8% dropped out at this point. The decision to quit was related to the students' personality types. On the basis of their responses to the Myers-Briggs Type Indicator (a Jungian measure of personal styles), those students classified as "thinking types" had a dropout rate of 11%, whereas "feeling types" had a dropout rate of 20%. The dropout rate was even higher (28.1%) for those feeling types who were especially idealistic and people oriented. In addition, this type of student was underrepresented in law school compared with the undergraduate population, implying that the high dropout rate may be a response to a problematic mix of personality style and occupational demands. In the thinking-versus-feeling classification used in the Myers-Briggs inventory, 75% of male lawyers and 60% of female lawyers are classified as "thinkers" rather than "feelers," compared to 60% and 40%, respectively, of the general population. Furthermore, feelers, who tend to make decisions based on personalized subjective values, tend to be the unhappiest lawyers (Moss, 1991).

A number of years ago, Roger Cramton, then dean of the Cornell Law School, wrote an article titled "The Ordinary Religion of the Law School Classroom" (1978). He wrote that the

> essential ingredients of the ordinary religion of the American law school classroom are: a skeptical attitude toward generalization; an instrumental approach to law and lawyering; a "tough-minded" and analytical approach toward legal tasks and professional roles; and a faith that man, by application of his reason and the use of democratic processes, can make the world a better place. (p. 248)

It follows, wrote Cramton, that "[t]he law teacher must stress cognitive rationality along with 'hard' facts and 'cold' logic and 'concrete' realities. Emotion, imagination, sentiments of affection and trust, a sense of wonder or awe at the inexplicable; these soft and mushy domains of the 'tender-minded' are off limits for law students and lawyers" (p. 250).

Law schools, concluded Cramton pessimistically, produce craftsmen rather than statesmen, "hired guns" rather than idealists, "thinkers" rather than "feelers." Writing 21 years later, Austin (1999) inveighed against what he called "womanly" legal education, a term he perjoratively used to describe "feeling" and "idealistic" educators. According to Austin, in the 1980s and 1990s, law schools gave up on "hard facts and "cold logic" and, to the detriment of future lawyers, adopted a canon of "emotion, imagination, sentiments of affection and trust." "Community has replaced individualism, while politically correct codes regulate speech and conduct. Feelings and emotions trump objectivity and rationality. Grade inflation is rationalized on the thesis that students deserve a sense of satisfaction. Kermit the Frog and Bill Cosby are featured commencement speakers" (Austin, 1999, p. A23). Austin believes that a soft approach to legal education poorly prepares putative lawyers for the rigors of law practice—where "cold facts" and "hard logic" usually carry the day.

## Women in Law School and the Legal Profession

In 1872, the Supreme Court of the United States upheld the state of Illinois's denial of a law license to a Vermont woman named Myra Bradwell. Justice Bradley's concurring opinion reflects the 19th-century view of a woman's place:

> Man is, or should be, woman's protector and defender. The natural and proper timidity and delicacy which belongs to the female sex evidently unfits it for many of the occupations of civil life. . . . The paramount destiny and mission of woman are to fulfill the noble and benign offices of wife and mother. This is the law of the Creator. And the rules of civil society must be adapted to the general constitution of things,

**BOX 4-5**   **Janet Reno, Elizabeth Dole, and the Harvard Law School**

When Janet Reno entered the Harvard Law School in the fall of 1960, she was 1 of only 16 women in a sea of more than 500 male students. Harvard had first admitted women only 13 years before, and some of the older professors evidently regarded legal coeducation as a failed experiment.

Professors like W. Barton Leach made little secret of their disdain for women. Leach, who taught property law, declared that "he wouldn't call on women in the big classrooms. He said their voices weren't powerful enough to be heard," recalled Charles Nesson,

one of two Reno classmates who now teach at the law school. So he scheduled Ladies' Day, and he made the five women in my section sit in front. Then he sat down close to the male students and questioned them.

"And we sat through that and laughed, without the thought ever occurring to us that something totally wrong was happening," Nesson said. "It had to have had some powerful effects on Janet and the others."

Ladies' Day infuriated Elizabeth Hanford Dole, class of 1965, who served as Secretary of Transportation in the Reagan administration

and Secretary of Labor in the Bush administration.

"Charles W. Kingsfield , the infamous law professor of the novel, movie, and television series *The Paper Chase,* at his most perverse could not have devised a more public humiliation," Dole later wrote. . . .

According to U.S. Senator Bob Graham, who graduated from Harvard Law School in 1962, "The pervasive attitude was that a woman in law school just took the position that should have been filled by a man who was going to practice the law and provide for a family." (Anderson, 1994, pp. 37–39)

---

and cannot be based upon exceptional cases. (*Bradwell v. State,* 1872)

Women were denied admission to elite law schools well into the 20th century. Yale did not admit women until 1918, and Harvard Law School did not become coeducational until 1947 (Stevens, 1983). (See ◆▶ **Box 4-5** for a picture of the latter law school in the 1960s.) As late as 1975, only 5% of American lawyers were women (Lentz & Laband, 1995). By 1980, however, women made up almost 40% of law students, a percentage that gradually increased to about 43% in 1996 (ABA, 1997). Because women came into the profession in large numbers only recently, the percentage of women lawyers trails the percentage of women law students. The *MacCrate Report* calculated the percentage of women lawyers in the United States during 1990–1991 to be 22% (ABA, 1992).

Are women in today's law schools disadvantaged? This question was addressed in 1996 by the ABA Commission on Women in the Profession. The commission's report, titled "The Experi-

ences of Women in Legal Education," is described in ◆▶ **Box 4-6.**

What kind of work experiences do female attorneys encounter? Do they face discrimination on the job? Overt pay discrimination based on gender was largely ended by Title VII and the Supreme Court case of *Hishon v. King & Spaulding* (1984), and male and female attorneys are now paid about the same for equal work. However, even in firms that have fewer than 15 employees and are not covered by Title VII, job satisfaction among men and women is not equal (Lentz & Laband, 1995). Women believe they are discriminated against "on intangible margins," involving factors such as work assignments, secretarial support, mentoring, invitations to social functions, and office camaraderie (Lentz & Laband, 1995).

In contrast, the hereafter described 1988 Stanford gender and law survey (in Box 4-6) found no significant differences between men and women in employment or job satisfaction. The sample of this study was 764 women (all the known living Stanford female graduates) and 764 men (who

## The Science of

### BOX 4-6    Women's experiences in law school

Based on reports and information gathered in a series of hearings, the ABA Commission on Women in the Profession has concluded that women still encounter serious gender-based problems in law school. The commission cited the following problems faced by women:

- Hostility and disrespect by male students
- Family care burdens
- Lack of role models
- Lack of confidence
- Sexual harassment
- Unequal classroom participation

Although many of the commission's findings are based on anecdotal evidence, some studies support the conclusion that female law students lack confidence relative to male students and do not participate in class equally with men. According to the gender and law project at the Stanford University Law School, male students participated more in class than females by asking more questions and volunteering more answers. The study noted that this pattern "supports our hypothesis that men are more likely than are women to participate in the classroom. This finding is important because it . . . confirms scholars' claims that professors are more likely to call on male students and that male students tend to dominate classroom discussions" (Taber, 1988, p. 1242).

Another study investigated gender bias in nine Ohio law schools. This study group was based on a 50% response to a questionnaire from a sample of 800 students. The items assessing class participation showed significant gender differences: 30% of the males but only 15% of the females reported asking questions "at least once a week"; 52% of the males and 66% of the females reported asking questions "never" or "only once a month" (Krauskopf, 1994). Of great concern were the responses to the survey item "Before law school I thought of myself as intelligent and articulate, but often I don't feel that way about myself now." Among these respondents, 16.5% of the men and 41% of the women agreed with this statement. A 25-percentage point difference is startling and indicates that—in this sample, at least—female law students tend to lose confidence to a substantially greater degree than male students do (Krauskopf, 1994).

were randomly selected). The return rate was 58%. The results indicated no statistically significant difference between female and male law students' or graduates' responses regarding their ultimate career goals or the setting in which they ultimately wanted to work. A gender difference was found for only one factor: 43% of the male graduates, but only 27% of the female graduates, considered the adversarial nature of the job important to job satisfaction. The survey also found that women (29%) were much more likely to interrupt a career than men (8%) and more likely to work part-time at some point in their careers (women, 31%; men, 9%) (Taber, 1988).

A survey of 1012 graduates of the University of New Mexico (with a return rate of 60%) indicated little difference between men and women in stress levels, job satisfaction, and hours worked. The study did reveal that women are more likely to be dissatisfied with a perceived lack of flexibility in their work schedules and with excessive time demands. The study indicated that women are somewhat more cooperative than men at work; they scored significantly higher on a "commitment to cooperation" question (Teitelbaum, 1991).

Although the New Mexico and Stanford studies indicate few gender differences in the professional lives of male and female lawyers, Lentz and Laband (1995) found that, by most indicators, women are less happy professionally than men. Other studies have also revealed that female attorneys continue to confront gender bias. A 1996

*National Law Journal* survey of women and minorities in 250 law firms revealed substantial gains in the number who had made partner between 1985 (6%) and 1995 (13.6%). However, women reported a new barrier: difficulty in making "equity partner"—that is, a partner who owns a share of the partnership assets:

> Often, however, women lawyers don't get a chance to build relationships in the firm or with the client. The days of institutional clients that are handed from one generation of partners to the next are over. Attaining new business, key to the coveted equity partnership, requires a fair amount of socializing. But social events tend to be male-centered: golf, ball games and "nights on the town when everyone ends up in a room smoking cigars," as one woman lawyer who asked not to be identified put it. (Klein, 1996, p. 1)

Like their male counterparts, female lawyers are often expected to work long hours. It is not uncommon for firms to expect the partners and associates to bill 2200 hours a year—about 45 hours a week, not including the hours spent commuting, eating lunch, or handling matters that do not create billable hours. A study of 584 female lawyers revealed a positive correlation between hours worked and stress-related ailments. Women lawyers working more than 45 hours per week were three times as likely to miscarry as those working fewer than 35 hours (Gatland, 1997). Balancing motherhood with a busy law practice isn't easy. Mothers in many law firms succeed through hard work, organization, and the support of husbands, friends, and baby-sitters. One mother described her life as one "without sleep," in which she gave her clients tax advice by cell phone while watching her children swim at the beach (Brennan, 1998).

## Minorities in Law School and the Legal Profession

In 1930, there were only six black lawyers in Mississippi, a state with a black population of more than 1 million (Houston, 1935). By 1966, the number of black lawyers in Mississippi had only grown to nine (Gellhorn, 1968). This rate reflected national trends; in 1988, only about 1% of the nation's lawyers were black (McGee, 1971). Jim Crow laws and practices barred blacks from southern law schools; Thurgood Marshall, who later became a justice on the U.S. Supreme Court, was denied admission to the University of Maryland Law School and attended Howard University, a predominately black school in the District of Columbia (Rowan, 1993).

Not until 1951 did the Association of American Law Schools take a position against racial discrimination in admissions (Cardozo, 1993), and not until 1964 could the AALS state that none of its member schools reported denying admission on the basis of race. Nonetheless, in that year, only 433 out of more than 50,000 students in predominately white law schools were black (ABA, 1992).

The number of African American and other minority law students has gradually risen over the past 30 years. In 1978–79, 9952 minorities were enrolled in 164 schools; in 1995–96, the figure was 25,554 in 175 schools out of a total of 135,518 students. The 1995–96 figures include 9779 African Americans, 6900 Hispanic Americans, 1085 Native Americans, and 7719 Asian Americans (ABA, 1995).

The increase in minority students, especially African Americans, has resulted largely from law schools' affirmative action programs since the mid-1960s. Recent cases, however, especially *Hopwood v. Texas* (◆ **Box 4-7**), have cast doubt on the constitutionality of affirmative action programs in higher education. In California, passage of Proposition 209 in 1995 required state law schools to admit on a color-blind basis. At highly rated Boalt Hall (the law school at the University of California at Berkeley), the number of African Americans admitted dropped sharply in the wake of Proposition 209's passage but rebounded when Boalt changed the way it looked at students' records (i.e., grades from all undergraduate institutions are now weighted the same) (Ward, 1998).

The number of minority lawyers in the United States has grown steadily since the mid-1960s, though the numbers still lag far behind the

## THE CASE OF

**BOX 4-7**   **Cheryl Hopwood and Heman Sweatt**

After working her way through a California state university, Cheryl Hopwood graduated in 1988 with a 3.8 undergraduate grade point average. She worked as a certified public accountant in California for a time and then moved to Texas with her husband, who was in the military. She took the LSAT and scored at the 83rd percentile of those taking the test. Hopwood applied for admission to the University of Texas Law School in the 1992 matriculating class.

As mentioned in Chapter 1, Heman Sweatt, an African American, had applied to the University of Texas Law School in 1946. He was initially denied admission but was then offered admission in a hastily arranged "Jim Crow" school—with no library, no permanent faculty, and no facilities. Sweatt took his case all the way to the U.S. Supreme Court, which unanimously ruled that Texas had denied him equal protection of the laws and ordered him admitted to the University of Texas Law School (*Sweatt v. Painter*, 1950). Sweatt left the law school in 1951 without graduating after being subjected to racial slurs, cross burnings, and tire slashings.

By the time of Cheryl Hopwood's application in 1992, the University of Texas Law School had attempted to improve access to legal education for all students. To remedy its discrimination against African Americans and other minorities, the law school had adopted and refined a system

of preferential admissions. In 1992, the system worked as follows: Minority applicants, predominately African Americans and Hispanic Americans, were put in one applicant "pool"; nonminority applicants went in another "pool." Based on combined LSAT and undergraduate grade point average, admission and denial scores were established for each pool. The admissions committee then made individual judgments about applicants whose scores were above the presumptive denial and below the presumptive admission lines. For the class for which Hopwood applied, the denial score for nonminorities was higher than the admission score for minorities.

In spite of her 3.8 college average, her working her way through college, her work as a CPA, and her 83rd percentile score on the LSAT, Hopwood was denied admission to the class matriculating in the fall of 1992.

With the assistance of the Center for Individual Rights, a public interest law firm, Hopwood and three other white applicants filed suit in a Texas federal court. Although sympathetic to their case, the judge denied the plaintiffs' claims. They then appealed to the federal appeals court in New Orleans.

In *Hopwood v. State of Texas* (1996), the federal appeals court agreed with the applicants' claim that they had been the objects of racial discrimination. The court read prior Supreme Court opin-

ions as allowing affirmative action in admissions for only one purpose: to remedy the effects of past discrimination. The court held that the law school's program was not "narrowly tailored" to undo the racial discrimination practiced in the Texas Law School more than 30 years before. The court found it especially significant that the Texas plan assured preferential treatment for Hispanic Americans, who had not been discriminated against in the past. The court rejected diversity in education as a legitimate goal for a racially preferential system. Although the court said that Texas could legitimately strive for diversity in its student body, it could not use race as a factor to enrich the student mix.

The appeals court remanded the case to the trial court to determine whether Hopwood and her fellow applicants would have been admitted under a nonpreferential system and to assess what damages, if any, the plaintiffs should receive from the state. Ironically, the trial court held that Cheryl Hopwood would not have been admitted under a colorblind system (*Hopwood v. Texas*, 1996).

*Hopwood* is not a Supreme Court case, but it may well portend the direction the Supreme Court will take when presented with a case in which the main justification for preferential admission is to increase the diversity of the student body.

percentage of minorities in the general population. In 1960, there were only 2102 African Americans out of 285,933 attorneys; in 1990, there were 25,704 African Americans out of 777,119 attorneys. However, only 3% of law firm partners were minorities.

## What Makes a Good Lawyer?

Students decide to go to law school for many different reasons: Some want to do well in the world, others seek to make money, a few want to satisfy parental expectations, and others elect law school because at the time there seems to be nothing better to do with a degree in history (or political science or English or economics).

John Hunter, a general practitioner in Raleigh, North Carolina, describes his decision to attend law school as follows:

> In my own case, I became interested in the law as a profession largely as a result of two factors which touched me entirely by chance. First, I was born and grew up in a neighborhood in which my family lived across the street from a very good lawyer who often talked with me about his profession, and secondly, I happened to take a course in public speaking during my first year in high school which led to a great interest in it and developed in me a skill in speaking in public which could be nicely worked in with the practice of law. In addition, I discovered in connection with the work I did in some of my English courses that I liked to work with words and particularly to express ideas in written or spoken language. The result was that by the time I entered college, I knew definitely that I wanted to be a lawyer, even though I had virtually no experience that touched upon the law itself or the type of work a lawyer does. (Love & Childers, 1963, pp. 75–76)

Hunter is representative of those who went to law school because of a perceived aptitude for the study and practice of law. Alan Dershowitz, the youngest professor to attain tenure at Harvard Law School and a frequent defender of unpopular clients, studied law out of a motivation to "argue and debate," a motive described as of great importance by 26% of the respondents in Stevens's (1983) survey. Dershowitz started talking about the law while growing up in a devout Jewish household in Brooklyn; he remembers his father and uncles spending hours discussing the Talmud, the basic treatise of Jewish law (Bayles, 1984). "The Jewish religion is a very argumentative religion," Dershowitz says. "You argue with everyone. You essentially put God on trial." The experience left him with "a problem with authority." He is quoted as saying, "Teachers were always telling me 'You're stupid, but you have a big mouth so you ought to be a lawyer'" (Bayles, 1984, p. 16).

As a young man, Clarence Darrow saw himself as a man of letters and sought the law as a medium in which he could express himself. He had also experienced farm work: "I was brought up on a farm. When I was a young man, on a very hot day, I was engaged in distributing and packing down the hay which a horse-propelled stacker was constantly dumping on top of me. By noon, I was completely exhausted. That afternoon, I left the farm, never to return, and I haven't done a day of hard work since" (quoted in Tierney, 1979, p. 21).

Supreme Court Justice Thurgood Marshall turned to the law after flunking anthropology, and abandoning his plans to be a dentist. Denied admission to the University of Maryland because he was black, Marshall attended Howard Law School in the District of Columbia. There Marshall came under the influence of Charles Houston, "who set a fire in Marshall's belly, a rage to go out into the legal profession immediately and reverse the myriad injustices of Maryland and America" (Rowan, 1993, p. 47).

Janet Reno's father was a crime reporter for the *Miami Herald*. "The courtrooms of the Dade County Courthouse, of that beautiful old federal building, were like magical places to me when I went with my father as he covered trials, both criminal and civil. And I thought that one of the most wonderful things anybody could do was to be a lawyer" (Anderson, 1994, p. 34). Her parents wanted her to be a doctor, and she graduated from Cornell University with a degree in chemistry. However, a summer job as a researcher convinced

*Two of America's most famous lawyers: Janet Reno and Thurgood Marshall*

her she wasn't cut out for a medical career, and she took her leadership skills to Harvard Law School in 1960 (Anderson, 1994).

Johnnie Cochran, who masterminded the successful defense of O. J. Simpson, put himself through school by selling insurance and working for the U.S. Postal Service. After a few years as a prosecutor, he began a criminal defense practice, which blossomed after the 1965 riots turned the Watts area of Los Angeles into a war zone. Early in Cochran's career he came to believe that his mission as a lawyer was to vigorously represent citizens, usually African Americans, who were the victims of police oppression or violence. Though paid handsomely for defending Simpson, Cochran sees himself as a champion of the downtrodden. "[M]y cases all have a component of official, under-color violence against a citizen who is usually poor, African-American, Haitian-American or some person of color" (Rovella, 1999, p. A1).

## Lawyers and Ethics

Lawyers are human, and it is inevitable that some will behave unethically or even criminally. Every state attempts to protect the public against un-ethical lawyers through a code of ethics (usually patterned after the ABA's "Model Rules of Professional Conduct"), enforced by a disciplinary body whose decisions are reviewed by the highest court of the state. The disciplinary body can censure, suspend, or even disbar unethical lawyers. In addition, most states have created "client security funds" to reimburse clients whose money has been embezzled by lawyers.

Public criticism of the disciplinary process for lawyers generally takes two forms: (1) an assumption that lawyers "get away with anything," based on the facts that disciplinary proceedings are often closed and the disciplinary tribunal is composed primarily of lawyers, and (2) a perception that the ethical rules—the lawyers' code—do not provide any relief for those who are over-charged or poorly represented. Both criticisms are just. The public can never be expected to accept a disciplinary process that takes place behind closed doors, and the failure of bar associations and disciplinary tribunals to come to grips with price gouging and/or inept lawyers explains in part why the public perception of lawyers is as low as it is. Gradually, states are opening the disciplinary process and are adding nonlawyers to the disciplinary panels that hear cases against lawyers. However, states rarely discipline lawyers who overcharge or perform poorly.

## THE MODEL RULES OF PROFESSIONAL CONDUCT AND ETHICAL TRAINING

ABA Standard 302(a)(iv) states as a condition for accreditation that law schools teach law students "the history, goals, structure, and responsibilities of the legal profession and its members, including the ABA Model Rules of Professional Conduct." In addition, many states require lawyers to take continuing legal education courses, including ethics courses. Lawyers often face ethical dilemmas in which the answer is less than obvious. Suppose, for example, a client tells the lawyer in confidence that he intends to burn down his business to collect the insurance proceeds. One might expect that the lawyer should inform the police of the impending arson. Because of the importance assigned to client confidences, however, the Model Rules require the lawyer to keep silent unless he or she reasonably believes that the fire might endanger someone within the building. The lawyer may, of course, try to talk the client out of the planned crime, but ultimately, the lawyer is required to keep the information confidential.

Take another example: Suppose a couple planning on an amicable divorce decide to hire a lawyer who has helped the husband with his business over the years. The couple ask the lawyer to "help them with the divorce." Can the lawyer represent both? The Model Rules allow the lawyer to represent both only if the lawyer reasonably believes that the husband and wife are in total agreement and that there is little likelihood that they will fall into conflict during the course of the divorce proceedings. Even then, the lawyer must be careful because the wife will need to know her husband's business transactions in order to enter into a fair property settlement. The lawyer cannot fairly represent the wife's interest unless the husband is willing to authorize the lawyer to tell the wife about matters earlier communicated to the lawyer in confidence.

One more example: Suppose a lawyer represents a client engaged in secret negotiations to buy a farm for development as a shopping center. Can the lawyer ethically buy the adjoining farm—which the client is not interested in buying—in anticipation of profiting when the shopping center is developed? The answer is only with the client's consent. As the client's agent, the lawyer cannot use confidential information to make a side profit unless the client consents.

Of course, other ethical conundrums exist in the law, many of which have been debated in legal ethics courses, law journal articles, and TV talk shows. Some of these problems have no satisfactory answers because the Model Rules do not resolve all questions and sound arguments can be advanced for contrary positions. You might try to develop arguments for different solutions to some of the best of these legal puzzles, such as the following:

◆ On examining her client's back tax returns, the lawyer tells the client that he probably will be charged with tax fraud. The client asks the lawyer for a list of countries that do not have extradition treaties with the United States. May the lawyer provide this information, knowing that the client may be planning to flee to escape prosecution?

◆ On being interviewed by his lawyer, the client tells a patently unbelievable story about the alleged crime. To what extent can a lawyer closely question the client in order to help the client develop an equally false, but more believable, story?

◆ In a criminal case, the defense lawyer knows that his client robbed the victim. In cross-examining the victim, may the lawyer ethically suggest that she is mistaken in her identification of the defendant as the assailant? May the lawyer ethically suggest that the victim is lying?

## Criticisms of Lawyers

The legal profession has been criticized for reasons other than its self-serving definition of ethics. Chief among these other criticisms are that the legal profession is relatively indifferent to the middle class, that it has a tendency to make the law overly complicated so that no one but a lawyer can understand it, that it tolerates or even encourages the practice of excessive billing, that it

**BOX 4-8    Abraham Lincoln and fees**

Lincoln would not charge more than his client could afford or more than he thought his services merited. Once he was hired to collect $650 owed to his client, Brokaw, by Stephen Douglas (Lincoln's opponent in the famous 1858 slavery debates). Lincoln sent the claim to a friend in Washington, where Douglas was a senator.

> Douglas sniffed and almost snorted [when shown the claim]; but he paid Brokaw, who remarked to his friends: "What do you suppose Lincoln charged me? Exactly three dollars and fifty cents for collecting nearly six hundred dollars." And Lincoln, asked about his low fee, replied: "I had no trouble with it. I sent it to my friend in Washington, and was only out the postage." (Sandburg, 1926, p. 63)

Lincoln teamed with another lawyer named Lamon to protect an incompetent woman from being swindled out of her life savings. The woman's brother had agreed to pay Lamon a fee of $250, but Lincoln gave half back to the woman.

> Judge Davis [a friend of Lincoln's] said, in the wheezing whisper of a man weighing 300 pounds, "Lincoln, you are impoverishing this bar by your picayune charges of fees, and the lawyers have reason to complain of you." Other lawyers murmured approval. Lincoln stuck to the point: "That money comes out of the pocket of a poor, demented girl, and I would rather starve than swindle her in this manner." In the evening at the hotel, the lawyers held a mock court and fined him; he paid the fine, rehearsed a new

line of funny stories, and stuck to his original point that he wouldn't belong to a law firm that could be styled "Catch 'em and Cheat 'em." (Sandburg, 1926, p. 51)

On the other hand, Lincoln demanded what he felt he was owed when the client could pay. He handled a tax case for the Illinois Central Railroad in 1855, obtaining a favorable decision in the Illinois supreme court that saved the railroad millions. When the Illinois Central refused to pay his bill of $2000, Lincoln sued for the value of his services; he received a verdict of $5000, a very sizable fee in those days (Sandburg, 1926).

---

often indulges the filing of frivolous lawsuits and that it disregards the truth.

### INDIFFERENCE TO THE MIDDLE CLASS

Lawyers, it is claimed, fail to adequately serve the "middle 70%" of the population. Rich criminal defendants can afford expensive law firms to represent them; corporations have the resources to pay for extensive legal research and preparation. At the other end of the economic scale, poor people are provided lawyers without cost if they are defendants in criminal trials, and they may rely on legal aid clinics, including volunteer private attorneys, if they are involved in civil suits. It is middle-income families who have difficulty obtaining legal assistance because attorneys' fees of $100 to $500 an hour quickly become prohibitive.

Lawyers typically respond that such cases demonstrate the merits of the contingency fee procedure, which is used for civil plaintiffs. In a **contingency fee system,** a plaintiff pays a lawyer a fee only if the plaintiff wins the case. For example, if you believe your physician's negligence has caused you a serious illness or injury, you can ask an attorney to represent you in a civil suit against the physician. If the case is settled in your favor, your attorney receives a percentage (usually 25% to 40%) of whatever is awarded to you. But if you lose, you do not have to pay your attorney any fee. However, contingency fees apply only to plaintiffs in civil cases; they are not ethical in criminal cases and are not used with civil defendants. See ◆ Box 4-8 to learn how Abraham Lincoln employed the contingency fee system in his law practice.

## UNNECESSARY COMPLICATIONS TO THE LAW

Lawyers are also charged with complicating the law unnecessarily so that consumers must hire an attorney to interpret the law for them. Lawyers' organizations will charge others with the unauthorized practice of law (UPL) if the latter carry out legal matters without being licensed to do so. Rosemary Furman, a Jacksonville, Florida, legal secretary, began dispensing do-it-yourself legal kits, mostly for couples seeking a divorce. She was prosecuted and sentenced to 30 days in jail for dispensing legal advice without a license. Shortly after this (and perhaps not independently of it), the Florida Bar Association developed a new procedure so that in Florida childless couples who agree to divide their assets and debts can receive a divorce at a cost of less than $100 in filing fees without the assistance of an attorney. In a similar case, Texas federal judge Barefoot Sanders declared that the sale of an interactive software program (Quicken Family Lawyer) was the unauthorized practice of law (*Unauthorized Practice of Law Committee v. Quicken Family Lawyer,* 1999). The Texas legislature responded to the decision by amending the unauthorized practice statute to exempt the sale of software programs, and, in light of the change in the state's law, the federal court of appeals reversed Judge Sanders's decision (*Unauthorized Practice of Law Committee v. Parsons Technology,* 1999).

*Furman* and *Quicken* are cases in which public institutions arguably protected consumers from lawyers' aggressive use of unauthorized practice statutes. Founded in 1978, HALT (not an acronym), "An Organization of Americans for Legal Reform," claims to be "dedicated to the principle that all Americans should be able to handle their legal affairs simply, affordably and equitably" (www.halt.org). Like others critical of suits such as *Quicken,* HALT believes that unauthorized practice prosecutions should be reserved for cases in which consumers are complaining about the services rendered by nonlawyers. Then it will be clear that the state bars are working for the public interest, rather than trying to protect lawyers' turf (Baker, 1999).

One of the legal profession's most serious challenges comes from the "Big Five" accounting firms, which provide legal services to their European clients and, for all practical purposes, do the same for their American clients. In 1999, recognizing the reality of the Big Five's practice of law, the ABA's Commission on Multi-disciplinary Practice recommended that lawyers be allowed to practice and share fees with other professionals, including accountants. If states adopt this recommendation, lawyers and accountants will work side by side in law and accounting firms, openly practicing both professions (Gibeaut, 1999).

If lawyers and accountants are permitted to work together, there is no reason why mental health specialists could not partner with attorneys. After speaking to the legal ethics class of one of the authors of this book, Charles Wolfram (2000), one of the most respected academicians in the field of legal ethics, commented in the *National Law Journal,*

> I recently met a Kentucky law student who had left his social work practice for law school and was keenly interested in the idea, post-law-school, of going into business with his spouse, also a social worker. The idea was that the two would practice together in the same two-person, multidisciplinary firm for the practice of divorce law (lawyer) and psychotherapy (social worker). (p. B1)

Professor Wolfram went on to point out the benefit to small-town lawyers, accountants, psychologists, and other professionals, who could then provide "one-stop shopping" to those whose problems cut across traditional professional boundaries.

## EXCESSIVE BILLING

Lawyers are often criticized for the way they charge fees for their services. These criticisms have been aimed at the practice of charging by the hour, which can encourage delays and extend debate. In large law firms, the associates must generate a certain number of "billable" hours a year; the average number of annual billable hours at some large New York City law firms increased from about 1700 in the late 1970s (Brill, 1978) to between 2300 and 2500 ten years later (Kingson, 1988). If we divide 2400 hours by 50 weeks (giving each associate a two-week paid vacation each year), we get the requirement of about 48 billable hours per week, every week—that is, 48 hours in which the young attorney meets with clients, conducts legal research on the clients' behalf, meets with opposing attorneys, takes depositions, litigates cases in court, talks on the telephone with or for clients, dictates correspondence, or prepares requested materials such as wills or contracts. This is a challenging standard, but young attorneys in large firms feel pressured to bill as many hours as are legitimate and possible.

Law firm partners surveyed in 1997 regretted the results of long stressful hours at the office: 73% overall, and 83% of the women, reported that their workloads prevented them from spending enough time with their families, and 66% reported that they have no time for hobbies or outside interests (Klein, 1997). Recent studies have indicated that lawyers' long hours often cause stress and sometimes even lead to suicide (Gatland, 1997).

Calculating fees by the billable hour sometimes results in fraud. One West Virginia lawyer billed the state 75 hours for one day's work representing indigent criminal clients. How is that possible? He charged the state travel and court time separately for each client—a total of 22 hours travel and 53 hours court time—though he traveled less than an hour and was in court only 4 hours. In censuring the lawyer, the West Virginia Supreme Court commented, "When an attorney spends one hour traveling to represent six clients at a hearing he does not actually travel six hours—he travels for one hour. When an attorney spends two hours representing six clients at a hearing, he does not actually work for 12 hours—he works for two hours" (*National Law Journal,* 1987). The late Edward Bennett Williams, one of the preeminent lawyers of the 20th century, bragged to reporters that he had billed 3200 hours in 1984—more than 60 hours per week—in spite of having undergone surgery twice in the year. According to his official

biographer, the fact that he billed 3200 hours did not mean that he worked 3200 hours. The way Williams calculated the number of hours to bill on a given case was to figure out what he was worth—an arbitrary figure—and divide by his hourly rate, which at the time of his death was $1000 an hour (Thomas, 1991).

Such abuses lead cynics to respond to the question "What do you call a lawyer who bills 2800 hours a year?" with this answer: "A liar." A litany of abuses has been cataloged in the legal and popular press: double billing (the prior example), minimum billing (in which every phone call, no matter how brief, is billed at some minimum multiple of an hour), value billing (in which research done for client A that benefits client B is billed to both), separate charges for overhead, and use of two (or three) lawyers when one will do (Rosner, 1992).

In 1993, the American Bar Association found it necessary to tell lawyers that it was unethical to charge one client for travel time and another client for work done while traveling for the first client and that it was unethical to charge clients for work already done for other clients (one lawyer charged 3000 times for the same 12 minutes of work) (ABA, 1993; Budiansky, 1995).

Because of such abuses, clients are increasingly shopping around before hiring a lawyer and demanding detailed invoices, cost estimates, and cost controls. Unhappy clients have found courts willing to slash excessive fees. In denying all fees, a Tennessee court concluded that a lawyer who overbills isn't entitled to anything; a Massachusetts court publicly censured a lawyer who charged a client $50,000 to defend a DUI case (Cox, 1996).

## FRIVOLOUS LAWSUITS

Another frequently heard criticism of lawyers is that they abuse the system by filing frivolous suits. Horror stories abound: pro football fans suing a referee over a bad call, umpires suing baseball managers over name calling, an adult man suing his parents for lack of love and affection, a man suing a woman over a broken date, one prisoner suing his guards for "allowing" him to escape, another inmate suing prison officials for denying him the chance to contribute to a sperm bank.

The reality, however, is that the extent of tort litigation involving claims of personal injury has been nearly constant since 1975 and has actually fallen since 1990. Most of the 10 million cases that clog the courts each year are divorce cases and contract and property claims. At the same time, there is considerable evidence that some litigants and their lawyers seek compensation for nonexistent injuries. From 1980 to 1989, rates of motor vehicle accidents fell, and the number of claims made for property damages per million miles traveled also fell 12%. With safer cars, the rate of claims for bodily injuries should have dropped even faster. Instead, the rate of bodily injury claims rose 15%. In Philadelphia, 75 bodily injury claims were made for every 100 property damage claims, but in Pittsburgh, 16 bodily injury claims were made for every 100 property claims (Budiansky, 1995).

## LAWYER ADVERTISING AND SOLICITATION

Of course, much of the criticism of lawyers is attributable to lawyer advertising and solicitation. In Lincoln's day, lawyers advertised and solicited as did any other tradespeople. As Carl Sandburg (1926) describes it, when McLean County, Illinois, attempted to tax the Illinois Central Railroad, Lincoln offered his services to both sides, because "in justice to myself, I cannot afford it, if I can help it, to miss a fee altogether." Lincoln represented the Illinois Central, won the case, and sued the railroad for his fee.

In the 20th century, however, the organized bar deemed advertising and solicitation to be "unprofessional." The Canons of Ethics promulgated by the ABA in 1908 forbade advertising, solicitation, and any form of "stirring up strife and litigation" (Canons 27 and 28). It was not until 1977 that lawyers were able to advertise, after the Supreme Court decided the case of *Bates v. State Bar of Arizona* (1977). The Court held that lawyers have a First Amendment right to advertise their services truthfully. The next year, the Court drew

a distinction between "advertising" and "in-person solicitation," holding that states could continue to ban face-to-face solicitation by lawyers. The case was *Ohralik v. Ohio State Bar Association* (1978), a classic "ambulance-chasing" case. The lawyer learned of an accident, raced to the hospital, found the injured driver, age 18, "lying in traction in her room," signed her (and a passenger) to fee contracts, and ultimately sued his own "client" for one-third of the recovery she received from an insurance company. Faced with such outrageous facts, the Court had no difficulty holding that Ohio could prohibit face-to-face solicitation.

In later cases, the Supreme Court continued to distinguish between advertising and solicitation. Advertising, so long as it is truthful, is protected by the First Amendment; solicitation is not.

Targeted mail would seem to fall on the advertising side of the line because the recipient can simply discard a solicitation letter. However, in *Florida Bar v. Went For It* (1995), the Court upheld Florida's 30-day ban on direct-mail solicitation of accident victims. Went For It was the wholly owned referral service of an attorney named McHenry, who had been disbarred by the time of the Supreme Court decision for exposing himself to female clients. Went For It obtained names and addresses from accident reports and mailed solicitation letters to victims and their families. The Florida bar proved that reading these letters was painful. Some of the recipients' reactions to the letters were as follows:

◆ "despicable and inexcusable";
◆ "rankest form of ambulance chasing and in incredibly bad taste";
◆ "appalled and angered by the brazen attempt" to solicit (115 S.Ct. at 2376).

In *Went For It*, the Supreme Court held that the state could constitutionally forbid mail solicitation during a 30-day grieving period.

***Disregard for the truth.*** The final criticism of lawyers to be mentioned here is the public's perception that lawyers, as a group, do not have the same regard for the truth as the public supposedly has. Sometimes the criticism focuses on some lawyers' willingness to hide behind legalisms to bend the truth. President Clinton (a skilled lawyer) amused us by contending that oral sex wasn't sex and by denying a sexual relationship with Monica Lewinsky because of the tense of the verb in the question. As noted by political scientist Austin Sarat, he "played into every stereotype of taking refuge in narrow legalisms. . . . He's a caricature of the overly prepared witness. As for the public view of lawyers, this does damage to the profession" (Carter, 1998, p. 42).

Although President Clinton escaped impeachment, on May 22, 2000, a disciplinary committee of the Arkansas Supreme Court recommended that he lose his license to practice law because of his perjury in the Paula Jones case (principally by denying that he had a sexual relationship with Monica Lewinsky). In January 2001, however, the reprimand was lessened officially to a five-year suspension of his license in Arkansas.

Often, lawyers are said to encourage falsity by consciously shaping a witness's recollection. Consider the following description of famed lawyer Edward Bennett Williams's interviewing technique:

> As a rule, Williams didn't bother to take notes of the initial interview because he knew the client

was lying. Slowly he'd probe for the truth. . . . The fact is, however, that Williams did not always want the truth—at least the whole truth. . . . He would . . . help the client come up with a plausible theory to explain away incriminating facts. This was done subtly, through leading questions and a certain amount of winking and nodding. (Thomas, 1991, p. 405)

The Dallas law firm of Baron & Budd sent clients allegedly suffering from asbestosis (a constellation of symptoms related to exposure to asbestos) instructions for depositions. The instructions went beyond the usual "make sure you understand the question" type advice and clearly were designed to tell the workers how to testify:

◆ It is important to emphasize that you had NO IDEA ASBESTOS WAS DANGEROUS when you were working around it.
◆ It is important to maintain that you NEVER saw any labels on asbestos products that said WARNING or DANGER. (Rogers, 1998 p. 49)

Examples such as these give the public good reason to believe that lawyers will twist the truth to win.

## SUMMARY

**1.** *What is the difference between the adversarial and inquisitorial models of trials?* The trial process in the United States is called the "adversarial model" because all the witnesses, evidence, and exhibits are presented by one side or the other. In contrast, in the inquisitorial model used in much of Europe, questioning of witnesses is done almost entirely by the judge. Although the adversarial model has been criticized for instigating undesirable competition between sides, in empir-

ical studies it has been judged to be fairer and lead to less biased decisions.

**2.** *What are the characteristics of courts, and how are judges selected?* Federal crimes are prosecuted in federal courts, and state crimes in state courts. Some civil cases may be brought in either federal or state court. Federal judges are appointed for life and may be removed only by the Senate on articles of impeachment voted by the House of Representatives. Some state judges are elected; in other states, judges are appointed and then run on their records in retention elections.

**3.** *What are the characteristics of juvenile courts?* Children under 18 who commit crimes are usually prosecuted in juvenile courts, where they are treated less harshly than adults who have committed the same crimes. Children over 14 who commit serious crimes may be transferred to adult crime and treated the same as adults. In some states, there is no minimum age for transfer. The public's attitude toward juveniles who commit crimes has become very punitive in recent years.

**4.** *What is alternate dispute resolution?* Alternate dispute resolution (ADR) refers to alternatives to the court and jury as a means of resolving legal disputes. The most common forms are mediation, in which a third party tries to facilitate an agreement between the disputants, and arbitration, in which a third party decides the controversy after hearing from both sides. The summary jury trial is another ADR mechanism.

**5.** *What are lawyers' characteristics?* Seventy percent of the world's lawyers live in the United States, three times as many per capita as in Great Britain and 25 times as many per capita as in Japan. Most lawyers are well paid. Contrary to their popular image, lawyers would rather settle a case than take it to trial.

**6.** *Are women and minorities accepted in the legal profession?* As we move into the 21st century, women are accepted in every facet of the legal profession, though many find that it is difficult to balance home and job. Women are not as adversarial in their approach to the practice of law as men. Minorities are underrepresented, and law schools' affirmative action programs are jeopardized by cases such as *Hopwood v. Texas*.

**7.** *What are some criticisms of the law and lawyers?* Criticisms include lawyers' efforts to keep nonlawyers from offering the same services at a lower price, the expense of legal services, the proliferation of lawyers, lawyers' disregard for the truth, and frivolous lawsuits.

## KEY TERMS

| | | | |
|---|---|---|---|
| adversarial system | contingency fee | Model Rules of | summary jury trial |
| alternate dispute | inquisitorial approach | Professional | *writ of certiorari* |
| resolution | juvenile court* | Conduct | |
| arbitration* | mediation* | retention election | |

---

**InfoTrac**
**College**
**Edition**

For additional readings go to **http://www.infotrac-college.com/wadsworth** and enter a search term related to your interest. The key terms that have been asterisked above will pull up several related articles. *See also:* for alternate dispute resolution, see DISPUTE RESOLUTION (LAW); for model rules of professional conduct, see ABA MODEL RULES OF PROFESSIONAL CONDUCT; for *writ of certiorari*, see CERTIORARI.

# *Theories of Crime*

## ORIENTING QUESTIONS

1. *Theories of crime can be grouped into four categories; what are they?*
2. *Among sociological explanations of crime, how does the subcultural explanation differ from the structural explanation?*
3. *What is emphasized in biological theories of crime?*
4. *What are the psychological factors explaining crime?*
5. *What is central to social-psychological theories of crime?*

Rates of serious crime have been steadily declining in the United States. This decrease is confirmed by both victimization studies and official police statistics; according to the National Crime Victimization Survey (Bureau of Justice Statistics, 1999), the rate of violent crime has been dropping since 1994, and the overall rate of violent and property crime is down almost 17% from the level of 1991 (FBI, 1998).

Despite this downturn in crime rates, many Americans continue to list crime and the fear of crime as one of their most serious concerns. Why, if the rate of crime is declining, do so many individuals continue to perceive crime as a major threat in their lives? One reason is that, despite recent decreases, the rate of violent crime is still relatively high: 51 out of every 1000 residents age 12 or older living in an urban area were victimized by violent crime in 1998—a rate much higher than most of the countries in Western Europe. The average citizen's fear of crime is also heightened by the highly publicized crimes of a few individuals that conjure up images of an epidemic of random violence beyond the control of a civilized society. Within a single one-month period in the summer of 1999, the headlines of America's newspapers covered:

- the slaying of nine people and wounding of more than a dozen others in two Atlanta brokerage firms by Mark Burton, after he had killed his wife and two children;
- the shooting rampage by white supremacist Burton Furrow that wounded several children in the Granada Hills, California, Jewish Community Center and resulted in the murder of a U.S. postal worker;
- the fatal shooting of three coworkers at two Alabama offices where disgruntled truck driver Alan Miller once worked.

Perhaps even more troubling than overall crime rates or highly publicized crime sprees is the frequency of serious crime activity among young people. In 1997, adolescents under 18 years of age were responsible for 17% of all arrests for violent crime and 35% of all property crime arrests; about

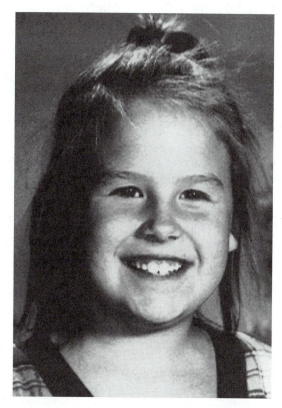

MEGAN KANKA
*In May 1996, President Bill Clinton signed legislation that requires law enforcement authorities to notify communities when convicted sex offenders move into their neighborhoods. The law was known as Megan's Law, after seven-year-old Megan Kanka who was murdered in 1994. The man charged with Megan's murder was a twice-convicted child molester who had settled in her neighborhood.*

a third of all juvenile arrests are of youths younger than 15 (Snyder, 1998). Between 1988 and 1997, arrests of offenders younger than 18 increased by 35%, but like adult crime, the juvenile crime rate began to level off or decline, particularly after 1995. As an illustration, the rate of homicides by youth under 17 tripled between 1984 and 1994 before declining steadily since 1994.

Finally, the public becomes especially fearful about crime when they perceive it to be occurring in environments that they traditionally have thought of as places of safety. In the 1990s, crime in the workplace and violence in our schools caused great national concern. Highly publicized acts of violence at school or in the workplace threaten fundamental assumptions about personal security and the safety of our children and have a major effect on how individuals feel about their quality of life. For that reason, policymakers and social scientists have begun to pay particular attention to workplace and school violence. A few of their discoveries are highlighted in ◆ **Box 5-1.**

The ups and downs of the crime rate give rise to much speculation about what factors are most responsible for causing and controlling crime. When crime is on the rise, the figures are used to justify requests for new policies and budget priorities. When the crime rate falls, the statistics are taken as an indication that one's favorite programs have been effective and need to be expanded.

The debate over the best means of crime control remains an impassioned social and political issue in the United States. Should we hire more police, increase the number of courts, build more and bigger prisons, execute more violent criminals? Should we encourage more aggressive, "zero tolerance" policing, aimed at apprehending individuals who commit even minor crimes such as vandalism and public intoxication? Should we impose curfews and school dress codes for adolescents? Is stricter gun control critical to curbing crimes of violence? Should parents be held legally liable for criminal assaults committed by their children?

Congress continues to pass anticrime bills that expand capital punishment to a wider spectrum of crimes, and, as noted in Chapter 1, many states have enacted so-called three-strikes legislation aimed at keeping repeat felons in prison for longer periods of time, sometimes for life. Other states have passed special anticrime measures that require a community to be notified whenever a former sex offender moves into its midst or that mandate the involuntary hospitalization of criminals still judged to be dangerous after they have completed their prison terms. The Supreme Court

has issued a series of rulings that strengthen the powers of law enforcement officials in the areas of search and seizure, interrogation of criminal suspects, and the pretrial detention of persons who have been arrested. All these steps have been justified, in part, as remedies for America's crime problem.

But to ease the crime problem, psychologists argue that we must first understand its causes. Why does crime happen? What motivates people to commit illegal acts? Bad genes? Inadequate parents? Failed schooling? Twisted impulses? Harsh environments? Delinquent friends? Social disadvantage? Drug addiction? Some combination of these factors? Can crime be predicted from knowledge of a person's early life? Or are many people capable of crime, given an unlucky mix of intoxication, anger, and unprotected victims, meeting, in the words of novelist Daniel Woodrell (1996), "like car wrecks that you knew would happen . . . almost nightly, at the same old crossroads of Hormones and Liquor" (p. 27)? Are some crimes so extreme that they defy scientific explanation (see ◆ **Box 5-2**)? These questions are the concern of **criminology,** which is the study of crime and criminal behavior. In this chapter, we summarize the major theories of crime, beginning with a brief review of the historical predecessors of 20th-century criminology.

# Theories of Crime as Explanations of Criminal Behavior

Theories of crime are as old as crime itself. Aristotle claimed that "poverty is the parent of revolution and crime," but most ancient explanations of crime took a religious tone; crime was either equivalent or due to sin, a view that was popular throughout the Middle Ages and lives on today in many religious belief systems.

In the 17th century, Sir Francis Bacon argued that "opportunity makes a thief." During the 1700s,

**The Science of**

**BOX 5-1**   **School violence: When kids kill**

Pearl, Mississippi. West Paducah, Kentucky. Jonesboro, Arkansas. Springfield, Oregon. Littleton, Colorado. These five communities share a common denominator that sets them apart from the thousands of other American towns that they resemble in so many other ways. In each of them, one or more deeply troubled boys went to school one day, armed with guns, and proceeded to kill and wound their classmates. The grizzly totals from these five incidents—all within only a single year of one another—were 30 dead and more than 60 wounded.

The spree of school shooting fatalities in the late 1990s has experts, parents, teachers, and youngsters themselves searching for answers about what motivates school shootings and what can be done to prevent them. Are school environments to blame? Is the ready availability of guns the explanation? Were the killers mentally ill misfits? Were they driven over the edge by violent music and gory video games? Or did their parents fail to support and supervise them adequately?

Statistics about school violence, and the case histories of those boys who have murdered their classmates at school, reveal some insights. First, according to a national survey of public schools (National Center for Education Statistics, 1998), about 10% of U.S. public schools reported experiencing at least one serious violent crime

(murder, rape, assault with a weapon, robbery, or suicide) during the prior school year. One out of five high schools reported a serious violent crime in the prior year; high schools reported experiencing 103 serious violent crimes per 100,000 students, a slightly higher rate than for middle schools. Although the rate of crime at schools is far outpaced by crime in the workplace, where nearly one million violent victimizations occur annually (Bureau of Justice Statistics, 1994), students admit to being afraid about their safety at school and often cite this fear as a justification for arming themselves. One survey (Center for Disease Control, 1991, reported by Small, 1997) revealed that 20% of high school students had carried a weapon (gun, knife, or club) to school at least once in the prior month.

School-ground homicides remain very rare, but they attract a great deal of speculation about the motives behind them. Based on the small sample of cases, a few common characteristics have been identified in the backgrounds of the boys responsible for recent killings (Cloud, 1998; Verlinden, Hersen, & Thomas, 2000). They tend to

- have had more than the usual experience with firearms, showing a persistent fascination with guns;
- have felt isolated from, rejected, or even tormented by class-

mates and to have had particular difficulty relating comfortably with girls;
- have been preoccupied with various forms of graphically violent media, including music, Internet sites, and video games;
- have suffered teasing because of their physical appearance—most of these assailants are either frail or somewhat obese;
- have had a history of angry brooding, often over their real or perceived status as social outcasts;
- have had a detailed plan for their aggression, which was often communicated to others in the days or weeks prior to the event.

Whether we will ever be able to explain this kind of crime is not clear. In retrospect, many of their classmates and teachers report that they now recognize there were warning signs about the danger to come. But how best to respond to these indicators in time remains the question. A number of reforms and programs have been attempted—requiring school uniforms, beefing up security measures, passing tougher gun laws, offering violence prevention programs, and restricting access to violent movies. Each of these interventions may exert some positive effects, but none has been proven to be uniquely successful.

# THE CASE OF

**BOX 5-2**   **Jeffrey Dahmer: Are all crimes explainable?**

When police entered apartment 213 at the Oxford Plaza Apartments in Milwaukee, Wisconsin, on July 22, 1991, they encountered one of the most horrifying crime scenes in this country's history: severed human heads stacked in the refrigerator, photographs of dismembered bodies tacked to the walls, and human body parts immersed in a vat of acid. Ultimately, police uncovered the remains of 11 male victims in and around the grimy, stench-filled one-bedroom apartment. Shortly after discovering these monstrosities, police arrested Jeffrey L. Dahmer, a 31-year-old chocolate factory worker who soon confessed to a total of 17 killings. Dahmer provided authorities with the details of his slayings, which typically involved luring men to his apartment where he would have sex with them, kill them, dismember their bodies, and horde the remains. He admitted to performing sex acts on his

corpses and also said he cut one man's heart out and stored it in his freezer so he could eat it later. He apparently ate body parts of the victims "he liked the most."

Can any theory of crime offer a reasonable explanation of this gruesome carnage? Does Jeffrey Dahmer's history, even viewed now with the full knowledge of his terrifying crimes, offer any satisfying account of how a human being could engage repeatedly in such conduct? Or is Dahmer's behavior so extreme that it embarrasses social science explanations as shallow, pale excuses that fail to confront the fundamental evil that seems to lurk in someone like Dahmer?

A review of Dahmer's life has not revealed the trauma, prolonged mistreatment, or environmental deprivations that would sufficiently explain his serial murders; neither is there convincing evidence that Dahmer suffered from a mental

*Jeffrey Dahmer*

illness serious enough to compel this conduct. Dahmer was raised in a middle-class family in a prosperous suburb. Neighbors recalled him and his younger brother as "very polite children." In high school, Dahmer showed erratic behavior, became gradually isolated from friends, and earned a reputation as an outcast. In 1978, Dahmer's parents went through a bitter divorce that led to a marked worsening of Dahmer's drinking

philosophers and social critics such as Voltaire and Rousseau emphasized concepts such as free will, hedonism, and flaws in the social contract to explain criminal conduct. These principles ultimately grew into the **classical school of criminology.**

The two leading proponents of classical criminology were the Italian intellectual Cesare Beccaria and the British philosopher Jeremy Bentham, who believed that lawbreaking occurred when people, faced with a choice between right and wrong, freely chose to behave wrongly. People made procrime decisions when they believed that

the gains of crime outweighed its losses. Classical theorists were interested in reforming the harsh administration of justice in post-Renaissance Europe, and they believed that punishment of criminals should be proportionate to the crimes committed: punishment should fit the crime. Classical theory influenced several principles of justice in Western societies (e.g., the U.S. Constitution's Eighth Amendment ban against "cruel and unusual punishment"), and, as we shall see in Chapter 17, it still exerts an important effect on modern correctional philosophy.

problems, which had begun in junior high school. Dahmer attended Ohio State University briefly in 1978, but he did poorly and dropped out to join the army in 1979. He was released early from the army in 1981 because of his drinking problems and then went to live with his grandmother in West Allis, Wisconsin. In 1985, he started a laborer's job at the Ambrosia Chocolate Factory, which he held until shortly before his arrest. In 1988, after moving out of his grandmother's house, Dahmer was arrested for molesting a 13-year-old boy and sentenced to five years' probation. Sometime later, he began his Milwaukee killing spree. Although Dahmer's acts seem beyond comprehension, a jury found that he was not insane during his crimes, and he was sentenced to life in prison. A few years after he began serving his prison term, Dahmer was bludgeoned to death by another inmate.

There is no doubt that Jeffrey Dahmer's life began to unravel in the late 1980s. But as his troubles unfolded, they did not appear very different from the marginal existence of many lonely alcoholic men who, despite the tragedies of their lives, did not lure multiple victims into traps of violent death. Although social scientists may try to link Jeffrey Dahmer's crimes with several factors in his life, including the diagnosis that he had a personality or sexual disorder or that he was sexually abused as a child, we doubt that any scientific theory can adequately come to terms with the enormity of these murders.

Although few criminals can match the sheer horror of Dahmer's deeds, many commit acts of enormous cruelty. Their crimes are all the more alarming because they too defy any type of rational understanding. How can we comprehend juveniles like Eric Harris and Dylan Klebold, the Columbine High School students whose well-planned Colorado massacre left 15 of their classmates dead, or Thomas Hamilton, a loner who stalked into a school in Dunblane, Scotland, with four handguns and slaughtered 16 first graders and their teacher before killing himself? Have you read any really satisfying explanation of why the so-called Unabomber carried out a 17-year string of bombings that killed 3 people and wounded 23 more? Attributing crimes like these to "evil" or Satan or basic moral failure is no more satisfying than most psychological theories because one must still answer why moral failure would be manifest in this excessive way.

The Jeffrey Dahmers and Thomas Hamiltons of the world are so frightening not only because of what they did but also because of our inability to comprehend why they did it.

Modern theories of crime developed from the **positivist school of criminology.** Rather than focusing on individuals' free will as previous philosophers had done, positivists emphasized factors that they believed determined criminal behavior. They sought to understand crime through the scientific method and the analysis of empirical data; some stressed sociological factors, whereas others preferred biological, psychological, or environmental explanations. Additionally, some positivistic theories try to explain how people choose between criminal and noncriminal behaviors, thereby sharing some common ground with classical theories. In practice, however, combinations of classical and positivist theories have been rare.

Cesare Lombroso, Enrico Ferri, and Raffaelo Garofalo were three early positivists. They were preceded by Adolphe Quetelet, a Belgian statistician, who, nearly 50 years before Lombroso, studied crime data and concluded that crime occurred more often in certain geographic areas and under specific social conditions. For various reasons, however, these early **ecological theorists** were not as influential as the Italian positivists.

Lombroso (1876) and Garofalo (1914) emphasized the physical characteristics of criminals and proposed a strong biological predisposition to crime. Ferri (1917) also acknowledged physical causes but stressed social and environmental factors. Although the early positivists thought of themselves as scientists, their science was crude by current standards and led to conclusions that are not taken seriously today. Positivists believed that punishment should fit the criminal rather than the crime, a position that foreshadowed rehabilitation as a correctional priority and the indeterminate sentence as a means for achieving it.

Most modern theories of criminal—including those of biology, genetics, psychology, sociology, economics, anthropology, and religion—are a legacy of the positivist tradition. The validity of these theories varies greatly. Most can account reasonably well for certain types of crime, but none of them explains all forms of criminality, and some explain very little. Empirical data, rational analyses, moral values, and political ideologies all play a role in shaping preferences for the leading theories in criminology.

For the most part, criminologists have concentrated on those crimes that frighten the average citizen—violent acts (e.g., robbery, rape, assault, and murder) or aggressive behavior against property (e.g., burglary, theft, and arson). But many other kinds of legally prohibited conduct—environmental plunder, price fixing, and business fraud—cause great damage to individuals and society. However, these crimes are not the typical focus of criminologists, nor are they the type of conduct the general public has in mind when it debates the "crime problem."

In addition, most theories of crime have concentrated on men. This focus is not unreasonable, given that about three-quarters of all arrests are of men and that almost 85% of violent crimes are committed by men. However, the factors that influence female criminality deserve more attention, at least in part because female crime has increased relative to male crime over the past decade (FBI, 1998). Females are most often arrested for larceny and theft; in most of these incidents, the

woman was collaborating with a male partner. One implication of this pattern is that explanations of female crime need to consider carefully the role of coercion, especially as it is exerted in close relationships.

In this chapter, we review criminological theories that attempt to explain aggressive crimes. We define these crimes as legally proscribed behavior in which one or more persons deliberately inflict or attempt to inflict physical injury on others or intentionally take or destroy the property of others. We group these theories into four categories: (1) sociological, (2) biological, (3) psychological, and (4) social-psychological. What are the most important distinctions among these four approaches?

**Sociological theories** explain crime as the result of social or cultural forces that are external to any specific individual, that exist prior to any criminal act, and that emerge from social class, political, ecological, or physical structures affecting large groups of people (Nettler, 1974). Individual differences are deemphasized in favor of factors that put groups of people at risk for crime.

Sociological theories can be subdivided into **subcultural** and **structural explanations.** (We describe a third type of sociological approach, control theory, under social-psychological theories.) Structural theories emphasize that most people have similar interests and motivations but differ dramatically in opportunities to employ their talents in socially legitimate ways. Discrepancies between individuals' aspirations and their means of attaining these aspirations create strains that lead to crime. Dysfunctional social arrangements (e.g., inadequate schooling, economic adversity, or community disorganization) thwart people from legitimate attainments and result in their breaking the law.

Subcultural theories hold that crime originates when various groups of people endorse cultural values that clash with the dominant, conventional rules of society. In this view, crime is the product of a subcultural deviation from the agreed-on norms that underlie the criminal law.

**Biological theories** stress genetic influences, chromosomal abnormalities, biochemical irregularities, or physical factors (body type) as causes of crime. Although biological theorists believe that biophysical factors predispose certain people to commit crime, they usually retain a healthy respect for environmental and social influences as well.

**Psychological theories** emphasize that crime results from personality attributes that are uniquely possessed, or possessed to a special degree, by the potential criminal. For example, psychoanalysts have proposed several variations on the theme that crime is the result of an ego and superego that are too weak to control the sexual and aggressive instincts of the id. Other psychologists have painted a psychological portrait of the "criminal type." Although a number of traits distinguish delinquent persons from nonoffenders, these findings do not necessarily mean that the traits in question caused the crimes observed.

**Social-psychological theories** (or **social-process theories**; Nettler, 1974; Reid, 1976) bridge the gap between the environmentalism of sociology and the individualism of psychological or biological theories. Social-psychological theories propose that crime is learned, but they differ about "what" is learned and "how" it is learned. **Control theory** assumes that people will behave antisocially unless they learn, through a combination of inner controls and external constraints on behavior, not to offend. **Learning theory** stresses how individuals directly acquire specific criminal behaviors through different forms of learning.

# Sociological Theories of Crime

## *Structural Explanations*

A key concept of structural approaches is that certain groups of people suffer fundamental inequalities in opportunities to achieve the goals valued by society. Living in an affluent society instills aspirations for wealth, success, education, and material possessions. Not all people can obtain these outcomes, however, through legally acceptable means. Some individuals—because of the good fortunes of education, family affluence, abilities, or good looks—have greater opportunities to achieve the goals that society prescribes. Other individuals, thwarted from reaching these goals through legitimate means, may turn to illegal means to do so.

Differential opportunity is the cornerstone of the structural theory of crime proposed by Cloward and Ohlin (1960) in their book *Delinquency and Opportunity*. This theory can be traced to Émile Durkheim's ideas about the need to maintain moral bonds between individuals in society. Durkheim thought that life without moral or social obligations becomes intolerable and results in **anomie,** a feeling of normlessness that often precedes suicide and crime. One implication of anomie theory was that unlimited aspirations pressure individuals to deviate from social norms.

According to Cloward and Ohlin, people in lower socioeconomic subcultures usually want to succeed through legal means, but society denies them legitimate opportunities to do so. Consider, for example, a person from Nicaragua who emigrates to the United States because of the sincere desire to make a better life for his family. He faces cultural and language differences, financial hardships, and limited access to the resources that are crucial for upward mobility. Poor people cannot, for example, afford advanced education. In addition, crowding in large cities makes class distinctions more apparent. When legal means of goal achievement are blocked, intense frustration results, and crime is more likely to surface. Youthful crime, especially in gangs, is one outgrowth of this sequence.

The theory of differential opportunity assumes that persons who grow up in crowded, impoverished, deteriorating neighborhoods endorse conventional, middle-class goals. Thus, crime is an illicit means to gain an understandable end. Consistent with this view, Gottfredson (1986) and Gordon (1986), a sociologist team, attempted to explain the higher crime rate of lower-class black youth by their less than satisfactory scholastic performance. Denied legitimate job opportunities because of low aptitude scores or grades, these youth discover they can make several hundred dollars a week dealing crack cocaine. In fact, with the advent of crack cocaine, arrests of juveniles in New York City, Detroit, Washington, and other cities tripled in the mid- to late 1980s.

The theory of differential opportunity has several limitations (Lilly, Cullen, & Ball, 1989). First, a great deal of research indicates that seriously delinquent youth display many differences from their law-abiding counterparts other than differing educational opportunities, and they tend to show these differences as early as the beginning of elementary school. Second, there is no evidence that lower-class youth find limited success in school to be more frustrating than do middle-class youngsters. On the contrary, the exact opposite is likely to be true. The assumption that lower-class juveniles typically aspire to middle-class membership is also unproved.

Furthermore, the major terms in the theory, such as *aspiration, frustration,* and *opportunity,* are defined too vaguely; the theory does not explicitly explain what determines how deprived individuals will adapt to blocked opportunities (Sheley, 1985).

Last and most apparent, crimes are often committed by people who have never been denied opportunities; in fact, they may have basked in an abundance of good fortune. Think of hotel magnate Leona Helmsley's conviction for income tax fraud or Michael Milken, the highly successful Wall Street stockbroker convicted of fraudulent business practices. Many other examples come readily to mind: the head of a local charity who pockets donations for personal enrichment, the pharmacist who deals drugs under the counter, the politician who accepts bribes for votes.

Albert Cohen's (1955) *Delinquent Boys: The Culture of the Gang* proposes a structural hypothesis that emphasizes the reaction of lower-class youth to the goals of the middle class, which, being judged to be unattainable, are ultimately repudiated through destructive vandalistic crime.

According to Cohen, lower-class youth are constantly evaluated by the "middle-class measuring rod," particularly in schools and jobs because most schools and jobs are controlled by middle-class individuals who insist on acceptance of their standards.

Lower-class juveniles lack the prior socialization necessary for successful middle-class achievement. Instead, they have been reared in an environment that values immediate gratification and physical aggression. Although they have been trained to endorse middle-class values, they are ill equipped to translate these aspirations into effective actions.

The frustration caused by these failures leads to a delinquent subculture that vigorously rejects the middle-class measuring rod. Cohen explains delinquent subcultures using the psychoanalytic concept of **reaction formation**—the norms of the previously accepted middle-class orientation are defied, or turned on their head, by replacing them with their most offensive opposites.

Delinquent subcultures allow gang members to express their resentment and anger toward middle-class respectability. Their crimes are *negativistic* ("the delinquent's conduct is right, by the standards of his subculture, precisely because it is wrong by the norms of the larger culture"; Cohen, 1955, p. 28) and *malicious* ("enjoyment in the discomfiture of others, a delight in the defiance of taboos itself"; p. 27).

Cohen's theory agrees with differential opportunity theory that social stratification, and the accompanying loss of status for lower-class persons, causes crime. However, Cohen describes crime that is nonutilitarian, gratuitous, and expressive (e.g., painting obscenities on storefronts or knocking down neighborhood mailboxes) rather than the "rational," utilitarian crime described by the differential opportunity theorist.

As with differential opportunity theory, empirical support for Cohen's theory is limited. The biggest problem is the assumption that members of the lower class adhere to middle-class values. If social class is as powerful as sociologists claim,

### BOX 5-3　Hate crimes in America

Hate crimes are crimes "in which the defendant intentionally selects a victim, or in the case of a property crime, the property that is the object of the crime, because of the actual or perceived race, color, national origin, ethnicity, gender, disability, or sexual orientation of any person" (Violent Crime Control and Law Enforcement Act, 1994). Although hate crimes have been a tragedy of human history, the 1990s marked the first time that they began to be studied, and in some cases prosecuted, as a specific category of crime. With this new focus has come an increasing awareness of the destructive effects hate crimes wreak on all of society. Whether they involve the burning of an African American church, the bombing of a lesbian bar, or a shooting spree by white supremacists who target minorities, hate crimes leave deep psychological scars on the victims (Herek, Gillis, Cogan, & Glunt, 1997) and threaten and intimidate entire communities.

The first piece of legislation devoted to hate crime violence was the Hate Crime Statistics Act of 1990. Since then, the federal government has passed several other hate crime laws—including the Church Arson Prevention Act of 1996—and is considering passage of the Hate Crimes Prevention Act, which would expand the jurisdiction of the government over bias-motivated crimes.

How frequent are hate crimes, and what do we know about the perpetrators? According to the FBI, more than 10,000 hate-crime offenses were reported in 1996, an increase of about 40% since 1991. Almost certainly, this figure is an underestimate because hate crimes are much less likely to be reported to the police probably because the victim fears additional retaliation. The police, in turn, are often reluctant to classify an offense as hate crime when a more traditional charge will suffice. Most hate crimes are directed against African Americans; antiblack crimes are twice as frequent as antiwhite crimes. Among offenses involving religious bias, anti-Semitic crimes account for over 80%. Attacks against gays and lesbians are increasing in number, and these attacks are becoming more violent, often involving mutilation and torture of the victims.

Contrary to popular belief, hate crimes are not usually committed by organized hate groups. Individual white males in their teens or early 20s are responsible for most of them. Although a history of antisocial behavior is found among those who commit extreme forms of hate crime, the most common motivation is personal prejudice supported by an environment that sanctions attacks on certain groups of people (APA, 1998). Increasingly, these sanctions are communicated through a variety of Internet sites and other electronic media, including hate hotlines and "Whitepower" music, that spread virulent hate propaganda. Although the full effects of this information are not known, excessive involvement with violent messages, chat rooms, and entertainment is likely to stimulate aggressive fantasies and create the impression that violence is not only an acceptable but a desirable way to solve problems.

why would it not be more reasonable to suppose that the socialization practices of the lower class insulate its members against being indoctrinated into middle-class preferences? In addition, Cohen's descriptions of typical gang-affiliated crime are not accurate (Kitsuse & Dietrick, 1959). Most lower-class delinquency has a functional quality to it; goods are stolen, drugs are peddled, property is defended. By contrast, it is middle-class crime that often involves random destruction of property and vandalism. Likewise, although so-called hate crimes (see ◆ Box 5-3) are often committed by young offenders (from all kinds of socioeconomic backgrounds), these crimes are not functional in nature, but neither are they randomly expressive. Instead, they are intended to express and aim strong emotions at specific kinds of people. Cohen's description may be partially right about the wrong people.

One last form of structural theory involves what has been termed **rational crime** (Nettler, 1974). Rational crime involves illegal behavior that "makes sense" because the person is rewarded for it, and it can be committed with a relatively low risk of detection. It is crime encouraged by some nearly irresistible "golden opportunity."

Rational crime is most likely in one of four contexts. First are situations in which objects or money are easy targets for theft. Shoplifting, theft by employees, and embezzlement are examples. Second are circumstances associated with otherwise legitimate work that "demand" certain crimes. Price fixing, fraud, and business crime are often rationalized as "just part of doing business." Third is crime as a preferred livelihood, including theft rings and "organized crime." The fourth context is crime organized as a business to offer illegal products: pornography, drugs, prostitution, and gambling.

Like other structural theories, rational crime applies only to certain offenses—in this case, those that are profitable. However, while most structuralists see crime as an understandable reaction to social disadvantage, the "rationalist" views crime as an understandable reaction to the advantages or invitations of particular social arrangements. We see two major problems with rational crime theory. First, it does not explain repeated, violent crimes; second, it does not explain why, given the same "golden opportunities," some people offend while the majority do not.

## Subcultural Explanations

The subcultural version of sociological theory claims that a conflict of norms held by different groups causes criminal behavior. This conflict arises when various groups endorse subcultural norms that pressure its members to deviate from the norms underlying the criminal law (Nietzel, 1979). Gangs, for example, enforce unique norms

about how to behave. For many youths, a gang supplants the young person's parents as the main source of norms, even when parents attempt to instill their own values.

This theme of cultural conflict is illustrated by Walter Miller's theory of **focal concerns.** Miller explains the criminal activities of lower-class adolescent gangs as an attempt to achieve the ends valued in their culture through behaviors that appear best suited to obtain those ends. Thus, youth must adhere to the traditions of the lower class. What are these characteristics? Miller (1958) lists six basic values: trouble, toughness, smartness, excitement, fate, and autonomy. For example, lower-class boys pick fights to show their toughness, and they steal to demonstrate their shrewdness and daring (Sheley, 1985). Hundreds of juvenile homicides occur each year; many are done for the sole purpose of demonstrating macho toughness or relieving sheer boredom (Heide, 1997). Table 5-1 summarizes the six focal qualities that are important to gang members and distinguishes between what the gangs consider to be desirable and undesirable alternatives.

The theory of focal concerns does not explain crime by individuals who are not socially disadvantaged, such as the rich hotel owner, the television evangelist, or the Wall Street swindler. In addition, key concepts in the theory are vague. How do cultural standards originate? How are they transmitted from one generation to the next? And how do they control the behavior of any one individual? The most troublesome concept is the main one—subculture. Some critics reject the assumption that different socioeconomic groups embrace radically different values.

Other social scientists question whether social class and urban living are strongly related to crime by youth. Based on self-reports of youth over a ten-year period, Elliott (1988) found very small differences in delinquency rates with respect to race and social class and very little difference between rural and urban young men with respect to self-reported criminal behavior. Although crimes in rural areas are less likely to be reported to the police, rural youth claim to have

*Miller's "focal concerns" of lower-class culture*

| | PERCEIVED ALTERNATIVES | |
|---|---|---|
| | Law-abiding behavior | Law-violating behavior |
| | Physical prowess; skill; "masculinity"; fearlessness; bravery; daring | Weakness; ineptitude; effeminacy, timidity; cowardice; caution |
| 3. Smartness | Ability to outsmart, dupe, "con"; gaining money by "wits"; shrewdness; adroitness in repartee | Gullibility, "conability"; gaining money by hard work; slowness, dull-wittedness, verbal maladroitness |
| 4. Excitement | Thrill; risk; danger; change; activity | Boredom; "deadness"; safeness; sameness; passivity |
| 5. Fate | Favored by fortune; being "lucky" | Ill omened; being "unlucky" |
| 6. Autonomy | Freedom from external constraint; freedom from superordinate authority; independence | Presence of external constraint; presence of strong authority; dependency; being "cared for" |

SOURCE: Adapted from Miller (1958).

committed almost as many crimes as urban youth (Rensberger, 1988).

# Biological Theories of Crime

Biological theories of crime search for genetic vulnerabilities, physiological excesses, or constitutional deficits that predispose people to criminal behavior. These dispositions are then translated into specific criminal behavior through environments and social interactions spanning long periods of time.

The early positivists advocated biological theories. For example, Lombroso championed the concept of **atavism,** which held that the criminal was a congenital throwback to a primitive, savage type of man. Another neo-Lombrosian view of crime was developed by the Harvard anthropologist Ernest A. Hooton in his controversial volume *Crime and the Man* (1939). Hooton searched for anatomical distinctions between different types of criminals and between criminals and "civilians" (his noncriminal controls). Hooton took physical measurements of about 14,000 criminals and more than 3000 civilians, and he reported a multitude of physical differences between these groups. Burglars were found to possess short heads, golden hair, and undershot jaws. Robbers were said to be conspicuous by their long wavy hair, high heads,

short ears, and broad faces. Sex offenders "include among the rapists no few of full-bodied and probably over-sexed ruffians, but also . . . a majority of shriveled runts, perverted in body as in mind, and manifesting the drooling lasciviousness of senile decay" (Hooton, 1939, p. 374).

Hooton's theory has been ridiculed by modern behavioral scientists, and deservedly so. The major objections concern the inadequacies and biases of his sampling procedures. But other theories that focus on the relationship between physique and specific categories of antisocial behavior have been proposed, and some have found a degree of empirical support.

## Constitutional Theories

Both a psychologist and a physician, William A. Sheldon (1942, 1949) proposed a somatic typology that was composed of three dimensions of physique and corresponding temperaments. Sheldon thought there are three **somatotypes,** or body builds: the **endomorph,** who tends to be obese, soft, and rounded; the **mesomorph,** who is muscular, athletic, and strong; and the **ectomorph,** who is tall and thin with a well-developed brain. Endomorphs are fun loving, sociable, and jolly. Ectomorphs are introverted, sensitive, and nervous. Mesomorphs are assertive, vigorous, and bold.

Based on a comparison of 200 delinquent and 200 nondelinquent men, Sheldon suggested that the mesomorph is best suited for criminal behavior. He thought the mesomorph's aggressiveness along with a lack of inhibitory controls on behavior produce a prime candidate for criminality. Sheldon did not believe that all mesomorphs became criminals; only those exposed to the wrong influences did. Neither did he believe that environment was unimportant; however, he was convinced that physical variables had to be considered when attempting to explain aggressive crimes.

Today, Sheldon's ideas are largely dismissed. His sampling methods were faulty. His definition of delinquency was too vague. The most common objection is that somatotypes are little more than stereotypes, not deserving serious scientific attention. However, the search for constitutional predispositions to delinquency has persisted. In their classic study, *Unraveling Juvenile Delinquency* (1950), Eleanor and Sheldon Glueck compared 500 chronic delinquents with 500 nondelinquents. The two samples were matched on a host of demographic variables (Glueck & Glueck, 1950, 1956). Using Sheldon's classification scheme plus a fourth typology they called "balanced," the Gluecks claimed that significantly more delinquent youth were mesomorphic than were nondelinquents. Nonetheless, a substantial percentage of delinquents was not mesomorphic, leading the Gluecks (1956) to suggest, "It is quite apparent that physique alone does not adequately explain delinquent behavior; it is nonetheless clear that, in conjunction with other forces, it does bear a relationship to delinquency" (p. 246).

Recent data do suggest that physique might be related to aggressive behavior. Dan Olweus, a psychologist in Norway, has studied the factors that tend to turn elementary schoolboys into bullies. Studying bullies is important for theories of crime because boys identified as bullies in grades 6 to 9 are about four times more likely to be arrested repeatedly as adults than boys not classified as bullies (Olweus, 1995). Olweus discovered that the typical bully was

- physically stronger than other boys of the same age;
- raised in a family that lacked warmth, was permissive about aggression, and used physical punishments as discipline; and
- someone with an active, hotheaded temperament.

Although a strong, mesomorphic, physique does not guarantee that a boy will be a bully, in combination with unpredictable or harsh child-rearing practices and an angry temperament, mesomorphy can be a risk factor that increases the chances that a boy will behave antisocially.

In summary, physical typologies have several limitations, and we must be cautious about giving them too much emphasis. When we use a few all-or-none categories, we force nature to fit into an oversimplified scheme. Even if an individual can be accurately described as an introvert or an aggressive type, such a description is incomplete. First, it ignores hundreds of other attributes by selecting only one or a few to use in categorizing a person. Second, it assumes that two individuals tossed into the same category have all the same attributes. Almost always, however, we find that human disposition is not a matter of black or white; it is a question of shadings.

When physique is proposed as the direct cause of criminal behavior, further problems emerge. Even if a correlation exists between the two, it does not necessarily mean that one causes the other. It is quite likely that boys with a mesomorphic physique have found that aggressive ways of demanding what they wanted tend to "work." Because of their body build and strength, they succeeded when they used physical intimidation. Having been rewarded for this bullying, they persist as adults in intimidating their peers (see ◆ Box 5-4). Thus, it may be that a social-learning theory explanation (described later in this chapter), rather than a constitutional one, is most appropriate for the findings of the Gluecks and Olweus.

## Genetic Theories

All sorts of conditions, good and bad, have been attributed to genetic inheritance. So it is with

## The Science of

**BOX 5-4    Bullying behavior: Once a bully, always a bully?**

A longitudinal study (Huesmann, Eron, & Yarmel, 1987) carried out over a 22-year period followed 870 children from Columbia County, New York, from the ages of 8 to 30. At age 8, the incipient bully was seen by other children as starting fights over nothing, being quick to anger, and taking things without asking (Goleman, 1987). He was often a social outcast who disliked school, expressing his defiance through tardiness and truancy. By age 19, he was likely to have dropped out of school. At that point, he was three times more likely than others to have been in trouble with the law (Goleman, 1987). At age 30, his wife saw him as aggressive, even abusive. His run-ins with the law ranged from drunken driving to crimes of violence. As a parent, he was uncaring and punitive; his children tended to follow his own earlier pattern of being a bully (Goleman, 1987). Likewise, females who were aggressors as children were more likely to punish their own children severely.

In fact, the bully's characteristics can be traced over three generations (Huesmann et al., 1987). The parents of incipient bullies discipline them severely, and when the younger generation becomes parents, their children also tend to be troublemakers, even in elementary school.

The researchers found that bullies did not have lower IQ scores than other children, but as teenagers and adults, they performed below their expected level on achievement tests and often held jobs below their levels of ability.

criminals who are thought to suffer a hereditary taint, which either by itself or in collaboration with a pernicious environment increases the risk of antisocial behavior.

The earliest methodology for studying genetic contributions to criminality was the **genealogy** or family study. This method requires tracing the ancestry of an individual or charting the descent of offspring from one common ancestor. Two famous genealogies in criminology are Henry Goddard's study (1916) of the fictitiously named Kallilak family and Richard Dugdale's (1877) examination of the Jukes. Both families were cursed by a large progeny of scoundrels, leading the investigators to suspect the influence of heredity. This suspicion was particularly strong for Goddard, who believed that "feeblemindedness" could be inherited and was associated 50% of the time with eventual criminality. The genealogical method suffers from several limitations, the major one being that it does not permit an unambiguous

conclusion about just what the family transmits—genetic predisposition, psychological characteristics, environmental influences, or all of these—a problem that is partially overcome by twin studies (see ◆ Box 5-5).

Another effective strategy for separating genetic from environmental influences, both of which are transmitted within families, is the **adoption study,** in which the adopted offspring of parents with a disorder are compared to their biological and adoptive parents or to the adopted offspring of parents without the disorder. For example, Cloninger, Sigvardsson, Bohman, and von Knorring (1982) studied the arrest records of adult males who had been adopted as children. They found that men whose biological parents had a criminal record were four times more likely to be criminal themselves (an incidence rate of 12.1%) than those adoptees who had no adoptive or biological criminal background (2.9%) and twice as likely to be criminal as adoptees whose adoptive parents

## The Science of

**BOX 5-5    Criminology: Crime and genetics**

In the twin study, the researcher compares the **concordance rate** (the percentage of pairs of twins sharing the behavior of interest) for **monozygotic twins** (identical twins) and **dizygotic twins** (commonly called fraternal twins). If the monozygotic concordance rate is significantly higher, the investigator concludes that the behavior in question is genetically influenced, because monozygotic twins are genetically identical whereas dizygotic pairs share, on average, only 50% of their genetic material. This method assumes that the environments of the twins in a dizygotic pair are no more different from each other than are the environments of the twins in a monozygotic pair; this assumption may not always be accurate. Of course, the discovery of any discordant monozygotic twins (twins that do not share the characteristic under study) indicates that some nongenetic factor influences the behavior being studied.

The first twin study of crime was conducted in Germany by Johannes Lange (1929). Lange ob-tained data on 13 monozygotic and 17 dizygotic pairs. In each twin pair, one member, the twin first studied, had been imprisoned. The criminality concordance rate for the monozygotic twins was 77% compared with the dizygotic rate of 12%; this sizable difference led Lange to conclude that inherited tendencies played a "preponder-ant part" in causing crime.

Kranz (1936) studied 32 mono-zygotic, 43 same-sex dizygotic, and 50 opposite-sex dizygotic twins and found that criminal concor-dance was 66% for monozygotics, 54% for same-sex dizygotics, and 14% for opposite-sex dizygotics. The difference between the iden-tical and same-sex fraternal twins was not statistically significant. A second study by Kranz (1937) replicated the lack of a significant difference in concordance rates for monozygotic versus same-sex dizygotic twins, although the rate was again higher for the identical twins. Christiansen (1977a) ob-tained data on 3586 pairs of twins born in Denmark and reported that 50% of the monozygotic twins were concordant for criminal be-havior compared with 21% of the same-sex dizygotic twins. After re-viewing twin studies conducted over four decades in Germany, Holland, the United States, Japan, Finland, and Norway, DiLalla and Gottesman (1990) concluded that the average concordance rate for adult criminality was 51% for monozygotic twins and 22% for dizygotic twins.

Most twin studies lump vio-lent and nonviolent criminals to-gether rather than calculate con-cordance rates separately for the two types of crime. Studies that distinguish between crimes against property versus violent crimes against persons have found that heredity and environment play important roles for both types of crime, but the influence of hered-ity is higher for aggressive types of antisocial behavior (assaults, rob-beries, sexual predation) than for nonaggressive crimes such as drug taking, shoplifting, and truancy (Eley, 1997).

were criminal but whose biological parents were not. Adoptees who had both biological and adop-tive criminal parents were 14 times more likely to be criminal (a 40% incidence rate) than men who had no criminality in their background.

The largest adoption study of criminality was conducted in Denmark on 14,427 adoptees and their biological and adoptive parents (Mednick, Gabrielli, & Hutchings, 1984b). Table 5-2 summa-rizes data for adopted boys having different combi-nations of criminal and noncriminal biological and adoptive parents. As shown, if neither set of par-ents had a conviction, 13.5% of their sons had been convicted of a crime. When the adoptive parents had a conviction but the biological parents did not, 14.7% of the sons were criminal. If their biological parents had been convicted but their adoptive par-ents had not, 20% of the boys had been convicted.

**TABLE 5.2** ◆ *Relationship of criminality among biological and adoptive parents and their sons*

| | ARE BIOLOGICAL PARENTS CRIMINAL? | |
| --- | --- | --- |
| | YES | No |
| *Are Adoptive Parents Criminal?* | | |
| Yes | 24.5% (of 143) | 14.7% (of 204) |
| No | 20.0% (of 1226) | 13.5% (of 2492) |

NOTE: The numbers in parentheses are the total number of adopted males for each cell.

SOURCE: From Mednick, Gabrielli, and Hutchings (1984b).

If both sets of parents had a conviction, the criminality in the sons increased to 24.5%. In addition, biological parents who were chronic offenders (three or more convictions) were three times more likely to have sons who were criminal than were biological parents with no convictions.

The bulk of the research evidence suggests that genetic factors influence criminal behavior (DiLalla & Gottesman, 1991). How large an influence is not yet clear, but it is enough to require our attention. And this is the issue where difficulties are encountered. Whenever a claim is made that an unwanted behavior (e.g., mental disorders or crime) is linked even to a small extent to genetic influences, controversy is almost certain to follow. In some cases, attempts to study the genetics of a problem behavior are condemned or blocked due to concerns that merely asking questions about genes and abnormality is improper. An example of this type of censorship was the fate of a national conference on the relationship between crimes and genes. Originally scheduled for 1992 by the University of Maryland with funding from the National Institutes of Health, the conference was postponed after critics charged that a meeting devoted to studying the genetics of crime might encourage racist views. The conference was ultimately held in 1995 despite continuing protests.

Why are genetic theories of crime so unpopular? What makes it difficult for some people to look objectively at the tangled issues involving possible genetic roots of criminal behavior? The first problem seems to be the fear that, if we attribute crime even partly to genetic factors, then social and environmental causes will be neglected. This concern reflects the misconception that genes and environment compete rather than interact to cause behavior. Just as a person who is genetically predisposed to high blood pressure might need to maintain a careful diet, the person who is genetically prone to aggression might require extra support to cope with problems nonaggressively.

A second concern about studying the genetics of crime is that it will lead to certain people being designated as genetically "inferior." Unfortunately, as exemplified by the Nazi regime in mid-20th-century Germany, genetic research has a history of grotesque abuses, including forced sterilization, racially based immigration policies, and genocide. Fears about the potential abuses of genetic discoveries have been intensified because of the rapid success of the Human Genome Project, which has achieved a preliminary mapping of the approximately 100,000 genes of human DNA. The new age of genomics promises (or threatens, depending on your point of view) to revolutionize many fields, including medicine, psychology, and criminology (Friedland, 1998). Nonetheless, contemporary behavioral geneticists emphasize that a person's genes should never be the basis for deciding whether that person is hired for a job, regarded as potentially dangerous, or stigmatized in any way. The study of behavioral genetics cannot explain the degree to which any given individual's behavior is due to genes or environment; it can only estimate the average influence that genes and environment exert on differences among a large group of people. Furthermore, as the following simple example illustrates, the extent to which any behavior—crime, intelligence, or athletic ability—is inheritable within one group of people cannot explain differences between groups of people.

Height is inheritable, much more so than criminal behavior. Assume that a group of people are raised in a culture in which they are chronically underfed; on average, the taller parents in this culture will still have the taller children. However, the children in this culture might be a few inches shorter than children raised in another culture where food is plentiful. Although height is genetically influenced in both cultures, the difference in height between the two cultures is not due to genetics. A similar situation exists for crime. Even though the evidence points to a possible influence of genes on crime, this does not diminish the importance of environmental factors.

A belief that crime is even partially determined by genetic factors still begs the obvious question: What, exactly, is inherited? There is a lengthy list of likely candidates (Brennan & Raine, 1997; DiLalla & Gottesman, 1991; Moffitt & Mednick, 1988), but five possibilities are emphasized:

1. *Constitutional predisposition.* The data are inconclusive about this factor and do not carry us much beyond the previously discussed finding that strong, athletic, muscular youth are more successful bullies than their portly or puny peers (Olweus, 1995). Physical stature is clearly influenced by genetic factors, and to the extent that a strong physique interacts with other variables to increase the likelihood of aggressive behavior early in life, genetics can contribute some risk of antisocial conduct.

2. *Neuropsychological abnormalities.* High rates of abnormal electroencephalogram (EEG) patterns have been reported in prison populations and in violent juvenile delinquents. These EEG irregularities may indicate neurological deficits that result in poor impulse control and impaired judgment. Unfortunately, in the general population, a high percentage of persons have EEG abnormalities, thus limiting the diagnostic utility of the EEG. Furthermore, some studies have not found a significant relationship between EEG pathology and delinquent behavior (Loomis, 1965). More promising results have been reported concerning abnormalities in four subcortical re-

gions of the brain—the amygdala, hippocampus, thalamus, and midbrain—specifically in the right hemisphere of the brain, which has been linked to the experience of negative emotions. In one study (Raine et al., 1998), brain scans of a group of murderers showed that, compared with normal controls, the murderers experienced excessive activity in the four subcortical structures. Excessive subcortical activity may underlie a more aggressive temperament that could, in turn, predispose an individual to violent behavior. Those individuals who also have impairments in the prefrontal cortex, the area of the brain responsible for planning and controlling behavior, would be prone to impulsive aggression. Individuals with normal prefrontal functioning would be more likely to use their aggressive tendencies to intimidate and threaten others to achieve what they want.

Other lines of research suggest that impaired functioning in the prefrontal cortex is a contributor to aggressive behavior. Offenders have about an eight- to ten-point lower IQ (intelligence quotient) than nonoffenders. This difference is mainly due to verbal (as opposed to performance) IQ scores, feeding speculation that offenders are less able to (1) postpone impulsive actions, (2) use effective problem-solving strategies (Lynam, Moffitt, & Stouthamer-Loeber, 1993), and (3) achieve academic success in schools as a route to socially approved attainments (Binder, 1988).

A frequent criticism of these findings is that incarcerated delinquents are not representative of delinquents at large. However, regardless of whether they are incarcerated or not, delinquent youth perform more poorly on IQ measures than their nondelinquent peers but do not differ among themselves (Moffitt & Silva, 1988). In addition, IQ deficits are reliably found before actual offending begins, suggesting that the causal relation runs from low IQ to antisocial behavior, not vice versa. In one longitudinal study of 411 London boys, low IQ at ages 8 through 10 was linked to persistent criminality and more convictions for violent crimes up to age 32 (Farrington, 1995). This relationship is still found even after controlling for the effects of social class, race, or motivation to do well on tests (Lynam et al., 1993).

**3. *Autonomic nervous system differences.*** The autonomic nervous system (ANS) carries information between the brain and all organs of the body. Because of these connections, emotions are associated with changes in the ANS. In fact, we can "see" the effects of emotional arousal on such ANS responses as heart rate, skin conductance, respiration, and blood pressure. One subset of criminals—those most repetitively in trouble—is thought to differ from noncriminals in that they show chronically low levels of autonomic arousal and weaker physiological reactions to stimulation (Mednick et al., 1977). These differences, which might also involve hormonal irregularities (see the next section), could cause this group of criminals to have (1) difficulties learning how to inhibit behavior likely to lead to punishment and (2) a high need for extra stimulation that they gratify through aggressive thrill seeking. These difficulties are also considered an important predisposing factor by some social-psychological theorists that we discuss later.

**4. *Physiological differences.*** A number of physiological factors might lead to increased aggressiveness and delinquency (Berman, 1997). Among the variables receiving continuing attention are (1) abnormally high levels of testosterone, (2) increased secretion of insulin, and (3) lower levels of serotonin (DiLalla & Gottesman, 1991). Research on testosterone has yielded inconsistent results (Archer, 1991), but depleted or impaired action of serotonin has received considerable support as a factor underlying impulsive aggression (Coccaro, Kavoussi, & Lesser, 1992). Low levels of serotonin might be linked with aggressiveness and criminal conduct in any of several ways— greater impulsivity and irritability, impaired ability to regulate negative moods, excessive alcohol consumption, or a hypersensitivity to provocative and threatening environmental cues (Berman, Tracy, & Coccaro, 1997).

**5. *Personality and temperament differences.*** Several dimensions of personality, known to be inheritable to a considerable degree, are related to antisocial behavior. Individuals with personalities marked by undercontrol, unfriendliness, irritability, low empathy, and a tendency to be easily frustrated are at greater risk for antisocial conduct (Nietzel, Hasemann, & Lynam, 1997). We discuss some of these characteristics more fully in the next section on psychological theories of crime.

# Psychological Theories of Crime

Psychological explanations of crime emphasize individual differences in the way people think or feel about their behavior. These differences, which can take the form of subtle differences or more extreme personality disturbances, might make some people more prone to criminal conduct by increasing their anger, weakening their attachments to others, or fueling their desire to take risks and seek thrills.

## *Psychoanalytic Theories of Crime*

Psychoanalysts believe that crime results from a weak ego and superego that cannot restrain the antisocial instincts of the id. Each individual's unique history should reveal the specific factors that produced a defective ego or superego, but the most commonly blamed factor is inadequate identification by a child with his or her parents.

Freud believed that the criminal suffers from a compulsive need for punishment to alleviate guilt feelings stemming from the unconscious, incestuous feelings of the oedipal period. He wrote, "In many criminals, especially youthful ones, it is possible to detect a very powerful sense of guilt which existed before the crime, and is therefore not its result but its motive. It is as if it was a relief to be able to fasten this unconscious sense of guilt onto something real and immediate" (1961, p. 52).

Franz Alexander (Alexander & Healy, 1935) proposed that the criminal does not orient his behavior with the **reality principle,** a task of the ego that requires a person to postpone immediate gratification to obtain greater rewards in the future. Alexander thought family and general social forces also contributed to criminality. In *Roots of Crime,* written with William Healy in 1935, Alexander argues that "criminal acts are not always committed by certain individuals who can be defined and characterized psychologically or in terms of personality as specifically inclined to crime, but neither are criminal acts restricted to certain social groups which can be characterized and defined sociologically . . . both personality and sociological factors are active at the same time; either of them may be predominant in one case, negligible in another" (p. 273).

Other psychoanalysts have suggested that criminal behavior is a means of obtaining substitute gratification of basic needs such as love, nurturance, and attention that have not been normally satisfied within the family. John Bowlby (1949, 1953; Bowlby & Salter-Ainsworth, 1965) believes that disruptions of the attachment between mother and infant or parental rejection of the developing child account for a majority of the more intractable cases of delinquency and repetitive crime (Bowlby, 1949, p. 37).

Psychoanalytic theories often trap their adherents in tautological circles, and, for the most part, they are no longer favored in modern criminology. What have been called "antisocial instincts" may simply be alternative names for the behaviors they are intended to explain. Another major problem with psychoanalytic interpretations of crime is that they are contradicted by patterns of real criminal conduct. Freud's idea that criminals commit crimes in order to be caught, punished, and have their guilt expiated ignores the obvious extremes to which most offenders go to avoid detection of their wrongdoing. Most offenders do not appear frustrated or guilt-ridden by the fact that their "crimes pay," at least some of the time. In fact, the success of their crimes seems to be a major source of gratification. Finally,

psychoanalytic descriptions are at odds with the observation that many forms of crime are more calculated than compulsed, more orchestrated than overdetermined, and more devised than driven.

## Criminal Thinking Patterns

In a controversial theory spawned from their frustration with traditional criminological theories, Samuel Yochelson and Stanton E. Samenow (1976; Samenow, 1984) have proposed that criminals engage in a fundamentally different way of thinking than noncriminals. They claim that the thinking of criminals, though internally logical and consistent, is erroneous and irresponsible. Consistent lawbreakers see themselves and the world differently from the rest of us.

Yochelson and Samenow reject sociological, environmental, and psychoanalytic explanations of criminality, such as a broken home, unloving parents, or unemployment. Rather, they argue that criminals become criminals as a result of choices they start making at an early age. These patterns, coupled with a pervasive sense of irresponsibility, mold lives of crime that are extremely difficult to change.

Yochelson and Samenow describe the criminals they studied as very much in control of their own actions, rather than being victims of the environment or being "sick." These criminals are portrayed as master manipulators who assign the blame for their behavior to others. They are such inveterate liars that they can no longer separate fact from fiction. They use words to manipulate, not to represent, reality.

Yochelson and Samenow's conclusions are based on intensive interviews with a small number of offenders, most of whom were incarcerated "hard-core" criminals or men who were hospitalized after having been acquitted of major crimes by reason of insanity. No control groups of any sort were studied. Yochelson and Samenow portray one type of criminal, but their analysis does not accurately represent the majority of lawbreakers. Furthermore, the "criminal thinking pattern" theory does not explain how these choices are made in the beginning (Pfohl, 1985), although in other publications Samenow hints at genetic predispositions to crime. In fact, in this way and others, this theory is similar to the notion of the psychopathic personality, which we turn to next.

## *Personality Defect as an Explanation of Criminality*

Many individuals attribute crime to personality defects, typically in the form of theories that posit a basic antisocial or psychopathic nature to the criminal. The concept of **psychopathy** has a long history. Generally, it refers to persons who engage in frequent, repetitive criminal activity for which they feel little or no remorse. Such persons appear chronically deceitful and manipulative; they seem to have a nearly total lack of conscience that propels them into repeated conflict with society, often from very early ages. They are superficial, arrogant, and do not seem to learn from experience; they lack empathy and loyalty to individuals, groups, or society (Hare, Hart, & Harpur, 1991). Psychopaths are selfish, callous, and irresponsible; they tend to blame others or to offer plausible rationalizations for their behavior.

The official diagnostic label for the psychopath is **antisocial personality disorder.** About 80% of psychopaths are men. Fortunately, psychopaths account for a small percentage of law violators, but they commit a disproportionately large percentage of violent crimes (McCord, 1982), and their acts often garner massive publicity (see ◆ Box 5-6). By some estimates, chronic antisocial personalities account for two-thirds of violent crime in the United States.

There are a multitude of theories for what causes psychopathic behavior. One view is that psychopathic persons suffer a cortical immaturity that makes it difficult for them to inhibit behavior. Robert Hare (Hare & McPherson, 1984) has proposed that psychopaths may have a deficiency in the left hemisphere of their brains that impairs what psychologists call **executive function,** the ability to plan and regulate behavior carefully (Moffitt & Lynam, 1994). Considerable research

supports the fact that there is a substantial correlation between antisocial behavior and impaired executive functioning (Morgan & Lilienfeld, 2000).

Compared to normal controls, psychopathic persons experience less anxiety subsequent to aversive stimulation and are relatively underaroused in the resting state as well. This low autonomic arousal generates, in turn, a high need for stimulation. Consequently, the psychopath prefers novel situations and tends to "shorten" stimuli, thereby being less controlled by them. Herbert Quay (1965) advanced a **stimulation-seeking** theory, which claims that the thrill-seeking and disruptive behavior of the psychopath serve to increase sensory input and arousal to a more tolerable level.

As a result of such thrill seeking, the psychopathic person becomes "immune" to many social cues that govern behavior. Eysenck (1964) proposed a theory that emphasizes the slower rate of classical conditioning for persons classified as psychopaths. Eysenck argues that the development of a conscience depends on acquiring classically conditioned fear and avoidance responses and that psychopathic individuals' conditioning deficiencies may account for their difficulties in normal socialization.

Another popular explanation for psychopathy involves being raised in a dysfunctional family (Loeber & Stouthamer-Loeber, 1986; Patterson, 1986). Arnold Buss (1966) identified two parental patterns that might foster psychopathy. First are parents who are cold and distant. The child who imitates these parents develops a cold, detached interpersonal style that conveys a superficial appearance of social involvement but lacks the empathy required for stable, satisfying relationships. The second pattern is parents who are inconsistent in their use of rewards and punishments, making it difficult for the child to imitate a stable role model and develop a consistent self-identity. A child in this situation learns to avoid blame and punishment but fails to know the difference between right and wrong behavior.

The major drawback of psychopathy as an explanation of crime is that it describes only a small

**THE CASE OF**

**BOX 5-6**   **Ted Bundy: Antisocial personality?**

Born in 1946, Theodore Robert Bundy seemed destined for a charmed life; he was intelligent, attractive, and articulate (Holmes & DeBurger, 1988). A Boy Scout as a youth and then an honor student and a psychology major at the University of Washington, he was at one time a work-study student at the Seattle Crisis Clinic. Later, he became assistant to the chairman of the Washington State Republican Party. It is probably around this time that he claimed his first victim; a college-age woman was viciously attacked while sleeping, left alive but brain damaged. From 1974 through 1978, Bundy stalked, attacked, killed, and then sexually assaulted as many as 36 victims in Washington, Oregon, Utah, Colorado, and Florida. Apparently, some of the women were distracted when the good-looking, casual Bundy ap-

proached, seeming helpless walking with crutches or having an apparent broken arm. He usually choked them to death and then sexually abused and mutilated them before disposing of their bodies in remote areas (Nordheimer, 1989).

It is characteristic of many people with antisocial personality disorder to maintain a facade of charm, so that acquaintances will describe them (as they did Bundy) as "fascinating," "charismatic," and "compassionate." As a matter of fact, beneath his surface charm, Bundy was deceitful and dangerous. Embarrassed by the fact that he was an illegitimate son and that his mother was poor, he constantly sought, as a youth, to create an impression of being an upper-class kid. He wore fake mustaches and used makeup to change his appearance. He faked a British accent

*Ted Bundy*

and stole cars in high school to help maintain his image. And he constantly sought out the company of attractive women, not because he was genuinely interested in them but because he wanted people to notice and admire him. As time went on, Bundy's snobbery and pretensions grew insatiable.

At his trial for the murder of two Chi Omega sorority sisters in their bedrooms at Florida State

percentage of offenders. It might be tempting to classify most offenders as psychopaths and feel content that their crimes had been explained with that terminology. In fact, however, most offenders are not psychopathic. We must look to other factors.

# Social-Psychological Theories of Crime

Social-psychological explanations view crime as being learned through social interaction. Sometimes called "social-process" theories in order to

draw attention to the processes by which an individual becomes a criminal, social-psychological theories fall into two subcategories: control theories and direct learning theories.

## Control Theories

Control theories assume that people will behave antisocially unless they are trained not to by others (Conger, 1980). Some people never form emotional bonds with significant others, so they never internalize necessary controls over antisocial behavior. For example, Hirschi's (1969, 1978) social-control model stresses four control variables, each

University, he served as his own attorney (Bundy had attended two law schools). But he was convicted; he was also found guilty of the kidnapping, murder, and mutilation of a Lake City, Florida, girl who was 12 years old.

Bundy was sentenced to death. Shortly before he was executed on January 24, 1989, Bundy gave a television interview to California evangelist James Dobson in which he blamed his problems on pornography. He said, "Those of us who are . . . so much influenced by violence in the media, in particular pornographic violence, are not some kind of inherent monsters. We are your husbands, and we grew up in regular families" (quoted by Lamar, 1989, p. 34). Bundy claimed that he spent his formative ages with a grandfather who had an insatiable craving for pornography.

He told Dr. Dobson, "People will accuse me of being self-serving but I am just telling you how I feel. Through God's help, I have been able to come to the point where I, much too late, but better late than never, feel the hurt and the pain that I am responsible for" (quoted by Kleinberg, 1989, p. 5A).

The tape of Bundy's last interview, produced by Dobson and titled "Fatal Addiction," has been widely disseminated, especially by those who seek to eliminate all pornography. (Dr. Dobson served on a federal pornography commission during the Reagan administration.) But Bundy's claim that pornography was the "fuel for his fantasies" should be viewed skeptically. It may merely have been one last manipulative ploy to gain further time. In none of his previous interviews, including extensive conversations in 1986 with Dorothy Lewis, a psychiatrist he had come to trust, did he ever cite "a pornographic preamble to his grotesqueries" (Nobile, 1989, p. 41). In all probability, Bundy had simply decided that he needed psychiatric testimony to escape the electric chair—by being diagnosed as incompetent to stand trial because he was supposedly too confused and irrational to assist in his own murder defense. Despite Dr. Lewis's testimony in 1986, the judge did not declare Bundy incompetent. Thus, perhaps at that time, Bundy decided that his last best option was to portray himself as a normal youth who had been corrupted by pornography (Nobile, 1989).

of which represents a major social bond: (1) attachment, (2) commitment, (3) involvement, and (4) belief. Young people are bonded to society at several levels. They differ in (1) the degree to which they are affected by the opinions and expectations of others, (2) the payoffs they receive for conventional behavior, and (3) the extent to which they subscribe to the prevailing norms.

Another example is Walter Reckless's (1967) **containment theory.** Reckless proposes that it is largely external containment (i.e., social pressure and institutionalized rules) that controls crime. If a society is well integrated, has well-defined limits on behavior, encourages family discipline and supervision, and provides reinforcers for positive accomplishments, crime will be contained. But if these external controls weaken, control of crime must depend on internal restraints, mainly an individual's conscience. Thus, a positive self-concept becomes an insulator against delinquency. Strong inner containment involves the ability to tolerate frustration, be motivated by long-term goals, resist distractions, and find substitute satisfactions (Reckless, 1967).

Containment theory is a good "in-between" view, neither rigidly environmental nor entirely psychological. Containment accounts both for the law-abiding individual in a high-crime environment as well as the law violator from a low-crime background. But containment theory explains only a part of criminal behavior. It does not apply to crimes within groups that are organized around their commitment to deviant behavior.

The British psychologist Hans Eysenck (1964) proposes a related version of containment theory in which "heredity plays an important, and possibly a vital, part in predisposing a given individual to crime" (p. 55). Socialization practices then translate these innate tendencies into criminal acts.

Socialization depends on two kinds of learning. First, **operant learning** explains how behavior is acquired and maintained by its consequences: Responses that are followed by rewards are strengthened, whereas responses followed by aversive events are weakened. Immediate consequences are more influential than delayed consequences. However, according to Eysenck (1964), in the real world, the effects of punishment are usually "long delayed and uncertain [while] the acquisition of the desired object is immediate; therefore, although the acquisition and the pleasure derived from it may, on the whole, be less than the pain derived from the incarceration which ultimately follows, the time element very much favors the acquisition as compared with the deterrent effects of the incarceration" (p. 101).

Because of punishment's ineffectiveness, the restraint of antisocial behavior ultimately depends on a strong conscience, which develops through **classical conditioning.** Eysenck believes that conscience is conditioned through repeated, close pairings of a child's undesirable behaviors with the prompt punishment of these behaviors. The taboo act is the **conditioned stimulus,** which, when associated frequently enough with the **unconditioned stimulus** of punishment, produces unpleasant physiological and emotional responses. Conscience becomes an inner control that deters wrongdoing through the emotions of anxiety and guilt.

Whether conditioning builds a strong conscience depends on the strength of the autonomic nervous system. According to Eysenck, conditioned responses have a genetically determined tendency in some people to develop slowly and extinguish quickly. In others, conditioning progresses rapidly and produces strong resistance to extinction. Underlying these differences are three major personality dimensions: **extroversion, neuroticism,** and **psychoticism** (Eysenck & Gudjonsson, 1989). Extroverted people are active, aggressive, and impulsive. Persons high in neuroticism are restless, emotionally volatile, and hypersensitive. Persons high in psychoticism are troublesome, lacking in empathy, and insensitive to the point of cruelty.

Extroversion, neuroticism, and psychoticism are inherited to a substantial degree and also are associated with important physiological differences, some of which we described in our previous discussion of psychopathy. High extroverts have relatively low levels of arousal that slow their ability to be conditioned and also render responses that are conditioned to be easily extinguished. Conditioning is also impaired because physiological arousal dissipates more slowly in extroverted people and psychopaths. As a result, avoiding a previously punished act may be less reinforcing for such people because they experience less reduction in fear following their avoidance of the taboo behavior (Mednick, Gabriella, & Hutchings, 1984a).

Persons high in neuroticism tend to overreact to stimuli. Therefore, high neuroticism interferes with efficient learning because of the irrelevant arousal that is evoked. In addition, high neuroticism leads to greater restlessness and drive to carry out behavior of all sorts, including crimes.

Eysenck believes that high extroversion and neuroticism result in poor conditioning and, consequently, inadequate socialization. Poor conditioning leads to a faulty conscience, which in turn produces a higher risk for criminality. Finally, if the person is high on psychoticism, he or she will be more of a primary, "toughminded" psychopath.

Research on the links between criminal offending and personality supports a positive association between high levels of extroversion and

**BOX 5-7**    **Postulates of differential association theory**

1. Criminal behavior is learned.
2. Criminal behavior is learned in interaction with other persons in a process of communication.
3. The influential aspect of the learning of criminal behavior occurs within intimate social groups.
4. When criminal behavior is learned, the learning includes (1) techniques of committing the crime, which are sometimes very complicated, sometimes very simple, and (2) the specific direction of motives, drives, rationalizations, and attitudes.
5. The specific direction of motives and drives is learned from definitions of the legal code as favorable or unfavorable.
6. A person becomes delinquent because of an excess of definitions favorable to violation of law over definitions unfavorable to violation of law.
7. Differential associations may vary in frequency, duration, intensity, and priority.
8. The process of learning criminal behavior by association with criminal and anticriminal patterns involves all the mechanisms that are involved in any other learning.
9. Although criminal behavior is an expression of general needs and values, it is not explained by those general needs and values, since noncriminal behavior is an expression of the same needs and values.

SOURCE: Adapted from Sutherland and Cressey (1974, pp. 75–76).

increased offending. However, the role of neuroticism and psychopathy is less clear; in fact, neuroticism may be lower in most psychopaths than in normal controls (Doren, 1987). Another problem is that Eysenck has not clearly separated the predisposition to be conditioned from the different conditioning opportunities that children experience. Genetic differences are accompanied by different conditioning histories. A family of extroverts can transmit a potential for crime not only through inherited personality traits but also through laissez faire discipline that is too scarce or inconsistent to be effective.

## Learning Theories

Learning theory focuses on how criminal behavior is learned. According to Edwin H. Sutherland's (1947) differential association approach, criminal behavior requires socialization into a system of values conducive to violating the law; thus, the potential criminal develops definitions of behavior that make deviant conduct seem acceptable. If definitions of criminal acts as being acceptable are stronger and more frequent than definitions unfavorable to deviant behavior, then the person is more likely to commit crimes (see ◆ Box 5-7). It is not necessary to associate with criminals directly to acquire these definitions. Children might learn procriminal definitions from watching their father pocket too much change or hearing their mother brag about exceeding the speed limit.

Sutherland's theory has been translated into the language of operant learning theory as developed by B. F. Skinner. According to **differential association reinforcement theory** (Akers et al., 1996; Burgess & Akers, 1966), criminal behavior is acquired through operant conditioning and modeling. A person behaves criminally when such behavior is favored by reinforcement contingencies that outweigh punishment contingencies. The major contingencies occur in families, peer groups, and schools, which control most sources of reinforcement and punishment and expose people to many behavioral models (Akers et al., 1996).

Differential association attempts to explain crime in places where it would not, on first blush, be expected (e.g., among lawbreakers who grew up in affluent settings). But it has difficulty explaining impulsive violence, and it does not explain why certain individuals, even in the same family, have the different associations they do. Why are some people more likely than others to form criminal associations?

## SOCIAL-LEARNING THEORY

Social-learning theory acknowledges the importance of differential reinforcement for developing new behaviors, but it gives more importance to cognitive factors and to observational or **vicarious learning.** Its chief proponent, Albert Bandura (1986), claims, "most human behavior is learned by observation through modeling" (p. 47). Learning through modeling is more efficient than learning through differential reinforcement. Sophisticated behaviors such as speech and complex chains of behavior such as driving a car require models. In all likelihood, so does crime.

Observational learning depends on (1) *attention* to the important features of modeled behavior, (2) *retention* of these features in memory to guide later performance, (3) *reproduction* of the observed behaviors, and (4) *reinforcement* of attempted behaviors, which determines whether they will be performed again.

The most prominent attempt to apply social-learning theory to criminal behavior is Bandura's (1973) book, *Aggression: A Social Learning Analysis* (see also Platt & Prout, 1987; Ribes-Inesta & Bandura, 1976). The theory emphasizes modeling of aggression in three social contexts.

*1. Familial influences.* Familial aggression assumes many forms, from child abuse at one extreme to aggressive parental attitudes and language at the other. It is the arena of discipline, however, in which children are exposed most often to vivid examples of coercion and aggression as a preferred style for resolving conflicts and asserting desires.

*2. Subcultural influences.* Some environments and subcultures provide a rich diet of aggression and an abundance of rewards for their most combative members. "The highest rates of aggressive behavior are found in environments where aggressive models abound and where aggressiveness is regarded as a highly valued attribute" (Bandura, 1976, p. 207).

*3. Symbolic models.* The influence of symbolic models on aggression has been attributed to the mass media, particularly television. A large number of studies have investigated the effects of televised violence on viewers, especially on children. Interpretations of this literature vary as to whether viewing televised violence causes later aggression in viewers. The consensus is that TV violence does increase aggression for children and adolescents, that this influence is small but meaningful in magnitude, that short-term effects have been demonstrated more clearly than long-term effects, that TV violence might have a larger impact on children who are initially more aggressive, and that children who watch a lot of televised violence are more likely to become fearful of the world around them at the same time they become less sensitive to the feelings of others (Friedrich-Cofer & Huston, 1986; Huston et al., 1992; Pearl, Bouthilet, & Lazar, 1982; Surgeon General's Scientific Advisory Committee on Television and Social Behavior, 1972; for the dissenting view that TV violence has not been shown to increase aggression, see Freedman, 1984, 1986). Of more recent interest is the question of whether movies, which often feature much more graphic depictions of violence than those allowed on TV, might exert stronger modeling effects on aggression.

Social-learning theory also points to several environmental cues that increase antisocial behavior. These "instigators" signal when it might be rewarding to behave antisocially versus when it might be risky to do so. Six instigators deserve special mention and are summarized in ◆ Box 5-8.

According to social-learning theorists, people also regulate their behavior through self-

___

## The Science of

**BOX 5-8** · **Criminology: Instigators to criminal behavior**

*Models.* Modeled aggression is effective in prompting others to behave aggressively, particularly when observers have been previously frustrated or when the modeled aggression is seen as justified.

*Prior aversive treatment.* Assaults, threats, reductions in available reinforcers, blocking of goal-directed behaviors, and perceptions of inequitable treatment can lead to increased aggression and can enhance the perceived rewards of aggression.

*Incentive inducements.* Antisocial behavior can be prompted by the anticipated rewards of misbehavior. Bandura (1976) suggests that aggression is sometimes stimulated and temporarily sustained by erroneously anticipated consequences. Habitual offenders often overestimate their chances of suc-

ceeding in criminal acts and ignore the consequences of failing.

*Instructions.* Milgram's (1963) famous experiment demonstrating widespread willingness to follow orders to inflict "pain" on another person suggests that antisocial behavior can be instigated by commands from authorities. The strength of instructional control is limited to certain conditions and is an infrequent source of instigation in most crimes. However, it may play a role in some hate crimes, in which the perpetrator believes he or she is doing the will of a religious or patriotic fanatic.

*Delusions.* Individuals occasionally respond aggressively to hallucinated commands or paranoid jealousies and suspicions. People who suffer delusional symptoms also tend to be socially isolated, a

factor that sometimes minimizes the corrective influences that a reality-based environment could have on them.

*Alcohol and drug use.* Alcohol and drugs must be reckoned with as potent instigators to antisocial conduct. A strong, positive association between crime and alcohol use is undeniable, especially in violent crime (Collins & Messerschmidt, 1993). By depressing a person's responsiveness to other cues that could inhibit impulsive or aggressive behavior, alcohol often leads to an increase in antisocial behavior even though it is not a stimulant (Chermack & Giancola, 1997). Narcotics use, by virtue of its cost and deviant status, also acts as a catalyst to or amplifier of criminality, especially property crime.

reinforcement. Individuals who derive pleasure, pride, revenge, or self-worth from an ability to harm or "rip off" others enjoy an almost sensual pleasure in the way criminal behavior "feels" (Katz, 1988). Conversely, people will discontinue conduct that results in self-criticism and self-contempt. People can also learn to exempt themselves from their own conscience after behaving antisocially. These tactics of "self-exoneration" assume many forms: minimizing the seriousness of one's acts by pointing to more serious offenses by others, justifying aggression by appealing to higher values, displacing the responsibility for

misbehavior onto a higher authority, blaming victims for their misfortune, diffusing responsibility for wrongdoing, dehumanizing victims so they are stripped of sympathetic qualities, and underestimating the damage of one's actions.

The major strength of social-learning theory is that it explains how specific patterns of criminality are developed by individual offenders. A second strength is that the theory applies to a wide range of crimes. The major limitation of social-learning theory is that little empirical evidence indicates that real-life crime is learned according to behavioral principles. Most of the data come from laboratory research where the experimental setting nullifies all the legal and social sanctions that actual offenders must risk. A second problem is that the theory does not explain why some people fall prey to "bad" learning experiences while others resist them. Learning might be a necessary ingredient for criminality, but it is probably not a sufficient one. Individual differences in the way people respond to reinforcement need to be considered, and they are by the theory we review next.

## WILSON AND HERRNSTEIN'S CONSTITUTIONAL-LEARNING THEORY

Some theorists have integrated several learning processes into comprehensive, learning-based explanations of criminality (e.g., Feldman, 1977). The most influential and controversial multiple-component learning theory is James Q. Wilson and the late Richard Herrnstein's (1985) book *Crime and Human Nature*. Wilson and Herrnstein begin by observing that criminal and noncriminal behavior have both gains and losses. Gains from committing crime include revenge, excitement, and peer approval. Gains associated with not committing crime include avoiding punishment and having a clear conscience. Whether a crime is committed depends, in part, on the net ratio of gains and losses for criminal and noncriminal behavior. If the ratio for committing a crime exceeds that for not committing it, the likelihood of the crime being committed increases (a proposition similar to what Cornish & Clarke [1986] call **rational choice theory**).

Wilson and Herrnstein argue that several individual differences influence these ratios and determine whether an individual is likely to commit a crime. Like Eysenck, they propose that individuals differ in the ease with which they learn to associate, through classical conditioning, negative emotions with misbehaviors and positive emotions with proper behaviors. These conditioned responses are the building blocks of a strong conscience that increases the gains associated with noncrime and increases the losses associated with crime.

Another important personality factor is what Wilson and Herrnstein call *time discounting*. All

reinforcers lose strength the more remote they are from a behavior, but persons differ in their ability to delay gratification and obtain reinforcement from potential long-term gains. More impulsive persons have greater difficulty deriving benefits from distant reinforcers. Time discounting is important for understanding crime because the gains associated with crime (e.g., revenge, money) occur immediately, whereas the losses from such behavior (e.g., punishment) occur later, if at all. Thus, for impulsive persons, the ratio of gains to losses shifts in a direction that favors criminal behavior.

Equity, a term we discussed in Chapter 3, is another important influence on criminality. Equity theory states that people compare what they feel they deserve with what they observe other people receiving. Inequitable transactions are perceived when one's own ratio of gains to losses is less than that of others. Judgments of inequity change the reinforcing value of crime. If one perceives oneself as being unfairly treated by society, this sense of inequity increases the perceived gains associated with stealing because such behavior helps restore one's sense of equity.

Another major component in Wilson and Herrnstein's theory is a set of constitutional factors, including gender, intelligence, variations in physiological arousal, and the aforementioned impulsivity, all of which conspire to make some persons more attracted to wrongdoing and less deterred by the potential aversive consequences of crime.

Of several social factors linked to criminal behavior, Wilson and Herrnstein believe that family influences and early school experiences are the most important. Families that foster (1) *attachment* of children to their parents, (2) *longer time horizons,* where children consider the distant consequences of their behavior, and (3) *strong consciences* about misbehavior will go far in counteracting criminal predispositions. The work of Gerald Patterson and his colleagues is pertinent here. Based on elaborate observations of families with and without aggressive and conduct-disordered children, Patterson (1982, 1986) has identified four family interaction patterns associated with later delinquency: (1) disciplinary techniques involving either excessive nagging or indifferent laxness; (2) lack of positive parenting and affection toward children, (3) ineffective parental monitoring of a child's behavior, and (4) failure to employ adequate problem-solving strategies, thereby increasing stress and irritability within a family.

The remedies to these harmful patterns involve warm supportiveness combined with consistent enforcement of clear rules for proper behavior. Unfortunately, these methods are least likely to be practiced by parents whose own traits reflect the predispositions they have passed to their children. Therefore, many at-risk children face the double whammy of problematic predispositions coupled with inadequate parental control and support.

Biological factors interact with family problems and early school experiences to increase the risks of poorly controlled behavior even more. Not only are impulsive, poorly socialized children of lower intelligence more directly at risk for criminality, but their interactions with cold, indifferent schools that do not facilitate educational success are an additional liability that pushes them away from traditional social conformity. Consistent with this part of the theory is a long line of research studies showing that children officially diagnosed with early conduct problems and/or attention deficit/hyperactivity disorder face a heightened likelihood of becoming adult offenders (Nietzel et al., 1997).

Because they took hereditary and biological factors seriously, Wilson and Herrnstein have come under heavy fire from critics who portray their ideas as a purely genetic theory. It is not. Instead, it is a theory that restores psychological factors (some inheritable, some not) and family interaction variables to a place of importance in criminology, which for decades was dominated by sociological concepts.

## The Social-Labeling Perspective

The most extreme version of a social-psychological theory of crime is the social-labeling perspective.

Its emergence as an explanation reflects (1) frustration about the inability of prior approaches to provide comprehensive explanations and (2) a shift in emphasis from why people commit crimes to why some people are labeled "criminals" (Sheley, 1985).

Some examples will illustrate this shift. In one study (Heussanstamm, 1975), during the turbulent 1970s, a group of college students in Los Angeles—each of whom had perfect driving records in the last year—had "Black Panther" bumper stickers put on their cars. Within hours, they began to get pulled over for traffic violations, such as improper lane changes, implying that the Los Angeles police officers were labeling behavior differently based on the presence of the bumper sticker.

A more contemporary and more troubling illustration of this phenomenon is the allegation that police use **racial profiling** as a basis for making a disproportionate number of traffic stops of minority motorists, particularly African Americans. As we discussed in Chapter 1, this practice has often been justified by police as a tool for catching drug traffickers, but arresting motorists for "driving while black" as a pretext for additional criminal investigations clearly raises the risk of harmful and inappropriate labeling, to say nothing of its discriminatory impact. The outcry over racial profiling has resulted in a call for federal legislation that would prohibit the practice as well as several lawsuits, including one in which the Maryland state police agreed to pay damages to four African American drivers who had been targets of profile stops.

The basic assumption of labeling theory is that deviance is created by the labels that society assigns to certain acts. Deviance is not simply based on the quality of the act; rather, it stems also from an act's consequences in the form of society's official reactions to the act. Social-labeling theory makes a distinction between **primary deviance,** or the criminal's actual behavior, and **secondary deviance,** or society's reaction to the offensive conduct (Lemert, 1951, 1972). With regard to primary deviance, offenders often rationalize their behavior as a temporary mistake, or

**BOX 5-9    Assumptions of the social-learning perspective**

1. Before persons can be labeled as criminals, their behavior must be noticed, or at least assumed to be noticed, by society.

2. Observation must be followed by reaction. Individuals cannot be labeled as criminals unless society reacts to their alleged offenses; that is, an act is devoid of social meaning until society attempts to give it meaning.

3. Society's attempt to label people as criminals may succeed or may fail. The attempt to label does not guarantee the successful imposition of a label.

4. The outcome of the negotiation of a label between society and individuals involves more than just the qualities of alleged criminal acts. Characteristics of the alleged violator, such as race, gender, or socioeconomic status, and the social or political climate in which the negotiation occurs will also influence the outcome.

5. Whether the effects of the labeling are long-lasting is also negotiable and depends on individuals' reactions to their labels, society's perceptions of those reactions, and society's willingness to negotiate.

SOURCE: Adapted from Sheley (1985, pp. 233–234).

---

they see it as part of a socially acceptable role (Lilly et al., 1989). Whether their self-assessment is accurate, secondary deviance serves to confer a more permanent "criminal" stigma on them.

◆ Box 5-9 lists the basic assumptions of this perspective. Its main point is that the stigma of being branded a deviant can create a self-fulfilling prophecy (Merton, 1968). Even those ex-convicts who seek an honest life in a law-abiding society are spurned by prospective employers and by their families and are labeled "ex-cons." Frustrated in their efforts to make good, they may adopt this label and ensure that it comes true by engaging in further lawbreaking (Irwin, 1970). According to this perspective, the criminal justice system produces much of the deviance it is intended to correct.

The social-labeling approach raises our awareness about the difficulties offenders face in returning to society. Moreover, it reminds us that some lawbreakers (e.g., those who live in crime-prone neighborhoods in which the police patrol often) are more likely to be caught and "criminalized" than are others. But the social-labeling approach does not explain most criminal behavior.

Primary deviance (i.e., a law violation in the first place) usually has to occur before secondary deviance takes its toll, and many lawbreakers develop a life of crime before ever being apprehended (Mankoff, 1971). Behavioral differences between people exist and persist despite the names we call them.

## Integration of Theories of Crime

Where do all these theories leave us? Do any of them offer a convincing explanation of crime? Do they suggest how we should intervene to prevent or reduce crime? Although many commentators decry the lack of a convincing theory of crime, an increasing fund of knowledge about the causes of serious crime has accumulated and now provides a set of valid explanations for how repeated, violent criminality develops.

Serious criminality is extraordinarily versatile, involving careers that include violent behavior, property offenses, vandalism, and substance abuse. One implication of this diversity is that persons travel several causal pathways to different brands of criminality. No single variable causes all crime, just as no one agent causes all fever or upset stomachs. However, several causal factors are associated reliably with many types of criminality. Any one of these factors will sometimes be a sufficient explanation for criminal behavior; more often, however, they act in concert to produce criminality.

Our attempt to integrate these various factors (see Figure 5-1) emphasizes four contributors to crime that occur in a developmental sequence. Our model emphasizes the causal factors that we believe are the best supported findings in criminological research.

*1. Antecedent conditions.* Chances of repeated offending are increased by biological, psychological, and environmental antecedents that make it easier for certain individuals to learn to behave criminally and easier for this learning to occur in specific settings.

The leading candidates for biological risk are genetic inheritance, strong physique, neurochemical abnormalities, brain dysfunction, and autonomic nervous system irregularities.

Among psychological variables, poor social skills; lower verbal intelligence; the personality traits of irritability, impulsiveness, and low empathy; and deficiencies in inner restraint (or conscience) leave some people well stocked in attitudes, thinking, and motivations that encourage antisocial behavior and that also render them relatively immune to negative consequences for misconduct. These psychological factors may accompany biological risks or may convey their own independent vulnerability to crime.

Finally, certain environments are rich in opportunities and temptations for crime and help translate biological or psychological predispositions to criminal behavior into ever-stronger antisocial tendencies. They achieve this quality because of social impoverishment and disorganization, fundamental economic inequalities, a tradition of tolerating if not encouraging crime, social dissension

and strife, and an abundance of inviting targets and easy victims of crime (Heide, 1997; Patterson, 1996). Crime-causing environments encourage offending because they are crammed full of antagonists who provoke violence, easy targets to be victimized by violence, and high rates of alcohol and substance abuse that lower inhibitions against violence (Chermack & Giancola, 1997).

Within family environments, high levels of mental disorders, criminality, parental absenteeism, and substance abuse also lead to more violence. These links may be forged through any one of several factors: genetic influence, modeling, increased hostility against a constant backdrop of harsh living conditions, disturbed attachments with parents, or lax or overly punitive discipline that does not teach youngsters how to control behavior. Recent research suggests that early exposure to harsh family living conditions can aggravate some of the biological factors that contribute to aggression, such as a child's physical and emotional reactions to threat (Gallagher, 1996).

*2. Early indicators.* Repetitive antisocial conduct is disconcertingly stable over time. Aggressive children often grow up to be aggressive adults, and the precedents for adult violence and substance abuse are often seen in early indicators of aggressiveness in preschool and elementary school-age children (Lynam, 1998; Slutske et al., 1998). Although not all chronic offenders are violent children, many repetitively aggressive adults are early starters; in fact, most psychologists studying aggression believe that severe antisocial behavior in adulthood is almost always preceded by antisocial behavior in childhood. These early indicators include officially diagnosed conduct disorder, oppositional defiant disorder, and attention deficit/hyperactivity disorder (Lynam, 1996; McGee, Feehan, Williams, & Anderson, 1992).

Long-term longitudinal studies have demonstrated that aggression in childhood predicts violence in adulthood. Recall the longitudinal study by Huesmann, Eron, and Yarmel (1987) (discussed in Box 5-4) in which the researchers measured aggression in childhood and tracked the boys and

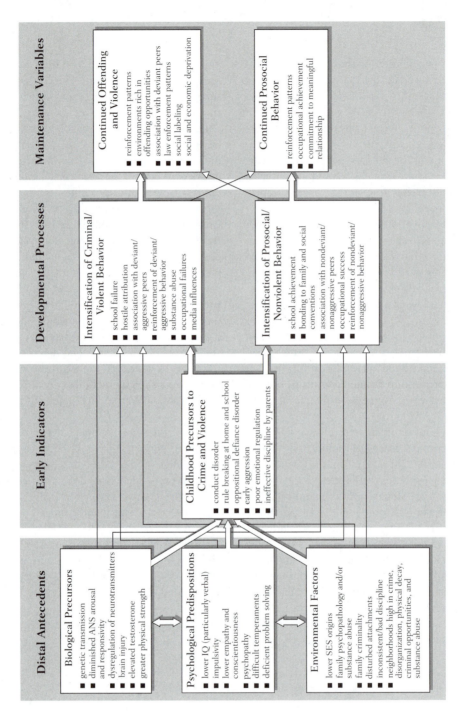

**FIGURE 5.1** *An integrated model for explaining repeated crime*

NOTE: Thick arrows indicate probable paths; thin arrows indicate less likely paths.

girls for 22 years. They found that aggression began to crystalize around the age of 8 and remained stable across three generations (Eron, 1990; Huesmann, Eron, Lefkowitz, & Walder, 1984). Aggressive boys turned into men who were more likely to commit serious crimes, abuse their spouses, and drive while intoxicated. Aggressive girls turned into women who were more likely to punish their children harshly.

3. *Developmental processes.* Whether early indicators of criminal offending harden into patterns of repeated adult crime or soften into prosocial nonviolent conduct depends on several developmental processes. These processes occur in families, schools, peer groups, the media, and in the thinking of the youth themselves.

Delinquency is often associated with poor school achievement. Grades in school begin to predict delinquency around age 15. As adolescent youth fall farther and farther behind in school, they have fewer and fewer opportunities or reasons to stay bonded to school and to strive for academic success (Cernkovich & Giordano, 1996). School failure seems to narrow the options for prosocial behavior because it decreases the chances of employability and job success.

Modeling and peer pressure also promote criminality. Crime increases when peers support it, as is sometimes the case in the criminal justice system itself when, by virtue of its official processing of offenders, "beginning" criminals are thrown together with more serious offenders. Furthermore, the more delinquent friends a youth has, the more likely he or she is to behave criminally (Elliott, Huizinga, & Ageton, 1985).

Modeling influences can also be mediated through the media. In Leonard Eron's (1987) large-scale study of aggression, children's viewing of TV violence at age 8 correlated 0.41 with several aggressive behaviors at age 30, even after controlling for baseline levels of aggressiveness, IQ, and socioeconomic status. TV and other media depictions of graphic violence could exert harmful effects by providing youngsters with opportunities to rehearse a lot of aggressive strategies. A steady diet of media violence might teach children to see their world as hostile and competitive. Repeated exposure to violence might also provide the "scripts" that youth elaborate into personal crime stories in which aggression and deceit are seen as necessary for surviving in a harsh world.

Another intensifier of aggression is alcohol and substance abuse (Murdoch, Pihl, & Ross, 1990). Numerous mechanisms could account for the tendency for substance abuse to lead to more crime. Alcohol is a depressant; therefore, it might suppress the ability of certain areas of the brain to inhibit behavior effectively. The more time a youth spends abusing drugs and alcohol, the less time he or she has for prosocial, academic activities. Substance abuse typically results in more associations with deviant peers, thereby increasing the opportunities for antisocial behavior to be reinforced. Repeated substance abuse during adolescence serves as one more "trap" that shuts off many youngsters' options for prosocial behavior. These limits, in turn, increase the reinforcing potential of antisocial conduct.

Unfortunately, these developmental processes tend to pile up on one another. The impulsive, low-IQ child is more likely to fail at school. School dropouts increasingly associate with antisocial peers. Parents who fail to monitor and sanction their children when they misbehave tend not to show much concern about what movies their children watch. Finally, early conduct and academic problems are strongly related to later substance abuse. When it comes to crime, at-risk youth stay at risk.

4. *Maintenance factors.* Violent offending can become an entrenched way of life when one or more of the following maintenance factors are in place:

The short-run positive payoffs for offending are stronger and more probable than the long-run risks of apprehension and punishment.
The person lives in environments that are rich in opportunities for offending and low in the chances of being detected.

As a result of the inevitable arrests and incarcerations that repeat offenders experience, their associations with aggressive peers increase as contacts with law-abiding citizens decrease.

As the long-run consequence of many earlier estrangements from conventional norms and values, delinquents begin to feel growing resentment and contempt for social rules.

These maintenance factors do not cause crime as much as they solidify it. Once they start to work their influence, the battle is often already lost because criminal conduct has become a basic part of a person's identity.

An implication of our integrative model is that preventing crime might be a better way of fighting the "crime problem" than rehabilitating criminals. Certainly, some people can "turn around" a life of violent offending with the help of treatment programs that strengthen their social skills, build better cognitive controls, model prosocial behavior, and reinforce law-abiding conduct (Andrews & Bonta, 1994). But despite these suc- cesses, interventions for lifelong offenders are frequently not successful (Lipton, Martinson, & Wilks, 1975; Palmer, 1984). This should not be surprising. After a protracted history of learning antisocial behavior, rejecting prosocial behavior, and facing closed doors to legitimate opportunity, repeat offenders will not yield easily to attempts to suppress criminal conduct. That is why prevention becomes so important. If most at-risk youth can be reliably identified, we can then intervene in multiple areas—with individuals, families, schools, peer groups, and neighborhoods—to stop those processes that eventually ensnare youth into antisocial lifestyles. Brought about by hostile environments and the decisions of youth themselves, these processes include experimenting with alcohol and drugs, dwelling on violent media and subcultures, dropping out of school, failing at legitimate employment, and associating with other lawbreakers. They are the pathways to deviance that must be blocked early before they become too well traveled for any change to occur.

# SUMMARY

**1.** *Theories of crime can be grouped into four categories; what are they?* The most common theories can be classified into four groups: sociological, biological, psychological, and social-psychological.

**2.** *Among sociological explanations of crime, how does the subcultural explanation differ from the structural explanation?* The structural explanation for crime emphasizes chronic barriers to conventional success that certain people face; these barriers include cultural and language differences, financial hardships, and limited access to those resources crucial for upward mobility. In contrast, the subcultural explanation proposes that certain groups, such as gangs, adhere to norms that conflict with the values of others in society and encourage criminal conduct.

**3.** *What is emphasized in biological theories of crime?* Both genetic and physiological factors are emphasized in biological explanations of criminal behavior. Hereditary factors influence criminal behavior, but it is still not clear what the mechanisms are through which this influence is exerted. The most likely candidates involve neurotransmitters such as serotonin and certain cortical and subcortical brain structures that regulate and generate arousal and emotions.

**4.** *What are the psychological factors explaining crime?* Psychological theories of criminal behavior emphasize the need to expiate unconscious guilt, criminal thinking patterns, or a personality defect.

**5.** *What is central to social-psychological theories of crime?* Social-psychological theories view criminal behavior as a learned response resulting from processes of classical conditioning, reinforcement, observation or modeling, and social labeling.

## KEY TERMS

adoption study

anomie*

antisocial personality
disorder

atavism

biological theories
of crime

classical
conditioning*

classical school of
criminology

concordance rate

conditioned stimulus

containment theory

control theory

criminology*

differential association
reinforcement
theory

dizygotic twins*

ecological theorists

ectomorph

endomorph

executive function

extroversion*

focal concerns

genealogy*

learning theory*

mesomorph

monozygotic twins*

neuroticism*

operant learning

positivist school of
criminology

primary deviance

psychological theories
of crime

psychopathy*

psychoticism*

racial profiling

rational choice theory*

rational crime theory

reaction formation

reality principle

secondary deviance

social-process theories

social-psychological
theory of crime

sociological theories
of crime

somatotypes*

stimulation-seeking
theory

structural explanations

subcultural explanations

unconditioned
stimulus

vicarious learning

---

**InfoTrac**
**COLLEGE**
**EDITION**

For additional readings go to http://www.infotrac-college.com/wadsworth and enter a
search term related to your interest. The key terms that have been asterisked above will
pull up several related articles.

_and the_

_ustice System_

_6, 7, 8, 9, 11, 12, 16_
_Review 12-(1-5)_
_12/(8-10) → Final_

**ORIENTING QUESTIONS**

1. _What is the role of the police in our society?_
2. _What procedures are used to select police?_
3. _How has the training of police officers expanded into new areas?_
4. _Describe the different activities of the police; is law enforcement central?_
5. _What stressors are faced by the police?_
6. _Is there a police personality?_
7. _What is the relationship between the police and the communities they
   serve?_

In any survey of public concerns, "crime" is usually near the top. This ranking stems from the pervasiveness of crime in our country as well as the fear that crime typically causes. Despite the declining rate of crime in the 1990s, nearly one out of four Americans older than age 12 was victimized by a crime in 1998 according to the National Crime Victimization Survey (Bureau of Justice Statistics, 1999). These figures also indicate that at least twice as many violent crimes and three times as many property crimes occur as are officially reported to the police. Only crimes that are detected and reported to the police find their way into the criminal justice system. But the physical, financial, and psychological effects of being a victim of crime persist even when the victimization is never reported to the police. Whether measured in lost cash, damaged property, medical expenses, emotional trauma, or lost pay due to injuries, the economic impact of crime runs to the billions of dollars.

The road from reporting a crime to convicting and punishing an offender can be long and tortuous, but in most cases the police are the officials in the criminal justice system with whom citizens have the most contact. Police are the frontline, face-to-face confronters of criminal activities, and we expect them to keep our streets safe and our homes secure. They are our "thin blue line" against public disorder. The visibility of the police is heightened by the uniforms they wear, the weapons they carry, and the special powers they are given. This visibility makes the police convenient targets for the public's frustrations with the criminal justice system. Many people place enormous trust in the police, and they are the first people called by most citizens in emergencies. Consequently, the public holds conflicting attitudes about the police. They demand protection by them at the same time that they resist interference from them. The major purpose of this chapter is to describe the selection, training, and behavior of police officers. This chapter also serves as an introduction to the next two chapters, on crime investigation and detection.

Police perform a complex set of tasks in the criminal justice system. Street officers must combine physical prowess, perceptual acuity, interpersonal sensitivity, and intelligent discretion to succeed at their jobs. They need to make quick judgments about all sorts of human behavior, often under very stressful conditions. They should be versed in the law and have at least some familiarity with the social sciences. In exchange for these demands, police are usually overworked and unappreciated. These factors, along with the job pressures they face, the criminal elements they encounter, and the isolation in which they often work, render the police subject to the lures of bribery, corruption, and abuses of power.

When we consider the police from a psychological perspective, we encounter each of the dilemmas introduced in Chapter 1. Many individuals see the police as intruding on their rights to privacy and freedom; yet, society recognizes that such an institution is necessary to protect society and to do its dirty work. Police officers investigate crime—their job is to find out what happened—but they also must make arrests and maintain an image of stability in society. In their quest for arrests, convictions, and the truth as they see it, police officers may exceed accepted legal procedures. In a dynamic society in which occasional injustices are inevitable, it is difficult to obtain efficient law enforcement and effective crime control from the police and at the same time assure due process and equal justice (Chevigny, 1969).

Another conflict arises when social scientists question the validity of techniques advocated by the police, such as lineup identifications, hypnotically refreshed memories, and the lie detector test. And last, but of great importance to the police, is the dilemma of equality versus discretion. When should an arrest be made, and when should only a warning be issued? How much force can legitimately be used in an arrest? Should all suspects be treated the same way?

# Selection of Police Officers

One purpose of this chapter is to examine the police officer from a psychological perspective. How are police officers selected? Do the selection criteria work? Is there a set of personality characteristics that police officers share? How are the police trained, and does their training improve actual performance on the job? Can the police officer's image in the community be improved?

These questions took on a special urgency in the 1990s when the spotlight was turned on the police as a result of several highly publicized cases in which police officers had brutally beaten suspects in their custody. Many of these cases involved white officers attacking black citizens, raising the possibility that racial animus was a motive. Beginning with the prosecution of the Los Angeles police officers who were videotaped beating Rodney King and followed by similar incidents in Detroit, New York, Lousiville, Pittsburgh, and Miami, concerns have grown over police brutality.

Perhaps no case sparked the national debate over the relationship between minorities and the police as much as the assault against Abner Louima, the Haitian immigrant who was beaten and sodomized with a bathroom plunger by New York City police officer Justin Volpe as a second officer, Charles Schwarz, held him down. After Volpe pled guilty, a federal jury convicted Schwarz of conspiracy to sodomize and of violating Louima's civil rights, but it acquitted three other officers who had also been charged in the beating. Although it is tempting to view this case as an isolated incident, similar cases have occurred often enough to suggest the possibility that they reflect a pervasive problem. Are certain police officers prone to these kinds of attacks; if so, can they be identified in advance and screened out of police work?

Psychological evaluation of police personnel began in 1916 when Lewis Terman, the Stanford University psychologist who revised Alfred Binet's intelligence scales to produce the Stanford-Binet intelligence test, tested the intelligence of 30 applicants for police and firefighter jobs in San Jose, California. Terman (1917) found that the average IQ among these applicants was 84 and recommended that no one with an IQ below 80 be accepted for these jobs. A few years later, L. L. Thurstone tested the intelligence of 358 Detroit policemen,

*The brutal police assault of Abner Louima by several New York City police officers led to their conviction on federal criminal charges.*

using the Army Alpha Intelligence Examination. Like Terman, he reported below-average IQ scores, but he also found that police of higher ranks scored lower than entry-level patrolmen.

Throughout the years, psychologists continued to assess police candidates, although their work was often unsystematic and poorly evaluated. As late as 1955, only 14 American cities with populations greater than 100,000 formally tested police candidates; by 1965, 27% of local police agencies reported some psychological evaluation of applicants (Ostrov, 1986). In the 1960s and 1970s, the period when police psychology became an established specialty, several national commissions, including the 1967 President's Commission on Law Enforcement and the Administration of

Justice and the 1973 National Advisory Committee on Criminal Justice Standards, called for formal psychological assessment of police personnel in all departments. By the mid-1980s, 11 states required psychological screening of police candidates, and more than 50% of the country's departments psychologically screened beginning police officers (Benner, 1986). By the 1990s, formal assessment of police candidates had become routine, due in part to attempts by municipal governments to prevent or defeat lawsuits claiming that they were liable for dangerous or improper conduct by their police employees.

Psychological evaluation of police applicants can focus on selecting those candidates who appear most psychologically fit or on eliminating individuals who appear least suited for police work. Most selection methods concentrate on screening out disturbed candidates because it is very difficult to agree on the "ideal" police profile (see ◆ Box 6-1). Despite serious concerns about the validity of psychological evaluations in police selection (Kent & Eisenberg, 1972; Levy, 1967), many experts (Bartol, 1983; Ostrov, 1986; Reiser & Klyver, 1987; Spielberger, 1979) believe that psychological screening is useful in the selection process and should be included. In general, the courts have upheld the legality of psychological screening of police candidates as long as the evaluation and testing involved do not violate the provisions of various civil rights acts or the Americans with Disabilities Act and are in compliance with federal guidelines.

Psychologists who evaluate police candidates rely on three tools: (1) personal interviews, (2) observations of candidates performing in special situations contrived to capture real-world characteristics of police work, and (3) psychological tests. How much emphasis different psychologists place on these tools depends on several factors including their professional background and training, the resources available for the evaluation, and the focus of the assessment (e.g., different strategies will be used for assessing mental disorders than for predicting what type of person will do best in which kind of position).

## The Interview

Personal interviews are the most widely employed tool despite evidence that interviews are subject to distortion, low reliability, and questionable validity. The extent to which an interview yields the same information on different occasions or with different interviewers (*reliability*) and the degree to which that information is accurately related to important criteria (*validity*) have not been clearly established for most police selection interviews. However, there is good evidence that reliability, at least, is increased by the use of **structured interviews,** those in which the wording, order, and content of the interview are standardized (Rogers, 1995). Work is under way on the Law Enforcement Candidate Interview—a structured interview for the psychological screening of law enforcement personnel—and preliminary research suggests that it is a modest predictor of performance in the training academy (Varela, Scogin, & Vipperman, 1999).

Interviews are a necessary evaluation ingredient according to guidelines recommended by police psychologists (Blau, 1994). They are also valuable as a rapport-building introduction to the evaluation process. They increase applicants' cooperation at the same time that they soothe anxiety and apprehension. Interviews are also popular because they are flexible and economical. However, because they are subject to distortions and impression management by candidates, interviews are still more useful for orienting candidates to the evaluation than for predicting subsequent performance.

## Situational Tests

Situational tests have been used from time to time in police selection. For example, Mills, McDevitt, and Tonkin (1966) administered three tests that simulated various police abilities to a group of Cincinnati police candidates. The Foot Patrol Observation Test required candidates to walk a six-block downtown route and then answer questions about what they remembered having just observed. In the Clues Test, candidates were

## BOX 6-1   Selection of "ideal" police officers

If it were your task to select police officers from a pool of applicants, what psychological qualities would you look for? Your answers probably reflect your values, as well as your image of what police officers do. Among the psychological characteristics usually generated in such a list are the following:

1. *Incorruptible:* A police officer should be of high moral character. Reports of officers taking bribes or framing innocent suspects are especially disturbing because the police officer must treat all citizens fairly within the rules of law.

2. *Well-adjusted:* A police officer should be able to carry out the stressful duties of the job without "cracking up." Officers are always in the public view. They need to

be thick-skinned enough to operate without defensiveness; yet they need to be sensitive to the needs of others. They also need to cope with the dangers of their jobs, including the constant realization that death may lurk around the corner. Throughout the 1990s, about 100 to 150 police officers were killed annually in the line of duty.

3. *People oriented:* A police officer's major duty is service to others. An officer needs to have a genuine interest in people and compassion for them. At a commencement program of the New York City Police Academy, new officers were told, "There is one thing we cannot teach you and that is about people. The bottom line is to treat people as people and you'll get by" (quoted by Nix, 1987, p. 15).

4. *Free of emotional reactions:* Although a degree of chronic suspiciousness may be desirable for the job, the police officer should be free of impulsive, overly aggressive reactions and other responses in which emotions overcome careful, thoughtful reactions. Restraint is essential because officers are trained to take an active position toward crime detection and are even encouraged by their superiors to be wary of what is happening around them (Greenberg & Ruback, 1982). A new police officer, reflecting on the effect of his training, said, "I've always been suspicious. [But now] I find myself looking up at the roofs of buildings to see if people are going to throw anything off" (quoted by Nix, 1987, p. 15). A study of police officers by Ruby and Brigham

given ten minutes to investigate a set of planted clues about the disappearance of a city worker from his office. They were observed as they performed this task and were graded on the information they assembled. The Bull Session was a two-hour group discussion of several topics important in police work. Performance on the Clues Test correlated significantly with class ranking in the police academy, but scores from the Foot Patrol Observation Test did not. Although "grades" for the Bull Session were not derived, it was viewed as an important measure of emotional and motivational qualities.

Despite the fact that situational tests have an intuitive appeal as selection devices, they have not proven to be superior predictors of performance compared to standardized tests. Because they are

time-consuming and expensive, they are used mainly to supplement psychological tests.

## Psychological Tests

Many standardized psychological tests have good reliability and can be objectively scored and administered to large groups of subjects at the same time; as a result, they are the backbone of police screening methods. Two types of tests are included in most selection batteries: tests of cognitive or intellectual ability and tests of personality traits, integrity, or emotional stability.

Police officers tend to score in the average to above-average range on intelligence tests (Poland, 1978), and intelligence tends to correlate fairly strongly with the performance of police recruits

(1996) confirms this police officer's reaction; they found that, compared to laypersons, police are more likely to view people's actions as more criminal in nature.

5. *Logical:* Police officers should be able to examine a crime scene and extract hypotheses about what happened and what characteristics might be present in the lawbreaker. An example of this deductive ability comes from the actions of Al Seedman, former chief of detectives of the New York City Police Department, who explained to an interviewer that he had been helping some detectives from a small Connecticut town investigate a case:

> In the woods just outside town they found the skeleton of a man who'd been dead for three months or so. They figured they'd find out who he was as soon as his family reported him missing, but it's been three months since he was found—which makes six months since he died—and nobody has claimed him. They don't know what to do. . . . Once I got the answer to one question I was able to give them a method. I asked whether this skeleton showed signs of any dental work, which usually can be identified by a dentist. But according to the local cops, they said no, although the skeleton had crummy teeth. No dental work at all. Now, if he'd been wealthy, he could have afforded to have his teeth fixed. If he'd been poor, welfare would have paid. If he was a union member, their medical plan would have covered it. So this fellow was probably working at a low-paying non-unionized job, but making enough to keep off public assistance. Also, since he didn't match up to any family's missing-person report, he was probably single, living alone in an apartment or hotel. His landlord had never reported him missing, either, so most likely he was also behind on his rent and the landlord probably figured he had just skipped. But even if he had escaped his landlord, he would never have escaped the tax man.
>
> The rest was simple. I told these cops to wait until the year is up. They can go to the IRS and get a printout of all single males making less than $10,000 a year but more than the welfare ceiling who paid withholding tax in the first three quarters but not the fourth. Chances are the name of their skeleton would be on that printout. (quoted in Seedman & Hellman 1974, pp. 4–5)

in their training programs. However, intelligence scores are only weakly related to actual police performance in the field (Bartol, 1983). These results point to the problem of predictive validity, which is a pervasive difficulty that we discuss in the next section.

The Minnesota Multiphasic Personality Inventory (MMPI; the 1989 revision of this test is called the MMPI-2) is the most often used test of personality in police screening, followed by the California Psychological Inventory (CPI) and the Sixteen Personality Factor Questionnaire (16PF). Evidence for the validity of these tests in screening out unsuitable candidates for police work is mixed. Several investigations support the validity of the MMPI (Bartol, 1991; Beutler, Storm, Kirkish, Scogin, & Gaines, 1985; Hiatt & Hargrave, 1988) and the CPI (Hogan, 1971; Spielberger, Spaulding, & Ward, 1978), but others (Lester, Babcock, Cassissi, & Brunetta, 1980; Mills & Stratton, 1982) have questioned the general value of psychological testing of police recruits.

One personality test designed specifically to identify psychologically unsuitable law enforcement candidates is the Inwald Personality Inventory (Inwald, 1992; Inwald, Knatz, & Shusman, 1983). It consists of 26 scales that tap past and present behaviors presumed to have special relevance for law enforcement applicants; examples include Lack of Assertiveness, Trouble with Law and Society, Undue Suspiciousness, and Driving Violations. This instrument has good reliability, but its predictive validity is not significantly better than that of the MMPI (Bolton, 1985; Swartz,

1985). Another new test developed to screen criminal justice employees is the 50-item National Criminal Justice Officer Selection Inventory; however, we were not able to find published norms or measures of validity for this instrument.

An excellent study of psychological test validity was conducted by Beutler et al. (1985), who examined the relationship between several tests (including the MMPI and five other standardized tests) and various measures of performance for 65 subjects who had been accepted for police work. Of these officers, 22 were employed in an urban police department, 27 worked in a department associated with a major state university, and 16 were from a community college police department. The researchers gathered an extensive list of criteria on how well each officer performed on the job. Ratings were obtained from supervisors, and seven criteria of performance (e.g., different kinds of reprimands, commendations, grievances, and suspensions) were collected from each officer's personnel record.

The results suggest that performance on the different criteria was predictable by psychological tests, and these predictions even generalized across different types of police departments. The MMPI profile was particularly effective in predicting reprimands, grievances, and suspensions. However, another discovery points out a difficulty in measuring police performance: Supervisors' ratings were not strongly related to criteria obtained from the personnel records (e.g., suspensions and reprimands). Beutler et al. (1985) suggest that supervisor bias might account for this result, and they caution against relying too heavily on supervisor ratings as measures of police job performance.

## The Validity of Police Screening

Although experts disagree on the usefulness of psychological screening of police, they all agree that good empirical research on this topic is difficult to conduct (Gaines & Falkenberg, 1998; In-

wald, 1986). Studies of predictive validity using actual police performance in the field as the criterion are so time-consuming and expensive that most departments cannot afford them. Instead, they settle for research that examines the relationship between screening results and performance by police recruits in police academies or training schools. This relationship is usually positive, but success or failure in training is not the criterion of real interest. One fairly inexpensive form of assessment is to gather peer ratings from trainees as they progress through their training classes together; these ratings have been shown to correlate with job retention of police officers, but not with most other measures of job performance or with supervisor ratings (Gardner, Scogin, Vipperman, & Varela, 1998).

Another problem with studies of validity is that the police candidates who do poorly on screening evaluations are eliminated from the pool of trainees and potential employees. Although this decision is reasonable, it makes it impossible to study whether predictions of poor performance by these individuals would have been valid.

In addition, applicants for police work, like applicants for most jobs, are likely to try to present an unrealistically positive impression of themselves. They may deny or underreport symptoms of mental illness, answer questions to convey a socially desirable impression, and respond as they believe a psychologically healthy individual generally would. If evaluators fail to detect such "fake good" test-taking strategies, they may mistakenly identify some psychologically disturbed candidates as well-adjusted applicants. For these reasons, tests such as the MMPI-2 and the Inwald include various **validity scales** intended to detect test takers who are trying to fake good (Baer, Wetter, Nichols, Greene, & Berry, 1995). Research on these scales has shown they are useful in detecting defensiveness and deception by some candidates for police positions (Borum & Stock, 1993).

Finally, selecting adequate criteria to measure effective police performance is notoriously difficult. Supervisor ratings are often inflated or biased by factors that are irrelevant to actual achievements or problems. In some departments, especially smaller ones, the individual police officer will be expected to perform so many diverse functions that it becomes unreasonable to expect specific cognitive abilities or psychological traits to be related in the same way to the multiple facets of performance. In addition, if we are interested in predicting which officers will act in risky, dangerous, or inappropriate ways, our predictions will be complicated by the fact that such behaviors occur only rarely in any group of people. As a consequence, these assessments will result in many erroneous predictions in which predicted events do not take place.

## Fitness-for-Duty Evaluations

Another type of psychological assessment of police officers is the fitness-for-duty evaluation. As a result of stress, a life-threatening incident, a series of problems, injuries, or other indicators that an officer is psychologically impaired, police administrators can order an officer to undergo an evaluation of fitness to continue duty.

These evaluations pose difficulties for everyone involved. Administrators must balance the need to protect the public from a potentially dangerous officer against the legal right of the officer to privacy and fair employment. Clinicians have to navigate a narrow path between a department's need to know the results of such an evaluation and the officer's expectation that the results will be kept confidential. Finally, the officers themselves face a dilemma: They can be honest and reveal problems that could disqualify them from service, or they can distort their responses to protect their jobs but, consequently, miss the opportunity for potentially beneficial treatment.

Two different models of fitness-for-duty evaluations have been used. In the first, departments use the same psychologist to perform the evaluation and to provide whatever treatment is necessary for the officer. In other departments, the psychologist who evaluates the officer does not provide

any treatment, thereby preventing an ethical conflict between keeping the therapy confidential and disclosing an officer's psychological functioning to supervisors. The second approach is endorsed in the "Guidelines for Fitness for Duty Evaluations" distributed by the Police Psychological Services Section of the International Association for Chiefs of Police; as such they constitute the closest thing to an official position on this question as is available. In-depth discussions of ethical dilemmas facing police psychologists are also provided by Dietz and Reese (1986) and Super (1997).

## Training of Police Officers

Once candidates have been selected, they participate in a course of police training that usually lasts several months. Many major American cities require 24 weeks of training, with 40 hours of training per week. Smaller jurisdictions have training programs averaging 14 to 16 weeks. An increasing number of departments are now requiring that police officers complete some amount of college education.

Two types of criticism of police training programs are common. One is that, after rigorous selection procedures, few trainees fail the training. For example, of 1091 recruits who began the training program in New York City in 1987, only 65 dropped out or were dismissed for a variety of reasons, including physical or academic inadequacies (Nix, 1987). Advocates count this rate of success as an indication that the initial selection procedures were valid, but critics complain that graduation is too easy, especially given the burnout rate of on-the-job police officers.

A second criticism is that there is insufficient training in the field, as well as a lack of close supervision of trainees during the time they spend on patrol. The limited time trainees spend with veteran training officers on patrol may give them a false sense of security (Beck, 1987) and may deprive them of learning different ways to respond to citizens from various cultural backgrounds or to resolve disputes other than through arrests. However, another side to this story, which we discuss later, argues against the benefits of extensive supervision by senior officers. It is possible that such contacts teach new officers to be cynical about law enforcement, to "cut corners" in their duties, and, above all, to identify almost exclusively with the norms of police organizations rather than the values of the larger, and more diverse, society (Tuohy, Wrennal, McQueen, & Stradling, 1993).

# Training in Crisis Intervention

The police are often asked to maintain public order and defuse volatile situations involving persons who are mentally ill, intoxicated, angry, or motivated by politically extreme views. Because of the instability of the participants in such disputes, they pose great risks to the police as well as to bystanders. In this section, we examine three types of crisis situations to which police are often called: incidents involving mentally ill citizens, family disturbances, and the taking of hostages. Psychologists have made important contributions to each of these areas by conducting research, designing interventions, and training the police in crisis intervention skills.

## Interactions with Mentally Ill Citizens

For the past two decades, several factors have forced mentally ill persons from the mental institutions in which they were formerly maintained to a variety of noninstitutional settings, including halfway houses, community mental-health centers, hospital emergency rooms, "flophouses," the streets, and local jails. Deinstitutionalization itself is an admirable goal; spending much of one's life in an institution breeds dependency, despair, and hopelessness. People with mental illness should receive treatment in the least restrictive situations possible, allowing them to function in and contribute to their local communities.

However, the reality of how people with mental illness have been deinstitutionalized in the United States has not achieved its lofty goals. The problems stem from two fundamental difficulties. First, even under ideal conditions, severe mental illness is difficult to treat effectively. The impairments associated with disorders such as schizophrenia, chronic substance abuse, and serious mood disorders can be profound, and relapses are common. For example, fewer than a third of nonhospitalized persons with schizophrenia are employed at any given time. Second, sufficient funding for alternative, noninstitutional care has not been provided in the United States. As a result, community-based treatment of severely mentally ill persons seldom takes place under proper circumstances, despite the fact that the economic costs of severe mental disorders rival those of diseases such as cancer and heart disease and could be reduced considerably if proper care were provided.

The deinstitutionalization movement resulted from four historical forces: (1) advances in antipsychotic medications, beginning in the 1950s, that allowed persons to function better outside of hospitals; (2) increased legal restrictions on the involuntary commitment of the mentally ill to hospitals; (3) reductions in the length of the average psychiatric hospitalization; and (4) decreased public funding for mental-health programs throughout the 1980s and 1990s (Kiesler, 1982; Teplin, 1984). The rise of the homeless or "street people" population, among whom problems of substance abuse and mental illness are frequent and severe (Fischer & Breakey, 1991), is also linked to declining availability of publicly supported mental-health treatment.

One consequence of deinstitutionalization is that supervising persons with mental illness has become a primary responsibility for the police. In medium- to large-sized police departments, about 7% of all police contacts involve citizens with mental illness, and it is estimated that the police are responsible for up to one-third of all mental-health referrals to hospital emergency rooms. In one recent survey, nine out of ten police officers had responded to a call involving a mentally ill individual in the past month, and eight out of ten had responded to two or more such calls in the same time period (Borum, Deane, Steadman, & Morrissey, 1998).

Research on how the police handle mentally ill persons has concentrated on the discretion that officers use in crisis incidents. Will they arrest the citizen, or will they have the person hospitalized? Will they offer on-the-spot counseling, refer the citizen to a mental-health agency, or return the person to a safe place, to relatives, or to friends? Early research on these questions suggested that the police were reluctant to arrest or to require emergency hospitalization of the mentally ill unless these people's behavior presented an obvious danger to themselves or others (Bittner, 1967). These findings are consistent with research on the use of discretion by police in general, which suggests that they tend to avoid an arrest in minor incidents unless the suspect is disrespectful to the officer, the complaining party prefers an arrest be made, or the officer perceives the benefits of arresting the subject to outweigh the perceived costs. Other studies, however, have shown that the police find the handling of mentally ill citizens to be among the most difficult cases they encounter. As a result, many may prefer arrest over hospitalization when dealing with mentally ill persons (Matthews, 1970), especially if they believe there will be less red tape in completing an arrest versus finalizing a hospitalization.

The best research on the question of how frequently mentally ill persons are arrested by the police has been conducted by Linda Teplin, a sociologist at Northwestern University. Teplin (1984) assembled a team of psychology graduate students and trained them to observe and code the interactions of police officers with citizens over a 14-month period in two precincts in a large U.S. city. Observers used a symptom checklist and a global rating of mental disorder to assess mental illness in the citizens observed. Teplin studied 884 non-traffic encounters involving a total of 1798 citizens, of whom 506 were considered suspects for arrest by the police. Arrest was relatively infrequent, occurring in only 12.4% of the encounters;

in terms of individuals (some incidents involved several suspects), 29.2% were arrested. The observers classified only 30 (5.9%) of the 506 suspects as mentally ill. The arrest rate for these 30 persons was 46.7% compared to an arrest rate of 27.9% for suspects who were not rated as having mental disorders. Mentally ill suspects were more likely to be arrested regardless of the type or seriousness of the incident involved.

Teplin concluded that the mentally ill were being "criminalized" and that this outcome was the result not only of the provocative nature of their psychological symptoms but also of the inadequacies of the mental-health system in treating such persons. As a result, the criminal justice system has become a "default option" for patients whom hospitals refuse to accept for treatment because they are too dangerous, are not dangerous enough, or suffer a disorder that the hospital does not treat. Not surprisingly, the rate of severe mental disorders in jail populations, often combined with diagnoses of substance abuse and personality disorder in the same individuals, is alarmingly high (Teplin, 1994; Teplin, Abram, & McClelland, 1996).

The jailing of mentally ill persons does not reflect improper behavior by the police as much as a failure of public policy regarding the treatment and protection of people with chronic mental illness. More and better training of police officers in the recognition and short-term management of mentally ill persons is necessary, but an adequate resolution of this problem requires better organization and funding of special services for those with serious mental illness (Abram & Teplin, 1991).

One possibility is to increase the use of **jail diversion programs,** in which mentally ill individuals who have been arrested and jailed are considered for supervised release to the community where they will presumably have better access to treatment and support services. One recent evaluation of a jail diversion program found that two months after arrest, approximately one in five diverted participants had been rearrested. By comparison, in the same time period, about 50% of nondiverted subjects had either been arrested or had never been released from jail (Steadman, Cocozza, & Veysey, 1999).

## Domestic Disturbances

When violence erupts in a family or between a couple, the police are often the first people called to the scene. What will they encounter when they arrive? Are the participants armed? Are they intoxicated or psychologically disturbed? How much violence has already taken place? What is certain is that responding to family disturbances is one of the most dangerous activities that police perform. The amount of time police devote to domestic disturbances exceeds the time they spend investigating murders, rapes, and aggravated assaults combined (Wilt, Bannon, Breedlove, Sandker, & Michaelson, 1977), and about 25% of police deaths and assaults on officers occur during police intervention in family disturbances (Ketterman & Kravitz, 1978).

Because of their danger and frequency, family disturbances pose a difficult challenge for the police. Can these encounters be handled in a manner that protects potential victims, reduces repeat offenses, and limits the risk of injury to responding officers?

The first project on crisis intervention with domestic disputes was developed by Morton Bard, a psychologist in New York City. Bard (1969; Bard & Berkowitz, 1967) trained a special group of New York City police officers (nine black and nine white volunteers) in family disturbance intervention skills for a project located in West Harlem. The month-long training program focused on teaching officers how to intervene in family disputes without making arrests. The training emphasized the psychology of family conflict and sensitivity to cross-racial differences. Role playing was used to acquaint officers with techniques for calming antagonists, lowering tensions, reducing hostilities, and preventing physical violence.

For two years after the training, all family crisis calls in the experimental precinct were answered by the specially trained officers. They performed 1375 interventions with 962 families. Evaluation of the project concentrated on six outcomes: (1) a decrease in family disturbance calls, (2) a drop in repeat calls from the same families, (3) a reduction of homicides in the precinct, (4) a decline in homicides among family members, (5) a reduction of assaults in the precinct, and (6) a decrease in injuries to police officers. The results indicated that the intervention affected only two of these outcomes. Fewer assaults occurred in the precinct, and none of the trained officers was injured (compared with three police officers who were not part of the program but who were injured while responding to family disturbances).

Evaluations of similar domestic crises units in other cities have yielded mixed results (Pearce & Snortum, 1983). Specially trained officers typically rate their resolutions of disturbance calls more favorably than do officers without special training. However, the long-term effects of the special interventions are less positive; sometimes they lead to an increase in repeat callers, but in other cases this effect is not observed.

In recent years, as more is learned about domestic violence (see ◆ Box 6-2 for elaboration), crisis intervention and other nonarrest alternatives for resolving family disturbances have come in for increased criticism. Women's rights groups have filed lawsuits against law enforcement agencies that have not arrested seriously assaultive domestic batterers. These critics maintain that, when actual assaults have taken place in a family, arrest is the most appropriate response to protect victims and reduce future violence (Dutton, 1987).

In response to these concerns and to their own evaluation of the problem of domestic assaults, many police departments have shifted policies and now advocate the arrest and prosecution of domestic batterers. Is this a better alternative than crisis intervention or counseling? The first well-controlled evaluation of the effects of arresting domestic batterers was the Minneapolis Domestic Violence Experiment (Sherman & Berk, 1984). In this experiment, police officers' responses to domestic violence were randomly assigned to be (1) arresting the suspected batterer, (2) ordering one of the parties to leave the residence, or (3) giving the couple immediate advice on reducing their violence. Based on official police records and interviews with victims, the occurrence of subsequent offending was reduced by almost 50% when the suspect was arrested, a significantly better outcome than that achieved by the two nonarrest alternatives. These findings quickly changed public and expert opinion about the value of arresting domestic batterers, and soon many cities had replaced informal counseling with immediate arrest as their response to domestic violence cases.

Since the initial Minneapolis experiment, at least five other jurisdictions—Charlotte, Colorado Springs, Miami, Omaha, and Milwaukee—have conducted experiments designed to test whether arresting batterers is the best deterrent to repeated domestic violence. The results of these projects, collectively known as the Spouse Assault Replication Program, have been mixed. In some cases, arrests reduced recidivism; in other cases, it increased recidivism; and in a few instances, the effect was different depending on whether official arrest records or victim interviews were considered (Garner, Fagan, & Maxwell, 1995). So far, the search for factors that could resolve the inconsistent results has not been fruitful, except that it does appear that whatever deterrent effects are associated with arrest, they tend to diminish over time (Mills, 1998). What conclusion should we reach about the value of arrest as a deterrent to future spouse abuse? At this point, the jury is still out. Deterrence is achieved in some cases, but it is too inconsistent an outcome to justify the enthusiastic claims that are often made for arrest programs.

Questions about how best to quell domestic violence illustrate an interesting phenomenon often encountered with social reforms. Social problems and well-intentioned efforts to modify them tend to revolve in cycles rather than moving in a straight line toward progress and increased sophistication. Today's reform, aimed at correcting some social evil, often develops its own difficulties or inequalities and ultimately becomes itself a problem in need of reformation. Crisis intervention was originally preferred over arrest as a more psychologi-

cally sophisticated response by police to family disturbances. However, this intervention fell out of favor and was criticized as an inadequate response to serious domestic violence. Official arrest was then championed as the most effective intervention, but as additional data are gathered about its effectiveness, new questions are raised about whether arrest and prosecution are the best answers for domestic violence.

## Hostage Negotiation

Although hostage incidents are at least as old as the description in Genesis of the abduction and rescue of Abraham's nephew Lot, most experts agree that the massacre of 11 Israeli athletes taken hostage at the 1972 Munich Olympic Games by Palestinian terrorists spurred the creation of new law enforcement techniques for resolving hostage incidents. Developed through extensive collaboration between military, law enforcement, and behavioral science experts, these hostage negotiation techniques are still being refined as more is learned about the conditions that lead to effective negotiations.

Soskis and Van Zandt (1986) have identified four types of hostage incidents that differ in their psychological dynamics and techniques for resolution (see also Gist & Perry, 1985; Hatcher, Mohandie, Turner, & Gelles, 1998). A large percentage of hostage incidents involve *persons suffering a mental disorder* or experiencing serious personal or family problems. In these situations, the hostage takers often have a history of depression, schizophrenia, or other serious mental illness, or they harbor feelings of chronic powerlessness, anger, or despondency that compel a desperate act. Disturbed hostage takers pose a high risk of suicide, which they sometimes accomplish by killing their hostage(s) and then themselves. In other situations, they try to force the police to kill them; such victim-precipitated deaths are termed **suicide by cop.**

A second common type of hostage situation involves the *trapped criminal*. Here, a person who is trapped by the police during the commission of

## The Science of

### BOX 6-2    Family violence

"People are more likely to be killed, physically assaulted, hit, beat up, slapped, or spanked in their own homes by other family members than anywhere else, or by anyone else, in our society" (Gelles & Cornell, 1985, p. 12). As the text indicates, police intervention into family violence is dangerous work. Because of the many risks and the few rewards for doing so, police officers are seldom motivated to get involved.

Not only is the dangerousness of the intervention a problem, but also many police officers—like many others among us—accept certain myths about the nature of family violence. Empirical research is shedding new light on the following five false assumptions, first described by Gelles and Cornell (1985):

*Myth 1: Family violence is rare.* It is difficult to get accurate statistics on child abuse and other forms of family violence because no agency systematically gathers such data. But it is not a rare phenomenon; it is estimated that 14% of children in the United States are abused within their families each year and that the lifetime in-

cidence of spouse abuse may be as high as 50% of married couples. Neither is family violence exclusively or even largely restricted to male perpetrators. In fact, recent surveys in both the United States and New Zealand suggest that women are as likely as men to be violent toward their partners (Magdol, Moffit, Caspi, Newman, Fagan, & Silva, 1997).

The question of how gender affects patterns of partner violence reveals an important characteristic of the methods uses to study such problems: The answers will vary—sometimes to a great extent—depending on the types of individuals who participate in the research. The initial studies of family violence relied on *clinical samples* of women who sought physical or psychological help for the injuries they suffered or male batterers who had been ordered into treatment or arrested because of their violence; not surprisingly, these studies suggested that male perpetrators far outnumbered females. More recent studies have used *community surveys* of large cohorts of people, and they tend to show that the rates of partner violence are substantial among both

male and female abusers. Neither approach is necessarily superior to the other; each addresses a slightly different question (Magdol et al., 1997). If one is interested in studying the consequences of especially severe partner violence, clinical samples would be preferred. If one is trying to outline the epidemiological patterns and general risk factors for partner violence, then community surveys would yield the most trustworthy answers.

*Myth 2: Family violence is confined to mentally disturbed or sick people.* When we hear or read that a woman has plunged her 2-year-old son into a tub of boiling water or that a man has had sexual intercourse with his 6-year-old daughter, our first reaction might be, "That person is terribly sick!" The way family violence is portrayed in the mass media (Steinmetz & Straus, 1974) leads to a conclusion that normal people do not hit their family members. Although family violence is too widespread to be adequately explained by mental illness per se, perpetrators of serious violence do tend to experience relatively high levels of depression and personality disorder

---

a crime takes, as a hostage, anyone who is available and then uses the hostage to bargain for freedom. Because these incidents are unplanned and driven by panic, they tend to be, especially at their early stages, very dangerous to the victims and the police.

The third type of hostage situation, also involving criminals, is the *takeover of prisons* by inmates who capture prison guards or take other inmates as hostages. In these incidents, the passage of time tends to work against nonviolent resolutions because the hostage takers are violent

as risk factors toward family violence (Andrews, Foster, Capaldi, & Hops, 2000).

*Myth 3: Family violence is confined to people in poor economic circumstances.* Violence and abuse are more common among families with fewer economic advantages, but these problems are by no means limited to such families. Among middle-class couples seeking a divorce, 23% mentioned violence as one of the reasons for wanting to end the marriage (Levinger, 1966). Nonetheless, unemployment, inadequate education, and sparse social support remain substantial risk factors for family violence (Magdol et al., 1997).

*Myth 4: Battered women like being hit; otherwise they would leave.* This belief reflects two myths in one. First, as we already discussed, family violence is perpetuated by both males and females although it is true that violence by men against women tends to produce more serious injuries. But faced with the fact that many female victims of partner violence do not leave even the most serious of abusers, people seek some type of rational ex-

planation. A common belief is that women who remain in violent relationships must somehow provoke or even enjoy the violence.

This form of "blaming the victim" (see Chapter 3) is not a very useful explanation. Instead, the concept of **learned helplessness** better explains why so many women endure such extreme violence for so long (Walker, 1979). Psychologist Lenore Walker observes that women who suffer continued physical violence at the hands of their partners have a more negative self-concept than women whose marriages are free from violence. She proposes that the repeated beatings leave these women feeling that they won't be able to protect themselves from further assaults and that they are incapable of controlling the events that go on around them (Gelles & Cornell, 1985). Under such circumstances, they give in to the belief that there is nothing they can do to change their circumstances and that any effort at a new life will not only be futile but also lead to even more violence against them.

*Myth 5: Alcohol and drug abuse are the real causes of violence in the*

*home.* "He beat up his children because he was drunk" is another popular explanation of domestic violence, and most studies do find a considerable relationship between drinking and violence (Magdol et al., 1997; Wolfgang, 1958), especially among male perpetrators. Perhaps as many as half the instances of violence and abuse involve alcohol or drugs (Gelles & Cornell, 1985); in the case of violence directed toward a spouse, both the offender and the victim may have been drinking extensively before the violence. But does the drug taking cause the violence? Some people assume that alcohol is a disinhibitor of behavior and that it therefore unleashes violent behavior. But in other societies, people drink and become more passive (MacAndrew & Edgerton, 1969). Reactions to drinking are largely a function of what we expect the reactions to be, and these expectations can provide an excuse to the violent offender: "I was drunk and didn't know what I was doing."

people, working as an undisciplined group with volatile leadership.

The fourth type of hostage taking, and the one that is most publicized, is **terrorism.** Terrorists use violence or the threat of violence "to achieve a social, political, or religious aim in a way

that does not obey the traditional rules of war" (Soskis & Van Zandt, 1986, p. 424). Terrorists usually make careful plans for their kidnapping of hostages or taking of property, and they are typically motivated by extremist political or religious goals. These goals may require their own deaths

*Recent sieges involving political and religious cults in the United States, such as the Branch Davidians, have tested conventional negotiation techniques pioneered by behaviorial scientists and law enforcement officials.*

as a necessary, but honorable, sacrifice for a higher cause. For this reason, terrorists are less responsive to negotiation techniques that appeal to rational themes of self-preservation.

The 1990s saw an outbreak of right-wing domestic terrorism and sieges in the United States. In the most visible of these incidents (e.g., the mass death of the Branch Davidian sect under the leadership of David Koresh; the three-month standoff between the FBI and the antigovernment Freemen group in Montana), conventional negotiation techniques did not prove to be effective. The reasons why negotiations were not successful are not clear; the American public seems divided between those who believe the government was too aggressive and those who think officials were too restrained in their handling of these incidents.

The new millennium is likely to bring additional forms of terrorism that redefine what it means to be "taken hostage." For example, *bioterrorism* in which biological "weapons" such as viruses and bacteria are released or threatened to

be released could hold far larger populations hostage than is the case with conventional guns or bombs. Effective countermeasures to such threats will require new collaborations among law enforcement officials, public health experts, and behavioral scientists

Successful hostage negotiation requires an understanding of the dynamics of hostage incidents so that these dynamics can be manipulated by the negotiator to contain and ultimately end the incident with a minimum of violence (Schlossberg & Freeman, 1974). For example, in many hostage situations, a strong sense of psychological togetherness and mutual dependency develops between the hostages and their kidnappers. These feelings emerge from (1) the close, constant contact between the participants, (2) their shared feelings of fear and danger, and (3) the strong feelings of powerlessness produced by prolonged captivity. This relationship, dubbed the **Stockholm syndrome,** involves positive feelings by the hostages toward their kidnappers as well as

## BOX 6-3 The Stockholm syndrome

The term *Stockholm syndrome* comes from a 1973 incident in which hostages held in a Swedish bank developed a close emotional attachment to their captors (Eckholm, 1985). Hostages may come to sympathize with the lawbreakers and even adopt, at least temporarily, their captors' ideological views. The behavior of Patricia Hearst, who was kidnapped in 1974 and later helped her captors rob a bank, has been explained through this syndrome. It resurfaced again in 1985 when 39 passengers from TWA Flight 847

were kept as hostages for 17 days by hijackers in Beirut. Allyn Conwell, the spokesperson for the hostages in the hijacking, was criticized for his statements expressing "profound sympathy" for his captors' Shiite position, but he explicitly denied that he was influenced by the Stockholm syndrome (Eckholm, 1985).

According to Martin Symonds, a New York psychiatrist and expert on terrorism, the syndrome, which is one of several that is known to form among hostages, hostage takers, and negotiators, is

more likely to emerge when the hostages are purely "instrumental" victims, of no genuine concern to the terrorists except as levers over a third party. In such situations, the captors say, "We'll let you go if our demands are met," and the captives begin "to misperceive the terrorist as the person who is trying to keep you alive" (Symonds, quoted in Eckholm, 1985, p. 6). For this reason, it is especially important for the police to determine the motivations of any hostage takers, as well as their specific goals.

reciprocated positive feelings by the kidnappers toward their hostages (see ◆ Box 6-3). Hostage negotiators try to take advantage of this dynamic by becoming a part of it themselves. First attempting to become a psychological member of the hostage group who maintains important ties to the outside world, negotiators will then try to use their outside contacts to persuade terrorists to bring the crisis to a peaceful end.

Successful negotiators make contact with hostage takers in as nonthreatening a manner as possible and then maintain communication with them for as long as necessary. Generally, the negotiator attempts to isolate the hostage takers from any "outside" communication in order to foster their dependency on the negotiator as the crucial link with other people. Once communication is established, the negotiator will try to reduce the hostage takers' fear and tension so that they will be more willing to agree to a reasonable solution. Negotiators will structure the situation in ways that maximize predictability and calmness. For example, they

may offer help with any medical needs the hostage group has, thereby fostering positive components of the Stockholm syndrome. Finally, through gradual prompting and reinforcement, the negotiator tries to encourage behaviors that promote negotiation progress. Examples of such behaviors include increased conversation between the negotiator and the hostage taker, the passage of deadlines without threatened violence taking place, and less violent content and fewer threats in the speech of hostage takers.

Increasingly, police departments have developed special crisis/hostage negotiation teams that usually include a psychologist as a consultant or adviser (Hatcher et al., 1998). In this capacity, the psychologist helps select officers for the team, provides on-the-scene advice during hostage incidents, profiles the hostage taker's personality, and assesses the behavior of the hostages themselves. Do psychologist-consultants make a difference? In the one study evaluating the effects of psychological consultation in hostage incidents, Butler,

Leitenberg, and Fuselier (1993) found that using a psychologist resulted in (1) fewer injuries and deaths to hostages and (2) more peaceful surrenders by hostage takers.

# The Police Officer's Job

In the eyes of most citizens, the job of the police officer is to catch criminals and enforce the law, just as the officers on *America's Most Wanted* and *Law and Order* do weekly on TV. But the police are responsible for more functions than these. The major duties of the police are divided into three general areas:

1. *Enforcing the law,* which includes investigating complaints, arresting suspects, and attempting to prevent crime. Although most citizens perceive law enforcement to be the most important function of the police, it accounts for only about 10% of police activity.

2. *Maintaining order,* including intervening in family and neighborhood disputes and keeping traffic moving, noise levels down, rowdy persons off the streets, and disturbances of the peace to a minimum. It is estimated that three out of every ten requests for police officers involve this type of activity.

3. *Providing services,* such as giving assistance in medical and psychological emergencies, finding missing persons, helping stranded motorists, escorting funerals, and rescuing cats from trees. Most studies indicate that the largest percentage of police activities fall into this category. In fact, according to one review (Klockars, 1985), the typical day's duty for a police officer in the high-crime areas of three of the nation's largest cities (Boston, Chicago, and Washington, D. C.) did not see the arrest of a single person!

Should the police spend so much time on community services? The major objections to community services are that they waste police resources and distract the police from the crucial roles of law enforcement and public protection for which

they are specially trained. In the 1990s, special initiatives were taken to increase the time police can commit to crime-fighting activities. Federal legislation providing funds for cities to hire thousands of new police officers was justified with the promise that additional police would lead to more arrests of criminals. And urban police forces have found that concentrating more police officers in high-crime areas and instructing them to arrest all lawbreakers (even for relatively minor offenses such as loitering and public drunkenness) have resulted in lowered crime rates. This **zero tolerance** policy demands that police officers concentrate more time on apprehension and arrest activities. Although it has been credited with bringing about reductions in crime, the zero tolerance policy has also been linked to increases in citizen complaints and lawsuits against the police (Greene, 1999).

There are two advantages to the police continuing to provide an array of social services. First, short of spending massive amounts of money to train and employ a new cadre of community service workers, no feasible alternative to the police in this capacity exists. Second, by providing these services, the police create a positive identity in the community that carries goodwill, respect, and cooperation over to their crime-fighting tasks. These "side effects" also serve as a buffer that gives the police opportunities to interact with people who are not behaving criminally, thereby decreasing the tendency of police to develop cynical, suspicious attitudes toward others. They also may encourage citizens to perceive the police in a less threatening and less hostile manner.

Not only is the police officer's job composed of multiple duties, but the requirements of these duties may lead to feelings of stress, personal conflicts, and eventually to psychological problems.

# Stress and the Police

Scores of books, technical reports, and journal articles have been written on the causes and treatment of police stress (e.g., Alkus & Padesky, 1983;

Ford, 1998; Kirschman, 1997; White, Lawrence, Biggerstaff, & Grubb, 1985), and entire Web sites (e.g., the Police Stressline: www.stressline.com) are devoted to this topic.

All of this begs the question: Is police work more stressful than other occupations? Although the stereotype of police work is that it must be extremely stressful because it entails a constant threat of danger and exposure to criminals, surprisingly little is known about whether policing is inherently stressful. The National Institute on Workers' Compensation lists police work among the "ten toughest jobs" (Miller, 1988, p. 43), but one large-scale survey of Australian police officers indicated that police felt no more stress as a group than the average citizen or college student (Hart, Wearing, & Headey, 1995). Whether this same finding would characterize American police officers is not certain. Also, the reasons for the relatively high level of psychological well-being reported by these officers are not clear. It might be because most of them were males, and males report fewer stressful feelings than females. It might be due to a reluctance of police officers to admit to feeling stressed. Or it could reflect the fact that preemployment screening of the police weeded out easily stressed individuals.

Regardless of this survey's findings, no one would suggest that a police officer's job is easy. Certain factors make the occupation particularly difficult. One problem that comes with being a police officer is the "life in a fishbowl" phenomenon. Officers are constantly visible to the public, and they realize that their every act is being evaluated. Often they perform their job differently than the public wants them to, and they are then likely to hear an outcry of protest and condemnation (Lefkowitz, 1975). Police are sensitive to public criticism, and this criticism also leads their spouses and children to feel isolated and segregated.

Several investigators have divided the stress of police work into different categories according to the sources of the stress or the type of problem involved (Ostrov, 1986; Spielberger, Westberry, Grier, & Greenfield, 1980). The leading example of a questionnaire designed to measure police stress is the Police Stress Survey (PSS; Spielberger et al., 1980), which in its original form consisted of 60 items. A revision of the PSS resulted in an additional 25 items derived from open-ended interviews with police officers (White, Lawrence, Biggerstaff, & Grubb, 1985). The following three categories of stress are most commonly encountered by the police:

1. *Physical and psychological threats.* Included here are events related to the unique demands of police work. Items referring to using force, being physically attacked, confronting aggressive people or grisly crime scenes, and engaging in high-speed chases load heavily on this factor (see ◆ Box 6-4 for further discussion). Danger can emerge from even apparently innocuous circumstances. Three police officers in Inkster, Michigan, made a routine call at a motel to serve a warrant for writing a bad check. They were met with a fusillade of gunfire; all three were killed. Patrolman Gary Lorenzen was one of the first officers to discover the bodies. "I haven't had anyone here I could talk to— I'm hurting like a son of a bitch inside but I have to be strong for the other officers," he said (Clancy, 1987, p. 1A).

2. *Evaluation systems.* These stressors include the ineffectiveness of the judicial system, court leniency with criminals, negative press accounts of the police, the public's rejection of the police, and put-downs and mistreatment of police officers in the courts. This source of stress is a major problem in countries other than the United States. For example, in France, where the public is particularly contemptuous of the police, the rate of suicide is 35 per every 100,000 officers, a rate that exceeds what is seen in most major U.S. cities. However, even in the United States, many more police officers die as a result of suicide than homicide.

3. *Organizational problems and lack of support.* Examples of these stressors include bureaucratic hassles, inadequate leadership by police administrators, weak support and confused feedback from supervisors, lack of clarity about job responsibilities, and poor job performance by fellow

## The Science of

### BOX 6-4   Police stress: The effects of deadly force incidents

Solomon and Horn (1986) studied 86 police officers who had been involved in line-of-duty shooting incidents. These officers, 53% of whom had been involved in a shooting in which a person was killed, were attending a three-day workshop on postshooting incident trauma at the time.

Here are the percentages of officers who experienced at least a moderate amount of each of 18 postincident reactions, followed by the percentage of officers who suffered certain perceptual distortions during or after the incident:

| REACTION | PERCENTAGE |
|---|---|
| 1. Heightened sense of danger | 58 |
| 2. Anger | 49 |
| 3. Nightmares | 34 |
| 4. Isolation/ withdrawal | 45 |

| REACTION | PERCENTAGE |
|---|---|
| 5. Fear and anxiety about future situations | 40 |
| 6. Sleep difficulties | 46 |
| 7. Flashbacks/ intruding thoughts | 44 |
| 8. Emotional numbing | 43 |
| 9. Depression | 42 |
| 10. Alienation | 40 |
| 11. Guilt/sorrow/ remorse | 37 |
| 12. Mark of Cain | 28 |
| 13. Problems with authority figures, rules, regulations | 28 |
| 14. Family problems | 27 |
| 15. Feeling of insanity/loss of control | 23 |
| 16. Sexual difficulties | 18 |

| REACTION | PERCENTAGE |
|---|---|
| 17. Alcohol/drug abuse | 14 |
| 18. Suicidal thoughts | 11 |

PERCEPTUAL DISTORTIONS

| | |
|---|---|
| 1. Slow motion (perceiving the event to occur in slow motion) | 67 |
| 2. Fast motion (perceiving the event to occur in rapid motion) | 15 |
| 3. Diminished sound during the event | 51 |
| 4. Intensified sound during the event | 18 |
| 5. Tunnel vision during the event | 37 |
| 6. Heightened detail during the event | 18 |

officers. In the survey of Australian police cited earlier (Hart et al., 1995) as well as other recent studies (Brown & Campbell, 1990), organizational problems proved to be the most important source of stress—more influential than physical danger, bloody crime scenes, and public scrutiny.

A certain degree of stress is inevitable, given the demands placed on the police. Yet, police officers often find it hard to admit that the stressful nature of their job is affecting them. A stigma exists about admitting a need for professional help. Too often, police officers believe that, if they acknowledge personal problems or ask for assistance, they will be judged to be unprofessional or inadequate. These fears are not entirely unreasonable. Officers found to have psychological problems are sometimes belittled by other officers or are relieved of their weapons and badges and assigned to limited-duty tasks. These consequences lead some officers to hide the fact that they are suffering from job-related stress.

Stressful working conditions also lead to **burnout,** which has been defined as "a syndrome of emotional exhaustion, depersonalization, and reduced personal accomplishment that can occur among individuals who work with people in some capacity" (Maslach & Jackson, 1984, p. 134). Emotional exhaustion reflects feelings of being emotionally overextended and "drained" by one's contact with other people. Depersonalization frequently takes the form of a callous or insensitive response to other people, particularly crime victims and others requesting police assistance. Reduced personal accomplishment is manifested in a decrease in one's feeling of competence at the end of a day's work with other people (Maslach & Jackson, 1984). Burnout also affects behavior off the job. In Jackson and Maslach's (1982) study of police officers and their families, emotional exhaustion was found more likely than any other factor to affect behavior at home. Police officers were described by their wives as coming home upset, angry, tense, and anxious. No wonder that high rates of substance abuse, domestic battering, and divorce are regarded as occupational hazards of police work.

Burnout may also result from working many years at the same job. Patrol officers sometimes speak of the "seven-year syndrome." Initially, officers are eager and anxious about their job performance. The tasks are initially interesting and challenging. But after several years, some officers lose interest; the job feels stale. Enthusiasm is lost.

What can be done to reduce stress and burnout in police officers? From their analysis of the research on organizational behavior, Jackson and Schuler (1983) have hypothesized four organizational qualities that increase employee burnout: (1) lack of rewards (especially positive feedback), (2) lack of control over job demands, (3) lack of clear job expectations, and (4) lack of support from supervisors. Although each of these is especially problematic for police officers, certain interventions can reduce the likelihood of burnout (see ◆ Box 6-5). For example, the police officer seldom hears when things go well but often hears of the complaints of enraged citizens. Police officials could create opportunities for citizens to express their appreciation of what police officers are doing daily. Officers often feel a lack of control in their jobs. They must react to calls; they cannot change the flow of demands. Furthermore, citizens expect them to respond immediately.

Although the level of demands cannot be changed, officers can be given greater flexibility in how they respond to these demands. Their daily duties can be restructured so as to increase a sense of choice of activities. The importance of discretion can be emphasized to the officers because they have a great deal of it when dealing with suspected offenders. Officers do not always make an arrest, even when they catch a suspect breaking the law. In one study, police officers did not make an arrest in 52% of the misdemeanors and 43% of the felonies, even when they had probable cause to believe that the suspect had committed a crime (Reiss, 1971). LaFave (1965) provides one illustration:

> A traffic officer stopped a car that had been going 15 m.p.h. over the speed limit. The driver was a youth, but he had a valid driver's license. Although the 15 m.p.h. excess was beyond the ordinary toleration limit for speeding violations, the officer only gave the youth a severe warning. The officer knew that the law required suspension of the license of a juvenile driver for any moving violation. (p. 138)

One strategy for decreasing burnout among police is the use of **team policing.** Team policing involves a partial shift of decision making from a centralized authority to front-line officers and their immediate supervisors, who share the responsibility of setting policing priorities and making management decisions. Teams are often organized around neighborhoods, where they focus their efforts for extended periods of time. Within a neighborhood team, members perform several different functions so that they come to realize how important each team member is to the overall success of the group. In addition, because the team stays in the neighborhood, citizens should come to know the officers more closely and develop a better understanding of them.

## Is There a Police Personality?

Given that the work of a police officer requires a number of challenging tasks and that the job is highly visible, the public has a tendency to label

## BOX 6-5    Stress reduction with the police

The negative consequences of stress can be especially troublesome for the police because they are exposed to dangerous situations, they are armed with deadly weapons, and they are given special powers to use force. All these facts add to the risks of serious consequences for police who experience high levels of stress and make it important that police receive effective treatment for stress-related disturbances.

In recognition of these concerns, many police agencies have developed their own stress management programs or referred their officers to other agencies for counseling. These programs emphasize the prevention of stress through various techniques, including relaxation training, stress inoculation, detection of the early signs of stress, and effective problem solving (Reiser & Geiger, 1984).

Another approach to stress-related problems is to change those aspects of police work that officers find the most frustrating. These system-level changes are usually aimed at organizational difficulties that complicate police work. One example of this type of change is *team policing*, which we describe in the text.

Despite attempts to prevent stress and to change organizations in positive ways, some officers will experience stress-related problems that require counseling. Psychological treatment of police officers is complicated because the police as a group are resistant to personal counseling. First, they tend to believe that really capable officers should be able to withstand any hardships and that failure to do so signals a lack of professionalism, machismo, or emotional control. Second, police fear that counsel-

ing attaches a stigma of mental disorder to them that will undercut respect from their peers. Finally, officers are justifiably concerned that the department's need to know their psychological status with respect to their fitness for continuing duty will override their rights of confidentiality and lead to embarrassing disclosures of personal information.

Police departments have developed several alternatives for providing psychological counseling to their officers. Although none of these options solves all the problems mentioned earlier, each tries to overcome the more common obstacles facing police counseling programs. One popular approach is peer counseling whereby police officers, with or without special training in peer-counseling methods, share their personal problems and discuss different ways of cop-

---

police officers as having a certain set of qualities. Is there a distinct "police personality," or is this just an inaccurate stereotype? Do police officers share a cluster of personality characteristics that differentiates them from other people?

If there is a police personality, how does it come about? Are police officers, by nature, a homogeneous group? Do they differ from other occupational groups and from the general population in terms of inherited personality traits? Or is the personality of police officers shaped gradually over their careers as a result of common occupational demands and experiences?

Different answers have been given to these questions, but the consensus is that career so-

cialization is a stronger influence than preexisting differences in temperament. Among the most influential conceptions of a police personality is Joel Lefkowitz's description of the psychology of the police. After studying a host of variables, Lefkowitz concludes that the police do not differ from other groups in terms of psychological disorders or intelligence, but he also suggests that there were other important differences. According to Lefkowitz (1975):

> there exists a constellation of traits and attitudes or a general perspective on the world which particularly characterizes the policeman. This constellation . . . presumably [comprises] such interrelated traits as authoritarianism, suspicious-

ing with the stress of their work. Describing their experiences with peer counseling in the Los Angeles Police Department, Reiser and Klyver (1987) report that 200 trained peer counselors conducted about 5000 hours of counseling with their fellow officers in one year alone. Most of this counseling was aimed at relationship problems and job dissatisfactions.

A second method is to provide counseling for specific problems that police officers suffer. The most noteworthy example of these focused interventions is with officers who have been involved in the use of deadly force (see Blau, 1986; also refer to Box 6-4). The emotional aftermath of shooting incidents is among the most traumatic experiences the police encounter and can often lead to symptoms of posttraumatic stress disorder (Reiser & Geiger, 1984; Solomon & Horn, 1986). Providing post-incident counseling is a common service of police psychologists; in many departments, counseling for officers involved in shooting incidents is mandatory (McManis, 1986). The goals of this counseling, which also often relies on peer support, are to reassure officers that their emotional reactions to incidents are normal, to give them a supportive place to express these emotions, to help them reduce stress, and to promote a well-paced return to duty. Many departments also try to make counseling services available to the family of officers who have been involved in traumatic incidents.

Although many ethical dilemmas are involved in psychological counseling for police officers (D'Agostino, 1986), the most difficult ones revolve around questions of confidentiality. Police counseling services are usually offered in one of two ways: by an "in-house" psychologist who is a full-time employee of the police department or by an "outside" psychologist who consults with the department on a part-time basis. In-house professionals are more available and knowledgeable about police issues. Outside consultants, because they're independent from the department, are better able to protect the confidentiality of their clients' disclosures.

ness, physical courage, cynicism, conservatism, loyalty, secretiveness, and self-assertiveness. (p. 6)

Lefkowitz and others (Charles, 1986; Muir, 1977) have identified two clusters of personality traits that have been viewed as distinctive of police officers, but not in any pathological way. Cluster 1 includes the traits of isolation and secrecy, defensiveness and suspiciousness, and cynicism. These traits portray a close-knit group of people whose occupational isolation and accompanying secrecy lead to strong feelings of being misunderstood by outsiders, who are in turn viewed with suspiciousness and cynicism by the police. Feelings of insecurity develop in response to this isolation and sense of being different and underlie the officers' desire for a uniform and badge as symbols to bolster their limited sense of personal adequacy to meet the extraordinary challenges of their jobs. In fact, feelings of being misunderstood by the public are one of the three most frequent problems reported by police officers. The segregation that results from wearing a uniform daily and from their role in the community leads to what Lefkowitz (1975) calls socio-occupational isolation, which only intensifies the solidarity with other police officers.

Another manifestation of this cluster is what has been called the "blue wall of silence," the

*A Los Angeles police officer on trial for corruption charges*

tendency for police officers to cover up the wrong-doings of fellow officers. The extent of this problem is unknown, but increased attention has been paid to it ever since Alan Dershowitz, one of O. J. Simpson's attorneys, charged that officers are routinely trained during police academy to lie on the witness stand. This charge is easier to make than to verify, but there is little doubt that some police officers shade the truth or ignore it all together to protect themselves and obtain convictions. In fact, allegations of police misconduct, including the planting of evidence, have become a mainstay argument among criminal defense attorneys. Moreover, this argument works; in the past couple of years, many convictions have been overturned because of police-faked or -suppressed evidence.

Lefkowitz's second cluster includes the qualities of **authoritarianism,** status concerns, and violence. This cluster is much more controversial than cluster 1 and includes a penchant for violence and several dimensions of authoritarianism. Authoritarianism, as conceived by Adorno, Frenkel-Brunswik, Levinson, and Sanford (1950), is a set

of beliefs that reflect identification with and submissiveness to authorities, an endorsement of power and toughness, intolerance of outgroups and minorities, pressure for conformity to group norms, and rejection of anything unconventional as "deviant" or "sick."

Although the police appear submissive to authority and tend to be politically conservative, they do not as a group score as particularly authoritarian on the California F Scale of Authoritarianism or as particularly rigid on Rokeach's Dogmatism Scale (Carlson, Thayer, & Germann, 1971; Fenster & Locke, 1973). In some studies, they score lower than college students and teachers. If police officers are authoritarian, it is primarily in the sense of enacting middle-class conventionality. Police may also become more aggressive when they perceive their personal authority to be questioned, and they work at a job that justifies (and sometimes overjustifies) the use of force.

Police also appear to be more responsive to politically powerful figures than to powerless ones. In a provocative investigation, Wilson (1978) asked police officers how they would respond if they saw a car with a very low license number (e.g., NY-2) speeding. Such low-number plates are offered to politicians in many states. Police officers in two New York communities, Amsterdam and Newburgh, responded without hesitation that they would "mind our own business." Police officers do not express similar concerns toward groups and individuals who lack political clout. Greenberg and Ruback (1982) summarize the relevant literature by stating:

> Several studies provide evidence of police discrimination against persons of lower socioeconomic status and members of minority groups (Cochran, 1971; Skolnick, 1975; Westley, 1970; Wilson, 1978). Chambliss and Seidman (1971), among others, contend that suspects of lower socioeconomic status are discriminated against by the police because they wield less political power than middle-class suspects. Chambliss and Seidman further contend that because the police associate minority-group membership with lower socioeconomic status, minority-group

members have become the objects of police discrimination. (p. 82)

The labels "authoritarian" and "violent" may be justified for police officers, but in a narrower sense than is usually applied. Police officers do tend to be a politically conservative, conventional group, very loyal to one another, and concerned with assertively maintaining the status quo. They are authoritarian, primarily in the sense of respecting the higher authority of the law, the nation, and the government they serve.

A primary psychological motivation to become a police officer appears to be the preference for order and security, which probably manifests the working-class backgrounds from which many police officers come (Gorer, 1955; Niederhoffer, 1967). A second important motive is a desire to provide social services to others. Police officers also report a desire for a job that allows them to exercise independent thought, to be creative, and to learn new things (Lurigio & Skogan, 1994).

Research indicates that police officers do not possess pathological extremes of personality. Most studies indicate that as a group they are "normal" or "healthy" in their adjustment. The group's average IQ is consistently within the high-average range.

# Police-Community Relations

Police officers are justified in feeling that they live in a "fishbowl." Their performance is constantly being reviewed by the courts and evaluated by the public. Several amendments to the U.S. Constitution impose limits on law enforcement officers; such limits are part of the first ten amendments, known as the Bill of Rights. The Fourth Amendment protects against unreasonable search and seizure of persons or property. The Fifth Amendment provides guarantees for persons accused of a crime; for example, no such person "shall be compelled in any criminal case to be a witness against himself, nor be deprived of life, liberty, or property, without due process of law." As we discuss in Chapter 9, limits on police activities are frequently reevaluated on the basis of current court interpretations of these amendments. The Sixth Amendment guarantees the accused "the right to a speedy and public trial" and "the assistance of counsel for his defense"; the way these provisions are interpreted also has implications for police procedures. Protection against "cruel and unusual punishment" is promised by the Eighth Amendment, and the Fourteenth Amendment guarantees all citizens "due process." These amendments also govern and constrain several police activities.

During the last two decades, citizens' groups have become increasingly critical of the police. Two types of concerns can be identified. The first deals with the manner in which the police conduct various investigative procedures. Historically, the interrogation practices used by the police to elicit confessions from suspects have been the major focus of this concern, and we discuss coercion of confessions extensively in Chapter 8. Briefly, the police are often criticized for using manipulative tactics to induce confessions from suspects. The most common approach is "to overwhelm the suspect with damaging evidence, to assert a firm belief in his or her guilt, and then to suggest that it would be easier for all concerned if the suspect admitted to his or her role in the crime" (Kassin & Wrightsman, 1985, p. 75). Along with this tactic, police often express concern for the suspect's welfare. Undue physical force is used far less than in the past, but promises of lowered bail, reduced charges, leniency by the judge, and vague threats about harsher treatment are common. These techniques are sometimes supplemented with exaggerated or trumped-up evidence to scare suspects into confessing (Kassin & Kiechel, 1996).

More recently, another police technique that has caused widespread concern and condemnation is racial profiling, the practice of making traffic arrests of an illegitimately larger percentage of minority than nonminority motorists. Although some law enforcement officials have defended this procedure (discussed in Chapter 5) as a reasonable crime control tool, the public outcry over its potential for abuse has led several states to abandon it.

A second major concern of community groups is excessive force or brutality by the police (Fyfe, 1988). During the protests of the 1960s that took place in Watts (a section of Los Angeles), in Detroit, and throughout the South, massive demonstrations were held by American citizens, mostly African Americans, against what they believed was racially motivated harassment by the police.

The police officer has come to be viewed in predominantly African American neighborhoods as a representative of an all-male, lily-white, overbearing colonial power that exerts economic, political, and social control over its inhabitants and who lies whenever it is expedient to do so. Although law enforcement officers are trained to act within legally prescribed boundaries and to do so equally toward all citizens, charges of "police brutality" have once again become all too frequent in the United States. During the late 1980s, it was estimated that approximately 2500 cases of police brutality were reported and investigated annually.

In the 1990s, the beating or killing of suspects by the police again commanded national attention. The most startling example of this phenomenon occurred in Los Angeles in March 1991, when police chased a black motorist who they alleged was speeding through an L.A. suburb in his 1988 Hyundai. As the unarmed man emerged from his car, a police officer felled him with a blast from a 50,000-volt stun gun, and three patrolmen proceeded to beat and kick him while a police helicopter hovered overhead. As a result of this attack, which was witnessed by at least 11 other police onlookers, Rodney King—a 25-year-old man who, it was later learned, was on parole—lay seriously injured with multiple skull fractures, a broken ankle, cracked cheekbone, and several internal injuries. One special feature of this attack was that a nearby citizen captured the entire episode on his videocamera; within hours, the tape of this terrifying beating was played across the country on network news programs. Soon thereafter, local, state, and federal agencies launched investiga-

tions into the beating and the entire Los Angeles Police Department. Three of the four officers who were charged with beating King were initially acquitted of all criminal charges, an outcome that shocked millions of Americans. But in a second trial, brought in federal court, two of the officers were found guilty of depriving King of his civil rights and were sentenced to prison.

Of course, more recent events confirm that the King case was not a completely isolated incident; minority citizens continue to have many cases to which they can point as justifications for their concerns that they are often not treated fairly by the police (Weitzer & Tuch, 1999). These cases, all of which were featured in the national media, include the shooting and killing of Amadou Diallo, an innocent West African immigrant, by four plainclothes New York City police officers; the sodomy and torture of Abner Louima by officers in a Brooklyn police station; and the shooting of Javier Franciso Ovando by two Los Angeles police officers, who then planted a gun on the paralyzed victim to frame him for a crime he did not commit. Even the U.S. Supreme Court has found it necessary to restrict the use of deadly force by police as discussed in ◆▶ Box 6-6.

What causes the police to act brutally? How can we explain incidents in which officers clearly have used excessive force? One popular explanation is that police excesses stem from the personality problems of a "few bad apples." In this view, brutality reflects the sadistic extreme of the aggressive, tough pole of the authoritarian personality that we have already discussed. An opposing explanation is that brutality is the unfortunate price occasionally paid for situations in which rising numbers of violent, even deadly, criminals demand forceful responses from the police. A third alternative is that police brutality reflects a fundamental sociological pathology, that the deep strains of racism are still endemic in society. Which view is correct?

Police brutality is another example of a problem for which psychology seeks explanations neither in individual personalities nor in environmental situations but in the interactions between

## THE CASE OF

**BOX 6-6** **Edward Garner**

In the 1985 case of *Tennessee v. Garner,* the Supreme Court struck down a Tennessee law that allowed police to shoot to kill, even when an unarmed suspect fleeing a crime scene showed no apparent threat (Duning & Hanchette, 1985; Fyfe, 1982). In October 1974, Edward Garner, then 15, fled when the police arrived just after Edward had broken the window of an unoccupied house. He was pursued by Officer Elton Hymon. As Edward scaled a 6-foot chain link fence at the back of the property, Officer Hymon yelled, "Police—halt!" Edward didn't halt,

and Officer Hymon, knowing that he was in no shape to catch the fleeing youth, shot and killed Edward with a bullet to the back of the head.

Edward's father sued public officials and the city of Memphis, alleging that the police had violated his son's civil rights by the use of excessive force. The city defended on the basis of a state statute giving peace officers the right to use deadly force if necessary to stop a fleeing felon. While the lower courts agreed with the city, 11 years later the United States Supreme Court struck down

the statute in a divided decision. The majority held that shooting a person, even one suspected of a felony, violates that person's Fourth Amendment right to be free from unreasonable searches and seizures. The majority said, however, that deadly force would be justified if the officer had reason to believe that the suspect posed an immediate threat to him or others. Three justices, Sandra Day O'Connor, Warren Burger, and William Rehnquist, dissented from the majority opinion, stating that it would give suspects a constitutional right "to flee unimpeded" from the police.

persons and the situations in which they function. From this perspective, we begin with police officers who, on average, are strongly committed to maintaining the conventional order and to protecting society. We repeatedly put them into potentially dangerous situations, we arm them well, we urge them to be "tough on crime," and we train and authorize them to use appropriate force. The result from mixing this type of person with these types of situations is predictable: In some encounters, the police will use excessive force against citizens who are suspected of wrongdoing that threatens public safety. Even more disturbing, however, is that the suspicions on which police force is based will sometimes be motivated by stereotypes, mistaken information, and the mutual mistrust that can develop between individuals from different cultural and ethnic backgrounds.

As it turns out, many episodes of police brutality occur following high-speed chases, when, as with Rodney King, police lose control of their

behavior after pursuing a suspect they think is belligerent or threatening. In such tension-charged situations, police are prone to let their emotions dictate their actions. Some police departments are now concentrating on the problem of high-speed pursuits as triggers for what they call "mad cop disease." They try to teach police to "keep their cool" during these incidents and not escalate their own fear and anger.

Since the 1970s, but particularly since the Rodney King episode, a number of attempts have been made to improve police relations with people in the community, especially in neighborhoods with large numbers of ethnic minorities. We have already described team policing as one effort to make the police officer's job less stressful and to respond to some community concerns about the way police perform. Evaluations of this type of innovation are inconsistent. In some cities, only minor changes were made, such as stenciling "Neighborhood Police Team" on several radio cars;

*Community policing is a philosophy designed to increase the amount and quality of specific police officers' contact with citizens and to involve police more in crime prevention and community maintenance activities.*

it is unlikely that such trivial actions will improve police-community relations. In other cities, proposed changes were thwarted by higher levels of police administration. But after team policing was introduced in Newark, New Jersey, crime rates decreased dramatically and officer morale was reported to be high.

Structural changes such as team policing must be accompanied by changes in operating philosophy, too (Skolnick & Bayley, 1986). Traditionally, police have been only reactive; they have responded to crime incidents. But now, police officials are asking whether they can reduce crime by managing—or even preventing—the problem rather than just responding to manifestations of it (Wilson & Kelling, 1989).

"Managing the problem" includes, for example, preventive maintenance. The philosophy behind this approach is that "if the first broken window in a building is not repaired, soon all the windows will be broken; likewise, when disorderly behavior is left unchallenged or neighborhood

decay is left unattended, the disorder escalates and the decay spreads" (Wilson & Kelling, 1989, p. 23). So police departments have organized local citizens' groups to paint out graffiti and have convinced city agencies to tow away abandoned cars. The goals are to (1) "harden the target" so that criminals have reduced opportunities to commit crime and (2) prevent physical deterioration so that citizens feel a larger stake in preserving order in their communities.

The city of Houston opened up storefront police stations, as another example of the community problem-solving orientation. In this approach, known as **community-based policing,** police officers develop a proactive, problem-solving approach with active collaboration from local citizens joining the police to combat crime, promote safety, and enhance the overall quality of neighborhoods. From a community-based policing perspective, officers combine their law enforcement techniques with the skills of a community organizer. Rather than nightly busting drunks who congregate in an empty lot, the police might elicit the help of business owners to convert the lot into a vest-pocket park (Anderson, 1988; Press, 1988).

In most versions of community policing, greater use is made of foot patrols by officers who stay in the same neighborhoods. As a result, community-based policing seeks to humanize police and citizens to one another and to broaden the roles that police play in a community. For example, Chicago's version of community policing, known as the Chicago Alternative Policing Strategy (CAPS), contains six basic features (Lurigio & Skogan, 1994):

1. *A neighborhood orientation,* in which officers make friendships with individual residents in a community, know where the "hot spots" for crime are, and develop partnerships with community organizations for fighting crime

2. *Increased geographic responsibility,* meaning that officers regularly walk a given neighborhood "beat" and become highly visible, well-known experts about problems in that area

3. *A structured response to call for police service,* in which emergency calls are handled by a special-response team, thereby permitting beat officers to stay available for routine calls and maintain a high-profile presence

4. *A proactive problem-oriented approach,* whereby more effort is devoted to crime prevention (e.g., closing down drug houses, breaking up groups of loitering youth) rather than responding to discrete disturbances or criminal activities

5. *Brokering more community resources for crime prevention,* such that police enlist the help of other city agencies to identify and respond to local community problems

6. *Anaylsis of crime problems,* which allows officers to target their attention to the highest-risk areas by using computer technology to keep accurate track of crime patterns

Does community policing work, or is it just a fad, long on rhetoric but short on success? As with most social reform projects, the results are mixed. Some cities that have introduced commu-

nity policing initiatives report large improvements in the public's attitude toward their police departments (Peak, Bradshaw, & Glensor, 1992) and sizable reductions in rates of serious crimes. Other evaluations indicate that police officers themselves remain skeptical about community policing. In Chicago's program, police officers initially doubted that community-based policing would reduce crime or improve relationships with racial minorities, but they believed it would require more work on their part and possibly undercut their authority in the community (Lurigio & Skogan, 1994). In general, police administrators endorse the value of community policing and believe that its advantages (improved physical environment, more positive attitudes by the public toward police, fewer citizen complaints) outweigh its disadvantages (displacement of crime to a non-community-policing area, more opportunities for officer corruption, resistance from rank-and-file officers). Currently, about three-quarters of police departments have some level of community policing in place.

Police administrators are also beginning to acknowledge the need for changes in attitudes in individual officers as well as in overall policing patterns. Recognizing the absence of dialogue between the police and the African American community in many cities, Teahan (1975b) used role playing and interpersonal feedback during police academy training to improve communication and relationships between black and white police officers. Black police officers are especially vulnerable to miscommunication problems because some white officers assume that a black person with a weapon must be a criminal and not an undercover cop (Lewis, 1996). An example of the role-playing situations that Teahan used to improve black-white relations is the following:

> Two officers representing scout car partners were chosen (or volunteered) from the group. A third officer was then assigned the role of citizen. The scout car men were given a card stating: "You are cruising in your scout car at 12 P.M. in the 13th precinct when you receive information over the car radio that an armed robbery has

just been committed a few blocks away. The suspect is described as a young adult male in his early twenties, dressed in a dark overcoat. Suddenly, you notice a young man fitting that description ahead of you. You pull up beside him and. . . .

The officer designated as the citizen received a similar card reading: "You are a black university student who has just finished seeing a movie a few blocks away. It is 12 P.M. and you are hurrying home to your apartment when a police squad car pulls up beside you." (Teahan, 1975b, p. 38)

The results were mixed. The black officers felt the workshops were beneficial; they showed greater concern over racial issues and felt that relationships between black and white officers were better than they had been at the beginning of training. But white officers became more prejudiced toward blacks. (White officers in control groups who did not participate in the workshops became less prejudiced.) Furthermore, they reported less contact with blacks at the end of the project. Similar results have been reported for police in other countries. One study assessed racial attitudes toward Aborigines by Australian police at the time of recruitment, after the completion of training, and after one year of service and found that training resulted in decreased authoritarianism and ethnocentrism. However, the police became more ethnocentric and prejudiced after a year in the

field, and this effect was greatest for those officers working in districts containing more Aborigines (Wortley & Homel, 1995).

Results were even more disappointing to Teahan when, in a second study, he followed up police officers 18 months after their participation in police academy workshops (Teahan, 1975b). He found radical increases in racial animosity between black and white officers over the 18 months. All officers seemed to become more impersonal and detached; they also more easily developed feelings of hostility toward authority figures. As black officers progressed through the academy and on to regular police work, they became increasingly negative toward whites and disillusioned with the department; they began to feel a greater sense of black unity and polarity against whites. Blacks saw greater preference being given to whites, but white officers perceived things to be the opposite. The result was that both groups became more ethnocentric and polarized.

One partial solution to the problem of race relations is greater representation of minorities on police forces. Many cities are now actively recruiting minorities, and the results are encouraging. According to the most recent estimates, about one in every five police officers represents a racial minority, and in cities with populations of 25,000 or more, about one in ten is African American (Zhao & Lovrich, 1998).

## SUMMARY

**1.** *What is the role of the police in our society?* Policing is necessary in any society concerned with maintaining public order, even though some people in our society see police activity as restricting individual freedom. Police officers daily face the dilemma of equality versus discretion: whether to treat all suspects or lawbreakers equally or whether to temper justice with mercy.

**2.** *What procedures are used to select police?* Selection of police officers usually includes the completion of psychological tests and a clinical interview.

Another assessment device is the use of situational tests, in which the candidate role-plays responses to real-life challenges that would face a police officer, such as intervening in a dispute between a wife and her husband or aiding an injured child in a public place. Although responses to these situational tasks are valuable additions to psychological testing and interviewing, they are costly and time-consuming.

**3.** *How has the training of police officers expanded into new areas?*    Training of police officers usually involves a variety of activities, including criminal law, human relations training, self-defense, and the use of firearms. Most training programs last at least six months. Police officers are now frequently trained in crisis intervention, including handling of the mentally ill, resolving family disputes, and responding to hostage-taking situations.

**4.** *Describe the different activities of the police. Is law enforcement central?*    The police officer's job is multifaceted. Law enforcement (including investigation of complaints, arrest and prosecution of suspects, and efforts at crime prevention) accounts for only about 10% of police activity. Maintaining order (intervening in family and neighborhood disputes, keeping traffic moving, responding to disturbances of the peace) accounts for about 30% of police activity. Providing social services to the community is even more time-consuming.

**5.** *What stressors do the police face?*    Three problems are especially significant: the "life in a fishbowl" phenomenon, job-related stress, and burnout. Job duties and perceptions of police work can be modified to reduce burnout. Special psychological interventions are also available to counteract stressful reactions suffered by the police.

**6.** *Is there a police personality?*    Whether a specific "police personality" exists is controversial, but research suggests that two clusters of traits exist: (1) isolation and secrecy, defensiveness and suspiciousness, and cynicism; and (2) authoritarianism, status concerns, and violence. The evidence for the existence or strength of the second cluster is less convincing than for the first, and there is no indication that police officers as a group possess pathological personalities.

**7.** *What is the relationship between the police and the communities they serve?*    In recent years, community groups have been very critical of police behavior. Manipulative tactics used to coerce confessions from criminal suspects have been documented. Brutal treatment of innocent citizens, especially those of racial minorities, has been highly publicized. Efforts to improve police-community relations include team policing, reorganization of the police department that restructures the traditional chain of command, community-based policing, interracial human relations workshops, and the hiring of more minority officers. These interventions have had a mixed degree of success.

## KEY TERMS

| | | | |
|---|---|---|---|
| authoritarianism* | jail diversion program | suicide by cop | zero tolerance* |
| burnout* | learned helplessness* | team policing | |
| community-based policing | Stockholm syndrome | terrorism* | |
| | structured interviews | validity scales* | |

**InfoTrac**
**College**
**Edition**       For additional readings go to http://www.infotrac-college.com/wadsworth and enter a search term related to your interest. The key terms that have been asterisked above will pull up several related articles.

### ORIENTING QUESTIONS

1. *What psychological factors contribute to the risk of mistaken identifications in the legal system?*

2. *How do courts regard the use of hypnotically refreshed memory? What procedures should be followed when using hypnosis in a forensic setting?*

3. *How do jurors evaluate the testimony of eyewitnesses, and can psychologists help jurors understand the potential problems of eyewitness testimony?*

4. *Can children accurately report on their experiences of victimization? What factors affect the accuracy of their reports?*

**5.** *What courtroom modifications are used in cases in which children must testify? What effects do these modifications have on jurors?*

**6.** *Can memories for trauma be repressed, and, if so, can these memories be recovered accurately?*

As we saw in Chapter 6, the tasks facing the police include investigating crimes and accumulating evidence so that suspects can be identified and arrested. Particularly at the early stages of an investigation, eyewitnesses to those crimes provide important information to police. In fact, sometimes they provide the only solid leads for the police. Based on their survey of prosecutors, Goldstein, Chance, and Schneller (1989) estimate that eyewitness evidence plays a major role in more than 75,000 cases in the United States each year.

But in their attempts to solve crimes—and especially in their reliance on eyewitness observers—police and prosecutors face the kinds of dilemmas described in Chapter 1. Witnesses make mistakes in their reports to police. The police may pressure them to point the finger at a suspect; sometimes the desire to get a case "nailed down" (the goal of conflict resolution and stability described in Chapter 1) dominates over the goal of discovering the truth. Hence, the reports of eyewitnesses can lead the police down blind alleys or cause them to arrest the wrong suspect; the testimony of mistaken observers can even lead to wrong verdicts by judges and juries. In fact, a leading researcher, Elizabeth Loftus, has stated, "Faulty eyewitness testimony, in my opinion, is the major cause of wrongful conviction in this country" (quoted in Leary, 1988, p. 23), a claim supported by other experts (Huff, Rattner, & Sagarin, 1996).

Concern about eyewitnesses' accuracy is not restricted to criminal cases or to the identification of persons (Wells & Loftus, 1984). The results of civil lawsuits are also often affected by the reports of eyewitnesses, and law enforcement officials know that eyewitness descriptions of unusual events cannot always be trusted. The potential unreliability of eyewitness accounts was a major

reason why the FBI discounted the theory that the July 1996 explosion of TWA Flight 800 was caused by a missile fired from the ground. Agents doubted the accuracy of at least 20 eyewitness reports of a streak of light shooting skyward seconds before the plane exploded into pieces over the Atlantic Ocean, killing all 230 passengers.

Many crimes have only one eyewitness. A rape, for example, is usually witnessed only by the victim; the same is true for the sexual abuse of children. But eyewitness testimony, even from one person, can still be very convincing to a judge or jury. In England, of cases in which the only evidence was eyewitness testimony, 74% resulted in conviction. Half of these (169 of 347) had only one eyewitness (Loftus, 1979). Society clamors for the prosecution of crimes and the punishment of lawbreakers, but innocent individuals deserve to be treated fairly by the criminal justice system. As you will discover in the next section, the latter goal is sometimes sacrificed through a combination of witness mistakes and faulty investigatory procedures.

# Examples of Mistaken Eyewitness Identification

Cases of proven wrongful convictions based on faulty eyewitness testimony abound. The ordeal of Calvin C. Johnson Jr. is illustrative. Johnson, a college graduate with a degree in communications, a job with Delta Air Lines, and some petty crimes under his belt, spent 16 years behind bars for a rape he did not commit. But he is not alone. In fact, Johnson was the 61st person in the United States to be exonerated through the use of DNA testing. (The introduction of DNA testing procedures in

*Wreckage of TWA Flight 800. Were eyewitnesses correct about the cause of the crash?*

the 1980s allowed a new look at previously decided cases in which DNA-rich evidence [e.g., blood, semen] had been preserved. We describe the outcome of other cases involving DNA testing later.) Tests in Johnson's case proved definitively that he could not have been the man who raped and sodomized a College Park, Georgia, woman in 1983. Yet, the victim had picked Johnson out of a photographic lineup two weeks after her attack and identified him as the rapist at trial. The all-white jury convicted Johnson, who is black, despite the fact that forensic tests excluded Johnson as the source of a pubic hair recovered from the victim's bed and serology tests conducted on blood found at the scene were inconclusive. The jury also apparently chose to disregard the testimony of four alibi witnesses, including Johnson's fiancée, the fiancée's mother, his employer, and his mother, who claimed Johnson was home asleep at the time. One of the jurors later stated that the victim's eyewitness testimony had been the most compelling evidence in the case.

One reason why such mistakes proliferate is that when eyewitnesses make a tentative identifi

cation, police often stop investigating other leads. The goal of finding the truth is submerged, often unintentionally, in the rush to find the cause of a crime. In Johnson's case, police pushed ahead with the case even after the victim picked someone else at a live lineup (conducted after the photographic lineup). She testified at trial that she had picked the wrong person at the lineup because looking at Johnson was too much for her: "I just pushed my eyes away and picked someone else," she reported (Boyer, 2000).

Although the Johnson case illustrates one type of eyewitness error—choosing the wrong person from a photographic lineup—other sources of error are possible. Richard M. Nance (notice the middle initial *M*) was arrested in Los Angeles. His was not a very serious charge, but he was found guilty and given a brief jail term. In the midst of his ten-day sentence, a nationwide computerized crime network spat out the information that a Richard Lee Nance was sought in Sonoma County, in northern California, on a burglary charge.

The Sonoma County Sheriff's Department warrant for Richard Lee Nance said he was born on July 3, 1946, was 5 feet 10 inches tall, and had brown hair and brown eyes. The L.A. prisoner's middle name was Marion, not Lee; he was born on July 6, 1946, not July 3; and his eyes were blue, not brown. Yet he was flown to Sonoma County and put in jail with bail set at $5000. During the pretrial hearing, the burglary victim even pointed to Richard M. Nance and identified him as the man who had stolen a valuable ring and $100 from his farmhouse. Because Richard M. Nance was there at the hearing, labeled as the defendant, the victim was quick to assume that Nance was the robber, even though his fingerprints differed from those left at the scene of the crime. As Nance said later, "I can laugh about it now but can you believe me sitting there in the bright orange jail jump suit. Who else is the guy going to point to? The judge?" Despite the inconsistencies in name, appearance, and fingerprints, it took an investigator from the public defender's office almost a month to unravel the case and get Nance released from jail.

Nance asked rhetorically, "Who else is the witness going to point to?" but witnesses *have* sometimes pointed to the wrong person. In a trial in Washington, D.C., two different U.S. Park police officers, on the witness stand, pointed to the defense attorney rather than the defendant when asked to identify the protester charged with assaulting a police officer. After the first witness erred, the defense attorney moved his note pad and papers in front of his client, who began to scribble furiously, thus contributing to the impression that the defendant was the attorney, and vice versa. After the second misidentification, the government dropped the charges (Strasser, 1989).

Wrongful convictions happen because eyewitnesses sometimes lie about crimes they claim to have seen. In March 1993, Walter McMillian was released from Alabama's death row, where he had been a prisoner for six years. Three witnesses had falsely identified him as having been present when a dry cleaning clerk was shot to death during a robbery; the witnesses had split $7000 in reward money for fingering McMillian.

Mistaken eyewitness identification is responsible for more wrongful convictions than all other

causes combined (Huff et al., 1996). A report commissioned by the National Institute of Justice examined 28 cases in which individuals who were convicted of crimes were later exonerated by DNA test results (Connors, Lundregan, Miller, & McEwan, 1996). More recently, a group of psychologists added 12 more cases (Wells, Small, Penrod, Malpass, Fulero, & Brimacombe, 1998). These 40 cases represent the first group of individuals who were convicted of serious crimes, imprisoned, and later exonerated by DNA testing. What role did eyewitness identification play in convicting them in the first place? Faulty eyewitness evidence was present in a staggering 90% of these cases! In one case, the innocent man was identified by five separate eyewitnesses. Eyewitness testimony may be the least reliable but most persuasive form of evidence presented in court (Wells et al., 1998).

You might suppose that people like Calvin Johnson, Richard M. Nance, and Walter McMillian who had been mistakenly identified and wrongly imprisoned would have some recourse, that they could get something back for the time they lost in prison. But Calvin Johnson got nothing for his years behind bars; Georgia does not have a law providing compensation for people who were wrongly imprisoned. In fact, the majority of people who are wrongly imprisoned get either nothing or a token sum (which may amount to a few hundred dollars for each of the years they spent behind bars) from state compensation funds. One commentator has suggested that the new crime is how little these lost lives are worth (Higgins, 1999). The case of James Newsome is illustrative (see ◆ Box 7-1).

## Points at Which a Mistaken Identification Can Occur

Jurors in a criminal trial see a victim take the witness stand and confidently identify the defendant as his or her attacker. Not only may the jurors assume that this identification is accurate, but they are likely to believe that the victim was just as confident about the initial description or identification.

## THE CASE OF

**BOX 7-1** **James Newsome: Tough luck for an innocent man**

James Newsome served 15 years of a life sentence because three witnesses identified him as the man who shot and killed a grocer in Chicago in 1979. They were all wrong. The real killer—identified several years later with the help of new fingerprint technology—was Dennis Emerson, a known killer who was free on parole at the time of the murder. Emerson even left fingerprints at the scene that clearly did not match Newsome's. But in this case, as in many others, the innocent person had no recourse after being exonerated. Thirty-six states have no compensation systems; the falsely imprisoned in these jurisdictions are likely to get nothing for their lost years. In the majority of states that do compensate the innocent, damages are lim-

ited. The federal government— perhaps the stingiest of all—caps payments at $5,000 regardless of the length of imprisonment.

Even though Illinois will ostensibly pay $140,000 to a person who was wrongly imprisoned, Newsome is unlikely to see even a penny. In his case, the police may have relied on witnesses who were mistaken, and the jurors may have believed these mistaken witnesses, but there was no deliberate misconduct, no grand scheme to frame Newsome. Without evidence of clear misconduct, Newsome cannot sue his accusers. So, despite the fact that Newsome spent 15 years in maximum-security prisons; was nearly killed when his cell was set on fire; and emerged from prison without a home, job, work

*James Newsome, the victim of mistaken identification, spent 15 years in prison for a crime he did not commit.*

history, or even a driver's license, the state owes him nothing. He now works as a part-time assistant for lawyers in Chicago (Higgins, 1999).

These assumptions fail to recognize the many problems that can plague the accuracy of a criminal identification (Wells, 1993).

Mistakes in the process of identification can occur the moment the crime is committed. It may be too dark, events may move too swiftly, or the encounter may be too brief for the victim to perceive the incident accurately. Yet, victims are forced to rely on their impressions about the criminal's height, hair color, voice, and other identifying features when questioned by police. These impressions are sometimes translated into sketches of suspects, usually drawn by police artists (see Figure 7.1).

Mistakes can also occur during the investigation of a crime. In cases that involve eyewitnesses, police often ask these witnesses to examine a se-

ries of photos or a lineup of suspects and say whether the perpetrator is present. During this process, the police may coax reactions from eyewitnesses. At this point, eyewitnesses want to help the police solve the crime; they may feel implicit pressure to identify someone, even if the police do not explicitly encourage them to do so.

Based on their research, psychologists have identified several factors that can influence the validity of identifications made from a lineup or photo spread. For example, it is preferable to ask witnesses, "Is he there? Do you see him?" rather than "Which one of these is he?" The last question suggests to the witness that the suspect is actually present in the lineup, whereas the first ones do not. Witnesses are less likely to choose someone from the lineup when informed that the per-

**FIGURE 7.1** *An example of a sketch drawn by a police artist*

petrator "might or might not be present" (Steblay, 1997).

But even if the preferred questioning is used, the viewer picks someone from the lineup or photo spread about 60% of the time. Is this a desirable outcome? We cannot say, because we do not know what percentage of lineups and photo spreads include the true criminal. Most lineups and photo spreads are composed of approximately six persons, one of whom is the suspect; the others—called "foils" or "fillers"—are people known to be innocent of the crime. (Often the foils are police officers or offenders in jail for other crimes.) However, even when the police avoid improper suggestions and use appropriate foils, many witnesses will assume that the police would not have scheduled a lineup or shown a photo spread if they did not have the suspect included in it (Malpass & Devine, 1984).

In a typical lineup or photo spread, the eyewitness sees the suspect and the foils simultaneously. (In a photo spread, the six photos are typically arrayed on a single page. In a live lineup, the suspect and foils are shown together, standing in a line.) This procedure is termed *simultaneous presentation.*

We now know that a better procedure is to show suspects and foils sequentially—one at a time (Lindsay, Lea, Nosworthy, Fulford, Hector, LeVan, & Seabrook, 1991)—in a procedure called **sequential presentation.** For example, Cutler and Penrod (1988) showed a one-minute videotape of a staged liquor store robbery and varied the way in which the lineup was constructed. When the six members of the lineup were shown simultaneously, witnesses falsely accused an innocent person 39% of the time. However, when suspects were shown individually,

### The Science of

**BOX 7-2**

### Relative judgments and the "removal without replacement" procedure

In a simultaneous presentation of individuals in a lineup or photo spread, eyewitnesses tend to identify the person who, in their opinion, looks most like the culprit *relative to* other members of the group. In other words, they make a **relative judgment.** But what happens when the actual culprit is not shown? Under this condition, the relative judgment process will still yield a positive identification because someone in the group will always look *most* like the culprit (Wells et al., 1998).

Contrast this situation with a lineup or photo spread in which the members are presented sequentially, one at a time. Here, the eyewitness compares each member in turn to his or her memory of the perpetrator and, on that basis, decides whether any person in the lineup is the individual who committed the crime. This is an

absolute judgment process. The value of sequential presentation is that it decreases the likelihood that an eyewitness will make a relative judgment in choosing someone from the lineup or photo spread.

Gary Wells (1993) cleverly demonstrated the use of relative judgment processes in his "removal without replacement" procedure. In this procedure, all eyewitnesses watch a staged crime. Some are shown a photo spread that includes the actual culprit and five foils; their identifications are recorded. Another group sees the same photo spread with one exception: the culprit's photo is removed and not replaced with another photo. If identifications of the culprit by the culprit-present group are based solely on their recognition of him, then the percentage of people in that group

who identified him *plus* the percentage who said "not there" should be exactly the same as the percentage in the culprit-absent group who said "not there."

Wells tested this idea by showing 200 eyewitnesses to a staged crime either a culprit-present lineup or a lineup in which the culprit was absent but was not replaced by anyone else (see Table 7.1). When the culprit was present in the lineup, 54% of eyewitnesses selected him and 21% said "not there." Did 75% of eyewitnesses in the "target-absent" lineup say "not there"? Unfortunately, no. The "not there" response was given by only 32% of people in that group; the others all mistakenly identified someone else from the lineup. Why? Through a process of relative judgment, eyewitnesses apparently select whomever looks most like the perpetrator.

**TABLE 7.1** ◆ *Rates of choosing lineup members when a culprit is present versus removed without replacement*

| | LINEUP MEMBER | | | | | | |
| | 1 | 2 | 3 (culprit) | 4 | 5 | 6 | NO CHOICE |
|---|---|---|---|---|---|---|---|
| Culprit present | 3% | 13% | 54% | 3% | 3% | 3% | 21% |
| Culprit removed (without replacement) | 6% | 38% | — | 12% | 7% | 5% | 32% |

SOURCE: From "What do we know from witness identification?" from G. Wells, *American Psychologist, 48,* 553–571.

witnesses picked the wrong individual only 19% of the time. Some police departments have adopted sequential lineup procedures, but many have not. The psychological evidence underlying the pref-

erence for sequential presentation is presented in ◆ Box 7-2.

Lineups are time-consuming to create, and adequate types or numbers of foils may not be available. Thus, police departments often use a book of photographs, or "mug book," to identify suspects. In fact, most identifications of criminal suspects are from mug books rather than live lineups. This procedure introduces a different kind of problem; victims may be asked to look at a large number of photographs in a short period of time (as many as 500 in an hour), and their memory of the perpetrator may blend with these images. Psychologists have developed photo-rating procedures that help reduce the total number of photos a witness has to view before making an identification in experimental settings and some police departments have adopted these procedures. Methods that attempt to retrieve and sort photographs based on descriptions provided by the witness are apparently the most successful (Pryke, Lindsay, & Pozzulo, 2000).

After a suspect is identified but before the trial, a preliminary hearing will be held, at which the suspect is present. At this hearing, the victims or other eyewitnesses might be asked whether the suspect is the person who committed the crime. It is hard for witnesses to change their public statement at this point. If they have picked the suspect out of a lineup or a photo spread, most would be very reluctant now, in front of a judge and the attorneys, to say, "I'm not so sure" or "I've changed my mind." Instead, witnesses who are repeatedly questioned about what they saw often become *more* rather than less confident about the accuracy of the details in their reports (Shaw, 1996). Also, their current identification of the suspect may now be determined more by their recognition of the mug-book picture than by their recall of the original crime.

# Procedural Guidelines for Lineups and Photo Spreads

Just as psychological research has shown how the procedures used in lineups and photo spreads can influence their validity, so, too, does it suggest alternative methods that will minimize false identifications. In fact, psychological research was at the core of a set of national guidelines issued by the U.S. Department of Justice in 1999 on recommended procedures for collecting eyewitness evidence. In her introduction to the published guidelines, Attorney General Janet Reno wrote, "Eyewitnesses frequently play a vital role in uncovering the truth about a crime. The evidence they provide can be critical in identifying, charging, and ultimately convicting suspected criminals. That is why it is absolutely essential that eyewitness evidence be accurate and reliable. One way of ensuring we, as investigators, obtain the most accurate and reliable evidence from eyewitnesses is to follow sound protocols in our investigations" (U.S. Department of Justice, 1999, p. iii). Reno also acknowledged the "growing body of research in the field of eyewitness identification" as support for the guidelines.

The guidelines issued by the Justice Department are recommended procedures for conducting lineups and photo spreads. All recommendations stem directly from the results of psychological research studies. Researchers have made other recommendations about how to improve lineups and photo spreads, such as videotaping the procedures (Kassin, 1998b) and making sure that the person who conducts them does not know who the real suspect is among the group (Wells et al., 1998), but for practical reasons, these suggestions have not yet been included in the published guidelines. Among these recommendations adopted by the Justice Department are the following:

1. When obtaining information from the witness(es), the investigating officer should use open-ended questions (e.g., "What can you tell me about the car?") and avoid leading questions (e.g., "Was the car red?"). Although open-ended questions can yield more information from witnesses, police tend to ask few open-ended questions and to interrupt witnesses who try to give narrative statements. Leading questions, in particular, can influence a witness's memory of the crime by suggesting features that were either not present or not remembered.

2. The investigator conducting the photo spread or lineup should instruct the witness that

the person who committed the crime may or may not be present. This rule is aimed at reducing the tendency for eyewitnesses to pick the person in a lineup who looks most like the culprit relative to the others, a judgment that encourages false identifications when the actual culprit is not included in the lineup. Despite this sensible advice, lineups are sometimes conducted without such instructions and, hence, lead to biased or inaccurate responses by eyewitnesses (Steblay, 1997). Furthermore, defense attorneys are often not aware of the potentially biasing nature of different types of lineup instructions, so they do not routinely understand how their clients might have been harmed by a given lineup procedure (Stinson, Devenport, Cutler, & Kravitz, 1996).

3. In composing a photo spread or lineup, the investigator should select fillers who generally fit the witness's description of the perpetrator. It would not be fair to create a photo spread or lineup in which only the suspect fit the prior description of "a man with acne." In such circumstances, if a nonwitness was simply told the description of the culprit and then saw the photographs showing only one man with acne, the nonwitness would be able to pick out the suspect.

Police departments differ in the care they give to creating photo spreads and lineups in which the foils resemble the suspect. They may place the suspect in a lineup of people who differ from that suspect in height, weight, physique, hair style, and other significant features mentioned in the witness's description of the offender. Here are some examples: "In one case . . . the defendant had been picked out of a line-up of six men, of which he was the only Oriental. In other cases, a black-haired suspect was placed among a group of light-haired persons, tall suspects have been made to stand with short suspects, and, in a case where the perpetrator of the crime was known to be a youth, a suspect under twenty was placed in a line-up with five other persons, all of whom were forty or over" (*United States v. Wade*, 1967).

4. After conducting an identification procedure, the investigator should record the witness's own words regarding how sure he or she is of any identification. This recommendation is based on the fact that eyewitnesses often express increased confidence in their identifications after they are told by the police that they picked out the real culprit or after they learn additional information that implicates the person they identified (Wells & Bradfield, 1998). This raised confidence is troubling because of the repeated finding that the confidence that eyewitnesses express during their trial testimony is one of the strongest reasons that jurors believe such identifications are accurate.

In response to being cross-examined at trial by an opposing attorney, many eyewitnesses become even more confident in their identifications. Additionally, they may try to justify their confidence and become more convincing by providing additional details and embellishments during subsequent steps in the process. For example, a defense attorney may propose a **suppression hearing,** in which the judge is asked to rule that the eyewitness cannot testify at the actual trial because of inaccuracies in his or her report or deficiencies in the way the lineup was conducted. (Judges rarely suppress such evidence, but defense attorneys try, anyway.) At the suppression hearing, the eyewitness may again be called on to make another identification of the accused and so again, of course, at the actual trial.

The problem with witness confidence and the large weight that it carries with juries is that many studies have shown that witness confidence is not a very strong predictor of whether the witness's identification is accurate (Sporer, Penrod, Read, & Cutler, 1995). Another problem with eyewitnesses' confidence is its apparent malleability: After making a false identification from a photo spread, witnesses who were told that a cowitness identified the same person became highly confident in their false identifications (Luus & Wells, 1994). One result of feedback from the person administering the lineup is a sense of false confidence.

Can the development of false confidence be prevented? Wells and Bradfield (1999) hypothesized that confidence inflation occurs because at the time that feedback is delivered by the investigator, the eyewitness has not yet formed an independent opinion about his or her confidence. If the eyewitness is encouraged to think privately about that identification decision and the degree of confidence about it before being given any feedback, however, the inflation of false confidence is reduced.

We have just seen some of the ways that the processes of crime detection and investigation can lead to mistaken identifications. But all of us, as observers, are prone to making errors in perception and memory. To illustrate these errors, we next consider the steps involved in acquiring information from the outside world and recalling it.

# Basic Information Processing: Perception and Memory

We have all had the experience of spotting someone we think we instantly recognize and realizing that he or she is a stranger only when we start to say hello. Similar mistakes can be made when crime is observed. To process information about a crime, we must first perceive a stimulus and then retain it in our minds at least momentarily. Failures and errors can emerge at any step along the way.

## Perception

Although our perceptual abilities are impressive (Penrod, Loftus, & Winkler, 1982), we do make errors. We tend to overestimate the height of criminals, and we overestimate the duration of brief events while underestimating the duration of prolonged incidents. When watching a short film, we notice more about the actions than about the persons doing the acting. If a weapon is present when a crime is committed, we devote our attention to it more than to the facial features or other physical aspects of the person who has the weapon. This **weapon focus effect** has been demonstrated even when people watch a film of a crime (Tooley, Brigham, Maass, & Bothwell, 1987). It appears to be caused not so much by emotional arousal as by the fact that witnesses narrow their attention to

the weapon, thereby limiting the amount of attention they can pay to other aspects of the situation, such as physical features of the perpetrator (Kramer, Buckhout, & Eugenio, 1990). This is particularly likely to occur in situations in which the presence of a weapon is surprising and unexpected (Pickel, 1999).

## Memory

Experimental psychologists subdivide the building of a memory into three processes: (1) encoding, (2) storage, and (3) retrieval. We describe the memory of eyewitnesses in each of these three stages.

*Encoding.* **Encoding** refers to the acquisition of information. Many aspects of a stimulus can affect how it is encoded; stimuli that are only briefly seen or heard are not encoded fully, of course. The complexity of a stimulus also affects its encoding, but the relationship is not a straightforward one. As the complexity of an event increases (e.g., consider an earthquake or an explosion), some portions of the event probably will be misremembered, whereas other aspects of the event will be accurately recalled.

Contrary to what many people believe, a stressful situation does not enhance the encoding of events. Although mild stress or arousal may indeed heighten alertness and interest in the task at hand, extreme stress usually causes the person to encode the information incompletely or inaccurately. This principle reflects an application of the **Yerkes-Dodson law,** which describes the effects of arousal on learning. Under extremely low levels of external stress, a person may be so relaxed and unalert that little learning takes place. On the other hand, if a person is facing an excessively stressful situation, perception is narrowed, information is funneled, and less learning occurs than under mild levels of stress. Performance on many tasks is best when the level of arousal is moderate enough to ensure adequate attention but not so high as to disrupt accuracy.

Characteristics of the witness also affect encoding. We all differ in visual acuity and hearing ability. If we have more experience perceiving a given kind of stimulus, we will usually notice its details better than when it is a novel experience. This is why experienced judges notice flaws in a gymnast's performance that the rest of us can only detect in a slow-motion replay. Different expectancies about upcoming events also influence how they are subsequently perceived; in general, we have a tendency to see what we expect to see.

*Storage.*    The second step in building a memory is the **storage** of stimulus information. How well do we retain what we encode? Many years ago, the experimental psychologist Hermann Ebbinghaus showed that early memory loss is rapid. Lipton (1977) illustrated this phenomenon in a setting relevant to the concerns of this chapter. Subjects were shown a film of an armed robbery and shooting without any prior knowledge that they would be serving as eyewitnesses. Those who were questioned after one week generated 18% less memory information than those who were questioned immediately after viewing the film.

A second phenomenon also occurs during the storage phase—a surprising and potentially disturbing one. Activities that eyewitnesses carry out or information they learn after they observe an event can alter their memory of the event. For example, viewing mug shots or photographs of suspects can alter an eyewitness's capacity to recognize faces that he or she viewed before the mug shots (Gorenstein & Ellsworth, 1980); that is, the new activity can interfere with memory of the old. In similar fashion, simply providing an eyewitness with information about what other witnesses have already said influences the first witness's recollection (Shaw, Garven, & Wood, 1997).

A similar conclusion derives from the ingenious studies of Elizabeth Loftus (1975, 1979; reviewed in Loftus, 1992, 1993). In one of her projects, subjects viewed a one-minute film of an automobile accident and were later asked a series of questions about it. The first question asked either how fast the car was going "when it ran the stop sign" or how fast it was going "when it turned right." Then, on the last question, all subjects were asked whether they had seen a stop sign in the film. In the first group, which had earlier been asked about the speed of the car "when it ran the stop sign," 53% said they had seen a stop sign, whereas only 35% of the second group said they had seen the sign. The effect of the initial question was to "prompt," or refresh, the memory for this part of the film. In a second study, Loftus included a misleading follow-up question that mentioned a nonexistent barn. When questioned one week later, 17% of the subjects reported seeing the barn in the original film! In essence, the new information conveyed simply as part of a question was added to the same memory store as the original stimulus.

*Retrieval.*    The third and last step in establishing memory is the **retrieval** of information. This is not as straightforward a process as you might at first think. For example, we all have experienced the "tip of the tongue" phenomenon, when we know an answer or a movie title or a person's name but can't dredge it out of our memory store.

Once again, the wording of questions can influence output at the retrieval phase (Wells, Wright, & Bradfield, 1999). For example, consider the question "What was the man with the mustache doing with the young boy?" Assume that the man in question had no mustache. This form of the question may not affect the eyewitness's report of the man's actions but it may influence memory of the man's appearance. Later, if asked to describe the man, eyewitnesses may incorporate the detail (i.e., the mustache) that was embedded in the original question (Loftus & Greene, 1980).

In recalling information from our memory store, we often generate memories that are, in a sense, accurate but are not relevant to the task at hand. For instance, victims will sometimes pick from a lineup or a photo spread the face of a person whom they have seen before but who is not the actual criminal. For example, a clerk at a convenience store who is the victim of a late-night robbery may mistakenly identify an innocent shopper who frequents the store. In an actual case, a Los Angeles judge who was kidnapped and attacked while she was jogging picked a suspect's picture from the police mug book after the attack, and on that basis, he was charged with the crimes. She later stated that she had not remembered at first that he had appeared before her in court four years earlier, for similar offenses, and that she had sentenced him to unsupervised probation (Associated Press, 1988). This phenomenon, called **unconscious transference,** was demonstrated by Robert Buckhout (1974), who staged a mock assault before an unsuspecting class of 141 students. Seven weeks later, when the students were asked to pick the assailant from a group of six photographs, 40% were able to select the assailant. But of the 60% who failed to make the correct identification, two-thirds selected a person who had been at the "crime scene" as an innocent bystander. This is one means by which innocent persons are thrust into a process that eventually convicts them of crime.

In summary, as Hall, Loftus, and Tousignant (1984) conclude, testing one's memory for an original event can alter the memory for that event; indeed, "the witness reacts as if original memory and postevent information had been inextricably integrated" (p. 127).

# Use of Hypnosis with Eyewitnesses

Most eyewitnesses cannot remember everything that happened during the crime; their memories are often fragmented and vague. Are there ways to enhance the memories of eyewitnesses, to help them accurately remember facts and details?

Law enforcement officials are eager to use techniques that will increase the detail, accuracy, and usefulness of recollections by victims and other witnesses. Hypnosis has been investigated as an aid to memory and has been credited with helping solve some notorious crimes. Hypnosis was used in the Sam Sheppard murder case, the trial of the Boston Strangler, and the investigation of the assassination of Robert Kennedy. Probably the most notorious example of its use was the 1976

Chowchilla, California, kidnapping case, in which a busload of 26 schoolchildren and their driver were abducted by three masked kidnappers and buried underground in a large tomb from which they later escaped. The driver had seen the license plate on one of the kidnappers' vans and had tried to memorize the numbers. However, he was unable to recall the numbers until he was hypnotized. At one point during the hypnotic session, he suddenly called out a license plate number he remembered seeing. Except for one digit, the number was correct and expedited the capture of the three culprits, who were later convicted and sentenced to life in prison.

## What Is Hypnosis?

Everyone is aware of hypnosis, and perhaps you have been hypnotized yourself. During the past two centuries, hypnotism has been used to treat a range of psychological and physical disorders (including obesity, smoking, addictions, pain, fears, asthma, and stress disorders) despite inconsistent findings about its effectiveness (Wadden & Anderton, 1982). Many different explanations exist for what occurs during a hypnotized state, as well as for the essential ingredients of hypnosis.

Explanations of hypnosis fall into one of two categories. First, some investigators think of hypnosis as a procedure delivered by a skilled practitioner who induces a special mental state in subjects, known as a *trance,* that provides them with unique mental abilities. The second perspective focuses on subjects' *suggestibility,* which is maximized during hypnotic inductions. We define hypnosis as a state of *extreme suggestibility,* in which the hypnotized subject is very relaxed, attentive to incoming stimuli, and responsive to suggestions from the hypnotist. In effect, the subject agrees to reduce logical judgment and yield to the hypnotist's instruction. Hypnosis often heightens subjects' attention and imagination, but it also sometimes leads to confusion between imagined memories and memories of real events.

Hypnosis is used by law enforcement officials and government agencies for two main purposes:

(1) generating investigative leads that can then be pursued through other means and (2) refreshing the memories of witnesses, victims, or defendants who have forgotten important details of events about which they might testify in court. The methods used to reach these two goals are basically identical, but their legal and professional status is different, as we discuss later.

## Dangers of Hypnosis as a Memory Refresher

*How the police use hypnosis.*    The use of hypnosis to uncover new leads or refresh memories usually follows one of two approaches. The first involves **age regression,** in which the hypnotized subject is asked to relive past events, even those that might have taken place years earlier. Age-regressed subjects often talk and act in a manner that is supposedly typical of them at the age to which they are regressed. They also report vivid memories of the past, sometimes with very strong emotions. Although some age-regressed subjects appear credible, empirical research has failed to support the conclusion that their recollections are accurate portrayals of the past (Orne, 1979).

The second memory enhancement technique, and the one favored by many hypnotists, involves giving hypnotic suggestions to subjects through the use of some metaphor such as a television, chalkboard, blank screen, or tape recorder. In the **television technique of retrieval,** the subject is told, before being hypnotized, that memories are stored in the subconscious mind and can be reached through hypnosis. Hypnotized subjects are asked to imagine that they are watching a televised documentary. They are told that their documentary can be slowed down, sped up, reversed, stopped, or played back and that close-ups of the people and objects involved are possible. The sound can be turned up so that everything can be heard clearly. The subject is told that the television will depict everything of importance vividly and the subject will remain calm while watching it so that he or she will now have an accurate memory of what took place.

*Effects of hypnosis on memory: Memory aid or altered memory?*    Few professionals find fault with forensic hypnosis when it is restricted to generating new leads for the police. However, the situation is different when hypnosis is used to help a witness recall details that may later be testified to in court or when hypnosis is used to help witnesses choose between conflicting versions of events that they have provided on different occasions. In these situations, many hypnosis researchers contend, the technique is fraught with so many problems that it should be allowed only under the strictest of safeguards or should be banned altogether (Diamond, 1980; Orne, 1979; Smith, 1983).

What are the dangers of hypnotically enhanced memory? Critics point to seven concerns, reflecting a theory of memory that is very different from that proposed by practitioners of forensic hypnosis. This view of memory is based on research (e.g., Loftus, 1979) that depicts memory as constantly changing and subject to reconstruction so that it "fits" with recently acquired information. From this perspective, memory is rewritten to help preserve existing knowledge and mental structures. The major concerns about the effects of hypnosis on memory are as follows:

1. Subjects often remember more material when hypnotized than when they are in a nonhypnotized state, an effect known as **hyperamnesia.** This additional material consists of a mixture of accurate and inaccurate recollections (Dywan & Bowers, 1983). False "recollections" can be implanted through suggestions from the hypnotist, or they can originate in other ways that are not yet completely understood. The addition of false information to accurate recollections is called **confabulation.** For example, an Illinois man was charged with first-degree murder after an eyewitness, under hypnosis, described his license plate. The witness claimed to have seen the car from 230 feet away, at night, with lights shining directly in his eyes. The charges were dropped, however, after an ophthalmologist testified that a person could not see more than 30 feet under such conditions. The net conclusion appears to be that hypnotized subjects do not show a reliable increase

in accurate recall compared to nonhypnotized subjects (Steblay & Bothwell, 1994).

2. One reason why confabulation occurs under hypnosis is that subjects relax their standards for reporting information. They become less critical and accept approximations of memory as "accurate enough." These approximations are then added to accurate memories to yield a version of events that is part fact and part fabrication. A second factor that contributes to confabulation is that hypnotized subjects are extremely suggestible and want to please the hypnotist by giving as full a report as possible. This motive encourages subjects to fill in the gaps in their memory with plausible details or with information they believe the hypnotist is expecting.

3. The greatest danger of confabulation is that persons who have been hypnotized find it difficult to separate actual memories from those generated under hypnosis. This problem can be compared to that of the basketball fan who watches a controversial play at an arena and then later watches TV replays of the same play. This fan develops a clear "picture" of the play in memory but is unable to separate which parts of the picture are from the actual game and which come from the TV replay.

4. Not only do hypnotized witnesses find it difficult to distinguish their original memories from those brought out under hypnosis, but they also tend to become more confident about their recall despite the fact that it might contain false recollections (Steblay & Bothwell, 1994). This confidence can persist long after the hypnosis session has ended. Hypnosis thus translates beliefs or expectations into "memories," a process called **memory hardening.**

5. It is not just hypnotized subjects who find it difficult to separate accurate from confabulated recall—hypnotists have the same problems. Even the most experienced hypnotist can be misled to accept confabulated recollections or to believe that a subject is hypnotized when in fact he or she is faking it.

6. Several studies have shown that hypnotized subjects are more responsive to the biasing influence of leading questions. For example, Zelig

and Beidleman (1981) showed subjects a short film of several bloody workshop accidents. After watching the film, the subjects were asked leading and nonleading questions about it while either hypnotized or not hypnotized. Hypnotized subjects made more mistakes on the leading questions, but they did not differ from the nonhypnotized subjects on the nonleading questions. Similar results were reported by Putnam (1979) with a film depicting an accident between a car and a bicycle. But a more recent experiment found no evidence that hypnosis increased the degree to which witnesses were misled by leading questions (Spanos, Gwynn, Comer, Baltruweit, & de Groh, 1989).

7. Posthypnotic testimony of witnesses in the courtroom is likely to affect the evaluation and weight given to this testimony by jurors. For example, Diamond (1980) warned that formerly hypnotized witnesses would become so confident about their testimony that they would be invulnerable to cross-examination. What little data are available on this matter suggest that this danger may be minimal (Spanos et al., 1989; Spanos, Quigley, Gwynn, Glatt, & Perlini, 1991).

Orne, Soskis, Dinges, and Orne (1984) reported that 96% of a sample of college students believed that hypnosis could help people remember material they otherwise could not recall. Wilson, Greene, and Loftus (1986) also found that a substantial proportion of a collegiate sample endorsed common myths about the power of hypnosis; however, these same students indicated that they would place *less* rather than *more* faith in the testimony of a witness who had been hypnotized. On the basis of additional mock jury research, Greene (1986) concludes, "it appears that hypnotic testimony is viewed by jurors with a certain amount of skepticism" (p. 71).

## Legal Status of Hypnosis

What if, as a result of being hypnotized, a victim claims to be able to identify her attacker—for example, by remembering his name or the license plate of his car? Can such information be introduced at a trial? The courts can be roughly divided into the following four camps concerning the admissibility of hypnotically refreshed testimony.

Up to about 1980, the majority view was that hypnotically assisted testimony was admissible (Diamond, 1980). According to this position, identified with the Maryland case of *Harding v. State* (1968), the fact that a witness has been hypnotized should apply to how much weight a jury should give that person's testimony and not to whether the testimony is admissible at trial. A number of courts followed *Harding's* line of thinking and ruled that hypnotically aided recall could be permitted in court but that the jury should consider the many problems of hypnosis when deciding how much weight to give such testimony.

The second camp, taking what has been called the "guidelines approach," requires that hypnotists follow specific precautions or guidelines if hypnotically aided testimony is to be admitted. The lead opinion in this category is *State v. Hurd* (1981), which was decided by the New Jersey Supreme Court. *Hurd* attempted to prevent most dangers of hypnotic memory refreshment by requiring the following safeguards: (1) the hypnosis should be conducted by a specially trained psychiatrist or psychologist; (2) the hypnotist should be independent of the prosecution, the police, or the defense; (3) information learned prior to the hypnosis should be written and retained so that it can be examined by other parties in the case; (4) the entire hypnosis session should be recorded, preferably on videotape; (5) only the hypnotist and the subject should be present during any phase of the hypnosis, including the posthypnosis interview; and (6) all of the subject's prehypnosis memories for the events in question should be recorded and preserved.

The third position is represented by decisions such as *People v. Hughes* (1983), in which the New York court of appeals awarded a new trial to a defendant who had been convicted of rape after having been identified by a victim who had undergone hypnosis to improve her memory. A man broke into a married woman's apartment, dragged her from bed, beat her, and raped her in the yard behind the apartment. When the woman's husband

arrived home, he found his wife lying naked outside their apartment. He called the police, who took the woman to the hospital, where she stayed several days. She was interviewed by police on numerous occasions, and while in the hospital, she spoke with her sister about the crime. Although her recall was not clear, she seemed to remember that her assailant was "Kirk" (the defendant's first name). In an attempt to improve her memory, the woman was hypnotized numerous times by a psychologist and a psychiatrist, who also administered a "truth serum" drug to her at the hospital. Following a videotaped hypnosis session, in which she identified Kirk Hughes as her attacker, she signed an affidavit indicating that Hughes was the man who beat and raped her. At the trial, the woman testified to the events as she recalled them both before and after the several sessions of hypnosis. Based in part on her identification, the jury convicted Hughes of rape, burglary, and assault.

The New York court stopped short of completely banning a hypnotized witness from testifying, ruling that "the pretrial use of hypnosis does not necessarily render the witness incompetent to testify to events recalled prior to being hypnotized." The court concluded that the admissibility of prehypnotic recollections should be decided on a case-by-case basis as courts evaluate whether the hypnosis was conducted in ways likely to contaminate prehypnotic memories.

The fourth, and most restrictive, position is that a witness who has been hypnotized to refresh recall cannot testify about either prehypnotic or posthypnotic recollections in the prosecution of that case. This view became increasingly popular in the 1980s beginning with the case of *State v. Mack* (1980), in which the supreme court of Minnesota, relying on the *Frye* test (discussed more fully in Chapter 8's description of the polygraph), ruled that hypnosis had not been generally accepted by the scientific community as a reliable method for enhancing accurate recall and that hypnotically refreshed recall was to be excluded from the trial.

This topic was revisited in the 1987 U.S. Supreme court decision of *Rock v. Arkansas* (see

# THE CASE OF

**BOX 7-3** **Vicki Rock: Hypnosis and defendants**

All the court decisions and changes in state laws described in the text refer to the hypnosis of witnesses, usually victims of a crime. What if a defendant who is charged with a crime claims he or she cannot remember what happened at a crucial time? Then, if the defendant is hypnotized before the trial and "remembers" facts that would help prove his or her innocence, should this testimony be admitted into evidence?

The U.S. Supreme Court faced this question in the case of *Rock v. Arkansas* (1987). Vicki Lorene Rock had been convicted of manslaughter in the shooting of her husband, Frank, in 1983 and was sentenced to ten years in prison. After the shooting, she could remember that she and her husband had been arguing, that he pushed her against a wall, and that she wanted to leave the house but he wouldn't let her. She recalled clutching the gun because she thought it would keep him from hitting her again. She also recalled phoning the police, who ar-

rived to find Frank lying on the floor, a bullet in his chest.

Only after Vicki had been hypnotized was she able to recall that she had not put her finger on the gun's trigger, that her husband had grabbed her from behind, that they struggled, and that the gun went off by accident. As a result of this new information, Vicki's attorney hired a gun expert to examine the handgun. This investigation revealed that the weapon was defective and prone to fire when hit, even without the trigger being pulled.

The judge at Mrs. Rock's trial, following the law in Arkansas, refused to let jurors hear anything Vicki remembered as a result of being hypnotized. In her appeal, Mrs. Rock contended that this ruling denied her the opportunity to present evidence crucial to her defense.

Note the dilemma facing the U.S. Supreme Court: On the one hand, hypnosis "is not generally regarded by the scientific community as reliable" (to quote the Ar-

kansas attorney general), and recent rulings had restricted its application. On the other hand, a defendant has a Fourteenth Amendment constitutional right to due process; in this case, the defendant's defense depended on the recollection of events that she could not remember before she was hypnotized.

The Supreme Court ruled 5–4 in favor of Mrs. Rock and struck down the Arkansas law prohibiting all hypnotically refreshed testimony. Mrs. Rock was granted a new trial. In the majority opinion, Justice Harry Blackmun acknowledged that hypnosis may produce "incorrect recollections" but said that the Arkansas court decision excluding all hypnotically refreshed testimony per se was "arbitrary." However, the decision did not open the door to all types of hypnotically enhanced testimony: Blackmun wrote, "We express no opinion on the admissibility of previously hypnotized witnesses other than criminal defendants."

◆ Box 7-3 for a summary of the facts of this case), in which the Court held that an automatic ban against hypnotically refreshed testimony violated previously hypnotized defendants' rights to testify on their own behalf.

By holding that hypnotically aided testimony is not to be automatically excluded, the *Rock* court reached a conclusion that is similar to the *Hurd* approach, in which each case is examined on the

merits of how the hypnosis was conducted. Many courts now follow the approach of *Rock* and decide whether to admit hypnotically assisted testimony based on the totality of the circumstances surrounding its use.

Law enforcement officials and victims of crime argue that it is unfair to permit defendants to have their memories refreshed by hypnosis but to deny this opportunity to prosecution witnesses.

At the same time, the evidence about the potentially biasing effects of hypnosis is becoming more and more persuasive, so we would not expect a large swing in the direction of relaxing the admissibility standards for hypnotically aided testimony.

In summary, although it generates additional information that the police can check out, hypnosis also increases the risks of inaccurate recall. Given the inconsistent court rulings, what can we say about the wisdom of relying on hypnotically aided memory?

The best use of hypnosis is during the early stages of a criminal investigation. Hypnosis can help witnesses provide clues: a license number, a piece of clothing, a description of a gun. These leads, even if they don't pan out, are better than no clues at all. At the first stage of a criminal investigation, inaccurate "facts" are not as damaging as they are at a trial.

Less desirable is the use of hypnosis by the police to *verify* previously obtained information, especially if such verification involves leading questions. Even riskier—in fact, undesirable—is to hypnotize a witness who has given several different stories in order to learn the "true" story. This step will simply fix in the witness's mind one particular version of the testimony, which he or she then will faithfully produce on demand.

If a witness is hypnotized during the investigatory phase, whatever is learned from that procedure should not be used as evidence in a trial. The American Medical Association has advocated the position that hypnotically induced memories are not accurate enough to be allowed on the witness stand. This seems a wise conclusion.

A potential substitute for hypnosis is a procedure called *context reinstatement* (Geiselman, Fisher, MacKinnon, & Holland, 1985), also referred to as a **cognitive interview** (McCauley & Fisher, 1995). Instead of a standard interview ("Tell me what happened"), witnesses participating in context reinstatement are encouraged to re-create the scene mentally and report everything they can remember. The interviewer may ask them to think about the surroundings, the smells and sound, the temperature, the location of the furniture, or anything else that may elicit new memories. The interviewer may suggest that they recall events in a reverse order or that they try to reexperience the moods they originally felt. All these activities help reinstate the context in which the crime occurred in the hopes that additional memories may appear spontaneously. Preliminary analyses show that interviews using context reinstatement lead to more recall than do standard interviews (Appavoo & Gwynn, 1996; O'Rourke et al., 1989), with fewer confabulations than in hypnosis (Fisher & Quigley, 1989; Leary, 1988).

# The Eyewitness in the Courtroom

Despite limitations in the reliability of their identifications, eyewitnesses are one of the most influential resources the prosecuting attorney uses to convict defendants in criminal trials. Jurors put a great deal of weight on testimony from an eyewitness. In a study showing this influence, Loftus (1974) gave subjects a description of an armed robbery that had resulted in two deaths. Of mock jurors who heard a version of the case that contained only circumstantial evidence against the defendant, 18% convicted him. But when an eyewitness's identification of the defendant was presented as well, 72% of the mock jurors convicted him. A third group of mock jurors was told that the eyewitness had very poor vision (20/400) and was not wearing eyeglasses on the day of the crime; still, 68% of the mock jurors found the defendant guilty! It is hard to overestimate the power of confident eyewitnesses to convince a jury of the correctness of their testimony.

Psychological research shows that jurors overestimate just how accurate eyewitnesses are. In one study, Wells, Lindsay, and Ferguson (1979) staged a "theft" under viewing conditions that were good, moderate, or poor for witnesses. As you might expect, eyewitnesses did a better job when the viewing conditions were good: 74% of them were accurate, compared with 50% in the moderate viewing conditions and 33% in the poor viewing conditions. Then, some mock jurors watched these eyewitnesses being cross-examined, after which the jurors indicated whether they believed the eyewitnesses. Belief rates for the good, the moderate, and the poor witnessing conditions were, respectively, 69%, 57%, and 58%. Thus, when the viewing conditions are only so-so or poor, jurors tend to overestimate how accurate the witnesses are.

Jurors overestimate the validity of eyewitnesses' testimony because they appear to be unaware of several of the factors that compromise eyewitness accuracy. For example:

◆ Jurors have little awareness of the factors that interfere with accurate retention, such as weapon focus, amount of violence in a criminal event, effects of prior exposures, and so on (Cutler, Penrod, & Dexter, 1990).

◆ Jurors show a lack of sophistication about the problems of typical lineups and photo spreads used by the police to test witness recognition (Cutler et al., 1990; Loftus & Wagenaar, 1990).

◆ Finally, jurors are usually not told about those eyewitnesses who could not identify a suspect; even the defendant's attorney may not be aware of these misses (Wells & Lindsay, 1980).

We also know that jurors pay attention to factors that may not help them distinguish accurate from inaccurate eyewitness testimony. One of these factors is the consistency in the eyewitness's reports. When asked whether various aspects of the eyewitness's testimony were indicative of accuracy, a group of 69 potential jurors tended to believe that a witness whose statement was inconsistent with previous statements was inaccurate (Brewer, Potter, Fisher, Bond, & Luszcz, 1999). Unfortunately, consistency is *not* related to identification accuracy, so jurors should probably not rely on inconsistencies as a basis for devaluing eyewitness testimony (Fisher & Cutler, 1996).

Jurors also put too much emphasis on witnesses' statements about the confidence of their identifications. In fact, Cutler, Penrod, and Stuve (1988) found that, for laypersons, the witness's level of confidence was the most important criterion for judging truthfulness. As we discuss in detail later, an eyewitness's confidence is not a strong indication of accuracy (Penrod & Cutler, 1995).

# Safeguards against Mistaken Identification

Much of the eyewitness research is motivated by a desire to increase the accuracy of eyewitnesses. If the validity of eyewitness testimony can be improved (careful adherence to the Department of Justice guidelines would certainly help), then there would be no need to caution jurors and judges about the potential fallibility of eyewitnesses (Seelau & Wells, 1995). Until that time, though, it would seem that truth would be better served if there were a means by which jurors and judges could be alerted and educated about some of the problems inherent in eyewitness reports. There are three ways this might be done.

## *Evaluating the Effectiveness of Cross-Examination*

First, eyewitnesses can be cross-examined in an attempt to reveal factors that might compromise their identification. But as we described earlier, studies of cross-examination suggest that this technique is not especially effective in increasing juror sensitivity to the factors that can affect eyewitness performance. For cross-examination to be effective, the following conditions must all be met:

1. Attorneys must have access to the information necessary to effectively cross-examine the eyewitness, including the conditions under which the crime was committed. Unfortunately, like everyone else, attorneys are forced to rely on the witness's memory of the crime, the perpetrator, and the conditions under which the crime

was committed. The quality of the information available to attorneys depends on the witness's memory and willingness to cooperate (Penrod & Cutler, 1999).

2. Attorneys must have knowledge of the factors that potentially influence eyewitnesses' performance. Do attorneys have this knowledge? In a survey designed to assess attorneys' knowledge of the factors that influence eyewitness identification accuracy, Brigham and Wolfskeil (1983) found that factors such as retention interval, the effect of disguises, weapon focus, and the suggestiveness of certain identification tests were generally not deemed important to identification accuracy. If attorneys are not aware of the results of empirical research studies, they may simply ask the wrong questions.

3. Judges and juries must be made aware during the trial, and discuss during the deliberations, the factors that influence the reliability of an eyewitness's memory (Penrod & Cutler, 1999). Cross-examination will only be effective if judges and jurors are sensitive to the factors that influence eyewitness performance. We have already seen that without guidance, jurors are often unable to discriminate between accurate and inaccurate eyewitness reports. How can jurors become better informed about the factors that influence eyewitness performance?

Two further remedies have been proposed. One solution would be to allow psychologists who are knowledgeable about the relevant research on perception and memory to testify to juries about their findings. As a second remedy, judges could instruct juries about potential weaknesses of eyewitness identifications and suggest how to interpret this testimony. We describe these two alternatives next.

## Evaluating the Testimony of Psychologists

Psychologists could have much to say to jurors about experimental research on eyewitness testimony: that eyewitnesses are sometimes inaccu-

rate, that extreme stress usually inhibits accurate and complete encoding, that the presence of a weapon deflects attention from the offender's appearance, that extremely confident eyewitnesses are not necessarily accurate, that differences in the way lineups are formed and presented to witnesses affect eyewitness accuracy, and that jurors' ability to discriminate between accurate and inaccurate identification is poor. Notice that the expert witness does not tell the jury what to believe about a particular eyewitness or whether the eyewitness is accurate. Even the eyewitness cannot always know this with certainty. Rather, the expert's task is to provide the jury with a scientifically based frame of reference within which to evaluate the eyewitness's evidence.

But as noted in Chapter 2, psychologists are sometimes not allowed to testify about these matters, and appellate courts have generally upheld such decisions. The decision is up to the presiding judge—another example of the breadth of discretion present in the legal system. This discretion challenges the goal of equality because sometimes psychologists are denied the right to testify in cases that are almost identical to others in which expert testimony is admitted.

Judges have usually been reluctant to let psychological experts testify for several reasons (Leippe, 1995). First, some judges believe that scientific research on eyewitness identification is not sufficiently established to provide valid research findings. As noted in Chapter 2, a few psychologists agree with this opinion (e.g., Egeth, 1995; Elliott, 1993; Konecni & Ebbesen, 1986), but most psychologists disagree (Tubb, Kassin, Memon, & Hosch, 2000). Second, judges may believe that such expert testimony would not provide facts that are beyond the common knowledge of most jury members and would therefore invade the province of the jury as finders and triers of fact. (In Chapter 2, we saw an example of such a judge's decision, reflecting the reluctance of the legal profession to yield part of the fact-finding process to other disciplines.) Third, judges fear that admitting such expert testimony would open the gates to conflicting expert testimony, leading to a confusing and uninformative "battle of the experts." (Such battles have occurred in some highly publicized trials involving a criminal defendant's claim of insanity; see Chapter 11.) Finally, judges worry that this type of testimony might lead jurors to give insufficient weight to eyewitness evidence, making them too skeptical of all eyewitnesses (Woocher, 1986). (We return to the question of juror skepticism in a moment.)

Recently, federal courts have become more receptive to expert testimony about eyewitness identification. For example, the courts are more likely to allow such testimony when a prosecutor's case against a defendant relies almost entirely on an eyewitness identification (*United States v. Jordan*, 1996).

One concern about expert testimony is that such testimony may make jurors skeptical of *all* eyewitnesses, even those who witnessed a crime or accident under good viewing conditions and who were not subjected to suggestive identification procedures. Indeed, expert testimony would be most useful if it could sensitize jurors to variations in witnessing and identification procedures that might threaten the reliability of the identifications. But can it have this limited function, or, instead, does it make jurors generally skeptical of all eyewitnesses? Recent studies that improved on earlier methodologies can answer that question (see ◆ Box 7-4).

A report of one actual crime also lends anecdotal support to the conclusion that the testimony of an expert witness has impact. Loftus (1984) described the trial of two Arizona brothers charged with the torture of three Mexicans. Two juries were in the courtroom at the same time, one deciding the verdict for Patrick Hanigan, the other deciding the fate of his brother, Thomas. Most of the evidence was from eyewitnesses, and it was virtually identical for the two defendants. However, expert testimony about the inaccuracy of eyewitnesses was introduced in Thomas's trial only. (The jury hearing Patrick Hanigan's case waited in the jury room while this evidence was presented.) Patrick Hanigan was convicted by one jury; his brother was acquitted by the other. This is as close

to a "natural experiment" as the legal system has come for assessing the influence of a psychologist in the courtroom.

To summarize, the bulk of research examining the effects of expert testimony about eyewitness identifications suggests that such testimony reduces mock juries' belief in eyewitnesses (Leippe, 1995). This increased sensitivity to the factors that influence eyewitness reliability is only a modest effect (Nietzel, McCarthy, & Kern, 1999); mock jurors exposed to expert testimony about the vagaries of eyewitness identifications do not reject all or even most such identifications, but they do tend to view them a bit more critically. Unfortunately, even when allowed, expert testimony is an expensive safeguard that is available in only a small fraction of the cases that come to trial each year (Wells et al., 1998). Are there other, more readily available remedies?

## Evaluating the Effectiveness of Cautionary Jury Instructions

The other major alternative for alerting jurors to the limitations of eyewitnesses is through a judge's instructions. Since the 1970s, both the federal courts and many state courts have encouraged trial judges to alert jurors to the possible mistakes and misinterpretations of eyewitnesses. In *Neil v. Biggers* (1972), the U.S. Supreme Court specified five conditions that jurors should consider in evaluating identification evidence:

1. The opportunity for witnesses to view the criminal at the time of the crime
2. The length of time between the crime and the later identification
3. The level of certainty shown by the witnesses at the identification
4. The witnesses' degree of attention during the crime
5. The accuracy of the witnesses' prior description of the criminal

These conditions were restated and reaffirmed five years later in *Manson v. Braithwaite* (1977).

## The Science of

BOX 7-4   Expert testimony on eyewitness reliability: Untangling confounds

Some early studies (e.g., Fox & Walters, 1986; Hosch, Beck, & McIntyre, 1980) manipulated the presence of expert testimony regarding eyewitnesses in a simulated jury study. Participants in those studies heard testimony from an eyewitness, and some also heard from a defense expert witness about the potential unreliability of eyewitness memory. What effect did the expert have? Generally, the expert testimony resulted in reduced belief in the eyewitness. Unfortunately, because of the design of those early studies, it is hard to know why. Did the expert testimony function to sensitize jurors to the factors that might impair the witness's ability to make a correct identification, or did it cause them to become skeptical of all eyewitnesses? Or were both factors—sensitivity and skepticism—at work? Because these studies did not *independently* vary the presence of expert testimony and evidence about the witness's viewing conditions and identification procedures, we cannot know for sure; sensitivity and skepticism were confounded. Would jurors who heard an expert become distrust-

ful of *all* witnesses (indicating general skepticism) or of only those witnesses whose viewing and identification conditions were poor (indicating sensitivity to the importance of these factors)?

As empirical scientists, psychologists can, and often do, build on the shortcomings of previous studies and refine their methods in order to untangle confusing effects. Brian Cutler and his colleagues were able to do that on the question of juror sensitivity versus skepticism in response to expert testimony on eyewitness reliability.

In perhaps the most comprehensive study of the effects of expert testimony on jurors' judgments, Cutler, Penrod, and Dexter (1989) showed undergraduate subjects a realistic videotaped trial that focused on the accuracy of an eyewitness's identification of an armed robbery defendant. Some subjects heard an expert testify about the effects of eyewitness and identification conditions on accuracy, whereas other jurors heard no expert testimony on these matters. In addition, some mock jurors heard evidence that the wit-

nessing and identification conditions were good, and others heard that they were bad. In other words, the researchers varied the presence of expert testimony and evidence about witnessing and identification factors *independently.*

What do the results say about sensitivity and skepticism? The results indicated that subjects who were exposed to the expert testimony more carefully evaluated the role of various factors (e.g., weapon focus, lineup procedures) on eyewitness reliability than did subjects who didn't hear such testimony. Subjects who heard an expert also gave less weight to the expressed confidence of eyewitnesses (a desirable finding in light of evidence that witness confidence and witness accuracy are only weakly related). These findings suggest that the effect of expert testimony was to generally sensitize jurors to the importance of witnessing and identification conditions. Finally, there was no evidence that mock jurors became more skeptical about the eyewitness when they heard an expert.

Although psychologists were pleased to see the Supreme Court take this action, they did not agree with all its strictures (Wells & Murray, 1983). Research supports consideration of the first two guidelines. The fourth and fifth conditions are plausible; however, limited research has been

done to substantiate the importance of these conditions as contributors to accuracy. It is recommendation 3—to take into account the witnesses' level of certainty—that is most in question as a factor in evaluating identification evidence. A great deal of research has examined the relation between the accuracy of an eyewitness's identification and the confidence expressed by the eyewitness. In an exhaustive review of those studies, Bothwell, Deffenbacher, and Brigham (1987) determined that the average correlation between confidence and accuracy is only 0.25, leading to a general conclusion that the relationship between witness accuracy and confidence is relatively weak. In other words, witnesses who are extremely confident are only somewhat more likely to be accurate than are witnesses who lack confidence.

Many states have followed the Supreme Court's lead in using a cautionary instruction similar to that from *Neil v. Biggers*. The instructions typically mention the eyewitness's degree of certainty as one of the factors that jurors should use to assess accuracy. Here we have another example of the conflict (discussed in Chapter 1) between the law and social science as ways of establishing truth.

Cautionary instructions have not been universally accepted in the courts. Some individual judges are reluctant to use such instructions. The defense typically requests that the instruction be given, but judges sometimes refuse. One reason is the concern that these instructions intrude on the jury's task. When asked whether they would use a cautionary instruction on eyewitness reliability in their courts, 78% of the judges polled said that it was improper to give to the jury. Only 12% approved; 10% did not respond (Greene, 1988). Disapproving judges felt that the instruction commented on the evidence too much and tended to take the decision out of the jury's hands.

What effects do cautionary instructions have on jurors' beliefs about eyewitness accuracy? One study compared the effectiveness of the so-called *Telfaire* instruction, a frequently used instruction based on the case of *U.S. v. Telfaire* (1972), and a set of instructions modeled after typical expert testimony regarding eyewitness reliability (Ramirez, Zemba, & Geiselman, 1996). The researchers were interested in the sensitivity versus skepticism concerns that we mentioned with regard to expert psychological testimony. The *Telfaire* instruction

reduced mock jurors' sensitivity to eyewitness evidence (probably because that instruction mentions only vague directives with little indication as to how jurors should evaluate the evidence) and produced either skepticism or overbelief in the eyewitness, depending on the timing of the instruction. An instruction that incorporated information likely to be delivered by an expert preserved jurors' sensitivity to the factors that influence eyewitness reliability, however.

One might think that judges should be willing to issue an instruction that apparently increases sensitivity to important witnessing conditions and that does not simultaneously cause jurors to question the truthfulness of *all* eyewitnesses. In general, though, judges will not deliver an instruction that provides the kind of detail that is inherent in expert testimony on eyewitness reliability. As a result, most jurors are not informed about the possibility of suggestive lineup procedures, weapon focus, the debilitating effects of stress on eyewitness memory, and a host of other factors that reduce the accuracy of eyewitness reports.

# Children as Witnesses

Sometimes a child is the only witness to a crime—or its only victim. Even in some civil cases, the only dispassionate observers to accidents may be children. A number of questions arise in cases in which children are witnesses. Is it appropriate for children to be asked about the precise details of these incidents? Is it appropriate for them to testify in a courtroom? Can children distinguish between fact and fantasy? Do young children know what it means to take an oath to tell the truth? Is it therapeutic for children to testify against people who may have hurt them?

In keeping with the initial dilemma posed at the beginning of this book, society's desire for criminals to be prosecuted and punished demands that all relevant witnesses be allowed to testify, but defendants also have the right not to be convicted on the basis of inaccurate testimony. Can we guarantee that right when the witnesses to crimes are children?

Two separate concerns emerge here: One deals with the accuracy of children as witnesses, and the other relates to threats to their well-being by subjecting them to the stress of testifying in court. We discuss the potentially traumatic impact of testifying later in this chapter and now turn to the issue of whether child witnesses are reliable.

## The Reliability of Children's Reports

Children may be called on to identify kidnappers and abuse perpetrators or to describe what they witnessed regarding other crimes. To test children's eyewitness capabilities, researchers have begun to test children's memory under conditions that closely match real-life events. In these studies, children typically interact with an unknown adult for some period of time in a school classroom or a doctor's office. They are later questioned about what they experienced and what the target person looked like, and they may attempt to make an identification from a lineup. Some of these studies have been designed to probe for memories of bodily touching and insinuations of sexual abuse. Of course, the challenge for researchers is to ask questions about sexual actions in an ethically permissible way.

Two general findings emerge from these studies. First, children's narrative accounts are more accurate when they participate in an incident rather than merely observe it (Tobey & Goodman, 1992). Second, children over the age of 6 can make reasonably reliable identifications from lineups provided that the perpetrator is actually in the lineup and that the child had extended contact with the perpetrator (Gross & Hayne, 1996). Yet, many of the factors that influence adult eyewitnesses—stress, weapon focus, leading questions—affect child witnesses as well. In fact, children are generally less accurate than adults when making an identification from a lineup in which the suspect is absent. In these situations, children are more likely than adults to select someone—usually a

foil—from the lineup, thereby making a false positive error (Lindsay, Pozzulo, Craig, Lee, & Corber, 1997). Such mistakes are troubling to the criminal justice system because they discourage police and prosecutors from using the identification evidence of a child witness in subsequent investigations.

Psychologists have attempted to devise identification procedures for children that will maintain identification accuracy when the suspect is present in the lineup but reduce false-positive choices when the suspect is absent. Unfortunately, training tasks and instructions about the risk of false identifications and the importance of choosing no one rather than making a false identification have not been effective in reducing false-positive selections (Pozzulo & Lindsay, 1997). Children tend to make false identifications even when viewing a sequential lineup (Lindsay et al., 1997). One procedure that has shown some success is the elimination lineup, in which witnesses are asked to eliminate all but one lineup member before being asked whether that person is the perpetrator. Elimination lineups decreased false-positive responding in a group of 10- to 14-year-old children without significantly affecting correct identification rates (Pozzulo & Lindsay, 1999).

## Children as Witnesses in Sexual Abuse Cases

The concern about the role of children as witnesses is perhaps most vexing in cases of child sexual abuse. Reflecting society's increased awareness of the problems of violence and abuse suffered by children, accusations of child sexual abuse increased dramatically in the 1980s and early 1990s. One conservative estimate is that there was an 83% increase in the number of sexually abused children between 1986 and 1993 (Sedlak & Broadhurst, 1996). (However, this trend may now be reversing: In 1994, there were 141,628 substantiated reports of child sexual abuse, whereas the figure for 1995 was reduced to 126,095 [U.S. Department of Health and Human Services, National Center on Child Abuse and Neglect, 1996; 1997]. This is still an enormous number and one that almost certainly underestimates the severity of the problem because many cases of abuse are never reported.)

Prompted by increased recognition of the incidence of child sexual abuse, most states and many countries in the Western world revised their criminal procedures to deal more effectively with the unique victims of this crime (Bottoms & Goodman, 1996; Myers, 1996). The most important procedural change has been a relaxing of the standards that had previously prevented many children from testifying in criminal or civil cases (Bruck, Ceci, & Hembrooke, 1998). So, for example, many jurisdictions have eliminated the competency requirement for child witnesses, allowing children as young as 3 or 4 to testify in court. Others now admit the uncorroborated testimony of a child victim in cases involving alleged sexual abuse. Still other reforms include allowing children who might be traumatized by the experience of testifying in court to testify instead via closed-circuit TV and to allow an adult to relay the child's story in court as hearsay evidence.

Two psychologists who have written extensively about the problems associated with child witnesses are Stephen Ceci and Maggie Bruck (Ceci & Bruck, 1995; Bruck et al., 1998). They contend that giving children their day in court has opened up a Pandora's box of questions about the reliability and credibility of child witnesses. Ceci and Bruck are not alone in their concern about the truthfulness of children involved in the legal system. Indeed, the reliability of children's testimony is now one of the "hot" empirical questions in the field of psychology and law (Bottoms & Goodman, 1996; McGough, 1994; Zaragoza et al., 1995).

Of prime concern is the extent to which children's reports can be influenced by suggestive interviewing techniques. This concern is most acute in cases of sexual abuse—as opposed to cases involving physical abuse or other forms of violence—because sexual abuse cases typically lack any physical evidence. (The typical forms of sexual abuse perpetrated on children are fondling, exhibitionism, and oral copulation.) Child sexual abuse cases often rest solely on the words of the victim. In some cases, the use of suggestive interviewing techniques may elicit false reports. Many people have speculated that suggestive questioning led to the notorious allegations of bizarre and ritualistic abuse in day care centers across the country in the 1980s, including the McMartin Preschool in California, Little Rascals Day Care Center in North Carolina, Wee Care Day Nursery in New Jersey, Old Cutler Presbyterian Day Care in Florida, and the Fells Acres Daycare Center in Massachusetts (see ◆ Box 7-5).

The problem of underreporting child sexual abuse is compounded by overreporting of abuse based on false allegations or false suspicions. Estimates of false-positive cases (cases in which a defendant is falsely accused of committing sexual abuse) range from 5% to 35% (Poole & Lindsay, 1998), suggesting that up to one-third of all claims of child sexual abuse may be invalid.

## Suggestive Interviewing Techniques

How can suggestive interviewing techniques lead to the false claim of child sexual abuse? In its decision in the Kelly Michaels case (*State v. Michaels,* 1994; Box 7-5), the New Jersey Supreme Court reasoned that the interrogations of the children revealed a lack of impartiality on the part of the interviewers and many instances in which children were asked leading questions that furnished information the children themselves had never mentioned. Consider the following exchange between an investigator and R.F., a 3-year-old girl:

*Detective:* Do you think Kelly can hurt you?
*R.F.:* No.
*Detective:* Did Kelly say she can hurt you? Did Kelly ever tell you she can turn into a monster?
*R.F.:* Yes.
*Detective:* What did she tell you?
*R.F.:* She was gonna turn into a monster.

Or this conversation between an investigator and B.M., a 6-year-old boy:

*Investigator:* I want to ask you something.

## THE CASE OF

**BOX 7-5**  **Margaret Kelly Michaels: Real or surreal?**

When 26-year-old Margaret Kelly Michaels resigned from her job at the Wee Care Nursery School in Maplewood, New Jersey on April 26, 1985, to take a better-paying position, she probably thought that her connection to Wee Care was over. Little could she have imagined the story that was about to unfold.

Four days later, while having his temperature taken rectally at a doctor's office, a 4-year-old former student of Michaels told the nurse, "That's what my teacher does to me at school." That afternoon, the boy's mother notified child protective services. Two days after that the boy was questioned by a prosecutor. During the course of the interview he inserted his finger into the rectum of an anatomical doll (a tool used by pro-

fessionals to help reluctant children enact sexual acts that were allegedly perpetrated on them) and stated that two other boys had also had their temperatures taken this way. Although neither boy confirmed this claim, one of them stated that Michaels had touched his penis. After the first child's mother disclosed her son's allegations to a member of the school board, this father questioned his own son, who reported that Michaels had touched his penis with a spoon.

The Wee Care Nursery distributed a letter to all parents, alerting them to the investigation of a former employee regarding "serious allegations made by a child." The school also invited parents to a talk given by a social worker who encouraged parents to examine

their children for genital soreness and to notice any incidents of bed wetting, masturbation, nightmares, or other changes in behavior.

Various therapists and investigators interviewed the children and their families over the next two months to determine the extent of the abuse. Many of the children were interviewed multiple times and, after persistent questioning, began to disclose some bizarre and horrifying details: that Michaels had licked peanut butter off their genitals, played the piano while nude, made children drink her urine and eat her feces, and raped children with knives, forks, spoons, and Lego blocks. These acts had allegedly occurred during regular school hours over the course of seven months. (Surprisingly, the acts had not been re-

---

B.M.: No.

*Investigator:* Don't be a baby. You're acting like a nursery school kid. Come here. Come here . . . we're not finished yet. Sit down.

B.M.: No.

*Investigator:* Come here. Seriously, we are going to need your help on this.

B.M.: No I'm not.

*Investigator:* How do you think she hurt boys and girls, with a fork? A fork in the face? Sticking on the legs? The arms or on the neck? Does that hurt?

Notice the suggestive nature of these last questions. The technique of **suggestive questioning** involves introducing new information into the in-

terview that the child has not already provided. Psychologists have known for many years that suggestive questions reduce children's accuracy (Cunningham, 1988) and now know that children become somewhat less susceptible to suggestion as they grow older (Cassel & Bjorklund, 1995). Keep in mind, however, that even adults are susceptible to suggestion, as we noted earlier in this chapter.

In the wake of the highly publicized cases of child sexual abuse in the 1980s and 1990s, researchers have focused considerable attention on how children's reports can be influenced by suggestive questioning. In particular, they have attempted to lend an empirical eye to the interview process itself in order to discover how various in-

ported by the children to their parents or noticed by other staff at the time they were alleged to have occurred; neither did any parents report unusual behavior, genital soreness, or any sign of urine or feces on their children at the time.) Even after three grand juries had convened and determined that the case should go to trial, the interviewing continued. One interviewer conducted five group therapy sessions with the children and assessed or treated 13 of the 20 children allegedly involved in the case. The children were also interviewed on multiple occasions by prosecutors and the prosecution's expert witness.

On August 2, 1988, Margaret Kelly Michaels was convicted of 115 counts of sexual abuse against 20 three- to five-year-old children

and was sentenced to 47 years in prison. She served 5 years of her sentence before her conviction was reversed on grounds that the interrogations of the children were coercive and highly suggestive. Ultimately, the Supreme Court of New Jersey ruled that if the prosecution decided to retry the case, they must first show at a pretrial "taint hearing" that despite the suggestive nature of the children's interviews, their statements were still reliable. In December 1994, the prosecution dropped all charges against Michaels. Ironically, though, when Michaels tried several years later to sue the Essex County prosecutors who had so badly botched the investigatory stages of the case, a judge ruled that Michaels can't hold prosecutors liable for abiding by the law

as they reasonably believed it to be. The judge noted that although the prosecutor's office had no internal instructions for interviewing child witnesses and few other guidelines for prosecutors to follow, they acted reasonably in light of the information they possessed at the time.

Still, the Michaels case, and other infamous child sex-abuse scandals of the 1980s, have forever changed the way that investigators question children. Several states now have laws on interviewing that limit the number of interviews and encourage the use of multidisciplinary teams to investigate and prosecute cases.

terviewing techniques can mold a child's responses. Although suggestive questioning is probably not the norm, it can have profound effects on a child's memory when it is used.

One factor that characterizes suggestive interviewing is **interviewer bias.** When interviewers have some preconceived notions about the occurrence or nonoccurrence of a certain event, they can frame their questions to elicit responses from the child that are consistent with their prior beliefs. Biased interviewers would probably not ask children open-ended questions such as "What happened?" Rather, they would use specific questions that presuppose the answer. The question asked of a child in the Michaels case is a good example: "How do you think she hurt boys and girls,

with a fork?" If the child does not immediately provide the expected answer, he or she may be repeatedly questioned until that answer is given (Ceci, Bruck, & Rosenthal, 1995).

**Social influence** can also play a role in these interviews. Regardless of the precise nature of the questions, the manner in which those questions are asked can vary greatly. Some interviewers may be warm and supportive; others may be hostile and intimidating. Although children interviewed by a highly supportive interviewer may be more resistant to leading questions than those interviewed in an environment of intimidation (Carter, Bottoms, & Levine, 1996), highly supportive interviewers can lose their impartiality if they begin selectively to reinforce statements that are consistent with their beliefs and ignore statements that are inconsistent. This can happen when the interviewer gives praise, rewards, approval, or agreement to a child who says something desirable and expresses disappointment when a child says something that is undesirable.

Yet another technique that can be used by professional interviewers involves **guided imagery** or memory work. An interviewer may first ask a child to try to remember whether a certain event occurred and then to pretend that the event *did* occur and to create a mental picture that provides details about the event. The concern here is that interviewers may ask children to imagine events that had not been reported by the children but that are suspected by the interviewer. The very act of imagining may make the event seem real (Garry & Polaschek, 2000).

At this point you may wonder whether investigative interviews of children really encompass these practices. Do interviewers really reward children who provide the desired answer and chastise those who don't? Do they really ask child witnesses to imagine events that the children themselves have never been reported? Apparently the answer is yes. Bruck and her colleagues (1998) describe their analysis of interview transcripts provided to them by attorneys, judges, parents, and medical and mental-health professionals who had concerns about the suggestive nature of a particular interview and its potential impact on a child's report. Although Bruck and colleagues acknowledge that their sample may not be representative of the vast number of interviews conducted with children, still their description is concerning. Other evidence suggests that interviewers sometimes do use specific and leading questions and introduce information into the interview that the child had not volunteered (Lamb, et al., 1996; Warren, Woodall, Hunt, & Perry, 1996). Interviews conducted in the McMartin Preschool case and the Kelly Michaels day care case included several suggestive procedures (see ◆ Box 7-6).

Obviously, not all interviews contain elements of suggestive questioning, and many interviewers are careful to avoid the controversial techniques we have described. What's more, professionals who interview, assess, and treat children have begun to receive training in interviewing techniques, child development, or both. But still more needs to be done. Some of the training programs have apparently fallen short (Doris, Mazur, & Thomas, 1995), and many interrogators lack up-to-date information about the latest scientific findings related to interviewing. Unfortunately, until professionals are familiar with this field of research and begin to incorporate that knowledge into their practices, we will continue to wonder about the competence of the interviewers and the reliability of the children's testimony.

## The Child Witness in the Courtroom

Although only a small percentage of sexual abuse cases filed with police actually result in a trial (many more end in admissions of guilt or plea bargains), tens of thousands of children have to testify in sexual abuse trials each year. Interestingly, a disproportionate number of them may be preschool children. In one study of child witnesses in sexual abuse cases, although only 18% of these cases involved children 5 years old or younger, 41% of all the cases that went to trial involved children of this age (Gray, 1993).

The traditional legal view of children, supported by early research that focused on children's *in*capacities, was that young children were not reliable witnesses because they had limited memory capabilities and could not distinguish truth from falsehood or fact from fantasy. So, for many years, American courts were reluctant to accept the uncorroborated statements of child witnesses. As a result, children under a certain age were not permitted to testify in court (Perry & Wrightsman, 1991). More recently, developmental psychologists have suggested that those early studies may have underestimated children's abilities because of the unnecessarily complicated assessment tasks that they used (Saywitz & Lyon, 1998). In fact, it appears that children as young as 3 years of age may be able to show that they understand the meaning of truth and lying if they can demonstrate that understanding in an age-appropriate way. Now, most jurisdictions allow children to testify regard-

## The Science of

**BOX 7-6  Content analyses and the interrogation of children**

Much of psychology proceeds by way of the experimental method: Research psychologists like to manipulate variables and measure outcomes. Psychologists who study the reliability of children's testimony are no different; many experimental studies have been conducted in recent years that manipulate the conditions under which children are questioned and measure their responses (Garven, Wood, & Malpass, 2000; Leichtman & Ceci, 1995; Schwartz-Kenney & Goodman, 1999). But there are other, complementary ways to understand what children remember and what they report about their experiences.

One such method, termed **content analysis,** involves careful, sometimes painstaking, analysis of the content of a discussion or a conversation. Some scholars of the jury have conducted sophisticated analyses of the content of mock jury deliberations, and psychologists interested in child interviewing techniques have begun to do the same with transcribed interviews of actual child witnesses. Content analyses of these interviews can provide a rich and complex picture of the techniques

used by interviewers to question children and can show us how the children think about and talk about these issues.

A group of researchers at the University of Texas in El Paso has undertaken a content analysis of 14 interview transcripts from the McMartin Preschool case, 20 interviews from the Kelly Michaels day care case, and 20 interviews from a child protective service (J. Wood, personal communication, April 20, 2000; Wood et al., 1998). The goal of the study was to assess the possibility that the allegations of ritualistic abuse that arose in the McMartin and Michaels cases could have been induced by suggestive interviewing techniques.

To measure the type of interviewing techniques that were used in these three situations, Wood and his colleagues coded each exchange (they defined an exchange as one interviewer "turn" in the interview transcript, followed by one child "turn"). They then scored each exchange for the presence or absence of several interviewing techniques, including

◆ positive consequences (giving, promising, or implying praise,

approval, or other reward to a child),

◆ negative consequences (criticizing or disagreeing with a child's statement),

◆ inviting speculation (asking the child to offer opinions or speculations about past events or to use imagination or solve a mystery), and

◆ suggestiveness (introducing information into the interview that goes substantially beyond what the child has already said).

Using this framework, Wood and his colleagues found that the interviews conducted in the McMartin case were characterized by positive consequences (19% of all exchanges), inviting speculation (8%), and suggestiveness (18%). Interviews in the Michaels case tended to involve positive consequences (10% of all exchanges), negative consequences (17%), and suggestiveness (18%). Contrast these numbers with interviews by child protective service: 7% of exchanges contained positive consequences, 4% implied negative consequences, 2% were suggestive, and less than 1% invited speculation.

less of the nature of the crime or the child's age and expect that juries will accord the child's testimony its appropriate weight.

How *do* jurors perceive child witnesses? Do they tend to doubt the truthfulness of children's testimony, reasoning that children often make things up and leave things out? Or do they tend

to "believe the children," as a popular bumper sticker would like us to do? To what extent do these impressions vary with the age and demeanor of the child witness and with the type of case?

In mock jury studies, child bystander witnesses are generally viewed as less credible than adult bystander witnesses, although the age of the witness apparently does not influence judgments of the defendant's guilt (Goodman, Golding, Helgeson, Haith, & Michelli, 1987). But something quite different happens in child sexual abuse cases. Here, younger victims are viewed as *more* credible than adolescents or adults, probably because jurors suspect that younger children lack the sexual knowledge to fabricate an allegation (Bottoms & Goodman, 1994).

## Procedural Modifications When Children Are Witnesses

We have already noted many issues related to the reliability of children's testimony. An equally troubling concern is the effect *on the child* of having to discuss these difficult issues in court. What happens when young children are scrutinized in court? Having to talk about atrocities in a public setting may increase the trauma for many children. Some children can, in private session, describe in graphic detail how they were abused. But when these children are put in a courtroom full of strangers, a judge in a long black robe, a jury, and the person accused of harming them, they often become speechless, evasive, or immobilized by fear (Goodman et al., 1992). They may feel that they are being made victims all over again. Especially when children know their abuser, they may experience tremendous conflict. They may be frightened by an attacker who has threatened them with further abuse. Defense lawyers may try to intimidate the child. In fact, one study found that 8- to 10-year-olds interviewed in a courtroom had poorer memory performance and gave higher stress ratings than children questioned at their school (Saywitz & Nathanson, 1993).

These concerns have been addressed in various ways. One strategy, allowed in 40 states, is to excuse the child from testifying and to introduce the evidence of abuse through **hearsay testimony** by a parent, physician, psychologist, teacher, police officer, or social worker who repeats the out-of-court statements that the child has previously made about the abuse. Typically, hearsay evidence is not admissible at trial; a witness cannot simply repeat another person's out-of-court statements. An exception to this general rule (and there are many) is made in cases in which children are victims (*Idaho v. Wright*, 1990). Suppose, for example, that a child reported to his father, "A man touched my private parts in the bathroom at the park." If the father were to repeat that statement in court to prove that the child had been abused, the child's words are hearsay. But under the child hearsay exception, the statement can be admitted into evidence anyway.

What effect do children's out-of-court statements have on jurors' perceptions of the witness's credibility? Previous studies on the impact of hearsay evidence showed that jurors perceive the hearsay witnesses as less credible than victims or witnesses who testify directly about what they experienced (Miene, Park, & Borgida, 1992). Is hearsay evidence also accorded less weight when the victims are children?

This question was addressed by John Myers and his colleagues (Myers, Redlich, Goodman, Prizmich, & Imwinkelried, 1999) in a questionnaire study of 248 jurors (representing 42 juries), all of whom had just served as jurors in child molestation or child exploitation trials. At least one child testified live in court in each of these trials, as did at least one adult who testified about the child's out-of-court disclosure of abuse. Thus, the study allowed for a direct comparison of perceptions of the child witness and the adult-hearsay witness.

In contrast to previous studies, jurors perceived adult-hearsay witnesses as *more* accurate, consistent, and confident than child witnesses. In addition, adult-hearsay witnesses' testimony was judged to be more complete and less likely to have been influenced by the attorneys' questions. One explanation of this finding is that jurors tend not to believe child witnesses who testify about their abuse experiences, favoring instead the testimony of adults to whom the children spoke. Another explanation is that many of the adults were police officers and teachers, who may have been afforded more credibility because of their professional status.

Jurors in these cases were highly attentive to the demeanor of the child witnesses and to the nature of their testimony. The children's facial expressions, gestures, eye contact, nervousness, and articulateness were all influential to jurors' verdicts. By contrast, the adult-hearsay witnesses' mannerisms had no effect on jurors' verdicts.

Another innovation to protect children from the potential stress of testifying is the placement of a one-way screen in front of the defendant so that he or she can't be seen by the child witness while the latter testifies. This type of screen was used in the trial of John Avery Coy, who was convicted of sexually assaulting two 13-year-old girls while they were sleeping outdoors in a tent. At the trial, a screen was placed in front of Coy when the two girls testified. (He was able to see the girls, but they could not see him.) Coy appealed his conviction on two grounds: (1) that the presence of the screen caused the jury to presume that he was guilty and (2) that the screen deprived him of the opportunity to confront the girls face to face. In a 1988 decision, the Supreme Court agreed with Coy about the second claim; by a 6–2 vote, it overturned his conviction, saying that the defendant's Sixth Amendment constitutional right to confront his accusers face to face was not outweighed "by the necessity of protecting the victims of sexual abuse" (*Coy v. Iowa*, 1988).

Justices Blackmun and Rehnquist dissented; they stated that the right to cross-examination (which Coy still had) was central to the Sixth Amendment's confrontation clause, whereas the right to a face-to-face confrontation was only peripheral (Hans, 1988). Their minority opinion reflected their interpretation of psychological research that child victims could be psychologically injured even more by having to testify as they faced their alleged abusers. The dissent also noted that such concerns "may so overwhelm the child as to prevent the possibility of effective testimony, thereby undermining the truth finding function of the trial itself."

In the *Coy* decision, the Court left the door open for a state to use one-way closed-circuit television (CCTV) to present the testimony of a child unable to testify in open court. In the case of *Maryland v. Craig* (1990), the Court upheld a Maryland law permitting such a procedure when the trial court has found that the child is likely to suffer significant emotional distress not just by testifying in court but specifically by being in the presence of the defendant. *Craig* thus modifies the rule of the *Coy* case.

Proponents of CCTV claim that aside from reducing the trauma experienced by the child, this technology will also provide more complete and accurate reports. Opponents claim that the use of CCTV erodes the presumption of innocence (the child witness does not need to be protected from the accused unless the accused is actually guilty) and violates the defendant's right to face-to-face confrontation of witnesses. (The Sixth Amendment right to confrontation is based in part on the assumption that the witness will find it more difficult to lie about the defendant in the presence of that defendant.)

Psychologists have now begun to assess the effects of CCTV when children take the stand. One of the most elaborate studies was conducted by Gail Goodman and her colleagues (Goodman et al., 1998). Each child in this study individually played with an unfamiliar male confederate. In the "defendant guilty" condition, the confederate helped the children place stickers on bare skin (e.g., the children's arm, toes, bellybutton). In the "defendant not guilty" condition, the confederate helped the children place stickers on their clothes. Each child then testified in a separate mock trial held in a courtroom. The child's testimony was presented either live in open court or via CCTV. Mock jurors viewed the trials, rated the child witness and the defendant, and deliberated to a verdict.

The use of CCTV had varying effects: It generally promoted more accurate testimony in children (young children who testified in open court made more errors to leading questions), it reduced the children's pretrial experience of stress, yet it had no effect on the likelihood of conviction or perceptions of fairness to the defendant. Based on these findings alone, one might argue for its use in every case in which a child feels anxious about testifying. But things aren't quite so simple. Children who testified via CCTV were viewed as less believable than children who testified in open court, despite the fact that they were more accurate! It appears as though jurors want to see children in the flesh and blood in order to assess the truthfulness of their reports.

Courts have made several other accommodations in cases in which children must testify. These include providing an advocate for the child who can familiarize the child with the courtroom setting, permitting a support person to sit with the child during testimony, making structural changes to the courtroom, and, on rare occasions, closing the courtroom to the public and the press (Myers, 1996).

Finally, we should note that although testifying has the potential for further trauma to the child, it can also provide a beneficial, therapeutic experience for some children. It can engender a sense of control over events and provide some satisfaction to the child if the defendant is found guilty. As an example, one 15-year-old girl said, "If I, as a young person, were a victim of a sexual abuse or rape case, I would *want* to testify before a full court. I might be scared at first or a little embarrassed, but I'd want to be present to make my assailant look like a complete fool. I'd want to see him convicted—with my own eyes. It would make me stronger" (quoted in Gunter, 1985, p. 12A).

# Repressed and Recovered Memories

Although the retrieval of memories over short time periods is a complex task, these complications pale in comparison to those involved in retrieving memories that have been forgotten over long time periods. Two basic processes need to be distinguished in discussing and understanding long-lost memories. The first is natural forgetting, which tends to occur when people simply do not think about events that happened years earlier. Just as you might have trouble remembering the names of your third- and fourth-grade teachers (or at least remembering which teacher taught which grade), witnesses to crimes, accidents, and business transactions are likely to forget the details of these events, if not the entire event, after the passage of months or years. Such forgetting or misremembering is even more likely when the target event is confused with prior or subsequent events that bear some resemblance to it.

No one disputes the reality of natural forgetting. However, much more controversy exists about a second type of lost memory: those that are presumed to have been repressed over long time periods. These scenarios involve events that are thought to be so traumatizing that, after they are experienced, individuals bury them deeply in their unconscious through a process of emotionally motivated forgetting called **repression.** For example, soldiers exposed to the brutal horrors of combat or citizens experiencing a natural disaster such as an earthquake are sometimes unable to remember the traumas they obviously suffered. In such cases, repression is thought to serve a protective function by sparing the individual from having to remember and relive horrifying scenes. Furthermore, it is often reported that these repressed memories stay unconscious, and hence forgotten, until and unless they are either spontaneously recalled or are retriggered by exposure to some aspect of the original experience such as the smell of gasoline that reminds one of the battlefield or the sight of a cloud formation that resembles the sky's appearance on the day of the earthquake.

A related unconscious process is **dissociation,** in which victims of abuse or other traumas are thought to escape the full impact of an event by psychologically detaching themselves from it. This process is thought to be particularly strong in children who, because they are still forming integrated personalities, find it easier to escape from the pain of abuse by fantasizing about made-up individuals and imagining that the abuse is happening to them. Many clinical psychologists believe that such early episodes of dissociation, involving unique ideas, feelings, and behavior, form the beginning of the altered personalities that are found in dissociative identity disorder (formerly called multiple personality disorder).

## Repressed Memories and Memory Recovery Therapy

In legal circles, the memory controversy that has received the most attention involves a set of claims by adults that they (1) suffered sexual/physical abuse as children (often at the hands of parents), (2) repressed or dissociated any memory of these horrors for many years as a form of unconscious protection, and then (3) recovered the long-lost memories of the abuse, only after entering "memory-focused" psychotherapy that uses techniques such as hypnosis, age regression, sodium amytal (the "truth serum"), guided visualization, diary writing, or therapist instructions to help clients remember past abuse (Lindsay & Read, 1995).

Such "de-repression" techniques have been advocated by popular books on incest (e.g., Bass & Davis, 1988) and by therapists who believe that, unless severe childhood traumas are recalled, confronted, and defused, they will cause mental problems (Blume, 1990). Some therapists who suspect clients of harboring repressed memories of abuse ask the clients highly suggestive questions such as, "You sound like you might have been abused; what can you tell me about that?" or "You show many of the signs of childhood sexual abuse; can you tell me some of the things you think might have happened to you when you were a very young child?" One book explicitly encourages women to believe that they were abused as infants by several perpetrators: "How old do you think you were when you were first abused? Write down the very first number that pops into your head, no matter how improbable it seems to you. . . . Does it seem too young to be true? I assure you it is not" (Fredrickson, 1992, pp. 59–66). In addition to being asked to dredge up memories of traumatic incidents, clients are often encouraged by therapists to join special support groups such as Survivors of Incest Anonymous that urge their members to search aggressively for buried memories of abuse.

Many researchers and therapists question the empirical and clinical validity of repressed memory techniques, especially when apparent memories of trauma resurface many years after the alleged incidents and then only after the individual has been in therapy that first presumes and then finds such memories (Loftus, 1993; Wakefield & Underwager, 1992). These skeptics point out that most people who suffer severe trauma do not forget the event; in fact, many of them suffer intrusive recollections of it for years afterward. Skepticism is also fueled by the fact that some alleged victims claim to have recalled traumas that happened when they were less than 1 year old, a feat contradicted by almost all research on childhood memory and amnesia.

One of the most widely cited studies on this topic confirms that it is possible for people to forget horrible events that happened to them in childhood, but it does not answer the question of how this forgetting occurs or how memories are usually recovered. Linda Williams (1994) interviewed 129 women who had experienced well-documented cases of childhood sexual abuse. She asked these women detailed questions about their childhood abuse histories, which had occurred an average of 17 years earlier. More than one-third of the women did not report the abuse they had experienced in childhood. But this figure does not prove that the forgetting was due to repression. It is possible that when the abuse occurred the women were too young to be fully aware of it; in addition, some of the women might have been unwilling to report sexual abuse to an interviewer, who was a relative stranger, even if they did remember it.

However, what should we make of the sudden recall of events that a person claims to have repressed for years? If recollections of past abuse do not stem from actual traumatic events, where else could they originate? Several sources are possible, including fantasies, distorted recollections, or even the unintentional planting of memories by therapists who try (perhaps too hard) to find reasons for clients' psychological problems.

The possibility that therapy clients can recover memories of childhood abuse that have been long repressed has led many states to pass legislation that allows victims of childhood sexual abuse to bring suit against their attackers long after the alleged abuse occurred. (Typically, all lawsuits must be filed within a prescribed "limitations period" dating from the occurrence of the act that caused harm. The defendant can bar a plaintiff's claim if the complaint was filed too late.) These **delayed reporting statutes** suspend the statute of limitations and grant abuse survivors, who claim to have repressed their memory of abuse and were therefore unaware it occurred, the right to bring a lawsuit within three years from the date of *recovering* the memory.

The fundamental questions are these: Are recovered memories true memories, consisting of vivid, albeit delayed, recalls of past horrors? Or are they pseudomemories, created by needy and suggestible clients responding to overzealous therapists who are trying to find a convincing explanation for their clients' current problems? Even psychologists are deeply divided on these questions. In fact, the Working Group on Investigation of Memories of Childhood Abuse, appointed by the American Psychological Association, was so disunited that the group was forced to issue two reports. One report, written by clinical psychologists (Alpert, Brown, & Courtois, 1998), suggests that intolerable emotional and physical arousal can lead a child victim to use numbing and/or dissociative coping strategies; that these strategies may interfere with or impair encoding, storage, and retrieval of memories, and that numbing responses may lead to delayed recall. A second report, authored by experimental research psychologists (Ornstein, Ceci, & Loftus, 1998), pointed out that suggestibility, memory distortions, and misleading information can work to degrade memory performance; that memory for traumatic experiences can be highly malleable; and that it is relatively easy to create pseudomemories for events that never occurred.

We are not, of course, suggesting that child abuse does not occur. Not only does it occur, but it occurs with horrifying frequency (Finkelhor, 1994), and it appears that children who were abused are at increased risk to suffer mental disorders in adulthood. The real question is whether allegations of childhood abuse that first surface only after intensive searching for them in therapy are trustworthy (Bottoms, Shaver, & Goodman, 1996; Bowers & Farvolden, 1996; Lindsay & Read, 1995).

Can we really be sure that these alleged abuses took place? Is it possible that some memories, especially those that appear to have been repressed for years only then to be recovered through aggressive "memory work" therapy, are imagined or made up? Although it is always difficult to know the authenticity of any one individual's memories, evidence is accumulating that false memories can be implanted, that people can be led through suggestion and misinformation to believe such memories are real, and that third parties such as therapists find it very difficult to distinguish authentic from unauthentic recollections (Loftus, 1993; Loftus & Ketcham, 1994; Ofshe & Watters, 1994). One wonders, for example, about the authenticity of Paul Ingram's memories (see ◆▶ Box 7-7).

## Creating Pseudomemories

In recent years, many psychologists have studied claims of repressed memories and the techniques used to retrieve them. They have used laboratory research and real-life cases to document how memories can be built from the suggestions of others.

One way that psychologists have been able to implant false memories is by enlisting the help of family members who suggest to adult research participants that these relatives recall a fabricated event. For example, with help from participants' relatives, Loftus and Pickrell (1995) constructed a false story that the participant had been lost during a shopping trip at the age of 5, was found crying by an elderly person, and was eventually reunited with family. After reading this story, participants wrote what they remembered about the event. Nearly 30% of participants either partially or fully remembered the made-up event, and 25% claimed that they remembered the fictitious situation in subsequent interviews. Other efforts to

## THE CASE OF

**BOX 7-7** **Paul Ingram: Real memories or fabricated memories?**

The case of Paul Ingram provides one chilling example of how false memories might be created (Ofshe, 1992). Ingram, a sheriff's deputy in Olympia, Washington, was arrested for child abuse in 1988. He steadfastly denied the allegations, but the police continued to question and pressure him over the next five months, despite the lack of much evidence to support the allegations of sexual abuse that two of Ingram's children had lodged against him. To help Ingram's memory, a psychologist or a detective would repeatedly describe to him an act of abuse, such as Ingram and a bunch of other men raping his daughter. At first, Ingram would have no memory for such incidents, but after concerted effort, including praying and being hypnotized to strengthen his memory,

he started "recalling" some details. Ultimately, Paul Ingram confessed not just to the charges of incest but to rapes, assaults, and participation in a satanic cult that was believed to have killed 25 babies (Wright, 1994).

To check the accuracy of Ingram's memory, sociologist Richard Ofshe, hired as a consultant to the prosecution, asked Ingram to recall an event that Ofshe totally fabricated—that Ingram had forced his son and daughter to have sex with each other in front of him. Just as with the police interrogation, Ingram could not remember anything at first, but after thinking and praying about it, he gradually formed images of the event and, within a matter of hours, endorsed a three-page confession to the scene Ofshe had made up.

Ofshe concluded that Paul Ingram was not a sex offender or satanic cult member, but a vulnerable man with a strong need to please authorities and a highly suggestible nature that made him fall easily into a trance.

Ultimately, Paul Ingram decided to plead guilty to six counts of third-degree rape. He is currently in prison and now insists that he never abused his children. Was Paul Ingram duped into confessing on the basis of false memories, or was he a guilt-ridden abuser who finally admitted his guilt? Questions such as these are at the heart of the controversy over whether therapists should aggressively try to help clients recover memories of abuse that they suspect have been repressed.

implant childhood memories have produced similar results, leading subjects to believe such fictitious experiences as being hospitalized overnight for a possible ear infection, attending a wedding reception and accidentally spilling punch on the parents of the bride, and evacuating a grocery store when the overhead sprinkler system erroneously activated (Hyman, Husband, & Billings, 1995; Hyman & Pentland, 1996). People with higher dissociative capacity and hypnotizability are apparently more susceptible to these suggestions than others (Loftus, 1997).

Still other experimental procedures have been used to examine the malleable nature of **autobiographical memory** (memory for one's past experiences). These include guided memory techniques

to plant "impossible" memories about experiences that occurred shortly after birth (Spanos, Burgess, Burgess, Samuels, & Blois, 1999) and interpretation of participants' dreams to suggest that they had experienced a critical childhood event such as being harassed by a bully before the age of 3 (Mazzoni, Loftus, Seitz, & Lynn, 1999). Simply imagining an event from one's past can affect the confidence that it actually occurred (Garry, Manning, Loftus, & Sherman, 1996). How can we account for this "imagination inflation" effect? One possibility stems from the notion of **source confusion.** The act of imagining may make the event seem more familiar, but that familiarity is mistakenly related to childhood memories rather than to the act of imagination itself. Other studies suggest that the frequency of imagining is important: the more times participants imagine a nonexistent event, the more likely they are to report having experienced it (Goff & Roediger, 1998). The creation of false memories is most likely to occur when people who are having trouble remembering are explicitly encouraged to imagine events and discouraged from thinking about whether their constructions are real.

Bear in mind that just because false childhood memories can be implanted in some people, the memories that result from suggestions are not always false. Unfortunately, without corroboration, it is indeed hard to know which distant memories are true and which were implanted via suggestion.

## False Memories in Court

Evidence that false memories are a significant problem for the law comes in two basic forms. First, several accusers have ultimately retracted their claims of repressed memories for abuse. One of the most highly publicized retractions involved a 1993 lawsuit filed by Stephen Cook, who alleged that he had been sexually abused as a teenager 17 years earlier by the late Joseph Bernardin, when he had been archbishop of the Catholic archdiocese in Cincinnati. Cook reported that he had repressed these memories for years only to then recover them while hypnotized as part of therapy. The allegations were forcefully denied by Cardinal Bernardin, who at the time of the lawsuit was the head of Chicago's archdiocese and the senior-ranking Roman Catholic official in the United States. Ironically, Bernardin was well known nationally for his work helping children who had been sexually abused by priests. Cook ultimately dropped the lawsuit after admitting that his charges were based on false memories. He and Bernardin reconciled shortly before Cook died of AIDS in 1995.

A second source of information about false memories comes from court cases in which parents sue therapists who have used aggressive memory recovery techniques to help the adult children of these parents recover supposedly repressed memories of childhood sexual abuse. The claims in

these malpractice lawsuits usually take the following form: (1) the abuse never took place, (2) the therapists created and implanted false memories of abuse through their uncritical use of memory retrieval techniques, and (3) the clients ultimately come to believe the false memories and accuse their parents of the abuse, sometimes suing them under delayed reporting statutes or even filing criminal charges against them.

The first case in which a parent successfully sued a therapist for implanting a false memory of abuse was brought by Gary Ramona, once a highly paid executive at a large winery in Napa County, California. Ramona accused family counselor Marche Isabella and psychiatrist Richard Rose of planting false memories of trauma in his daughter, Holly, while she was their 19-year-old patient. In his suit, Ramona claimed that the therapists told Holly that her bulimia and depression were caused by having been repeatedly raped by her father when she was a child. They also told her, he claimed, that the memory of this molestation was so traumatic that she had repressed it for years. According to Ramona, Dr. Rose then gave Holly sodium amytal to further confirm the validity of her "recovered memory." Finally, Isabella was said to have told Holly's mother that up to 80% of all bulimics had been sexually abused (a statistic for which no scientific support exists).

At their trial, the therapists claimed that Holly suffered flashbacks of what seemed to be real sexual abuse. She also became increasingly depressed and bulimic after reporting these frightening images. In addition, Holly's mother, Stephanie, who had divorced her husband after Holly's allegations came to light, testified that she suspected her husband might have abused Holly. She listed several pieces of supposedly corroborating evidence: that Holly had complained of vaginal pains during childhood, that she always feared gynecological exams and disliked her father touching her, and that Gary had seemed overeager to baby-sit Holly and their two other daughters when they were little. She also recalled once coming home to find young Holly wandering around the house wearing no underwear; she said she found the underwear along with bedsheets in the clothes dryer. During his testimony, Gary Ramona emotionally denied ever sexually abusing his daughter.

The mental-health experts who testified on Ramona's behalf criticized the therapists for using risky and dangerous techniques. Elizabeth Loftus (1993), an expert called by Gary Ramona and a leading critic of therapists who aggressively pursue the recovery of long-buried traumatic memories, charged that these therapists often either suggest the idea of trauma to their clients or are too uncritical in accepting clients' reports of trauma. Another defense witness, Martin Orne, a renowned authority on hypnosis, condemned the use of sodium amytal interviews as "inherently untrustworthy and unreliable" and concluded that Holly's memory had been so distorted by her therapists that she no longer knew what the truth was.

The jury decided that Holly's therapists had, indeed, acted improperly and, in May 1994, awarded Gary Ramona damages in the amount of $500,000. Since then, the number of false memory cases against therapists appears to be growing. In its first two years of operation, the False Memory Syndrome Foundation received more than 13,000 reports from people who said they were victims of false accusations; most were parents whose grown children had charged them with long-past abuse. This organization has also received reports from scores of former therapy patients who admit that their original charges of abuse were false and had resulted from therapists encouraging them to "remember" events that never happened.

The threat of false memory lawsuits adds to the already-difficult challenges therapists face when trying to help adult clients cope with a traumatic childhood. It is obvious that recovered memory therapy has led to very real damage to some clients and their families (Ofshe & Watters, 1994). It is also obvious that the trauma of child abuse does occur and can leave deep and long-lasting emotional scars. Accordingly, therapists must be sympathetic listeners for clients who remember the real horrors of their childhood. At the same time, therapists must be cautious to avoid suggesting that clients' problems come from traumas that might never have happened. In the words of Gary Ramona's attorney, Richard Harrington, "If [therapists] use nonsensical theories about so-called repressed memories to destroy people's lives, they will be held accountable."

# SUMMARY

**1.** *What psychological factors contribute to the risk of mistaken identifications in the legal system?* Evidence produced by eyewitnesses often makes the difference between an unsolved crime and a conviction. In the early stages of a crime investigation, eyewitness accounts can provide important clues and permit suspects to be identified.

But witnesses often make mistakes, and mistaken identifications have led to the conviction of numerous innocent persons. Errors can occur at the moment the crime is committed or at any of the three phases of the memory process: encoding, storage, and retrieval. Furthermore, subsequent questioning and new experiences can alter what has been remembered from the past. Errors can also result from biased identification procedures, unconscious transference or excessive focus on a weapon.

**2.** *How do courts regard the use of hypnotically refreshed memory? What procedures should be followed when using hypnosis in a forensic setting?* The courts have taken different positions about the admissibility of hypnotically induced testimony. Three cautions seem paramount: (1) The hypnosis should be carried out by a psychiatrist or a psychologist (not a police officer) who is unaware of the facts of the case, (2) the procedures should be recorded so that they can be scrutinized by others, and (3) the products of such a hypnosis during the investigation of a crime should either not be used as evidence during the trial or be admitted only under exceptional circumstances. A context-reinstatement technique has recently been suggested as a substitute for forensic hypnosis.

**3.** *How do jurors evaluate the testimony of eyewitnesses, and can psychologists help jurors understand the potential problems of eyewitness testimony?* Psychological tests of eyewitnesses' accuracy conclude that eyewitnesses can be erroneous, although rates of accuracy depend on many factors—some environmental, some personal, and some related to the interval between the crime and the recall. Despite these limitations, jurors are heavily influenced by the testimony of eyewitnesses, and they tend to overestimate the accuracy of such witnesses, relying to a great extent on the confidence of the eyewitness.

To alert jurors to these problems, two types of special interventions have been tried (in addition to the routine use of cross-examination of witnesses). Some trial judges permit psychologists to testify as expert witnesses about the problems in being an accurate eyewitness. Laboratory evaluations of mock juries find that such testimony generally sensitizes jurors to factors that affect an eyewitness's reliability. The other intervention, encouraged by the U.S. Supreme Court and several state courts, is for the judge to give the jurors a "cautionary instruction," sensitizing them to aspects of the testimony of eyewitnesses that they should especially consider.

**4.** *Can children accurately report on their experiences of victimization? What factors affect the accuracy of their reports?* Psychologists are concerned by the possibility that suggestive interviewing techniques can influence the accuracy of a child's report of abuse. When children are questioned in a nonsuggestive manner, asked open-ended questions, and given little or no reinforcement for their answers, the resulting report will be more accurate than if suggestive interrogation procedures are used.

**5.** *What courtroom modifications are used in cases in which children must testify? What effects do these modifications have on jurors?* Many children are anxious about having to testify in a courtroom. The setting is formal and unfamiliar, the children may be asked intimate questions about embarrassing matters, and the alleged perpetrator is present. On occasion, when a child would experience further trauma by testifying, an adult will instead testify about the child's prior out-of-court statements. Jurors tend to put more weight on the adult-hearsay testimony than on the testimony of a child victim/witness. Other modifications include the use of a screen to shield the defendant from the child/victim and closed-circuit TV that allows the child to testify out of the presence of the alleged perpetrator. Although the defendant apparently suffers no ill effects of these protective devices, jurors tend to believe the in-court testimony of a child more than the testimony presented via CCTV.

**6.** *Can memories for trauma be repressed, and, if so, can these memories be recovered accurately?* The problems that threaten accurate memories are compounded in cases in which an individual claims to have recovered memories for traumatic childhood events that have been repressed or dissociated for long periods. The accuracy of repressed and then recovered memories is particularly suspect when the recollections occur in the context of therapies that use suggestive memory retrieval techniques such as hypnosis. Litigation involving the recovery of repressed memories involves lawsuits brought by victims claiming that therapists led them to believe that they were abused in the past and by the accused claiming that therapists promoting such false recollections are guilty of malpractice.

# KEY TERMS

absolute judgment

age regression

autobiographical
 memory*

cognitive interview

confabulation

content analysis*

delayed reporting
 statutes

dissociation*

encoding*

guided imagery

hearsay testimony

hyperamnesia

interviewer bias

memory hardening

relative judgment

repression*

retrieval

sequential presentation

social influence*

source confusion

storage

suggestive questioning

suppression hearing

television technique of
 retrieval

unconscious
 transference

weapon focus effect

Yerkes-Dodson law

---

**InfoTrac**
**COLLEGE**
**EDITION**
For additional readings go to **http://www.infotrac-college.com/wadsworth** and enter a search term related to your interest. The key terms that have been asterisked above will pull up several related articles. *See also:* HEARSAY EVIDENCE.

# *Identification and Evaluation of Criminal Suspects*

## ORIENTING QUESTIONS

1. *What are some psychological investigative techniques used by the police?*
2. *What is criminal profiling?*
3. *Is the polygraph a valid instrument for lie detection?*
4. *When is the best time to use a polygraph?*
5. *Why is the "voluntariness" of a confession important?*
6. *What are the main legal definitions of entrapment?*

In Chapter 7, we discussed how psychological findings and techniques contributed to assessments of the accuracy of eyewitness reports, reliability of children's testimony, and veracity of claims of repressed memory. In this chapter, we discuss three other activities in which psychology can assist law enforcement: the profiling of criminal suspects, the use of polygraphy in evaluating the truthfulness of suspects, and the evaluation of confessions from suspects. The common thread that ties these topics together is the assumption that psychological theory and techniques can be used to improve police officers' identification or evaluation of criminal suspects.

These contributions occur in a logical sequence. Psychological profiling is usually performed at the beginning of a criminal investigation, when the police need help focusing their investigation on certain types of people who might be the most likely suspects. Once suspects have been identified, law enforcement officials use other procedures to determine which, if any, of these suspects should be charged. The police often encourage suspects to confess, because confessions make it more likely that suspects will be bound over for trial (and eventually convicted). But confessions can be coerced, and, as a result, individual rights may be submerged in the quest for conviction. Courts have tried to clarify when a confession is truly voluntary, but, as we see in this chapter, psychological findings often conflict with the courts' evaluations of confessions—again reflecting the final dilemma described in Chapter 1.

The police may also suspect specific persons of criminal behavior but lack firm evidence of their lawbreaking. Hence, the police may create situations in which these suspicious persons have the opportunity to commit crimes. Often, when lawbreakers are caught in such actions, they claim entrapment as a defense. Confusion exists in the legal world over the meaning of this term, and further problems become evident when entrapment is examined from a psychological perspective, as we do later in this chapter.

Suspects are often given so-called lie detection tests to provide more information about their guilt or innocence and, sometimes, to encourage them to confess. Here again, the legal system's belief about the efficacy of lie detection procedures conflicts with some psychological findings about their accuracy. Some states permit the results of a lie detection test to be admitted into evidence under limited circumstances, whereas many psychologists question the objectivity of the procedure as it is usually administered and, hence, the validity of its results. Thus, a consistent theme throughout this chapter is the conflict between the legal system and psychological science regarding ways of gaining knowledge and evaluating truth. A subsidiary conflict is the subordination of the goal of truth to the desire to resolve conflict and maintain the stability of the system.

# Profiling of Criminal Suspects

Do criminals commit their crimes or choose their victims in distinctive ways that leave clues to their psychological makeup—much as fingerprints point to their physical identity or ballistics tests reveal the kind of gun they used? Evidence is accumulating that psychological characteristics are linked to behavioral patterns and that these links can be detected by a psychological analysis of crime scenes. **Criminal profiling** is used by behavioral scientists and police to narrow criminal investigations to suspects who possess certain behavioral and personality features that are revealed by the way a crime was committed. Profiling, also termed *criminal investigative analysis*, does not identify a specific suspect. Instead, profilers sketch a general psychological description of the most likely type of suspect so that the police can concentrate their investigation of difficult cases in the most profitable directions. (Profiles are also used to help investigators search for persons who fit descriptions known to characterize hijackers, drug couriers, and illegal aliens; Monahan & Walker, 1990).

Many famous fictional detectives have been portrayed as excellent profilers because they could interpret the meaning of a small detail or find a common theme among seemingly unrelated features of a crime. Lew Archer, the hero in Ross MacDonald's popular series of detective novels, often began his search for a missing person (usually a wayward wife or a troubled daughter) by looking at the person's bedroom, examining her reading material, and rummaging through her closet to discover where her lifestyle might have misdirected her. Helen McCloy's Dr. Basil Willing, the psychiatrist/detective featured in novels such as *The One That Got Away*, boasts, "Every criminal leaves psychic fingerprints and he can't wear gloves to hide them." Profiling even infiltrated popular culture through TV programs such as *Profiler*.

One of the earliest cases of criminal profiling involved the 1957 arrest of George Metesky, otherwise known as the Mad Bomber of New York City. Over an eight-year period, police had tried to solve a series of more than 30 bombings in the New York area. They finally consulted Dr. James Brussel, a Greenwich Village psychiatrist, who, after examining pictures of the bomb scenes and analyzing letters that the bomber had sent, advised the police to look for a heavyset, middle-aged, Eastern European, Catholic man who was single and lived with a sibling or aunt in Connecticut. Brussel also concluded that the man was very neat and that, when found, would be wearing a buttoned double-breasted suit. When the police finally arrested Matesky, this composite turned out to be uncannily accurate—even down to the right type of suit.

Not all early profiles were so useful. For example, the committee of experts charged with the task of profiling the Boston Strangler predicted that the killer was not one man but two, each of whom lived alone and was a schoolteacher. They also suggested that one of the men would be homosexual. When Albert De Salvo ultimately confessed to these killings, police discovered that he was a married construction worker who lived with his wife and two sons and was not homosexual (Porter, 1983).

The major source of research and development on criminal profiling has been the FBI's Be-

havioral Science Unit, which has been working on criminal profiles since the 1970s and currently analyzes about 1000 cases per year (Homant & Kennedy, 1998). This unit—now known as the Profiling and Behavioral Assessment Unit—is composed of about a dozen profilers with training in behavioral science (suggesting just how rare it is to have a career in this field) as well as consultants from the mental health professions. It has amassed large amounts of data on the backgrounds, family characteristics, current behaviors, and psychological traits of different types of criminals. The unit has concentrated on the study of violent offenders, especially those who commit bizarre or repeated crimes (Jeffers, 1991). Special attention has been given to rapists (Ressler, Burgess, & Douglas, 1988), arsonists (Rider, 1980), sexual homicides (Hazelwood & Douglas, 1980), and mass and serial murderers (Porter, 1983). A key to this research has been to interview offenders of a given type in order to learn how they select and approach their victims, how they react to their crimes, what demographic or family characteristics they share, and what personality features might predominate among them. For example, as part of its study of mass and serial killers, the FBI conducted detailed interviews with some of this country's most notorious killers—among them Charles Manson, Richard Speck, and David Berkowitz—to determine the similarities among them (see ◆ Box 8-1).

## Steps Involved in Criminal Profiling

Douglas, Ressler, Burgess, and Hartman (1986) divide the FBI's profiling strategy into five stages, with a final, sixth stage being the arrest of the correct suspect. The five phases, as they evolve in a murder investigation, are as follows:

1. *Profiling inputs.* The first stage involves collecting all information available about the crime, including physical evidence, photographs of the crime scene, autopsy reports and pictures, complete background information on the victim, and police reports. The profiler does not want to be

told about possible suspects at this stage, because such data might prejudice or prematurely direct the profile.

2. *Decision process models.* In this stage the profiler organizes the input into meaningful questions and patterns along several dimensions of criminal activity. What type of homicide has been committed? (See Box 8-1 for a discussion of different styles of murder.) What is the primary motive for the crime—sexual, financial, personal, or emotional disturbance? What level of risk did the victim experience, and what level of risk did the murderer take in killing the victim? What was the sequence of acts before and after the killing, and how long did these acts take to commit? Where was the crime committed? Was the body moved, or was it found where the murder was committed?

3. *Crime assessment.* Based on the findings of the previous phase, the profiler attempts to reconstruct the behavior of the offender and the victim. Was the murder *organized* (suggesting an intelligent killer who carefully selects victims against whom to act out a well-rehearsed fantasy) or *disorganized* (indicating an impulsive, less socially competent, possibly even psychotic killer)? Was the crime staged to mislead the police? What motivation was revealed by such details as cause of death, location of wounds, and position of the body? For example, criminal profilers often are guided by the following hypotheses: (1) brutal facial injuries point to killers who knew their victims, (2) murders committed with whatever weapon happens to be available are more impulsive than murders committed with a gun and may reveal a killer who lives fairly near the victim, and (3) murders committed early in the morning seldom involve alcohol or drugs.

4. *Criminal profile.* In this stage, profilers formulate an initial description of the most likely suspects. This profile includes the perpetrator's race, sex, age, marital status, living arrangements, and employment history; psychological characteristics, beliefs, and values; probable reactions to the police; and past criminal record, including the possibility of similar offenses in the past. This stage also contains a feedback loop whereby profilers check their predictions against stage 2 information to make sure that the profile fits the original data.

5. *Investigation.* A written report is given to investigators, who concentrate on suspects matching the profile. If new evidence is discovered in this investigation, a second feedback process is initiated, and the profile can be revised.

6. *Apprehension.* The intended result of these procedures, arrest of a suspect, allows profilers to evaluate the validity of their predictions. The key element in this validation is a thorough interview of the suspect to assess the influences of background and psychological variables.

## The Validity of Criminal Profiles

Is there any evidence that psychological profiling is valid? Are profilers more accurate than other groups in their descriptions of suspects, or is this activity nothing more than a reading of forensic tea leaves? Do profilers use a different process in evaluating information than other investigators?

In a recent review of criminal profiling, Homant and Kennedy (1998) conclude that different kinds of crime scenes can be classified with reasonable reliability and that differences in these crimes do correlate with certain offender characteristics such as murderers' prior relationships and interactions with victims (Salfati & Canter, 1999), organized versus disorganized approaches, and serial versus single offenders (e.g., Knight, Warren, Reboussin, & Soley, 1998). At the same time, this research suggests several reasons for caution: (1) inaccurate profiles are quite common, (2) many of the studies have been conducted in-house by FBI profilers studying a fairly small number of offenders, and (3) the concepts and approaches actually used by profilers have often not been objectively and systematically defined.

One study by Pinizzotto and Finkel (1990) investigated the effectiveness of criminal profiling as practiced by real-life experts. In this investigation, four different groups of subjects evaluated two criminal cases—a homicide and a sex offense—

## The Science of

**BOX 8-1    Classifying mass murderers**

Experts agree that the portrait of the contemporary American murderer is changing. Historically, most murders have been committed by killers who were well acquainted with their victim, had a personal but rational motive, killed once, and were then arrested. In the past two decades, however, increased attention is being paid to patterns of homicide involving killers who attack multiple victims, sometimes with irrational or bizarre motives, and who are much less likely to be apprehended than in former days. The criminal trail of these murderers may center on one locale and period of time or cross through different locations and stretch over a longer period of time.

Mass murderers have become a favorite subject of lurid true-crime books such as *The Only Living Witness* (Ted Bundy), *The Co-Ed Killer* (Edmund Kemper), and *Killer Clown* (John Gacy), as well as of more scholarly, comparative studies of multiple homicides (Fox & Levin, 1998; Levin & Fox, 1985; Leyton, 1986; Ressler, Burgess, & Douglas, 1988). On the basis of such studies, multiple killers have been classified into one of three categories, based on the pattern of their murders.

Although experts differ on the precise number of victims to use in defining multiple homicides, Fox and Levin's (1998) criterion of "the slaying of four or more victims, simultaneously or sequentially, by one or a few individuals" is probably the most widely accepted opinion. How many multiple homicides are committed each year is very difficult to estimate, but the consensus is that they are increasing, and this increase does not reflect merely greater media attention or police apprehension rates.

The **mass murderer** kills four or more victims in one location during a period of time that lasts anywhere from a few minutes to several hours. It is estimated that about two mass murders are committed every month in the United States, resulting in the deaths of 100 victims annually (Fox & Levin, 1998). Although most mass murderers are not severely mentally ill people, they do tend to harbor strong feelings of resentment and are often motivated by revenge against their victims. Contrary to popular myth, the majority of mass murderers do not attack strangers at random; in almost 80% of studied mass murders, the assailant was related to or was well ac-

quainted with the victims, and in many of these cases, the attack was a carefully planned assault rather than a crazy rampage. For every Charles Whitman, who shot and killed 16 people and wounded more than 30 other strangers from a tower on the University of Texas campus, there are many more people like Thomas McIlvane, who shot four coworkers in Royal Oak, Michigan before killing himself. Most mass murders are solved by law enforcement; the typical assailant is killed at the location of the crime, commits suicide, or surrenders to police.

**Spree killers** are a special form of mass murderer in which the attacker kills victims at two or more different locations with no "cooling-off"" interval between the murders. The killing constitutes a single event, but it can last either a short time or go on for a day or more.

Serial murderers kill four or more victims, each on separate occasions. Unlike mass murderers, **serial killers** usually select a certain type of victim who fulfills a role in the killer's fantasies. There are cooling-off periods between serial murders, which are usually better planned than mass or spree

that had already been solved but that were completely unknown to the subjects. The first group consisted of four experienced criminal profilers who had a total of 42 years of profiling experience and six police detectives who had recently been trained by the FBI to be profilers. The second group consisted of six police detectives with 57 years of total experience in criminal investigations but with no profiling experience or training. The third group was composed of six clinical psychol-

killings. Some serial killers (e.g., Angel Maturino Resendiz, the so-called Railway Killer because the murders he was charged with took place by railroad tracks) travel frequently and murder in several locations; others (e.g., Wayne Williams, the man convicted of killing the Atlanta children) are geographically stable and kill within the same area. The Unabomber, who apparently remained in one place but chose victims for his carefully constructed mail bombs who lived in different parts of the country, reflected an unusual combination of serial killer characteristics.

Because they are clever in the way they plan their murders, are capable of presenting themselves as normal members of the community, kill for idiosyncratic reasons, and frequently wait months between killings, serial murderers are difficult to apprehend. However, social scientists have gained some knowledge about these criminals, who may number as many as 100 in the United States. In general they are white males, aged 25 to 34, of at least average intelligence, and often charming in nature. Many were illegitimate and experienced abuse as children. They tend to select vulnerable vic-

tims of some specific type who gratify their need to control people. Consistent with the motive of wanting to dominate people, they prefer to kill with "hands-on" methods such as strangulation and stabbing, rather than with guns, which is the preferred weapon for mass murderers. They are often preoccupied with sadistic fantasies involving capture and control of their victims; these fantasies are frequently sexualized, as was the case with Jeffrey Dahmer. Many serial killers obsessively use pornography and violent sexual fantasies as "rehearsals" for and "replays" of their crimes, and they often keep souvenirs (sometimes in the form of body parts from victims) to commemorate their savage attacks. Despite the apparent craziness of their behavior, serial killers are not typically psychotic individuals. Most of them are antisocial personalities who are incapable of empathizing with anyone and who feel no genuine remorse for their aggression. In fact, serial killers often revel in the publicity that their crimes receive. Over the course of their criminal careers, serial killers may become less organized in how they plan and commit their murders.

Ronald Holmes, a criminologist at the University of Louisville who specializes in the study of serial murder, has identified four subtypes of serial killers (Holmes & De Burger, 1988). The *visionary* type feels compelled to murder because he hears voices or sees visions ordering him to kill certain kinds of people. An exception to the typical profile of serial killers, the visionary type is often psychotic. The *mission-oriented* type seeks to kill a specific group of people who he believes are unworthy to live and without whom the world would be a better place. His everyday acquaintances frequently will describe him as a fine citizen. The *hedonistic* type kills for the thrill of it. Such killers enjoy the physical sensations and sadistic gratification of killing. Sexual arousal is commonly associated with this type of murder. Finally, the *power-oriented* type kills because he enjoys exerting ultimate control over his victims. These murderers are obsessed with capturing and controlling their victims and forcing them to obey their every command.

ogists who had no profiling or criminal investigation experience. The final group consisted of six undergraduates drawn from psychology classes.

All subjects were given, for each case, an array of materials that profilers typically use. These ma-

terials included crime scene photographs, crime scene descriptions by uniformed officers, autopsy and toxicology reports (in the murder case), and descriptions of the victims. After studying these materials, subjects were asked to write all the details of each crime they could recall and to indicate the importance of these details to completing a profile. Three tests of profiling quality were used: all subjects prepared a profile of a suspect in each case, they answered 15 questions about the identity (e.g., gender, age, employment) of the suspects, and they were asked to rank-order a written "lineup" of five suspects from most likely to least likely to have committed each of the crimes.

The results indicated that, compared with the other three groups, the profiler group wrote longer profiles that contained more specific predictions about suspects, included more accurate predictions, and were rated as more helpful by other police detectives. Although they did not differ substantially in the way they thought about the evidence, profilers were more accurate in answering specific questions about the sex-offense suspect than the other groups; the groups did not differ in their accuracy about the homicide suspect. Similar results were found with the "lineup" identification; profilers were the most accurate for the sex offense, whereas there were no differences for the homicide case.

This study suggests that profilers can produce more useful and valid criminal profiles, even when compared to experienced crime investigators. This advantage may be limited, however, to certain kinds of cases or to the types of information made available to investigators. How do psychologists themselves view criminal profiling? In a survey of 152 police psychologists, 70% had serious questions about the validity of crime scene profiling (Bartol, 1996). Nonetheless, despite such reservations, profiling is gaining popularity among law enforcement officials and is now practiced, in some form or the other, in several countries (Homant & Kennedy, 1998).

## "Lie Detection" through Use of the Polygraph

Throughout history, many societies have assumed that criminals can be detected by the physical manifestations of their denials. Ever since King Solomon tried to discover which of two women who claimed to be the mother of an infant was lying by watching their emotions when he threatened to cut the baby in half and divide it between them, people have believed that the body will reveal in some way that the mind is lying when the mouth protests innocence. Who knows how many children have been scared into truthfulness by the prospect that their noses, like Pinocchio's, will give away their deceits?

Suspects in India were once required to submit to "trial by sacred ass." After mud had been put on the tail of an ass in a tent, the potential suspects were required to enter the tent one by one and pull the ass's tail; they were told they would be judged innocent if it didn't bray. The logic of this method was that, because the innocent knew they had nothing to hide, they would immediately yank the tail and get mud on their hands. A guilty suspect, however, would try to shield guilt by not pulling the tail. In the end, the guilty suspect was the one with the clean hands.

The ancient Hindus forced suspects to chew rice and spit it out on a leaf from a sacred tree. If the rice was dry, the suspect was considered guilty. The Bedouins of Arabia required conflicting witnesses to lick a hot iron; the one whose tongue was burned was thought to be lying (Kleinmuntz & Szucko, 1984). Both of these procedures reflect activity of the sympathetic nervous system (under emotional states, salivation usually decreases) and thus are crude measures of emotion, though not necessarily of lying. But emotion and lying are not the same, even if they are correlated to some extent (Saxe, 1991). The failure to appreciate this distinction is at the root of many mistaken ideas about the polygraph, as well as its unacceptably high rate of misclassifying persons as honest or deceitful.

### Emergence of the Polygraph

Despite this long history, the **polygraph,** or lie detector, was not developed until around 1917 with the work of William Moulton Marston, a complex and colorful figure who originated the

*A polygraph test*

term *lie detector*. Marston had studied at Harvard University with Hugo Munsterberg, who directed the experimental psychology laboratory there. Marston claimed that he could detect lying by noting increases in systolic blood pressure when subjects told untruths. He was an avid publicist for his new technique; he even tried to get permission to test Bruno Hauptmann, the alleged kidnapper of the Lindbergh baby, on his new lie detector machine (Lykken, 1981).

Marston's technique was the procedure under question in the landmark U.S. Supreme Court case, *Frye v. United States* (1923). In this case, James Frye appealed his murder conviction on the ground that the trial judge did not allow a polygrapher to testify about the results of a physiological deception test that supported Frye's claim of innocence. Because of his extravagant claims, Marston was repudiated not only by the courts but also by serious investigators. (Marston was a man of many talents; using the name "Charles Moulton," he created the comic strip *Wonder Woman*.)

A solid step forward in the use of the polygraph was taken by John A. Larson (1932) of the Berkeley, California, Police Department. He built

a forerunner of the modern polygraph that could measure pulse rate, blood pressure, and respiratory changes during questioning. Here we see the origins of the polygraph concept (*poly-* meaning "many"). What is commonly called the lie detector does not measure lies as such; it measures *emotion*. It is more properly called a polygraph because it employs several physiological measures—usually blood pressure, heart rate, breathing rate, and the galvanic skin response (or skin resistance to an electrical current). Unfortunately for Marston, Larson, and others who sought a specific "lie response," the physiological manifestations of various negative emotions (e.g., fear, guilt, anger) are all very similar (physiological differences between positive and negative emotions are more apparent; Zajonc & McIntosh, 1992).

Larson also developed the first systematic way of questioning suspects. The R/I procedure (standing for **relevant/irrelevant procedure**) intersperses relevant questions about the crime under investigation ("Did you steal Mrs. Riley's cow?") with irrelevant questions that are unrelated to the crime and are not stressful ("What did you do on your last birthday?"). Larson compared suspects' physiological reactions on these two types of questions to determine whether greater emotion was shown in response to the relevant questions. He assumed that truthful subjects would respond with equivalent reactions to all questions, whereas guilty, and dishonest, subjects would react more to the relevant questions.

Because one negative emotion can't be reliably distinguished from another on physiological grounds, Larson was forced to infer lying. But such an inference is unacceptable. Simply being a suspect in a crime, even if you are innocent, may generate a great deal of surplus emotion, but that should not be taken as a sign of guilt. Regardless of whether you are guilty or innocent, you are more likely to be aroused by relevant questions; these questions are obviously related to the crime being investigated, whereas the irrelevant questions are just as obviously unrelated to it. Despite these problems, the polygraph procedure, during the 1930s and later, was enthusiastically and uncritically employed by law enforcement officials. In fact, from 1915 to 1965, Larson himself was the only investigator to report an objective study of the diagnosis of deception using polygraph recordings obtained from criminal suspects (Lykken, 1985).

*The Control Question Test.*   A further refinement was made by criminologists associated with the Northwestern University Law School. In the 1930s, the Keeler polygraph, the prototype of current instruments, was developed by Leonard Keeler and his colleagues. During the mid–20th century, lie detectors were quite the topic of interest. In the movie *Northside 777,* it was Keeler himself who administered the R/I test to Richard Conte in Joliet Prison, proving what reporter Jimmy Stewart had suspected all along: that Conte was innocent of the crime for which he had been imprisoned. Such media portrayals contributed to the public's belief that lie detectors could infallibly distinguish between honesty and dishonesty.

While at Northwestern University, Keeler met Fred Inbau and John Reid. Reid had also developed a polygraph, and they established schools to train investigators to use polygraph techniques.

Most present examiners have been trained through outgrowths of these schools.

In the 1940s, John Reid pioneered the **Control Question Test,** which became the most popular approach to polygraphic examinations. This exam begins with an interview in which the examiner gathers biographical information from the subject and attempts to impress on the subject that he or she must be honest at all times during the test. The examiner tries to convince the subject that the polygraph is an infallible instrument; this strategy is meant to threaten guilty subjects at the same time that it reassures the innocent. Polygraphers often use a stim test to instill respect for the instrument. (See ◆ **Box 8-2** for a description of the stim test.)

Next the subject is asked a series of two kinds of questions. *Relevant questions* inquire about the crime under investigation (e.g., "Did you steal the law school's TV set?"). *Control questions* are not directly concerned with the crime under investigation but are calculated to induce an emotional reaction because they cover common misdeeds that almost all of us have committed at some point (e.g., "Have you ever stolen anything?" or "Prior to the age of 21, did you ever try to hurt someone you disliked?"). Most polygraphers consider these "known lies." They are assumed to have occurred, but subjects will deny them, thereby providing a characteristic physiological response to a lie. Guilty subjects should be more aroused by the relevant questions (to which they must lie to maintain their innocence), whereas innocent subjects should be more aroused by the control questions (because they will worry that admitting to a past misdeed might make them look more like a criminal at the present time). Therefore, this procedure works best when innocent subjects lie to the control questions (or at least show greater emotional turmoil over them) and the guilty subject lies (and becomes more emotionally aroused) to the relevant questions.

Reid also introduced "guilt complex" questions. In this procedure, the examiner pretends to be equally interested in whether the suspect is also guilty of some fictitious crime. Since this other

## The Science of

**BOX 8-2   Using intimidation to elicit confessions**

Some polygraph examiners will readily acknowledge that a basic goal in giving the test is to encourage lawbreakers to confess. Reid and Inbau (1966), leading experts in the development of the procedure, advise:

> After the subject's questions, if any, about the instrument and test procedure have been answered . . . he should be told something like the following: "You know, of course, that we're checking on the death of John Jones at First and Main Street the other night. . . . If you did do this thing . . . I'm going to know about it as soon as this investigation is over. If you did do this, therefore, I suggest you tell me about it now, before the test." (p. 13)

Examiners will use tricks to intimidate suspects and to convince them that the machine is infallible. A favorite is the "stim test." The subject is shown seven playing cards and told to take one, look at it, and put it back in the deck without showing it to the examiner. Reid and Inbau (1966) write, "After the selection is made, the examiner proceeds to shuffle the cards and instructs the subject to answer 'no' to each question concerning the cards, even when asked the number of the card he selected. In other words, the subject's answer to one of the questions will be a lie" (p. 27).

At the end of this exercise, the examiner tells the subject which card he or she picked, leaving the implication that the apparatus detected lying. But Reid and Inbau (1966) advise examiners that "the cards are arranged and shown to the subject in such a way that the examiner will immediately know which card has been picked by the subject" (p. 27). Another variant of this shoddy procedure is to use a deck of 52 replications of the same playing card (Lykken, 1981).

Reid and Inbau (1966) even acknowledge that the polygraph is not completely accurate; one of the reasons for the card trick deception is that "the polygraph record itself may not actually disclose the card 'lie'" (p. 27).

---

crime is imaginary, the examiner knows that the suspect's denial is truthful and therefore can compare the subject's physiological responses to the guilt complex questions with the responses to the questions about the actual crime. However, the "measurement" of lying still rests here on a shaky assumption that differences in intensity of physiological reactions are based on guilt.

The final step in the Control Question Test is to interpret the polygraphic charts. Most polygraphers reach a conclusion about the subject's honesty on subjective grounds that include the physiological record as well as the interviewers' observations of the subject's behavior throughout the test (Gale, 1988). A second approach, known as the *zone of comparison* method (Backster, 1974), involves a quantified comparison of physiological reactions to the relevant and control questions.

*The Directed Lie Test.*   The **Directed Lie Test** is a variation of the Control Question Test. In the pretest interview, the examiner will direct the examinee to lie in response to certain questions. As explained in *United States v. Galbreth* (1995):

> The examiner tells the subject that the . . . test enables the examiner to determine the subject's characteristic response patterns when lying and when answering truthfully. The examiner then explains that the directed lie questions will ensure that the subject will be correctly classified as truthful or deceptive on the subsequent polygraph test. [The expectation that the examiner] can detect when the subject is practicing deception . . . causes the guilty person to be more concerned with the relevant questions than with the directed lie questions. As he answers the relevant questions, which are the questions that

have put him in great jeopardy, he will think to himself, "Oh the examiner knows what my pattern looks like when I'm lying because she can see it on those questions to which she told me to lie and she's going to see that this is the same pattern and I am going to be in big trouble." On the other hand, the innocent subject's concern is focused very hard on the directed lie questions and the subject often thinks very hard to make sure he has something in mind when he answers those questions falsely so that it produces an enhanced reaction. (p. 885)

*The Guilty Knowledge Test.* The **Guilty Knowledge Test** (GKT) was developed by David Lykken (1981), a University of Minnesota psychologist who has also been one of the staunchest critics of standard procedures such as the Control Question Test. Both the procedure and the purposes of this method are fundamentally different from the control question approach. The goal is to detect the presence of guilty knowledge in the suspect's mind, not to detect lying. The procedure relies on the accumulation of facts that are known only by the police, the criminal, and any surviving victims. For example: In what room was the victim's body found? What was the murder weapon? What strange garment was the victim wearing? What was clutched in the victim's hand?

A series of multiple-choice questions is created based on this information, and the suspect is presented with each question in order and asked to respond to each choice. Was it the bedroom? Was it the kitchen? Was it the living room? Although each alternative would appear equally plausible to an innocent person, the true criminal will be revealed by physiological reactions that accompany recognition of guilty knowledge. Imagine that the suspect has been asked five questions about the crime, each of which has five choices, and that on question 1 his physiological reaction is much stronger to the "correct" response than to any of the others. Just by coincidence, that would happen 20% of the time (i.e., one time out of five choices). So we can't make any strong inference about his knowledge of the crime from his responses to just one question. But let us say further

that for each of the five questions his emotional reaction to the correct response is much greater than to the other choices. By coincidence, this latter set of reactions would be unlikely; its probability is $1/5 \times 1/5 \times 1/5 \times 1/5 \times 1/5$, or $1/3125$. One in 3125 is a probability of .0003, or very, very unlikely by chance. If this pattern of reactions occurs, we can be confident that the suspect has detailed and accurate knowledge of the crime. That, in itself, is suggestive, but not direct, evidence that the suspect committed the crime.

Notice that the goal of the Guilty Knowledge Test is not to detect emotions that might accompany deception; rather, it is to detect knowledge possessed by subjects. The underlying assumption is that people are more physiologically aroused when they perceive a meaningful stimulus. This well-established pattern is known as the *orienting response* (Ben-Shakhar, Bar-Hillel, & Lieblich, 1986).

Obviously, this technique can be used only when the details of the crime have been kept from the public. Even then, it is conceivable that the suspect is not the perpetrator but, rather, was told about the crime by the true criminal and therefore possesses "guilty" knowledge. Moreover, it is possible that some guilty subjects are so distraught or pay so little attention to the details of their crimes that they actually lack the requisite knowledge that this method requires. Some skeptics of the GKT suggest that it can be conducted properly in only a small percentage of real-life cases.

## Validity of Polygraph Procedures

Advocates of polygraph procedures claim very high rates of accuracy. Reid and Inbau (1966) asserted that their success rate was 99%. F. Lee Bailey proposed on national television that, out of every 100 polygraph tests administered, 96 are accurate, 3 are inconclusive, and only 1 will be in error (quoted in Lykken, 1985, p. 96). Critics of the polygraph argue that most of the techniques are based on implausible psychological assumptions and that errors of classification are too frequent. Within psychology, this debate has been waged vigorously by David Lykken (1981, 1985), who strongly criticizes most polygraphic techniques, and David Raskin (1982, 1989), a former University of Utah psychologist who argues that the polygraph yields valid indications of deception when used correctly.

Before summarizing the results of empirical studies of polygraphic accuracy, we highlight five problems that complicate scientific study of criminal polygraphy and that must be kept in mind when evaluating evidence about the polygraph.

1. Clearly, the polygraph is useful in inducing suspects to confess their crimes. This outcome, produced presumably by suspects' being convinced that the polygraph is infallible and that they can best mitigate their sentences by confessing their crimes, is no small accomplishment. But false confessions can and do occur. Therefore, the utility of the polygraph in prompting confessions should not be confused with its accuracy in determining truth versus deceit. This latter issue is at the heart of the validity question.

2. A vexing problem in evaluating polygraph results is the difficulty of finding a decisive criterion of accuracy, sometimes known as **ground truth.** In some studies, ground truth is defined by a panel of judges who review all the evidence in a case and conclude who is the guilty culprit. In other studies, ground truth is established through subsequent confessions. A third choice is to use the official judicial outcome (e.g., jury verdict) as the criterion. All these alternatives have some methodological limitations.

3. In the context of criminal investigations, detecting a liar is a *true positive* and believing a truthful suspect is *a true negative*. Believing a liar is truthful is *a false negative,* whereas disbelieving a truthful subject is *a false positive*. The frequency of these errors depends on both the accuracy of the technique and the **base rate** (how often something happens) of liars and honest subjects among a tested sample. The following example illustrates this relationship. Assume that the overall accuracy of the polygraph is 80%; also assume that the base rate of guilt and accompanying deception among criminal suspects is 75% (a reasonable fig-

ure if we grant that the police usually arrest and charge the right suspects). If 1000 people are arrested, 750 will be guilty in our example. The polygraph will catch 600 (750 $\times$ 0.80), but it will make 150 false negatives. Of the 250 innocent suspects, the polygraph will exonerate 200, but it will falsely implicate 50 persons. Given a constant level of polygraphic accuracy, as the base rate of liars increases, false negatives also increase. More false positives will occur when the base rate of lying by suspects is low.

The problem of base rates also indicates how a claim of "96% correct" can be misleading. Let us say a major theft has occurred in a factory with 50 employees. One is the thief; 49 are honest. The polygrapher gives a lie detection test to each of the employees, and each denies being the thief. The polygrapher misclassifies one of the innocent people as the thief (false positive). He also fails to detect lying by the true thief (false negative). So he has erred in two cases, but he has been correct in classifying the 48 others as truthful. His accuracy rate is 48 of 50, or 96%. But he has still erred on the crucial determination; despite the inflated overall "accuracy rate," his basic test result is invalid.

4. **Field studies** of the polygraph are based on real-life investigations of subjects who have a large stake in being cleared of suspicion. **Analog studies** involve investigations of mock crimes staged, usually in the laboratory, by an experimenter who also arranges for some subjects (often, college students) to be "guilty" and others to be "innocent." Field studies face the problem of locating ground truth, but their use of subjects who are motivated to avoid detection is a methodological advantage (Kircher, Horowitz, & Raskin, 1988). In addition, analog studies may overestimate polygraphic accuracy because "innocent" analog subjects will probably not experience the emotional arousal that a vulnerable but innocent subject feels in a real crime investigation.

5. A final threat to the polygraph is that deceptive subjects will "beat" the test by using countermeasures to avoid detection (Honts, Raskin, Kircher & Hodes, 1984). Deliberate physical

movements, drugs, and cognitive or psychological maneuvers have all been suggested as possible countermeasures. Effective countermeasures should increase false negatives, but they should have negligible effects on false positives. In fact, the evidence does not strongly support the fear that countermeasures can consistently distort polygraph results (Raskin, 1989).

The most thorough review of the polygraph's validity was a report in 1983 by the Office of Technology Assessment (OTA), directed by Leonard Saxe and entitled *Scientific Validity of Polygraphic Testing: A Research Review and Evaluation*. A brief version of OTA's report by Saxe, Dougherty, and Cross (1985) reports that, of 250 empirical studies of polygraphic testing, only 10 field studies met adequate scientific standards. All 10 studies investigated the Control Question Test (CQT). The average rate of false negatives across these 10 studies was 11.5% (ranging from 0% to 23%). The average range of false positives was 18.3% (range: 0% to 53%). Saxe et al. (1985) interpret these outcomes as follows: "on average, in field studies polygraphic test results reduced 64% of the error of chance prediction" (p. 360), "although the data also suggest that substantial rates of false positives, false negatives, and inconclusives are possible" (p. 364). Since the OTA review, a major field study of the polygraph using U.S. Secret Service examiners indicated that, across a three-year period, these examiners correctly identified 95% of the 76 deceptive suspects and 96% of the truthful subjects they polygraphed (Raskin, 1989). Further research is needed to determine why these examiners were more successful than other polygraphers.

Twelve analog studies of the CQT met adequate scientific standards and showed an average 47% reduction in efforts from chance predictions. OTA located no field studies of the Guilty Knowledge Test (GKT). However, Lykken (1985) argues that analog evaluations of the GKT are acceptable since this procedure does not rely on the emotional arousal that can be dependably elicited only in the field. For eight analog studies of the GKT cited

by Lykken (1985), 88.2% of 161 "guilty" subjects were detected, whereas 96.7% of 152 "innocents" were cleared.

Even severe critics of the polygraph, such as Lykken, acknowledge that the technique has overall accuracy rates of 65% or better. But is this figure high enough to permit polygraphic data as evidence at a trial or high enough to base the prosecution of a suspect on it as the primary evidence? We think not. The best use of the polygraph remains at the investigatory stages of a criminal prosecution and as a "stage prop" to encourage confessions from suspects against whom other incriminating evidence has been gathered.

## Other "Lie Detection" Methods

As controversy about the polygraph has continued to swirl, other "lie detection" procedures have been advocated. The **psychological stress evaluator** (PSE) uses the speaking voice as the determinant of lying. Advocates of the PSE claim that it can measure variations in emotional stress and that it can distinguish words and phrases spoken in periods of high and low stress. Despite claims of accuracy by its users, no evidence has been published in any scientific journal showing that the psychological stress evaluator is effective (Lykken, 1985).

A second approach is to judge lying on the basis of facial, bodily, nonverbal, and vocal cues. For example, when subjects lie, their voice pitch tends to increase, they illustrate their language with gestures less frequently, and they may attempt to lengthen the time they gaze at persons to whom they lie (Ekman, 1985). However, the ability of observers to use this information to catch liars is fairly limited (Ekman & O'Sullivan, 1991).

Several systems have been developed for differentiating the verbal content of truthful accounts from nontruthful reports. For example, because it is difficult to fabricate details that do not exist in memory, a large amount of reported detail should be indicative of truthful reports. Likewise, reports of sensory impressions (e.g., "the smell of freshly cut hay was in the air") are more common in truthful accounts, while hedging (e.g., "it seems to me") is more typical of fabrications. In a test of how well these cues discriminated between honest and deceptive alibis given by subjects who were told that they were trying to fool an interrogator investigating a theft, only three cues (of a possible 17) proved useful: truthful subjects (1) gave more detailed descriptions of their actions, (2) provided more coherent accounts of their behavior, and (3) were more likely to admit that they could not remember certain aspects of the event in question (Porter & Yuille, 1996).

A third approach to lie detection involves measuring cortical activity rather than physiological responses. Based on findings in the field of **cognitive psychophysiology,** these techniques, which have only recently been applied to lie detection problems, analyze the brain waves that are evoked when a subject attends to a stimulus (Bashore & Rapp, 1993). Certain components of these brain waves, termed **event-related brain potentials,** vary depending on whether the person is confronted with a familiar, meaningful stimulus or a novel, nonmeaningful stimulus. Different components of evoked potentials also can be elicited if a subject is exposed to a stimulus that is inconsistent with the subject's expectations or personal knowledge. The logic of these findings is that electroencephalogram (EEG) measures could serve as an index of the brain activity that occurs specifically when people are attempting to conceal information that they possess; therefore, these brain activity measures might be used to identify people who are denying guilty knowledge. Whether brain waves can serve as a valid physiological index of deceptive behavior is still not widely accepted, in part because of uncertainty about what exactly is indexed by different types of brain activity.

## Admissibility of Polygraph Records

New Mexico stands alone as the only state in which polygraph evidence is routinely admitted in court. (Other states allow its admission, but only under limited circumstances that we describe later.) In 1975, the New Mexico Supreme Court held that polygraph evidence should be admitted if the operator was qualified and followed testing procedures designed to produce reliable results (*State v. Dorsey,* 1975). In 1983, the court adopted an evidence rule that regulates the admission of polygraph evidence. The rule requires that

◆ polygraph examiners must have at least five years' experience in administration or interpretation of tests and must have satisfied continuing education requirements;

◆ scoring must be in a manner generally accepted as reliable by polygraph experts;

◆ at least two relevant questions must be asked;

◆ at least three charts must be analyzed;

◆ the pretest interview and actual test must be recorded; and

◆ the report, charts, and recording of the interview must be given to the opponent at least 30 days prior to trial.

In *United States v. Scheffer* (1998), the United States Supreme Court upheld the constitutionality of Military Rule of Evidence 707, which declares that polygraph results and opinions shall not be admitted into evidence. This case is described in ◆ **Box 8-3.**

While binding only on military courts, the Supreme Court's decision in *Scheffer* reinforces the general reluctance of courts to admit polygraph results and opinions. Only in New Mexico may polygraph evidence be admitted as a matter of course. In other states, and in the federal courts, polygraph evidence is sometimes admitted if both parties in the trial **stipulate,** or agree, that the evidence can be used. Less often, results of a polygraph are admitted when a judge is convinced that the evidence is reliable and necessary for a fair determination.

In *United States v. Galbreth* (1995), for example, a federal trial judge allowed psychologist David Raskin to testify that a defendant in a tax fraud case was not being deceptive when he said that he didn't know certain items should have been reported as taxable income. In a 19-page opinion, the judge applied the factors set out in *Daubert v.*

## THE CASE OF

**BOX 8-3**

### Airman Scheffer and the admissibility of polygraph examination results

Airman Edward Scheffer had tested positive for methamphetamine. To buttress his claim that he unwittingly took the drug (one wonders how), Airman Scheffer sought to introduce the results of a polygraph administered by the Office of Special Investigations (OSI) that indicated that he had not been deceptive when he answered no to the question "Since you've been in the Air Force have you used any illegal drugs?" Relying on Military Rule of Evidence 707, the military court refused to admit the polygraph evidence and convicted Airman Scheffer.

Writing for the majority of justices in *United States v. Scheffer*, Justice Thomas stated that "there is simply no consensus that polygraph evidence is reliable. To this day, the scientific community remains extremely polarized about the reliability of polygraph techniques" (*United States v. Scheffer*, 1998, p. 1265). According to Justice Thomas, given the lack of consensus, it was reasonable for the authorities to exclude polygraph evidence in all military trials. He went on to opine that, unlike other types of expert testimony, polygraph evidence invades the province of the jury: "A fundamental premise of our criminal trial system is that the '*jury* is the lie detector'" (*United States v. Scheffer*, 1998, p. 1266). To allow polygraph evidence, said Justice Thomas, might cause a jury to abandon its traditional role of determining credibility.

*Merrell Dow Pharmaceuticals* (1993; described in Chapter 2) to the "directed lie control question technique" used by Dr. Raskin. The judge found that the technique (1) had been tested, (2) had been subjected to peer review, (3) had a sufficiently low known rate of error, (4) was subject to existing standards, and (5) was generally (80%) accepted by the relevant scientific community. The judge noted that Dr. Raskin's charts had been independently reviewed and scored by a second examiner and that even the prosecutor conceded that the charts did not indicate deception. (The prosecutor challenged the test because of the possibility that Galbreth used countermeasures to affect the results.)

*Galbreth* is one of a very few decisions allowing polygraph evidence to be introduced. Most courts are hostile to this type of evidence. In addition to the argument that polygraph evidence undermines the jury's role to determine credibility, judges share many of the same concerns that have been discussed by psychologists (Saxe & Ben-Shakhar, 1999).

Concerning countermeasures, consider the following commentary:

[A]t least one study has shown that a group of subjects given a mere fifteen minutes of instruction on the proper physical countermeasures techniques were successful in producing false negative results in nearly 89% of the cases. Using the same simple countermeasures, almost one-half the students participating in a mock-crime study were able to defeat the polygraph. The utilization of easily taught and learned physical countermeasures seriously undermines the accuracy of polygraph test results. (Hensler, 1997, p. 1282)

Another area of concern—lack of examiner standards—indicates evidence of improvement, however. The American Polygraph Association (APA) accredits 14 polygraph schools, publishes a quarterly journal, and posts a Web site (www.polygraph.org) that exudes respectability. Almost all polygraphers are graduates of APA-accredited schools, in which they are taught ethical standards and the techniques of administering and scoring the various tests. In addition, 29 states license polygraphers, with licensing requirements varying from state to state.

How do juries react to such polygraph evidence? Do they blindly accept polygraph evidence? Cavoukian and Heslegrave (1980) conducted two studies to find out. In the initial study, mock jurors reacted to one of three versions of a trial. In the first version, they were given a summary of the major points in the case and the judge's instructions. In the second, they also had polygraph evidence showing the defendant to be innocent. In the third, they had these materials plus an additional instruction from the judge that polygraph tests were about 80% accurate, so jurors should be cautious in deciding verdicts on the basis of such tests. The percentages of jurors who acquitted the defendant in the three conditions were 48%, 72%, and 60%, respectively. The judge's cautionary instruction reduced some of the effect of the polygraph evidence. Moreover, even when the polygraph results were presented, the subjects did not follow them blindly. In a second study, using a different case, Cavoukian and Heslegrave (1980) found that the judge's cautionary instruction was even more influential; it reduced the acquittal rate below what it was without any polygraph evidence at all.

Recently, the legality of the polygraph has been challenged in another way. The administration of a polygraph examination as part of an employment application has been outlawed in the case of most jobs (see ◆ Box 8-4).

The federal Employee Polygraph Protection Act of 1988 prohibits most private employers from using polygraphs (as well as PSE machines) to screen employees for honesty or past offenses. Ironically, most firms that previously used polygraph examinations are now using other devices, especially "integrity tests," to detect potentially dishonest employees. These paper-and-pencil tests are intended to measure employees' attitudes toward thefts or other crimes, but the evidence to date indicates that such tests are probably inferior to the polygraph as "honesty tests." They ap-

pear to be easily faked and to be trivially related to actual honest or dishonest behavior (Guastello & Rieke, 1991).

# Use of Confessions

Throughout history, confessions have been accorded enormous importance. Confession is valued as an indicator of truth and also as an act that benefits confessors because it relieves them of guilt and earns them forgiveness from their fellow citizens. Many religions maintain that confession is the first step toward redemption and have evolved special rituals to encourage it.

When the police capture suspects, one of their first acts is to encourage them to confess to the crime. A confession will, of course, permit a district attorney or grand jury to bring charges. Even if the suspect later denies the confession and pleads not guilty to charges, the confession can be introduced into evidence at the trial (Gudjonsson, 1988).

Although disputed "confessions" by defendants occur more often than most of us would guess (Rattner, 1988) and many false confessions have been documented (e.g., Gudjonsson, 1992; Parloff, 1993), the number of false confessions is actually a matter of contention (Cassell, 1999; Leo & Ofshe, 1998). Prosecutors claim that defendants can easily recant confessions by alleging that police had coerced them, but defense attorneys say that false confessions happen more often than prosecutors acknowledge.

The confessions that do prove false often occur in highly publicized cases, frequently involving violent acts in which the police have few leads and are under pressure to make an arrest. For example, four suspects confessed to murdering nine people at a Buddhist temple outside Phoenix in 1991. All were innocent (Parloff, 1993). According to court documents, 17-year-old Michael Rene Pardue confessed to three murders that had occurred in his small Alabama town in 1973. After he was convicted, he claimed that a detective

## The Science of

BOX 8-4    **Detecting liars on job applications**

This chapter focuses on polygraph techniques in criminal investigations, but until recently, more polygraph examinations were administered in employment screening than in criminal cases. Probably 80% of the two million tests given each year in the United States were job related. Beginning in December 1988, however, the use of the polygraph as part of a job interview was banned for all private businesses except those manufacturing or dispensing drugs, those employing security guards, and those doing sensitive work on government contracts. However, the law did not prohibit federal, state, or local governments from continuing to use preemployment polygraph tests.

Before this law, whenever a crime occurred in a business, its management might routinely administer polygraph tests to all employees. Some companies would randomly test some employees each month, even if a crime had not occurred. According to the new law, an employer can ask a current employee to take the test only if

the employer provides written reasons for suspecting the worker was involved in a theft or other crime and the employee had access to any missing materials. Furthermore, an employee may not be fired solely on the basis of the results of a polygraph examination.

Given the void created by this important law, some firms have begun to substitute "integrity tests" in the employment process. These are paper-and-pencil personality questionnaires that try to assess the honesty of job applicants. In 1990, an estimated 5.5 million integrity tests were administered. Firms such as Stop'n'Go stores and certain Kentucky Fried Chicken restaurants have required all their applicants to take integrity tests (Caprino, 1989). Questions elicit self-reports about shoplifting, drug use, drinking, petty theft, and financial problems, as well as behaviors less obviously related to honesty on the job. These straightforward questions (e.g., "Have you ever taken something from a store without paying for it?") are quite easy to fake, but adherents of

integrity testing claim that many job applicants will freely reveal their past transgressions (Gorman, 1989).

The validity of integrity tests has been a topic of considerable research, and the studies to date indicate that these tests can predict counterproductive behavior on the job such as theft and absenteeism moderately well (Ones, Viswesvaran, & Schmidt, 1993). They tend, however, to do a better job of predicting disruptive employee behavior in general rather than theft or dishonesty specifically.

Despite these results, integrity tests still receive sharp criticism, and several states have introduced legislation that would ban their use (Massachusetts already prohibits them) (Camara & Schneider, 1994). In addition to concerns about the qualifications of those who use and interpret these tests, the concept of integrity itself is still not well understood psychologically, resulting in lingering skepticism about the overall value of these tests (U.S. Congress, 1990).

---

known for beating confessions out of suspects had interrogated him nonstop for more than 78 hours and scared him into confessing. More than 20 years later, the Alabama Supreme Court agreed that his confession had been coerced. Ironically, Pardue will never see the light of day; under the "three-strikes" law, his three escapes from custody mandate a life sentence despite the fact that he never should have been imprisoned (Bragg, 1998).

If jurors hear a police detective testify about a confession by the defendant, even though they know the defendant now is pleading not guilty, their eventual verdicts often are affected by the incriminating testimony, whatever counterevidence is presented later. In fact, leading legal scholars (e.g., McCormick, 1983; Wigmore, 1970) rank confessions as the most powerful kind of evidence offered at trial.

*Police removing bodies of victims killed at a Buddhist temple near Phoenix in 1991. Four people confessed to the murders; all were innocent.*

A study by Saul Kassin and Katherine Neumann (1997) demonstrates the power of such evidence. Mock jurors in this study read summaries of four criminal trials (concerning murder, rape, assault, and theft). Each summary contained a confession, eyewitness testimony, character testimony, or none of these. After reading each case, the jurors rendered verdicts. Confession evidence proved to be the most incriminating: in three of four cases (the exception was the theft case), confessions produced the highest conviction rates. In a follow-up study, Kassin and Neumann asked mock jurors to rate the relative influence of confessions, eyewitness testimony, and character evidence on their verdicts. Confessions were deemed the most incriminating.

## The Validity of Confessions

Knowledge of a prior confession apparently pushes a juror's verdict in the guilty direction. But are confessions always valid? A study by Kassin and Kiechel (1996), described in ◆ **Box 8-5**, raises the possibility of false confessions in the real world.

## The Voluntariness of Confessions

Many "confessions" do not come spontaneously from the defendant; rather, they result from intense questioning by the police—interrogation that may involve promises, threats, harassment, or even brutality (Wrightsman & Kassin, 1993). Sometimes the coercion is very subtle. In Chapter 1, we mentioned that a Texas appeals court overturned the conviction of LaCresha Murray who, at age 11, was found guilty of beating a 2-year-old to death. The appellate court found that her conviction was tainted by a confession in which police did not tell her she could leave or consult with an adult. In fact, many police departments use a manual called *Criminal Interrogation and Confessions* (Inbau, Reid, & Buckley, 1986) that suggests the use of tricks, deceptions, and lies to extract confessions. Do the police ever go too far in obtaining confessions? Are there safeguards against their going too far?

The courts have ruled that a confession must be voluntary for it to be admitted into evidence. But it is not always easy to categorize a confes-

## The Science of

BOX 8-5   **False confessions: Can studies generalize to the real world?**

As this chapter indicates, most people assume that if a person confesses to a crime during a police interrogation, it means he or she committed the crime—unless the suspect has been tortured, beaten, or otherwise coerced into confessing. In fact, when we asked undergraduates whether they would ever confess to committing a crime that they hadn't committed, only 3% acknowledged that they might. We now know that at least some of these people are deceiving themselves: Kassin and Kiechel have shown that undergraduate research subjects not only will confess to an action they did not take but may actually come to believe what they confessed to.

In this study, 75 students participated in what was described as a reaction-time study. Two subjects took part in each session, but one was really an assistant to the experimenter. This assistant, or research confederate, read a list of

letters, and the real participant was required to type them as quickly as possible on the keyboard of the experimenter's computer. Before they started, the typists were warned not to hit the ALT key near the space bar; if that happened, the program would crash and the experimenter's data would be lost.

Not surprisingly, soon after the experiment started, the computer suffered an apparent malfunction. Frantically, the experimenter entered the room and accused the subject of hitting the wrong key and causing the damage. In all cases, the subject rightly denied this accusation. But then, the confederate demurely commented that yes, the subject had in fact struck the wrong key.

Faced with the "evidence" against them and the possibility of facing an angry professor, most subjects signed a "confession" hastily drafted by the experimenter. In one experimental condition, in

which the confederate had read the letters to the subject at a very rapid rate, all the subjects confessed, and 65% came to believe that they really had hit the wrong key (This internal acceptance of a false belief was assessed by having someone else later question the subject about the experiment.)

Do the results of this study tell us anything about the possibility of false confessions in the real world? The answer is a definite "maybe." Confessing to striking the wrong key and "ruining" a psychology experiment is a far cry from confessing to a major crime during a grueling police interrogation. Certainly the consequences that follow from the confession are different in those two circumstances. But this research should cause each of us to give second thought to the belief that we would be invincible to interrogation pressures.

sion as voluntary or involuntary. Figure 8.1 proposes a continuum of voluntariness.

Confessions ought to be voluntary. The truthfulness of an involuntary confession is questionable; therefore, the confession is not trustworthy evidence for jurors who are mandated to assume the innocence of the defendant and to require the prosecution to prove guilt. Illustrating one of the dilemmas of Chapter 1, the assumption of innocence standard conflicts with practices that allow government officials to question an accused person and introduce into evidence statements that

the accused has made under possibly coercive conditions.

In England 400 years ago, that dilemma was not considered a legitimate question. All confessions were routinely admitted into evidence. In fact, a confession was treated as a plea of guilt (i.e., as a criminal pleading rather than as a matter of evidence; Wigmore, 1970). One statement, in 1607, pointedly said, "A confession is a conviction." Even confessions extracted by torture—and they were numerous—were accepted into evidence without question.

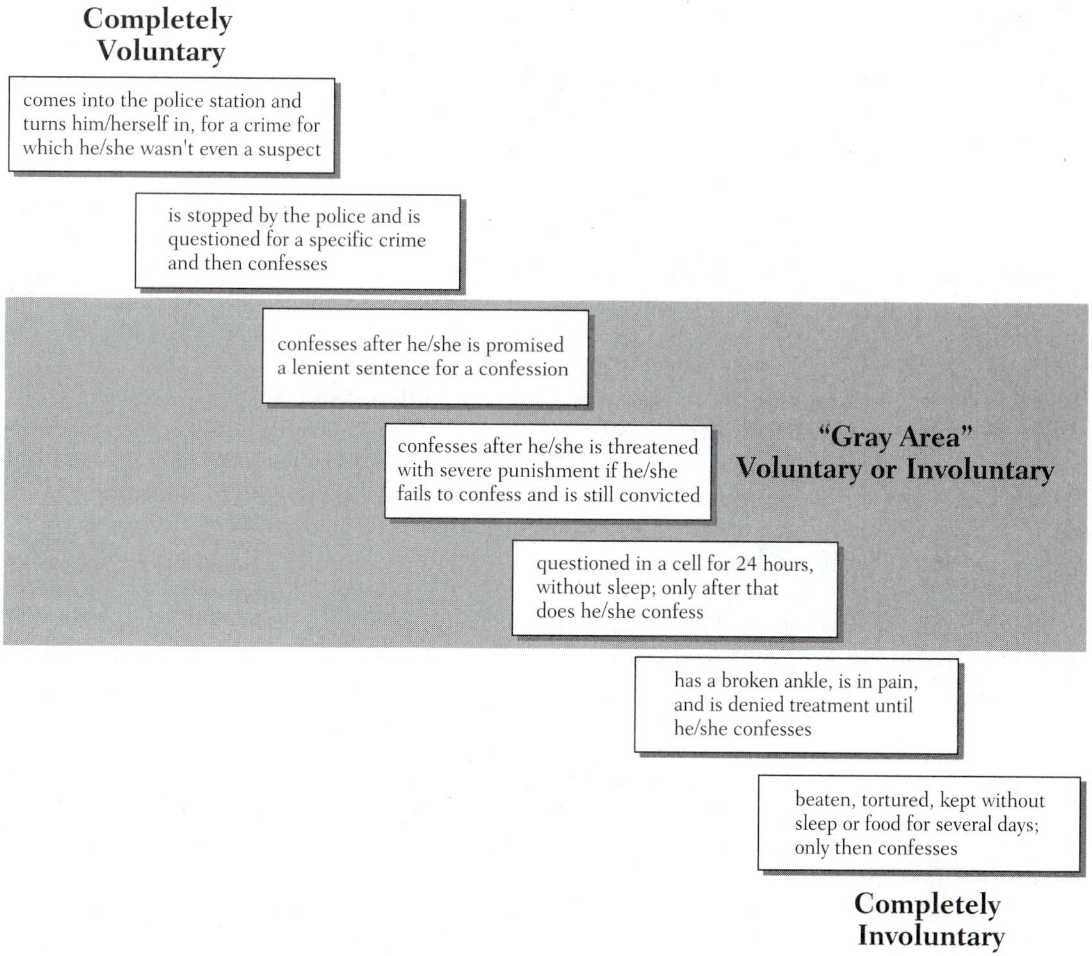

**Completely
Voluntary**

comes into the police station and
turns him/herself in, for a crime for
which he/she wasn't even a suspect

is stopped by the police and is
questioned for a specific crime
and then confesses

confesses after he/she is promised
a lenient sentence for a confession

**"Gray Area"
Voluntary or Involuntary**

confesses after he/she is threatened
with severe punishment if he/she
fails to confess and is still convicted

questioned in a cell for 24 hours,
without sleep; only after that
does he/she confess

has a broken ankle, is in pain,
and is denied treatment until
he/she confesses

beaten, tortured, kept without
sleep or food for several days;
only then confesses

**Completely
Involuntary**

**FIGURE 8.1** *What is a voluntary confession?* How can we tell whether a particular confession is voluntary and, hence, likely to be truthful or whether it is involuntary, coerced, and, hence, possibly false? Some cases lead to subjective opinions, but we could probably agree generally to the relative position of the above specific examples on a continuum of voluntary to involuntary confessions.

We have come a long way since then, but, as this section will show, jurors' evaluations of confessions are still problematic. Slowly over the centuries, the place of confessions in the legal system shifted. In the mid-1600s, the right against self-incrimination emerged in English common law. A century later, the admissibility into evidence of ordinary confessions was first limited. By the mid-dle to late 1700s, coerced confessions began to be excluded as evidence because, as in the later case of *Hopt v. Utah* (1884), the trustworthiness of a confession was believed to be lost when it was obtained through threat or inducement. A general viewpoint developed that a confession should be "reliable" (i.e., an accurate representation of the truth) before it is used in evidence. A few judges therefore began to scrutinize confessions more carefully: What is the nature of the witness who testifies that a confession occurred? Is the witness a paid informer? An overzealous police officer? But in reality, few confessions were excluded from evidence during this time period.

By the late 1800s, judicial opinions tended to agree that confessions vary in their trustworthiness but that they should be admitted as evidence and then left to the jury for an evaluation of their utility. This laissez-faire approach would not last for long. In the early 1900s, courts in the United States were increasingly faced with cases of African American defendants who had "confessed" to crimes after being beaten by the police. *Brown v. Mississippi*, a 1936 Supreme Court case, was a landmark decision on this matter.

This case involved three black defendants who had been convicted of the murder of a white man entirely on the basis of "confessions" procured after one of the defendants had been severely whipped and hung twice from a tree and the other two defendants had been stripped naked and beaten until they signed a confession the police had written. The Supreme Court reversed these convictions on the ground that the police had violated the defendants' rights to due process of law; the Court ruled that evidence procured through torture must be excluded from trials.

What emerged after *Brown* was a distinction between coerced confessions—hence, involuntary ones—and voluntary confessions. The courts said that coerced confessions could not be included as evidence for three reasons: (1) coerced confessions were untrustworthy, (2) their use would offend the community's sense of fair play and decency, and (3) the exclusion of coerced confessions from evidence would, it was hoped, reduce the use of brutality and other undue pressures when police question suspects (Wigmore, 1970, p. 324). What constituted "coercion" remained a thorny question. As early as the Supreme Court case of *Bram v. United States* (1897), the courts recognized that sheer physical brutality was not the only means of coercion. Other factors considered were use of drugs (*Townsend v. Swain*, 1963),

sleep deprivation (*Ashcraft v. Tennessee*, 1944), lack of food (*Reck v. Pate*, 1961), and prolonged interrogations (*Davis v. North Carolina*, 1966).

A case-by-case approach to assessing the voluntariness of confessions proved difficult for many reasons. The task was highly subjective, and it resulted in countless "swearing contests" between police and suspects about what went on behind the closed doors of interrogation rooms. The case of *Miranda v. Arizona* (which we discuss in the next chapter) was in part an attempt to remedy the foregoing problems by creating a rule, based on the Fifth Amendment privilege against self-incrimination, that any confessions obtained without suspects having been advised of their legal rights to obtain counsel and to remain silent were inadmissible at trial.

However, *Miranda* does not solve all problems about the validity of confessions. Many suspects waive their Miranda rights and once a suspect voluntarily enters the interrogation room, investigators can use any number of tactics to extract a confession. For their part, the police may believe that a waiver of Miranda rights gives them greater latitude in how they question suspects. The result may be a statement that the defendant later claims should not be admitted because it was coerced. Finally, there are suspects whose intellectual disability or psychological instability renders them especially vulnerable to certain tactics of interrogation. Although an individual's special vulnerabilities must be considered in assessing voluntariness, the Supreme Court has stated, in *Colorado v. Connelly* (1986), that a suspect's mental limitations or psychological problems alone are not sufficient for concluding that a confession was involuntary.

The Supreme Court, in *Jackson v. Denno* (1964), made explicit the exclusion of confessions obtained against the will of the accused. In fact, the Court in this case held that criminal defendants are entitled to a pretrial hearing that determines whether any confession they have made to officials was voluntarily given and not the outcome of physical or psychological coercion, which the U.S. Constitution forbids. Only if the fact

**THE CASE OF**

BOX 8-6

**Oreste Fulminante: Was it "harmless error" to admit his confession?**

While incarcerated in New York for possession of a firearm, Oreste Fulminante befriended an FBI informant named Anthony Sarivola who was masquerading in prison as an organized crime figure. Sarivola questioned Fulminante about rumors that the latter had killed a child in Arizona, but Fulminante repeatedly denied these allegations. All that changed in October 1983. One evening as the two walked together around the prison track, Sarivola said that he knew Fulminante had been getting rough treatment from other inmates and offered to protect him, but only if Fulminante "told him about it." Fulminante then admitted that he sexually assaulted his 11-year-old stepdaughter before shooting her

twice in the head. Two years later, the state of Arizona introduced this confession as evidence at Fulminante's trial. He was convicted of first-degree murder and sentenced to death.

On appeal to the United States Supreme Court, Fulminante argued that his confession was coerced and should not have been admitted into evidence. Although the Court conceded that the confession was indeed coerced, they ruled that its introduction at trial amounted to **harmless error.** (In an earlier case, the Supreme Court ruled that erroneously admitted testimony can be considered harmless if the State can show that "the error complained of did not contribute to the verdict obtained";

*Chapman v. California,* 1967, p. 24).

What effect will the *Fulminante* decision have on other cases? Some commentators (e.g., Kamisar, 1995) believe it will encourage the police to use ever-increasing coerciveness in their interrogation practices. Because judges must determine the voluntariness and admissibility of a disputed confession, others (e.g., Mueller & Kirkpatrick, 1995) wonder whether judges can accurately gauge the "harmless" nature of a coerced confession. And finally, one wonders whether jurors are sensitive to the pressures of an interrogation procedure and whether they can correctly evaluate testimony about a coerced confession.

finder (usually the judge) at this hearing determines, by a preponderance of the evidence, that the confession was voluntary may it then be introduced to the jury at the trial.

The *Jackson v. Denno* decision explicitly acknowledged the possibility of coerced confessions. However, in a 1991 case, *Arizona v. Fulminante,* the Rehnquist Court held that admission of an involuntary confession does not automatically taint a conviction (see ◆ Box 8-6).

## Do Jurors Really Discount a Possibly Coerced Confession?

If a defendant confesses while under severe threat during an interrogation, that confession may be viewed either as a reflection of the defendant's true guilt or as a means of avoiding the negative

consequences of silence. Ideally, jurors would employ what a leading attribution theorist (Kelley, 1971) has called the **discounting principle:** They would have more doubts about the truth and reliability of a confession elicited by threat than about one made in the absence of threat. In other words, they would "discount," or give less weight to, the confession—and perhaps even disregard it—because it was generated by threat of force.

But discounting doesn't always occur. A number of social-psychological studies have reported that, when making attributions about the causes of another's behavior, people often commit the **fundamental attribution error:** They do not give sufficient importance to the external situation as a determinant; instead, they believe the behavior is caused by stable, internal factors unique to the actor (Jones, 1990). Thus, in the present situation, they would conclude, "He confessed, so he must be guilty."

Does the fundamental attribution error apply to situations in which jurors must judge the validity of a confession? Apparently, yes. In a series of jury simulation studies, Wrightsman and Kassin (1993; see also Kassin & Wrightsman, 1980, 1981) showed that when mock jurors read transcripts of a trial in which the defendant had confessed in response to a threat of punishment, they judged the confession to be involuntary and disregarded it in their verdict decisions. When the confession was induced by a promise of leniency or favored treatment, however, mock jurors responded inconsistently: They conceded that the defendant had confessed involuntarily, but they judged him to be guilty anyway. These subjects accepted the defendant's confession as probative (i.e., as useful evidence) despite acknowledging that it had been induced through a promise of leniency.

More subtle forms of obtaining confessions show similar effects. When confessions are "noncoercively" encouraged by interrogators who sympathetically attempt to minimize the severity of the charges or the culpability of suspects during questioning, subjects show the same strong **positive coercion bias:** They are willing to vote guilty even when they see the confessions as being involuntary (Kassin & McNall, 1991).

Another interpretation of these results is possible: Maybe jurors associated the differences between positive and negative *kinds* of constraint with differences in the perceived *degree* of cause. People often assume that punishment is a more powerful form of behavioral inducement than reward (Wells, 1980). For example, threatening a child with a spanking if she doesn't clean her room is usually seen as a stronger motivator than offering her money if she does. In the studies just described, subjects may have accepted the leniency-induced confessions not simply because the constraint was positive but because a promise of leniency or suggestion of sympathy seemed like a relatively weak inducement.

The Supreme Court deemed the use of an involuntary confession to be "harmless error" in the *Fulminante* case. In direct response to this opinion, Kassin and Sukel (1997) conducted a study to assess whether erroneously admitted coerced confessions are actually discounted by jurors, whether their use truly constitutes "harmless error."

Mock jurors read a murder trial transcript that involved a suspect who confessed either in a high-pressure or low-pressure interrogation. (In addition, in a control condition, there was no evidence concerning a confession.) In the high-pressure interrogation, the defendant testified that he was handcuffed, questioned, and verbally abused by an armed detective and that he felt pressured to confess after the detective began brandishing his weapon. In the low-pressure situation, the defendant was not handcuffed, threatened with a weapon, or intimidated.

In both of the confession conditions, half of the jurors learned that the judge allowed the confession to be entered as evidence, and half learned that the judge ordered the confession to be stricken from the trial record after jurors had heard about it; the confession was ruled either admissible or inadmissible. Playing the role of jurors, participants gave a verdict at the conclusion of the trial and answered various questions.

To get a preliminary indication of the impact of a coerced confession, Kassin and Sukel asked jurors whether the defendant had confessed voluntarily and whether the confession influenced their verdicts. Participants were quite good at distinguishing high-pressure from low-pressure interrogation situations and judged the confession to be significantly less voluntary under the former situation than the latter. Furthermore, they stated that their verdicts were more influenced by the admissible confession than by the inadmissible and by a confession resulting from low-pressure interrogation procedures than from an interrogation that was high in pressure. So far, these data seem to justify the Court's faith in juries. Unfortunately, that's not the whole picture.

When Kassin and Sukel analyzed the impact of the confession on verdicts, a troubling result came to light: the presence of a confession increased the conviction rate dramatically, even when jurors believed that it was coerced (obtained by high-pressure tactics) and when it was ruled inadmissible. In contrast to the 19% conviction rate in the no-confession control condition, 47% of jurors in the high-pressure condition voted to convict the defendant, as did 47% of jurors in a condition in which the confessions had been stricken from the record.

What do these findings mean for the "harmless error" analysis? At least in the context of confessions, the admission of this evidence might indeed constitute "harmful error": Even when mock jurors deemed a confession to be coerced, when the judge ruled the confession inadmissible, and when jurors said that the confession did not influence their verdicts, still they did not adequately discount that coerced confession. As the authors state, "The mere presence of a confession was thus sufficient to turn acquittal into conviction, irrespective of the contexts in which it was elicited and presented" (p. 42).

## Judge's Instructions as an Effort to Rectify Matters

How might the courts deal with this inconsistency between the legal assumptions and the empirical findings? It would seem that the courts should exercise special caution when a confession has apparently resulted from an offer of a lighter sentence or some other form of leniency. One way to try to curb this bias is through the use of a judge's instruction. As indicated earlier, some states provide the opportunity, after the confession has been admitted into evidence, for the judge to instruct the jurors that they should also determine the voluntariness issue before rendering a verdict.

Another study in Kassin and Wrightsman's program of research tested the effects of judicial instructions that have actually been used in different jurisdictions (Kassin & Wrightsman, 1985; Wrightsman & Kassin, 1993). In this mock jury study, subjects received from the judge a brief confession-related instruction, a more detailed instruction, or no instruction at all. After reading a trial transcript, mock jurors judged the voluntariness of the defendant's confession, rendered their verdicts, and answered other case-related questions.

The manipulation of instructions had two interesting effects. First, compared with the uninstructed subjects, those who had received the elaborate judicial instruction generally conceded that more pressure to confess had been exerted on the suspect. Yet, the instruction did not affect a more practically important variable: judgments of voluntariness. Second, and perhaps more disturbing, these instructions also had no influence on verdicts even though subjects claimed they had been influenced by the instruction. This pattern thus reveals a fascinating discrepancy between the actual impact of the judge's charge and subjects' self-reported beliefs about that effect.

Overall, these results suggest that a judge's instructions do not dissipate the positive coercion bias. The negligible impact of the judge's instructions in this area is consistent with other research suggesting that jurors are relatively unaffected by all sorts of judicial instructions and admonitions (Nietzel, McCarthy, & Kern, 1998). It is still premature, however, to dismiss totally the potential utility of instructions, since they did affect certain reactions by the mock jurors. Instead, it would be helpful to speculate about why they failed and to explore how they could be improved.

## "Unfairness" and "Untrustworthiness" of Coerced Confessions: Which Is More Influential?

Recall two of the reasons why coerced confessions are deemed inadmissible as evidence: (1) they are unconstitutional and unfair to the accused, and (2) they are unreliable and untrustworthy. A close look at the elaborate, or long-form, judge's instruction shows that it emphasizes the latter and neglects to advance the "fairness" justification. Yet Kalven and Zeisel (1966), citing real-world examples, suggest that "the jury may not so much consider the credibility of the confession as the impropriety of the method by which it was obtained" (p. 320). This observation implies that one promising approach to improving the elaborate instruction is to shift its emphasis. Perhaps an argument that emphasizes what Kalven and Zeisel call the "sympathy hypothesis" rather than the "credibility hypothesis" might prove effective.

Hence, Kassin and Wrightsman (1985) conducted another experiment to evaluate and compare a "sympathy instruction" (i.e., one that emphasizes the unfairness of the coerced confession). Specifically, mock jurors read the transcript of a hypothetical assault case that included testimony about either an unconstrained confession or a confession induced through the promise of lenient treatment. Subjects then received the standard instruction about evaluating the truthfulness of the confession, an instruction pointing out the unfairness of a coerced confession (a sympathy instruction), an instruction that encompassed both arguments, or no instruction.

Again there emerged the conflicting influence of a confession induced through a promise of leniency; that is, even though subjects acknowledged that the leniency-induced confession was relatively involuntary, they did not disregard that evidence when rendering their verdicts. The sympathy appeal, presented either alone or combined with other instructions, significantly increased mock jurors' perceptions that the defendant had been unfairly treated. But it failed to lower the conviction rate. Here again, mock jurors are unduly influenced by the "what" of behavior rather than the "why."

### Jurors' Inability to Fulfill the Court's Expectations

Throughout the last four centuries, the legal definition of coercion has progressed through a series of stages: (1) negative/physical pressure; (2) negative/physical or psychological pressure; (3) positive or negative/physical or psychological pressure. But Kassin and Wrightsman's program of research suggests that the layperson (the potential juror) is stuck at the second stage. Subjects readily acknowledge that a mere threat, even without signs of physical brutality, is coercive enough to elicit an untruthful confession. Yet, they seem unable or unwilling to excuse defendants whose confessions are propelled by a promise or hint of a lighter sentence—this despite the recognition that accused persons might plausibly have "confessed" to acts they had not committed.

Clearly, up to this point, efforts to use judicial instructions to reduce the positive coercion bias have not been totally successful. Subjects' responses to some questions are affected by which instructions they are given, but not on the most important variable—verdicts.

# Entrapment

In their zeal to catch criminals, the police sometimes induce law-abiding people to commit crimes they otherwise would not have committed. This practice is called **entrapment.** Defendants who claim they were entrapped are offering two explanations: (1) They were induced to break the law by a person or persons working for the police (often an informant), and (2) they were not predisposed to break that law—the police created a crime that otherwise would not have occurred.

The defense of entrapment is recognized in all states. There are two general approaches to the defense. One asks whether the police methods would have induced a reasonable, law-abiding citizen to commit the offense; this so-called *objective approach* is followed in a minority of states. The other position asks whether the defendant was ready to commit the offense in the absence of inducement or encouragement (i.e., was "otherwise disposed to engage in the conduct") and is termed the *subjective approach*. The latter approach is followed in a majority of states and in the federal courts.

Proactive law enforcement often necessitates deception. We understand that the police must sometimes pose as drug buyers (or sellers) to catch those dealing in illegal drugs. We want the police to infiltrate conspiracies to prevent criminal activity. We expect the police to "troll the net" to identify pedophiles who might use the Internet to perpetrate sex crimes (see ◆ Box 8-7). But we do not want the police to induce law-abiding folks to commit crimes. The trick, as the Supreme Court stated in *Sherman v. United States,* is to distinguish between a "trap for the unwary innocent and the trap for the unwary criminal" (*Sherman v. United States,* 1958, p. 372).

In states following the subjective approach, defendants must prove that they were induced or persuaded to commit the crime by someone working for the police. If the defendant is successful in meeting this burden, the prosecution then has the burden of responding to the claim of entrapment. The prosecution may respond by proving one or both of the following: (1) The police didn't induce the defendant to commit the offense but rather just provided an opportunity; or (2) even though police induced the defendant to commit the offense, he or she was predisposed to commit it anyway.

An example of the first response is the *passive sting*. The police put an officer dressed like a prostitute on the corner and wait for would-be "johns" to take the bait. In such a case, the court and jury will likely say that there is no inducement—the police simply provided an opportunity for criminal activity.

An *active sting,* such as that described in Box 8-7, involves inducement and persuasion. The crucial question in such a case is whether the defendant was predisposed to commit the offense and, if so, at what point in time was the predisposition present—before or after police contacts. The leading case on this issue is *Jacobson v. United States* (1992).

In *Jacobson,* the Supreme Court held that the trial court erred in refusing to direct a verdict on the lack of predisposition in a case in which the defendant ordered child pornography through the mail after a lengthy cultivation of the defendant's prurient interest by the Postal and Customs Services. Before such acts were illegal, the defendant

had obtained nude photos of young boys from a mail-order bookstore. After such acts were made criminal, postal authorities found Jacobson's name on the bookstore's mailing list and started a campaign of phony surveys, circulars, and letters designed to pique the defendant's interest in preteen sex. After being aroused by this lengthy cultivation (some of the come-ons flaunted the First Amendment), Jacobson placed an order for child pornography from a brochure mailed to him by the postal authorities.

Jacobson was convicted, but the Supreme Court reversed the conviction because the government had failed to show that Jacobson was predisposed to engage in illegal activity before the postal authorities started their campaign to induce him to order child pornography. His interest in child pornography at a time when it was not illegal did not give the authorities reason to believe that he would break the law in this regard.

In her dissenting opinion, Justice O'Connor argued that the majority opinion effectively requires law enforcement officials to have some basis for targeting individuals in a sting operation (as opposed to passive sting operations in which law enforcement officials set the trap and wait for someone to take the bait). If there is no basis for targeting an individual, any resulting prosecution is at risk because of a potential lack of evidence proving that the predisposition existed prior to contact. Targeted individuals may supply the evidence of predisposition—perhaps by bragging about their criminal exploits—but an individual who merely responds to the attention of the undercover agent has not clearly shown predisposition to commit the offense. Although it is consistent with the subjective approach, *Jacobson* furthers the major goal of the objective approach: to deter police from the kind of overreaching that might induce law-abiding citizens to break the law.

The goal of the objective approach, like the exclusionary rule, is to deter police misconduct. Can governmental conduct ever be so outrageous that an admittedly predisposed defendant is entitled to be acquitted as a matter of due process? A

## THE CASE OF

**BOX 8-7**   **Billy Burgess: Entrapment on the Internet**

When Billy Burgess (computer name "LandofAhz") logged onto an America Online chat room for men interested in "barely legal females," he might have thought "Maggie284," his cyberpal's computer persona, was a 13-year-old girl—a female of an age not "legal" in any state. After all, Maggie284 repeatedly referred to "Mom," misspelled words, and mentioned not only her age but her weight (92 pounds) and her inexperience in sexual matters. Intrigued by Maggie284's responses to his sexually explicit messages, LandofAhz told Maggie284 that he would be coming to Orlando, where Maggie284 purported to live, and asked her what size clothing she wore. Perhaps unprepared for the question, Maggie284 told him, "size 10" (hardly the correct size for a 92-pound 13-year-old), and LandofAhz replied that he would meet her in a limousine with lingerie, champagne, and other gifts. Maggie284 asked him to "e-mail me," and LandofAhz promised to do so before logging off.

Did Billy Burgess really believe he was corresponding with a 13-year-old girl, or was he merely engaged in fantasy play? In the world of Internet chat rooms, reasonable people should assume their cyber penpals might not be what they purport to be (Sheetz, 2000). Even if Burgess did believe he was corresponding with a 13-year-old, little evidence indicates he intended to pursue the matter by going to Orlando—until Maggie-284 contacted him two weeks later.

Of course, Maggie284 was not a budding teenager. Maggie284 was a 26-year-old man named Randall Sluder, on probation for the felony of attempting to evade a police officer, who had created Magge284 to identify and apprehend individuals who use the Internet to engage in cybersex with underage teenagers.

After communicating with LandofAhz on March 30, 1997, Sluder printed out the salacious e-mails and took them to the Kissimmee, Florida police, who assumed the identity of Maggie284

and e-mailed LandofAhz on April 14 to ask him to come to Orlando for a meeting. Over the next few days Maggie284 and LandofAhz exchanged e-mails, and LandofAhz promised to come to Orlando bearing gifts on April 16. Maggie284 e-mailed a phone number, LandofAhz called, and a female police officer successfully simulated the voice of a 13-year-old girl. Again, LandofAhz asked what size dress he should buy, and this time was told "size 12"—far too large for a 92-pound 13-year-old.

On the evening of April 16, LandofAhz, aka Billy Burgess, arrived at the Enterprise Hotel in a Lincoln Town Car (but without gifts) and was arrested. He was charged in federal court with attempting, through the Internet, to induce a minor to have sex and with traveling in interstate commerce to have sex with a minor.

Burgess claimed that he was entrapped—that he was induced to come to Orlando by Maggie-284's e-mail to him two weeks after the initial correspondence, had no

majority of the Supreme Court acknowledged the possibility in *Hampton v. United States* (1976), although there have been no Supreme Court cases in which a majority was sufficiently offended by the government's conduct to overturn a conviction.

*United States v. Twigg* (1978) is the case most often referred to as authority for the due process defense. In *Twigg*, an informant contacted Neville, an old friend, and proposed they set up a "speed"

laboratory. Neville agreed and assumed responsibility for the capital and the distribution of the product. With the government's financial backing, the informant supplied the chemicals, apparatus, and expertise required to make the drug. Twigg, one of Neville's creditors, was drawn into the operation. The federal court of appeals reversed the convictions of Neville and Twigg, because of the government's extraordinary level of

intention of trying to meet Maggie284, and would not have come to Orlando had the Kissimmee police not contacted him.

The jury seriously considered the entrapment defense, as evidenced by the following question it sent to the judge: "Need clarification on entrapment, the jury instruction seems contradictory. There is some reasonable doubt that the Defendant would have pursued this further if the police did not send the first E-mail on 4/11/97, is this nothing more than the Govt. offering an opportunity" (*United States v. Burgess,* 1999, p. 1268).

After being reinstructed, the jury convicted Burgess on all counts. Did the jury believe he was "merely offered an opportunity"? Or did the jury think he was induced to commit the offense but was predisposed to commit it? We don't know, though clearly Maggie284's reopening of the correspondence went beyond "offering an opportunity." On appeal, the federal court of appeals de-

scribed the evidence that Burgess was not entrapped as less than "overwhelming," but it reversed the conviction on other grounds (the trial judge had failed to instruct the jury not to draw an "adverse inference" from Burgess's failure to testify in his own behalf) (*United States v. Burgess,* 1999). If the court of appeals had not reversed, the court might have grappled with the interesting question of how *Jacobson*—which seems to suggest that the government must show predisposition before contacting a defendant—applies to trolling chat rooms.

Is it fair for the police to assume that one who responds to sexually oriented chatter from purportedly underage correspondents is predisposed to engage in illegal sexual activity? As Michael Sheetz describes, a police investigator will assume a suggestive name (e.g., Rachel-12) and wait for hits. "It has been my experience as an investigator that when using a female sounding name and a youthful persona, so many requests for

private chat occur within five minutes that immediate response to all would be impossible" (Sheetz, 2000, p. 410).

Although acknowledging that some of the correspondents are "offending pedophiles," Sheetz contends that most of those who would want to chat with "Rachel-12" are merely curious or are "non-offending pedophiles," whose fantasy role playing involves clandestine sexual encounters with underage children. There is no sharp psychological distinction between offending and nonoffending pedophiles, and the police might push a nonoffending pedophile over the line through the apparent eagerness of "Rachel-12" to engage in real sexual activity. In such a case, the police have created a crime that otherwise would never have occurred (Sheetz, 2000).

involvement—the government had, in fact, manufactured the drug the defendants were accused of conspiring to sell.

Although not decided on due process grounds, an old Kentucky case shows that convictions obtained by unfair police practices will not be allowed to stand. In *Scott v. Commonwealth* (1946), the police trapped a bootlegger after they were ordered to return whiskey they had seized in an il-

legal search. The police gave the whiskey back to the bootlegger and then obtained a search warrant for the very same whiskey. The Kentucky court reversed the resulting conviction because of the police conduct, even though the defendant clearly was predisposed to commit the offense.

In cases in which the police create the crime, courts may be inclined to overlook evidence of predisposition and find that the defendant was entrapped as a matter of law. This result may be reached by application of the due process clause or by limited acceptance of the objective approach. *United States v. Twigg* is one example: Supplying a person who harbors general criminal tendencies with the means and opportunity of committing a crime that he or she otherwise could not have committed is not acceptable. Another example is the offer that is "too good to refuse." Suppose the police advertise a willingness to pay $1000 for a basketball ticket in a jurisdiction where "ticket scalping" is illegal. Perhaps a judge would dismiss the charges without regard to the predisposition of the one who took the bait, on the ground that the nature of the offer is such that normal law-abiding citizens would be inclined to accept, and such an offer therefore serves no legitimate law enforcement goal.

How do average citizens react to the defense of entrapment? First, they have difficulty understanding the judge's instructions about the definition of entrapment, especially when the objective definition is used (Borgida & Park, 1988; Morier, Borgida, & Park, 1996). Second, if the subjective definition is used and the defendant has a prior conviction, this admission heightens the likelihood of guilty verdicts (Borgida & Park, 1988). In general, laypersons react harshly to an entrapment claim. They respond as jurors do to a confession elicited by positive coercion. They say, "He got caught, so he must be guilty." Moreover, use of entrapment as a defense usually doesn't work. Jurors have a hard time believing that otherwise honest people could be so easily induced into criminal behavior.

## SUMMARY

**1. What are some psychological investigative techniques used by the police?** The police use a variety of devices to increase the likelihood that suspects will be prosecuted and convicted. Among these are criminal profiling, the so-called lie detector (technically, the polygraph technique), and procedures to induce confessions. Police may even create crime situations to tempt suspects to commit new crimes. When the latter is done, the accused may claim entrapment as a defense against the charge.

**2. What is criminal profiling?** Criminal profiling is an attempt to use what is known about how a crime was committed to infer what type of person might have committed it. Preliminary evidence about profiling suggests that it may have some validity as a means of narrowing police investigations to the most likely suspects.

**3. Is the polygraph a valid instrument for lie detection?** Lie detection has a long history but a short career as a standardized technique. Early attempts to be rigorous still confused "lying" with the display of any emotion. No measure of physiological reactions can precisely distinguish between guilt and other negative emotions, such as fear, anger, or embarrassment. Nevertheless, examiners using the Keeler polygraph (which measures pulse rate, breathing rate, and electrical resistance of the skin) claim high rates of accuracy (96%–99%) in distinguishing between subjects who are lying and those who are not. Several problems arise in accepting such claims, including the lack of real follow-ups, the question of adequate criteria, and the misleading nature of "accuracy rates." There is also the problem of lack of consistency in the conclusions of different examiners. Critics of the procedure acknowledge, however, that the polygraph has accuracy rates of 65% or higher. New approaches to lie detection or the concealment of guilty knowledge are being developed and tested.

**4. When is the best time to use a polygraph?** The best use of the polygraph appears to be during the investigatory stages of a criminal prosecution. Its results may excuse some suspects; however, polygraph examiners often use the technique to intimidate their subjects and trick them into confessing. In some states, polygraph examiners are allowed to testify about the results of their examinations. This appears to be a dangerous procedure if jurors are convinced of a defendant's guilt on the basis of this testimony alone.

Recently the use of polygraph examinations as part of screening for employment in private businesses has been outlawed.

**5. *Why is the "voluntariness" of a confession important?*** The police encourage suspects to confess. Sometimes, after a suspect "confesses" to the police, he or she will later deny this; recanted confessions occur in about 20% of all criminal cases. Therefore, it is important to assess the voluntariness of a confession because the Supreme Court has ruled that the prosecution can introduce a confession into trial evidence only if it was truly voluntary (i.e., not coerced).

But jurors have difficulty evaluating confessions that were elicited by a promise of lenient treatment. Many jurors still judge the defendant guilty in these circumstances.

**6. *What are the main legal definitions of entrapment?*** Entrapment, as a defense to charges of lawbreaking, rests on two different legal standards. The objective test of entrapment focuses entirely on the propriety of investigative methods. It asks whether the actions of the authorities were so compelling that they elicited a criminal act in a person not otherwise ready and willing to commit it. In contrast, the subjective standard (used in most states and by the federal government) emphasizes the defendant's state of mind—whether he or she was predisposed to commit an offense. Jurors have not generally been sympathetic to a defendant's claim of entrapment; they react much like jurors who are evaluating a coerced confession.

## KEY TERMS

| | | | |
|---|---|---|---|
| analog studies | entrapment | harmless error | serial killer* |
| base rate | event-related brain | mass murderer* | spree killer |
| cognitive |    potentials | polygraph | stipulate |
|    psychophysiology | field studies | positive coercion bias | |
| Control Question Test | fundamental | psychological stress | |
| criminal profiling |    attribution error |    evaluator | |
| Directed Lie Test | ground truth | relevant/irrelevant | |
| discounting principle | Guilty Knowledge Test |    procedure | |

**InfoTrac**
**College**
**Edition**

For additional readings go to **http://www.infotrac-college.com/wadsworth** and enter a search term related to your interest. The key terms that have been asterisked above will pull up several related articles. *See also:* EVOKED POTENTIALS.

# The Rights of Victims and the Rights of the Accused

## ORIENTING QUESTIONS

1. *During the 1960s, several Supreme Court decisions established important rights for criminal suspects. What were the principles in these decisions?*
2. *A number of Supreme Court decisions since the 1960s have strengthened the powers of law enforcement officials. What were the principles in these decisions?*
3. *What is the status of the Fourth Amendment today?*
4. *Does the criminal justice system treat victims of crime fairly? What can be done to improve crime victims' beliefs that the justice system works for them as well as for criminal defendants?*
5. *What advantages do the prosecution and defense each have in a criminal trial?*

A fundamental task of our society, extending from the dilemmas of Chapter 1, is to balance the claims of individuals to just treatment and presumed innocence against organized society's expectation that public order will be maintained. Since the 1960s, the U.S. Supreme Court has been the battleground for continuing efforts to achieve both goals. The Supreme Court in the 1960s, led by Chief Justice Earl Warren, believed that a number of earlier Court decisions had abused the rights of accused persons. So the Warren Court tried to redress the balance in a series of cases that, in the words of the Chief Justice, "dislodged old law enforcement practices that had become tainted with brutal intimidation of prisoners and suspects along with other injustices" (Warren, 1977, p. 316). The first section of this chapter reviews some of these decisions. With the shifts in the membership of the Supreme Court that took place in the early 1970s and again in the late 1980s and early 1990s, more recent decisions have shifted toward the crime control model described in Chapter 1.

A psychological analysis of these Court decisions is appropriate because these judgments, either directly or indirectly, reflect current values in American society. As we will see later in this chapter, in some recent cases, the Supreme Court has recognized the difficulty of balancing the competing goals identified at the beginning of this book.

# Fairness to the Accused: The Warren Court Decisions

The 1960s unleashed permissive and democratic forces that influenced the Supreme Court in its decision making. The first four cases in this section are the most important criminal procedure decisions of the Warren Court; these cases altered the balance between the powers of the police and the rights of the accused. As we will see in the next section, the protections guaranteed by these four cases have been trimmed back in re-

cent years by the Burger and Rehnquist courts. We discuss two other cases in this section: *In re Gault* (1967) and *Jackson v. Denno* (1964). These cases establish important protections for defendants and have not been weakened by the Burger and Rehnquist courts.

## Mapp v. Ohio *(1961):* *The Exclusionary Rule*

Although the *Mapp* case began as a bombing investigation, it led to the conviction of Dolree Mapp on a charge of possession of obscene materials. The case is now known primarily because of its effect on the methods police may use for obtaining evidence. On May 23, 1957, seven Cleveland, Ohio, police officers forcibly opened a door to Ms. Mapp's house after she refused to admit them because they had no search warrant. A paper, purported to be a warrant, was held up by one of the officers. Ms. Mapp grabbed it and placed it "in her bosom" (to use the phrasing of the Supreme Court). A struggle ensued, the police retrieved the paper, and they handcuffed Ms. Mapp because she was being "belligerent." They then searched the entire house, including her child's bedroom, and eventually found the obscene materials leading to her conviction. (There was no indication that she knew anything about the bombing.) At her trial, no search warrant was produced by the prosecution, nor was the failure to produce one explained. Still, she was found guilty.

What if the police exceed the limits of the law in their law enforcement activities and yet, in doing so, discover evidence of criminal behavior? Should evidence, such as a murder weapon or stolen property, obtained during an illegal search and seizure be admitted in court? In its decision in *Mapp v. Ohio* (1961), the Warren Court said no, that it was inadmissible in both state and federal courts. Until this decision, about half the states had admitted illegal evidence into testimony.

The *Mapp* case deals with the **exclusionary rule**—that is, what must be excluded from the evidence admitted in court. As we will see later in this chapter, the exclusionary rule continues to be controversial because, to many people, in the words of former Supreme Court Justice Benjamin Cardozo, it makes little sense for "the criminal to go free because the constable has blundered" (*People v. Defore*, 1926).

The Fourth Amendment of the U.S. Constitution guarantees to citizens the right "to be secure in their persons, houses, papers, and effects, against unreasonable searches and seizures." However, the Fourth Amendment does not state what the remedy should be for the victim of an illegal search or seizure. *Mapp* held that exclusion of the evidence illegally seized was necessary because the Court believed that other remedies (e.g., suing the police) did not deter police misconduct.

*Mapp v. Ohio* is considered a landmark case because the Supreme Court ruled that the exclusionary rule is part and parcel of the Fourth Amendment and also because it stated that the Fourteenth Amendment to the Constitution "incorporated" the provisions of the Fourth Amendment and thus made binding on the states all the provisions of the Fourth Amendment (Kerper, 1972). This aspect of the *Mapp* decision is reflected in subsequent cases discussed in this section.

## Fay v. Noia (1963): *The Writ of Habeas Corpus*

In 1942, Santo Caminito, Frank Bonino, and Charles Noia were convicted in a New York State court of the murder of Murray Hammeroff and sentenced to prison in Sing Sing for the rest of their lives. Caminito and Bonino appealed their convictions to the New York appellate courts; Noia did not appeal. Caminito and Bonino complained that their confessions had been coerced and should not have been allowed into evidence. In New York at the time, the jury, not the judge, decided whether a confession had been coerced (a procedure later held unconstitutional in *Jackson v. Denno*, 1964, discussed later in this section), and the jury had decided that the confessions were not coerced.

The New York state courts rejected the appeals of Caminito and Bonino, and Caminito filed a petition for a writ of **habeas corpus** (Latin for

"you have the body") in federal district court. In a habeas corpus petition, a defendant typically alleges that his or her continued confinement is unlawful. The primary function of the writ is not to assess a prisoner's guilt or innocence but, rather, to release the accused from unlawful imprisonment. Caminito asked the federal court to hold that his confession was coerced and that he had been convicted in violation of the due process clause of the U.S. Constitution. The federal district court denied the claim, but the court of appeals granted Caminito's petition. The state of New York conceded that Caminito, Bonino, and Noia were kept incommunicado, denied access to their lawyers and families, and questioned continuously for 27 hours before confessing. Caminito testified to his innocence at trial and explained that, to stop the interrogation, he finally told the police what they wanted. The federal court of appeals held that Caminito's confession was coerced and should not have been considered by the jury. The state trial court then dismissed the indictment because there was no substantial evidence against Caminito other than his confession.

Heartened by Caminito's victory, Bonino successfully sought his release from prison and, by 1956, joined Caminito on the streets. Noia, too, asked the state trial court to order his release because his confession, like those of Caminito and Bonino, was the result of a lengthy secret interrogation. The state district attorney opposed Noia's claim because Noia, unlike Caminito and Bonino, had not appealed his conviction. The state's attorney argued that, by not appealing, Noia had "waived" any right to complain about the admission of his confession. To this argument, Judge Joyce, the state trial judge, eloquently said:

> It is true that Noia did not at any time seek appellate review anywhere of the judgment of conviction upon this indictment. The question thus arises whether or not he must serve out a life sentence imposed on what is now determined to have been a manifestly unlawful conviction, merely because he did not so appeal.
>
> In the light of the developments in the highest courts of the states and nation with respect

to the cases of Caminito and Bonino, the reasons for Noia's failure to press an appeal, whatever they may have been, have now become unimportant. What remains of paramount importance is the question whether substantial—even elemental—justice is to be denied him merely by reason of an omission to take certain procedural steps.

Here we have this defendant sitting out a life sentence in one of the state prisons on a conviction [based on] facts and law which it is conceded are identical with those of his co-defendants Caminito and Bonino, on a conviction that our highest courts held in the Caminito and Bonino decisions to be an unlawful one and in violation of due process. (*People v. Noia*, 1956)

The New York appeals court, however, held that Noia had waived any complaint about his confession by failing to appeal. Like Caminito, Noia filed a petition for writ of habeas corpus in federal court, and his case eventually found its way to the U.S. Supreme Court in 1963, 22 years after the slaying of Murray Hammeroff. Justice William Brennan wrote the opinion of the Court. He held that federal courts should issue writs whenever it appeared that someone in federal or state custody had been convicted in violation of the U.S. Constitution. Furthermore, he held that a defendant was not barred by his failure to appeal (or make use of any other available state procedures) unless the defendant "deliberately bypassed" the state procedure. Brennan found Noia's failure to appeal wholly understandable and excusable. He had exhausted his money and didn't want to saddle his family with added costs. Furthermore, he faced the "grisly choice" (the words of Justice Brennan) of risking a death sentence if he appealed. If he appealed and his conviction were reversed, he could be sentenced to death if convicted after a retrial. *Fay v. Noia* swung the door of the federal courthouse wide open to state prisoners, who were complaining that their convictions were tainted by illegally seized evidence, bad confessions, or other violations of the Bill of Rights. As we will see in the next section, it did not take long for the door to start to close.

## Gideon v. Wainwright *(1963)*: *The Right to Counsel during a Trial*

Clarence Earl Gideon was a small-town thief who lived on the fringes of society; yet his case made legal history. At age 51, Gideon was tried for breaking and entering the Bay Harbor Pool Room in Panama City, Florida, and stealing money from a cigarette machine and a jukebox. At his trial, Gideon asked the judge to appoint an attorney to defend him because he had no money to pay for one. The judge, following the laws in Florida, refused. Free attorneys were provided only if there were special circumstances in the case—if, for instance, the offense was a very serious one or if the defendant's mental abilities were limited.

Gideon did not have a lawyer during his trial and although he was no stranger to a courtroom—having been convicted on four previous occasions—he lost this case, too. Eventually, from his prison cell, Gideon filed a pauper's appeal to the U.S. Supreme Court. His contention, laboriously printed in pencil, was that the U.S. Constitution guaranteed the right of every defendant in a criminal trial to have the services of a lawyer. Gideon's effort was a long shot; well over 1500 pauper's appeals are filed each term, and the Supreme Court agrees to consider only about 3% of them. Furthermore, 20 years earlier, in the case of *Betts v. Brady* (1942), the Supreme Court had rejected the very proposition that Gideon was making by holding that poor defendants had a right to free counsel only under "special circumstances" (e.g., if the defendant was very young, illiterate, or mentally ill).

Yet, ever since its adoption, the doctrine of *Betts v. Brady* has been criticized as inconsistent and unjust. The folly of requiring a poor person to represent himself is exemplified by Gideon's cross-examination of the most important witness for the prosecution:

Q. Do you know positively I was carrying a pint of wine?
A. Yes.
Q. How do you know that?
A. Because I seen it in your hand. (Lewis, 1964)

When the Supreme Court agreed to hear Gideon's appeal, four of the justices had already declared, in other cases, that they believed *Betts v. Brady* should be overturned. When Gideon's case was argued before the Supreme Court in January 1963, he was represented by Abe Fortas, a Washington attorney later named a Supreme Court justice. Fortas argued that it was impossible for defendants to have a fair trial unless they were represented by a lawyer. He also observed that the "special circumstances" rule was very hard to apply fairly.

On March 18, 1963, the Supreme Court ruled unanimously that Gideon had the right to be represented by an attorney, even if he could not afford one. Justice Hugo Black stated, "That the government hires lawyers to prosecute and defendants who have the money hire lawyers to defend are the strongest indications of the widespread belief that lawyers in criminal cases are necessities, not luxuries" (*Gideon v. Wainwright*, 1963, p. 344). Although *Gideon* applied only to defendants accused of felonies, nine years later, the Supreme Court extended the right to counsel to persons accused of misdemeanors (*Argersinger v. Hamlin*, 1972).

Nearly two years after he was sentenced, Clarence Gideon was given a new trial. With the help of a free court-appointed attorney, he was found not guilty. The simple handwritten petition of a modest man had changed the procedures of criminal trials, perhaps forever. Gideon lived the rest of his life almost free of legal tangles; his only subsequent difficulty came two years later, when he pleaded guilty to a charge of vagrancy in Kentucky. He died in 1972.

## Miranda v. Arizona (1966):
### The Right to Remain Silent

The most famous of all the Supreme Court cases decided during the 1960s, *Miranda v. Arizona*, dealt with the problem of coerced confessions. The case started in an all too typical fashion with an all too disturbing outcome. Late on a Saturday night, May 2, 1963, an 18-year-old woman finished her job at the refreshment stand at the Para-

mount Theater in downtown Phoenix, Arizona. After riding the bus to a stop near her home, she started walking the remaining distance. But a man grabbed her, dragged her to a parked car, tied her hands behind her, laid her down in the back seat, tied her ankles together, and told her to lie still. She felt a cold, sharp object—she was never sure what it was—at her neck. Her abductor drove her to the desert, where he raped her. Then, as he waited for her to get dressed, he demanded whatever money she had. She gave him the four $1 bills in her purse.

The Phoenix police had the victim look at a lineup on Sunday morning. She had described her attacker as a Hispanic American male; 27 or 28; 5 feet, 11 inches tall; and weighing 175 pounds. He was slender, she said, and had a medium complexion, with short black hair. She remembered him as having a tattoo and wearing Levis, a white T-shirt, and dark-rimmed glasses. The police composed a lineup of likely-looking choices, but the victim failed to identify anyone. She was very shy; apparently of limited intelligence, she had dropped out of school after failing for several years.

But a week after the rape, the victim's brother-in-law spotted a car like the one she had described. He pointed it out, and she said yes, it did look like her assailant's car. As the car sped away, they were able to remember enough of the license plate for the police to trace the registration to a young woman who had a friend named Ernest Miranda. He fit the description; he was a Mexican American in his early 20s.

When the police located the car, they saw a rope strung along the back of the front seat, just as the young woman had described. Police records also confirmed that Miranda had several previous criminal convictions, including one for assault with intent to commit rape. A man with a long criminal history going back to age 14, he had been charged with attempted rape at the age of 15. So the police put together a new lineup, selecting three Hispanic Americans, all about the same height and build, to stand with Miranda. But he was the only person wearing a short-sleeved T-shirt, the only one with eyeglasses, and the only tattooed man in the lineup. Still, the young woman couldn't identify her assailant, although she felt that number one—Miranda—had a similar build and features.

Frustrated, the police then took Miranda to an interrogation room for what they thought was routine questioning. But the exchanges that occurred in that tiny chamber forever changed the way that police interact with citizens. Miranda asked, "How did I do?" "You flunked," a police officer replied, and he began to question Miranda about the rape of the young woman. No attorneys, witnesses, or tape recorders were present. The police later reported that Miranda voluntarily confessed, that he "admitted not only 'that he was the person who had raped this girl' but that he had attempted to rape another woman and to rob still another" (Baker, 1983, p. 13).

Miranda described the interrogation differently:

> Once they get you in a little room and they start badgering you one way or the other, "You better tell us . . . or we're going to throw the book at you." . . .They would try to give me all the time they could. They thought there was even a possibility that there was something wrong with me. They would try to help me, get me medical care if I needed it. . . . And I haven't had any sleep since the day before. I'm tired. I just got off my work, and they have me and they are interrogating me. They mention first one crime, then another one; they are certain I am the person. . . . Knowing what a penitentiary is like, a person has to be frightened, scared. And not knowing if he'll be able to get back up and go home. (quoted in Baker, 1983, p. 13)

Whichever story one believes, Ernest Miranda emerged from the questioning a confessed rapist. Because the young woman had been unsure of her identification, the police summoned her to the interrogation room to hear Miranda's voice. As she entered, one of the officers asked Miranda, "Is that the girl?" "That's the girl," he replied, believing that she had already identified him in the lineup.

Miranda was brought to trial in June 1963. The jury of nine men and three women convicted him of rape and kidnapping, and he was sen-

tenced to 20 to 30 years for each charge. But Miranda appealed his conviction all the way to the U.S. Supreme Court, and the Court—by a 5–4 vote—concluded that his right against self-incrimination had been violated. Henceforth, they stated, the police must warn suspects of certain rights before starting a custodial interrogation. If these procedures are not followed, any damaging admissions made by suspects cannot be used by the prosecution in a trial. These *Miranda* rights are the following:

1. Suspects must be warned that they may remain silent, that anything they say may be used against them, that they have the right to have a lawyer present during questioning, and that a lawyer will be appointed if they cannot afford one.

2. If suspects waive their right to counsel and later change their minds, all questioning must stop until the lawyer arrives.

3. If suspects waive their right to an attorney and then confess, the prosecution must show that they knew what they were doing when they waived their rights.

By unintentionally giving his name to the warning that police officers must give suspects, Ernest Miranda became a footnote to history. His own history took an ironic twist, as ◆ Box 9-1 illustrates.

## In re Gault (1967): *The Rights of Juvenile Offenders*

A 15-year-old boy named Gerald Francis Gault was committed to a state industrial school in Arizona for six years for making lewd remarks over the phone. If he had been an adult in Arizona and had done the same thing, he could have been jailed for no more than two months and fined from $5 to $50.

Gault had not been advised of his right to a lawyer or his right to remain silent when questioned by the police. Initially, his parents were not informed that he had been detained. When this decision was appealed to the Supreme Court, the attorneys for the state of Arizona explained that juvenile offenders were not given these and other

### BOX 9-1     What ever happened to Ernest Miranda?

Ernest Miranda was given a new trial as a result of the Supreme Court's ruling in his appeal. But even though his confession was excluded, he was convicted again in 1966 because the prosecution had uncovered new evidence against him.

Between that time and 1976, Miranda served some prison time, was released, but had several run-ins with the law. By the age of 34, he had been an ex-con, an appliance store delivery man, and, probably, a drug dealer. On the night of January 31, 1976, he was playing poker in a flophouse section of Phoenix. A drunken fight broke out involving two illegal Mexican immigrants. As he tried to take a knife away from one of them, Mi-

randa was stabbed in the stomach and again in the chest. He was dead on arrival at the hospital.

Miranda's killer fled, but his accomplice was caught. Before taking him to police headquarters, two Phoenix police officers read to him—one in English, one in Spanish—from a card:

> You have the right to remain silent.
> Anything you say can be used against you in a court of law.
> You have the right to the presence of an attorney to assist you prior to questioning and to be with you during questioning, if you so desire.
> If you cannot afford an attorney, you have the right to have an attorney appointed for you prior to questioning.

*Ernest Miranda*

> Do you understand these rights?
> Will you voluntarily answer my questions?

Thus ironically ended the life, but not the legacy, of Ernest Miranda.

---

criminal safeguards because they were not formally charged with crimes.

For years, as we discussed in Chapter 4, juvenile courts had been given wide freedom to disregard the standard procedures used in trials of adults, supposedly so that these courts could concentrate on rehabilitation rather than punishment of wayward children. But the *Gault* decision stopped such practices. In the majority opinion in this case, Abe Fortas declared that juveniles had the right to a lawyer, to cross-examination of witnesses, and to protection against self-incrimination. The way things were then, wrote Justice Fortas, "the child receives the worst of both worlds; he gets neither the protections accorded to adults nor the solicitous care and regenerative treatment postulated for children" (*In re Gault*, 1967, p. 1428). The only significant right denied to children after *Gault* is the right to a jury; juveniles are tried by judges. The abil-

ity of juveniles to understand their legal rights is a separate matter that we consider in Chapter 11.

*Gault* held that juveniles are entitled to most of the procedural rights of adults. As discussed in Chapter 4, it is apparent that a majority of the public wants children who commit serious crimes tried as adults and given adult sentences if convicted. For example, a 13-year-old boy who beat a 4-year-old child to death with rocks was tried as an adult and sentenced to the maximum—nine years to life—in New York state in 1993 (Pressley, 1996).

## Jackson v. Denno *(1964): The Right to Have a Confession Judged Voluntary or Involuntary*

As noted in Chapter 8, a defendant often makes and then withdraws an out-of-court confession. The legal admissibility of such a confession into evidence has been controversial. In *Jackson v. Denno* (1964), the Supreme Court held that criminal defendants are entitled to a pretrial determination that any confession they make to officials was voluntary and was not obtained through physical or psychological coercion, which the Constitution forbids. Only if the judge determines at the hearing that a confession was in fact voluntary may it then be introduced at trial to the jury.

*Jackson* is based on the Court's assumptions about the way jurors think when asked to decide the voluntariness of a confession that establishes the defendant's guilt:

> Under the New York procedure, the fact of a defendant's confession is solidly implanted in the jury's mind, for it not only hears the confession, but it has been instructed to consider and judge its voluntariness and is in a position to assess whether it is true or false. If it finds the confession involuntary, does the jury—indeed, can it—then disregard the confession in accordance with its instructions? If there are lingering doubts about the sufficiency of the other evidence, does the jury unconsciously lay them to rest by resort to the confession? Will uncertainty about the sufficiency of the other evidence to prove guilt beyond a reasonable doubt actually result in acquittal when the jury knows the defendant has given a truthful confession? (*Jackson v. Denno*, 1964, p. 388)

As noted in Chapter 8, there are other problems in the way that juries interpret confessions, but *Jackson v. Denno* at least reflected the Warren Court's view of the dangers of confessions.

# The Shift in Supreme Court Decisions

As the composition of the Supreme Court shifted in the 1970s, reflecting several Court appointments made by Presidents Nixon and Ford, so did the direction of the Court's decisions. Although the Supreme Court headed by Warren Burger (Earl Warren's successor) was less ideologically consistent than the Warren Court, one of its primary emphases was to provide victims more safeguards under the law. Wrote Chief Justice Burger, "I refuse to join in what I consider an unfortunate trend of judicial decisions in this field which strain and stretch to give the guilty not the same but vastly more protection than the law-abiding citizen." Appointment by President Reagan of three justices (O'Connor, Scalia, and Kennedy) and by President G. H. W. Bush of two (Souter and Thomas) gave a second wind to decisions that restricted the rights provided suspects and defendants by the Warren Court.

Changes in the direction of Court decisions do not happen by chance. A psychological analysis of the causes of this shift in judicial decisions focuses on the values, attitudes, and behavior of individuals. One reason why the Supreme Court has moved toward restricting the rights of the accused over the last 25 years is that the justices reflect the conservative political values of the presidents who chose them (Nixon, Ford, Reagan, and Bush). President Clinton's two appointees—Justices Ginsburg and Breyer—are "centrists." On matters of criminal procedure, they, along with Justices Souter and Stevens, tend to favor the accused in close cases. The other justices—Rehnquist, Scalia, Thomas, Kennedy, and O'Connor—tend to favor the police.

All of our recent presidents, including President Clinton, have been strong advocates of law and order. These presidents were elected—and hence were able to make the appointments—because of shifts in the concerns of individual voters and society at large. Crime, particularly street crime, became a highly publicized issue in the United States in the late 1960s and early 1970s. "Law and order" was the rallying cry heard during the presidential campaign of 1968. The election of Richard Nixon as president in that year symbolized a shift in the sympathies of the general population. More than three decades later, crime remains a prime concern of many U.S. citizens. In the 1988 presidential campaign, G. H. W. Bush effectively used the fact that his opponent, Michael Dukakis, when governor of Massachusetts, had furloughed a criminal, Willie Horton, who then raped a woman. In the 1996 presidential election, both President Clinton and Senator

## THE CASE OF

BOX 9-2    **Bernhard Goetz: Subway vigilante**

A few days before Christmas in 1984, newspaper reports began to appear about a New York City subway incident that resembled a Charles Bronson movie. Eventually, Bernhard Goetz came forward as the white man who had shot and wounded four black youth when they approached him in a subway car and asked for five dollars. One of the young men was shot in the back. The case became news throughout the country and the world.

Polls taken by the New York *Daily News* two weeks after the confrontation on the subway train found that 49% of respondents approved of Goetz's shooting the youth and 31% disapproved (Lichtenstein, 1985). Only 28% felt that he should be charged with at-

tempted murder; 58% disapproved of his being charged. Other polls produced similar results: About twice as many respondents supported his actions as criticized them. Bernhard Goetz became a mythic hero for many Americans, despite the fact that he was to stand trial on four counts of attempted murder and on criminal possession of an unregistered gun. In keeping with this sentiment, Goetz's jury found him guilty only of gun possession, not of attempted murder. He was sentenced to one year in prison.

Nine years later, however, Goetz received a different reception from a Bronx jury, which returned a verdict of $43 million for Darrell Cabey, one of the injured youth. The 1996 verdict represented a

*Bernhard Goetz*

change in mood in a city where crime had dropped markedly and the subway system had been much improved. When Goetz was on the witness stand in his civil trial, he was hardly the subway vigilante of 1987; even his own lawyer saw him as a "clown" and a "geek" (Gladwell, 1996).

---

Dole were determined not to be outdone in their devotion to law and order. Running for president in 2000, Texas Governor George W. Bush seemed almost proud of his state's record of leading the nation in the number of people executed.

The bizarre 1984 case of Bernhard Goetz, the "subway vigilante," reflects the public's fear and condemnation of criminal behavior (see ◆ Box 9-2). The year 1996 saw the passage of several examples of anticrime measures: "three strikes and you're out" legislation in many states, a law requiring a national registry of sex offenders, and "chemical castration" of sex offenders in California (Drummond, 1996).

As early as 1968, the courts began to redress the perceived imbalance between suspects' rights and society's rights. In that year, the U.S. Supreme Court upheld the authority of the police to stop

and frisk suspicious-looking people; however, the police officer had to have a "reasonable and articulable" suspicion, supported by objective facts, that the suspect was about to commit a crime or had just done so. The decision was *Terry v. Ohio*, and the author of the majority opinion was none other than Chief Justice Warren, the person most responsible for the expansion of individual rights in the early 1960s.

Perhaps unwittingly, Chief Justice Warren provided the framework for the Burger Court to rely on a cost/benefit analysis in which the possibility of freeing a "clearly guilty" offender is balanced against the effect of excluding evidence because of misconduct by police (Schwartz, 1988). As discussed in the following section, a cost/benefit approach to search and seizure tends to undermine the deterrent effect of the exclusionary rule. Such an approach reflects the crime control orientation described in Chapter 1 and puts more value on efficient police action than on deterring police from making mistakes. This emphasis fits with the basic cognitive processes of most people; for example, Casper, Benedict, and Kelly (1988) found that mock jurors' decisions about whether police acted inappropriately in search-and-seizure cases depended on whether the police actually had found anything illegal during their warrantless search, a tendency known as **hindsight bias.** Courts also are influenced by hindsight bias; they may be more likely to approve of questionable police procedures when those procedures uncover important evidence of criminal activity (Saks & Kidd, 1986).

In the preceding section we discussed six decisions of the Warren court. The first four—*Mapp, Noia, Gideon,* and *Miranda*—have been chipped away by decisions of the Burger and Rehnquist courts over the past 30 years. We summarize these decisions next.

## The Attack on the Exclusionary Rule

Remember that *Mapp v. Ohio* (1961) held that in order to deter police from violating the Fourth Amendment, illegally obtained evidence could not be admitted at trial. Although controversial, because it may result in reliable evidence being excluded from a jury's consideration, the exclusionary rule has not been overruled by the Burger/Rehnquist Court. It has, however, been modified substantially:

1. *The "good faith" exception.* In *United States v. Leon* (1984), the Court held that evidence obtained by officers who relied on a search warrant issued by a neutral judge may be used in court, even if the warrant is ultimately found not to be supported by probable cause. The same reasoning applies when the police rely in good faith on a computer printout (later determined to be incorrect) maintained by a court clerk (*Arizona v. Evans,* 1995).

2. *The standing requirement.* To object to an illegal search or seizure, the defendant must have "standing"—that is, a "legitimate expectation of privacy" in the place searched (*Rakas v. Illinois,* 1978) or in the thing seized (*United States v. Payner,* 1980). No matter how outrageous the police conduct, there will be no exclusion of illegally obtained evidence if the defendant lacks standing. In *Payner,* FBI agents illegally removed private papers from the briefcase of a bank official and used them to prosecute Payner, one of the bank's customers. The Court held that Payner could not object because he owned neither the briefcase nor the papers.

3. *The inevitable discovery exception.* *Nix v. Williams* (1984) holds that illegally seized evidence need not be excluded if it would inevitably have been found by legal means. *Williams* has become known as the "Christian burial speech" case. On Christmas Eve in 1968, a former mental patient named Robert Williams abducted a 10-year-old girl in Des Moines, Iowa. Williams's car was found abandoned in Davenport, 160 miles away. The day after Christmas, his lawyer arranged for Williams, then in Davenport, to surrender to local police, who would turn him over to Des Moines detectives for the return trip to Des Moines. The detectives agreed that they would not question Williams during the trip.

Knowing that Williams was deeply religious and a former mental patient, the detectives used the return trip to work on Williams's psyche. One of them engaged Williams in a wide-ranging conversation. Addressing Williams as "Reverend," the detective said:

> I want to give you something to think about while traveling down the road. . . . Number one, I want you to observe the weather conditions. It's raining; it's sleeting; it's freezing; driving is very treacherous; visibility is poor; it's going to be dark early this evening. They are predicting several inches of snow for tonight, and I feel that you yourself are the only person that knows where this little girl's body is, that you yourself have only been there once, and if you get a

snow on top of it you yourself may be unable to find it. And, since we will be going right past the area on the way into Des Moines, I feel that we could stop and locate the body, that the parents of this little girl should be entitled to a Christian burial for the little girl who was snatched away from them on Christmas Eve and murdered. And I feel we should stop and locate it on the way in rather than waiting until morning and trying to come back out after a snow storm and possibly not being able to find it at all. (*Brewer v. Williams,* 1977, pp. 392–393)

The detective then stated, "I do not want you to answer me. I don't want to discuss it any further. Just think about it as we're riding down the road."

As the car approached Grinnell, Iowa, Williams asked whether the girl's shoes had been found. When the detective said he wasn't sure, Williams directed the officers to a service station where he said he had left the shoes; a search for the shoes was unsuccessful. As they continued toward Des Moines, Williams asked whether the police had found the blanket and directed them to a rest area where he said he had disposed of the blanket. Nothing was found. They continued toward Des Moines, and as the car approached Mitchellville, Williams said he would show the officers where the body was. He then directed the police to the body of the 10-year-old girl.

Ultimately, the Supreme Court held that the "Christian burial speech" violated Williams's right to counsel because the police had employed trickery to coerce a confession, violating their agreement with Williams's lawyer (*Brewer v. Williams,* 1977). The question then was whether the evidence connected with the body had to be suppressed, since the body was discovered as a result of Williams's illegally obtained statement. At the second trial, the prosecutor convinced the judge that the body would have been discovered anyway, in essentially the same condition as it was found, because the search teams were moving toward the area at the time Williams led the police to the body. This holding was upheld by the Supreme Court in *Nix v. Williams* (1984) and

stands for the "inevitable discovery" exception to the exclusionary rule.

### Limiting the Right to Appointed Counsel

Even though the basic principle of the *Gideon* decision remains intact today, the Supreme Court has limited its application in several respects. For example, in *Ross v. Moffitt* (1974), the Court held that the constitutional right to free counsel does not apply beyond the trial and one appeal. Many (but not all) states provide attorneys for what are termed "**collateral attacks**" (i.e., efforts to get appellate courts to reverse convictions that have become final), but they are not required to do so by the federal Constitution. In *Murray v. Giarratano* (1989), the Court held that the state of Virginia was not obligated to provide lawyers for death row inmates who wished to attack their sentences collaterally in state or federal court. In the opinion of the Court, the state discharged its constitutional obligation to the death row prisoners by providing them with a law library.

In *Coleman v. Thompson* (1991), a Virginia lawyer attempted to help a death row inmate by filing a petition for habeas corpus in a Virginia state court. The judge denied the petition, and the lawyer appealed to the Virginia court of appeals *three days late*. The Virginia appeals court refused to hear the case, and the U.S. Supreme Court held that Coleman's claims were waived because he had not filed the appeal on time. The mistake was the attorney's, not Coleman's, but the Court said Coleman could not complain of ineffective assistance of counsel because the state of Virginia was not obligated to provide a lawyer for a state habeas corpus petition. Many advocates of defendants' rights believe that it is unfair to hold that one cannot complain about his or her attorney's mistakes just because the state was not constitutionally obligated to provide the attorney in the first place. Roger Coleman was subsequently executed.

In *Gideon,* the Court held that a state must provide effective assistance of counsel for a defen-

## THE CASE OF

**BOX 9-3     Glen Ake: Indigent defendants' right to assistance at trial**

Glen Burton Ake had been convicted of the 1979 murder of an Oklahoma minister and his wife. (This case is also notorious in the area of victim's rights, as we describe in this chapter.) Ake's sole defense was insanity. Four months before the trial, a state psychiatrist found him not competent to stand trial and recommended that he be committed to a state mental hospital. But he was found competent to stand trial a month later, after being sedated with Thorazine three times a day. In spite of Ake's obvious mental illness, the court refused to appoint a psychiatrist (at state expense) to examine Ake on the question of criminal responsibility (insanity at the time of the offense). As a result, there was no psychiatric testimony for the jury to consider. The jury convicted Ake and sentenced him to death.

In reversing the decision, the Supreme Court observed that the testimony of a psychiatrist or a psychologist as an expert witness for the defense was a "virtual necessity" if the plea was to have any chance of success. Thurgood Marshall, writing the majority opinion, stated, "Without the assistance of a psychiatrist to conduct a professional examination on issues relevant to the defense, to help determine whether the insanity defense is viable, to present testimony, and to assist in preparing cross-examination of a state's psychiatric witnesses, the risk of an inaccurate resolution of sanity issues is extremely high" (quoted in Turkington, 1985, p. 2).

At Ake's second trial in 1986, a court-appointed psychiatrist testified that he had diagnosed Mr. Ake as a paranoid schizophrenic who had been hearing voices since 1973. He said that Mr. Ake had gone to the victims' home to find the source of the voices and make them stop. Despite this testimony, the jury in the second trial also found the defendant guilty. However, the jury sentenced him to life, not death, in the second trial.

dant who could not afford to hire his or her own counsel. Twenty years later, the Court defined "effective assistance of counsel" to mean that an attorney's representation must meet an "objective standard of reasonableness" (*Strickland v. Washington*, 1984). Unfortunately, there is evidence that some poorly paid appointed attorneys do not meet this standard and serve as nothing more than warm bodies at the side of defendants in court. In two cases—*Javor v. United States* (1984) and *Tippins v. Walker* (1995)—for example, the attorneys in question slept through much of the trials. In a recent development, defense lawyers joined with county governments to force the state of Mississippi to start a statewide public defender system or otherwise adequately fund defense attorneys for indigent defendants. One of the lawsuits involved a capital trial in a small county that forced the

county to raise taxes and borrow money to pay $250,000 in defense costs in a multiple-murder case (Rovella, 2000).

Although most of the decisions of the Burger/Rehnquist Court have gone against the defendant, one significant decision runs the other way. In 1985, the Burger Court extended the Gideon decision by ruling in *Ake v. Oklahoma* that poor defendants must be given free psychiatric help in preparing an insanity defense if a serious question about their sanity has arisen (Turkington, 1985) (see ◆ Box 9-3).

*Ake* is significant because it establishes the principle that an indigent defendant is entitled not only to an attorney at the state's expense but also to the assistance of experts at the state's expense if there are grounds to believe that expert testimony is necessary for a fair determination of the facts at trial. The principle in *Ake* has been extended to other areas of expert assistance. For example, an indigent defendant against whom DNA evidence is offered is entitled to his or her own DNA expert to assist counsel in understanding the evidence (*Dubose v. State*, 1995). Unfortunately, according to some attorneys, it is not clear that the *Ake* decision is followed conscientiously in most courts (Perlin, 1992).

## Whittling Away at Miranda

*Miranda v. Arizona* was the most controversial criminal procedure decision of the Warren Court. "Impeach Earl Warren" billboards were widely seen, and the Chief Justice was castigated in congressional committees and on the floor of Congress (Warren, 1977). Although *Miranda* has survived the Burger and Rehnquist courts, the case remains controversial to this day.

Miranda faced a major challenge from University of Utah law professor Paul Cassell through the case of *Dickerson v. United States* (2000). For many years Professor Cassell has claimed that *Miranda* was an illegitimate exercise of judicial power that freed thousands of guilty defendants on technicalities. He railed at the Department of Justice for refusing to rely on 18 U.S.C. 3501, a statute Congress had passed in 1968 in an attempt to overrule *Miranda*. In 1999, the Court of Appeals for the Fourth Circuit responded to Professor Cassell's call and used the statute to admit a confession that had been taken in violation of *Miranda*. With the support of the Justice Department (which had prosecuted him), the defendant sought a review by the United States Supreme Court. The Court granted review and appointed Professor Cassell to argue in support of the Fourth Circuit's decision. To the surprise of many, however, the Supreme Court emphatically reaffirmed *Miranda*. In a 7–2 decision striking down 18 U.S.C. 3501 as unconstitutional, Chief Justice Rehnquist pointed out that *Miranda* warnings do not significantly deter people from confessing and that *Miranda* has become part of the national culture (*Dickerson v. United States*, 2000, p. 2336). This case is a good example of **stare decisis**—the court's preference

for maintaining stability in its decisions whenever possible. Given *Miranda's* longtime acceptance in the United States, the Court opted not to change the law of confessions.

Since the 1960s, however, the Supreme Court has weakened *Miranda* through a series of decisions hostile to the spirit of the case. Ironically, these decisions were a factor in saving *Miranda* when the case was challenged by Professor Cassell. The police are able to live with *Miranda*, in large part because the following decisions have weakened the case.

*1. Confessions that violate Miranda may be used to impeach a defendant.*   Suppose a person confesses when arrested, and the confession is taken in violation of the *Miranda* warnings. If the defendant testifies to his or her innocence at trial, the prosecutor may use the confession to show that the defendant should not be believed (*Harris v. New York*, 1971).

*2. Confessions by defendants who don't fully understand the warnings may still be admissible.*   The privilege against self-incrimination requires that, before custodial interrogation begins, an accused must be advised as follows:

1.   You have the right to remain silent.
2.   Anything you say may be used against you.
3.   You have the right to speak with an attorney before answering questions and to have an attorney present during questioning.
4.   An attorney will be appointed for you if you cannot afford one.

To validate a subsequent confession, it is enough that the police give the warnings and the defendant responds affirmatively when asked whether he or she wishes to make a statement. Although inability to understand the warnings as a result of very low IQ or mental illness might lead to suppression of a confession, any misimpression or incomplete understanding, even by a young or uneducated person, will rarely invalidate a confession. Psychological research on the ability of people to comprehend the full meaning of *Miranda* warnings indicates that those with mental retardation have great difficulty understanding the warning and the meaning of a waiver; these deficiencies are particularly strong for someone who has no prior experience in the criminal justice system (Fulero & Everington, 1995). Thus, the police can take advantage of a suspect who thinks that an oral confession is not admissible (*North Carolina v. Butler*, 1979). Similarly, the police need not tell the defendant that they suspect him of additional crimes and plan to question him about those matters if he agrees to be questioned about the crime with which he is charged (*Colorado v. Spring*, 1987).

**3. To stop an interrogation, a request for a lawyer must be unequivocal.** In *Davis v. United States* (1994), the Court held that the police were not obligated to stop the questioning or clarify an equivocal request by a suspect ("Maybe I should get a lawyer").

**4. Miranda does not apply unless the suspect is in the custody of the police.** The Court has treated "custody" as a term of art, with recent decisions emphasizing the various evils that *Miranda* was designed to prevent: station house questioning, in which suspects fear they will be subjected to indeterminate isolation and interrogation. Thus, the Court held that roadside questioning of a motorist stopped for drunk driving is noncustodial, even though the motorist is not free to go (*Berkemer v. McCarty*, 1984). Warnings are not required in this circumstance. "Stop and frisk" questioning is also usually viewed as noncustodial because such questioning merely accompanies temporary detentions in public places. Confessions obtained through "jail plants" also do not implicate *Miranda* because the defendant, though incarcerated, believes he or she is talking to a fellow inmate (*Illinois v. Perkins*, 1990).

**5. Miranda does not apply unless the defendant is being interrogated.** A volunteered confession is always admissible. Suppose the police arrest a robbery suspect and decide, for whatever reason, not to interrogate him. On the way to the station, however, the accused volunteers that he wouldn't have been caught if he'd kept his mask on. This confession is admissible because it was not in response to police questioning (*Rhode Island v. Innis*, 1980).

**6. The police are not required to tell the defendant anything more than what is contained in the Miranda warnings.** They are not required to tell the defendant what he is suspected of doing (*Colorado v. Spring*, 1987). They are not required to tell him that a lawyer hired by his family wants to see him (*Moran v. Burbine*, 1986). They are not required to tell him that his silence cannot be used against him.

**7. The police can mislead defendants about the evidence in order to get them to confess (Frazier v. Cupp, 1969).** Trickery is permissible so long as the police do not lie about the *Miranda* warnings themselves.

**8. Miranda warnings are not required in situations in which public safety might be endangered by giving the warnings.** In *New York v. Quarles* (1984), a woman told the police that she had been raped by an armed man who had just run into a supermarket. Officer Kraft entered the market and spotted Quarles running to the rear of the store. Kraft gave chase and caught him in the storage area. After frisking Quarles and finding no gun, Kraft asked where the gun was. Quarles nodded in the direction of some empty cartons and said, "The gun is over there." The police found the gun, and Quarles was prosecuted for criminal possession of the weapon (the rape charge was not pursued). The New York courts suppressed the defendant's statement (and the gun) because Quarles had not been given the *Miranda* warnings. The Supreme Court, however, used the case to create a "public safety" exception to *Miranda*; warnings do not have to be given when police questioning is reasonably motivated by a concern for public safety.

9. *The exclusionary rule does not apply to "derivative evidence" obtained as a result of a confession taken in violation of* **Miranda.** In *Michigan v. Tucker* (1974) and *Oregon v. Elstad* (1985), the defendants' confessions were suppressed because of *Miranda* violations, but other evidence that was ultimately derived from the confessions was admitted into evidence. The *Tucker* and *Elstad* cases were heavily relied on by Professor Cassell in his attack on the *Miranda* holding.

## Gutting the Writ of Habeas Corpus

After *Fay v. Noia* (1963), federal trial courts could hear the habeas corpus petitions of state prisoners who claimed that they had been convicted in violation of the U.S. Constitution. Many important Supreme Court decisions in the 1960s and 1970s came in cases filed as habeas corpus petitions attacking state convictions. In recent years, however, both Congress and the Court have been hostile to habeas corpus claims.

1. *The writ may not be used to claim that a search or seizure violated the Fourth Amendment if the state has already provided an opportunity for a full and fair hearing on the claim* (**Stone v. Powell**, *1976*).

2. *The writ of habeas corpus may not be used to make "new" law* (**Teague v. Lane**, *1989*). In this controversial case, the Court held that the writ should be available only to those whose claims were based on "settled law." A state prisoner could not thereafter use the writ to argue for an expansion of existing rights. The writ was thus rendered impotent as a tool for changing the law.

3. *The writ of habeas corpus is not available to one who "procedurally defaulted" in the state courts* (**Wainwright v. Sykes**, *1977*). *Fay v. Noia* held that the writ was available unless the defendant "deliberately bypassed" a state procedure under which the claim might have been heard. In *Sykes,* the Court applied a strict "waiver" rule: One waives one's rights by not using whatever state procedure is available. In the years since

*Sykes,* which involved the failure to object to evidence, the waiver rule has been applied with a vengeance. In *Engle v. Isaac* (1982), the failure to object to the trial court's instructions to the jury resulted in the defendant's waiver of rights, as did the failure to file a notice of appeal in *Coleman v. Thompson* (1991). It is significant that in all these cases the error was made by a defense attorney. However, the defendant, not the attorney, pays for the mistakes. The Court has provided a very narrow means of escape from the consequences of a procedural default. It has suggested that the writ may be issued to one who establishes "actual innocence," but it has yet to find that anyone has met this burden (*Sawyer v. Whitley,* 1992).

4. *Habeas corpus claims must comply with the strict requirements of the 1996 Antiterrorist and Effective Death Penalty Act (AEDPA).* The AEDPA requires federal courts to defer to state courts' reasonable interpretations of the Constitution, and it imposes strict time limits on filing petitions. Primarily aimed at death penalty cases, the AEDPA applies whenever a state court conviction is challenged in a federal habeas corpus proceeding.

# The Fourth Amendment Today

What is an *unreasonable* search or seizure under the Fourth Amendment? Although this is an enormously complex subject, the following generalizations may be useful.

1. *The accused must have a legitimate expectation of privacy, which was violated by the search or seizure.* A legitimate expectation of privacy is one that society is willing to protect, but the Supreme Court defines what society is willing to protect. The average person might be surprised to learn that the Court does not believe there is a legitimate expectation of privacy in bank records (*United States v. Miller,* 1976), fenced fields (*Oliver v. United States,* 1984), garbage bagged and set out at a curb (*California v. Greenwood,* 1988), or a backyard visible (as all backyards are)

to low-flying planes (*California v. Ciraola*, 1986). In general, the Court has refused to recognize a legitimate expectation of privacy when the item seized could be seen or handled by strangers.

**2. *More protection is afforded in the home than elsewhere.*** Except in emergencies, police must have a warrant to enter a home without consent. A *warrant* is an authorization signed by a judge on the basis of an affidavit that establishes probable cause to believe that criminal evidence is in the home. Furthermore, the police must ordinarily knock and announce their presence—to give the occupants a chance to open the door—before forcing an entry (*Wilson v. Arkansas*, 1995). However, warrants are not needed to stop and search cars, boats, or planes. **Probable cause** is generally thought to imply at least a 50% probability. As long as officers have probable cause to stop a car, their true motivations are irrelevant. Stopping a driver who has committed a minor traffic violation so the police can look inside the car is not unconstitutional (*Whren v. United States*, 1996).

**3. *"Reasonable suspicion" will support a temporary detention or protective search.*** In *Terry v. Ohio* (1968), the Court upheld a "stop and frisk" of three men apparently preparing to rob a jewelry store, on the basis of the officer's **reasonable suspicion** that criminal activity was afoot. This principle is central to day-to-day law enforcement. The police cannot stop a car or pedestrian on a mere hunch, but they can stop a car or pedestrian if there are factors, which they can later explain to a judge, supporting a reasonable suspicion of criminal activity. After making the stop, the officer may frisk the person (or conduct a limited search of the car) if there is reasonable suspicion that the person is armed. The *Terry* test asks whether the officer's actions were reasonable under the "totality of the circumstances." It is a flexible test, requiring an analysis of the factual setting that caused the officer to act as he or she did. *Illinois v. Wardlow* (2000) (see ◆ Box 9-4), in which the Court held that a stop and frisk of a fleeing suspect was justified, is an excellent example of the totality of the circumstances test.

In addition to a stop (and sometimes frisk), a brief period of detention may follow to gather additional information. A DUI (driving under the influence) stop illustrates these principles. A weaving car gives the officer reasonable suspicion that the driver is intoxicated. The officer pulls the car over, thereby "seizing" the car and driver. The officer further detains the car and driver to perform sobriety tests and check the car's registration. A "frisk" of the driver or a search of the driver's seat would be necessitated if the driver threatened bodily harm to the officer.

**4. *The general principles are complicated by special "rules" that affect certain kinds of searches and seizures.*** The Court has treated searches and seizures differently if they are incident to arrest (*United States v. Robinson*, 1973), pursuant to a legitimate inventory (*Illinois v. Lafayette*, 1983), pursuant to a health and safety regulation (*New York v. Burger*, 1987), at the border (*United States v. Montoya de Hernandez*, 1985), of schoolchildren (*Vernonia School District v. Acton*, 1995), and of parolees (*Griffin v. Wisconsin*, 1987).

As the Court enters the 21st century, with Reagan/Bush appointees giving Chief Justice Rehnquist a solid law-and-order majority on most issues, the Court's lack of sympathy for the privacy interests protected by the Fourth Amendment is obvious. In *Florida v. Bostick* (1991), for example, the Court held that the Fourth Amendment is not violated by a police officer boarding a bus, arbitrarily picking out a passenger, and asking for permission to search the passenger's bag. The Court said the passenger had not been "seized," because he was "free" to leave the bus or refuse the officer's request. Would the Court have been more sympathetic if the passenger had been a middle-aged businessperson and the confrontation had taken place on a plane waiting for takeoff?

In the view of the present Supreme Court, a person loses a substantial amount of personal privacy upon entering an automobile. Warrants are not required to search a car on probable cause (*United States v. Ross*, 1982). Suppose the police have probable cause to believe that an arriving airline passenger's bag contains cocaine. As the passenger walks

## THE CASE OF

BOX 9-4

### William a.k.a. "Sam" Wardlow: Does fleeing suggest criminal activity?

From the police's point of view, some inner-city neighborhoods are "high-crime areas," the young men standing on corners are presumed to be up to no good, and flight is a sure sign of guilt. From the perspective of the young men on the corners, the police are to be feared, and flight means nothing more than a desire to avoid an unpleasant encounter. In *Illinois v. Wardlow,* a young man, carrying a white opaque bag under his arm, fled when police cars rolled into the neighborhood. The police chased and caught him and found a gun, which led to his conviction on gun possession charges.

The state of Illinois asked the Supreme Court for a "bright line" rule—that is, a rule that would authorize the police to stop anyone who ran from them. The state argued that flight is evidence of a guilty mind, and the police can reasonably infer that a fleeing person is engaged in criminal activ-

ity. As stated in Illinois's brief to the Supreme Court, "a person's unprovoked flight at the mere sight of a policeman undeniably demonstrates and exposes that person's consciousness of guilt and is a sure signal that criminal activity may be afoot. Accordingly, in the interest of crime detection and prevention, an officer should be entitled to briefly stop that person and make inquiry."

Wardlow's counsel, on the other hand, argued that a person has a constitutional right to be left alone and is under no obligation to submit to a police encounter in the absence of probable cause or reasonable suspicion. The defense argued for a different bright line rule—that flight may not be considered in determining whether reasonable suspicion of criminal activity exists.

The Supreme Court rejected both bright line rules and applied *Terry's* "totality of the circumstances" test to uphold the stop and

frisk. Justice Rehnquist held that the police were justified in considering flight, along with other factors—the high-crime area and the defendant's opaque bag—in deciding to pursue Wardlow. This analysis is not surprising, but note the practical effect of the *Wardlow* case: An inner-city youth living in a high-crime area runs from the police, not because he is committing a crime but because he doesn't want to be questioned and frisked. He is pursued and tackled, but no Fourth Amendment violation has occurred because the police could legitimately consider flight and the neighborhood as evidence of criminal activity. Meanwhile, a suburban youth in an upscale neighborhood flees at the sight of the police because he has an illegal gun in his pocket. He is pursued and tackled, and the gun found. But in this case, a Fourth Amendment violation has occurred because nothing but flight suggested criminal activity.

through the airport, any search of the bag requires a search warrant. As soon as the passenger puts the bag in the trunk of a car, however, the police may seize and search the bag without a warrant. Furthermore, the Court has said that when a person consents to the search of a car, it may be assumed that he or she has consented to the search of anything (e.g., a briefcase) found in the car (*Florida v. Jimeno,* 1991).

The police often conduct searches without warrants when, for example, a third party (e.g., a landlord, a spouse, or a roommate) consents to let

them search an area that the third party controls or shares with the suspect. The courts have assumed that people who share space with others yield their expectation of privacy with respect to the shared space. Therefore, the third party can consent to a police search of this space. Furthermore, the police can rely on the consent of the third party to search the suspect's possessions if it appears reasonable that the third party has authority to consent (*Illinois v. Rodriguez,* 1990).

Are these assumptions valid? Do people believe that they relinquish their rights to privacy when they share space with others? For that matter, do people's expectations of privacy decrease when they sit in their cars, discard objects in their garbage, or place items in their backyards? The courts have often based their decisions on an assumption that people hold different privacy expectations for different situations. However, judges have seldom considered scientific research on these topics despite the availability of pertinent studies. Psychologists have conducted empirical research on these questions, and their preliminary results challenge many of the courts' assumptions.

For example, Kagehiro, Taylor, Laufer, and Harland (1991) asked college students whether they believed a coresident in a condominium could consent to the police searching for evidence against a suspect (the other coresident) without a warrant. Depending on the experimental condition, subjects read that (1) the suspect just happened to be absent during the search, (2) the police had waited to search the condo until they knew the suspect had left, or (3) the suspect was present during the search and was protesting it. Half of the subjects read that the search uncovered the incriminating evidence the police were after; the other half read that the police did not find incriminating evidence.

Results indicated that people hold more complex expectations about privacy in shared living arrangements than the courts have assumed. When incriminating evidence was discovered, subjects were more likely to believe that the consenter had a right to allow the police search when the suspect was gone just by chance (92%) than when the suspect was present and protested the search (67%). When the police discovered no evidence, subjects were more likely to believe that the consenter could permit a police search when the suspect was present and protesting (83%) than when the suspect happened to be absent by chance (42%). Additional research on how citizens rate the intrusiveness of different types of searches and seizures (see ◆ Box 9-5) suggests that the courts consistently misread the intrusiveness of many search-and-seizure methods, at least as they are perceived by the public.

# The Rights of Victims and Potential Victims

As suspects were being granted more rights, society began to question whether victims were being treated fairly. This concern stemmed partly from greater awareness of crime rates in the United States. On an annual basis, approximately one out of every four households in the United States is a target of a violent crime or theft. In a recent year, 37 million Americans were crime victims, and among these, 2 million were victims of violent crime—rape, robbery, assault, attempted murder. Advocates of law and order and critics of court rulings in the late 1960s and early 1970s claimed that the government offered innocent victims little or no support, even though ostensibly the criminal justice system was established to serve them (Karmen, 1984).

Crimes are sometimes thought of only as abstract, hostile acts against the state, that represents all the people, rather than as events that hurt a specific person. As Ellison and Buckhout (1981) note, the victim of a crime is often referred to as the "complaining witness" and might be regarded as a bit player or just a piece of evidence. In fact, however, being the victim of a crime—especially a violent crime—is one of the most traumatic experiences a person can suffer.

Victims are often dissatisfied with the criminal justice system. A study released by the National Institute of Justice asked 249 victims of major crimes in six cities how satisfied they were with the handling of their cases (Meddis, 1984). It discovered that 77% said the courts were "too slow" and wasted time; even more (86%) felt that offenders weren't punished enough. In contrast, only 30% felt that the courts care about victims' needs. Increasingly, legislators, prosecutors, and court systems are trying to respond to the concerns of crime victims. What are some of the main initiatives in this area?

*1. Compensating crime victims.* In most cases, judges will order the defendant to compensate

## The Science of

BOX 9-5  **Public opinion about search and seizure**

Christopher Slobogin and Joseph Schumacher (1993) hypothesized that people would perceive searches and seizures of their own property or person to be more intrusive than those of other people's. They also predicted that searches conducted without a specific objective in mind would be perceived as more intrusive than searches aimed at uncovering a specific piece of evidence (e.g., frisking someone to see whether they are carrying a concealed weapon). They asked subjects to read 50 different search-and-seizure scenarios and rate the intrusiveness of each, depending on whether it was their property or someone else's that was searched and whether there was a specific evidentiary target of the search.

In general, the subjects rated many searches and seizures to be

intrusive and to violate expectations of privacy, contradicting the Supreme Court's approval of these same procedures on the grounds that they were minimally intrusive. Consistent with the hypotheses, a given procedure was seen as more intrusive when (1) it was aimed at the subject rather than a third party and (2) it did not target a specific objective. Individual subject characteristics also affected these ratings. Subjects who were more committed to the due process model of criminal justice described in Chapter 1 perceived greater intrusiveness in many types of search and seizure than did subjects who were less committed to due process protections.

Finally, the subjects' ratings were not significantly related to most demographic characteristics,

but ethnic minorities did tend to perceive some of the procedures as more intrusive than did nonminority subjects (C. Slobogin, personal communication, 1996). However, the original sample did not include many ethnic minorities, so it is not clear how well these findings would generalize to America's increasingly diverse society. We suspect that Hispanic Americans or African Americans, who tend to report a greater number of adverse encounters with the police, might on this basis perceive higher levels of intrusiveness and privacy violations for many kinds of police procedures than do European Americans.

---

the victim for any losses. This payment is often termed **restitution.** In addition to helping recompense victims, restitution is intended to help offenders appreciate how their crimes have hurt someone else. Of course, in many cases, there is no defendant because the crime has not been solved or the defendant has been acquitted. In other cases, the defendant is financially unable to reimburse the victim, so restitution is often a hollow promise.

About three-fourths of the states now also have special crime victim compensation funds to pay for lost wages and medical expenses of crime victims. These funds usually do not cover property losses (payment for thefts would quickly bankrupt the funds) and have fairly low caps on how much compensation will be provided. New

York will pay victims unlimited medical costs (beyond those reimbursed by insurance) and up to $20,000 in lost wages at a rate of up to $250 weekly. New Jersey limits financial aid to $10,000. Kentucky pays lost wages and medical expenses up to $25,000. Kansas has a small fund administered through a Victims Reparation Board. California now has what is called a "reverse *Miranda* law," in which the police must inform victims that they have the right to apply for state assistance.

The federal government has also provided assistance to victims. President Reagan signed the Victims of Crime Act of 1984, establishing a Crime Victims Fund, which provides federal assistance to the states' crime victim compensation programs. The fund is financed through fines collected from prisoners convicted of federal offenses.

### 2. Participation by victims in crime proceedings.

Many states provide that victims have a right to be notified of and attend court proceedings and a right to make their views known, either to the prosecutor or directly to the judge, on significant issues in their cases. Victims are concerned that important decisions are made without their input and, in some cases, without their knowledge. Some important developments aimed at addressing these concerns have occurred.

In *Payne v. Tennessee* (1991), the defendant killed a young mother and her 2-year-old daughter and injured her 3-year-old son. The Supreme Court upheld a death penalty imposed after a sentencing hearing in which the mother of the victim (and grandmother of the surviving boy) provided **victim impact evidence** that described for the jury the effects the crime had on the young boy. The Court held that the defendant was not denied due process by the impact this testimony may have had on the jury. Indeed, victim impact evidence has been shown to influence mock jurors' sentiments about victims and victims' survivors (Greene, 1999).

When Timothy McVeigh was tried in Denver for the bombing of the Oklahoma City federal building, Judge Richard Matsch anticipated that victim impact testimony might cause the trial to become a "lynching party." Even though the judge limited the number of witnesses, two days of victim impact evidence caused jurors, spectators, and even the judge to weep as family members, rescue workers and others took the stand to describe their suffering. Earlier, Congress had intervened to undo one of Judge Matsch's rulings. The judge had ruled that witnesses who intended to present victim impact evidence at the penalty phase must stay out of the courtroom during the guilt phase of McVeigh's trial. Congress took an extraordinary step: it passed legislation allowing those witnesses to attend the trial (Gibeaut, 1997).

The bizarre case of Colin Ferguson, the gunman who shot up a commuter car on the Long Island Railway in 1995, brought national attention to victims' rights. Despite the fact that Ferguson's mental competency was questionable, he represented himself at his trial. Claiming that he didn't

*Seventeen years after watching his parents murdered at the hands of Glen Ake and Steven Hatch, Brooks Douglass, now a state legislator in Oklahoma, wrote the law that gave him and his sister, Leslie Frizzell, the right to watch the state execute Hatch for his role in the murders. According to Douglass, giving victims a role in the criminal justice system helps them feel that they have some control over the factors that affect their own destinies.*

shoot anyone, Ferguson stood face to face with his victims in a Long Island courtroom, forcing them to respond to his absurd "cross-examination" questions. However, instead of being a frightening and painful experience, it "turned out to be an unexpected victory for them [the victims] to be able to say, 'I saw you shoot me'" (Lambert, 1995, p. B10).

As one final example of victims' opportunity to participate in criminal proceedings, we describe the case of Steven Hatch, the codefendant of Glen Ake, who was executed by lethal injection in the Oklahoma state penitentiary on August 9, 1996. Watching through a tinted glass partition were the son and daughter who survived the attack that had killed their parents 17 years earlier. Brooks Douglass, the son and an Oklahoma state legislator, sponsored the bill allowing the families of victims to attend executions. At his request, the prison constructed a private enclosure so he and his sister could view the execution firsthand, rather than on closed-circuit television. Watching the execution of the man convicted of murdering his parents afforded Douglass and his sister a sense of closure. "I do believe that it's the end of a very long ordeal that's dominated our lives. He's gone, it's over. I can get back to my law practice, my family" (Romano, 1996 p. A3).

**3. *Legislative changes protecting victims' rights.*** Thirty-two states have amended their constitutions in recent years to protect victims' rights (Feinstein, 2000), and almost all the other states have passed special laws protecting victims' rights. In 1999, Senators Dianne Feinstein (D-CA) and Jon Kyl (R-AZ) reintroduced bipartisan legislation (first proposed in 1996) to create a Victims' Rights Constitutional Amendment that would establish for victims of violent crimes the right

- to be notified of proceedings;
- not to be excluded from the trial and other proceedings;
- to be heard at crucial stages such as the release of an offender, plea bargaining, and sentencing;
- to be notified of the offender's release from custody;
- to be freed from unreasonable delay in the proceedings; and
- to receive restitution from the convicted offender (Feinstein, 2000).

Voter approval for victims' rights initiatives has been overwhelming: 70% to 90% of voters in different states have supported such amendments (Westbrook, 1998).

**4. *Reconciling victims and offenders.*** A different approach to victims' rights is to attempt to reconcile the victim and the offender. Such reconciliation programs, although controversial, can cause the offender to realize the victim's pain and the victim to understand why the offender committed the crime. These programs, often called "**restorative justice**," are supported by the Department of Justice and many prosecutors and corrections officials. The following information is provided

*Pope John Paul II reconciling with Mehmet Ali Acga, the man who tried to kill him*

on the Web site of an organization that trains mediators to help offenders and their victims understand one another (www.Realjustice.org, 2000):

> The U.S. Department of Justice's Guide for Implementing the Balanced and Restorative Justice Model says conferencing—also called "community conferencing" and "family group conferencing"—provides benefits in the areas of accountability, competency development and community safety.

ACCOUNTABILITY

- Offenders must take personal responsibility for their actions.
- Offenders face those they have harmed.
- Offenders take steps to repair harm and make amends.

COMPETENCY DEVELOPMENT

- Offenders develop empathy.
- Offenders learn affective communication skills.
- Offenders learn conflict resolution skills.

COMMUNITY SAFETY

◆  Victims and community members have an opportunity to tell the offender how they feel.
◆  Victims have a say in how the harm should be repaired.
◆  Victims have an opportunity to ask questions.
◆  Victims and community members can regain a sense of safety, bringing healing and closure to the incident.

# Advantages to the Prosecution and to the Defense in a Criminal Trial

As society continues to struggle over the appropriate balance between the rights of victims and the rights of the accused, it is meaningful to consider the advantages to each side in a criminal trial. Although full discussion of the procedures and psychology of trials is taken up in later chapters, a listing of the elements relevant to the balance between the two sides is warranted now because it is part of the continuing tension between the rights of individuals and society's needs for public safety.

## Advantages to the Prosecution

The state, in its efforts to convict wrongdoers and bring justice to bear, has several benefits:

1. It has the full resources of the government at its disposal to carry out a prosecution. Detectives can locate witnesses and subpoena them. The state can call on testimony from chemists, fingerprint examiners, medical examiners, psychiatrists, photographers, or whoever is an appropriate expert.

2. The prosecution can produce its evidence in a virtually unfettered way if a grand jury system is used to bring down indictments. (Chapter 10 describes the grand jury.)

3. In the trial itself, the prosecution presents its evidence before the defense, getting "first crack" at the jury. In presenting opening statements, which

are not evidence but do provide a structure for the entire trial, the prosecution always goes first. And at the end of the trial, when both sides are permitted closing arguments (again, not part of the evidence), the prosecution usually gets to go first and then is permitted to offer a last-word rebuttal to the defense attorney's closing argument. Therefore, the prosecution has the advantages of both *primacy* and *recency* in its attempts at jury persuasion.

## Advantages to the Defense

The courts also provide defendants certain safeguards in addition to those described earlier in this chapter:

1. The defense is entitled to "discovery"; the prosecution must turn over exculpatory evidence, but the defense does not have to turn over incriminating evidence.

2. If a trial is before a jury, the defense may have more peremptory challenges—that is, opportunities to remove potential jurors without giving a reason (see Chapter 14)—than the prosecution.

3. Defendants do not have to take the stand as witnesses on their own behalf. In fact, they do not have to put on any defense at all; the burden of proof is on the prosecution to prove beyond a reasonable doubt that the defendant is guilty of the crime.

4. Defendants who are found not guilty can never be tried again for that specific crime. For example, O. J. Simpson was found not guilty of killing his ex-wife, Nicole Brown, and her friend, Ron Goldman. Even if uncontrovertible evidence of his guilt comes to light, he can never be retried for murder. (He was, however, forced to defend himself in a civil suit by the families of the victims and was found liable for their deaths.)

# The Future of the Dilemma

Times change. Matters are never settled in a complex society. A constant quest continues for fairness to all parties—to crime victims and to criminal suspects, who are assumed to be innocent until proven guilty. Although it is futile to expect that the issues examined in this chapter will ever be completely re-solved, we should be encouraged that the quest continues.

Right now, the balance weighs in one direc-tion; Chief Justice Rehnquist has wanted to over-turn *Mapp v. Ohio,* describing the decision as a "basic unconstitutional mistake." The public and the courts strongly favor the prosecution and the police. But a decade or two from now, the bal-ance may shift again. There is always conflict and reconciliation.

Despite the differences, society benefits ulti-mately from the continued quest to guarantee the rights of the accused and the rights of victims. We should avoid an extreme "either-or" orientation, in which the rights of one group always come at the expense of the rights of the other. Civil liberties ac-tivists, concerned that suspects receive their due rights, and conservatives, threatened by Warren Court decisions, both are assisted by the scrutiny devoted to this issue. Rights that are won by the "unworthy" are won for all of us (Lewis, 1984). As Karmen (1984) notes, "What the critics of the civil liberties movement fail to appreciate is the contri-bution these reforms have made toward easing the plight of crime victims" (p. 21). Likewise, judicial attempts to encourage the professionalism and the responsibility of the police will benefit all of us; the Warren Court decisions led to better training, closer supervision, and higher qualifications for po-lice officers. The implicit promise behind these changes was that everyone—suspects and vic-tims—would be more likely to receive nonsexist,

nonracist treatment and effective responses from the police. In addition, we should benefit because these court decisions have extended guarantees of equal protection of the law to victims who were formerly neglected and previously ignored because they were powerless (Walker, 1982).

However, it is not clear that the promise of fairer justice and more equitable law enforcement is a reality for all Americans. Do the poor, ethnic minorities, and women actually have greater ac-cess to and receive better treatment from the law enforcement system than before? Highly publi-cized cases of the police targeting black motorists for traffic stops or prosecutors pursuing more prosecutions of black than white defendants for drug possession call some of these cherished as-sumptions into question.

By the same token, it is not necessary to as-sume that every restriction on the exclusionary rule means that the rights of criminal suspects will au-tomatically be trampled. A Columbia University law professor (Uviller, 1988) spent his sabbatical leave with the police on patrol in the crime-ridden ninth precinct in Manhattan. He reports that, even though many police officers don't like some of the rules, they have learned to live with them. He ob-served occasional violations by the police—for ex-ample, when officers would casually question suspects in the back of the police car, saving the reading of their *Miranda* rights for the police sta-tion (Jacoby, 1988). But sometimes the police were even more scrupulous than the court required with regard to respecting the rights of suspects.

## SUMMARY

**1.** *During the 1960s, several Supreme Court decisions established important rights for criminal suspects. What were the principles in these decisions?* As-suring both the rights of suspects and the rights of crime victims and potential victims is one of the most challenging tasks of any society. Sus-pects are assumed to be innocent until proven guilty; yet, as shown in the previous chapter con-

cerning the inducement of confessions and the use of the polygraph to intimidate sus-pects, the opposite assumption has often been made in the law enforcement system.

During the 1960s, the U.S. Supreme Court, led by Chief Justice Earl Warren, made a number of pivotal decisions that extended the rights accorded to suspects and defendants. Among these were (1) *Mapp v. Ohio* (1961), which restricted state courts from admitting evidence that had been obtained by the police through illegal means; (2) *Gideon v. Wainwright* (1963), which provided indigent defendants with an attorney during any criminal trial; (3) *Fay v. Noia* (1963), which opened the door to challenge state court convictions by habeas corpus petitions in federal court; and (4) *Miranda v. Arizona* (1966), which permitted suspects to remain silent after being arrested and also established that the police must demonstrate that suspects are aware of their rights.

**2.** *A number of Supreme Court decisions since the 1960s have strengthened the powers of law enforcement. What were the principles in these decisions?* As a result of publicity over some Warren Court decisions and of citizens' increasing concern over the crime rate, the Supreme Court in more recent years has relaxed some restrictions on the activities of police officers as they apprehend criminals. These relaxations have dealt primarily with the exclusionary rule, the use of writ of habeas corpus, the appointment of counsel, and *Miranda* rights.

**3.** *What is the status of the Fourth Amendment today?* The Supreme Court's opinions about what are unreasonable police searches and seizures have undergone several changes in recent years, generally in the direction of permitting greater police latitude in how they conduct searches and seizures and in defining privacy interests more narrowly. Psychological research examining people's expectations of privacy and views of intrusiveness have often conflicted with the assumptions reflected by Supreme Court decisions.

**4.** *Does the criminal justice system treat victims of crime fairly? What can be done to improve crime victims' beliefs that the justice system works for them as well as for criminal defendants?* Several programs have been developed to address the needs and rights of crime victims. Included in this category are victim restitution and compensation programs, guarantees that victims can participate in legal proceedings, and legislative initiatives designed to protect victim rights.

**5.** *What advantages do the prosecution and defense each have in a criminal trial?* Rights of defendants and victims are also illustrated through the advantages given the respective sides in a criminal trial. For example, the prosecution has the advantage of access to extensive government resources. At the trial, it goes first, thus providing the initial structure for jurors. In the closing arguments at the end of the trial, the prosecution has both the first word and the last word. In contrast, defendants enjoy several special rights during trials. Defendants are entitled to know whether the prosecution has uncovered evidence that supports a conclusion of innocence. No defendant is required to testify; in fact, the defense is not required to present any evidence.

## KEY TERMS

| | | | |
|---|---|---|---|
| collateral attacks | hindsight bias | restitution* | victim impact evidence |
| exclusionary rule* | probable cause* | restorative justice* | |
| *habeas corpus** | reasonable suspicion* | *stare decisis** | |

---

InfoTrac COLLEGE EDITION   For additional readings go to **http://www.infotrac-college.com/wadsworth** and enter a search term related to your interest. The key terms that have been asterisked above will pull up several related articles.

## ORIENTING QUESTIONS

1. *What are the major legal proceedings between arrest and trial in the criminal justice system?*
2. *What is bail, and what factors influence the amount of bail set?*
3. *What is the role of the grand jury?*
4. *Why do defendants and prosecutors agree to plea bargain?*
5. *Does pretrial publicity pose a danger to fair trials? If so, can these dangers be reduced?*

Previous chapters presented psychological perspectives on the actions of law enforcement officials as they investigate crimes and make arrests. Between these events and the eventual trial of a suspect are several other steps with psychological implications. These steps also reflect the dilemmas posed in Chapter 1.

The grand finale in our adversary system of justice is the trial, a public battle waged by two combatants (prosecution versus defense in a criminal trial or plaintiff versus defendant in a civil trial), each fighting for a favorable outcome. To the victors go the spoils of this contest; criminal defendants seek their freedom through an acquittal, and civil plaintiffs seek compensation for wrongs they have suffered. Although the trial may be the most dramatic conflict in our system, many skirmishes come before it that play large—and often decisive—roles in determining victors. In the adversarial system, both sides seek numerous tactical advantages and favorable ground rules before they fight the trial/battle. Attorneys wage these struggles vigorously because they know they are crucial in shaping the contours of the adversarial contest.

In this chapter and the next, we concentrate on these pretrial proceedings. This chapter examines four pretrial activities with psychological significance: (1) bail setting, (2) grand jury actions, (3) plea bargaining, and (4) motions to change venue to minimize the effect of pretrial publicity. Then, in Chapter 11, we discuss the legal concept of *competence*, with emphasis on its assessment by psychiatrists and psychologists. In the criminal justice system, competence refers to a defendant's capacity to understand and participate meaningfully in legal proceedings; it covers mental and psychological abilities that the criminal justice system requires of defendants in order for court actions to be applied to them. Questions of competence are usually raised between the time of arrest and the formal trial, and they typically are concerned with two issues: competence to plead guilty and competence to stand trial.

Before we discuss bail, the grand jury, plea bargaining, and change of venue in detail, it will

be useful to provide a framework for these topics by describing the usual sequence of pretrial activities in the criminal justice system.

# Steps between Arrest and Trial

If the police believe probable cause exists that a suspect committed a crime, they will in all likelihood arrest the suspect. However, being arrested for a crime and being charged with a crime are two different events. A person may be arrested without being charged; for example, the police may arrest drunks to detain them and sober them up, but formal charges may never be filed. Charging implies a formal decision to continue with the prosecution, and that decision is made by the prosecuting attorney rather than the police.

## The Initial Appearance

The initial appearance is an important step in the criminal process that must be taken soon after arrest. Important players—the judge and the defense counsel—become participants in a process in which the defendant has previously been in the control of the police and prosecutor. In the United States, extended detention of those charged with a crime violates the Fourth Amendment proscription against "unreasonable" seizures (*Gerstein v. Pugh*, 1975); thus, defendants must be taken before a judge or released.

This appearance is not an occasion for testifying or challenging the state's proof but, rather, an organizational meeting in a judicial setting. The purposes of this meeting are for the judge to do the following:

1. Inform suspects of the charges against them.

2. Review the evidence summarized by the prosecutor to determine whether probable cause exists for believing that the suspects committed the crimes charged (the Supreme Court has held that this *probable cause determination* must be held within 48 hours of a person's arrest; *Riverside County v. McLaughlin*, 1991).

3. Inform suspects of their constitutional rights, especially their right to counsel and their privilege against self-incrimination.

4. Inform suspects that they have a right to counsel. If they cannot afford a lawyer, either the public defender's office will provide a lawyer, or the judge will recruit a private lawyer to represent the accused for a modest compensation by the state. (See ◆ Box 10-1 for a discussion of public defenders.)

5. Consider the issue of whether suspects should be kept in custody or released from jail while they await their trial. If the judge decides to release a suspect, he or she will usually set conditions on the release designed to protect the community and ensure that the suspect will appear in court when required. These conditions usually involve a "setting of bail," in which suspects must arrange for a sum of money to be deposited with the court as security to ensure subsequently required appearances.

6. Schedule further court proceedings as required.

## The Preliminary Hearing

The next step after the initial appearance is the preliminary hearing; one of its purposes is to filter out those cases in which the prosecution's proof is insufficient. At a preliminary hearing, the prosecution must offer some evidence on every element of the crime charged. **Hearsay** is admissible at this hearing, meaning that one witness may summarize what another said earlier. Thus, a victim's account of a crime can be presented through the testimony of the investigating officer. The judge must decide whether the prosecutor has presented evidence sufficient to support a finding of probable cause on all elements of the crime. Cross-examination by defense lawyers is limited to the issue of probable cause. No jury is present, and the judge has no authority to choose between competing versions of the events.

For these reasons, the defendant rarely testifies or offers any evidence at a preliminary hearing. Furthermore, defense attorneys often waive the preliminary hearing because they are afraid

that the publicity in newspapers or on television will harden community attitudes against their clients and make it more difficult to seat an impartial jury. At times, however, the preliminary hearing serves as an opportunity for defense attorneys to glimpse the prosecution's case and size up its chief witnesses.

At the preliminary hearing, the judge will bind the defendant over to the grand jury if the judge finds probable cause exists to believe the defendant committed the crimes charged. It is also possible that the judge will reduce the charges, either because he or she believes the evidence does not support the level of crime charged by the prosecutor or because of a plea bargain between the prosecutor and the defense attorney. Generally, the judge also reconsiders the amount of bail originally set if the defendant is still being held in custody. (A later section of this chapter describes bail setting in detail.)

## The Grand Jury

Consisting of citizens drawn from the community, the **grand jury** meets in secret with the prosecutor to investigate criminal activity and return indictments. In theory, the grand jury functions both as a "sword," issuing subpoenas and compelling reluctant witnesses to testify, and as a "shield," protecting those accused of crime from unjust prosecution. About one-third of the states require that a criminal defendant cannot be prosecuted unless a grand jury has found grounds to do so. The remaining states permit the prosecutor to proceed either by grand jury **indictment** or by **information** (e.g., a complaint prepared and signed by the prosecutor describing the crime charged).

In states that require grand jury review, the prosecutor presents those cases that have been "bound over" from preliminary hearings for consideration by the grand jury. The grand jury meets secretly and listens to the witnesses called by the prosecutor (who may relate what other witnesses said) and votes whether to indict and, if so, for what offenses. The grand jury may call witnesses on its own initiative if it is dissatisfied with the witnesses presented by the prosecutor and may

**BOX 10-1**

## "Did you have a lawyer?" "No, I had a public defender."

Public defenders are underpaid and overworked. Heavy caseloads and low salaries sap the energy of all but the most dedicated lawyers. James Kunen, a former public defender, described his experience in a book whose title asks the question posed sooner or later to every public defender: *How Can You Defend Those People?* (1983):

> [Y]ou get tired of the pressure—someone's freedom always riding on you. And you get tired of what the exertion and the pressure is all about; you're defending the Constitution; you're defending *everybody's* rights, but you're also, more often than not—defending a criminal. That needs to be done, but it doesn't need to be done *by you,* not all your life. After a while, it's somebody else's turn. (p. 142)

While public defenders might be young, inexperienced, and overworked, they at least know the law. The same cannot always be said of "appointed counsel"—lawyers appointed to handle often serious cases for little or no fee. Stephen Bright, director of the Southern Center for Human Rights, describes some of these lawyers in his aptly titled journal article, "Counsel for the Poor: The Death Sentence Not for the Worst Crime but for the Worst Lawyer" (1994):

I. a lawyer appointed in a Georgia capital case who was paid $15 an hour, did not request funds to hire an expert to challenge the state's hair-identification evidence; his closing argument was only 225 words long

II. a lawyer appointed in a Texas capital case, who was paid $11.84 an hour, failed to interview witnesses and misinterpreted the law

III. a lawyer appointed to defend a capital case in Alabama and given only $500 to investigate the case, later admitted that he had not properly investigated the facts

IV. a lawyer, who when asked to name some criminal cases, could name only *Miranda* and *Dred Scott* (the latter, of course, is not a criminal case). (pp. 1835–1838)

In many states, public defender systems (and appointed counsel systems as well) are improving, thanks to changing public opinion and litigation aimed at forcing states to increase funding. The Spangenberg Group, a nationally recognized criminal justice research and consulting firm, has worked with many states over the last 15 years to raise public defender salaries and reduce caseloads to manageable levels. In Connecticut, the state drastically increased funding for defender services in order to settle a lawsuit brought by the American Civil Liberties Union on behalf of indigent defendants. And in Mississippi, three counties sued the state in an attempt to force the state to create a statewide public defender system in order to relieve the counties of financial burdens, such as the one experienced by one small Mississippi county that was forced to raise taxes and borrow money to pay the cost of prosecuting two men for a quadruple homicide (Rovella, 2000b, p. A1).

Occasionally one reads of a public defender or appointed counsel who goes far beyond what can reasonably be expected of someone who is overworked and underpaid—a person such as Annette Lee of the Bronx (NY) Defenders. Appointed to defend a 15-year-old charged with selling drugs, Ms. Lee went to her client's home to find proof of his age in order to keep him out of adult court. Based on what she found during the home visit—a drug-addicted single mother—Ms. Lee persuaded the court to put the boy in a drug treatment program and then kept tabs on him while in the program, visiting him, bringing him clothes, and ultimately helping him obtain a small grant to pay for technical college (Rovella, 2000b, p. A1).

vote to indict or not to indict for any reason. Its decision is not appealable to a court, although a prosecutor disgruntled over a jury's refusal to indict may resubmit a case to a second grand jury.

If the grand jury decides that sufficient evidence exists to justify the defendant being tried, it issues an indictment, signed by the foreperson of the grand jury. The indictment is a written accusation by the grand jury accusing one or more persons of one or more crimes. Its function is to inform defendants clearly of the nature of the charges against them, so that they have the opportunity to prepare a defense.

## Arraignment

A grand jury gives its indictments to a judge, who brings those indicted to court for arraignment on the indictment. At the arraignment, the judge makes sure that the defendant has an attorney and appoints one if necessary. The indictment is then read to the defendant, and the defendant is asked to plead guilty or not guilty. It is customary for defendants to plead not guilty at this time, even if they contemplate ultimately pleading guilty. The reason is to provide opportunities both for **discovery** (which means that the defendant's attorney gets to examine some of the evidence against the defendant) and for plea bargaining. At arraignment, the judge again reviews the issue of pretrial release (bail) and sets a date for the trial. Often, the judge also fixes a date by which pretrial motions must be filed.

## Discovery and Pretrial Motions

Defendants and their attorneys want to be aware of the materials the prosecution will use to prove its case. In civil trials, each side is entitled to *discovery*—meaning a right to depose (ask questions) the witnesses on the other side and to look at and copy documents the other side might use at trial. In criminal trials, however, just how much the prosecution has to reveal to the defense is controversial. Some states require prosecutors to turn over all reports, statements by witnesses, and physical evidence to the defense. Most states, however, require only that the prosecutor share certain evidence (e.g., laboratory reports) and evidence that is **exculpatory** (i.e., that tends to show the defendant to be not guilty as charged). In the case of *Brady v. Maryland* (1963), the U.S. Supreme Court ruled that the prosecution must disclose to the defense evidence in its possession favorable to the defendant. Beyond the constitu-

tional obligation to disclose exculpatory evidence (called *Brady* material), however, the extent to which discovery occurs in criminal cases is determined by local statutes, not constitutional right.

In many cases, prosecutors provide "open file" discovery to defense attorneys even though not obligated to do so; one reason is to encourage a guilty plea and avoid a trial. A prosecutor, knowing that defense counsel will find it difficult to recommend a guilty plea without knowing the strength of the prosecution's case, will turn over most evidence, expecting that defense counsel, made aware of the prosecutor's firepower, will talk sense to the defendant and encourage a quick plea. At the same time, prosecutors must remain sensitive to witnesses who may not want their identities or statements given to defense counsel.

Discovery is a two-way street. In general, states require the defense to turn over materials that the prosecution is required to turn over. If the prosecution is required to reveal laboratory reports, the defense will likewise be required to share such reports. In many states, the defense is required to notify the prosecution if it intends to rely on certain defenses, notably insanity and alibi defenses. The reason for requiring such pretrial notice is to give the state an opportunity to investigate the claim and avoid being surprised at trial. The Supreme Court has upheld the constitutionality of pretrial notice requirements, provided the state is required to notify the defendant of witnesses it would call to refute the defense (*Williams v. Florida*, 1970).

During the discovery phase of the case, pretrial motions are filed by both sides. The defense will often move for dismissal of the charges. Both sides will seek favorable rulings on the admissibility of evidence. Both sides will explore the possibility of a negotiated plea—a plea bargain. Although it is impossible to list all pretrial motions, the following are the most common:

*1. Defense motion for separate trials.* When two or more defendants are jointly indicted, one of them can be counted on to move for a separate trial, claiming that to be tried together would be prejudicial. When some of the prosecution's evidence is admissible against one defendant but not against the other, the motion is often granted, as in the case of Timothy McVeigh and Terry Nichols, convicted in separate trials of bombing the federal building in Oklahoma City, killing 168 people. McVeigh was convicted of murder and sentenced to death, but Nichols was convicted of a lesser charge (conspiracy) and sentenced to life imprisonment.

**2. Defense motion to sever counts.** Suppose the indictment charges the defendant with robbing a convenience store on April 13 and burglarizing a house on April 15. The defendant may move for separate trials on these offenses. A defendant will argue that it is prejudicial for the same jury to hear evidence about separate crimes because the jury will be tempted to combine the evidence introduced on the separate crimes to find the defendant guilty of each crime.

**3. Defense motion for change of venue.** The defendant may move for a **change of venue** on the ground that community opinion, usually the product of prejudicial pretrial publicity, makes it impossible to seat a fair-minded jury. We discuss the involvement of psychologists in such motions later in this chapter.

**4. Defense motion to dismiss on speedy trial grounds.** The Sixth Amendment of the U.S. Constitution guarantees defendants a right to a "speedy trial." A delay in trial is cause for dismissal if the prosecutor was attempting to obtain an unfair advantage and the defendant was harmed by the delay, as would happen if a crucial defense witness died (*Barker v. Wingo,* 1972). Dismissals **with prejudice** are rarely granted. The term *with prejudice* refers to a dismissal that bars any subsequent attempt to reinstate the prosecution; a dismissal without prejudice allows the possibility for the state to prosecute the defendant at a later time.

**5. Defense motion to dismiss on grounds of selective prosecution.** Often, a crime involves many participants, but only a few of them are charged. Generally speaking, indictments will not be dismissed simply because the defendants were selected for prosecution. Effective use of limited resources often requires that police and prosecutors direct their efforts toward the most culpable offenders or those whose convictions will best deter others (*Wayte v. United States,* 1985), as, for example, in drug-trafficking crimes. Selective enforcement and prosecution are unconstitutional, however, when the selection is made on racial or gender grounds or when the selection impermissibly interferes with First Amendment rights. For example, it would be unconstitutional for the police to give speeding citations only to out-of-state motorists because such a selection would interfere with the First Amendment right to travel freely within the United States. Dismissal on this ground is rare because the defense must prove that others similarly situated were not prosecuted, that the selection was purposeful, and that the selection was for an impermissible reason.

One lingering controversy concerning allegations of selective prosecution involves the fact that, although African Americans make up only about 12% of the U.S. population, 90% of the defendants prosecuted in federal courts for trafficking in crack cocaine are African American. These defendants face much longer prison sentences than offenders trafficking in the same amount of powdered cocaine, for which about equal percentages of white and black defendants are prosecuted. Is this a case of racial discrimination in which prosecutors are treating black defendants more severely than whites, or is it, as prosecutors claim, a case of zeroing in on crime problems where they exist—inner-city gangs made up predominantly of minorities? In 1996, the Supreme Court rejected a claim by black defendants that the U.S. attorney had selectively prosecuted them for crack cocaine offenses (*United States v. Armstrong,* 1996). The Court held that a mere disparity does not support a claim that defendants were selected for prosecution on the basis of race.

**6. Defense motion to dismiss on double jeopardy grounds.** The Fifth Amendment to the

U.S. Constitution states that no person shall be "subject for the same offense to be twice put in jeopardy of life or limb." The Court has interpreted this clause to mean that the state is entitled to one, but only one, "fair chance" to convict the defendant. If the state loses—or if the trial is aborted without reason—the defendant cannot be retried. Most litigation over the double-jeopardy clause involves the question of whether the second charge is for the "same offense" for which the defendant previously was tried (*Grady v. Corbin,* 1990). The issue reflects the first dilemma described in Chapter 1. Does society's right to be protected overcome the rights of individuals to be freed from extended harassment by the state? For example, Los Angeles police officers Stacey Koon and Laurence Powell were found not guilty in a California state court of beating Rodney King after they stopped King for speeding. Koon and Powell were later tried a second time—this time in a federal court—on charges of violating King's civil rights. Much of the same evidence was used. In the second trial, the two police officers were found guilty and sentenced to several years in prison. Double jeopardy did not bar the second prosecution because it took place in federal court, rather than in a California state court.

*7. Defense motion to suppress evidence on Fourth Amendment grounds.* The *exclusionary rule,* which we discussed in Chapter 9, requires courts to suppress evidence obtained in violation of a defendant's right under the Fourth Amendment to be free from unreasonable searches and seizures. Suppression motions are often filed to test the prosecution's case and to obtain information with which to plea bargain.

*8. Defense motion to suppress a confession or other statement by the defendant.* The Fifth Amendment protects against self-incrimination, the due process clauses of the Fifth and Fourteenth Amendments protect against the use of confessions extracted by duress or promise, and the Sixth Amendment forbids the use of a statement taken in violation of the right to counsel.

One or more of these constitutional provisions potentially become relevant any time the prosecution offers a confession or other statement by a defendant as evidence of guilt. Typically, defense counsel files a motion alleging that the confession was obtained in violation of the defendant's constitutional rights, the prosecutor files a written response, and the court holds a hearing at which the defendant and police give their versions of the circumstances under which the confession was obtained. The judge hears the testimony without a jury and decides the issue based on what was said and the credibility of the witnesses. Questions of who is telling the truth are usually resolved in favor of the police.

*9. Discovery motions.* When disputes arise in the discovery process, either side can ask the trial court for assistance. The typical dispute involves a sweeping defense request (e.g., a request for the names of all persons who saw the robbery) and a prosecutor who interprets the *Brady* rule (the obligation to turn over exculpatory information) narrowly.

*10. Motions in limine.* Perhaps the most common pretrial motions are those that seek advance rulings on evidentiary issues that will arise at trial. Suppose, for example, that the defendant was previously convicted of burglary; it is within the discretion of the judge whether to allow the conviction into evidence in order to discredit the defendant if he chooses to testify. The defendant obviously wants a pretrial ruling on this issue. to plan the questioning of the jurors and to decide whether to testify. Similarly, the prosecutor may want a pretrial ruling on the admissibility of a certain piece of evidence to plan the opening statement (a cardinal sin of trial practice is to refer to a matter in the opening statement that is later deemed inadmissible). A **motion in limine** is simply a request for a pretrial ruling. Although judges are not constitutionally required to grant such a request, most trial judges will cooperate with attorneys who are trying to avoid midtrial problems.

# The Decision to Set Bail

As we have already discussed, judges routinely decide whether to keep defendants in custody during the often lengthy process between arrest and trial. Judges have many options. In some cases (capital cases and cases in which the defendant poses a serious risk to flee or commit other crimes), they can deny bail altogether; short of denying bail, judges can require that money (or a bail bondsman's pledge) be deposited with the court or that a third person sign for and be responsible for the defendant's future appearances. Minor offenders are often released on their own recognizance (their promise to appear). Bail setting evolved in the American legal system as an attempt to resolve the basic conflict between individual and societal rights (as discussed in Chapter 1).

## *The Purposes of Bail*

The bail decision determines whether defendants are detained or released before trial. When bail is higher than defendants can afford, they have no choice but to remain in jail. And often, bail can be quite high. In the case of John Emil List, who was arrested after his crimes of 17 years before were portrayed on the TV program, *America's Most Wanted,* the judge set bail at $5 million. A similar amount was set for Imelda Marcos's bail, after she was charged with fraud and embezzling $100 million from the Philippine government.

The Eighth Amendment to the U.S. Constitution says that excessive bail shall not be required, but the Supreme Court has ruled that this provision does not guarantee a right to bail; it simply requires that bail, if any, should not be excessive (*United States v. Salerno,* 1987).

In 1998, of the almost 600,000 inmates confined in local jails in the United States, 57% were in custody waiting to be arraigned, to be tried, or to have their trials conclude (U.S. Department of Justice, 1998). They were in jail not because they had been convicted of a crime but because either they had been denied bail, or they had not been able to

raise the bail that had been set for them. Is this fair, given the fundamental value in U.S. society that defendants are innocent until proven guilty?

## *What Considerations Affect the Decision to Set Bail?*

Traditionally, the justification for requiring bail has been the degree of risk that the defendant will not appear for his or her trial. Defendants who are believed not to pose this risk are often **released on their own recognizance** (called ROR), those for whom some doubt exists are allowed to post a bail bond as a kind of insurance that they will appear, and those who are considered very high risks are kept in custody. Whether bail bonds actually reduce the risk of nonappearance is not clear. Studies of jurisdictions where defendants are given ROR reveal that very few defendants fail to appear (Ares, Rankin, & Sturz, 1963; Feeley, 1983).

Should the dangerousness of the defendant or his or her likelihood of committing other crimes in the interim also be a consideration? Around 1970, a push began for legislation that would increase the use of preventive detention—the detention of arrested persons who pose a risk of flight or dangerousness. Most citizens approve of preventive detention, opting for society's need to be protected from possible future dangerousness over the rights of individual suspects to be free until proven guilty—an aspect of the presumption of innocence guaranteed by the Constitution.

The Bail Reform Act of 1984 was introduced by Congress in part to ensure that community safety is considered by judges when they set bail for criminal defendants. Despite challenges to the constitutionality of the preventive detention authorized by this act, it was upheld by the U.S. Supreme Court. In the 1987 case of *United States v. Salerno,* the Court upheld the provision in this law permitting the detention of defendants charged with serious crimes if prosecutors could establish probable cause that the defendants committed the crimes charged and could convince the judge that "the safety of any other person and the community" would be jeopardized if the defendants were released on bail (Taylor, 1987a). (The standard to be used was "clear and convincing evidence.") Thus, preventive detention on the grounds of perceived dangerousness is not only a federal law but on the books (in some form) in many states as well. Reflecting the dilemma in Chapter 1 between individual rights and society's needs, Chief Justice Rehnquist wrote, "We have repeatedly held that the Government's regulatory interest in community safety can, in appropriate circumstances, outweigh an individual's liberty interest" (quoted in Taylor, 1987a, p. 9). Crucial to the Court's opinion, however, was the assumption that the defendant would be tried promptly in accordance with the Federal Speedy Trial Act.

Preventive detention requires two procedures: (1) determining which persons pose threats of committing additional crimes if released from jail and (2) detaining these persons prior to their trials. In practice, preventive detention assumes that valid assessments of risk and accurate predictions of future dangerous conduct can be made, an assumption that is uncertain (Douglas & Webster, 1999; Lidz, Mulvey, & Gardner, 1993; Monahan, 1984; Mossman, 1994). Judges have difficulty knowing which defendants are dangerous and which can be trusted. In Shepherd, Texas, Patrick Dale Walker tried to kill his girlfriend by putting a gun to her head and pulling the trigger. The loaded gun failed to fire. Walker's original bail was set at $1 million, but after he had sat in jail for four days, the presiding judge lowered his bail to $25,000. This permitted Walker to be released; four months later, he fired three bullets at close range and killed the same woman. Afterward, the judge did not think he was wrong in lowering the bail, even though, since 1993, Texas has had a law that permits the safety of the victim and the community to be considered in determining the amount of bail. In fact, Patrick Walker had no previous record, was valedictorian of his class, and was a college graduate. Would a psychologist have done any better in predicting Walker's behavior?

The answer to this question is uncertain. Although psychologists might make valid predictions of future dangerousness for 50% or more of

the persons they evaluate (Douglas & Webster, 1999; Gardner et al., 1996; Lidz et al., 1993; Mossman, 1994), this level of accuracy (or inaccuracy) has led some scholars to argue that mental-health professionals simply should not make such predictions because they lack adequate scientific validity (Ewing, 1991). We will return to this issue in a later chapter on forensic assessment, but for now we would simply note that assessing risks and predicting dangerousness are very difficult tasks and that even the best clinicians still have trouble making accurate long-term predictions of dangerous behavior.

Psychologists and other social scientists can play a helpful role in this area by conducting research on the determinants and fairness of bail-setting decisions (Goldkamp & Gottfredson, 1979; Goldkamp, Gottfredson, Jones, & Weiland, 1995). Psychologists have evaluated the following topics: (1) What factors most strongly influence whether defendants released from pretrial custody appear when they are required (e.g., which is more important: ties to the local community or the amount of money posted as bond?)? (2) Can defendants who pose a high risk of fleeing if they are released from pretrial custody be identified at the time of bail setting? (3) What effect does pretrial detention have on defendants' trials? (4) What criteria influence a judge's decision to set bail? A research team housed at Temple University (Goldkamp et al., 1995) has developed a set of guidelines to assist courts in deciding on detention or release of defendants prior to trial.

## Does Bail Ensure Defendants' Appearance, and Is It Discriminatory?

Across many studies in several different communities, researchers have discovered that ROR as a form of release is as effective in guaranteeing defendants' return for trial as requiring them to post bail. In these studies, the "skip rate" for ROR defendants has averaged less than 10% (Ares et al., 1963; Feeley, 1983; Nietzel & Dade, 1973). One reason why the decision about detention versus cash bail versus release on recognizance is important is the possibility that the setting of bail un-

## BOX 10-2 The cybersearch for defendants on the run

Bail bond agents are renowned for their diligence in tracking down defendants who have skipped bail and failed to return to court as required. Bonding agents stand to lose the value of the bond posted if the defendant cannot be located, so their financial incentive for locating and returning the defendant to custody is considerable.

Although bonding agents have been criticized in the past for strong-arm search-and-return tactics, they increasingly are turning to modern technology to catch defendants on the run. An example is a Web site entitled "The World's Most Wanted—Bail Jumpers" (www.mostwanted.org/BailJumpers. html). The 21st century's counterpart to the old "Wanted Dead or Alive" posters of the western frontier, this Web page lists the names, pictures, last known locations, and characteristics of scores of defendants who are being pursued by a host of private bail bond companies. Warning that these defendants have "Nowhere to Run! Nowhere to Hide!" the subscribing companies typically offer $1000 and $2000 cash rewards for information that leads to the apprehension of the most wanted bail fugitives. They also caution would-be bounty hunters that most of the suspects are armed and should be considered dangerous.

justly discriminates against certain people, particularly if bail is not essential for ensuring required appearances. If the judge sets bail at $15,000, the defendant must come up with this amount of money as a security deposit or remain in jail until the trial is completed. (The defendant receives this security deposit back when he or she appears for trial.) The more affluent the defendant, the more capable he or she is to provide the money and obtain temporary freedom. This difference conflicts with our society's goal that people be treated equally before the law, regardless of their occupation, income, or status.

In many communities, bonding agents (or "bail bondsmen") serve as intermediaries between courts and defendants. For a percentage of the bail (usually 10%) the bonding agent provides the total bail as a surety bond. If the defendant fails to appear for trial, the agent pays the entire amount of the bail to the court. The 10% is the fee paid by defendants for their temporary freedom. If bail is set at $15,000 and the defendant hires an agent, the defendant does not have to post the $15,000 to get his freedom (often an impossible task), but he is out the $1500 fee to the bonding agent, even if he does appear in court.

Furthermore, most bonding agents require the defendant to provide collateral (personal property—e.g., jewelry, a car, or a mortgage on real estate); if the defendant fails to appear, the agents use this property to recoup some of their loss. So bail is costly to defendants, especially those who can least afford it. (See ◆ **Box 10-2** for a description of modern bail bond agent techniques.)

### Can High-Risk Defendants Be Identified?

The major concerns about defendants once they are released from pretrial custody are that they will commit more crimes or will fail to return for trial as required. If those defendants who pose the greatest risk for new offenses following their release could be accurately identified, guidelines could be developed for judges to use in their bail-setting decisions. In one extensive study (Goldkamp & Gottfredson, 1988), the researchers followed the status of 2200 persons who had been arrested for felonies and were then released from custody prior to their trials. Within 90 days of their release, 17% of these defendants had been arrested either for a new crime or for failing to appear as required in court.

## The Science of

**BOX 10-3**

### Bail setting and the factors that determine judges' decisions

Faced with a bail determination, judges must balance two concerns that reflect the prongs of our first dilemma: that society's interest in the defendant's appearing in court is satisfied and that the defendant's rights will be protected. Ordinarily, the judge hears the prosecuting attorney and the defendant's lawyer each recommend different amounts of bail, or even different actions, because bail recommendations can be conceptualized along a monetary continuum from zero (accused is released on ROR) to infinite (accused is held in jail without bail). Attorneys experienced in trial advocacy claim they can assess, from the defendant's record, what the judge will decide as appropriate bail. Frank Citrano, a New York City trial attorney who handles as many as 20 arraignments a day, says, "In a matter of seconds, I can read the complaint and the defendant's record and get an immediate sense if I can argue for release without bail or ask for one low enough that my client can make it immediately" (quoted in Sullivan, 1991, p. A16).

Social psychologists Ebbe Ebbesen and Vladimir Konecni (1975) studied the decision processes that judges use in setting bail. They conducted two studies, with differing outcomes. In the first, 18 municipal and superior court judges in San Diego, California, were given eight fictitious case records. Some aspects of these records were consistent; they all involved robberies, and the accused was always an unmarried white male between the ages of 21 and 25 who claimed he was innocent. The type of stolen property differed, but its value was always between $850 and $950.

In contrast to these constant factors, Ebbesen and Konecni varied four independent variables in order to determine their relative importance to judges' decisions about appropriate bail:

1. *Prosecuting attorney's recommendation*. In actual robbery cases in San Diego, the average recommendation for bail by the district attorney had been $2850. The researchers established three levels of recommended bail: low ($1500–$1700), medium ($2000–$2500), or high ($5000–$7500).

2. *Defense attorney's recommendation*. In actual cases, the average recommendation by defense attorneys was $747. Again, three levels were established, but as you would expect, they were

lower than the prosecutor suggested: low ($0; i.e., ROR), medium ($500–$600), or high ($1000–$1200).

3. *Prior record*. In actual bail hearings, prosecuting attorneys usually refer to the prior criminal record of the accused to bolster their recommendations; two levels were embedded in the district attorney's statement. In one, the defendant had no prior record; in the other, he had a past history of felony convictions and was currently on probation.

4. *Local ties*. Defense attorneys, trying to make the best possible case that their clients deserve less bail, often portray them as responsible persons. One means is to refer to the defendant's local ties: He has lived in that city for a long time, or he is employed there. Two extremes were created: The defendant had either strong local ties (he had lived in San Diego for four to six years, he was employed there, and his family also lived in San Diego) or weak ones (he had lived in San Diego only one or two months, he was unemployed, and his family lived several hundred miles away).

Thus, there were 36 possible combinations of these four fac-

Among the factors that predicted new offenses or failure to appear were the following: the defendant lived alone, the original criminal charge was for robbery or a property offense, the defendant previously had failed to show up for a required court appear-ance, and the arresting police officer noted factors at the time of arrest suggesting a risk of fleeing. Based on these factors, defendants were classified into four groups representing increasing levels of risk. The failure rates (defined as a new offense or

tors; that is, 3 (prosecutor's recommendation) × 3 (defense recommendation) × 2 (prior record) × 2 (local ties). Each judge reviewed eight cases, so that each of the 36 cases was reviewed by four judges. Judges were asked what bail they would set for each case they reviewed. Table 10.1 presents the average decisions. Judges were influenced most by the degree to which the defendant was tied to the area and by a previous criminal record. Weak local ties led to higher bail amounts, as did a prior criminal record. But remember that this was a simulation study; the judges were aware that these were not real cases, and some of them even commented that certain combinations of the four factors would never occur in real bail hearings. Consequently, Ebbesen and Konecni decided to observe actual bail-setting hearings.

In this second study, trained observers attended the hearings of five judges. Decisions involving 106 defendants, including four charged with homicide, were studied. The observers recorded information about five independent variables:

1. *Severity of the crime.* There were six categories: (1) homicide; (2) violent crimes not resulting in death (kidnapping, rape, and assault); (3) crimes with the potential of violence or death (armed robbery or possession of a deadly weapon); (4) nonviolent major crimes with specific victims (sale of drugs or robbery); (5) nonviolent minor crimes with unspecified victims (forgery); and (6) victimless crimes (possessing drugs or being AWOL).

2. *Prior record.* The accused's criminal record was categorized as (1) none; (2) only traffic violations; (3) a moderate record (no more than one prior felony

*(continued)*

**TABLE 10.1** ◆ *Mean bail set by judges in a controlled simulation of the bail-setting situation*

| | | DEFENSE ATTORNEY'S RECOMMENDATION | | | | | |
| | | $0 | | $550 | | $1100 | |
| | | STRENGTH OF LOCAL TIES | | | | | |
| DISTRICT ATTORNEY'S RECOMMENDATION | PRIOR RECORD | STRONG | WEAK | STRONG | WEAK | STRONG | WEAK |
|---|---|---|---|---|---|---|---|
| $1600 | No | $687 | $2775 | $937 | $1550 | $2000 | $1550 |
| | Yes | 2500 | 2125 | 1312 | 1900 | 2550 | 2550 |
| $2250 | No | 1625 | 2375 | 750 | 2312 | 1750 | 2625 |
| | Yes | 1250 | 2375 | 1387 | 3000 | 1750 | 2875 |
| $6250 | No | 1125 | 3250 | 2125 | 2875 | 1550 | 3300 |
| | Yes | 2750 | 5687 | 3125 | 3375 | 1600 | 4250 |

SOURCE: From Ebbesen and Konecni (1975, Table 1, p. 809).

a failure to appear) of these four groups were 6%, 12%, 23%, and 30%. Many courts now use similar empirical guidelines in denying bail to defendants or setting different levels of bail. (Note, however, the large number of false positives among the highest-risk group; 70% of the persons in this group did not commit a new crime or fail to appear after being released.) ◆ Box 10-3 describes the "science" of bail setting as studied in San Diego, California, some years ago.

## The Science of

### BOX 10-3

### Bail setting and the factors that determine judges' decisions

*(continued)*

conviction, and that for a nonviolent crime); or (4) a severe prior record (consisting of more than one felony conviction or one violent-crime felony conviction).

3. *Local ties.* Three levels of local ties were distinguished based on whether the defendant was employed and had relatives in the San Diego area and on how long he or she had lived there.

4. *Defense attorney's recommendation.* The actual monetary recommendations were recorded. These ranged from $0 to $25,000 (in one murder case).

5. *Prosecutor's recommendation.* The recommended bail from the district attorney's office for these 106 cases ranged from $0 to $100,000.

The researchers used a statistical procedure called *multiple regression* to determine how the five independent variables interacted to affect the judges' decisions about bail. In combination, the five independent variables ac-

counted for 80% of the variance in the decisions.

The district attorney's recommendation was the single strongest predictor of the judges' decisions. One reason is that this recommendation incorporated aspects of two of the other variables (severity of crime and prior record). For example, when the crime was more severe and there was a prior record, the prosecutor suggested higher bail. Interestingly, local ties did not play a consistent role in the prosecuting attorney's recommendation; in fact, when the crime was severe, the attorney proposed that higher bail be set when there were strong local ties.

The mean bail amount set by the judges ($2162 without the murder cases) fell between the district attorney's ($2820) and the defense attorney's ($583) mean recommendations. And although the defense attorney's recommendation did influence the judge, it had less influence than the prosecutor's. In fact, Ebbesen and Konecni (1975) concluded:

Even though a hearing is held in which both attorneys make a major point of discussing the prior record and local ties of the accused, the judges set bail almost in complete accord with the district attorney's recommendations. This decision strategy seems inconsistent with the traditional claim that the accused is presumed innocent until proven guilty, especially since in the adversary system the district attorney's goal is to prove that the accused is guilty. Furthermore, since the district attorneys always seem to recommend a higher bail than the defense attorneys, following the former's recommendations is more likely to lead to discrimination against the poor. (p. 820)

A later survey in Philadelphia, using a larger number of cases (Goldkamp & Gottfredson, 1979), also concluded that community ties had very little impact on bail setting. Seriousness of the offense was most important, accounting for 29% of the variance in judges' decisions to release defendants on their own recognizance.

## Does Pretrial Release Affect Trial Outcome?

What if the defendant cannot provide bail and remains in jail until the time of trial? Does this pretrial incarceration affect the trial's outcome? Clearly, yes. Defendants who are detained in jail are more likely to be convicted and to receive higher sentences than those who can afford bail,

even when the seriousness of their offenses and the evidence against them are the same (Goldfarb, 1965). An accused person who is free on bail finds it easier to gather witnesses and prepare a defense. Jailed defendants cannot meet with their attorneys in the latter's office, have less time with their attorneys to prepare for trial, and have less access to records and witnesses. In addition, pretrial detention is likely to cost defendants their jobs, making it harder for them to pay attorneys. Detention also corrodes family and community ties. Casper's (1972) interviews with convicted defendants who were serving prison sentences revealed that, for many of them, the time spent in local jails prior to trial was worse than the time in prison; the conditions were terrible, there was nothing to do, and the guards were hostile.

Civil libertarians oppose pretrial detention because it conflicts with our society's fundamental assumption that a defendant is innocent until proven guilty. The Supreme Court has taken a somewhat different view—that the "presumption of innocence" refers to the rule of trial procedure that places the burden of demonstrating a defendant's guilt on the government, and that pretrial detention is not a punishment but rather a regulation (like a quarantine) for the public's protection. In other words, the presumption of innocence allows a judge to consider evidence that a defendant is dangerous. However, numerous surveys (reported in Goldfarb, 1965) have shown that defendants who are detained because they could not pay bail are frequently found not guilty (or have their charges dismissed). In Philadelphia, of 1000 people detained an average of 33 days, 67% were later acquitted or, if convicted, not given any prison sentences. Another survey of 114,653 people in pretrial detention reported that 73% were later acquitted or not given jail or prison sentences. A partial explanation for these outcomes is that charges are sometimes dismissed (or the defendant is credited with time already served in jail) when the prosecutor believes that the pretrial incarceration has been sufficient punishment for the crime.

# The Role of the Grand Jury

In the federal system and in many states, a defendant cannot be convicted of a felony unless a grand jury has first returned an indictment. Thus, the grand jury's job is to determine whether enough evidence exists to bring the defendant to trial: Is there probable cause that the defendant committed the crime? In theory, the grand jury should therefore serve as a shield against unwarranted prosecutions. But although the grand jury can serve as a buffer against hasty prosecution of innocent suspects, it also can be used by prosecutors as a tool to implement their wishes to "put criminals behind bars." For example, if a given grand jury decides not to indict the defendant despite the prosecutor's desire to do so, the prosecutor can submit the case to new grand juries repeatedly, as long as the statute of limitations has not been exceeded (Taylor, 1993).

Sometimes the grand jury is used for the political aims of the prosecuting attorney, who for various reasons, does not want to indict a suspect. After Mary Jo Kopechne drowned in Senator Ted Kennedy's car off Chappaquiddick Bridge in July 1969, the grand jury—according to its foreperson, Leslie Leland—was denied access to witnesses and the transcript of the inquest. "I felt I had been set up by the D.A. so that they could claim there was a grand jury investigation; we had been used," Leland is quoted as saying (Kunen, Mathison, Brown, & Nugent, 1989, p. 36). A grand jury can thus be used as a "dumping ground" by prosecutors who don't want to take the heat for a decision not to prosecute.

Historically, the grand jury arose out of a struggle between King Henry II of England and the Roman Catholic Church. In 1164, the church reluctantly agreed to accept an organization that represented the earliest forerunner of the modern grand jury. At this point, the grand jury served as an instrument of the king; "grand jurors were penalized if they failed to return an indictment against someone considered indictable by the Crown" (Clark, 1975, p. 9). An equivalent concern, that the grand jury serves as a "rubber stamp" for the prosecutor, remains today. Clark (1975) observes, for example, that "in periods of severe political stress, or when a locality or the nation has been caught up in some intense ideological struggle, the grand jurors have shared the political sympathies of the prosecuting agent, and unpopular accused people have not been protected against improper or politically inspired charges" (p. 26).

At the same time, the grand jury can serve as a useful investigative tool. The grand jury can subpoena witnesses to give testimony, and it can require that documents be brought forth. The grand jury has been extremely effective in gathering evidence in cases involving organized crime.

## Problems with the Grand Jury

Because public procedures could injure the reputations of innocent parties (people bound over to the grand jury but ultimately not indicted) and inhibit potential witnesses, grand jury procedures are conducted in secret. Furthermore, they are one-sided in that those people facing possible indictment have no right to be present or to cross-examine witnesses. The grand jury can consider any evidence it chooses to hear, including hearsay and evidence produced by illegal searches. These practices have led to problems with the way some grand juries have functioned, causing them at times to be more of a threat to, than a protector of, the innocent.

For a number of reasons, two-thirds of the states do not require the use of grand juries; O. J. Simpson's case did not include a grand jury indictment. In contrast, New York still requires that every person accused of a felony is entitled to have a grand jury decide whether there should be an indictment (Collins, 1996). States also differ on whether the suspect is permitted access to the minutes of the grand jury deliberations. Some permit ready access; others (and the federal government) do not consider this necessary, concluding that once indicted, "a defendant is adequately protected by the requirement of proof beyond a reasonable doubt before a unanimous trial jury may convict" (Frankel & Naftalis, 1977, pp. 24–25).

## Use of the Grand Jury as a Political Weapon

During the administration of President Richard Nixon (1969–1974), the executive branch of the federal government used federal grand juries as weapons against political opponents. Leroy D. Clark (1975), a law professor and observer of the

process, noted at the time that "there are strong indications that the Justice Department has used the grand jury to gather intelligence against groups deemed 'radical,' to harass and deplete the resources of political opponents, and generally to discredit and intimidate people from continuing to support and participate in groups that the administration differs with politically" (p. 6). When people refused to tell these grand juries about their friends and associates, they were jailed for contempt. More recently, Kenneth Starr, the independent counsel investigating President Clinton's affair with Monica Lewinsky, impaneled a grand jury to gather evidence for the House of Representatives to use in deciding whether to impeach the president.

# Plea Bargaining

No better example exists of the dilemma between truth and conflict resolution as goals of our legal system than the extensive use of **plea bargaining** in the U.S. criminal justice system. Most criminal cases—at least 85%—end between arrest and trial, primarily when the defendant pleads guilty to some charge, usually in exchange for a concession by the prosecutor. For example, between March 27 and April 21, 1989, the largest county in New York State disposed of 1256 felony cases. A total of 82.5% were plea-bargained, 6.8% were resolved through jury trials, 9.1% were dismissed, and the remaining 1.6% had other dispositions (Lee, 1989). In 1996, 80% of all federal charges were disposed of by guilty pleas; after acquittals and dismissals are removed from this figure, 92% of federal convictions were secured by guilty pleas (Dressler & Thomas, 1999).

Often serious cases are resolved by plea bargains. Ted Kaczynski, the "Unabomber," accepted life imprisonment without possibility of parole to avoid facing the death penalty. James Earl Ray, the assassin of Martin Luther King, died in prison while serving a life sentence as a result of a plea bargain with state prosecutors. In Kaczynski's case, the plea bargain satisfactorily resolved the controversy. Kaczynski had acted alone, the victims agreed to the resolution, and Kaczynski received what the public accepted as a fair disposition for one who was mentally ill. In the case of James Earl Ray, however, the plea bargain was not well received. Many thought Ray had not acted alone, and the plea bargain meant that the facts would never be aired in a public forum. Years after Martin Luther King's death, the King family was still searching for answers, going so far as to visit with James Earl Ray in the hope that he would reveal what lay behind the assassination. After Ray's death in 1998, the King family released a statement expressing regret that Ray had never had his day in court and stating, "The American people have a right to the truth about this tragedy and we intend to do everything we can to bring it to light" (www.cnn.com, April 23, 1998).

Not all guilty pleas are reached through bargaining; some defendants plead guilty with no promise of leniency because they choose to end the process as quickly as possible and get on with serving their sentences. However, most defendants plead guilty as a result of a negotiation process that leads them to expect a concession or benefit from the prosecutor in exchange for not contesting guilt.

The defendant's part of the bargain requires an admission of guilt. This admission relieves the prosecutor from any obligation to prove that the defendant committed the crimes charged. It is usually a formal plea of guilty to a judge, who, if he or she accepts the plea, imposes a sentence. In addition, most states allow **deferred prosecution** for minor crimes, in which first-time offenders who admit guilt are placed on probation and have the charges against them dismissed if they stay out of trouble during probation. By admitting guilt—through either a guilty plea or a deferred-prosecution agreement—the defendant saves the prosecution the time, expense, and uncertainty of a trial.

The prosecutor's part of the bargain may involve an agreement to allow the defendant to plead guilty to a charge less serious than the evidence supports. For example, manslaughter is a lesser charge to murder, and many murder prosecutions are resolved by a plea of guilty to manslaughter. In one year in Brooklyn, of 6621 people charged with narcotics felonies, 2983 charges were ultimately reduced to misdemeanors (Kurtz, 1988).

In a common procedure known as *charge bargaining,* the prosecutor drops some charges in return for a plea of guilty. Laboratory research using role-playing procedures (Gregory, Mowen, & Linder, 1978) indicates that "overcharging" is effective; subjects were more likely to accept a plea bargain when relatively many charges had been filed against them. Charge bargaining may lead prosecutors to charge the defendant with more crimes or a more serious crime than they could prove at trial as a strategy for motivating guilty pleas. The defendants who engage in this type of bargaining may win only hollow victories. Cases in which prosecutors offer to drop charges are likely to be ones for which judges would have imposed concurrent sentences for the multiple convictions anyway. Judges and parole boards also tend to pay more attention to the criminal act itself than to the formal charge when making sentencing decisions.

Plea bargaining may also take the form of *sentence bargaining,* in which prosecutors recommend reduced sentences in return for guilty pleas. Sentencing is the judges' prerogative, and judges vary in their willingness to follow prosecutors' recommendations. Judges can rubber-stamp prosecutorial sentencing recommendations, and some judges do just that. On the other hand, judges should consider many factors when imposing a sentence—seriousness of the crime, harm to the victim, background of the offender, to name a few—and some judges believe that simply going along with every recommendation from the prosecutor compromises their duty to consider these factors sufficiently. In general, most defendants can expect that judges will usually follow the sentences that have been recommended by a prosecutor. Prosecutors can promote this expectation and earn the trust of judges by recommending sentences that are reasonable and fair.

Defendants try to negotiate a plea to obtain less severe punishment than they would receive if they went to trial and were convicted. But why do prosecutors plea-bargain? What advantages do they seek, given that they hold the more powerful position in this bargaining situation? Prosecutors are motivated to plea-bargain for one or more of the following reasons: (1) to dispose of cases in which the evidence against the defendant is weak or the defense attorney is a formidable foe, (2) to obtain the testimony of one defendant against a more culpable or infamous codefendant, (3) to expedite the flow of cases for an overworked staff and a clogged court docket, (4) to maintain a cordial working relationship with defense attorneys from whom the prosecutor may want certain favors in the future, or (5) to avoid trials that might be unpopular because the defendant is a well-liked figure in the community or the crime charged might be seen as morally justified.

## Evaluations of Plea Bargaining

Plea bargaining remains a controversial procedure. During the 1970s, two national commissions reviewed its value; one concluded that it was a necessary device for keeping cases moving through the courts, but the other called for its abolition. Plea bargaining has been practiced in the United States since the middle of the 19th century, although some states purport to forbid (Alaska) or restrict (California) the practice. The Supreme Court has upheld plea bargaining, calling it "an essential component of the administration of justice" (*Santobello v. New York*, 1971). However, several rules must be followed for guilty pleas to be valid. First, as we discuss in the next chapter, pleas of guilty must be voluntary, intelligent, and knowing. A plea of guilty is voluntary even if it is induced by a promise of leniency, so long as the defendant is represented by an attorney (*Brady v. United States*, 1970). Likewise, a plea can be voluntary even if encouraged by the threat of additional charges should the defendant insist on trial. In *Bordenkircher v. Hayes* (1978), the Court held that forcing a defendant to choose between unpleasant alternatives (e.g., pleading guilty or facing a trial in which a more severe sen-

tence would be sought) does not mean that the choice is involuntary, provided that the choices advance legitimate social goals and do not impose unconstitutional restrictions on the defendant. However, some pressures will not be tolerated. In *Bordenkircher,* for example, the Court expressed reservations about offers not to prosecute third parties in exchange for a guilty plea from a defendant. Also, prosecutors cannot renege on their "deals" and require a more severe sentence than their original negotiated offer (*Santobello v. New York,* 1971).

Plea bargaining has been defended as a necessary and useful part of the criminal justice system (American Bar Association, 1993), and it has been condemned as a practice that should be abolished from our courts (Alschuler, 1968; Kipnis, 1979; Langbein, 1978; National Advisory Commission on Criminal Justice Standards and Goals, 1973). Advocates cite the following justifications for the procedure: (1) the defendant's admission of guilt is an important first step in rehabilitation; (2) guilty pleas relieve the backlog of cases that would otherwise engulf the courts; (3) outcomes are reached promptly and with a sense of finality; (4) other criminal justice participants benefit from the process—from the police officer who doesn't have to spend hours in court testifying to the victim who is spared the trauma of a trial; and (5) the defendant's cooperation may facilitate prosecution of others.

Critics urge the abolition of plea bargaining on the following grounds: (1) improper sentences—sometimes too harsh but more often too lenient—are likely, (2) the process encourages defendants to surrender their constitutional rights, (3) prosecutors exert too much power in negotiating guilty pleas, (4) the process is private and encourages "shady" deals not available to all defendants, and (5) innocent defendants might feel coerced to plead guilty because they fear the more severe consequences of being convicted by a jury.

Data on these contentions are limited, but what evidence exists suggests that plea bargaining is not as evil as the abolitionists claim or as essential as its defenders believe. Rates of plea bargaining are surprisingly consistent across rural and urban jurisdictions as well as across understaffed and well-funded prosecutors' offices (Heumann, 1978; Silberman, 1978). After Alaska ended plea bargaining in 1975, defendants continued to plead guilty at about the same rate, court proceedings did not slow down, and a modest increase in the number of trials occurred—though not as great as had been feared (Rubinstein, Clarke, & White, 1980). On the other hand, when El Paso, Texas, abolished plea bargaining in 1975, it experienced a serious backup of cases. This result occurred largely because defendants perceived no benefit of pleading in comparison to waiting for their trials in the hope that witnesses would not be available or other weaknesses in the prosecution's case would develop, making acquittal more likely (Greenberg & Ruback, 1984). The risk of innocent parties pleading guilty is uncertain; however, data from laboratory simulation experiments suggest that "guilty" parties are more likely to plea-bargain than are the "innocent" (Gregory et al., 1978). Experimental research also suggests that "defendants" (college students or prisoners asked to imagine themselves plea bargaining) prefer to participate in the bargaining process and perceive it as being fairer when they do (e.g., Houlden, 1981).

Plea bargaining serves the need of the defense attorney to appear to gain something for his or her client and the need of the prosecutor to appear fair and reasonable. Both prosecutors and defense attorneys believe they are making the "punishment fit the crime" by individualizing the law to fit the circumstances of the case, and both are comfortable with a system in which most cases are resolved without a clear winner or clear loser. Experienced prosecutors and defense attorneys teach plea bargaining to the rookies in their offices, and lawyers from both sides engage in a ritual of give and take, with changing facts and personalities but with the same posturing and rationalizations. In fact, the procedures are so well known that in some cases no formal bargaining even takes place; everyone involved—prosecutor, defense attorney, defendant, and judge—knows

the prevailing "rate" for a given crime, and if the defendant pleads guilty to that crime, the rate is the price that will be paid.

Defense attorneys appeal to prosecutors' inclination to bargain through two approaches. First, they try to offer something of benefit to the prosecutor, enhancing the value of the benefit as much as possible without misstating facts. Benefits for prosecutors have already been described, but one constant advantage of guilty pleas is that they eliminate the uncertainty of a trial's outcome (a benefit whenever the prosecutor believes an acquittal is possible because of weak evidence). The second strategy is to offer the prosecutor the chance to "do the right thing" for a client who deserves a break. The duty of prosecutors is to "seek justice, not merely to convict" (ABA Standards for Criminal Justice, "The Prosecution Function," 1993, 3-1.2). Many prosecutors are open to alternatives to incarceration and will look for opportunities to mitigate the harshness of punishments that could be imposed if a defendant stood trial and was convicted. Community service and restitution to victims are attractive dispositions, particularly when related meaningfully to the offense. When the crime results from mental illness, supervised probation coupled with therapy for the offender can be an appropriate resolution.

Of course, there is a "dark side" to plea bargaining when dispositions are not commensurate with the gravity of the offense. When these "errors" are in the direction of sentencing leniency, they often are attributed to a perceived overload in the prosecutor's office or the courts. It is wrong for a defendant to be able to plead to a greatly reduced charge simply because the criminal justice system lacks the resources to handle the case. However, the answer to problems of unwarranted leniency is not the abolition of plea bargaining; rather, adequate funding must be provided for the court system as well as for the correctional system so that, when severe penalties are necessary, severe penalties can be given. In the long run, if plea bargaining serves primarily as a method for balancing the underfunded budgets of our courts and correctional systems, it will cease to be a bargain in the larger sense and will become, instead, too great a price for our society to pay.

## Ethical Issues in Plea Bargaining

Plea bargaining may work against the long-range goal of achieving justice. When some lawbreakers bargain a guilty plea, the agreement may permit other lawbreakers to escape prosecution.

Sidney Biddle Barrows, a 33-year-old New York socialite, was arrested on charges of running a 20-woman prostitution ring from a brownstone house on Manhattan's Upper West Side. In 1985, she pled guilty to promoting prostitution. Her penalty: a $5000 fine and no prison sentence. As a result of the plea bargain, she was not required to reveal the names of the 3000 clients of her "escort service." If, in fact, Barrows was operating a house of prostitution, her customers were breaking the law, too.

Plea bargaining also may prevent the families of victims from seeing the defendants "get justice" or hearing them acknowledge full responsibility for their offenses. In the so-called Preppie Murder Case, Robert Chambers agreed to plead guilty to a lesser charge of manslaughter *while the jury was deliberating* whether to convict him of the 1986 murder of Jennifer Levin (Taubman, 1988). The family of Ms. Levin was not consulted, although the victims' rights legislation that was discussed in Chapter 9 increasingly ensures that the victim or his or her family has a say in plea bargaining.

Another problem in plea bargaining involves the use of criminals as prosecution witnesses, which occurs when lawbreakers turn state's evidence to avoid prosecution or to reduce their own penalties. Under the federal sentencing guidelines, a defendant is entitled to a downward departure (a more lenient sentence) "upon motion of the government that the defendant has provided substantial assistance in the investigation or prosecution of another person who has committed an offense." This means that the only way in which a defendant can get out from under the guidelines is by turning on his codefendants or by becoming an informant. After evaluating the in-

formation or cooperation provided by the defendant, the prosecutor decides whether to ask the judge to give the defendant a sentence below that prescribed by the guidelines. In *Wade v. United States* (1992), the Supreme Court held that, in the absence of a motion by the government, a judge is powerless to find that the defendant has provided "substantial assistance" and, further, that a prosecutor is under no legal duty to file a motion even if the facts, objectively viewed, indicate that substantial assistance was provided. A defendant who bargains in the federal courts assumes the risk that the prosecutor will not be pleased with the assistance provided and will refuse to ask the judge to give the defendant a break.

# Pretrial Publicity

## Change of Venue and Other Remedies

Two cherished rights guaranteed by the U.S. Constitution are freedom of speech (the First Amendment) and the right to a speedy, public trial before an impartial jury (the Sixth Amendment). The right to free speech applies to the written as well as the spoken word. It also applies to the institution of the press, not just to individuals. The press is expected to be the government watchdog, a role encouraged by constitutional protection. The right to an impartial jury and a fair trial is also a fundamental expectation of Americans. The fairness of our adversarial system of justice rests in large part on the decision making of an unbiased group of jurors.

In the vast majority of cases, the liberties ensured by the First and Sixth Amendments are compatible and even complementary. The press informs the public about criminal investigations and trials, and the public not only learns the outcomes of these proceedings but often gains increased appreciation for both the justness and the foibles of our system of justice.

For a few trials, however, the First and Sixth Amendments clash. The press publishes information that, when disseminated among the public, threatens a defendant's right to a trial by impartial jurors. These problem cases can involve defendants and/or victims who, because of their fame or infamous acts, gain a national reputation. The trials of O. J. Simpson, Mike Tyson, and Timothy McVeigh are examples. A more common problem occurs when local media release incriminating information about a defendant that is later ruled inadmissible at trial. Once made public, this information can bias opinion about the defendant. Examples include publication of details about a prior criminal record, a confession made by the accused, or unfavorable statements regarding the defendant's character. In general, local news coverage of trials exerts a greater impact in small towns than in large cities because a larger percentage of the population in small towns knows the parties; also, serious crimes occur less frequently in smaller towns, thereby increasing attention and rumor when they do occur.

But potentially biasing information can also be released by a national organization and, hence, create a nationwide problem. When Theodore Kaczynski was identified as the Unabomber in 1996, the FBI leaked to the media detailed information about the contents of his cabin, including a potentially incriminating typewriter, a partially assembled bomb, and lists of potential victims.

In cases with extensive pretrial publicity (e.g., the Unabomber's), the courts must answer two basic questions. First, does the publicity threaten the fairness of a defendant's trial? Second, if the answer to this question is yes, what steps should be taken to remedy the situation? Psychologists have conducted research on both queries and can offer guidance to judges who are willing to listen.

## Court Decisions on Pretrial Publicity

The history of the "free press/fair trial" controversy divides into several phases, differing in the ways the courts assessed pretrial publicity and the steps they favored to remedy any prejudice that was created (Loh, 1984). Phase 1 began with the famous trial in 1807 of Aaron Burr, third vice

president of the United States, who was charged with treason. Burr claimed that he could not get a fair trial because inflammatory newspaper articles had prejudiced the public against him. Chief Justice Marshall ruled that the law did not require a jury "without any prepossessions whatever respecting the guilt or innocence of the accused" and that finding such a jury would be impossible anyway. However, the Court did consider "those who have deliberately formed and delivered an opinion on the guilt of the prisoner as not being in a state of mind to fairly weigh the testimony, and therefore as being disqualified to serve as jurors in the case" (*United States v. Burr,* 1807). In phase 1 therefore, the question of pretrial publicity was evaluated in terms of the effects jurors reported it to have on their minds.

In phase 2, the Supreme Court began to question whether jurors' own assurances of impartiality in the face of massive amounts of prejudicial publicity constituted a sufficient protection for defendants subjected to this publicity. *Irvin v. Dowd* (1961) was the first case in which the U.S. Supreme Court struck down a state conviction on the ground of prejudicial pretrial publicity. In this case, six murders had been committed around Evansville, Indiana, between December 1954 and March 1955. The defendant, Leslie Irvin, was arrested on April 8, 1955. Shortly thereafter, the prosecutor and local police issued extensively publicized press releases saying that Irvin had confessed to the present crimes as well as to 24 other burglaries; that he had been previously convicted of arson, burglary, and AWOL charges; and that he was a parole violator, a bad-check artist, and a remorseless and conscienceless person. Irvin's attorney obtained a change of venue to adjoining Gibson County, which was saturated by the same publicity that tainted the original venue. He petitioned to have the trial moved again, but this motion was denied. At Irvin's trial, 430 prospective jurors were examined; 268 were excused because they were convinced of Irvin's guilt. Eight members of the jury that was seated admitted that they thought he was guilty prior to his trial. At the trial, Irvin was convicted of murder and sentenced to death.

Following *Irvin,* the Supreme Court considered several cases in which defendants claimed that their right to an impartial jury had been destroyed by inflammatory pretrial publicity. For example, in *Rideau v. Louisiana* (1963), the Court decided that exposure to news that included information strongly pointing to the defendant's guilt in the case was a violation of due process. A local TV station broadcast at three different times a 20-minute clip of Rideau, surrounded by law enforcement officials, confessing in detail to charges of robbery, kidnapping, and murder. A request for a change of venue was denied, and Rideau was convicted and sentenced to death by a jury, of which at least three members had seen the televised confession. The Supreme Court reversed this decision.

In *Sheppard v. Maxwell* (1966), the Court reviewed the famous trial of Dr. Sam Sheppard, a prominent Cleveland physician charged with the murder of his wife. News coverage of this trial was unrestrained and turned the proceeding into a media carnival. The Court overturned Sheppard's conviction, concluding that "where there is a reasonable likelihood that prejudicial news prior to a trial will prevent a fair trial, the judge should continue the case until the threat abates, or transfer it to another county not so permeated with publicity" (p. 363). The Court also discussed several options to prevent a trial where "bedlam reigned at the courthouse." This attention to remedies for adverse publicity heralded the beginning of phase 3.

Phase 3, spanning the 1970s and 1980s, was concerned with various preventive or remedial techniques for adverse pretrial publicity. It is important to recognize at the outset that these methods are usually rejected by the courts. One such measure is for a judge to order the press not to publish pretrial information likely to be prejudicial, a procedure known as prior restraint or **gag order.** The leading case is *Nebraska Press Association v. Stuart* (1976), in which the Supreme Court ruled that a trial judge could not order the press to refrain from publishing information likely to be prejudicial to a defendant unless it could be shown that a fair trial would be denied the defendant without such prior restraint. In 1990, however, the Supreme Court refused to lift a gag order barring CNN from disseminating tape recordings of telephone conversations between deposed Panamanian dictator Manuel Noriega and his attorneys. In general, gag orders are usually quickly overturned on appeal in most cases.

Likewise, the press cannot be barred from attending and reporting a trial because the First Amendment guarantees public access to criminal trials (*Richmond Newspapers, Inc. v. Virginia,* 1980). However, the press can be excluded from pretrial hearings in which potentially prejudicial material might be at issue (*Gannett Co. v. DePasquale,* 1979). The press can also volunteer to put off publishing incriminating information, and responsible members of the media often will limit their disclosures, especially when the police are investigating possible suspects in unsolved crimes.

We would prefer that the history of the free press/fair trial debate had ended with phase 3. However, there is a phase 4, initiated by the 1984 Supreme Court case of *Patton v. Yount.* The case of Jon Yount (see ◆ **Box 10-4**) represents a return to the standards of *Burr* or even something less than this standard.

Finally, in its more recent look at the potentially prejudicial effects of pretrial publicity (*Mu'Min v. Virginia,* 1991), the Supreme Court compounded the problem of jurors promising impartiality. In this case, the Court held that defendants do not have a constitutional right to ask prospective jurors about the specifics of the pretrial publicity to which they have been exposed. Under such circumstances, it is difficult to know how much trust to place in jurors' assurances that they are impartial, but the Supreme Court concluded that such assurances are all that the Constitution requires. This is the reason why there are better remedies for ensuring fair trials in light of heavy pretrial publicity. (We discuss these remedies later in this chapter.)

Many judges believe in jurors' promises of impartiality. For that reason (and for matters of

## THE CASE OF

### Jon Yount: When pretrial publicity does not warrant a change of venue

BOX 10-4

In 1966, Jon Yount confessed that he had killed Pam Rimer, an 18-year-old Pennsylvania high school student. His confession was published in two local papers and was admitted into evidence at trial, where, despite his plea of temporary insanity, he was convicted. However, his conviction was overturned because his confession had been obtained in violation of his *Miranda* rights. A second trial was held in the same county in 1970. Yount moved for a change of venue because of the continuing publicity about the case, including his confession, which was not going to be admissible at the second trial. The motion for a change of venue was denied. Of 163 prospective jurors questioned, all but two said they had heard about the case, and 77% admitted they had an opinion about Yount's guilt. Eight of the final jurors acknowledged having at some time formed an opinion as to Yount's guilt. Yount did not testify at the second trial, nor did he claim insanity. The jury convicted him of murder and sentenced him to life imprisonment.

Yount appealed, claiming that the jury was not impartial—that the publicity had made a fair trial impossible in the venue county. Nonetheless, by a 5–2 majority,

the Supreme Court held that the passage of time between the two trials had cured the prejudice that existed at the first trial and that there was not a "wave of public passion" that made a fair trial unlikely by the second jury. In addition, the Court reasoned that a "presumption of correctness" should be given to the trial judge's opinion on this matter because, being present at the trial, the judge was in a better position to evaluate the demeanor, the credibility, and, ultimately, the competence of prospective jurors. Unless the record shows that the judge made a "manifest error," reviewing courts should defer to the trial judge.

From a psychological standpoint, several deficiencies exist in this decision. The Court trusted the passage of time to erase bad memories. It speaks of time as "softening or effacing opinion." As a matter of fact, remembering and forgetting are enormously complex phenomena that depend on several factors, including how well new information is integrated with old knowledge, what new learning takes place in intervening periods of time, what type of contexts surrounded the initial learning and later retrieval, what emotional state a subject was in when the

material was originally learned, what state the subject is in at the time of attempted recall, and what type of material is to be remembered (facts, attitudes, sensations, or feelings). Time can dull a memory. But time can also enlarge it until a person "remembers" more than he or she learned in the first place. Time can enable memories to be reconstructed to fit new information, a process almost certain to work to the detriment, not the advantage, of a person being tried for the same crime a second time. Our prior discussions of hypnotically aided recall and the vagaries of eyewitness testimony also illustrate this problem.

A second problem with this decision was the Court's willingness to accept, at face value, what jurors say about their own opinions. The problem is not that jurors lie about their beliefs (although some probably do). The issue is that many reasons explain why people might not admit the full measure of their prejudice in public. People might not recognize the extent of their biases (Ogloff & Vidmar, 1994); even if completely aware, they might not disclose them in an open courtroom before a judge who encourages them to be fair and open-minded.

expediency, a point to which we return later), they are hesitant to grant change of venue requests. On rare occasions, though, when the volume of publicity has been overwhelming and when a

crime has touched the lives of many local residents, a judge will have no option but to move the trial. The Oklahoma City bombing case described in ◆ Box 10-5 is a good example.

# THE CASE OF

## Timothy McVeigh: Demonstrating the prejudicial effects of massive pretrial publicity

At 9:02 A.M. on April 19, 1995, a massive explosion destroyed the Murrah Federal Building in Oklahoma City. The bombing killed 163 people in the building (including 15 children in the building's day care center visible from the street) as well as 5 people outside. The explosion trapped hundreds of people in the rubble and spewed glass, chunks of concrete, and debris over several blocks of downtown Oklahoma City. It was the country's most deadly act of domestic terrorism.

Approximately 75 minutes after the blast, Timothy McVeigh was pulled over while driving north from Oklahoma City because his car lacked license tags. After the state trooper discovered a concealed, loaded gun in his car, McVeigh was arrested and incarcerated for transporting a loaded firearm. Two days later, on April 21, 1995, the federal government filed a complaint against McVeigh on federal bombing charges. By August 1995, McVeigh and co-defendant Terry Nichols had been charged with conspiracy, use of a weapon of mass destruction, destruction by explosives, and eight counts of first-degree murder in connection with the deaths of eight federal law enforcement officials who had been killed in the blast.

The bombing, the heroic actions of rescue workers, and the arrest of McVeigh all generated massive amounts of publicity. The image of an exhausted and despondent rescue worker, emerging from the wreckage with a dead baby in his arms, was flashed across the country. Millions of Americans saw images of McVeigh wearing orange jail garb and a bulletproof vest, being led through an angry crowd outside the Noble County Jail in Perry, Oklahoma. One wondered, at that time, whether any location in the country was not saturated with news of the bombing. Predictably, McVeigh requested a change of venue from Oklahoma City to a more neutral (or at least a less emotionally charged) locale.

As part of a motion to change venue, McVeigh enlisted the help of a team of psychologists to provide information to the court about the extent and type of publicity in the Oklahoma City newspaper and in the papers from three other communities (Lawton, Oklahoma, a small town 90 miles from Oklahoma City; Tulsa; and Denver) (Studebaker & Penrod, 1997). The psychologists identified all articles pertaining to the bombing in these four papers between April 20, 1995, and January 8, 1996, and coded the content of the text including negative characterizations of the defendant, reports of a confession, and emotionally laden publicity. They also measured the number of articles printed in each paper and the amount of space allotted to text and pictures. By February 1996, data analysis was complete and a hearing was held on the issue of moving the trial (*U.S. v. McVeigh*, 1996).

The data were compelling: During the collection period, 939 articles about the bombing had appeared in the Oklahoma City newspaper and 174 in the *Denver Post*. By a whopping 6312 to 558 margin, the *Daily Oklahoman* had printed more statements of an emotional nature (e.g., emotional suffering, goriness of the scene, economic impact to Oklahoma, helping themes, emotional pictures) than had the *Denver Post* (Studebaker & Penrod, 1997). On the basis of this analysis and other evidence presented at the hearing, Judge Richard Matsch moved the trial to Denver. In support of his decision, Matsch cited "(a) the development of differences over time in both the volume and focus of media coverage in Oklahoma compared with local coverage and national coverage, (b) the demonization of the defendant in the local pretrial publicity versus the humanization of the victims, and (c) the frequency of televised interviews of Oklahoma citizens emphasizing the importance of ensuring a verdict of guilty, with an evident implication that death would be the appropriate punishment" (Studebaker & Penrod, 1997, pp. 452–453.) In June 1997, McVeigh was convicted on all 11 counts and sentenced to death. He was executed in June 2001.

## *Effects of Pretrial Publicity*

Does pretrial publicity influence public opinion? Does adverse publicity produce negative opinions about defendants? If so, do these negative opinions continue despite efforts to control them?

When Carroll et al. surveyed the social science literature on these questions in 1986, they concluded, "It is surprising that so little is known" (p. 190). Since then, several new, more realistic studies have been conducted that measure the effects of various kinds of pretrial publicity presented in different media. Taken together, these studies fairly convincingly point to the conclusion that jurors may be adversely affected by pretrial publicity.

### FIELD STUDIES OF THE EFFECTS OF NATURALLY OCCURRING PUBLICITY

Serious crimes attract extensive news coverage, typically from the prosecutor's view of the case. A number of studies have examined effects of pretrial publicity by polling samples of people exposed to varying media coverage about actual crimes. These studies, whether surveying opinions about notorious crimes (Freedman & Burke, 1996) or cases of only local interest (Costantini & King, 1980; Moran & Cutler, 1991; Nietzel & Dillehay, 1982), consistently find that persons exposed to pretrial publicity possess more knowledge about the events in question, are more likely to have prejudged the case, and are more knowledgeable of incriminating facts that would be inadmissible at the trial. (An example of incriminating facts comes from the rape trial of William Kennedy Smith, a nephew of Edward Kennedy. Prior to trial, a number of newspapers published reports by unnamed earlier victims; the judge did not allow this information to be presented at the trial.).

These studies were conducted using survey methodology; participants are typically asked about their knowledge of the crime in question, their perceptions of the defendant's culpability, and their ability to be impartial in light of their knowledge. The studies have several strengths. For example, they use large and representative samples of prospective jurors, and they rely on naturally occurring publicity about actual cases (Moran & Cutler, 1991). They also have a significant weakness: the data are correlational in nature. As such, they cannot decipher the direction of the relationship between exposure to publicity and prejudice. For example, does exposure to publicity lead to prejudicial sentiments about the defendant, or, alternatively, are people with an antidefendant bias likely to expose themselves to such publicity (Moran & Cutler, 1991)? We have some reason to believe that the publicity influences jurors' beliefs. When persons are asked what has most influenced their opinions about a given crime, they reliably report as leading sources what they read in the papers and what they discuss with other people (Nietzel & Dillehay, 1982).

Some scholars (e.g., Carroll et al., 1986) have suggested another weakness in these field surveys. They argue that courts should not conclude that pretrial publicity biases jurors just because it affects their attitudes; to be truly prejudicial, it must also affect their verdicts. (Unfortunately, no studies have examined the relationship between naturally occurring exposure to publicity and verdicts in a real trial.) According to this logic, we do not know whether pretrial publicity effects persist through the presentation of trial evidence.

This concern may actually be irrelevant to the legal system, however. Biased persons are not qualified to serve as jurors. So, for example, in *Rideau v. Louisiana* (1963), the Supreme Court reversed a lower court conviction on the basis of *presumed* prejudice, without inquiring as to effect of the publicity on the outcome. In addition, evidence from other sources suggests that antidefendant biases held at the beginning of the trial may persist through the presentation of evidence and may even color the way that the evidence is remembered (Moran & Cutler, 1991).

### EXPERIMENTAL STUDIES OF THE EFFECTS OF PRETRIAL PUBLICITY

In experimental studies of pretrial publicity effects, subjects (often college students) are first exposed (or not exposed) to some form of prejudicial publicity, shown a videotape or written transcript meant to simulate a trial, and then they are asked their opinions about a verdict and their use of the evidence. These procedures ensure that the only differences between the two sets of jurors (i.e., those who have seen pretrial publicity and those who have not) involve the nature and extent of the publicity. Thus, researchers can be fairly confident that differences in responding are related to the impact of the pretrial information.

Early studies using this methodology studied the impact of pretrial information that would have been inadmissible at trial (e.g., confessions [Padawer-Singer & Barton, 1975] and prior criminal records [Hvistendahl, 1979]). More recent studies have looked at the effects of varying amount of negative information included in the pretrial publicity, pretrial publicity effects in different types of crimes, and whether the interval between exposure to the pretrial information and the juror's judgment affects the impact of that information (Stebaly, Besirevic, Fulero, & Jiminez-Lorente, 1999). Pretrial publicity has also been shown to affect mock jurors' judgments of negligence in a civil trial (Otto, Penrod, & Hirt, 1990).

These studies generally show that jurors' sentiments about a defendant's guilt can be influenced by case-specific information made available before trial. Other studies have shown that mock jurors can also be influenced by media coverage of issues that are not specifically related to a particular case but that are thematically relevant to the issues at hand. Greene and Wade (1988) termed this **general pretrial publicity.** They showed that subjects who read the inflammatory facts about a series of heinous crimes were more likely to judge a defendant guilty in an unrelated case than were subjects who instead first read about a miscarriage of justice. Similarly, Polvi, Jack, Lyon, Laird, and Ogloff (1996) showed that subjects previously exposed to inflammatory publicity about a sexual abuse case rendered more guilty verdicts, were more likely to believe the complainants, and assigned longer prison sentences to a defendant in an unrelated case than

did subjects who had not been exposed to the general publicity. Vidmar (1997) has distinguished prejudices arising from publicity about a specific trial from more generic prejudices that can result from stereotyped beliefs and that can cause prejudgments about a defendant's culpability.

Two methodological issues related to case-specific pretrial publicity have garnered psychologists' attention in recent years. One concerns the distinction between factual pretrial publicity and emotional pretrial publicity. **Factual pretrial publicity** typically consists of nonsensational but damaging information about the defendant that raises potential jurors' subjective certainty about the defendant's guilt (Wilson & Bornstein, 1998). Information that the defendant has a reputation for being violent is an example. **Emotional pretrial publicity,** on the other hand, typically involves lurid details about the crime that may or may not be admissible at trial but that has the effect of arousing jurors' emotions. Descriptions of a victim's suffering constitute one example.

Kramer, Kerr, and Carroll (1990) exposed subjects to either factual or emotional pretrial publicity followed by a videotaped reenactment of an actual armed robbery trial. Emotional pretrial publicity produced a 20% increase in conviction rates over the factual publicity conditions. Some data suggest that emotional publicity effects may be particularly difficult to undo and may influence the kinds of attributions jurors make about defendants (Otto, Penrod, & Dexter, 1994). More recent data (Wilson and Bornstein, 1998) have shown that if the amount, duration, and degree of bias inherent in the two types of pretrial publicity are held constant, then there are no significant differences in the impact of these different forms of pretrial publicity, however. All of these studies agree that exposure to pretrial publicity increases jurors' prejudgment of the defendant, however.

Another methodological issue of importance concerns the way that the pretrial information is conveyed (by print, televised, or both). In one experiment, subjects were randomly assigned to one of three conditions that varied the format by which pretrial media information was presented about the Mount Cashel Orphanage Cases, a highly publicized case in Canada concerning alleged sexual abuse by a group of Roman Catholic men who ran an orphanage in Newfoundland (Ogloff & Vidmar, 1994). The damaging pretrial material was presented to subjects through (1) television, (2) newspaper articles, or (3) both TV and newspapers; a fourth control group received only minimal information about the case. Presentation of publicity via television had a greater biasing impact than the same information presented in print, but the combined effects of TV and newspaper publicity had the greatest impact of all. Of additional interest was the finding that the subjects were generally unaware that their opinions had been biased by this material; subjects who had formed opinions about the trial were just as likely to say that they could be fair as were those who had not formed opinions.

Although videotaped presentations have been shown to be more persuasive in this context and in others (Chaiken & Eagly, 1983), the effect does not always hold. For example, Wilson and Bornstein (1998) have shown that pretrial publicity presented via video did not produce higher guilt ratings among mock jurors than written pretrial publicity, provided that the content was the same for both groups and that the jurors were exposed to trial evidence.

Why the conflicting findings? They could be a result of different measurement techniques, different fact patterns, or both. These varied approaches are invaluable for defining the limits of any effect (i.e., the conditions under which an effect holds) but complicate our understanding of the relationship between exposure to pretrial publicity and jurors' judgments. Fortunately, other research techniques (see ◆ Box 10-6) can shed light on these uncertainties.

## Remedies for the Effects of Pretrial Publicity

If pretrial publicity adversely affects juror impartiality, the next question is, What procedures should

be used to restore the likelihood of a fair trial for the defendant? Five alternatives are available.

*1. Continuance.* The trial can be postponed until a later date with the expectation that the passage of time will lessen the effects of the prejudicial material. This view remains in vogue with the current Supreme Court. However, research indicates that although continuances may decrease jurors' recall of factual evidence (and hence their reliance on factual pretrial publicity), they do not dampen jurors' recall or use of emotionally biasing information (Kramer et al., 1990).

*2. Expanded voir dire.* The most popular method for rooting out pretrial prejudice is to conduct a thorough voir dire (questioning) of potential jurors. Standard 8-3.5 of the American Bar Association's (1993) "Standards for a Fair Trial and Free Press" recommends that, in cases in which jurors have been exposed to prejudicial publicity, an intensive, thorough questioning of each prospective juror be conducted outside the presence of other chosen and prospective jurors. Although thorough voir dire can be a valuable protection against partiality, it may not always be adequate. Jurors may not recognize their own biases, and they can hide their true feelings from an examiner if they so choose.

Dexter, Cutler, and Moran (1992) have conducted the most compelling study to date on the effectiveness of extended voir dire as a remedy to pretrial publicity effects. A week before their participation in the study, some mock jurors were sent a packet of fictitious news articles, including information about the defendant's prior criminal record and retracted confession. After undergoing either a brief (15-minute) or extended (60-minute) voir dire, participants watched a 6-hour videotaped murder trial. The conviction rates for the groups that read the pretrial publicity were approximately 15% higher than for the group that had no exposure to the pretrial information, and the extended voir dire was not effective in eliminating the biasing effect of pretrial publicity.

## The Science of

**BOX 10-6**   **Meta-analysis and the impact of prejudicial pretrial publicity**

A *meta-analysis* is a statistical technique that combines the results of many small studies into one large study. It allows researchers to identify underlying patterns across studies and provides information about variables that may moderate an apparent effect (Rosenthal, 1991). In the context of pretrial publicity, a meta-analysis can address the effect of such publicity on prejudgments of the defendant, as well as the conditions under which this prejudgment is likely to occur. Steblay et al. (1999) conducted a meta-analysis of studies on pretrial publicity.

Their analysis involved 44 separate tests of the effect, published in articles between 1966 and 1997 and representing 5755 subjects. For each study, researchers coded as many of the following characteristics as possible: sample size, type of study (survey vs. experimental), information provided to

control group, origin of stimulus trial (real vs. fabricated), origin of the pretrial publicity (real vs. fabricated), type of information provided in the pretrial publicity (e.g., confession, arrest record), medium (newspaper, video, both), extent of delay between exposure and jurors' decisions, type of crime, and time of verdict (pretrial, posttrial before deliberations, posttrial after deliberations).

Steblay et al. first examined the hypothesis that negative pretrial publicity increases judgments of the defendant's guilt. They found strong support for this notion: Across the 44 studies, subjects who were exposed to negative pretrial publicity were more likely to judge the defendant guilty than were subjects exposed to less or to no negative publicity.

Other analyses examined the conditions under which this effect is more or less pronounced.

Results of the meta-analysis showed that pretrial publicity effects are stronger in the following conditions: (1) when subjects are potential jurors rather than students; (2) when multiple points of information about the crime and defendant are publicized; (3) when the pretrial publicity is real, as opposed to fabricated; and (4) when the delay between exposure to the pretrial information and jurors' judgments exceeds one week. Finally, the effect is apparently stronger in cases involving drugs, sexual abuse, and murder as compared to rape, embezzlement, armed robbery, or disorderly conduct. Interestingly, these are the features that most commonly occur in an actual case. The findings raise concerns about (1) the likelihood that pretrial publicity will prejudice jurors and (2) how to combat the harmful effects of the pretrial information.

*3. Judicial instructions.*   A fairly simple remedy for the bias that can result from pretrial publicity involves an instruction from the judge to the jury, admonishing members to base their decision on the evidence rather than on nonevidentiary information. Kramer et al. (1990) found that a judicial instruction was unable to reduce the biasing effect of exposure to either factual or emotional pretrial publicity, a conclusion that is consistent with a recent meta-analysis (Nietzel, McCarthy, & Kerr, 1999). A judge's instruction to disregard certain in-

formation may have the unintended consequence of drawing jurors' attention to it—a so-called boomerang effect. In addition, jurors may have a difficult time complying with such an order.

Some work by Steven Fein and his colleagues (Fein, McCloskey, & Tomlinson, 1997) may help us understand the role of judicial instructions in this context. Participants in this study read the transcript of a case in which the defendant was charged with killing his estranged wife and a neighbor who was in her home. Before trial, half of the mock jurors read a series of articles about the murders and the evidence. Some of these subjects also read an article that called into question the motives of the media covering the case. In this article, the defense attorney complained about the negative publicity: "The coverage of this case serves as another fine example of how the media manipulates information to sell papers, and knowingly ignores acts which would point toward a defendant's innocence" (p. 1219).

Despite judicial instructions to ignore the pretrial information, jurors' verdicts were significantly influenced by it, unless they had been made suspicious of the media's motives. So, although judicial instructions had no effect on conviction rates per se, mock jurors could follow the instruction when given some reason to suspect the source of the pretrial information.

**4. Imported jurors.** Prospective jurors can be imported to the venue from another county "whenever it is determined that potentially prejudicial news coverage of a given criminal matter has been intense and has been concentrated primarily in a given locality in a state" (ABA, 1993). These foreign venires allow the trial to be conducted in the original venue but before a group of jurors presumably less affected by prejudicial material than local jurors would be. Judges are often reluctant to exercise this alternative because of the inconvenience to jurors and the expense.

Of the four previous remedies, the first three alternatives appear, on the basis of existing research, to be largely ineffective, and the fourth—importing jurors from another area—is seldom used because of its perceived impracticality. Why do the most commonly relied-on methods tend to fail as safeguards? The answer is probably because of several basic features in the way that human beings remember and use information to form impressions and overall judgments (Studebaker & Penrod, 1997). Unless they have some reason to discount or ignore pretrial publicity when it is first encountered, most people will use it to help them interpret subsequent information and to make various pieces of information "fit" to-

gether in a coherent theme. Therefore, once the idea of a guilty perpetrator is established, it may become an organizing principle for the processing of additional information about the person. Furthermore, if people try to suppress forbidden thoughts, they often find that the thoughts actually become stronger or more frequent (Wegner & Erber, 1992).

For these reasons, safeguards that attempt to remove an existing bias may never work as well as trying to seat jurors who never had a bias to start with. This goal is why changes of venue are preferred by most social scientists.

**5. Change of venue.** A change of venue involves the most extreme remedy for pretrial prejudice. Changing venue requires that the trial be conducted in another geographic jurisdiction altogether and that jurors for the trial be drawn from this new jurisdiction. Because venue changes are expensive, inconvenient, and time-consuming, courts are reluctant to use them.

Venue changes can result in significant variations in characteristics of the communities involved, as was illustrated by the case of William Lozano, a Hispanic police officer who was convicted of killing an African American motorist in Miami. After his conviction was reversed because of pretrial publicity, the case was moved to Tallahassee (which has a much smaller Hispanic population than Miami) and finally to Orlando (where the Hispanic population is more sizeable). The Florida appellate court reasoned that in cases in which race may be a factor and changes of venue are appropriate, trials should be moved to locations where the demographic characteristics are similar to those of the original venue (*State v. Lozano,* 1993).

Psychologists can be enlisted to support a lawyer's motion for one or more of these protections against pretrial prejudices by testifying about the psychological evidence that pertains to each one. When pretrial contamination is extensive, a professionally conducted public opinion survey is the technique of choice for evaluating the degree of prejudice in a community. Public opinion surveys gauge how many people have read or heard about a case, what they have read or heard, whether they have formed opinions, what these opinions are, and how they affect the way the case is perceived.

## Change of Venue Surveys

A growing body of literature exists on ways to conduct venue surveys, as well as on the practical, methodological, legal, and ethical issues involved in them (Arnold & Gold, 1978–1979; Costantini & King, 1980; Hans & Vidmar, 1982; Moran & Cutler, 1997; Nietzel & Dillehay, 1982; Pollock, 1977). In this section, we outline the steps involved in these surveys.

*1. Planning the survey and designing the questionnaire.* Scripts for the survey questionnaires are written for telephone interviews, which usually take about 15 minutes to complete. The content is based on an analysis of the media to which the community has been exposed, and the wording of the survey questions is aligned with the key words and phrases used repeatedly in the media.

One criticism of past surveys has been that they might overestimate the public's exposure to pretrial publicity by not controlling for various response biases. Obviously, awareness of pretrial publicity will be overestimated if respondents report they are aware of a media report when in fact they are not. Gary Moran and Brian Cutler (1997) measured the degree to which such overreporting might invalidate public opinion surveys by including a bogus item (i.e., a plausible-sounding item from the media that in fact never happened and was never reported) in two telephone public opinion surveys. In surveys using bogus media items, anywhere from less than a tenth to about a third of respondents reported awareness of news items that never appeared. In Moran and Cutler's study, they deleted the data from any respondent who claimed knowledge of a bogus item and found that dropping these data did not change the over-

all relationship in the sample between having greater awareness of real publicity items and holding antidefendant biases.

*2. Training the interviewers.* The persons who conduct the telephone interviews are trained to administer the questionnaire in a standardized fashion. Interviewers should be "blind" to the purpose of the survey as much as possible. Therefore, the callers do not construct the questionnaire or interpret the results.

*3. Drawing the sample.* Respondents to venue surveys must be drawn at random for the results to be valid. Usually, persons are surveyed in at least two jurisdictions: the original venue county and at least one other "comparison" county. Data about the differences between the surveyed counties are then presented to show the relative levels and effects of pretrial influence in the different jurisdictions.

*4. Presenting the results.* Survey results are presented in one of two ways. The expert can prepare an **affidavit,** which is a written report sworn to be truthful. A stronger presentation results when the expert testifies about the design, results, and meaning of the survey at a change of venue hearing. Such testimony is subject to cross-examination by the opposing side.

Public opinion surveys are time-consuming, hectic activities that often demand more resources than the typical client can afford. However, they usually yield valuable information. Obtaining a change of venue for a highly publicized case is probably the most effective procedure available for improving the chances for a fair trial. Moreover, even if the venue is not changed, the results of the survey can often be used to assist the defense in jury selection. Because of the multiple purposes for which they can be used, public opinion surveys are a popular tool among litigation consultants. We discuss some of these additional uses in the next chapter.

# SUMMARY

**1.** *What are the major legal proceedings between arrest and trial in the criminal justice system?*

1. An initial appearance, at which defendants are informed of the charges, of their constitutional rights, and of future proceedings
2. A preliminary hearing, in which the judge determines whether there is enough evidence to hold the defendant for processing by the grand jury
3. Action by the grand jury, which decides whether sufficient evidence exists for the defendant to be tried
4. An arraignment, involving a formal statement of charges and an initial plea by the defendant to these charges
5. A process of discovery, requiring that the prosecutor reveal to the defense certain evidence, and pretrial motions, or attempts by both sides to win favorable ground rules for the subsequent trial

**2.** *What is bail, and what factors influence the amount of bail set?* Bail is the provision of money or other assets by a defendant that is forfeited if the defendant fails to appear at trial. In determining whether to release a defendant between the indictment and trial, the judge should consider the risk that the defendant will not show up for his or her trial. Most judges also consider the potential danger to the community if the defendant is released. Predictions of dangerousness, however, are often unreliable.

A simulation study of the determinants of bail found that judges were most influenced by the degree to which defendants were tied to the local area and by whether they had a previous criminal record. But in observing judges' bail setting in actual cases, researchers concluded that the district attorney's recommendation was the single strongest predictor.

**3.** *What is the role of the grand jury?* The grand jury theoretically operates to shield citizens from unwarranted prosecutions, but often it functions as a rubber stamp for prosecutors who seek community endorsement for their recommendations. Because they can subpoena uncooperative witnesses and force them to testify, grand juries are sometimes used to investigate criminal activity.

**4.** *Why do defendants and prosecutors agree to plea-bargain?* Plea bargaining is an excellent example of the dilemma between truth and conflict resolution as goals of our legal system. At least 80% of criminal cases end between arrest and trial with the defendant pleading guilty to some (often reduced) charges. Prosecutors claim that the system would break down if all cases went to trial. When El Paso, Texas, abolished plea bargaining, court delays became intolerable, although in Alaska the processing of court cases actually speeded up.

Plea bargaining poses risks for both defendants and prosecutors. Defendants accept some penalty and give up the chance that, after a trial, they might be acquitted of all charges. Prosecutors want to "win," but they realize that frequent plea bargains allow their prosecution skills to deteriorate.

**5.** *Does pretrial publicity pose a danger to fair trials? If so, can these dangers be reduced?* The rights to a free press and a fair trial are usually complementary, but some criminal trials generate extensive publicity to the point that the defendant's right to an impartial jury is jeopardized. Psychologists have studied the effects of pretrial publicity on potential fact finders and have also evaluated different mechanisms for curbing or curing the negative effects of pretrial publicity.

# KEY TERMS

| | | | |
|---|---|---|---|
| affidavit | exculpatory* | grand jury* | released on |
| change of venue | factual pretrial | hearsay* | recognizance (ROR) |
| deferred prosecution | publicity | indictment* | with prejudice |
| discovery | gag order* | information | |
| emotional pretrial | general pretrial | motion in limine | |
| publicity | publicity | plea bargaining* | |

---

**InfoTrac**
**COLLEGE**
**EDITION**

For additional readings go to **http://www.infotrac-college.com/wadsworth** and enter a search term related to your interest. The key terms that have been asterisked above will pull up several related articles. *See also:* for discovery, see DISCOVERY (LAW).

# Forensic Assessment in Criminal Cases: Competence and Insanity

## ORIENTING QUESTIONS

1. *What is the scope of forensic psychology?*
2. *What is meant by competence in the criminal justice process?*
3. *How do clinicians assess competence?*
4. *What are the consequences of being found incompetent to proceed in the criminal justice process?*
5. *What is the legal definition of insanity?*
6. *How frequently is the insanity defense used, and how successful is it?*
7. *What are the major criticisms of the insanity defense, and what attempts have been made to reform it?*

*John E. du Pont*

On January 26, 1996, multimillionaire John du Pont, a 58-year-old heir to the du Pont chemical fortune, went for a tour of his Foxcatcher estate near Philadelphia with his private security expert, Patrick Goodale. According to Goodale, du Pont wanted to survey the damage that recent winter storms had done to his property. In a matter of minutes, du Pont drove his Lincoln Town Car up to the driveway of David Schultz, an Olympic gold-medal wrestler, who had a home on du Pont's property and was one of several wrestlers who trained at the state-of-the-art athletic training facility du Pont had built. Schultz was sitting half-in and half-out of his Toyota Tercel, tinkering with the car's radio. Suddenly, du Pont pulled out a long-barreled .44 magnum revolver and fired three shots into Schultz, killing him almost instantly.

No one disputes that John du Pont killed David Schultz. Goodale was an eyewitness to the crime, as was Schultz's horrified wife, Nancy. The question that dominated du Pont's criminal trial in early 1997 was whether he was insane at the time of the killing and, therefore, not criminally responsible for murder. Was John du Pont, as described by his lawyer, a man trapped "in the abyss of insanity," so disturbed by paranoid schizophrenia that he could not be held accountable for his actions? Or was he, as prosecutors maintained, merely an eccentric man driven by envy and anger who knew exactly what he was doing on the day he killed David Schultz in his driveway?

Both sides had plenty of ammunition for their respective arguments. According to friends and relatives, du Pont had displayed bizarre behavior over several years, causing many acquaintances to grow afraid of him. He was prone to rages, hallucinations, and a paranoia that led him to line his estate with secret tunnels and mechanical trees that he operated with switches from his home. At one point, he ordered Goodale to check the billiard balls in a recreation room because he suspected someone had installed eavesdropping transmitters in them. When he appeared at one of his first court hearings and was asked by the judge to identify himself, he replied that he was "the Dalai Lama." Du Pont was also rumored to have serious drug and alcohol problems that compounded his mental problems. Prosecutors, on the other hand, pointed out that du Pont continued to manage his financial affairs during the time he was alleged to be psychotic, noted that he regularly consulted with his lawyers, and argued that he was using his eccentricities simply as an excuse to escape conviction.

The question of whether John du Pont—or any criminal defendant—was insane at the time of a criminal offense is probably the most controversial question that forensic psychologists and psychiatrists are called on to assess. It is also a question that has attracted extensive research by forensic specialists. In this chapter, we survey how insanity is defined, how claims of insanity are assessed by mental-health professionals, and what some of the implications of the insanity defense are. We also discuss one other concept—criminal competence—which is often confused with insanity. Because competence is usually assessed at or near the same time that an insanity evaluation is performed (Heilbrun & Collins, 1995), we cover both of these issues in this chapter.

In the next chapter, we explore several other forensic questions that clinicians also assess. These questions arise in criminal trials, civil litigation, divorce and child custody disputes, commitment hearings, and many other types of legal proceedings.

# The Scope of Forensic Psychology

Forensic psychologists use knowledge and techniques from psychology, psychiatry, and other behavioral sciences to answer questions about individuals involved in legal proceedings. In most cases, forensic assessment activities are performed by clinical psychologists, and the field of forensic psychology has prospered and matured considerably in the last 30 years (Nicholson, 1999; Nicholson & Norwood, 2000). For example, forensic psychology is officially recognized as a specialty by the American Board of Professional Psychology, specialty guidelines for the practice of forensic psychology have been approved (Committee on Ethical Guidelines for Forensic Psychologists, 1991), forensic psychology training programs have been developed, and the research and clinical literature on forensic practice has increased dramatically.

Despite both public concerns and professional skepticism about whether forensic psychology should be afforded as much credibility and stature as it now appears to enjoy, the field continues to expand. It is estimated that psychologists and psychiatrists testify in about 8% of all federal civil trials and that mental-health professionals participate as experts in as many as a million cases per year (O'Connor, Sales, & Shuman, 1996). If anything, this level of participation will increase because of three forces at work that encourage forensic activities.

First, mental-health experts claim to have expertise on a long list of clinical and social issues. As scientists learn more about human behavior, attorneys will find new ways to use this informa-

tion in various legal proceedings; in this chapter and Chapter 12, we focus on several topics that mental health professionals are called on to assess for individuals involved in court proceedings.

Second, forensic psychology is flourishing because the law permits, and even encourages, the use of expert testimony in a host of areas, including psychology, engineering, toxicology, genetics, and medicine. Expert testimony of all types is used increasingly often, but psychological topics have enjoyed an especially large increase in prominence.

In general, a qualified expert can testify about a topic if such testimony is relevant to an issue in dispute and if the usefulness of the testimony outweighs whatever prejudicial impact it might have. If these two conditions are satisfied—as they must be for any kind of testimony to be admitted—an expert will be permitted to give opinion testimony if the judge believes that "scientific, technical, or other specialized knowledge will assist the trier of fact to understand the evidence or to determine a fact in issue" (Federal Rule of Evidence 702). As was discussed in Chapter 2, the U.S. Supreme Court ruled in the 1993 case of *Daubert v. Merrell Dow* that federal judges are allowed to decide when expert testimony is based on sufficiently relevant and reliable scientific evidence to be admitted into evidence. This opinion, which applies to all federal courts and any state courts that have adopted it, encourages the consideration of innovative opinions, and many critics, including experts themselves, fear that some judges—especially those who cannot accurately distinguish valid from invalid research—will allow jurors to hear "expert" testimony that is based on little more than "junk science" (Goodman-Delahunty, 1997; Shuman & Sales, 1999). As we noted in Chapter 2, in the case of opinions offered by behavioral scientists and mental-health experts, the *Daubert* standard suggests that for expert testimony to be admitted, the expert should have relied on methods and knowledge that are scientifically based (Penrod, Fulero, & Cutler, 1995; Rotgers & Barrett, 1996).The Supreme Court has decided that this requirement also applies to opinions that are tied to the technical or professional skills of practitioners and clinicians (*Kumho Tire Co., Ltd v. Carmichael,* 1999).

Finally, expert testimony by forensic psychologists thrives because, quite simply, it can be very lucrative. At an hourly rate of anywhere between $100 and $500, forensic experts can earn thousands of dollars per case. If one party in a lawsuit or criminal trial hires an expert, the other side usually feels compelled to match that expert. Consequently, the use of psychological experts feeds on itself, and it has become a significant source of income for many professionals.

# Competence

Prior to John du Pont's trial, the question of his competence had to be resolved. Du Pont's lawyers and several mental-health experts claimed that he was incompetent to stand trial, and after a three-day hearing on the matter, the trial judge agreed. Du Pont was then committed to Pennsylvania's Norristown State Hospital where he was treated with medication to restore his competence. Early in December 1996, at another hearing, the judge concluded that du Pont's psychosis had been treated successfully, and du Pont was declared competent. In late January 1997, almost one year after the fatal shooting of David Schultz, John du Pont stood trial for murder. After a week's deliberation, the jury concluded that he was mentally ill but also guilty of third-degree murder.

What do we mean by competence to stand trial? How do clinicians assess competence? What legal standards should be applied?

The question of a defendant's competence is the psychological issue most frequently assessed in the criminal justice system. Basically, **competence** refers to a defendant's capacity to function meaningfully and knowingly in a legal proceeding; defendants are typically declared incompetent if they are seriously deficient in one or more abilities, such as understanding the legal proceedings, communicating with their attorneys, appre-

ciating their role in the proceedings, and making legally relevant decisions. Concerns about a defendant's competence are tied to one fundamental principle: Criminal proceedings should not continue against someone who cannot understand their nature and purpose. This rule applies at every stage of the criminal justice process, but it is raised most often at pretrial hearings concerned with two topics: competence to plead guilty and competence to stand trial.

Why is competence an important doctrine in our system? The law requires defendants to be competent for several reasons (Melton, Petrila, Poythress, & Slobogin, 1997). First, competent defendants must be able to understand the charges against them so that they can participate in the criminal justice system in a meaningful way and make it more likely that legal proceedings arrive at accurate and just results. Second, punishment of convicted defendants is morally acceptable only if they understand the reasons they are being punished. Finally, the perceived fairness and dignity of our adversary system of justice requires participation by defendants who have the capacity to defend themselves against the charges of the state. As Grisso and Siegel (1986) observed, "there is no honor in entering a battle in full armor with the intention of striking down an adversary who is without shield or sword" (p. 146).

## Adjudicative Competence

When defendants plead guilty, they waive several constitutional rights: the right to a jury trial, the right to confront their accusers, the right to call favorable witnesses, and the right to remain silent. The Supreme Court has held that waiving such important rights must be knowing, intelligent, and voluntary (*Johnson v. Zerbst,* 1938), and trial judges are required to question defendants about their pleas in order to establish clearly that they understand that they are waiving their constitutional rights by pleading guilty. A knowing, intelligent, and voluntary guilty plea also includes understanding the charges and the possible penalties that can be imposed, and it requires the judge to examine any plea bargain to ensure that it is "voluntary" in the sense that it represents a considered choice between constitutionally permissible alternatives. For example, prosecutors can offer lighter sentences to a defendant in exchange for a guilty plea, but they cannot offer money to the defendant to encourage a guilty plea.

The accepted national standard for **competence to stand trial,** as we discuss next, is a "sufficient present ability to consult with [one's] attorney with a reasonable degree of rational understanding, and . . . a rational, as well as factual understanding of the proceedings against him" (*Dusky v. United States,* 1960). Logically, **competence to plead guilty** would require that defendants understand the alternatives they face and have the ability to make a reasoned choice among them. Such a test, theoretically at least, is more exacting than competence to stand trial. Defendants standing trial need only be aware of the nature of the proceedings and be able to cooperate with counsel in presenting the defense. Defendants pleading guilty, on the other hand, must understand the possible consequences of pleading guilty instead of going to trial and be able to make a rational choice between the alternatives.

In the past, even though several courts recognized a difference between competence to stand trial and competence to plead guilty (*United States v. Masthers,* 1976), the majority used the *Dusky* standard (cited earlier) for both competencies. There were two reasons for this practice. First, a separate standard for competence to plead guilty cuts too fine a distinction between different types of legal understanding; it is doubtful that mental-health professionals could make such distinctions reliably. Second, a separate standard could create the difficult situation of having a class of defendants who are competent to stand trial but incompetent to plead guilty and who thereby could not participate in the possibly advantageous plea-bargaining process.

The American Bar Association has suggested a compromise between those who say that the tests for competence to stand trial and competence to plead guilty should be the same and those who would require a separate finding of competence to plead guilty. Criminal Justice Mental Health Standard 7-5.1 (ABA, 1989) provides in part:

> a) No plea of guilty or **nolo contendere** should be accepted from a defendant who is mentally incompetent to enter a plea of guilty.
> i) Ordinarily, absent additional information bearing on defendant's competence, a finding that the defendant is competent to stand trial should be sufficient to establish the defendant's competence to plead guilty.
> ii) The test for determining mental competence to plead guilty should be whether the defendant has sufficient present ability to consult with the defendant's lawyer with a reasonable degree of rational understanding and whether, given the nature and complexity of the charges and the potential consequences of a conviction, the defendant has a rational as well as factual understanding of the proceedings relating to a plea of guilty.

Despite these recommendations and the belief by many psychologists that competence cannot be separated from the specific decisions a defendant must make, the Supreme Court resolved this debate in its 1993 decision of *Godinez v. Moran.* In this opinion, the Court ruled that the standard for competence to stand trial will be used in federal courts for assessing other competence questions that arise in the criminal justice process. In so doing, it rejected the idea that competence to plead guilty involves a higher standard than competence to stand trial.

As a result of this decision, the terms *competence to plead guilty* and *competence to stand trial* have become somewhat misleading. Instead, many scholars are now suggesting that **adjudicative competence** is a better concept for describing the multiple abilities that criminal defendants are expected to exercise in different legal contexts (Bonnie, 1993; Hoge et al., 1997).

The ABA Standards also require prosecutors and defense attorneys to alert the court if they have information that bears on a defendant's adjudicative competence. Imposing this requirement

**TABLE 11.1**   *Foundational and decisional components of adjudicative competence*

FOUNDATIONAL COMPETENCE

1. Can the defendant *understand* the basic elements (e.g., prosecutor, defense attorney, judge, jury, guilty plea) of the adversarial process?
2. Can the defendant use *reasoning* to relate relevant information to his or her attorney?
3. Can the defendant *appreciate* his or her legal predicament?

DECISIONAL COMPETENCE

1. Can the defendant *understand* information that is relevant to decisions, such as pleading guilty or waiving a jury trial?
2. Can the defendant use *reasoning* about alternative courses of action in making decisions about his or her defense?
3. Can the defendant *appreciate* the decisions that need to be made in his or her own best interest?
4. Can the defendant make a *choice* among the alternative defense strategies available?

on defense attorneys may work to the defendant's detriment, but the ABA Standards reason that attorneys have an obligation of candor to the court that overrides loyalty to the client. Thus, lawyers must inform a trial judge that their clients might not be competent to plead guilty, even though the client does not want to raise the issue and even though a lengthy incarceration could result from a competence evaluation. This principle has led to the censure of a defense attorney who hid evidence of his client's mental illness because neither the client nor the lawyer wanted a competence evaluation (*State v. Johnson,* 1986).

In evaluating adjudicative competence, the mental-health professional focuses on two basic components. First, there is the basic, *foundational* question of whether the defendant has the capacity to assist counsel. As Table 11.1 summarizes, this foundational component has three requirements: (1) the ability to understand the basic elements of the adversary system, (2) the ability to relate information to one's attorney that is relevant to the case, and (3) the ability to understand one's situation as a criminal defendant. The second component consists of a *decisional competence,* which consists of four interrelated abilities: (1) understanding the information relevant to decisions the defendant must make, (2) thinking rationally about the alternatives involved in these decisions, (3) ap-

preciating the specific legal questions one must resolve as a defendant, and (4) making and expressing a choice about one's legal alternatives.

If an evaluator believes a defendant is competent, the evaluator will prepare a report that states this opinion and the reasons for it (see ◆ Box 11-1). However, if the evaluator believes the defendant is incompetent, the report will also discuss possible treatments that might render the defendant competent. The evaluator's report should not be changed at the request of an attorney, although it may be supplemented in response to questions from an attorney. In the real world of the criminal justice system, attempts by attorneys to influence the content, style, or conclusions of these reports are not uncommon.

As we have already discussed, the standard for competence to stand trial was defined by the U.S. Supreme Court in *Dusky v. United States* (1960):

> "whether [the defendant] has sufficient present ability to consult with [his] attorney with a reasonable degree of rational understanding—and whether he has a rational as well as factual understanding of the proceedings against him."

With minor modifications, this standard is used in all American courts. It establishes the basic criterion of competence as the capacity to know and do the things that a trial requires of a

## THE CASE OF

### BOX 11-1    Jamie Sullivan: Assessing competence

Jamie Sullivan was a 24-year-old clerk charged with arson, burglary, and murder in connection with a fire he had set at a small grocery store in Kentucky. The evidence in the case was that after closing hours, Sullivan had returned to the store where he worked and forced the night manager, Ricky Ford, to open the safe and hand over $800 in cash that was in it. Sullivan then locked Ford in a back-room office, doused the room in gasoline, and set the store on fire. Ford was killed in the blaze. On the basis of a lead from a motorist who saw Sullivan running from the scene, police arrested him at his grandmother's apartment a few hours later. If convicted on all charges, Sullivan faced a possible death sentence.

Jamie Sullivan was mentally retarded. He had dropped out of school in the eighth grade, and a psychologist's evaluation of him at that time reported his IQ to be 68. He could read and write his name and a few simple phrases, but nothing more. He had a history of drug abuse and had spent several months in a juvenile correctional camp at the age of 15 after vandalizing five homes in his neighborhood. The army refused his attempt to volunteer for service because of his limited intelligence and drug habit. His attorney believed that Sullivan's mental problems might render him incompetent to stand trial and therefore asked a psychologist to

evaluate him. After interviewing and testing Sullivan and reviewing the evidence the police had collected, the psychologist found the following: Sullivan's current IQ was 65, which fell in the mentally retarded range; he did not suffer any hallucinations or delusions, but he expressed strong religious beliefs that "God watches over his children and won't let nothing happen to them." The psychologist asked Sullivan a series of questions about his upcoming trial, to which he gave the following answers:

Q. What are you charged with?
A. Burning down that store and stealing from Ricky.
Q. Anything else?
A. They say I killed Ricky too.
Q. What could happen to you if a jury found you guilty?
A. Electric chair, but God will watch over me.
Q. What does the judge do at a trial?
A. He tells everybody what to do.
Q. If somebody told a lie about you in court, what would you do?
A. Get mad at him.
Q. Anything else?
A. Tell my lawyer the truth.
Q. What does your lawyer do if you have a trial?
A. Show the jury I'm innocent.
Q. How could he do that best?
A. Ask questions and have me tell them I wouldn't hurt Ricky. I liked Ricky.

Q. What does the prosecutor do in your trial?
A. Try to get me found guilty.
Q. Who decides if you are guilty or not?
A. That jury.

At a hearing to determine whether Jamie Sullivan was competent to stand trial, the psychologist testified that Sullivan was mentally retarded and that, as a result, his understanding of the proceedings was not as accurate or thorough as it might otherwise be. However, the psychologist also testified that Sullivan could assist his attorney and that he did understand the charges against him as well as the general purpose and nature of his trial. The judge ruled that Jamie Sullivan was competent. A jury convicted him on all the charges and sentenced him to life in prison.

It is estimated that, much like Jamie Sullivan, as many as 30,000 defendants are evaluated annually to determine their competence to stand trial (Nicholson & Kugler, 1991). Among those mentally disordered offenders who are committed to nonfederal hospitals, the single largest category are defendants being evaluated for or already judged to be incompetent to stand trial (IST) (Steadman, Rosenstein, MacAskill, & Manderscheid, 1988).

defendant. The criterion refers to *present* abilities rather than the psychological state of the defendant at the time of the alleged offense, which, as you will learn later, is the focus of evaluations of a defendant's sanity.

A problem with the *Dusky* standard is that it does not specify how the evaluator should judge the sufficiency of rational understanding, ability to consult, or factual understanding when assessing competence. A number of courts and mental-health groups have expanded on *Dusky* by listing more specific criteria related to competence. For example, evaluators are sometimes urged to consider these 11 factors:

1. Defendant's appreciation of the charges
2. Defendant's appreciation of the nature and range of penalties
3. Defendant's understanding of the adversary nature of legal process
4. Defendant's ability to disclose to attorney pertinent facts of the alleged offense
5. Defendant's ability to relate to attorney
6. Defendant's ability to assist attorney in planning a defense
7. Defendant's capacity to realistically challenge prosecution witnesses
8. Defendant's ability to manifest appropriate courtroom behavior
9. Defendant's capacity to testify relevantly
10. Defendant's motivation to help him- or herself in the legal process
11. Defendant's capacity to cope with the stress of incarceration prior to trial

## Raising the Issue of Competence

The question of a defendant's competence can be raised at any point in the criminal process, and it can be raised by the prosecutor, the defense attorney, or the presiding judge. The issue is typically raised by the defense attorney, but prior to the 1970s, it was common for prosecutors to question a defendant's competence because, up until that time, defendants found incompetent were often confined in mental hospitals for excessive periods of time. (Sometimes such confinements were

even longer than their sentences would have been had they stood trial and been convicted.) However, this practice was stopped, at least in theory, in 1972 when the U.S. Supreme Court decided the case of *Jackson v. Indiana*. This decision ordered that defendants who had been committed because they were incompetent to stand trial could not be held "more than a reasonable period of time necessary to determine whether there is a substantial probability that [they] will attain that capacity in the foreseeable future." As a result of this decision, the length of time a defendant found incompetent can be confined is now limited, although such limitations are often still exceeded.

Once the question of incompetence is raised, the judge will order an evaluation of the defendant if a "bona fide doubt" exists that the defendant is competent. The circumstances of each case and the behavior of each defendant are considered when judges make this determination. However, if the question of competence is raised, an examination will usually be conducted. Because it is relatively easy to obtain such evaluations, attorneys often seek them for reasons other than a determination of competence. Competence evaluations are used for several tactical reasons: to discover information about a possible insanity defense, to guarantee the temporary incarceration of a potentially dangerous person without going through the cumbersome procedures of involuntary civil commitment (see Chapter 12), to deny bail, and to delay the trial as one side tries to gain an advantage over the other (Berman & Osborne, 1987; Winick, 1996). Defense attorneys have questions about their clients' competence in up to 15% of felony cases (approximately twice the rate for defendants charged with misdemeanors); in many of these cases, however, the attorney does not seek a formal evaluation (Hoge et al., 1997; Poythress, Bonnie, Hoge, Monahan, & Oberlander, 1994).

## The Evaluation of Competence

After a judge orders a competence examination, arrangements are made for the defendant to be evaluated by one or more mental-health profes-

John C. Salvi

Todd Hall

*Being psychotic or mentally retarded does not guarantee that a defendant will be found incompetent to stand trial. Despite an apparent psychosis, John Salvi was found competent to stand trial and was convicted of murdering two people and wounding five others during a shooting spree at two Massachusetts medical clinics that performed abortions. Salvi later committed suicide in prison. Todd Hall, on the other hand, was found incompetent to stand trial on charges that he murdered nine people after starting a fire in an Ohio fireworks store. Hall had suffered severe brain damage earlier in his life and was seriously retarded.*

sionals. Although traditionally, these evaluations were conducted in a special hospital or inpatient forensic facility, recent surveys suggest that most evaluations are now conducted in the community on an outpatient basis (Grisso, Cocozza, Steadman, Fisher, & Greer, 1994; Nicholson & Norwood, 2000). The transition from inpatient to outpatient has occurred because inpatient exams are more costly, require more time, and are seldom clinically necessary compared to local, outpatient evaluations (Winick, 1985, 1996).

Physicians, psychiatrists, psychologists, and social workers are authorized by most states to conduct competency examinations, but psychologists are the professional group responsible for the largest number of reports (Nicholson & Norwood, 2000).Existing data suggest that nonmedical professionals prepare equivalent, if not superior, reports of competence evaluations to those prepared by physicians (Petrella & Poythress, 1983).

Prior to 1970, the usual evaluation of competence involved a standard psychiatric or psychological examination of a defendant and consisted of assessing current mental status, administering psychological tests, and taking a social history. If the examiner diagnosed a serious disorder such as schizophrenia or a paranoid state or if the defendant was seriously mentally retarded, the expert would often conclude that the defendant was incompetent to stand trial. The problem with this approach was that it ignored the legal definition of competence as the capacity to understand and function as a defendant, and it often neglected crucial information that was available in existing records or could be obtained by interviewing third parties who had recently interacted with the defendant. Psychosis or mental retardation may or may not render a defendant IST. The crucial question is whether the psychological disorder impairs a defendant's ability to participate knowingly and meaningfully in the proceedings and to cooperate with the defense attorney. A psychotic defendant might be competent to stand trial in a relatively straightforward case but be incompetent to participate in a complex trial that would demand more skill and understanding. As we saw with Jamie Sullivan, his mental retardation did not make him incompetent because he still was able to understand the charges against him and the basic nature of his trial.

Current competence evaluations focus on the defendant's present ability to function adequately in the legal process. This focus has been aided by the development of several structured tests or

> ## BOX 11-2
>
> ### The Competency Screening Test
>
> 1. The lawyer told Bill that _____
> 2. When I go to court, the lawyer will _____
> 3. Jack felt that the judge _____
> 4. When Phil was accused of the crime, he _____
> 5. When I prepare to go to court with my lawyer _____
> 6. If the jury finds me guilty, I _____
> 7. The way a court trial is decided _____
> 8. When the evidence in George's case was presented to the jury _____
> 9. When the lawyer questioned his client in court, the client said _____
> 10. If Jack had to try his own case, he _____
> 11. Each time the DA asked me a question, I _____
> 12. While listening to the witnesses testify against me, I _____
> 13. When the witness testifying against Harry gave incorrect evidence, he _____
> 14. When Bob disagreed with his lawyer on his defense, he _____
> 15. When I was formally accused of the crime, I thought to myself _____
> 16. If Ed's lawyer suggests that he plead guilty, he _____
> 17. What concerns Fred most about his lawyer is _____
> 18. When they say a man is innocent until proven guilty _____
> 19. When I think of being sent to prison, I _____
> 20. When Phil thinks of what he is accused of, he _____
> 21. When the jury hears my case, they will _____
> 22. If I had a chance to speak to the judge, I _____
>
> SOURCE: From Lipsitt, Lelos, and McGarry (1971).

instruments specifically aimed at assessing competence to stand trial. Psychological testing remains a common ingredient in competency evaluations, and although clinicians have begun to use one or more of these specially designed competence assessment instruments in their practice, their use is not as typical as would be desirable (Skeem, Golding, Cohn, & Berge, 1998). The leading examples of these instruments are described in the following paragraphs.

*Competency Screening Test (CST).*   Developed by A. Louis McGarry, Paul Lipsitt, and their colleagues at the Harvard Laboratory of Community Psychiatry, the CST is a 22-item sentence com-

pletion task designed as an initial screening test for incompetence (Lipsitt, Lelos, & McGarry, 1971). Because the majority of defendants referred for competence evaluations are later determined to be competent (Nicholson & Kugler, 1991; Roesch & Golding, 1987), an instrument that can quickly identify those referred defendants who are competent is especially useful because it can save the time and expense of many unnecessary, full evaluations.

In the CST, the defendant answers each of the 22 sentence stems (see ◆ Box 11-2), and each response is then scored as 2 (a competent answer), 1 (a questionably competent answer), or 0 (an incompetent answer). Total scores can range from 0 to 66; generally, a score of 20 or less suggests possible IST.

Despite widespread use, the CST has several weaknesses. First, the scoring of the sentence completions reflects what some observers (Roesch & Golding, 1987) claim is a naively positive view of the legal process. For example, on the item "Jack felt that the judge . . . ," the answer "would be fair to him" would be scored 2, whereas a response of "would screw him over" would be scored 0. As a matter of fact, defendants might have encountered judges for whom the second answer was more accurate than the first, and such a response should not be regarded as a sign of incompetence.

A second difficulty is that the CST produces a large number of false positives (defendants called incompetent who, with fuller evaluations, are judged to be competent). Although a false positive is less troubling than mistakenly forcing to trial a defendant who is incompetent (a false negative), too many false positives robs the CST of its claim to be an effective screening instrument.

Finally, despite evidence for excellent interrater reliability and internal consistency (Lipsitt et al., 1971; Randolph, Hicks, & Mason, 1981, Melton et al., 1997), the high levels of agreement between raters appear to require extensive training and experience with the instrument.

*Competency Assessment Instrument (CAI).* Also developed by the Harvard group as a more in-depth instrument for assessing competence, the CAI is a structured, one-hour interview that covers 13 functions relevant to competent functioning at trial (Laboratory for Community Psychiatry, 1974; ◆ Box 11-3). A defendant is rated on each function with a score from 1 (total incapacity) to 5 (no incapacity). A specific cutoff score has not been used, although a substantial number of scores of 3 or less is cause for concern. Although few studies of reliability have been conducted, Roesch and Golding's (1980) study of North Carolina defendants evaluated with the CAI revealed adequate interrater agreements on the separate functions and a 90% agreement with separate decisions about competence rendered after a lengthy hospital evaluation.

*Interdisciplinary Fitness Interview (IFI).* Golding and Roesch's IFI is a semistructured interview that evaluates a defendant's abilities in specific legal areas (five items). It also assesses 11 categories of psychopathological symptoms. Each area is rated from 0 to 2 in terms of the degree of capacity the defendant demonstrates. Evaluators also rate the weight they attached to each item in reaching their decision about competence. These weights vary depending on the nature of the defendant's case; for example, hallucinations might impair a defendant's ability to participate in some trials, but they would have minor effects in others and would therefore be given slight weight. The IFI is designed to be given jointly by a mental-health professional and an attorney, although it is probably administered by a mental-health professional only in most cases. A related instrument, the *Fitness Interview Test* (FIT; Roesch, Zapf, Eaves, & Webster, 1998), is a 30-minute screening test and is the only instrument designed to assess competence as defined in Canadian law.

Golding, Roesch, and Schreiber (1984) found that interviewers using the IFI agreed on final judgments of competence in 75 of 77 cases evaluated. These judgments agreed 76% of the time with independent decisions about competence made later at a state hospital. Preliminary research on the FIT (e.g., Zapf & Roesch, 1997) suggests that it is a promising screening tool.

*Georgia Court Competency Test (GCCT).* Consisting of 21 questions, the GCCT has been found to be a highly reliable instrument that taps three dimensions: general legal knowledge (e.g., the jobs of the judge, the lawyer, etc.), courtroom layout (e.g., where the judge or the jury are located in the courtroom), and specific legal knowledge (e.g., how to interact with defense counsel) (Bagby, Nicholson, Rogers, & Nussbaum, 1992). The GCCT does not do as good a job of measuring the less cognitive aspects of competence such as defendants' ability to cooperate with counsel and assist in their defense, but it shows significant correlations with a variety of independent criteria of competency (Nicholson, 1999).

## BOX 11-3 The Competency Assessment Instrument

1. *Appraisal of available legal defenses:* This item calls for an assessment of the accused's awareness of possible legal defenses and how consistent these are with the reality of the particular circumstances.

2. *Unmanageable behavior:* This item calls for an assessment of the appropriateness of the current motor and verbal behavior of the defendant and the degree to which this behavior would disrupt the conduct of a trial. Inappropriate or disruptive behavior must arise from a substantial degree of mental illness or mental retardation.

3. *Quality of relating to attorney:* This item calls for an assessment of the interpersonal capacity of the accused to re-

late to an attorney. Involved are the ability to trust and to communicate relevantly.

4. *Planning of legal strategy, including guilty pleas to lesser charges where pertinent:* This item calls for an assessment of the degree to which the accused can understand, participate, and cooperate with counsel in planning a defense that is consistent with the reality of the circumstances.

5. *Appraisal of role of:*
   a. Defense counsel
   b. Prosecuting attorney
   c. Judge
   d. Jury
   e. Defendant
   f. Witnesses
   These items call for a minimal understanding of the adversary process by the ac-

cused. The accused should be able to identify prosecuting attorney and prosecution witnesses as foe, defense counsel as friend, the judge as neutral, and the jury as the determiners of guilt or innocence.

6. *Understanding of court procedure:* This item calls for an assessment of the degree to which the defendant understands the sequence of events in a trial and their importance (e.g., the different purposes of direct and cross-examination).

7. *Appreciation of charges:* This item calls for an assessment of the accused's concrete understanding of the charges and to a lesser extent the seriousness of the charges.

8. *Appreciation of range and nature of possible penalties:* This

---

*The MacArthur Measures of Competence.* Growing out of the concept of adjudicative competence, which describes several interrelated components that need to be considered in the evaluation of competence, the *MacArthur Structured Assessment of the Competence of Criminal Defendants* (MacSAC-CD; Hoge et al., 1997) is a new but already highly regarded instrument. Most of the 82 items in the MacSAC-CD rely on a hypothetical vignette about which the defendant is asked questions that tap foundational and decisional abilities. Defendants are asked the questions in a sequence: open-ended questions come first; in the event of a wrong answer, correct information is provided to the defendant; de-

fendants are then asked additional open-ended questions to determine whether they now have the necessary understanding based on this disclosure; a series of true-false questions conclude each area of assessment. This format has several advantages, including the possibility of a more standardized evaluation across different defendants and the ability to assess separately defendants' preexisting abilities as well as their capacity to learn and apply new information.

One major disadvantage of the MacSAC-CD is that it was developed as a research instrument and takes about two hours to complete, far too long to be used in clinical practice. To overcome this limitation, a 22-item clinical version of this

item calls for an assessment of the accused's concrete understanding and appreciation of the conditions and restrictions that could be imposed and their possible duration.

9. *Appraisal of likely outcome:* This item calls for an assessment of how realistically the accused perceives the likely outcome and the degree to which impaired understanding contributes to a less-than-adequate participation in the defense. Without adequate information on the part of the examiner regarding the facts and circumstances of the alleged offense, this item would be unratable.

10. *Capacity to disclose to attorney available pertinent facts surrounding the offense, in-* *cluding the defendant's movements, timing, mental state, and actions at the time of the offense:* This item calls for an assessment of the accused's capacity to give a basically consistent, rational, and relevant account of the motivational and external facts.

11. *Capacity to challenge prosecution witnesses realistically:* This item calls for an assessment of the accused's capacity to recognize distortions in prosecution testimony. If false testimony is given, the degree of activism with which the defendant informs the attorney of inaccuracies is important.

12. *Capacity to testify relevantly:* This item calls for an assessment of the accused's ability to testify with coherence, rel- evance, and independence of judgment.

13. *Self-defeating versus self-serving motivation (legal sense):* This item calls for an assessment of the accused's motivation to adequately and appropriately utilize legal safeguards. Of particular concern here are the pathological seeking of punishment and the deliberate failure by the accused to rely on appropriate legal protections. Passivity or indifference do not justify low scores on this item. Actively self-destructive manipulation of the legal process arising from mental pathology does justify low scores.

measure, called the *MacArthur Competence Assessment Tool—Criminal Adjudication* (MacCAT-CA) is being field-tested. The preliminary validation studies of the MacCAT-CA have been very promising (e.g., Otto et al., 1998), and we anticipate that once adequate norms are available the clinical version of this test will become a popular tool among forensic practitioners.

***Other Competence Instruments.*** Several additional specialized competence tests have been developed in the past decade and are finding their way into forensic practice.For example, the *Computer-Assisted Determination of Competence to Proceed* (CADCOMP; Barnard et al., 1991) is a 272-item instrument that uses interactive computer technology to simulate a competency assessment by a clinician. Studies of this instrument's reliability and validity suggest its potential value (e.g., Nicholson, Robertson, Johnson, & Jensen, 1988), but a number of questions still remain about several of this test's subscales. At the present time, most evaluators who use a specialized instrument rely on the CST, CAI, IFI, GCCT, or some local variation of one of them. These different tests of competence show moderate agreement in how they classify defendants; in other words, a defendant classified as competent with one test is usually—but not always—similarly classified with another of the tests (Ustad, Rogers, Sewell, & Guarnaccia, 1996).

Another new test, the *Competence Assessment for Standing Trial for Defendants with Mental Retardation* (CAST-MR; Everington & Luckasson, 1992) was developed specifically for assessing defendants with mild to moderate mental retardation. Preliminary studies have indicated its potential usefulness, but it has not been employed with a large enough sample of mentally retarded defendants to assess its overall effectiveness (Nicholson, 1999).

One other issue being studied by forensic clinicians is the extent to which defendants can successfully fake incompetence on these tests. Preliminary results suggest that although offenders can simulate incompetence, they often take such simulations to extremes, scoring much more poorly on competence tests than their truly incompetent counterparts (Gothard, Rogers, & Sewell, 1995; Gothard, Viglione, Meloy, & Sherman, 1995). Therefore, very low scores should make evaluators suspicious that a defendant might be exaggerating his or her deficiencies.

Following the collection of assessment data, evaluators communicate their findings to the judge. Often, a written report is submitted that summarizes the evidence pertaining to IST as well as the likelihood of appropriate treatment being able to restore competence. In controversial or strongly contested cases, such as the Jamie Sullivan trial, a formal competence hearing is held at which the experts testify and are questioned by attorneys from both sides. The proper content of such testimony and written reports is a hotly debated topic. Some (Morse, 1978) believe that experts should restrict themselves to a description of the referral questions and the techniques used to answer these questions, followed by a thorough summary of the findings and a discussion of the defendant's mental difficulties and the possible consequences of these impairments. They recommend that the expert not offer an opinion on the ultimate question of whether the defendant is IST because it is the court's responsibility to make that legal decision. On the other hand, courts require the expert to state just such a conclusion, believing, along with many mental-health experts, that no one is better suited for such a

judgment than a qualified mental-health professional (see Poythress, 1982; Rogers & Ewing, 1987).

In formal competence hearings, who bears the burden of proof? Do prosecutors have to prove that defendants are incompetent, or do defendants have to overcome a presumption of competence? In the 1992 case of *Medina v. California,* the U.S. Supreme Court held that a state can require a criminal defendant to shoulder the burden of proving that he or she is incompetent. But how stringent should that burden be? Most states established the criterion to be a "preponderance of the evidence," meaning that the defendant had to show that it was more likely than not that he or she was incompetent. But four states—Oklahoma, Pennsylvania, Connecticut, and Rhode Island—required a higher standard of proof that was "clear and convincing." In 1996, the Supreme Court found in the case of *Cooper v. Oklahoma* that this standard was too stringent because it could lead to situations in which a defendant proved that he or she was probably incompetent yet, failing to provide clear and convincing evidence, still was forced to trial. The Court reasoned that, although the higher standard might prevent some instances of defendants faking their incompetence, the risks of forcing a certain number of incompetent defendants to trial were constitutionally unacceptable.

## Results of Competence Evaluations

About 70% of the defendants referred for evaluation are ultimately found competent to stand trial (Nicholson & Kugler, 1991); when very rigorous examinations are conducted, the rate of defendants found competent approaches 90%. Judges seldom disagree with clinicians' decisions about competence (Steadman, 1979), and opposing attorneys often will **stipulate** (agree without further examination) to clinicians' findings (Melton et al., 1997). As a result, mental-health professionals exert great, perhaps excessive, influence on this legal decision.

What sort of person is most often judged to be incompetent? In his study of more than 500

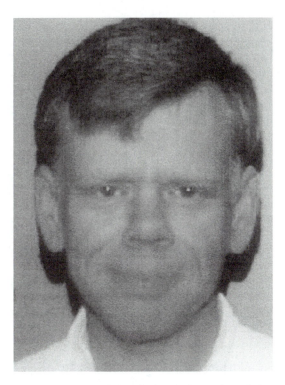

*Russell Weston, Jr. whose July 1998 rampage through the U.S. Capitol left two Capitol guards dead and led to questions about his mental competence.*

defendants found IST, Steadman (1979) found them often to be "marginal" men who were undereducated and deficient in job skills, with long histories of involvement in both the legal and mental-health systems (see also Williams & Miller, 1981). Problems of substance abuse were common. Minorities were overrepresented. Others report relatively high percentages of psychosis, lower intelligence, and more problems with certain aspects of memory among IST defendants (Nestor, Daggett, Haycock, & Price, 1999; Nicholson, Briggs, & Robertson, 1988; Roesch & Golding, 1980; Ustad et al., 1996). One other consistent finding is that IST defendants are charged with more serious crimes than defendants in general. After an extensive review of competence research, Nicholson and Kugler (1991) described the typical defendant found IST to (1) have a history of psychosis for which previous treatment had been received; (2) exhibit symptoms of current serious mental disorder; (3) be single, unemployed, and poorly educated; and (4) score poorly on specific competence assessment instruments.

If a defendant referred for a competence evaluation is found competent, the legal process resumes and the defendant again faces the possibility of trial. If the defendant is found IST, the picture becomes more complicated. For crimes that are not serious, the charges might be dropped, sometimes in exchange for requiring the defendant to receive treatment. If the charges are serious, as they were in the case of John du Pont, the defendant usually will be returned to an institution to be treated for restoration of competence, which, if successful, will result in the defendant ultimately standing trial. Outpatient treatment of incompetent defendants is used less often, even though it might often be justified.

How successful are efforts to restore defendants' competence? One study evaluated an experimental group treatment for a sample of incompetent defendants sent to one of three Philadelphia facilities (Siegel & Elwork, 1990). In addition to receiving the psychiatric medication, defendants assigned to these special treatment groups watched videotapes and received special instructions on courtroom procedures. They also discussed different ways of resolving problems that a defendant might face during a trial. A matched control group received treatment for their general psychiatric needs, but no specific treatment relevant to incompetence. Following their treatment, defendants participating in the special competence restoration group showed significant increases in their CAI scores compared to the controls. In addition, hospital staff judged 43% of the experimental subjects to be competent to stand trial after treatment compared to 15% of the control subjects. In general, most defendants have their adjudicative competence restored, usually with about six months of treatment (Melton et al., 1997).

The real dilemma for IST defendants occurs when treatment is not successful in restoring competence and holds little promise of success in the future. At this point, all options are problematic. Theoretically, the previously described *Jackson* ruling prohibits the indefinite commitments common in the past; many states limit the period of treatment to restore competence to six months (four months in the federal system), after which a reevaluation of competence is conducted. If the defendant is still found IST, a six-month extension of treatment is usually permitted.

One solution for permanently incompetent defendants is to have them committed to a hospital through involuntary civil commitment proceedings (see Chapter 12). Standards for this type of commitment are stricter than for being found IST, however. The state must show that the person is mentally ill and either imminently dangerous to self/others or so gravely disabled as to be unable to care for him- or herself. Furthermore, civil commitments cannot generally last longer than one year, although they can be renewed by holding new commitment hearings when necessary. Should an incompetent defendant not meet the criteria for a civil commitment, what happens? One possibility is that permanent incompetence might immunize this person from standing trial for future crimes. In response to this fear, it appears that, despite the ruling in the *Jackson* case, some states simply continue to confine incompetent defendants for indefinite periods. Although this "solution" might appease the public, we believe it jeopardizes defendants' due process rights and results in lengthy periods of punishment (disguised as treatment) without a trial.

Several alternative procedures have been proposed to solve this catch-22, including proposals to abolish the IST concept altogether (Burt & Morris, 1972), to allow defendants to seek trial continuances without going through an elaborate evaluation, or to waive their right to be competent under certain circumstances (Fentiman, 1986; Winick, 1996). One solution that we find promising is the American Bar Association's (1984) proposal that a provisional trial be held for a defendant who is likely to be declared permanently incompetent. This hearing would decide the question

of guilt or innocence. If the defendant is found not guilty, he or she is formally acquitted and could be further confined only through civil commitment. If proven guilty, the defendant would be subject to a special form of commitment that would recognize society's needs for secure handling of these persons.

## Amnesia and Competence to Stand Trial

Are defendants with amnesia incompetent to stand trial? Not necessarily. Loss of memory might render a defendant incompetent, but the law does not presume that amnesia per se is incapacitating. Most courts believe this question should be answered on a case-by-case basis, with consideration given to the severity of the amnesia and the extent to which it interferes with preparation of a defense. A leading decision in this area, *Wilson v. United States* (1968), lists six factors to be considered when deciding whether amnesia produces IST:

a. The extent to which the amnesia affected the defendant's ability to consult with and assist counsel.
b. The extent to which the amnesia affected the defendant's ability to testify at trial.
c. The extent to which evidence concerning the crime could be reconstructed by others.
d. The extent to which the prosecution assisted the defendant and counsel in that reconstruction.
e. The strength of the prosecution's case; if there is a substantial possibility that the accused could, but for the amnesia, establish an alibi or other defense, it should be presumed that [s]he would have been able to do so.
f. Any other facts and circumstances that would indicate whether the defendant had a fair trial.

Most judges are skeptical about claims of amnesia, believing that it can be easily faked. Consequently, claims of amnesia will not usually lead to a finding of incompetence, but they might result in the prosecution having to cooperate more with the defense attorney in reconstructing the facts and exploring possible defenses.

## Competent with Medication, Incompetent Without

For most defendants found IST, psychoactive medication has been the treatment of choice because it is assumed to be the best intervention for bringing defendants to a level of competence in a reasonable period of time. Can incompetent defendants refuse this treatment? If medicated, will defendants be found competent to stand trial even though the medication, through its temporarily tranquilizing effects, might undercut a defense such as insanity?

Few courts have considered the first question, but most of those that have tend to affirm compulsory treatment to restore competence. The answer to the second question is usually yes; most states allow the trials of defendants who are taking medication to help them remain competent. In one case on this topic, the New Hampshire Supreme Court, recognizing the possible tactical disadvantages faced by a medicated (and therefore artificially subdued) defendant claiming insanity as a defense, ruled that "defendants should be allowed to appear at trial without medication, provided they are medicated and competent when they make the decision to appear at trial unmedicated, thereby insuring a valid waiver of their right to be tried while incompetent" (Melton et al., 1987, p. 78; commenting on *State v. Hayes,* 1978).

In 1992, the U.S. Supreme Court considered the case of *Riggins v. Nevada.* In this case, the defendant, David Riggins, was being tried for murder and robbery. As he awaited trial, Riggins started to hear voices and have trouble sleeping. A psychiatrist prescribed Mellaril for Riggins, who was then found competent to stand trial. However, Riggins asked that the Mellaril be stopped during his trial so that he could show the jurors his true mental state, thereby bolstering the credibility of his insanity defense. The trial judge refused his request. However, the Supreme Court ruled that forcing Riggins to receive the antipsychotic medication violated his Sixth and Fourteenth Amendment rights *unless* it could be shown that the medicine was medically appropriate and was necessary to ensure Riggins's safety or the safety of others or that a fair trial could not be conducted unless Riggins was medicated. This finding requires that, before a defendant can be medicated against his or her will, the court must find the treatment to be medically appropriate and necessary for accomplishing an "essential state interest." The use of nonmedical "treatments" for incompetence can solve some of the foregoing problems. Educational, problem-solving approaches that teach incompetent defendants how to communicate effectively with their attorneys and how to understand and participate better in legal proceedings have shown that competence skills can be learned (Siegel & Elwork, 1990).

## Other Competence Issues

Because questions about competence can be raised at any point in the criminal process, several other competencies are at issue in deciding whether a defendant can participate knowingly in different functions. Competence for any legal function involves (1) determining what functional abilities are necessary, (2) assessing the context where these abilities must be demonstrated, (3) evaluating the implication of any deficiencies in the required abilities, and (4) deciding whether the deficiencies warrant a conclusion that the defendant is incompetent (Grisso, 1986). Mental-health professionals are asked, on occasion, to evaluate each of the following competencies (see also Melton et al., 1997; Chapter 7). Other questions about competencies arising in civil law are discussed in Chapter 12.

*Competence to confess.*   Discussed previously in Chapter 8, competence to confess requires that defendants, once in police custody, make a confession only after having waived their *Miranda* rights knowingly, intelligently, and voluntarily. A clinician's assessment of these abilities is difficult because, in most cases, the waiver and confession occur months before the professional's evaluation, requiring many assumptions about the defendant's psychological condition at the time. As a result of these difficulties, professional evaluations of competence to confess are given less weight than evidence about the police methods used to obtain the confession.

### Competence to waive the right to an attorney.
Can defendants decide they do not want a lawyer to represent them at trial? The Supreme Court has held that defendants have a constitutional right to waive counsel and represent themselves at trial, providing that this decision is made competently (*Faretta v. California,* 1975). Theoretically, the standard for this competence is the same as for defendants to stand trial. In addition, the presiding judge must be convinced that the waiver of counsel is both voluntary (uncoerced) and intelligent (with understanding). Defendants do not have to convince the court that they possess a high level of legal knowledge, although some legal knowledge is probably important.

Competence to waive the right to counsel was at issue in the trial of Colin Ferguson, charged with murdering 6 passengers and wounding 19 more when, on a December 1993 evening, he went on a killing rampage aboard the Long Island Railroad train. Ferguson insisted on serving as his own attorney, after rejecting the "black rage" defense suggested by his two lawyers, Ron Kuby and the late William Kunstler. At first, Ferguson proved effective enough to have several of his objections to the prosecutor's case sustained. But then, giving new meaning to the old saying that a defendant who argues his own case has a fool for a client, Ferguson opened his case by claiming that, "There were 93 counts to that indictment, 93 counts only because it matches the year 1993. If it had been 1925, it would been a 25-count indictment." This was a prelude to Ferguson's attempt at cross-examining a series of eyewitnesses, who, in response to his preposterous suggestion that someone else had been the murderer, answered time after time to the effect, "No, I saw the murderer clearly. It was you."

### Competence to refuse the insanity defense.
In cases with a likelihood that the defendant was insane at the time of the offense, can the defendant refuse to plead insanity? If there is evidence that a defendant was not mentally responsible for criminal acts, do courts have a duty to require that the defendant plead insanity when the defendant does not want to do so? Courts are divided on this question. In some cases, they have suggested that society's stake in punishing only mentally responsible persons requires the imposition of an insanity plea even on unwilling defendants (*Whalen v. United States,* 1965). Other decisions (*Frendak v. United States,* 1979) use the framework of competence to answer this question—if the defendant understands the alternative pleas available and the consequences of those pleas, the defendant should be permitted to reject an insanity plea. This latter approach, which is followed in most courts, recognizes that an acquittal on grounds of insanity is not always a "better" outcome for a defendant than a conviction and criminal sentence.

This question was at the heart of the prosecution of Theodore Kaczynski for his two-decade-long "Unabomber" attacks. Although the consensus of several experts was that Kaczynski suffered from paranoid schizophrenia, he adamantly refused to let his attorneys use an insanity or diminished capacity (see Box 11-9 later) defense, arguing that he did not want to be stigmatized, in his words, as a "sickie." Was Kaczynski competent to make this decision, or was Judge Garland E. Burrell Jr. correct in ordering that Kaczynski's lawyers could control his defense, even over the defendant's persistent objections? It is doubtful that either an insanity or diminished capacity defense would have been successful—Kaczynski's own diary proved that he understood and intended to commit his crimes—but we will never know for sure. Ultimately, to avoid the possibility of the death penalty, Kaczynski pled guilty to murder and was sentenced to life in prison. (A portion of Kaczynski's handwritten motion concerning his objections to a mental-status offense is reproduced in Figure 11.1.)

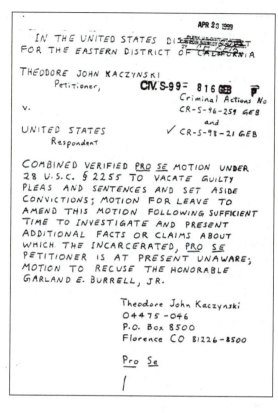

**FIGURE 11.1** *Portions of Theodore Kaczynski's handwritten motion objecting to the use of an insanity defense in his case and requesting that he be allowed to represent himself at trial*

SOURCE: Portion of a motion handwritten by Ted Kaczynski.

*Competence to be sentenced and punished.* For legal and humanitarian reasons, convicted defendants are not to be sentenced to punishment unless they are competent. In general, the standard for this competence is that the defendant can understand the punishment and the reasons it is being imposed. It is often a more straightforward question for the clinician to evaluate than adjudicative competence, which involves issues of whether the accused can interact effectively with counsel and appreciate alternative courses of action.

The most controversial aspect of this area is determining whether a defendant is competent to be executed. The U.S. Supreme Court decided, in the case of *Ford v. Wainwright* (1986), that the Eighth Amendment ban against cruel and unusual punishments prohibits the execution of defendants while they are incompetent. Therefore, mental-health professionals will at times be called on to evaluate inmates waiting to be executed to determine whether they are competent to be put to death. The practical problems and ethical dilemmas involved in these evaluations are enormous (Heilbrun, 1987; Mossman, 1987; Susman, 1992) and have led some psychologists to recommend that clinicians should not perform such evaluations.

## The Competence of Juveniles

When juveniles are arrested, they are often subjected to police interrogations, just like adults. Also like adults, juveniles are encouraged to confess to crimes for which they are suspects. This practice raises two basic questions: Are juveniles able to understand their *Miranda* rights, and are they competent to waive them and offer valid confessions to the police?

Prior to the decision *In re Gault* (1967; see Chapter 9), the courts had treated juvenile defendants differently from adults under the theory that the state should assume a parental interest in rehabilitating youthful offenders rather than punishing them. In exchange for this presumably less adversarial attitude (known as the theory of **parens patriae**), juveniles relinquished some constitutional rights given to adult defendants because they were deemed not necessary. The *Gault* decision replaced the former parental stance toward juveniles with a more adversarial posture in which juveniles were to be accorded many of the same constitutional protections given adults. As more and more states change their laws to make it easier to transfer juveniles to adult courts and to increase the punishment of juveniles, questions about juveniles' competence abilities become more pressing (Grisso, 1997). Constitutional rights need to be understood if they are to protect accused persons fully. Thus, a major question is whether juveniles possess adequate capacities to waive their *Miranda* rights knowingly, intelligently, and voluntarily and make a confession during interrogations by the police.

Thomas Grisso (1981), the leading expert on juveniles' comprehension of the *Miranda* warning, describes two approaches to evaluating the competence of a juvenile's waiver of *Miranda* rights. First, the totality of the circumstances surrounding the waiver can be considered. Included in such an evaluation would be the juvenile's age, intelligence, and prior experience in criminal proceedings as well as the methods used by the police in obtaining the waiver and in questioning the youth. A second strategy, known as the *per se approach,* assumes that juveniles are limited in their understanding of these matters; it requires that they be given special assistance from an interested adult to help them grasp the meaning of the rights and the implications of waiving them. If

such assistance were not given, regardless of the court's assessment of the totality of circumstances, the waiver would be judged incompetent.

The totality approach prevails in most U.S. courts, although some states follow the *per se* approach. The leading case on this topic is *Fare v. Michael C.* (1979), in which the Supreme Court adopted the totality approach as the constitutional standard. The defendant was a 16-year-old boy taken into custody by police and questioned about the murder of a man in Van Nuys, California. The boy had a long record of legal trouble and had been on probation in juvenile court since he was 12. Before questioning him, the police read Michael C. his *Miranda* rights, but they then refused his request to see his probation officer. He finally agreed to talk to them without an attorney being present, and he went on to make statements and draw pictures that incriminated him in the murder. The Supreme Court held that "the totality of circumstances surrounding the interrogation" made it clear that Michael had knowingly and voluntarily waived his rights and that the statements he made could be admitted into evidence against him. The Court based its decision partly on the fact that Michael had an extensive prior police record and, therefore, the Court assumed, possessed sufficient knowledge about police methods.

To evaluate adults' and juveniles' comprehension of *Miranda* warnings, Grisso (1981) conducted a series of studies that measured subjects' understanding of (1) the vocabulary and phrases used in the warnings and (2) the purposes of the rights involved. He also examined the relationships between these measures and several background characteristics of juveniles. Grisso developed three different measures of vocabulary and phrase comprehension. In addition, subjects' perceptions of the function and significance of the warnings were assessed through a structured interview in which they described their understanding of four drawings, depicting scenes such as a police questioning a suspect or a suspect consulting with an attorney. These measures have recently been published in a manual so that clinicians now have a standardized format for assessing juveniles' understanding and appreciation of the *Miranda* warnings (Grisso, 1998). Among the most important findings were the following:

1. At least one of the four crucial elements of the *Miranda* warning was inadequately paraphrased by 55% of the juveniles and by 23% of the adults.
2. At least one of six crucial vocabulary words was completely misunderstood by 63% of the juveniles versus 37% of the adults.
3. The majority of juveniles younger than 15 years had significantly poorer comprehension of the significance or function of the warnings than did the adults.
4. Prior court experience was not related to an understanding of the vocabulary and phrases in the warnings, but juveniles with more court experience had a greater appreciation of the significance of *Miranda* rights.

Based on these results, Grisso (1981) concluded that juveniles younger than 15—and especially those who are 13 or younger—do not understand all of their *Miranda* rights and that they would require assistance to waive these right knowingly. He recommends a *per se* approach that would rely on one of four special protections: (1) using a simplified *Miranda* warning appropriate for juveniles, (2) requiring a preinterrogation screening of juveniles to assess whether they comprehend the warnings adequately, (3) requiring the presence of an interested adult during the interrogation to advise the juvenile, or (4) requiring that an attorney for the juvenile be present during interrogation. Grisso prefers the last alternative.

Although juveniles 15 or older comprehended better than younger juveniles, they still showed gaps in their *Miranda* understanding (as did a substantial percentage of adults). Therefore, a *per se* approach even for older juveniles may be justified, especially if we heed the admonition in *Gault* that other courts give the "greatest care" to evaluating juveniles' waivers of rights. On the other hand, if priority is given to efficient, vigorous police investigation of crime, courts' general satisfaction with the totality standard will continue. Currently, unless a juvenile is so severely retarded or mentally disordered that he or she couldn't understand what a waiver meant, or unless it can be shown that the police took improper advantage of a suspect's psychological disorder in their interrogation methods, a waiver of *Miranda* rights will probably be judged a competent act.

Preference for a *per se* verus totality standard will also reflect the personal emphasis one places on the competing values in the dilemma introduced in Chapter 1: the belief that extra protections are owed people who have special needs, even if these protections handicap society in certain ways, versus the belief that individual rights must sometimes give way to society's interest in identifying criminals and protecting itself from them.

## The Insanity Defense

The issue of insanity intensifies each of the dilemmas of Chapter 1. Any society that respects the rights of individuals recognizes the possibility that some of its citizens cannot comprehend the consequences or the wrongfulness of their actions. Yet, the highly publicized "success" of defendants who claimed insanity as an explanation for their actions (e.g., John Hinckley) has caused lawmakers to introduce new legislation intended to make it more difficult for jurors to acquit defendants by reason of insanity.

The quest for equality is also threatened by great discretion in how the insanity defense is used. It is much harder to find a defendant not guilty by reason of insanity in some states than in others because of differing definitions of insanity. Five states do not allow a formal insanity defense (Borum & Fulero, 1999), even though they do allow defendants to introduce evidence about their mental condition at the time of an offense. In addition, the federal government has revised its definition of this defense three times since 1950.

Likewise, truth is an ideal that is very hard to implement when a defendant uses insanity as an explanation for his or her actions. The jury or judge must answer the question "Why did he fire the gun?" rather than "Did he fire the gun?" How can we determine whether a defendant is truly insane? Can we know a person's state of mind while he or she committed an antisocial act? The task of truth finding becomes even more formidable when we acknowledge that the fact finders—juries and judges—must determine not whether the person is currently insane but, rather, whether he or she was insane at the time of the crime, possibly months or years before.

This problem is further complicated by the fact that unlike the assessment of competence, forensic clinicians do not have many instruments available that are designed specifically to assess insanity. One brief screening instrument—the Mental Status Examination at the Time of the Offense (Slobogin, Melton, & Showalter, 1984)—has been developed, but research on its reliability and validity is limited to one study. More research has been conducted on the Rogers Criminal Responsibility Scales (RCRAS; Rogers, 1986), a set of 25 scales that organize the many factors and points of decision that clinicians need to consider when assessing criminal responsibility. Although the RCRAS is not without limitations, it is the only formal instrument with some proven reliability and validity for guiding clinicians' decision-making process in insanity evaluations (Nicholson, 1999).

Another reason why truth is so elusive in cases of alleged insanity stems from the conflict between law and behavioral sciences as alternative pathways to knowledge. As noted in Chapter 1, insanity is a legal concept, not a medical or psychological one. In many states, a defendant could be hallucinating, delusional, and diagnosed as schizophrenic, but if the individual knew the difference between right and wrong, he or she would be classified as legally sane. Thus, psychiatrists and clinical psychologists are called on as expert witnesses to make absolute judgments about a concept that is beyond their professional/scientific framework. Their goals—clinical diagnoses that are probabilistic and complex—compete with the legal system's demand for a straightforward yes or no answer. Furthermore, although psychiatrists and other mental-health experts can give names to disorders, these labels do not make the jury's task any easier or its decision any more accurate.

Some mental-health professionals even argue that the law and the behavioral sciences are incompatible (Winslade & Ross, 1983). The law assumes that we are free agents, and if we act illegally, we should be punished. The behavioral sciences assume that behavior is caused both by conditions within the person and by the environment acting on the person. With such an assumption, the concept of "responsibility" is diluted, and the justification for punishment can be called into question.

## Rationale for the Insanity Defense

Why do we have laws about insanity at all? Wouldn't it be simpler to do away with insanity in the legal system? Allowing a criminal defendant to plead not guilty by reason of insanity reflects a fundamental belief that a civilized society should not punish persons who do not know what they are doing or who are incapable of controlling their conduct. Thus, on occasion, the state must tell the victim's friends and family that, although it abhors the defendant's acts, some offenders do not deserve punishment. Before it can do that, however, a judgment about whether such persons were responsible for their actions must be made.

As we have already discussed, in many cases in which an insanity defense is used, a decision about a defendant's competence must be reached first. If the defendant is declared incompetent to stand trial, the trial is delayed until the defendant is found competent to proceed. Therefore, a judgment that a defendant is not competent does not relieve the individual of responsibility for an illegal act; it only delays the determination. Furthermore, competence refers exclusively to the defendant's mental abilities at the time of the proceeding, whereas insanity relates to the defendant's mental state at the time the offense was committed.

In trying to define insanity, the courts back in the 1700s used phrases such as, "did not know what he did" or "[did not know more] than an infant, than a brute, or a wild beast." By the 1800s, "knowing the difference between right and wrong" was the predominant legal definition. At that time, it was assumed that juries could decide whether a defendant was insane without the help of professional witnesses. But the more we learn about psychological disorders, the more difficult we find the task to be.

What is the legal standard for insanity? There is no one answer. The following sections describe several definitions currently in use. The legal standards that define criminal responsibility vary from state to state, but in all states, the defendant is initially presumed to be responsible for his or her alleged act. Therefore, if pleading insanity, defendants have the duty to present evidence that would disprove the presumption of criminal responsibility in their case—a requirement known as an **affirmative defense.** A related legal issue is the assessment of **mens rea** or the mental state of knowing the nature and quality of a forbidden act. To be a criminal offense, an act must not only be illegal but also must be accompanied by the necessary mens rea, or guilty mind.

## The McNaughton Rule: An Early Attempt to Define Insanity

In 1843, an Englishman named Daniel McNaughton shot and killed the private secretary of the British prime minister. Plagued by paranoid delusions, McNaughton believed that the prime minister, Robert Peel, was part of a conspiracy by the Tory party against him. At first, McNaughton sought to escape his imagined tormentors by traveling through Europe. When that didn't work, he stalked the prime minister and, after waiting in front of the prime minister's residence at No. 10 Downing Street, shot the man he thought was Peel.

McNaughton was charged with murder, and his defense was to plead not guilty by reason of insanity. Nine medical experts, including the American psychiatrist Isaac Ray, testified for two

days about his mental state, and all agreed that he was insane. On instructions from the lord chief justice, the jury brought forth a verdict of not guilty by reason of insanity without even leaving the jury box to deliberate. McNaughton was committed to the Broadmoor asylum for the insane, where he remained for the rest of his life.

The public was infuriated, as was Queen Victoria, who had been the target of several attempts on her life. She demanded a tougher test of insanity. Subsequent debate in the House of Lords led to five questions, presented to 15 high court judges. Their replies constitute what has come to be called the *McNaughton* rule, which was announced in 1843, long before *psychiatry* became a household word. The McNaughton rule defines insanity as follows:

> The jury ought to be told in all cases that every man is to be presumed to be sane, and to possess a sufficient degree of reason to be responsible for his crimes, until the contrary be proved to their satisfaction; and that to establish a defense on the grounds of insanity it must be clearly proved that, at the time of committing the act, the accused was laboring under such a defect of reason, from disease of the mind, as not to know the nature and quality of the act he was doing, or, if he did know it, that he did not know what he was doing was wrong. (quoted in Post, 1963, p. 113)

The McNaughton rule, which became the standard for defining insanity in Great Britain and the United States, thus "excuses" criminal conduct if the defendant, as a result of a "disease of the mind": (1) did not know what he was doing (e.g., believed he was shooting an animal rather than a human) or (2) did not know that what he was doing was wrong (e.g., believed killing unarmed strangers was "right"). In some jurisdictions, an *irresistible impulse* test was added to try to deal with individuals who might have known that an act was wrong but lacked the capacity to avoid performing it. However, it has proven very difficult to distinguish between an irresistible impulse and an impulse that simply is not resisted.

## THE CASE OF

**BOX 11-4    Monte Durham: Was he insane?**

In 1945, when he was 17, Monte Durham was discharged from the U.S. Navy after a psychiatric examination had diagnosed a "profound personality disorder" that left him unfit for military service. Two years later, he was convicted of stealing a car and was placed on probation for up to three years. He attempted to commit suicide and was committed to St. Elizabeth's Hospital in Washington, D.C. But after two months, he was released.

A year later, in 1948, Durham was found guilty of passing bad checks, his probation was revoked, and he began serving his prison sentence for the earlier car theft. In prison, he behaved so bizarrely that he was given another mental examination. Found to be of "unsound mind," he was

sent back to St. Elizabeth's Hospital, where he was diagnosed as suffering from "psychosis with psychopathic personality." After a little over a year, he was discharged as "recovered" and sent back to prison to complete his sentence. Released on parole, he almost immediately violated one of the conditions by leaving the District of Columbia.

Finally captured—and having passed some more bad checks while he was a fugitive—Durham was again diagnosed as being of unsound mind and once more admitted to St. Elizabeth's. Three months later, he was discharged for the third time. Within a couple of months, he was arrested for housebreaking. The police had discovered him in an apartment, cowering in a corner with a T-shirt

over his head and with property worth about $50 in his pockets (Maeder, 1985). Another psychiatric examination concluded that he should be committed to a mental hospital, but after being there for 16 months, he was judged competent to stand trial. Durham claimed the defense of insanity, but the judge refused to admit such testimony, and Durham was convicted.

Was Monte Durham insane? It depends on the standard of insanity. The appeals court found the prevailing standard inadequate, which is why Durham's case took on more than local interest. Ironically, Durham was tried three times for this same crime of housebreaking because of appeals. At his third trial, he pleaded guilty (Maeder, 1985).

---

The American Psychiatric Association describes the line between an irresistible impulse and an impulse not resisted as "no sharper than that between twilight and dusk" (APA, 1982). One proposed solution, known as the "police at the elbow test," asks, in effect, Would the impulse have been so overwhelming that the individual would have committed the crime even if a police officer had been standing at his or her elbow, thereby assuring that he or she would be caught? Neither legal experts nor forensic clinicians are satisfied with the concept, and it is now used rarely.

The McNaughton rule remains the standard for defining insanity in roughly one-third of the states, but it has often been criticized by mental-health professionals, who contend that the defi-

nition is too restrictive and that the relevant issue is more a motivational question of being able to control wrongful actions than a cognitive one of distinguishing right from wrong. Thus, modifications were inevitable.

### The Durham Rule

Monte Durham had little going for him, as ◆▶ Box 11-4 illustrates. He was in and out of mental hospitals and prisons, and, in 1954, his case provided the impetus for the first major change in the standard for insanity used in U.S. federal courts.

When Durham was originally tried, his defense was that he "was of unsound mind" (i.e., insane) when he robbed a house on July 13, 1951.

But the judge rejected this defense, saying, "I don't think it has been established that the defendant was of unsound mind as of July 13, 1951, in the sense that he didn't know the difference between right and wrong or that even if he did, he was subject to an irresistible impulse by reason of derangement of mind" (*Durham v. United States,* 1954, pp. 865–866). Durham was found guilty.

But Durham's lawyer appealed his conviction, claiming that the existing standards of criminal responsibility were obsolete and should be replaced. Judge David Bazelon of the U.S. Court of Appeals, District of Columbia Circuit, used the case to reform the McNaughton rule. In his decision, Judge Bazelon reviewed the century-long history of the right/wrong test and presented the opinions of scientists, physicians, and various commissions. He quoted one of the founders of the American Psychiatric Association, who called knowledge of right and wrong a "fallacious" test of criminal responsibility. He cited Supreme Court justices' complaints about the standard ("Everyone concedes that the present legal definition of insanity has little relation to the truths of mental life"). And he summarized the report of the Royal Commission on Capital Punishment, which stated that the McNaughton test "is based on an entirely obsolete and misleading conception of the nature of insanity."

The U.S. Court of Appeals overturned the conviction of Monte Durham and ordered a new trial in which the standard for insanity would not be the right/wrong test. Instead, the court specified the rule to be "that an accused is not criminally responsible if his unlawful act was the product of mental disease or mental defect." This became known as the Durham rule or the **product rule,** and it was adopted by some federal courts in 1954.

Mental-health professionals approved of the Durham rule initially; in fact, it led to an influx of psychiatrists and clinical psychologists into the courtroom as expert witnesses. But many judges and prosecutors did not like the Durham standard. Some believed it permitted the testimony of psychiatrists to usurp the jury's fact-finding

function. In fact, even some judges in Washington, D.C., did not appreciably modify their instructions after the Durham rule was instituted there. Judges tended to retain the language of the McNaughton instructions, reflecting their disapproval of the Durham rule. Furthermore, alcoholics and drug addicts charged with crimes could claim that their acts were the result of a mental disease, and they should thus be ruled insane. A former jewelry store manager claimed the insanity defense in a case involving the theft of $500,000 worth of diamonds. He insisted that, being a compulsive gambler, he couldn't help himself.

Although adopted by some federal courts, the Durham rule was never accepted by more than a few states. Finally, in 1972, the Bazelon court unanimously repealed the Durham standard in the federal system and replaced it with the Brawner rule.

## The Brawner Rule, Stemming from the Model Penal Code

In response to problems with the Durham rule, a committee of legal scholars sponsored by the American Law Institute (ALI) developed the Model Penal Code, which led to what is now called the **Brawner rule** (or ALI rule). This rule states that a defendant is not responsible for criminal conduct if he, "at the time of such conduct as a result of mental disease or defect, [lacks] substantial capacity either to appreciate the criminality [wrongfulness] of his conduct or to conform his conduct to the requirements of the law."

This standard, or a variation of it, is now used in about half the states; in a drastically altered form (which we will describe later), it is also used in all federal courts. It may be the best solution yet, because the key concepts are general enough to allow the jury some latitude and yet solid enough to provide ground for the testimony of expert witnesses. It differs from the McNaughton rule in three substantial respects. First, by using the term *appreciate,* it acknowledges the emotional determinants of criminal actions. Second, it does not require a total lack of appreciation by offenders for the nature of their conduct—only a lack of "substantial capacity." Finally, it includes both a cognitive element and a volitional element, making defendants' inability to control their actions an independent criterion for insanity.

In theory, varying rules for insanity should influence jurors to reach different verdicts, but psychologists have questioned whether the typical juror can comprehend the legal language of these definitions and then apply them as intended by the courts. (Further evaluation of the effectiveness of the judge's instructions to the jury can be found in Chapter 15.) Elwork, Sales, and Suggs (1981) found jurors only 51% correct on a series of questions testing their comprehension of instructions regarding the McNaughton rule. Arens, Granfield, and Susman (1965) and Ogloff (1991) obtained similar results: Regardless of what insanity rule was used, college students showed very low rates of accurate recall and comprehension of crucial components in various insanity definitions.

The limited empirical evidence indicates that different standards of insanity make little difference in verdicts. Simon (1967) presented mock juries with re-creations of two actual trials in which the insanity defense had been used; one was a charge of housebreaking, the other incest. A third of the juries received the McNaughton rule, a third the Durham rule, and a third no instructions about how to define insanity (although they knew the defendant was using this as his defense). In both trials, jurors operating with the McNaughton rule were less likely to vote for acquittal (although the differences between conditions were not large). The Durham rule seemed to produce verdicts more in keeping with the jurors' "natural sense of equity," as reflected in their judgments without any instructions at all. Interestingly, at least half of the uninstructed and Durham juries brought up the defendant's ability to distinguish between right and wrong—the McNaughton standard—during their deliberations. This latter finding suggests that, although instructions have some effect on jury decision making in insanity cases, they tell only part of the story—and perhaps a minor part at that (Finkel, 1989,

1991; Finkel & Slobogin, 1995; Ogloff, 1991; Roberts & Golding, 1991; Roberts, Golding, & Fincham, 1987).

Probably more important than formal instructions are jurors' own views or schemata through which they interpret and filter the evidence and then reach verdicts that are compatible with their own personal sense of justice. This decision process is yet another example of how jurors are prone to interpret "facts" in the context of a personal story or narrative that "makes the most sense" to each of them subjectively. Differences among jurors in the individual narratives they weave about the same set of trial "facts" may be related in turn to the different attitudes they hold about the morality of the insanity defense and the punishment of mentally ill offenders (Roberts & Golding, 1991).

In general, it appears that jurors are more likely to find a defendant not guilty by reason of insanity when they (1) believe the defendant is seriously mentally ill, to the point of lacking the capacity to plan and control his or her behavior; (2) hear expert testimony, uncontradicted by a prosecution expert, about the defendant's mental illness; and (3) find no logical or evil motive for the defendant's actions (see, e.g., Bailis, Darley, Waxman, & Robinson, 1995). In addition, jurors are flexible in how they use such personal constructs, emphasizing different variables in different cases rather than seeing all insanity cases in the same way. As an example, jurors appear more likely to believe that defendants are insane if they hear evidence that an offense was committed in a particularly unusual or bizarre manner (Pickel, 1998).

## Famous Trials and the Use of the Insanity Plea

Is the insanity plea a frequent problem in the American criminal justice system? Are many defendants getting off scot-free by using it? One reason for the congressional action to alter the federal standard was the public perception, generated largely by the verdict in John Hinckley's trial, that too many criminals were escaping punishment through this defense. Several surveys over the last 20 years have concluded that most U.S. citizens view the insanity defense as a legal loophole through which many guilty people escape conviction (Bower, 1984; Hans & Slater, 1983). Before reporting on the actual frequency and effectiveness of attempts to use the plea, we review the results of several highly publicized trials that have molded public opinion about insanity pleas.

*Trials in which the insanity plea failed.* Among murder defendants who have pleaded insanity as a defense were Jack Ruby, who millions saw kill Lee Harvey Oswald, President John F. Kennedy's alleged assassin, on television; Sirhan Sirhan, charged with the assassination of Robert F. Kennedy; and John Wayne Gacy, who was convicted of killing 33 boys in Chicago. All these defendants were convicted of murder despite their pleas of insanity.

More recently, in the sensational case of Jeffrey Dahmer (described in Chapter 5), jurors rejected a plea of insanity as a defense against murder charges. Dahmer admitted killing and dismembering 15 young men over about a ten-year period, but his attorney, Gerald Boyle, claimed that Dahmer was insane at the time: "This is not an evil man, this is a sick man." Predictably, prosecutor E. Michael McCann disagreed, arguing that Dahmer "knew at all times that what he was doing was wrong." After listening to two weeks of evidence and expert testimony about Dahmer's mental condition, the jury ruled, by a 10–2 margin, that Jeffrey Dahmer was sane. He was subsequently sentenced to life in prison for his crimes, only to be beaten to death in prison by a fellow inmate.

Wisconsin defines insanity with the ALI rule; consequently, to have found Dahmer insane, the jury would have had to conclude that he suffered a mental disorder or defect that made him unable either to appreciate the wrongfulness of his conduct or to control his conduct as required by the law. The jury rejected both conclusions, perhaps because of evidence that Dahmer was careful to kill his victims in a manner that minimized his chances of being caught. This cautiousness suggested that he appreciated the wrongfulness of his behavior *and* could control it when it was opportune to do so.

In the case of Herbert Mullin, there seemed to be a basis for an acquittal on the ground of insanity, but the jury convicted him nonetheless (Lunde & Morgan, 1980). Between October 1972 and February 1973, Mullin killed 13 persons in the environs of Santa Cruz, California. There was no pattern among the victims: a derelict, a hitchhiking young woman, a priest in a church, four teenaged campers, a family. Mullin reported hearing voices. For example, on the day he was caught, before delivering a load of wood to his parents, he was "instructed" to kill a man he had never seen before.

Mullin also had a history of hospitalizations (one in 1969, another in 1970) and diagnoses of schizophrenia. A social psychologist, David Marlowe, had administered the Minnesota Multiphasic Personality Inventory and found that Mullin scored at very high levels on six out of ten clinical scales, suggesting a severe mental disorder. Marlowe concluded that Mullin suffered a "schizophrenic reaction, paranoid type." But at Mullin's trial, a psychiatrist, Joel Fort, testified for the prosecution that Mullin was legally sane at the time of the killings. Fort stated, "He knew the nature and quality of his actions and did specifically know that they were wrong" (quoted in Lunde & Morgan, 1980).

On the third day of deliberations, the jury found Mullin guilty of two counts of first-degree murder and eight counts of second-degree murder. The judge sentenced him to concurrent life terms for the first-degree murders and imposed consecutive sentences of five years to life for the eight second-degree murder convictions. He will be eligible for parole in the year 2020.

Another defendant who claimed insanity was Richard Herrin, the Yale graduate who brutally murdered his college sweetheart, Bonnie Garland, by splitting her head open with a hammer as she slept at her parents' home. Herrin claimed a "transient situational reaction," which his psychiatrist said was so different from his otherwise normal personality that the jury should not hold him responsible for murder (Gaylin, 1982). Although the jury rejected his plea, it found him guilty of manslaughter, not of murder—a verdict that left persons on both sides frustrated with the outcome (Meyer, 1982).

Richard Herrin's trial points up a key dilemma of the insanity defense. Herrin was a good person—modest, tolerant, and good humored. He had risen above his illegitimate birth and his upbringing in an East Los Angeles barrio to graduate from Yale University. When Bonnie Garland, his sweetheart for almost three years, told him that she wanted to date other men, he suddenly decided to kill her and then commit suicide. Afterward, he could describe the act with amazing precision, but he reported no emotion while committing it and no understanding of why he had done it.

To many people, Herrin's behavior was incomprehensible; "he must have been crazy" was their gut reaction to the bludgeoning. Some kind of psychiatric explanation for this type of behavior is almost inevitable. But in succumbing to the temptation to always define extreme behavior in psychological terms, we lose sight of the legal responsibility that juries have to assess criminality and provide justice (Robinson, 1982). Thousands of seriously mentally ill people live disoriented and disrupted lives, but they never murder anyone. Yet, when we think of their behavior exclusively in psychological terms, we are tempted to sympathize and perhaps overlook the fact that psychological problems do not usually rob individuals of responsibility for their actions.

Several other famous defendants who might have attempted to escape conviction through use of the insanity plea did not do so. Among these are Son of Sam serial murderer David Berkowitz, cult leader Charles Manson, and Mark David Chapman, who killed John Lennon.

*Trials in which the insanity plea "succeeded."* Occasionally, when a jury concludes that the defendant is not guilty by reason of insanity, the defendant spends only a short period of time in a treatment program. After being acquitted on charges of malicious wounding (for cutting off her husband's penis), Lorena Bobbitt was released from the mental hospital after only several weeks of evaluation.

But sometimes when the insanity plea "works," the defendant spends more time in an institution than he or she would have spent in prison if found guilty. In fact, this outcome has led defense attorneys to request that judges be required to instruct jurors that, if the defendant is found not guilty by reason of insanity, he or she will probably be committed to a mental hospital (Whittemore & Ogloff, 1995). The Supreme Court, however, has refused to require such an instruction (*Shannon v. United States*, 1994).

Anthony Kiritsis was an Indianapolis businessman who in 1977 strapped a shotgun to the head of a mortgage banker who was planning to foreclose on Kiritsis's real estate project. Kiritsis was found not guilty of kidnapping by reason of insanity and committed to the hospital ward of the Indiana State Reformatory at Pendleton. As of last report, Kiritsis remained in the state institution; he regards himself as a "political prisoner." Had he been convicted of kidnapping or plea-bargained for a lesser charge, it is quite likely he would be a free man today.

Ed Gein, another serial killer from Wisconsin, was acquitted by reason of insanity on multiple charges involving the mutilation, skinning, and murder of at least two women in the 1950s around Plainfield, Wisconsin. Gein admitted to other atrocious crimes, including robbing bodies from graves; he later made the corpse parts into ornaments and clothes that he wore to re-create the image of his dead mother. Gein, who was the real-life inspiration for several Hollywood films (including *Psycho* and *Silence of the Lambs*), was committed to a state psychiatric hospital, where he remained until his death in 1984.

The trial of John W. Hinckley Jr. is, of course, the single case that triggered much of the court reform and legislative revision regarding the insanity plea. Television replays show his March 30, 1981, attempt to kill President Ronald Reagan.

## THE CASE OF

**BOX 11-5**  John W. Hinckley Jr.

The defense in John Hinckley's trial made several claims:

1. Hinckley's actions had reflected his pathological obsession with the movie *Taxi Driver,* in which Jodie Foster starred as a 12-year-old prostitute. The title character, Travis Bickle, is a loner who is rejected by Foster; he stalks the president and engages in a bloody shootout to rescue the Foster character. It was reported that Hinckley had seen the movie 15 times and that he so identified with the hero that he had been driven to reenact the fictional events in his own life (Winslade & Ross, 1983).

2. Although there appeared to be planning on Hinckley's part, it was really the movie script that provided the planning force.

The defense argued, "A mind that is so influenced by the outside world is a mind out of control and beyond responsibility" (Winslade & Ross, 1983, p. 188).

3. The expert witnesses generally agreed that Hinckley was suffering from schizophrenia.

4. The defense tried to introduce the results of a CAT scan—an X ray of Hinckley's brain using computerized axial tomography—to support its contention that he was schizophrenic. The admissibility of this evidence became a controversy at the trial. The prosecution objected, claiming that all the apparent scientific rigor of this procedure—the physical evidence, the numerical responses—would cause the jury to place undue importance on it. The

*John W. Hinckley Jr.*

prosecution also contended that there are no grounds for concluding that the presence of abnormal brain tissue necessarily denotes schizophrenia. Initially, the judge rejected the request to admit this testimony, but he later reversed the decision on the ground that it might be relevant.

When Hinckley came to trial 15 months later, his lawyers didn't dispute the evidence that he had planned the attack, bought special bullets, tracked the president, and fired from a shooter's crouch. But he couldn't help it, they claimed; he was only responding to the driving forces of a diseased mind. (◆ Box 11-5 summarizes the details of the defense's case.) Dr. William Carpenter, one of the defense psychiatrists, testified that Hinckley did not "appreciate" what he was doing; he had lost the ability to control himself.

Even though the Hinckley case is one in which the insanity defense was successful in the narrow sense of the word, that outcome was largely a result of a decision by the presiding judge

regarding the burden of proof. Judge Barrington Parker instructed the jury in accordance with then-existing federal law, which required the prosecution to prove the defendant sane beyond a reasonable doubt, rather than with the law of the District of Columbia (which has its own penal code), which would have placed the burden on the defendant to prove insanity. After listening to two months of testimony, the Hinckley jury deliberated for four days before finding the defendant not guilty by reason of insanity. Afterward, several jurors said that, given the instruction that it was up to the government prosecutors to prove Hinckley sane, the evidence was too conflicting for them to agree. They thought his travel meanderings raised a question about his sanity, and both sides' expert psychiatric witnesses had testified that he suffered from some form of mental disorder.

What types of defendants use the insanity plea successfully? The public tends to assume such people are of three types: "mad killers" who attack victims without provocation; "crafty cons" who fake symptoms to escape conviction; or "desperate defendants," aware of the strength of the evidence, who use the insanity defense as a last resort (Sales & Hafemeister, 1984). The empirical data do not support these assumptions. The insanity defense is not used only for murder or attempted murder charges, as assumed (Pasewark & Pantle, 1981); one study noted that in Oregon and Missouri, only one of ten such pleas was for the crime of murder (Sales & Hafemeister, 1984). Usually, the charges do involve violent felonies, but this is not always the case.

The crafty con charge is also questionable. Available research consistently suggests that the majority of defendants found not guilty by reason of insanity (NGRI) have been diagnosed as psychotic, suggesting severe and probably chronic mental impairments (Melton et al., 1997). Insanity acquittees do not appear to be especially "crafty"; in fact, one study revealed that defendants found NGRI had significantly lower IQ scores than men who pleaded insanity but were convicted (Boehnert, 1989).

Another approach to the crafty con question is to study how often criminal defendants being assessed for insanity try to fake a mental disorder. On the basis of his research, Rogers (1986, 1988) estimates that about one of four or five defendants being assessed for insanity engages in at least moderate malingering of mental disorders. This figure suggests that crafty conning is not rampant, but it is frequent enough to cause concern. As a result, psychologists have developed a number of assessment methods to detect persons who are trying to fake a mental disorder. These methods include special structured interviews (Rogers, Gillis, Dickens, & Bagby, 1991), individual psychological tests (Wetter, Baer, Berry, Smith, & Larsen, 1992), and batteries of differ-

ent tests (Schretlen, Wilkins, Van Gorp, & Bobholz, 1992).

In several laboratory studies, these techniques have shown promising results in differentiating between subjects who were trying to simulate mental illness (to win monetary incentives for being the "best" fakers) and those who were reporting symptoms truthfully. In a careful study that was limited to the court records of a single county, Steadman, Keitner, Braff, and Arvanites (1983) were able to compare defendants who were successful and unsuccessful in their pleas of insanity. The factor most strongly associated with success was the outcome of a court-authorized mental examination before the trial. When this evaluation concluded that the defendant was insane, in 83% of cases the charges were dismissed or the defendant was later found at a trial to be not guilty by reason of insanity. If the mental examination concluded that the offender was sane, in only 2% of the trials did the insanity defense "work." ◆ **Box 11-6** lists several other characteristics that are typical of defendants who have been acquitted on the basis of an insanity defense.

## Facts about the Insanity Plea

The American public has repeatedly expressed its dissatisfaction with the insanity defense. After John Hinckley was found NGRI for the shooting of President Reagan and four other men in 1982, a public opinion poll conducted by ABC News showed that 67% of Americans believed that justice had not been done in the case; 90% thought Hinckley should be confined for life, but 78% believed he would eventually be released back into society.

The public's disapproval of the insanity defense appears to be stimulated by trials such as Hinckley's that receive massive publicity. Melton et al. (1997) report the following four beliefs to be prevalent among the public: (1) a large number of criminal defendants use the insanity defense, (2) most of those defendants who use the insanity defense are acquitted by juries who are too gullible about it, (3) those defendants found

## The Science of

**BOX 11-6    The insanity defense: Characteristics of insane defendants**

On the basis of research studies, we are beginning to replace misconceptions about defendants found NGRI with more accurate portrayals of these defendants. This research paints the following picture of the typical insane defendant:

1.  Most NGRI defendants have a record of prior arrests or convictions, but this rate of previous criminality does not exceed that of other felons (Boehnert,

1989; Cohen, Spodak, Silver, & Williams, 1988).

2.  Most NGRI defendants come from lower socioeconomic backgrounds (Nicholson, Norwood, & Enyart, 1991).

3.  Most NGRI defendants have a prior history of psychiatric hospitalizations and have been diagnosed with serious forms of mental illness, usually psychoses (Nicholson et al., 1991).

4.  Most NGRI defendants have previously been found incom-

petent to stand trial (Boehnert, 1989).

5.  Although most studies have concentrated on males, female defendants found NGRI have similar socioeconomic, psychiatric, and criminal backgrounds to their male NGRI counterparts (Heilbrun, Heilbrun, & Griffin, 1988).

NGRI are released back into society shortly after their trials, and (4) persons found insane are extremely dangerous.

How accurate are these views? Are they myths or realities? We'll now review data concerning each of these questions.

*How often is the plea used, and how often is it successful?*    The plea is used a lot less than people assume. A study in Wyoming showed that people assumed that the insanity plea was a ploy used in nearly half of all criminal cases and that it was successful in one of five cases (Pasewark & Pantle, 1981). The actual figures: It was pleaded by only 102 of 22,102 felony defendants (about 1 in every 200 cases) and was successful only once in those 102 times. A survey of the use of the insanity defense in eight states between 1976 and 1985 found that although the public estimated that the insanity defense was used in 37% of the cases, the actual rate was only 0.9% (Silver, Cirincione, & Steadman, 1994).

Juries appear especially reluctant to find violent offenders NGRI out of fear that they will be

released and repeat their violent acts. Although few individual states keep complete records on the use of the insanity plea and its relative success, Silver et al.'s (1994) survey found that the overall success rate of the insanity defense was 26%. This means that of the nine insanity pleas raised in every 1000 cases, about two will be successful. Given the interest and debate that swirls around the insanity defense, it is surprising that so few empirical studies have been conducted about its actual outcomes. One recent attempt to study this issue is summarized in ◆ Box 11-7.

*What happens to defendants who are found NGRI?*    People mistakenly assume that defendants who are found NGRI go scot-free. We have seen Anthony Kiritsis's situation. It is doubtful that John Hinckley will be released from custody in the near future (although a federal court has ruled that he be allowed to make brief home visits to his family). Steadman and Braff (1983) found that defendants acquitted on the basis of the insanity plea in New York had an average hospital stay of three years. During the period studied, the

# The Science of

### BOX 11-7    The insanity defense: How successful is it?

To answer the question of how many people are acquitted by reason of insanity each year, Carmen Cirincione and Charles Jacobs (1999) contacted officials in all 50 states and asked for the number of insanity acquittals statewide between the years 1970 and 1995. After dogged attempts to collect these data from a variety of sources, they received at least partial data from 36 states. Few states could provide information for the entire 25-year period, but the following results were obtained:

◆ The median number of insanity acquittals per state per year was 17.7.

◆ California and Florida had the highest annual averages (134 and 111, respectively); New Mexico (0.0) and South Dakota (0.1) had the lowest.

◆ Most of the acquittals were for felonies rather than misdemeanors.

Of greatest interest is whether there has been any trend in the frequency of insanity acquittals. Are they becoming more common, or is the volume decreasing? Figure 11.2 shows the median number of successful insanity defenses per 100,00 people between 1970 and 1995. There appears to

be a steady increase from 1970 to 1981, followed by a gradual decline. Might this finding point to a "Hinckley effect"—a decrease in insanity acquittals that can be traced to reforms in insanity defense laws and the public outcry that followed John Hinckley's insanity acquittal in 1982? Whatever the interpretation, we can safely conclude that the number of insanity acquittals represents an extremely small percentage of defendants on trial.

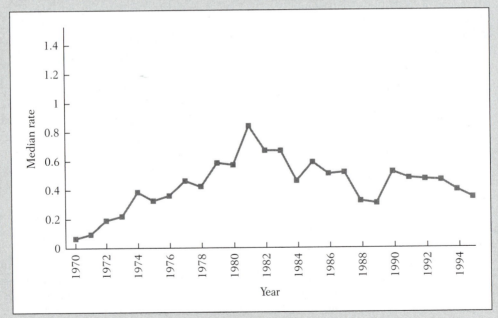

**FIGURE 11.2**  *Insanity acquittals per 100,000 people*
SOURCE: Cirincione and Jacobs (1999, p. 494).

average length of hospitalization was increasing. These researchers also found a clear trend for longer detentions of defendants who had committed more serious offenses.

In general, researchers are interested in finding answers to two basic questions: Are defendants who are acquitted of crimes on the basis of insanity released from confinement after a verdict more often that those who are convicted? Are defendants found not guilty by reason of insanity confined for shorter periods than defendants who are found guilty of similar crimes? The previously described survey of the use of the insanity defense across several states, covering nearly one million felony indictments between 1976 and 1985, sought answers to these two questions (Silver, 1995). Based on more than 8000 defendants who pleaded insanity during this period, Silver (1995) found that

- defendants found guilty were actually more likely to be released from confinement than were defendants acquitted on the grounds of insanity;
- compared to convicted defendants, insanity acquittees spent less time in confinement in four states and more time in confinement in three states;
- in all seven states, the more serious the crime, the longer the confinement for those found not guilty by reason of insanity.

One reason why insanity acquittees do not usually serve shorter terms of confinement than those convicted of comparable crimes is that many states follow a procedure of automatically committing persons found NGRI to a mental institution and then releasing them only when a judge is convinced that they can be released safely. A problem with these procedures is that the criteria for release are often more restrictive than those for the usual civil commitment and perhaps intentionally guarantee longer confinements. In the 1992 case of *Foucha v. Louisiana,* however, the Supreme Court held that it is unconstitutional for a state to continue to hold a de-

fendant who is no longer mentally ill and dangerous. This is the usual test for civil commitment.

Some states use a procedure known as *conditional release,* in which persons found NGRI are released to the community (following a period of hospital confinement) and are monitored and supervised by mental health personnel. Conditional release is the mental-health system's counterpart to parole; it functions essentially like a form of outpatient commitment. According to one four-state follow-up of 529 persons found NGRI, about 60% of these individuals were conditionally released within five years of their confinement. Of those released, the median period of hospital confinement was 3.6 years for violent offenders and 1.3 years for those charged with less serious offenses.

*How dangerous are defendants found NGRI?*
Because most defendants who are found NGRI are quickly committed to an institution following their acquittal, it is difficult to assess how dangerous they are at that time. In addition, they are likely to receive treatment in the hospital to which they are committed, further complicating the question of how dangerous they would have been without this treatment. What evidence is available on this question points to either no difference in recidivism rates between NGRI defendants and "regular" felons or slightly lower recidivism rates among the NGRI group (Cohen, Spodak, Silver, & Williams, 1988; Melton et al., 1997). Nicholson, Norwood, and Enyart (1991) collected data on 61 defendants found NGRI in Oklahoma; this group constituted the entire population of NGRI defendants over a five-year period who had been treated in the state forensic hospital. Follow-up of persons released from custody indicated that, within two years, half of the discharged patients had been either rearrested or rehospitalized. Thus, insanity acquittees continue to have legal and/or psychiatric problems, but their overall rate of criminal recidivism falls in the range found for criminals in general.

Whether the period of hospital commitment and treatment following an acquittal has any benefits for persons found NGRI is not certain; some studies show that individuals who complete a treatment program do better than those who go AWOL from the institution (Nicholson et al., 1991), but another study reported no differences between regularly discharged acquittees and those who escaped from the institution (Pasewark, Bieber, Bosten, Kiser, & Steadman, 1982).

## Current Criticisms of the Insanity Defense

Even if the insanity defense is not successful as often as presumed, legitimate concerns remain about its continued use. Several of these will now be evaluated.

### It sends criminals and troublemakers to hospitals and then frees them.    For example, E. E. Kemper III murdered his grandparents and then spent five years in a California hospital for the criminally insane. He was released in 1970; three years later, he petitioned to have his psychiatric records sealed. After psychiatrists examined Kemper and found him sane, the judge agreed to the request. The authorities were not aware that, since his release, he had murdered his mother and seven other women—one of them only three days before the court decision. Most of the bodies had been dismembered. Kemper, it was later claimed, had memorized the responses to 28 standardized psychological tests so that he could appear to give "well-adjusted" answers (Gleick, 1978, p. 23).

Psychopathic killers can try to capitalize on the insanity plea to escape prison and eventually get released from the hospital. How often this happens is unknown, but as we have already discussed, the available data indicate that persons found NGRI may be confined more frequently and for longer periods than defendants convicted of similar crimes (Perlin, 1996). After such confinement, they also may undergo an additional period of conditional release. In addition, NGRI defendants tend to be no more or no less dangerous following their release than non-NGRI felons (NGRI persons who escape from the hospital may pose a higher risk of danger to the community).

Some would say that, even if the preceding examples were the only ones, they would be too many. The real problem with such incidents is that they contribute to the public's perception that these outcomes "happen all the time" and that the insanity defense is therefore a constant threat to justice. Such incidents do not happen all the time; in fact, they are rare. Furthermore, in the interest of protecting society, if all NGRI defendants were kept hospitalized until they no longer showed symptoms of mental illness, then society would have to be willing to violate the rights of many mentally ill persons to protect against the violence of a few.

### It is a defense only for the rich.    The parents of John W. Hinckley Jr. spent between $500,000 and $1,000,000 on psychiatric examinations and expert psychiatric testimony in their son's trial—an amount that contributes to the perception of the insanity defense as a jail dodge for the rich. Of all the criticisms leveled at the insanity defense, this one is perhaps most contradicted by the data. A long line of studies have failed to find socioeconomic or racial bias in the use or the success of the insanity defense (Boehnert, 1989; Howard & Clark, 1985; Nicholson et al., 1991; Pasewark & Pantle, 1981; Steadman et al., 1983). In addition, this criticism is further weakened by the Supreme Court's 1985 ruling, in the case of *Ake v. Oklahoma,* that poor defendants who plead insanity are entitled to psychiatric assistance at state expense in pursuing this defense. Although defendants who can afford more than one expert might be more likely to benefit from raising the issue of insanity, this is not a problem unique to the insanity defense. Defendants who can afford to hire ballistic experts, chemists, and their own private detectives also have an advantage over poor defendants, but no one suggests that a defense relying on ballistic evidence, blood analyses, or mistaken identity should be prohibited because of the expense.

### It relies too much on psychiatric experts.    Several issues are pertinent here. One criticism is that testifying about insanity forces psychiatrists

and clinical psychologists to give opinions about things they are not competent or trained to do—for example, to express certainty rather than probability about a person's mental condition, to predict future dangerous behavior, and to claim greater knowledge about the relationship between psychological research and legal questions than is justified.

Psychologists themselves are sharply divided on these matters. Their debate centers on three related questions: (1) Can clinicians reliably and validly diagnose mental illness? (2) Will these diagnoses permit accurate opinions about a defendant's criminal responsibility for acts committed in the past? (3) Assuming that the answers to the first two questions are yes, are psychologists any more expert or capable of answering these questions than nonprofessionals? A number of respected psychologists are skeptical about psychology's expertise on these issues and have challenged their forensic colleagues to provide whatever supporting evidence they have (Dawes, 1994; Dawes, Faust, & Meehl, 1989; Ziskin & Faust, 1988).

Additionally, critics are concerned over the intrusion of psychiatry into the decision-making process. They want to reserve the decision for the judge or jury, the fact finder in the trial. This criticism is an example of the general concern (discussed in Chapter 2) over the use and willingness of experts to answer legal questions for which they possess limited scientific evidence. Again, some psychologists vigorously oppose the courts' reliance on mental-health experts' opinions about a defendant's status as insane or sane (Bonnie & Slobogin, 1980; Morse, 1978). In general, this opposition is grounded on the belief that psychology has not established its scientific expertise on the three questions just mentioned. Obviously, if one cannot show expertise, one should not testify as an expert. But even if we were to grant special expertise to psychologists, critics raise the additional objection that questions about a defendant's criminal responsibility for an act are properly answered only by jurors, not by expert witnesses.

One remedy proposed to solve this problem is to prevent experts from giving what is often called **ultimate opinion testimony;** that is, they could describe a defendant's mental condition and the effects it could have had on his or her thinking and behavioral control, but they could not state conclusions about whether the defendant was sane or insane. As we discuss next, the federal courts, as part of their reforms of the insanity defense, now prohibit mental-health experts from offering ultimate opinion testimony about a defendant's insanity. But does this prohibition solve any problems, or is it, in the words of Rogers and Ewing (1989), merely a "cosmetic fix" that has few effects (see ◆ Box 11-8)?

Finally, there is the feeling that the process holds mental-health professionals up to ridicule. When the jury sees and the public reads about a parade of mental-health experts representing one side and then the other, their confidence in the behavioral sciences is jeopardized (Slater & Hans, 1984). Further, some experts, in an effort to help the side that has retained them, offer explanations of such an untestable nature that their profession loses its credibility with jurors and the public. However, in many cases involving claims of insanity, the experts retained by each side basically agree on the question of insanity. These cases receive less publicity because they often end in a plea agreement.

## Revisions and Reforms of the Insanity Defense

Several reforms in the rules and procedures for implementing the insanity defense have been introduced, but they have led to mixed outcomes. Proposals have ranged from abolition of the insanity defense (as has already been done in five states), to provision of a "guilty but mentally ill" verdict, to reform of insanity statutes, to maintenance of the present procedures. We review three reforms in this section.

### The guilty but mentally ill (GBMI) verdict.
Since 1976, about a quarter of the states have passed laws allowing juries to reach a verdict of guilty but mentally ill (GBMI) in cases in which

## The Science of

### BOX 11-8   The insanity defense: Do expert opinions matter?

In a study designed to answer the question of whether prohibiting ultimate opinion testimony affects jury decisions (Fulero & Finkel, 1991), subjects were randomly assigned to read one of ten different versions of a trial, in all of which the defendant was charged with murdering his boss and was pleading insanity as a defense. For our purposes, the comparisons among three different versions of the trial are of greatest interest: Some subjects read transcripts in which the mental- health experts for both sides gave only *diagnostic testimony* (that the defendant suffered a mental disorder at the time of the offense); a second group read a version in which the experts gave a diagnosis and then also offered differing *penultimate opinions* about the effects this disorder had on the defendant's understanding of the wrongfulness of his act; a final group read a transcript in which the experts offered differing diagnoses, penultimate opinions, and *ultimate opinion testimony* about whether the defendant was sane or insane at the time of the killing.

Did ultimate opinion testimony affect the subjects' verdicts? Not in this case; subjects' verdicts were not significantly different regardless of the type of testimony they received. The lack of difference could be interpreted as evidence that the prohibition of ultimate opinion testimony is unnecessary, or it could indicate that the ban streamlines the trial process without sacrificing any essential information.

---

a defendant pleads insanity. These GBMI rules differ from state to state, but generally they give a jury the option of finding a defendant who is pleading insanity the following verdict alternatives: (1) guilty of the crime, (2) not guilty of the crime, (3) NGRI, or (4) GBMI. Typically, a judge will sentence a defendant found GBMI exactly as he or she would the same defendant found guilty of the same offense. The intent is for the prisoner to start his or her term in a hospital and then be transferred to prison after treatment is completed.

Proponents of GBMI verdicts hoped that this compromise verdict would decrease the number of defendants found NGRI. Whether insanity acquittals have actually decreased as a result of GBMI legislation is highly questionable. Mock jury research consistently reveals that adding the GBMI option decreases NGRI verdicts (Roberts & Golding, 1991; Roberts, Sargent, & Chan, 1993). However, actual GBMI statutes have not produced decreases in NGRI verdicts in South Carolina or Michigan, although decreases were noted after GBMI laws were enacted in Georgia (Callahan, McGreevey, Cirincione, & Steadman, 1992) and Pennsylvania (see Roberts & Golding, 1991, for a discussion of the effects of this legislation on jury decisions).

Other problems have provoked a "second look" at the GBMI reform, leading to growing skepticism about its value (Borum & Fulero, 1999). If regular insanity instructions are confusing to jurors, the GBMI verdict only adds to the confusion by introducing the very difficult distinction for juries to make between mental illness that results in insanity and mental illness that does not. One possible effect of the GBMI verdict is that it raises jurors' threshold for what constitutes insanity, leading to a more stringent standard for acquitting defendants who use this defense (Roberts et al., 1993). Also, the claim that the GBMI option will make it more likely that mentally ill offenders will receive treatment is largely a bogus promise. Overcrowding at hospitals in most states has impeded implementation of this part of the GBMI option. In one Michigan study, 75% of GBMI offenders went straight to prison with no treatment (Sales & Hafemeister, 1984).

In Kentucky, in spite of a statute that appears to promise treatment to those found GBMI, the chair of the parole board filed an affidavit in 1991 stating that "from psychological evaluations and treatment summaries, the Board can detect no difference in treatment or outcome for inmates who have been adjudicated as 'Guilty But Mentally Ill,' from those who have been adjudicated as simply 'guilty'" (Runda, 1991).

Finally, the opportunity to be found GBMI and then treated (in states where there is a difference in treatment opportunities) is available only to defendants who themselves first raise an insanity defense. An equally disturbed defendant who does not claim insanity cannot be found GBMI. Somewhat similar to the GBMI concept is the diminished-capacity defense, which is discussed in ◆ Box 11-9.

*The Insanity Defense Reform Act.* In the wake of the John Hinckley trial, the U.S. Congress enacted the Insanity Defense Reform Act (IDRA) in 1984. The main purpose of this law was to limit the insanity defense so that fewer defendants would be able to use it successfully. The law did not abolish the insanity defense, but it changed the way the defense could be used in the federal system in the following three ways:

1. It did away with the so-called volitional prong of the Brawner rule. Therefore, the definition of insanity in the federal system and in several states is now restricted to the cognitive portion of the defense; that is, as a result of mental illness the defendant lacks the capacity to appreciate the nature and quality or the wrongfulness of his or her acts. Without the volitional part of the defense, the test is now essentially a restatement of McNaughton.

2. It prohibited experts from giving ultimate opinions about insanity. The rule states, "[N]o expert witness testifying with respect to the mental state or condition of a defendant in a criminal case may state an opinion or inference as to whether the defendant did or did not have the mental state or condition constituting an element of the crime charged or of a defense thereto. Such ultimate issues are matters for the trier of fact alone." Although this prohibition may have little effect on jurors, reformers believed it would prevent expert witnesses from usurping the province of the jury.

3. It placed the burden on the defendant to prove insanity by clear and convincing evidence rather than on the prosecution to disprove insanity. What little research has been conducted on the Insanity Defense Reform Act suggests that it does not accomplish either what its proponents envisioned or what its critics feared. At least in mock jury studies, verdicts do not significantly differ regardless of whether the jurors have heard IDRA instructions, ALI (Brawner) instructions, or no instructions (Finkel, 1989).

*Elimination of the insanity plea.* Winslade and Ross (1983) reviewed seven trials (mostly for murder) in which the insanity defense was used and psychiatric testimony was introduced to justify it. They conclude that the possibility of an insanity defense often leads to injustice for the following reasons:

1. Juries are asked to decide questions that predispose them to make arbitrary and emotional judgments because of either overidentification with or alienation from the defendant;
2. Psychiatrists and other mental-health professionals are encouraged to parade their opinions, guesses, and speculations under the banner of scientific expertise; and
3. Society's views about criminality and craziness are so intertwined that an insanity defense to a crime does not make much sense. (p. 198)

On the basis of their analysis of the outcomes of these trials, Winslade and Ross recommend that the insanity defense be eliminated.

A workable solution would require the elimination of the insanity plea; the elimination of any testimony by psychiatrists about the actual or theoretical state of the defendant's mind at the

**THE CASE OF**

BOX 11-9   Dan White: The law of diminished capacity

Several states allow a defense of **diminished capacity,** which is a legal doctrine that applies to defendants who lack the ability to commit a crime purposely and knowingly. Like the insanity defense, diminished capacity often involves evidence that the defendant suffers a mental disorder. It differs from insanity in that it focuses on whether defendants had the state of mind to act with the purpose and intent to commit a crime—that is, to think through the consequences of their contemplated actions—not on whether they knew the crime was wrong or whether they could control their behavior. Suppose McNaughton knew that murder was wrong but, because of his mental condition, wasn't thinking clearly enough to intend to kill Peel's secretary. Under these conditions, he would not be insane, but he would lack the *mens rea* for first-degree murder; so he probably would have been convicted of second-degree murder or manslaughter.

The rationale for this defense is simple: Offenders should be convicted of the crime that matches their mental state, and expert testimony should be offered on the issue of their mental state. Even when the diminished-capacity defense "works," it still usually leads to a prison sentence.

In 1979, the Dan White trial brought national publicity to the plea of diminished capacity. Dan White was tried for killing George Moscone, the mayor of San Fran-

cisco, and Harvey Milk, a San Francisco city supervisor. The killings were clearly premeditated. White had resigned his $9600-a-year supervisor position because of its low pay and then decided he wanted it back, only to learn from the mayor that it was no longer available. Several days later (on November 27, 1978), he loaded the .38 Smith & Wesson revolver that he had owned since his days on the police force, wrapped ten extra bullets in a handkerchief, and headed for the mayor's office. He slipped through a city hall window to avoid a metal detector at the main entrance. He pumped nine bullets into Moscone and Milk, his opponent on the board. Some shots were fired point-blank as White leaned over their prostrate bodies.

Although Dan White did not take the witness stand in his own defense, his attorneys argued that his mental abilities had been impaired by a steady diet of junk food that produced a chemical imbalance in his brain—the so-called Twinkie defense. He was also depressed, they said, because of his financial status and the political maneuvering. His "diminished capacity" left him unable to premeditate, deliberate, or harbor malice. Therefore, he lacked the *mens rea,* or criminal intent, necessary to be convicted of first-degree murder. Four psychiatrists and one psychologist testified to this effect.

After the jury found him guilty of voluntary manslaughter—the

least serious charge possible—there were angry protests, especially in the homosexual community, for which Harvey Milk had been an advocate. White was sentenced to seven years and eight months in prison, but he served less than five years. (Had he been found guilty of premeditated murder, his actual time served in prison would probably have been about 13 years.) He was released from Soledad Prison on January 6, 1984, and ordered to live in Los Angeles County (and avoid San Francisco) during his one-year parole. White committed suicide in October 1985.

In June 1982, a proposition to abolish the diminished-capacity defense was overwhelmingly passed by the voters of California (that state still permits defendants to use a McNaughton-based insanity defense), and several other states have either outlawed the diminished-capacity defense or do not allow expert testimony about it. In general, however, the majority of states permit expert testimony about a defendant's *mens rea,* thereby allowing clinicians to present testimony that could be used in support of a diminished-capacity defense (Melton et al., 1997). As long as proof of a defendant's *mens rea* is required, defendants are likely to put forward expert evidence about it, especially in those states that have abolished an affirmative insanity defense.

time of the crime; the elimination of psychiatric expert witnesses in the guilt phase of the trial; and the requirement of a two-phase trial that would, in its first phase establish guilt or innocence of the commission of the crime with no concern for the individual's state of mind in terms of mental illness at the time the crime was committed. The second phase of the trial, if guilt were found, would address itself to the appropriate disposition of the defendant. (p. 219)

In the second part of the trial, if a defendant claimed mental illness, he or she would be required to testify. The judge would permit psychiatrists to testify as expert witnesses, but only to report on previous clinical assessments, not to predict the defendant's future behavior. Psychiatrists representing state institutions would also be required to testify about the likelihood of rehabilitating the defendant; they would be asked to specify at least a minimum duration of treatment. Combinations of hospitalization and incarceration, in Winslade and Ross's proposal, would be based on the defendant's amenability to treatment.

*Arguments against eliminating the plea.* At the opposite end of the continuum is the position of James Kunen (1983), a former public defender, who proposes that "guilty but mentally ill" is logically impossible. He explains his opposition to states that have adopted this verdict, such as Michigan (the first, in 1975) and Georgia:

> Such legislation represents a radical departure from Anglo-American legal tradition, which for centuries has required that to convict someone of a crime, the prosecution must prove not only that he did a particular act—such as pulling a trigger—but that he did it with a particular state of mind. . . . "Guilty but insane" is a contradiction in terms, because insane means not capable of forming a criminal intent, not responsible, and, therefore, not guilty. (p. 157)

Kunen's comments are especially useful in distinguishing between commission of an act and guilt. Winslade and Ross (1983) confound these

terms when, in their proposal quoted earlier, they advocate an initial phase of a trial to "establish guilt or innocence of the commission of the crime with no concern for the individual's state of mind" (p. 219). As Kunen notes, we cannot talk about guilt without bringing in the person's state of mind. If a defendant slashes his victim's throat, thinking that he is slicing a cucumber, we say that he committed an act but not that he was guilty of the intent to commit a crime. This is why even in those few states that have abolished the insanity defense defendants may still introduce evidence that they lacked the mental state required for the crime.

Some offenders are truly "not guilty by reason of insanity"; they do not know the "nature and quality of their acts"—they literally do not know what they are doing. Harvard law professor Alan Dershowitz has said, "I almost would be in favor of abolishing the insanity defense, except there really are a few genuinely crazy people who believe they're squeezing lemons when they're actually squeezing throats" (quoted in Footlick, 1978, p. 108). The actual number of such people is much smaller, of course, than the number who raise the NGRI defense.

We believe that the NGRI plea should be maintained as an option, and modifications of the system should be restricted to those that clarify the rule and later evaluate those for whom it is successful. For example, the federal government has already acted to change the law that formerly put the burden of proof on the prosecution to prove beyond a reasonable doubt that John Hinckley was not insane. If an act similar to Hinckley's were committed today in a federal jurisdiction and in the vast majority of states, the defendant, not the prosecution, would bear the responsibility of proving his plea; otherwise, he would be found guilty.

It is legally acceptable for an NGRI defendant to be confined to a hospital longer than a guilty defendant remains in prison for the same crime. Michael Jones was accused of shoplifting a coat in 1974; he "successfully" used the NGRI defense. He was still in St. Elizabeth's Hospital in 1983 when the Supreme Court, hearing his appeal, ruled that such commitments in excess of the maximum sentence are legal. States should carefully monitor people committed after NGRI verdicts to ensure that they are not released while still mentally ill and dangerous. All indications are that this is being done. In fact, it is likely that some NGRI defendants are now unconstitutionally locked up because they are no longer mentally ill and dangerous (*Foucha v. Louisiana*, 1992).

## SUMMARY

**1.** *What is the scope of forensic psychology?* Forensic psychology is a specialty involving the application of knowledge and techniques from the behavioral sciences to answer questions about individuals involved in legal proceedings. The range of topics about which psychological and psychiatric experts are asked to testify continues to grow despite both professional concerns and public skepticism about the validity of such testimony.

**2.** *What is meant by competence in the criminal justice process?* Adjudicative competence requires having a sufficient present ability to consult with one's attorney with a reasonable degree of rational understanding and with a rational, as well as factual, understanding of the proceedings. This same standard is applied to the question of whether a defendant is competent to plead guilty and whether a defendant is competent to stand trial.

**3.** *How do clinicians assess competence?* When mental-health professionals assess a defendant's competence, they should use one of several special instruments designed specifically for the purpose of evaluating how well a defendant understands the charges and potential proceedings. These specific tests and structured interviews have made competence assessments more reliable, valid, and useful. Competency evaluations are sometimes complicated by such factors as malingering, amnesia, and the problem of whether incompetent defendants can be treated against their will. Other competence questions can arise at different points in the criminal process, and assessing the competence of juveniles is a special concern.

**4.** *What are the consequences of being found incompetent to proceed in the criminal justice process?* When defendants are found incompetent to stand trial, they can be committed for a period of treatment designed to restore their competence. If later found competent, they will stand trial. If treatment is not successful in restoring competence, the state will usually attempt to commit the person to a mental hospital for a period of time. Some proposed alternatives for how to deal with the permanently incompetent criminal defendant include waiving the right to be found incompetent to proceed to trial or using a special form of commitment for incompetent defendants who are judged at a provisional trial to be guilty of the crimes with which they are charged.

**5.** *What is the legal definition of insanity?* Two major definitions of insanity are used currently. The McNaughton rule defines insanity as not knowing the difference between right and wrong: "To establish a defense on the grounds of insanity it must be clearly proved that, at the time of committing the act, the accused was laboring under such a defect of reason, from disease of the mind, as not to know the nature and quality of the act he was doing, or, if he did know it, that he did not know what he was doing was wrong." In some jurisdictions, an "irresistible impulse" test has been added to the McNaughton rule.

In response to criticism of McNaughton, the federal government, from 1954 to 1972, used the

Durham rule: "that an accused is not criminally responsible if his unlawful act was the product of mental disease or mental defect." The Durham rule was supplanted by the Brawner rule, which states that a person is not responsible for a criminal act if, as a result of mental disease or defect, the person lacked "substantial capacity either to appreciate the criminality of his conduct or to conform his conduct to the requirements of the law."

The Brawner rule or a variation of it is the standard in about half the states. Until 1984, it was also the federal standard, but the federal system now requires the defense to show that, as a result of a severe mental disease or defect, the defendant was unable to appreciate the nature and quality or the wrongfulness of his or her acts. Five states have outlawed insanity as a defense, although these states still allow the defendant to put on evidence about his or her mental condition that is relevant to determining *mens rea*. Some highly publicized trials have led to "successful" use of the insanity defense. But many others who used this defense were found guilty.

**6.** *How frequently is the insanity defense used, and how successful is it?* The insanity plea is used much less frequently than people assume; it is tried in only about 9 of every 1000 cases, and it succeeds in only about 25% of these cases. When it does succeed, there is no guarantee that the defendant will be released from the hospital any more often or any sooner than he or she would have been paroled from prison.

**7.** *What are the major criticisms of the insanity defense, and what reforms have been attempted?* Some examples of early release of NGRI defendants have led to justified criticism of the procedure. Other criticisms are that insanity cannot be reliably and validly assessed and that the insanity defense relies too much on psychiatric testimony.

Reforms include the Insanity Defense Reform Act and the adoption in several states of a "guilty but mentally ill" verdict, resulting (at least in theory) in the defendant's being treated in a state hospital until releasable and then serving the rest of the sentence in prison. A number of states also allow the diminished-capacity plea, a partial defense based on mental condition. But it also has been controversial, and at least one state (California) that formerly allowed the defense no longer does so.

## KEY TERMS

| | | | |
|---|---|---|---|
| adjudicative competence | competence to plead guilty | insanity* | stipulate |
| affirmative defense | competence to stand trial | *mens rea* | ultimate opinion testimony |
| Brawner rule | | *nolo contendere* | |
| competence | diminished capacity | *parens patriae* | |
| | | product rule | |

---

 InfoTrac COLLEGE EDITION For additional readings go to **http://www.infotrac-college.com/wadsworth** and enter a search term related to your interest. The key term that has been asterisked above will pull up several related articles. *See also:* for *mens rea*, see CRIMINAL INTENT.

# Forensic Assessment in Civil Cases

## ORIENTING QUESTIONS

1. *Under what conditions can a plaintiff be compensated for psychological damages?*
2. *What is workers' compensation, and how do mental-health professionals participate in such cases?*
3. *What abilities are involved in civil competence?*
4. *What are psychological autopsies, and how are they used?*
5. *What criteria are used for decisions about child custody and parental fitness disputes?*
6. *How well can clinicians assess the risk of dangerousness, a key criterion for civil commitments?*
7. *What are the problems with expert testimony, and what reforms have been proposed?*

Whether a defendant is mentally competent to stand trial or was insane at the time of an alleged criminal offense are the most visible and controversial legal questions asked of mental-health professionals, but they are by no means the only questions. Throughout earlier chapters, we have examined other questions arising in the legal system that psychologists are often asked to assess. Is a given individual a good candidate for police work? Will a person who is suffering mental illness be dangerous in the future? How accurate is one's memory for, and testimony about, highly traumatic events likely to be? These questions—like those of competence and insanity—are often asked of forensic psychologists and psychiatrists, and they are usually answered based on a combination of research knowledge and the results of individual assessments performed by forensic clinicians.

Litigation of all sorts is making increased use of scientific knowledge and expert opinion. Psychology and psychiatry are two fields in which the use of experts has become most prolific. ◆ Box 12-1 gives just a partial listing of some of the topics that courts have permitted psychologists to testify about in recent years. Therefore, judges now find themselves more and more often in the position of having to decide whether the expert testimony that an attorney seeks to introduce at trial passes the criteria that the *Daubert* and *Kumho* cases (discussed in Chapters 2 and 11) have established as the modern standard for admitting scientific evidence and expert testimony.

In general, a qualified expert can testify about a topic if such testimony is relevant to an issue in dispute and if the usefulness of the testimony outweighs whatever prejudicial impact it might have. If these two conditions are met, an expert will be permitted to testify if the judge believes that the testimony is based on sufficiently relevant and reliable scientific evidence to be admitted. In other words, under the *Daubert/Kumho* criteria, the judge serves as a "gatekeeper" who must determine whether the theory, methodology, and analysis that are the basis of the expert's opinion measure up to scientific standards. If they

pass this standard, the judge will probably admit relevant expert testimony; if they do not, the judge should not allow the testimony. How well judges can perform this gatekeeper function is not certain (Mark, 1999). Many, if not most, judges lack the scientific training that *Daubert/ Kumho* appears to require; even with such training, the range of expert topics about which judges will need to be informed is staggering. As a result, many critics, including experts and judges themselves, believe that the difficulty of distinguishing valid from invalid scientific evidence will result in jurors too often being exposed to "expert" testimony that is based on little more than "junk science" (Grove & Barden, 1999; see also ◆ Box 12-2).

In this chapter, we describe six areas of forensic assessment in which forensic psychologists and psychiatrists are increasingly involved: (1) psychological damages to civil plaintiffs, (2) workers' compensation claims, (3) the assessment of civil competence, (4) psychological autopsies, (5) child custody and parental fitness, and (6) civil commitment and risk assessment. Although these areas do not rival the publicity commanded by criminal competence or claims of insanity, which were discussed in Chapter 11, they do illustrate several ways in which psychological expertise can be brought to bear on important legal questions. For each of the six areas, we will:

◆ Discuss the basic psycholegal questions experts are expected to address
◆ Describe the techniques typically used by forensic clinicians to evaluate these questions
◆ Summarize the empirical evidence and legal status associated with the forensic activity

## Psychological Damages to Civil Plaintiffs

When one party is injured by the actions of a second party, the injured individual can sue the second party to recover monetary damages as compensation for the injury. This action is covered by an area of civil law known as torts. A **tort**

**BOX 12-1**  **Topics for expert testimony in civil cases**

The following list contains some of the questions on which psychological testimony has been permitted in civil cases. This list continues to expand as attorneys and forensic experts create new opportunities to apply behavioral science knowledge to litigation issues.

1. Civil commitment — Does a mentally ill person present an immediate danger or threat of danger to self or others that requires treatment no less restrictive than hospitalization?

2. Psychological damages in civil cases — What psychological consequences has an individual suffered as a result of tortious conduct?

3. Psychological autopsies — How treatable are these consequences? To what extent are the psychological problems attributable to a preexisting condition?

4. Negligence and product liability — How do environmental factors and human perceptual abilities affect an individual's use of a product or ability to take certain precautions in its use?

5. Trademark litigation — Is a certain product name or trademark confusingly similar to a competitor's? Are advertising claims likely to mislead consumers?

6. Discrimination — What psychological evidence is there that equal treatment is being denied or that certain procedures and decisions discriminate against women or minorities in the schools or in the workplace?

---

is a wrongful act that causes harm to an individual. The criminal law also exacts compensation for wrong acts, but it does so on behalf of society as a whole; by punishing an offender, the criminal law attempts to maintain society's overall sense of justice. Tort law, on the other hand, provides a mechanism for individuals to redress the harms they have suffered from the wrongful acts by another party.

As illustrated by the O. J. Simpson case, both criminal punishment and civil remedies can be sought for the same act. Simpson was prosecuted by the state under the criminal law for murder;

he was also sued for money damages by the surviving relatives of the victims who alleged he caused the wrongful deaths of Nicole Brown Simpson and Ronald Goldman.

Many kinds of behavior can constitute a tort. Slander and libel are torts, as are cases of professional malpractice, invasion of privacy, the manufacture of defective products that result in a personal injury, and intentional or negligent behavior producing harm to another person.

Four elements are involved in proving a tort in a court of law. First, torts occur in situations in which one individual owes a **duty,** or has an obli-

| | | | |
|---|---|---|---|
| 7. Guardianship and conservatorship | Does an individual possess the necessary mental ability to make decisions concerning living conditions, financial matters, health, and so forth? Is the person competent to draw up a "living will"? These questions probably come up most often with older individuals who are suffering from various forms and degrees of dementia. | 9. Adoption and termination of parental rights | What psychological factors affect the best interests of a child whose parents' disabilities may render them unfit to raise and care for the child? |
| | | 10. Professional malpractice | Did a defendant's professional conduct fail to meet the standard of care owed to a plaintiff? |
| 8. Child custody | What psychological factors will affect the best interests of the child whose custody is in dispute? What consequences are these factors likely to have on the family? | 11. Social issues in litigation | What are the effects of pornography, violence, spouse abuse, and so forth, on the behavior of a person who claims that his or her misconduct was caused by one of these influences? What constitutes sexual harassment or a hostile work environment? |

SOURCE: Nietzel and Dillehay (1986).

gation, to another; a physician has a duty to treat patients in accordance with accepted professional standards, and individuals have a duty not to harm others physically or psychologically. Second, a tort typically requires proving that one party breached or violated a duty that was owed to other parties. The **breached duty** can be due to negligence or intentional wrongdoing. **Negligence** is behavior that falls below a standard for protecting others from unreasonable risks; it is often measured by asking whether a "reasonable person" would have acted as a civil defendant acted in similar circumstances. **Intentional be-**

**havior** refers to conduct in which a person meant the outcome of a given act to occur. In a third kind of tort, a party can be held strictly liable even without acting negligently or intentionally. This standard is often used in product liability cases. For example, if a company manufactures a product that harms an innocent user, it can be held liable for the harm even though the company was without fault.

Third, the violation of the duty had to constitute the proximate cause of the harm suffered by a plaintiff. A **proximate cause** is one that constitutes an obvious or substantial reason why a

## BOX 12-2  The Judas Priest trial: Expert opinion or junk science?

Can subliminal messages cause someone to commit suicide? This was the question at the center of a widely publicized 1990 trial involving the British heavy metal rock band Judas Priest. Two teenage boys, James Vance and Ray Belknap, had attempted suicide by shooting themselves. Belknap died immediately from the gunshot wounds he inflicted, but Vance survived, only to die three years later as a result of drug complications. The boys' parents sued the band and its record company, claiming that the band had embedded provocative lyrics—below the conscious threshold of recognition—in its 1978 album *Stained Class* and that these lyrics had led to their sons' suicidal impulses. The specific phrase in question consisted of only two words—"do it"—which allegedly were hidden in the song "Better by You Better Than Me."

Among the plaintiffs' witnesses was Dr. Howard Shevrin, a well-known and well-respected psychologist on the faculty at the University of Michigan. Dr. Shevrin had published a number of scholarly articles on unconscious learning and subliminal influence. He testified that subliminal messages are particularly powerful be-

cause their hidden nature makes them seem to reflect the individual's own motivation and are therefore harder to resist. He stated his opinion that the subliminal "do it" message had triggered the boys' suicidal actions.

Although Dr. Shevrin's claims seem logical, empirical support for the notion that subliminal messages can compel behavior or influence motivation is lacking. In fact, when asked by defense attorneys to cite a single study that supported his theory that subliminal messages could motivate impulsive or harmful behavior, Dr. Shevrin cited a handful of references, none of which actually involved evidence that subliminal communications motivated behavior.

In addition to denying that any subliminal messages were planted on the album, the defense presented evidence that both boys had personal histories marked by petty

*Judas Priest band members*

crime, drug abuse, learning disabilities, and family difficulties and that these factors were much more likely to blame for the shootings than any rock music lyrics. The defense also countered Dr. Shevrin with three experts of its own—Drs. Timothy Moore, Anthony Pratkanis, and Don Read—who testified that, although subliminal stimuli had been demonstrated to have small and fleeting effects on perception and memory, there was no scientific evidence to show that they could influence intentional behavior such as suicide.

The judge ultimately rejected the plaintiffs' claims and rendered a verdict in favor of the defendants. He stated that there was little scientific evidence establishing that subliminal stimuli were a strong influence on behavior, a conclusion that is close to what most experimental psychologists believe. However, perhaps the more important questions growing out of this case are these: (1) Was there any credible scientific basis for Dr. Shevrin's opinions? and (2) Should he have been permitted to express his opinion on this matter without being able to document a stronger scientific foundation for it?

given harm occurred. It is sometimes equated with producing an outcome that is "foreseeable"—that is, that a given event would be expected to cause a given outcome.

Fourth, a **harm,** or loss, must occur, and the harm has to involve a legally protected right or interest for which the person can seek to recover damages that have been suffered; if it does, then it is compensable and can be the subject of a civil lawsuit.

The damages a person suffers from a tort can involve destruction of personal property, physical injuries, and/or emotional distress (sometimes called "pain and suffering"). Historically, the law has always sought to compensate victims who are physically hurt or sustain property losses, but it was reluctant to compensate emotional distress, largely out of concerns that such damages are too easy to fake and too difficult to measure. In cases in which recovery for emotional damages was allowed, the courts often required that a physical injury had to accompany the psychological harm or that a plaintiff who was not physically injured had at least to be in a "zone of danger" (e.g., even if the plaintiff was not injured by the attack of an escaped wild animal, she was standing next to her children when they were attacked) (Weissman, 1985).

One case that received extensive international coverage illustrates this historical approach to emotional damages. On the afternoon of March 22, 1990, the *Aleutian Enterprise,* a large fishing boat, capsized in the Bering Sea. Within ten minutes, the boat sank, killing nine crew members. Twenty-two sailors survived the disaster; of these men, 2 returned to work in a short time, but the other 20 filed a lawsuit against the company that owned the ship. Of the 20 plaintiffs, 19 consulted a psychologist or psychiatrist, and every one of these 19 individuals was subsequently diagnosed with posttraumatic stress disorder (PTSD) by his mental-health professional (Rosen, 1995). (The defendant company hired its own psychologist who evaluated plaintiffs and diagnosed PTSD in only five of them and some other postincident disorder in three others.) The surviving sailors were entitled to recover for their psychological injuries because they had been in the "zone of danger."

In recent years, the courts have progressed to a view in which psychological symptoms and mental distress are more likely to be compensated regardless of whether the plaintiff suffered physical injuries. Two types of "purely" psychological injuries are now claimed in civil lawsuits: those arising from "extreme and outrageous" conduct that is intended to cause distress, and those arising from "negligent" behavior. In the latter type of case, plaintiffs are often allowed to sue for psychological damages if they are bystanders to an incident in which a loved one is injured (e.g., a parent sees her child crushed to death when a defective roller coaster on which the child was riding derails).

In the case of intentional torts causing psychological distress, a plaintiff must prove that a defendant intentionally or recklessly acted in an extreme and outrageous fashion (sometimes defined as "beyond all bounds of decency") to cause emotional distress. In addition, the plaintiff must prove that the distress is severe; in other words, the effects must be something more than merely annoying or temporarily upsetting (Merrick, 1985). What kinds of behavior might qualify? Courts have found that a debt collector who was trying to locate a debtor acted outrageously when he posed as a hospital employee and told the debtor's mother that her grandchildren had been seriously injured in a wreck and he needed to find the debtor to inform him of this fact (*Ford Motor Credit Co. v. Sheehan,* 1979).

In recent years, an increasing number of cases have dealt with the tort of sexual harassment, usually in the workplace. A plaintiff who claims to have been sexually harassed at work can sue the workers responsible for the harassment and the company itself, if the plaintiff can show that the company knew (or should have known) about the harassment and failed to stop it. These cases can be filed either in state courts or in federal courts in which Title VII of the federal Civil Rights Act of 1991 applies to companies with at least 15 employees. Plaintiffs can seek both **compensatory damages** (payment for emotional harm and damages suffered) as well as **punitive damages** (punishing the company for its failure to respond properly to the misconduct).

Of course, the tort of harassment is not always based on gender. In a case in which one of us was involved, a car salesman sued his employer for permitting—and even participating in—the repeated "goosing" of the salesman at work. The plaintiff, whom we will call Lyle, had been disabled since his teenage years with a left leg that was four inches shorter than the right leg and a left hip that had about 30% of the usual range of motion. Consequently, Lyle walked slowly and with a severe limp. It was a regular practice of the sales personnel at the dealership where Lyle worked to amuse themselves during slow business hours by goosing one another. They took special pleasure in goosing Lyle, particularly after discovering that he could not easily avoid them and that he would shriek loudly each time he got goosed. Lyle testified that he was goosed several times an hour and estimated that it had happened as many as 1500 times during his employment. His coworkers even gave him the nickname "Oops" because of the sound he would make each time he was the recipient of a surprise attack. On one occasion, Lyle was goosed by a coworker while talking with a couple to whom he was selling a car. Soon, the other sales personnel began making $2 bets on who could goose him in the presence of other customers. On another instance, Lyle was goosed while he was standing next to a vehicle in the showroom, causing him to bang his left knee against the vehicle and miss two weeks of work because of the subsequent injury. After returning to work, he was chided by his colleagues for drawing "gooseman's compensation."

Lyle attempted several strategies to deal with the harassment. For a time, he joined in the goosing, hoping the other men would stop picking on him. He would stay seated in his chair or with his back to a wall to reduce the opportunities for goosing, but this resulted in a severe loss of sales commissions. He repeatedly complained to his sales manager but obtained no relief. After learning that his prosthesis had been fractured—as a result of his goose-propelled bump into the showroom vehicle—Lyle quit his job and sued his employer for outrageous conduct causing physical and psychological damages.

At trial, Lyle testified how angry and humiliated he felt over the treatment and admitted that he often felt suicidal and fantasized about getting revenge against his protagonists. A clinical psychologist testified that Lyle suffered a mixed anxiety and mood disorder brought on by the repeated harassment. The jury returned a verdict for Lyle and awarded him $795,000 for his physical and psychological injuries.

When a mental-health professional assesses a plaintiff, the clinician will typically conduct an evaluation that, like most evaluations, includes a social history, a clinical interview, and a number of psychological tests (Boccaccini & Brodsky, 1999). One major difference, however, between standard clinical evaluations and forensic assessments is the much greater use of the third-party interviews and review of available records in forensic examinations. This practice is based on two basic considerations (Melton et al., 1997). First, forensic experts must be sure that their opinions are based on accurate information; other witnesses might be testifying about this information, and if this testimony contradicts what the clinician has learned, the value of any expert opinion is largely lost. Second, forensic experts are often asked to evaluate an individual's psychological condition at some specific moment or in some particular situation in the past. Therefore, clinicians are obligated to use independent sources of information, when possible, to verify their descriptions and judgments about such matters.

Based on the data from these sources, the clinician arrives at an opinion about the psychological condition of the person in question. With the exception of greater reliance on third-party interviews and records, this much of the evaluation is not too different from how a clinician would assess any client, regardless of whether the person was involved in a lawsuit. The more difficult question the clinician must answer in litigation is whether the psychological problems were caused by the tort, aggravated by the tort, or existed before the tort. In fact, based on research showing that psychological problems make people more prone to accidents, the clinician even needs to consider whether certain psychological conditions might have contributed to the fact that the plaintiff was injured in the first place.

There is no established procedure for answering these questions, although most clinicians will try to locate records and other sources of data that will help date the development of any disorder that is diagnosed. In some situations, a plaintiff might allege that he or she was selected for harassment precisely because the defendants knew of some prior difficulty that made the plaintiff vulnerable to a particular kind of harassment. In such cases, the clinician must factor in this additional piece of information before reaching a conclusion about the significance of the prior psychological problem.

One other complication affects many evaluations of individuals claiming to have suffered psychological damages: Plaintiffs are often motivated to exaggerate their claims in order to improve their chances of winning large awards. In some cases, the distortion is so large as to constitute outright lying. In other more subtle instances of **malingering,** a real psychological disturbance is present, but the plaintiff exaggerates the seriousness of the complaints. In some cases, no deception is intended at all; the plaintiff has simply become convinced that he or she is suffering a disorder and responds to the evaluation in a way that is meant to convince the examiner to reach the same conclusion. One meta-analysis found that the possibility for receiving compensation for an injury increased subjects' reports of pain by an effect size of .60 (Rohling, Binder, & Langhin-richsen-Rohling, 1995). Based on results like these and estimates by experienced clinicians that malingering and self-serving presentations are not at all uncommon in forensic evaluations (Rogers, Sewell, & Goldstein, 1994), some commentators have recommended that, when conducting forensic evaluations, clinicians must be vigilant to the special motives held by litigants and take extra steps to scrutinize their claims (Williams, Lees-Haley, & Djanogly, 1999).

---

# Workers' Compensation

When a worker is injured during the course of his or her job, the law provides for the worker to be compensated through a streamlined system that avoids the necessity of proving a tort. This system is known as *workers' compensation law;* all 50 states and the federal government have some type of workers' compensation system in place. Prior to workers' compensation, a person who was injured at work had to prove that the employer was responsible for a tort in order to receive compensation. This requirement proved difficult because employers had several possible defenses they could use to defeat the worker's claim. They often blamed the employee's negligence or the negligence of another worker for the injury. In other cases, employers said that a worker's injuries were simply the unavoidable risks of particular jobs and that the worker was well aware of these risks at the time of employment. As a result, up to the early part of the 20th century, many seriously injured workers and their families were denied any compensation for their work-related injuries.

Workers' compensation systems were developed around the beginning of the 20th century to provide an alternative to the tort system. In workers' compensation systems, employers contribute to a large fund that insures workers who are injured at work, and employers also waive their right to blame the worker or some other individual for the injury. For their part, workers give up their right to pursue a tort case against their employers, and if they are compensated, the size of the award they receive is determined by (1) the type and duration of the injury and (2) their salary at the time of the injury. Workers can seek compensation for

- physical and psychological injuries suffered at work,
- the cost of whatever treatment is given,
- lost wages, and
- the loss of future earning capacity.

Determining how much impairment in future earning capacity a given mental disorder or psychological condition might produce is very difficult. Physicians can assess the degree of impairment from a ruptured disc or a paralyzed arm, but how can we measure the degree or permanence of a mental disability? To bring some uniformity to these determinations, many states require evaluators to use the American Medical Association's *Guide to the Evaluation of Permanent Impairment.* The latest edition of the *Guide* does not provide an objective rating system for quantifying psychological impairments, but it does include five categories of impairment, ranging from "no impairment" to "extreme impairment" that clinicians can use to organize their descriptions of a claimant (Spaulding, 1990). In general, however, ratings of psychological impairments are difficult to quantify reliably.

Both employers and employees should benefit from a process in which workers' claims can be resolved fairly quickly, which is a major goal of the workers' compensation system. Formal trials are not held, and juries do not resolve these cases; they are heard and decided by a hearing officer or commissioner. (These decisions can be appealed). In theory workers' compensation cases should be handled expeditiously, but they often drag on for years as both sides go through a process of hiring one or more experts to examine the worker and give opinions about the injuries and any disability suffered.

How do mental-health professionals become involved in workers' compensation claims? Because psychological injuries or mental disorders arising from employment can be compensated, clinicians are often asked to evaluate workers and render an opinion about the existence, cause, and implications of any mental disorders. Claims for mental disability usually arise in one of two ways. First, a physical injury can lead to a mental disorder and psychological disability. A common pattern in these *physical-mental* cases is for a worker to sustain a serious physical injury (e.g., a broken back or severe burns) that leaves the worker suffering chronic pain. As the pain and the disability associated with it continue, the worker begins to experience an overlay of psychological problems, usually depression and anxiety. These problems worsen until they become full-fledged mental disorders, resulting in further impairments in the worker's overall functioning.

The second work-related pathway to mental disability is for an individual either to suffer a traumatic incident at work or to undergo a long period of continuing stress that leads to substantial psychological difficulties. A night clerk at a convenience store who is the victim of an armed robbery and subsequently develops posttraumatic stress disorder is an example of such *mental-mental* cases. Another example is the clerical worker who, following years of overwork and pressure from a boss, experiences an anxiety disorder. In a third kind of case, known as *mental-physical,* work-related stress leads to the onset of a physical disorder such as high blood pressure. Many states have placed restrictions on these types of claims, and psychologists are seldom asked to evaluate them.

In recent years, the number of psychological claims in workers' compensation litigation has increased dramatically, and much of the increase can be attributed to a surge in mental-mental cases (Barth, 1990). In the 1980s, stress-related mental disorders became the United States' fastest-growing occupational disease category (Hersch & Alexander, 1990). Although it is not clear what accounts for the increase in psychological claims, at least three explanations have been proposed. First, because more women have entered the workforce and because women are more often diagnosed with anxiety and depression disorders than men, the rise in psychological claims might be due to the growing percentage of female workers (Sparr, 1995). A second possibility is that a shift in the job market from manufacturing and industrial jobs to service-oriented jobs has produced corresponding increases in job-related interpersonal stressors and decreases in physical injuries. A third possibility is that claims of psychological impairments are motivated primarily by financial incentives, producing a range of cases in which genuine impairments are mixed in with exaggerated or false claims of disability.

Very few empirical studies have been conducted on the assessment of psychological damages in worker compensation cases. What little research does exist has usually addressed one of the following questions:

◆ How do worker compensation claimants score on standard psychological tests such as the Minnesota Multiphasic Personality Inventory (MMPI)?

◆ Are certain injuries or stressors associated with a particular pattern of psychological test scores?

◆ Can psychological tests distinguish claimants who are suffering from a bona fide disorder from those who are faking or exaggerating their problems?

One study investigated the most common pattern of scores on the MMPI for 200 individuals filing worker compensation claims (Repko & Cooper, 1983). Seventeen percent of the profiles did not show any significant elevations, but over one-third of the MMPIs involved elevated scores on one or more of the scales measuring depression, fatigue and physical complaints, worrying, and a general lack of insight into psychological symptoms. These results have been replicated in other studies that have found, in addition to these psychological test patterns, a tendency for claimants to receive elevated scores on the MMPI scale measuring feelings of disorientation, isolation, alienation, and confusion (Hersch & Alexander, 1990). Of course, these high scores do not prove that the psychological distress was caused by a work-related difficulty; it is possible that already-existing psychological problems make it more likely that a person will suffer stressful or harmful experiences at work.

The research does not suggest that particular injuries or claims are reliably linked with different patterns of test scores (e.g., Snibbe, Peterson, & Sosner, 1980). One reason for the lack of distinguishing patterns might be that regardless of the injury or the stressor, most people manifest psychological distress through a mixture of physical complaints and negative emotions such as anxiety, depression, and feelings of isolation.

The objectivity of psychological evaluations performed in workers' compensation cases is

threatened by several factors (Tsushima, Foote, Merrill, & Lehrke, 1996). Chief among these problems is that attorneys often retain the same expert over and over again to conduct evaluations. An expert who is repeatedly hired by the same attorney, whether it be a plaintiff or defense attorney, runs the risk of merely advocating the opinions the expert knows is desired by the attorney rather than rendering objective decisions about each case. We discuss this "hired gun" problem more fully in the last section of the chapter and in ◆ **Box 12-3.** In addition, it is possible that a worker being evaluated answers test items and interview questions differently depending on who is conducting the evaluation. One study suggests that plaintiffs who were referred for evaluations by their attorneys or who sought evaluations on their own tended to exaggerate their symptoms or respond inconsistently on the MMPI more often than did plaintiffs who were evaluated at the request of defense attorneys (Fox, Gerson, & Lees-Haley, 1995).

As we discussed in Chapter 6, the MMPI contains sets of items that are sometimes used to assess the test-taking attitudes of a respondent. These **validity scales** can be examined to determine whether respondents might have tried to fool the examiner by exaggerating or denying psychological problems. In workers' compensation cases, a main concern is that some plaintiffs might "fake bad" by exaggerating or inventing symptoms to improve their chances for an award. A growing body of research focuses on whether existing or new validity scales on the MMPI-2 can distinguish respondents who have bona fide problems from those who are malingering. New tests are also being developed to detect malingering on cognitive and neuropsychological measures (Frederick & Crosby, 2000).

The typical case of a person trying to fake insanity involves the individual answering many items in the "bad" direction, thereby attempting to look as disturbed as possible. However, the strategy might be more complicated in the case of a person who is faking or exaggerating a disorder in a worker compensation case. These individuals

## The Science of

BOX 12-3   **Forensic evaluations: Does the adversarial system bias experts?**

A frequent criticism of expert testimony is that the adversarial system encourages partiality on the part of experts. According to this view, experts hired by plaintiffs reach conclusions favorable to that side, and defense experts show a similar predisposition to the defense side. Does the adversarial system bias experts? Does it create "hired guns" who render the most favorable opinions that large fees can buy?

One recent study investigated these questions by examining whether psychological assessments of worker compensation claimants were related to the side that had retained the expert. Dawn Hasemann (1997) collected and compared 385 reports that have been prepared by various mental-health professionals. Of these reports, 194 had been conducted by defense-hired experts, 182 were completed by plaintiff-hired experts, and 9 evaluations could not be classified.

Did plaintiff and defense experts differ in their opinions in these cases? Several results indicate that they did and that they might have been unduly influenced by the adversarial system. Consider these three results:

1. Plaintiff experts gave impairment ratings to claimants that were nearly four times larger than the impairments rated by defense experts.
2. Defense experts concluded that MMPIs completed by claimants were invalid or malingered in 72% of their evaluations, whereas plaintiff experts reached this conclusion in 31% of their evaluations.
3. Of the 19 experts who had conducted three or more evaluations, 17 tended to do so almost exclusively for one side. Ten showed partiality toward plaintiffs, conducting a total of 107 plaintiff evaluations and only 8 defense evaluations.

Seven experts completed 147 assessments for the defense and only 36 for the plaintiffs.

Although these data do not prove that forensic experts cannot be impartial, they clearly raise concerns that experts are influenced by the adversarial nature of the legal process. It is conceivable that the experts were accurately describing claimants who behaved differently depending on who was evaluating them. Or it might be that the experts are objective but that the attorneys selectively introduce expert opinions depending on whether those opinions support their side. Of course, either of these two explanations poses additional challenges to the overall validity of expert opinion. Whatever the interpretation, the results of the Hasemann study call into question whether the adversarial system encourages or discourages rigorously objective expert testimony.

usually want to appear honest, virtuous, and free of any psychological problems that might have existed prior to the injury, while at the same time endorsing many symptoms and complaints that would establish that they had been harmed by a work-related incident. In other words, their motivation involves a combination of faking good and faking bad. A special validity scale composed of MMPI-2 items that tap this simultaneous fake-good/fake-bad strategy has been developed and has proven successful in distinguishing between

genuine and faked psychological injury claims (Lees-Haley, 1991, 1992).

## Civil Competencies

The concept of mental competence extends to many kinds of decisions that individuals are called on to make throughout their lives. When we discussed competence to stand trial in Chapter 11, we focused on the knowledge and decisions that criminal defendants are required to make. However, the question of mental competence is raised in several noncriminal contexts as well; we refer to these other situations with the general term **civil competencies.**

The question of civil competence focuses on whether an individual has the capacity to understand information that is relevant to decision making in a given situation and then make an informed choice about what to do in that situation. Examples of civil competence include the following questions:

◆ Is a person competent to manage his or her financial affairs?

◆ Can an individual make competent decisions about his or her medical or psychiatric treatment?

◆ Is a person competent to execute a will and decide how to distribute property to heirs or other beneficiaries?

◆ Can a person make advance decisions about the kind of medical treatment he or she wants or does not want to receive if terminally ill or seriously injured?

The legal standards used to define competence have evolved over many years. Scholars who have studied this issue usually point to four abilities that contribute to competent decision making (Appelbaum & Grisso, 1995). A competent individual is expected to be able to

1. understand basic information that is relevant to making a decision,

2. apply that information to a specific situation in order to anticipate the consequences of various choices,

3. use logical—or rational—thinking to evaluate the pros and cons of various strategies and decisions, and

4. communicate a personal decision or choice about the matter under consideration.

As indicated in ◆ **Box 12-4,** the specific abilities associated with each of these general criteria vary depending on the decision that a person must

make. Deciding whether to have risky surgery demands different information and thinking processes than does deciding whether to leave property to children or to a charitable organization.

Decisions about medical treatment that one might receive in the future, including the desire to have life-sustaining medical treatments discontinued, involve a special level of planning that has been encouraged by a 1990 federal statute known as the Patient Self-Determination Act. Planning about future medical treatments is formalized through what are known as **advance medical directives,** in which patients indicate the kinds of treatment they want should they later become incapacitated and incompetent to make treatment decisions. The most controversial of these advance directives is the "living will," in which a patient essentially asserts that he or she prefers to die over being kept alive on a ventilator or feeding tubes. The ethical and practical issues involved in determining patients' competence to issue advance medical directives are enormous, but the trend, revealed in Supreme Court decisions such as *Cruzan v. Director, Missouri Department of Health* (1990) is to recognize that patients have great autonomy in accepting or rejecting a variety of treatments and health-care provisions (Cantor, 1998; Rich, 1998)

The question of competence to consent to treatment usually arises when a patient refuses treatment that seems to be medically and psychologically justified. Under these circumstances, the first step might be to break down the explanation of the treatment decisions facing the patient into smaller bits of information (results from the MacArthur Treatment Competence Study have shown that patients are capable of significantly better understanding when treatment information was presented to them one element at a time). Using this kind of presentation might facilitate a patient's appreciation of how a recommended treatment would be in his or her best interests. Should an impasse between the patient and treating professionals still exist after such a presentation, it would be important to have a clinical assessment instrument that could be administered

# The Science of

## BOX 12-4    Competence: Assessing competence for treatment decisions

One area in which psycholegal researchers have focused attention is on the competence of individuals with severe mental disorders to make decisions and give informed consent about their own psychiatric treatment. Can persons with serious mental disorders make competent treatment decisions for themselves? Do their decision-making abilities differ from persons who do not suffer mental disorders? These questions have been the focus of the MacArthur Treatment Competence Study, which has led to the development of a series of structured interview measures to assess the four basic abilities—understanding information, applying information, thinking rationally, and expressing a choice—involved in legal competence (Grisso, Appelbaum, Mulvey, & Fletcher, 1995). For example, this is an item that taps a person's ability to apply information to the question of whether he or she has a condition that could be effectively treated:

> "Most people who have symptoms of a mental or emotional disorder like your doctor believes you have can be helped by treatment. The most common treatment is medication. Other treatments some-

times used for such disorders are having someone to talk to about problems, and participating in group therapy with other people with similar symptoms."

". . . [D]o you believe that you have the kind of condition for which some types of treatment might be helpful?"

"All right, you believe that . . . (paraphrase of the patient's expressed opinion). Can you explain that to me? What makes you believe that . . . (again paraphrase as above)?"

For a patient who believes that treatment will not work because he or she is "just too sick," the interviewer would ask:

"Imagine that a doctor tells you that there is a treatment that has been shown in research to help 90% of people *with problems just as serious as yours*. Do you think this treatment might be of more benefit to you than getting no treatment at all?" (Grisso et al., 1995, p. 133)

Standardized interviews, using items of this type, were conducted with three groups of patients—those with schizophrenia, major depression, and heart disease—and with groups of nonill persons from the community who were demographically matched to the patient groups (Grisso & Appelbaum, 1995). Only a minority of

the persons in all the groups showed significant impairments in competent decision making about various treatment options. However, the patients with schizophrenia and major depression tended to have a poorer understanding of treatment information and used less adequate reasoning in thinking about the consequences of treatment than did the heart patients or community sample. These impairments were more pronounced and consistent across different competence abilities for patients with schizophrenia than for patients with depression, and the more serious the symptoms of mental disorder (especially those involving disturbed thinking), the poorer the understanding.

These results obviously have implications for social policies involving persons with mental disorders. First, contrary to popular impressions, the majority of patients suffering from severe disorders such as schizophrenia and major depression appear to be capable of competent decision making about their treatment. On the other hand, a significant number of patients—particularly those with schizophrenia—show impairments in their decision-making abilities.

in a brief period of time to determine whether a given patient lacks the necessary ability to reach a competent decision. The development of such an instrument—the MacArthur Competence Assessment Tool for Treatment Decisions (MacCAT-T)—is under way.

# Psychological Autopsies

Like most clinical assessments, the typical forensic assessment involves a clinician interviewing, observing, and testing a client to arrive at an understanding of the case. However, in a few unusual circumstances, clinicians may be called on to give an opinion about a deceased person's state of mind as it existed at a specific time before death. Obviously, in these cases, the clinician must conduct an evaluation without any participation by the individual whose prior condition is in question. These evaluations—termed **psychological autopsies** (or **equivocal death analyses**)—involve an investigation by a clinician to determine the psychological condition of a decedent at some previous point in time (Ogloff & Otto, 1993).

Psychological autopsies originated in the 1950s when a group of social scientists in the Los Angeles area began assisting the coroner's office in determining whether suicide, murder, or accident was the most likely mode of death in some equivocal cases. Their use has spread over the years, and now they are encountered most often in the following kinds of cases:

◆ determining whether a death was due to a suicide or an accident in cases in which the question is raised by an insurance company that could deny death benefits if it is shown that the policy holder committed suicide;

◆ assessing claims in workers' compensation cases that stressful working conditions or work trauma contributed to a worker's death or suicide;

◆ evaluating a deceased individual's mental capacity to execute or modify a will;

◆ supporting the argument occasionally made by criminal defendants that a victim's mode of death was suicide rather than homicide.

Although there is no standard format for psychological autopsies, most of them rely on information from two sources: past records and interviews with third parties who knew the decedent. In some sense, psychological autopsies resemble the technique of criminal profiling (see Chapter 8); both approaches attempt to infer an individual's motives and state of mind by collecting and assessing archival information or other data a person has "left behind." In the case of the psychological autopsy, the identity of the person in question is known, but the nature of his or her behavior remains in question; in the case of the criminal profile, the behavior is known, but the identity of the culprit is not.

General guidelines for what should be included in psychological autopsies have been published (Ebert, 1987). Some investigators concentrate on more recent data, generated close in time to the person's death. What was the person's mood? How was the person doing at work? Were there any pronounced changes in the person's behavior? Others—especially those who take a psychodynamic perspective on behavior—look for clues early in the person's life. As a child, how did the person interact with his or her parents? What was the individual's approach to school? To competition with peers?

As with any assessment technique, the first question to be considered is the reliability of the psychological autopsy. There are several reasons to suspect that the reliability of psychological autopsies is low. The person in question is not available to be interviewed or tested. The persons who are interviewed might not remember the past accurately, or they might have reasons to distort their answers.

We are aware of only one study that has addressed the question of reliability, and it did so in a very indirect fashion, using data from the investigation of the *U.S.S. Iowa* explosion (see ◆ Box 12-5).

No empirical information exists concerning the validity of psychological autopsies—that is, do they accurately portray a person's state of mind at the time of death? Obviously, a major problem is that the decedent's "true" state of mind is unknown; in fact, were this not the case, the autopsy would be unnecessary. However, it might still be possible

## THE CASE OF

BOX 12-5 The *U.S.S. Iowa*

On April 19, 1989, 47 sailors were killed when an explosion ripped through turret 2 of the *U.S.S. Iowa*. The U.S. Navy's investigation of this tragedy initially concluded that the explosion was caused by the suicidal acts of Gunner's Mate Clayton Hartwig, who was himself killed in the explosion. The major foundation for this conclusion was a psychological autopsy conducted by FBI agents working at the National Center for the Analysis of Violent Crime. The navy's conclusions were later evaluated by a congressional committee, which commissioned its own panel of 14 psychological and psychiatric experts to

review the FBI's analysis. Based in part on this panel's input, the congressional committee rejected the FBI analysis as invalid. Ultimately, the U.S. Navy also concluded that the cause of the explosion could not be determined.

Randy Otto and his colleagues asked 24 psychologists and psychiatrists to rate the reports pre-

*The* U.S.S. Iowa, *damaged in an explosion*

pared by the 14 experts commissioned by the U.S. House of Representatives to review the FBI analysis of the *U.S.S. Iowa* explosion (Otto, Poythress, Starr, & Darkes, 1993). Three raters judged each of the 14 reports, and although they failed to show precise agreement in how they thought the reports should be interpreted, they did achieve a moderate amount of broad agreement in their ratings of the 14 reports. Note, however, that this agreement pertains only to how the raters interpreted the 14 panelists' reports rather than the contents or opinions in the reports themselves.

to examine the validity of psychological autopsies by giving reputed experts background information in cases that appear ambiguous (but in which the cause of death is actually known) and studying the opinions offered and the reasons for them.

How has testimony about psychological autopsies fared in court? In cases involving workers' compensation claims and questions of whether insurance benefits should be paid, the courts have usually admitted psychological autopsy testimony; in criminal cases or in cases involving the question of whether a person had the mental capacity to execute a will, the courts have been more reluctant to permit the testimony (Ogloff & Otto, 1993). Judges are more hesitant to allow expert testimony in criminal cases than in civil ones perhaps because the risks of prejudicial testimony

are greater when one's liberties can be taken away. One reason for the courts' hesitancy in permitting psychological autopsy testimony in cases involving the validity of wills might be that, in such cases, the state of mind of the deceased is the critical question for the jury. Allowing expert testimony on this matter might, therefore, be viewed as invading the province of the jury, a perception that judges usually want to avoid.

## Child Custody and Parental Fitness

One of the fastest-growing areas of forensic psychology is the evaluation of families for the purpose of recommending the particular custodial arrangement that is in the best interests of a child whose parents are divorcing or separating. The increase in these cases is attributable to two facts. First, half of all marriages in the United States now end in divorce. As a result, over one-third of children in the United States will spend some time living in a stepfamily, and more than half will spend some time in a single-parent household (Bray, 1991). Therefore, the issue of custody is a practical concern for millions of families. Second, from the end of the 19th century to about the middle of the 20th century, the prevailing assumption was that awarding custody of young children (sometimes called children of "tender years") to their mothers was usually in their best interests. This preference for maternal custody has weakened as we enter the 21st century; now many courts want to know about the parenting abilities of each parent before making a decision about custody (Liss & McKinley-Pace, 1999).

Currently, the prevailing standard for custody decisions is the **future best interests of the child,** but an alternative standard—the **primary caretaker standard**—has been applied in a few states. By this standard, custody is awarded to the parent who has been primarily responsible for caring for and supervising the child. Although the child's "best interests" must be assessed on a case-by-case basis, the Uniform Marriage and Divorce Act indicates that courts should consider the following criteria: (1) the wishes of the child; (2) the wishes of the child's parents; (3) the relationships between the child and the parents, siblings, and significant others who interact with the child; (4) the child's adjustment at home and school and in the community; and (5) the physical and mental health of the parties involved.

Child custody evaluations usually arise in situations in which divorcing parents disagree about which of them can best meet the needs of their children and should therefore have custody. Most states permit two kinds of custodial arrangements. In **sole custody,** one parent is awarded legal custody of the child and the other parent is granted rights of visitation and other types of contact with the child. In **joint custody,** both parents retain parental rights concerning decisions about the child's general welfare, education, health care, and other matters. Joint custody does not necessarily mean that the child spends equal time with each parent. Usually, one parent is designated the residential parent, and the child spends more time living at the home of that parent. The three main differences between sole and joint custody are as follows:

1. Joint custody distributes the frequency of interaction more evenly between the children and each parent.

2. Joint custody requires more interactions between the divorced parents and generates more demands for cooperation concerning the children.

3. Joint custody results in more alterations in caregiving arrangements along with more separations and reunions between children and parents (Clingempeel & Reppucci, 1982).

Evaluations of parental fitness involve different questions from the typical custody dispute (Azar & Benjet, 1994). In every state, the Department of Child Welfare will intervene if it receives a credible report that a child is being abused or neglected. After an investigation, the department might file a petition asking a court to remove the child from the home and arrange placement with a relative or in foster care. In such cases, the issue before the court is whether the child should be left with the parents or removed from the home because of parental unfitness. The issue for the evaluator is different from the issue in a custody case. In a custody case, the matter to be determined is what arrangement with the parents is in the best interests of the child. In abuse/neglect cases, the issue is what arrangement protects the child's well-being, while properly respecting the right of the parents. Although parental rights are important, the state must protect children from parents who cannot or will not provide adequate food, shelter, and supervision. The state must also protect children from parents who abuse them, physically or psychologically. A clinician might

*Elizabeth Morgan (right), whose child custody case made national news after she was jailed for refusing to disclose to a court the location of her daughter. Morgan claimed that her ex-husband had previously molested their daughter and hid her whereabouts to protect her.*

recommend that the child be placed temporarily in foster care and that the parents be taught parenting skills as a condition of having the child returned to them. In extreme cases—those in which parents abandon a child or are clearly incapable of caring for a child—the state might seek to terminate parental rights. This is done most often in cases in which relatives or others wish to adopt the child.

Many mental-health professionals regard child custody cases to be the most ethically and clinically difficult forensic evaluations they perform. First, the emotional stakes are extremely high, and both parents are often willing to spare no expense or tactic in the battle over which of them will win custody. The children involved are usually forced to live—for months, if not years—in an emotional limbo where they do not know in whose home they will be residing, where they will be going to school, or how often they will see each parent. Second, a thorough competence evaluation requires that the clinician evaluate the chil-

dren, both parents, and—when possible—other people who have interacted with the child such as other relatives, teachers, and family health care providers. Often, not all the parties agree to be evaluated or do so only under coercion, resulting in a lengthy and sometimes unfriendly process. Third, to render a truly expert opinion, a clinician must possess a great deal of knowledge not just about the children and parents under evaluation but also about child development, bonding and attachment, family systems, the effects of divorce on children, adult and childhood mental disorders, and several different kinds of testing. Added to these factors are variations in what we have traditionally defined as a family. With increasing acceptance of different lifestyles and family structures, clinicians must often confront questions about whether parents' sexual orientation or ethnicity should have any bearing on custody decisions. Finally, child custody evaluations are often highly adversarial processes in which each parent tries to expose all the faults of the other and each side challenges any procedures or opinions by an expert with which it disagrees. Clinicians who conduct custody evaluations need to brace themselves for aggressive attacks directed at their clinical methods, scholarly competence, personal character, and professional ethics.

In disputed custody cases, clinicians can conduct a custody evaluation under any of three scenarios: (1) a judge can appoint one clinician to conduct a custody evaluation that is available to all the parties, (2) each side can retain its own expert to conduct independent evaluations, or (3) the sides can agree to share the expenses of hiring an expert to conduct one evaluation (Weissman, 1991). Most clinicians prefer either the first or third option because they do not want to be subjected to the hostilities and adversarial pressures that arise when separate experts are hired by each side (Keilin & Bloom, 1986). Attorneys tend to agree with this preference, believing that option 2 leads to greater bias (LaFortune, 1997, cited in Nicholson & Norwood, 2000).

Specific guidelines for conducting custody evaluations have been developed by the American Psychological Association and the Association of Family and Conciliation Courts. Although the methods used in custody evaluations vary a great deal depending on the specific issues in each case, most evaluations include the following components:

1. Clinical, social history, and mental status interviews of the parents and the children

2. Standardized testing of the parents and the children

3. Observation of interactions between each parent and the children, especially when the children are minors

4. Assessments or interviews with other people who have had opportunities to observe the family (adult children of the parents, grandparents, neighbors, the family physician, school teachers, etc.)

5. Documents or records that might be relevant to the case (medical records of children and parents, report cards, arrest records)

In a national survey of mental-health professionals who conducted child custody evaluations, Ackerman and Ackerman (1997) found that experts devoted about 30 hours to each custody evaluation. Much of this time was devoted to interviewing and observing the parties in various combinations. In fact, more than two-thirds of the respondents indicated that they conducted individual interviews with each parent and each child, observed each parent interacting (separately) with each child, and conducted formal psychological testing of the parents and the children. The MMPI was the test most often used with parents; intelligence tests and projective personality tests were the most common instruments used with the children. An increasing number of clinicians report using one of two instruments specifically designed for child custody evaluations: the Bricklin Perceptual Scales (Bricklin, 1984) and the Ackerman-Schoendorf Scales for Parent Evaluation of Custody (ASPECT; Ackerman & Schoendorf, 1992). Both instruments have been criticized for serious psychometric

**TABLE 12.1 *Preferred custodial recommendations***

| RECOMMENDATION | MEAN % TIME ACTUALLY RECOMMENDED |
|---|---|
| Single-parent custody without visitation | 4.6 |
| Single-parent custody with visitation | 30.4 |
| Limited joint custody | 42.8 |
| Joint custody | 21.7 |
| Other arrangement[a] | 0.3 |

[a]Includes placement in foster homes, with relatives, and so on.
SOURCE: Keilin and Bloom (1986).

problems, but the ASPECT currently enjoys a bit better empirical support (Nicholson, 1999).

These experts also reported how often they recommended different kinds of custodial arrangements. As shown in Table 12.1, limited joint custody (parents share the decision making, but one parent maintains primary physical custody) was the most common recommendation, and single parent custody without visitation was the least recommended alternative.

One question addressed by several research studies is whether children raised in joint custody arrangements function better than children in sole custody. One could predict that, to the extent that joint custody allows the child to maintain close ties to both parents, better child adjustment would be promoted by joint custody arrangements. Alternatively, one might argue that because sole custody simplifies custodial arrangements, minimizes the child's confusion over where his or her home is, and keeps still-angry parents away from each other, better adjustment will occur with sole custody.

Based on several criteria, most studies report either no major differences between children in the two types of custody or somewhat better adjustment by joint custody children (Bender, 1994). For example, in her study of 78 stepfamilies with adolescent children, Margaret Crosbie-Burnett (1991) found that joint custody was associated with greater family cohesion, improved adjustment by the adolescents, and better relationships with their stepparents. However, the gender of the child moderated the impact of the custodial arrangement on adjustment. Girls felt more upset in sole custody families; boys expressed more anxiety in joint custody families. Consistent with earlier research (Emery, 1982; Hetherington & Arasteh, 1988), continuing hostility and conflicts between the parents—regardless of the type of custody—were associated with poorer adjustment on the part of the children. At this point, most research suggests that the quality of the relationship between divorced parents is more important to the adjustment of their children than whether the children are raised in sole custody or joint custody.

Because divorce is a potent stressor for children and because protracted custody battles tend to leave a trail of emotionally battered family members in their wake, increasing attention is being given to helping parents and children cope with these transitions or to finding alternatives to custody fights (Grych & Fincham, 1992; Kelly, 1991). Many judges require divorcing couples to attempt to settle issues of custody, visitation, and support through **mediation,** a form of alternative dispute resolution that minimizes the adversarial quality of the typical custody dispute (Mediation is discussed further in Chapter 4.). If mediation fails, the couple can return to court and have the judge decide the issues. The benefits of custody mediation are that resolutions are reached more quickly, and with better compliance among the participants than with adversarial procedures.

It is not clear, however, that mediation always leads to better adjustment by divorcing parents or by their children. To assess the impact of mediated versus adversarial child custody procedures, Robert Emery and his colleagues at the University of Virginia randomly assigned divorcing couples to settle their custody disputes either through mediation or through litigation. They found that mediation reduced the number of hearings necessary and the total amount of time to reach a resolution. Parents who mediated did

not differ in terms of psychological adjustment from those who litigated, but a consistent gender difference in satisfaction with the two methods did emerge. Fathers who went through mediation were much more likely to report feeling satisfied with the process than did fathers who litigated; mothers who went through mediation, on the other hand, were less likely to express satisfaction with its effects, and some dependent measures actually favored mothers who litigated their dispute (Emery, Matthews, & Kitzmann, 1994; Emery, Matthews, & Wyer, 1991). Mediation is most likely to be harmful when "domestic violence, child abuse, or substance abuse have resulted in drastic inequalities between partners [so that] a truly consensual mutual decision may be impossible" (Liss & McKinley-Pace, 1999, p. 362).

# Civil Commitment and Risk Assessment

All 50 states and the District of Columbia have **civil commitment** laws that authorize the custody and restraint of persons who, as a result of mental illness, are a danger to themselves or others or who are so gravely disabled that they cannot care for themselves. This restraint is usually accomplished by compulsory commitment to a mental hospital. The courts also provide rules and safeguards for how these involuntary commitments are to be accomplished.

Many of these procedures were instituted in the 1970s in response to a concern that, in the 1950s and 1960s, it was too easy to commit people to state psychiatric facilities. At that time, persons who were mentally ill could be involuntarily committed whenever the state believed they needed treatment. Beginning around 1970, commitment proceedings began to be reformed, resulting in more legal rights for the mentally ill to resist compulsory commitment. A key case in this reform movement was *O'Connor v. Donaldson* (1975), in which the Supreme Court held that mental illness and a need for treatment were insufficient justifications for involuntarily committing mentally ill persons who were not dangerous. Similar limits on involuntary hospitalizations have been upheld by the Supreme Court more recently (e.g., *Foucha v. Louisiana*, 1992). The standard for commitment changed from mere mental illness to mental illness that was associated with dangerousness or a grave lack of ability to care for oneself. Ironically, today many people believe "it's too hard to get people in and much too easy to get them out" of mental hospitals (Riechmann, 1985, p. 6). Mental-health activists and patients' families feel that patients are often "dumped," without concern for their fate on the outside. Some of these people end up in the courts and jails after being on the streets (Teplin, 1984). Although the legislative changes of the 1970s were intended to protect the rights of the mentally ill, an exclusive concern with rights can sometimes leave patients without adequate care, housing, or the effective psychiatric treatment that can be provided in some hospitals (Turkheimer & Parry, 1992; Wexler, 1992).

## Three Types of Commitment Procedures

The laws permit three types of civil commitment: (1) without a court order, (2) by court order, and (3) outpatient.

Commitment without a court order is the means by which most mental patients are initially admitted to hospitals; that is, detention is permitted under emergency or temporary commitment statutes. A police officer, a mental-health professional, or sometimes a private citizen can initiate involuntary detention of another person. Usually, the cause is actual or anticipated harmful behavior by the patient either against self (e.g., attempted suicide) or against others. The examination is performed by a physician or a qualified mental-health professional. A few states require approval by a judge before emergency detention can be implemented. But usually, the decision is left in the hands of professionals; judges defer to their expertise because the goal is to protect individuals incapable of taking care of themselves (Hiday &

Suval, 1984). Hearings are usually perfunctory; one observer found the average length to be 17 minutes (Swenson, 1993).

On admission, patients are read their rights, much as criminal suspects are read their rights from a *Miranda* card (Goodman, 1982). Patients committed on an emergency basis are told that they can be detained for only a specified length of time before a review takes place, usually a matter of two or three days. Then a preliminary hearing must be held before the patient can be confined any longer.

Of course, a person may volunteer to enter a mental institution. But while there, the patient may find that the hospital has instigated commitment proceedings to challenge or delay his or her release. Schwitzgebel and Schwitzgebel (1980) note, "In actual practice, 'voluntary' admission is seldom as benign as the formalities make it appear. Usually there is considerable pressure from relatives, civil authorities, and mental health personnel who are becoming worried or angry about a person's deviant behavior" (p. 8). A research investigation by David Rosenhan (1973), described in ◆ Box 12-6, illustrates the tendency for patients, once committed to the hospital, to be seen as deserving to be there, whether they really are or not.

The second type of commitment is through court order. The criteria for obtaining a formal civil commitment vary from state to state; in general, however, the person must be mentally ill and fulfill both of the following conditions:

1. be dangerous to self and others or so gravely disabled as to be unable to provide for his or her own basic needs, and
2. need treatment that is available in a setting no less restrictive than a hospital.

Although the criterion of "dangerousness" is the most often discussed standard and therefore is deemed the most important for involuntary hospitalization, grave disability is the standard that determines most commitments (Turkheimer & Parry, 1992).

## The Science of

**BOX 12-6**   **Psychiatric diagnosis: Mistakes in the mental hospital**

In 1973, David Rosenhan tested the ability of psychiatric-hospital staff members to distinguish "normal" from "insane" behaviors. He and seven other normal persons gained admission to hospitals (in five states on the East and West Coasts) by complaining of hearing voices that repeated the word *one*. The pseudopatients were a psychology graduate student, three psychologists, a pediatrician, a psychiatrist, a painter, and a homemaker—three women and five men.

Seven were diagnosed as schizophrenic and one as manic-depressive. Immediately after being admitted, the pseudopatients stopped saying they heard voices. They gave false names and employment data, but otherwise they responded honestly to questions about their lives and tried to interact normally with the staff. It became apparent to them that a psychiatric label, once attached, distorted the staff's interpretations of patients' behavior. For example, the pseudopatients had been told to keep detailed notes about life in the wards. Members of the staff, in observing this be-

havior, concluded that they were obsessive-compulsive.

None of the pseudopatients was detected as such by the staff of any of the hospitals. In fact, the only ones who sometimes recognized the pseudopatients as normal were other patients. But the pseudopatients were eventually released. The hospital stays averaged 19 days, with a range of 7 to 52 days. Each of the pseudopatients who had been diagnosed as schizophrenic was eventually discharged with the label of "schizophrenia in remission." Thus, the diagnostic label stuck, despite changes in behavior.

---

For a court order to be obtained, the concerned persons must petition the court for a professional examination of the individual in question. A formal court hearing usually follows the examination. In most states, the hearing is mandatory, and persons whose commitment is sought can call witnesses and have their lawyer cross-examine witnesses who testify against them.

A third type of commitment procedure, known as outpatient commitment, is available in almost all states and allows a patient to be mandated to receive treatment in an outpatient setting, such as a community mental-health center, rather than in a hospital (Hiday & Goodman, 1982). Outpatient commitments often involve conditional releases from a hospital; that is, formerly hospitalized patients are ordered to continue treatment in the community. Several legal and clinical complications arise with this approach. For example, what should be done with patients who refuse medication? Are therapists treating these patients liable for any dangerous

acts the patients might commit? And, most important, is effective community-based treatment available?

## Dangerousness and Risk Assessment

Dangerousness is one of the central constructs of mental-health law. Determining whether a person is now or could in the future be dangerous is a question that underlies many decisions in our system of justice. For our purposes, we define **dangerousness** as involving acts of physical violence or aggression by one person against another; verbal threats and destruction of property are not included in this definition.

Dangerousness is a major justification for involuntarily committing the mentally ill to hospitals. As we saw in Chapter 2 when we discussed the *Tarasoff* case, dangerousness is the basis for requiring therapists to protect third parties from possible acts of violence against them by the patients of these therapists. Chapter 10 identified dangerousness as a reason for denying bail to certain defendants. In Chapter 11, we learned that dangerousness is the justification for hospitalizing defendants after they have been found not guilty by reason of insanity. And as you will learn in Chapter 17, some states use future dangerousness as one factor a jury can consider when deciding whether to sentence a convicted murderer to life in prison or death by execution. In Chapter 17, we also discuss the related question of predicting whether certain sex offenders will reoffend.

## Difficulties in Assessing Dangerousness

Can mental-health experts accurately assess a person's present dangerousness and then predict whether that person will be dangerous in the future? Is mental illness a sign that a person is likely to be dangerous? Do certain types of mental illness make a person more prone to dangerous conduct? These questions have been examined extensively by researchers for more than three decades, and they are at the heart of many real-life cases. For example, should the mental-health professionals who treated John Hinckley in the past have predicted that he posed a danger to President Reagan? What about Jeffrey Dahmer? Was his brutal behavior predictable, given his early psychological problems? Clinicians who attempt to answer these questions perform what are called **risk assessments;** using the best available data and research, they try to predict which persons are and are not likely to behave violently in certain circumstances, give some estimate of the probability of the risk for violence, and offer suggestions on how to reduce the risks (Webster, 1998).

The original consensus of researchers was that mental illness was not linked to a risk of violence. Leading scholars such as John Monahan (1984) of the University of Virginia had traditionally concluded that clinicians could not assess risks for future dangerousness with any acceptable degree of accuracy. The following summary of this research is typical: "In one study after another, the same conclusion emerges: for every correct prediction of violence, there are numer-

ous incorrect predictions" (Pfohl, 1984). Another early summary of the research on clinicians' ability to predict dangerousness was that their predictions were wrong in two of every three cases.

More recent research has modified the early pessimism about clinicians' ability to predict dangerousness. Researchers have learned that these predictions can sometimes reach moderate to good levels of accuracy when certain conditions are present (Borum, 1996). Specifically, clinicians who consider a set of factors that years of research have shown to be related to future violence (see ◆ Box 12-7 for a summary) can predict the risk for violence considerably better than was the case 20 years ago (Douglas & Webster, 1999). Specifically, when clinicians are given information about a range of historical, personal, and environmental variables related to violence, when they limit their predictions to specific kinds of dangerous behavior, and when they concentrate on predicting risks in certain settings rather than in all situations, they can predict dangerousness with a fair degree of accuracy. Although they still make a large number of errors, they do significantly better than chance.

Many factors can lower the accuracy of predictions of dangerousness. For example, the base rate of dangerous behavior is generally very low, so clinicians are being asked to predict a phenomenon that rarely occurs. The clinical assessments of persons suspected of being dangerous are usually conducted in hospitals or prisons, whereas the environment where dangerousness is likely to occur is "on the streets." The predictions have often been for long-term dangerousness, which is harder to predict than dangerousness over a shorter time frame such as two weeks.

However, if we examine clinicians' ability to predict dangerous behavior on a short-term basis, particularly when they are familiar with whether a person has a history of prior violence or has stated an intention to behave violently, we find the predictions to be much more accurate (Klassen & O'Connor, 1988). Thus, reasonable accuracy in predictions can be expected under the following conditions: (1) the predictions are

## The Science of

### BOX 12-7

### Risk assessment: What are the most important predictors of violence?

Based on a review of risk assessment research, Kevin Douglas and Christopher Webster (1999) identified 20 predictor variables that are related to the risk of violence. Ten of these variables are *static predictors*, meaning that they are features about an individual or an individual's past that do not change. Five variables are termed *dynamic predictors* because they involve features about the individual such as psychological condition, emotional state, and involvement in treatment that can and do change over time. The final five variables, known as *risk management predictors*, are concerned with the nature of the environments in which a subject will live in the future.

*Static Predictors;* in general, these variables tend to be the strongest predictors of future violence:

1. A *history of prior violence*
2. *The younger a person's age,* particularly if the person's first incidence of violence was committed at a young age
3. A *history of relationship instability or hostility*
4. A *history of employment instability* involving frequent unemployment or job terminations
5. A *pattern of drug or alcohol abuse*
6. A *major mental disorder* such as schizophrenia or severe mood disturbances

7. A diagnosis of *psychopathy or antisocial personality disorder*
8. A *history of early maladjustment at home or school*
9. A *diagnosis of any personality disorder,* but especially antisocial personality disorder and borderline personality disorder
10. A history of *attempted or actual escapes from custody or confinement*

*Dynamic Predictors;* the following clinical variables have been shown to often correlate with increased risks for dangerous behavior

11. A *lack of insight* into one's own personality and capacity for violent behavior as well as a tendency to misunderstand the intentions of others
12. A tendency to be *angry and hostile* in multiple situations
13. Experiencing *psychotic symptoms such as delusions and hallucinations that threaten a person's self-control*
14. Tendencies toward *impulsivity and unstable negative emotions*
15. *Resistance or unresponsiveness to psychiatric treatment*

*Risk Management Predictors;* these factors involve characteristics of social and physical environments that can elevate risks for violence:

16. A *lack of adequate supervision and monitoring for persons released from institutions*

17. *Easy access to victims, weapons, alcohol, and drugs*
18. *Lack of social support and tangible resources for effective living*
19. *Noncompliance with medication and other mental health treatments*
20. *Excessive stress in the areas of family, employment, and peers*

Based on this list, several risk assessment instruments have been developed to help clinicians utilize the most important variables for assessing risk and predicting violence. For example, the HCR-20 (meaning 20 historical, clinical, and risk management variables; Webster, Douglas, Eaves, & Hart, 1997) predicts violent behavior by released psychiatric patients. The Violence Risk Appraisal Guide (VRAG; Harris, Rice, & Quinsey, 1993) and a related instrument known as the Violence Prediction Scheme (VPS; Webster, Harris, Rice, Cormier, & Quinsey, 1994) have been used to predict violent recidivism among offenders. New instruments designed to predict violence in specific subgroups, such as sex offenders (Hanson & Thornton, 2000) and spouse abusers (Kropp & Hart, 2000) have also been developed recently. Each of these instruments relies heavily on the collection and combination of the static variables that have proven to be the strongest predictors of violence.

for the short term, (2) they are made for environmental settings for which the clinician has data about the person's past behavior, (3) they consider the person's history of past violent behavior, and (4) they are made for individuals belonging to groups with relatively high base rates of violence (Litwack & Schlesinger, 1987; Mossman, 1994).

As accustomed as psychologists once were to claiming that mental illness and violence are not associated, recent evidence suggests that this opinion may, in fact, be wrong. Monahan himself has revised his stance on this issue. Whereas he once dismissed any link between mental illness and violence, he now believes that a small but reliable connection exists. After reviewing recent studies that surveyed the prevalence of violent behavior among mentally ill people in the community and that measured levels of mental illness among violent citizens, Monahan (1992) concluded, "there appears to be a relationship between mental disorder and violent behavior. Mental disorder may be a robust and significant risk factor for the occurrence of violence" (p. 519).

# Experts in the Adversarial System

Judges, lawyers, and mental-health professionals themselves have expressed great concern about the reliability, validity, propriety, and usefulness of expert testimony. Former federal appellate judge David T. Bazelon (1974) once complained that "psychiatry . . . is the ultimate wizardry . . . in no case is it more difficult to elicit productive and reliable testimony than in cases that call on the knowledge and practice of psychiatry." This view was echoed by Warren Burger (Burger, 1975), a past Chief Justice of the Supreme Court, who chided experts for the "uncertainties of psychiatric diagnosis." Sharply worded critiques of psychologists' expert testimony can be found in several sources (Bonnie & Slobogin, 1980; Ennis & Litwack, 1974; Morse, 1978), and one well-known guidebook by Ziskin and Faust (1988) has been devoted entirely to the subject of how to cross-examine mental health professionals who are giving expert testimony. So popular is this resource that experts who have been cross-examined according to its principles are often said to have been "Ziskinized."

What are the main problems with or objections to testimony by psychological or psychiatric experts? Smith (1989) lists the following eight concerns:

1. The scientific foundations for much of the testimony offered in court is often less than adequate, leading to unreliable information and therefore potentially incorrect verdicts.

2. Much of the testimony is of limited relevance, therefore wasting court time and burdening an already crowded docket.

3. Experts are too often permitted to testify about "ultimate issues" (e.g., Is the defendant insane? Was the plaintiff emotionally damaged?), which should be left to juries to decide.

4. Expert testimony is frequently used to introduce information that would otherwise be prohibited because it is hearsay. (Experts are permitted to share this information with juries if it is the kind of information they routinely rely on in reaching expert opinions.)

5. The adversarial system compromises experts' objectivity. Experts readily testify to opinions that favor the side that retained them, becoming little more than "hired guns" whose testimony can be bought.

6. Expert testimony is very expensive, and relying on experts gives an advantage to the side with the most money.

7. Testing the reliability and validity of expert opinions through cross-examination is inadequate because attorneys are usually not well equipped to conduct such cross-examination, and juries often fail to understand the significance of the information that is uncovered during the cross-examination.

8. The spectacle of experts disagreeing with one another in trial after trial ultimately reduces the public's esteem for mental-health professionals.

BOX 12-8 **Limiting instructions for the jury**

The following instructions are to be given by the court upon qualification of an opinion witness by Judge Charles R. Richey:

## OPINION WITNESS TESTIMONY

Ladies and Gentlemen, please note that the Rules of Evidence ordinarily do not permit witnesses to testify as to their opinions or conclusions. Two exceptions to this rule exist. The first exception allows an ordinary citizen to give his or her opinion as to matters that he or she observed or of which he or she has firsthand knowledge. The second exception allows witnesses who, by education, training and experience, have acquired a certain specialized knowledge in some art, science, profession or calling to state an opinion as to relevant and material matters.

The purpose of opinion witness testimony is to assist you in understanding the evidence and deciding the facts in this case. You are not bound by this testimony and, in weighing it, you may consider his or her qualifications, opinions and reasons for testifying, as well as all other considerations that apply when you evaluate the credibility of any witness. In other words, you should give it such weight as you think it fairly deserves and consider it in light of all the evidence in this case.

In response to these concerns, some of which are also supported by empirical research (see Box 12-3), several reforms of expert testimony have been proposed. Most of these suggestions are aimed at reducing the undue influence or excessive partisanship that can adversely affect expert testimony. As a result, federal courts and some state courts do not allow experts to testify about the "ultimate issue" (e.g., Is a person competent? Was a death accidental or the result of suicide?) in forensic cases. As you will recall from Chapter 11, this change was part of the overall reform of federal laws concerning insanity that occurred in the 1980s. There is little evidence that limiting experts' testimony in this way has had much impact on the use or success of the insanity defense (Borum & Fulero, 1999), and it is not at all certain that it would have any larger impact in the kinds of cases we discussed in this chapter.

Other suggestions have been to reduce the overly adversarial nature of expert testimony by limiting the number of experts on a given topic, by requiring that the experts be chosen from an approved panel of individuals reputed to be objective and highly competent, and by allowing testimony only from experts who have been appointed by a judge rather than hired by opposing attorneys. Although these changes would appear to reduce the hired gun problem, it is not clear that consensus could be easily reached on which experts belong on an approved list or that being appointed by a judge guarantees an expert's objectivity. Furthermore, recent research suggests that jurors might already be inclined on their own to discount the testimony of experts who they perceive to be "hired guns" because of the high fees they are paid and a history of testifying frequently (Cooper & Neuhaus, 2000).

Several scholars have suggested that courts not permit clinical opinion testimony unless it can be shown that it satisfies standards of scientific reliability. The standard required by the *Daubert/Kumho* decisions have now made this recommendation more realistic (Faust & Ziskin, 1988; Imwinkelried, 1994). Such a requirement might produce a decline in testimony by forensic psychologists and psychiatrists, but unless lawyers are educated more thoroughly about scientific methodology, it is not clear that they can make informed distinctions between "good" and "bad" science (Gless, 1995).

A more modest reform, but one we believe has merit, is simply to ban any reference to witnesses as providing *expert* testimony, a term that suggests that jurors should pay extra deference to it. Instead, judges would always refer—in the presence of juries—to *opinion* testimony or witnesses. In addition to deleting any mention of expert testimony, Federal Judge Charles R. Richey (1994) recommends that juries be read a special instruction (see ◆ **Box 12-8**) before hearing any opinion testimony in order to reduce its possible prejudicial impact.

## SUMMARY

**1. *Under what conditions can a plaintiff be compensated for psychological damages?*** Plaintiffs can seek damages in civil trials if they are a victim of a tort, which is a wrongful act that can be proven to have caused them harm. Although the law has historically been skeptical of claims for psychological harm and emotional distress unless also accompanied by physical injuries, the recent trend has been to allow plaintiffs to be compensated for emotional damages (without any physical injuries) resulting from intentionally outrageous or negligent conduct.

**2. *What is workers' compensation, and how do mental-health professionals become involved in such cases?*** Workers' compensation is a no-fault system now used by all states and the federal system to provide a streamlined alternative for determining the compensation of workers who are injured in the course of their jobs. Although formal trials are not held or juries used in workers' compensation cases, it is not clear that these cases are handled as expeditiously as intended. Psychologists often testify in workers' compensation hearings about the extent, cause, and likely prognosis for psychological problems that have developed following a physical injury and/or work-related stress.

**3. *What abilities are involved in civil competence?*** Questions of civil competence focus on whether an individual has the mental capacity to understand information that is relevant to decision making in a given situation and then make an informed choice about what to do. The issue of civil competence is raised in instances in which it is not clear that an individual is capable of managing his or her financial affairs, giving informed consent to current or future medical treatments, or executing a will.

**4. *What are psychological autopsies, and how are they used?*** A psychological autopsy, also called an *equivocal death analysis,* involves a clinical assessment of the psychological condition of a now-deceased individual at some previous point in time. They are used in cases in which there are questions about the cause of death (suicide vs. accident) or the mental state of someone who executed a will.

**5. *What criteria are used in making decisions about child custody disputes?*** The best interest of the child is the main criterion applied to disputes about which parent should have custody of a child following divorce. Evaluations of parental fitness address a different question: Should a parent's custody of a child be terminated because of indications of parental unfitness? Many mental-health professionals regard custody and parental fitness assessments to be the most difficult evaluations they perform. For this reason, as well as an attempt to reduce the stress of custody battles, custody mediation has been developed as a less adversarial means of resolving these disputes.

**6. *How well can clinicians assess the risk of dangerousness, a key criterion for civil commitment?*** Persons who are considered gravely disabled or dangerous to themselves or others may be committed to a state mental hospital against their will, but they have the right to a hearing shortly thereafter to determine whether they should be retained. After being hospitalized, some patients may continue on outpatient commitment. Long-term predictions of dangerousness cannot be made with any acceptable degree of accuracy, but there is a reliable association among several static, dynamic, and environmental factors and dangerous behavior that provides a basis for reasonably accurate short-term assessments of risk.

**7.** *What are the problems with expert testimony, and what reforms have been proposed?*

The main objections to expert testimony are that it invades the province of the jury, is too adversarial and therefore not sufficiently objective, takes too much court time, introduces irrelevant information, and is often founded on an insufficient scientific base. Reforms have focused on limiting the scope of expert testimony, reducing the partisanship involved in adversaries retaining their own experts, requiring judges to examine more strictly the scientific foundation of expert testimony, and referring to it as opinion testimony rather than *expert* testimony.

## KEY TERMS

advance medical
   directives
breached duty*
civil commitment
civil competence
compensatory damages
dangerousness

duty*
equivocal death
   analysis
future best interests of
   the child
harm
intentional behavior*

joint custody
malingering
mediation*
negligence*
primary caretaker
   standard
proximate cause

psychological autopsy*
punitive damages*
risk assessment
sole custody
tort*
validity scales*

---

**InfoTrac**
**COLLEGE**
**EDITION**

For additional readings go to **http://www.infotrac-college.com/wadsworth** and enter a search term related to your interest. The key terms that have been asterisked above will pull up several related articles.

# The Trial Process

### ORIENTING QUESTIONS

1. *What is the purpose of a trial?*
2. *What are the steps the legal system follows in bringing a case to trial?*
3. *What is the order of procedures in the trial itself?*
4. *Do juries' verdicts differ from those of judges?*
5. *What is jury nullification?*
6. *How has race played an issue in the debate over jury nullification?*

# THE CASE OF

**BOX 13-1   Bruno Richard Hauptmann: Arguments and evidence**

Even though the trial occurred about 70 years ago, people still talk about it, books are still being published about it, and critics still speculate whether the verdict was just (Behn, 1995; Berg, 1998). The act that led to it has been termed one of the "crimes of the century" (Geis & Bienen, 1998). The violent treatment of the victim sickened our society, which then sought revenge and retribution.

Sometime during the night of March 1, 1932, the young son of Colonel Charles A. Lindbergh was kidnapped from a crib in the nursery of his parents' estate in Hopewell, New Jersey. Lindbergh, who ironically had been called "Lucky Lindy," was the quintessential American hero; in 1927, piloting the *Spirit of St. Louis,* he had become the first person to complete a solo flight from the United States to Europe.

A month after the baby's kidnapping, Colonel Lindbergh, through a go-between, paid $50,000 to a shadowy figure he had arranged to meet in a Bronx, New York, cemetery; Lindbergh had been assured that the child would then be returned unharmed. But he was not. On May

12, 1932, two months after the kidnapping, the baby's body was found in a shallow grave about five miles from Lindbergh's home. His skull had been bashed in, probably on the night he was kidnapped.

For more than two years, the police and the FBI sought the criminal. They had found several physical clues, including ransom notes, footprints under a first-floor window, and a makeshift ladder apparently used to climb to the second-floor nursery, but it was not until September 19, 1934, that the police arrested Bruno Hauptmann and charged him with the crime.

Bruno Richard Hauptmann, 34 at the time of his arrest, was German born and in the United States illegally. Through dogged persistence, he had entered the United States without money, passport, or source of income and successfully adapted to a new country and a new language.

The trial began in Flemington, New Jersey, the day after New Year's in 1935. Public interest was unquenchable; hundreds of reporters crowded into the small courthouse to cover the trial. Some media representatives went beyond calm, objective reporting; "no harm-

*Charles and Anne Lindbergh*

less rumor was too wild to print, no conjecture too fantastic to publish" (Whipple, 1937, pp. 46–47). Radio stations retained well-known attorneys daily to broadcast their opinions about the progress of the case and about Hauptmann's likelihood of conviction.

The public hoped that those chances were good; the whole country seemed to harbor a deep-felt desire that the defendant be convicted and executed. And he was. After a trial that lasted 40 days, the jury unanimously voted that Bruno Richard Hauptmann was guilty of murder; there was no recommendation of mercy from

# What Is the Purpose of a Trial?

Every trial, civil or criminal, presents two contrasting versions of the truth, just as the Hauptmann trial did (see ◆ Box 13-1). Both sides try

to present the "facts" of the matter in question in order to convince the fact finder (the judge or the jury) that their claims are the truth. The fact finder must render judgments on the probable truth or falsity of each side's statements and evidence.

the death sentence. After several unsuccessful appeals, he was electrocuted on April 3, 1936.

Was Bruno Hauptmann guilty? Here are the arguments and evidence used by each side in his trial. What do you think?

In the Lindbergh kidnapping trial, the prosecution presented the following evidence and arguments:

1. One of the ransom bills was found in a bank deposit from a gasoline station. In examining the bill, the FBI discovered written on it an automobile license plate number—that of a car registered to Hauptmann.

2. A thorough search of Hauptmann's garage revealed $14,600 of the Lindbergh ransom money secreted in an extraordinary hiding place.

3. Written on a strip of wood in a closet in Hauptmann's house was the telephone number of the man who served as an intermediary in the transport of the ransom money.

4. When the police dictated to Hauptmann the contents of the ransom notes and asked him to transcribe them, he misspelled certain words, just as the author

of the notes had. (The wording of the notes, such as "The child is in gut care," implied that they had been composed by a German-speaking person.)

5. Hauptmann stopped work on the very day the ransom was paid and never thereafter resumed steady employment. He bragged to friends that he could live without working because he knew how to beat the stock market, although in actuality he was losing money (Whipple, 1937).

6. Wood from the makeshift ladder could have come from a portion of the floorboards of Hauptmann's attic that had been removed.

The defense presented the following responses:

1. Several witnesses testified that they saw Hauptmann in the Bronx, New York, on the night of the kidnapping, implying that he could not have kidnapped the baby.

2. Expert witnesses claimed that the wood on the makeshift ladder did not match that from the attic.

3. The ransom money in his garage, he said, had belonged to

his friend Isidor Fisch. Fisch had returned to Germany and then died, and so Hauptmann had kept the money safely hidden.

4. Hauptmann claimed that, when the police had dictated the ransom notes to him, they insisted that he spell the words as they were spelled in the notes. He knew, for example, that *boat* was not spelled *boad*, as it was on the notes.

Hauptmann proclaimed his innocence to the day he died; so did his wife, who for 60 years sought to reverse the decision. As recently as 1985, the U.S. Third Circuit Court of Appeals rejected her request to reinstitute a lawsuit against the state of New Jersey for wrongfully trying and convicting her husband. In that same year, a book by Ludovic Kennedy (1985) concluded that the prosecution withheld unfavorable evidence, perjured its witnesses, and capitalized on the public mood in order to frame Hauptmann. A more recent review of the case (Behn, 1995) reconsiders early speculation that Mrs. Lindbergh's sister was the real murderer.

---

If we were asked what the purpose of a trial is, our first response might be "to determine the truth, of course." Conflicts over the purposes of the legal system, however, raise the question of whether this is the prime function of a trial. In fact, trials serve many purposes in our society. In line with one of the dilemmas described in Chapter 1, trials also serve the function of providing a sense of stability and a way to resolve conflicting issues so that the disputants can get some satisfaction. Miller and Boster (1977) have identified three images of the trial that reflect these contrasting conceptions.

## The Trial as a Rational, Rule-Governed Event

Many people see a trial as a "rational, rule-governed event involving the parties to a court-room controversy in a collective search for the truth" (Miller & Boster, 1977, p. 23). This view assumes that what really happened can be clearly ascertained—that witnesses are capable of knowing, remembering, and describing events completely and accurately. Although this image of the trial recognizes that the opposing attorneys present only those facts that buttress their positions, it assumes that the truth will emerge from the confrontation of conflicting facts. It also assumes that judges or jurors, in weighing these facts, can "lay aside their prejudices and preconceived views regarding the case and replace such biases with a dispassionate analysis of the arguments and evidence" (Miller & Boster, 1977, p. 25).

## The Trial as a Test of Credibility

The image of the trial as a rational, rule-governed event has been challenged on several grounds. Chapter 7 questioned the assumption that eyewitnesses are thorough and accurate reporters, as the legal system would like to believe they are. We saw in Chapter 8 that interrogations can sometimes result in false confessions and that jurors are not particularly good at distinguishing false confessions from true ones. Sections of Chapters 14 and 15 review the limitations of jurors and judges as they seek to put aside their own experiences and prejudices. Although this image remains as an aspiration, other images need to be considered.

A second conception, that the trial is a test of credibility, acknowledges that facts and evidence are always incomplete and biased. Hence, the decision makers, whether judge or jury, "must not only weigh the information and evidence, but must also evaluate the veracity of the opposing evidential and informational sources" (Miller & Boster, 1977, p. 28). Fact finders must focus on the way evidence is presented, the qualifications of witnesses, the omissions from a body of testimony, and the inconsistencies between witnesses. Competence and trustworthiness of witnesses take on added importance in this image.

These two images share the belief that the primary function of a trial is to produce the most nearly valid judgment about the guilt of a criminal defendant or the responsibility of a civil defendant. The difference between the two images is one of degree, not of kind; Miller and Boster (1977) observe that "where the two images diverge is in the relative emphasis they place on weighing information and evidence per se as opposed to evaluating the believability of the sources of such information" (p. 29).

This image of the trial also has problems. Fact finders often make unwarranted inferences about witnesses and attorneys based on race, gender, mannerisms, or style of speech. Judges' and jurors' judgments of credibility may be based more on stereotypes, folklore, or "commonsense intuition" than on the facts.

## The Trial as a Conflict-Resolving Ritual

The third image shifts the function of the trial from determining the truth to providing a mechanism to resolve controversies. Miller and Boster (1977) express it this way: "At the risk of oversimplification we suggest that it removes primary attention from the concept of doing justice and transfers it to the psychological realm of *creating a sense that justice is being done*" (p. 34).

Chapter 1 posed the dilemma between two needs of society: achieving truth and providing a way to resolve conflicts. This third image gives priority to maintaining a shared perception that "our legal system provides an efficient means of resolving conflict peacefully" (p. 34). Truth remains a goal, but participants in the trial process also need both the opportunity to have their "day in court" and the reassurance that, whatever the outcome, "justice was done."

In 1935, the nation wanted to know the identity of the Lindbergh baby's kidnapper. Did Bruno Hauptmann really do it? But people also needed to know that the killer had been captured, tried, and convicted. The nation could not indefinitely tolerate any uncertainty in this matter. Thus, trials serve to stabilize society, provide answers, and give closure so that people can resume their normal business. They are necessary rituals in our process of ensuring that evil acts are punished in a just manner.

This stabilizing function is worthless, of course, if the public doubts that justice was done in the process. Sometimes a sense of closure is not the result; the widespread dissatisfaction in some segments of our society with the outcome of O. J. Simpson's criminal trial meant continued media interest and public fascination with his actions and statements. The belief that "he got away with murder" even led to proposals to reform and restrict the jury system, which we review in Chapter 15. However, other segments of society were equally dissatisfied with the verdict in Simpson's civil trial, when he was found liable for the deaths of his ex-wife and her friend, Ronald Goldman. Perhaps together, the verdicts in the two trials converged on a reasonable outcome—Simpson probably was the killer, but this couldn't be proven to the level of certainty required for a criminal conviction.

These three contrasting images are guideposts for interpreting the findings presented in this and the next two chapters. Truth is elusive, and in the legal system, all truth seekers are subject to human error, even though the system seems to assume that they approach infallibility. The failure to achieve perfection in our decision making will become evident as we review the steps in the trial process.

# Steps in the Trial Process

The usual steps in a trial are sketched out here as a framework for issues to be evaluated in this and the next two chapters.

## Preliminary Actions

In Chapter 10, we discussed **discovery,** the pretrial process by which each side tries to gain vital information about the case that will be presented by the other side. This information includes statements by witnesses, police records, documents, material possessions, experts' opinions, and anything else relevant to the case.

Statements from parties involved in a case may be taken in written form, called **written interrogatories**. These do not permit cross-examination. In carrying out discovery, particularly in civil cases, attorneys may also collect **depositions** from witnesses expected to testify at trial. A deposition is usually an oral statement by a potential witness, given under oath in the presence of a court reporter and attorneys from both sides. (A judge is seldom present.) It is taken in question-and-answer form, like testimony in court, with the opportunity for the opposing lawyer (or "adversary") to cross-examine the witness. In his now-famous deposition in the Paula Jones sexual harassment case, President Clinton stated that he had not had sexual relations with Monica Lewinsky. And in her equally famous deposition given in the Senate impeachment trial of President Clinton, Lewinsky swore under oath that she had not been asked to lie about their relationship.

Before any trial, the decision must be made whether a judge or a jury will hear the evidence and render the verdict. The U.S. Constitution provides criminal defendants with the right to have the charges against them judged by a jury of their peers. In addition, the defendant is entitled to be acquitted unless the jury finds his guilt beyond a reasonable doubt. Though a judge may consider evidence not heard by the jury in imposing a sentence, a judge may not increase the maximum penalty for the offense based on matters not considered by the jury. In *Apprendi v. New Jersey*, 99-478 (June 26, 2000), the United States Supreme Court struck down a New Jersey statute that authorized judges to increase the maximum penalty for "hate crime" offenses—that is, crimes motivated by the victim's race, national origin, or sexual orientation. After the defendant pled guilty to a firearms violation, the judge in *Apprendi* held a hearing and determined that the crime was racially motivated. He then increased the maximum sentence from 20 to

30 years. In reversing the sentence, the Supreme Court held that the defendant was entitled to have a jury, applying the reasonable doubt standard, decide his motivation.

Although most defendants opt for a jury trial, some will, in certain cases, choose to waive a jury trial and, if the prosecutor agrees, have a judge decide the case. Does it make any difference? We answer this important question in a later section of this chapter.

Civil lawsuits may also be decided by either a jury or a judge, depending on the preferences of the opposing parties. Many states have revised the size and **decision rule** from the traditional 12-person jury requiring a unanimous verdict. In some states, for some kinds of cases, juries as small as six persons and decision rules requiring only a three-fourths majority are in effect. We assess the history of these changes and their psychological impact in Chapter 15.

## Jury Selection

If the trial is before a jury, the identification of jurors involves a two-step process. The first step is to draw a panel of prospective jurors, called a **venire,** from a large list (usually based on voter registration lists and lists of licensed drivers).

Once the venire for a particular trial has been selected—this may be anywhere from 30 to 200 people, depending on the customary practices of that jurisdiction and the nature of the trial—a process known as **voir dire** is employed to select the actual jurors. (*Voir dire,* in French, means "to tell the truth.") In actuality, prospective jurors who reveal biases and are unable to be open-minded about the case are dismissed from service, so that the task is one of elimination rather than selection. Prospective jurors who appear free of these limitations are thus "selected." Voir dire can have important effects on the outcome of the trial; the process is described in detail in Chapter 14.

## The Trial

At the beginning of the trial itself, lawyers for each side are permitted to make **opening statements.**

These are not part of the evidence (if the trial is before a jury, the jurors are instructed that these opening statements are not to be considered evidence), but they serve as overviews of the evidence to be presented. The prosecution or plaintiff usually goes first, as this side is the one that brought charges and bears the burden of proof. Attorneys for the defendant, in either a criminal or civil trial, can choose to present their opening statement immediately after the other side's or wait until it is their turn to present evidence.

After opening statements, the prosecution or plaintiff calls its witnesses. Each witness testifies under oath, with the threat of a charge of **perjury** if the witness fails to be truthful. That witness is then cross-examined by the adverse counsel, after which the original attorney has a chance for **redirect questioning.** Redirect questioning is likely if the original attorney feels the opposition has "impeached" his or her witness; **impeach** in this context refers to a cross-examination that has effectively called into question the credibility (or reliability) of the witness.

The purpose of redirect examination is to "rehabilitate" the witness, or to salvage his or her original testimony. The defense, however, has one more chance to question the witness, a process called **recross** (for "recross-examination").

After the prosecution's or plaintiff's attorneys have presented all their witnesses, it is the defense's turn. The same procedure of direct examination, cross-examination, redirect, and recross is used.

After both sides have presented their witnesses, one or both may decide to introduce additional evidence and witnesses and petition the judge's permission to do so—that is, to present **rebuttal evidence,** which attempts to counteract or disprove evidence given by an earlier adverse witness.

Once all the evidence has been presented, each side is permitted to make a **closing argument,** also called a *summation*. Although jurisdictions vary, ordinarily the prosecution or plaintiff gets the first summation, followed by the defense, after which the prosecution or plaintiff has an opportunity to rebut.

The final step in the jury trial is for the judge to give instructions to the jury. (In some states, instructions precede the closing arguments.) The judge informs the jury of the relevant law. For example, a definition of the crime is given, as well as a statement of what elements must be present for it to have occurred—that is, whether the defendant had the motive and the opportunity to do so. The judge also instructs jurors about the standard they should use to weigh the evidence (see ◆ Box 13-2).

With criminal charges, the jurors must be convinced **"beyond a reasonable doubt"** that the defendant is guilty before they vote to convict. Although the concept of "reasonable doubt" is difficult to interpret, generally it means that jurors should be strongly convinced (but not necessarily convinced beyond all doubt). Each of us interprets such an instruction differently, and, as Chapter 15 illustrates, this instruction is often a source of confusion and frustration among jurors.

In a civil trial, in which one party brings a claim against another, a different standard is used. The **preponderance of the evidence** is all that is necessary to find in favor of one side. Usually, judges and attorneys translate this to mean, "Even if you find the evidence favoring one side to be only slightly more convincing than the other side's, rule in favor of that side." Preponderance is often interpreted as meaning at least 51% of the evidence.

The jury is sometimes given instructions on how to deliberate, but these are usually sparse. Jurors are excused to the deliberation room, and no one—not even the bailiff or the judge—can be present or eavesdrop on their deliberations. When the jury has reached its verdict, its foreperson informs the bailiff, who informs the judge, who reconvenes the attorneys and defendants (and plaintiffs in a civil trial) for the announcement of the verdict.

## Sentencing

If the defendant in a criminal trial is judged guilty, at some later point a punishment must be decided.

In many jurisdictions, the judge makes this decision, but in some states, the jury is reconvened, evidence relevant to the sentencing decision is presented by both sides, and the jury deliberates until it agrees on a recommended punishment.

In cases involving the death penalty (described in Chapter 17), states differ with respect to the requirements for the judge to follow the jury's decision on a sentence; in several states, judges are permitted to override a jury's judgment and impose a death sentence when the jury has recommended life in prison (Greenhouse, 1995; Morier, 1995). Likewise, in a civil trial, in cases in which the jury has awarded damages to the plaintiff, the judge may reduce the award if he or she finds it excessive (Fisk, 1998).

## The Appellate Process

Treatment of guilty defendants within the legal system does not end when they are sentenced to a prison term or to probation. To protect the rights of those who may have been convicted unjustly, society grants any defendant the opportunity to appeal a verdict to a higher level of courts. Appeals are also possible in virtually every civil suit.

As in earlier steps in the legal process, a conflict of values occurs as appeals are pursued. One goal is equality before the law—that is, to administer justice consistently and fairly. But appellate courts also try to be sensitive to individual differences in what at first appear to be similar cases. Appellate courts recognize that judges and juries can make errors. The appellate procedure is used to correct mistakes that substantially impair the fairness of trials; it also helps promote a level of consistency in trial procedures.

When a decision is appealed to a higher court, the appellate judges read the record (transcript of the trial proceedings), the pleadings (motions and accompanying documents filed by the attorneys), and the briefs (written arguments, which are rarely brief, from both sides about the issues on appeal) and then decide whether to overturn the original trial decision or let it stand. Appellate judges rarely reverse a verdict based on

## The Science of

**BOX 13-2**    **Jury instructions: How well do studies generalize to real juries?**

Before the jury adjourns to deliberate, the judge gives instructions regarding the law in the case. In a typical criminal case, these instructions will include such matters as the functions of the judge and the jury, the presumption of innocence, the burden of proof, a definition of the offense including the elements that must be proved, defenses that are proper in the case (e.g., insanity plea, entrapment claims), and the procedures to be followed in the jury room.

A great deal of research has focused on jurors' ability to understand and apply their instructions and has consistently shown that jurors do not understand a large portion of the instructions presented to them (Lieberman & Sales, 1997). It is common to find over half the instructions misunderstood, and some studies have reported that less than 10% of the important parts of judicial in-

structions can be recalled after a brief interval (Hastie, Schkade, & Payne, 1998). Although many studies document jurors' difficulties in comprehending their instructions, few changes have been introduced in the way that judges instruct juries despite empirical evidence that a few modifications, such as simplifying the language of the instructions, giving them in writing as well as orally, or giving them on more than one occasion, would improve jurors' recall and understanding. One reason for the slow implementation of psychological research findings is that legal policymakers may not trust the data, most of which has been generated by mock jurors who hear or read mock cases in a laboratory setting (Reifman, Gusick, & Ellsworth, 1992). Judges in particular, not trained in the rigors of experimental methodologies, may be skeptical of research

that attempts to simulate what happens in an actual courtroom.

To rectify this situation, Alan Reifman, Spencer Gusick, and Phoebe Ellsworth (1992) conducted a study to test the generalizability of the laboratory demonstrations of poor juror comprehension by examining real jurors' ability to understand the law. Unlike mock jurors, the participants in this study were actually called for jury duty: all of them were questioned (and instructed) by attorneys during voir dire, and some were selected to serve on juries (and as a result, also received formal instructions delivered by the judge at the end of the trial). After either being excused during voir dire or after completing their jury service, jurors were mailed a questionnaire designed to test their knowledge of the substantive and procedural law that applied in the case. Sixty-three percent of respondents had

---

the facts of the case or the apparent legitimacy of that verdict. When they do reverse, it is usually because they believe that the trial judge made a procedural error, for example, by allowing controversial evidence to be presented or by failing to allow the jury to consider some evidence that should have been included.

If a verdict in a criminal trial is overturned or reversed, the appeals court will either order a retrial or order the charges thrown out. In reviewing the decision in a civil case, an appellate court can let the decision stand, reverse it (i.e., rule in favor of the side that lost rather than the side that won),

or make some other changes in the decision. One possible conclusion in either civil or criminal appeals is that certain evidence should not have been admitted or certain instructions should not have been given; hence, a new trial may be ordered.

## Judges' Decisions versus Juries' Decisions

As noted earlier, defendants in criminal trials ordinarily opt for a jury to decide their guilt or inno-

actually served on a jury, and 37% had been questioned and dismissed. Reifman and his colleagues wanted to know whether the poor showing jurors make on comprehension tests in laboratory studies would be replicated in this more realistic situation.

The questionnaire included ten questions related to jurors' duties and procedural rules. As these data show, instructed jurors scored significantly higher than noninstructed jurors, suggesting that instructions do provide some understanding of procedural law.

*Mean number correct for ten questions involving jurors' duties and procedural rules:*

Jurors instructed
   in criminal cases = 4.78

Jurors instructed
   in civil cases = 4.18

People who did
   not sit in a trial = 3.81

Researchers also assessed knowledge of the substantive law (the laws that specifically apply to the case at hand—e.g., the elements of a crime) and found that 35% of questions were answered correctly by individuals who had not heard the instructions bearing on particular crimes, and 41% of questions were answered correctly by jurors who had actually heard the instructions. This small percentage difference was not statistically significant, indicating that the instructions were ineffective in conveying important aspects of the law to jurors. There was some glimmer of hope in these results, however; jurors who requested help from the judge performed better than those who did not, particularly when the judge provided supplemental information.

Most important, these findings are generally similar to those of laboratory experiments, suggesting that the vast number of experimental studies that assess jurors' abilities to understand and apply instructions generalize to real juries and should be taken seriously. Appellate judges cite errors in instructions in a large number of cases that are reversed on appeal, and jury instructions are constantly being rewritten to state the law more precisely. But ironically, few legal policymakers seem concerned about whether jurors actually understand the law as conveyed in their jury instructions. Perhaps the more realistic setting of this study and its replication of many previous findings will convince them that the law as understood by jurors is worthy of their attention.

cence, but if the prosecutor consents, they can choose to have a judge decide (called a **bench trial**). The parties involved in a civil case can also opt for a bench trial. Federal Judge Thomas Penfield Jackson decided the landmark case brought by the government against the software giant, the Microsoft Corporation. In late 1999, after a year-long trial, Judge Jackson said that Microsoft had used its monopoly power to stifle innovation, reduce competition, and hurt consumers.

Why do some plaintiffs and defendants choose to have their case decided by a jury or by a judge? And does it make any difference? A survey (Mac-Coun & Tyler, 1988) found that citizens believe a jury decision offers more procedural fairness (i.e., greater thoroughness, better representation of the community, fewer personal biases affecting decisions) than a decision by a judge.

We know that juries and judges sometimes disagree, but we don't know how frequently. When they do disagree, can we say which made the better decision? After all, jury verdicts are not systematically compared against some "correct," back-of-the-book answer—even if there were one.

Jury verdicts are almost never "second-guessed" and reversed by the judge. One prominent

**TABLE 13.1** ◆ *Agreement of judges' and juries' verdicts based on 3576 trials (in percentage of all trials)*

| | JURY | | | |
|---|---|---|---|---|
| JUDGE | ACQUITS | CONVICTS | HANGS | TOTAL, JUDGE |
| Acquits | **13.4** | 2.2 | 1.1 | 16.7 |
| Convicts | 16.9 | **62.0** | 4.4 | 83.3 |
| Total, jury | 30.3 | 64.2 | 5.5 | 100.0 |

SOURCE: Adapted from Kalven and Zeisel (1966, p. 56). Figures in bold show judge/jury agreements on verdict.

exception is the case of Louise Woodward, discussed in Chapter 1, that riveted both sides of the Atlantic Ocean in the fall of 1997. Woodward, a young English au pair, was convicted by a Massachusetts jury of second-degree murder and sentenced to life imprisonment for the death of Matthew Eappen, age eight and a half months. Declaring that the penalty was too harsh, the judge reduced her conviction to that of manslaughter and the life sentence to time already served, 279 days. The judge stated that he was seeking a "compassionate conclusion" to the case. On review of this case, the Massachusetts Supreme Court chastised the judge for not making the manslaughter verdict available as one option for the jury.

Such reversals are unusual; jury verdicts are rarely overturned on appeal because they were wrong, and not-guilty verdicts are final regardless of their validity. So we must rely on the social sciences and survey data to get some estimate of how frequently judges and jurors agree.

Harry Kalven and Hans Zeisel (1966), professors at the University of Chicago, carried out the most extensive survey of the outcomes of jury trials. It is a classic application of the methods of social science to the understanding of juries' decisions. Kalven and Zeisel asked each district court judge and federal judge in the United States to provide information about recent jury trials over which he or she had presided. Of approximately 3500 judges, only about 500 responded to a detailed questionnaire. But some judges provided information about a large number of trials—some, amazingly, about more than 50 trials—so that the database for this analysis consisted of ap-

proximately 3500 trials. Although one might question whether judges can recall accurately the details of as many as 50 different cases, the Kalven and Zeisel study remains the most extensive investigation of judge/jury agreement that has been conducted.

Of basic concern were two questions: What was the jury's verdict? And did the judge agree? By looking at the frequency of agreement, we can get hints about the extent of juries' deviations from application of the law.

In criminal trials, the judges reported that their verdict would have been the same as the jury's actual verdict 75% of the time (see Table 13.1 for detailed results). Thus, in three-fourths of the trials, two independent fact-finding agents would have brought forth the same result. Similar consistency was found for civil trials, as illustrated in Table 13.2. Although each of us may have our own opinion of the desirability of this degree of agreement, it does suggest that jurors are not deviating to an inappropriate degree from the narrow mandate to follow the judge's instructions about the law and use only that information plus the actual evidence to reach their verdict.

In fact, we might speculate on what is an optimal degree of agreement between judge and jury. What if they agreed 100% of the time? That would be undesirable, indicating that the jury was a rubber stamp of the judge. But if they agreed only 50% of the time, given only two possible outcomes of guilty and not guilty (putting aside "hung" juries momentarily), it would reflect no real agreement at all. (Two independent agents, choosing yes or no at random, would agree 50%

**TABLE 13.2** ◆ *Agreement of judges' and juries' decisions in civil cases (in percentage of all trials)*

| JUDGE FINDS FOR: | JURY FINDS FOR: | | |
|---|---|---|---|
| | PLAINTIFF | DEFENDANT | TOTAL, JUDGE |
| Plaintiff | **47** | 10 | 57 |
| Defendant | 12 | **31** | 43 |
| Total, jury | 59 | 41 | 100 |

SOURCE: Adapted from Kalven and Zeisel (1966, p. 63). Figures in bold show judge/jury agreements on verdict.

of the time by chance alone.) Appropriately enough, the 75% level of agreement is halfway between chance and perfect agreement. And what is most important, all this speculation after the fact should not obscure the basic conclusion that in *the vast majority of cases, juries base their verdicts on the evidence and the law* (Visher, 1987).

Among the 25% of the criminal cases in which there was disagreement, 5.5% resulted in hung juries; that is, the jury members could not agree on a verdict. Thus, it is more appropriate to say that in 19.5% of the criminal cases the jury provided a guilty verdict where the judge would have ruled not guilty, or vice versa.

*Vice versa* needs to be emphasized because in most of these discrepant decisions the jury was more lenient than the judge. The judge would have convicted the defendant in 83.3% of these cases, whereas the jury convicted in only 64.2% of them. For every trial in which the jury convicted and the judge would have acquitted, there were almost eight trials in which the reverse was true. In only 2% of the cases would the judge have ruled not guilty when the jury found the defendant guilty; in contrast, in 17% of cases the opposite was true.

## Judge/Jury Differences and Types of Charges

The foregoing results would lead to a conclusion that, other things being equal, defendants are better off putting their case in the hands of a jury. But we need to remember that Kalven and Zeisel's conclusions were drawn only from those

trials in which the defendants had chosen the jury to hear their case. To verify the conclusions, it would be necessary to deny defendants the choice between a jury trial and a bench trial, randomly assign them to one versus the other, and then see for a large sample of trials whether juries were still more lenient. Such a study is, of course, not legally possible given the rights that society, appropriately, provides to defendants.

Other qualifications must be made to a conclusion of overall jury leniency. For example, the jury is much more lenient than the judge in certain types of cases, mostly minor offenses such as gambling or hunting-law violations. In contrast, juries in libel trials are more likely to find the defendant (e.g., a newspaper or a television station) at fault than judges are; one survey found that when such cases were tried before juries, the media lost almost nine of every ten (Associated Press, 1982). In serious crimes, such as murder or kidnapping, the judge and the jury were in closer agreement. This is a useful finding because often, in trials for capital offenses, the prosecuting attorney will remind the jury that its standard of reasonable doubt should not be looser just because a guilty verdict would determine the rest of a defendant's life—or death. In actuality, juries in cases involving serious or capital crimes seem to adjust their standard of reasonable doubt so that it is more in keeping with the judge's.

## Determinants of Discrepancies

Type of case aside, what else accounts for the discrepancies between judge and jury? For their sample of cases, Kalven and Zeisel unfortunately have only one source to answer this: the judge's opinion. Yet on this basis, they offer a classification of cases. Through an analysis of these cases, we may be able to shed more light on the subject.

A few of these discrepancies—about 2% of all the trials—apparently resulted from facts that one party knew but the other did not. For example, in several cases, the judge was aware of the defendant's prior arrest record (a matter not introduced into evidence) and would have found him guilty, but the jury acquitted him. Or, especially in a small community, a member of the jury might share with fellow jurors some information about a witness or the defendant that was not part of evidence and not known to the judge at the time. In cases like this, it is hard to make a blanket indictment of the jury for basing its verdict on something beyond the evidence. One or more of the jurors may possess knowledge—not brought out during the trial—that the only eyewitness to the crime is a known liar in the community. Judgments of the credibility of witnesses are legitimate parts of the jury's function.

A second source of judge/jury discrepancies was the relative effectiveness of the two attorneys. In about 1% of Kalven and Zeisel's sample of trials, the jury was swayed by the apparent superiority of one lawyer over the other and produced a verdict that was, at least in the judge's opinion, contrary to the weight of the evidence. If this is a generalizable finding, it is a matter of some concern. At the same time, it is not surprising that some portion of jury verdicts would have such determinants, in light of findings on the impact of nonevidentiary aspects (to be described in the next two chapters).

Another reason for judge/jury discrepancies is that the two disagree about the evidence. It is inevitable that, in cases in which the evidence is balanced and the decision rests on the evidence (i.e., issues of law are straightforward), the judge may occasionally disagree with the jury. In such disagreements, it is often unclear whether the judge or the jury has reached the "correct" verdict (MacCoun, 1999).

Consider a case of theft in which there is a solitary eyewitness and the accused person claims mistaken identity. In a bare-bones case like this, the issue boils down to "Whom do you really believe?" The judge may trust the eyewitness more; the jurors, though initially in disagreement, may eventually come to give the defendant the benefit of their collective doubt. In such cases, judge and jury may differ in their estimates of the probability that the defendant committed the crime or in their standards of reasonable doubt or in both. And on such matters, there can be honest disagreement. (In fact, two judges could disagree over these issues.) Although any inconsistency between judge and jury may, to some, imply unreliability in the fact-finding process, this type of disagreement seems to rest on differences in standards for the acceptability of evidence. Judge/jury discrepancies based on "Whom do you believe?" are of less concern to us than are some of Kalven and Zeisel's other explanations.

## Jury Sentiments

Perhaps the most important explanation of judge/jury differences involves what Kalven and Zeisel called **jury sentiments** (they account for 9% or roughly half of the disagreements). Kalven and Zeisel, after reviewing the multitude of discrepancies, used this term to cover all trials in which, in *the judge's view,* the jury's verdict was detrimentally determined by factors beyond the evidence and the law. (There is an implicit assumption here that the judge's decision was free of sentiments—a dubious claim given that some judges admitted favoring conviction for defendants who the judge, but not the jurors, knew had a prior arrest!)

Sometimes, the judge concluded, the jurors felt that the "crime" was just too trivial for any punishment or at least for the expected punishment, and hence, they found the defendant not guilty, thus making sure that he or she would not be punished. In one case, a man was brought to trial for stealing two frankfurters. Since this was his second crime, if he had been convicted, it would have been considered a felony conviction, and he would have been sentenced to prison. Whereas the judge would have found him guilty, the jury voted 10–2 for acquittal.

In other cases, the jury seemed to believe that a law was unfair and hence voted to acquit. In trials for the sale of beer and liquor to minors who were in the military, juries have concluded that there was minimal social harm. Apparently they felt that, if a young man can be forced to die for his country, "he can buy and consume a bottle of beer" (Kalven & Zeisel, 1966, p. 273).

In actuality, jury sentiments surfaced in many types of cases involving "unpopular" crimes—for example, in small misdemeanors such as gambling or in so-called victimless crimes such as prostitution. Often the jurors' brusque announcement of a not guilty verdict, when technically the defendant most certainly had committed a crime, was their way of expressing frustration. "Why waste our time over such minor affairs?" they might have been thinking.

More relevant to the question of whether jury sentiments are sources of jury error or expressions of a different definition of justice are cases in which the jury, after due deliberation, concluded that the defendant had already been sufficiently sanctioned and that punishment by the legal system was hence unnecessary. Here are two examples.

In one case, the defendant had fired a shot into the family home of his estranged wife. The judge would have found him guilty of shooting with the intent to kill; the jury convicted him only on the lesser charge of pointing and discharging a firearm. The decisive circumstance appears to be that, although the defendant's shot hadn't hurt anyone, his brother-in-law had shot back in self-defense and had seriously injured the defendant.

In a second example, the pivotal circumstances were unrelated to the crime. In a case of income tax evasion, the following series of misfortunes plagued the defendant between the crime and the trial: "His home burned, he was seriously injured, and his son was killed. Later he lost his leg, his wife became seriously ill, and several major operations were necessary . . . his wife gave birth to a child who was both blind and spas-

tic" (Kalven & Zeisel, 1966, p. 305). The jury found the defendant not guilty of income tax evasion, apparently concluding that he had already suffered divine retribution. The judge would have found him guilty.

As noted in Table 13.2, in civil trials the level of agreement between the jury and the judge is also satisfactorily high. Judges report that their verdict would have favored the side favored by the jury in 78% of the civil suits analyzed by Kalven and Zeisel. Also of importance is the lack of meaningful difference in the likelihood of finding for the plaintiff; the jury ruled for the plaintiff in 59% of the cases, whereas the judge did in 57%.

These figures are a healthy empirical response to the critics (Huber, 1990; Olson, 1991) who conclude that in civil suits, especially those involving personal injury claims, juries are overly sympathetic to victims. In fact, in certain kinds of cases plaintiffs who go to trial before juries win infrequently, a matter that we address further in Chapter 15.

For example, Stephen Daniels and Joanne Martin (1997) have done a thorough analysis of the results of medical malpractice cases. Their findings challenge the notion that the civil justice system—at least in malpractice cases—has run amok and that plaintiffs stand to gain vast fortunes by suing their doctors. First, most injured patients do not even file a malpractice claim; rather, they "lump it." Second, most claims that are made end without adjudication and without payment to the plaintiff. Third, the amount of any compensation received is strongly tied to the severity of the injury sustained. Finally, awarded compensation often falls short of the losses suffered by the plaintiff.

But do juries decide malpractice cases differently than judges would? When they find for the plaintiff, do they award more money for damages? Using federal court verdict statistics, Clermont and Eisenberg (1992) have provided some answers. Plaintiffs in medical malpractice cases are more likely to win at trial if the case is tried to a judge than a jury. In these cases as well as other personal injury lawsuits, judges apparently award more money than jurors. Unfortunately, it is diffi-cult to interpret these results because of selec-tion effects: Cases that are selected for bench trials may differ in important ways from cases se-lected for jury trials. There is also evidence that lawyers try cases differently depending on whether the fact finder is a judge or jury and that judges may have access to information that is kept from the jury. For these reasons, comparing bench trials to jury trials may be like comparing apples and oranges (Vidmar, 1994).

A better test of the comparison between judges' and jurors' decisions in malpractice cases would involve the two groups responding to ex-actly the same evidence. Vidmar approximated those conditions by comparing the awards of mock jurors with experienced legal professionals (not judges) and found no important differences. The legal professionals in the first study (done by Vid-mar in association with Jeffrey Rice and David Landau) were 21 lawyers who served as arbitra-tors for personal injury, contract, or labor disputes; five had previously been judges. In a case involv-ing an accidentally scarred knee that occurred during bunion removal, the lawyers gave the plain-tiff a median award of $57,000, whereas 89 mock jurors gave her a median award of $47,850, almost $10,000 less than the professionals. However, the awards by individual jurors were much more vari-able than those of the lawyers; jurors awarded the plaintiff anywhere between $11,000 and $197,000, whereas the lawyers' awards only ranged from $22,000 to $82,000. Similarly, in an automobile negligence case in the second study, awards by jurors did not significantly differ from those by legal professionals.

Juries occasionally make outlandishly high awards to injured plaintiffs, and these are the de-cisions that are publicized in newspapers and on talk shows (Bailis & MacCoun, 1996). But in controlled studies, juries make decisions—ver-dicts and awards—quite akin to those made by judges and experienced lawyers, and there is little evidence that juries are especially proplaintiff, as several critics have claimed. In fact, some would argue that because the jury can apply its sense of community standards to a case, their award of damages in a civil case might actually be more fit-ting than a judge's award: "The appreciation of pain and suffering, and the likely impact on an in-dividual's life and his or her ability to earn a liv-ing, are not matters which judges are any more qualified to assess than is a member of the public applying his or her life experience" (Watson, 1996, p. 457). Any disagreement between judge and jury that does exist might be better attributed to the jury's interest in equity, its application of commonsense justice (see Chapter 3), its consid-eration of a range of sensible factors that might be broader than those considered by an individ-ual judge, or its emotional closeness to the par-ties in the case rather than to its incompetence (Shuman & Champagne, 1997).

## A Critique of the Kalven and Zeisel Study

The study by Kalven and Zeisel described in *The American Jury* (1966) was certainly a massive un-dertaking, supported by a $1.4 million grant from the Ford Foundation (Hans & Vidmar, 1991). But the actual data were collected between 1954 and 1961, and in the intervening decades, the methodological limitations of the study have be-come increasingly apparent:

1. Judges were permitted to choose which trial or trials they reported. Did they tend to pick those cases in which they disagreed with the jury, thus causing the sample's result to misrepresent the true extent of judge/jury disagreement? We do not know. (Judges were requested by the re-searchers to indicate their "verdicts" before the jury gave its, but the researchers have no way of knowing the extent of compliance.) Furthermore, what does a judge's hypothetical verdict mean?

2. Only 555 judges out of 3500 provided re-sponses to the survey; half of the cases in the study were provided by only 15% of the judges—a very unbalanced sampling of possible responses.

3. The focus is on disagreements in criminal trials; little information is provided on civil cases.

4. Juries have changed in many ways. No longer do they have to be unanimous in all jurisdictions, and many states have shifted to smaller-sized juries (see Chapter 15). The absence of a requirement for unanimous verdicts would probably decrease the percentage of "hung" juries.

5. Furthermore, the membership of juries has changed; "juries are today more representative and heterogeneous than in the 1950s when Kalven and Zeisel conducted their research" (Hans & Vidmar, 1986, p. 142). The increased heterogeneity in contemporary juries might increase their rate *of disagreement* with the judge's position because their broader experiences and cultural diversity might give them insights or perspectives on the trial evidence that judges do not have access to (Hans & Vidmar, 1986). For example, does a jury of African Americans believe a white police officer's testimony that a drug dealer "dropped" a bag of cocaine to the degree that a white judge accepts such testimony?

6. As for *causes* of discrepancies between verdicts by the judge and jury, we have only the judge's attribution of what the jurors' feelings and sentiments were (Hans & Vidmar, 1991).

As Hans and Vidmar (1991, p. 347) observe, replication of this classic study is long overdue. And, although no direct replications have been reported, several recent studies that compare judges and juries show how well Kalven and Zeisel's conclusions have withstood the test of time.

As part of a larger evaluation of how various procedural variations affected jury performance, Larry Heuer and Steven Penrod (1994) studied agreements between jury verdicts and judges' opinions in a total of 160 trials (75 civil and 85 criminal) from 33 states. In general, the rate of agreement between jury verdicts and judges' verdict preferences was comparable to what Kalven and Zeisel had reported. The main exception to this trend was that judges in the Heuer and Penrod study were a bit more likely to convict defendants and find for civil plaintiffs than were the Kalven and Zeisel judges.

A Colorado judge, Rebecca Bromley (1996), compared the verdicts of judges and juries in drinking and driving cases in 1958 and 1993 and found a slight decline in judge-jury agreement rates, with jurors continuing to be more lenient. Finally, with respect to sentencing in four moderately severe criminal cases, jurors are apparently still more lenient than judges (Diamond & Stalans, 1989). Taken together, these studies point to a small increase in the degree to which jury decisions are more lenient than judges' preferred outcomes.

# Jury Nullification

Do jurors have the right to disregard the judge's instructions and disobey the law when they render their verdicts? Laura Kriho apparently thought so (see ◆ Box 13-3).

Laura Kriho is not alone in her desire to ignore the law. A 1998 survey conducted by the *National Law Journal* showed that the vast majority of potential jurors would disregard the judge and the law and do what they thought was right (www.ljextra.com/njl/1998/upcoming/1102a.html). For example, a Kentucky jury acquitted actor Woody Harrelson on a misdemeanor charge of marijuana possession after deliberating only 25 minutes. Four years before, Harrelson had planted four hemp seeds, knowing that he would be arrested, in order to challenge a Kentucky law that outlawed possession of any part of the cannabis plant. Harrelson argued that the statute was unconstitutional because it didn't distinguish marijuana from hemp. According to Harrelson, the jury sent a very strong message that it's not right for someone to go to jail for growing industrial hemp.

Jurors who have, on several occasions, sat in judgment of Dr. Jack Kevorkian, also apparently believed that they had the right to disregard the law as instructed by the judge. The first three times that Kevorkian was tried for assisting in a terminally ill patient's suicide, jurors refused to convict him. In these cases, despite incontrovertible evidence that Kevorkian supervised a procedure that led to the death of his patients, he

**THE CASE OF**

BOX 13-3   **The case of Laura Kriho: Jury nullifier**

A 32-year-old University of Colorado researcher, Laura Kriho was a juror in the 1997 felony drug possession trial of a young woman charged with possession of methamphetamines. During deliberations, a fellow juror sent an anonymous note to the judge that Kriho had stated "the criminal court system is no place to decide drug charges." The judge, Kenneth Barnhill, had no alternative but to declare a mistrial. He told the lawyers who assembled in his courtroom that May afternoon that he was "more than a little bit ticked" (www.fija.org/kriho/kriho1.htm).

Judge Barnhill also launched an investigation of Kriho that uncovered an arrest 12 years earlier for possession of LSD and membership in a hemp legalization organization. Because Kriho had not disclosed this information during jury selection, nor had she dis-

cussed her views of drug laws, she was charged with criminal contempt.

At her trial in a small Gilpin County, Colorado, courtroom packed with her supporters, seven fellow jurors revealed her comments during their private deliberations—comments that were not denied by Kriho: "I can't send this girl to prison. . . . I'm against the drug laws and won't vote for guilt. . . . Drug cases should be handled by family and community. . . . Jurors can vote their conscience. . . . Jurors have the right to nullify laws they don't like." They also acknowledged that following the mistrial, Kriho had shared a pamphlet on jury nullification she had gotten from the Libertarian party.

Although the prosecutor argued that Kriho was on trial not for her beliefs but for her disobedience of a court order and her

failure to tell the truth when questioned during jury selection, Kriho's testimony had a ring of truth: "If I had voted guilty, I would not be sitting here now," she stated. Her attorney declared, "If Laura Kriho can be prosecuted for contempt, no juror who thinks for himself can safely speak in the jury room. The court is trying to intimidate anybody with an independent mind. The government cannot tell its citizens not to think critically of the law or the government. The government cannot order a juror to violate her own conscience. And the court cannot banish all jurors who have consciences." Notwithstanding these pleas, Kriho was convicted and fined $1200, although her conviction was later overturned by a Colorado appellate court, and the case was eventually dismissed.

escaped punishment because jurors refused to enforce the Michigan law that prohibits doctor-assisted suicide. Kevorkian's good luck ran out in 1999, however, after he appeared on national television with a videotape that showed him administering a lethal injection to a 52-year-old man who was suffering from Lou Gehrig's disease. This time, the jury convicted Kevorkian of second-degree murder and the judge sentenced him 10 to 25 years in prison, stating that "No one, sir, is above the law. No one."

The Kevorkian case makes us aware that different conceptions of justice make different demands on, and ask different questions of, the

evidence. The traditional approach asks about the defendant's "intent" in a way that isolates intent from the larger context in which the event took place. If we focus only on the issue of Dr. Kevorkian's intent, the case is open and shut: obviously Kevorkian planned his actions both before and during the assisted suicides. Whatever his altruistic values, if the legal elements of the crime (e.g., forming and acting with intent) can be associated with his actions (actually assisting in the suicide), he is guilty of murder.

A contrasting view of justice focuses on different issues and asks different questions: What evidence is there that the assisted suicides

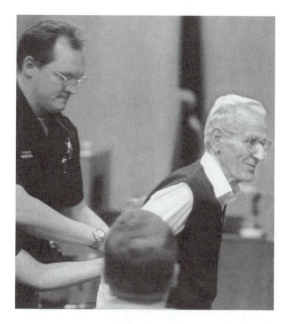

*Dr. Jack Kevorkian*

to the decision by the jurors" (Horowitz, 1988, pp. 439–440).

The concept of jury nullification reflects society's awareness that we have juries for a variety of reasons. Not only do we entrust them to resolve the facts and apply the law in a given case, but we also value juries because they represent the breadth of community values. This latter function manifests their historical role of serving as the conscience of the community (Abramson, 1994) and of bringing their common sense to bear on matters between the government and private individuals. Even though juries in the United States are instructed that their task is only to evaluate the facts and then apply the law as described by the judge, the opportunity to apply a community perspective has existed for centuries, even if it ignores or "violates" the law. In fact, juries have sometimes been praised for their willingness to ignore, rather than enforce the law, particularly when the law is perceived as unjust.

For example, in a precedent-setting trial during colonial times, the printer John Peter Zenger was charged in 1735 with printing material that had not been authorized by the government; hence, he had committed sedition. The British law stated that the truth of the unauthorized material was irrelevant (Alexander, 1963). But Zenger's attorney, Andrew Hamilton, the foremost attorney in colonial times, told the jurors that they "had the right beyond all dispute to determine both the law and the facts." They did; they went against the judge's instructions and acquitted Zenger. The philosophy of "the jury as the judge," at least in criminal cases, was very prominent in post-Revolutionary America, partly in keeping with the resentment felt toward Crown-appointed judges (Rembar, 1980, p. 362). It even extended to the mid-1800s, when juries found defendants not guilty of aiding slaves to escape from the South, even though by doing so, these abolitionists had violated the fugitive slave law.

Up until that time, federal and state judges often instructed juries that they had the right to disregard the court's view of the law. But after northern juries began acquitting abolitionists,

were intended as harmful or malicious acts? Do Kevorkian's actions before and during the act reflect an ethic of care for others? Were his acts intended to relieve the pain and suffering of others? From this perspective, Kevorkian's actions can be seen in a new light. He has helped dying patients who requested assistance to end their lives. So, although Kevorkian's intent and conduct fit the elements that the law requires for guilt to be proven, jurors in the early cases apparently focused more on the morality of his behavior (and, perhaps, on their disdain of the Michigan law that prohibits assisted suicide). Jurors in the last trial apparently focused on the strict illegality of Kevorkian's actions.

Juries do, in fact, have the implicit power to acquit defendants despite evidence and judicial instructions to the contrary. This power, termed **jury nullification,** has permitted juries to acquit defendants who were legally guilty but morally upright (Horowitz & Willging, 1991). The jury's power to deliver a verdict that is counter to the law "resides in the fact that a general verdict of guilty or not guilty requires no other revelation as

judges started questioning jurors to find out whether they were prejudiced against the government, dismissing those who were. In 1895, the Supreme Court ruled in a bitter split decision (*Sparf and Hansen v. United States*) that criminal juries were obligated to apply the law as set out by the judge; they had no right to deviate from that law (Scheflin, 1972). But as Horowitz and Willging note (1991) note, the controversy resurfaced in the turbulent Vietnam War period when the government began to prosecute antiwar activists, usually on charges of conspiracy. Defense attorneys sought ways that jurors could, within the law, consider the morality of such actions. Several cases reached the federal appellate level, although none progressed as far as the Supreme Court for review. However, in a 1968 decision (*Duncan v. Louisiana*), the Supreme Court recognized the jury's power to decide cases *as a matter of conscience* as a characteristic so "fundamental to the American scheme of government that a state violates due process of law in eliminating a jury trial" (Kadish & Kadish, 1971, p. 204).

The U.S. Court of Appeals for the D.C. Circuit decided another important nullification case in 1972 (*U.S. v. Dougherty*). Several members of the Catholic clergy had been found guilty of ransacking the Dow Chemical Company's offices to protest the company's manufacture of napalm. The trial judge had refused their attorney's request that he instruct the jurors that they could acquit the defendants whether or not there had been a violation of criminal law. The appellate court, by a 2–1 vote, upheld this decision by the trial judge. In the majority opinion, Judge Harold Leventhal suggested that the jurors "knew quite well through informal channels that they could nullify without fear of reprisal. To make this power explicit would loosen any restraints jurors may feel" (Horowitz & Willging, 1991, p. 171). Thus, the court acknowledged a curious irony: Jurors can thumb their noses at the law, but ordinarily they aren't told they can.

The real issue in the debate over jury nullification is whether jurors should be informed of this power. State and federal judges do not tell jurors they have the power to disregard the law. What might happen if they did? Would we have anarchy and "runaway" juries, as opponents of nullification suggest? How would juries behave if they were informed that they have the option to disregard the law? Would they be less likely to convict? Possibly so; in two trials of Vietnam war protesters who broke into offices and destroyed records, the judge in one trial of the Camden 28 allowed a jury nullification defense and the jury acquitted all the defendants, whereas the judge in the other trial did not, and all nine defendants were convicted (Abramson, 1994).

Another way to assess the effects of nullification instructions is to look to the empirical evidence on this topic. Irwin Horowitz has conducted a number of important studies on this matter, one of which is detailed in ◆ **Box 13-4**.

Other studies, different from Horowitz's in several respects, corroborate his general conclusion that personal sentiments can determine verdicts when they disagree with the law and jurors are told they can disregard the law (Hill & Pfeifer, 1992; Kerwin & Schaffer, 1991).

Jury nullification instructions encourage the application of "sentiments," to use Kalven and Zeisel's term, in the jury's decision making. But they are not without their problems, of course (Rembar, 1980). For example, prosecutions of police officers for using excessive force in the course of their duties are an example of charges that are often unpopular and prone to nullification. Some people have suggested the 1992 acquittal of four Los Angeles police officers charged with the assault of black motorist Rodney King shows that jurors may be reluctant to convict police officers for actions that they see as "just part of the job" of fighting crime. In fact, verdicts like the ones rendered in the King beating case might be one cause for judges' hesitation to formally recognize or encourage nullification. Confident judgments about "what happened" in the jury deliberations are also complicated by possible racial influences. King was beaten by four white police officers, and the first jury, which deliberated the charges for seven days, contained no black persons.

As another example, some observers have labeled the verdict in the criminal trial of O. J. Simpson for double murder as an example of jury nullification in that the jury—composed predominantly of African American and other minority jurors—chose to respond primarily to the claims that white police officers tampered with the evidence. But a claim that this verdict was an act of nullification per se fails to recognize the weaknesses in the prosecution's case and its failure to marshal evidence that overcame the burden of proving guilt beyond a reasonable doubt. Furthermore, we believe that jury nullification needs to be reserved for cases in which the jury, as the conscience of the community, believes a *law* is wrong. As Rosen (1996) observes, "Nobody on the defense team ever suggested there is anything unjust about the laws prohibiting intentional homicide. Instead [ Johnny] Cochran called on the jurors to refuse to apply a *just* law in order to punish the police and to express solidarity with the defendant" (p. 42, italics in original).

## Jury Nullification and Racial Considerations

Although the Simpson verdict probably had more to do with the prosecution's failure to convince a predominantly African American jury than with jury nullification, the issue of race is a subtext to the nullification debate as well. There are notorious cases of nullification in which white southern juries refused to convict members of the Ku Klux Klan and others who terrorized blacks during the early years of the civil rights movement. One such case concerns Byron de la Beckwith and the murder of civil rights leader Medgar Evers (◆ Box 13-5).

Was jury nullification a factor in these trials? Did some of the jurors in the early trials of Beckwith and other Ku Klux Klan members set aside the law and refuse to convict these defendants because they supported the defendants' racist dogma? Because we can't talk to the jurors, we will never know for sure. Yet, it is telling that a racially mixed jury convicted Beckwith for the murder of Medgar Evers 30 years after two all-white juries were unable to agree on a verdict.

In an ironic twist, much of the nullification debate today centers around the recommendation, championed primarily by law professor Paul Butler, that African American jurors should nullify the law in cases in which black men are the defendants. The rationale for this idea is not that the law is unjust but that a racist criminal justice system targets black men as perpetrators of crime. Black jurors are not so much "judging" the law as preventing its unfair application to members of their own race (Butler, 1995). As a result, prosecutors in cities with large African American populations have come to expect to lose their cases against black defendants even when they persuade the jury beyond a reasonable doubt. Why? Because some black jurors refuse to convict black defendants whom they know are guilty.

Finally, to bring the story full-circle from the days when segregationists refused to apply the law, members of extremist groups that support militia and white-supremacist movements are now calling for jurors to fight the government by essentially ignoring the law in cases they judge.

## Some Final Thoughts on Jury Nullification

Jury nullification has garnered significant attention in recent years. In January 1990, members of the antiabortion group Operation Rescue went on trial for attempting to shut down several family planning clinics in San Diego; they were charged with trespassing and resisting arrest. As one of the trials was to start, a newspaper urged potential jurors to use their right of nullification to find the defendants not guilty. The ad's headline read, "You can legally acquit anti-abortion 'trespassers' even if they're guilty" (Abramson, 1994, p. 57). Arguing that the defendants had performed acts of civil disobedience, the advertisement reminded jurors that they had the right to act as the conscience of the community.

The city attorney and judges presiding over the trials were outraged; one judge admonished the jurors to "pay no attention to the ad, to ignore it" (Abramson, 1994, p. 58). Apparently they did;

*The Science of*

BOX 13-4   Jury nullification: Factorial design

What effect does explicit instruction about the jury's right to nullify have on verdicts in criminal cases? What if, rather than hearing from the judge about their power to acquit, jurors hear explicit nullification instructions embedded in the defense attorney's arguments? Will challenges to this power by prosecutors influence jurors' judgments? These questions were addressed by Irwin Horowitz (1988) in an elegant study of the impact of judicial instructions, arguments, and challenges concerning jury nullification.

The mock jury study used a four-way factorial design (four variables were manipulated). Each mock juror was exposed to (1) one of three criminal cases, (2) either nullification or nonnullification instructions from the judge, (3) either nullification or nonnullification arguments from the defense attorney, and (4) either challenges or no challenges to nullification information from the prosecuting attorney.

By combining these four variables, Horowitz devised 24 different trials, only one of which was shown to each juror. Jurors participated in groups of six and delivered a group verdict on the defendant's guilt. (They used a six-point bracketed scale to indicate their verdict. Points 1 to 3 were bracketed as a not-guilty verdict, with point 1 indicating strong confidence in innocence and point 3 indicating little confidence in innocence. Points 4 to 6 were bracketed as a guilty verdict, with point 4 signifying little confidence in guilt and point 6 signifying strong con-

fidence in guilt.) There were six juries in each condition.

In all three cases, the weight of the evidence indicated that the defendant was guilty. In a drunk driving case, the defendant, while driving home from a party during which he was seen consuming numerous alcoholic drinks, killed one pedestrian and injured another. In the euthanasia case, a male nurse who had cared for a terminal cancer patient over a long period was tried for mercy killing. The defendant was portrayed sympathetically, reflecting his compassion for the patient and the family. In the illegal weapon possession case, a mentally disabled convicted felon stood trial for illegally obtaining a revolver that he thought was necessary for a mail-order detective course he wished to take.

The judge's instructions took one of two forms: either the standard, nonnullification instruction or a nullification instruction in which jurors were told that although they must give respectful attention to the laws, they have the final authority to decide whether to apply a given law to the acts of the defendant on trial. They were also instructed that nothing would bar them from acquitting the defendant if they felt that the law, as applied to the fact situation before them, would produce an inequitable or unjust verdict.

Defense attorney arguments paralleled the judge's instructions—they either did or did not refer to the nullification defense. When present, the nullification

arguments were given both in opening statements and during closing arguments.

Finally, the prosecutor either did or did not remind jurors, in both opening statements and closing arguments, of their obligations to follow the law as it was delivered to them, regardless of their personal sentiments about the law.

What effects did these experimental manipulations have on jury verdicts? First, there were clear differences in the frequency that jurors convicted the defendant as a function of the case they heard. Juries who heard the drunk driving case were much harsher in their verdicts than were juries in either of the other two cases. Both the judge's nullification instructions and the defense attorney's arguments also mattered and in a dramatic way: pronullification information from either of these sources increased the likelihood of conviction in the drunk driving case and decreased the likelihood of conviction in the euthanasia and illegal possession cases. When informed of the nullification option, jurors are more likely to acquit a sympathetic defendant and less likely to acquit a culpable, dangerous defendant.

The effectiveness of the defense attorney's arguments also depended on the kind of case, as shown by the data in Figure 13.1. In the drunk driving case, nullification arguments resulted in a more confident guilty verdict than when nullification was not requested; whereas in the euthanasia and illegal possession cases, nullification arguments increased the confidence of a not guilty verdict. The prosecutor's challenges to nullification information were also effective in dampening jurors' tendencies to act on their sentiments.

What seems to drive the verdicts of juries with nullification instructions? Apparently, nullification instructions change the way the evidence is weighed (Horowitz & Willging, 1991). The presence of these instructions shifts the focus of discussion away from the evidence per se and in the direction of extraevidentiary factors such as concerns about what is just rather than what is lawful. However, according to other studies, the shift of focus has its limits; nullification does not cause jurors to ignore evidence or give full sway to their biases (Niedermeier, Horowitz, & Kerr, 1999). Nullification instructions seem to encourage jurors to think about what is moral and to fashion internal stories that help them interpret the evidence in light of this morality. Such stories alter the perception of the evidence in ways that will be described in Chapter 15.

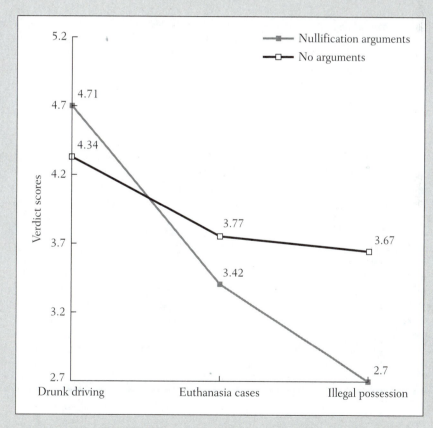

**FIGURE 13.1** *Verdicts given by mock jurors in different kinds of cases when nullification arguments were presented and when they were not.* The higher the score, the greater the confidence in a "guilty" verdict. From Horowitz (1988).

## THE CASE OF

**BOX 13-5    Byron de la Beckwith: Jury nullification and race**

Eager to see his children after a long day at work, civil rights leader Medgar Evers stepped out of his car in Jackson, Mississippi, on a hot June night in 1963 and, in the blink of an eye, was gunned down from behind by an assassin. The shooting set off a firestorm of protest that ended in several more deaths and galvanized the civil rights movement.

The case against Byron de la Beckwith was strong but circumstantial. His rifle with his fingerprint was found at the scene and a car similar to his was seen in the vicinity of Evers's home. But no one saw Beckwith pull the trigger, and his claim that he was 90 miles away at the time of the shooting was substantiated by two former police officers.

Beckwith was tried twice in 1964; both times the all-white, all-male jury deadlocked and failed to reach a verdict. This was an era of volatile race relations in which blacks were excluded from jury service and attorneys for Ku Klux Klan members charged with killing civil rights leaders openly appealed to white jurors for racial solidarity. The defense attorney for the alleged murderer of Emmet Till (a 12-year-old black youth allegedly killed by a group of white boys) appealed to an all-white jury by say-

*Byron de la Beckwith*

*Medgar Evers*

ing that he was sure that "every last Anglo-Saxon one of you has the courage to free [the defendants]" (www.intellectualcapital.com/issues/97/0109/icopinions1.html). In fact, Beckwith's segregationist views were a common bond between himself and the juries that failed to convict him in 1964.

But things would be different in 1994. Despite the burdens presented by stale evidence, dead witnesses, and constitutional questions, prosecutors tried Beckwith for the third time. They presented several witnesses who testified that Beckwith suggested—and in some cases bragged—of murdering Evers. Witnesses also described Beckwith's racist views, including his description of blacks as "beasts of the field" and his belief that NAACP leaders should be exterminated.

This time, Beckwith's racist ideology was a liability. Despite pleas from defense attorneys that jurors not focus on Beckwith's sensational beliefs, a jury of eight blacks and four whites convicted Beckwith of murder in February 1994. He was immediately sentenced to life in prison. Darrell Evers, son of the slain civil rights leader who was nine at the time of the shooting, said he attended the trial to confront Beckwith: "He never saw my father's face. All he saw was his back. I wanted him the see the face, to see the ghost of my father come back to haunt him" (http://newslibrary.krmediastream.com/cgi-...document/). National leaders of the NAACP called for other civil rights cases to be reopened, and charges against aging Klansmen have been revived in several other cases.

the defendants were convicted and sentenced to brief periods in the county jail. But the episode gave new publicity to the possibility of jury nullification and focused attention on an organization

devoted to lobbying for laws to protect and extend the right of nullification; founded in 1989, it is the Fully Informed Jury Association (FIJA). This organization advocates that judges be required to inform jurors of their inherent right to bring in a verdict according to their conscience and suggests that defendants' motives be admissible evidence in all trials.

An instruction that would explicitly permit jurors to disregard the law puts a heavy burden of responsibility on them. And if jurors have a license to acquit despite the facts and the law, do they equivalently have the license to convict when the facts and the law fail to support that decision?

If the nullification procedure is ever implemented nationally, it must be available only in cases in which a jury wants to acquit in the face of law and evidence to the contrary. It should not be available to a jury that vindictively wants to convict even though the evidence would lead to acquittal. As noted, it is most applicable in cases

of civil disobedience, in which community sentiment points to a moral responsibility to disobey unjust laws.

So, in the end, what should we think about jury nullification? Should it be condemned as an inappropriate takeover of legislative authority by juries that have run wild? Or instead as an example of the "democratic and populist role of the jury in shaping the application of legal rules to the living norms of the commmunity" (Casper, 1993, p. 418)? Without a doubt, one person's jury nullification is another's "tempering of justice with equity" (Casper, 1993, p. 418). As we described in Chapter 1, jury nullification exemplifies the equality versus discretion dilemma and shows the powerful role that community preference for discretion can play in individual cases.

## SUMMARY

**1. What is the purpose of a trial?** Every trial presents two contrasting views of the truth. Although on first glance the purpose of a trial is seen as determining truth, it has also been argued that agreed-on conflict resolution is an equally valid purpose. This debate is exemplified by three contrasting images of a trial: (1) as a rational, rule-governed event; (2) as a test of credibility; and (3) as a conflict-resolving ritual.

**2. What are the steps the legal system follows in bringing a case to trial?** When a case is brought to trial, the legal system employs a series of steps. Pretrial procedures include discovery, or the process of obtaining the information about the case held by the other side. Interviews of potential witnesses, called *depositions,* are a part of the discovery procedure. Before the trial, attorneys may make motions to exclude certain witnesses or testimony from the trial. The decision whether a judge or jury will render the verdict is also made at this point.

**3. What is the order of procedures in the trial itself?** After the jury, if any, is selected (a process called *voir dire*), the following sequence of steps unfolds in the trial itself:

a. Opening statements by attorneys for the two sides (prosecution or plaintiff goes first)

b. Direct examination, cross-examination, and redirect and recross-examination of witnesses, with prosecution witnesses first, then defense witnesses

c. Presentation of rebuttal witnesses and evidence

d. Closing statements, or summations, by the two sides, usually in the order of prosecution, then defense, then prosecution again

e. Judge's instructions to the jury (in some jurisdictions, these come before the closing statements)

f. Jury deliberations and announcement of a verdict

g. If guilty, determination of the punishment

**4. Do juries' verdicts differ from those of judges?** The question of whether juries' and judges' verdicts differ significantly has been answered in a massive empirical study by Harry Kalven and Hans Zeisel. In actual trials, 75% of the time the jury came to the same verdict that the judge would have reached. With respect to the discrepancies, in 5.5% of the cases the jury was hung. In the remaining 19.5% the judge and jury disagreed. In the vast majority of these disagreements, especially those involving minor offenses, the jury was more lenient than the judge would have been.

Among the sources of the discrepancies were facts that the judge possessed and the jury did not (accounting for a small percentage of disagreements), the relative effectiveness of the two attorneys (again, a small percentage), disagreements over the weight of the evidence, and what Kalven and Zeisel call "jury sentiments," or factors beyond the evidence and the law.

**5.** *What is jury nullification?*   The doctrine of jury nullification provides a way for a jury to acquit a defendant in, for example, a mercy-killing case, even when the evidence would lead to a conviction. Jury nullification instructions give the jurors the explicit right to disregard the weight of the evidence and the law if, in their judgment, community standards argue for compassion.

**6.** *How has race played an issue in the debate over jury nullification?*   Abolitionists who helped slaves during the Civil War were found not guilty of violating the fugitive slave laws, even though their actions indicated they were breaking the law. During the turbulent civil rights movement of the 1960s, jurors refused to convict white defendants who had murdered black civil rights leaders, perhaps because they supported the defendants' racist beliefs. Today, some African American jurors refuse to apply the law in cases in which black men are defendants. Obviously, different racial groups have embraced the notion of jury nullification at different periods in our history to further their personal political agendas.

## KEY TERMS

| | | | |
|---|---|---|---|
| bench trial | depositions* | opening statements | recross |
| beyond a reasonable doubt | discovery | perjury* | redirect questioning |
| closing argument | impeach | preponderance of the evidence | *venire* |
| decision rule | jury nullification* | rebuttal evidence | *voir dire* |
| | jury sentiments | | written interrogatories |

**InfoTrac COLLEGE EDITION**   For additional readings go to **http://www.infotrac-college.com/wadsworth** and enter a search term related to your interest. The key terms that have been asterisked above will pull up several related articles. *See also:* REASONABLE DOUBT; for *voir dire,* see JURY SELECTION.

# Jury Trials I: Jury Representativeness and Selection

## ORIENTING QUESTIONS

1. *What does the legal system seek in trial juries?*
2. *What stands in the way of jury representativeness?*
3. *What procedures are used in voir dire?*
4. *What personality characteristics of jurors, if any, are related to their verdicts?*
5. *Are lawyers and psychologists effective in jury selection?*

**BOX 14-1    Peremptory challenges and challenges for cause**

Technically, opposing counsel do not select a jury; rather, the judge gives them the opportunity to exclude a number of potential jurors from the eventual jury without having to give any reasons. These exclusions are called **peremptory challenges;** their number is determined in advance by the judge, and, as we discuss in the text, varies from one jurisdiction to another.

In addition, in any trial, each side can claim that particular jurors should be excluded from service because they are inflexibly biased or prejudiced or because the relationship of the prospective juror to the parties or the issues seems to raise the appearance of bias. These exclusions are known as **challenges for cause.** (For example, a relative or business associate of a party will be excused for cause.) Additionally, the judge may excuse a panelist for cause without either attorney requesting

it. In contrast to the finite number of peremptory challenges, the number of challenges for cause is theoretically unlimited. However, in real life, few prospective jurors are excused for prejudice. In a survey of New Mexico courts over a three-year period, only about 1 of every 20 jurors was dismissed for cause (Hans & Vidmar, 1986).

# The O. J. Simpson Criminal Trial as an Illustration of Jury Selection

The murder trial of O. J. Simpson could stake several claims on being the most influential trial of the 20th century. The defendant was a former Heisman Trophy winner, a beloved and glamorous sports hero to millions. His assemblage of high-priced lawyers, dubbed the "dream team," included several of America's most successful trial attorneys. The trial, televised daily for over a year, became the nation's favorite soap opera and made overnight celebrities out of expert witnesses, prosecutors, and several bit players in the Simpson saga. Highly technical, scientific evidence was often on center stage, and the courtroom oratory and legal arguments were frequently spellbinding. But perhaps the most distinctive element of the Simpson trial was the jury—how it was selected, the way it performed, and, ultimately, the verdict of not guilty that it returned.

Although the trial of O. J. Simpson was by no means typical of all trials with respect to the jury's selection and its deliberations, it still merits a detailed review as an illustration of how juries are composed and how they function in our justice system. (◀▶ Box 14-1 clarifies some the procedures in what is usually called "jury selection" but in actuality involves the *exclusion* of prospective jurors.)

## Drawing a Panel, or Venire

Jury selection begins with the drawing of a panel, or **venire,** of prospective jurors. In the Simpson case, an unusually large number, 304, was included on this "jury list." But Judge Lance Ito excluded a significant percentage of these prospects for "hardship" reasons, including poor health, job demands, and the presence of small children in the home. Hence, even if the original panel had been drawn in a manner that would have made it representative of the community, the exemption of hardship jurors threatened the representativeness of the remainder of the panel.

When it came time to "select" the jury in the criminal trial of O. J. Simpson, each side initially considered the input of a trial consultant. Donald Vinson, a founder of two jury consulting firms, Litigation Sciences and DecisionQuest, volunteered his services to the prosecution. But his advice about "ideal jurors" clashed with the preconceptions of prosecutor Marcia Clark, who believed that if black women were on the jury, they would be sympathetic to the prosecution's contention that the murder of Nicole Brown was related to the history of domestic violence between her and O. J. Simpson.

Vinson's interviews with simulated jurors led to an opposite conclusion: Blacks in the jury simulation overwhelmingly voted for acquittal; in fact, African American women were Simpson's strongest supporters. When asked to assume that Simpson had beaten, threatened, and stalked his ex-wife, the uniform reaction of the African American women was that the use of physical force was not always inappropriate in a marriage; they said: "In every relationship, there's always a little trouble"; "People get slapped around. That just happens"; "It doesn't mean he killed her" (quoted by Toobin, 1996b, p. 62).

Marcia Clark's gut reactions prevailed, Dr. Vinson's recommendations were dismissed, and the prosecution welcomed the presence of black women on the jury. The prosecution did not even exercise all of its 20 peremptory challenges. According to Jeffrey Toobin (1996b, p. 66), Clark allowed Vinson to attend only a day and a half of the jury selection and then told him that his advice was no longer needed.

In contrast, the defense eagerly sought the assistance of a trial consultant. Late in the summer of 1994, Robert Shapiro, who was then still the lead attorney for the defense, hired Jo-Ellan Dimitrius of Forensic Technologies, Incorporated; her previous successes had included assisting the defendants in the McMartin Preschool case and the police officers charged with beating Rodney King. Dimitrius not only conducted surveys and focus groups, as Vinson did, but she was in the courtroom every day to observe the extended process of jury selection.

## Did the Jury Selection "Work"?

The eventual jury included one African American man, one Hispanic American man, two white women, and eight African American women. According to Vinson's analysis of their voir dire questionnaires, they possessed the following characteristics:

All twelve were Democrats.
Only two were college graduates.
Not one juror read a newspaper regularly. (One juror said she read nothing at all "except the horse sheet.")
Two had supervisory or management responsibilities at work; ten did not.
Eight watched evening television tabloid news, like "Hard Copy." (Vinson's polling data found a predilection for the tabloids to be a reliable predictor of belief in Simpson's innocence.)
Five said that they or a family member had personally had a negative experience with law enforcement.
Five thought that using physical force on a family member was sometimes justified.
Nine—three-quarters of the jury—thought that O. J. Simpson was unlikely to have committed murder because he excelled at football. (quoted by Toobin, 1996b, pp. 66–67)

Analysis of the juror questionnaires led the defense team's jury consultant to the same conclusion as Vinson's: This group of jurors leaned heavily toward the defense from the very beginning (Miller, 1995). Furthermore, the black women on the jury did not like Marcia Clark. They saw her as a "castrating bitch" who "was attempting to demean this symbol of black masculinity" (Toobin, 1996b, p. 67).

After listening to nine months of evidence, this jury deliberated for less than four hours before unanimously finding the defendant not guilty of each murder. A number of explanations have been offered for this outcome, but it was clearly a triumph for the jury selection decisions made by the defense team.

When William Kennedy Smith was accused of raping a woman on the grounds of Senator Edward Kennedy's Florida estate, he also employed a team of jury experts, who developed jury questionnaires and assisted counsel in jury selection. As reported in the *American Bar Association Journal* (1992a), husband-and-wife consultants Cathy Bennett and Robert Hirschhorn later explained their techniques to an audience of lawyers, saying that "some of the least promising prospects on paper went on to become some of their favorite candidates for the jury" (p. 29).

Take the 44-year-old married man who said he was a churchgoing Catholic with children the same age as the alleged victim's child, for example. On his questionnaire, the man also indicated that a member of his family was in law enforcement and his daughter had been the victim of a crime. Based on his answers to the questionnaire, a majority of the audience said they would have quickly rejected him as a juror for the defense in the Smith trial. But the consultants revealed how the man won them over during voir dire. Under questioning, the man came across as sensitive, warm, and caring. He spoke softly and looked directly at Smith in a nonjudgmental way. And he said he admired his own father because his dad worked hard and never quit on his family (p. 29).

The defense team spent nearly four weeks helping select the jury; the jury spent only 77 minutes in deliberations before acquitting William Kennedy Smith.

# General Problems in Forming a Jury Panel

Were the selection procedures in these trials fair? Were the outcomes just? These trials highlight some of the challenges to the legal system's goal of forming juries that are both representative *and* fair. When implementing this first step of forming a venire, each state—as well as the federal government—has its own procedures about how the sample of prospective jurors will be drawn.

But each method must share the goal of not systematically eliminating or underrepresenting any subgroups of the population. To encourage representativeness, U.S. Supreme Court cases going back to 1880 (*Strauder v. West Virginia,* 1880) have forbidden systematic or intentional exclusion of religious, racial, and other **cognizable groups** (who, because of certain shared characteristics, might also hold unique perspectives on selected issues) from jury panels. Despite these rulings, until about 40 years ago, the composition of most venires did not achieve this goal. Middle-aged, better-educated white men were usually overrepresented (Beiser, 1973; Kairys, 1972). In some cities and counties, every jury was composed exclusively of white men. Furthermore, 40 years ago no consistent standard for composing jury pools existed. In 1961, according to the Department of Justice, 92 federal courts employed 92 different methods of establishing the venire (Hyman & Tarrant, 1975). In some local jurisdictions, representativeness was totally ignored. It was the custom in some towns to use as jurors those retired or unemployed men who hung around the courthouse all day.

## *Judicial and Legislative Reforms*

In a series of decisions, the Supreme Court and the U.S. Congress established the requirement that the pool from which the jury is selected must be a representative cross section of the community. One of the most noteworthy of these decisions, the Jury Selection and Service Act of 1968, led federal courts to seek uniform criteria for determining what groups are to be excused from jury service.

These decisions were propelled by two policy concerns, each of which entails psychological assumptions (Hans & Vidmar, 1982). First, the government believed that, if the pools from which juries are drawn represent a broad cross section of the community, the resulting juries would be more heterogeneous; that is, they would be composed of people who were more diverse with respect to age, gender, ethnic background, occupation, and education. The courts assumed that this diversity would produce two benefits: (1) heterogeneous juries would be better fact finders and problem solvers, and (2) juries composed of a diverse collection of people would be more likely to include minority-group members, who might discourage majority-group members from expressing prejudice.

This second assumption seems logically valid; casting a wider net will yield members of smaller religious and ethnic groups. But the first expectation—that more heterogeneous juries are better problem solvers—is an empirical question. Extensive research on the dynamics of groups studied in the psychological laboratory shows that, other things being equal, groups composed of people with differing abilities, personalities, and experiences are better problem solvers than groups made up of people who share the same background and perspective (Hoffman, 1965). The first type of group is more likely to evaluate facts from different points of view and have richer discussions. But the tasks carried out by these laboratory groups are very different from the jury's task. For the lab groups, the task usually involves a solution that can be judged as clearly correct or incorrect; in the case of the jury, the correctness of the decision is difficult to assess. In addition, the speed of solution is often used as a measure of superior decision making in laboratory groups. Although almost everybody in the courtroom would prefer juries to hold speedy deliberations, few would argue that speed should substitute for accuracy. In summary, the initial reason the legal system offers for requiring representative venires seems justified, both logically and empirically, although the applicable psychological findings must be highly qualified.

The second policy reason for the Court's and Congress's decisions on representativeness is more concerned with the *appearance* of legitimacy than with the jury's actual fact-finding and problem-solving skills (Hans & Vidmar, 1982). Juries should reflect the standards of the community. When certain components of the community are systematically excluded from jury service, the community is likely to reject both the criminal justice process and its outcomes as invalid. It has been said that "justice must not only be done; it must be seen to be believed," and the different elements of the community must see that they are well represented among those entrusted with doing justice—that they have a voice in the process of resolving disputes (Hans, 1992a).

The violent aftermath of the first trial of four white Los Angeles police officers who were acquitted of assault for their role in beating black motorist Rodney King illustrates this problem as dramatically as any event in our nation's history. The panel eventually selected for the trial of these officers contained no black jurors (◆ Box 14-2). After the jury found the police officers not guilty, the black community rejected the validity of the verdict and angrily challenged the legitimacy of the entire criminal justice system for black people. Shaken by the surprising verdicts and shocked by the ensuing riots, many Americans, regardless of their race, questioned the fairness of the jury's decision, in part because of the absence of black citizens from its membership.

So, too, might defendants reject the fairness of decisions made by juries whose members share few, if any, social or cultural experiences with them. Consider, for example, the likely reaction of a college sophomore, on trial for possession of marijuana, who is found guilty by a jury composed entirely of people in their 50s and 60s. Representative juries not only preserve the legitimacy of the legal process, but they also solidify participants' positive feelings toward the process. If members of underrepresented groups—the poor, the elderly, blacks, youth—do not serve on juries, they are more likely to become angry and impatient with the legal process. For some participants, at least, the net result of serving on a jury is an increased appreciation for the jury as a worthwhile institution.

## Devices Used for Drawing a Pool

Thus, representativeness of jury pools is an eminently worthwhile goal. Given the guidelines from the federal courts and the legislature, how should local courts go about forming the "jury list" in order

# THE CASE OF

**BOX 14-2   Rodney King**

When the four white police officers were acquitted of beating Rodney King in their first trial, most people who had seen excerpts of the videotaped confrontation on television were surprised and appalled. The jury was severely criticized, and observers sought to understand the outcome. Critics sometimes fail to concentrate on just what was and was not included in the evidence that the jury considered. Often a major cause of a surprising verdict by a jury (especially an acquittal) is that the prosecution was not effective in arguing its case or presenting its evidence. Or it may be that what the public hears or reads through the mass media is different from what the jury is exposed to. For example, before O. J. Simpson's criminal trial began, the public heard allegations that Simpson had slapped his wife at a beach, had pushed her out of a moving car, and had caused a distraught Nicole to make her now-famous 911 call. But in the trial, Judge Ito allowed little of this evidence to be admitted, including only one example of physical violence (Dershowitz, 1996). Even conceding the importance of such rulings to trial outcomes, the composition of the jury needs to be ex-

amined as a determinant of verdicts, too.

The first trial of the police officers in the King case was moved from urban Los Angeles to neighboring Ventura County as a result of pretrial publicity. The demographics of Ventura County favored the defense—suburban, white, a bedroom community with more than 2000 police families, a place to which people move to escape urban problems. It could be expected that jurors would empathize with the defendants—the "thin blue line" regarded by many as protecting the citizenry from drugs and gang violence—rather than with Rodney King, a large, black, drunk driver. As one legal specialist put it, "I think the case was lost when the change of venue was granted. I don't think Terry White [the prosecutor] had a chance, and it doesn't do a lot of good to debate whether they should have called Rodney King and all that stuff, because I think from that point on these people approached the case with a mindset" (National Law Journal, 1992, p. 15).

The six-man, six-woman jury, whose verdict of acquittal sparked one of the worst riots in this nation's history, consisted of ten

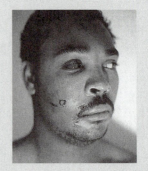

*Rodney King*

whites, one Hispanic, and one Asian, but no African Americans. The median age of the jurors was 50 years. Five jurors were registered as Republicans and five as Democrats, one did not indicate a party preference, and one was not registered. Three were members of the National Rifle Association, and two others had law enforcement backgrounds. Most of the jurors were married and owned or were purchasing their own homes.

As a possible indication of the role played by juror characteristics, the more racially diverse jury that was seated in the subsequent federal trial found two Los Angeles police officers, Stacy Koon and Laurence Powell, guilty of violating King's civil rights.

to reach this goal? (It is important to note that these laws do not require any one pool to be representative; they require that a series of jury pools drawn over a period of several years be representative of the community's composition; Farmer,

1976.) The 1968 law required that voter registration lists be used as "the primary source" for jury pool selection. But such lists underrepresent certain segments of the community. Compared with the general population, people who have recently reached voting age are less likely to have registered to vote. People who move frequently may not have registered, and smaller percentages of the poor, blacks, and other minorities register to vote. Consequently, representative pools require that voters' lists be supplemented by other sources, such as lists of licensed drivers, persons receiving public assistance, and unemployment lists (Kairys, Kadane, & Lehoczky, 1977). Another option is to stratify the selection procedures so that historically underrepresented groups in a jurisdiction receive a larger number of jury summons, thereby increasing the ultimate yield of prospects from these groups (King & Munsterman, 1996). Unfortunately, the Jury Selection and Service Act of 1968 did not make these recommendations into requirements. Even though half the states have added more sources (usually driver's license lists), others were slow to broaden the source for potential jurors. For example, a study conducted almost a decade after the new law was passed documented the continued use of outdated voter registration lists, failure to contact those who had not returned their questionnaires, and very liberal application of exemptions (Alker, Hosticka, & Mitchell, 1976).

Furthermore, some local courts have ruled that underrepresentation of such groups—in a 1973 Louisiana test case, it was the poor—does not violate the purpose of the Jury Selection and Service Act (Handman, 1977). The courts have still not agreed about what "representativeness" means in practice.

## Exclusions and Exemptions: Threats to Representativeness?

Once a pool of potential jurors has been drawn, each individual is sent a questionnaire to assess his or her qualifications and ability to serve. Some people may be excluded by law because of personal limitations, although these restrictions are changing. For example, deaf people have recently been permitted to serve on juries in several jurisdictions (Rothfeld, 1991). Although the rationale for prohibiting the service of certain groups (the visually impaired, persons who are not mentally competent,

those who do not speak English, people who have felony convictions, those who are not U.S. citizens) may be justified, a number of factors during this phase can further erode the representativeness of the eventual jury. For example, there is a lower return rate of the questionnaire by some segments of the community (the highly mobile, the less educated), and in some jurisdictions, this failure to respond results in these people being excluded from jury service (Macauley & Heubel, 1981). The courts play an indirect role in these exclusions when they fail to recruit such people zealously.

Among those persons who are eligible for jury service and who return the questionnaire, members of the jury panel are randomly selected and summoned to appear for jury service on a designated date. One county estimates that about 20% of those called ignore the jury duty summons, further eroding the representativeness (Dauner, 1996). Often, as long as enough prospective jurors appear to fill the needed juries, those no-shows are never contacted or punished.

Is it permissible for a court to remove non–African Americans from the jury pool in order to increase the likelihood that African Americans will be represented in the panel? The Detroit federal court did exactly that. African Americans were consistently underrepresented on jury venires in Detroit. The reason? A mobile population and a high percentage of individuals who did not respond to their jury summonses. To remedy the resulting disparity, the jury commissioners removed one out of every five non–African Americans from the potential pool in order to make the venires more accurately reflect a cross section of the greater Detroit area. However, when two Hispanic defendants appealed their convictions on the grounds that increasing the percentage of African Americans disadvantaged other groups, specifically Hispanics, the appeal court agreed. The court ruled that while the desire to increase African Americans on Detroit juries was commendable, the district court's actual plan was fatally flawed because it eliminated persons from jury service solely on the basis of race (*United States v. Ovalle,* 1998).

## BOX 14-3    Are women a "cognizable" group?

Women were not allowed on juries in the United States until 1898, when Utah did so. Prior to 1920, only four other states granted this right to women. Connecticut did not do so until 1937! This discrimination against women was tolerated for many years by the courts; the 1880 *Strauder v. West Virginia* decision ruled that jury selection could not discriminate on the basis of race but that it was acceptable to limit jury service to men.

In 1957 in Florida, Gwendolyn Hoyt was convicted of the murder of her husband. Her jury was composed entirely of men; at that time in Florida, a woman's name was added to the jury pool only if she took the trouble to go to the county courthouse and register her willingness to be considered eligible.

In 1966, the Mississippi Supreme Court held, "The legislature has the right to exclude women so they may contribute their services as mothers, wives, and homemakers, and also to protect them from the filth, obscenity, and noxious atmosphere that so often pervades a courtroom during a jury trial" (quoted by Hans & Vidmar, 1986, p. 53).

It was not until 1975 (in *Taylor v. Louisiana*) that the Supreme Court ruled that jury service could not be confined to men and that the use of special exemptions for women resulted in depriving a defendant of a fair and impartial jury. This decision also forbade the practice like that in New York, in which the court refused to pay women for jury service but did pay men.

Discrimination against female jurors persisted, however. In the early 1980s in New York City, a prospective juror named Carolyn Bobb was asked during voir dire whether there was a "Mr. Bobb" and, if so, what his occupation was. She refused to answer, saying that it was her perception that only female members of the jury panel had been asked questions about their spouse and, hence, the procedure reflected sex discrimination. The municipal court judge sentenced Ms. Bobb (an attorney) to one day in jail for refusing to answer the question.

In contrast to the exclusions or disqualifications required by law, many prospective jurors avoid service by claiming personal hardship. In some communities, the judge will exempt anyone whose jury service might inconvenience the community (e.g., a physician). Many judges are also sympathetic to claims of ill health, business necessity, vacation plans, and the like. Because only those who make the request are excused, the result is a winnowing out of many who don't want to serve. Does this change the representativeness of the pool? Intuitively, it would seem that those who remain are more likely to regard jury service as a civic responsibility important enough for them to endure personal inconvenience. Until recently, all members of certain occupations were automatically exempted from jury service in some jurisdictions. For example, the state of New York gave automatic exemptions to physicians, firefighters, veterinarians, podiatrists, phone operators, and embalmers. Why? The rationale extends back a hundred years, when each of these occupations played a vital role in small-town life, and the person (usually there was only one physician or one telephone operator) had to remain available to the community.

One reform, now implemented in over a third of the states, to lessen the hardship of jury service and therefore eliminate the need for automatic exemptions is the **one day/one trial system,** in which prospective jurors are "on call" for only one day or one trial and are then dismissed rather than being eligible to serve on multiple trials over a month or longer term (Munsterman, 1996). By shrinking the length of required service, courts are also able to call on a wider diversity of prospects without threatening their employment or the community's well-being.

Until 1979, Missouri offered *all* women an automatic exemption, which allowed them to opt out of jury service simply by signing their name on the jury questionnaire. Before this policy was changed, women constituted only about 15% of the jurors in the Kansas City, Missouri, area. A ruling by the Supreme Court in 1979, stating that the procedure violated the aspiration of the jury to be a "fair cross-section of the community," led to a fourfold increase in the percentage of Missouri jurors who are women (Mills, 1983; see also ◆ Box 14-3).

Thus, even before the formal jury selection in a trial is under way—that is, choosing from among the people who are physically present in the courtroom—a selection process has already begun that removes some people from the panel of prospective jurors from which the final jury will be drawn. These removals distort the representativeness of panels whenever certain groups of people are overrepresented among those removed. As Hans and Vidmar (1982) stated after reviewing the evidence, "The ideal of a jury panel as a representative cross-section of the community is seldom realized" (p. 46).

Fortunately, several states are revising their laws to reduce exemptions; New Jersey has eliminated nearly all of its automatic jury exemptions; many states no longer give blanket exemptions to lawyers, doctors, police officers, or judges. When the name of Texas governor and presidential candidate George W. Bush, was drawn for the jury pool, he showed up on the appointed day, saying no one is too important to be excused.

Judges are also becoming less willing to dismiss individual jurors because of perceived "hardships." During the jury selection for the O. J. Simpson civil trial, Judge Hiroshi Fujisaki responded to one prospective juror who had requested dismissal because she suffered from claustrophobia, "How big is your living room? Is it as big as this courtroom?" She remained in the pool. Another prospective juror complained of the likelihood of getting stiff from sitting too long. "That's why we take breaks," replied the unsympathetic judge.

# Voir Dire: A Reasonable Process with Unreasonable Outcomes?

As if the previous steps in the empaneling of juries had not already compromised their representativeness, the **voir dire** process may accentuate the resulting jury's bias, as we saw in the chapter-opening example. Paradoxically, the purpose of the voir dire questioning is to eliminate biased jurors. As part of the constitutional right to be tried by a "fair and impartial" jury, a defendant is afforded the opportunity to screen prospective jurors to determine whether any of them are prejudiced (*Dennis v. United States,* 1966). (See ◆ Box 14-4 for examples of questions posed to potential jurors during the voir dire.)

As for procedures, the ways in which voir dire is conducted are almost as numerous as the judges who hold trials (Bermant, 1982). Who asks the questions, what questions are asked and how they are phrased, how long the questioning goes on, and whether the questions are posed to individual jurors or to jurors as a group are all matters left to judges' discretion. In federal courts, judges tend to interrogate jurors themselves and to direct their questions to the entire group rather than to individuals (Bermant, 1977, 1982). Some federal judges will accept additional questions from the opposing attorneys. But even here there is variation; some federal judges delegate almost all of the voir dire to the attorneys. In state courts, judges are more likely to permit the attorneys to ask most of the questions with only minimal supervision. Examination of jurors is usually conducted in open court, but if very sensitive topics are raised, the questioning may be done at the judge's bench or in the judge's chambers.

## BOX 14-4    Examples of voir dire questions

Prospective jurors are under oath to tell the truth when questioned during voir dire. Thus, they have no place to hide when asked embarrassing questions. If the charge is rape, prospective jurors may be asked whether they have ever been sexually assaulted or raped, and if they have, they may have to describe the circumstances in detail. Matters that are ordinarily private—credit ratings, health problems, religious beliefs, and one's history of domestic violence—are fair game to prying attorneys if it is the judge's opinion that the information is relevant to an assessment of the prospective juror's fairness.

Can a potential juror refuse to answer questions that, in the juror's opinion, are invasive or irrelevant? Dianna Brandborg tried. As a potential juror in a trial for the murder of two teenagers, she was given a 100-item questionnaire to complete. She answered "not applicable" to 12 questions dealing with her income, religion, political affiliation, and preferences in TV shows and books.

Judge Sam Houston, in a state court in Denton, Texas, told her that her response was insufficient, and he gave her a chance to reconsider. She refused, upon which he sentenced her to three days in jail. His view is that a prospective juror's right to privacy must defer

to the urgency of a fair trial, particularly in an important case such as a murder trial. However, a federal magistrate thought otherwise and set aside Ms. Brandborg's contempt citation. He held that she had a constitutional right to refuse to answer questions that unnecessarily pried into her personal life (*Brandborg v. Lucas*, 1995).

Beyond the specifics of each case, certain types of questions are asked. Among the questions that prospective jurors might be asked in voir dire are the following:

Have you ever served on a jury before, either in a criminal or a civil case, or as a member of a grand jury, either in federal or state courts?

Have you or any members of your family or close friends ever been the victims of this type of crime?

Can you set aside any personal beliefs or feelings and any knowledge you have obtained outside the court and decide this case solely on the evidence you hear from the witness stand?

Do you have any opinion at this time as to the defendant's guilt or innocence?

Do you understand that all the elements of the crime must be proven beyond a reason-

able doubt, and if any element is not proven, would you then vote not guilty?

Notice that most of these questions can be answered with a simple yes or no. These are the types of close-ended questions attorneys are taught to ask in the courtroom. They are effective in controlling the answers of witnesses, but they are not very useful in learning about jurors' beliefs and attitudes. This goal requires open-ended questions that encourage jurors to talk more about their feelings and experiences. Psychologists who aid attorneys in voir dire teach them to use open-ended questions when they need to discover a juror's true feelings about something. Examples of these questions are the following:

When you read about these crimes in the paper, what did you think about the person accused of committing them?

What experiences have you had in your life that caused you to believe that a person was being discriminated against because of the color of his skin?

If there were evidence that Mr. Wallace had been drinking alcohol that night, how would that affect your ability to listen to the rest of the evidence about his behavior?

Voir dire varies in other important aspects as well, such as how long the process takes and how the peremptory challenges are applied. As noted in Box 14-1, the questioning may reveal that certain

prospective jurors are biased and hence should be excluded from jury participation for cause. A prospective juror is excused from jury duty on a specific case if the judge accepts the challenge for cause; this "stricken" juror will be eligible for potential jury service on other cases.

## Use of Peremptory Challenges

Potential jurors who are prejudiced against either party in a trial should be stricken from service, and that is the purpose of judges granting challenges for cause. But additionally, as Box 14-1 explained, each side may exclude a designated number of prospective jurors "without a reason stated, without inquiry, and without being subject to the court's control" (*Swain v. Alabama,* 1965). The purpose of providing this opportunity is to make sure that the jurors will decide on the basis of the evidence placed before them, not on irrelevant factors that either side might believe will color the opinion of a given juror (*Swain v. Alabama,* 1965). The number of peremptory challenges allocated to each side varies from one jurisdiction to another and also on the basis of the type of case (civil or criminal) and the seriousness of the charge. In criminal trials, the defense will have either the same number or a greater number than the prosecution. In civil litigation, the defense and the plaintiff are granted the same number of peremptories, which are usually fewer than those granted in criminal trials in the same jurisdiction. In felony cases, the federal government gives the prosecution six challenges and the defense ten, but the defense can be awarded more if special circumstances warrant.

Peremptory challenges are the vehicle that attorneys use to challenge potential jurors who they believe will not be sympathetic, for whatever reason, to their client. Their use raises an interesting dilemma. Are *only* truly biased panelists eliminated from service by peremptory challenges, or do opposing attorneys manage to obtain jurors who might be *biased in their favor?* Most attorneys seek to build a jury of individuals who are sympathetic to their side of the case. For such lawyers, the goals of voir dire are threefold: (1) to identify and eliminate—preferably through challenges for cause but, if need be, through peremptory challenges—those prospective jurors unfavorable to their side and to "select" those they think will look favorably on their arguments; (2) to indoctrinate prospective jurors

and influence those who ultimately will make up the actual jury; and (3) to create positive impressions about themselves and their client.

Do these goals match the legal system's goals for voir dire? Basically, these latter goals are also threefold: (1) to determine whether a prospective juror meets the statutory requirements for jury service, (2) to discover any grounds for a challenge for cause, and (3) to discover information that can lead to the intelligent exercise of peremptory challenges (*United States v. Dellinger,* 1972). These goals direct voir dire to one overall aim: ensuring that an impartial jury is empaneled. However, lawyers are well aware that jury selection, as practiced in an adversarial system, permits them to achieve other goals.

Textbooks on trial advocacy instruct attorneys that jurors are prejudiced in one way or another; hence, attorneys should try to capitalize on jurors' biases. These texts, plus lawyers' workshops and the use of trial consultants, many of whom are psychologists, provide advice about how to indoctrinate those jurors who are chosen. For example, Holdaway (cited in Blunk & Sales, 1977, p. 44) gives the following example of how counsel can introduce a question that will acquaint the juror with rules of law expected to arise in the case but introduce it in such a way that it allies the juror with the attorney's position. The question is "Do you agree with the rule of law that requires acquittal in the event there is reasonable doubt?" The real purpose of this question is, of course, to alert the prospective juror right from the start that reasonable doubt could exist in the case and to make the juror aware of the rule in the hope that he or she will thus look for reasonable doubt and then vote to acquit.

As you will learn in the next section, the Supreme Court has imposed more and more limits on the exercise of peremptory challenges. As a result, the overall status of this jury selection tool is in doubt. Although opinions about the importance of the peremptory challenge remain divided—some experts favor its elimination altogether, and others argue that it is crucial for fair trials—surprisingly few data have been published about how peremptory challenges are used in real trials. Are they used to remove minority jurors or other specific groups, a major

## The Science of

**BOX 14-5    Peremptory challenges: Who strikes whom?**

To answer fundamental questions about the use of peremptory challenges by prosecutors and defense attorneys, Mary Rose (1999) studied 13 felony trials in North Carolina involving the questioning of 348 juror prospects (32% African American; 53% female) by the attorneys. A total of 147 peremptory challenges were exercised, and the defense used the majority (66%) of them. The following pattern of dismissals was uncovered:

- African American jurors were no more likely to be peremptorily challenged than white jurors.
- However, 71% of the African Americans who were dismissed were challenged by the prosecution, while 81% of the white jurors who were dismissed were challenged by the defense.
- Men were more likely to be dismissed than women, but there was no association between gender and the proba-

bility of being removed by one side or the other.

- On most juries, the percentage of African American and female jurors mirrored their level of representation in the community.
- When discrepancies in representation were observed, it was usually in the direction of African Americans and women being *overrepresented* on juries relative to their share of the population.

---

concern that is addressed in the next section? Do the prosecution and defense repeatedly strike different types of jurors? Some preliminary answers are presented in ◆ **Box 14-5.**

## The Batson Decision

As a result of a series of Supreme Court decisions, it is forbidden to exercise peremptory challenges solely on the basis of a juror's race or gender. Consequently, there is nothing particularly "peremptory" about these challenges any longer. The first decision was triggered by an appeal by James Batson, a black man convicted of second-degree burglary by an all-white jury. During the voir dire, the prosecuting attorney had used four of his six peremptory challenges to dismiss all the black persons from the venire. In *Batson v. Kentucky,* decided in 1986, the Court held that a black defendant was denied his Fourteenth Amendment right to equal protection by the prosecution's strikes against black members of the panel (Pizzi, 1987). In *Holland v. Illinois* (1990), the Court held that a white defendant could also complain about the exclusion of blacks because the principle of

representativeness was violated by the arbitrary exclusion of any racial group. Finally, and most significantly, the Court in 1991 held that striking jurors solely on the basis of race violates the Equal Protection rights of the jurors (*Powers v. Ohio; Edmonson v. Leesville Concrete Co.*). The *Edmonson* decision makes it clear that race-based peremptory strikes are forbidden in civil cases, and in the 1992 case of *Georgia v. McCollum,* the Supreme Court also prohibited race-based strikes by the defense in criminal cases (Bonora, 1995).

In a case in which a peremptory challenge is exercised against a black juror, the judge will ask the attorney for an explanation. The attorney must then advance a race-neutral explanation for the strike—for example, that the juror has a brother in prison or has filed a suit against the police. The judge then determines whether the explanation is genuine, considering the other jurors who were not struck by the attorney. For example, if an attorney were to explain that she struck a black juror because he had been robbed, the judge would want to know why she had not struck a white juror who also had been robbed. (See ◆ **Box 14-6** for an example.)

## BOX 14-6   Peremptories after *Batson:* Discriminatory or race-neutral?

In *Branch v. State* (Alabama, 1986), decided soon after the *Batson* case, the court accepted as genuine the prosecutor's "race-neutral" explanations for striking six black jurors:

Potential juror Harris:

> One of the prosecutors had participated in a "bust" five months before, at a home close to Harris's residence, and saw Harris during the "bust"; he could not recall Harris's relationship to the person arrested, so he thought it best to strike him. Moreover, Harris was similar in age and physical appearance to Branch.

Potential juror Manor:

> As an employee of Gold Kist, Manor was not desirable as a juror because it was the prosecutor's general experience that Gold Kist's employees had not been attentive as jurors and because a number of employees were being investigated for a variety of crimes.

Potential juror Meadows:

> Meadow's background as an unemployed former student was not attractive, and she "appeared . . . to have kind of a dumbfounded or bewildered look on her face, as if she didn't know why she was here, or what she was supposed to do."

Potential juror Montgomery:

> Being a scientist, Montgomery's presence on the jury

would have put too great a burden on the prosecution, considering the background of the case and "knowing the problems with one hundred percent mathematical aspects of a case like this"; the prosecutors did not want "a scientific application in the decision."

Potential juror Parmer:

> Parmer's general appearance was unkempt. Moreover, he worked in "credit management," and because the prosecutors were not able to question him about his specific job, they deemed it too risky to leave Parmer on the jury. Parmer appeared to be a gruff individual, and the prosecution did not want a juror who would be at odds with anyone else on the jury.

Potential juror Kelley:

> A single female who was about the same age as Branch, Kelley "might feel as though she were a sister, or that type thing and have some pity on the person." Moreover, Kelley was observed frowning, and the prosecutors did not want a person who was in a bad mood on the jury. Finally, her response to defense counsel was much more favorable than her response to the prosecutors.

Not only did the trial judge accept these as "race-neutral," but the appeals court concluded that

the judge had applied *Batson* "with caution and sensitivity." Do these results indicate that a judge will always accept a lawyer's race-neutral explanation for striking a juror? If so, *Batson* is a paper tiger. In fact, a minority of the Supreme Court justices used a similar label in reacting to an unsigned Court decision (*Purkett v. Elem,* 1995), based on a *Batson*-like appeal. In a Missouri trial, a prosecutor had dismissed two prospective black jurors. Because the defendant, Jimmy Elem, charged with robbery, was black, the attorney was instructed to give a race-neutral reason for his strikes; he told the judge that the jurors' long hair, beards, and mustaches "look suspicious to me." An appeals court had decided that such explanations had to be not only race-neutral but also "plausible," but the Supreme Court decided that was too stringent; the trial judge must only decide whether the reason denies equal protection. By giving trial judges such broad latitude, this procedure—in the dissenting opinion by Justices Stevens and Breyer—turned the inquiry into a "meaningless charade" in which "silly, fantastic, and implausible" explanations had to be tolerated. It appears that creative prosecutors can always find so-called race-neutral reasons for excluding minorities from the jury.

The Supreme Court has also extended the logic of *Batson* to peremptory challenges based on another cognizable characteristic—gender. The case is *J. E. B. v. Alabama ex rel. T. B* (Alabama, 1994). The facts are these: Teresia Bible gave birth to a child in May 1989; she named the child Phillip Rhett Bowman Bible, claimed that James E. Bowman Sr. was the father, and filed a paternity suit against him to obtain child support. Even though a blood test showed that there was a 99.92% probability that he was the father, Mr. Bowman refused to settle, and so a trial was held. The jury pool was composed of 24 women and 12 men; after three prospective jurors were dismissed for cause, the plaintiff used nine of its ten peremptory challenges to remove males; the defendant used ten of his eleven to remove women (he also removed one man). So the resulting jury was composed of 12 women; note that this is a case in which men were systematically excluded from the jury. The jury concluded that Mr. Bowman was the child's father and ordered him to pay child support of $415.71 per month. Because the judge had dismissed his challenge to the procedure of striking male jurors, Bowman appealed to the higher courts. The U.S. Supreme Court ruled that peremptory challenges that were used to eliminate one gender were, like those excluding a race, unacceptable, and other grounds had to be justified.

How many different cognizable groups are there? A judge in the state of New York, named Dominic Massaro, decided that Italian Americans were entitled to *Batson*-type protection (Alden, 1996), and a California law bans attorneys from removing jurors simply because they are gay. But in other trials, attempts to apply the rule to obese jurors (*United States v. Santiago-Martinez*, 1995) and bilingual jurors (*Hernandez v. New York*, 1991; Restrepo, 1995) were denied. Arguments have also been offered on behalf of making religion a cognizable characteristic that should enjoy *Batson*-like protection, but the Supreme Court has yet to hold that it is unconstitutional to base peremptory challenges on religious affiliation.

Sometimes, trial attorneys attempt to extend the principle of "a jury of your peers" to an extreme degree. In Houston, Texas, the attorney for accused murderer Jeffrey Leibengood asked to include only those people shorter than five feet tall in the jury pool because his client's height was four feet six inches. The attorney told the judge, "We say a short person is subject to discrimination, and we hope to have two or three short people end up on the jury. *Batson* should be extended to include the little people" (quoted by Taylor, 1992, p. 43).

There is an irony to court-ordered limitations on the use of peremptory challenges that harkens back to the dilemmas introduced in the first chapter. Cognizable groups are defined in part by the fact that their members share certain attributes and points of view. But if this is the case, and if these views tend to be adverse to one side or the other (e.g., compared to white jurors, African Americans tend to be more skeptical of the police), why shouldn't individual litigants be allowed to remove certain types of prospects who might be biased against them?

It is true that if members of cognizable groups are systematically underrepresented on juries, the community at large might lose confidence that the jury system is fair and sufficiently inclusive. But is it not inconsistent to argue that particular demographically defined segments of a community need to be included on jury panels in general to promote minority points of view while at the same time denying attorneys the opportunity to base their peremptory challenges on these characteristics if they are linked to negative opinions of their specific clients? Are these two arguments logically incompatible? In the end, both sides of this debate may have only a slim empirical leg to stand on. As discussed in the next sections, demographic variables tend not to be very powerful predictors of jury verdicts.

## Lawyers' Theories: Stereotypes in Search of Success

Do the trial strategies of attorneys conflict with the goal of having unprejudiced fact finders? Do they perpetuate or extend the bias that might occur in the impaneling and questioning of prospective jurors? Before we answer these questions, we need to answer a more basic one: How do lawyers go about selecting or excluding jurors, and do their strategies work?

In everyday life, our impressions about others are governed largely by what psychologists have termed **implicit personality theories.** An implicit personality theory is a person's organized network of preconceptions about how certain attributes are related to one another and to behavior. Trial lawyers often apply their implicit personality theories to jury selection. For example, William J. Bryan (1971) advised prosecutors to "never accept a juror whose occupation begins with a P. This includes pimps, prostitutes, preachers, plumbers, procurers, psychologists, physicians, psychiatrists, printers, painters, philosophers, professors, phoneys, parachutists, pipe-smokers, or part-time anythings" (p. 28). We know of another attorney who vowed to always use a peremptory strike against any prospect who wore a hat indoors. Implicit personality theories lead to stereotypes when a person believes that all members of a distinguishable group (e.g., a religious, racial, sexual, age, or occupational group) have the same attributes. They also produce assumptions that two qualities are associated—for example, when a lawyer assumes that slow-talking jurors are also unintelligent.

We all tend to link qualities together and form our implicit personality theories. Sometimes these judgments are rationally based; we may have had enough consistent experiences to draw a valid conclusion about the relationship. Other theories, however, like the examples just presented, are only intuitive or are based on limited experiences and purely coincidental relationships. But of such material are stereotypes often formed.

Even though implicit personality theories can stem from snap judgments, they can become well developed, detailed, and entrenched. An example comes from a book, published in 1920, entitled *Characterology: An Exact Science,* which related individuals' characters to their head shape, body shape, coloring, facial features, and the like. The author concluded, for example, that small ears indicate a poor memory, whereas bushy eyebrows are a sign of a harsh, inflexible mentality.

These examples now sound exaggerated and almost charmingly outdated. But the emergence of implicit personality theories is almost inevitable when we form impressions of others and make interpersonal decisions. After all, human behavior is very complex. We must simplify it in some way. Richard "Racehorse" Haynes, a highly successful lawyer, was once defending two white Houston police officers charged with beating a black prisoner to death. Like all lawyers, Haynes had his ideas about the kind of juror who would be sympathetic to his police officer clients, but his candor was a surprise. After the trial was over, Haynes was quoted as saying, "I knew we had the case won when we seated the last bigot on the jury" (Phillips, 1979, p. 77).

The use of implicit personality theories and stereotypes was reflected by the jury selection decisions shown by each side in the trial that led to the *J. E. B. v. T. B.* appeal. Ms. Bible's attorney struck male jurors, assuming they would be sympathetic to the man alleged to be the baby's father, whereas female jurors were struck by the opposing attorney because of equivalent beliefs that women would be biased in favor of another woman. But the courts are beginning to prohibit the use of such stereotypes; in his majority opinion in the *J. E. B.* case, Justice Harry Blackmun wrote, "Virtually no support [exists] for the conclusion that gender alone is an accurate predictor of [jurors'] attitudes," and if gender does not predict a juror's predisposition, then there is no legitimacy in dismissing jurors on the basis of it only (quoted by Greenhouse, 1994, p. A10).

Despite such admonitions, books of advice for trial lawyers continue to perpetuate gender stereotypes as a basis for evaluating jurors. A jury selection primer, published in 1985 with endorsements by prestigious trial lawyers F. Lee Bailey and Melvin Belli, stated, "Women are born skeptics, generally as curious as the cat. . . . And they are skeptical in direct proportion to the physical beauty of a female witness" (quoted in Ruben, 1995, p. 188).

CLARENCE DARROW
*"I try to get a jury with little education but with much human emotion. The Irish are always best for the defense. I don't want a Scotchman, for he has too little human feelings; I don't want a Scandinavian, for he has too strong a respect for law as law. In general, I don't want a religious person, for he believes in sin and punishment. The defense should avoid rich men who have a high regard for the law, as they make and use it. The smug and ultra-respectable think they are the guardians of society, and they believe the law is for them."* (Quoted in Sutherland & Cressey, 1974, p. 417.)

Lawyers must choose which prospective jurors to strike with their quota of peremptory challenges. Hence, their own implicit personality theories come into play. Typically, their decisions are based on little information beyond the juror's race, sex, street address, appearance, and occupation. Even if they are allowed to question jurors individually, lawyers cannot know for certain whether they are being told the truth. By necessity, they fall back on their own impressions. What attributes do lawyers find important? Textbooks and journal articles on trial advocacy provide a wealth of folklore about jurors' characteristics. Not

surprisingly, characteristics that are visible or easily determined—age, gender (as noted earlier), race, religion, occupation, country of origin—receive special attention.

In addition to applying their own theories of personality to juror selection, some attorneys use their understanding of group structure. For example, they play hunches about which jurors will be the most dominant during the deliberations. Who will be selected as foreperson (if, as in most jurisdictions, that choice is left up to the jury)? What cliques will form? Although an understanding of group dynamics is more sophisticated than simple stereotypes of individual jurors, lawyers who use such conceptions are still relying on their own assumptions about human behavior. Keeton (1973) has noted that a significant number of lawyers maintain a simple "one-juror verdict theory"—that is, they believe that the final group decision is usually determined by the opinions of one strong-willed, verbal, and influential juror. Lawyers who adhere to this maxim look for one juror who is likely to be both sympathetic and influential and then concentrate their influence attempts during the trial on that individual. In pursuing this search for a "key juror," the typical attorney follows one basic rule of thumb: "In general, an individual's status and power within the jury group will mirror his status and power in the external world" (Christie, 1976, p. 270). If jurors themselves are asked who among them was most influential during their deliberations, three characteristics tend to emerge: male gender, an extroverted personality style, and height taller than their fellow jurors (Marcus, Lyons, & Guyton, 2000).

Another common attorney strategy is based on the assumption that jurors who are demographically or socially similar to a litigant will be predisposed to favor that litigant, a belief known as the **similarity-leniency hypothesis** (Kerr, Hymes, Anderson, & Weathers, 1995). Does this rule of thumb hold true? Are jurors more likely to favor litigants with whom they share certain characteristics? One could make the opposite prediction in some cases—being similar to another might make a juror more skeptical of that person's excuses or justifications for behavior that the juror dislikes. The so-called **black sheep effect** may apply: Although people generally favor individuals who are part of their in-group, they may sometimes strongly sanction those fellow members who reflect negatively on and could embarrass the in-group. Recent studies have produced conflicting evidence about this issue. Religious similarity between a defendant and mock jurors has been found to increase leniency, but when the evidence against the defendant was very strong, a black sheep effect was discovered whereby the religiously similar defendant was treated more harshly than an out-group defendant (Kerr et al., 1995).

Finally, some attorneys follow the "first 12 called" rule. Frustrated by past attempts to predict how jurors will behave based on their background, they simply accept the first prospects called to the jury box, sometimes deliberately drawing jurors' attention to their willingness to believe that everyone is fair and can be trusted to decide the case "correctly."

## Demographic Characteristics of Jurors

Trial attorneys must make informed guesses about which prospective jurors will be more favorable to their side. They are ethically bound to defend their client "zealously." Given their task, the nature of the adversarial system, and the availability of peremptory challenges, failure to make choices among potential jurors may reflect lawyers' inflated opinion of their own persuasiveness, but it would not indicate effective trial advocacy. But on what basis should these choices be made? Are juror demographics the answer?

Demographic characteristics of jurors are related to their verdicts only some of the time, and even then, the relationships are weak and inconsistent from one type of trial to another (Feild, 1978b; Fulero & Penrod, 1990; Penrod, 1979). The relationships that emerge are usually small; they permit researchers to claim "there's something there!" but offer no guarantee of success to the attorney who deals with only a few individuals and one trial at a time.

For example, research on the relationship between jurors' gender and their verdicts has often focused on the type of crime. Simon (1967) had subjects listen to a simulation of a trial for either housebreaking or incest. She found that women were more lenient toward the housebreaking defendant than men but somewhat harsher toward the incest defendant than men. In civil trials, the gender of jurors can be an influential variable when a topic involving gender is at the center of the litigation. For example, women are more inclined than men to perceive that sexual harassment has occurred in the workplace (Weiner, Hurt, Russell, Mannen, & Gasper, 1997). Even here, however, the gender effect is not particularly large (Blumenthal, 1998).

The most consistent gender difference involves social influence rather than content; men play a more active role in the jury room than women. A man is more frequently selected as foreperson (Dillehay & Nietzel, 1985; Strodtbeck, James, & Hawkins, 1957), men speak more often during deliberations (James, 1959), and men are generally perceived by other jurors as more influential than women (Marcus et al., 2000). Men seem to be chosen more often to head the jury for two reasons: (1) they are more likely to make a personal statement about their status by choosing the end seat at the deliberation table, and (2) they are seen by other jurors as more experienced in such decisions (Strodtbeck & Lipinski, 1985).

Jurors' socioeconomic status and occupational level are related to their verdicts in only a very general way. In a survey of how jurors voted in 100 criminal trials, Adler (1973) found that jurors who voted to convict the defendant were of higher socioeconomic status (indicated by variables such as income, occupational level, and education) than those who voted for acquittal. This tendency for "well-off" jurors to be harsh on criminal defendants has been confirmed in controlled laboratory studies (Simon, 1967). And like men, jurors of higher economic status are more likely to be elected foreperson (Strodtbeck et al., 1957). One demographic variable—education—has been shown to predict antilibertarian attitudes that are in turn associated with a tendency to convict defendants (Moran, Cutler, & Loftus, 1990).

Attempts to relate jurors' ethnic origin to their verdicts have led some to a few tentative conclusions—for example, that jurors of German and British descent favor the prosecution, whereas those of Slavic and Italian descent favor the defense (Broeder, 1959)—but these generalizations must be viewed with great caution. For example, other factors such as socioeconomic differences among ethnic groups may provide a better explanation for their different reactions. When other demographic characteristics are studied (e.g., race, level of education, or place of residence), they are often found to interact so much with ethnicity, with one another, and with characteristics of the case that it is impossible to make even the most tentative of conclusions about the influence of any one variable.

Some psychologists have concluded that black jurors are more lenient than whites in the typical criminal case but that black jurors tend to treat corporate defendants more severely than white jurors (Bothwell, 1999). This general conclusion might not be warranted in the majority of cases, however. Rather, the severity or leniency of verdicts is affected by the interaction of characteristics of jurors (e.g., their race and social class) with aspects of the trial (e.g., type of crime), race of the defendant, and race of the victim. Simon (1967) reported that black mock jurors were more likely than white mock jurors to acquit defendants who used an insanity defense. On the other hand, upwardly mobile black middle-class jurors may, in fact, be harsher toward black defendants in violent crimes such as murder and rape than white jurors (Nietzel & Dillehay, 1986).

## Personality Characteristics of Jurors

If demographic qualities have an uncertain relationship to jury verdicts, what about the personality characteristics of the individual juror? Do attorneys' implicit personality theories and stereotypes work here? A number of studies have concluded that enduring aspects of personality may

influence a person's courtroom decisions, but usually only to a modest degree. Many commentators suggest that personality factors typically do not predict more than 10% of the variance in jury verdicts, but other researchers claim that in certain cases these variables can account for as much as 30% of the variance (Moran et al., 1990).

Psychological research using simulated juries in laboratory settings has indicated that certain personality attributes of mock jurors, such as authoritarianism, internal or external locus of control, and belief in a just world, may at times be related to verdicts in a jury simulation. Lawyers might improve their outcomes to a slight degree when they select jurors on the basis of those dispositions. But we need to remember that the trials used in these studies were "close calls"; that is, the evidence for each side was manipulated to be about equally persuasive, and it is in such cases that individual juror characteristics may have their greatest influence (Hepburn, 1980; Nietzel & Dillehay, 1986; Penrod, 1990). In the real world, the evidence is often so conclusive for one side that the jurors' personality dispositions have no appreciable impact. And equally important—yet often overlooked—is the interaction between the jurors' personality characteristics and aspects of the specific trial.

Authoritarianism is one personality characteristic of jurors that is correlated with their verdicts (Dillehay, 1999). Authoritarian subjects are more likely to vote for conviction in mock jury experiments (Narby, Cutler, & Moran, 1993) and impose more severe sentences than less authoritarian jurors (Bray & Noble, 1978).

Psychologists measure authoritarianism using the California F Scale, which identifies people who rigidly adhere to traditional values, identify with and submit to powerful figures, and are punitive toward those who violate established norms. However, when highly authoritarian jurors encounter a defendant who symbolizes authority, their usual tendency to punish the defendant is reversed (Nietzel & Dillehay, 1986). In fact, about the only time that more authoritarian mock jurors are not more conviction-prone might be in trials in which the defendant is a police officer. In such cases, the more authoritarian jurors tend to identify with the powerful and punitive image of the officer.

Beliefs about what determines our outcomes in life form another personality variable that sometimes affects jurors' verdicts. Clinical psychologist Julian Rotter (1966) proposed that people differ in their beliefs about whether their lives are controlled by internal factors, such as skill and effort, or external factors, such as luck, fate, or the actions of others. Research has shown that this **internal/external locus of control** (or I-E, as it is abbreviated) is a potent determinant of behavior in a variety of settings (Phares, 1976). In their verdicts, jurors seem to project their own orientations onto the behavior of defendants; jurors with an internal locus of control (seeing themselves as responsible for their own outcomes) tend to perceive defendants as more responsible for their predicaments, especially when the evidence is ambiguous (Phares & Wilson, 1972). Hence, they may be harsher jurors than those who hold external beliefs and who are more likely to attribute criminal acts to forces beyond the defendant's control.

Jurors' locus-of-control beliefs could influence their verdicts in some civil trials. Consider, for example, a longtime cigarette smoker who sues the tobacco company after he develops lung cancer. Some jurors might feel sympathy toward this plaintiff, but those high in internal locus of control, believing him to be responsible for his own outcomes in life, might be reluctant to award him any damages. Studies by the National Jury Project (1990) find that people differ a great deal in whether they hold individuals or outside forces responsible for negative happenings. Some prospective jurors hold a "personal responsibility" viewpoint, believing that individuals are completely responsible for their own "adversity," whereas others lean toward "social responsibilities," arguing that social and environmental factors are the key determinants of behavior. Such a variable is relevant to a number of personal injury and medical malpractice cases—an older woman

slipping on the ice in front of a grocery store, a hunter who accidently shoots himself and then sues his emergency physician for improper treatment. Jurors who hold a personal responsibility perspective take special notice whenever the plaintiff has assumed a risk and has contributed in even a minor way to the harm (Hans, 1992a).

A third relevant personality characteristic of jurors is called "belief in a just world" (Lerner, 1970). As indicated in Chapter 3, individuals differ in the extent to which they believe that people get what they deserve (and deserve what they get) in life. A person who believes in a just world has a need for explanation and justification; such a person is threatened by the possibility that events happen by chance. Imagine that someone is killed in what appears to be a completely coincidental accident; he is walking along a sidewalk when a truck careens out of control and runs him down. Those who believe in a just world are so threatened by the idea that the victim died just by chance that they will conclude that he must have deserved such a fate by having done something wrong to cause his misfortune. Relatives and friends of rape victims, instead of providing sympathy, often will derogate them on the assumption that, if they were raped, they must somehow have provoked, invited, or caused it. Consistent with this view, researchers have found that persons who believe in a just world will berate the victim of a crime or be tougher on the defendant in order to maintain their belief system (Gerbasi, Zuckerman, & Reis, 1977; Moran & Comfort, 1982).

One final juror characteristic that has been linked to jury outcomes is not a personality variable at all; it is the amount of prior experience jurors have had deciding other cases. Although the results of studies about the effects of prior juror experience on jury verdicts are inconsistent (Dillehay & Nietzel, 1999), most criminal defense attorneys prefer jurors who have never served on a jury before, whereas attorneys for civil defendants prefer experienced jurors (Bailey & Rothblatt, 1985; Belli, 1954)—a preference with some empirical support, as indicated in ◆ Box 14-7.

In an effort to learn whether prior jury service influences later verdicts, Dillehay and Nietzel (1985) studied 175 consecutive criminal trials across one calendar year in Lexington, Kentucky. Because jurors in this jurisdiction are "on call" for service for 30-day terms, they have the opportunity to serve on several trials in one month. Two indices of juror experience correlated with a greater likelihood of conviction: (1) the number of jurors per jury who had served on at least one prior jury and (2) the total number of juror experiences represented on each jury. Guilty verdicts increased when a majority of jurors on a given case had prior jury experience. Although a follow-up study of 169 trials in the next 18 months did not find any relationship, a third study of these cases (Himelein, Nietzel, & Dillehay, 1991) found that juries with more experienced members handed down more severe sentences than did inexperienced juries (Kentucky is one of the states where jurors sentence convicted defendants). The results of studies in other states have been mixed; in some cases, no relationship is found, but when a relationship is discovered, it has always been in the direction of juries with more experience being more conviction-prone (Dillehay & Nietzel, 1999).

Although many psychologists doubt that personality and demographic characteristics can predict individual jurors' verdicts sufficiently well to be useful, other legal experts believe that specific attitudes and beliefs can be important influences in certain trials (Gayoso, Cutler, & Moran, 1994). With a few exceptions, practicing attorneys and authors of trial advocacy textbooks state that a case can be won or lost during voir dire. Attorneys take pride in their skill in selecting a proper jury. For example, a president of the Association of Trial Lawyers in America wrote, "Trial attorneys are acutely attuned to the nuances of human behavior, which enables them to detect the minutest traces of bias or inability to reach an appropriate decision" (Begam, 1977, p. 3). Yet Kalven and Zeisel (1966), two experts on jury decision making, suggest that, in general, lawyers overestimate their own abilities to turn a jury verdict in a favorable direction. Others are even more skeptical about how much lawyers can accomplish in voir dire. One social scientist observed the jury selection process in 23 consecutive trials in a federal court in the Midwest and concluded that "the *voir dire* was grossly ineffective not only in weeding out 'unfavorable' jurors but even in eliciting the data which would have shown particular jurors as very likely to prove 'unfavorable'" (Broeder, 1965, pp. 505–506).

In a test of this question (Olczak, Kaplan, & Penrod, 1991), experienced trial attorneys were observed to use juror selection strategies that were not different from or better than those of inexperienced college and law students who were asked to evaluate mock jurors. As with other comparisons of experts and novices, trial attorneys do not appear to think any more accurately when making personality judgments than do nonprofessionals. Even when asked to perform a more realistic task—rating jurors from the videotapes of a previous voir dire—attorneys did not do better than chance in detecting jurors who were biased against them (Kerr, Kramer, Carroll, & Alfini, 1991).

In another studying evaluating the effectiveness of voir dire, Cathy Johnson and Craig Haney (1994) observed the full voir dires used in four felony trials in Santa Cruz, California. As part of this study, they collected information on the criminal justice attitudes held by the jurors by administering Boehm's (1968) Legal Attitudes

Questionnaire to prospective jurors. By comparing the attitudes of persons who were retained as jurors with those who were challenged by the prosecutor or defense attorneys, they were able to gauge the effectiveness of each side's peremptory challenge strategy. Jurors who were peremptorily excused by prosecutors held stronger prodefense attitudes than jurors excused by the defense, and jurors excused by the defense were more proprosecution than jurors excused by the prosecution. However, the overall score of the retained jurors was not significantly different from the average score of the first 12 jurors questioned or of a group of prospective jurors sampled at random. Apparently, although each side succeeded in getting rid of jurors most biased against it, the end result was a jury that would not have differed appreciably from just accepting the first 12 people called or empaneling 12 jurors at random.

A few other findings are a bit more favorable to attorneys. In one experiment involving a simulated personal injury case, a social scientist (Strodtbeck, reported in Zeisel & Diamond, 1978) asked experienced civil attorneys to rank jurors according to the size of the damage award that each might advocate in the jury deliberations. He then compared their rankings with the actual awards proposed by these jurors. Both plaintiff and defense attorneys were good at predicting the variations in awards. Another study by a team of psychologists and lawyers (Padawer-Singer, Singer, & Singer, 1974) also concluded that the voir dire served its purpose for the attorneys; compared with jurors who were not questioned by attorneys, those selected were more sympathetic about mitigating circumstances, less influenced by negative pretrial information, and more concerned about following the law set forth by the judge.

In a more sophisticated study, two social scientists (Zeisel & Diamond, 1978) assessed lawyers' selection skills by looking at how prospective jurors who were challenged and excused would have voted. For 12 criminal trials conducted at the U.S. District Court of Northern Illinois, the researchers had those venire members who had been excused remain as "shadow jurors," watch the trial from the spectator section of the courtroom, and then render their own verdicts. In this way, the researchers could compare the decisions of actual juries composed of those who had survived the voir dire with the verdicts of hypothetical juries composed simply of the first 12 venire members. (The latter, reconstituted juries were thus made up of both real jurors and those who had been excused.) Zeisel and Diamond estimated that, in 3 of the 12 cases, the actual verdicts were affected by the defense attorney's effective use of peremptory challenges. They concluded that trial attorneys apparently do win some of their cases because of their decisions during the voir dire. Interestingly, defense attorneys seem to exercise more peremptory challenges than do prosecutors, even when the number granted to each side is equal (a finding replicated in other studies; Rose, 1999). This "zealous" representation of clients may be one reason for their relative effectiveness in the preceding survey (Van Dyke, 1977).

# "Scientific Jury Selection": Does It Work Any Better?

As this chapter has noted, for years trial lawyers have been "picking" jurors on the basis of their own theories about how people behave. To the extent that these hunches, superstitions, and stereotypes have validity—and sometimes they do—the process can increase attorneys' chances of winning some cases they might have lost if decided by a jury with a different composition.

Many attorneys, convinced of the importance of jury selection but skeptical of their ability to do it well or limited in the time they can devote to it, have hired social scientists as jury selection consultants. These consultants try to use empirically based procedures, including focus groups and shadow juries, systematic ratings of prospective jurors, and surveys of the community, to detect bias (Strier, 1999). This collection of techniques is known by the label of "scientific" or "systematic jury selection." Although these techniques were

## The Science of

### BOX 14-8   Jury selection: Trial consultants and the death penalty

In an attempt to evaluate the effectiveness of the defense's use of jury consultants in a series of death penalty cases, Nietzel and Dillehay (1986) examined the 35 outcomes of 31 capital trials (a couple of trials had two defendants). Juries recommended the death sentence in 61% of the trials in which consultants were not employed by the defense versus 33% of the verdicts in trials with defense jury consultants. The correlation between use of a consultant and an outcome other than the death penalty was 0.26. The small number of cases in the sample rendered this correlation statistically nonsignificant. Of course, these cases differed on many variables besides the use of consultants, so it is not possible to conclude that any differences were due to their presence alone. But the results are consistent with claims that jury consultants might be effective in cases in which jurors' attitudes are particularly important, as they are when a jury is asked to choose between life and death.

first used to aid defendants in several highly publicized "political" trials (McConahay, Mullin, & Frederick, 1977; Schulman, Shaver, Colman, Emrich, & Christie, 1973), they are now frequently practiced in the full range of criminal and civil trials. (Chapter 2 discussed the use of scientific jury selection in a high-profile case.)

Jury consultants also attempt to predict the power structure and sociometric network within the eventual jury; that is, they try not only to eliminate the "wrong" individuals but also to arrange the composition of the jury so that their preferred individual is elected foreperson.

Earlier, in considering whether lawyers' strategies "work," we concluded that they do, to a slight degree, when the legal evidence is equivocal. Similarly, when the defense in criminal trials has relied on the more empirically grounded scientific jury selection, it has often been victorious. At first glance, the procedure seems to work, but the success rate may be inflated by any of the following factors: (1) many of the more widely discussed cases involved weak or controversial evidence against defendants, (2) the trials have often been lengthy and complex, increasing the opportunity for juror characteristics to color perceptions of the evidence, and (3) attorneys who make the extra effort to enlist jury consultation resources may also be more diligent and thorough in other areas of their case preparation.

How does scientific jury selection compare to traditional attorney methods when the two approaches are used to select jurors for the same trials? Horowitz (1980) carried out one empirical comparison using four criminal cases. Conventional jury selection methods used by attorneys, including their past experience, interactions with similar jurors in prior trials, and conventional wisdom, were pitted against social science methods. Neither approach was superior for all four trials. Scientific jury selection was more effective in cases in which there were clear-cut relationships between personality or demographic variables and jurors' votes, but when these relationships were weak, scientific selection lacked accuracy and precision. Reviewing a collection of studies that contrasted scientific jury selection with attorney methods, Fulero and Penrod (1990, p. 252) concluded, "If a defendant has his or her life . . . at stake, the jury selection advantages conferred by scientific jury selection techniques may well be worth the investment."

How effective is scientific jury selection? Psychologists disagree about its usefulness (Hans

& Vidmar, 1986; Nietzel, in press; Saks, 1976; Strier, 1999), and few empirical studies have been conducted investigating this question. Often, the research that has been published involves only simulated—mock jury—experiments, which may limit the extent to which the results apply to actual juries (Bornstein, 1999). ◆ **Box 14-8** describes one study of scientific jury selection as it was practiced in a series of actual capital murder trials.

Recognizing that jurors' demographic and personality characteristics do not correlate strongly with verdicts in general, jury consultants have shifted their focus to the intensive study of specific cases (Smith & Malandro, 1986; Strier, 1999; Vinson & Anthony, 1985). This new strategy emphasizes the following methods:

1. Conducting public opinion surveys, small-group discussions (or focus groups), and jury simulation studies in which subjects hear abbreviated versions of the evidence, discuss it, and make individual and group decisions about it as the consultant watches and listens to their deliberations. The consultant tries to discover whether any individual characteristics of subjects are systematically related to the different reactions they have to the evidence. If so, these relationships will guide the use of peremptory challenges in the subsequent trial and will also help the attorneys craft their presentation of the evidence so that it has the greatest appeal possible to jurors. Software programs have been developed to calculate correlations between juror background characteristics and their likely verdicts.

2. Analyzing how different jurors form a narrative or private story that summarizes the evidence into a coherent, compelling account (Pennington & Hastie, 1986, 1988). This analysis is followed by an attempt to relate the narratives to the demographic characteristics, personality traits, and attitudinal differences of subjects.

3. Developing a consistent case theme suggested by the results of the study groups used in steps 1 and 2. This theme is then reinforced by voir dire questions, evidence presentation, open-

ing statements, and closing arguments so that the most salient psychological factors of the case are repeatedly presented to the jurors in a manner that best supports the attorney's desired interpretation of the facts.

# Lawyers, Psychologists, and Ethics: Problems with Jury Selection

The legal system promulgates an idealized assumption that all members of the community have an equal chance of serving on juries, but prevalent practices prevent that. All segments of the community are not fairly represented in the jury pools of many jurisdictions across the nation. Furthermore, attorneys do not seek neutral jurors; they seek those favorable to their own side. Proponents of the current system acknowledge this tendency but assume that, if both parties are successful in rejecting those who are unfavorable to them, their respective challenges will balance out. In theory, both extremes will be eliminated, leaving those who are less biased and more open-minded.

This assumption is required by the logic of our adversarial system, which holds that fair process and just outcomes are achieved when two opponents work zealously to win outcomes favorable to themselves. But, unfortunately, actual trials don't usually work out that way. Because some lawyers don't really care about jury selection ("Give me any 12 people and I'll convince 'em!") and because others are inept in their selection of favorable jurors, this theoretical balance is seldom if ever achieved. As the O. J. Simpson criminal trial reflects, the effective use of jury consultants by one side but not the other adds to the imbalance. In effect, when one of the attorneys is more motivated or more capable at jury selection, the outcome is equivalent to giving that side a larger number of peremptory challenges. Of course, this imbalance is not restricted to adversarial systems; resources are not equally distributed in education, medicine, government, or any of our other social institutions. But the adversarial system may magnify the impact of unequally qualified participants; when opponents are not evenly matched, the superior one will win more often.

As the practice of scientific jury selection has expanded, so, too, have legal and ethical objections to it. Critics often condemn these techniques as "jury rigging" that undermines public confidence in the jury system and allows rich litigants an unfair edge over poor or average-income citizens. Fueled by these criticisms, public concern has led to several suggested reforms, including (1) a ban on the use of jury consultants, (2) greater restrictions on voir dire questioning, (3) curtailing or eliminating altogether the use of peremptory challenges, (4) requiring jury consultants to share with the other side any information on prospective jurors that they gather, and (5) regulating jury consultants through professional licensure and practice standards (Strier, 1999).

Few, if any, of these reforms have been implemented in the United States, nor is it clear that they would necessarily yield fairer justice. The American system of justice remains fundamentally adversarial. As long as litigants are expected to present their version of the case as

zealously as possible, they should be expected to use every legal means available to woo the jury and counter the opposition in order to win the dispute. To single out jury consultation for special restrictions is a slippery slope premised on the faulty notion that each side in a trial can be required to be equal.

As previously discussed, it is paradoxical that the legal system insists that jurors first be drawn so as to be typical of their communities and then often allows this representativeness to be undone at the stage of voir dire. The jury selection process does sometimes conflict with the goals of representativeness. The "12 good 'men' and true" who found O. J. Simpson not guilty of murder were themselves not representative of their community. Neither was the civil trial's jury, on which no African Americans deliberated, who found Simpson liable for killing his ex-wife and Ronald Goldman. But then, representativeness as a goal may have its limits. In cases in which the local community is biased but a change of venue is not granted, justice is sacrificed to the goal of representativeness. And although the legal system seeks with equal fervor to achieve both representativeness and fairness, it fails to recognize that these ideals may be incompatible.

# SUMMARY

**1. What does the legal system seek in trial juries?** Among its goals for juries, the legal system seeks that they be representative and unbiased. Each of these goals is hard to achieve. The jury selection process can, in some instances, create an unrepresentative jury.

**2. What stands in the way of jury representativeness?** Reforms have not been very successful in creating juries that are representative of local populations. Too many people are excused from service. Furthermore, the traditional source of names, voter registration lists, excludes too many people. To make jury pools representative,

jurisdictions need (1) to broaden the sources, by using lists of licensed drivers, and (2) to reduce automatic exemptions to persons in a number of occupations.

**3. What procedures are used in voir dire?** The process of selecting a jury from the panel of prospective jurors is called *voir dire*. Its goal is to end up with a jury that is unbiased. Each side may discharge a certain number of prospective jurors without giving any reasons; these are called *peremptory challenges*. Prospective jurors who have biases or conflicts of interest can be challenged for cause and discharged. Questioning of the prospective jurors is done at the discretion of the judge. In most local courts, the attorneys do the questioning; in federal courts, judges typically interrogate the jurors. When questioning jurors, most attorneys will also try to sway jurors to their viewpoint through various ingratiation and indoctrination techniques.

**4.** *What personality characteristics of jurors, if any, are related to their verdicts?* In choosing jurors, lawyers often base their decisions on their implicit personality theories and stereotypes of what is a "good" juror. A few personality characteristics are weakly to moderately related to juror verdicts: authoritarianism, locus of control, and belief in a just world.

**5.** *Are lawyers and psychologists effective in jury selection?* Whether lawyers' choices of ju-

rors actually improve their chances of winning is controversial. Clearly, the relative weight of the evidence is the most important determinant of the jury's verdict. Initially, practitioners of "scientific jury selection" used community surveys to determine which demographic characteristics of jurors were related to their being sympathetic to one side or the other in trials. More recently, trial consultants have concentrated on studying how specific individual characteristics may be related to the psychological themes and interpretation of evidence in a specific case. There is some evidence that science-oriented consultation may be useful in cases in which the evidence is equivocal or jurors' attitudes about the evidence is important.

## KEY TERMS

| | | | |
|---|---|---|---|
| black sheep effect | implicit personality | one day/one trial | similarity-leniency |
| challenges for | theories | systems | hypothesis |
| cause | internal/external locus | peremptory | *venire* |
| cognizable groups | of control | challenges* | *voir dire* |

---

**InfoTrac**
**College**
**Edition**

For additional readings go to **http://www.infotrac-college.com/wadsworth** and enter a search term related to your interest. The key term that has been asterisked above will pull up several related articles.

# *Jury Trials II: Concerns and Reforms*

## ORIENTING QUESTIONS

1. Describe the concern related to the competence of jurors and juries.
2. What is the impact of opening statements on jurors?
3. What is the impact of extralegal information on jurors?
4. Can jurors disregard inadmissible evidence?
5. How can jurors be helped to understand their instructions?
6. What is meant by the statement that "bias is inevitable in jurors"?
7. What reforms of the jury system are suggested by psychologists?

The right to trial by jury is protected by state constitutions and by the Sixth (for criminal cases) and Seventh (for civil cases) Amendments to the U.S. Constitution. The U.S. Supreme Court underscored the importance of the jury by stating that "[t]he guarantees of jury trial in the state and federal constitutions reflect a profound judgment about the way in which the law should be enforced and justice administered" (*Duncan v. Louisiana*, 1968, p. 149).

Trial by jury is an institution that routinely, on every working day, draws ordinary citizens into the working apparatus of the justice system. More than one-fourth of all American adults report that they've served on a jury (Gallup Organization, 1989). Three million U.S. citizens are called for jury duty every year. For many jurors, their participation demands major sacrifices of income, time, and energy. In a massive class-action lawsuit against the Ford Motor Corporation, one juror continued to attend the trial even after suffering injuries in a hit-and-run accident and requiring constant pain medication; another juror whose family moved out of the county opted to live in a hotel near the courthouse in order to continue hearing the case.

The jury system casts its shadow well beyond the steps of the courthouse, however, because predictions about how juries would decide cases influence decisions to settle civil lawsuits and to accept plea bargains in criminal cases. So the jury trial is an important and influential tradition; no other institution of government places power so directly in the hands of the people and allows average citizens the opportunity to judge the actions of their peers (Abramson, 1994).

Antecedents of the contemporary jury system stretch back to English law established 700 years ago and beyond. Even the ancient Greeks had a form of citizen jury. Throughout its history, however, the jury system has been under attack. One critic described the jury as, at best, 12 people of average ignorance. The esteemed Judge Jerome Frank, who served on the federal appeals court, complained that juries apply law they don't understand to facts that they can't get straight. Even

Mark Twain took a swing at the jury system. In *Roughing It,* he called the jury "the most ingenious and infallible agency for defeating justice that wisdom could contrive." One anonymous commentator asked rhetorically, "How would you like to have your fate decided by twelve people who weren't smart enough to get out of jury duty?" (cited by Shuman & Champagne, 1997). Others have noted that when a judge makes an unpopular decision, that particular judge is criticized, but when a jury reaches an unpopular verdict, the entire jury system is indicted (Ellsworth & Mauro, 1998).

Many people cite the 1995 acquittal of O. J. Simpson on charges of murder as the prime example of flaws in the jury system. A public opinion poll taken exactly a year after the verdict found that only 25% of 3400 adults felt that it was the right decision (Price & Lovitt, 1996). However, 62% of the blacks questioned felt that Simpson was not guilty, compared to 20% of the whites. One of the many consequences of that trial has been a renewed call for jury reforms including greater limits placed on peremptory challenges, bans against the use of jury consultants, the end of jury sequestration, and the elimination of the requirement that jury verdicts be unanimous (Nietzel, McCarthy, & Kern, 1999; Strier, 1999). We discuss jury reforms later in this chapter.

The civil jury, in particular, has been resoundingly vilified. In fact, one prominent scholar of the civil jury points out that "so many writings, both scholarly and journalistic have been devoted to criticizing the institution of the civil jury that it becomes boring to recite the claims" (Vidmar, 1998, p. 849). According to Vidmar, civil juries have been criticized as incompetent, capricious, unreliable, biased, sympathy-prone, confused, gullible, hostile to corporate defendants and excessively generous to plaintiffs. We examine some of these claims later in this chapter.

Much of the public outcry focuses on the seemingly excessive nature of jury damage awards. For example, Katie Brophy, of Louisville, Kentucky, won a $15,000 jury award because her dog died after being spayed. The judge in this case instructed the jury that the intrinsic value of the animal can supplement its market value, analogizing it to the "heirloom value of wedding photos or a grandmother's brooch." (At least one commentator has argued that paying a person for the loss of a pet's companionship puts the animal on the same footing as a child and so cheapens human life.)

In a case that captured the public's attention because of the sheer size of the jury damage award, an Alabama jury awarded an eye-popping $581 million to a family who claimed they were overcharged $1200 for two satellite dishes. Most of the award was intended to punish the company. In this case, as in most cases that result in large damages, the award is likely to be reduced by the judge or renegotiated during posttrial settlement conferences.

The jury system has been described as an expensive and time-consuming anachronism. Some critics want to restrict the use of juries; others would prefer to abandon them altogether. Advocates of radical revision of the jury have even included former Chief Justice Warren Burger of the U.S. Supreme Court, who publicly questioned the abilities of jurors to understand and sort out the complexities of protracted civil cases.

Not all the criticism comes from the outside. From the perspective of jurors themselves, the satisfaction of doing their civic duty often does not offset their apprehensions or discomforts about jury service. After their verdict in the first Rodney King police brutality trial was announced, the jurors were warned not to open their mailboxes because officials feared that bombs might have been placed inside them. Some trials challenge human endurance; the Los Angeles trial concerning the sexual abuse of children in the McMartin preschool took more than three years to complete. Other trials result in serious financial hardship for jurors. David Olson, a single father of two and a juror in a complex lawsuit between the state of Minnesota and major U.S. cigarette manufacturers, lost all his credit cards and nearly lost his home after serving on the jury for four months. The small contracting company

he worked for was unable to pay him while he was away and the state paid only $30 per day. (To jurors' dismay, the case settled just prior to closing arguments, but the judge granted the jury's unusual request to hear the plaintiffs' closing argument anyway.)

To be sure, the jury system also has its defenders. Many authors point out that claims about juries are often based on anecdotes that are unrepresentative or fabricated and on studies that lack scientific validity (see, e.g., Daniels, 1989; Vidmar, 1998, 1999). Indeed, most of us never hear about the hundreds of thousands of juries that each year toil out of the spotlight and, after careful deliberation, reach reasonable verdicts.

Proponents further argue that the notion of trial by jury epitomizes what is special about the justice system in that it ensures public participation in the process. Verdicts reached by representative juries can and often do increase the legitimacy of the process in the eyes of the public, particularly in controversial trials. Juries can serve as a check on the arbitrary or idiosyncratic nature of a judge. Because juries do not give a reason for their verdicts as judges are required to do, they retain a flexibility denied judges: They can nullify the law to achieve justice in particular cases. Finally, participating on a jury can both educate and enhance regard for the justice system. Alexis de Tocqueville (1900), a 19th-century French statesman, wrote, "I do not know whether the jury is useful to those who are in litigation, but I am certain it is highly beneficial to those who decide the litigation; and I look upon it as one of the most efficacious means for the education of the people which society can employ" (p. 290).

Who's right? Are juries capable of making fair and intelligent decisions, or is the jury system so flawed that its use should be restricted or possibly even eliminated? Are criticisms of the jury justified? If so, can the legal system do anything to improve the functioning of juries?

Over the past several decades, researchers have subjected the jury to careful scientific scrutiny. In fact, studies of juror and jury decision making have become so plentiful that they occupy a center seat in psychology and law research. Knowledge of how juries operate comes from simulation studies, archives, court documents, appellate opinions, and actual jurors who have granted interviews or written books about their experiences. From these sources, we have been able to obtain a better, though still somewhat incomplete, picture of how the jury system works.

What have we learned from these many studies? In this chapter, we focus on two broad categories of concern: first, that juries are not competent to execute their duties properly, and, second, that juries are biased and prejudiced. Within each of these broad categories we consider several related issues and rely on research studies to address the criticisms. Finally, we consider various proposals to reform the institution of the jury.

# The Concern That Juries Are Not Competent

In reaching their verdicts, jurors are expected to rely only on the evidence and to disregard that which is not evidence (e.g., irrelevant information about the defendant, victim, plaintiff, or witnesses as well as information that the judge asks them to disregard). They are expected to listen attentively to expert testimony but not to give it undue weight. The legal system assumes that jurors will understand and correctly apply the judge's instructions on the law and that they have the necessary reasoning skills to understand protracted and complex cases. The concern related to these issues is that jurors are lacking in all areas and that they are generally not competent to carry out their defined duties.

## Concern about the Effects of Extralegal Information

Perhaps the most fundamental criticism about the jury is that its decisions will be determined *not* by the evidence presented in court but instead by irrelevant information about the defen-

dant's background or appearance, by what jurors read in the newspaper or by other sources of irrelevant information, all of which constitute **extralegal information.**

Is this critique warranted? How capable are jurors of basing their verdicts only on the evidence that is brought out in court? Answers to these questions may be hard to come by because it is not obvious when juries incorporate extralegal information into their decision-making process. If they do so, no one necessarily knows the difference. For example, some jury decisions may be based on irrelevant considerations rather than the evidence. But checking the reasons for a verdict following a trial is done only very infrequently, and the real reasons for a verdict or even for trends in jury verdicts are often impossible to assess (Vidmar, 1994). Much of what we know about jurors' attention to the evidence and disregard for the irrelevant comes from jury simulation studies in which some extralegal information is introduced by the researcher who then measures the extent to which that information influenced jurors' reasoning and their verdicts.

## Impact of Opening Statements

As part of a trial, attorneys for the two sides are allowed to make opening statements, which usually take the form of pledges to show certain facts and conditions. In some courts, the statement must be limited to a general outline; in others, lawyers are permitted to recite in detail the evidence that will be put forth by each of their witnesses. Judges have discretion to permit wide diversity in both the content and the length of opening statements. In some lengthy cases, an opening statement may last for an entire day!

On occasion, a defense attorney will use the opening statement to admit some damaging facts about the defendant. Lawyers using this approach hope to take the sting out of inflammatory accusations by the prosecutor. When Thomas Capano, the oldest son of one of Delaware's wealthiest real estate families, was tried for murdering his mistress, his lawyer took a risky gamble: He told the

*Thomas Capano being led into court. He was convicted of murder and sentenced to death.*

jury that Capano had lied to everyone for 28 months when he said he had nothing to do with the disappearance of the governor's secretary, Anne Marie Fahey. According to the lawyer, Capano had, in fact, dumped Fahey's lifeless body from a boat into the Atlantic Ocean. The lawyer promised that an unnamed witness would testify about how Fahey had died. Apparently the gamble failed; Capano was convicted of first-degree murder and sentenced to death.

In a civil trial, the person or organization filing charges (i.e., the plaintiff) is permitted to make the first opening statement. In a criminal trial, the prosecution ordinarily makes the initial statement, and the defense then has the option of either giving its overview immediately or waiting until the other side has presented its evidence. Textbooks on trial advocacy and legal experts differ on which of these is the wiser procedure (Tigar, 1996). Some argue that the defense should make its opening statement immediately after the other side's in order to try to negate any one-sided bias, but others argue

that it is better not to "show your hand" to the opposition until the last minute. Regardless of when the defense chooses to make its opening statement, it would seem that the prosecution or plaintiff has several psychological advantages by presenting its side first.

Even though opening statements are not evidence, they can exert great influence on jurors, occurring as they do at the beginning of the trial. As we know, the legal system insists that jurors should not form their decisions on the basis of opening statements. Judges will often instruct the jury that "statements and arguments of counsel are not evidence. They are only intended to assist the jury in understanding the evidence and the contentions of the parties" (LaBuy, 1963, p. 41).

Is this kind of instruction necessary? Are lawyers' statements and arguments a significant source of extralegal influence? Apparently so. In a Miami trial, two lawyers disagreed over a point of law right after the completion of the opening statements and before the introduction of any testimony. The judge asked the jury to leave the courtroom while the legal point was discussed. When the jury was brought back a few minutes later, the foreperson announced, "We've arrived at a verdict, Your Honor" (quoted in Kassin & Wrightsman, 1988, p. 105).

Trial lawyers often believe that a case may be won or lost on the basis of their statements and arguments to the jury. Louis Nizer (1961) has written, "By a skillful presentation of what he intends to prove the attorney can convert a mere informative exercise into a persuasive plea . . . the opportunity to condition the jury favorably is as limitless as the attorney's art" (p. 42).

The psychological findings support these claims to a disturbing degree. One set of studies (Pyszczynski, Greenberg, Mack, & Wrightsman, 1981; Pyszczynski & Wrightsman, 1981; Wells, Miene, & Wrightsman, 1985) demonstrated that opening statements can even overrule the impact of the evidence. Sometimes, though, this effect is not immediate; rather, it affects jurors' sentiments over the course of the entire trial. We describe one such study in ◆ Box 15-1.

Why does the first strong opening statement carry such impact? Consider the juror's situation. Called for jury service, the prospective juror is anxious and yet conscientious. Many prospective jurors dread the responsibility; they fully expect that they will be serving in some sleazy murder trial, and they abhor the task of deciding another's fate. Some also fear retaliation from disgruntled defendants. Yet they are attracted to the suspense and the importance of the jury trial. Most jurors want to do a good job; they take their responsibilities seriously. All these concerns combine to make jurors very eager to "get a handle" on the case. The judge may have told them a little about the charge; during voir dire there may have been hints about the evidence and the witnesses. But it is not until the opening statements that jurors get their first systematic overview of the nature of the case.

All of us reject ambiguity to one degree or another. We seek explanations for behavior. The opening statements provide these; they create what social psychologists have called a thematic

framework, or **schema** (Lingle & Ostrom, 1981), which guides jurors in their processing and interpretation of actual testimony that is presented later in the trial. Jurors apparently use the theories developed by the attorneys in opening statements as plausible scenarios of what took place on the day of the crime or accident. These frameworks assist jurors in their attempts to make sense of the rather disjointed array of information that is presented in a typical trial.

Experimental psychologists have demonstrated the usefulness of thematic frameworks in memory. For example, recall of sentences and of prose is improved when the material is preceded by a thematic title (Bransford & Johnson, 1972). After exposure to a list of 15 common everyday behaviors, participants who had been asked to form an impression of a hypothetical target person who enacted those behaviors recalled more of the behaviors than did participants who had been instructed to memorize the list (Hamilton, Katz, & Leirer, 1980).

The oft-repeated conclusion that first impressions affect later reactions reflects the operation of thematic frameworks. In a typical study (Langer & Abelson, 1974), subjects listened to a tape of two men interacting. Half the subjects had been told that the tape was of a job interview and the other half that it was of a psychiatric intake interview. Subjects who believed the tape to be of a psychiatric interview reported more pathology in the interviewee's behavior; they distorted background information to make it fit better with their impressions. Thematic frameworks affect not only the encoding of information and its retrieval from memory but also the interpretation that is placed on that information (Brewer & Nakamura, 1984; Taylor & Crocker, 1981). This is especially true when the thematic framework is concrete rather than abstract (Pryor, McDaniel, & Kott-Russo, 1986), such as the description of the criminal as wearing a certain type of shirt or having a mustache.

But how far should lawyers go in opening statements? Lawyers are often faced with a situation in which they are not sure exactly what the

## The Science of

**BOX 15-1**   **Multiple measures and the impact of opening statements**

In one study (Pyszczynski & Wrightsman, 1981), mock jurors from the community watched a videotape of a case involving a charge of transporting a car across state lines. Some mock jurors were shown brief opening statements; in these, the attorneys only introduced themselves and whatever witnesses they had and then promised that their evidence would be convincing. Other mock jurors heard much more extensive opening statements, which consisted of a full preview of what the attorney expected the evidence to be and the way he believed the evidence should be interpreted. Then all the mock jurors watched the same evidence and closing arguments. To gauge the ways that the opening statements affected jurors' judgments as the trial progressed, these researchers asked jurors to give their individual verdicts not once but, rather, at 12 points during the trial presentation, as well as at the end.

Psychologists often take multiple measures of the effects they are studying. Sometimes, as in this study, the multiple measures involve asking one question (e.g.,

"Is the defendant guilty?") several times over the course of the study to see how sentiments change as the study progresses. Other times, different, but related, questions are posed to participants. For example, researchers evaluating the effect of an injury on a plaintiff in a civil case might ask the following set of questions: "To what extent was the plaintiff disabled by the accident?" "To what extent was the plaintiff disfigured?" "To what extent has the plaintiff suffered physically?" "To what extent has the plaintiff suffered emotionally?" The benefit of multiple questions is that they allow the researcher to gain a more sophisticated understanding of the behavior or cognition of interest, even if this sometimes seems annoying (or at least redundant) to the research participant!

The use of multiple measures by Pyszczynski et al. illustrated the mutable impact of opening statements, particularly when they were brief. When both sides' opening statements were brief, there was substantial shift in preferences for a verdict over the 12 data points. In this situation, jurors

seemed to give the defendant the benefit of doubt and hence started out leaning toward a not-guilty verdict. After hearing the prosecution's first witness testify, however, they began to shift toward a guilty verdict and stayed there until the conclusion of the trial.

The opening statement exerted a more powerful influence when it was lengthy. Most jurors who heard an elaborate statement from the prosecution began by believing the defendant to be guilty and then maintained that verdict throughout the trial presentation. If the defense made an extensive opening statement (and if the prosecution made only a brief introduction), then jurors were more likely to respond with not-guilty verdicts. Nowhere is the power of first impressions more clearly demonstrated than in these differences. In fact, a follow-up study (Wells et al., 1985) found that, if the defense was permitted to make its extensive opening statement before the prosecution's (a procedure not usually allowed by the courts), jurors were more likely to find the defendant not guilty.

testimony of a particular witness will be. Should they run the risk of promising more than can be delivered? If so, how might a jury react? Would the lawyer who promised too much lose all credibility?

From an information-processing viewpoint, the dangers of making too extensive an opening statement may not be as great as some observers have

assumed. Social psychologists using the concept of thematic frameworks argue that, in most situations, people's inferences and verdicts are affected more by their initial judgments in response to information set than by the set itself. After hearing a persuasive, extensive opening statement, jurors may make tentative decisions about guilt or responsibil-

*An attorney arguing his case to a jury*

ity and begin to view the evidence in light of these early "hunches." Even if the subsequent evidence is not exactly as promised, these initial impressions may strongly influence the final verdicts.

To test these ideas, Pyszczynski and his colleagues (1991) compared the effects of three versions of a trial transcript. In one, the defense attorney claimed—inaccurately—that the defendant would present an alibi that would rule him out as the perpetrator. In a second version of the transcript, some mock jurors were promised the alibi in the defense's opening statement and also were reminded by the prosecution at the end of the trial that the defense had not fulfilled its promise. The remaining third of the mock jurors were exposed to a trial transcript that contained neither a promise from the defense nor a reminder from the prosecution. The actual evidence was the same for all three types of jurors.

Of course, the greatest danger to the attorney who makes a promise that cannot be fulfilled is for the opposing counsel to make the jury aware of the discrepancy, as was done here. And it had

the expected effect. Jurors exposed to the opposing attorney's reminder apparently began to question other aspects of the overzealous attorney's case; they were more confident that the defendant was guilty than were subjects who had not been exposed to the dashing of this promise.

But more important, if the jurors were given an unfulfilled promise and were never reminded of it by the opposition, they were more likely to acquit the defendant than if they had not been given such a false promise. A completely unsubstantiated claim worked when unchallenged.

These disturbing results need to be qualified. First, the respondents were mock jurors, not actual ones; second, they did not engage in any deliberation. (The process of deliberating may weaken any tendency of individual jurors to give precedence to the opening promise over the actual evidence.) And in real trials, any opposing attorney who is at all alert will remind the jurors of his or her adversary's omission.

Even though we doubt that a blatant lie in an opening statement could be an effective strategy, some attorneys may opt to take the risk to make the strongest, most extensive opening statement that is plausible. By doing so, the attorney may provide a favorable framework that jurors will use to interpret later evidence. Even if this later testimony does not fully substantiate the lawyer's claims, the final verdicts may be more favorable than if such strong claims had not been made. Indeed, in their closing arguments, clever defense attorneys could even admit that such factors as capricious witnesses may have prevented them from fulfilling their claims, thereby eliminating the opportunity for prosecutors to discredit those claims.

Of course, an ethical issue also needs to be considered in this area. An attorney who deliberately refers to inadmissible or unavailable evidence violates the codes that govern the profession: the Model Code of Professional Conduct and the Model Rules of Professional Responsibility. This practice may lead to censure by the trial court or reversal by an appellate court. In one such case, the prosecutor said in his opening that the killing was "gang related." However, he failed to introduce any proof to support this claim, and the appellate court reversed the defendant's conviction (*Alexander v. State*, 1998).

## Impact of Extralegal Information in Criminal Cases

*The influence of prior record evidence.* In 1993, Maria Ohler was convicted of possessing a small amount of methamphetamine and was sentenced to three years of probation. Four years later, customs inspectors found 84 pounds of marijuana behind a loose panel in the van Ohler was driving into the United States from Mexico. When she was tried on the marijuana charge, evidence of her prior conviction was admitted at the trial in order to attack her credibility as a witness.

Once jurors have heard evidence about a defendant's prior criminal record, they may no longer be able to suspend judgment about that defendant and decide his or her fate based solely on the evidence at trial. Therefore, the prosecution is often not permitted to introduce evidence of a defendant's criminal record for fear that jurors would be prejudiced by it and judge the current offense in light of those past misdeeds. However, if defendants take the witness stand, then prosecutors may be able to question them about certain types of past convictions in order to impeach their credibility as witnesses. In that circumstance, the judge may issue a **limiting instruction** to the effect that evidence of a defendant's prior record can be used for limited purposes only: to gauge the defendant's credibility but not to prove the defendant's propensity to commit the charged offense. (Defense attorneys are decidedly suspicious of jurors' ability to follow this rule, however, and often recommend to their clients with prior records that they not take the witness stand to testify on their own behalf. Ohler opted to testify, and even mentioned the conviction on direct examination in order to soften its effects.)

An early study showed that attorneys' hunches were valid: Mock jurors informed of a defendant's prior conviction were more likely than jurors who had no information about a prior record to convict the defendant on subsequent charges (Doob & Kirshenbaum, 1972). More recent research found that the similarity of the charges was an important variable: Conviction rates were higher when the prior conviction was for an offense similar to the one being decided (Wissler & Saks, 1985). One study found that deliberating juries spend considerable time talking about a defendant's prior record, not for what it suggests about credibility but, rather, to decide whether the defendant has a criminal disposition (Shaffer, 1985).

Why does evidence of a prior conviction increase the likelihood of conviction on a subsequent charge? For some jurors, the prior record, in combination with allegations related to the subsequent charge, may show a pattern of criminality; together they point to an individual who is prone to act in an illegal or felonious manner. Other jurors, upon hearing evidence of a prior conviction, may need less evidence to be convinced of the defendant's guilt beyond a reasonable doubt on the subsequent charge. Prior record evidence may lead a juror to think that because the defendant already has a criminal record, an erroneous conviction would not be serious. This juror might therefore be satisfied with a slightly less compelling demonstration of guilt.

On some occasions, a jury will hear evidence not of a prior *conviction* but of a prior *acquittal* (i.e., the defendant was previously tried and found not guilty of charges unrelated to the present case.) The U.S. Supreme Court has held that the admission of prior acquittal evidence does *not* unfairly prejudice the defendant (*Dowling v. U.S.*, 1990). In the *Dowling* case, the defendant, Reuben Dowling, was tried for armed robbery of a bank in the Virgin Islands. During his trial, the prosecutor introduced evidence from an unrelated home break-in—a charge on which Dowling had previously been acquitted. The judge admitted the evidence to prove that Dowling was present in the community in which the bank was located. Theoretically, jurors should disregard evidence of a prior acquittal when deciding whether a defendant is guilty in a subsequent case. But do they?

To test whether jurors conform to this expectation, Greene and Dodge (1995) presented a summary of the facts in the *Dowling* case to three groups of mock jurors who were deciding whether the defendant should be found guilty of armed robbery. One third of the jurors learned that the defendant had been previously tried and convicted of charges stemming from the home break-in. Another third was informed that the defendant had been acquitted of the home break-in charges, and the final group had no information about the defendant's prior record. The results supported the Supreme Court's reasoning: Jurors who heard evidence of a prior acquittal were no more likely to convict the defendant than were jurors who had no information about a prior record, and both groups were less likely to convict than jurors who had evidence of a prior conviction. These findings suggest that jurors may exercise some restraint in their use of prior acquittal evidence and may indeed not be prejudiced by it.

### The impact of evidence on multiple charges.
Can jurors show the same restraint when multiple charges are tried together in the same trial? Consider the case of Toby Dudley. Dudley was to be tried in Breckenridge, Colorado, in late 1999 on two sets of charges stemming from two robberies of souvenir shops on October 6, 1998. Most courts permit a criminal defendant to be tried for two or more charges at the same time as long as the offenses are similar or are connected to the same act. This procedure, called **joinder,** exists primarily for purposes of efficiency: It is more efficient to try similar cases together than to stage separate trials. But does trying someone for two or more charges at the same time increase the likelihood that the jury will convict the defendant of at least one of these crimes? Was Dudley more likely to be convicted of either robbery because it was tried in conjunction with a second robbery? A recent meta-analysis of simulation studies that have examined the effects of joinder (Nietzel et al., 1999) concluded that such a procedure was clearly to the defendant's disadvantage. Criminal defendants are more likely to be convicted of any single charge when it is tried in combination with other charges than when it is tried alone. Some evidence indicates that jurors who hear multiple cases misremember and confuse evidence against the defendant across charges and conclude that the defendant has a criminal disposition because of the multiplicity of charges (Nietzel et al., 1999).

### The impact of character and propensity evidence.
Historically, evidence about a defendant's character could not be used in court to prove that the defendant committed a crime. Likewise, evidence of other crimes or wrongdoing (so-called **propensity evidence**) is typically not admissible to suggest that because a defendant had the propensity to act in a criminal manner, he is guilty of the charge now at issue. Sex crimes, however, are treated differently in federal court and in some states. In 1994, Congress passed a law making evidence of other sex offenses admissible to show a defendant's propensity to commit the charged sex offense. The California legislature enacted a similar law in 1995, and the California

Supreme Court upheld the law in the following case (*People v. Falsetta,* 1999).

When Charles Falsetta was tried for rape and kidnapping in Alameda County Court, the prosecutor introduced evidence of two prior uncharged sexual assaults allegedly committed by Falsetta. In the first, the defendant allegedly began jogging beside a woman, asked her where she was going, and then tackled and raped her. In the second incident, the defendant allegedly blocked the path of a woman as she walked to work and later jumped out from behind some bushes, grabbed her, threw her into the bushes, and sexually assaulted her. These incidents bore a striking resemblance to the Alameda County case in which the defendant allegedly stopped a 16-year-old girl as she was walking to her house from a convenience store. After initially refusing a ride, the girl eventually accepted and was driven to a darkened parking lot and raped. The defendant was convicted and appealed his conviction, contending that the admission of evidence of other uncharged rapes violated his rights.

On appeal to the California Supreme Court, Richard Rochman, the deputy attorney general who argued the case on behalf of the state of California, stated that because victims of sex offenses often hesitate to speak out and because the alleged crimes occur in private, prosecutors are often faced with a "he said, she said" credibility problem. Allowing prosecutors to present propensity evidence in these cases would give jurors the full picture of the defendant's past sexual misconduct, reasoned Rochman. The California Supreme Court agreed.

What effect might propensity evidence have on jurors? In its argument in the *Falsetta* case, the state of California assumed that jurors could properly use propensity evidence to gauge the defendant's possible disposition to commit sex crimes. Furthermore, according to Rochman, concerns about defendants' rights would be appeased by a judge's caution that jurors not convict merely on the weight of the propensity evidence. At least one study raises questions about jurors' abilities to use propensity evidence

properly, however. In their study of jury decision making in sexual assault cases, Bette Bottoms and Gail Goodman exposed some mock jurors to a defendant's past criminal acts and other negative defendant character evidence. These jurors perceived the victim to be more credible and the defendant to be more likely guilty than did jurors not exposed to this character evidence (Bottoms & Goodman, 1994).

## Impact of Extralegal Information in Civil Cases

When individuals have a dispute with their landlord, insurance company, or the manufacturer of a product that allegedly caused them harm, they can attempt to resolve that dispute through the workings of the civil justice system. Although the vast majority of civil cases are resolved outside the courtroom, typically in settlement discussions between the opposing lawyers, still thousands of civil cases are tried before juries each year. Juries in these cases typically make two fundamental decisions: whether the defendant (or, in some instances, the plaintiff) is **liable** or responsible for the alleged harm and whether the injured party (typically the plaintiff) should receive any money to compensate for his or her losses, and if so, in what amount. These monies are called **damages.**

Although the vast majority of scholarly research on juror and jury decision making has focused on criminal cases, in recent years psychologists have devoted considerable attention to the workings of civil juries and are increasingly able to address the concern that juries are incompetent to decide civil cases fairly and rationally. Do jurors determine liability and assess damages in a rational way, or are they swayed by emotion and prejudice?

*Determining liability.*    An important decision that jurors must make in civil cases concerns the parties' respective responsibility for the harm that was suffered. When psychologists study juries' liability judgments, they are really asking how people assign responsibility for an injury. When a baby is stillborn, do jurors perceive the doctor to be at fault for not performing a cesarean section? Would the child have died anyway? When a smoker dies from lung cancer, do jurors blame the cigarette manufacturer for elevating the nicotine level in its product or the smoker who knowingly exposed herself to a dangerous product over the course of many years? Or do they blame both?

The severity of an injury or accident, sometimes referred to as **outcome severity,** is legally relevant to decisions about the damage award in a civil case, but it should be irrelevant to a judgment concerning liability or legal responsibility. The defendant should not be saddled with a liability judgment against him simply because the plaintiff was seriously injured. Rather, jurors should decide liability on the basis of the defendant's conduct. Were his actions reckless? Were they negligent? Were they malicious and evil? These are the questions that jurors should ask themselves in the course of deliberating on the defendant's liability. Are jurors able to use the evidence concerning outcome severity for the limited purposes for which it is intended—namely, to assess damages? Or, instead, do they factor it into their calculations of responsibility?

In an important early study, Elaine Walster sparked an interest in examining how the consequences of an accident affect judgments of responsibility for that accident (Walster, 1966). She presented participants with the facts of an accident and asked them to rate the responsibility of the actor who was potentially at fault. Some participants learned that the actor's conduct resulted in a dented fender (a low-severity outcome), and others learned that his actions resulted in major property damage or personal injury (a high-severity outcome). Walster found that participants assigned more responsibility to the actor in the high-severity condition than in the low-severity condition.

Why would we assign more responsibility to an individual as the consequences of his or her conduct become more serious? One explanation is **defensive attribution** (Fiske & Taylor, 1991): As the consequences of one's actions become more severe, they also become more unpleasant, and the notion that they might be accidental becomes less tolerable. Thus, we are likely to blame a person for their occurrence because doing so makes the incident somehow more controllable and avoidable. This idea also underlies the belief in a just world, discussed in Chapter 3.

Walster's study was conducted with college students who read a brief description of an accident and assigned responsibility judgments. One wonders whether the same or similar results occur in the real world of a jury deliberation room. When information concerning injury severity is presented in combination with other testimony and when this complex set of evidence is discussed during deliberations, will jurors continue to focus inappropriately on the outcome of the incident? Will their liability judgments be improperly influenced?

This question was recently addressed by Greene and her colleagues (Greene, Johns, & Bowman, 1999; Greene, Johns, & Smith, 2001) in a reenactment of an automobile negligence case in which the defendant, a truck driver hauling 22 tons of asphalt, crashed into a highway median. Remarkably, one of the truck's axles took flight and landed on the cab of a small pickup truck being driven in the opposite direction by the plaintiff. These researchers manipulated the defendant's conduct that led to the accident by varying information about the driver's speed and the number of lane changes he undertook prior to the accident as well as his braking technique and his use (or nonuse) of an available engine retarder. They also varied the severity of the injuries to the plaintiff by describing either a catastrophic head injury coupled with paraplegia (high-severity outcome) or a concussion with accompanying soft-tissue injury (low-severity outcome). In theory, jurors' judgments of liability should be affected by evidence of the defendant's conduct but not by evidence related to outcome severity.

As is legally appropriate, the defendant's conduct had a strong impact on citizen-jurors' judgments of the defendant's liability, but evidence about the severity of the plaintiff's injuries mattered, too: The defendant was perceived to be more negligent when the plaintiff suffered more serious injuries. Perhaps most troubling, these effects were not erased during deliberation. (One might hope that jurors could correct each other's misuse of the evidence as they discuss it during deliberation.) Rather, individual jurors were more likely to rely on irrelevant information regarding the plaintiff's injuries *after* deliberating than they had been *before* deliberations.

When asked various questions about factors that influenced their verdicts, jurors who heard that the plaintiff had been severely injured were more likely than those with evidence of mild injuries to say that their negligence judgments were fueled by a desire to compensate the plaintiff for economic losses and his pain and suffering. In situations in which a plaintiff has suffered emotionally and financially (and in which the defendant had acted carelessly), jurors may decide to find the defendant liable so that the plaintiff can be compensated for his losses. These results are consistent with a recent meta-analysis (Robbennolt, 2000) showing that people attribute greater responsibility for the outcome of a negative incident when that outcome is more severe than when the outcome is minor.

*Assessing damages.*   Pity the poor man. Michael Brennan, a St. Paul bank president, was simply responding to nature's call when he was sprayed with more than 200 gallons of raw sewage as he sat on the toilet in the bank's executive washroom. The geyser of water came "blasting up out of the toilet with such force that it stood him right up," leaving Brennan "immersed in human excrement." He sued a construction company working in the bank at the time, but the jury awarded Brennan nothing. Why, then, did a jury award $300,000 to a workman who slipped from a ladder and fell into a pile of manure (a story aired on CBS's *60 Minutes*)?

One of the most perplexing issues for trial attorneys is how jurors assess damages (Hastie, Schkade, & Payne, 1999). This complex decision seems especially subjective and unpredictable because people value money and injuries differently

and because jurors are given scant guidance on how to award damages. The awards for punitive damages—intended to punish the defendant and deter future malicious conduct—are especially of concern because the jury receives little instruction about how those awards should be determined. Consider the staggering $145 billion punitive damage award against the tobacco industry in 2000. Even the judge in the case was amazed. "A lot of zeros," he observed dryly, after reading the verdict.

Recently, psychologists have begun to study this issue. What have they learned? First, few people get rich by suing for damages. The median award in tort cases—involving injury to persons or property—was $30,000 in 1996; the median award in automobile accident cases was a mere $18,000. Although the media are eager to tell us about multimillion-dollar damage awards, these colossal awards are far from the norm. Second, in general, the more a plaintiff asks for, the more that plaintiff receives. Jurors tend to adjust their awards toward "anchor points," the most obvious of which is the plaintiff's requested damages.

What factors do jurors consider in their decisions about damages? Data from interviews with actual jurors and from experimental studies show that at least some juries consider attorneys' fees, the possible taxation of a damage award, whether the plaintiff is a resident of the local community or lives in a distant location, and whether any loss is covered by insurance—issues that are all theoretically irrelevant to decisions about the amount of damages to award. A common assumption is that if jurors believe the actions of a civil defendant were covered by insurance, any award to the plaintiff would be increased. But whether this knowledge has any actual effect on the resulting damage award is uncertain: In some interviews, jurors indicated that deliberation about these matters occurred but that jurors decided the issue was irrelevant. On other occasions, jurors who believed that a defendant lacked insurance may have reduced the award out of concern for the defendant's ability to pay.

Attorneys who represent plaintiffs in personal injury cases (a kind of civil case that is sometimes tried before a jury) typically work on a contingent fee basis. Plaintiffs do not pay their attorneys up front to represent them. Rather, if successful in securing a settlement or damage award for the client, the attorney will take some percentage (typically 25% to 35%) of it as a fee. If unsuccessful, the attorney (and the plaintiff as well) will receive nothing. Neil Vidmar and Jeffrey Rice compared the awards of legal professionals (senior lawyers and judges) to those of jurors in medical malpractice cases and found that the professionals explicitly calculated a fair award for the plaintiff and then increased it to account for attorney fees; few jurors said that they did this (Vidmar & Rice, 1993). One other study (Goodman, Greene, & Loftus, 1989) found that most jurors are unlikely to supplement the damage award to account for attorneys' fees.

Oftentimes, both the plaintiff and defendant share responsibility for the alleged wrongdoing. Consider a situation in which a home furnace malfunctions, setting fire to a house and injuring the homeowner. One might suspect that the furnace manufacturer was partially at fault for any injuries suffered. However, if the homeowner had rushed back into the burning house to retrieve some cherished possessions, many of us would also believe that he was partially at fault. This is one of the situations investigated by Neil Feigenson and his colleagues (Feigenson, Park, & Salovey, 1997).

In cases like this, called **comparative negligence** cases because the jury compares and apportions the blame between the two parties, jurors are instructed to compensate the plaintiff fully for his losses and are informed that the award will be reduced in proportion to the plaintiff's fault. (If the jury determines that 60% of responsibility rests with the defendant and 40% with the plaintiff, any damages they award would be reduced by 40%.) If jurors are supposed to compensate the plaintiff fully, they should not further discount their awards to reflect their sentiments about the plaintiff's liability, a practice termed *double discounting*.

A question of considerable interest to psychologists is whether jurors are able to do this.

Some recent research (e.g., Feigenson et al., 1997; Wissler, Kuehn, & Saks, 2000; Zickafoose & Bornstein, 1999) suggests that they may have trouble not making a double discount. In each of these studies, the experimenters manipulated the comparative fault of the plaintiff and found evidence of double discounting: Mock jurors intuitively and inappropriately lowered their damages award when the plaintiff was partially at fault. This diminished award would then have been discounted again by the judge to reflect the degree to which the plaintiff was responsible. Even when jurors were instructed to disregard the plaintiff's level of fault and were informed that the judge would reduce the award, their awards were apparently influenced by the level of the plaintiff's responsibility (Wissler et al., 2000; Zickafoose & Bornstein, 1999).

## Instructions to Disregard Inadmissible Evidence: How Effective?

Research on **inadmissible evidence** is also relevant to the assumption that jurors can separate evidence from nonevidence. All fans of *Perry Mason* are familiar with the attorney's "I object." If the judge sustains an objection, the opposing attorney's objectionable question or the witness's objectionable response will not be recorded, and the judge will instruct or admonish the jury to disregard the material. But are jurors able to do so?

Most of the empirical evidence indicates not only that they are not but, even more disturbing, that a judge's admonition to disregard inadmissible evidence may boomerang (Tanford, 1990). For example, Pickel (1995) presented mock jurors with information that a defendant in a theft trial had a prior conviction. That information was admitted as evidence, ruled inadmissible with a simple admonition for the jury to disregard it, or ruled inadmissible and accompanied by an explanation of this ruling by the judge. Results showed that when the judge gave a legal explanation of why the jurors were to disregard information about the defendant's prior conviction, they were *more* likely to convict him.

Broeder (1959) found a similar effect in a civil case in which mock jurors learned either that the defendant had insurance or that he did not. Half the subjects who were told that he had insurance were admonished by the judge to disregard that information. Juries who believed that the defendant had no insurance awarded damages to the plaintiff in an average amount of $33,000. Juries believing that he did have insurance awarded an average of $37,000. But those juries that were aware of the insurance but had been admonished to disregard it gave the highest average award, $46,000.

These findings imply that admonishments to disregard certain testimony may serve instead to sensitize jurors to the inadmissible evidence. Several theoretical explanations have been offered for this process. A theory that relies on motivation as an explanation, **reactance theory** (Brehm, 1966; Brehm & Brehm, 1981) would propose that instructions to disregard evidence may threaten jurors' freedom to consider all available evidence. When this happens, jurors may respond by acting in ways that will restore their sense of decision-making freedom.

Alternatively, jurors' overreliance on evidence they are admonished not to use may reflect a cognitive process described in Wegner's (1989, 1994) **thought suppression** studies. Wegner and his associates (Wegner & Erber, 1992; Wegner, Schneider, Carter, & White, 1987) found that asking people "not to think of a white bear" increased the tendency to do just that. In fact, the harder that people try to control a thought, the less likely they are to succeed (Wegner, 1994). Likewise, jurors may think more about inadmissible evidence as a direct consequence of their attempts to follow the judge's request to suppress thoughts of it (Clavet, 1996).

A third theoretical explanation emphasizes the phenomenon of **belief perseverance,** or the tendency for beliefs to persist even after the evidence on which they were based has been rejected or discredited (Kassin & Studebaker, 1998). In a provocative study, Anderson, Lepper, and Ross (1980) had their subjects read a case study about firefighters. Half of the subjects were given information that the best firefighters were risk takers; the other half were informed that the best firefighters were cautious types. Then each subject had to generate a reason for whichever relationship that subject had been given. Later, all the subjects were told that the information they had been given was totally false, created specifically for the study. But when questioned about the relationship of risk taking and firefighting ability, subjects clung to their newly created beliefs. How is this study relevant to jurors' decision making? As Kassin and Studebaker (1998) observe, instructions by the judge to disregard evidence may fail when the invalidated information has already activated the formation of some explanatory structure, such as a schema.

Psychologists emphasize that, in contrast to the stated view of the legal system, jurors are active information processors. Their goal is to make a decision based on what they believe is just, not necessarily one that reflects what the judge says. (We discussed the notion of commonsense justice in Chapter 3.) So, for example, when mock jurors were told to disregard certain evidence because of a legal technicality, they still allowed that evidence to influence their verdicts when they thought that it enhanced the accuracy of their decisions (Kassin & Sommers, 1996). Because jurors want to be correct in their judgments, they may rely on information that *they* perceive to be relevant, regardless of whether that information meets the law's technical standards of admissibility.

Not all the empirical evidence indicates such a boomerang effect (Kagehiro & Werner, 1977; Mitchell & Byrne, 1972; Simon, 1966). But the overall pattern of findings makes us very suspicious of an assumption that jurors are able to disregard inadmissible evidence, especially when such evidence would lead to conviction of the defendant (Nietzel, McCarthy, & Kern, 1999; Thompson, Fong, & Rosenhan, 1981). After a very thorough review of the experimental evidence, Tanford (1990) concluded, "the empirical research clearly demonstrates that instructions to disregard are ineffective in reducing the harm caused by inadmissible evidence and improper arguments" (p. 95).

But what happens when individual jurors come together to deliberate? Will the process, or even the expectation of discussion with other jurors, motivate jurors to follow the judge's instructions (Kerwin & Shaffer, 1994)? Limited research on mock juries indicates that jury deliberations modified but did not eliminate the impact of inadmissible evidence (London & Nightingale, 1996). In fact, audiotapes of jury deliberations in one mock jury study (Carretta & Moreland, 1983) showed that the jurors discussed the inadmissible evidence—and even the judge's ruling—during their deliberations.

Inadmissible evidence thus is information that has been ruled legally irrelevant but still has potentially great influence on jurors' opinions. Many other irrelevant factors in the trial presentation also could influence the jury's decision, including the gender, race, age, physical appearance, and attractiveness of the litigants and other witnesses, the personal style and credibility of attorneys, and the order of presentation of evidence. For example, Zebrowitz and McDonald (1991) discovered that, as civil plaintiffs increased in physical attractiveness, they were more likely to win their case.

Are jurors able to eliminate such irrelevant considerations from their decisions about verdicts, liability, and damage awards? An early review by Gerbasi, Zuckerman, and Reis (1977) offered a summary that is, unfortunately, still relevant today: "It appears that extraevidential factors, such as defendant, victim, and juror characteristics, trial procedures, and so forth, can influence the severity of verdicts rendered by individual jurors" (p. 343). More recently, after reviewing a variety of extralegal influences ranging from speculative questions during cross-examination (Kassin, Williams, & Saunders, 1990) to hearsay as communicated by an expert witness (Schuller, 1995), two researchers concluded that "indeed, mock jury research has shown that verdicts can be influenced by a wide range of nonevidentiary factors presented both

inside and outside the courtroom" (Kassin & Studebaker, 1998, p. 3).

The findings in this section offer a serious challenge for those who want to reform jury procedures so that jurors do pay attention only to the evidence, as they are assumed to do. In their current form, instructions and admonishments by judges do not seem to work.

To deal with the effects of inadmissible evidence, a radical reform has been proposed: to videotape the whole trial before the jurors are present, edit out any references to inadmissible evidence, and then play it for jurors (Miller & Fontes, 1979). But such a procedure has limitations of its own: Jurors may be less motivated to do a conscientious job, and the tape restricts their freedom to observe what they want to (e.g., watching the defendant's face when the victim's widow testifies). In addition, practical problems involving excessive expense and court time make this reform problematic.

A less radical suggestion is for judges to provide juries at the start of every trial with a general warning that some of the information they will receive will be inadmissible (Kassin & Studebaker, 1998). A study in a nonlegal setting by Schul (1993) concluded that such an early warning, along with a later reminder, permitted subjects both to suspend the processing of evidence and to think more critically about information that was later discredited. As will be described in detail later in this chapter, jury instructions that come before the evidence are more effective than those that come after the evidence. An added boost would be for the judge to secure a public commitment from the jurors during voir dire that they will disregard any information ultimately judged to be inadmissible (Tanford, 1990).

## Concern about the Effects of Expert Testimony

As society has become increasingly specialized and technical knowledge has accumulated at a feverish pace, the judicial system has had to rely more often on expert witnesses to inform jurors

## THE CASE OF

**BOX 15-2**   **Orville Lynn Majors and the use of expert testimony**

In 1994, Orville Lynn Majors was employed as a nurse at the Vermillion County Hospital in Indiana. Five years later, he stood trial for killing seven patients under his care with lethal doses of potassium chloride. One of the witnesses called by the defense was Dr. Rory Childers, a multiboard-certified doctor, professor, and researcher at the University of Chicago. Childers provided dramatic testimony about the highly specialized area of medicine involved in determining the cause of death. He spent considerable time

testifying about the difficult task of reading rhythm strips produced when a patient is on electro-cardiomonitoring. According to Childers, most of the patients died

*Orville Lynn Majors, seated with his attorney, on trial for multiple murders*

at the hospital as a result of heart failure, not poisoning. He called one patient's existence "nothing short of a pulmonary miracle," described another as "extraordinarily emaciated and debilitated," and remarked that a third patient suffered from a "monstrous infection" that ultimately led to death. Despite his impressive performance, Dr. Childers's expert testimony was not enough to sway the jury: Majors was convicted of killing six of the seven patients and was sentenced to 360 years in prison.

of this professional information. Experts typically testify about scientific, technical, or other specialized knowledge with which most jurors are not familiar. Dr. Rory Childers took on that role in a well-publicized case described in ◆ **Box 15-2.**

A concern that arises when experts testify is that because jurors lack rigorous analytical skills, they may resort to irrational decision-making strategies when faced with highly specialized or technical testimony. Some people suspect, for example, that jurors will rely on superficial aspects of the expert's demeanor, including his or her appearance, personality, or presentation style to determine how much weight to put on the expert's testimony. Others fear that expert testimony would mesmerize jurors, causing them to discount their own common sense and rely too heavily on the opinions of the experts. The opposite result has been forecast as well: that because jurors

"know it all along," they do not need to hear from a supposed "expert" whose testimony they view as meaningless and gratuitous. The "battle of the experts"—a situation that arises when opposing sides each present their own experts—is thought to compound problems for the jury: "An especially perplexing task for lay jurors is to assimilate and select in some rational manner from the competing testimonies of expert witnesses. This battle of the experts tends to confound factfinders, especially juries" (Strier, 1996, p. 112).

Do jurors place undue weight on testimony from experts? How are their verdicts affected by expert testimony? Dan Shuman and Anthony Champagne addressed these issues in a questionnaire study of jurors, judges, attorneys, and experts in Dallas, Baltimore, Seattle, and Tucson (Shuman & Champagne, 1997). Lawyers and experts in all four cities expressed confidence in jurors' abilities to understand expert testimony, ranking jurors only slightly less able than judges in this department. And, contrary to the critics' concerns, the votes of confidence were warranted: Factors such as an expert's personality and appearance—thought by critics to play a significant role in jurors' assessments of experts—were not significant considerations. Rather, jurors stated that they evaluated the testimony of the experts based on the professionalism and quality of the experts' testimony. Neither did jurors mechanistically defer to the experts because of the experts' proven qualifications and knowledge base. Instead, jurors were somewhat skeptical, even demanding, of the experts. Finally, jurors were conscious of the possibility that experts could be biased and expressed skepticism of partisan experts.

Taken together, these findings and those of other research teams (e.g., Hans & Ivkovich, 1994; Kovera & Borgida, 1997; Vidmar, 1995) suggest that jurors give balanced consideration to experts and base their decisions about the believability of experts on a sensible set of considerations: the expert's qualifications, factual familiarity, reasoning abilities, and impartiality. A recent meta-analysis (Nietzel et al., 1999) lends further support to this position. Examining the effects of psychological expert testimony in 22 studies, Nietzel and his colleagues found little support for the concern that expert testimony will dominate jurors' decision making. Nor is it an expensive waste of time. Jurors appear to give reasoned and balanced consideration to experts whom they perceive to be fair and professional.

## Concern about Jurors' Abilities to Understand and Apply Their Instructions

Jury instructions, provided by the judge to the jury near the end of a trial, play a crucial role in every case. They explain the laws that are applicable to the case and direct jurors to reach a verdict in accordance with those laws. Ironically, jurors are often treated like children during the testimonial phase of the trial—they are expected

to sit still, pay attention, and not ask questions—but like accomplished law students during the reading of the judge's instructions—they are expected to understand the complicated legal terminology of the instructions. Unfortunately, the greatest weakness for many juries is their inability to understand these instructions (Ellsworth, 1999; Lieberman & Sales, 1997).

One source of confusion is the legal language itself. Often, the instructions simply repeat statutory language and therefore are full of legal terms that are unfamiliar to laypeople (e.g., in most civil cases, jurors are informed that the burden of proof is on the plaintiff to establish his case by a *preponderance* of the evidence; the word *preponderance* appears 0.26 times per million words in the English language (Zeno, Ivens, Millard, & Duvvuri, 1995)! And here's an example of how jurors are instructed about the meaning of "proximate cause," an important concept in civil trials: "a cause which, in a natural and continuous sequence, produced damage, and without which the damage would not have occurred." If you were a juror, would you now be confident that you know the meaning of that term? Despite the fact that juries work hard to understand their instructions—spending 20% or more of their deliberation time trying to decipher the meaning of the judge's instructions (Ellsworth, 1989)—they sometimes get it wrong simply because they do not understand the legal jargon.

Another source of confusion lies in the way that the instructions are conveyed to jurors. Typically, the jury listens passively as the judge reads the instructions aloud. Jurors may or may not be provided with a written copy of the instructions, and they are almost never given the opportunity to ask questions in the courtroom to clarify misunderstandings they may have about the law. When jurors ask for assistance with the instructions in the course of deliberating, the judge often is unwilling to help, reasoning that rewording or clarifying the instructions could be grounds for appeal. In one of the cases studied by a Special Committee of the American Bar Association (1991), during deliberations the jury asked the judge to define the word *tortious*. His response: "Take away the *-ious*." Not exceedingly helpful, we suspect! (Incidentally, a *tort* is an injury to persons or to property.)

Judges generally assume that the instructions will have their intended effects of guiding jurors through the thicket of unfamiliar legal concepts. That was the sentiment of the U.S. Supreme Court in *Weeks v. Angelone* (2000). Lonnie Weeks confessed to killing a Virginia state trooper in 1993 and was tried for capital murder. During the penalty phase deliberations, jurors sent the judge a note asking for clarification of their instructions. The judge simply repeated the instruction. Two hours later the jurors, some in tears, sentenced Weeks to death. Weeks appealed, citing the jury's apparent confusion about the instructions. But the appeal fell on deaf ears. Chief Justice William Rehnquist, author of the opinion, wrote that there was only a "slight possibility" that jurors had been confused by the trial judge's instructions. Ironically, a study conducted by Cornell law professor Stephen Garvey and his colleagues challenges that assumption. Simulating the Weeks case, Garvey and his colleagues concluded that the jury might not have sentenced Weeks to death had they received clarification of their instructions (Garvey, Johnson, & Marcus, 2000).

Can this situation be rectified? Could the instructions be rewritten, or could their presentation be revised so that jurors have a better chance of understanding and implementing them properly? The answer appears to be yes. Borrowing principles from the field of **psycholinguistics** (the study of how people understand and use language), psychologists have been able to simplify jury instructions by minimizing or eliminating the use of abstract terms, negatively modified sentences, and passive voice and by reorganizing the instructions in a more logical manner. These simplified instructions are easier for jurors to understand and use (English & Sales, 1997; Steele & Thornburg, 1988).

Another method for improving jurors' understanding of the instructions is to restructure how they are presented. Although instructions are typi-

cally read at the close of the trial, after the evidence has been presented and just before the jury retires to deliberate, some judges are willing to provide preliminary instructions before any of the evidence is presented. In a survey on the feasibility of instructing jurors about the law at the beginning of the trial (Smith, 1991), a group of California judges was divided into those who favored such pretrial instructions (42%) and those who opposed them (57%). Judges who favored preinstructions did so because they believed jurors' ability to process trial information and integrate these facts with the law would be improved. Judges who opposed preinstructions doubted any beneficial effects and claimed that they could not know before the trial what instructions would be appropriate because they had not heard the evidence.

Instructing the jury at the conclusion of the trial reflects a belief in the **recall readiness hypothesis** (Jones & Goethals, 1971). This hypothesis predicts a recency effect, suggesting that the judge's instructions will have a more powerful impact on a jury's decision when they are given late in the trial, after the presentation of evidence. The reasoning behind the recall readiness hypothesis reflects an assumption that immediate past events are generally remembered better than more remote ones, especially when the earlier events have unfolded over a longer period of time. Presenting the instructions after the evidence should thus increase the salience of the instructions and make the judge's directives more available for recall during deliberations. Having just heard the judge's instructions, deliberating jurors would have them fresh in their minds and be more likely to make references to them.

Logical as the recall readiness hypothesis might seem, it has been questioned by a number of authorities. Two lines of reasoning guide such criticism. First, Roscoe Pound, former dean of the Harvard Law School, and others have proposed what is essentially a "schema" theory—that jurors should be instructed before the presentation of testimony because this gives them a mental set to appreciate the relevance or irrelevance of testimony as it unfolds and thus to make selective use of the

## The Science of

BOX 15-3 **Field research and the timing of jury instructions**

Some research questions can be studied in a laboratory; other research begs for answers from the real world. A psychologist studying the effects of television or video violence on aggressiveness in children could ask the children's parents to comment on their behavior, or she could actually observe the children on a playground after they had viewed some violent programming. The latter, because it takes place "in the field," is called a **field experiment.** The value of a field experiment is that it provides an opportunity to observe the behavior in question in the setting in which it occurs.

Heuer and Penrod conducted a field experiment in which they examined the effectiveness of preinstructions in 67 trials in Wisconsin circuit courts. In 34 of these trials, judges preinstructed the juries on procedural law and any substantive issues they thought would be helpful. In the other 33 trials, no preinstructions were given. All jurors were also instructed after the evidence was presented. Following the trials, judges, lawyers, and jurors answered questionnaires about the use of pretrial instructions.

Results showed small but positive effects of preinstructions: Ju-

rors reported that preinstructions helped them understand the law and apply it to their evaluation of the evidence. Preinstructed jurors also reported greater satisfaction with the trial experience. Pretrial instructions did not assist jurors with recall of the evidence or of the judge's instructions, however. Yet, taken together, these findings (and the absence of any negative effects of pretrial instructions) suggest that the procedure has merit and should be seriously considered in other trials.

---

facts. This line of reasoning gains support from research findings in experimental psychology showing (1) that people learn more effectively when they know in advance what the specific task is and (2) that schematic frameworks facilitate comprehension and recall (Bartlett, 1932; Neisser, 1976).

Second, a number of judges (e.g., Frank, 1949) have objected to the customary sequence on the ground that instructions at the end of the trial are given after the jurors have already made up their minds. Research has shown that, despite cautionary instructions, jurors often form very definite opinions before the close of the trial (Kalven & Zeisel, 1966). This argument is an example of the **primacy hypothesis,** and Judge E. Barrett Prettyman's (1960) position reflects it:

> It makes no sense to have a juror listen to days of testimony only then to be told that he and his conferees are the sole judges of the facts, that the accused is presumed to be innocent, that

the government must prove guilt beyond a reasonable doubt, etc. What manner of mind can go back over a stream of conflicting statements of alleged facts, recall the intonations, the demeanor, or even the existence of the witnesses, and retrospectively fit all these recollections into a pattern of evaluations and judgments given him for the first time after the events; the human mind cannot do so. (p. 1066)

So there is a clear-cut contrast between the recall readiness hypothesis and the primacy hypothesis concerning predicted effects if the judge's instructions are delayed until the end of the trial. Psychologists believe this leads to an empirical question: At what point in the trial proceedings *should* the judge instruct the jury in order to maximize the jurors' adherence to that instruction? Using field experimentation, Larry Heuer and Steven Penrod (1989) attempted to answer this question (see ◆ Box 15-3).

Using a different methodology, Vicki Smith (1991) addressed the same question about the benefits of pretrial instruction. She conducted a simulated trial in which 125 mock jurors were instructed about the requirements of proof and the substantive law before they heard any evidence, after the evidence, or both before and after the evidence. One important finding was that preinstructed jurors were more likely than postinstructed jurors to defer their verdict decisions until after the trial. Jurors who were instructed both before and after the presentation of evidence were better able to integrate the facts of the case with the relevant law, suggesting that both pre- and postinstruction may be beneficial to jurors (Lieberman & Sales, 1997).

The beneficial effects of preinstruction apparently also extend to civil cases. In one study (ForsterLee, Horowitz, & Bourgeois, 1993), the timing of the instructions affected mock jurors' assignment of damages in a toxic tort case. Jurors who had been preinstructed on the elements of compensation made clearer differentiation among several plaintiffs than did jurors who had not been preinstructed: When jurors had been preinstructed, the most severely injured plaintiff received the highest award and the least severely injured plaintiff received the lowest award. There were no differences in compensatory awards as a function of injury severity for jurors who had received posttrial instructions.

What practical applications can we draw from these findings? A number of states give judges discretion as to when to instruct the jury. Some states go further. In Arizona, judges are required to give jurors both oral and written instructions at the beginning of trial. In Indiana, jurors hear a preliminary instruction on the manner of weighing testimony. The jury is then advised that it will receive further instructions at the close of the trial. In Missouri, the state Supreme Court's Committee on Jury Instructions recommends:

> that the jury be instructed before the trial begins about its duty to determine the facts solely from the evidence, how it shall determine the believability of evidence, and its obligation to give each party fair and impartial consideration without sympathy or prejudice. The committee believes that it is better to draw the jury's attention to these matters before the trial rather than waiting until after the jurors may have reached a decision.

We agree and would argue that judicial use of preinstructions is vastly underutilized. There is no reason why general instructions about the law (e.g., burden of proof, assessment of the credibility of witnesses) should not be given at both the beginning and end of trials; instructions that depend on the specific evidence in a trial could be given at the end (Kassin & Wrightsman, 1979).

Other procedural remedies have been proposed to enhance jurors' comprehension of the instructions including providing a written copy of the instructions and taping the instructions for later playback by the jurors. Traditionally, judges have instructed jurors orally. There is good reason to expect that written or taped instructions would improve comprehension. Trial-related information is processed more efficiently and recalled better when it is presented in writing in addition to being read aloud (Elwork, Sales, & Alfini, 1982). In addition, less confusion about the instructions may arise when they are in writing, which in turn should lead to a reduction in the number of questions about the instructions during deliberation (Dann, 1993).

Studies of the effects of written instructions show that some of these expectations are met but that written jury instructions may not be the panacea that many envision. Although the presence of written instructions increases jurors' satisfaction with the trial process and aids in settling disputes that arise during deliberation (Heuer & Penrod, 1989), there is conflicting evidence as to whether written instructions enhance jurors' understanding of the law. Some studies (e.g., Kramer & Koening, 1990) suggest that they might; others (e.g., Greene & Johns,

2001; Reifman, Gusick, & Ellsworth, 1992) find no improved comprehension.

## Concern about Jurors' Abilities to Decide Complex Cases

Judge John V. Singleton looked up as his law clerk leaned against his office door as if to brace it closed. "You won't believe this," she said breathlessly, "but there are 225 lawyers out there in the courtroom!" (Singleton & Kass, 1986, p. 11). Judge Singleton believed it. He was about to preside over the first pretrial conference in *In re Corrugated Container Antitrust Litigation,* one of the largest and most complicated class action cases ever tried to a jury. (A **class action case** involves many plaintiffs who collectively form a "class" and claim that they suffered similar injuries as a result of the defendants' actions. The plaintiffs portrayed in the popular movie *Erin Brockovich* constituted a class.)

The case actually entailed three trials: a 15-week criminal trial that involved four major paper companies, 27 corporate officers, scores of witnesses, and hundreds of documents; a four-month-long class action trial with 113 witnesses and 5,000 exhibits; and a second class action trial involving plaintiffs who had opted out of the original class action lawsuit. Discovery and trials took five years. In the midst of this organizational nightmare, Judge Singleton wondered whether the framers of the Constitution had ever imagined a case of such magnitude when they drafted the Sixth and Seventh Amendments, guaranteeing the right to trial by jury in criminal and civil cases. He also worried about the "unsuspecting souls out there in the Southern District of Texas whose destiny was to weigh the facts under the complex antitrust law" (Singleton & Kass, 1986, p. 11.)

Some of the loudest and most vehement criticisms of the jury center on its role in complex cases. In product liability and medical malpractice cases, for example, there are difficult questions related to causation (i.e., who or what actually caused the claimed injuries), and in business cases there are intricate financial transactions that must be dissected and evaluated. These cases often require the jury to render decisions on causation, liability, and damages for multiple plaintiffs, multiple defendants, or both (Vidmar, 1998).

Many arguments have been made against the use of juries in complex cases: The evidence is too difficult for a layperson to understand; the general information load on juries is excessive because of the large number of witnesses, particularly expert witnesses who testify in these cases; and, because of the length of these trials, there is a tendency for better-educated jurors to be excused from service, leaving these important cases to be decided by less capable individuals (cited by Vidmar, 1988). Many judges have gone on record expressing concerns about jurors' abilities in these cases: "I remain convinced that the highly complicated issues presented by this litigation are such that an attempt to dispose of them in a jury trial would result in nothing short of judicial chaos" (dissent of Judge Kilkenny in *In re U.S. Securities Litigation,* 1979, p. 431).

The two primary methods for assessing the abilities of jurors to decide complex cases are to conduct mock jury studies and to interview jurors after they have served in these cases. A third technique—to select a group of jurors who function, for all intents and purposes, like the real jury (i.e., they sit in the jury box throughout the entire trial and mingle with the actual jurors during the breaks) until the end of the case when they become "research jurors" whose deliberations are videotaped—was used by a Special Committee of the American Bar Association in the late 1980s but, regrettably, has not been tried since.

Interview studies (e.g., ABA Special Committee, 1990; Sanders, 1993) consistently point to a substantial spread in individual jurors' abilities to understand and summarize the evidence. Some jurors are willing and able to attend to the complicated nature of the testimony and the sometimes-arcane questions of law that they raise; other jurors are overwhelmed from the outset. Whether some capable jurors can atone for others' failings is unclear. Sanders (1993) interviewed jurors in a products liability case against Merrell Dow Pharmaceuticals and concluded that the jury's deliberation appeared to fall short of full understanding of the case. But the Special ABA Committee (1990) that studied four complex cases in different jurisdictions across the country (involving sexual harassment, criminal fraud, antitrust, and the misappropriation of trade secrets) concluded that the stronger, more capable jurors, even when not designated as forepersons, were able to direct the deliberations and defensible verdicts resulted. Richard Lempert, professor of law at the University of Michigan, systematically examined the reports of 12 complex trials including those reported by Sanders and the ABA Committee (Lempert, 1993). He concluded that in 2 of the 12 cases, the expert testimony was so complicated and esoteric that only professionals in the field could have understood it. On the other hand, Lempert found little evidence of jury befuddlement and that, on balance, the juries' verdicts were defensible.

Oregon State University professor Irwin Horowitz and his colleagues have conducted several sophisticated studies of mock juror decision making in complex cases. These studies are inherently difficult to do because the conditions of a complex case (e.g., its length, the large number of expert witnesses, and the complicated nature of the testimony) are not easily simulated. Horowitz and his team dealt with this problem by basing their simulation studies on an actual toxic tort case involving manufacture of a chemical known as "DBX," or dibenzodioxin. (The facts of their case resembled those described in the popular book and movie *A Civil Action*.) Residents adjacent to a chemical plant sued the chemical manufacturer for injuries allegedly caused when the company allowed DBX to leach from the plant into the surrounding drainage ditches and waterways, thus entering the plaintiffs' drinking water, contaminating the fish and wildlife they consumed, and threatening their recreational facilities. The studies typically involved multiple plaintiffs, all of whom complained, in varying degrees, of health problems such as skin rashes, chloracne, and elevated blood pressure; psychological distress; a fear of contracting cancer and future illnesses; as well as economic loss. Attorneys for the defendant chemical manufacturer refuted the allegations. Using these facts and manipulating the structure of the trial and nature of the testimony, Horowitz and his colleagues have been able to examine, among other things, the effects of the number and order of decisions required of jurors, complexity of the language, number of plaintiffs, and the role of preliminary instructions and group deliberations.

The picture that emerges from this vast set of data is of a jury whose abilities and whose verdicts are significantly impacted by nuances in trial procedure. For example, jurors who received preliminary instructions from the judge at the beginning of the trial recalled more legally relevant evidence and less irrelevant information than jurors who were instructed at the end of the trial (ForsterLee et al., 1993), preinstructed jurors made more appropriate distinctions among different plaintiffs who suffered different degrees of injury (ForsterLee et al., 1993), access to a trial transcript reduced jurors' reliance on inappropriate testimony (Bourgeois, Horowitz, & ForsterLee, 1993), and complex language lessened jurors' ability to compensate appropriately plaintiffs who suffered injuries of varying severity (Horowitz, ForsterLee, & Brolly, 1996).

None of these findings suggests that jurors are inherently unable to decide matters of complexity. As psychologist Phoebe Ellsworth has noted, there is little support for the popular idea that bad jury decisions are caused by bad jurors (Ellsworth, 1999). Rather, the findings point to the need for care and consideration in the manner in which a complex case is presented to the jury. A judge has wide discretion to set the tone and pacing of the trial and to implement procedures to assist the jury and, ultimately, to assure equal justice under law. Indeed, there *is* no justice unless the jury understands the facts and the law in each case they decide.

We would not expect a college student to pass a course without taking any notes, asking questions to seek clarification or discussing an interesting concept with a fellow student. Yet, too often, we handicap jurors by forcing trial procedures on them that discourage or even forbid these simple steps toward better understanding. We suspect that jurors would have an easier time of it, and that their verdicts would be more reasoned, if judges were willing to structure jurors' tasks so that they were more conducive to their learning (e.g., preinstruction and simplifying the language of the instructions). Fortunately, some courts have begun that process, and we will discuss these jury reforms later in the chapter.

# The Concern That Juries Are Biased

## The Assumption of a Blank Slate

Jurors are assumed to enter a trial as "blank slates," free of overwhelming biases. Courts assume that jurors can put aside any preconceptions about the guilt of a criminal defendant or the merits of civil defendants and plaintiffs when forming their judgments. If jurors cannot set aside their biases, they should be excused for cause. (In criminal cases, the "blank slates" should be tinted by a presumption that the defendant is innocent of the charges at the outset.)

Olivia Brodsky, summoned for jury duty in Connecticut, might have had difficulty setting aside her preconceptions. When asked what she would do as a juror, Brodsky responded, "I would wait until the bad guy talks. Then I would put him in jail." Brodsky was 4 years old at the time. In Connecticut, potential jurors can be culled from state income tax records that lack birth dates; the tax return on Olivia's trust fund was the likely reason she was summoned to appear.

As we noted in Chapter 14, the judge and the attorneys inquire about a prospective juror's biases during the jury selection process. A frequent question during voir dire takes the following form; "Sir, do you believe that you, as a juror, can set aside any negative feelings you might have toward

the defendant because he is black or a police officer or a used-car salesman [whatever the group membership that possibly elicits prejudice] and make a judgment based on the law and the facts of this case?" If the prospective juror says yes, the judge usually believes him, and he is allowed to serve as a juror.

Less frequently, prospective jurors may have positive feelings about the defendant that could influence their ability to be impartial. Consider the lawsuit filed against Michael Jordan (see ◆ Box 15-4).

Prospective jurors who admit to discernible and resolute prejudices or vested interests in the outcome of the case can be identified and dismissed. But what can be done about prospective jurors who, during the jury selection process, consciously or unconsciously misrepresent their views?

In John Grisham's novel *The Runaway Jury* (1996), a central character develops a scheme by which he is impaneled on a jury in a huge lawsuit against a tobacco company; he then gets the tobacco industry to pay him for influencing the jury to decide in its favor. Jurors who proclaim neutrality while they possess and conceal a bias are called *stealth jurors* (Bodaken & Speckart, 1996); they may possess a number of reasons to misrepresent themselves, not just for the possibility of financial gain, as in people who seek to be chosen for jury service on highly publicized trials, but also for revenge against one of the parties.

The courts assume that individual jurors can divest themselves of any improper "leaning" toward one side or the other and that through detailed, sometimes time-consuming, jury selection procedures the ideal of open-minded jurors can be achieved. Because prospective jurors whose preconceptions would affect their verdicts are identified and dismissed, the trial can begin with the expectation that the jury will reach a fair verdict. But this aspiration faces at least four types of challenges. First, attorneys are motivated to select jurors who are favorable to their own side, rather than those who are neutral and unpredictable. Second, as we discuss in detail later, it is impossible for anyone to be completely uninfluenced by

## THE CASE OF

**BOX 15-4**    Michael Jordan and the search for unbiased jurors

When 36 prospective jurors filed into a drab, windowless courtroom in Chicago, a big surprise awaited them: Seated at the defense table was basketball star, Michael Jordan, undoubtedly the biggest sports hero in Chicago history. Jordan was being sued for allegedly reneging on a deal to star in the basketball film *Heaven Is a Playground.* The movie flopped without him. Dean Dickie, attorney for the plaintiff production company, anticipated difficulties in finding jurors who were not partial toward Jordan. Indeed, after five long hours of jury selection, only three jurors had been selected. Nearly all of the other prospective jurors stated that their admiration and adoration of Jordan would interfere with their neutrality in the case. In the end, the jury returned a judgment in Jordan's favor. In fact, jurors determined that the corporation that made the film owed Jordan $50,000 for failing to live up to its financial obligation to him.

*Basketball star Michael Jordan*

past experiences and resulting prejudices. Third, as seen in the foregoing examples, if people systematically misrepresent their views during jury selection, no sure way exists to detect it. And finally, as illustrated in Chapter 14, trial lawyers often deliberately attempt to bias the panel through the use of suggestive questions during voir dire.

### Inevitability of Juror Bias

Bias is an inevitable human characteristic. But even though the word *bias,* in this case **juror bias,** conjures up many unfavorable associations, we should not focus exclusively on its negative qualities. Rather, bias is simply part of the human condition, and, as such, it colors all our decisions, including jury verdicts.

Bias, as used here, refers to a human predisposition to make interpretations based on past experience—to try to fit new stimuli and information into one's already-developed system for looking at the world. When we are exposed to a new event, we respond to it by relying on past experiences.

For example, when we view a traffic accident, it is hard to separate our perceptions from our interpretations. We may make judgments that one car was going too fast or that another car was in the wrong lane. We may assume a particular driver was at fault simply because we happen to have a negative stereotype about, for example, teenage drivers or drivers from a particular state.

Bias in our responses to the actions of others is inevitable because people account for so many outcomes in our lives, and we must make assumptions about the causes of their behavior. Why was Emily so abrupt when she spoke to me this morning? Why did Juan decide to buy a new car? Why did the defendant refuse to take a lie detector test? Every day, we make decisions based on our assumptions about other people. Criminal defense lawyers make recommendations to their clients on how to plead based on their expectations about the reactions of prosecuting attorneys, judges, and jurors. College administrators decide who will be admitted as students on the basis of applicants' credentials and academic promise. Choices are always necessary, and our expectations about the outcomes of our choices rest partly on our biases.

Why do we have expectations? We probably could not tolerate life if people were constantly surprising us. We need assumptions about people to help in predicting what they will do. Our expectations often help simplify our explanations for people's behavior.

Such processes apply to the behavior of jurors too. When Dallas Cowboys wide receiver Michael Irvin appeared before the grand jury with regard to a charge of cocaine possession, he was wearing a mink coat, a lavender suit, and a bowler hat. Did the jurors form any impressions of him based on his attire? Virtually all the legal and psychological conceptions of how a juror makes decisions in a criminal case propose that verdicts reflect the implicit operation of two judgments on the part of jurors.

One judgment is an estimate of the probability of commission—that is, how likely it is that the defendant actually committed the crime. Most jurors base their estimates of this probability mainly on the strength of the specific evidence, but their previous beliefs and experiences also have an impact on how they interpret the evidence (Finkel, 1995). Although jurors must arrive at subjective estimates of this probability, they are reluctant to use more objective probabilities about the occurrence of the events in question to guide them to a conclusion (Cohen, 1986). Psychologists have begun to study the reasons why people in general are hesitant to use "naked statistical evidence" to answer questions of liability or causation (Wells, 1992).

A second judgment by the criminal juror concerns reasonable doubt. Judges instruct jurors in criminal cases that they should bring back a verdict of not guilty if they have any reasonable doubt of the defendant's guilt. Yet the legal system has difficulty defining and operationalizing reasonable doubt; a common, but not very informative, definition is that it is a doubt for which a person can give a reason. Jurors apply their own standards for the threshold of certainty deemed necessary for conviction.

On the basis of these factors, many jurors can be classified as having a proprosecution bias or a prodefense bias. (These generally resemble, respectively, the crime control model and due process model described in Chapter 1.) Jurors with a proprosecution bias view the conflicting evidence through the filter of their own past experiences and beliefs, which make them more likely to think that the defendant committed the crime. Consider, for example, the statement "Any suspect who runs from the police probably committed the crime." Agreement with this statement reflects a bias in favor of the prosecution. But persons with prodefense biases also filter the evidence as a result of their past experiences and reactions. For example, agreement with the statement "Too many innocent people are wrongfully imprisoned" reflects filters leading to biases sympathetic to the defense.

Even if we accept the proposition that bias is inevitable, we must still ask whether such biases color the judgments of jurors. That is the bottom line. To determine whether bias affects one's verdicts, Kassin and Wrightsman (1983) measured potential jurors' biases by having them complete a 17-statement attitude inventory containing statements such as those just given as examples. Later, these mock jurors watched videotapes of reenacted actual trials or read transcripts of simulated trials. Five types of criminal trials were used. After being exposed to the trial, each mock juror was asked to render an individual verdict about the defendant's guilt or innocence. Jurors voting guilty were then compared with those voting not guilty to see whether their preliminary biases differed. In four of the five cases, they did. Even though everyone was exposed to the same evidence and judge's instructions, mock jurors holding a proprosecution bias were more likely to find the defendant guilty. The average rate of conviction was 81% for the prosecution-biased jurors compared with only 52% for defense-biased ones. It appears that, at least in a majority of cases, each juror's reaction to the evidence is filtered through personal predispositions. Pretrial beliefs and values may influence and, on occasion, even overwhelm the evidence presented in court.

Pretrial beliefs may also affect the very way that the evidence is evaluated. Jane Goodman-Delahunty and her colleagues found that mock jurors' beliefs about the death penalty influenced more than the penalty they imposed in a capital murder case; they also influenced jurors' perceptions of the evidence (Goodman-Delahunty, Greene, & Hsiao, 1998). Mock jurors in this study watched the videotaped murder of a convenience store clerk that had been filmed by a camera mounted on a wall of the store. When asked questions about the defendant's motive and intentions, jurors who favored the death penalty were more likely than those who opposed capital punishment to "read" criminal intent into the actions of the defendant. For example, pro–death penalty jurors were more likely than those opposed to infer from the videotape that the defendant intended to murder the victim, that his specific actions indicated premeditation, and that he would be a future threat to society. These findings remind us of the common situation in which two people experience the same event—a movie or a play, for example—and interpret the actions in very different ways, partly because of the "mind-set" with which they watched or experienced that event. These beliefs, or schemas, can apparently influence the way that jurors make sense of the evidence in a trial.

Do jurors' biases predispose them to favor one side over another in a civil case? A common perception is that jurors are generally biased in favor of injured plaintiffs. Are they? Was the Miami jury's decision to award $37 million to the family of 12-year-old honor student Jill Goldberg, killed in a 1997 car accident, fueled by feelings of sympathy for her grieving family members? It seems natural for people to have feelings of compassion for injured persons and for these feelings to translate into favorable verdicts and lavish damage awards for plaintiffs. But do they?

Surprisingly, perhaps, a variety of studies using different methodologies suggest that the answer is no. From posttrial juror interviews, we have learned that although elements of sympathy play *some* role in deliberations (and that feelings of anger toward a defendant matter, too), this happens relatively infrequently. In her study of cases involving claims by individuals against corporate defendants, Valerie Hans (1996) interviewed jurors who decided these cases, conducted surveys of jurors' attitudes, and launched experimental studies that manipulated variables related to this **sympathy hypothesis.** All these sources of data pointed to the same conclusion—namely, that the general public is "quite suspicious of, and sometimes downright hostile to, civil plaintiffs" (p. 244). A survey conducted by the consulting firm DecisionQuest found similar results: Eighty-four percent of the 1012 people polled agreed with the statement "When people are injured, they often try to blame others for their carelessness."

According to the same survey, potential jurors do not think highly of civil defendants, either. For example, more than 75% of respondents believe that corporate executives often try to cover up evidence of wrongdoing by their companies, and more respondents say that product warnings are intended to protect manufacturers than say they are intended to keep consumers safe.

These opinions beg the next question: Do juries give larger awards when a defendant is wealthy? Some data would seem to support this so-called deep pockets effect: Jury damage awards *are* consistently higher in products liability and medical malpractice cases than in automobile negligence cases. (The former group typically involves wealthy defendants and the latter does not.) But a number of studies (Hans & Ermann, 1989; Mac-Coun, 1996) suggest that the wealth of the defendant alone is not the important variable. Rather, the public believes that businesses and corporations should be held to a higher standard of responsibility than individual defendants. Any inflation of awards against corporate defendants apparently relates to their status as a corporation and not to their wealth.

The jury that awarded $37 million to the family of Jill Goldberg clearly focused on the duties and responsibilities of the defendant, Florida Power and Light (FPL) Company. The victim was killed when a car driven by her mother, Rosalie, sailed through an intersection and was struck by a Ford Expedition on a rainy September afternoon. The role of the defendant? Ten minutes before the accident occurred, an FPL lineman pulled a fuse from a transformer box about 100 feet away from the intersection, cutting power to the traffic light. At trial, FPL lawyers told the jury that the utility couldn't be obligated to ensure that every traffic light in the county worked when it terminated power. The lineman testified that he never looked to see whether the traffic light had been affected. Neither of these contentions sat well with jurors. Said jury foreman, Juan Perez, "To them, power outages were a fact of life and they throw switches all the time. But to say that in front of a jury is almost suicidal to the defense." After a week-long trial, the jury deliberated for three hours and determined that FPL was entirely at fault. But for the power outage, they reasoned, the accident would never have happened. They awarded $17 million to Walter Goldberg, Jill's father, and $20 million to Rosalie Goldberg, Jill's mother—far more than the plaintiffs had requested.

*Judge B. Michael Dann, advocate of jury reform in Arizona*

## Jury Reform

Psychologists and other social scientists began suggesting reforms to the jury system in the 1970s. Until very recently, though, not many people listened. For example, in 1991, Alexander Tanford, a professor of law at Indiana University, reviewed the impact of research on pretrial instructions and written instructions on state court judges, legislatures, and rule-making commissions and concluded that the research had very little impact: Lawmakers were not being persuaded about the need for reform on the basis of empirical research studies alone. (This raises some interesting and difficult questions about whether psychologists, armed with sophisticated theories and well-honed research techniques, can effectively influence the landscape of the law. This concern is reminiscent of the "science versus the law" dilemma that we discussed in Chapter 1).

Many observers of the jury (e.g., Ellsworth, 1999; Marder, 1999) now suspect that intense media coverage of a series of dramatic trials and controversial verdicts has accomplished for jury reform what decades of social science research could not do. As the names Lorena Bobbitt, Rodney

King, Lyle and Erik Menendez, and O. J. Simpson became household terms, as sensational trials were being broadcast in living rooms across the country, and as the media splashed news of a $2.7 million award to an 81-year-old New Mexico grandmother who was burned by hot coffee at McDonald's (the award was reduced by the judge to $480,000 and the grandmother eventually settled for even less—something that the media generally failed to report), the public grew increasingly dissatisfied and occasionally even outraged about the failure of the jury system. Calls for reform became more frequent and more urgent. (One notable exception to the public's general disapproval of juries comes from the trials of Timothy McVeigh and Terry Nichols, convicted of bombing the Murrah Federal Building in Oklahoma City in 1995. Perhaps because the defendants were both convicted and McVeigh was sentenced to death—appropriate results, according to many people [www.ljx.com/1998/decisionquest_survey/]—or perhaps because

## The Science of

### BOX 15-5    Jurors' inferences: The story model

In many ways, the juror's task is like that of the reader of a mystery story. The juror is bombarded with many pieces of evidence, often incomplete and conflicting, just as the mystery reader is tantalized by hints, clues, and coincidences. The joy of reading a mystery comes from savoring each clue, bouncing it off prior clues, and then evaluating its significance in the overall puzzle of who committed the crime. That is how most jurors operate. They form a schema, a mental structure that aids in the processing and interpretation of information. As indicated earlier, such schemata—precisely because they provide a cognitive framework—can produce a skewed perception and recall of reality. Just like mystery readers who remember those clues that fit their hypothesis and forget others that do not, jurors construct their own private stories about the evidence so that it makes sense to them; in the process, they pay inordinate attention to certain pieces of evidence while ignoring others.

Good lawyers know this. In fact, really great lawyers know that an important task for them at trial is to convince the jury that their story, and not their opponent's story, is the right one. Famed criminal defense attorney "Racehouse" Haynes once said, "The lawyer with the best story wins"; Gerry Spence, another well-known defense attorney, stated, "When I make an opening statement, I always do it as a story."

Psychologists Reid Hastie and Nancy Pennington developed the story model to describe inferences that individual jurors make when reaching a decision in a case (see, generally, Pennington & Hastie, 1993). Hastie and Pennington dubbed their theory the "story model" because they suspect that the core cognitive process involved in juror decision making is construction of a story or narrative summary of the events in dispute.

To illustrate the role of narrative evidence summaries in juror decision making, Hastie and Pennington interpret the dramatic differences between white Americans' and African Americans' reactions to the verdict in the O. J. Simpson case. They suspect that because of their life experiences and beliefs, African Americans can more easily construct a story about police misconduct and police brutality than can white Americans. Thus, African Americans were more likely than whites to accept the "defense story" that racist police detective, Mark Fuhrman, planted incriminating evidence on Simpson's property (Hastie & Pennington, 1996).

In one of their early empirical studies, Pennington and Hastie (1986) interviewed mock jurors who had seen a filmed reenactment of a murder trial and who were asked to talk out loud while making a verdict decision. The evidence summaries constructed

the trials were not televised, public reaction to these verdicts was decidedly mute.)

Determined that the time was right for serious discussion of reform to the jury system, the University of Michigan sponsored a symposium that brought together judges, lawyers, legal academics, social scientists, and even a thoughtful and experienced juror to share their concerns and to suggest solutions. Despite the diversity in intellectual backgrounds and practical experience, there was remarkable convergence of opinion among participants about how to improve the jury system. For example, none of them sub-scribed to the "bad juror" theory—that bad jury decisions are caused by bad jurors. Rather, all shared the view, long advocated by psychologists, that the system is primarily to blame. According to the "bad system" theory, deficiencies in the performance of jurors reflect deficiencies in the jury system, and any jury reform should be directed at how the task is presented to jurors, rather than at how people are selected to serve. As Phoebe Ellsworth (1999), one of the participants at the Michigan forum, aptly noted, "Before deciding that jurors are governed by their hearts, we should consider the possibility that

by jurors had a definite narrative story structure, and, importantly, jurors who reached different verdicts had constructed different stories.

Pennington and Hastie (1988) wondered whether these stories were constructed spontaneously in the course of jurors' decision making and how jurors represent the evidence in memory. To answer these questions, Pennington and Hastie asked mock jurors to read a written description of the murder case that included sentences from different verdict stories gleaned from the previous interview study (e.g., sentences from stories that resulted in guilty verdicts as well as sentences from stories that led to not-guilty verdicts). All participants then determined a verdict and were asked to say whether various sentences had been included in the trial evidence or had not been presented before. Mock jurors were more likely to "recognize" as having been presented those sentences that were associated with their chosen verdict than sentences from stories associated with other, rejected verdicts.

Does the order of evidence presentation influence jurors' judgments? Apparently, yes. In that same study, Pennington and Hastie (1988) found that stories were easy to construct when the evidence was presented in a temporal order that matched the occurrence of the original events ("story order") but harder to construct when the evidence was presented in an order that did not match the sequence of the original events ("witness order"). Prosecutors and defense attorneys might be wise to familiarize themselves with these findings; the study has significant implications for the practice of actual trials. When Pennington and Hastie manipulated the order of evidence, they affected the likelihood of a guilty verdict. For example, mock jurors were *most* likely to convict a criminal defendant when the prosecution evidence was presented in story order and the defense evidence was presented in witness order. They were *least* likely to convict when the prosecution evidence was in witness order and the defense evidence was in story order.

Is the story model a complete and accurate description of how jurors organize themselves to decide the verdict in a trial? Decidedly not. For starters, it focuses only on *jurors* and does not address the complex nuances that come into focus when individual jurors deliberate as a jury. But as a mechanism for understanding the cognitive strategies used by individual jurors to process trial information prior to deliberations, it is highly useful. Indeed, several other studies (e.g., Fulero & Penrod, 1990; Hastie, Schkade, & Payne, 1998; Olsen-Fulero & Fulero, 1997) have been inspired by its elegant theorizing.

the system does very little to encourage the intelligent use of their minds."

Arizona Judge Michael Dann reports that at the conclusion of a two-month murder trial, a juror told him that she had felt "gagged and bound and treated more like a hostage than a responsible adult decision maker." Not coincidentally, Judge Dann has become one of the leading proponents of jury reform, criticizing the traditional legal model that treats jurors as passive recipients of information who, like tape recorders, record a one-way stream of communication. Dann (1993) contrasts this model with his perception that jurors actively evaluate the evidence through their personal experiences and frames of reference, pose questions to themselves, and construct narratives or stories to help them understand the evidence and make a judgment about it. His notions fit well with research showing that jurors are active interpreters of trial information rather than passive recipients of the evidence (Diamond & Casper, 1992). They are also consistent with an influential model of juror decision making devised by University of Colorado psychologists Reid Hastie and Nancy Pennington. Their "**story model**" is described in ◆ Box 15-5.

## The Science of

### BOX 15-6  Jury reform

In 1995, the Arizona Supreme Court implemented a radical innovation in the jury system. For the first time, jurors in civil trials were permitted to discuss the evidence during the trial, rather than to wait until their formal deliberations began. The rules were simple: All jurors must be present in the deliberation room during these discussions, and jurors must keep an open mind and avoid debating verdict options.

Psychologists have described a number of potential advantages of such midtrial discussions based on fundamental principles of cognitive and social psychology. For example, juror discussions about the evidence can

◆ improve juror comprehension by permitting jurors to sift through and organize the evidence into a coherent framework over the course of the trial;
◆ improve juror recollection of the evidence and testimony by

emphasizing and clarifying points made during trial; and
◆ promote greater cohesion among jurors, thereby reducing the time needed for deliberations (Hans, Hannaford, & Munsterman, 1999).

There are also several potential drawbacks to the use of jury discussions during trial, also based on well-established psychological principles, including the possibility that jury discussions may

◆ facilitate the formation or expression of premature judgments about the evidence,
◆ detract from the ideal of the juror as a neutral decision maker,
◆ diminish the quality of the deliberations as jurors become more familiar with each other's views, and
◆ produce more interpersonal conflicts prior to formal deliberations (Hans et al., 1999).

Because of the many potential benefits and drawbacks of this technique and because Arizona was the first jurisdiction to expressly permit jury discussions during trial, it is important to evaluate the effects of this reform. Staff at the National Center for State Courts, including psychologist Valerie Hans, were entrusted with this work. They conducted a field experiment in which they randomly assigned approximately 100 civil jury trials to an experimental "trial discussion" condition and an equal number to a control "no discussion" condition (Hannaford, Hans, & Munsterman, 2000; Hans et al., 1999). For both conditions, questionnaires were distributed to jurors, judges, attorneys, and litigants.

What did the researchers learn about the effects of this reform? Surprisingly perhaps (given their general tendency to adhere to traditional courtroom procedures), judges were the most enthusiastic group. Three-quarters of the

Although jurors apparently construct stories to help them interpret the evidence, the courts expect something different. They envision a juror who does not form hunches or fill in the blanks but instead passively processes all incoming information without immediate interpretation until finally instructed by the judge to decide. Are human beings capable of such detached information processing? Can they separate the acquisition of information from its

evaluation? Should the court's ideals and procedures be revised to bring them in line with jurors' actual abilities?

Many scholars of the jury say yes; the time has come to enact reforms that take advantage of jurors' natural inclinations and to provide tools to encourage jurors' active involvement in the trial. Some of the reforms are relatively uncontroversial and benign: Provide notebooks that list the witnesses and summarize their testimony in long or

judges indicated that they supported the reform, and only 15% opposed it (others were neutral). Another large percentage (75%) agreed that juror discussions helped jurors understand the evidence; only 30% expressed concern that jurors who engaged in these discussions were likely to prejudge the evidence.

Attorneys and litigants were more negative, however. Only approximately half of each group thought that trial discussions improved juror understanding of the evidence, and approximately half agreed that trial discussions might also encourage premature decision making.

How did the innovation affect jurors' experiences and views? Of the 686 jurors who were permitted to discuss the evidence, approximately 70% reported that their jury had at least one such discussion, suggesting that even when permitted to talk about the case, a sizeable minority of juries opt not to. Experience with the reform apparently increases support for it. Jurors who reported having these discussions were quite positive about them: They said that trial evidence was remembered very accurately during these discussions, that discussions helped them understand the evidence in the case, and that all jurors' points of view were considered during the course of the discussions. The perceived drawbacks were mostly logistical: Jurors said that there were difficulties in attempting to get all jurors together at the same time. (After all, these short breaks represent the only time in the course of several hours that jurors may use the rest rooms or smoke a cigarette. For some people, their desire for these comforts undoubtedly outweighed their interest in talking about the evidence!)

Some of the jurors expressed concern that extensive discussions might encourage premature decision making or improper influence. For example, one juror noted:

I think I had this strong feeling that if I talked about it a lot before all the facts were in I might get some biases; once you've said something you kind of feel that you've made a proclamation that you have to stand behind. If you haven't said anything it's easier to change your mind. I think most of us there seemed to have that same feeling. We'll talk about it when we get all the facts.

Are this juror's concerns warranted? We will soon have an answer to that question as a team of researchers has recently been permitted to videotape civil jury trials in Arizona, including all of the midtrial discussions and the deliberations. These data will provide a fascinating and previously unseen picture of the jury at work as it discusses the evidence in the midst of the trial and reaches a final verdict at its conclusion.

complex cases; have judges give preinstructions or interim instructions during the course of a lengthy trial; allow jurors to take notes; designate alternate jurors only after the trial is completed; provide a written copy of the judge's instructions to each juror; allow jurors to examine the demonstrative evidence during their deliberations. Other reforms are more radical: Allow jurors to pose questions to witnesses (questions would still be screened by the judge who decides whether they are appropri-

ate); simplify the language of the jury instructions; require judges to clarify instructions or to answer jurors' questions during the deliberations. Perhaps the most controversial reform is one that would allow jurors to discuss the evidence in the midst of trial. (Traditionally, jurors are forbidden from talking about the case until they begin deliberations.) Some preliminary studies of the effects of this reform are now complete, and we describe them in ◆ Box 15-6. Although many of these reforms remain controversial, judges are slowly awakening to the realization that changes in trial procedures must be enacted so that jurors can be empowered to make the best decisions possible.

# The Jury: Should It Be Venerated or Vilified? Revered or Reviled?

The American trial jury is a remarkable institution and, in important ways, almost a unique one. Four-fifths of all the criminal-case jury trials in the world are held in the United States. Kalven and Zeisel (1966) make the following comments about the jury system:

> It recruits a group of twelve lay people, chosen at random from the widest population; it convenes them for the purpose of a particular trial; it entrusts them with great official powers of decision; it permits them to carry out deliberations in secret and report out their final judgment without giving reasons for it; and, after their momentary service to the state has been completed, it orders them to disband and return to private life. (p. 3)

The use of average citizens to determine outcomes for rich or politically powerful figures such as John duPont, O. J. Simpson, or even President Clinton manifests our country's commitment to egalitarian values. It is no exaggeration to claim that the trial jury is sanctified as one of our fundamental democratic institutions. Political scientist Jeffrey Abramson (1994), author of *We, the Jury,* put it eloquently:

> [T]here are all the jurors we never read about, who toil out of the limelight every day, crossing all kinds of racial and ethnic lines to defend a shared sense of justice. These examples convince me that the jury, far from being obsolete, is more crucial than ever in a multiethnic society struggling to articulate a justice common to [all] citizens. Though the jury system is a grand phenomenon—putting justice in the hands of the people—we still have lessons to learn about how to design an institution that gathers persons from different walks of life to discuss and decide upon one justice for all. (p. 5)

Although we do have many lessons left to learn, we now know a good deal about how juries function. We know that juries don't always get it right; on occasion, jurors are overwhelmed by the sheer volume of evidence, they misunderstand their instructions, they use evidence in inappropriate ways, and their biases and prejudices rise to the surface and color their judgments. But by and large, we find little support for the extreme claims charging juries with poor and irresponsible performance. On the contrary, we believe that the institution of the jury is worth defending and worth improving.

# SUMMARY

**1.** *Describe the concern related to the competence of jurors and juries.* Some critics have expressed concern that jurors and juries are overly attentive to extralegal information that, in theory, is irrelevant to the guilt decision in criminal cases and to the liability judgment in civil cases. Others have voiced concerns that jurors will be mesmerized by the testimony of an expert or, conversely, that they will not understand such testimony and dismiss it out-right. Whether jurors and juries are able to understand and apply their instructions is another concern. Finally, critics of the jury system claim that jurors are poorly equipped to decide the complicated issues that arise in so-called complex cases.

**2.** *What is the impact of opening statements on jurors?* Opening statements in a trial are not part of the evidence but provide an overview of the facts in the case. Jurors' verdicts can be greatly influenced by opening statements, especially those that come first. Longer opening statements are more influential on jurors than are brief ones.

**3.** *What is the impact of extralegal information on jurors?* Research studies suggest that on occasion, jurors may be influenced by evidence of a defendant's prior record, multiple charges, or character and propensity to commit crimes. In civil cases, evidence related to an accident victim's injury may influence the judgment of a defendant's liability, and evidence related to the plaintiff's negligence may inappropriately deflate damage awards.

**4.** *Can jurors disregard inadmissible evidence?* When a question or an answer during a trial is ruled inadmissible by the judge, jurors are instructed to disregard it. Psychological evidence indicates that it is difficult for jurors to disregard this testimony; in fact, the stronger the judge's admonition, the less effective it may be.

**5.** *How can jurors be helped to understand their instructions?* Jurors can be instructed before the trial begins about the relevant elements of the law that they will apply to the facts they hear. Judges can provide written copies of the instructions for all jurors. Unfortunately, judges rarely answer jurors' questions about their instructions.

**6.** *What is meant by the statement that "bias is inevitable in jurors"?* Bias, as used here, refers to the human predisposition to make interpretations based on past experience. Bias is inevitable because of the human requirement to make assumptions about behavior.

**7.** *What reforms of the jury system do psychologists suggest?* The information-processing demands placed on jurors should be simplified. More clearly worded instructions, in written as well as oral form, delivered at the beginning and at the conclusion of the trial would be helpful. In complex trials in which multiple verdicts must be decided, preinstruction, access to a trial transcript, and simplifying complex language may be especially helpful. During the trial, jurors can pose questions that the judge would ask of the witnesses. Finally, there may be benefits to midtrial discussion of the evidence; such discussion may help jurors to organize the evidence in a thematic framework and to improve their memory of the testimony.

## KEY TERMS

belief perseverance
class action case*
comparative negligence
damages*
defensive attribution
extralegal information

field experiment
inadmissible
  evidence
joinder
juror bias
liable*

limiting instruction
outcome severity
primacy hypothesis
propensity evidence
psycholinguistics*
reactance theory

recall readiness
  hypothesis
schema
story model
sympathy hypothesis
thought suppression

InfoTrac
COLLEGE
EDITION
For additional readings go to **http://www.infotrac-college.com/wadsworth** and enter a search term related to your interest. The key terms that have been asterisked above will pull up several related articles. *See also:* for comparative negligence, see NEGLIGENCE, COMPARATIVE.

## ORIENTING QUESTIONS

1. *What is the frequency of victimization?*
2. *What are two types of sexual harassment recognized by the courts?*
3. *What are the components of the battered woman syndrome?*
4. *What types of research have psychologists conducted on crime victimization?*
5. *What factors predict the development of PTSD after being a crime victim?*
6. *How have the laws about rape changed?*
7. *How may rape be prevented?*

# Perception of Victims

What is common to almost every crime is the presence of at least one victim. Even so-called victimless crimes—referring to crimes such as prostitution, ticket scalping, and gambling—have victims, even if they do not immediately recognize it or would not describe themselves that way. The social burdens and psychological costs of these offenses are often delayed—the squandering of a person's income due to the inevitable losses from repeated gambling or the physical abuse and underworld crimes that surround prostitution—but ultimately society and individuals feel victimized by these crimes nonetheless.

Society has conflicting feelings toward victims. At the same time that most individuals feel sympathy toward them, we also tend to question why they became victims and sometimes even blame them for their plight. Chapter 3 described one reason for this inclination to blame; the need to believe in a "just world" suggests that the thought of becoming victims ourselves is so threatening that we feel compelled to justify why other people are victimized (Lerner, 1980). These justifications often take the form of singling victims out as the primary cause for their plight.

Such judgments are predicted by the perspective known as **attribution theory,** which originated with the work of Fritz Heider (1958). Heider stated that persons operate as "naive psychologists"; they reach conclusions about what caused a given behavior by considering both personal and environmental factors. Generally, when considering someone else's actions, we use *dispositional attributions* that rely on the person's ability level, personality, or even temporary states such as fatigue or luck as explanations for the conduct in question. To explain a person's misfortune on the basis of his or her physical disabilities, lack of effort, or loose morals reflects a kind of defensive attribution that puts the onus for bad outcomes on the person rather than the environment. Such reactions help shape our responses to victims. The norms of our society demand that we help others if they deserve our help. But if people are responsible for their own suffering, we do not feel so obligated to help them (Mulford, Lee, & Sapp, 1996).

Since 1970, the term *blaming the victim* has increased in popularity. The term was first popularized in a widely read book by William Ryan (1970), in which the author observed that people on welfare were often seen as lazy or shiftless and hence responsible for their fate. A literature search (cited by Downs, 1996) found no use of the term *blaming the victim* before 1970, but there was a steep increase from the early 1980s up through 1993, with more than 1000 references that year.

An extreme example of blaming the victim was given by trial attorney Robert Baker, who represented O. J. Simpson in his civil trial for the wrongful deaths of Nicole Brown and Ronald Goldman. His opening statement for the defense included a scorching attack on Nicole Brown, whom he portrayed as a heavy-drinking party girl whose dangerous lifestyle often included companions who were prostitutes and drug dealers. Sometimes by implication and sometimes by direct comment, he communicated that she had many boyfriends and at least one abortion. As a trial observer noted, "it was as close to calling her a slut without using the word" (quoted by Reibstein & Foote, 1996, p. 64). Baker demeaned the victim for a reason, of course; he wanted to leave the implication that her sordid lifestyle had led her to become involved with someone other than O. J. Simpson as her killer (Toobin, 1996a). For his part, Simpson has echoed this claim, stating that he feels angry at Nicole because he believes her careless lifestyle contributed to her being murdered.

# Offenders as Victims

When offenders are at the same time victims, or claim to be victims, society's reaction becomes even more complex, and decisions made by the legal system become even more controversial. Consider the trials of Bernhard Goetz, Lorena Bobbitt, and the Menendez brothers, Lyle and Erik. What do these trials have in common? In each case, the defendant or defendants, charged with serious crimes, claimed the role of victim and argued that they were retaliating against an unwanted act or trying to prevent a feared attack. Bernhard Goetz, when confronted by four youths asking for five dollars, was convinced that they were going to beat him up, so he pulled out a gun and shot each of them. Lorena Bobbitt was outraged over an act earlier that evening that she considered to be spousal rape by her husband, John, so while he was sleeping, she cut off his penis. At their trials, the Menendez brothers described episodes of physical and sexual abuse from their father, with their mother as a passive accomplice; fearing the worst, they decided to kill their parents first.

How did the juries react to these defenses? Bernhard Goetz's jury found him not guilty of attempted murder and assault; he was convicted only for the illegal possession of a firearm. Lorena Bobbitt was essentially found not guilty by reason of insanity. Jurors' reactions in the Menendez brothers' trials were more complicated. In the first trials, the jurors could not agree and hence were hung. Contrary to comments by some critics of these verdicts, the jurors agreed that each brother was guilty of a crime, but they split on whether he should be convicted of murder or manslaughter (Thornton, 1995). With each jury deadlocked over the appropriate charge for conviction, the result was a mistrial. At the second trial, both brothers were found guilty of murder and sentenced to life in prison.

In cases like those of Bobbitt and the Menendezes, in which a defendant claims to be a victim, critics are concerned that jurors will be tempted to accept what has been called the **abuse excuse**—"the legal tactic by which criminal defendants claim a history of abuse as an excuse for violent retaliation" (Dershowitz, 1994, p. 3). Although Dershowitz concludes that more

and more defense lawyers are using the abuse excuse and that juries increasingly are accepting it, evidence in support of the latter claim is sparse at best. In fact, such defenses seem to be met with increasing skepticism and a willingness to blame the offender, exactly as the "just world" theory predicts they would be.

# Types of Victims

There is no shortage of victims in our society. Estimates of the numbers of children who are sexually abused, the adults who are battered by their partners, and women and men who are assaulted, robbed, or raped run into the millions each year.

The primary source of information on crime victims in the United States is the Bureau of Justice Statistics' National Crime Victimization Survey, which can be found at *www.ojp.usdoj.gov/bjs/*. Each year, data are collected from a national sample of 50,000 households on the frequency and consequences of criminal victimization from rape and other sexual assaults, robbery, theft, assault, household burglary, and car theft. From these figures, the rate of victimization nationwide can be calculated. For example, in 1998, approximately 31 million criminal victimizations were estimated to occur; more than 22 million involved property crimes (a rate of 217 incidents per 1000 persons), and over 8 million were crimes of violence (39 incidents per 1000 persons). Additional statistics on the frequency, consequences, and prevention of criminal victimization can be found at the National Center for Victims of Crime Web site (www.nvc.org/).

For other offenses, it is difficult to assess the frequency of victimization, but what we do know is that they happen all too often. Included here, for example, are acts of racial or religious discrimination in which the recipient is denied rights that others receive. Homophobic attitudes are frequently expressed (Herek, 1987; Larsen, Reed, & Hoffman, 1980); 90% of gay men report having been threatened or subjected to verbal abuse, and more than 33% were victims of violence (Segell,

1997). Persons diagnosed with AIDS are frequently stigmatized in our society (Crandall, Glor, & Britt, 1997); not only laypersons but even medical professionals rate people with AIDS more negatively than they rate people with cancer, diabetes, or heart disease (Katz et al., 1987). In fact, society's reaction to victims of serious diseases is another reflection of how being threatened by the risk of illness can harden our attitudes toward seriously ill people and cause us to stigmatize them (Jones et al., 1984). We often come to believe that someone's disease is not just a consequence of his or her behavior or physical predisposition but that the illness comes to reflect the afflicted person's intrinsic value (Sontag, 1978).

Technological advancements and cultural changes have brought new forms of victimization to the fore. "Cyberstalking" is a recently emerged technique favored by some sexual predators as a way to target victims. "Identity theft," in which information about an individual's personal and financial life is stolen by computer hackers and then used fraudulently, has become a major fear of people in the 21st century. Nationwide, 9% of all students in secondary schools report feeling afraid that they will be attacked at school and avoid certain locations within their schools because they believe them to be unsafe (Verlinden, Hersen, & Thomas, 2000); millions more are traumatized by bullying and other forms of peer victimization that cause them to dread going to school (Hanish & Guerra, 2000).

This chapter concentrates on three types of victims and the effects of victimization on them: targets of sexual harassment, battered women, and victims of violent crime—particularly rape, the violent crime that has been studied most often. For each of these, the field of psychology has produced theory and research relevant to the laws and court decisions instituted to protect such victims. The responses of the legal system reflect conflicting views in our society about the nature of victims, especially victims of sex-related offenses. For example, how extreme does a situation need to be before we conclude that sexual harassment exists, and how distressed does the

response of the victim need to be? In the case of a battered woman who kills her batterer, will a claim of self-defense be accepted by a jury? And why do as many as two-thirds of rape victims never report the attack to the police?

# Sexual Harassment

Even though sexual harassment is a significant problem in educational and work environments, the term didn't come into use until 1974. A group of women at Cornell University, faced with the fact that several of their female colleagues had been forced to quit because of unwanted advances from their supervisors, began to speak out against such harassment (Brownmiller & Alexander, 1992). Also, in the early 1970s, the United States Equal Employment Opportunity Commission (EEOC) emerged as a major tool for redressing sexual harassment by employers.

*Incidence rates.* Within the past decade two cases involving sensational charges of sexual harassment made international headlines and directed people's attention to the problem of sexual harassment. The first case was the highly publicized confirmation hearings for Clarence Thomas to become a justice of the U.S. Supreme Court. During the hearings, Anita Hill, an attorney who worked for Thomas while he was head of the EEOC, testified that he had pressured her for dates and repeatedly made lewd comments to her. The second case involved the four-year legal battle in which Paula Jones, a former secretary in Arkansas state government, charged that then-governor Bill Clinton had pressured her to perform oral sex in a Little Rock hotel room. Although he admitted no wrongdoing and refused to apologize to Jones, President Clinton finally paid her $850,000 to drop the lawsuit. Of course, the consequences of this case stretched far beyond sexual harassment; the nearly universal recognition that Clinton had testified in a less than complete and truthful manner in a deposition taken during the Jones case led to his becoming only the second president in U.S. history to be impeached.

*Clarence Thomas*

*Anita Hill*

How frequent is sexual harassment? A survey of 20,000 federal employees found that 42% of the female workers had experienced sexual harassment on the job in the previous two years (Brownmiller & Alexander, 1992). Similarly, 43% of the women lawyers in large law firms reported that they had been recipients of deliberate touching, pinching, or cornering in the office (Slade, 1994). One survey of female graduate students reported that 60% had experienced some form of everyday harassment by male faculty members, and 22% had been asked out on dates by them (Schneider, 1987). A nationwide survey of female psychologists revealed that over half of them had experienced sexual harassment from a psychotherapy client at some point in their careers (deMayo, 1997).

Sexual harassment is typically assumed to involve a male perpetrator and a female victim, but men also experience sexual harassment, and the Supreme Court has ruled in the case of *Oncale v. Sundowner Offshore Industries* (1998) that intragender harassment is also prohibited. Although

Michael Crichton's novel *Disclosure,* and the movie based on it, suggest that sexual harassment of men usually involves an aggressive female boss demanding sex from a male subordinate, the reality is that men report that other men are more likely than women to sexually harass them. One survey of nearly 1000 male workers found that just under 50% of the men had experienced at least one incident involving potential sexual harassment at work and that other men were the perpetrators in over half of these incidents (Waldo, Berdahl, & Fitzgerald, 1998). Although lewd sexual comments, negative comments about men, and unwanted sexual attention were the most common types of harassment, the form of harassment that these men found to be the most upsetting involved statements or actions that belittled them for acting too "feminine" or that pressured them to adopt stereotypical "masculine" behavior.

*Defining sexual harassment.*   Title VII of the Civil Rights Act of 1964 prohibits discrimination in the workplace because of a person's gender. It therefore provides the legal basis for outlawing sexual harassment. Even though more cases are coming forward, confusion remains as to just how sexual harassment is defined. "Can I tell my assistant that she looks especially nice today?" "What kinds of jokes are okay at the office party?" Questions of this sort reflect the uncertainty men in particular seem to have about the possibility that a comment will be viewed by a woman as sexually harassing if it attempts to reflect a compliment or to be humorous (Gutek, 1985; Terpstra & Baker, 1987). The U.S. EEOC (1980) defines harassment as follows:

> unwelcome sexual advances, requests for sexual favors, and other verbal or physical conduct of a sexual nature when: (1) submission to such conduct is made either explicitly or implicitly a term or condition of an individual's employment, (2) submission to or a rejection of such conduct by an individual is used as a basis for employment decisions affecting such individual, or (3) such conduct has the purpose or effect of unreasonably interfering with an individual's work performance or creating an intimidating, hostile, or offensive work environment. (p. 74677)

One problem with this definition is that it still leaves key terms such as *unwelcome* or *unreasonably interfering* open to varying interpretations. When men and women differ in their evaluations of potential harassing interactions, women are more likely to classify a specific act as harassing than are men (Frazier, Cochran, & Olson, 1995), but, on average, this gender difference is small (Blumenthal, 1998). So who determines when an act is harassing—the alleged victim, the alleged perpetrator, or an outside, "neutral" observer?

What can psychology and other social sciences contribute to understanding sexual harassment? As Frazier et al. (1995) note, one contribution of psychological research is to provide information about just what behaviors people consider to be sexual harassment. The research summarized in ◆ Box 16-1 indicates that a gen-

der difference is one factor that is relevant to the question of what legal standard should be used in evaluating claims of sexual harassment, but it is not the only factor.

Structured measures of sexual harassment, such as the Sexual Experiences Questionnaire (Fitzgerald, Gelfand, & Drasgow, 1995), identify three forms of sexual harassment: (1) *gender harassment,* which involves lewd comments and negative comments directed at a person's gender; (2) *unwanted sexual attention,* which involves overtures for sexual contact ranging from flirting to uninvited touching; and (3) *sexual coercion,* which involves the offer of bribes or the threat of retaliation in exchange for sexual contact. As you would expect, reactions to these behaviors vary widely; fewer than 10% of respondents consider staring, flirting, or nonsexual touching to be harassment, but almost 100% believe that pressure for sexual favors or sexual bribery constitutes harassment (Frazier et al., 1995).

The courts, following the EEOC guidelines, have recognized two types of sexual harassment. The *quid pro quo* type involves sexual demands that are made in exchange for employment benefits; it is comparable to sexual coercion on the Sexual Experiences Questionnaire. Quid pro quo harassment is reflected in an implicit or explicit bargain whereby the harasser promises a reward or threatens punishment, depending on the victim's response (Hotelling, 1991). When a teacher says to a student, "Sleep with me or you fail this course," it qualifies as quid pro quo sexual harassment (McCandless & Sullivan, 1991).

The second type of harassment, usually referred to as *hostile workplace* harassment, involves the other two dimensions of the Sexual Experiences Questionnaire—gender harassment and unwanted sexual attention. Under Title VII, it is illegal for employers to create or tolerate "an intimidating, hostile, or offensive working environment" by the use of harassment. In Paula Jones's lawsuit against President Clinton, the plaintiff claimed that Clinton's behavior constituted hostile workplace harassment. How is this defined? How disabling for the victim must such an

## The Science of

BOX 16-1   **Defining sexual harassment: What factors matter?**

When psychologists study the way individuals define sexual harassment, they usually employ the following methodology: Subjects are presented a set of facts and are then asked to evaluate whether they believe those facts prove that sexual discrimination occurred. In some studies, the subjects read a summary of the facts; in others they watch or listen to a taped description of the events. Some fact patterns are taken from cases that have previously been tried in court; others are "made up" by the experimenters and may bear little or no resemblance to real cases. These methodological variations can affect the results. For example, most studies use college students as subjects, which is a potential problem because undergraduates tend to define sexual harassment more leniently than older adults (Blumenthal, 1998). Along these same lines, studies that use real legal scenarios tend to find smaller effects due to subjects' gender than do studies employing other kinds of stimuli (Blumenthal, 1998).

Some studies examine the impact of subject characteristics other than, or in addition to, gender. For example, Richard Wiener and his colleagues conducted a complex experiment that simultaneously assessed the impact of

subject gender, sexist attitudes, and the legal standard used to define harassment (Wiener, Hurt, Russell, Mannen, & Gasper, 1997). In addition to replicating the finding that females were more likely than men to find that sexual harassment had occurred in two workplace situations, Wiener et al. (1997) also examined the impact of a psychological variable—sexist attitudes—on perceptions of sexual harassment.

Subjects were classified as being either high or low in *hostile sexism* or *benevolent sexism*. Hostile sexism is an attitude of antipathy toward women; it reflects a belief that males are superior to women and should be dominant over them. Benevolent sexism is an attitude of protection toward women; it reflects a belief that as the "weaker sex," women need to be shielded from the world's harshness. Wiener and his colleagues hypothesized that subjects who scored high on a measure of benevolent sexism would be more likely to find that sexual harassment had occurred, especially when they were directed to judge the behavior from the perspective of the woman. Conversely, they predicted that subjects high in hostile sexism would be less inclined to conclude that sexual harassment had occurred. The results supported most

of their predictions. Subjects high in hostile sexism were less likely than subjects who scored low on this dimension to find that the defendant's behavior constituted sexual harassment. However, this effect was eliminated for those subjects who were also high in benevolent sexism; benevolent sexism appears to soften the impact of hostile sexism to the point that it no longer substantially influences judgments of harassment.

Much stronger than the effect of gender on perceptions of sexual harassment is the influence of the harasser's status relative to the victim. In his meta-analysis of 111 empirical studies examining how sexual harassment is evaluated by different observers, Blumenthal (1998) found that both men and women were more likely to perceive behavior directed by someone of higher status at someone of equal or less rank in the workplace as harassment than similar behavior occurring between peers. This is a reassuring result given that the law also tends to assume greater liability on behalf of a defendant in cases in which harassment by a supervisor or manager, as opposed to a peer or coworker, is alleged (Goodman-Delahunty, 1998).

environment be? The courts have answered these questions in a couple of recent decisions.

In the 1986 case of *Meritor Savings Bank v. Vinson,* the U.S. Supreme Court recognized for

the first time that sexual harassment that creates a hostile work environment also violates Title VII of the 1964 Civil Rights Act. Isolated incidents of sexual misconduct do not necessarily involve sex-

*Five army women being interviewed after recanting testimony about sexual harassment at Aberdeen Proving Grounds*

ual harassment; it usually requires repeated of-fensive behavior or behavior of a severe nature to qualify. But it took another decision, *Harris v. Forklift Systems, Inc.* (1993; see ◆ **Box 16-2**), to clarify how extreme the effects had to be.

Experts remain divided about whether sexual harassment should be viewed from the perspec-tive of the "reasonable woman" or the "reasonable person" (Wiener & Gutek, 1999). One point of view is that the latter standard ignores the differ-ent perspective of women, who are more likely to be victims than are men and who therefore can provide the more appropriate perspective. The other viewpoint concludes that use of a reason-able woman standard would perpetuate a stereo-type that women are less able to cope with ordinary job pressures than are men.

It was noted earlier that although women are more likely than men to describe an act as sexual harassment, the gender difference is usually small. Extreme behaviors, such as coercive threats to have sex or lose one's job, are rated as sexual ha-rassment by 99% of each gender; it is the more am-biguous behaviors from which gender differences

emerge. For this reason, Gutek and O'Connor (1995) argue that a reasonable woman standard is not advisable in sexual harassment cases. That standard can focus attention on the recipient's be-havior and away from the perpetrator's, as well as perpetuate the very sexist attitudes it seeks to elim-inate. On the other hand, using a reasonable woman standard should cause workers to be more sensitive to the perspective of potential victims, thereby possibly preventing some acts of sexual ha-rassment (Wiener & Hunt, 1999). As a compro-mise, some commentators have recommended a "reasonable victim" standard that would encourage jurors to examine several factors—including gen-der of the victim—in evaluating claims of sexual harassment (Goodman-Delahunty, 1999).

*Applying psychological knowledge to detecting harassment.* Psychological approaches con-tribute to our understanding of sexual harassment in two other ways. First, some psychologists have attempted to predict when sexual harassment will occur. Other psychologists have tried to deter-mine the likelihood of a favorable outcome in

## THE CASE OF

**BOX 16-2** **Teresa Harris**

Teresa Harris was the rentals manager at Forklift Systems in Nashville; her boss (the company president) made a number of suggestive and demeaning comments to her. At first she tried to ignore him, and then she confronted him. He promised to stop, but a month later, in public, he asked if she had slept with a client to get his account. This was the last straw; after working there two years, she quit. She sought relief from the EEOC and the courts, claiming that the boss's behavior had created a hostile workplace; she asked for back wages.

Unable to get satisfaction from the lower courts, she brought her appeal to the U.S. Supreme Court, which agreed to hear the case because different circuit courts had been inconsistent in their decisions in such cases. Some courts had adopted a subjective approach, focusing on the impact of the alleged harassment on the plaintiff. But others, taking an objective ap-

proach, had asked whether a reasonable person would have found the environment to be abusive. Also unclear was the question of degree of impact: Was it sufficient that the environment interfered with the complainant's work performance, or was it necessary for "psychological injury" to have occurred? Even though there is ample evidence that sexual harassment produces psychological damages (Fitzgerald, Buchanan, Collinsworth, Magley, & Ramos, 1999), should plaintiffs be forced to prove that they were psychologically harmed in order to persuade a jury the sexual harassment has occurred?

The unanimous decision of the Court, announced by Justice O'Connor, ruled in favor of Harris and held that it was not always necessary for plaintiffs to prove that they had suffered psychological injuries. The case was returned to the lower court, which was instructed to examine the ruling and decide how much back pay, if any,

Harris deserved. (Several months later, Forklift Systems settled with Harris out of court, for an unpublicized amount.) The decision listed a menu of factors indicative of illegal harassment, including the frequency and severity of the behavior. Also covered was behavior that was physically threatening or humiliating or that would unreasonably interfere with an employee's work performance.

Noteworthy in Justice O'Connor's decision was her use of the "reasonable person" standard. For example, she ruled out as sexual harassment conduct that is not so severe and pervasive as to create an "objectively hostile" work environment, as defined by a reasonable person. Her decision reflected a middle-of-the-road position; on the one hand, no longer was the behavior defined by responses of the "reasonable man," but Justice O'Connor did not go so far as to permit the victim to define what is hostile, either.

court when a person alleging sexual harassment files a complaint. We consider these issues next.

When does sexual harassment occur? Pryor, Giedd, and Williams (1995) propose that certain individuals possess proclivities for sexual harassment and that the norms in specific organizations function to encourage the expression of harassment. For example, a factory that permits its workers to display *Playboy* centerfolds or nude calendars in their work areas may encourage the expression of harassment by a worker who, in an-

other environment, would not do so. Similarly, a company that provides sexually oriented entertainment at office parties or has work-related parties that exclude one gender is expressing a norm that gives tacit approval to at least some forms of harassment.

But men also differ in their likelihood to harass. Pryor (1987) asked men to imagine themselves in a series of scenarios in which they had power over an attractive woman. In one scenario, for example, the man is a college professor, meeting with a female student who is seeking to raise her grade in the class. The subjects were asked to rate how likely they were to engage in an act of quid pro quo sexual harassment in each scenario, given that they could do so without being punished. Men who scored relatively high on the Likelihood to Sexually Harass (LSH) Scale were more accepting of myths about rape, possessed more coercive sexual fantasies, and endorsed more stereotypical beliefs about male sex roles (Pryor et al., 1995). They had strong needs to dominate women and to seek sex for sexual gratification. In a series of laboratory experiments, Pryor and his colleagues found that men high in likelihood to sexually harass engaged in harassment in social situations in which harassing behavior was convenient and not conspicuous and under conditions in which local norms encouraged such behavior.

Which type of harassment claims succeed, and which ones fail? Terpstra and Baker (1988) examined 81 sexual harassment charges filed with the Illinois State Equal Employment Opportunity Commission agency over a two-year period to determine what factors influenced their outcomes. About 31% of these cases were settled in favor of the complainant. The researchers identified three characteristics that were significantly related to EEOC decisions; sexual harassment charges were more likely to be resolved in favor of the complainant when

1. the harassing behaviors were serious,
2. the complainant had witnesses to support the charges, and
3. the complainant had given notice to management prior to filing formal charges.

This analysis was repeated for another sample of 133 court decisions between 1974 and 1989 (Terpstra & Baker, 1992). A total of 38% of these cases were decided in favor of the complainants—higher than the 31% of the EEOC cases—even though the complainants' cases were generally not as strong as those heard by the EEOC agency. In these cases, complainants were more likely to win their cases if

1. the harassment was severe,
2. witnesses supported their claims,
3. documents supported their claims,
4. they had given notice to management prior to filing charges, and
5. their organization had taken no action.

If a complainant had none of these factors in his or her favor, the odds of winning the case were less than 1%; if he or she had all five, the odds of winning were almost 100% (Terpstra & Baker, 1992).

# Battered Women

*Incidence rate.* The extent of physical abuse directed toward spouses and romantic partners in American society is difficult to estimate, but all experts agree that it is extensive. Lenore Walker (1992) concluded that between one-third and one-half of all American women will be abused at some point in their lives. Other experts have estimated that some form of physical aggression occurs in one-fourth to one-third of all couples (Straus & Gelles, 1988). Although relationship aggression by women against men is as frequent as male-to-female aggression (Magdol et al., 1997), male aggression is significantly more likely to result in serious injuries than female aggression. About 30% of all the women murdered in the United States each year are killed by their male partners; in fact, women are 3.7 times more likely to be killed by their partner than by a stranger (Kellerman & Mercy, 1992). For this reason, most of the research on relationship aggression has concentrated on male aggression against female partners (Rosenbaum & Gearan, 1999); we maintain that same emphasis in this chapter.

Despite these disturbing statistics and the increased research on relationship aggression that is being conducted, myths about battered women still abound. The mass media often gloss over this kind of violence, and some professionals, such as physicians and police, fail to ask appropriate questions when a battered woman reports an attack by her intimate partner. Arrest and prosecution of perpetrators of partner violence remain unpredictable, and protective restraining orders against batterers are often not consistently enforced.

*Myths and exaggerated beliefs.*   Experts emphasize that many simplified beliefs, exaggerations, and myths are held about battered women. Follingstad (1994, p. 15) identified the following misconceptions:

1. Battered women are masochists.
2. They provoke the assaults inflicted on them.
3. They get the treatment they deserve.
4. They are free to leave these violent relationships any time they want to.
5. Violence among intimate partners is not common.
6. Men who are nonviolent in their dealings with outsiders behave the same way in their dealings with their intimates.
7. Middle-class and upper-class men don't batter, and middle-class and upper-class women don't get beaten.
8. Battering is a lower-class, ethnic-minority phenomenon, and such women don't mind because this is a part of their culture.
9. "Good" battered women are passive and never try to defend themselves.

Although these statements do not fit with the reality of domestic violence, surveys conducted to determine the pervasiveness of such myths conclude that a clear majority of adult subjects subscribed to some of these myths, and about one-third of the subjects endorsed most of them (Ewing & Aubrey, 1987; Ewing, Aubrey, & Jamieson, 1986). These myths serve to obscure several truths about the plight of battered women: They face many real obstacles that make it difficult for them to leave their abusers, and, when they do attempt to leave abusive relationships— and many women do—they often suffer further threats, recriminations, attacks.

*The causes of battering.*   What are the main risk factors for battering? Researchers who have stud-

ied the causes of battering have focused on ecological factors, the characteristics of the battering victim, the nature of violent intimate relationships, and the psychological makeup of batterers. A recent review of this literature points to several risk factors as important (Rosenbaum & Gearan, 1999).

Although batterers come from all socioeconomic backgrounds, they are more likely to be unemployed, less educated, members of minority groups, and of lower socioeconomic status than nonbatterers. Batterers tend to have been raised in families in which they either suffered physical abuse as children or observed an abusive relationship between the parents. Adolescents who later become batterers have experienced a higher rate of conduct problems and are more likely to have engaged in early substance abuse; early experiences with coercive or aggressive behavior may set the stage for similar strategies in adult relationships (Magdol, Moffitt, Caspi, & Silva, 1998). Batterers usually have poor self-concepts, are not very good problem solvers, and often have inferior verbal skills. They are prone to extreme jealousy and fear being abandoned by their partners. As a result they monitor their partners' activities closely and try to exercise excessive control over their partners' whereabouts and activities. They overreact to signs of rejection and alternate between rage and desperation toward their partner.

*The cycle of violence.*   Batterers are sometimes described as being locked in a "cycle of violence," involving a Jekyll-and-Hyde pattern of emotional and behavioral instability that makes their victims all the more fearful of the battering they believe is inevitable. A man may be loving and attentive to a woman's needs early in their relationship as he cultivates her affection and relies on her to satisfy his dependency needs. However, when disappointments or disagreements occur in the relationship, as they invariably will in any relationship, a *tension-building phase* begins, involving increased criticism of the partner and maybe even some minor physical assaults.

This phase leads to a second stage in the cycle, an *acute battering incident.* By the time this more serious form of aggression occurs, the woman has become too dependent on the man to break off the relationship easily. He has succeeded in controlling her behavior and curtailing her contact with friends who could have possibly helped extract her from her plight. The woman also tends to believe that if only she can find the right way to mollify the man's anger and reassure him of her faithfulness and obedience, he will reform his behavior.

Following a battering incident, a third stage, called the *contrite phase,* often occurs in which the battterer apologizes for his attacks, promises never to do it again, and entices the woman to believe that he is a changed man. Typically, of course, this is an empty pledge. Sometimes the humiliation that the man feels over having apologized so profusely to his partner simply fuels more intense anger and violence. The cycle then repeats itself.

How frequent is the cycle of violence? Even though Walker (1979) portrays it as a significant dynamic faced by battered women, she did not identify it in about a third of the 400 women she studied. What the *cycle of violence* term may actually be describing is an underlying personality disorder that typifies a certain category of batterer. According to Donald Dutton (1995, 2000), a psychologist at the University of British Columbia and one of the experts who testified for the prosecution in O. J. Simpson's murder trial, as many as 40% of batterers have the features of **borderline personality disorder,** a severe disturbance that is characterized by unstable moods and behavior. People with borderline personality disorder are drawn into intense relationships in which they are particularly unable to tolerate negative emotions. They are demandingly dependent, which causes them to feel easily slighted, which leads to jealousy, which leads to rage, which leads to extreme behavior, which leads to guilt. These emotional cycles repeat themselves over and over, providing the underlying motivation for the cycle of violence. In addition to emotional instability, batterers also are prone to believing the worst about others; for example, they are quick to attribute hostile intentions to their partners (Eckhardt, Barbour, & Davison, 1998). Dutton traces the origin of this personality disorder to insecure attachments that batterers experienced with their parents that later cause them to feel intense anger toward partners whenever things go awry in a relationship.

*Responses to victims of battering.* The prevalence of many myths about battered women reflects the negative feelings toward crime victims described earlier in this chapter. A deep uneasiness, even a hostility, exists toward some victims of battering (Jones, 1994). They are often seen as pathological "doormats" or delusional alarmists "crying wolf" over minor disagreements. When victims retaliate against their abusers—when battered women kill their batterers—they may receive a greater punishment than do men committing acts with similar outcomes. Do women receive harsher sentences for homicide than men do? The question is difficult to answer because the circumstances may be quite different. Jenkins and Davidson (1990) analyzed the court records of ten battered women charged with the murder of their abusive partners in Louisiana between 1975 and 1988; all pleaded guilty or were found guilty at trial. Their sentences ranged from five years' probation to life in prison, with half getting the latter sentence.

Ewing (1987) surveyed a larger number of women who had killed their batterers. All 100 were charged with murder, manslaughter, or some form of criminal homicide. The outcomes were as follows: 3 were found not guilty by reason of insanity; 3 had their charges dropped; 9 pleaded guilty; 85 went to trial, using the defense of self-defense; 63 were convicted. For those convicted, 12 were given life in prison, 1 was sentenced to 50 years without parole, and the others received anywhere from 4 years' probation to 25 years in prison. A total of 17 of the 63 received prison sentences greater than 10 years.

*The battered woman syndrome as a defense.* Only a very small minority of battered women kill their attackers, but these victims receive a great deal of public scrutiny, usually in connection with their standing trial on murder charges. If they go to trial, most battered women use either insanity or self-defense as a defense; in either type of defense, the **battered woman syndrome** is likely

JUNE BRIAND

*Conflicts between the values of discretion and equality often surface in cases in which a woman is charged with murdering a partner who has been abusive to her throughout their relationship. For example, the last three pardons granted in New Hampshire—a state in which pardons are rarely given—were for women who had been victims of domestic abuse and had killed their husbands, the latest being for June Briand, 33, who had served nearly ten years in prison for killing her physically and emotionally abusive husband.*

to be part of the defense. The battered woman syndrome is defined as a collection of symptoms and reactions by a woman to a pattern of continued physical and psychological abuse inflicted on her by her mate. Lenore Walker (1984a), the psychologist who is recognized for advancing this term, emphasizes the following elements of the battered woman syndrome:

1. As a result of chronic exposure to repeated incidents of battering, the woman develops a sense of *learned helplessness,* in which she comes to believe that there is nothing she can do to escape from the batterer or improve her life; finally, she gives up trying to make a change.

2. As a result of her social isolation and often her economic dependence on the batterer, the woman falls more and more under his domination. She believes that she has diminished alternatives for solving her problem.

3. As she restricts her outside activities and has less contact with friends or relatives, the woman grows more and more fearful of the threats and attacks of the batterer. Most of the women Walker interviewed stated that they believed that their batterer would eventually kill them.

4. Trapped in this existence, the woman experiences several emotional and psychological reactions—her self-esteem is shattered, she feels guilty and ashamed about what she sees as her multiple failures and shortcomings, and she feels increasing rage and resentment toward her partner, whose control over her seems to grow relentlessly over time.

5. After years of victimization, the woman grows *hypervigilant;* she notices subtle things—reactions by the batterer that others wouldn't recognize as a signal of upcoming violence (e.g, her partner's words come faster, he assumes a specific posture, or his eyes get darker). This heightened sensitivity to danger cues often motivates the woman to kill her assailant and accounts for her genuine belief that she acted in self-defense.

*Evaluating the battered woman syndrome.* How have claims of battered woman syndrome fared in court? Does the battered woman syndrome really exist? And does it advance the cause of victims who feel they are forced to retaliate?

A battered woman's claim of self-defense often faces both legal hurdles and the skepticism of jurors (Dodge & Greene, 1991; Schuller, 1994). These obstacles might account for the fact that the majority of battered women charged with murdering their abusive partner are convicted.

Historically, a claim of **self-defense** applied to killings in which at the time of the killing, the individual reasonably believed that he or she was in imminent danger of death or great bodily harm from an attacker. The defense was usually invoked in cases in which a specific attack or fight put defendants in fear for their lives. However, the typical case in which a battered woman relies on a theory of self-defense to exculpate her from charges of murdering her partner is much different. The violence does not involve a specific episode; rather, it is ongoing. And the woman's response may seem disproportionate to what a "reasonable" person believes was necessary; often she kills her abuser while he is unarmed or even sleeping. To help jurors understand how the battered woman syndrome leads to a woman's perception that she is acting in self-defense, defendants often try to introduce expert testimony about the characteristics and consequences of the syndrome. The impact of this testimony is not clear. Schuller's (1994) review of studies on the impact of expert testimony about battered woman syndrome found that the testimony was sometimes associated with juror opinions that were more favorable to the woman's claim, and sometimes it had little or no effects.

It is important to remember that no single set of reactions or characteristics can describe all battering victims. One study (Button, Perrin, Chrestman, & Halle, 1990) that investigated the characteristics of battered women seeking help at a counseling program identified five distinct personality types, indicating different patterns of psychological functioning among them, including profiles that were "normal."

Although battered women share the experience of being victimized by a violent partner, their reaction to this aggression and the way they cope with it takes many different forms. This variation has implications for developing the most effective types of intervention for these women. Rather than assuming that they need traditional services such as psychotherapy or couple counseling, it might be more helpful to provide battered women with assistance from special advocates who would assist and support these survivors to find the resources they need to improve their lives. Just such

an intervention has proven very effective in helping bring about changes that allowed battered women to become violence-free. After providing battered women with a personal advocate who helped them gain access to the resources that each woman needed to reduce her risk of partner abuse, Sullivan and Bybee (1999) found that the women who received advocacy services were twice as likely across a two-year time period to have been free of any battering than women without such a service.

# Victims of Violent Crime

The dilemmas confronted throughout this book, especially the quest to preserve both the rights of suspects and the rights of victims, are highlighted when we consider the victims of crime, particularly victims of violent crimes such as rape. Until recently, society had not paid much attention to crime victims. Their trial testimony was necessary to obtain convictions, but most of the legal rights formally protected in the adversarial system are extended to defendants, not victims. As a result, the needs and rights of crime victims have often been ignored. This imbalance began to change in the late 1970s and early 1980s as victim advocacy groups, mental-health professionals, police, and court officials all began to realize the need to better recognize and serve crime victims. Several developments reflect the growing stature and influence of the victims rights movement, such as:

◆ the emergence of the interdisciplinary field of **victimology,** which concentrates on studying the process and consequences of victimization experiences and how victims (or survivors, which is the term preferred by many) recover;

◆ the increasing availability of services to crime victims, including compensation and restitution programs (see Chapter 9), victim assistance programs in the courts, self-help programs, and formal mental-health services;

◆ the expanded opportunity for victims to participate in the trials of their victimizers through mechanisms such as victim impact statements (see Chapter 9);

◆ the heightened focus on victims brought about by new journals (*Victimology, Violence and Victims*), organizations such as the National Organization for Victim Assistance, and commissions such as the President's Commission on Victims of Crime (1982) and the American Psychological Association's Task Force on the Victims of Crime and Violence.

For their part, psychologists have conducted research on and delivered clinical services to a diverse array of crime victims. Three areas have received special attention: the consequences of physical/sexual abuse on child victims; the role of violent victimization as a cause of psychological disorders, particularly posttraumatic stress disorder; and the psychology of rape. We review each of these topics in the remainder of this chapter.

# Physical/Sexual Abuse of Children

Over the past 20 years, psychologists as well as the general public have become increasingly aware of the problem of childhood physical and sexual abuse. How widespread these problems are is difficult to know for sure because of the many problems involved in documenting their occurrence. Some experts point to frequencies of epidemic proportions, claiming that one-fifth to one-third of all women and about one-seventh of men are sexually abused before they turn 18 (Finkelhor, Hotaling, Lewis, & Smith, 1990). Others question these figures, in part because they are based on long-term retrospective reports and in part because they sometime involve reports by people who claim that their memories of abuse were repressed for years.

Nonsexual, physical abuse of children is equally prevalent. By the time they are 18, about one of every five children has experienced physical abuse that is serious enough to have caused injuries (Elliott, 1997), and about 1500 children

die from abuse annually, with 80% of these deaths caused by actions of their parents (Warner-Rogers, Hansen, & Hecht, 1999). Add to these figures the problem of victimization by peers in which boys and girls are bullied, attacked, or singled out for other forms of prolonged abuse while at school (Crick & Bigbee, 1998), and it is obvious that the majority of youth have had one or more potentially serious victimization experiences by the time they reach adulthood.

What are the effects of the physical/sexual abuse of children? The direct effects include short-term consequences such as increased mood and anxiety disorders among children as well as inappropriate sexual behavior and impaired school performance (Prentky, 1999). But even more concern has been raised by the possibility of long-term effects from physical/sexual child abuse—effects that include a much greater risk for developing mental disorders, for suffering subsequent revictimization experiences, and for engaging in criminal conduct as adults.

Does being abused as a child actually cause criminal behavior in later years? This question is controversial because studies that report a higher incidence of abuse in the childhoods of aggressive adults have usually relied on retrospective methods, often using self-reported memories of abuse. It would be better, of course, to base any conclusions about the relationship of childhood abuse to adult violence on long-term prospective studies in which abused children are identified and then repeatedly assessed into adulthood. As ◆ Box 16-3 summarizes, just such a study has been conducted, and it has led to some disturbing results.

Several risk factors have been discovered for child abuse (Nietzel, Speltz, McCauley, & Bernstein, 1998). As examples, compared to nonabusers, abusive parents tend to

◆ possess less knowledge about normal child development;

◆ hold unrealistic expectations for their children, such as the age by which they should be toilet trained;

### The Science of

**BOX 16-3    Victimization: Is violence inherited?**

Cathy Spatz Widom (1989, 1992) used court records to identify a group of 908 children in a midwestern American city who had suffered abuse (i.e., sexual abuse or physical assault leading to injury) or severe neglect (i.e., inadequate food, clothing, shelter, or medical care) between 1967 and 1971. This "abuse/neglect" group was matched to a group of 667 children who had not been exposed to abuse or neglect but who were similar in gender, age, ethnicity, and family socioeconomic status. Matching the abused and nonabused groups on these variables was important because it allowed Widom to assure that any differences between the groups in terms of violent behavior in adolescence or adulthood were not due to differences in demographic characteristics.

Widom's analysis of police and court records showed that, as earlier research had suggested, abused or neglected children were significantly more likely than the comparison group to have been arrested for violent crimes as juveniles or as adults. In addition, the abused or neglected individuals were, on average, 1 year younger than comparison subjects at the time of their first arrest and had committed twice as many total offenses over the 15- to 20-year period studied. These differences were seen in boys and girls and in European Americans and African Americans; however, the relationship between abuse and violence was particularly strong among African Americans.

As disturbing as these results are, they may actually *underestimate* the risks created by childhood abuse. For one thing, only incidents that resulted in arrest or trial were included in this study. Many other undetected or unreported crimes may have been committed by the abused/neglected group. Furthermore, this aspect of the study did not assess group differences in mental disorders, substance abuse, educational and occupational difficulties, or other possible long-term consequences of childhood abuse. In a second phase of Widom's research, the groups are being interviewed about such consequences, and preliminary results indicate that they may be as common in the abused/neglected group as the delinquency and violent crime already identified.

---

- become easily annoyed when under stress;
- choose aggressive means of resolving conflicts;
- have limited access to social support and help with child care; and
- disagree with each other about child rearing and discipline.

Parents who are poor, were abused themselves as children, give birth to children with congenital defects, have children while they are still teenagers, or are embroiled in their own marital conflicts are also at greater risk to be abusers (Nietzel & Himelein, 1986). Can these risks be reduced or overcome?

Several studies have shown that parents can learn more effective child management skills and that abusive interactions with children can also be reduced. For example, Joseph Denicola and Jack Sandler (1980) developed a 12-session program that (1) taught parents basic principles of child management, such as using reinforcement rather than punishment to control children's behavior, and (2) helped parents reduce their own feelings of stress, anger, and frustration through the use of relaxation training exercises and stress inoculation. In general, interventions that include these components are somewhat successful in decreasing abusive behavior and increasing positive interactions.

Abusive parents can be taught to change their behavior, if they learn the necessary skills for managing their children. However, child abuse is not caused solely by the problems of individual parents. Social factors play a role as well. A comprehensive plan to reduce child abuse should combine parent training with larger-scale interventions aimed at helping families. Community day care centers to relieve mothers of child care demands and crisis intervention to help parents cope with personal stress are two examples of needed social services.

# Violent Victimization and Posttraumatic Stress Disorder

Individuals who suffer a severe trauma and, weeks or months later, continue to experience intense, fear-related reactions when reminded of the trauma, may be experiencing **posttraumatic stress disorder** (PTSD). Usually, the trauma must be of sufficient severity to have threatened the victim, or someone close to the victim, with mortal danger or serious bodily harm. Most examples of violent crime qualify as trauma that are severe enough to trigger PTSD in at least some victims.

The symptoms of PTSD fall into three broad classes:

1. frequent reexperiencing of the event through intrusive thoughts, flashbacks, and repeated nightmares and dreams;
2. persistent avoidance of stimuli associated with the trauma and a general numbing or deadening of emotions (feeling detached or estranged from others); and
3. increased physiological arousal resulting in exaggerated startle responses or difficulty sleeping.

The case of Jim (◆ Box 16-4) reveals how these diagnostic criteria apply to a real-life case. Shot and left to die, Jim suffered an extreme traumatic event; guns and related stimuli would trigger a reexperiencing of the trauma; he avoided stimuli associated with the trauma; and he was hyperaroused and reactive. These symptoms must last longer than one month to qualify as PTSD.

Trauma-related symptoms beginning within one month after the trauma and lasting more than two days but less than one month are diagnosed as *acute stress disorder*. In some cases of PTSD, the symptoms may not emerge for months or even years following the actual event.

How common is PTSD? As part of the Epidemiological Catchment Area studies, door-to-door diagnostic interviews of thousands of residents of the United States found PTSD in about 0.5 percent of males, most of whom were veterans of the Vietnam War. About 1.3% of females carried this diagnosis, most of whom had suffered sexual or physical assault or had witnessed others being assaulted (Helzer et al., 1987). However, estimates of PTSD prevalence from other studies are much higher. For example, Heidi Resnick and her colleagues (1993) conducted a diagnostic survey of 4008 females and found that 12% of the sample had symptoms of PTSD at some time in their lives, and 4.6% were currently suffering PTSD symptoms. These percentages suggest that, in the United States alone, 11,800,000 women have had PTSD at some time in their lives and that 4,400,000 currently suffer from it (Resnick et al., 1993). Resnick et al. (1993) found that 26% of women whose trauma was crime related developed PTSD, whereas only 9% of noncriminal trauma victims developed PTSD symptoms. The extent of injury during trauma also predicts whether PTSD symptoms will develop. Women who were injured by a trauma are more likely to develop PTSD symptoms than those who were not. Victims' perceptions of trauma are also important in determining the likelihood of PTSD. The belief that the victim's life is in danger and that he or she has no control over the trauma increases risk for PTSD (Foa & Kozak, 1986; Green et al., 1990; Kushner et al., 1992).

Although traumas are unfortunate facts of life, there is reason to believe that PTSD—in some trauma victims, at least—can be prevented. For one thing, although many persons experiencing severe trauma may develop acute stress disorder, most do not go on to develop PTSD. One reason

## THE CASE OF

**BOX 16-4** Jim

When Jim appeared for treatment at age 40, he had been suffering from anxiety and depressive symptoms for 8 years. He dated his problems to one fall day when he foiled a burglary attempt across the street from where he worked. A distance runner, Jim decided to pursue the fleeing burglar and to attract help along the way. After a chase, Jim slowed and looked around for help. Turning again to the burglar, he found himself staring down the barrel of a handgun. The burglar shot him. Jim was hit in the legs with three bullets and immobilized. He begged the young man to spare his life. Instead, the assailant continued firing until the gun was empty. He then fled, leaving Jim to die.

Fortunately, Jim was found and rushed to surgery. After eight days in the hospital, he knew he would recover. He felt elated just to be alive. Soon, the elation wore off, and Jim began thinking of what might have occurred had he not been found in time. More and more frequently, sights and sounds began to evoke the memory of the shooting and the panic he had experienced. The sight of guns or depictions of violence on TV triggered waves of strong emotion. Sirens and the sight of ambulances would startle him, then panic and despair would set in. By the following year, even the cool dampness of autumn could reactivate the event in his mind. He had frequent nightmares of looking into a gun barrel.

As time went on, Jim felt more on edge. He became wary of people, and he kept to himself. He no longer experienced life's joy and excitement. Due to injury-related leg pain, he was forced to stop running, giving up one of his major pleasures and outlets for stress. Leg pain brought up images of the shooting that, in turn, brought fear, hyperventilation, and a racing heart. Episodes in which Jim felt deeply depressed and suicidal would sometimes follow exposure to various triggering stimuli. After eight years of nightmares and daily reminders of the trauma, Jim sought treatment and was able to make substantial improvements in his condition.

---

may be that those experiencing trauma, but not PTSD, tend to receive high levels of social support from family, friends, or counselors immediately following the event (e.g., Sutker et al., 1995). Thus, providing immediate social support for trauma victims may prevent their experiences from progressing into a posttraumatic stress disorder.

Two other characteristics distinguish people who develop PTSD from those who do not. Individuals who suffer PTSD often perceive the world as a dangerous place from which they must retreat, and they come to view themselves as helpless to deal with stressors. If these two misconceptions can be eliminated, full-blown cases of PTSD might be prevented in many victims. Edna Foa has developed a four-session prevention course

designed to attack these two misconceptions in women who have been raped or assaulted. Foa includes the following elements in her PTSD prevention course:

1. education about the common psychological reactions to assault in order to help victims realize that their responses are normal,
2. training in skills such as relaxation so that the women are better prepared to cope with stress,
3. emotionally reliving the trauma through imaginal exposure methods to allow victims to defuse their lingering fears of the trauma, and
4. cognitive restructuring to help the women replace negative beliefs about their competence and adequacy with more realistic appraisals.

Ten women who had recently been raped or assaulted completed the four-week course. Their PTSD symptoms were then compared with ten other women who had also been assaulted or raped but who did not take part in the course. At 2-month and 5.5-month postassault assessments, victims who completed the prevention course had fewer PTSD symptoms that did the no-treatment controls. Two months after their trauma, 70% of the untreated women but only 10% of the treated women met the criteria for PTSD (Foa, Hearst-Ikeda, & Perry, 1995). These results suggest that a brief program that facilitates emotionally reexperiencing trauma *and* correcting beliefs about personal inadequacy can reduce the incidence of PTSD.

# The Psychology of Rape

Until recently, rape victims had been singled out for misunderstanding, harassment, and neglect. For example, if a rape victim did not resist her attacker, people may incorrectly assume that she wanted to be raped; in contrast, people never raise the question of whether a robbery victim wanted to be robbed, even when he or she didn't resist (Scroggs, 1976). Furthermore, society struggles over how to deal with convicted rapists. Is rape a sexual crime or an act of violence? Is it the act of a disordered mind or a normal one?

Among serious crimes, rape is perhaps the most appropriate for psychological analysis (Allison & Wrightsman, 1993). Myths abound about the nature of rapists and their relationship to their victims. Rape is a crime in which the interaction between the criminal and his prey is central to attributions of responsibility and blame (Stormo, Lang, & Stritzke, 1997). Since the 1970s, there has been an explosion of psychological research directed toward the understanding of sexual assaults (Ellis, 1991; Hall & Hirschman, 1991; Marshall, Fernandez, & Cortoni, 1999). For these reasons, we devote special attention to the crime of rape and its victims. We focus on female rape victims, but the fact that men are also raped

should not be overlooked, even though the law has only recently recognized them as victims.

*Myths about rape.*   Myths and incorrect stereotypes about rape, rapists, and rape victims take three general forms: (1) women cannot be raped against their will, (2) women secretly wish to be raped, and (3) most accusations of rape are faked. For example, we are told, "Only bad girls get raped." But we are also told, "All women want to be raped" and "Women ask for it." We also learn that "any healthy woman can resist a rapist if she really wants to." These falsehoods create a climate hostile to rape victims, often portraying them as willing participants in or even instigators of sexual encounters. In fact, these attitudes often function as self-serving rationalizations and excuses for blaming the victim.

*Rape attitude surveys.*   Rape means different things to different people, and these differing attitudes and perceptions affect behaviors toward both offenders and their victims (Feild, 1978a). Some respondents feel more empathy toward rape victims than others do; some feel empathy toward defendants charged with the crime of rape (Deitz, Blackwell, Daley, & Bentley, 1982; Deitz, Littman, & Bentley, 1984; Deitz, Russell, & Hammes, 1989; Weir & Wrightsman, 1990). Thus, the measurement of attitudes about rape can clarify what different people believe about this crime, its victims, and its perpetrators.

In his groundbreaking studies of rape attitudes, Herbert S. Feild (1978a, 1979; Barnett & Feild, 1977; Feild & Barnett, 1978; Feild & Bienen, 1980) hypothesized that a person's view of rape cannot be summarized by one score on a single scale. After constructing a 75-item Attitudes toward Rape questionnaire and analyzing responses to it, Feild concluded that seven different attitude clusters contribute to our overall perspective. Among these factors were

1.  the degree to which women were seen as responsible for preventing their own rape,

2. the degree to which a desire for sex is seen as the main motive for rape,

3. the degree to which severe punishment is advocated for rapists, and

4. the degree to which a woman is seen as instigating rape through flirtatious behavior or provocative dress.

*What accounts for stereotypes and myths about rape?* Individuals who, on the basis of answers to Feild's questionnaire, are unsympathetic to victims and tolerant of rapists also tend to believe in many of the rape myths described earlier. Such persons have developed a broad ideology that encourages the acceptance of myths about rape (Burt, 1980). This ideology embraces the following beliefs:

1. *Sexual conservatism.* This attitude emphasizes restrictions on the appropriateness of sexual partners, sexual acts, and circumstances under which sexual activity should occur. Burt (1980) observes, "Since many instances of rape violate one or more aspects of this conservative position, a sexually conservative individual might feel so strongly threatened by, and rejecting of, the specific circumstances of rape that he or she would overlook the coercion and force involved, and condemn the victim for participating" (p. 218).

2. *Adversarial sexual beliefs.* This component refers to the belief that sexual relationships are fundamentally exploitive—that participants in them are manipulative, unfaithful, and not to be trusted. To a person holding this ideology, "rape might seem the extreme on a continuum of exploitation, but not an unexpected or horrifying occurrence, or one justifying sympathy or support" (Burt, 1980, p. 218).

3. *Acceptance of interpersonal violence.* Another part of the ideology is the belief that force and coercion are legitimate behaviors in sexual relationships. This ideology approves of men dominating women and overpowering passive partners with violence and control.

4. *Sex-role stereotyping.* The last component of Burt's ideology casts each gender into the traditional mold of behaviors associated with that gender.

Burt constructed a set of attitude statements and administered them to a sample of 598 Minnesota adults to determine whether each of these components contributed to acceptance of myths about rape. When subjects' responses on the ideology clusters were compared to their answers on a scale measuring beliefs in myths about rape, Burt found that three of the four clusters had an impact (sexual conservatism did not). The strongest predictor of believing the myths was the acceptance of interpersonal violence. The subjects, both men and women, who felt that force and coercion were acceptable in sexual relationships, were the ones who agreed with items such as, "Women who get raped while hitchhiking get what they deserve" and "Any healthy woman can successfully resist a rapist if she really wants to."

A review of more than 70 studies that used a variety of measures of attitudes about rape supports Burt's conclusions (Anderson, Cooper, & Okamura, 1997). Those subjects who are more tolerant of rape are more likely to have traditional beliefs about gender roles, more adversarial sexual beliefs, greater needs for power and dominance, and heightened expressions of aggressiveness and anger.

*Facts about rape.* As we have seen, mistaken beliefs about rape are related to general attitudes about law and crime. But what are the facts about rape?

The United States has one of the highest rates of forcible rape among the world's industrialized counties (Marshall et al., 1999). Between 75 and 85 forcible rapes are reported annually to the police for every 100,000 females (Butterfield, 1997). This rate is three times that of England and twice that of countries such as France, Norway, and Spain (Kutchinski, 1988; Quinsey, 1984; Russell, 1984). However, experts estimate that reported rapes are only a minority of all those that occur, maybe only a

## The Science of

**BOX 16-5    Rape statistics: The National Women's Study**

A major study of rape published in 1992 provided valuable data on the frequency of rape and women's reactions to it. This study, known as the National Women's Study, was organized and funded by several governmental agencies and crime victim organizations. A nationwide, stratified sample of 4008 adult women were interviewed over the telephone about their experiences as victims of sexual aggression. Because men, children, and adolescents were excluded from the sample, the figures, of course, underestimate the total number of rapes, but they do give us a picture of the magnitude of the problem with adult women. Among the study's findings are the following:

1. Based on the sample of women surveyed, an estimated 683,000 women were raped during 1990; this is more than six times as many rapes as were reported to the police during the same year.
2. Among rape victims, over two-thirds reported that they re-ceived no physical injuries during the rape, 24% reported minor injuries, and 4% reported serious physical injuries.
3. An estimated 12.1 million women in the United States have been raped at least once in their lifetime.
4. Among rape victims, 61% report having been raped before the age of 18.

---

fifth or a tenth of actual rapes (Koss, 1992; Russell, 1984). Estimates are that between 20% and 30% of females in the United States suffer at least one rape or rape attempt in their lifetime (Ellis, 1989; Koss & Oros, 1982; Muehlenhard & Linton, 1987; see also ◆ Box 16-5).

Several factors account for the low report rates (Feldman-Summers, & Ashworth, 1981): the woman believes that reporting won't do any good, that she will suffer further embarrassment as a result of reporting, and that she will not be believed by law enforcement officers. Many victims are afraid that the attacker will retaliate if charges are made, and these expectations are sometimes fulfilled. According to FBI figures, only about half of reported rapes result in an arrest. And if a suspect is charged and the victim is a witness at his trial, his defense attorney may ridicule her testimony and impugn her character.

Females of all ages, social classes, and ethnic groups are vulnerable to rape. According to a study by the U.S. Bureau of Justice Statistics, the high-risk age groups are children and adolescents, with victims younger than age 12 accounting for 15% of those raped and victims aged 12 to 17 accounting for an additional 29% (Butterfield, 1997). Other surveys report that between 1% and 12% of victims are over 50 years of age.

*Motivations and characteristics of rapists.* Not all rapists have the same motives. Rape involves diverse combinations of aggressive and sexual motivation and deviant lifestyles for different offenders (Barbaree & Marshall, 1991). Experts have developed typologies of rapists, some proposing as many as nine types (Prentky & Knight, 1991), others as few as two or three (Groth, 1979). Most typologies have emphasized four factors that distinguish different types of rapists: (1) the amount and type of aggression the rapist used; (2) when the level of aggression was high, whether it heightened sexual arousal in a sadistic manner; (3) whether the offender showed evidence of psychopathy or antisocial personality disorder; and (4) whether the offender relied on deviant sexual fantasies to produce sexual arousal.

Recent theories of sexual aggression combine several causal factors into an integrated scheme that accounts for the different types of rapists (Sorenson & White, 1992). For example, Hall and Hirschman (1991) rely on four factors, similar to those just identified, to describe most rapists: (1) high levels of sexual arousal that are not inhibited by aggression, (2) attitudes toward women that justify aggressiveness toward females, (3) loss of control over emotions such as anger and hostility that are acted out in sexual aggression, and (4) long-standing antisocial personality disorder.

Ellis (1989) identified three theories of rape: the *feminist theory,* emphasizing rape as a pseudo-sexual act of male domination and exploitation of women (Donat & D'Emilio, 1992; White & Sorenson, 1992); the *social-learning approach,* suggesting that sexual aggression is learned through observation and imitation; and the *evolutionary theory,* holding that natural selection favors men who use forced sexual behavior (Buss & Malamuth, 1996). Ellis (1991) also suggests that high levels of testosterone increase the proclivity to rape by increasing a man's sexual urges and by decreasing the man's sensitivity to aversive outcomes such as a victim's suffering.

These different approaches illustrate that rape cannot be easily explained by any one theory. However, every one of these classification systems still fails to capture the full spectrum of behavior and motivations that typify rapists. Some of these systems are also limited by the fact that they are based on studies of convicted rapists who have been sentenced to prison. The majority of rapists are never imprisoned for their offenses; fewer than 10% of the rapes result in convictions or prison sentences (Frazier & Haney, 1996).

*Acquaintance rape and "date rape."* Over three-fourths of rapes are committed by acquaintances (Koss, 1992; Warshaw, 1988), and these are the assaults that women are least likely to report. Sometimes these actions are not even interpreted as rape. Kanin (1957, 1971) found that, over a 20-year period, between one-fourth and one-fifth of college women he had surveyed reported forceful attempts at sexual intercourse by their dates, during which the women resorted to such reactions as screaming, fighting, crying, and pleading. But usually they did not label the event as attempted rape. More recent surveys draw similar conclusions; 22% of college females in Yegidis's (1986) survey reported being a victim at least once of an attempted or a completed rape; 25.3% of a sample of undergraduates in New Zealand reported being raped or having a rape attempted against them (Gavey, 1991). Muehlenhard and Linton (1987) reported that 78% of females had experienced some kind of unwelcome sexual initiative during a date. Even among college males, 6% in one study reported having been sexually assaulted at least once (Lott, Reilly, & Howard, 1982).

The 1992 National Women's Study reported that only 22% of rapes were committed by a stranger to the victim; 29% were committed by a nonrelative acquaintance; 27% by a relative; 9% by a boyfriend or former boyfriend; and 9% by a husband or former husband. In general, date rapes differ from sexual assaults by a stranger in several ways. They tend to occur on weekends, between 10:00 P.M. and 1:00 A.M., and they usually take place at the assailant's home or apartment. Date rapes tend to involve situations in which both the attacker and the victim have been using alcohol or drugs. But they are less likely to involve the use of weapons; instead, the date rapist employs verbal threats and physical prowess to overpower his victim.

## Responding to Rape Victims

Chapter 9 described some of the rights recently provided by the courts and legislatures to victims of violent crimes. Providing psychological assistance to crime victims is an equally important goal. Rape victims suffer physical injuries, emotional pain and humiliation, and sometimes severe psychological aftereffects. Recovery from the trauma of rape can be very slow, and victims often describe a sense that they will never be the same again.

The plight of rape victims has received increased attention through a number of highly publicized cases in which females have come forward to report their experiences. As these cases have unfolded in the public eye, sexual aggression has become a topic of increased discussion among men and women. The gang rape of the Central Park jogger during a "wilding" spree, Patricia Bowman's claim that she was raped by William Kennedy Smith after meeting him in a bar, Desiree Washington's rape charges that resulted in the conviction of former heavyweight boxing champion Mike Tyson, and the arrest of more than a dozen men for a string of daylight sexual assaults on scores of women in Central Park during Puerto Rican National Day celebrations have focused this nation's attention on matters of sexual conduct and on the plight of the victims of sexual aggression.

One part of this discussion has been a debate about whether the names of victims of sexual assault should be made public. The tradition in this country has been to protect the identity of rape victims by not using their names in media coverage. However, in the trial of William Kennedy Smith, both NBC News and the *New York Times* broke with this tradition and published the name of Smith's accuser: Patricia Bowman. Defenders of this decision argued that not naming rape victims perpetuates the stigma, making it more difficult in the long run for victims to come forward and confront their attackers. Critics of the practice claimed that publishing the victim's name invaded her privacy and perhaps ruined her future because she will forever be branded as a rape victim. According to the National Women's Study, most rape victims prefer not to have their names published; 86% of the respondents said they would be less likely to report a rape if they knew their names would be made public.

How do women react to being raped? Burgess and Holmstrom (1974, 1979) describe a collection of symptoms experienced by many rape victims. This pattern—the **rape trauma syndrome**—contains three kinds of reactions: emotional responses, disturbances in functioning, and changes in lifestyle. The primary emotional response is fear, including fear of being left alone

and fear of situations similar to the one in which the rape occurred (Calhoun, Atkeson, & Resick, 1982). Even the most general of associations with the rape or rapist may trigger an emotional response. Judith Rowland (1985), a deputy district attorney, describes a reaction of a white rape victim, Terri Richardson, as the trial of her alleged attacker began. Her attacker was a black man.

> Now, in the summer of 1979 the San Diego Municipal Court had one black judge among its numbers. As it happened . . . his chambers were next door. As Terri and I stood . . . while the bailiff scurried out to reassemble the jury, this lone black judge was also preparing to take the bench. I was aware of him standing in his doorway, wearing his ankle-length black robes. It was only when his bailiff held the courtroom door open for him and he was striding toward it that Terri saw him. In less than the time it took him to get through the door, Terri had bolted from the corridor, through the courtroom, and into the main hallway. By the time I got to the outside corridor, I found only a group of startled jurors. I located Terri in a nearby ladies' room, locked in a stall, crying. With a bit more comforting, she was able to regain her composure and get through both my direct and the defense's cross-examination with only minor bouts of tears, particularly while describing the attack itself. (pp. 166–167)

Guilt and shame are also frequent emotional responses. Victims may blame themselves: "Why was I at a bus stop in a strange part of town?" "Did I check that the back door was locked that night?" They may worry that they didn't resist the attacker strongly enough. The victim often feels a loss of autonomy and control over her body. She may no longer trust others, a loss that may never be fully repaired throughout her lifetime. One victim describes the feeling this way: "I never feel safe. I couldn't stand the apartment where I lived, but I'm so afraid to be alone anywhere. I never was like that before. I carry things with me, like kitchen knives and sticks, when I go out" (quoted in Rowland, 1985, p. 146).

The second type of reaction, a disturbance in functioning, is also frequent among rape victims.

Specific disturbances include changes in sleep patterns (insomnia, nightmares, and early awakening), social withdrawal, changes in appetite, and problems in sexual functioning. Feldman-Summers, Gordon, and Meagher (1979) studied the impact of rape on victims' sexual satisfaction. Although the sample was small, consisting of 15 victims, the study did include a comparison group of women who had not been sexually assaulted. Compared with them, the rape victims reported no difference in frequency of sexual behavior or degree of satisfaction with sexual activities before the rape. However, the victims reported less satisfaction with most areas of sexual functioning one week after the rape than during the period before the rape. The level of dissatisfaction diminished somewhat over the next two months, but women who had been raped did not, during this period, approach the level of sexual satisfaction they had experienced before the attack.

Changes occur not only in emotions and in general functioning but also in lifestyle. Some victims report obsessively checking doors to make sure they are double-locked; one of the victims whose attacker was prosecuted by Rowland (1985) took 45-minute showers two or three times daily, trying to remove the rapist's odor from her body. Other women make major changes in lifestyle, breaking up with their boyfriends, changing jobs, and moving to new residences. The overall socioeconomic impact of rape can be profound; victims of sexual assault are at greater risk of subsequently losing income, becoming unemployed, and going through a divorce (Byrne, Resnick, Kilpatrick, Best, & Saunders, 1999). Women who have been sexually assaulted in the past or who were sexually abused as children are two to three times more likely to suffer a subsequent sexual attack than women without prior sexual victimizations (Nishith, Mechanic, & Resick, 2000). Although the reasons for the heightened risk are not clear, one possibility is that some women who have been victimized before are slower to recognize when they are at risk and therefore are more likely to remain in situations where they are vulnerable (Wilson, Calhoun, & Bernat, 1999).

Women with more than one sexual victimization across their childhood and adult years are more likely to report unplanned and aborted pregnancies (Wyatt, Guthrie, & Notgrass, 1992).

The impact of rape trauma tends to change over time as well. In fact, observers (Burgess & Holmstrom, 1974; Ellison & Buckhout, 1981) have described the typical rape victim's response as a crisis reaction that follows a series of discrete phases.

The *acute phase* begins with the attack and lasts a few hours or a day. During this acute phase, the primary needs of the victim are to understand what is happening, regain control over her life, predict what will happen next, and ventilate her feelings to someone who will listen without passing judgment (Ellison & Buckhout, 1981). At this point, police officers investigating the crime can either help or hinder the victim. For example, a pelvic examination and the collection of any semen samples are necessary at this point; it is unlikely that the suspect can be prosecuted otherwise. But the examination may cause a resurgence of the initial feelings of disruption, helplessness, hostility, and violation, a reaction known as *secondary victimization*. In fact, negative experiences with legal and medical authorities has been shown to increase rape victims' symptoms of posttraumatic stress disorder (Campbell et al., 1999).

Within a few hours or days of the attack, many victims slip into a period of false recovery. Denial occurs: "I'm OK; everything is the same as before." Then a secondary crisis occurs—a sort of "flashback"—in which some of the symptoms of the acute crisis phase, particularly phobias and disturbances in eating and sleeping, return (Ellison & Buckhout, 1981, p. 59). This phase may last for hours or days before another "quiet period" emerges in which the victim feels a range of negative emotions such as loneliness, anger, and guilt.

Because of increased public awareness of the needs of rape victims, rape crisis centers have been established in many cities. These centers provide crisis counseling to victims. Most follow up with at least one further interview (usually by phone), and a third of their clients have from two to six follow-up interviews. The crisis center also checks for pregnancy and sexually transmitted disease.

Long-term counseling for rape victims is more difficult to provide because of the lack of staff at some rape crisis centers and, in some cases, because of a feeling that it is no longer needed. Burgess and Holmstrom (1979), in a follow-up of their earlier sample, found that 74% of rape victims felt that they had recovered and were "back to normal" four to six years after the rape. But 26% did not. A longitudinal study of 20 rape victims (Kilpatrick et al., 1981) measured the personality and mood of these victims and of a matched control group at three time intervals: one month, six months, and one year after the rape. Even at a one-year follow-up, many victims continued to suffer emotionally from the sexual assault. Among the major problems were fear and anxiety, often severe enough to constitute a diagnosis of posttraumatic stress disorder. Several factors contributed to the severity of the victim's reaction. Providing social support is one of the most helpful interventions that can be made. The therapeutic power of social support may derive in part from the fact that women, in particular, tend to react to stress by seeking opportunities for attachment and caregiving—or what psychologist Shelley Taylor has termed the "tend-and-befriend" response (Taylor et al., 2000). (Men, on the other hand, are more likely to respond to stress with the well-known "fight-or-flight" strategy.) Therefore, it might be especially useful to female crime victims to have ample opportunities for social support so that their preference to be with others in times of need can be fully answered.

*Rape trauma syndrome in court.*  Psychologists, along with psychiatrists and other physicians, often testify as expert witnesses in rape trials, especially about the nature and consequences of rape trauma syndrome (Fischer, 1989; Frazier & Borgida, 1985, 1988). This syndrome is usually thought of as an example of a posttraumatic stress disorder, similar to that experienced by veterans of combat, survivors of natural disasters, and victims of other violent crimes. The expert can be of special use to the prosecution in those trials in which the defendant admits that sexual intercourse took place but claims that the woman was a willing participant; evidence of rape trauma syndrome can be used to corroborate the complainant's version of the facts (Frazier & Borgida, 1985). In addition, jurors are often not familiar with the reactions that rape victims frequently experience (Borgida & Brekke, 1985), and so psychological experts can educate the jury. Courts around the country are divided, however, on the admissibility of such testimony, and the resulting controversy has generated considerable debate.

The main argument against admitting expert testimony on the rape trauma syndrome is as follows: The psychological responses of rape victims are not unique to rape and are not uniform; thus, it is impossible to say with certainty that a woman exhibiting any given set of responses has been raped. Therefore, a psychologist should not be allowed to testify that a woman is suffering from rape trauma syndrome because to do so is tantamount to telling the jury that she has been raped, which should remain a matter for the jury to decide. Many courts also reject expert testimony on the rape trauma syndrome on the ground that the reliability of the syndrome has not been established.

## Legislation and Court Decisions

Throughout history, rape has had a rather uncertain status within whatever legal system was in effect. Laws about rape in the United States, rooted in English common law, changed little for three centuries (Harper, 1984). The first American law about rape, created in Massachusetts, imposed the death penalty on the rapist except when the victim was unmarried, reflecting a view that women belonged to their husbands (Estrich, 1987). But beginning in the 1970s, legislation about rape began to undergo dramatic review and revision. Since Michigan initiated its reform in 1974, most of the other states have modified their rape statutes or passed new ones. These changes are correlated with our increased knowledge about rape, generated by social science research and feminist groups. The revisions have usually involved replacing the term *rape* with the term *sexual assault,* reflecting the view that this crime primarily involves the sexual expression of violence (Harper, 1984). This term also eliminates any lingering requirements that the state provide corroborating evidence for the victim's testimony, and it devotes more attention to the extent of physical and psychological injury inflicted on the victim.

The basic definition of sexual assault is non-consenting sexual contact (e.g., intercourse) that is obtained by using force or coercion against the victim. But how do we distinguish between rape and a consensual sexual act? No single standard defines what is meant by *nonconsent,* which is why, despite the legal reforms, the nature of the victim's conduct in a sexual assault often remains an issue.

*Shifts in rape laws.*    How much does the victim's behavior contribute to the determination of nonconsent? Is resistance relevant or necessary?

Until the 1980s, about four-fifths of the states still imposed a resistance standard—it had to be shown that the victim attempted to resist a sexual assault—in their definition of rape (Largen, 1988). But most states now concentrate their sexual assault statutes more on the behavior of the assailant and have expanded their definition of force to include coercion or intimidation by the alleged assailant. The standard of resistance has been weakened or eliminated almost entirely.

A second shift in sexual assault laws has been to define several different crime levels. Previously, some states found that with only one degree of offense, which carried possibly severe penalties, juries saw the sentence (which could be life in prison) as too extreme for some cases; hence, they opted for not-guilty verdicts. Many of the newer laws divide sexual assault into degrees according to the extent of force or threat that was used. For example, a *first-degree* sexual assault (rape) would involve sexual intercourse by forcible compulsion

under aggravated circumstances (e.g., using a deadly weapon or kidnapping the victim). A *second-degree* rape would require sexual intercourse by forcible compulsion. A *third-degree* rape would be defined as sexual intercourse without consent or with threat of substantial harm to property rights.

One other legislative change is that up until approximately 1980, most states did not consider the sexual assault of a spouse to be rape. Now, all the states have eliminated this exception and recognize **spousal rape** as a crime. In Florida in 1984, a 41-year-old man was found guilty of kidnapping and raping his wife. He was the first man to be convicted of a sexual assault that occurred while the couple was married and living together. Even though spousal rape is now considered a crime in every state, it is not always treated the same as a sexual assault involving unmarried persons. For example, some states impose a shorter "reporting period" on victims of spousal rape compared to victims of other violent crimes. If a victim does not report the assault within this period, the spouse cannot be prosecuted. Another difference between spousal rape and nonspousal rape is the requirement that force or threat of force by the spouse must be proved rather than the lack of consent by the victim, which is the requirement in many nonspousal sexual assault statues.

*The rape victim as a trial witness.*    Shifts in the rape laws have also addressed a persistent problem in the trials of alleged rapists. Defense attorneys have often tried to make the rape victim look like the instigator of the sexual act. The overriding effect of this cross-examination strategy has been to punish innocent victims for asserting their rights to bring charges and to testify against their alleged attackers.

Some defense attorneys use cross-examination to attack the victim's truthfulness and her general morality. They try to portray the victim as sexually promiscuous by graphically inquiring about her past sex life and even bringing forth a string of past lovers to testify about the breadth and frequency of her sexual experiences. Jurors can be influenced by testimony about the woman's character, reputation, and lifestyle (Lee, 1985). In one savage rape, the victim's jaw was fractured in two places, but the jury acquitted the defendant because it found that there may have been sexual relations on previous occasions and the two persons had been drinking together on the night of the incident (Kalven & Zeisel, 1966, p. 251). As a result of this type of problem, all states have adopted **rape shield laws** to provide victims with more protection as trial witnesses. In addition, the Privacy Protection for Rape Victims Act of 1978 amended the federal rules of evidence with regard to the admissibility of testimony on the victim's sexual history with parties other than the defendant.

Although these laws differ from jurisdiction to jurisdiction (Borgida, 1981), they usually prohibit inquiries about the victim's previous sexual conduct unless it can be shown that the questions are relevant to specific issues of the case. In Connecticut, for example, testimony about prior sexual activity is admissible only if it does one of the following:

1. Raises the issue of consent by showing prior sexual conduct between the victim and the defendant
2. Shows that the defendant was not the source of semen, pregnancy, or sexually transmitted disease
3. Attacks the victim's credibility, provided she has testified on direct examination about her past sexual conduct
4. Is otherwise so relevant to a critical issue in the case that excluding it would violate the defendant's constitutional rights

An example of evidence that is so relevant that excluding it would violate the defendant's constitutional rights is found in *Commonwealth v. Wall* (1992). A child victim had been placed in an aunt's home following a sexual assault by her mother's boyfriend. The child was unhappy in the aunt's home and allegedly fabricated a sexual-assault claim against her uncle in an attempt to

be removed. The Pennsylvania court held that it was relevant to the defense to introduce evidence of the earlier sexual assault.

Wide latitude is still allowed in questioning rape victims, and in some jurisdictions, rape shield laws may not shield the victim from very much. Borgida (1980, 1981) classified these laws into three categories, based on the extent to which evidence is excluded, and then assessed how mock jurors reacted to different versions of a rape trial reenactment reflecting each of these categories. Consider, for example, the following:

> The complainant testifies that she met the defendant at a singles bar, danced and drank with him, and accepted his offer to drive her home. She testifies that at the front door he refused to leave, forced his way into her apartment, and raped her. The defendant wants to prove that the complainant had previously consented to intercourse with casual acquaintances she had met at singles bars. Is the evidence relevant? (Borgida, 1981, p. 234)

In a few states, a judge would likely rule that the evidence of the victim's past liaisons is relevant to the fact at issue and admit the evidence. But, under the more restrictive statutes of most states (Borgida, 1981, p. 213), such evidence probably would be excluded. These states have concluded that such evidence would be prejudicial (against the victim). As it turns out, Borgida's (1981) study supported this expectation. The "jurors" were reluctant to convict the defendant when testimony was introduced regarding the victim's past sexual relationships with other men. Although no state permits defense attorneys to offer evidence of the victim's sexual history in all situations, some states recognize defense arguments that the victim's sexual history can bear directly on the crime charged in certain situations. For example, North Carolina allows evidence of "a pattern of sexual behavior so distinctive and so closely resembling the defendant's version of the alleged encounter with the complainant as to tend to prove that such complainant consented to the acts charged, or behaved in such a manner as to lead the defendant to reasonably believe that the complainant consented" (*North Carolina Evidence Rule 412*, 1983).

Even if stringent rape shield laws are in force, some jurors will continue to doubt the testimony of rape victims or will use the testimony to make attributions about the witnesses' honesty. For example, mock jurors who are relatively lacking in empathy for rape victims are less likely to see an attacker as responsible for a rape (Deitz, Littman, & Bentley, 1984). Mock jurors who are low on rape victim empathy will take the fact that an alleged victim stares intently at the defendant throughout her testimony and conclude from that behavior that she is lying (Weir, Willis, & Wrightsman, 1989; Weir & Wrightsman, 1990).

One experience that increases empathy for rape victims is to be personally acquainted with a woman who has been raped. In a laboratory study in which subjects read summaries of witness testimony and then rated the responsibility of a man charged with rape, men and women who themselves knew a rape victim were twice as likely to find the accused guilty of rape as were men and women who did not personally know a rape victim (Wiener, Wiener, & Grisso, 1989).

As can be seen, the recent changes in rape laws cover several aspects of the crime. Although these changes are impressive, their impact on the courts is unclear. One thorough review of the effects of rape law reforms (Goldberg-Ambrose, 1992) concluded that some have been quite successful but others have had little impact. Myths and false assumptions held by judges, juries, and trial attorneys remain an obstacle; it is easier to change laws than to change attitudes (Largen, 1988).

## Preventing Rape

As more is learned about the frequency and consequences of rape, a primary goal of concerned citizens, law enforcement officials, and social scientists has been to develop effective interventions for preventing rape. Two basic strategies have been emphasized: (1) training potential victims how best to protect themselves against rape and (2) designing effective treatment for rapists so that they do not repeat their crimes.

*Training potential victims to reduce the risk of rape.* If a woman finds herself in a situation in which a man begins to sexually assault her, what should she do? Should she scream? Should she fight back, or should she try to reason with him? Should she submit to the attack, especially if the assailant has a weapon, all the while trying to notice as many identifying features of the attacker as possible? There is no uniformly correct response, just as there is no one type of rapist. However, on the issue of passive compliance, a Justice Department survey of over a million attacks (quoted in Meddis & Kelley, 1985) found that women who did not resist a rape attack were twice as likely to suffer a completed rape as women who tried to protect themselves.

As we have already seen, national surveys suggest that between one-fifth to one-quarter of college women have suffered a sexual assault and that the majority of victims were acquainted with their assailants before the assault. Research has also uncovered several risk factors associated with sexual assault. For example, rape victims tend to have suffered a disproportionately high number of sexual assaults prior to their most recent assault. Acquaintance rapes are more frequent (1) when both the victim and the assailant have been drinking or using drugs, (2) when on dates in which the man pays all the expenses, and (3) when the date is at an isolated location. Several colleges and universities have incorporated this information about risk factors into rape prevention programs aimed at changing attitudes about sexuality, challenging rape myths and sex-role stereotypes, and improving women's coping responses in potentially dangerous situations.

In the typical rape prevention program, participants discuss several facts and myths about rape, learn how to avoid situations involving heavy use of alcohol, practice resisting pressure for unwanted sexual activity, and role-play other strategies for protecting themselves. The programs try to help women change behaviors and to dispel the notion that victims cause sexual assault. They also strive to minimize the blaming of women as the cause of sexual trauma. Evaluation of the success of these programs in preventing assaults is just beginning.

In one large experimental study (Hanson & Gidycz, 1993), 181 college women participated in a nine-week acquaintance rape prevention program while 165 others were assigned to a no-program control group. The prevention program was designed to debunk common myths about rape, educate women about how to protect themselves against rape, alter risky dating practices, improve communication between men and women concerning sexual behavior, and prevent sexual assaults. Participants discussed rape myths and protective behaviors, watched videotapes that depicted risky situations and the protective behaviors that women can use in these situations, and shared general information about how to prevent acquaintance rape.

The effects of the program were assessed nine weeks later. The prevention program appeared effective for women who had never been victimized before the study; 14% of the women in the control group reported that they had suffered a sexual victimization during the period studied compared with only 6% of the women in the prevention program. However, among women who had histories of sexual victimization, there was no difference in the victimization rates of the program and control groups.

These results confirm that previous sexual assaults are a potent risk factor for future assaults. What they do not explain is why prior sexual assault is such a strong risk for repeated victimization. Perhaps victimization lowers self-esteem so that a woman thinks she has already been so damaged that subsequent victimizations don't matter. Alternatively, victimization may convince a woman that she will not be wanted for any reason other than sex so she continues to place herself in sexually risky situations. Whatever the explanation, these results send a clear message for other prevention programs: the earlier the attempt at prevention, the better. If women partici-

pate in assault prevention services before they are ever victimized, it appears that the success of such services will be substantially greater.

*Designing effective treatments for rapists.*   Society is rightfully concerned about the likelihood of sex offenders repeating their crimes (Quinsey, Lalumiere, Rice, & Harris, 1995). In some states, men convicted of sex crimes are required to complete a sex-offender program before being considered for parole (see Chapter 17). In such programs, the offender must acknowledge responsibility for his actions and participate in special treatment programs (Glamser, 1997).

The treatment of rapists can involve psychological, physical, and medical procedures; in many treatment programs, different interventions are often combined. On the international scene, psychosurgery and surgical castration have been used, but their effectiveness is unclear. Because of the ethical controversies that surround these procedures, few experts advocate their use in the United States (Marshall, Jones, Ward, Johnston, & Barbaree, 1991).

In the United States it is not uncommon to prescribe antiandrogen drugs to sex offenders in order to reduce their sex drive, a procedure sometimes referred to as *chemical castration.* The most common treatment involves giving offenders a synthetic female hormone, MPA, which has the trade name of Depo-Provera. MPA decreases the level of testosterone in the body, thereby decreasing sexual arousal in most men. Its use with sexually aggressive offenders has met with mixed success (Marshall et al., 1991). But the drug has also been associated with a number of negative side effects, including weight gain, hair loss, feminization of the body, and gall bladder problems.

In some cases, men were told they would not have to serve any time in prison if they agreed to submit to drug treatments. In 1983, Joseph Frank Smith, 30, of San Antonio, Texas, became the first convicted rapist actually to receive drug treatments as a condition of his ten-year probation. Feminists, on the one side, and defense attorneys, on the other, have raised a number of concerns and criticisms regarding this procedure. For instance, its effectiveness has yet to be fully assessed, even though its advocates claim a very high success rate.

Antiandrogen treatments have problems other than negative side effects. The rate of men dropping out of such treatment prematurely is very high, and failure to complete treatment is one of the strongest predictors of recidivism for sex offenders (Hanson & Bussiere, 1998). Of greater concern is the fact that the treatment does not always reduce sexual arousal and sexual offenses. In some men, arousal is not dependent on their level of testosterone, so the drugs have minimal effects on their sexual behavior. This point relates to the fact that rape is often an act of violence, not of inappropriate sexual arousal; consequently, drugs aimed at reducing sexual desire may be pointing at the wrong target. Even if the drugs inhibit sexual appetites, they may not control violent outbursts. Hence, they would not truly rehabilitate these offenders.

Another major approach to treating aggressive sexual offenders involves combining several behavior therapy techniques into an integrated treatment package designed to increase offenders' self-control, improve their social skills, modify their sexual preferences, and teach them how to prevent relapses of their offenses. These programs are usually situated in institutions because of the prison sentences imposed on offenders, but they have also been implemented in the community. Some programs are run in a group format; others rely on individual treatment (Hall, 1996).

These integrated programs employ a wide range of treatment techniques. Sex education and training in social skills are common ingredients because of the widespread belief that sex offenders are often socially incompetent. Biofeedback and aversive conditioning are often used to decrease inappropriate sexual arousal and replace it with arousal to nonaggressive sexual cues. Existing programs appear able to produce short-term decreases in recidivism, but longer-term improvements have been difficult to achieve. As a result, relapse prevention techniques (which have proven useful in

the treatment of drug addictions and cigarette smoking) have been added to some programs.

## Detecting the Rapist

What methods exist to prove whether a given suspect committed a rape? The late 1980s saw the introduction of a device that initially was acclaimed as the greatest advance in the science of crime detection in a century (Lohr, 1987). The technique, sometimes informally called "genetic fingerprinting," relies on genetic X-ray analyses of DNA (or deoxyribonucleic acid) samples, which produce patterns for each of us as distinctive as our fingerprints. DNA samples can be taken from any kind of biological material, including hair or skin, as well as from substances such as blood, saliva, and semen. Geneticists have claimed that the identifying patterns are absolutely specific for each individual.

An early use of the procedure in a highly publicized case in Great Britain was described in a nonfiction book by Joseph Wambaugh, *The Blooding* (1989). On separate occasions, three years apart but in the same location, two 15-year-old girls were sexually assaulted and strangled to death. For several years, despite intensive efforts by the police, no killer was found. But with the development of DNA technology, the Leicestershire police decided to obtain blood samples from every possible perpetrator of the crimes and compare these with the analyses of the semen taken from the bodies of the victims. All men living in the vicinity who had been born between 1953 and 1970—which turned out to be thousands of men—were asked to present themselves for a "blooding"; if they did not appear, the police searched them out. Despite the trampling of civil liberties involved in forcing thousands of innocent people to submit to the test, and even though the killer tried to cheat, the police found their man (Walker, 1989). When confronted, the murderer ultimately confessed.

Genetic fingerprinting is a rapidly growing industry in the United States. The FBI uses the procedure in its crime lab, as do most state crime labs. The results of DNA testing proved to be one of the most controversial elements of the O. J. Simpson criminal trial, and it is increasingly being used, as we discuss in the next chapter, to evaluate prisoners' claims that they are innocent of crimes for which they were convicted and in some cases sentenced to capital punishment. An increasing number of states require genetic profiling of people convicted of sex offenses before they are released.

However, there are concerns about genetic fingerprinting, even beyond the possible violations of civil rights that compulsory testing might involve. For example, the crime laboratory at the Orange County, California, sheriff's de-

partment sent about 50 blood and semen samples drawn from about 20 people to each of three labs. The labs were asked to identify which specimens came from the same people. One lab was wrong on 1 of the 44 matches it found; a second was wrong on 1 out of 50. The third, more cautious lab offered no conclusions on about 14 of the samples but got all 37 of its reported matches correct (M. Thompson, 1989). Across the board, the accuracy rate was 98%, but not absolutely perfect. It may be that current technology is unable to make matches perfectly, or it may be that certain assumptions about the characteristics of DNA identification are false (Thompson & Ford, 1989).

# SUMMARY

**1. What is the frequency of victimization?** According to the National Crime Victimization Survey, crime victimization occurs at a rate of 217 incidents per 1000 persons. But this figure underestimates the true extent of victimization that befalls an unknown number of individuals in homes, schools, and the workplace

**2. What are two types of sexual harassment recognized by the courts?** The first type of harassment, quid pro quo harassment, refers to sexual demands made in exchange for benefits or threats of punishment if the respondent does not comply. The second type is harassment that creates a hostile work environment; it often involves demeaning comments, acts of touching or attempted intimacy, or the display of provocative photographs or artwork.

**3. What are the components of the battered spouse (woman) syndrome?** The battered woman syndrome refers to a collection of responses, many of which are displayed by individuals who are repeatedly physically abused by their intimate partners. These include learned helplessness, lowered self-esteem, impaired functioning, fear or terror, loss of the assumption of invulnerability, and anger or rage.

**4. What types of research have psychologists conducted on crime victimization?** Three areas of crime victimization have received special attention from psychologists: physical/sexual abuse of children, violent victimization and posttraumatic stress disorder, and the psychology of rape.

**5. What factors predict the development of PTSD following a crime victimization?** The extent of injury suffered in the crime and the belief that the victim has no control over his or her life heightens the risk of developing PTSD. Treatments that help restore a sense of control and that help victims reexperience the trauma so that its emotional power is drained are the most effective interventions for preventing and reducing PTSD after a crime victimization.

**6. How have the laws about rape changed?** Beginning in the 1970s, state legislatures and the courts began to modify long-standing laws about rape. One general type of shift was to deemphasize resistance as a requirement in showing that a rape took place. A second shift was to divide rape into several degrees of offense, permitting juries to render guilty verdicts more frequently. Virtually all states now permit a husband to be charged with rape against his wife; most states now have rape shield laws that restrict the defense attorney's questioning of the victim about her sexual history.

**7.** *How can rape be prevented?* Prevention of rape has taken two routes. One is to determine what responses by potential victims are most effective in warding off a sexual assault. The other is to use effective treatments for convicted rapists. Antiandrogen drugs, which reduce sex drive, and a combination of various behavior therapy techniques have shown some effectiveness as treatment for convicted rapists.

## KEY TERMS

| | | | |
|---|---|---|---|
| abuse excuse | borderline personality | rape shield laws | victimology |
| attribution theory* |    disorder* | rape trauma syndrome | |
| battered woman | posttraumatic stress | self-defense | |
|    syndrome |    disorder | spousal rape | |

---

**InfoTrac**
**College**
**Edition**

For additional readings go to **http://www.infotrac-college.com/wadsworth** and enter a search term related to your interest. The key terms that have been asterisked above will pull up several related articles.

**ORIENTING QUESTIONS**

1. *What are the purposes of punishment?*
2. *How are the values of discretion and fairness reflected in sentencing decisions?*
3. *What factors influence sentencing decisions?*

**4.** *What special factors are considered in the sentencing of offenders repeatedly convicted of sex crimes?*

**5.** *How is the sentence of death decided by juries?*

**6.** *What legal rights do prisoners have?*

Although crime rates have declined in recent years, no other industrialized country except Russia incarcerates its citizens at the rate of that in the United States. In 1997, the U.S. rate of incarceration was 645 inmates per 100,000 residents, more than four times what it had been in 1970. Two-thirds of those incarcerated were in prisons, the rest in city and county jails (Caplow & Simon, 1999). Drug offenders account for much of the increase; in just 17 years, from 1980 to 1997, the rate of incarceration of drug offenders increased tenfold (Blumstein & Beck, 1999). Expanded use of mandatory prison sentences and longer prison sentences in general have also fed the increase in incarceration. The average sentence for a person sent to prison in 1997 was 43 months, compared to a term of 38 months in 1990.

What can be done about crime? How should we respond to individual criminals? The nation's inmate population is over 1.8 million. Does it make sense to lock up more and more offenders? Incarceration comes at a price. Every dollar spent on corrections means one less dollar for other programs. As an example, adjusting for inflation, state spending for prisons increased 30% from 1987 to 1995, while state spending on higher education declined 18% in the same period (Caplow & Simon, 1999).

# Responses to Crime: The Issue of Crime Control

Chapter 1 described Packer's (1964) two models of the criminal justice system: the due process model and the crime control model. These models differ in their views of punishment. The crime control model, which has dominated the thinking of police officers, prosecutors, and many judges

in the past 25 years, sees the sole aim of law enforcement to be the apprehension and punishment of criminals. Its major purpose is to punish offenders so that they will not repeat their offenses and so that others will be deterred from similar acts.

Punishment of criminals, whether by community service, fines, or imprisonment, can have several purposes. At least seven different goals have been identified (see, e.g., Greenberg & Ruback, 1984):

1. *General deterrence.* The punishment of one offender and the publicity given to it are assumed to discourage other potential lawbreakers. Some advocates of the death penalty, for example, believe that fear of death may be our strongest motivation; hence, they believe the death penalty will serve as a general deterrent to serious crime.

2. *Individual deterrence.* Punishment of the offender is assumed to keep that person from committing other crimes in the future. Some theories assume that many criminals lack adequate internal inhibitors; hence, punitive sanctions must be used to teach them that their behavior will be controlled—if not by them, then by society.

3. *Incapacitation.* If a convicted offender is sent to prison, society can feel safe while the felon is confined there. One influential position (Wilson, 1975) sees a major function of incapacitation simply to age the criminal—an understandable, but very limited goal, given that many more crimes are committed by the young than by the old and that the rate of offending declines as offenders grow older.

4. *Retribution.* Society believes that offenders should not benefit from their crimes; rather, they should receive their "just desserts." The moral cornerstone of punishment is that it

should be delivered to people who deserve it as a consequence of their misdeeds.

5. *Moral outrage.* Punishment can give society a means of catharsis and relief from the feelings of frustration, hurt, loss, and anger that result from being victims of crime; what emerges is thought to be a sense of satisfaction that offenders have paid for what they have done to others.

6. *Rehabilitation.* One hope in sentencing has always been that offenders will recognize the error of their ways and develop new skills, values, and lifestyles so that they can return to normal life and become law abiding. Rehabilitation as a goal received a boost from an influential book by the psychiatrist Karl Menninger (1966), *The Crime of Punishment,* which proposed that criminals are capable of change if they are placed in humane prisons. However, the data generally indicate that correctional rehabilitation has not been as effective as Menninger first suggested.

7. *Restitution.* Wrongdoers should compensate victims for their damages and losses. Typical statutes require judges, in imposing a criminal sentence, to make defendants pay for victims' out-of-pocket expenses, property damage, and other monetary losses. Restitution is often a condition of probation.

Most of these goals are utilitarian. They look forward to accomplishing a useful outcome: to compensate the victim, to deter crime, to incapacitate or rehabilitate the defendant. Two of the goals, however, are retributive and look backward toward the offense. Those are retribution (or "just desserts") and moral outrage, a close cousin of retribution (Kaplan, 1996).

Although the original purpose of prisons was to rehabilitate (the root of *penitentiary* is *penitent,* and many prisons are still called *correctional* institutions), it is now assumed that prisons are not very effective at rehabilitating offenders. This opinion, sometimes dubbed the "nothing works" position, originated with a review article about rehabilitation by Robert Martinson (1974) who, after reviewing scores of outcome studies, concluded that most attempts at offender rehabilita-

tion were failures. Although it is now recognized that this conclusion was too pessimistic—Martinson (1979) himself revised his opinion and acknowledged that there was more evidence favoring rehabilitation than he originally believed—the "nothing works" view has prevailed among many politicians, policymakers, and the public at large (Haney, 1997b).

When rehabilitation was the dominant goal, criminal sentences were expected to accomplish something other than incarceration and punishment. In the 21st century, however, rehabilitation as a goal of sentencing has lost much of its popular appeal. And as the goal of rehabilitation has fallen into decline, criminal sentences have become longer, and prison conditions have grown more harsh. It now appears that the public wants to punish convicts, and politicians are happy to respond. An example: Sheriff Joe Arpaio of Maricopa County, Arizona, puts prisoners in "leaky, dilapidated military-surplus tents set on gravel fields surrounded by barbed wire" and feeds them "bologna streaked with green and blue packaging dye" (Morrison, 1995). He puts men—and women—on chain gangs, to humiliate offenders and deter others. His philosophy, which has gained him national publicity and notoriety, is to make jail so unpleasant no one would want to come back—while saving money at the same time. Allegedly to conserve funds, coffee is no longer served in the Niagara County, New York, jail; smoking is banned entirely in Texas, Utah, and Arizona facilities (Curriden, 1995a).

First introduced in the House of Representatives in 1995, and kept alive in subsequent Congresses, the "No Frills Prisons Act" would require states receiving federal money to eliminate "luxurious" prison conditions, defined as including unmonitored telephone calls, in-cell television viewing, personally owned computers, in-cell coffee pots, weight-lifting equipment, and practice on any musical instrument for more than one hour a day! For violent offenders, the bill would require states to deny all television and more than an hour a day spent in sports or exercise (HR 370, 1999). Because they have to administer the institutions in which these punitive measures would be implemented, correctional officials are appalled at the prospect of prisons seething with idle men denied opportunities for recreation, education, and entertainment. "Take away television, they say, and you take away a legitimate means of occupying an inmate's time and mind. Without that diversion . . . prisons will have to hire more guards, which means more money from taxpayers" (Curriden, 1995a, p. 74).

Jails and prisons are generally designed to punish, not to rehabilitate. Authority is centralized, communication is formalized, and rules are strictly maintained. The original purpose of prisons included the goal of creating a controlled environment that would separate the offender from corrupting influences of the real world. Now, overcrowded prisons appear best suited to giving inmates enriched opportunities to learn new criminal behaviors and attitudes from one another. Given this state of affairs, it is worthwhile to examine the system of assigning criminal punishments.

## Sentencing: Difficult Choices

The sentencing of a convicted criminal lies at the very center of society's efforts to ensure public order. Hoffman and Stone-Meierhoefer (1979) go so far as to state, "Next to the determination of guilt or innocence, a determination waived by a substantial proportion of defendants who plead guilty (around 90%), the sentencing decision is probably the most important decision made about the criminal defendant in the entire process" (p. 241).

Sentencing is a judicial function, but sentencing decisions are largely controlled by the legislative branch—Congress and state legislatures. The legislative branch dictates the extent of judges' discretion, and many legislators argue that judges should have little or no discretion. They emphasize retribution and argue that the punishment should fit the crime. Mandatory sentences, sentencing guidelines, and the abolition of parole

are the primary ingredients in these "get tough" schemes. On the other hand, a few legislators still maintain that the sentence should fit the offender—that judges should have discretion to make the sentence fit not only the crime but the criminal as well.

In some states and the federal system, the legislative branch has imposed a **determinate sentencing** system on the judiciary. In these systems, sentences are determined (fixed) by statutes and sentencing guidelines. Judges have little discretion over the sentences, and there is no parole. In such systems, the primary goals are retribution and moral outrage. There is little concern for the offender's personal characteristics, other than his criminal record.

In other states, judges have wide discretion, and parole is available. All seven of the sentencing goals listed earlier are taken into account. The focus tends to be more on the offender than on the offense. Judges (and parole boards) consider the reasons why the offender committed the crime and the likelihood of rehabilitation if the offender is probated or paroled.

Many sentencing systems are mixed. Judges and parole boards have discretion in some cases, but not in others. Statutes fixing mandatory minimums to be served are often used in a system in which judges otherwise have wide discretion. These sentencing statutes must be complied with, even when their results seem unconscionable. For example, in *United States v. Goff* (1993), a federal judge was forced to sentence a wheelchair-bound quadraplegic to ten years in prison for sale of LSD; one of the appellate judges in the case commented that "common sense is removed from the sentencing process when a judge is barred from fashioning a punishment that fits the unique circumstances presented by a defendant in a particular case" (*Goff*, p. 367). Recently, a number of groups, including the American Psychological Association, have spoken out against mandatory minimums. "[T]hey have done nothing to reduce crime or put big-time drug dealers out of business. What they have done . . . is to fill prisons with young, nonviolent, low-level drug offenders serving long sentences at enormous and growing cost to taxpayers" (Hansen, 1999, p. 14).

## Discretion Justified as a Value

Discretion allows judges to capitalize on their perceptions of the crime, the criminal, and the circumstances so that their decisions can "serve, within limits set by law, that elusive concept of justice which the law in its wisdom refuses to define" (Gaylin, 1974, p. 67). Those who advocate individually tailored sentences note that each offender is different and deserves to be treated as an individual. As Tonry (1996) observes: "[B]ecause dessert theories place primary emphasis on linking deserved punishments to the severity of crimes, in the interest of treating cases alike, they lead to disregard of other ethically relevant differences between offenders—like their personal backgrounds and the effects of punishments on them and their families—and thereby treat unlike cases alike" (p. 15).

As we enter the 21st century, some states (but not the federal government) are beginning to embrace the concept of **intermediate sanctions** for nonviolent offenders (Carlson, Hess, & Orthmann, 1999). Intermediate sanctions serve utilitarian goals—rehabilitation, deterrence, restitution—and are tailored to fit the offender. An example of an intermediate sanction is intensively supervised probation. A probationer serving such a sentence might be required to report daily to the probation officer, submit to random drug tests, stay away from certain people, and work or go to school. Intermediate sanctions are individualized; they focus on the offender, rather than the offense. State legislatures adopt intermediate sanctions to save money and, in so doing, give trial judges alternatives to prison. For example, the 1998 Kentucky legislature adopted a two-track system. Violent offenders are sent to prison to serve at least 85% of their sentences; most nonviolent offenders receive an intermediate sanction in one of the following: a halfway house; home incarceration; jail with work release; community service; residential treatment program; intensive probation supervision; and "any

other specified counseling program, rehabilitation or treatment program, or facility."

In Vermont, although violent offenders still go to prison, community boards fix the sanctions for people convicted of nonviolent misdemeanors and low-level felonies. A woman who wrote bad checks was ordered to write letters of apology and an essay on what she had learned. A reckless driver was ordered to issue a public apology and spend time with brain-damaged children. This approach, called "**restorative justice**," is designed to repair the damage caused by the offender (Hansen, 1997). Restorative justice emphasizes three basic principles:

- ◆ Crimes injure victims, communities, and offenders; therefore the criminal justice system should repair those injuries,
- ◆ Victims, offenders, and communities—not just the government—should be actively involved in the criminal justice process,
- ◆ In promoting justice, the government should keep order and the community should keep the peace (Carlson, Hess & Orthmann, 1999, p. 31).

Restorative justice and intermediate sanctions both reflect a sentencing philosophy that is utilitarian and values discretion. Although public opinion is usually assumed to be unsympathetic to this philosophy, the public appears to be much more attuned to these values when it is adequately informed about the costs and effects of alternatives to imprisonment. ◆ Box 17-1 summarizes one study illustrating this point.

A leading advocate of alternatives to imprisonment, Professor Dan Kahan, argues that, to be acceptable to the public, a sentence must *express* society's outrage. He maintains that the expressive dimension of punishment is not satisfied by "straight" probation, "mere" fines, or direct community service. Probation appears to be no punishment, a fine appears to be a means to "buy one's way out," and community service is something everyone ought to do. Kahan argues that attaching a **shaming penalty** to an intermediate

## The Science of

**BOX 17-1    Sentencing: Public opinion about alternatives to prison**

A 1989 public opinion study by the Public Agenda Foundation (Doble & Klein, 1989) found that citizens, after being informed about prison costs and alternative sentences, often softened their views of imprisonment as the only adequate punishment for crime. The researchers asked a cross section of 422 Alabama residents to complete a detailed questionnaire about their preferred "sentences"— either prison or probation—in 23 hypothetical cases ranging from shoplifting to rape and armed robbery. The participants then watched a videotape that discussed prison costs, described problems of over-

crowding in Alabama prisons, and presented five alternatives to incarceration: strict probation, strict probation plus restitution, strict probation plus community service, house arrest, and "boot camp." The video presented arguments for and against these alternatives.

After watching the video, participants convened in groups to discuss how the alternatives would work for various types of offenders. The subjects then filled out a second questionnaire for the 23 hypothetical cases, selecting sentences from the original two options (probation and prison) and the five "alternative sentences." Their atti-

tudes changed dramatically. On the initial questionnaire a majority of participants would have sent 18 of the 23 defendants to prison; after the video and discussion, they would have sentenced only 4 of the 23 to prison. However, after learning of the alternatives, respondents would have imposed restrictions greater than straight probation on 18 of the 19 defendants not sent to prison. The participants favored sentences that required defendants to take active responsibility for their actions; thus, restitution and community service were preferred over house arrest or strict probation.

---

sanction will make it more acceptable to the public and more meaningful to offenders.

Shaming is a traditional means by which communities punished offenders. In colonial days, those who committed minor offenses were put in stocks in a public place for several hours for all to see and ridicule. Serious offenders were branded or otherwise marked so they would be "shamed" for life. In Williamsburg, Virginia, thieves were nailed to the stocks by the ear; after a period of time the sheriff would rip the offender from the stocks, thus "ear-marking" the offender for life (Book, 1999). Increasingly employed in state courts, the modern counterpart to shaming (without mutilation) is to allow offenders to avoid all or part of a jail sentence by publicly renouncing their crimes in a humiliating way. In Atlanta, a thief was given a choice: six months in jail, or five weekends in jail and 30 hours walking around the Fulton County courthouse wearing a sign

reading, "I AM A CONVICTED THIEF." The offender chose the latter and endured the honks and catcalls of passers-by (Book, 1999).

Kahan argues that the public is not satisfied with intermediate sanctions in which offenders merely "pay their debt to society" by doing good deeds through community service. He would require those performing community service to do so in distinctive clothing—so that it is clear they are not volunteers or paid workers (Kahan, 1996). Shaming has intuitive appeal as a penal sanction, because everyone has experienced shaming in childhood. Parents teach their children "to be good" by making them ashamed of their bad behavior. A child forced to confess to the store owner that he stole a piece of candy should associate embarrassment with theft from that time on (Book, 1999). Shaming may be effective in deterring bad conduct, and it is a remedy that should be considered in many cases.

**BOX 17-2**    **Innovative sentences: Clever, cute, or cruel?**

Local and state judges have wide discretion in the punishments they give. Here are examples of innovative punishments, many of which inject an element of shaming into the penalty:

1. A judge in Sarasota County, Florida, required drunk drivers to place a bumper sticker saying "Convicted DUI" on their cars if they wish to drive to work (*Goldschmitt v. State,* 1986).

2. A circuit court judge in South Dakota sentenced convicted cattle rustlers to shovel manure for a week.

3. A construction manager who was an avid golfer was convicted of diverting $300,000 in material and labor from a California building project in order to build a house near the famous Pebble Beach golf course. The judge ruled that for nine months he had to go to a busy public golf course and schedule tee-off times for other golfers. He was not allowed to play himself and was incarcerated except during working hours (Neff, 1987).

4. The punishment that dentist Michael Koplik received for sexually abusing a heavily sedated female patient was to provide free treatment for six AIDS patients who had been rejected by other dentists (Sachs, 1989).

5. Houston judge Ted Poe ordered a piano teacher who molested two students not to play the piano for 20 years and to give his piano to a school (Reske, 1996).

6. Judge Poe ordered a teenager who had stolen and damaged a woman's car to turn over his car to the woman while her car was being fixed (Reske, 1996).

---

Of course, shaming can be excessive or counterproductive (see ◆ **Box 17-2**), and if it is used too often, it might even lose some of its power to embarrass offenders (Massaro, 1997). In *People v. Meyer* (1997), the judge placed a 62-year-old man convicted of aggravated battery on probation and then required him to put 4' × 8' signs on his property reading, "Warning! A Violent Felon lives here. Enter at your own Risk!" The Illinois Supreme Court overturned the probation condition as an abuse of judicial discretion. In the Court's view, ridicule is not a legitimate condition of probation, which is intended to rehabilitate offenders and integrate them into the community.

## Sentencing Disparity and the Quest for Equal Treatment

**Sentencing disparity** is the term critics use to describe the practice of sentencing similar defendants in a dissimilar fashion. Disparity is one byproduct of individualized sentences. The current federal sentencing system was developed to remedy problems of sentencing disparity. By the 1970s, the ideal of rehabilitation was in collapse, and many commentators blamed sentencing disparity for much of the United States' prison unrest and discontent (Stith & Cabranes, 1998). Therefore, the Sentencing Reform Act of 1984 abolished parole and established a Sentencing Commission charged with the responsibility of developing mandatory sentencing guidelines. While the act acknowledged the goals of deterrence, incapacitation, just punishment, and rehabilitation, Congress did not want the Sentencing Commission to allow the goal of rehabilitation to undermine the overriding goal of sentencing uniformity.

The commission's guidelines are very complicated. Each offense is graded—from 1 (least severe) to 43 (most severe); the higher the level, the longer the term of imprisonment. The offense level can be adjusted up or down in the grid depending on the characteristics of the offense and the offender's criminal history. The judge then must sentence within a narrow range prescribed by the grid. For example, if the adjusted offense level is 20 and the defendant has no criminal history, the judge has discretion to impose a sentence of a length between 33 months and 41 months.

The Sentencing Guidelines take into account not only the charged crime but also the circumstances of the crime. For example, section 3A1.1 provides that "if the defendant knew or should have known that a victim of the offense was unusually vulnerable, due to age, physical or mental condition, or that a victim was otherwise particularly vulnerable to the criminal conduct, increase by 2 levels" (Federal Sentencing Guidelines, 1995). In other words, all other things being equal, a longer sentence will be given for a robbery of an elderly and infirm person than for a robbery of a young and healthy person.

Although applications of mandatory guidelines result in injustices at times, proponents of guideline sentencing point to our society's tradition of equal treatment under the law. Writing in 1997, Charles Sifton, chief judge of a New York federal court, praised the guidelines for having brought rationality to sentencing—making the sentencing decision less dependent on personalities and "gut instincts" and more dependent on the facts of the case (Sifton, 1997).

Even under the guidelines, federal judges retain some discretion. They still can decide the particular sentence within a range, and they have discretion in deciding the facts on which the guideline calculation will be made. For example, it is for the judge to decide whether an offender's role in a crime was major or minor. This decision can mean a difference of months, or even years, in the sentence (Stith & Cabranes, 1998).

# Determinants of Sentencing: Relevant and Irrelevant

Punishment, to be morally acceptable, should be consistent with the seriousness of the crime. And punishment correlates strongly with the severity of the crime; even in systems in which judges retain wide sentencing discretion, graver crimes earn greater punishments.

However, factors other than seriousness of crime influence sentencing. Should they? What is relevant and what is irrelevant in determining punishment? Should a criminal's past history be taken into account? Should it matter that a convicted offender was deprived as a child, always hungry, abused, and denied opportunities to go to school or to look for work? The Federal Sentencing Guidelines do not consider such factors, but many states still do. How about a criminal's past record? This is a relevant factor in every jurisdiction. In fact, most states require those with prior records to serve longer terms. California's famous "three strikes and you're out" law is an example. A third-time offender with two prior convictions for violent felonies can be sentenced to life imprisonment without parole.

What other factors might affect the sentence? It shouldn't matter whether a defendant convicted of burglary is a man or a woman (Dane & Wrightsman, 1982), but Nagel (1969) found sentences to be more lenient for women than for men when the crime was grand larceny or burglary. A survey of the sentences of more than 10,500 felony defendants in Los Angeles found that male judges gave more lenient punishments to women than to men, especially when the defendants were nonwhite (Associated Press, 1984). Even though women plead guilty and are convicted at about the same rate as men, they are more likely to receive suspended sentences and less likely to be incarcerated. "Judges . . . treat women more leniently than men because they do not want to subject the supposedly physically weaker sex to the harsh conditions of prison," concluded the authors of the survey, John Gruhel, Susan Welch, and Cassia Spohn, political scientists at the University of Nebraska (quoted by Associated Press, 1984). Judges apparently also give women offenders lighter punishments because they assume that many women are the sole care providers of young children and that placing them in jail may leave the children homeless. However, after controlling for other factors, such as the offender's past criminal record and the seriousness of the crime, a good deal of the leniency toward women disappears.

What about characteristics of the victim, including the victim's race? Green (1961) found that black offenders with black victims got the mildest penalties, with half as many penitentiary sentences and four times the number of probations as either black-white or white-white offender-victim combinations. In Georgia, a 1989 *Atlanta Journal-Constitution* study concluded that, throughout two-thirds of Georgia, black men were at least twice as likely to go to jail as whites convicted of the same offense (Anderson, 1990). We will consider the race of the victim again later in this chapter, in the section on the death penalty.

Demographic characteristics such as the race or socioeconomic status of the victim often show inconsistent relationships with severity of sentence. But these influences should not be cavalierly disregarded; as Dane and Wrightsman (1982) note, their effects are often indirect but real. For example, special characteristics of the victim may create anger toward the offender or sympathy toward the victim. Austin, Walster, and Utne (1976) found that more suffering by the victim led to more severe sentences. Often, of course, offenses are graded in part by the suffering of the victim. For example, in Kentucky it is a misdemeanor to strike and injure someone; it is a felony to strike and *seriously* injure someone.

## Disparities in Judges' Sentences

As indicated earlier, the majority of sentencing decisions are made by judges, rather than juries. It has always been assumed that judges will reflect the values of the society they represent. Likewise, it has been assumed that, when a judge's "values differ from those defined by law, he [or she] would, as a judge, serve the interests of the law over his personal interests" (Gaylin, 1974, p. 7). Do judges conform to the requirements of the law, or do their own values enter in? One way to approach this question is to determine how serious the problem is. What is the ex-

tent of disparity in sentences for the same crime given by different judges?

By the early 1970s, disparity in sentencing had reached an appalling extreme. One of the authors was a federal public defender in Los Angeles in the early 1970s. At that time a judge could sentence a person convicted of bank robbery to any term between probation and 20 years in prison. One judge was so lenient he would probate an armed bank robber, while two other judges were so strict they would always sentence a bank robber to the maximum 20 years in prison. For an accused, the most crucial event in the criminal justice process was the clerk's draw of the card assigning him to 1 of the 16 judges on the federal bench.

It was against this background of unbridled judicial discretion that the Federal Sentencing Guidelines were adopted. In the federal system in the 21st century, judges have very limited discretion in sentencing. Discretion has passed largely to prosecutors—the United States Attorneys—who decide what charges to file.

A certain amount of variation in sentencing practices among the states is inevitable because the 50 state legislatures will view certain crimes differently. But state-to-state discrepancies can be dramatic. For example, in Michigan possession of more than 650 grams of cocaine (about a pound and a half) is punishable by imprisonment for life without possibility of parole; in Kentucky possession of a like amount of cocaine is punishable by a sentence of 5 to 10 years with eligibility for probation and parole. Variations occur even within the same state. Lunden (1957) found one judge in Iowa who gave ten times more suspended sentences than did his colleagues. Judge Marvin Frankel (1972) has written that the situation as it once existed was "a wild array of sentencing judgments without any semblance of the consistency demanded by the ideal of equal justice" (p. 5).

Are claims of unfair sentencing justified? Science, as a way of gaining knowledge, can help answer this question by comparing different judges' reactions to the same case, as was done in the study described in ◆ Box 17-3.

## The Science of

**BOX 17-3**  **Sentencing disparity**

In one study of sentencing disparity, Austin and Williams (1977) asked Virginia district court judges attending an educational workshop to respond to the same hypothetical cases by recommending a verdict and sentence. For example, in one case the judges read:

Debbie Jones, 18 years of age, appears in court. She was apprehended with her boyfriend in the apartment of an acquaintance of theirs. There were seven boys and girls present. Seven roaches, or butts, were found, none in Debbie's hands, and ten unused marijuana cigarettes were found in a paper bag on the coffee table.

Debbie is charged with "Possession of Marijuana." Is she guilty or not guilty? As charged or what?

Debbie has no previous record. She attends high school regularly as a senior. She does not appear particularly apologetic for her alleged use of marijuana, but neither does she appear rebellious against the "establishment." Her father, in court with her, is branch manager of a national manufacturer of duplicating equipment.

Punishment?

Judges' reactions on this case varied greatly, as the following summary shows:

VERDICTS:
Not guilty: 29 judges
Guilty: 18 judges

SENTENCES (based on the 18 judges ruling guilty):
Probation: 8 judges
Fine: 4 judges
Fine plus probation: 3 judges
Jail term: 3 judges

The lack of consensus on both the verdict and the sentence is obvious. What is even more surprising is that the data illustrating this example of sentencing disparity were gathered at a judicial workshop "designed, among other things, as a forum for judges and 'experts' to discuss the complexities of sentencing because a number of observers have called for such workshops as one way to reduce sentencing disparity" (Austin & Utne, 1977, pp.173–174).

---

Sometimes differences in sentencing are justified on the ground that they reflect the norms and feelings of the community. A humorous example is provided by Judge Edward Lumbard:

A visitor to a Texas court was amazed to hear the judge impose a suspended sentence where a man has pleaded guilty to manslaughter. A few minutes later the same judge sentenced a man who pleaded guilty to stealing a horse and gave him life imprisonment. When the judge was asked about the disparity of the two sentences, he replied, "Well, down here there is some men who need killin', but there ain't no horses that need stealin'!" (quoted in Gaylin, 1974, p. 8).

## Possible Sources of Bias in Judges

Judges are human. When latitude exists in the punishments they can give, their backgrounds and personal characteristics may influence their decisions (Hogarth, 1971). They may be prejudiced for or against certain groups—racial minorities, war resisters, homosexuals. A Dallas judge told a reporter that he was giving a lighter sentence to a murderer because the victims were "queers." A judge in Jackson County, Missouri, said in court that he would like to shoot people who vandalize automobiles "in the head so they can't testify"

(Blakeman, 1988, p. A1) . Both judges later apologized; the Dallas judge was censured by the Texas State Commission on Judicial Conduct. This section discusses some characteristics of judges that might affect their decisions, but in general, as the wave of mandatory and guidelines sentencing sweeps across the country, we would expect there are fewer opportunities for these qualities to affect judges' sentencing decisions than in the past.

## Age and Experience

How does a judge's experience affect his or her sentencing behavior? Are new judges more lenient? Or harsher? Seymour Wishman (1981a), in *Confessions of a Criminal Lawyer,* writes:

> I knew Judge Mangione well. Twelve years earlier I had been prosecuting in his court when he was first assigned to handle criminal cases. . . . I remembered how hard he had worked in those early trials to be fair to defendants, not only in making sure he had conducted fair trials, but also in sentencing those who had been convicted. About 11 years after Judge Mangione had started handling criminal trials, a client of mine had pleaded guilty to a charge of possessing marijuana with the intention of distributing it. My client was a 19-year-old college student . . . ; it had been his first problem with the law, and from the way the young man's hand shook, it was clear he wasn't going to get into any trouble again. The D.A. wouldn't offer a plea bargain guaranteeing that the boy wouldn't go to jail, but it was inconceivable to me that Mangione would send him away. He did.
>
> After the sentencing, I went to see the judge in his chambers. "Judge, I can't believe what you did with that boy today. They'll rip him to pieces in jail. . . ."
>
> "Seymour, I felt I had to do it. I've been giving young people breaks for years now, and they laugh at me. The crime rate only gets worse. We've got to do something."
>
> . . . That afternoon, as I talked to the judge, it was clear to me that he had undergone a dramatic change since I first met him. He must have been hardened by the constant exposure to so many vicious criminals and to all the atrocities they had committed. He must have

felt impotent over the years to do anything that would have any appreciable effect on the violence that appeared in his courtroom. From earlier conversations, I also knew of another aspect in his reaction to the defendants brought before him—he felt personally betrayed by the false promises of the many who had said that if they had just one more break, they would not get in trouble again. (pp. 107–108)

But not all judges respond the way Judge Mangione did. Some become more lenient in their sentencing. It is impossible to make a general statement about the effects of judicial experience on sentencing. Perhaps older judges are *selectively* punitive; "that is, they impose harsher sanctions on certain offenders with whom, because of their age, they are least able to sympathize. Drug offenders are the most obvious possibility" (Myers, 1988, p. 654).

## Previous Employment as a District Attorney

Judges who have been district attorneys may maintain their sympathy for the prosecution, and some research finds them to be selectively more punitive than judges who have not been prosecutors (Myers, 1988). Seymour Wishman (1981a) writes, "What juries don't know is that many judges were once prosecutors and that they sometimes forget that it is no longer their duty to get convictions. A number of judges—admittedly fewer than a majority—want to 'beat' defense lawyers and are much more dangerous and difficult to deal with than prosecutors" (pp. 206–207).

A California state judge, "speaking as a former prosecutor," publicly criticized the United States Court of Appeals for setting aside a state conviction. He accused the federal court of having an anti–death penalty bias and called on Congress to prevent federal courts from reviewing death penalty cases. Another former prosecutor taped a photograph of the "hanging saloon" of Texas Judge Roy Bean on the front of his bench with his own name superimposed over Judge Bean's and referred to the judges of the Texas Court of Criminal Appeals as "idiots" and "liberal bastards" (Bright & Kennen, 1995, pp. 811, 813).

## Politics

Judges are public officials, and although the judiciary should be above the political fray, as a practical matter judges find their careers influenced by politics. Dissatisfied with the California Supreme Court, then-governor George Deukmejian warned the justices in 1986 that he would oppose them in an upcoming retention election (a proceeding in which the justices run "against their records") if they continued to reverse death penalty convictions. He carried out his threat, and three justices, including Chief Justice Rose Bird, lost their seats (see the discussion in Chapter 4). Governor Deukmejian appointed conservative replacements, and, as of 1995, the "new" court had affirmed death penalty convictions 97% of the time (Bright & Kennen, 1995, p. 761).

Bright and Kennan (1995) cite many examples of political attacks on judges and many examples of judges seeking political advantage by appearing "tough on crime":

◆ In Louisville, Kentucky a judge sought to have a colleague preside over the arraignment of an African American charged with the slaying of a white police officer. The judge on whose docket the case appeared told defense counsel that his colleague would preside because "Jim's on the ballot Tuesday" (p. 787).

◆ Federal judges are nominated by the president and confirmed by the Senate; if confirmed, the appointments are for life. In 1994, Oliver North, running for the U.S. Senate from Virginia, made a political issue of Senator Charles Robb's votes to confirm two "liberal" judges. In another 1994 unsuccessful race for the Senate, Michael Huffington of California attacked Senator Diane Feinstein with commercials stating, "Feinstein judges let killers live after victims died" (p. 790).

When judges are constantly subjected to the political process, they understand that upholding the Bill of Rights for controversial or unpopular defendants can cost them reelection. In general, the impact of politics on the judiciary is to undermine the rule of law.

## Philosophy about the Purpose of the Penalty

How would a given judge describe the objective of a sentence in a specific case? What is a specific judge's "theory of punishment"? "Should the offender be punished to deter crime in general? To deter the specific offense for which he or she was convicted? To establish equity? To gain retribution for society and the victim? To rehabilitate the offender?" (Austin & Utne, 1977, p. 168). Judges' views on these matters can affect their sentencing decisions (Gottfredson, Gottfredson, & Conly, 1989).

Some judges give more severe sentences in order to punish the offender for lying on the stand as well as for committing the initial crime. Paul A. Bilzerian, a Florida investor who was one of the most successful corporate raiders of the 1980s, was sentenced to four years in prison and fined $1.5 million for conspiracy to violate securities laws. Federal Judge Robert Ward stated that the sentence was stiff in part because he believed that Bilzerian had perjured himself when he testified in his own defense: "I do believe that if Mr. Bilzerian had not testified at all at the trial, his sentence would not be what it was" (quoted in Eichenwald, 1989, p. 29).

In *Grayson v. United States* (1978), the trial judge said, "[I]t is my view that your defense was a complete fabrication without the slightest merit whatsoever. I feel it is proper for me to consider that fact in the sentencing and I will do so" (p. 44). In upholding the conviction, the Supreme Court rejected the defendant's contention that allowing a judge to penalize someone for perceived perjury chilled the right to testify on one's own behalf. Not so, said the Court, for the right to testify is the right to testify *truthfully.*

## The Sentencing Process

The procedure used in most courts for sentencing has several components. The judge receives a file on the offender, prepared by the probation officer. It contains the probation officer's written report on the case, the offender's personal history, the offender's prior convictions (if any), and a number of documents describing various procedures (e.g., the date of the arraignment, the formal indictment). The judge reviews the file before the sentencing hearing.

## The Sentencing Hearing

At the hearing, recommendations for a sentence are presented to the judge by the prosecutor and by the attorney representing the offender. The judge has at hand the probation officer's recommendation. The judge may ask the offender questions and will usually permit the offender to make a statement.

Two social psychologists, Ebbe Ebbesen and Vladimir Konecni (1981), observed more than 400 sentencing hearings in San Diego in 1976 and 1977 in order to determine which factors seemed to influence judges' decisions. (Chapter 10 reviewed these researchers' work on the determinants of bail setting by judges.) They discovered that very few of the sentencing hearings in San Diego lasted more than *five minutes*. On average, judges took 42% of this time, and defense attorneys took the next biggest chunk of time—38%. Participation by offenders averaged only 3% of these hearings' total time. Usually anything said by the offender came at the end of the hearing, in response to the judge asking whether the offender wanted to make a statement.

## What Predicts the Sentence?

In Ebbesen and Konecni's (1981) sample, four factors accounted for almost all the systematic variations among sentences:

1. Type of crime
2. Extent of the offender's past record
3. Status of the offender between arrest and conviction—that is, whether the offender was released on his or her own recognizance, freed on bail, held in jail, or originally held in jail and then released on bail
4. Probation officer's sentence recommendation. The judge's sentence agreed with the proba-

tion officer's recommendation in more than 84% of the cases. When they disagreed, the judge was more lenient 10% of the time and more severe 6% of the time. Over the eight judges who supplied most of the data for this study, the range of agreement with probation officers was from 93% to 75%, with a median of 87% agreement with the recommendation. Another, more recent, study in New Zealand found similar levels of agreement, with judges agreeing with the probation officer's recommendation 77% of the time (Rush & Robertson, 1987).

Ebbesen and Konecni conclude that sentencing works this way: The probation officer's recommendation is determined by the prior record, the seriousness of the current crime, and the offender's present status. An extensive past criminal record strongly increases the likelihood that a severe sentence will be recommended. The probation officer incorporates all these factors into his or her recommendation, which is one reason why the judge's agreement with this recommendation is so high.

# Special Punishments: The Sentencing of Sex Offenders

In Chapter 1, we described the case of Leroy Hendricks, a pedophile who was involuntarily committed under Kansas's Sexual Predator Act after he served his prison sentence. Although his confinement was called a "civil" commitment, Hendricks was locked up—potentially for the rest of his life—because he had committed a criminal offense and was judged to pose a substantial risk of reoffending. The state of Kansas treated Hendricks differently than it treats other offenders because he had committed sex crimes, and sex offenders—at least those convicted of predatory offenses—are believed to pose a greater risk of recidivism than other offenders (Doren, 1998).

We discuss three ways in which sex offenders are treated differently than other offenders, based largely on the belief that sex offenders are particularly likely to reoffend: (1) requirements that sex offenders register with state officials and that these officials publicly notify the community about the location of the offender's residence; (2) a greater use of involuntary commitment of sex offenders following the completion of their criminal incarceration; and (3) increased endorsement of extraordinary sanctions, including mandatory treatments and chemical castration of repeat sex offenders.

Sentencing for sex crimes, particularly those against children, has been singled out for special attention by the states. Probation for serious sex offenses is no longer an option in most states; in fact, sentences for sex offenses against children can be as severe as sentences for murder. As discussed later in this chapter, rape of a child is considered a capital offense in Louisiana.

## Registration and Notification

Most sex offenders are required to register with local law enforcement and to notify the authorities of subsequent changes of address. The period of required registration depends on the classification of the offender, which is a product of a formal risk assessment. In Kentucky, for example, high-risk offenders are required to register for life, while moderate- or low-risk offenders are required to register for ten years after their formal sentence is completed. Mandatory registration is based on the premise that sex offenders are more likely to reoffend than those convicted of other crimes, a premise that is the subject of much debate among researchers and mental-health professionals (Becker & Murphy, 1998; Doren, 1998). The fact of the matter is that it is very difficult to measure the recidivism rates for sexual offenses because calculating accurate base rates and recidivism estimates has not yet been done with great precision. Nonetheless, the logic behind mandatory registration is that it will deter potential reoffenders and assist law enforcement in solving crimes and apprehending offenders.

Notification is even more controversial than registration. Typically, a state will classify offenders according to the severity of the offense and the predicted risk for offending in the future. For example, in New Jersey, only law enforcement is notified of the presence of Tier 1 (low-risk) offenders, community groups are additionally notified about Tier 2 (moderate-risk) offenders, and the community—those likely to come in contact with the offender—are notified about Tier 3 (high-risk) offenders.

Community notification—sometimes involving far-reaching attempts to inform the public about the whereabouts of sex offenders—has the effect, if not the objective, of branding the offender as *persona non grata,* isolating him in the community, and often forcing him to flee to some other community—where, of course, he is supposed to reregister so that this additional community can be notified. Examples of this phenomenon abound. In Danville, Kentucky, a recently released parolee, classified as a "high-risk offender," was taken in by a middle-class couple who wanted to put their newfound Christian faith to work. The couple wasn't prepared for their neighbors' reaction when notified there was a high-risk sex offender in their suburban neighborhood. Fliers appeared in mailboxes and on light poles, anonymous letters were written, children were kept in their homes and off the streets, and the couple was shunned by the neighbors. When a crew from the television program *Extra* showed up, the ex-offender packed his bags and left without a word (Breed, 1999). After the community was notified about a released offender in Waterloo, Iowa, children started carrying bats and sticks as they walked to school; the recently released offender was threatened and ultimately hounded out of the community (VanDuyn, 1999).

Some states have begun to use the World Wide Web as a medium for notification. Typically, all offenders are placed on the Web for the period of their required registration, and law enforcement officials take no further steps to notify the community. Web site notification appears to be plagued by the worst of two extremes. On the one hand, it is overinclusive; the entire world can learn about the offender even though only one or a few communities really have any need to know.

*Home page of a sex offender registry on the World Wide Web*
SOURCE: www.dps.state.ak.us

At the same time, Web notification is underinclusive; persons who cannot or do not regularly access the Web site will not be made aware of a sex offender living in the neighborhood. Not surprisingly, most Web site hits appear to involve idle browsers, not people who are afraid an offender might be living in the neighborhood.

Web site posting involves an astounding invasion of privacy. No matter how minor the offense, in most states an offender's personal information, including photo, is posted on the Web for all to see during the period of required registration. What information is available? In Alaska, for example, one can search by name or by ZIP code; a ZIP code inquiry yields all offenders currently living in that ZIP code. Clicking on a name pulls up a photo, home and work address, and the crime for which the offender was convicted (www.dps.state.ak.us, 2000). It appears that Alaska puts all sex offenders on the state Web site, most for life. Offenders must inform law enforcement of changes in address so that postings can be updated. An offender posted on the Web will live under the shadow of his conviction in a way that no other type of offender must endure. A murderer could move to a new community safe in the knowledge that his past, while a matter of public record, is not readily accessible to friends and neighbors. On the other hand, a sex offender, even though the offense might be minor, will know that his past is available to anyone in the world with the click of the mouse.

## Involuntary Commitment

Leroy Hendricks was "every parent's nightmare" (Kolebuck, 1998, p. 537). In his 60s at the time he was scheduled to be released from a Kansas state prison where he had served ten years for molesting his stepdaughter, Hendricks had repeatedly molested children throughout his adult life. Kansas had recently passed a Sexually Violent Predator Act (SVP), allowing for the involuntary commitment of offenders suffering from a "mental abnormality" making them likely to commit predatory acts of sexual violence. The Kansas court found Hendricks to be a sexually violent predator and committed him to a mental hospital. As recounted in Chapter 1, the United States Supreme Court rejected Hendricks's constitutional challenges (double jeopardy, substantive due process, and ex post facto) and upheld the commitment.

Predictably, other states have now passed statutes similar to the Kansas statute upheld in *Hendricks*. Arizona, California, Florida, Illinois, Iowa, Minnesota, Missouri, New Jersey, South Carolina, Washington, and Wisconsin now provide for involuntary commitment of sex offenders. In 2000, the California court of appeals upheld the California SVP statute (*People v. Green*, 2000). According to a 1997 survey, 240 sex offenders had been civilly committed in Arizona, California, Illinois, Kansas, Washington, and Wisconsin (Becker & Murphy, 1998).

While the assessment of risk for purposes of registration and notification can be done at the time of sentencing, civil commitment evaluations are conducted around the time the offender is scheduled to be released from prison. The first type of assessment typically relies on one of a growing number of actuarial instruments such as the Sex Offender Risk Appraisal Guide (SORAG; Quinsey, Harris, Rice, & Cormier, 1998), the Minnesota Sex Offender Screening Tool—Revised (MnSOST-R; Epperson, Kaul, & Hesselton, 1998), the Rapid Risk Assessment for Sex Offense Recidivism (RRASOR; Hanson, 1997), and the Structured Anchored Clinical Judgment (SACJ; Grubin, 1998). A recent study of results of the RRASOR and SACJ concluded that these instruments were capable of predicting sex offense recidivism with moderate degrees of accuracy. However, a combination of the RRASOR and SCAJ scales—termed the Static-99—was even more accurate than either of the original scales in isolation and identified a subset of high-risk offenders with an observed recidivism rate of over 50% at one end of the scale and a low-risk subset with a recidivism rate of under 10% (after 15 years) at the other end of the scale (Hanson & Thornton, 2000).

Unfortunately, in evaluations made for the purposes of involuntary commitments, the assessments rely on the judgments of examining clinicians, in which the psychologist or psychiatrist often goes beyond the actuarial data to opine whether the defendant is suffering from a mental abnormality (or illness) that will render him a substantial risk to reoffend. Compared to actuarial prediction schemes, such clinically based predictions of dangerousness are notoriously inaccurate (Falk, 1999) and should not be used as the basis for risk-based decisions concerning involuntary commitment.

## Castration and Other Treatments

Unlike other offenders, sex offenders are often required to undergo treatment designed to "cure"

them of their antisocial tendencies. Most states order sex offenders to participate in counseling sessions as a condition of probation or parole. In these counseling sessions, offenders are required to acknowledge their wrongdoing and are taught to recognize situations that might lead them to reoffend. These sessions often also include an assortment of behavior modification techniques, including aversive conditioning and, in some cases, medications designed to diminish the sex drive (Becker & Murphy, 1999).

The most controversial form of treatment is **chemical castration**—the administration of drugs such as medroxyprogesterone acetate (MPA), known by its brand name Depo-Provera. This drug reduces testosterone levels and lowers most men's sex drives. In the past some courts have given convicted sex offenders a choice: prison or MPA; and it is not surprising that some men have opted for the drug, even though the possible side effects include lethargy, hot flashes, nightmares, hypertension, and shortness of breath (Keene, 1997). The effectiveness of MPA as a treatment for repeat sex offenders (sometimes called *paraphiliacs*) is still in question. Some studies report dramatic decreases in recidivism by male sex offenders following MPA treatment (Beckman, 1998), but others report that the drug is effective only for sex offenders who want to control their behavior but feel unable to do so; that it does not inevitably suppress erections or prevent sexual arousal; and that it is less effective than a combination of interventions involving counseling, medication, and behavior modification (Bund, 1997).

California was the first state to pass a law requiring repeat child molesters to be treated with MPA as a condition of parole. Recognizing that not all pedophiles are paraphiliacs, the California statute requires that a clinician conclude that the offender will benefit from the treatment. This issue is similar to the question that a clinician must answer in civil commitment proceedings for sexually violent predators: Does the offender suffer from a condition (**paraphilia**) that creates a substantial risk of reoffending? If so, the California legislature reasoned, it makes sense to deny parole unless the offender agrees to the treatment. At the time the California Chemical Castration Bill was being considered, Assemblyman Bill Hoge, one of the sponsors, was quoted as saying:

> What we're up against is the kind of criminal who, just as soon as he gets out of jail, will immediately commit this crime again at least 90% of the time. So why not give these people a shot to calm them down and bring them under control, or alternatively, give them the option of going under the knife? (Ayres, 1996, p. A1)

Unfortunately, Assemblyman Hoge had his facts wrong, and critics were quick to point out that the rate of recidivism he quoted was a substantial exaggeration. In addition, the assumption that forcing offenders to take MPA (through making it a condition of parole) will be as effective as if it were taken voluntarily is contradicted by a considerable amount of clinical evidence (Keene, 1997).

Florida has gone one step further than California. In the Sunshine State, judges may order MPA in any sexual battery case, and they are required to do so for repeat offenders. Florida's statute is not limited to child molesters or to cases in which there is some evidence that MPA treatment has been effective.

## The Death Penalty: The Ultimate Punishment

In 1976, in the case of *Gregg v. Georgia,* the Supreme Court reinstituted the possibility of the death penalty. Previously, in the case of *Furman v. Georgia* (1972), the Court had in effect abolished the death penalty throughout the United States on the grounds that, as it had been administered in the mid-1960s, it constituted "cruel and unusual punishment." After the *Furman* case, state legislatures revised their death penalty laws to answer the Court's concern that capital punishment was being applied in an arbitrary and discriminatory fashion due to the "unbridled discretion" in sentencing given to juries.

To address this criticism, the states passed statutes that narrowed and guided the capital-sentencing discretion of juries. First, they made only certain crimes eligible for the death penalty. If a defendant is charged with one of these crimes, the trial is conducted in two phases. The jury decides the guilt or innocence of the defendant in the first phase. If the defendant is found guilty, the second, or sentencing, phase of the trial is held. During this phase, the jury (in a few states, the judge, not the jury, makes the decision at the sentencing phase) hears evidence of **aggravating factors** (facts that argue for a death sentence) and **mitigating factors** (facts that argue for a sentence less than death). Specific aggravating and mitigating factors are listed in the statutes, but a jury is not limited to only those factors in its deliberations. Before reaching a sentencing decision, the jurors hear instructions from the judge on how they are to weigh the aggravating and mitigating factors. Generally, a jury cannot vote for a sentence of death unless it finds at least one aggravating factor to be present. However, even if it finds one or more aggravating circumstances to be present, it may still, after considering the mitigating factors, return a sentence of less than death.

Although the *Gregg* decision allowed states to reinstitute the death penalty, it was unclear whether crimes other than murder could be punishable by death. The year after *Gregg,* the Supreme Court decided *Coker v. Georgia* (1977). An escapee from prison, Coker robbed and raped a woman after stealing the family car and kidnapping her. Rape was a capital offense in Georgia, and a jury sentenced Coker to death on the basis of the aggravating factor of having committed the crime while on escape status. In reversing Coker's conviction, the Supreme Court applied the Cruel and Unusual Punishment Clause of the Eighth Amendment and held that the death penalty is a grossly disproportionate penalty for the rape of an adult woman.

Five years after *Coker,* the Court decided *Enmund v. Florida* (1982), a case in which the driver of a getaway car was sentenced to death under Florida's "felony-murder" rule. His accomplices had shot and robbed two people. The driver, however, did not intend the deaths, and the Supreme Court held that giving the death penalty to the driver was grossly disproportionate to his criminal conduct. Although *Coker* and *Enmund* seem to limit the death penalty to murder, several states have extended the penalty to nonhomicide crimes. In *State v. Wilson* (1996), the Louisiana Supreme Court upheld a statute making rape of a child under 12 a capital offense. However, in *State v. Gardner* (1997), the Utah Supreme Court struck down a statute providing for the death penalty for aggravated assaults in prison. In the near future, the United States Supreme Court will likely decide what nonhomicide cases, if any, may be the proper subject of a capital indictment.

Since its 1976 and 1977 decisions, the Supreme Court has issued many death penalty opinions. The Court has paid particular attention to the way the penalty phase is conducted and the manner by which capital juries are impaneled and then reach their decisions (Costanzo & Costanzo, 1992; Luginbuhl, 1992; Nietzel, Hasemann & McCarthy, 1998). ◆ Box 17-4 lists several of the most important Supreme Court decisions regarding death penalty litigation.

Following the *Gregg* decision, state after state began to execute those convicts who had been sentenced to death. The first to be executed, on January 17, 1977, was Gary Gilmore, in Utah, who gave up his right to challenge his conviction and resisted the efforts of his relatives to save him from the firing squad (Gilmore is the only person to be executed in the United States by firing squad since the death penalty was reinstituted). Gilmore was the first of many to die at the hand of the executioner. Between 1977 and 2000, more than 600 defendants have been executed in the United States, the largest number occurring in 1999, when 98 individuals were executed.

How many of those executed were innocent we cannot say with precision; all we can say with confidence is that some executed defendants surely were. As we begin the 21st century, recognition of this problem is increasing; and as a result, the American public's support of the death penalty has begun to erode a bit. A number of factors are responsible. First, a fairly large number of death row inmates have been found to be innocent. In Illinois, for example, 13 men waiting to be put to death were exonerated during the same 12-year period that 12 were executed, a ratio so troubling that Governor George Ryan, a death penalty supporter, imposed a moratorium on executions in his state. According to the Death Penalty Information Center (www.deathpenaltyinfo. org), at least 87 people have been freed from death rows since 1973. Some of these condemned convicts were cleared when new evidence came to light or when witnesses changed their stories. However, the major source of exoneration has been the use of more sophisticated DNA testing. DNA evidence has been credited with proving the innocence of scores of death row inmates in the United States and Canada in the years since capital punishment was reinstated (Shapiro, 1998). Many of these cases involved defendants who had been originally convicted on the basis of faulty eyewitness identifications (see Chapter 7) or false confessions (see Chapter 8). As a result of such cases, a number of states, including Illinois, Oklahoma, Washington, and New York, have passed laws that give death row inmates the right to postconviction DNA testing, and federal legislation—the National Death Penalty Moratorium Act—has been introduced in Congress that would suspend all executions in the United States while a national commission examines the problems in how the death penalty is being administered.

The moratorium on executions has gained further momentum from a monumental Columbia University Law School study, "A Broken System: Error Rates in Capital Cases" (Liebman, 2000). This study analyzed every capital conviction in the United States between 1973 and 1995 and discovered that serious mistakes had been made in two-thirds of the cases, a startling indictment of the criminal justice system. The most common mistakes included incompetent defense attorneys (37%), faulty jury instructions (20%), and misconduct on the part of prosecutors (19%).

## BOX 17-4    Death penalty trials: The Supreme Court's views

Because it is the ultimate punishment a society can deliver, because of its enormous symbolic importance, and because of the impassioned rhetoric it inspires in both advocates and opponents, the death penalty has received special scrutiny from the Supreme Court in the past three decades. The Court has reviewed and regulated the procedures of capital trials very closely, reflecting the opinion that society may tolerate the death penalty only when its use is carefully monitored. Along with the cases of *Witherspoon, Witt,* and *Lockhart,* which are discussed at length in the text, the following Supreme Court cases have helped define what is acceptable and what is not in death penalty litigation across the United States.

CASE

1. *Lockett v. Ohio* (1978) — The jury is allowed to consider as a mitigating factor any aspect of the defendant's background or the offense that the defendant introduces.

2. *Payne v. Tennessee* (1991) — The jury is allowed to consider evidence about the impact a crime had on the victim before it reaches a sentencing decision.

3. *Mu'Min v. Virginia* (1991) — A judge does not have to ask prospective jurors about the content of the pretrial publicity to which they have been exposed.

4. *Mc Cleskey v. Kemp* (1987) — A disparity in death sentences linked to racial differences of murder victims does not make the death penalty unconstitutional.

5. *Enmund v. Florida* (1982); *Tison v. Arizona* (1987) — If a defendant commits a felony in the course of which a murder is committed by another defendant, the first defendant cannot be sentenced to death if he or she did not kill or intend that killing or lethal force would take place (*Enmund*). However, if this defendant's participation in the crimes was major or if the defendant showed a "reckless indifference to the value of human life," the defendant could be sentenced to death (*Tison*).

6. *Ford v. Wainwright* (1986) — A defendant sentenced to death must be competent before his or her execution can be carried out.

Of those defendants whose capital sentence was overturned because of an error, 82% received a sentence less than death at their retrials, including 7% who were found not guilty of the capital crime with which they had originally been charged.

Other defendants who had been sentenced to death received reprieves. For example, Johnny Ross was sentenced for rape in 1975 in Louisiana but was released in 1981 when it was shown that his blood type did not match that of the rapist. Robert Henry McDowell was a North Carolina black man sentenced to death for the murder of a 4-year-old white girl. He received a stay of his execution only days before it was scheduled, when the victim's mother implicated the victim's stepfather. McDowell's conviction was ultimately reversed. Edgar Labat and Clinton Poret, two black

## THE CASE OF

BOX 17-5   Gary Graham: Executing an innocent man?

On June 22, 2000, Texas executed Gary Graham for the murder of a man during a stickup in a grocery store parking lot. Protesting his innocence to the end, Graham was forcibly hauled to the execution chamber and strapped to the gurney with extra restraints. The only evidence against Graham was an eyewitness who said she saw the killer through her car windshield. Two eyewitnesses who would have testified that Graham was not the killer did not testify, and three jurors, after watching the videotaped statements of the two potential witnesses, signed affidavits that they would have acquitted had the witnesses been called. The Texas Board of Pardons wasn't convinced that an injustice had been done and voted not to recommend clemency. Without a recommendation of clemency, Governor (and then presidential candidate) George W. Bush was powerless to stop the execution (Duggan, 2000).

*Gary Graham*

men, were sentenced to death in Louisiana in 1953 for raping a white woman. After a dozen stays of execution and 16 years on death row, they were released because prosecution witnesses' testimony unraveled, alibi witnesses came forward, and evidence showed that one defendant had been beaten into confessing.

In 1992, Roger Dale Coleman was executed by the state of Virginia for the brutal rape and slaying of his sister-in-law. Coleman maintained his innocence to the last, but the courts refused to consider evidence, discovered after the trial, pointing to Coleman's innocence—because Coleman's attorneys failed to file a motion on time! What is unusual about the case is that, in the week before his death, Coleman became a media celebrity—appearing on the cover of *Time* magazine (under the headline "This Man May Be Innocent") and participating in extraordinary live interviews on CNN's *Larry King Live* and NBC's *Today* show.

Would the death penalty still be justified if we knew that innocent people were executed? Some proponents insist that it would, invoking the analogy that a vaccine is justified even though some child might have an adverse, even lethal, reaction to it. Whatever one's position on this issue, new cases involving the execution of possibly innocent persons continue, as ◆ Box 17-5 indicates.

### Reasons for the Death Penalty

According to a February 2000 poll, 66% of U.S. citizens support the death penalty, the lowest figure in 20 years and 20% lower than the peak support in 1994 (Hansen, 2000). However, the number of executions in the United States continues to increase; the 98 people put to death in 1999 was the highest number since 1951, when 105 people met the executioner.

Many reasons have been advanced for endorsing the irrevocable penalty of death. While he was the mayor of New York City, Ed Koch contended that the death penalty "affirms life." By failing to execute murderers, he said, we "signal a lessened regard for the value of the victim's life" (quoted in Bruck, 1985, p. 20). Capital punishment is thus justified as the ultimate retribution—the best

**BOX 17-6    Arguments for and against the death penalty as a deterrent**

ARGUMENTS FAVORING THE
DEATH PENALTY

1. The death penalty accomplishes general deterrence.

2. "Potential murderers" who committed other crimes report they did not carry a gun out of fear of capital punishment.

3. Abolishing capital punishment would increase the homicide rate.

4. Execution of a criminal, if highly publicized, has at least a short-term deterrent effect.

5. Murderers are dangerous individuals, and allowing them to live increases the risk to inmates and prison guards; that is, they will kill in prison because they have nothing to lose.

RESPONSE BY ABOLITIONISTS
TO EACH OF THE PRECEDING
ARGUMENTS

1. Most homicides are emotional, spontaneous acts, not premeditated ones. Among premeditated murders, many offenders are convinced that they can escape detection. Hence, many murderers do not consider the consequences of their act. Furthermore, a study of 110 nations by Dane Archer (1984) finds that the death penalty does not deter homicidal criminals (Wilkes, 1987).

2. Careful comparisons of states with and without the death penalty reflect no differences in homicide rates (Sellin, 1968).

3. Abolition or reintroduction of the death penalty has no effect on established trends in homicide rates, regardless of whether rates are increasing or decreasing (Lempert, 1981; Zeisel, 1976).

4. No empirical evidence exists for this conclusion. If anything the opposite might happen (Bruck, 1985).

5. The evidence contradicts this view. Research has repeatedly shown that capital murderers tend to commit fewer violent offenses and prison infractions of any type compared to prison inmates in general (Cunningham & Reidy, 1998).

SOURCE: Based on Baum (1985).

---

means we have of doing justice in response to particularly heinous crimes.

Most justifications for the death penalty reflect value choices and thus extend beyond the capacity of empirical research to prove or disprove them. But a major argument for capital punishment offered by the public—and a reason endorsed by a few experts—is the belief that it deters others from performing criminal acts.

A variety of empirical approaches has been used to evaluate the deterrent effects of the death penalty. As ◆ Box 17-6 shows, these methods and findings consistently lead to a conclusion that the death penalty does not affect the incidence rate for crimes of violence. In fact, some researchers contend that capital punishment actually enhances crime, an effect known as **brutalization.** Brutalization theorists argue that executions increase violent crime by sending the message that

it is acceptable to kill those who have wronged us. However, the evidence in support of brutalization effects is no stronger than the data in favor of deterrence (Radelet & Akers, 1996).

## The Future of the Death Penalty

Whether a society should extract the ultimate punishment of death for serious crimes has troubled judges, philosophers, theologians, and social scientists for centuries. The future of capital punishment is enmeshed in the dilemmas introduced in Chapter 1. The principle of the social good demands that we ask what we, as a society, want. We have the right to expect our government to provide us with safety and protection, yet we need to demonstrate a respect for human life as best we can. As Foley (1983) observed, an absolute moratorium on killing would seem to violate an

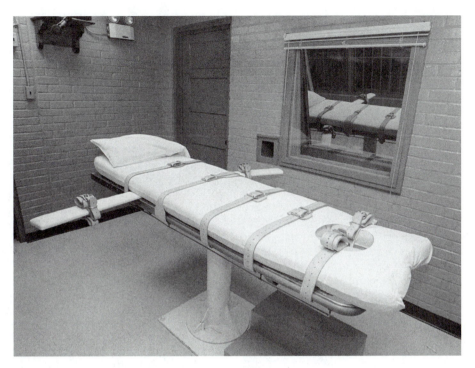

*Gurney on which the prisoner is executed by lethal injection*

optimal balance in these goals; for example, it may be necessary to kill a sniper if we are convinced that he will continue to kill people. But capital punishment is not the same as killing in self-defense, and society must ask whether the death penalty achieves the social good.

Does the death penalty achieve the goal of equal treatment before the law? About a fourth of the states, plus the District of Columbia, do not permit it, and vastly different rates of execution occur in those states that do. For example, even though the state of New Hampshire has the death penalty, no one has been executed or even sent to death row in that state since the penalty was reestablished. In contrast, about a third of all executions in the United States since 1977 have taken place in one state—Texas. If discretion is the operating principle, it is discretion run amok. The death penalty is administered in only a minority of eligible cases, and its determinants often seem inconsistent and unpredictable. As one example, there

are dramatic regional differences in the application of the penalty, with most executions taking place in southern states. Furthermore, some of the decisions seem prejudicial; for instance, the victims of intentional homicide are equally divided between blacks and whites, and yet the chances of a death sentence are much greater for criminals who kill whites than those who kill blacks (U.S. General Accounting Office, 1990).

The possibility that the race of a defendant or of a victim might play a role in capital sentencing has become a key topic of legal appeals and scientific research. For example, the Supreme Court refused to overturn the death sentence of a Utah man who claimed that the jury that had decided his case was racially biased. The appellant and another man (since executed) were charged with entering an Ogden store in 1974, forcing five people to drink liquid drain cleaner, and then shooting three of them. During the trial a juror handed a bailiff a drawing of a man on a gallows

## THE CASE OF

**BOX 17-7**   **Warren McCleskey: Does race matter?**

Warren McCleskey was a black man who had been convicted of a 1978 armed robbery and the murder of a white police officer who had responded to an alarm while the robbery was in progress. McCleskey was sentenced to die in Georgia's electric chair. With the assistance of the NAACP Legal Defense and Educational Fund, he challenged the constitutionality of the death penalty on the ground that it was administered in a racially discriminatory manner in Georgia. In the words of one of his attorneys, "When you kill the organist at the Methodist Church, who is white, you're going to get the death penalty, but if you kill the black Baptist organist, the likelihood is that it will be plea-bargained down to a life sentence" (quoted in Noble, 1987, p. 7).

The foundation for Walter McCleskey's appeal was a comprehensive study of factors that determined whether capital sen-tencing in the state of Georgia was influenced by extralegal factors. David Baldus, a law professor at the University of Iowa, and his colleagues analyzed the race of the offender and race of the victim for about 2000 murder and manslaughter convictions from 1973 to 1979 and concluded that those who killed whites were 11 times more likely to receive the death penalty than those who killed blacks (Baldus, Pulaski, & Woodworth, 1983).

In Georgia, juries (in line with the Supreme Court guidelines we discussed earlier) must weigh aggravating and mitigating circum-stances before deciding to sentence a convicted murderer to death rather than life in prison. Aggravating circumstances would include killing a police officer, killing for hire, killing that is es-pecially cruel, or killing that is committed during other law-breaking activities. Mitigating cir-cumstances could include a defendant's mental illness or voluntary intoxication at the time of the offense. Anticipating the argument that some murders were typically more heinous than others, Baldus identified 230 different aggravating or mitigating factors. Then he eliminated cases in which extreme violence or other aggravating circumstances virtually ensured the death penalty. He also eliminated those in which overwhelming mitigating circumstances almost guaranteed a life sentence. For the remaining cases—which permitted the greatest jury discretion—he found that defendants were about four times more likely to be sentenced to death if their victims were white. Similar patterns have been reported for capital sentencing in Arkansas, North Carolina, Illinois, Ohio, Texas, Mississippi, and several other states (Nietzel, Hasemann, & McCarthy, 1998).

with the inscription "Hang the niggers" (Beissert, 1988).

As another example, in Missouri, within a two-year period, two state troopers were killed in separate but similar incidents. (Both were killed during routine traffic checks.) Each defendant was found guilty of murder. David Tate, a white man, was sentenced to life in prison; Jerome Mallett, a black man, was given the death penalty.

In *McCleskey v. Kemp* (1987), the Supreme Court considered the impact of racial differences in capital sentencing. At issue was the question of whether the death penalty discriminated against blacks—or, more specifically, whether it discriminated against persons who murdered whites. The details of this case and the research associated with it are summarized in ◆ Box 17-7.

It is very unlikely that the Supreme Court will reject the death penalty in the near future. For example, with regard to the issue of deter-rence as a justification for the death penalty, we have already seen that social science has found

What factors might account for this difference? One possibility is that death sentences are more likely when defense counsel is appointed by the court rather than privately retained. Appointed counsel in capital cases covered by the Baldus study tended to be inexperienced and lacking the resources necessary to mount a vigorous defense for their clients. A recent reanalysis of 606 trials from the original Baldus data (Beck & Shumsky, 1997) confirmed that type of defense counsel was related to sentencing; prosecutors were more likely to seek a death penalty after they discovered that a defendant would be represented by appointed counsel. Not surprisingly, death sentences were more likely for defendants represented by appointed versus privately retained counsel.

A second factor that might contribute to the results is the difficulty that juries have giving proper attention to possible mitigating factors in reaching their penalty verdicts. Several studies indicate that jurors do not adequately comprehend the instructions they receive about mitigating factors because much like other types of judicial instructions, mitigation instructions are often couched in legal jargon and are unusually lengthy and grammatically complex (Haney & Lynch, 1994,1997; Lynch & Haney, 2000). If jurors do not understand a judge's instructions about mitigation, they are more likely to rely on other more familiar factors to guide their verdicts, such as the heinousness of the crime or extralegal considerations such as racial stereotypes, sympathy for victims, or the expertise of the lawyers. The race of the defendant and the victim do appear to affect sentences to a significantly greater extent when comprehension of instructions is low versus when it is high. In a study by Lynch and Haney (2000), jury-eligible subjects who scored low on their comprehension of instructions recommended death 68% of the time for black defendant/white victim cases versus 36% of the time for white defendant/black victim cases. Among subjects who comprehended the sentencing instructions well, neither the race of the defendant nor the victim affected sentences.

Despite the mass of statistical evidence, the Supreme Court upheld McCleskey's death sentence. The Court's majority opinion found no proof of arbitrary dispensation of justice (prohibited by the Eighth Amendment) or of deliberate racial prejudice in this specific case. Justice Lewis Powell, in the majority opinion, wrote that discretion is bound to lead to disparities, but statistical disparities were not proof enough. Powell noted: "At most, the Baldus study indicates a discrepancy that appears to correlate with race."

no solid evidence to support this claim. However, the Supreme Court, in its 1976 decision upholding Georgia's capital punishment statute, concluded that for many potential murderers the possibility of execution "is undoubtedly a significant deterrence." This discrepancy illustrates the sometimes-stark conflict between legal assumptions and social science observations.

Finally, regarding the dilemma between truth and stability as goals of law enforcement, the controversy over the propriety of capital punishment is again illustrative. Community standards often support capital punishment because society demands a sense of final justice after a heinous crime has been committed; the cathartic effect of learning that a murderer has himself been executed cannot be denied. For example, Morris Odell Mason was electrocuted in Virginia in 1985. He had been convicted of raping and murdering two elderly women, raping a 12-year-old girl, and maiming her 13-year-old sister. But Mason was a retarded black man with an IQ of

66 who had been diagnosed on three occasions as suffering from paranoid schizophrenia. He was found guilty of acts committed only *after* he had vainly pleaded with the state to be taken off the streets and put back into custody (Wicker, 1985). Was Morris Mason so clearly responsible for his behavior that it was appropriate for the state to kill him? Or would detention in a state hospital for the criminally insane have been more just? In a similar case, Justice Sandra Day O'Connor's majority opinion stated, "There is insufficient evidence of a national consensus against executing mentally retarded people convicted of capital offenses for us to conclude that it is categorically prohibited by the Eighth Amendment."

## Voluntary Executions

Some defendants "volunteer" to be executed. Gary Gilmore, the first person executed after *Furman,* resisted all efforts to save him and willingly faced the firing squad (Mailer, 1979). Recently, Indiana upheld a plea bargain in which the defendant agreed to plead guilty if he would receive the death penalty! The trial court accepted the plea bargain, the state proved an aggravating circumstance, the defendant produced no mitigating evidence, and the judge imposed the death penalty, which was upheld on automatic appeal to the state supreme court (*Smith v. State,* 1997).

A competent defendant might rationally decide that death is preferable to lengthy imprisonment, and then the question arises as to whether society should force defendants to attempt to prevent their own executions. Free will is a premise of our criminal justice system, and the right to make basic decisions is a corollary of that premise. Consistent with those principles, a competent defendant should not be forced to present mitigating evidence or to appeal a death sentence. On the other hand, there probably should be a presumption that a defendant is incompetent to choose death. The prospect of lengthy imprisonment, perhaps on death row, might cause a prisoner to become suicidal. Those already on death row might have a strong urge to forego appeals

and "get it over with." For these reasons, the state should be required to show that the defendant voluntarily and knowingly is "choosing death" (Chandler, 1998). For example, after his murder conviction was affirmed on appeal, Alan Willett elected to waive his postconviction remedies and be executed. A psychiatrist examined Willett and found that he was competent to elect between life and death. The trial court accepted Willett's waiver of further proceedings, and the Supreme Court of Arkansas affirmed the decision (*Willett v. State,* 1999).

Society should also have an interest in preventing the imposition of a death penalty that is not warranted by the facts. Suppose a man, drunk and distraught over the loss of his job, kills his wife and children and attempts to kill himself. Failing in his attempt at suicide, he is arrested and charged with capital murder. He then asks for the death penalty and refuses to allow his lawyer to present mitigating evidence or to argue that the death penalty would not be the correct sentence. In such cases, we believe that the judge should appoint an **amicus curiae** (friend of the court) to investigate the case and present relevant mitigating evidence. The jury should not be required to decide the case on an incomplete record.

# Death Qualification and "Death-Qualified" Jurors

In most states, sentencing decisions are made by the trial judge, except in capital cases, for which juries usually decide the sentence. (As we discussed in Chapter 13, a few states give the jury responsibility for allocating other punishments, but even in these states, momentum is building to abolish jury sentencing).

When jurors are impaneled to serve on cases in which the death penalty is being sought, they are required to answer voir dire questions about their attitudes toward capital punishment. Are some prospective jurors so in favor of the death penalty that they would vote for it regardless of

**BOX 17-8**   **Reactions to voting for the death penalty**

Jurow's (1971) Capital Punishment Attitude Questionnaire contained a section in which respondents were to assume that they were "on a jury to determine the sentence for a defendant who has already been convicted of a very serious crime." Then they were asked to choose among the following five answers:

1. I could not vote for the death penalty regardless of the facts and circumstances of the case.
2. There are some kinds of cases in which I know I could not vote for the death penalty even

if the law allowed me to, but others in which I would be willing to consider voting for it.
3. I would consider all the penalties provided by the law and the facts and circumstances of the particular case.
4. I would usually vote for the death penalty in a case when the law allows me to.
5. I would always vote for the death penalty in a case when the law allows me to.

Option 1 resembles the criterion established in *Witherspoon v.*

*Illinois* for exclusion of prospective jurors. Fitzgerald and Ellsworth (1984) found that about one-sixth of their respondents would be eliminated from jury service because they chose option 1.

Before *Witherspoon*, a general "scruples" question was used, such as "Do you have any conscientious scruples that would cause you to hesitate about sentencing the defendant to death?" Under that rule, an even higher percentage was excluded.

the weight of the evidence? Ironically, the law has been much more concerned about those potential jurors who are opposed to the death penalty than about those who, because of their personal beliefs, might apply it even when it would be much too harsh a penalty. Until 1968, persons who indicated they had any "scruples" against the death penalty were routinely prohibited from sitting as jurors in trials for capital crimes (Haney, 1984). In this sense, *scruples* meant moral reservations or hesitancy because of conscientious feelings.

In 1968, in the case of *Witherspoon v. Illinois,* the U.S. Supreme Court concluded that having "scruples" was too broad a guideline because it excluded too many people from jury service. In the *Witherspoon* decision, the Court ruled that the standard for excluding a juror from a capital case was that the juror had to express unequivocal opposition of the sort that would prevent the juror from ever considering the death penalty, regard-

less of the crime. (This distinction is illustrated by the attitude survey questions in ◆ Box 17-8.)

The procedure of **death qualification** occurs during the voir dire portion of a capital trial, when jurors are questioned about their beliefs regarding the death penalty. If, on the basis of their answers, jurors indicate extreme beliefs about the death penalty, they may be excused "for cause"—that is, dismissed from serving in that case. The procedures and standards for determining which jurors should be excused for cause in capital trials have undergone substantial changes in the past 25 years. These changes began with the *Witherspoon* case.

*Witherspoon* limited the reasons jurors could be excused for cause to the following two situations: (1) those prospective jurors who indicated that they would automatically vote against imposing capital punishment, without regard to any evidence they might hear at the trial, should be excluded; and (2) those prospective jurors who indicated that their beliefs about capital punishment would prevent them from making an impartial decision about the defendant's guilt should be excused for cause. As a result of this standard, most defendants facing the death penalty have been convicted and sentenced to die by what are known as "death-qualified" juries. Such decisions remain suspect because of the nature of the juries that rendered them: "in capital trials, unlike other criminal cases, the issue of guilt and innocence is decided exclusively by jurors who have stated a willingness to impose a death sentence" (W. C. Thompson, 1989, p. 185).

When Witherspoon appealed his conviction and death sentence to the Supreme Court, he did so on the ground that the jury selection procedures were arranged to produce a jury that would be "biased in favor of conviction" (*Witherspoon v. Illinois,* 1968, p. 516). But the jury selection procedures had other problems; early in the voir dire of Witherspoon's trial, the presiding judge had said, "Let's get those conscientious objectors out of the way without wasting any time on them." In rapid succession, 47 members of the venire were successfully challenged for cause on the basis of their attitudes toward the death penalty.

To support his claims of bias, Witherspoon presented three unpublished studies showing that those jurors who survived the selection regarding attitudes about the death penalty were biased toward the *guilt* of the defendants; that is, they were not representative of all prospective jurors with regard to a verdict, which should be made independently of any later decision about punishment. But the Supreme Court balked; it concluded that the data were "too fragmentary and tentative . . . to establish that jurors not opposed to the death penalty tend to favor the prosecution in the determination of guilt" (p. 527). So, with respect to the claim that the selection procedure had affected the verdict, Witherspoon lost his appeal; his conviction was upheld.

But on his claim that the sentencing procedure was inappropriate, Witherspoon won. The Supreme Court wrote, "It is self-evident that, in its role as arbiter of the punishment to be imposed, this jury fell woefully short of that impartiality to which the petitioner was entitled under the Sixth and Fourteenth Amendments" (p. 518). The Court agreed that excluding all jurors with any scruples about the death penalty produced a jury that was unfairly biased against the defendant in the penalty phase of the trial.

However, the Supreme Court left open the question of whether death-qualified jurors were conviction-prone, and from 1968 to 1980 the lower courts followed suit. They refused to consider the findings of newer, better-designed social science studies on the topic (Gross, 1984). It was not until 1985 that the U.S. Supreme Court considered the issue again.

The first major development since the *Witherspoon* decision was an appeal to the California Supreme Court (*Hovey v. Superior Court,* 1980). As we noted, *Witherspoon* had allowed two types of prospective jurors to be excused for cause: (1) those unequivocally against the death penalty in any case and (2) those who could not be fair and impartial in determining a capital defendant's guilt or innocence. The logic behind these exclusions was understandable: Jurors must be willing and able to follow the law and to apply their judgment to the evidence (Gross, 1984).

The petitioner in *Hovey* argued, "Prospective jurors, who would automatically vote against death at the *penalty* phase, cannot constitutionally be excused from sitting at the *guilt* phase, if they can be fair and impartial at that phase." *Hovey* forced the California court to face two constitutional issues: (1) Are death-qualified juries prone to convict? (2) Are they less representative of the community than non-death-qualified juries? (Specifically, do they include fewer blacks and women?)

The brief prepared for Hovey's appeal reported several new empirical studies that had been conducted in 1979 but were not published until 1984, in a special issue of the journal *Law and Human Behavior.* Employing a better methodology than the earlier unpublished studies, these studies produced results that were consistent with one another and with the earlier studies that the Supreme Court had disregarded. They showed that death-qualified jurors were conviction-prone (Gross, 1984).

Phoebe Ellsworth (then at Stanford University) and her colleagues were the authors of this integrated set of empirical studies that demonstrated the effect of death qualification on verdicts as well as sentences. In the first study, Fitzgerald and Ellsworth (1984) surveyed a random sample of 811 eligible jurors in Alameda County, California. A total of 64% favored the death penalty (37% did so "strongly"). Another 17% said they could never vote to impose the death penalty and thus were excludable under the *Witherspoon* decision. This group included a higher percentage of the blacks than of the whites (25% vs. 15%) and more of the women than of the men (21% vs. 13%). Twice as many Democrats as Republicans were excluded.

The 17% representing the "excludables" may be higher than in other parts of the country. Palladino and his colleagues (1986) found in a telephone interview of a sample of prospective jurors in southern Indiana that only 9% would qualify as "Witherspoon excludables." This study found that, *if* the jury's vote is a recommendation to the judge, as it is in Indiana, a greater percentage of prospective jurors will be willing to vote for the death penalty. However, this study, like the one in California, found that a greater percentage of women (12%) than of men (4%), as well as a greater percentage of blacks than of whites, were "excludables." Another study (Luginbuhl & Middendorf, 1988), using North Carolina jurors, found 10% strongly opposed to the death penalty, with the same race and gender differences as in the previous two studies.

In contrast, death-qualified jurors were more prone to favor the prosecutor's viewpoint, more likely to mistrust criminal defendants and their counsel, more in sympathy with a punitive approach toward offenders, and more concerned with crime control than with due process (see Chapter 1 for Packer's distinction between these two orientations).

In a follow-up study, Cowan, Thompson, and Ellsworth (1984) showed a two-hour videotape of a murder trial reenactment to 288 mock jurors who were either death qualified or excludable, using the *Witherspoon* ruling. (Thirty of the 288 were excludable.) These adults were divided into juries. About half of the juries were composed entirely of death-qualified jurors; the others contained from two to four excludables, with the majority being death qualified. Three-fourths of the death-qualified jurors found the defendant guilty; only 53% of the excludables did. The "mixed" juries took a more serious approach to their deliberation task; they were more critical of witnesses and better able to remember the evidence.

Ellsworth, Bukaty, Cowan, and Thompson (1984) predicted that those persons who were excluded from jury service on capital cases because they opposed the death penalty would be more likely to accept an insanity defense in a homicide case than death-qualified subjects would. This prediction was confirmed when the insanity defense was based on a diagnosis of schizophrenia. When disorders involving brain damage (epilepsy or mental retardation) were given as the causes of the purported insanity, death-qualified jurors were as likely as the excludables to find the defendant insane.

In a final study, Thompson, Cowan, Ellsworth, and Harrington (1984) studied why death-qualified jurors voted guilty more often than excludable jurors. The researchers found that the death-qualified jurors tend "to interpret evidence in a way more favorable to the prosecution and less favorable to the defense" (p. 104). The two groups expressed different kinds of regret over making a mistaken decision; death-qualified jurors were more upset about acquitting a guilty defendant, whereas excludables were more disturbed about convicting an innocent one. Subsequent research has added to these findings; subjects who strongly favor the death penalty are more likely to attribute criminal intent to a defendant and are more inclined to perceive the defendant as a danger to society (Goodman-Delahunty, Greene, & Hsiao, 1998).

But the California Supreme Court did not provide relief to Hovey. The court was concerned with a category of jurors not yet mentioned: those who would *always* vote to impose the death penalty in every capital case, regardless of the weight of the evidence. Such persons can be thought of as "automatic death penalty jurors" or, more colloquially, "hanging jurors." In California this type of prospective juror, who is the mirror opposite of the juror irrevocably opposed to capital punishment, is also excluded from juries in capital cases, but none of the empirical studies identified this group. Frankly, the researchers considered the number of people with such attitudes to be too small to be of any practical importance. Ironically, the court expressed concern about excluding the same end of the continuum of prospective jurors that initiated our discussion of this topic—those who are ready to sentence a defendant to death no matter what the evidence is. Thus, the court concluded that, because of this omission, the studies had made the wrong comparisons; the death-qualified jury that they had described was not the *true* "California death-qualified jury" from which automatic death penalty jurors are excluded. The court acknowledged that this latter group may exist only "in theory," but the burden of proof was on the petitioner, Hovey, to show why excluding this type of juror would not offset the effects of excluding those who would never consider voting for the death penalty under any circumstances. So Hovey's appeal was denied.

The courts remained sensitive about the possible problems of using death-qualified jurors, even though they have not prohibited the procedure. For example, in the case of *Grigsby v. Mabry* (1980), the U.S. Supreme Court raised the concern that prosecutors may ask for the death penalty in order to get a death-qualified jury, knowing full well that such a jury is more likely to convict. In the Grigsby trial, as soon as the prosecutor obtained a "guilty" verdict, he withdrew his request for the death penalty.

In 1985, the U.S. Supreme Court used the case of *Wainwright v. Witt* to change the standard for death-qualifying jurors and thereby broadened even further its acceptance of death-qualified juries. By a 7–2 vote, it reinstated the death sentence of convicted Florida child killer Johnny

Paul Witt; it overturned an 11th U.S. Circuit Court of Appeals decision that had thrown out Witt's sentence because one potential juror had been improperly dismissed for having doubts about capital punishment. Justice William H. Rehnquist, writing for the majority, stated that it was not necessary to show that a juror was automatically opposed to the death penalty in order to exclude that juror. Instead, Rehnquist wrote, a judge may bar the prospective juror if the judge concluded that the juror's views would "prevent or substantially impair the performance of his duties as a juror in accordance with his instructions and his oath." Furthermore, he stated, "We do not think . . . a defendant is entitled to a legal presumption or standard that allows jurors to be seated who quite likely will be biased in his favor." The Witt standard increases the percentage of prospective jurors who are excludable (Neises & Dillehay, 1987) beyond the previous estimates of 9% to 29%. A thorough review of research on this topic estimates that as many as 40% may be excluded (W. C. Thompson, 1989).

Reflecting his general mistrust of social science methodology, Justice Rehnquist commented, "Determinations of juror bias cannot be reduced to question-and-answer sessions which obtain results in the manner of catechism." He added that a trial judge should have broad discretion in deciding which prospective jurors may be seated for capital cases because the judge is able to observe each juror closely and is in a position to analyze whether jurors are trying to hide their true feelings. Justice Rehnquist is more sanguine about the ability of judges to detect deception than social scientists are on the basis of their findings from empirical studies. But Justice Rehnquist's decision is the law as it applies to the acceptability of death-qualified jurors—despite the opinions of the social scientists and of some of his Supreme Court colleagues. Justice William Brennan, in a written dissent, reflected the conclusions of the social science research that the ruling will lead to "a jury biased against the defendant, at least with respect to penalty."

For social scientists who had hoped that their empirical findings would influence the courts, the

Supreme Court decision in the case of *Lockhart v. McCree* (1986; Bersoff, 1987) seemed to be the final nail in the coffin. Ardia McCree was an Arkansas man who had been convicted of robbery and murder. At his trial the judge had excluded eight prospective jurors who said that they could not under any circumstances impose a death sentence (Taylor, 1986). The American Psychological Association submitted an *amicus curiae* brief in support of McCree's position. It summarized three decades of social science research showing that the process of death qualification produced juries that were likely to be conviction-prone and that were unrepresentative of the larger community (Bersoff, 1987).

But, in spite of this concerted effort, the Supreme Court, in a 6–3 vote, held that the jury in McCree's trial was not an improper one. Chief Justice Rehnquist wrote the majority opinion. On the issue of unrepresentativeness of death-qualified juries, he noted that the only requirement was to have representative jury panels. Exclusion of groups who were "defined solely in terms of shared attitudes" was not improper.

Furthermore, the majority rejected the claim that death-qualified juries were less than neutral. An impartial jury, Justice Rehnquist wrote, "consists of nothing more than jurors who will conscientiously apply the law and find the facts"; he noted that McCree had conceded that each of the jurors who convicted him met that test. So the Supreme Court reversed the appellate decision and upheld the state's use of a death-qualified jury for the decision at the guilt/innocence phase; the defendant had argued for two juries: a guilt/innocence jury that was not death qualified and, if necessary, a penalty jury that was death qualified.

In effect, the majority opinion dismissed 30 years of research as irrelevant (W. C. Thompson, 1989). The conflict between social science and the law was never more sharply represented than in the majority opinion's final view:

> We will assume for purposes of this opinion that the studies are both methodologically valid and adequate to establish that "death-qualification" in fact produces juries somewhat more "conviction-prone" than "non-death-qualified juries." We hold, nonetheless, that the Constitution does not prohibit the states from "death-qualifying" juries in capital cases. (p. 1764)

To summarize, many social scientists who have studied death qualification are concerned that these Supreme Court decisions condone trial juries that are slanted toward both conviction and capital punishment. Although a few scholars question whether the evidence linking death penalty beliefs and conviction-proneness is strong (Elliott, 1991), the consensus is that death qualification disadvantages defendants (Allen, Mabry, & McKelton, 1998; Ellsworth, 1991; Nietzel, McCarthy, & Kerr, 1999) and that alternative approaches to impaneling juries in capital cases could probably overcome these disadvantages (Cox & Tanford, 1989).

If, during the voir dire, a prospective juror were to state that he or she would automatically vote for the death penalty if the defendant were found guilty, this prospective juror also should be excluded by the judge. But in an Oklahoma case (*Ross v. Oklahoma,* 1988), the judge refused to exclude such a man. The jury in the trial convicted Ross, and he was sentenced to death. In responding to Ross's appeal, the Supreme Court, in a 5–4 vote, upheld the conviction and the death sentence. Justice Rehnquist wrote that it was true that the trial judge had erred, but this error had not deprived Ross of an impartial jury because his attorney later excluded this man from the jury by using one of the defense's peremptory challenges (Taylor, 1988a). The dissenting opinion—consistent with the reaction of many social scientists—said that the defendant's rights had been violated; his attorney had been forced to use one of the limited number of peremptory challenges to dismiss someone who should have been dismissed for cause. In the 1992 case of *Morgan v. Illinois,* the Supreme Court did rule that defendants' due process rights are violated if they are forced to trial with a jury that includes an individual who so favored the death penalty that he or she would vote for it automatically in every case.

# The Rights of Prisoners

Although the first jail in America was established in the Massachusetts Bay Colony in 1632, it wasn't until the 19th century that imprisonment became the preferred penalty for convicted criminals. In colonial times, jails were used only to hold people awaiting trial. After conviction, depending on the severity of the crimes, they were fined, whipped, put in stocks, branded, or hung (Carlson, Hess, & Orthmann, 1999). The Quakers were appalled at these barbaric penalties and pressured the Pennsylvania legislature to provide more humane punishments. In 1794, the legislature funded a separate wing of the Philadelphia Walnut Street Jail to hold convicted felons, thus establishing the first prison in the United States.

Prisoners in the Walnut Street Jail and other early U.S. prisons were kept in solitary confinement with only the Bible for companionship. The hope was that the felons would read the Bible and repent of their sins (hence the word *penitentiary*) so they would emerge from prison as changed men. The reality, of course, was much different.

From the beginning, prisons were places of strict confinement in which prisoners were punished, often brutally, for violations of prison rules. Prison administrators had free rein to abuse the inmates as they wished. There were no "prisoner's rights." In 1871 a Virginia judge stated that a prisoner has "forfeited not only his liberty, but all his personal rights except that which the law in its humanity accords to him. He is for the time being the slave of the State" (*Ruffin v. Virginia,* 1871, p. 794). The courts deferred to the supposed expertise and "tender mercies" of prison officials and largely maintained a "hands-off" policy toward prisoners' complaints (Bronstein, 1980).

But word began to spread about abuses—including, as Bronstein (1980) notes, "abuses of the cruelest sort: physical brutality, gross medical neglect, the silence rules, racial discrimination, kangaroo courts for disciplinary matters, incredible tortures . . . , chain gangs, bread and water diets and worse, economic exploitation by the convict lease system . . . , along with meaningless and brutally hard work" (p. 20). Slowly, the courts' "hands-off" policy was replaced by a willingness to intervene to stop the worst of the abuses. Though prison administrators are still accorded much discretion (*Bell v. Wolfish,* 1979), prisoners do have rights that will be protected by the courts. For example, a recent decision involving the notorious Pelican Bay State Prison in California (*Madrid v. Gomez,* 1995) illustrates the willingness of some courts to intercede in matters of prison management.

The Pelican Bay State Prison was opened in 1989. It is a maximum-security prison with a special unit—the Security Housing Unit (SHU) built to house the "worst of the worst," inmates with serious disciplinary infractions in other institutions, habitual criminals, and prison gang members. A class action was filed in federal court over the conditions within Pelican Bay and the SHU. The case was assigned to Judge Thelton Henderson, who presided over the lengthy and complex lawsuit. After hearing from 57 witnesses who provided more than three months of testimony, looking at more than 6000 exhibits, and spending two days touring Pelican Bay, Judge Henderson issued a 120-page opinion examining every aspect of Pelican Bay and the SHU. He agreed with many of the plaintiffs' complaints and ordered the state to revise its procedures for the use of physical force, improve physical and mental health care, and afford fair hearings before assigning alleged gang members to the SHU.

## Due Process Rights

In *Wolff v. McDonnell* (1974), the Supreme Court held that prisoners charged with a serious disciplinary offense have a right to call witnesses and present evidence at their disciplinary hearings. However, the Court held that "procedural due process" does not require that prison officials

*The maximum-security prison at Pelican Bay*

allow the prisoner to confront or cross-examine the witnesses against him. A prisoner might never know what information was considered by the hearing committee. For example, in the Pelican Bay case, Judge Henderson ruled that it was constitutionally permissible for prison officials to assign alleged gang members to the SHU on the basis of hearsay statements and statements by confidential informants.

*Washington v. Harper* (1990) is an important case involving due process rights. A competent person has a constitutionally protected liberty interest to refuse unwanted medication, and the Court held in *Harper* that prisoners also are entitled to due process protection against forcible administration of psychoactive medication. Only after it has been determined that the drug is medically appropriate and essential to the safety of the prisoner or others can it be administered against the will of the prisoner.

## Cruel and Unusual Punishment

The Eighth Amendment to the United Constitution protects us from "cruel and unusual" punishments, but in general, the Supreme Court has not been very sympathetic to Eighth Amendment attacks on U.S. prison conditions (Haney & Zimbardo, 1998). In the 1992 case of *Hudson v. McMillian,* the Supreme Court held that prison officials violate the Eighth Amendment when they intentionally or with "deliberate indifference" subject prisoners to *unnecessary* pain or hardship. In the Pelican Bay case, for example, Judge Henderson found that caging a naked prisoner outside and exposed to the elements was cruel and unusual (p. 1171).

The Supreme Court, however, has tended to focus less on prison conditions themselves and more on the expressed motivations or justification of the officials in charge of these conditions. As a result, prison officials' explanations for any of a number of extreme measures will usually be accepted by judges. In *Bass v. Perrin* (1999), for example, the federal court accepted a Florida prison administrator's explanation for keeping two prisoners in solitary confinement for two years: the official claimed that both men were serious security risks—one had killed a guard, and the other had attempted to escape five times. It is only at the extreme—where the use of force or the conditions of confinement "shock the conscience"— that a judge will interfere with the administration of a prison.

The effect of solitary confinement on prisoners' mental health should be cause for concern. After extensive testimony, including testimony that a SHU prisoner was found sitting on the floor in a catatonic state, staring "bug-eyed" at the walls and ceiling, Judge Henderson ordered the state to increase its mental health staffing, keep adequate records, and provide adequate mental health care to the Pelican Bay inmates (pp. 1224, 1258). Rebman (1999) describes studies of solitary confinement conducted by Dr. Stuart Grassian and others in the early 1980s. Grassian studied prisoners incarcerated in the maximum-security unit at Massachusetts's Walpole prison. He found them to suffer strikingly consistent symptoms, including sensory disturbances, primitive aggressive fantasies, and disturbances of memory and attention (p. 580). Since it is apparent that solitary confinement can cause extreme suffering, the courts should require particularly stringent justification for such confinement.

As damaging as solitary confinement can be, the negative effects of average prison life are surprisingly powerful also. The most famous demonstration of these effects—indeed, one of the most celebrated examples of psychological research in the 20th century—was the Stanford Prison Project (Haney, Banks, & Zimbardo, 1973), a study that we also briefly described in Chapter 2. In an attempt to study the dynamics among prison guards and prisoners, the authors recruited a group of college student volunteers to play the roles of guards and inmates in a simulated prison environment. Twenty-five years after the experiment, the authors summarized their dramatic discoveries as follows:

> The outcome of our study was shocking and unexpected to us, our professional colleagues, and the general public. Otherwise emotionally strong college students who were randomly assigned to be mock-prisoners suffered acute psychological trauma and breakdowns. Some of the students begged to be released from the intense pains of less than a week of merely simulated imprisonment, whereas others adapted by becoming blindly obedient to the unjust authority of the guards. The guards, too—who also had been carefully chosen on the basis of their normal-average scores on a variety of personality measures—quickly internalized their randomly assigned role. Many of these seemingly gentle and caring young men, some of whom had described themselves as pacifists or Vietnam War "doves," soon began mistreating their peers and were indifferent to the obvious suffering that their actions produced. Several of them devised sadistically inventive ways to harass and degrade the prisoners, and none of the less actively cruel mock-guards ever intervened or complained about the abuses they witnessed. Most of the worst prisoner treatment came on the night shifts and other occasions when the guards thought they could avoid the surveillance and interference of the research team. Our planned two-week experiment had to be aborted after only six days because the experience dramatically and painfully transformed most of the participants in ways we did not anticipate, prepare for, or predict. . . .
>
> [E]ven in this minimalist prison setting, all of our "guards" participated in one way or another in the pattern of mistreatment that quickly developed. Indeed, some escalated their definition of "role-appropriate" behavior to become highly feared, sadistic tormentors. Although the prisoners' terms of incarceration were extremely abbreviated (corresponding, really, to very short-term pretrial detention in a

county jail), half of our prisoner–participants left before the study was terminated because they could not tolerate the pains of this merely simulated imprisonment. The pains were as much psychological—feelings of powerlessness, degradation, frustration, and emotional distress—as physical—sleep deprivation, poor diet, and unhealthy living conditions. Unlike our participants, of course, many experienced prisoners have learned to suppress such outward signs of psychological vulnerability lest they be interpreted as weakness, inviting exploitation by others. (Haney & Zimbardo, 1998, pp. 709, 719)

## Rights to Free Communication

Inmates have the right to communicate with others, but this right may be limited in the name of "legitimate penological interests." In *Turner v. Safley* (1987), the Supreme Court set out three factors to be considered in right-to-communicate claims by prisoners: (1) whether there is a clear connection between regulations on inmates' communication and the prison's legitimate interest in ensuring the security of the institution, (2) whether there are alternative means by which the inmate can exercise the right of communication (e.g., by mail rather than by phone), and (3) whether the regulation represents an "exaggerated response" to the prison's concerns about matters such as security. Applying this standard, prisons (and the courts) often distinguish between incoming and outgoing mail: Incoming mail is much more subject to being opened and inspected because it might contain contraband; outgoing mail normally will be opened only if the officials suspect that criminal activity is being planned. Mail between an inmate and his or her attorney is generally treated differently. Incoming mail is opened in the presence of the inmate to check for contraband but is not read; outgoing attorney mail is not opened (Palmer & Palmer, 1999).

Most prisoners are allowed to have visitors, but the courts have not recognized a constitutional right to visitation for persons other than attorneys. Contact visitation is generally restricted to prisoners who do not pose a security risk or a serious risk of introducing contraband.

## Religious Rights

Courts are increasingly sympathetic to inmates' claims that prison regulations unconstitutionally interfere with their right to free exercise of their religion. However, prisons are not required to go to great expense and trouble to accommodate inmates' religious beliefs. In *Hamilton v. Schirro* (1996), for example, a federal court refused to require a prison to provide a "sweat lodge" to Native Americans, who believed that their prayers must be proceeded by sweating impurities out in a sauna-type structure. The court accepted the prison's argument that allowing prison inmates to congregate around a fire in a tent was impractical and potentially dangerous.

# SUMMARY

**1. What are the purposes of punishment?** Punishment is associated with seven purposes: general deterrence, individual deterrence, incapacitation, retribution, expression of moral outrage, rehabilitation, and restitution. Although rehabilitation originally played a stronger role as a justification, deterrence, incapacitation, and retribution are now advocated as the major justifications for punishment.

**2. How are the values of discretion and fairness reflected in sentencing decisions?** The allocation of punishments is second only to the determination of guilt or innocence in importance to the criminal defendant. The sentencing process raises again the conflicts that permeate a psychological approach to the legal system. Until recently, judges (and, in some states, juries) were allocated broad discretion in sentencing. Some judges are much more severe than the norm; others, more lenient. In recent years, concern over sentencing disparity has led to greater use of determinate sentencing and tighter controls over judicial discretion in sentencing.

**3.** *What factors influence sentencing decisions?* Determinants of sentencing can be divided into relevant and irrelevant factors. For example, seriousness of the crime is a relevant factor, and there is a general relationship between it and the severity of the punishment. But a number of other, less relevant, factors also are related to severity of sentence, such as the race and gender of the offender and of the victim.

Possible sources of bias in judges' sentencing decisions include their age, experience, and background in the legal system. The sentencing hearing is usually a brief, routinized procedure. Factors that predict the sentence include (1) type of crime, (2) extent of the offender's past record, (3) status of the offender between arrest and conviction, and (4) the recommendation by the probation officer.

**4.** *What special factors are considered in the sentencing of repeated sex offenders?* Because they are believed to be at high risk for reoffend-

ing, sex offenders have been singled out for three types of special punishment: (1) mandatory registration and community notification, (2) involuntary commitment, (3) extreme treatments such as chemical castration.

**5.** *How is the death sentence decided by juries?* Jurors who oppose the death penalty regardless of the nature of the crime or the circumstances of the case are excluded from both the guilt phase and the sentencing phase of capital trials. Social science research has shown that the remaining so-called death-qualified jurors are not only unrepresentative of the entire population of potential jurors (fewer women and blacks) but also conviction-prone. But the Supreme Court has not been responsive to these findings.

**6.** *What legal rights do prisoners have?* Convicted prisoners have fewer rights than other institutionalized persons because the courts have generally assumed that prison officials should be granted considerable latitude in the way they administer their institutions. Prisoners do retain the right to avoid "cruel and unusual punishment," to express religious beliefs, and to have certain due process protections.

## KEY TERMS

| | | | |
|---|---|---|---|
| aggravating factors | chemical castration | intermediate sanctions | restorative justice* |
| *amicus curiae** | death qualification | mitigating factors | sentencing disparity |
| brutalization | determinate sentencing | paraphilia | shaming penalty |

---

 InfoTrac COLLEGE EDITION

• For additional readings go to **http://www.infotrac-college.com/wadsworth** and enter a search term related to your interest. The key terms that have been asterisked above will pull up several related articles. *See also:* for intermediate sanctions, see ALTERNATIVES TO IMPRISONMENT.

# Glossary

**abuse excuse**   A legal tactic by which a person charged with a crime claims that past victimization justified his or her retaliation.

**absolute judgment**   An eyewitness's process of deciding, when looking at a sequential lineup, whether any of the people shown in the lineup match the perpetrator.

**adoption study**   A procedure used to evaluate the effects of heredity versus environment in determining behavior, specifically criminal behavior.

**adjudicative competence**   The set of abilities necessary for a criminal defendant to understand the proceedings in which he or she is participating and make rational decisions about the alternative courses of action that are available to be pursued.

**advance medical directives**   Legal documents in which patients indicate the kinds of future medical treatments they will agree to should they later become incapacitated and therefore be incompetent to make treatment decisions for themselves at the time.

**adversarial system**   A system of resolving disputes in which the parties, usually represented by counsel, argue and present evidence to a neutral fact finder, who makes a decision based on the evidence and arguments presented by the parties; as distinguished from an *inquisitorial system,* in which the fact finder takes an active part in determining what occurred.

**advocate**   A professional person whose goal is to represent the interests of another party.

**affidavit**   A signed, written statement by a potential witness, bearing on issues relevant to a dispute or trial.

**affirmative defense**   In a trial, a position by the defendant that places the burden on the defendant to prove his or her claim. Insanity or self-defense is an example of an affirmative defense.

**age regression**   A procedure in hypnosis in which it is claimed that the subject can be returned to an earlier time in his or her life.

**agency**   A striving for achievement and success.

**aggravating circumstances**   Conditions that make a criminal act more serious—for example, to knowingly create a risk of death or serious injury to other persons as well as to the victim.

**alternative dispute resolution**   Any legal mechanism used to settle a conflict without going to trial.

**amicus curiae**   "Friend of the court"; someone not a party to the action (i.e., not the defendant or plaintiff) who files a brief to argue a particular point relevant to the case.

**analog studies**   Studies that simulate real-life situations.

**anomie**   A sense of alienation or meaninglessness.

**antisocial personality disorder**   A personality disorder characterized by repeated rule breaking, chronic manipulativeness, impulsive and irresponsible behavior, callous attitudes toward others, and a lack of guilt or remorse for wrongdoing.

**applied scientist**   Scientists who apply their knowledge to solving real-world problems.

**arbitration**   A form of dispute resolution in which a neutral third party makes a decision that is binding on the two disputants.

**atavism**   The view that crime is due to a genetic throwback to a more primitive and aggressive form of human being.

**attribution theory**   A theory in social psychology that deals with the explanations people make for the causes of their behavior and the behavior of others.

**authoritarianism**   A set of beliefs and characteristics that include submissiveness to authorities, demands for obedience from subordinates, intolerance of minorities and other outgroups, and endorsement of the use of power and punishment to ensure conformity to conventional norms.

**autobiographical memory**   Memory for one's own life experiences.

**base rate**   The frequency with which some event occurs.

**basic scientist**   Scientists who study a phenomenon in order to understand it, without concern for whether their work will be used in solving real-world problems.

**battered woman syndrome**   A collection of symptoms many of which are manifest in women who have suffered prolonged and extensive abuse from their spouses.

**belief in a just world**   The belief that justice exists in the world and that people get what they deserve.

**belief perseverance**   An explanation for why jurors disregard instructions to disregard inadmissible testimony.

**bench trial**   A trial in which the judge, rather than the jury, makes the decision.

**beyond a reasonable doubt**   The standard of proof required in a criminal trial; generally means that jurors (or the judge) should be strongly convinced (but not necessarily convinced beyond all doubt) that the defendant is guilty before they convict.

**biological theory of crime**   An explanation for the causes of criminal behavior that uses heredity and constitutional characteristics of the lawbreaker.

**black sheep effect**   The tendency to be more punitive toward those members of one's group who violate the norms of the group.

**borderline personality disorder**   A personality disorder characterized by impulsivity and instability in moods, behavior, self-image, and interpersonal relationships.

**Brawner rule**   States that a defendant is not responsible for criminal conduct when, as a result of a mental disease or defect, he or she lacks substantial capacity either to appreciate the criminality (wrongfulness) of the conduct or to conform his or her conduct to the requirements of the law. (Also known as the *ALI rule*.)

**breached duty**   The violation, either through negligence or intentional wrongdoing, of a duty that one party legally owes to another party.

**brutalization**   The proposition that the use of capital punishment actually increases the crime rate by sending a message that it is acceptable to kill those who have wronged us.

**burn-out**   A syndrome that occurs in people who work with other people; symptoms include emotional exhaustion, depersonalization, and reduced personal accomplishment.

**case law**   A law made by rulings by judges in individual cases.

**challenge for cause**   Occurs when individuals are interviewed during any jury selection. If the judge agrees that there is a justification for the attorney's claim of bias, a juror may be excused for cause. Also, a judge may excuse a prospective juror for cause without a request to do so from either attorney.

**change of venue**   A decision by a trial judge to move a trial to another locality, usually done because extensive pretrial publicity has prevented the paneling of an open-minded jury.

**chemical castration**   The use of injections of a female hormone into male rapists as a method of lowering their sex drive.

**civil commitment**   The legal proceeding by which a person who is mentally ill and imminently dangerous is involuntarily committed to a psychiatric hospital.

**civil competence**   The ability of a person to act appropriately in such noncriminal decisions as executing a will or determining medical treatment.

**class action case**   A case that involves many plaintiffs who collectively form a "class" and who claim that they suffered similar injuries as a result of a defendant's actions.

**classical conditioning**   A procedure in which one learns to associate a new response with a stimulus.

**classical school of criminology**   The point of view that evolved in the 1700s and 1800s, emphasizing the role of free will and cost-benefit analysis in determining criminal behavior.

**closing argument**   A summation of evidence, made by an attorney at the end of a trial.

**cognitive interview**   A procedure used to assist victims to recall aspects of a crime or other traumatic event.

**cognitive psychophysiology**   The measurement of mental activity during physiological responses.

**cognizable group**   A group of persons, usually defined by demographic characteristics such as race or gender.

**collateral attacks**   A request by defendants that their convictions be thrown out for some reason after the case is over. A collateral attack is different from an appeal, which is a request to a higher court to reverse a conviction; a collateral attack on a conviction might occur years after the conviction has apparently become final; a petition for a writ of habeas corpus is a form of collateral attack.

**commonsense justice**   Ordinary citizens' basic notions of what is just and fair in contrast to the dictates of formal, statutory law.

**communion**   A concern with intimacy and interpersonal relationships.

**community-based policing**   A policy that increases direct police/citizen contacts within a neighborhood.

**comparative negligence**   A doctrine in civil law under which the negligence of the plaintiff and defendant are measured in terms of percentages.

**compensatory damages**   The payment or restitution owed to a plaintiff for the damages and harm that have been determined to have been caused by a civil defendant.

**competence**   The ability to understand implications of making legal decisions.

**competence to plead guilty**   The ability of a defendant to understand the possible consequences of pleading guilty to criminal charges instead of going to trial and to make a rational choice between the alternatives.

**competence to stand trial**   Sufficient ability to understand the legal proceedings in which one is involved and to consult with one's attorney.

**concordance rate**   The extent of similarity in a behavior or characteristic between two twins.

**conditioned stimulus**   An act that, through association, comes to elicit a learned response.

**confabulation**   One effect of hypnosis, in which the hypnotized subject adds false information to accurate recollections.

**confounding variables**   Variables that distort the results of a study or that compete with the independent variable as explanations of a result.

**containment theory**   The proposition that societal pressure controls the rate of crime.

**content analysis**   Scientific analysis of the content of a conversation or discussion.

**contingency fee**   An agreement between a plaintiff in a civil suit and the plaintiff's attorney by which the attorney receives a portion of any award to the plaintiff but otherwise is not paid by the plaintiff.

**Control Question Test**   A polygraph technique in which the subject is asked a question that elicits an emotional response.

**control theory**   The proposition that people will act in an antisocial way unless they are prevented from doing so.

**correlation**   A measure of the degree to which one variable is related to another.

**crime control model**   A point of view that emphasizes procedures that detect suspects and prosecute defendants.

**criminal profiling**   The use of psychological principles as a crime investigation technique to guide police toward suspects who possess certain personal characteristics as revealed by the way a crime was committed.

**criminology**   The study of crime and criminal behavior.

**critical legal studies**   A philosophical approach to the study of law that proposes that the law is an instrument used by the powerful in society to maintain their control.

**damages**   Money awarded to a person injured by the unlawful act or negligence of another.

**dangerousness**   Behavior that involves acts of physical violence or aggression by one person against another.

**death-qualified jury**   A jury panel that excludes persons whose attitudes about capital punishment would prevent them from performing their sworn duty as jurors.

**decision rule**   The requirement whether a jury must reach a unanimous verdict or whether a majority vote will suffice for a verdict.

**defensive attribution**   An explanation for behavior that enables people to deal with perceived inequities in others' lives and to avoid feelings of vulnerability.

**deferred prosecution**   A procedure whereby offenders (usually first-time offenders) who admit their guilt are placed on probation and the charges against them are dismissed if they successfully complete probation.

**delayed reporting statutes**   Those laws that suspend the statute of limitations to permit alleged victims of child sex abuse to report this after their memory for it has been reinstated.

**deposition**   A witness's pretrial statement given under oath.

**determinate sentencing** The provision of strict limits for the sentences that judges can give for particular crimes.

**dialectic analysis** A scholarly dialogue that focuses on tension or opposition between interacting ideas.

**differential association reinforcement theory** A learning-theory approach that asserts that criminal behavior is the result of socialization into a system of values that is conducive to violations of the law.

**diminished capacity** A variation of the insanity defense that is applicable if the defendant (in the words of the law) lacks the ability to "meaningfully premediate the crime."

**Directed Lie Test** A polygraph technique in which the subject is directed to lie in response to a question.

**discovery** A procedure in which the attorney for one side seeks to become aware of the materials being used by the other side to form its case.

**discounting principle** The notion that jurors should put less weight on information provided under threat than on information given in the absence of threats.

**discretion** The application of judgment to temper a response after having weighed the circumstances.

**dissociation** The act of a person "escaping" from a traumatic event by detaching himself or herself from it.

**dizygotic twins** Fraternal twins; that is, those who share about half of the same genes.

**double jeopardy** A second prosecution for the same offense, prohibited by the Fifth Amendment.

**due process model** A view that proposes the goal of the criminal justice system is to protect innocent suspects from prosecution and conviction.

**duty** The obligation that one party legally owes to another party.

**duty to assist laws** Laws that authorize the criminal prosecution of an individual who fails to render assistance to a victim who is in obvious peril.

**ecological theorists** A group of criminologists who believed that crime was caused primarily by a combination of social, environmental, and cultural factors.

**ectomorph** In Sheldon's typology, a tall, thin physique.

**emotional pretrial publicity** Lurid accounts of a crime that stir emotions and make it difficult for prospective jurors to look at the evidence dispassionately.

**empowerment** The process of increasing power to affect change in one's life.

**encoding** The process of entering a perception into memory.

**endomorph** In Sheldon's typology, a soft rounded physique.

**entrapment** A defense used by criminal defendants, claiming that the government used procedures to encourage criminal activity in otherwise law-abiding persons.

**equality** The goal of treating people in the legal system the same, regardless of their eminence, income, or power.

**equity** The award of resources to participants on the basis of their contributions.

**equivocal death analysis** An application of psychological procedures to determine whether the mode of death was accident, suicide, homicide, or due to natural causes.

**event-related brain potential** Components of brain waves that are affected by stimuli.

**euthanasia** The act of killing an individual for reasons that are considered merciful.

**exclusionary rule** The principle that rules as off limits any material that was obtained illegally.

**exculpatory** Evidence that clears a defendant of fault or guilt.

**executive function** The cognitive ability to plan and regulate behavior carefully.

**experiment** A scientific technique for understanding a phenomenon that usually involves manipulating variables and measuring an outcome.

**ex post facto** Something that is done or formulated after the fact.

**extralegal information** Information about a particular case that is not presented in a legal context.

**extroversion** The personality cluster characterized by outgoing orientation, enthusiasm, and optimism.

**factual pretrial publicity** Nonsensational but damaging information about the defendant that might cause prospective jurors to believe the defendant committed the crime in question; an account of a defendant's criminal record is factual pretrial publicity.

**feminist jurisprudence** An approach to the study of law that is an alternative to portraying the law as an expression of masculine values.

**field experiment** An experiment that is conducted in the real world, rather than in a laboratory setting.

**field studies** Studies conducted in real-life situations.

**focal concerns theory** A theory that relates the criminal activities of lower-class gangs to their need to achieve those ends that are most culturally valued through the simplest possible means.

**forensic psychology** The application of the methods, theories, and concepts of psychology to the legal system. Forensic psychologists may serve as expert witnesses, carry out competence evaluations, and otherwise assist litigators and fact finders.

**fundamental attribution error** The belief that behavior is caused by stable factors internal to a person rather than by situational factors external to a person.

**future best interests of the child** The legal standard by which most child custody decisions are made in the United States.

**gag order** A trial judge's order to the press not to print or broadcast certain information; gag orders of this type are usually found to violate the First Amendment. More common are court orders to attorneys and witnesses not to talk to the press about an upcoming trial; gag orders are entered to prevent pretrial publicity from affecting prospective jurors.

**genealogy** The tracing of the ancestry of an individual; an early method of studying genetic contributions to criminality.

**general pretrial publicity** Media coverage of issues not specifically related to a particular case but which are thematically relevant to the issues at hand; jurors exposed to pretrial publicity about other crimes are more likely to judge a defendant guilty than jurors who have not been exposed to such publicity.

**good Samaritan laws** Laws that encourage altruistic behavior by granting immunity from civil lawsuits to passersby who render assistance to victims in an emergency.

**grand jury** A group of citizens who receive evidence in closed proceedings and decide whether to issue an indictment.

**ground truth** A clear-cut criterion of accuracy.

**guided imagery** The technique of helping a person to form a mental picture of an experience.

**Guilty Knowledge Test** A polygraph technique in which the subject is asked a series of questions whose answers would only be known by the perpetrator.

**habeas corpus** After direct appeals have been exhausted, the defendant may petition the trial court claiming that his or her continued detention is unlawful. If sufficient basis exists, the government may be asked to establish the legality of the detention.

**harm** The losses or adversities suffered by a person who is the victim of wrongdoing.

**harmless error** The legal notion that although an error may have occurred during trial, it did not substantially affect the outcome of the trial.

**hate crimes** Criminal acts that are intended to harm or intimidate people because of their race, ethnicity, sexual orientation, religion, or other minority group status.

**hearsay testimony** Testimony by one person about what another person said.

**hindsight bias** The proposition that knowledge about the outcome of an action influences one's memory or evaluation of the acceptability of the action.

**hyperamnesia** One effect of hypnosis, in which the subject remembers more material than when he or she was not hypnotized.

**hypothesis** A tentative assumption that is tested in a scientific study.

**impeach** To cross-examine a witness with the purpose of calling into question his or her credibility or reliability.

**implicit personality theory** A person's preconceptions about how certain attributes are related to one another and to behavior.

**impossible acts** Behavior that is motivated by criminal intent, but, through an accident or mistake, results in no objective harm to the intended victim.

**inadmissible evidence** That testimony which the judge rules is not proper and, hence, instructs the jury to disregard.

**indictment** An accusation issued by a grand jury charging the defendant with criminal conduct.

**information** A complaint filed by a prosecutor against a defendant.

**inquisitorial approach** The procedure used in Europe, in which questioning is the responsibility solely of the judge.

**insanity** A legal term for a mental disease or defect that, if proved to be present at the time a person committed a criminal act, can result in the person being found not criminally responsible for the act.

**intention** The purpose for an act.

**intentional behavior** Conduct in which an actor means for the outcomes of his or her behavior to occur.

**intermediate sanctions**   A probationary sanction, tailored to the offender, with rehabilitation, deterrence, and restitution as its goals.

**internal/external locus of control**   The tendency for people to believe that their lives are controlled by internal factors such as skill and effort or external factors such as luck or the actions of others.

**interviewer bias**   Bias sometimes exhibited by an interviewer who has some knowledge or preconceived ideas about the topic in question.

**jail diversion programs**   Programs that attempt to keep special populations of citizens, such as the mentally ill, out of jail by providing special forms of supervision and treatment in lieu of incarceration.

**joinder**   The joining together of multiple defendants or multiple charges in one trial.

**joint custody**   A legal outcome in which divorcing parents share or divide various decision-making and control responsibilities for their children.

**juror bias**   The tendency of any juror to evaluate the facts of the case such that the juror favors one side or the other.

**jury nullification**   An option for the jury that allows it to disregard both the law and the evidence and acquit the defendant if the jury believes that an acquittal is justified.

**jury sentiments**   Factors beyond the evidence and the law that jurors may rely on to decide a case.

**justice**   Fairness, or providing outcomes to each party in line with what they deserve.

**juvenile court**   A court to decide criminal charges brought against children under 18; these courts often handle cases of abused or neglected children.

**law and economics**   A point of view in legal philosophy that analyzes legal procedures and doctrine from the framework of economics.

**learned helplessness**   A condition in which people come to believe that they have no personal influence over what happens to them and consequently they passively endure aversive treatment rather than to try to control it.

**learning theory**   A form of criminological theory that emphasizes how specific criminal behaviors are learned directly from reinforcement and modeling influences.

**liable**   Responsible or answerable for some action.

**limiting instruction**   A jury instruction that allows a prior record to be used only to gauge the defendant's credibility.

**malingering**   The intentional fabrication or exaggeration of physical or psychological symptoms in order to gain an incentive or advantage.

**mass murderer**   A person who kills four or more victims in one location during a period of time that lasts anywhere from a few minutes to several hours.

**mediation**   A form of alternative dispute resolution in which a neutral third party helps the disputing parties agree on a resolution to their conflict.

**memory hardening**   A process sometimes associated with hypnotically aided recall whereby a subject transforms a belief or experience into a "memory" that he or she is convinced is accurate.

**mens rea**   A guilty mind; the mental state accompanying a forbidden act.

**mercy killing**   The killing of an individual for compassionate or altruistic motives.

**mesomorph**   In Sheldon's typology, a muscular physique.

**mitigating circumstances**   Factors such as age, mental capacity, motivations, or duress that lessen the degree of guilt in a criminal offense and thus the nature of the punishment.

**Model Rules of Professional Conduct**   A code promulgated by the Americal Bar Association to regulate lawyers' ethical behavior; the Model Rules have been adopted in most states.

**monozygotic twins**   Commonly called identical twins.

**moral dilemmas**   Hypothetical scenarios that require an individual to choose a specific moral action and then justify why that particular resolution was the right thing to do; used to assess levels of moral reasoning.

**motion in limine**   A legal request for a judge to make a pretrial ruling on some matter of law expected to arise at the trial.

**negligence**   Behavior that falls below the legal standard for acting in a way that would protect others from unreasonable risks.

**neuroticism**   A major dimension of personality involving the tendency to experience negative emotions such as anxiety, anger, and depression, often accompanied by distressed thinking and behavior.

**nolo contendre**   A plea of no contest.

**notification law**   A law that notifies citizens that a sex offender has been released in their area.

**one day/one trial systems**   Jury systems in which potential jurors are called for only one day of service or one trial rather than being "on call" for multiple trials for a month or more.

**opening statements**   Not part of the evidence, these orations made by the lawyers on each side give an overview of the evidence that will be presented.

**operant learning**   A form of learning in which the consequences of a behavior influence the likelihood of it being performed in the future.

**operational definition**   The definition of a variable according to the operations or means used to measure it.

**outcome severity**   The severity of an accident or injury.

**paraphilia**   A condition in which sexual arousal and gratification is dependent on fantasizing about and engaging in sexual behavior that is atypical and extreme; it is thought that sexual offenders who are paraphiliacs are likely to reoffend.

**parens patriae**   The parent-like role of guardian assumed by the state to protect the interests of persons with disabilities.

**peremptory challenge**   The opportunity to exclude a certain number of potential jurors from the eventual jury without having to give any reasons; their number, determined by the judge, varies from one jurisdiction to another.

**perjury**   Lying while under oath.

**plea bargain**   In exchange for the defendant's promise to forgo a trial, the government may promise to charge the defendant with a lesser crime or ask the judge for a reduced sentence. When the "bargain" is reached, the defendant pleads guilty and no trial is held.

**policy evaluation**   An activity performed by a psychologist in the role of evaluation researcher, in which the effectiveness of some governmental or other intervention is determined.

**polygraph**   "Lie detector"; an instrument for recording variations in several physiological functions that may indicate whether a person is telling the truth or lying.

**positive coercion bias**   The tendency for jurors to conclude that a suspect is guilty when he or she has been promised leniency for confessing to the crime.

**positivist school of criminology**   A point of view that emphasized that criminal behavior by a person was determined, rather than a product of free will.

**posttraumatic stress disorder**   An anxiety disorder in which the victim experiences a pattern of intense fear reactions after being exposed to a highly stressful event.

**preponderance of the evidence**   The standard for a verdict in a civil suit; the evidence for one side outweighs that of the other by even a slight margin.

**primacy hypothesis**   In this context, the assumption that jurors have often formed definite opinions before the close of the trial.

**primary caretaker standard**   An alternative to the best-interests-of-the-child standard, it states that custody of a child should be awarded to the parent who has been primarily responsible for caring for and supervising that child.

**primary deviance**   Behavior that violates a law or norm for socially acceptable conduct.

**principle of proportionality**   A legal principle that the severity of punishment should be consistent with the seriousness of the offense.

**probable cause**   Reasonable ground for believing that a crime has been committed or that the person committed a crime. Probable cause is required to support the issuance of a search warrant or arrest warrant.

**procedural justice**   A sense that the methods for resolving a dispute have been fair.

**product rule**   Another name for the Durham rule, a legal definition of insanity that states that the accused is not criminally responsible if his or her unlawful conduct was the product of mental disease or defect.

**propensity evidence**   Evidence of a defendant's past wrongdoings that suggest the defendant had the propensity, or inclination, to commit a crime.

**proximate cause**   A cause that constitutes an obvious or substantial reason why a given harm occurred.

**psycholinguistics**   The psychological study of how people use and understand language.

**psychological autopsy**   An attempt to determine the mode of death (whether an accident, suicide, homicide, or natural causes) by an examination of what was known about the deceased.

**psychological stress evaluator**   A device that analyzes vocal characteristics to determine if the person is lying.

**psychological theory of crime**   The approach to explaining criminal behavior that uses factors within the person such as motivation, ability level, and aspirations.

**psychopathy**   A long-term pattern of unsocialized or criminal behavior by a person who feels no guilt about such conduct.

**psychoticism**   A major element in Eysenck's theory of personality, characterized by insensitivity, trouble-making, and lack of empathy.

**punitive damages**   Financial compensation as a form of punishment for failure to respond to a misconduct.

**quasi-experiment**   A study that "comes close" to being a true experiment but lacks one or more of the crucial elements of an experiment, such as random assignment of participants to groups.

**racial profiling**   The police practice of using race as a factor in determining actions such as traffic stops, arrests, and questioning of suspects.

**rape shield laws**   Laws that prevent or restrict the questioning of an alleged rape victim during that person's time on the witness stand; specifically, questioning about the alleged victim's past sexual activities is prohibited or limited.

**rape trauma syndrome**   A collection of behaviors or symptoms that are frequent aftereffects of having been raped.

**rational choice theory**   A proposition that, if the rationale for committing a crime exceeds that for not committing it, the likelihood of the crime being committed increases.

**rational crime theory**   The theory that some illegal behavior "makes sense" because of the reward and unlikelihood of detection.

**reactance theory**   A theory proposing that, if something is denied or withheld from a person, the person's desire for it will increase.

**reaction formation**   The acceptance of whatever is opposite to the norm.

**reality principle**   In psychoanalysis, the task of the ego to reach rational compromises between the instincts of the id and the moral demands of the superego.

**reasonable suspicion**   A term of art referring to police officers' justification for stopping and, perhaps, frisking persons; a reasonable suspicion is one which can be described in terms of specific facts which a judge deems to be reasonable; a mere hunch is not reasonable suspicion.

**rebuttal**   The presentation of evidence to counter or disprove facts previously introduced by the adverse party.

**recall readiness hypothesis**   The assumption that immediate past events are generally remembered better than more remote ones.

**recross**   To cross-examine a witness a second time, after redirect examination.

**redirect questioning**   Questioning by the original attorney that follows the opposing counsel's cross-examination.

**relative judgment**   An eyewitness's process of deciding, when looking at a simultaneous lineup, which of the people shown in the lineup looks most like the perpetrator.

**release on recognizance**   A court order releasing a defendant from custody on the defendant's written promise to appear in court when the defendant's case is scheduled for a hearing, trial, or other proceeding; a defendant who is released on recognizance is not required to deposit money or other property with the court in order to be released.

**relevant/irrelevant procedure**   A polygraph technique in which the subject is asked a series of questions, some of which are relevant to the crime and some of which are not.

**replication**   The repetition of a study to determine if results are similar to those of a previous study.

**repression**   The removal of certain unpleasant thoughts or memories into the unconscious.

**restitution**   The act of giving back what has been taken.

**restorative justice**   Programs to reconcile offenders with their victims; are designed to cause the offender to realize the victim's pain and the victim to understand why the offender committed the crime.

**retention election**   An election in which a judge runs on his/her record; there is no opponent—voters are simply asked whether or not they want to retain the judge in office.

**retrieval**   The process in which a memory is returned to a conscious state.

**risk assessment**   The assessment of the probability that a person will behave violently in certain circumstances, often accompanied by suggestions for how to reduce the likelihood of violent conduct.

**sampling**   The methods used to select research participants.

**schema**   A mental structure that aids in the processing and interpretation of information.

**scientific method** A set of research principles and methods that allow scientists to reach valid conclusions.

**secondary deviance** Creating or increasing the deviant identity of a person through the use of official labels or formal legal sanctions.

**self-defense** A legal defense relied upon by criminal defendants typically charged with homicide; it asserts that the defendant's actions were justified by a reasonable belief that he or she was in imminent danger of death or bodily harm from an attacker.

**sentencing disparity** The tendency of different judges to administer a variety of penalties for the same crime.

**sequential presentation** A lineup presentation in which the choices are shown one at a time.

**serial killer** A person who kills four or more victims on separate occasions, usually in different locations.

**settlement negotiation** In civil cases, the pretrial process whereby plaintiffs and defendants agree to an outcome that ends their legal disagreement.

**sexual predator laws** Laws that allow the government to sentence certain sex offenders (those deemed likely to reoffend) to psychiatric hospitals after they have served their prison sentences.

**shaming penalty** A criminal sanction designed to embarrass an offender by publicizing the offense; shaming penalties are thought to express the community's moral outrage and to deter others from committing this type of crime.

**similarity-leniency hypothesis** The proposal that fact finders will treat those like themselves differently from those they perceive as different.

**social influence** The influence of other people and the social context on behavior.

**social-process theories** A broad category of criminological theory that emphasizes how different types of learning involved in social interactions lead to crime.

**social-psychological theory of crime** The theory that proposes that criminal behavior is learned through social interaction.

**sociolegal studies** A multidisciplinary framework for the study of law.

**sociological theory of crime** An examination of the institutions and norms of society as they determine adherence to the law and lawbreaking.

**sole custody** Awarding custody of a child to one parent, with the other parent being granted rights of visitation and other types of contact with the child.

**somatotypes** Different types of human physiques that Sheldon originally hypothesized were linked to distinct types of personality.

**source confusion** Confusion about the origin of a memory.

**spousal rape** Sexual assault (rape) against a spouse.

**spree killer** A person who kills victims at two or more different locations with no "cooling-off" interval between the murders.

**stare decisis** To stand on the decisions of the past. A principle that holds that courts and judges should follow prior decisions and judicial rulings in the interest of predictability, fairness, and certainty.

**stimulation-seeking theory** A theory that psychopathic behavior is due to individuals' attempts to raise their sensory and arousal experiences to an optimal level through repeated thrill-seeking and risk-taking.

**stipulate** To agree about a fact in a legal proceeding without further argument or examination.

**Stockholm syndrome** Feelings of dependency and emotional closeness that hostages sometimes develop toward their kidnappers in prolonged hostage situations.

**storage** That phase of the memory process referring to the retention of information.

**story model** The notion that people construct a story or narrative summary of the events in a dispute.

**structural explanations** A type of sociological theory of crime that emphasizes similar interests and motivations, but differences in opportunities.

**structured interviews** Interviews in which the wording, order, and content of the questions are standardized in order to improve the reliability of the information an interviewer obtains.

**subcultural explanations** A type of sociological theory of crime that emphasizes class differences in values.

**suggestive questioning** Questioning that suggests an answer.

**suicide by cop** A crisis situation in which a citizen precipitates his or her own death by behaving in such a fashion that a police officer is forced to use lethal force.

**summary jury trial**   A brief presentation of both sides of the case, usually lasting only one day, in which a jury renders a verdict that is only advisory to a judge.

**suppression hearing**   A hearing before a judge, in which one of the attorneys argues that certain evidence should not be admitted at trial.

**sympathy hypothesis**   The assumption that jurors' decisions will be influenced by feelings of sympathy.

**team policing**   A policy of less centralized decision making within police organizations.

**television technique of retrieval**   The notion that memories are stored as television images that can later be replayed.

**terrorism**   The use of threat of violence to achieve certain organizational goals.

**theory**   A set of propositions and related hypotheses used to predict and explain a phenomenon.

**therapeutic jurisprudence**   A position that one aspect of the study of the law should be a consideration of the mental health impact of the legal system upon its participants and clients.

**thought suppression**   The attempt to avoid thinking about something.

**"three-strikes" law**   A law that mandates severe penalties for those who are multiple offenders.

**tort**   A tort is a civil suit that does not involve a contract; thus, tort litigation would be illustrated by a suit by one automobile driver against another, most medical malpractice cases, and other personal injury suits.

**trial consultants**   Individuals who provide assistance to trial lawyers about effective ways to try cases.

**ultimate opinion testimony**   Testimony that offers a conclusion about the specific defendant or a specific witness, in contrast to testimony about a general phenomenon.

**unconditioned stimulus**   An original stimulus, not associated with a new or conditioned response.

**unconscious transference**   Generation of a memory that is based on the recall of several past occurrences, so that an innocent person may be confused with an offender.

**validity scales**   Those measures whose goal is to access whether the test taker is telling the truth.

**venire**   A panel of prospective jurors drawn from a large list.

**vicarious learning**   Learning by observing the actions of another person and their outcomes.

**victim impact evidence**   Evidence offered at sentencing to show the impact on the victim of the crime for which the defendant has been convicted; the victims' testimony in the Oklahoma City bombing case is a good example of victim impact evidence.

**victimology**   The study of the process and consequences of victim's experiences, including recovery.

**voir dire**   The process by which the judge and/or attorneys ask potential jurors questions and attempt to uncover any biases.

**weapon focus effect**   When confronted by an armed attacker, the victim's tendency to focus attention on the weapon and fail to notice other stimuli.

**with prejudice**   When a suit is dismissed, a judicial dismissal "with prejudice" means that it cannot be resubmitted.

**writ of certiorari**   An order by an appellate court allowing an appeal from a lower court; used in cases when the appellate court may, but is not required to, allow the appeal.

**written interrogatories**   Questions given to a witness, and the responses, in writing, prior to a trial.

**Yerkes-Dodson law**   A psychological law stating that increased stress lowers eyewitnesses' accuracy.

**zero tolerance**   An approach to law enforcement in which the police attempt to arrest all lawbreakers, even those who have committed what are traditionally viewed as petty or nuisance crimes.

# References

Abram, K. M., & Teplin, L. A. (1991). Co-occurring disorders among mentally ill jail detainees: Implications for public policy. *American Psychologist, 46,* 1036–1045.

Abramson, J. (1994). *We, the jury.* New York: Basic Books.

Ackerman, M. J., & Ackerman, M. (1997). Custody evaluation practices: A survey of experienced professionals (revisited). *Professional Psychology: Research and Practice, 28,* 137–145.

Ackerman, M. J., & Schoendorf, K. (1992). *The Ackerman-Schoendorf Parent Evaluation of Custody Test* (ASPECT). Los Angeles: Western Psychological Services.

Adler, F. (1973). Socioeconomic factors influencing jury verdicts. *New York University Review of Law and Social Change, 3,* 1–10.

Adler, S. J. (1994). *The jury: Trial and error in the American courtroom.* New York: Times Books.

Adorno, T., Frenkel-Brunswik, E., Levinson, D., & Sanford, N. (1950). *The authoritarian personality.* New York: Harper & Row.

Age of accountability. (1981, December 14). *Time,* p. 80.

*Ake v. Oklahoma,* 105 S.Ct. 977 (1985).

Akers, R. L., Krohn, M. D., Lanz-Kaduce, L., & Radosevich, M. (1996). Social learning and deviant behavior: A specific test of a general theory. In D. G. Rojek & G. F. Jensen (Eds.), *Exploring delinquency: Causes and control* (pp. 109–119). Los Angeles: Roxbury.

Alden, B. (1996, September 9). Italian-Americans win *"Batson"* shield. *National Law Journal,* p. A8.

Alexander, F., & Healy, W. (1935). *Roots of crime.* New York: Knopf.

Alexander, J. (Ed.). (1963). *A brief narration of the case and trial of John Peter Zenger.* Boston: Little, Brown.

*Alexander v. State,* 509 S.E. 2d 56 (Ga. 1998).

Alker, H. R., Jr., Hosticka, C., & Mitchell, M. (1976). Jury selection as a biased social process. *Law and Society Review, 11,* 9–41.

Alkus, S., & Padesky, C. (1983). Special problems of police officers: Stress-related issues and interventions. *Counseling Psychologist, 11,* 55–64.

Allen, D., & Wall, D. (1993). Role orientations and women state supreme court justices. *Judicature, 77,* 156–165.

Allen, M., Mabry, E., & McKelton, D. (1998). Impact of juror attitudes about the death penalty on juror evaluations of guilt and punishment: A meta-analysis. *Law and Human Behavior, 23,* 715–731.

Allison, J. A., & Wrightsman, L. S. (1993). *Rape: The misunderstood crime.* Thousand Oaks, CA: Sage.

Alpert, J. L., Brown, L. S., & Courtois, C. A. (1998). Symptomatic clients and memories of childhood abuse: What the trauma and child sexual abuse literature tells us. *Psychology, Public Policy, and Law, 4,* 941–995.

Alschuler, A. W. (1968). The prosecutor's role in plea bargaining. *University of Chicago Law Review, 36,* 50–112.

American Bar Association. (1978). *Standards relating to the administration of criminal justice, fair trial and free press.* Chicago: Author.

American Bar Association. (1979). *Approval of law schools: American Bar Association standards and rules of procedure, as amended, 1979.* Chicago: Author.

American Bar Association. (1989). *ABA criminal justice mental health standards.* Washington, D.C.: Author.

American Bar Association Special Committee. (1991). *Jury comprehension in complex cases.* Washington, D.C.: American Bar Association.

American Bar Association. (1992a, April). Finding sympathetic jurors. *American Bar Association Journal,* p. 29.

American Bar Association. (1992b). *Narrowing the gap.* St. Paul, MN: West.

American Bar Association. (1993). *ABA formal opinion 93379.* Chicago: Author.

American Bar Association. (1995). *A review of legal education in the United States.* Chicago: Author.

American Bar Association. (1996). *The experiences of women in legal education.* Chicago: Author.

American Bar Association. (1997). *The official guide to U.S. law schools.* Newton, PA: Law School Admission Council.

American Judicature Society. (1999). www.ajs.org/fire1.html.

American Psychiatric Association. (1982). APA statement on the insanity defense. *American Journal of Psychiatry, 140,* 681–688.

American Psychological Association. (1990). Ethical principles of psychologists. *American Psychologist, 45,* 390–395.

American Psychological Association. (1992). Ethical principles of psychologists and code of conduct. *American Psychologist, 47,* 1597–1611.

American Psychological Association. (1998). *Hate crimes today: An age-old foe in modern dress* [On-line]. Available: http://www.apa.org/pubinfo/hate/

Anderson, C. A., Lepper, M. R., & Ross, L. (1980). Perseverance of social theories: The role of explanation in the persistence of discredited information. *Journal of Personality and Social Psychology, 39,* 1037–1049.

Anderson, D. (1988). *Crimes of justice.* New York: Times Books.

Anderson, G. (1990). Sentencing, race and rapport. *America,* p. 508.

Anderson, K. B., Cooper, H., & Okamura, L. (1997). Individual differences and attitudes toward rape: A meta-analytic review. *Personality and Social Psychology Bulletin, 23,* 295–315.

Anderson, P. (1994). *Janet Reno: Doing the right thing.* New York: Wiley.

Andrews, D. A., & Bonta, J. (1994). *The psychology of criminal conduct.* Cincinnati, OH: Anderson.

Andrews, J. A., Foster, S. L., Capaldi, D., & Hops, H. (2000). Adolescent and family predictors of physical aggression, communication, and satisfaction among young adult couples. *Journal of Consulting and Clinical Psychology, 68,* 195–208.

*Apodaca, Cooper, and Madden v. Oregon,* 32 L. Ed. 2d 184 (1972).

Appavoo, P. M., & Gwynn, M. I. (1996, August). *Effectiveness of the cognitive interview on delayed eyewitness recall.* Paper presented at the meeting of the American Psychological Association, Toronto.

Appelbaum, P. S., & Grisso, T. (1995). The MacArthur Treatment Competence Study. I: Mental illness and competence to consent to treatment. *Law and Human Behavior, 19,* 105–126.

*Apprendi v. New Jersey,* 530 U.S. 466 (2000).

Archer, D. (with Gartner, R.). (1984). *Violence and crime in cross-national perspective.* New Haven, CT: Yale University Press.

Archer, J. (1991). The influence of testosterone on human aggression. *British Journal of Psychology, 82,* 128.

Arens, R., Granfield, D. D., & Susman, J. (1965). Jurors, jury charges, and insanity. *Catholic University Law Review, 14,* 129.

Ares, C. E., Rankin, A., & Sturz, H. (1963). The Manhattan bail project: An interim report on the use of pre-trial parole. *New York University Law Review, 38,* 67–95.

*Argersinger v. Hamlin,* 407 U.S. 25 (1972).

*Arizona v. Evans,* 115 S.Ct. 1185 (1995).

*Arizona v. Fulminante,* 111 S.Ct. 1246 (1991).

Arnold, S. & Gold, A. (1978–1979). The use of a public opinion poll on a change of venue application. *Criminal Law Quarterly, 21,* 445–464.

*Ashcraft v. Tennessee,* 322 U.S. 143 (1944).

Aspin, L., & Hall, W. (1994), Retention elections and judicial behavior. *Judicature, 77,* 306–315.

Associated Press. (1982, August 29). Juries tough on media in libel suits. *Kansas City Times,* p. A5.

Associated Press. (1984, November 23). Judicial leniency toward women found. *Kansas City Times,* p. A15.

Associated Press. (1988, January 13). Former Kansas woman identifies man in attack. *Kansas City Times,* p. B5.

Astin, A. W. (1984). Prelaw students: A national profile. *Journal of Legal Education, 34,* 73–85.

Attorney General's Commission on Pornography. (1986, July). *Final report.* Washington, D.C.: U.S. Department of Justice.

Austin, A. (1998). *The empire strikes back.* New York: New York University Press.

Austin, A. (1999, May 18). Womanly approach harms future lawyers. *National Law Journal,* p. A23.

Austin, W. (1980). Friendship and fairness: Effects of type of relationship and task performance on choice of distribution rules. *Personality and Social Psychology Bulletin, 6,* 402–408.

Austin, W., & Utne, M. K. (1977). Sentencing: Discretion and justice in judicial decision-making. In B. D. Sales (Ed.), *Psychology in the legal process* (pp. 163–194). New York: Spectrum.

Austin, W., Walster, E., & Utne, M. K. (1976). Equity and the law: The effect of a harmdoer's "suffering in the act" on liking and assigned punishment. In L. Berkowitz & E. Walster (Eds.), *Advances in experimental social psychology* (Vol. 9, pp. 163–190). Orlando, FL: Academic Press.

Austin, W., & Williams, T. (1977). A survey of judges' responses to simulated legal cases: A research note on sentencing disparity. *Journal of Criminal Law and Criminology, 68,* 306–310.

Ayres, B. D. (1996, August 27). California child molesters face "chemical castration." *New York Times,* p. A1.

Azar, S. T., & Benjet, C. L. (1994). A cognitive perspective on ethnicity, race, and termination of parental rights. *Law and Human Behavior, 18,* 249–267.

Backster, C. (1974). The anticlimax dampening concept. *Polygraph, 3,* 28–50.

Baer, R., Wetter, M., Nichols, J., Greene, R., & Berry, D. (1995). Sensitivity of MMPI-2 validity scales to underreporting of symptoms. *Psychological Assessment, 7,* 419–423.

Bagby, R. M., Nicholson, R. A., Rogers, R., & Nussbaum, D. (1992). Domains of competency to stand trial: A factor analytic study. *Law and Human Behavior, 16,* 491–508.

Bailey, F. L., & Rothblatt, H. B. (1985). *Successful techniques for criminal trials* (2nd ed.). Rochester, NY: Lawyers Cooperative.

Bailis, D., & MacCoun, R. (1996). Estimating liability risks with the media as your guide: A content analysis of media coverage of tort litigation. *Law and Human Behavior, 20,* 419–429.

Bailis, D. S., Darley, J. M., Waxman, T. L., & Robinson, P. H. (1995). Community standards of criminal liability and the insanity defense. *Law and Human Behavior, 19,* 425–446.

Bakan, D. (1966). *The duality of human existence.* Chicago: Rand McNally.

Baker, D. (1999, June). Is this woman a threat to lawyers? *American Bar Association Journal, 85,* 54.

Baker, L. (1983). *Miranda: Crime, law, and politics.* New York: Atheneum.

Baldus, D., Pulaski, C., & Woodworth, G. (1983). Comparative review of death sentences: An empirical study of the Georgia experience. *Journal of Criminal Law and Criminology, 74,* 661–753.

Baldus, D., Woodworth, G., Zuckerman, D., Weiner, N. A., & Broffitt, B. (1998). Race discrimination and the death penalty in the post-*Furman* era: An empirical and legal overview with recent findings from Philadelphia. *Cornell Law Review, 83,* 1638–1770.

Bales, J. (1988, June). New laws limiting duty to protect. *APA Monitor,* p. 18.

Bandura, A. (1973). *Aggression: A social learning analysis.* Englewood Cliffs, NJ: Prentice Hall.

Bandura, A. (1976). Social learning analysis of aggression. In E. Ribes-Inesta & A. Bandura (Eds.), *Analysis of delinquency and aggression* (pp. 203–232). Hillsdale, NJ: Erlbaum.

Bandura, A. (1977). *Social learning theory.* Englewood Cliffs, NJ: Prentice Hall.

Bandura, A. (1986). *Social foundations of thought and action: A social cognitive theory.* Englewood Cliffs, NJ: Prentice Hall.

Barbaree, H. E., & Marshall, W. L. (1991). The role of male sexual arousal in rape: Six models. *Journal of Consulting and Clinical Psychology, 59,* 621–630.

Bard, M. (1969). Family intervention police teams as a community mental health resource. *Journal of Criminal Law, Criminology, and Police Science, 60,* 24.

Bard, M., & Berkowitz, B. (1967). Training police as specialists in family crisis intervention: A community psychology action program. *Community Mental Health Journal, 3,* 209–215.

*Barefoot v. Estelle,* 463 U.S. 880 (1983).

*Barker v. Wingo,* 407 U.S. 514 (1972).

Barnard, G. W., Thompson, J. W., Freeman, W. C., Robbins, L., Gies, D., & Hankins, G. L. (1991). Competency to stand trial: Description and initial evaluation of a new computer-assisted assessment tool. *Bulletin of the American Academy of Psychiatry and Law, 19,* 367–381.

Barnett, N., & Feild, H. S. (1977). Sex differences in attitudes toward rape. *Journal of College Student Personnel, 18,* 93–96.

Barovick, H. (1998, June 15). DWB: Driving while black. *Time,* p. 35.

Barr, W. (1992, March). *Comments by the attorney general of the United States.* Speech delivered at the University of Kansas, Lawrence.

Barth, P. S. (1990). Workers' compensation for medical stress cases. *Behavioral Sciences and the Law, 8,* 349–360.

Bartol, C. (1983). *Psychology and American law.* Belmont, CA: Wadsworth.

Bartol, C. (1996). Police psychology: Then, now, and beyond. *Criminal Justice and Behavior, 23,* 70–89.

Bartol, C. R. (1991). Predictive validation of the MMPI for small-town police officers who fail. *Professional Psychology: Research and Practice, 22,* 127–132.

Bartlett, F. C. (1932). *Remembering: A study of experimental and social psychology.* New York: Cambridge University Press.

Bashore, T. R., & Rapp, P. E. (1993). Are there alternatives to traditional polygraph procedures? *Psychological Bulletin, 113,* 3–22.

*Bass v. Perrin,* 170 F.3d 1312 (11th Cir. 1999).

Bass, E., & Davis, L. (1988). *The courage to heal: A guide for women survivors of child sexual abuse.* New York: Harper & Row.

*Bates v. State Bar of Arizona,* 433 U.S. 350 (1977).

*Batson v. Kentucky,* 476 U.S. 79 (1986).

Baum, L. (1985). *The Supreme Court* (2nd ed.). Washington, D.C.: Congressional Quarterly.

Bayles, F. (1984, May 7). Law professor has a taste for controversial cases. *Lawrence Journal-World,* p. 16.

Bazelon, D. (1974). Psychiatrists and the adversary process. *Scientific American, 230,* 18–23.

Beauchamp, T. (1997). Opposing views on animal experimentation: Do animals have rights? *Ethics and Behavior, 7,* 113–121.

Beck, A. (1987, July 25). Recruits graduate to police duties. *Lawrence Journal-World,* p. 3A.

Beck, J. C., & Shumsky, R. (1997). A comparison of retained and appointed counsel in cases of capital murder. *Law and Human Behavior, 21,* 525–538.

Becker, J. V. & Murphy, W. D. (1998). What we know and do not know about assessing and treating sex offenders. *Psychology, Public Policy and Law, 4,* 116–137.

Beckman, L. (1998). Chemical castration: Constitutional issues of due process, equal protection, and cruel and unusual punishment. *West Virginia Law Review, 100,* 853–859.

Begam, R. (1977). Voir dire: The attorney's job. *Trial, 13,* 3.

Behn, N. (1995). *Lindbergh: The crime.* New York: Onyx.

Beiser, E. N. (1973). Are juries representative? *Judicature, 57,* 194–199.

Beissert, W. (1988, March 1). Stateside. *USA Today,* p. 9A.

Belkin, L. (1988, June 10). Expert witness is unfazed by "Dr. Death" label. *New York Times,* p. 23.

*Bell v. Wolfish,* 99 S.Ct. 1861 (1979).

Belli, M. (1954). *Modern trials.* Indianapolis, IN: Bobbs-Merrill.

Bender, W. N. (1994). Joint custody: The option of choice. *Journal of Divorce and Remarriage, 21,* 115–131.

Benner, A. W. (1986). Psychological screening of police applicants. In J. T. Reese & H. A. Goldstein (Eds.), *Psychological services for law enforcement* (pp. 11–20). Washington, D.C.: U.S. Government Printing Office.

Ben-Shakhar, G., Bar-Hillel, M., & Lieblich, I. (1986). Trial by polygraph: Scientific and juridical issues in lie detection. *Behavioral Sciences and the Law, 4,* 459–479.

Benton, A. A. (1971). Productivity, distributive justice, and bargaining among children. *Journal of Personality and Social Psychology, 18,* 68–78.

Berg, A. S. (1998). *Lindbergh.* New York: Putnam.

Berk, L. E. (1991). *Child development* (2nd ed.). Boston: Allyn & Bacon.

*Berkemer v. McCarty,* 468 U.S. 420 (1984).

Berman, L. M., & Osborne, Y. H. (1987). Attorneys' referrals for competency to stand trial evaluations: Comparisons of referred and nonreferred clients. *Behavioral Sciences and the Law, 5,* 373–380.

Berman, M. E. (1997). Biopsychosocial approaches to understanding human aggression: The first 30 years. *Clinical Psychology Review, 17,* 585–588.

Berman, M. E., Tracy, J. I., & Coccaro, E. F. (1997). The serotonin hypothesis of aggression revisited. *Clinical Psychology Review, 17,* 651–665.

Bermant, G. (1977). *Conduct of the voir dire examination: Practices and opinions of federal district judges.* Washington, D.C.: Federal Judicial Center.

Bermant, G. (1982). *Jury selection procedures in United States district courts.* Washington, D.C.: Federal Judicial Center.

Bersoff, D. N. (1987). Social science data and the Supreme Court: Lockhart as a case in point. *American Psychologist, 42,* 52–58.

*Betts v. Brady,* 316 U.S. 455 (1942).

Beutler, L. E., Storm, A., Kirkish, P., Scogin, F., & Gaines, J. A. (1985). Parameters in the prediction of police officer performance. *Professional Psychology: Research and Practice, 16,* 324–335.

Bevan, W. (1991). Contemporary psychology: A tour inside the onion. *American Psychologist, 46,* 475–483.

Binder, A. (1988). Juvenile delinquency. In M. R. Rosenzweig & L. W. Porter (Eds.), *Annual review of psychology* (pp. 253–282). Palo Alto, CA: Annual Reviews.

Bittner, E. (1967). Police discretion in emergency apprehension of mentally ill persons. *Social Problems, 14,* 278–292.

Black, D. (1972). The boundaries of legal sociology. *Yale Law Journal, 81,* 1086–1100.

Black, D. (1976). *The behavior of law.* Orlando, FL: Academic Press.

Blackman, J. (1986). Potential uses for expert testimony: Ideas toward the representation of battered women who kill. *Women's Rights Law Reporter, 9*(3 & 4), 227–238.

Blau, T. H. (1986). Deadly force: Psychosocial factors and objective evaluation: A preliminary effort. In J. T. Reese & H. A. Goldstein (Eds.), *Psychological services for law enforcement* (pp. 315–334). Washington, D.C.: U.S. Government Printing Office.

Blau, T. H. (1994). *Psychological services for law enforcement.* New York: Wiley.

Blume, E. S. (1990). *Secret survivors: Uncovering incest and its aftereffects in women.* New York: Ballantine.

Blumenthal, J. A. (1998). The reasonable woman standard: A meta-analytic review of gender differences in perceptions of sexual harassment. *Law and Human Behavior, 22,* 33–58.

Blumstein, A., & Beck, A. J. (1999). Population growth in U.S. Prisons, 1980–1996. *Crime and Justice: A Review of Research, 26,* 17–61.

Blunk, R., & Sales, B. (1977). Persuasion during the voir dire. In B. Sales (Ed.), *Psychology in the legal process* (pp. 39–58). New York: Spectrum.

Boccaccini, M. T., & Brodsky, S. L. (1999). Diagnostic test usage by forensic psychologists in emotional injury cases. *Professional Psychology: Research and Practice, 30,* 253–259.

Bodaken, E. M., & Speckert, G. R. (1996). To down a stealth juror, strike first. *National Law Journal,* pp. B7, B9, B13.

Boehm, V. (1968). Mr. Prejudice, Miss Sympathy, and the authoritarian personality: An application of psychological measuring techniques to the problem of jury bias. *Wisconsin Law Review, 1968,* 734–750.

Boehnert, C. (1989). Characteristics of successful and unsuccessful insanity pleas. *Law and Human Behavior, 13,* 31–40.

Boersema, C., Hanson, R., & Keilitz, S. (1991). State court-annexed arbitration: What do attorneys think? *Judicature, 75,* 28–33.

Bolton, B. (1985). Review of Inwald Personality Inventory. In J. V. Mitchell (Ed.), *The ninth mental measurements yearbook* (pp. 711–713). Lincoln: Buros Institute of Mental Measurements, University of Nebraska.

Bonnie, R., & Slobogin, C. (1980). The role of mental health professionals in the criminal process: The case for informed speculation. *Virginia Law Review, 66,* 427–522.

Bonnie, R. J. (1993). The competence of criminal defendants: Beyond Dusky and Drope. *University of Miami Law Review, 47,* 539–601.

Bonora, B. (1995, February 27). Bias in jury selection continues. *National Law Journal,* pp. B8–B9.

Book, A. S. (1999). Shame on you: An analysis of modern shame punishment as an alternative to incarceration. *William and Mary Law Review, 40,* 653–686.

*Bordenkircher v. Hayes,* 434 U.S. 357, 363 (1978).

Borgida, E. (1980). Evidentiary reform of rape laws: A psycholegal approach. In P. D. Lipsitt & B. D. Sales (Eds.), *New directions in psycholegal research* (pp. 171–197). New York: Litton.

Borgida, E. (1981). Legal reform of rape laws. In L. Bickman (Ed.), *Applied social psychology annual* (Vol. 2, pp. 211–241). Newbury Park, CA: Sage.

Borgida, E., & Brekke, N. (1985). Psycholegal research on rape trials. In A. Burgess (Ed.), *Research handbook on rape and sexual assault* (pp. 313–342). New York: Garland.

Borgida, E., & Park, R. (1988). The entrapment defense: Juror comprehension and decision making. *Law and Human Behavior, 12,* 19–40.

Bornstein, B. H. (1999). The ecological validity of jury simulations: Is the jury still out? *Law and Human Behavior, 23,* 75–92.

Borum, R. (1996). Improving the clinical practice of violence risk assessment: Technology, guidelines, and training. *American Psychologist, 51,* 945–956.

Borum, R., Deane, M. W., Steadman, H. J., & Morrissey, J. (1998). Police perspectives on responding to mentally ill people in crisis: Perceptions of program effectiveness. *Behavioral Sciences and the Law, 16,* 393–406.

Borum, R., & Fulero, S. M. (1999). Empirical research on the insanity defense and attempted reforms: Evidence toward informed policy. *Law and Human Behavior, 23,* 375–394.

Borum, R., & Stock, H. V. (1993). Detection of deception in law enforcement applicants: A preliminary investigation. *Law and Human Behavior, 17,* 157–166.

Bothwell, R. K. (1999). The ethnic factor in voir dire. In W. F. Abbott & J. Batt (Eds.), *A handbook of jury research.* (pp. 10.1–10.11). Philadelphia: ALI-ABA.

Bothwell, R. K., Deffenbacher, K. A., & Brigham, J. C. (1987). Correlation of eyewitness accuracy and confidence: Optimality hypothesis revised. *Journal of Applied Psychology, 72,* 691–695.

Bottoms, B., & Goodman, G. (1994). Perceptions of children's credibility in sexual assault cases. *Journal of Applied Social Psychology, 24,* 702–732.

Bottoms, B., & Goodman, G. (Eds.). (1996). *International perspectives on child abuse and children's testimony.* Thousand Oaks, CA: Sage.

Bottoms, B. L., Shaver, P. R., & Goodman, G. S. (1996). An analysis of ritualistic and religion-related child abuse allegations. *Law and Human Behavior, 20,* 1–34.

Boulding, K. E. (1975). Truth or power. *Science, 190,* 423.

Bourgeois, M. J., Horowitz, I. A., & ForsterLee, L. (1993). Effects of technicality and access to trial transcripts on verdicts and information processing in a civil trial. *Personality and Social Psychology Bulletin, 19,* 220–227.

Bower, B. (1984). Not popular by reason of insanity. *Science News, 126,* 218–219.

Bowers, K. S., & Farvolden, P. (1996). Revisiting a century-old Freudian slip: From suggestion disavowed to the truth repressed. *Psychological Bulletin, 119,* 355–380.

Bowlby, J. (1949). *Report of the conference on the scientific study of juvenile delinquency.* London: National Association for Mental Health.

Bowlby, J. (1953). *Child care and the growth of love.* Baltimore: Penguin.

Bowlby, J., & Salter-Ainsworth, M. D. (1965). *Child care and the growth of love.* London: Penguin.

Boyer, P. J. (2000, January 17). DNA on trial. *The New Yorker,* pp. 42–53.

Bradsher, K. (1999). Canoeist goes to court, fighting for right to curse. *New York Times* [On-line]. Available: http://www.nytimes.com/yr/mo/day/news/national/michigan-swearing.html

*Bradwell v. State,* 83 U.S. 130 (1872).

*Brady v. Maryland,* 373 U.S. 83 (1963).

*Brady v. United States,* 397 U.S. 742 (1970).

Bragg, R. (1998, May 30). Conviction set aside, but in prison for life. *New York Times* [On-line]. Available: www.nytimes.com/yr/mo/day/news/national/ala-prisoner.html

*Bram v. United States,* 168 U.S. 532 (1897).

*Branch v. State,* 40 Cr.L. Rpts. (BNA) 2215 (Ala. 1986).

*Brandborg v. Lucas,* 891 F. Supp. 352 (E.D. Tx. 1995).

Bransford, J. D., & Johnson, M. D. (1972). Contextual prerequisites for understanding: Some investigations of comprehension and recall. *Journal of Verbal Learning and Verbal Behavior, 11,* 717–726.

Bray, J. H. (1991). Psychological factors affecting custodial and visitation arrangements. *Behavioral Sciences and the Law, 9,* 419–437.

Bray, R. M., & Noble, A. M. (1978). Authoritarianism and decisions of mock juries: Evidence of jury bias and group polarization. *Journal of Personality and Social Psychology, 36,* 1424–1430.

Breed, A.G. (1999, September 2). "Love thy neighbor" tested in Danville. *Lexington* (Ky.) *Herald-Leader,* pp. 1, 13.

Brehm, J. W. (1966). *A theory of psychological reactance.* Orlando, FL: Academic Press.

Brehm, S. S., & Brehm, J. (1981). *Psychological reactance.* New York: Academic Press.

Brennan, A. (1998, August 17), Women having it all. *National Law Journal,* p.1.

Brennan, P. A. & Raine, A. (1997). Biosocial bases of antisocial behavior: Psychophysiological, neurological, and cognitive factors. *Clinical Psychology Review, 17,* 589–604.

Brenner, J. F. (1995, December 24). A verdict for the system. *Book World,* p. 7.

*Brewer v. Williams,* 430 U.S. 387 (1977).

Brewer, N., Potter, R., Fisher, R.P., Bond, N., & Luszcz, M. A. (1999). Beliefs and data on the relationship between consistency and accuracy of eyewitness testimony. *Applied Cognitive Psychology, 13,* 297–313.

Brewer, W. F., & Nakamura, G. V. (1984). The nature and function of schemas. In R. S. Wyer & T. K. Srull (Eds.), *Handbook of social cognition* (Vol. 1). Hillsdale, NJ: Erlbaum.

Bricklin, B, (1984). *Bricklin Perceptual Scales: Child perception of parent series.* Furlong, PA: Village.

Brigham, J. C., & Wolfskeil, M. P. (1983). Opinions of attorneys and law enforcement personnel on the accuracy of eyewitness identification. *Law and Human Behavior, 7,* 337–349.

Bright, S. (1997). Political attacks on the judiciary. *Judicature, 80,* 165–173.

Bright, S. (1997). Political attacks on the judiciary: Can justice be done amid efforts to intimidate and remove judges from office for unpopular de-

cisions? *New York University Law Review, 72,* 308–336.

Bright, S., & Kennan, P. (1995). Judges and the politics of death: Deciding between the Bill of Rights and the next election in capital cases. *Boston University Law Review, 75,* 759–835.

Bright, S. B. (1994). Counsel for the poor: The death sentence not for the worst crime but for the worst lawyer. *Yale Law Journal, 103,* 1835–1883.

Brill, S. (1978, March 14). When lawyers help villains. *Esquire,* p. 21.

Broderick, R. (1991), Court-annexed compulsory arbitration is providing litigants with a speedier and less expensive alternative to the traditional courtroom trial. *Judicature, 75,* 41–44.

Broeder, D. W. (1959). The University of Chicago jury project. *Nebraska Law Review, 38,* 744–760.

Broeder, D. W. (1965). Voir dire examinations: An empirical study. *Southern California Law Review, 38,* 503–528.

Bromley, R. (1996). Jury leniency in drinking and driving cases: Has it changed? 1958 versus 1993. *Law and Psychology Review, 20,* 27–55.

Bronstein, A. J. (1980). Prisoners' rights: A history. In G. P. Alpert (Ed.), *Legal rights of prisoners* (pp. 14–45). Newbury Park, CA: Sage.

*Brown v. Board of Education,* 347 U.S. 483 (1954).

*Brown v. Mississippi,* 297 U.S. 278 (1936).

Brown, J. M., & Campbell, E. A. (1990). Sources of occupational stress in the police. *Work and Stress, 4,* 305–318.

Brown, R. (1992). *Before and after.* New York: Farrar, Straus & Giroux.

Browne, A. (1987). *When battered women kill.* New York: Free Press.

Brownmiller, S., & Alexander, D. (1992, January/February). From Carmita Wood to Anita Hill. *Ms.,* pp. 70–71.

Bruck, D. (1985, May 20). The death penalty: An exchange. *New Republic,* pp. 20–21.

Bruck, M., Ceci, S. J., & Hembrooke, H. (1998). Reliability and credibility in young children's reports: From research to policy and practice. *American Psychologist, 53,* 136–151.

Brussel, J. A. (1968). *Casebook of a crime psychiatrist.* New York: Bernard Geis Associates.

Bryan, W. J. (1971). *The chosen ones.* New York: Vantage.

Buckhout, R. (1974). Eyewitness testimony. *Scientific American, 231,* 23–31.

Budiansky, S. (1995, January 30). How lawyers abuse the law. *U.S. News & World Report,* pp. 50–53.

Bund, J. M. (1997). Did you say chemical castration? *University of Pittsburgh Law Review, 59,* 157.

Bureau of Justice Statistics. (1994). *Violence and theft in the workplace.* NCJ148199. Annapolis Junction, MD: Bureau of Justice Statistics Clearinghouse.

Bureau of Justice Statistics. (1999). *National Crime Victimization Survey.* Washington, D.C.: U.S. Department of Justice.

Burger, W. E. (1975). Dissenting opinion in *O'Connor v. Donaldson. U.S. Law Week, 42,* 4929–4936.

Burger, W. E. (1982). Isn't there a better way? *American Bar Association Journal, 68,* 274–277.

Burgess, A. W., & Holmstrom, L. L. (1974). *Rape: Victims of crisis.* Bowie, MA: Brady.

Burgess, A. W., & Holmstrom, L. L. (1979). Rape: Sexual disruption and recovery. *American Journal of Orthopsychiatry, 49,* 648–657.

Burgess, R. L., & Akers, R. L. (1966). A differential-reinforcement theory of criminal behavior. *Social Problems, 14,* 128–147.

*Burnet v. Coronado Oil and Gas Co.,* 285 U.S. 393, 406, 52 S.Ct. 443, 447, 76 L.Ed. 815 (1932).

Burt, M. R. (1980). Cultural myths and supports for rape. *Journal of Personality and Social Psychology, 38,* 217–230.

Burt, R., & Morris, N. (1972). A proposal for the abolition of the incompetency plea. *University of Chicago Law Review, 40,* 66–95.

Buss, A. H. (1966). *Psychopathology.* New York: Wiley.

Buss, D. M., & Malamuth, N. M. (Eds.). (1996). *Sex, power, conflict: Evolutionary and feminist perspectives.* New York: Oxford University Press.

Butler, P. (1995). Racially based jury nullification: Black power in the criminal justice system. *Yale Law Journal, 105,* 677–725.

Butler, W. M., Leitenberg, H., & Fuselier, D. G. (1993). The use of mental health consultants to police hostage negotiation teams. *Behavioral Sciences and the Law, 11,* 213–221.

Butterfield, F. (1996, March 8). Tough law on sentences is criticized. *New York Times,* p. A8.

Butterfield, F. (1997, February 3). '95 data show sharp drop in reported rapes. *New York Times*, pp. A1, A14.

Byrne, C. A., Resnick, H. S., Kilpatrick, D. G., Best, C. L., & Saunders, B. E. (1999). The socioeconomic impact of interpersonal violence on women. *Journal of Consulting and Clinical Psychology, 67*, 362–366.

Calhoun, K., Atkeson, B., & Resick, P. (1982). A longitudinal examination of fear reactions in victims of rape. *Journal of Counseling Psychology, 29*, 656–661.

*California v. Byers*, 402 U.S. 424 (1971).

*California v. Ciraola*, 476 U.S. 207 (1986).

*California v. Greenwood*, 108 S.Ct. 1625 (1988).

Callahan, V. A., McGreevey, M. A., Cirincione, C., & Steadman, H. J. (1992). Measuring the effects of the guilty but mentally ill (GBMI) verdict: Georgia's 1982 GBMI reform. *Law and Human Behavior, 16*, 447–462.

Camara, W. J., & Schneider, D. L. (1994). Integrity tests: Facts and unresolved issues. *American Psychologist, 49*, 112–118.

Campbell, D. T. (1969). Reforms as experiments. *American Psychologist, 24*, 409–429.

Campbell, R., Self, T., Barnes, H. E., Ahrens, C. E., Wasco, S. M., & Zaragoza-Diesfeld, Y. (1999). Community services for rape survivors: Enhancing psychological well-being or increasing trauma? *Journal of Consulting and Clinical Psychology, 67*, 847–858.

Cantor, N. L. (1998). Making advance directives meaningful. *Psychology, Public Policy, and Law, 4*, 629–652.

Caplow, T., & Simon, J. (1999). Understanding prison policy and population trends. *Crime and Justice: A Review of Research, 26*, 63–120.

Caprino, M. (1989, May 7). Employers use tests to head off work force problems. *Lawrence (KS) Journal-World*, p. 11D.

Cardozo, M. (1993). Racial discrimination in legal education. *Journal of Legal Education, 43*, 79–84.

Carlson, H., Thayer, R. E., & Germann, A. C. (1971). Social attitudes and personality differences among members of two kinds of police departments (innovative vs. traditional) and students. *Journal of Criminal Law, Criminology, and Police Science, 62*, 564–567.

Carlson, N. A., Hess, K. M., & Orthmann, C. M. (1999). *Corrections in the 21st century.* Belmont CA: West/Wadsworth.

Carretta, T. R., & Moreland, R. L. (1983). The direct and indirect effects of inadmissible evidence. *Journal of Applied Social Psychology, 13*, 291–309.

Carroll, J. S., Kerr, N. L., Alfini, J. J., Weaver, F. M., MacCoun, R. J., & Feldman, V. (1986). Free press and fair trial: The role of behavioral research. *Law and Human Behavior, 10*, 187–201.

Carter, C. A., Bottoms, B. L., & Levine, M. (1996). Linguistic and socioemotional influences on the accuracy of children's reports. *Law & Human Behavior, 20*, 335–358.

Carter, T. (1998, August). Superstars or falling stars? *American Bar Association Journal, 84*, 28.

Carter, T. (1998, November). Terms of embitterment. *American Bar Association Journal, 84*, 42.

Carter, T. (2000, March). The man who would undo *Miranda. American Bar Association Journal, 86*, 44–47, 108.

Casper, J. (1993). Restructuring the traditional civil jury: The effects of changes in composition and procedures. In R. Litan (Ed.), *Verdict: Assessing the civil jury system* (pp. 419–459). Washington, D.C.: Brookings Institute.

Casper, J. D. (1972). *American criminal justice: The defendant's perspective.* Englewood Cliffs, NJ: Prentice Hall.

Casper, J. D., Benedict, K., & Kelly, J. R. (1988). Cognitions, attitudes, and decision-making in search and seizure cases. *Journal of Applied Social Psychology, 18*, 93–113.

Cassel, W., S., & Bjorklund, D.F. (1995). Developmental patterns of eyewitness memory and suggestibility. *Law and Human Behavior, 19*, 507–532.

Cassell, P. G. (1999). The guilty and the "innocent": An examination of alleged cases of wrongful convictions from false confessions. *Harvard Journal of Law and Public Policy, 22*, 523–603.

Cate, F. H. (1996). Cybersex: Regulating sexually explicit expression on the Internet. *Behavioral Sciences and the Law, 14*, 145–166.

Cavoukian, A., & Heslegrave, R. J. (1980). The admissibility of polygraph evidence in court. *Law and Human Behavior, 4*, 117–131.

Ceci, S. J., & Bruck, M. (1995). *Jeopardy in the courtroom: A scientific analysis of children's testimony.* Washington, D.C.: American Psychological Association.

Ceci, S. J., Bruck, M., & Rosenthal, R. (1995). Children's allegations of sexual abuse: Forensic and scientific issues: A reply to commentators. *Psychology, Public Policy, and Law, 1*, 494–520.

Cernkovich, S. A., & Giordano, P. C. (1996). School bonding, race, and delinquency. In D. G. Rojek & G. F. Jensen (Eds.), *Exploring delinquency: Causes and control* (pp. 210–218). Los Angeles: Roxbury.

Chaiken, S., & Eagly, A. H. (1983). Communication modality as a determinant of persuasion: The role of communicator salience. *Journal of Personality and Social Psychology, 45*, 241–256.

Chambliss, W. J., & Seidman, R. B. (1971). *Law, order, and power.* Reading, MA: Addison-Wesley.

Chandler, C., (1998). Voluntary executions. *Stanford Law Review, 50*, 1897–1927.

*Chapman v. California*, 386 U.S. 18 (1967).

Charles, M. T. (1986). *Policing the streets.* Springfield, IL: Thomas.

Chermack, S. T., & Giancola, P. R. (1997). The relation between alcohol and aggression: An integrated biopsychosocial conceptualization. *Clinical Psychology Review, 17*, 621–649.

Chevigny, P. (1969). *Police power: Police abuse in New York City.* New York: Vintage.

*Chicago v. Morales*, 527 U.S. 41 (1999).

Chodorow, N. (1978). *The reproduction of mothering: Psychoanalysis and the sociology of gender.* Berkeley: University of California Press.

Christiansen, K. O. (1977a). A preliminary study of criminality among twins. In S. A. Mednick & K. O. Christiansen (Eds.), *Biosocial bases of criminal behavior.* New York: Wiley.

Christiansen, K. O. (1977b). A review of studies of criminality among twins. In S. A. Mednick & K. O. Christiansen (Eds.), *Biosocial bases of criminal behavior.* New York: Wiley.

Christianson, S. (1998). *With liberty for some.* Boston: Northeastern University Press.

Christie, R. (1976). Probability v. precedence: The social psychology of jury selection. In G. Bermant, C.

Nemeth, & N. Vidmar (Eds.), *Psychology and the law: Research frontiers* (pp. 265–281). Lexington, MA: Lexington.

Cirincione, C., & Jacobs, C. (1999). Identifying insanity acquittals: Is it any easier? *Law and Human Behavior, 23,* 487–497.

Clancy, P. (1987, July 22). Cops battle stress; "I'm hurting . . ." *USA Today,* pp. 1A–2A.

Clark, L. D. (1975). *The grand jury: The use and abuse of political power.* New York: Quadrangle.

Clavet, G. J. (1996, August). *Ironic effects of juror attempts to suppress inadmissible evidence.* Paper presented at the meeting of the American Psychological Association, Toronto, Canada.

Clermont, K., & Eisenberg, T.(1992) Trial by jury or judge: Transcending empiricism. *Cornell Law Review, 77,* 1124–1177.

Clingempeel, W. G., & Reppucci, N. D. (1982). Joint custody after divorce: Major issues and goals for research. *Psychological Bulletin, 91,* 102–127.

Cloninger, C., Sigvardsson, S., Bohman, M., & von Knorring, A. (1982). Predisposition to petty criminality in Swedish adoptees. II: Cross-fostering analysis of gene-environment interaction. *Archives of General Psychiatry, 39,* 1242–1249.

Cloud, J. (1998). Of arms and the boy. *Time,* p. 152.

Cloward, R. A., & Ohlin, L. E. (1960). *Delinquency and opportunity: A theory of delinquent gangs.* New York: Free Press.

Cobb, A. T., & Frey, F. M. (1996). The effects of leader fairness and pay outcomes on supervisor/subordinate relations. *Journal of Applied Social Psychology, 26,* 1401–1426.

Coccaro, E., Kavoussi, R. & Lesser, J. (1992). Self- and other-directed human aggression: The role of the central serotonergic system. *International Clinical Psychopharmacology, 6,* 70–83.

Cochran, P. A. (1971). A situational approach to the study of police-Negro relations. *Sociological Quarterly, 12,* 232–237.

Coggins, M. H., & Pynchon, M. R. (1998). Mental health consultation to law enforcement: Secret service development of a mental health liaison program. *Behavioral Sciences and the Law, 16,* 407–422.

Cohen, A. K. (1955). *Delinquent boys: The culture of the gang.* Glencoe, IL: Free Press.

Cohen, L. J. (1986). The role of evidential weight in criminal proof. *Boston University Law Review, 66,* 635–649.

Cohen, M. I., Spodak, M. K., Silver, S. B., & Williams, K. (1988). Predicting outcome of insanity acquittees released to the community. *Behavioral Sciences and the Law, 6,* 515–530.

Cohn, E. S., & White, S. O. (1990). *Legal socialization: A study of norms and rules.* New York: Springer.

*Coker v. Georgia,* 433 U.S. 584 (1977).

Colby, A., Kohlberg, L., & collaborators (1987). *The measurement of moral judgment. Vol. 1: Theoretical foundations and research validation.* Cambridge: Cambridge University Press.

Colby, A., Kohlberg, L., Gibbs, J., & Lieberman, M. (1983). A longitudinal study of moral judgment. *Monographs of the Society for Research in Child Development, 48* (12, Serial No. 200).

*Coleman v. Thompson,* 501 U.S. 722 (1991).

Collins, G. (1996, April 2). The small world of grand juries. *New York Times,* p. A12.

Collins, J. J., & Messerschmidt, P. M. (1993). Epidemiology of alcohol-related violence. *Alcohol Health and Research World, 17,* 93–100.

*Colorado v. Connelly,* 107 S.Ct. 515 (1986).

*Colorado v. Spring,* 479 U.S. 564 (1987).

Committee on Ethical Guidelines for Forensic Psychologists. (1991). Specialty guidelines for forensic psychologists. *Law and Human Behavior, 15,* 655–665.

*Commonwealth v. Wall,* 606 A.2d 449 (Pa. 1992).

Conger, R. (1980). Juvenile delinquency: Behavior restraint or behavior facilitation? In T. Hirschi & M. Gottfredson (Eds.), *Understanding crime: Current theory and research* (pp. 131–142). Newbury Park, CA: Sage.

Congressional Research Service. (1982). *The Constitution of the United States of America: Analysis and interpretation.* Washington, D.C.: U.S. Government Printing Office.

Connors, E., Lundregan, T., Miller, N., & McEwan, T. (1996). *Convicted by juries, exonerated by science: Case studies in the use of DNA evidence to* establish innocence after trial. Alexandria, VA: National Institute of Justice.

Cook, B. (1993). Moral authority and gender difference, Georgia Bullock and the Los Angeles Women's Court. *Judicature, 77,* 144–153.

Cook, S. W. (1984, August). *Participation by social scientists in litigation regarding school desegregation: Past contributions and future opportunities.* Paper presented at the meeting of the American Psychological Association, Toronto.

*Cooper v. Oklahoma,* 116 S.Ct. 1373 (1996).

Cooper, J., & Neuhaus, I. M. (2000). The hired gun effect: Assessing the effect of pay, frequency of testifying, and credentials on the perception of expert testimony. *Law and Human Behavior, 24,* 149–172.

*Copelin v. State,* 659 P.2d 1206 (Alaska, 1983).

Cornish, D. B., & Clarke, R. V. (1986). *The reasoning criminal: Rational choice perspectives on offending.* New York: Springer.

Costantini, E., & King, J. (1980). The partial juror: Correlates and causes of prejudgment. *Law and Society Review, 15,* 9–40.

Costanzo, M., & Costanzo, S. (1992). Jury decision making in the capital penalty phase: Legal assumptions, empirical findings, and a research agenda. *Law and Human Behavior, 16,* 185–202.

Cowan, C. L., Thompson, W. C., & Ellsworth, P. C. (1984). The effects of death qualification on jurors' predispositions to convict and on the quality of deliberation. *Law and Human Behavior, 8,* 53–79.

Cox, D. (1999, June 28). Arbitration is no simple matter. *National Law Journal,* p. 1.

Cox, G. (1996, November 4). Excessive fees are attacked across the board. *National Law Journal,* p. 1.

Cox, G. D. (1989, June 26). Trial by ordeal. *National Law Journal, 1,* 42–43.

Cox, M., & Tanford, S. (1989). An alternative method of capital jury selection. *Law and Human Behavior, 13,* 167–184.

*Coy v. Iowa,* 108 S.Ct. 2798 (1988).

Cramton, R. (1978). The ordinary religion of the law school classroom. *Journal of Legal Education, 29,* 247–263.

Crandall, C. S., Glor, J., & Britt, T. W. (1997). AIDS-related stigmatization: Instrumental and symbolic attitudes.

*Journal of Applied Social Psychology,* 27, 95–123.

Crano, W. D., & Messe, L. A. (1982). *Social psychology: Principles and themes of interpersonal behavior.* Pacific Grove, CA: Brooks/Cole.

Cressey, D. R. (1965). Prison organization. In J. G. March (Ed.), *Handbook of organizations.* Skokie, IL: Rand McNally.

Cressey, D. R. (1979). Fifty years of criminology. *Pacific Sociology Review,* 22, 457–480.

Crick, N. & Bigbee, M. (1998). Relational and overt forms of peer victimization: A multi-informant approach. *Journal of Consulting and Clinical Psychology,* 66, 337–347.

Crosbie-Burnett, M. (1991). Impact of joint versus sole custody and quality of co-parental relationship on adjustment of adolescents in remarried families. *Behavioral Sciences and the Law,* 9, 439–449.

*Cruzan v. Director, Missouri Department of Health,* 497 U.S. 261 (1990).

Cunningham, J. L. (1988). Contribution to the history of psychology: XLVI. The pioneer work of Alfred Binet on children as eyewitnesses. *Psychological Reports,* 62, 271–277.

Cunningham, M. D., & Reidy, T. J. (1998). Integrating base rate data in violence risk assessment at capital sentencing. *Behavioral Sciences and the Law,* 16, 71–96.

Curriden, M. (1995a, July). Hard time. *American Bar Association Journal,* 81, 72–74.

Curriden, M. (1995b, December). Judicial barriers quickly breaking down. *American Bar Association Journal,* 81, 24.

Cutler, B. L., & Penrod, S. D. (1988). Improving the reliability of eyewitness identification: Lineup construction and presentation. *Journal of Applied Psychology,* 73, 281–290.

Cutler, B. L., Penrod, S. D., & Dexter, H. R. (1989). The eyewitness, the expert psychologist, and the jury. *Law and Human Behavior,* 13, 311–332.

Cutler, B. L., Penrod, S. D., & Dexter, H. R. (1990). Juror sensitivity to eyewitness identification evidence. *Law and Human Behavior,* 14, 185–192.

Cutler, B. L., Penrod, S. D., & Stuve, T. E. (1988). Juror decision making in eyewitness identification cases. *Law and Human Behavior,* 12, 41–55.

D'Agostino, C. (1986). Police psychological services: Ethical issues. In J. T. Reese & H. A. Goldstein (Eds.), *Psychological services for law enforcement* (pp. 241–248). Washington, D.C.: U.S. Government Printing Office.

Dane, F. C., & Wrightsman, L. S. (1982). Effects of defendants' and victims' characteristics on jurors' verdicts. In N. L. Kerr & R. Bray (Eds.), *Psychology of the courtroom* (pp. 83–115). Orlando, FL: Academic Press.

Daniels, S. (1989). The question of jury competence and the politics of civil justice reform: Symbols, rhetoric, and agenda-building. *Law and Contemporary Problems,* 52(4), 269–310.

Daniels, S., & Martin, J. (1997). Persistence is not always a virtue: Tort reform, civil liability for health care, and the lack of empirical evidence. *Behavioral Sciences and the Law,* 15, 3–19.

Dann, B. M. (1993). Learning lessons and speaking rights: Creating educated and democratic juries. *Indiana Law Journal,* 68, 1229–1279.

*Daubert v. Merrell Dow Pharmaceuticals, Inc.* 113 S.Ct. 2786 (1993).

Dauner, J. T. (1996, March 20). Potential juries fail to appear. *Kansas City Star,* p. C-4.

*Davis v. North Carolina,* 384 U.S. 737 (1966).

*Davis v. United States,* 411 U.S. 233 (1994).

Davis, L. V. (1985). Female and male voices in social work. *Social Work,* 30(2), 106–113.

Davis, R. C., & Meteu-Gelabert, P. (1999). *Respectful and effective policing: Two examples in the South Bronx.* New York: Vera Institute of Justice.

Davis, S., Haire, S. & Songer, D. (1993). Voting behavior and gender on the U.S. courts of appeal. *Judicature,* 77, 129–133.

Dawes, R. M. (1994). *House of cards: Psychology and psychotherapy built on myth.* New York: Free Press.

Dawes, R. M., Faust, D., & Meehl, P. E. (1989). Clinical versus actuarial judgment. *Science,* 243, 1668–1674.

de Botton, A. (2000). *The consolations of philosophy.* New York: Pantheon.

Degoey, P., & Tyler, T. R. (1994, August). *Understanding when and why procedural justice matters: A test of the group-value model.* Paper presented at the meeting of the American Psychological Association, Los Angeles.

Deitchman, M. A., Kennedy, W. A., & Beckham, J. C. (1991). Self-selection factors in the participation of mental health professionals in competency for execution evaluations. *Law and Human Behavior,* 15, 287–303.

Deitz, S. R., Blackwell, K. T., Daley, P. C., & Bentley, B. J. (1982). Measurement of empathy toward rape victims and rapists. *Journal of Personality and Social Psychology,* 43, 372–384.

Deitz, S. R., Littman, M., & Bentley, B. J. (1984). Attribution of responsibility for rape: The influence of observer empathy, victim resistance, and victim attractiveness. *Sex Roles,* 10, 261–280.

Deitz, S. R., Russell, S. A., & Hammes, K. M. (1989, August). *Who's on trial? Information processing by jurors in rape cases.* Paper presented at the meeting of the American Psychological Association, New Orleans.

deMayo, R. A. (1997). Patient sexual behavior and sexual harassment: A national survey of female psychologists. *Professional Psychology: Research and Practice,* 28, 58–62.

Denicola, J., & Sandler, J. (1980). Training abusive parents in child management and self-control skills. *Behavior Therapy,* 11, 263–270.

*Dennis v. United States,* 384 U.S. 855 (1966).

Dershowitz, A. M. (1994). *The abuse excuse.* Boston: Little, Brown.

Dershowitz, A. M. (1996). *Reasonable doubts: The O. J. Simpson case and the criminal justice system.* New York: Simon & Schuster.

*DeShaney v. Winnebago County,* 109 S.Ct. 998 (1989).

De Tocqueville, A. (1900). *Democracy in America* (Henry Reeve, Trans.). New York: Colonial Press.

Deutsch, M. (1975). Equity, equality, and need: What determines which value will be used as the basis for distributive justice? *Journal of Social Issues,* 31(3), 137–149.

Dexter, H. R., Cutler, B. L., & Moran, G. (1992). A test of voir dire as a remedy for the prejudicial effects of pretrial publicity. *Journal of Applied Social Psychology,* 22, 819–832.

Diamond, B. L. (1980). Inherent problems in the use of pretrial hypnosis on a prospective witness. *California Law Review,* 68, 313–349.

Diamond, S., & Casper, J. (1992). Blindfolding the jury to verdict consequences: Damages, experts, and the civil jury. *Law & Society Review, 26,* 513–563.

Diamond, S. S., & Stalans, L. J. (1989). The myth of judicial leniency in sentencing. *Behavioral Sciences and the Law, 7,* 73–89.

*Dickerson v. United States,* 120 S.Ct. 2326 (2000).

Dietz, P. E., & Reese, J. T. (1986). The perils of police psychology: 10 strategies for minimizing role conflicts when providing mental health services and consultation to law enforcement agencies. *Behavioral Sciences and the Law, 4,* 385–400.

DiLalla, L. F., & Gottesman, I. (1991). Biological and genetic contributors to violence: Widom's untold tale. *Psychological Bulletin, 109,* 125–129.

Dillehay, R. C. (1999). Authoritarianism and jurors. In W. F. Abbott & J. Batt (Eds.), *A handbook of jury research* (pp. 13.1–13.18). Philadelphia: ALI-ABA.

Dillehay, R. C., & Nietzel, M. T. (1985). Juror experience and jury verdicts. *Law and Human Behavior, 9,* 179–191.

Dillehay, R. C., & Nietzel, M. T. (1999). Prior jury service. In W. Abbott & J. Batt (Eds.), *Handbook of jury research.* Philadelphia: American Law InstituteAmerican Bar Association.

Doble, J., & Klein, J. (1989). *Punishing criminals: The public's view: An Alabama survey.* New York: Edna McConnell Clark Foundation.

Dodge, M., & Greene, E. (1991). Jurors and expert conceptions of battered women. *Violence and Victims, 6,* 271–282.

Donat, P. L. N., & D'Emilio, J. (1992). A feminist redefinition of rape and sexual assault: Historical foundations and change. *Journal of Social Issues,* 48(1), 9–22.

Doob, A., & Kirschenbaum, H. (1972). Some empirical evidence on the effect of S. 12 of the Canada Evidence Act upon the accused. *Criminal Justice Quarterly, 15,* 88–96.

Doren, D. M. (1987). *Understanding and treating the psychopath.* New York: Wiley.

Doren, D. M. (1998). Recidivism base rates, predictions of sex offender recidivism, and the "sexual predator" commitment laws. *Behavioral Sciences and the Law, 16,* 97–114.

Doris, J., Mazur, R., & Thomas, M. (1995). Training in child protective

services: A commentary on the amicus brief of Bruck and Ceci (1993/1995). *Psychology, Public Policy, and Law, 1,* 479–493.

Dornstein, M. (1988). Pay equity evaluations of occupations and their bases. *Journal of Applied Social Psychology, 18,* 905–924.

Douglas, J. E., Ressler, R. K., Burgess, A. W., & Hartman, C. R. (1986). Criminal profiling from crime scene analysis. *Behavioral Sciences and the Law, 4,* 401–421.

Douglas, K. S., & Webster, C. D. (1999). Predicting violence in mentally and personality disordered individuals. In R. Roesch, S. D. Hart, & J. R. P. Ogloff (Eds), *Psychology and law: The state of the discipline* (pp. 175–239). New York: Kluwer/Plenum.

Dowd, M. (1983, September 5). Rape: The sexual weapon. *Time,* pp. 27–29.

*Dowling v. U.S.,* 110 S.Ct. 668 (1990).

Downs, D. A. (1996). *More than victims: Battered women, the syndrome society, and the law.* Chicago: University of Chicago Press.

Dressler, J. & Thomas, G. C. (1999). *Criminal procedure: Principles, policies, and perspectives.* St. Paul, MN: West.

Drummond, B. D. (1996, August 27). California child molesters face chemical castration. *New York Times,* p. A1.

*Dubose v. State,* 662 So.2d 1189 (Ala. 1995).

Dugdale, R. (1877). *The Jukes: A study in crime, pauperism, and heredity.* New York: Putnam.

Duggan, P. (2000, 23 June). Texas executes Graham after appeals fail: Death penalty case dogs Bush in his bid for the presidency. *Washington Post,* p. A1.

*Duncan v. Louisiana,* 391 U.S. 145 (1968).

Duning, C., & Hanchette, J. (1985, March 28). Don't shoot, Court tells police. *USA Today,* p. 2A.

*Durham v. United States,* 214 F.2d 862 (1954).

*Dusky v. United States,* 362 U.S. 402 (1960).

Dutton, D. G. (1987). The criminal justice response to wife assault. *Law and Human Behavior, 11,* 189–206.

Dutton, D. G. (1995). Male abusiveness in intimate relationships. *Clinical Psychology Review, 15,* 567–582.

Dutton, D. G. (2000). *The domestic assault of women* (3rd ed.). Vancouver: University of British Columbia Press.

Dutton, M. A. (1992). *Empowering and healing the battered woman: A model for assessment and intervention.* New York: Springer.

Dywan, J., & Bowers, K. S. (1983). The use of hypnosis to enhance recall. *Science, 222,* 184–185.

Ebbesen, E. B., & Konecni, V. J. (1975). Decision making and information integration in the courts: The setting of bail. *Journal of Personality and Social Psychology, 32,* 805–821.

Ebbesen, E. B., & Konecni, V. J. (1981). The process of sentencing adult felons: A causal analysis of judicial decision. In B. D. Sales (Ed.), *The trial process* (pp. 413–458). New York: Plenum.

Ebert, B. W. (1987). Guide to conducting a psychological autopsy. *Professional Psychology: Research and Practice, 18,* 52–56.

Ebreo, A., Linn, N., & Vining, J. (1996). The impact of procedural justice on opinions of public policy: Solid waste management as an example. *Journal of Applied Social Psychology, 26,* 1259–1285.

Eckhardt, C. L, Barbour, K. A., & Davison, G. C. (1998). Articulated thoughts of maritally violent and nonviolent men during anger arousal. *Journal of Consulting and Clinical Psychology, 66,* 259–269.

Eckholm, E. (1985, July 4). Stockholm syndrome: Hostages' reactions. *Lawrence (KS) Journal-World,* p. 6.

*Edmonson v. Leesville Concrete Co.,* 111 S.Ct. 2077 (1991).

*Edwards v. Arizona,* 451 U.S. 477 (1981).

Egeth, H. (1995). Expert psychological testimony about eyewitnesses: An update. In F. Kessel et al. (Eds.) *Psychology, science, and human affairs: Essays in honor of William Bevan* (pp. 151–166). Boulder, CO: Westview.

Eichenwald, K. (1989, September 28). Bilzerian gets four years in jail, stiffest in stock crackdown. *New York Times,* pp. 29, 36.

Eisele, G.T. (1991), The case against mandatory court-annexed ADR programs. *Judicature, 75,* 34–40.

Ekman, P. (1985). *Telling lies.* New York: Norton.

Ekman, P., & O'Sullivan, M. (1991). Who can catch a liar? *American Psychologist, 46,* 899–912.

Eley, T. C. (1997). General genes: A new theme in developmental psychopathology. *Current Directions in Psychological Science, 6,* 90–95.

Elliott, D. M. (1997). Traumatic events: Prevalence and delayed recall in the general population. *Journal of Consulting and Clinical Psychology, 65,* 811–820.

Elliott, D. S. (1988, August). *Is there a common etiology for multiple problems in youth?* Paper presented at the meeting of the American Psychological Association, Atlanta.

Elliott, D. S., Huizinga, D., & Ageton, S. S. (1985). *Explaining delinquency and drug use.* Thousand Oaks, CA: Sage.

Elliott, G. C., & Meeker, B. F. (1986). Achieving fairness in the face of competing concerns: The different effects of individual and group characteristics. *Journal of Personality and Social Psychology, 50,* 754–760.

Elliott, R. (1991). Social science data and the APA: The Lockhart brief as a case in point. *Law and Human Behavior, 15,* 59–76.

Elliott, R. (1993). Expert testimony about eyewitness identification: A critique. *Law and Human Behavior, 17,* 423–436.

Ellis, L. (1989). *Theories of rape: Inquiries into the causes of sexual aggression.* New York: Hemisphere.

Ellis, L. (1991). A synthesized (biosocial) theory of rape. *Journal of Consulting and Clinical Psychology, 59,* 631–642.

Ellison, K., & Buckhout, R. (1981). *Psychology and criminal justice.* New York: Harper & Row.

Ellsworth, P. C. (1989). Are 12 heads better than one? *Law and Contemporary Problems, 52*(4), 205–224.

Ellsworth, P. C. (1991). To tell what we know or wait for Godot? *Law and Human Behavior, 15,* 77–90.

Ellsworth, P. C. (1999). Jury reform at the end of the century: Real agreement, real changes. *University of Michigan Journal of Law Reform, 32,* 213–225.

Ellsworth, P. C., Bukaty, R. M., Cowan, C. L., & Thompson, W. C. (1984). The death-qualified jury and the defense of insanity. *Law and Human Behavior, 8,* 81–93.

Ellsworth, P. C. & Mauro, R. (1998). Psychology and law. In D. Gilbert, S. Fiske, et al. (Eds.), *The handbook of social psychology* (Vol. 2, pp. 684–732), Boston: McGraw-Hill.

Elwork, A., Alfini, J. J., & Sales, B. D. (1982). Toward understandable jury instructions. *Judicature, 65,* 433–442.

Elwork, A., Sales, B. D., & Suggs, D. (1981). The trial: A research review. In B. D. Sales (Ed.), *The trial process* (pp. 1–68). New York: Plenum.

Emery, R. E. (1982). Interparental conflict and the children of discord and divorce. *Psychological Bulletin, 92,* 310–330.

Emery, R. E., Matthews, S. G., & Kitzmann, K. M. (1994). Child custody mediation and litigation: Parents' satisfaction and functioning one year after settlement. *Journal of Consulting and Clinical Psychology, 62,* 124–129.

Emery, R. E., Matthews, S. G., & Wyer, M. M. (1991). Child custody mediation and litigation: Further evidence on the differing views of mothers and fathers. *Journal of Consulting and Clinical Psychology, 59,* 410–418.

*Engle v. Isaac,* 456 U.S. 107 (1992).

English, P. W., & Sales, B. D. (1997). A ceiling or consistency effect for the comprehension of jury instructions. *Psychology, Public Policy, and Law, 3,* 381–401.

*Enmund v. Florida,* 458 U.S. 782 (1982).

Ennis, B. J., & Litwack, T. R. (1974). Psychiatry and the presumption of expertise: Flipping coins in the courtroom. *California Law Review, 62,* 693–752.

Epperson, D. L., Kaul, J. D., & Hesselton, D. (1998, October). *Final report of the development of the Minnesota Sex Offender Screening Tool-Revised (MnSOST-R).* Presentation at the 17th Annual Research and Treatment Conference of the Association for the Treatment of Sexual Abusers, Vancouver.

Eron, L. (1987). The development of aggressive behavior from the perspective of a developing behaviorism. *American Psychologist, 42,* 435–442.

Eron, L. (1990). Understanding aggression. *Bulletin of the International Society for Research on Aggression, 12,* 59.

Eron, L. D., & Redmount, R. S. (1957). The effect of legal education on attitudes. *Journal of Legal Education, 9,* 431–443.

Estrich, S. (1987). *Real rape.* Cambridge, MA: Harvard University Press.

Estrich, S. (1996, June 27). Three strikes: Judges' discretion advised. *USA Today,* p. 13A.

Etzioni, A. (1974a, September). On the scientific manipulation of juries. *Human Behavior,* pp. 10–11.

Etzioni, A. (1974b, May 26). Science: Threatening the jury trial. *Washington Post,* p. C3.

Everington, C. T., & Luckasson, R. (1992). *Competence assessment for standing trial for defendants with mental retardation (CASTMR) test manual.* Columbus, Ohio: International Diagnostic Systems.

Ewing, C. (1987). *Battered women who kill: Psychological self-defense as legal justification.* Lexington, MA: Lexington.

Ewing, C. (1991). Preventive detention and execution: The constitutionality of punishing future crimes. *Law and Human Behavior, 15,* 139–164.

Ewing, C. P., & Aubrey, M. (1987). Battered women and public opinion: Some realities about the myths. *Journal of Family Violence, 2,* 257–264.

Ewing, C. P., Aubrey, M., & Jamieson, L. (1986, August). *The battered woman syndrome: Expert testimony and public attitudes.* Paper presented at the meeting of the American Psychological Association, Washington, D.C.

Eysenck, H. J. (1964). *Crime and personality.* Boston: Houghton Mifflin.

Eysenck, H. J., & Gudjonsson, G. H. (1989). *The causes and cures of criminality.* New York: Plenum.

Eysenck, H. J., & Gudjonsson, G. H. (1991). Crime, personality, and punishment. *Contemporary Psychology, 36,* 575–577.

Faigman, D. L. (1995). The evidentiary status of social science under Daubert: Is it "scientific", "technical", or "other" knowledge? *Psychology, Public Policy, and Law, 1,* 960–979.

Falk, A. J. (1999). Sex offenders, mental illness and criminal responsibility: The constitutional boundaries of civil commitment after *Kansas v. Hendricks. American Journal of Law and Medicine, 25,* 117–147.

*Fare v. Michael C.,* 21 Cal. 3d 471, 519 p.2d 7 (1979).

*Faretta v. California,* 422 U.S. 806 (1975).

Farmer, M. W. (1976). Jury composition challenges. *Law and Psychology Review, 2,* 45–74.

Farrington, D. P. (1985). The development of offending and antisocial behavior from childhood: Key findings from the Cambridge Study in Delinquent Development. *Journal of Child Psychology and Psychiatry, 360,* 929–964.

Faust, D., & Ziskin, J. (1988). The expert witness in psychology and psychiatry. *Science, 241,* 31–35.

*Fay v. Noia,* 372 U.S. 391 (1963).

Federal Bureau of Investigation (1998). *Uniform crime reports, 1997.* Washington, D.C.: U.S. Government Printing Office.

*Federal sentencing guidelines.* (1995). St. Paul, MN: West.

Feeley, M. M. (1983). *Court reform on trial.* New York: Basic Books.

Feigenson, N., Park, J., & Salovey, P. (1997). Effect of blameworthiness and outcome severity on attributions of responsibility and damage awards in comparative negligence cases. *Law and Human Behavior, 21,* 597–617.

Feild, H. S. (1978a). Attitudes toward rape: A comparative analysis of police, rapists, crisis counselors, and citizens. *Journal of Personality and Social Psychology, 36,* 156–179.

Feild, H. S. (1978b). Juror background characteristics and attitudes toward rape: Correlates of jurors' decisions in rape trials. *Law and Human Behavior, 2,* 73–93.

Feild, H. S. (1979). Rape trials and jurors' decisions: A psycholegal analysis of the effects of victim, defendant, and case characteristics. *Law and Human Behavior, 3,* 261–284.

Feild, H. S., & Barnett, N. J. (1978). Simulated jury trials: Students vs. "real" people as jurors. *Journal of Social Psychology, 104,* 287–293.

Feild, H. S., & Bienen, L. B. (1980). *Jurors and rape: A study in psychology and law.* Lexington, MA: Heath.

Fein, S. (1996). The effects of suspicion on attributional thinking and the correspondence bias. *Journal of Personality and Social Psychology, 70,* 1164–1184.

Fein, S., McCloskey, A. L., & Tomlinson, T. M. (1997). Can the jury disregard that information? The use of suspicion to reduce the prejudicial effects of pretrial publicity and inadmissible testimony. *Personality and Social Psychology Bulletin, 23,* 1215–1226.

Feinstein, D., (2000). Victim rights amendment [On-line]. Available: http://www.senate.gov/feinstein/body_victims

Feld, B. (1997). Abolish the juvenile court: Youthfulness, criminal responsibility and sentencing policy. *Journal*

*of Criminal Law and Criminology, 88,* 68–136.

Feldman, M. P. (1977). *Criminal behavior: A psychological analysis.* New York: Wiley.

Feldman-Summers, S., & Ashworth, C. D. (1981). Factors related to intentions to report rape. *Journal of Social Issues, 37,* 71–92.

Feldman-Summers, S., Gordon, P. E., & Meagher, J. R. (1979). The impact of rape on sexual satisfaction. *Journal of Abnormal Psychology, 88,* 101–105.

Fenster, G. A., & Locke, B. (1973). Neuroticism among policemen: An examination of police personality. *Journal of Applied Psychology, 57,* 358–359.

Fentiman, L. (1986). Whose right is it anyway? Rethinking competency to stand trial in light of the synthetically sane insanity defendant. *University of Miami Law Review, 40,* 1109–1169.

Ferri, E. (1917). *Criminal sociology* (Joseph I. Kelley & John Lisle, Trans.). Boston: Little, Brown.

Finkel, N. (1995). *Commonsense justice: Jurors' notions of the law.* Cambridge, MA: Harvard University Press.

Finkel, N., & Groscup, J. L. (1997). When mistakes happen: Commonsense rules of culpability. *Psychology, Public Policy, and Law, 3,* 65–125.

Finkel, N., Hurabiell, M., & Hughes, K. (1993). Right to die and euthanasia: Crossing the public/private boundary. *Law and Human Behavior, 17,* 487–506.

Finkel, N. (1989). The Insanity Defense Reform Act of 1984: Much ado about nothing. *Behavioral Sciences and the Law, 7,* 403–419.

Finkel, N. (1991). The insanity defense: A comparison of verdict schemas. *Law and Human Behavior, 15,* 533–556.

Finkel, N., Maloney, S. T., Valbuena, M. Z., & Groscup, J. L. (1995). Lay perspectives on legal conundrums: Impossible and mistaken act cases. *Law and Human Behavior, 19,* 609–630.

Finkel, N., & Slobogin, C. (1995). Insanity, justification, and culpability toward a unifying theme. *Law and Human Behavior, 19,* 447–464.

Finkelhor, D. (1994). Current information on the scope and nature of child sexual abuse. *The Future of Children, 4,* 31–53.

Finkelhor, D., Hotaling, G., Lewis, I. A., & Smith, C. (1990). Sexual abuse in a national survey of adult men and women: Prevalence, characteristics,

and risk factors. *Child Abuse and Neglect, 14,* 19–28.

Firestone, D. (1996, November 5). For one day, the jury pool welcomes a big fish named Giuliani. *New York Times,* p. B15.

Fischer, K. (1989). Defining the boundaries of admissible expert psychological testimony on rape trauma syndrome. *University of Illinois Law Review, 1989,* 691–734.

Fischer, P. J., & Breakey, W. R. (1991). The epidemiology of alcohol, drug, and mental disorders among homeless persons. *American Psychologist, 46,* 1115–1128.

Fisher, R. P., & Cutler, B. L. (1996). Relation between consistency and accuracy of eyewitness testimony. In G. M. Davies, S. Lloyd-Bostock, M. McMurran, & C. Wilson (Eds.), *Psychology and law: Advances in research.* Berlin: DeGruyter.

Fisher, R. P., & Geiselman, R. E. (1992). *Memory enhancing techniques for investigative interviewing: The cognitive interview.* Springfield, IL: Thomas.

Fisher, R. P., & Quigly, K. L. (1989, August). *The cognitive interview, person description, and person recognition.* Paper presented at the meeting of the American Psychological Association, New Orleans.

Fisk, M. C. (1998, September 28). Now you see it, now you don't. *National Law Journal,* pp. C1–C2.

Fiske, S., & Taylor, S. (1991). *Social cognition* (2nd ed.). New York: McGraw-Hill.

Fiske, S. T., Bersoff, D. N., Borgida, E., Deaux, K., & Heilman, M. E. (1991). Social science research on trial: Use of sex stereotyping research in *Price Waterhouse v. Hopkins. American Psychologist, 46,* 1049–1060.

Fitzgerald, L. F., Buchanan, N. T., Collinsworth, L. L., Magley, V. J., & Ramos, A. M. (1999). Junk logic: The abuse defense in sexual harassment litigation. *Psychology, Public Policy, and Law, 5,* 730–759.

Fitzgerald, L. F., Gelfand, M., & Drasgow, F. (1995). Measuring sexual harassment: Theoretical and psychometric advances. *Basic and Applied Social Psychology, 17,* 425–445.

Fitzgerald, R., & Ellsworth, P. C. (1984). Due process vs. crime control: Death qualification and jury attitudes. *Law and Human Behavior, 8,* 31–51.

*Florida v. Bostick,* 501 U.S. (1991).

*Florida v. Jimeno,* 111 S.Ct. 1801 (1991).

*Florida Bar v. Went for It*, 115 S.Ct. 2371 (1995).

Foa, E. B., Hearst-Ikeda, D., & Perry, K. J. (1995). Evaluation of a brief cognitive behavioral program for the prevention of chronic PTSD in recent assault victims. *Journal of Consulting and Clinical Psychology, 63*, 948–955.

Foa, E. B., & Kozak, M. J. (1986). Emotional processing of fear: Exposure to corrective information. *Psychological Bulletin, 99*, 20–35.

Foley, M. (1983). Confessions of a retributivist. *Social Action and the Law, 9*(1), 16–17.

Folger, R., Cropanzano, R., Timmerman, T. A., Howes, J. C., & Mitchell, D. (1996). Elaborating procedural fairness: Justice becomes both simpler and more complex. *Personality and Social Psychology Bulletin, 22*, 435–441.

Folger, R., & Greenberg, J. (1985). Procedural justice: An interpretive analysis of personnel systems. In K. Rowland & G. Ferris (Eds.), *Research in personnel and human resources management* (Vol. 3, pp. 141–183). Greenwich, CT: JAI.

Folger, R., Sheppard, B. H., & Buttram, R. T. (1995). Equity, equality, and need: Three faces of social justice. In B. B. Bunker & J. Z. Rubin and Associates (Eds.), *Conflict, cooperation, and justice* (pp. 261–289). San Francisco: Jossey-Bass.

Follingstad, D. R. (1994, March 10). *The use of battered woman syndrome in court.* Workshop for the American Academy of Forensic Psychology, Santa Fe, NM.

Footlick, J. (1978, May 8). Insanity on trial. *Newsweek*, pp. 108–112.

*Ford v. Wainwright*, 477 U.S. 399 (1986).

*Ford Motor Credit Co. v. Sheehan*, 373 So.2d 956 (Fla. App. 1979).

Ford, W. (1998). *Managing police stress.* Walnut Creek, CA: Management Advantage.

ForsterLee, L., Horowitz, I. A., & Bourgeois, M. J. (1993). Juror competence in civil trials: Effects of preinstruction and evidence technicality. *Journal of Applied Psychology, 78*, 14–21.

ForsterLee, L., Horowitz, I. A., & Bourgeois, M. (1994). Effects of note-taking on verdicts and evidence processing in a civil trial. *Law and Human Behavior, 18*, 567–578.

*Foucha v. Louisiana*, 112 S.Ct. 1780 (1992).

Fox, D., Gerson, A., & Lees-Haley, P. (1995). Interrelationship of MMPI-2 validity scales in personal injury claims. *Journal of Clinical Psychology, 51*, 42–47.

Fox, D. R. (1993). Psychological jurisprudence and radical social change. *American Psychologist, 48*, 234–241.

Fox, D. R. (1999). Psycholegal scholarship's contribution to false consciousness about injustice. *Law and Human Behavior, 23*, 9–30.

Fox, J. A., & Levin, J. (1998). Multiple homicide: Patterns of serial and mass murder. *Crime and Justice, 23*, 407–455.

Fox, S. G., & Walters, H. A. (1986). The impact of general versus specific expert testimony and eyewitness confidence upon mock juror judgment. *Law and Human Behavior, 10*, 215–228.

Frank, J. (1949). *Courts on trial.* Princeton, NJ: Princeton University Press.

Frankel, M. E. (1972). *Criminal sentences.* New York: Hill & Wang.

Frankel, M. E., & Naftalis, G. P. (1977). *The grand jury: An institution on trial.* New York: Hill & Wang.

*Frazier v. Cupp*, 394 U.S. 731 (1969).

Frazier, P., & Borgida, E. (1985). Rape trauma syndrome evidence in court. *American Psychologist, 40*, 984–993.

Frazier, P., & Borgida, E. (1988). Juror common understanding and the admissibility of rape trauma syndrome evidence in court. *Law and Human Behavior, 12*, 101–122.

Frazier, P., & Borgida, E. (1992). Rape trauma syndrome: A review of case law and psychological research. *Law and Human Behavior, 16*, 293–311.

Frazier, P. A., Cochran, C. C., & Olson, A. M. (1995). Social science research on lay definitions of sexual harassment. *Journal of Social Issues, 51*(1), 21–37.

Frazier, P. A., & Haney, B. (1996). Sexual assault cases in the legal system: Police, prosecutor, and victim perspectives. *Law and Human Behavior, 20*, 607–628.

Frederick, R. I., & Crosby, R. D. (2000). Development and validation of the Validity Indicator Profile. *Law and Human Behavior, 24*, 59–82.

Fredrickson, R. (1992). *Repressed memories: A journey to recovery from sexual abuse.* New York: Simon & Schuster.

Freedman, J. L. (1984). Effect of television violence on aggressiveness. *Psychological Bulletin, 96*, 227–246.

Freedman, J. L. (1986). Television violence and aggression: A rejoinder. *Psychological Bulletin, 100*, 372–378.

Freedman, J., & Burke, T. (1996, July). The effect of pretrial publicity: The *Bernardo* case. *Canadian Journal of Criminology*, pp. 253–270.

*Frendak v. United States*, 408 A.2d 364 (D.C. 1979).

Freud, S. (1961). *The complete psychological works of Sigmund Freud* (Vol. 19). London: Hogarth.

Friedland, S. I. (1998). The criminal law implications of the human genome project: Reimagining a genetically oriented justice system. *Kentucky Law Journal, 86*, 303–366.

Friedrich-Cofer, L., & Huston, A. C. (1986). Television violence and aggression: A rejoinder. *Psychological Bulletin, 100*, 364–371.

*Frye v. United States*, 293 F. 1013, 34 A.L.R. 145 (D.C. Cir. 1923).

Fulero, S. M. (1987). The role of behavioral research in the free press/free trial controversy: Another view. *Law and Human Behavior, 11*, 259–264.

Fulero, S. M., & Everington, C. (1995). Assessing competency to waive *Miranda* rights in defendants with mental retardation. *Law and Human Behavior, 19*, 533–543.

Fulero, S. M., & Finkel, N. J. (1991). Barring ultimate issue testimony: An "insane" rule? *Law and Human Behavior, 15*, 495–508.

Fulero, S. M., & Penrod, S. D. (1990). Attorney jury selection folklore: What do they think and how can psychologists help? *Forensic Reports, 3*, 233–259.

*Furman v. Georgia*, 408 U.S. 238 (1972).

Fyfe, J. J. (1982). Blind justice: Police shootings in Memphis. *Journal of Criminal Law and Criminology, 73*, 707–722.

Fyfe, J. J. (1988). Police shooting: Environment and license. In J. E. Scott & T. Hirschi (Eds.), *Controversial issues in crime and justice* (pp. 79–94). Newbury Park, CA: Sage.

Gaines, L. K., & Falkenberg, S. (1998). An evaluation of the written selection test: Effectiveness and alternatives. *Journal of Criminal Justice, 26*, 175–183.

Gale, A. (Ed.). (1988). *The polygraph test: Lies, truth and science.* London: Sage.

Gallagher, W. (1996). *I.D.: How heredity and experience make you who you are.* New York: Random House.

Gallup Organization. (1989, June 23). A jury of one's peers. *Lawrence (KS) Journal-World*, p. 1B.

*Gannett Co. v. DePasquale*, 443 U.S. 368 (1979).

Gardner, J., Scogin, F., Vipperman, R., & Varela, J.G. (1998). The predictive validity of peer assessment in law enforcement: A 6-year follow-up. *Behavioral Sciences and the Law, 16,* 473–478.

Gardner, W., Lidz, C. W., Mulvey, E. D., & Shaw, E. C. (1996). A comparison of actuarial methods for identifying repetitively violent patients with mental illness. *Law and Human Behavior, 20,* 35–48.

Garner, J., Fagan, J., & Maxwell, C. (1995). Published findings from the spouse assault replication program: A critical review. *Journal of Quantitative Criminology, 11,* 3–28.

Garofalo, R. (1914). *Criminology* (R. W. Millar, Trans.). Boston: Little, Brown.

Garry, M., Manning, C. G., Loftus, E. F., & Sherman, S. J. (1996). Imagination inflation: Imagining a childhood event inflates confidence that it occurred. *Psychonomic Bulletin & Review, 3,* 208–214.

Garry, M., & Polaschek, D. L. (2000). Imagination and memory. *Current Directions in Psychological Science, 9,* 6–9.

Garven, S., Wood, J. M., & Malpass, R. S. (2000). Allegations of wrongdoing: The effects of reinforcement on children's mundane and fantastic claims. *Journal of Applied Psychology, 85,* 38–49.

Garvey, S. P., Johnson, S. L., & Marcus, P. (2000). Correcting deadly confusion: Responding to jury inquiries in capital cases. *Cornell Law Review, 85,* 627–655.

Gatland, L. (1997, December). Dangerous dedication. *American Bar Association Journal, 83,* 28.

Gavey, N. (1991). Sexual victimization prevalence among New Zealand University students. *Journal of Consulting and Clinical Psychology, 59,* 464–466.

Gaylin, W. (1974). *Partial justice: A study of bias in sentencing.* New York: Vintage.

Gaylin, W. (1982). *The killing of Bonnie Garland: A question of justice.* New York: Simon & Schuster.

Gayoso, A., Cutler, B. L., & Moran, G. (1994). Assessing the value of social scientists as trial consultants: A consumer research approach. *Forensic Reports.*

Geiselman, R. E., Fisher, R. P., MacKinnon, D. P., & Holland, H. L. (1985). Eyewitness memory enhancement in the police interview. *Journal of Applied Psychology, 70,* 401–412.

Geis, G. & Bienen, L. B. (1998). *Crimes of the century.* Boston: Northeastern University Press.

Gelles, R. J., & Cornell, C. P. (1985). *Intimate violence in families.* Newbury Park, CA: Sage.

Gellhorn, E. (1968). The law schools and the Negro. *Duke Law Journal, 1968,* 1069–1099.

*Georgia v. McCollum,* 112 S.Ct. 2348 (1992).

Geraghty, T., & Rhee, W. (1998). Learning from tragedy: Representing children in discretionary hearings. *Wake Forest Law Review, 33,* 595–650.

Gerbasi, K. C., Zuckerman, M., & Reis, H. T. (1977). Justice needs a new blindfold: A review of mock jury research. *Psychological Bulletin, 84,* 323–345.

Gergen, K. J. (1994). Exploring the postmodern: Perils or potentials? *American Psychologist, 49,* 412–416.

Gershman, B. L. (1982). Abscam, the judiciary, and the ethics of entrapment. *Yale Law Journal, 91,* 1565–1591.

*Gerstein v. Pugh,* 420 U.S. 103 (1975).

Gibeaut, J. (1997, September). The last word. *American Bar Association Journal, 83,* 42–44.

Gibeaut, J. (1999, July), Share the wealth. *American Bar Association Journal, 85,* 14.

*Gideon v. Wainwright,* 372 U.S. 335 (1963).

Gilligan, C. (1977). In a different voice: Women's conceptions of the self and of morality. *Harvard Educational Review, 47,* 481–517.

Gilligan, C. (1982). *In a different voice: Psychological theory and women's development.* Cambridge, MA: Harvard University Press.

Gilligan, C., Ward, J. V., & Taylor, J. McL. (Eds.). (1988). *Mapping the moral domain.* Cambridge, MA: Harvard University Press.

Gist, R. M., & Perry, J. D. (1985). Perspectives on negotiation in local jurisdictions. Part 1: A different typology of situations. *FBI Law Enforcement Bulletin, 54*(11), 21.

Glaberson, W. (1989, February 1). Challenge for jurors. *New York Times,* p. 46.

Gladwell, M. (1996, April 24). Goetz loses $43 million jury verdict: "Subway vigilante" victim victorious in Bronx trial. *Washington Post,* p. A1.

Glamser, D. (1997, January 27). Washington State testing therapy for sex felons. *USA Today,* p. 3A.

Glaser, R., & Chi, M. T. H. (1988). Overview. In M. T. H. Chi, R. Glaser, & M. J. Farr (Eds.), *The nature of expertise* (pp. xv–xxvii). Hillsdale, NJ: Erlbaum.

Gleick, J. (1978, August 21). Getting away with murder. *New Times,* pp. 21, 27.

Gless, A. G. (1995). Some post-Daubert trial tribulations of a simple country judge: Behavioral science evidence in trial courts. *Behavioral Sciences and the Law, 13,* 261–292.

Glueck, S., & Glueck, E. (1934). *One thousand delinquents.* Cambridge, MA: Harvard University Press.

Glueck, S., & Glueck, E. (1950). *Unraveling juvenile delinquency.* Cambridge, MA: Harvard University Press.

Glueck, S., & Glueck, E. (1956). *Physique and delinquency.* New York: Harper & Row.

Goddard, H. (1916). *The Kallilak family: A study in the heredity of feeblemindedness.* New York: Macmillan.

*Godinez v. Moran,* 113 S.Ct. 2680 (1993).

Goff, L.M. & Roediger, H.L. (1998). Imagination inflation for action events: Repeated imaginings lead to illusory recollections. *Memory & Cognition, 26,* 20–33.

Goldberg-Ambrose, C. (1992). Unfinished business in rape law reform. *Journal of Social Issues, 48*(1), 173–186.

Goldfarb, R. L. (1965). *Ransom.* New York: Harper & Row.

Golding, J. M., Warren, A. R., & Ross, D. F. (1997). On legal validity, internal validity, and ecological validity: Comment on *Wasby* and *Brody. Law and Human Behavior, 21,* 693–695.

Golding, S. L., Roesch, R., & Schreiber, J. (1984). Assessment and conceptualization of competency to stand trial: Preliminary data on the Interdisciplinary Fitness Interview. *Law and Human Behavior, 8,* 321–334.

Goldkamp, J. S., & Gottfredson, M. R. (1979). Bail decision making and pretrial detention. *Law and Human Behavior, 3,* 227–249.

Goldkamp, J. S., & Gottfredson, M. R. (1988). *Guidelines for bail and pretrial release in three urban courts.* Unpublished final report.

Goldkamp, J. S., Gottfredson, M. R., Jones, P. R., & Weiland, D. (1995). *Personal liberty and community safety: Pretrial release in the criminal court.* New York: Plenum.

Goldman, S. & Saronson, M. (1994). Clinton's nontraditional judges: Creating a more representative bench. *Judicature, 78*, 68–73.

Goldman, S., & Slotnick, E. (1997). Clinton's first-term judiciary: Many bridges to cross. *Judicature, 80*, 254–273.

*Goldschmitt v. State*, 490 So.2d 123 (Fla. App. 1986).

Goldstein, A. G., Chance, J. E., & Schneller, G. R. (1989). Frequency of eyewitness identification in criminal cases: A survey of prosecutors. *Bulletin of the Psychonomic Society, 27*, 71–74.

Goleman, D. (1987, April 7). The bully: New research depicts a paranoid, lifelong loser. *New York Times*, p. 23.

Goodman, G. S., Golding, J. M., & Haith, M. M. (1984). Jurors' reactions to child witnesses. *Journal of Social Issues, 40*(2), 139–156.

Goodman, G. S., Golding, J., Helgeson, V., Haith, M., & Michelli, J. (1987). When a child takes the stand: Jurors' perceptions of children's eyewitness testimony. *Law and Human Behavior, 11*, 27–40.

Goodman, G. S., Pyle-Taub, E., Jones, D., England, P., Port, L., Rudy, L., & Prado, L. (1992). Emotional effects of criminal court testimony on child sexual assault victims. *Monographs of the Society for Research in Child Development, 75* (Serial No. 229).

Goodman, G. S., Tobey, A., Batterman-Faunce, J., Orcutt, H., Thomas, S., Shapiro, C., & Sachsenmaier, T. (1998). Face-to-fact confrontation: Effects of closed-circuit technology on children's eyewitness testimony and jurors' decisions. *Law and Human Behavior, 22*, 165-203.

Goodman, H. (1982, August 9). Mental patients' rights clash with public's desire for safety. *Kansas City Times*, pp. A1, A4.

Goodman, J., Greene, E., & Loftus, E. F. (1989). Runaway verdicts or reasoned determinations: Mock juror strategies in awarding damages. *Jurimetrics Journal, 29*, 285–309.

Goodman-Delahunty, J. (1997). Forensic psychological expertise in the wake of *Daubert. Law and Human Behavior, 21*, 121–140.

Goodman-Delahunty, J. (1998). Approaches to gender and the law: Research and applications. *Law and Human Behavior, 22*, 129–143.

Goodman-Delahunty, J. (1999). Pragmatic support for the reasonable victim standard in hostile workplace sexual harassment cases. *Psychology, Public Policy, and Law, 5*, 519–555.

Goodman-Delahunty, J., Greene, E., & Hsiao, W. (1998). Construing motive in videotaped killings: The role of jurors' attitudes toward the death penalty. *Law and Human Behavior, 22*, 257–271.

Gordon, M., & Dutton, M.A. (1996). *Validity of "battered woman syndrome" in criminal cases involving battered women*. U.S. Department of Justice and Health and Human Services report. National Criminal Justice Reference Service #160972.

Gordon, R. (1995, January 1). On trial: Parallels of the profession. *The Recorder* (American Lawyer Media). Web.lexis-nexis.com/universe/docum...

Gordon, R. A. (1986, August). *IQ commensurability of black-white differences in crime and delinquency*. Paper presented at the meeting of the American Psychological Association, Washington, D.C.

Gorenstein, G. W., & Ellsworth, P. C. (1980). Effect of choosing an incorrect photograph on a later identification by an eyewitness. *Journal of Applied Psychology, 65*, 616–622.

Gorer, G. (1955). Modification of national character: The role of police in England. *Journal of Social Issues, 11*(2), 24–32.

Gorman, C. (1989, January 23). Honestly, can we trust you? *Time*, p. 44.

Gothard, S., Rogers, R., & Sewell, K. W. (1995). Feigning incompetency to stand trial: An investigation of the Georgia Court Competency Test. *Law and Human Behavior, 19*, 363–374.

Gothard, S. Viglione, D. J., Jr., Meloy, J. R., & Sherman, M. (1995). Detection of malingering in competency to stand trial evaluations. *Law and Human Behavior, 19*, 493–506.

Gottfredson, D. M., Gottfredson, S. D., & Conly, C. H. (1989). Stakes and risks: Incapacitative intent in sentencing decisions. *Behavioral Sciences and the Law, 7*, 91–106.

Gottfredson, L. (1986, August). *IQ versus training: Job performance and black-white occupational inequality*. Paper presented at the meeting of the American Psychological Association, Washington, D.C..

*Grady v. Corbin*, 495 U.S. 508 (1990).

Gray, E. (1993). *Unequal justice: The prosecution of child sexual abuse*. New York: Macmillan.

*Grayson v. United States*, 438 U.S. 41 (1978).

Green, B., Grace, M., Lindy, J., Gleser, G., & Leonard, A. C. (1990). Risk factors for PTSD and other diagnoses in a general sample of Vietnam veterans. *American Journal of Psychiatry, 147*, 729–733.

Green, E. (1961). *Judicial attitudes in sentencing*. London: Macmillan.

Green, S. (1984). Victim-offender reconciliation program: A review of the concept. *Social Action and the Law, 10*(2), 43–52.

Greenberg, M. S., & Ruback, R. B. (1982). *Social psychology of the criminal justice system*. Pacific Grove, CA: Brooks/Cole.

Greene, E. (1986). Forensic hypnosis to lift amnesia: The jury is still out. *Behavioral Sciences and the Law, 4*, 65–72.

Greene, E. (1988). Judge's instruction on eyewitness testimony: Evaluation and revision. *Journal of Applied Social Psychology, 18*, 252–276.

Greene, E. (1999). The many guises of victim impact evidence and effects on jurors' judgments. *Psychology, Crime, and Law, 5*, 331–348.

Greene, E., & Dodge, M. (1995). The influence of prior record evidence on juror decision making. *Law and Human Behavior, 19*, 67–78.

Greene, E., & Johns, M. (2001). Jurors' use of instructions on negligence. *Journal of Applied Social Psychology, 31*, in press.

Greene, E., Johns, M., & Bowman, J. (1999). The effects of injury severity on jury negligence decisions. *Law and Human Behavior, 23*, 675–693.

Greene, E., Johns, M., & Smith, A. (2001). The effects of defendant conduct on jury damage awards. *Journal of Applied Psychology, 86*, 228–237.

Greene, E., & Wade, R. (1988). Of private talk and public print: General pretrial publicity and juror decision making. *Applied Cognitive Psychology, 2*, 123–135.

Greene, J. A. (1999). Zero tolerance: A case study of police policies and practices in New York City. *Crime and Deliquency, 45*, 171–187.

Greenhouse, L. (1994, April 20). High court bars sex as standard of picking jurors. *New York Times*, pp. A1, A10.

Greenhouse, L. (1995, February 23). Judges may overrule juries, court rules. *New York Times*, p. A12.

*Gregg v. Georgia,* 428 U.S. 153 (1976).

Gregory, W. L., Mowen, J. C., & Linder, D. E. (1978). Social psychology and plea bargaining: Applications, methodology, and theory. *Journal of Personality and Social Psychology, 36,* 1521–1530.

*Griffin v. Wisconsin,* 107 S.Ct. 3164 (1987).

*Grigsby v. Mabry,* 483 F.Supp. 1372 (E.D. Ark. 1980). Modified and remanded, 637 F.2d 525 (8th Cir. 1980).

Grisham, J. (1996). *The runaway jury.* New York: Doubleday.

Grisso, T. (1981). *Juveniles' waivers of rights: Legal and psychological competence.* New York: Plenum.

Grisso, T. (1986). *Evaluating competencies: Forensic assessments and instruments.* New York: Plenum.

Grisso, T. (1997a). The competence of adolescents as trial defendants. *Psychology, Public Policy, and Law, 3,* 3–32.

Grisso, T. (1987b). The economic and scientific future of forensic psychological assessment. *American Psychologist, 42,* 831–839.

Grisso, T. (1998). *Instruments for assessing understanding and appreciation of Miranda rights.* Sarasota, FL: Professional Resource Press.

Grisso, T., & Appelbaum, P. S. (1995). The MacArthur Treatment Competence Study. III: Abilities of patients to consent to psychiatric and medical treatments. *Law and Human Behavior, 19,* 149–174.

Grisso, T., Appelbaum, P. S., Mulvey, E. P., & Fletcher, K. (1995). The MacArthur Treatment Competence Study. II: Measures of abilities related to competence to consent to treatment. *Law and Human Behavior, 19,* 127–148.

Grisso, T., Cocozza, J. J., Steadman, H. J., Fisher, W. H., & Greer, A. (1994). The organization of pretrial forensic evaluation services: A national profile. *Law and Human Behavior, 18,* 377–394.

Grisso, T., & Saks, M. J. (1991). Psychology's influence on constitutional interpretation: A comment on how to succeed. *Law and Human Behavior, 15,* 205–211.

Grisso, T., & Siegel, S. K. (1986). Assessment of competency to stand criminal trial. In W. J. Curran, A. L. McGarry, & S. A. Shah (Eds.), *Forensic psychiatry and psychology* (pp. 145–165). Philadelphia: Davis.

Gross, J. & Hayne, H. (1996). Eyewitness identification by 5- to 6-year old children. *Law and Human Behavior, 20,* 359–373.

Gross, S. R. (1984). Determining the neutrality of death-qualified juries: Judicial appraisal of empirical data. *Law and Human Behavior, 8,* 7–30.

Groth, A. N., with Birnbaum, H. J. (1979). *Men who rape.* New York: Plenum.

Grove, W, M., & Barden, R. C. (1999). Protecting the integrity of the legal system: The admissibility of testimony from mental health experts under *Daubert/Kumho* analyses. *Psychology, Public Policy, and Law, 5,* 224–242.

Grubin, D. (1998). *Sex offending against children: Understanding the risk.* Police Research Series Paper 99. London: Home Office.

Grych, J. H., & Fincham, F. D. (1992). Interventions for children of divorce: Toward greater integration of research and action. *Psychological Bulletin, 111,* 434–454.

Guastello, S. J., & Rieke, M. L. (1991). A review and critique of honesty test research. *Behavioral Sciences and the Law, 9,* 501–523.

Gudjonsson, G. H. (1988). How to defeat the polygraph tests. In A. Gale (Ed.), *The polygraph test: Lies, truth and science* (pp. 126–136). London: Sage.

Gudjonsson, G. H. (1992). *The psychology of interrogations, confessions, and testimony.* London: Wiley.

Gunter, G. (1985, Jan. 25). Voices across the USA. *USA Today,* p. 12A.

Gutek, B. (1985). *Sex and the workplace.* San Francisco: Jossey Bass.

Gutek, B. A., & O'Connor, M. (1995). The empirical basis for the reasonable woman standard. *Journal of Social Issues, 51*(1), 151–166.

Hagen, M. (1997). *Whores of the court: The fraud of psychiatric testimony and the rape of American justice.* New York: HarperCollins.

Hall, D. F., Loftus, E. F., & Tousignant, J. P. (1984). Postevent information and changes in recollection for a natural event. In G. L. Wells & E. F. Loftus (Eds.), *Eyewitness testimony: Psychological perspectives* (pp. 124–141). New York: Cambridge University Press.

Hall, G. C. (1996). *Theory-based assessment, treatment, and prevention of sexual aggression.* New York: Oxford University Press.

Hall, G. C., & Hirschman, R. (1991). Toward a theory of sexual aggression: A quadripartite model. *Journal of Consulting and Clinical Psychology, 59,* 662–669.

*Hamilton v. Schirro,* 74 F.3d 1545 (9th Cir. 1996).

Hamilton, D. L., Katz, L. B., & Leirer, V. O. (1980). Cognitive representation of personality impressions: Organizational processes in first impression formation. *Journal of Personality and Social Psychology, 39,* 1050–1063.

*Hampton v. United States,* 424 U.S. 484 (1976).

Handman, L. R. (1977). Underrepresentation of economic groups on federal juries. *Boston University Law Review, 57*(1), 198–224.

Haney, C. (1984). Editor's introduction. *Law and Human Behavior, 8,* 1–6.

Haney, C. (1997a). Commonsense justice and capital punishment: Problematizing the "will of the people." *Psychology, Public Policy, and Law, 3,* 303–337.

Haney, C. (1997b). Psychology and the limits to prison pain: Confronting the coming crisis in Eighth Amendment law. *Psychology, Public Policy, and Law, 3,* 499–588.

Haney, C., Banks, W., & Zimbardo, P. (1973). Interpersonal dynamics in a simulated prison. *International Journal of Criminology and Penology, 1,* 69–97.

Haney, C., & Lynch, M. (1997). Clarifying life and death matters: An analysis of instructional comprehension and penalty phase closing arguments. *Law and Human Behavior, 21,* 575–596.

Haney, C., & Zimbardo, P. (1998). The past and future of U.S. prison policy: Twenty-five years after the Stanford Prison Experiment. *American Psychologist, 53,* 709–727.

Hanish, L. D., & Guerra, N. G. (2000). The roles of ethnicity and school context in predicting children's victimization by peers. *American Journal of Community Psychology, 28,* 201–224.

Hannaford, P., Hans, V., & Munsterman, G.T. (2000). Permitting jury discussions during trial: Impact of the Arizona reform. *Law and Human Behavior, 24,* 359–382.

Hans, V., Hannaford, P., & Munsterman, G. T. (1999) The Arizona jury reform permitting civil jury trial discussions: The views of trial participants, judges, and jurors. *University of Michigan Journal of Law Reform, 32,* 349–377.

Hans, V. P., (1988, November). Confronting the accused. *APA Monitor,* p. 35.

Hans, V. P. (1992a). Judgments of justice. *Psychological Science, 3,* 218–220.

Hans, V. P. (1992b). Jury decision making. In D. K. Kagehiro & W. S. Laufer (Eds.), *Handbook of psychology and law* (pp. 56–76). New York: Springer.

Hans, V. P. (1996). The contested role of the civil jury in business litigation. *Judicature, 79,* 242–248.

Hans, V. P. (2000). *Business on trial: The civil jury and corporate responsibility.* New Haven, CT: Yale University Press.

Hans, V. P., & Ermann, M. D. (1989). Responses to corporate versus individual wrongdoing. *Law and Human Behavior, 13,* 151–166.

Hans, V. P., & Ivkovich, S. K. (1994, March). *Civil jurors' evaluations on expert testimony.* Paper presented at the meeting of the American Psychology-Law Society, Santa Fe, NM.

Hans, V. P., & Slater, D. (1983). John Hinckley, Jr., and the insanity defense: The public's verdict. *Public Opinion Quarterly, 47,* 202–212.

Hans, V. P., & Vidmar, N. (1982). Jury selection. In N. L. Kerr & R. M. Bray (Eds.), *The psychology of the courtroom* (pp. 39–82). Orlando, FL: Academic Press.

Hans, V. P., & Vidmar, N. (1986). *Judging the jury.* New York: Plenum.

Hans, V. P., & Vidmar, N. (1991). The American jury at 25 years. *Law and Social Inquiry, 16,* 323–351.

Hansen, M. (1997, September). Repairing the damage. *American Bar Association Journal, 83,* 20.

Hansen, M. (1999, April). Mandatories going, going, . . . going. *American Bar Association Journal, 85,* 14.

Hansen, M. (2000). Death knell for the death penalty? *American Bar Association Journal, 86,* 40–48.

Hanson, K. A., & Gidycz, C. A. (1993). Evaluation of a sexual assault prevention program. *Journal of Consulting and Clinical Psychology, 61,* 1046–1052.

Hanson, R. K. (1997). *The development of a brief actuarial risk scale for sexual offense recidivism.* User Report 97-04. Ottawa: Department of the Solicitor General of Canada.

Hanson, R. K., & Bussiere, M. T. (1998). Predicting relapse: A meta-analysis

of sexual offender recidivism studies. *Journal of Consulting and Clinical Psychology, 66,* 348–362.

Hanson, R. K., & Thornton, D. (2000). Improving risk assessments for sex offenders: A comparison of three actuarial scales. *Law and Human Behavior, 24,* 119–136.

*Harding v. State (of Maryland),* 5 Md.App. 230, 246, A.2d, 302 (1968), 252 Md. 731, Cert. denied, 395 U.S. 949, 89 S.Ct. 2030, 23 L.Ed.2d 468 (1969).

Hare, R. D., Hart, S. D., & Harpur, T. J. (1991). Psychopathy and the DSM-IV criteria for Antisocial Personality Disorder. *Journal of Abnormal Psychology, 100,* 391–398.

Hare, R. D., & McPherson, L. M. (1984). Violent and aggressive behavior by criminal psychopaths. *International Journal of Law and Psychiatry, 7,* 35–50.

*Harmelin v. Michigan,* 111 S.Ct. 2680 (1991).

Harper, T. (1984, April 29). State rape laws see decade of change. *Lawrence (KS) Journal-World,* p. 1B.

*Harris v. Forklift Systems, Inc.,* 114 S.Ct. 367 (1993).

*Harris v. New York,* 401 U.S. 222 (1971).

Harris, G. T., Rice, M.E., & Quinsey, V. L. (1993). Violent recidivism of mentally disordered offenders: The development of a statistical prediction instrument. *Criminal Justice and Behavior, 20,* 315–335.

Hart, P. M., Wearing, A., & Headey, B. (1995). Police stress and well-being: Integrating personality, coping, and daily work experiences. *Journal of Occupational and Organizational Psychology, 68,* 133–156.

Harvey, J. H., & Smith, W. P. (1977). *Social psychology: An attributional approach.* St. Louis: Mosby.

Hasesmann, D. (1997). *Practices and findings of mental health professionals conducting workers' compensation evaluations.* Unpublished doctoral dissertation, University of Kentucky, Lexington.

Hastie, R., & Pennington, N. (1996). The O. J. Simpson stories: Behavioral scientists' reflections on *The People of the State of California v. Orenthal James Simpson. University of Colorado Law Review, 67,* 957–976.

Hastie, R., Schkade, D., & Payne, J. (1999). Juror judgments in civil cases: Effects of plaintiff's requests and plaintiff's identity on punitive

damage awards. *Law and Human Behavior, 23,* 445–470.

Hastie, R., Schkade, D. A., & Payne, J. W. (1998). A study of juror and jury judgments in civil cases: Deciding liability for punitive damages. *Law and Human Behavior, 22,* 287–314.

Hatcher, C., Mohandie, K., Turner, J., & Gelles, M. G. (1998). The role of the psychologist in crisis/hostage negotiations. *Behavioral Sciences and the Law, 16,* 455–472.

Haugaard, J. J. (1988). Judicial determination of children's competency to testify: Should it be abandoned? *Professional Psychology, 19,* 102–107.

Hazelwood, R. R., & Douglas, J. E. (1980). The lust murderer. *FBI Law Enforcement Bulletin, 49*(4), 18–22.

Heide, K. M. (1997). Juvenile homicide in America: How can we stop the killing? *Behavioral Sciences and the Law, 15,* 203–220.

Heider, F. (1958). *The psychology of interpersonal relations.* New York: Wiley.

Heilbrun, K. S. (1987). The assessment of competency for execution: An overview. *Behavioral Sciences and the Law, 5,* 383–396.

Heilbrun, K. S. (1992). The role of psychological testing in forensic assessment. *Law and Human Behavior, 16,* 257–272.

Heilbrun, K., & Collins, S. (1995). Evaluation of trial competency and mental state at the time of offense: Report characteristics. *Professional Psychology: Research and Practice, 26,* 61–67.

Heilbrun, K. S., Heilbrun, P., & Griffin, N. (1988). Comparing females acquitted by reason of insanity, convicted, and civilly committed in Florida: 1977–1984. *Law and Human Behavior, 12,* 295–312.

Helzer, J. E., Robins, L. N., & McVay, L. (1987). Posttraumatic stress disorder in the general population. *New England Journal of Medicine, 317,* 1630–1634.

Hengstler, G. (1992, June). Looking back: Reflections on a life well spent. *American Bar Association Journal, 78,* 57–66.

Hensler, T. (1997). A critical look at the admissibility of polygraph evidence in the wake of *Daubert. Catholic University Law Review, 46,* 1247–1297.

Hepburn, J. R. (1980). The objective reality of evidence and the utility of systematic jury selection. *Law and Human Behavior, 4,* 89–102.

Herbert, W. (1998, March 23). Behind bars: We've built the largest prison system in the world. Here's a look inside. *U.S. News and World Report* [On-line]. Available: http://www.usnews.com/usnews/issue/980323/23pris.htm

Herek, G. M. (1987). Can functions be measured? A new perspective on the functional approach to attitudes. *Social Psychology Quarterly, 50,* 285–303.

Herek, G. M., Gillis, J. R., Cogan, J. C., & Glunt, E. K. (1997). Hate crime victimization among lesbian, gay, and bisexual adults: Prevalence, psychological correlates, and methodological issues. *Journal of Interpersonal Violence, 12,* 195–215.

Herek, G. M., Gillis, J. R., & Cogan, J. C. (1999). Psychological sequelae of hate-crime victimization among lesbian, gay, and bisexual adults. *Journal of Consulting and Clinical Psychology, 67,* 945–951.

*Hernandez v. New York,* 111 S.Ct. 1859 (1991).

Hersch, P. D., & Alexander, R. W. (1990). MMPI profile patterns of emotional disability claimants. *Journal of Clinical Psychology, 46,* 795–799.

Hetherington, E. M., & Arasteh, J. D. (Eds.). (1988). *Impact of divorce, single parenting, and step-parenting on children.* Hillsdale, NJ: Erlbaum.

Heuer, L., & Penrod, S. (1988). Increasing jurors' participation in trials: A field experiment with jury notetaking and question asking. *Law and Human Behavior, 12,* 231–262.

Heuer, L., & Penrod, S. (1989). Instructing jurors: A field experiment with written and preliminary instructions. *Law and Human Behavior, 13,* 409–430.

Heuer, L., & Penrod, S. (1994). Juror notetaking and question asking during trials: A national field experiment. *Law and Human Behavior, 18,* 121–150.

Heumann, M. (1978). *Plea bargaining.* Chicago: University of Chicago Press.

Heussanstamm, F. K. (1975). Bumper stickers and the cops. In D. J. Steffensmeier & R. M. Terry (Eds.), *Examining deviance experimentally: Selected readings* (pp. 251–255). Port Washington, NY: Alfred.

Hiatt, D., & Hargrave, G. E. (1988). Predicting job performance problems with psychological screening. *Journal*

of *Police Science and Administration, 16,* 122–125.

Hiday, V. A., & Goodman, R. R. (1982). The least restrictive alternative to involuntary hospitalization, outpatient commitment: Its use and effectiveness. *Journal of Psychiatry and Law, 10,* 81–96.

Hiday, V. A., & Suval, E. M. (1984). Dangerousness of the mentally ill and inebriates in civil commitment. In L. A. Teplin (Ed.), *Mental health and criminal justice* (pp. 227–250). Newbury Park, CA: Sage.

Higgins, M. (1999, March). Tough luck for the innocent man. *ABA Journal, 85,* 46–52.

*Hill v. Colorado,* 120 S. Ct 2480 (2000).

Hill, E. & Pfeifer, J. (1992). Nullification instructions and juror guilt ratings: An examination of modern racism. *Contemporary Social Psychology, 16,* 6–10.

Himelein, M. J., Nietzel, M. T., & Dillehay, R. C. (1991). Effects of prior juror experience on jury sentencing. *Behavioral Sciences and the Law, 9,* 97–106.

Hirschi, T. (1969). *Causes of delinquency.* Berkeley: University of California Press.

Hirschi, T. (1978). Causes and prevention of juvenile delinquency. In H. M. Johnson (Ed.), *Social systems and legal process.* San Francisco: Jossey-Bass.

*Hishon v. King & Spaulding,* 467 U.S. 69 (1984).

Hoffman, L. R. (1965). Group problem solving. In L. Berkowitz (Ed.), *Advances in experimental social psychology* (Vol. 2, pp. 99–127). Orlando, FL: Academic Press.

Hoffman, P. B., & Stone-Meierhoefer, B. (1979). Application of guidelines to sentencing. In L. E. Abt & I. R. Stuart (Eds.), *Social psychology and discretionary law* (pp. 241–258). New York: Van Nostrand Reinhold.

Hogan, R. (1971). Personality characteristics of highly rated policemen. *Personnel Psychology, 24,* 679–686.

Hogarth, J. (1971). *Sentencing as a human process.* Toronto: University of Toronto Press.

Hoge, S. K., Bonnie, R. J., Poythress, N., Monahan, J., Eisenberg, M., & Feucht-Haviar, T. (1997). The MacArthur adjudicative competence study: Development and validation of a research instrument. *Law and Human Behavior, 21,* 141–179.

*Holland v. Illinois,* 493 U.S. 474 (1990).

Holmes, R. M., & DeBurger, J. (1988). *Serial murder.* Newbury Park, CA: Sage.

Homant, R. J., & Kennedy, D. B. (1998). Psychological aspects of crime scene profiling. *Criminal Justice and Behavior, 25,* 319–343.

Honts, C. R., Raskin, D. C., Kircher, J. C., & Hodes, R. L. (1984). Effects of spontaneous countermeasures on the detection of deception. *Psychophysiology, 21,* 583.

Hooton, E. A. (1939). *Crime and the man.* Cambridge, MA: Harvard University Press.

*Hopt v. Utah,* 110 U.S. 574 (1884).

*Hopwood v. State of Texas,* 78 F.3d 932 (5th Cir. 1996).

*Hopwood v. Texas,* 999 F.Supp. 872 (W.D. Tex., 1998).

Horgan, D. D. (1988, August). *The ethics of unexpected advocacy.* Paper presented at the meeting of the American Psychological Association, Atlanta.

Horowitz, I. A. (1980). Juror selection: A comparison of two methods in several criminal cases. *Journal of Applied Social Psychology, 10,* 86–99.

Horowitz, I. A. (1998). The impact of judicial instructions, arguments, and challenges on jury decision making. *Law and Human Behavior, 12,* 439–453.

Horowitz, I. A., ForsterLee, L., & Brolly, I. (1996). Effects of trial complexity on decision making. *Journal of Applied Psychology, 81,* 757–768.

Horowitz, I. A., & Willging, T. E. (1984). *The psychology of law.* Boston: Little, Brown.

Horowitz, I. A., & Willging, T. E. (1991). Changing views of jury power: The nullification debate, 1787–1988. *Law and Human Behavior, 15,* 165–182.

Hosch, H. M., Beck, E. L., & McIntyre, P. (1980). Influence of expert testimony regarding eyewitness accuracy on jury decisions. *Law and Human Behavior, 4,* 287–296.

Hostetler, A. J. (1988, June). Indictment, Congress send message on fraud. *APA Monitor,* p. 5.

Hotelling, K. (1991). Sexual harassment: A problem shielded by silence. *Journal of Counseling and Development, 69,* 497–501.

Houlden, P. (1981). Impact of procedural modifications on evaluations of plea bargaining. *Law and Society Review, 15,* 267–292.

Houston, C. (1935). The need for Negro lawyers. *Journal of Negro Education, 4,* 49–52.

*Hovey v. Superior Court of California,* 28 Cal.3d 1 (1980).

Howard, P. K. (1994). *The death of common sense: How law is suffocating America.* New York: Random House.

Howard, R. C., & Clark, C. R. (1985). When courts and experts disagree: Discordance between insanity recommendations and adjudications. *Law and Human Behavior, 9,* 385–395.

Huber, P. (1988). *Liability: The legal revolution and its consequences.* New York: Basic Books.

*Hudson v. McMilian,* 112 S.Ct. 995 (1992).

Huesmann, L. R., Eron, L. D., Lefkowitz, M. M., & Walder, L. O. (1984). Stability of aggression over time and generations. *Developmental Psychology, 20,* 1120–1134.

Huesmann, L. R., Eron, L. D., & Yarmel, P. W. (1987). Intellectual functioning and aggression. *Journal of Personality and Social Psychology, 52,* 232–240.

Huff, C. R., Rattner, A., & Sagarin, E. (1996). *Convicted but innocent: Wrongful conviction and public policy.* Thousand Oaks, CA: Sage.

Huston, A. C., Donnerstein, E., Fairchild, H., Feshbach, N. D., Katz, P. A., Murray, J. P., Rubinstein, E. A., Wilcox, B., & Zuckerman, D. (1992). *Big world, small screen: The role of television in American society.* Lincoln: University of Nebraska Press.

Hvistendahl, J. (1979). The effect of placement of biasing information. *Journalism Quarterly, 56,* 863–865.

Hyman, H. M., & Tarrant, C. M. (1975). Aspects of American trial jury history. In R. J. Simon (Ed.), *The jury system in America: A critical overview* (pp. 21–44). Newbury Park, CA: Sage.

Hyman, I., & Pentland, J. (1996). The role of mental imagery in the creation of false childhood memories. *Journal of Memory and Language, 35,* 101–117.

Hyman, I. E., Husband, T.H., & Billings, F.J. (1995). False memories of childhood experiences. *Applied Cognitive Psychology, 9,* 181–197.

Hyman, J., & Huemann, M. (1996). Minitrials and matchmakers. *Judicature, 80,* 123–129.

*Idaho v. Wright,* 497 U.S. 805 (1990).

*Illinois v. Lafayette,* 462 U.S. 640 (1983).

*Illinois v. Perkins,* 110 S.Ct. 2394 (1990).

*Illinois v. Rodriguez,* 497 U.S. 177 (1990).

*Illinois v. Wardlow,* 120 S.Ct. 673 (2000).

Imwinkelreid, E. J. (1994). The next step after *Daubert:* Developing a similarly epistemological approach to ensuring the reliability of nonscientific expert testimony. *Cardozo Law Review, 15,* 2271–2294.

Inbau, F. E., Reid, J. E., & Buckley, J. P. (1986). *Criminal interrogation and confessions* (3rd ed.). Baltimore: Williams & Wilkins.

*In re Corrugated Container Antitrust Litigation,* 614 F.2d 958 (5th Circuit, 1980).

*In re Gault,* 387 U.S. 1, 87 S.Ct. 1428 (1967).

*In re U.S. Securities Litigation,* 609 F2d 411 (9th Circuit, 1979).

*In re Winship,* 397 U.S. 358 (1970).

Inwald, R. E. (1986). Issues and guidelines for mental health professionals conducting pre-employment psychological screening programs in law enforcement agencies. In J. T. Reese & H. A. Goldstein (Eds.), *Psychological services for law enforcement* (pp. 47–50). Washington, D.C.: U.S. Government Printing Office.

Inwald, R. E. (1992). *Inwald Personality Inventory technical manual* (rev. ed.). Kew Gardens, NY: Hilson Research.

Inwald, R. E., Knatz, H., & Shusman, E. (1983). *Inwald Personality Inventory manual.* New York: Hilson Research.

*Irvin v. Dowd,* 366 U.S. 717 (1961).

Irwin, J. (1970). *The felon.* Englewood Cliffs, NJ: Prentice Hall.

*J. E. B. ex rel. T. B.,* 114 S.Ct. 1419 (1994).

*Jackson v. Denno,* 378 U.S. 368 (1964).

*Jackson v. Indiana,* 406 U.S. 715 (1972).

Jackson, S. E., & Maslach, C. (1982). After-effects of job-related stress: Families as victims. *Journal of Occupational Behavior, 3,* 63–77.

Jackson, S. E., & Schuler, R. S. (1983, March–April). Preventing employee burnout. *Personnel,* pp. 58–68.

*Jacobson v. United States,* 112 S.Ct. 1535 (1992).

Jacoby, T. (1988, July 18). Fighting crime by the rules. *Newsweek,* p. 53.

James, R. (1959). Status and competence of juries. *American Journal of Sociology, 64,* 563–570.

*Javor v. United States,* 724 F.2d 831 (9th Cir. 1984).

Jeffers, H. P. (1991). *Who killed Precious?* New York: Pharos.

Jefferson, J. (1994, April). Doing soft time. *American Bar Association Journal,* p. 63.

Jenkins, J. A. (1983, February 20). A candid talk with Justice Blackmun. *New York Times Magazine,* p. 20.

Jenkins, P., & Davidson, B. (1990). Battered women in the criminal justice system: An analysis of gender stereotypes. *Behavioral Sciences and the Law, 8,* 161–170.

*Johnson v. Louisiana,* 32 L.Ed.2d 152 (1972).

*Johnson v. Zerbst,* 304 U.S. 458 (1938).

Johnson, C., & Haney, C. (1994). Felony voir dire: An explanatory study of its content and effect. *Law and Human Behavior, 18,* 487–506.

Johnson, J., & Kamlani, R. (1991). August 26). Do we have too many lawyers? *Time, 138,* p. 54–55.

Jones, A. (1994). *Next time, she'll be dead: Battering and how to stop it.* Boston: Beacon Press.

Jones, E. E. (1990). *Interpersonal perception.* New York: Freeman.

Jones, E. E., Farina, A., Hastorf, A. H., Markus, H., Miller, D. T., & Scott, R. A. (1984). *Social stigma: The psychology of marked relationships.* New York: Freeman.

Jones, E. E., & Goethals, G. R. (1971). *Order effects in impression formation: Attribution context and the nature of the entity.* Morristown, NJ: General Learning Press.

Jurow, G. (1971). New data on the effect of a death-qualified jury on the guilt determination process. *Harvard Law Review, 84,* 567–611.

Kadish, M. R., & Kadish, S. H. (1971). The institutionalization of conflict: Jury acquittals. *Journal of Social Issues, 27*(2), 199–218.

Kagehiro, D. K., Taylor, R. B., & Harland, A. T. (1991). Reasonable expectation of privacy and third-party consent searches. *Law and Human Behavior, 15,* 121–138.

Kagehiro, D. K., Taylor, R. B., Laufer, W. S., & Harland, A. T. (1991). Hindsight bias and third-party consentors to warrantless police searches. *Law and Human Behavior, 15,* 305–314.

Kagehiro, D. K., & Werner, C. M. (1977, May). *Effects of authoritarianism and inadmissibility of evidence on jurors' verdicts.* Paper presented at the meeting of the Midwestern Psychological Association, Chicago.

Kahan, D. (1996). What do alternative sanctions mean? *Chicago Law Review, 63,* 591–653.

Kahn, A., Nelson, R. E., & Gaeddert, W. P. (1980). Sex of subject and sex composition of the group as determinants of reward allocations. *Journal of Personality and Social Psychology, 38,* 737–750.

Kairys, D. (1972). Juror selection: The law, a mathematical method of analysis, and a case study. *American Criminal Law Review, 10,* 771–806.

Kairys, D., Kadane, B., & Lehoczky, P. (1977). Jury representativeness: A mandate for multiple source lists. *California Law Review, 65,* 776–827.

Kalven, H., & Zeisel, H. (1966). *The American jury.* Boston: Little, Brown.

Kamisar, Y. (1988, March 16). The *Gideon* case 25 years later. *New York Times,* p. 27.

Kamisar, Y. (1995). On the "fruits" of *Miranda* violations, coerced confessions, and compelled testimony. *Michigan Law Review, 93,* 929–1010.

Kamisar, Y., LaFave, W. R., & Israel, J. (1999). *Basic criminal procedure: Cases, comments and questions.* St. Paul, MN: West.

Kanin, E. (1957). Male aggression in dating-courtship situations. *American Journal of Sociology, 63,* 197–204.

Kanin, E. (1971). Sexually aggressive college males. *Journal of College Student Personnel, 12*(2), 107–110.

*Kansas v. Hendricks,* 117 S.Ct. 2106 (1997).

Kaplan, J. (1972). A legal look at prosocial behavior: What can happen for failing to help or trying to help. *Journal of Social Issues, 28*(3), 218–226.

Kaplan, J. (1996). *Criminal law.* Boston: Little, Brown.

Karmen, A. (1984). *Crime victims: An introduction to victimology.* Pacific Grove, CA: Brooks/Cole.

Kassin, S. (1998a). Clinical psychology in court: House of junk science? *Contemporary Psychology, 43,* 321–324.

Kassin, S. (1998b). Eyewitness identification procedures: The fifth rule. *Law and Human Behavior, 22,* 649–653.

Kassin, S. & Neumann, K. (1997). On the power of confession evidence: An experimental test of the fundamental difference hypothesis. *Law and Human Behavior, 21,* 469–484.

Kassin, S. & Sukel, H. (1997). Coerced confessions and the jury: An experimental test of the "harmless error" rule. *Law and Human Behavior, 21,* 27–46.

Kassin, S. M. (1985, August). *Juries and the doctrine of entrapment.* Paper presented at the meeting of the American Psychological Association, Los Angeles.

Kassin, S. M., Ellsworth, P. C., & Smith, V. L. (1989). The "general acceptance" of psychological research on eyewitness testimony: A survey of the experts. *American Psychologist, 44,* 1089–1098.

Kassin, S. M., Ellsworth, P.C., & Smith, V. L. (1994). Deja vu all over again: Elliott's critique of eyewitness experts. *Law & Human Behavior, 18,* 203–210.

Kassin, S. M., & Kiechel, K. L. (1996). The social psychology of false confessions: Compliance, internalization, and confabulation. *Psychological Science, 7,* 125–128.

Kassin, S. M., & McNall, K. (1991). Police interrogations and confessions: Communicating promises and threats by pragmatic implication. *Law and Human Behavior, 15,* 233–251.

Kassin, S. M., & Sommers, S. (1997). Inadmissible testimony, instructions to disregard and the jury: Substantive vs. procedural considerations. *Personality and Social Psychology Bulletin, 23,* 1046–1054.

Kassin, S. M., & Studebaker, C. A. (1998). Instructions to disregard and the jury: Curative and paradoxical effects. In J. M. Golding & C. M. MacLeod (Eds.), *Intentional forgetting: Interdisciplinary approaches* (pp. 413–434). Hillsdale, NJ: Erlbaum.

Kassin, S. M., Tubb, V., Hosch, H., & Memon, A. (2001). On the "general acceptance" of eyewitness testimony research: A new survey of the experts. *American Psychologist, 56,* 405–416.

Kassin, S. M., Williams, L. N., & Saunders, C. L. (1990). Dirty tricks of cross-examination: The influence of conjectural evidence on the jury. *Law and Human Behavior, 14,* 373–384.

Kassin, S. M., & Wrightsman, L. S. (1979). On the requirement of proof: The timing of judicial instructions and mock juror verdicts. *Journal of Personality and Social Psychology, 37,* 1877–1887.

Kassin, S. M., & Wrightsman, L. S. (1980). Prior confessions and mock juror verdicts. *Journal of Applied Social Psychology, 10,* 133–146.

Kassin, S. M., & Wrightsman, L. S. (1981). Coerced confessions, judicial instruction, and mock juror verdicts. *Journal of Applied Social Pshchology, 11,* 489–506.

Kassin, S. M., & Wrightsman, L. S. (1983). The construction and valida-

tion of a juror bias scale. *Journal of Research in Personality, 17,* 423–441.

Kassin, S. M., & Wrightsman, L. S. (1985). Confession evidence. In S. M. Kassin & L. S. Wrightsman (Eds.), *The psychology of evidence and trial procedure* (pp. 67–94). Newbury Park, CA: Sage.

Kassin, S. M., & Wrightsman, L. S. (1988). *The American jury on trial: Psychological perspectives.* New York: Hemisphere.

Katz, I., Hass, R. G., Parisi, N., Astone, J., Wackenhut, G., & Gray, L. (1987). Lay people's and health care personnel's perceptions of cancer, AIDS, cardiac and diabetic patients. *Psychological Reports, 60,* 615–629.

Katz, J. (1988). *Seductions of crime.* New York: Basic Books.

Katz, L. (1996). *Ill-gotten gains: Evasion, blackmail, fraud, and kindred puzzles of the law.* Chicago: University of Chicago Press.

Keene, B. (1997). Chemical castration: An analysis of Florida's new "cutting-edge" policy towards sex criminals. *Florida Law Review, 49,* 803–820.

Keeton, R. E. (1973). *Trial tactics and methods* (2nd ed.). Boston: Little, Brown.

Keilin, W. G., & Bloom, L. J. (1986). Child custody evaluation practices: A survey of experienced professionals. *Professional Psychology: Research and Practice, 17,* 338–346.

Kellerman, A. L., & Mercy, J. M. (1992). Men, women, and murder: Gender-specific differences in rates of fatal violence and victimization. *Journal of Trauma, 33,* 1–5.

Kelley, H. H. (1971). *Attribution in social interaction.* Morristown, NJ: General Learning Press.

Kelly, J. B. (1991). Parent interaction after divorce: Comparison of mediated and adversarial divorce processes. *Behavioral Sciences and the Law, 9,* 387–398.

Kennedy, J. (1998). Personality type and judicial decision making. *The Judges' Journal, 3,* 4–10.

Kennedy, L. (1985). *The airman and the carpenter: The Lindbergh kidnapping and the framing of Richard Hauptmann.* New York: Viking.

Kent, D. A., & Eisenberg, T. (1972). The selection and promotion of police officers: A selected review of recent literature. *Police Chief, 39,* 20–29.

Kerper, H. B. (1972). *Introduction to the criminal justice system.* St. Paul, MN: West.

Kerr, N., Kramer, G. P., Carroll, J. S., & Alfini, J. J. (1991). On the effectiveness of voir dire in criminal cases with prejudicial pretrial publicity: An empirical study. *American Law Review, 40,* 665–701.

Kerr, N. L., Hymes, R. W., Anderson, A. B., & Weathers, J. E. (1995). Defendant-juror similarity and mock juror judgments. *Law and Human Behavior, 19,* 545–568.

Kerwin, J., & Shaffer, D. R. (1991). The effects of jury dogmatism on reactions to jury nullification instructions. *Personality and Social Psychology Bulletin, 17,* 140–146.

Kerwin, J., & Shaffer, D. R. (1994). Mock jurors versus mock juries: The role of deliberations in reactions to inadmissible testimony. *Personality and Social Psychology Bulletin, 20,* 153–162.

Ketterman, T., & Kravitz, M. (1978). *Police crisis intervention: A selected biography.* Washington, D.C.: U.S. Government Printing Office.

Kiel, D., Funk, C., & Champagne A.(1994). Two-party competition and trial court elections in Texas. *Judicature, 77,* 290–293.

Kiesler, C. A. (1982). Public and professional myths about mental hospitalization: An empirical reassessment of policy-related beliefs. *American Psychologist, 37,* 1323–1339.

Kilpatrick, D. G., Resick, P., & Veronen, L. (1981). Effects of a rape experience: A longitudinal study. *Journal of Social Issues, 37*(4), 105–112.

King, N. J., & Munsterman, G. T. (1996). Stratified juror selection: Cross-sections by design. *Judicature, 79,* 273–279.

Kingson, J. A. (1988, August 8). Women in the law say path is limited by "mommy track." *New York Times,* pp. 1, 8.

Kipnis, K. (1979). Plea bargaining: A critic's rejoinder. *Law and Society Review, 13,* 555–564.

Kircher, J. C., Horowitz, S. W., & Raskin, D. C. (1988). Meta-analysis of mock crime studies of the control question polygraph technique. *Law and Human Behavior, 12,* 79–90.

Kirschman, E. (1997). *I love a cop: What police families need to know.* New York: Guilford.

Kitsuse, J. I., & Dietrick, D. C. (1959). Delinquent boys: A critique. *American Sociological Review, 24,* 208–215.

Klassen, D., & O'Connor, W. (1988a). Crime, inpatient admissions, and violence among male mental patients. *International Journal of Law and Psychiatry, 11,* 305–312.

Klassen, D., & O'Connor, W. A. (1988b). A prospective study of predictors of violence in adult male mental health admissions. *Law and Human Behavior, 12,* 143–158.

Klein, C. (1996, May 6). Women's progress slows at top firms. *National Law Journal,* p. 1.

Klein, C. (1997, May 26). Law-firm partners: Profession sinking. *National Law Journal,* p. 1.

Kleinberg, H. (1989, January 29). It's tough to have sympathy for Bundy. *Lawrence (KS) Journal-World,* p. 5A.

Kleinmuntz, B., & Szucko, J. J. (1984). Lie detection in ancient and modern times: A call for contemporary scientific study. *American Psychologist, 39,* 766–776.

Klockars, C. (1985). *The idea of police.* Thousand Oaks, CA: Sage.

Knight, R. A., Warren, J. I., Reboussin, R., & Soley, B. J. (1998). Predicting rapist type from crime-scene variables. *Criminal Justice and Behavior, 25,* 30–45.

Kohlberg, L. (1958). *The development of modes of thinking and choices in years 10 to 16.* Unpublished doctoral dissertation, University of Chicago.

Kohlberg, L. (1963). The development of children's orientations toward a moral order: I. Sequence in the development of moral thought. *Vita Humana, 6,* 11–33.

Kohlberg, L. (1973). Stages and aging in moral development: Some speculations. *Gerontologist, 13,* 497–502.

Kohlberg, L. (1981). *The philosophy of moral development.* San Francisco: Harper & Row.

Kohlberg, L., Levine, C., & Hewer, A. (1983). Moral stages: A current formulation and response to critics. *Monographs of Human Development, 10,* 11–78.

Kolebuck, M. D. (1998). *Kansas v. Hendricks:* Is it time to lock the door and throw away the key for sexual predators? *Journal of Contemporary Health Law and Policy, 14,* 537–561.

Konecni, V. J., & Ebbesen, E. B. (1986). Courtroom testimony by psychologists on eyewitness identification issues: Critical notes and reflections. *Law and Human Behavior, 10,* 117–126.

Koss, M. P. (1985). The hidden rape victim: Personality, attitudes and situational characteristics. *Psychology of Women Quarterly, 9,* 193–212.

Koss, M. P. (1992). The underdetection of rape: Methodological choices influence incidence estimates. *Journal of Social Issues, 48*(1), 61–75.

Koss, M. P., Gidycz, C.A., & Wisniewski, N. (1987). The scope of rape: Incidence and prevalence of sexual aggression and victimization in a national sample of higher education students. *Journal of Consulting and Clinical Psychology, 55,* 162–170.

Koss, M. P., & Oros, C. (1982). Sexual experiences survey: A research instrument investigating sexual aggression and victimization. *Journal of Consulting and Clinical Psychology, 50,* 455–457.

Kovera, M. B., & Borgida, E. (1997). Expert testimony in child sexual abuse trials: The admissibility of psychological science. *Applied Cognitive Psychology, 11,* S105–S129.

Kramer, G., & Koening, D. (1990). Do jurors understand criminal jury instructions? Analyzing the results of the Michigan juror comprehension project. *University of Michigan Journal of Law Reform, 23,* 401–437.

Kramer, G. P., & Kerr, N. L. (1989). Laboratory simulation and bias in the study of juror behavior. *Law and Human Behavior, 13,* 89–99.

Kramer, G. P., Kerr, N. L., & Carroll, J. S. (1990). Pretrial publicity, judicial remedies, and jury bias. *Law and Human Behavior, 14,* 409–438.

Kramer, T. H., Buckhout, R., & Eugenio, P. (1990). Weapon focus, arousal, and eyewitness memory: Attention must be paid. *Law and Human Behavior, 14,* 167–184.

Kranz, H. (1936). *Lebenschicksale krimineller Zwillinge.* Berlin: Springer.

Kranz, H. (1937). Untersuchungen an Zwillingen in Furosorgeer-jiehungsanstalten. *Zeitschrift für Induktive Abstammungs-Vererbungslehre, 73,* 508–512.

Krauskopf, J. (1994). Touching the elephant: Perceptions of gender issues in nine law schools. *Journal of Legal Education, 44,* 311–340.

Kropp, P. R., & Hart, S. D. (2000). The Spousal Assault Risk Assessment (SARA) Guide: Reliability and validity in adult male offenders. *Law and Human Behavior, 24,* 101–118.

*Kumho Tire Co. v. Carmichael,* 526 U.S. 137 (1999).

Kunen, J. (1983). *"How can you defend those people?" The making of a criminal lawyer.* New York: Random House.

Kunen, J. S., Mathison, D., Brown, S. A., & Nugent, T. (1989, July 17). Frustrated grand jurors say it was no accident Ted Kennedy got off easy. *People,* pp. 34–36.

Kurtz, H. (1988, December 511). Take a number, cop a plea. *Washington Post National Weekly Edition,* pp. 9–10.

Kushner, M., Riggs, D., Foa, E., & Miller, S. (1992). Perceived controllability and the development of post-traumatic stress disorder (PTSD) in crime victims. *Behavior Research & Therapy, 31,* 105–110.

Kutchinski, B. (1988, June). *Pornography and sexual violence: The criminological evidence from aggregated data in several countries.* Paper presented at the 14th International Congress on Law and Mental Health, Montreal.

Laboratory for Community Psychiatry. (1974). *Competency to stand trial and mental illness.* Northvale, NJ: Aronson.

LaBuy, W. J. (1963). *Jury instructions in federal criminal cases.* St. Paul, MN: West.

Lacayo, R. (1986, August 11). Rattling the gilded cage. *Time,* p. 39.

LaFave, W. (1965). *Arrest: The decision to take a suspect into custody.* Boston: Little, Brown.

LaFortune, K. A. (1997). *An investigation of mental health and legal professionals' activities, beliefs, and experiences in domestic court: An interdisciplinary survey.* Unpublished doctoral dissertation, University of Tulsa, Tulsa, OK.

Lamar, J. V. (1989, February 6). "I deserve punishment." *Time,* p. 34.

Lamb, M. E., Hershkowitz, I., Sternberg, K. J., Esplin, P. W., Hovav, M., Manor, T., & Yudilevitch, L. (1996). Effects of investigative utterance types on Israeli children's responses. *International Journal of Behavioral Development, 19,* 627–637.

Lambert, W. (1995, February 27). LIRR gunman's trial has given fresh focus to victims' rights. *Wall Street Journal,* p. B10.

Lambros, T. (1993). The summary jury trial: An effective aid to settlement. *Judicature, 77,* 6–8.

Lane, I. M., & Messe, L. A. (1971). Equity and the distribution of rewards. *Journal of Personality and Social Psychology, 20,* 1–17.

Langbein, J. H. (1978). Torture and plea bargaining. *University of Chicago Law Review, 46,* 12–13.

Lange, J. (1929). *Verbrechen als Schiskal.* Leipzig: Thieme.

Langer, E. J., & Abelson, R. P. (1974). A patient by any other name . . . : Clinical group differences in labeling bias. *Journal of Consulting and Clinical Psychology, 42,* 4–9.

Largen, M. A. (1988). Rape-law reform: An analysis. In A. W. Burgess (Ed.), *Rape and sexual assault* (Vol. 2, pp. 271–292). New York: Garland.

Larsen, K. S., Reed, M., & Hoffman, S. (1980). Attitudes of heterosexuals toward homosexuality: A Likert-type scale and construct validity. *Journal of Sex Research, 16,* 245–257.

Larson, J. A. (1932). *Lying and its detection.* Chicago: University of Chicago Press.

Leary, W. E. (1988, November 15). Novel methods unlock witnesses' memories. *New York Times,* p. 23.

Lee, F. (1985, May 16). Women are put "on trial" in rape cases. *USA Today,* p. 1A.

Lee, F. R. (1989, May 22). Bad crack, waiting witnesses, low pay—A prosecutor's day. *New York Times,* p. 14.

Lees-Haley, P. (1991). A fake bad scale on the MMPI-2 for personal injury claimants. *Psychological Reports, 68,* 203–210.

Lees-Haley, P. (1992). Efficacy of MMPI-2 validity scales and MCMI-2 modifier scales for detecting spurious PTSD claims: F, F-K, Fake Bad Scale, Ego Strength, Subtle-Obvious subscales, DIS, and DEB. *Journal of Clinical Psychology, 48,* 681–689.

Lefkowitz, J. (1975). Psychological attributes of policemen: A review of research and opinion. *Journal of Social Issues, 31*(1), 3–26.

Leichtman, M. & Ceci, S. (1995). The effects of stereotypes and suggestions on pre-schoolers' reports. *Developmental Psychology, 31,* 568–578.

Leippe, M. R. (1995). The case for expert testimony about eyewitness memory. *Psychology, Public Policy, and Law, 1,* 909–959.

Lemert, E. M. (1951). *Social pathology.* New York: McGraw-Hill.

Lemert, E. M. (1972). *Human deviance, social problems, and social control*

(2nd ed.). Englewood Cliffs, NJ: Prentice Hall.

Lempert, R. (1993). Civil juries and complex cases: Taking stock after twelve years. In R. E. Litan (Ed.), *Verdict: Assessing the civil jury system* (pp. 181–247). Washington, D.C.: Brookings Institution.

Lempert, R. O. (1981). Desert and deterrence: An assessment of the moral bases of the case for capital punishment. *Michigan Law Review, 79,* 1177–1231.

Lentz, B., & Laband, D. (1995). *Sex discrimination in the legal profession.* Westport, CT: Quorum.

Leo, R. E., & Ofshe, R. J. (1998). The consequences of false confessions: Deprivations of liberty and miscarriages of justice in the age of psychological interrogation. *Journal of Criminal Law and Criminology, 88,* 429–496.

Lerner, M. J. (1970). The desire for justice and reactions to victims. In J. Macaulay & L. Berkowitz (Eds.), *Altruism and helping behavior* (pp. 205–229). Orlando, FL: Academic Press.

Lerner, M. J. (1974). Social psychology of justice and interpersonal attraction. In T. L. Huston (Ed.), *Foundations of interpersonal attraction* (pp. 331–351). Orlando, FL: Academic Press.

Lerner, M. J. (1977). The justice motive in social behavior: Some hypotheses as to its origins and forms. *Journal of Personality, 45,* 1–52.

Lerner, M. J. (1980). *The belief in a just world.* New York: Plenum.

Lerner, M. J., & Simmons, C. H. (1966). The observer's reaction to the "innocent victim": Compassion or rejection? *Journal of Personality and Social Psychology, 4,* 203–210.

Lester, D., Babcock, S. D., Cassissi, J. P., & Brunetta, M. (1980). Hiring despite the psychologists' objections. *Criminal Justice and Behavior, 7,* 41–49.

Leventhal, G. S. (1976). The distribution of rewards and resources in groups and organizations. In L. Berkowitz & E. Walster (Eds.), *Advances in experimental social psychology* (Vol. 9). Orlando, FL: Academic Press.

Leventhal, G. S., & Lane, D. W. (1970). Sex, age and equity behavior. *Journal of Personality and Social Psychology, 15,* 312–316.

Levin, J., & Fox, J. A. (1985). *Mass murder.* New York: Plenum.

Levine, F. J., & Tapp, J. L. (1977). The dialectic of legal socialization in community and school. In J. L. Tapp & F. L. Levine (Eds.), *Law, justice, and the individual in society* (pp. 163–182). New York: Holt, Rinehart & Winston.

Levinger, G. (1966). Marital dissatisfaction among divorce applicants. *American Journal of Orthopsychiatry, 36,* 803–807.

Levy, C. J. (1996, April 10). Minority defendants handed harsher sentences, study says. *New York Times,* p. A13.

Levy, R. J. (1967). Predicting police failures. *Journal of Criminal Law, Criminology, and Police Science, 58,* 265–276.

Lewin, T. (1994, October 21). Outrage over 18 months for a killing. *New York Times,* p. A18.

Lewis, A. (1964). *Gideon's trumpet.* New York: Knopf.

Lewis, A. (1984, November 16). Rights won by "unworthy" are won for all. *Kansas City Times,* p. A17.

Lewis, C. (1996, April 3). Keep trying to improve relations between black and white police officers. *Kansas City Star,* p. C–11.

*Lexington (KY) Herald-Leader.* Get tough Arizona sheriff puts first women's chain gang to work. (1996, September 20) p. A3.

Leyton, E. (1986). *Compulsive killers.* New York: New York University Press.

Lichtenstein, A. (1985). Polls, public opinion, pre-trial publicity and the prosecution of Bernhard H. Goetz. *Social Action and the Law, 10,* 95–102.

Lichtman, J. L. (1993, June 7). Equal pay: Women still don't get it. *USA Today,* p. 13A.

Lidz, C. W., Mulvey, E. P., & Gardner, W. P. (1993). Reconsidering the violent and illegal behavior of mental patients. *American Sociological Review, 57,* 1229–1236.

Lieberman, J., & Sales, B. (1997). What social science teaches us about the jury instruction process. *Psychology, Public Policy, and Law, 3,* 589–644.

Liebman, J. S., Fagan, J., West, V., & Lloyd, J. (2000). Capital attrition: Error rates in capital cases, 1973–1995. *Texas Law Review, 78,* 1839–1865.

Lilly, J. R., Cullen, F. T., & Ball, R. A. (1989). *Criminological theory: Context and consequences.* Newbury Park, CA: Sage.

Lind, E. A. (1975). The exercise of information influence in legal advocacy.

*Journal of Applied Social Psychology, 5,* 127–143.

Lind, E. A. (1982). The psychology of courtroom procedure. In N. L. Kerr & R. M. Bray (Eds.), *Psychology in the courtroom* (pp. 13–37). Orlando, FL: Academic Press.

Lind, E. A., Erickson, B. E., Friedland, N., & Dickenberger, M. (1978). Reactions to procedural models for adjudicative conflict resolution. *Journal of Conflict Resolution, 22,* 318–341.

Lind, E. A., Thibaut, J., & Walker, L. (1973). Discovery and presentation of evidence in adversary and nonadversary proceedings. *Michigan Law Review, 71,* 1129–1144.

Lind, E. A., & Tyler, T. R. (1988). *The social psychology of procedural justice.* New York: Plenum.

Lindsay, D. S., & Read, J. D. (1995). "Memory work" and recovered memories of childhood sexual abuse: Scientific evidence and public, professional, and personal issues. *Psychology, Public Policy, and Law, 1,* 846–908.

Lindsay, R. C., Lea, J., Nosworthy, G., Fulford, J., Hector, J. LeVan, V., & Seabrook, C. (1991). Biased lineups: Sequential presentation reduces the problem. *Journal of Applied Psychology, 76,* 796–802.

Lindsay, R. C., Pozzulo, J. D., Craig, W., Lee, K., & Corber, S. (1997). Simultaneous lineups, sequential lineups, and showups: Eyewitness identification decisions of adults and children. *Law and Human Behavior, 21,* 391–404.

Lingle, J. H., & Ostrom, T. M. (1981). Principles of memory and cognition in attitude formation. In R. E. Petty, T. M. Ostrom, & T. C. Brock (Eds.), *Cognitive responses in persuasion.* Hillsdale, NJ: Erlbaum.

Lipsitt, P. D., Lelos, D., & McGarry, A. L. (1971). Competency for trial: A screening instrument. *American Journal of Psychiatry, 128,* 105–109.

Lipton, D., Martinson, R., & Wilks, J. (1975). *The effectiveness of correctional treatment: A survey of treatment evaluation studies.* New York: Praeger.

Lipton, J. P. (1977). On the psychology of eyewitness testimony. *Journal of Applied Psychology, 62,* 90–95.

Liss, M. B., & McKinley-Pace, M. J. (1999). Best interests of the child: New twists on an old theme. In R. Roesch, S. D. Hart, & J. R. P. Ogloff (Eds.), *Psychology and the law: The state of the discipline* (pp. 339–372). New York: Kluwer Academic/Plenum.

Litwack, T. R., & Schlesinger, L. B. (1987). Assessing and predicting violence: Research, law and applications. In I. B. Weiner & A. K. Hess (Eds.), *Handbook of forensic psychology* (pp. 205–257). New York: Wiley.

*Lockett v. Ohio,* 438 U.S. 586 (1978).

*Lockhart v. McCree,* 106 S.Ct. 1758 (1986).

Loeber, R & Farrington, D. (1998). *Serious and violent juvenile offenders.* Thousand Oaks, CA: Sage.

Loeber, R., & Stouthamer-Loeber, M. (1986). Family factors as correlates and predictors of juvenile conduct problems and delinquency. In M. Tonry & N. Morris (Eds.), *Crime and justice: An annual review of research* (Vol. 7, pp. 291–249). Chicago: University of Chicago Press.

Loftus, E. F. (1974). Reconstructing memory: The incredible witness. *Psychology Today, 8,* 116–119.

Loftus, E. F. (1975). Leading questions and the eyewitness report. *Cognitive Psychology, 7,* 560–572.

Loftus, E. F. (1979). *Eyewitness testimony.* Cambridge, MA: Harvard University Press.

Loftus, E. F. (1983). Silence is not golden. *American Psychologist, 38,* 564–572.

Loftus, E. F. (1984). Expert testimony on the eyewitness. In G. L. Wells & E. F. Loftus (Eds.), *Eyewitness testimony: Psychological perspectives* (pp. 273–282). New York: Cambridge University Press.

Loftus, E. F. (1992). When a lie becomes memory's truth: Memory distortion after exposure to misinformation. *Psychological Science, 1,* 121–123.

Loftus, E. F. (1993). Psychologists in the eyewitness world. *American Psychologist, 48,* 550–552.

Loftus, E .F. (1997). Creating childhood memories. *Applied Cognitive Psychology, 11,* S75–S86.

Loftus, E. F., & Davies, G. M. (1984). Distortions in the memory of children. *Journal of Social Issues, 40*(2), 51–67.

Loftus, E. F., & Greene, E. (1980). Warning: Even memory for faces may be contagious. *Law and Human Behavior, 4,* 323–334.

Loftus, E. F., & Ketcham, K. (1994). *The myth of repressed memory.* New York: St. Martin's.

Loftus, E .F., & Pickrell, J. E. (1995). The formation of false memories. *Psychiatric Annals, 25,* 720–725.

Loftus, E. F., & Wagenaar, W. (1990). Ten cases of eyewitness identification: Logical and procedural problems. *Journal of Criminal Justice, 18,* 291–305.

Loftus, E. F., & Zanni, G. (1975). Eyewitness testimony: The influence of the wording of a question. *Bulletin of the Psychonomic Society, 5,* 86–88.

Loh, W. D. (1984). *Social research in the judicial process.* Newbury Park, CA: Sage.

Lohr, S. (1987, November 30). For crime detection, "genetic fingerprinting." *New York Times,* p. 5.

Lombroso, C. (1876). *L'uomo delinquente.* Milan: Hoepli.

London, K., & Nightingale, N. N. (1996, March). *The impact of incriminating inadmissible evidence on jury deliberations.* Paper presented at the meeting of the American Psychology-Law Society, Hilton Head, SC.

Loomis, S. D. (1965). EEG abnormalities as a correlate of behavior in adolescent male delinquents. *American Journal of Psychiatry, 121,* 1003.

Lott, B., Reilly, M. E., & Howard, D. R. (1982). Sexual assault and harassment: A campus community case study. *Signs: Journal of Women in Culture and Society, 8,* 296–319.

Lou, H. (1927). *Juvenile courts in the United States.* Chapel Hill: University of North Carolina Press.

Love, A., & Childers, J. (1963). *Listen to leaders in law.* New York: Holt, Rinehart & Winston.

Lovitt, J. T., & Price, R. (1997, January 28). Simpson defense lashes out. *USA Today,* p. 1A.

Lowe, R. H., & Wittig, M. A. (Eds.). (1989). Approaching pay equity through comparable worth. *Journal of Social Issues, 45*(4) (Special Issue), 11–246.

Luginbuhl, J. (1992). Comprehension of judges' instructions in the penalty phase of a capital trial: Focus on mitigating circumstances. *Law and Human Behavior, 16,* 203–218.

Luginbuhl, J., & Middendorf, K. (1988). Death penalty beliefs and jurors' responses to aggravating and mitigating circumstances in capital trials. *Law and Human Behavior, 12,* 263–281.

Lunde, D. T., & Morgan, J. (1980). *The die song: A journey into the mind of a mass murderer.* New York: Norton.

Lunden, W. A. (1957). *The courts and other criminal justice in Iowa.* Ames: Iowa State University Press.

Lurigio, A. J., & Skogan, W. G. (1994). Winning the hearts and minds of police officers: An assessment of staff perceptions of community policing in Chicago. *Crime and Delinquency, 40,* 315–330.

Luus, C. A. E. & Wells, G. L. (1994). The malleability of eyewitness confidence: Co-witness and perseverance effects. *Journal of Applied Psychology, 79,* 714–724.

Lykken, D. T. (1981). *A tremor in the blood: Uses and abuses of the lie detector.* New York: McGraw-Hill.

Lykken, D. T. (1985). The probity of the polygraph. In S. M. Kassin & L. S. Wrightsman (Eds.), *The psychology of evidence and trial procedure* (pp. 95–123). Newbury Park, CA: Sage.

Lynam, D. (1996). Early identification of chronic offenders: Who is the fledgling psychopath? *Psychological Bulletin, 120,* 209–234.

Lynam, D., Moffitt, T., & Stouthamer-Loeber, M. (1993). Explaining the relation between IQ and delinquency: Class, race, test motivation, school-failure, and self-control. *Journal of Abnormal Psychology, 102,* 187–196.

Lynam, D. R. (1998). Early identification of the fledgling psychopath: Locating the psychopathic child in the current nomenclature. *Journal of Abnormal Psychology, 107,* 566–575.

Lynch, M., & Haney, C. (2000). Discrimination and instructional comprehension: Guided discretion, racial bias, and the death penalty. *Law and Human Behavior, 24,* 337–358.

Lyons, D. (1995, September 18). Deal cited in Noriega trial. *National Law Review,* p. A6.

MacAndrew, C., & Edgerton, R. B. (1969). *Drunken comportment: A social explanation.* Chicago: Aldine.

Macauley, W. A., & Heubel, E. J. (1981). Achieving representative juries: A system that works. *Judicature, 65*(3), 126–135.

MacCoun, R. J. (1996). Differential treatment of corporate defendants by juries: An examination of the "deep pockets" hypothesis. *Law and Society Review, 30,* 121–161.

MacCoun, R. J. (1999). Epistemological dilemmas in the assessment of legal decision making. *Law and Human Behavior, 23,* 723–730.

MacCoun, R. J., & Tyler, T. R. (1988). The basis of citizens' perceptions of the criminal jury: Procedural fairness, accuracy, and efficiency. *Law and Human Behavior, 12,* 333–352.

Mack, J. (1909). The juvenile court. *Harvard Law Review, 23,* 104–122.

MacKinnon, C. A. (1993). *Only words.* Cambridge, MA: Harvard University Press.

*Madrid v. Gomez,* 889 F.Supp. 1146 (N.D. Cal. 1995).

Maeder, T. (1985). *Crime and madness: The origins and evolution of the insanity defense.* New York: Harper & Row.

Magdol, L., Moffitt, T. E., Caspi, A., Newman, D. L., Fagan, J., & Silva, P. A. (1997). Gender differences in rates of partner violence in a birth cohort of 21-year-olds: Bridging the gap between clinical and epidemiological approaches. *Journal of Consulting and Clinical Psychology, 65,* 68–78.

Magdol, L., Moffitt, T. E., Caspi, A., & Silva, P. A. (1998). Developmental antecedents of partner abuse: A prospective-longitudinal study. *Journal of Abnormal Psychology, 107,* 373–389.

Maguire, K., & Flanagan, T. J. (Eds.). (1991). *Sourcebook of criminal justice.* Washington, D.C.: U.S. Department of Justice, Bureau of Justice Statistics.

Mailer, N. (1979). *The executioner's song.* Boston, MA: Little, Brown.

Major, B., McFarlin, D. B., & Gagnon, D. (1984). Overworked and underpaid: On the nature of gender differences in personal entitlement. *Journal of Personality and Social Psychology, 47,* 1399–1412.

Malpass, R. S., & Devine, P. G. (1984). Research on suggestion in lineups and photospreads. In G. L. Wells & E. F. Loftus (Eds.), *Eyewitness testimony: Psychological perspectives* (pp. 64–91). New York: Cambridge University Press.

Mankoff, M. (1971). Societal reaction and career deviance: A critical analysis. *Sociological Quarterly, 12,* 204–218.

*Manson v. Braithwaite,* 432 U.S. 98 (1977).

*Mapp v. Ohio,* 367 U.S. 643 (1961).

Marcus, D. R., Lyons, P. M., & Guyton, M. R. (2000). Studying perceptions of juror influence in vivo: A social relations analysis. *Law and Human Behavior, 24,* 173–186.

Marcus, R. (1992, March 16–22). So many defendants, so little time. *Washington Post National Weekly Edition,* p. 33.

Marder, N. S. (1999). The interplay of race and false claims of jury nullification. *University of Michigan Journal of Law Reform, 32,* 285–321.

Mark, M. M. (1999). Social science evidence in the courtroom. *Psychology, Public Policy, and Law, 5,* 175–193.

Marshall, J. (1968). *Intention in law and society.* New York: Minerva.

Marshall, W. L., Fernandez, Y. M., & Cortoni, F. (1999). Rape. In V. Van Hasselt & M. Hersen (Eds.), *Handbook of psychological approaches with violent offenders* (pp. 245–266) New York: Kluwer Academic/Plenum.

Marshall, W. L., Jones, R., Ward, T., Johnston, P., & Barbaree, H. E. (1991). Treatment outcome with sex offenders. *Clinical Psychology Review, 11,* 465–485.

Martinson, R. (1974). What works? Questions and answers about prison reform. *Public Interest, 35,* 22.

Martinson, R. (1979). New findings, new views: A note of caution regarding sentencing reform. *Hofstra Law Review, 7,* 243–258.

*Maryland v. Craig,* 110 S.Ct. 3157 (1990).

Maslach, C., & Jackson, S. E. (1984). Burnout in organizational settings. In S. Oskamp (Ed.), *Applied social psychology annual* (pp. 133–154). Newbury Park, CA: Sage.

Massaro, T. M. (1997). The meanings of shame: Implications for legal reform. *Psychology, Public Policy, and Law, 3,* 645–704.

Matthews, A. (1970). Observations on police policy and procedures for emergency detention of the mentally ill. *Journal of Criminal Law, Criminology, and Police Science, 61,* 283–295.

Mazzoni, G. A., Loftus, E. F., Seitz, A., & Lynn, S.J. (1999). Changing beliefs and memories through dream interpretation. *Applied Cognitive Psychology, 13,* 125–144.

McCandless, S. R., & Sullivan, L. P. (1991, May 6). Two courts adopt new standard to determine sexual harassment. *National Law Journal,* pp. 18–20.

McCarthy, T. (1997). A stunning verdict: A trial that riveted both Britain and American ends in more contention. *Time* [On-line]. Available: http://cgi.pathfinder.com/time/magazine/1997/dom/971110/nation.a_stunning_ve.html)

McCauley, M. R., & Fisher, R. P. (1995). Facilitating children's eyewitness recall with the revised cognitive interview. *Journal of Applied Psychology, 80,* 510–516.

*McCleskey v. Kemp,* 107 S.Ct. 1756 (1987).

McConahay, J. B., Mullin, C., & Frederick, J. (1977). The uses of social science in trials with political and racial overtones: The trial of Joan Little. *Law and Contemporary Problems, 41,* 205–229.

McCord, W. (1982). *The psychopath and milieu therapy: A longitudinal study.* Orlando, FL: Academic Press.

McCormick, C. T. (1983). *Handbook of the law of evidence* (2nd ed.), St Paul, MN: West.

McGee, H. (1971). Black lawyers and the struggle for racial justice in the American social order. *Buffalo Law Review, 20,* 423–433.

McGee, R., Feehan, M., Williams, S., & Anderson, J. (1992). DSM III disorders from age 11 to age 15 years. *Journal of the American Academy of Child and Adolescent Psychiatry, 31,* 50–59.

McGough, L. (1995). *Child witnesses: Fragile voices in the American legal system.* New Haven, CT: Yale University Press.

*McKay v. Ashland Oil Inc.,* 120 F.R.D. 43, 49 (E.D.Ky. 1988).

*McKeiver v. Pennsylvania,* 403 U.S. 528 (1971).

*McLaurin v. Oklahoma State Regents for Higher Education,* 339 U.S. 637 (1950).

McManis, M. J. (1986). Post shooting trauma: Demographics of professional support. In J. T. Reese & H. A. Goldstein (Eds.), *Psychological services for law enforcement* (pp. 361–364). Washington, D.C.: U.S. Government Printing Office.

Meddis, S. (1984, August 27). Victims rate judges low in crime cases. *USA Today,* p. 2A.

Meddis, S. S., & Kelley, J. (1985, April 8). Crime drops but fear on rise. *USA Today,* p. 1A.

*Medina v. California,* 112 S.Ct. 2572 (1992).

Mednick, S. A., & Christiansen, K. O. (Eds.). (1977). *Biosocial bases of criminal behavior.* New York: Gardner.

Mednick, S. A., Gabrielli, W. F., Jr., & Hutchings, B. (1984a). Genetic factors in the etiology of criminal behav-

ior. In S. A. Mednick, T. E. Moffitt, & S. A. Stack (Eds.), *The causes of crime: New biological approaches* (pp. 74–91). Cambridge: Cambridge University Press.

Mednick, S. A., Gabrielli, W. F., & Hutchings, B. (1984b). Genetic influences in criminal convictions: Evidence from an adoption cohort. *Science, 234,* 891–894.

Melani, L., & Fodaski, L. (1974). The psychology of the rapist and his victim. In New York Radical Feminists (Eds.), *Rape: The first sourcebook for women* (pp. 82–93). New York: New American Library.

Melton, G. B. (1987). Legal regulation of adolescent abortion: Unintended effects. *American Psychologist, 42,* 79–83.

Melton, G. B., Bulkley, J. A., & Wulkan, D. (1985). Competency of children as witnesses. In J. A. Bulkley (Ed.), *Child sexual abuse and the law* (pp. 125–145). Washington, D.C.: American Bar Association.

Melton, G. B., Petrila, J., Poythress, N. G., & Slobogin, C. (1987). *Psychological evaluations for the courts.* New York: Guilford.

Melton, G. B., Petrila, J., Poythress, N.G., & Slobogin, C. (1997). *Psychological evaluation for the courts: A handbook for mental health professionals* (2nd edition). New York: Guilford.

Menninger, K. (1966). *The crime of punishment.* New York: Viking.

*Meritor Savings Bank v. Vinson,* 106 S.Ct. 2399 (1986).

Merrick, R. A. (1985). The tort of outrage: Recovery for the intentional infliction of mental distress. *Behavioral Sciences and the Law, 3,* 165–175.

Merton, R. K. (1968). *Social theory and social structure.* New York: Free Press.

Meyer, P. (1982). *The Yale murder.* New York: Empire.

*Michigan v. Tucker,* 417 U.S. 433 (1974).

Miene, P., Park, R C., & Borgida, E. (1992). Juror decision making and the evaluation of hearsay evidence. *Minnesota Law Review, 76,* 683–701.

Milgram, S. (1963). Behavioral study of obedience. *Journal of Abnormal and Social Psychology, 67,* 371–378.

Miller, A. (1988, April 25). Stress on the job. *Newsweek,* pp. 40–45.

Miller, D. T. (1999). The norm of self-interest. *American Psychologist, 54,* 1053–1060.

Miller, G. R., & Boster, F. J. (1977). Three images of a trial: Their implications for psychological research. In B. D. Sales (Ed.), *Psychology in the legal process* (pp. 19–38). New York: Spectrum.

Miller, G. R., & Fontes, N. E. (1979). *Videotape on trial: A view from the jury box.* Thousand Oaks, CA: Sage.

Miller, M. (1995, October 30). The road to Panama City. *Newsweek,* p. 84.

Miller, P. V. (1967). Personality differences and student survival in law school. *Journal of Legal Education, 19,* 460–467.

Miller, W. B. (1958). Lower-class culture as a generating milieu of gang delinquency. *Journal of Social Issues, 14,* 5–19.

Mills, K. (1983, September 19). Some lawyers alter tactics as more women take seats on juries. *Kansas City Times,* p. A1.

Mills, L. G. (1998). Mandatory arrest and prosecution policies for domestic violence: A critical literature review and the case for more research to test victim empowerment approaches. *Criminal Justice and Behavior, 25,* 306–318.

Mills, M. C., & Stratton, J. G. (1982). MMPI and the prediction of job performance. *FBI Law Enforcement Bulletin, 51,* 10–15.

Mills, R. B., McDevitt, R. J., & Tonkin, S. (1966). Situational tests in metropolitan police recruit selection. *Journal of Criminal Law, Criminology, and Police Science, 57,* 99–104.

*Miranda v. Arizona,* 384 U.S. 486 (1966).

Mitchell, H. E., & Byrne, D. (1972, May). *Minimizing the influence of irrelevant factors in the courtroom: The defendant's character, judge's instructions, and authoritarianism.* Paper presented at the meeting of the Midwestern Psychological Association, Cleveland.

Mitchell, P. (1976). *Act of love: The killing of George Zygmanik.* New York: Knopf.

Moehringer, J. (1998, August 12). Boys sentenced for Arkansas school murders. *Los Angeles Times,* p. A1.

Moffitt, T., & Lynam, D. (1994). The neuropsychology of conduct disorder and delinquency: Implications for understanding antisocial behavior. In D. Fowles, P. Sutker, & S. Goodman (Eds.), *Psychopathy and antisocial behavior: A developmental perspective* (pp. 233–262). New York: Springer.

Moffitt, T. E., & Mednick S. A. (1988). *Biological contributions to crime causation.* New York: Martinus Nijhoff.

Moffitt, T. E., & Silva, P. A. (1988). IQ and delinquency: A direct test of the differential detection hypothesis. *Journal of Abnormal Psychology, 97,* 330–333.

Monahan, J. (1977). Community psychology and public policy: The promise and the pitfalls. In B. D. Sales (Ed.), *Psychology in the legal process* (pp. 197–213). New York: Spectrum.

Monahan, J. (1984). The prediction of violent behavior: Toward a second generation of theory and practice. *American Journal of Psychiatry, 141,* 10–15.

Monahan, J. (1992). Mental disorder and violent behavior: Perceptions and evidence. *American Psychologist, 47,* 511–521.

Monahan, J., & Walker, L. (1990). *Social science in law: Cases and materials* (2nd ed.). Westbury, NY: Foundation Press.

*Moran v. Burbine,* 475 U.S. 412 (1986).

Moran, G., & Comfort, J. C. (1982). Scientific juror selection: Sex as a moderator of demographic and personality predictors of impaneled felony juror behavior. *Journal of Personality and Social Psychology, 43,* 1052–1063.

Moran, G., & Cutler, B. L. (1991). The prejudicial impact of pretrial publicity. *Journal of Applied Social Psychology, 21,* 345–367.

Moran, G., & Cutler, B. L. (1997). Bogus publicity items and the contingency between awareness and media-induced pretrial prejudice. *Law and Human Behavior, 21,* 339–349.

Moran, G., Cutler, B. L., & Loftus, E. F. (1990). Jury selection in major controlled substance trials: The need for extended voir dire. *Forensic Reports, 3,* 331–348.

*Morgan v. Illinois,* 112 S.Ct. 2222 (1992).

Morgan, A. B., & Lilienfeld, S. O. (2000). A meta-analytic review of the relation between antisocial behavior and neuropsychological measures of executive function. *Clinical Psychology Review, 20,* 113–136.

Morier, D. (1995, February). Can a judge overrule a jury's sentence? *APA Monitor,* p. 17.

Morier, D., Borgida, E., & Park, R. C. (1996). Improving juror comprehension of judicial instructions on the entrapment defense. *Journal of Applied Social Psychology, 26,* 1838–1866.

Morrison, P. (1995, August 21). The new chain gang. *National Law Journal,* pp. A1, A22.

Morse, S. J. (1978). Law and mental health professionals: The limits of expertise. *Professional Psychology, 9,* 389–399.

Morse, S. J. (1998). Fear of danger, flight from culpability. *Psychology, Public Policy, and Law, 4,* 250–267.

Moss, D. (1991). Lawyer personality. *American Bar Association Journal, 79,* 34.

Mossman, D. (1987). Assessing and restoring competency to be executed: Should psychiatrists participate? *Behavioral Sciences and the Law, 5,* 397–410.

Mossman, K. (1994). Assessing predictors of violence: Being accurate about accuracy. *Journal of Consulting and Clinical Psychology, 62,* 783–792.

Muehlenhard, C. L., & Linton, M. A. (1987). Date rape and sexual aggression in dating situations: Incidence and risk factors. *Journal of Counseling Psychology, 34,* 186–196.

Mueller, C. B. & Kirkpatrick, L. C. (1995). *Modern evidence: Doctrine and practice.* Boston: Little, Brown.

Muir, W. K., Jr. (1977). *Police: Streetcorner politicians.* Chicago: University of Chicago Press.

Mulford, C. L., Lee, M. Y., & Sapp, S. C. (1996). Victim-blaming and society-blaming scales for social problems. *Journal of Applied Social Psychology, 26,* 1324–1336.

*Mu'Min v. Virginia,* 111 S.Ct 1899 (1991).

Munsterman, G. T. (1996). A brief history of state jury reform efforts. *Judicature, 79,* 216–223.

Murdoch, D., Pihl, R., & Ross, R. (1990). Alcohol and crimes of violence: Present issues. *International Journal of Addiction, 25,* 1065–1081.

*Murray v. Giarratano,* 492 U.S. 1 (1989).

Myers, J. (1996). A decade of international reform to accommodate child witnesses. *Criminal Justice and Behavior, 23,* 402–422.

Myers, J., Redlich, A., Goodman, G., Prizmich, L., & Imwinkelried, E. (1999). Jurors' perceptions of hearsay in child sexual abuse cases. *Psychology, Public Policy, and Law, 4,* 1025–1051.

Myers, J., Saywitz, K., & Goodman, G. (1996). Psychological research on children as witnesses: Practical implications for forensic interviews and courtroom testimony. *Pacific Law Review, 28,* 3–90.

Myers, M. A. (1988). Sentencing behavior of judges. *Criminology, 26,* 649–675.

Nagel, R. (1989, April 24). The no-bail solution. *New Republic,* pp. 13–14.

Nagel, S. (1962). Judicial backgrounds and criminal cases. *Journal of Criminal Law, Criminology, and Police Science, 53,* 333–339.

Nagel, S. (1969). *The legal process from a behavioral perspective.* Pacific Grove, CA: Brooks/Cole.

Narby, D. J., Cutler, B. L., & Moran, G. (1993). A meta-analysis of the association between authoritarianism and jurors' perceptions of defendant culpability. *Journal of Applied Psychology, 78,* 34–42.

National Advisory Commission on Criminal Justice Standards and Goals. (1973). *Corrections.* Washington, D.C.: U.S. Government Printing Office.

National Center for Education Statistics (1998). *Violence and discipline problems in U.S. public schools: 1996–97.* NCES 98-030. Washington, D.C.: U.S. Government Printing Office.

National Jury Project. (1990). *Jurywork: Systematic techniques.* Release No. 9. New York: Boardman.

National Law Journal. (1987, August 3). West Virginia bar claims attorney billed a 75-hour day. *National Law Journal,* p. 13.

*Nebraska Press Association v. Stuart, 427* U.S. 539 (1976).

Neff, C. (1987, April 8). Scorecard. *Sports Illustrated,* p. 28.

*Neil v. Biggers,* 409 U.S. 188 (1972).

Neises, M. L., & Dillehay, R. C. (1987). Death qualification and conviction proneness: Witt and Witherspoon compared. *Behavioral Sciences and the Law, 5,* 479–494.

Neisser, U. (1976). *Cognition and reality: Principles and implications of cognitive psychology.* San Francisco: Freeman.

Nestor, P. G., Daggett, D., Haycock, J., & Price, M. (1999). Competence to stand trial: A neuropsychological inquiry. *Law and Human Behavior, 23,* 397–412.

Nettler, G. (1974). *Explaining crime.* New York: McGraw-Hill.

Neubauer, D. W. (1988). *America's courts and the criminal justice system* (3rd ed.). Pacific Grove, CA: Brooks/Cole.

*New Jersey Statutes Annotated* 2C:7-1 et seq. (1998).

Newman, J. (1997). Correspondence from the House, Senator Dole, congressmen, and judges. *Judicature, 80,* 156–164.

*New York v. Burger,* 107 S.Ct. 2636 (1987).

*New York v. Quarles,* 467 U.S. 649 (1984).

Nicholson, R. A. (1999). Forensic assessment. In R. Roesch, S. D. Hart, & J. R. Ogloff (Eds.), *Psychology and law: The state of the discipline* (pp. 122–173). New York: Kluwer Academic/Plenum.

Nicholson, R. A., Briggs, S. R., & Robertson, H. C. (1988). Instruments for assessing competency to stand trial: How do they work? *Professional Psychology: Research and Practice, 19,* 383–394.

Nicholson, R. A., & Kugler, K. E. (1991). Competent and incompetent criminal defendants: A quantitative review of comparative research. *Psychological Bulletin, 109,* 355–370.

Nicholson, R. A., & Norwood, S. (2000). The quality of forensic psychological assessments, reports, and testimony: Acknowledging the gap between promise and practice. *Law and Human Behavior, 24,* 9–44.

Nicholson, R. A., Norwood, S., & Enyart, C. (1991). Characteristics and outcomes of insanity acquittees in Oklahoma. *Behavioral Sciences and the Law, 9,* 487–500.

Nicholson, R. A., Robertson, H., Johnson, W., & Jensen, G. (1988). A comparison of instruments for assessing competency to stand trial. *Law and Human Behavior, 12,* 313–321.

Niederhoffer, A. (1967). *Behind the shield: The police in urban society.* New York: Anchor.

Niedermeier, K. E., Horowitz, I. A., & Kerr, N. L. (1999). Informing jurors of their nullification power: A route to a just verdict or judicial chaos? *Law and Human Behavior, 23,* 331–352.

Nietzel, M. T. (1979). *Crime and its modification: A social learning perspective.* New York: Pergamon.

Nietzel, M. T. (in press). Psychology and courtroom consultation. In N. J. Smelser & P. B. Baltes (Eds.), *International encyclopedia of the social and behavioral sciences.* Oxford: Elsevier Sciences.

Nietzel, M. T., & Dade, J. (1973). Bail reform as an example of a community psychology intervention in the criminal justice system. *American Journal of Community Psychology, 1,* 238–247.

Nietzel, M. T., & Dillehay, R. C. (1982). The effects of variations in voir dire procedures in capital murder trials. *Law and Human Behavior, 6,* 1–13.

Nietzel, M. T., & Dillehay, R. C. (1986). *Psychological consultation in the courtroom.* New York: Pergamon.

Nietzel, M. T., & Dillehay, R. C. (1999). Prior jury service. In W. F. Abbott & J. Batt (Eds.), *A handbook of jury research* (pp. 11.1–11.17) Philadelphia: ALI-ABA.

Nietzel, M. T., Hasemann, D., & Lynam, D. (1997). Behavioral perspectives on violent behavior. In J. B. Van Hasselt & M. Hersen (Eds.), *Handbook of psychological approaches with violent criminal offenders: Contemporary strategies and issues.* New York: Plenum.

Nietzel, M. T., Hasemann, D., & McCarthy, D. (in press). Psychology and capital litigation: Research contributions to courtroom consultation. *Applied and Preventive Psychology: Current Scientific Perspectives.*

Nietzel, M. T., & Himelein, M. (1986). Prevention of crime and delinquency. In L. Michelson & B. Edelstein (Eds.), *Handbook of prevention* (pp. 195–221). New York: Plenum.

Nietzel, M. T., McCarthy, D., & Kern, M. (1999). Juries: The current state of the empirical literature. In R. Roesch, S. D. Hart, & J.R.P. Ogloff (Eds.), *Psychology and law: The state of the discipline* (pp. 25–52). New York: Kluwer Academic/Plenum.

Nietzel, M. T., Speltz, M., McCauley, E., & Bernstein, D. (1998). *Abnormal psychology.* Boston: Allyn & Bacon.

Nishith, P., Mechanic, M. B., & Resick, P. A. (2000). Prior interpersonal trauma: The contribution to current PTSD symptoms in female rape victims. *Journal of Abnormal Psychology, 109,* 20–25.

*Nix v. Williams,* 467 U.S. 431 (1984).

Nix, C. (1987, July 9). 1000 new officers graduate to New York City streets. *New York Times,* p. 15.

Nizer, L. (1961). *My life in court.* New York: Pyramid.

Nobile, P. (1989, July). The making of a monster. *Playboy,* pp. 41–45.

Noble, K. B. (1987, March 23). High court to decide whether death penalty discriminates against blacks. *New York Times,* p. 7.

Nolo Press. Web site, www.nolo.com (2000).

Nordheimer, J. (1989, January 25). Bundy is put to death in Florida, closing murder cases across U.S. *New York Times,* pp. 1, 11.

*North Carolina v. Butler,* 441 U.S. 369 (1979).

*O'Connor v. Donaldson,* 422 U.S. 563 (1975).

O'Connor, M., Sales, B. D., & Shulman, D. (1996). Mental health professional expertise in the courtroom. In B. D. Sales & D. W. Shulman (Eds.), *Law, mental health, and mental disorder* (pp. 40–60). Pacific Grove, CA: Brooks/Cole.

Office of Juvenile Justice and Delinquency Prevention. (1999). Web site: http://ojjdp.ncjrs.org.

Office of Technology Assessment. (1983). *Scientific validity of polygraph testing: A research review and evaluation.* Washington, D.C.: U.S. Government Printing Office.

*Official Guide to U.S. Law Schools, 1997 version,* 5, 6, 15.33. (1996).

Ofshe, R. (1992). Inadvertent hypnosis during interrogation: False confession due to dissociative state; misidentified multiple personality and the satanic cult hypothesis. *International Journal of Clinical and Experimental Hypnosis, 40*(3), 125–156.

Ofshe, R., & Watters, E. (1994). *Making monsters: False memories, psychotherapy, and sexual hysteria.* New York: Scribner's.

Ogloff, J. R. P. (1991). A comparison of insanity defense standards on juror decision making. *Law and Human Behavior, 15,* 509–532.

Ogloff, J. R., & Finkelman, D. (1999). Psychology and law: An overview. In R. Roesch, S. D. Hart, & J. R. Ogloff (Eds.), *Psychology and law: The state of the discipline* (pp. 1–20). New York: Kluwer.

Ogloff, J. R. P., & Otto, R. (1993). Psychological autopsy: Clinical and legal perspectives. *Saint Louis University Law Journal, 37,* 607–646.

Ogloff, J. R. P., & Vidmar, N. (1994). The impact of pretrial publicity on jurors: A study to compare the relative effects of television and print media in a child sex abuse case. *Law and Human Behavior, 18,* 507–525.

*Ohralik v. Ohio State Bar Association,* 436 U.S. 447 (1978).

Olczak, P. V., Kaplan, M. F., & Penrod, S. (1991). Attorneys' lay psychology and its effectiveness in selecting jurors: Three empirical studies. *Journal of Social Behavior and Personality, 6,* 431–452.

*Oliver v. United States,* 466 U.S. 170 (1984).

Olsen-Fulero, L. & Fulero, S. (1997). Commonsense rape judgments: An empathy-complexity theory of rape juror story making. *Psychology, Public Policy, and Law, 3,* 402–427.

Olson, W. K. (1991). *The litigation explosion.* New York: Dutton.

Olson-Raymer, G. (1984). National juvenile justice policy: Myth or reality? In S. H. Decker (Ed.), *Juvenile justice policy: Analyzing trends and outcomes* (pp. 19–57). Newbury Park, CA: Sage.

Olweus, D. (1987). Testosterone and adrenaline: Aggressive antisocial behavior in normal adolescent males. In S. A. Mednick, T. E. Moffitt, & S. A. Stack (Eds.), *The causes of crime: New biological approaches* (pp. 263–282). Cambridge: Cambridge University Press.

Olweus, D. (1995). Bullying or peer abuse at school: Facts and interventions. *Current Directions in Psychological Science, 4,* 196–200.

*Oncale v. Sundowner Offshore Services, Inc.,* 118 S. Ct. 998 (1998).

Ones, D. S., Viswesvaran, C., & Schmidt, F. L. (1993). Meta-analysis of integrity test validities: Findings and implications for personnel selection and theories of job performance. *Journal of Applied Psychology, 78,* 679–703.

*Oregon v. Elstad,* 470 U.S. 298 (1985).

O'Reilly, J., & Sales, B. D. (1987). Privacy for the institutionalized mentally ill: Are court-ordered standards effective? *Law and Human Behavior, 11,* 41–53.

Orne, M. T. (1979). The use and misuse of hypnosis in court. *International Journal of Clinical and Experimental Hypnosis, 27,* 311–341.

Orne, M. T., Soskis, D. A., Dinges, D. F., & Orne, E. C. (1984). Hypnotically induced testimony. In G. L. Wells & E. F. Loftus (Eds.), *Eyewitness testimony: Psychological perspectives* (pp. 171–213). New York: Cambridge University Press.

Ornstein, P. A., Ceci, S. J., & Loftus, E. F. (1998). Adult recollections of childhood abuse: Cognitive and developmental perspectives. *Psychology, Public Policy, and Law, 4,* 1025–1051.

O'Rourke, T. E., Penrod, S. D., Cutler, B. L., & Stuve, T. E. (1989). The external validity of eyewitness identification research: Generalizing across subject populations. *Law and Human Behavior, 13,* 385–396.

Ostrov, E. (1986). Police/law enforcement and psychology. *Behavioral Sciences and the Law, 4,* 353–370.

Otto, A. L., Penrod, S. D., & Dexter, H. D. (1994). The biasing impact of pretrial publicity on juror judgments. *Law and Human Behavior, 18,* 453–470.

Otto, A., Penrod, S., & Hirt, E. (1990). *The influence of pretrial publicity on juror judgments in a civil case.* Unpublished manuscript, University of Minnesota, Minneapolis.

Otto, R., Poythress, N., Starr, K., & Darkes, J. (1993). An empirical study of the reports of APA's peer review panel in the congressional review of the USS *Iowa* incident. *Journal of Personality Assessment, 61,* 425–442.

Otto, R. K., Poythress, N. G., Nicholson, R. A., Edens, J. F., Monahan, J., Bonnie, R. J., Hoge, S. K., & Eisenberg, M. (1998). Psychometric properties of the MacArthur competence assessment tool—Criminal adjudication. *Psychological Assessment, 10,* 435–443.

Packer, H. L. (1964). Two models of the criminal process. *University of Pennsylvania Law Review, 113,* 1–68.

Padawer-Singer, A. M., & Barton, A. H. (1975). The impact of pretrial publicity on jurors' verdicts. In R. J. Simon (Ed.), *The jury system in America: A critical overview* (pp. 123–139). Newbury Park, CA: Sage.

Padawer-Singer, A. M., Singer, A., & Singer, R. (1974). Voir dire by two lawyers: An essential safeguard. *Judicature, 57,* 386–391.

Palladino, J. J., van Giesen, S., Emerson, R., Pitzer, T., Price, T., Crowe, G., & Fisher, R. (1986, May). *Effects of death qualification on attitudes and demographics of the potential jury pool.* Paper presented at the meetings of the Midwestern Psychological Association, Chicago.

Palmer, J., & Palmer, S.E. (1999). *Constitutional rights of prisoners.* Cincinnati: Anderson.

Palmer, T. (1984). Treatment and the role of classification: A review of basic issues. *Crime and Delinquency, 30,* 245–267.

Parloff, R. (1993). False confessions: Standard interrogations by Arizona law enforcement officials led to four matching confessions to the murders of nine people at a Buddhist temple. But all four suspects were innocent. *American Lawyer,* pp. 58–62.

Pasewark, R. A., Bieber, S., Bosten, K. J., Kiser, M., & Steadman, H. J. (1982). Criminal recidivism among insanity acquittees. *International Journal of Law and Psychiatry, 5,* 365–374.

Pasewark, R. A., & Pantle, M. L. (1981). Opinions about the insanity plea.. *Journal of Forensic Psychology, 8,* 63.

Patterson, E. B. (1996). Poverty, income inequality, and community crime rates. In D. G. Rojet & G. F. Jensen (Eds.), *Exploring delinquency: Causes and control* (pp. 142–149). Los Angeles: Roxbury.

Patterson, G. R. (1982). *Coercive family process.* Eugene, OR: Castalia.

Patterson, G. R. (1986). Performance models for antisocial boys. *American Psychologist, 41,* 432–444.

*Patton v. Yount,* 467 U.S. 1025 (1984).

*Payne v. Tennessee,* 498 U.S. 21 (1991).

Peak, K., Bradshaw, R., & Glensor, R. (1992). Improving citizen perceptions of the police: "Back to the basics" with a community policing strategy. *Journal of Criminal Justice, 20,* 24–40.

Pearce, J. B., & Snortum, J. R. (1983). Police effectiveness in handling disturbance calls: An evaluation of crisis intervention training. *Criminal Justice and Behavior, 10,* 71–92.

Pearl, D., Bouthilet, L., & Lazar, J. (Eds.). (1982). *Television and behavior: Ten years of scientific progress and implications for the eighties* (Vols. 1 & 2). Washington, D.C.: U.S. Government Printing Office.

Penn, S. (1985, April 22). Offenders face victims in program that's an alternative to jail. *Kansas City Times,* p. B2.

Pennington, N., & Hastie, R. (1986). Evidence evaluation in complex decision-making. *Journal of Personality and Social Psychology, 51,* 242–258.

Pennington, N., & Hastie, R. (1988). Explanation-based decision making: Effects of memory structure on judgment. *Journal of Experimental Psychology: Learning, Memory, and Cognition, 14,* 521–533.

Pennington, N., & Hastie, R. (1993). The story model for juror decision making. In R. Hastie (Ed.), *Inside the juror: The psychology of juror decision making* (pp. 192–221). New York: Cambridge University Press.

Penrod, S. D. (1979). *Study of attorney and "scientific" jury selection models.* Unpublished doctoral dissertation, Harvard University, Cambridge, MA.

Penrod, S. D. (1990). Predictors of jury decision making in criminal and civil cases: A field experiment. *Forensic Reports, 3,* 261–278.

Penrod, S. D., & Cutler, B. (1995). Witness confidence and witness accuracy: Assessing their forensic relation. *Psychology, Public Policy, and Law, 1,* 817–845.

Penrod, S. D., & Cutler, B. (1999). Preventing mistaken convictions in eyewitness identification trials: The case against traditional safeguards. In R. Roesch, S. D. Hart, & J. Ogloff (Eds.), *Psychology and law: The state of the discipline* (pp. 89–118). New York: Kluwer Academic/Plenum.

Penrod, S. D., Fulero, S. M., & Cutler, B. L. (1995). Expert psychological testimony on eyewitness reliability before and after *Daubert*: The state of the law and the science. *Behavioral Sciences and the Law, 13,* 229–260.

Penrod, S. D., Loftus, E. F., & Winkler, J. (1982). The reliability of eyewitness testimony: A psychological perspective. In N. L. Kerr & R. M. Bray (Eds.), *The psychology of the courtroom* (pp. 119–168). Orlando, FL: Academic Press.

*People v. Defore,* 150 N.E. 2d 585 (N.Y. 1926).

*People v. Falsetta,* 986 P.2d 182 (1999).

*People v. Garcia,* 99 C.D.O.S. 4094 (California Supreme Court, 1999).

*People v Green,* (A086488, Cal. App. 4/7/00).

*People v. Hughes,* 453 N.E.2d 484 (N.Y. App. 1983).

*People v. Meyer,* 680 N.E. 2d 315 (Ill. 1997).

*People v. Noia,* 158 N.Y.S. 2d 683 (1956).

Perlin, M. L. (1992). Fatal assumption: A critical evaluation of the role of counsel in mental disability cases. *Law and Human Behavior, 16,* 39–60.

Perlin, M. (1996). The insanity defense: Deconstructing the myths and reconstructing the jurisprudence. In B. D. Sales & D. W. Shulman (Eds.), *Law, mental health, and mental disorder* (pp. 341–359). Pacific Grove, CA: Brooks/Cole.

Perry, N. W., & Wrightsman, L. S. (1991). *The child witness.* Newbury Park, CA: Sage.

Petty, R. E., Fleming, M. A., & White, P. H. (1999). Stigmatized sources and persuasion: Prejudice as a determinant of argument scrutiny. *Journal of Personality and Social Psychology, 76,* 19–34.

Petrella, R. C., & Poythress, N. G. (1983). The quality of forensic evaluations: An interdisciplinary study. *Journal of Consulting and Clinical Psychology, 51,* 76–85.

Pfohl, S. J. (1984). Predicting dangerousness: A social deconstruction of psychiatric reality. In L. A. Teplin (Ed.), *Mental health and criminal justice* (pp. 201–225). Newbury Park, CA: Sage.

Pfohl, S. J. (1985). *Images of deviance and social control: A sociological history.* New York: McGraw-Hill.

Phares, E. J. (1976). *Locus of control in personality.* Morristown, NJ: General Learning Press.

Phares, E. J., & Wilson, K. G. (1972). Responsibility attribution: Role of outcome severity, situational ambiguity, and internal-external control. *Journal of Personality, 40,* 392–406.

Phillips, D. A. (1979). *The great Texas murder trials: A compelling account of the sensational T. Cullen Davis case.* New York: Macmilan.

Phillips, S. (1977). *No heroes, no villains: The story of a murder trial.* New York: Random House.

Pickel, K. L. (1995). Inducing jurors to disregard inadmissible evidence: A legal explanation does not help. *Law and Human Behavior, 19,* 407–424.

Pickel, K. L. (1998). The effects of motive information and crime unusualness on jurors' judgments in insanity cases. *Law and Human Behavior, 22,* 571–584.

Pickel, K .L. (1999). The influence of context on the "weapon focus" effect. *Law and Human Behavior, 23,* 299–311.

Pinizzotto, A. J., & Finkel, N. J. (1990). Criminal personality profiling: An outcome and process study. *Law and Human Behavior, 14,* 215–234.

Pipkin, R. M. (1982). Moonlighting in law school: A multischool study of part-time employment of full-time students. *American Bar Foundation Research Journal, 1982(4),* 1109–1162.

Pizzi, W. T. (1987). *Batson v. Kentucky*: Curing the disease but killing the patient. In P. K. Kurland, G. Casper, & D. Hutchinson (Eds.), *The Supreme Court review, 1987* (pp. 97–156). Chicago: University of Chicago Press.

*Planned Parenthood v. Casey,* 112 S.Ct. 2791 (1992).

Platt, J. J., & Prout, M. F. (1987). Cognitive-behavioral theory and interventions for crime and delinquency. In E. K. Morris & C. J. Braukmann

(Eds.), *Behavioral approaches to crime and delinquency: A handbook of application, research, and concepts* (pp. 477–497). New York: Plenum.

*Plessy v. Ferguson,* 163 U.S. 537 (1896).

Podgers, J. (1999, July). Confidence game. *American Bar Association Journal, 85,* 86–87.

Poland, J. M. (1978). Police selection methods and the prediction of police performance. *Journal of Police Science and Administration, 6,* 374–393.

Pollock, A. (1977). The use of public opinion polls to obtain changes of venue and continuance in criminal trials. *Criminal Justice Journal, 1,* 269–288.

Polvi, N., Jack, L., Lyon, D., Laird, P., & Ogloff, J. (1996). *Mock jurors' verdicts in a child sexual abuse case: The effects of pretrial publicity.* Paper presented at the Biennial Convention of the American Psychology-Law Society, Hilton Head, SC.

Poole, D. A., & Lindsay, D. S. (1998). Assessing the accuracy of young children's reports: Lessons from the investigation of child sexual abuse. *Journal of Applied and Preventive Psychology, 7,* 1–26.

Porter, B. (1983). Mind hunters. *Psychology Today, 17,* 44–52.

Porter, S., & Yuille, J. C. (1996). The language of deceit: An investigation of the verbal clues to deception in the interrogation context. *Law and Human Behavior, 20,* 443–458.

Posner, R. A. (1992). *Economic analysis of law* (4th ed.). Boston: Little, Brown.

Posner, R. A. (1996, July 15 & 22). The immoralist. *New Republic,* pp. 38–41.

Post, C. G. (1963). *An introduction to the law.* Englewood Cliffs, NJ: Prentice Hall.

*Powers v. Ohio,* 111 S.Ct. 1364 (1991).

Pozzulo, J. D., & Lindsay, R. C. (1997). Increasing correct identifications by children. *Expert Evidence, 5,* 126–132.

Pozzulo, J. D., & Lindsay, R. C. (1998). Identification accuracy of children versus adults: A meta-analysis. *Law and Human Behavior, 22,* 549–570.

Pozzulo, J. D., & Lindsay, R. C. (1999). Elimination lineups: An improved identification procedure for child eyewitnesses. *Journal of Applied Psychology, 84,* 167–176.

Poythress, N. (1982). Concerning reform in expert testimony. *Law and Human Behavior, 6,* 39–43.

Poythress, N. (1994). Procedural preferences, perceptions of fairness, and compliance with outcomes: A study of alternatives to the standard adversary trial procedure. *Law and Human Behavior, 18,* 361–376.

Poythress, N. G., Bonnie, R. J., Hoge, S. K., Monahan, J., & Oberlander, L. B. (1994). Client abilities to assist counsel and make decisions in criminal cases: Findings from three studies. *Law and Human Behavior, 18,* 437–452.

Prentky, R. A. (1999). Child sexual molestation. In V. B. Van Hasselt & M. Hersen (Eds.), *Handbook of psychological approaches with violent offenders* (pp. 267–302). New York: Kluwer Academic/Plenum.

Prentky, R. A., & Knight, R. A. (1991). Identifying critical dimensions for discriminating among rapists. *Journal of Consulting and Clinical Psychology, 59,* 643–661.

President's Commission on Law Enforcement and Administration of Justice. (1967). *Toward a just America.* Washington, D.C.: U.S. Government Printing Office.

Press, A. (1988, May 2). Helping the cops and jails. *Newsweek,* p. 67.

Pressley, S. A. (1996, August 6). Adolescent on trial in toddler's death. *Washington Post,* p. A3.

Prettyman, E. B. (1960). Jury instructions—First or last? *American Bar Association Journal, 46,* 10–66.

Price, R., & Lovitt, J. T. (1996, October 4). Poll: More now believe O. J. is guilty. *USA Today,* p. 3A.

*Price-Waterhouse v. Hopkins,* 109 S.Ct. 1775 (1989).

Pryke, S., Lindsay, R. C., & Pozzulo, J. D. (2000). Sorting mug shots: Methodological issues. *Applied Cognitive Psychology, 14,* 81–96.

Pryor, J. B. (1987). Sexual harassment proclivities in men. *Sex Roles, 17,* 269–290.

Pryor, J. B., Giedd, J. L., & Williams, K. B. (1995). A social psychological model for predicting sexual harassment. *Journal of Social Issues, 51*(1), 69–84.

Pryor, J. B., McDaniel, M. A., & Kott-Russo, T. (1986). The influence of the level of schema abstractness upon the processing of social information. *Journal of Experimental Social Psychology, 22,* 312–327.

*Purkett v. Elem,* SIS U.S. 1170 (1995).

Putnam, W. H. (1979). Hypnosis and distortions in eyewitness memory. *International Journal of Clinical and Experimental Hypnosis, 27*(4), 437–448.

Pyszczynski, T., Greenberg, J., Mack, D., & Wrightsman, L. S. (1981). Opening statements in a jury trial: The effect of promising more than the evidence can show. *Journal of Applied Social Psychology, 11,* 434–444.

Pyszczynski, T., & Wrightsman, L. S. (1981). The effects of opening statements on mock jurors' verdicts in a simulated criminal trial. *Journal of Applied Social Psychology, 11,* 301–313.

Quay, H. C. (1965). Personality and delinquency. In H. C. Quay (Ed.), *Juvenile delinquency.* Princeton, NJ: Van Nostrand.

Quinsey, V. L. (1984). Sexual aggression: Studies of offenders against women. In D. Weisstub (Ed.), *Law and mental health: International perspectives* (Vol. 1, pp. 84–121). New York: Pergamon.

Quinsey, V. L., Harris, G.T., Rice, M.E., & Cormier, C.A. (1998). *Violent offenders: Appraising and managing risk.* Washington, D.C.: American Psychological Association.

Quinsey, V. L., Lalumiere, M. L., Rice, M. E., & Harris, G. T. (1995). Predicting violent offenses. In J. C. Campbell (Ed.), *Assessing dangerousness: Violence by sexual offenders, batterers, and child abusers* (pp. 114–137). Thousand Oaks, CA: Sage.

Rabasca, L. (1998). Indians need for access to behavioral medicine. *American Psychological Association Monitor, 29,* Available: www.apa.org/monitor/aug98/indian.html

Radelet, M., & Akers, R. (1996). *Deterrence and the death penalty: The views of the experts* [On-line]. Available: http://sun.socio.niu.edu/

Raine, A., Meloy, J., & Buchshaum, M. (1998). Reduced prefrontal and increased subcortical brain functioning using positron emission tomography in predatory and affective murderers. *Behavioral Sciences and the Law, 16,* 319–332.

*Rakas v. Illinois,* 439 U.S. 128 (1978).

Ramirez, G., Zemba, D., & Geiselman, R. E. (1996). Judges' cautionary instructions on eyewitness testimony. *American Journal of Forensic Psychology, 14*(1), 31–66.

Randolph, J. J., Hicks, T., & Mason, D. (1981). The Competency Screening Test: A replication and extension. *Criminal Justice and Behavior, 8,* 471–482.

Rappaport, J. (1981). In praise of paradox: A social policy of empowerment over prevention. *American Journal of Community Psychology, 9,* 125.

Rappaport, J. (1987). Terms of empowerment/exemplars of prevention: Toward a theory of community psychology. *American Journal of Community Psychology, 15,* 121–144.

Raskin, D. C. (1982). The scientific basis of polygraph techniques and their uses in the judicial process. In A. Trankell (Ed.), *Reconstructing the past: The role of psychologists in criminal trials* (pp. 317–371). Stockholm: Norstedt & Soners.

Raskin D. C. (1989). *Psychological methods in criminal investigation and evidence.* New York: Springer.

Rattner, A. (1988). Convicted but innocent: Wrongful conviction and the criminal justice system. *Law and Human Behavior, 12,* 283–293.

Rebman, C. (1999). The Eighth Amendment and solitary confinement: The gap in protection from psychological consequences. *DePaul Law Review, 49,* 567–619.

*Reck v. Pate,* 367 U.S. 433 (1961).

Reckless, W. C. (1961). *The crime problem.* New York: Appleton-Century-Crofts.

Reckless, W. C. (1967). *The crime problem* (4th ed.). New York: Meredith.

Rehnquist, W. (1992). *Grand inquest.* New York: Morrow.

Reibstein, L., & Foote, D. (1996, November 4). Playing the victim card. *Newsweek,* pp. 64, 66.

Reid, J. E., & Inbau, F. E. (1966). *Truth and deception: The polygraph ("lie-detector") technique.* Baltimore: Williams & Wilkins.

Reid, S. T. (1976). *Crime and criminology.* Hinsdale, IL: Dryden.

Reifman, A., Gusick, S., & Ellsworth, P. (1992). Real jurors' understanding of the law in real cases. *Law and Human Behavior, 16,* 539–554.

Reis, H., & Jackson, L. (1981). Sex differences in reward allocation: Subjects, partners and tasks. *Journal of Personality and Social Psychology, 40,* 465–478.

Reiser, M., & Geiger, S. (1984). Police officer as victim. *Professional Psychology: Research and Practice, 15,* 315–323.

Reiser, M., & Klyver, N. (1987). Consulting with police. In I. B. Weiner & A. K. Hess (Eds.), *Handbook of forensic psychology* (pp. 437–459). New York: Wiley.

Reiss, A. J., Jr. (1971). *The police and the public.* New Haven, CT: Yale University Press.

Rembar, C. (1980). *The law of the land.* New York: Simon & Schuster.

*Reno v. American Civil Liberties Union,* 117 S.Ct. 2329 (1997).

Rensberger, B. (1988, August 29–September 4). New findings on the crime rate of urban black youths. *Washington Post National Weekly Edition,* p. 39.

Repko, G. R., & Cooper, R. (1983). A study of the average workers' compensation case. *Journal of Clinical Psychology, 39,* 287–295.

Reppucci, N. D., & Haugaard, J. J. (1989). Prevention of child sexual abuse: Myth or reality. *American Psychologist, 44,* 1266–1275.

Reske, H. (1996, January). Scarlet letter sentences. *American Bar Association Journal,* pp. 16–17.

Resnick, H. S., Kilpatrick, D. G., Dansky, B. S., Saunders, B., & Best, C. L. (1993). Prevalence of civilian trauma and posttraumatic stress disorder in a representative national sample of women. *Journal of Consulting and Clinical Psychology, 61,* 984–991.

Resnick, R. (1992, June 1). Grand jury witnesses get help. *National Law Journal,* pp. 3, 48.

Ressler, R. K., Burgess, A. W., & Douglas, J. E. (1988). *Sexual homicide: Patterns and motives.* Lexington, MA: Lexington.

Rest, J. R. (1988). *DIT manual* (3rd ed., rev.). Minneapolis: University of Minnesota Press.

Rest, J. R., Cooper, D., Coder, R., Masanz, J., & Anderson, D. (1974). Judging the important issues in moral dilemmas: An objective measure of development. *Developmental Psychology, 10,* 491–501.

Restrepo, L. F. (1995, April 17). Excluding bilingual jurors may be racist. *National Law Journal,* pp. A21, A22.

Reuben, R. (1996, August). The lawyer turns peacemaker. *American Bar Association Journal, 82,* 54–55.

*Rhode Island v. Innis,* 446 U.S. 291 (1980).

Ribes-Inesta, E., & Bandura, A. (Eds.). (1976). *Analysis of delinquency and aggression.* Hillsdale, NJ: Erlbaum.

Rich, B. A. (1998). Personhood, patient-hood, and clinical practice: Reassessing advance directives. *Psychology, Public Policy, and Law, 4,* 610–628.

Richey, C. R. (1994). Proposals to eliminate the prejudicial effect of the use of the word "expert" under the federal rules of evidence in civil and criminal jury trials. *Federal Rules Decisions, 154,* 537–562.

*Richmond Newspapers, Inc. v. Virginia,* 448 U.S. 555 (1980).

*Rideau v. Louisiana,* 373 U.S. 723 (1963).

Rider, A. O. (1980). The firesetter: A psychological profile. *FBI Law Enforcement Bulletin, 49,* 123.

Riechmann, J. (1985, May 21). Mental illness: Parents of deranged children suffer private tragedies. *Lawrence (KS) Journal-World,* p. 6.

*Riggins v. Nevada,* 112 S.Ct. 1810 (1992).

Ring, K. (1971). *Let's get started: An appeal to what's left in psychology.* Unpublished manuscript, University of Connecticut.

*Riverside County v. McLaughlin,* 111 S.Ct. 1661 (1991).

Robbennolt, J. (2000). Outcome severity and judgments of "responsibility": A meta-analytic review. *Journal of Applied Social Psychology, 12,* 2575–2609.

Roberts, C. F., & Golding, S. L. (1991). The social construction of criminal responsibility and insanity. *Law and Human Behavior, 15,* 349–376.

Roberts, C. F., Golding, S. L., & Fincham, F. D. (1987). Implicit theories of criminal responsibility: Decision making and the insanity defense. *Law and Human Behavior, 11,* 207–232.

Roberts, C. F., Sargent, E. L., & Chan, A. S. (1993). Verdict selection processes in insanity cases: Juror construals and the effects of guilty but mentally ill instructions. *Law and Human Behavior, 17,* 261–275.

Robinson, P. (1982, June 9). Criminals and victims. *New Republic,* pp. 37–38.

*Rock v. Arkansas,* 107 S.Ct. 2704 (1987).

*Roe v. Wade,* 410 U.S. 113 (1973).

Roesch, R., & Golding, S. L. (1980). *Competency to stand trial.* Urbana: University of Illinois Press.

Roesch, R., & Golding, S. L. (1987). Defining and assessing competence to stand trial. In I. Weiner & A. Hess (Eds.), *Handbook of forensic psychology* (pp. 378–394). New York: Wiley.

Roesch, R., Zapf, P. A., Eaves, D., & Webster, C. D. (1998). *The fitness inter-*

view test (rev. ed.). Burnaby, Canada: Mental Health, Law, and Policy Institute, Simon Fraser University.

Rogers, J. (1998). Special report: Witness preparation memos raise questions about ethical limits. *ABA/BNA Manual on Lawyers' Professional Conduct, 14,* 48–54.

Rogers, R. (1986). *Conducting insanity evaluations.* New York: Van Nostrand.

Rogers, R. (1988). *Clinical assessment of malingering and deception.* New York: Guilford.

Rogers, R. (1995). *Diagnostic and structural interviewing: A handbook for psychologists.* New York: Psychological Assessment Resources.

Rogers, R., & Ewing, C. P. (1989). Ultimate opinion proscriptions: A cosmetic fix and a plea for empiricism. *Law and Human Behavior, 13,* 357–374.

Rogers, R., Gillis, J. R., Dickens, S. E., & Bagby, R. M. (1991). Standardized assessment of malingering: Validation of the structured interview of reported symptoms. *Psychological Assessment: A Journal of Clinical and Consulting Psychology, 3,* 89–96.

Rogers, R., Sewell, K. W., & Goldstein, A. (1994). Explanatory models of malingering: A prototypical analysis. *Law and Human Behavior, 18,* 543–552.

Rohling, M. L., Binder, L. M., & Langhrinrichsen-Rohling, J. (1995). Money matters: A meta-analytic review of the association between financial compensation and the experience and treatment of chronic pain. *Health Psychology, 14,* 537–547.

Romano, L. (1996, August 10). Execution closes a tragic circle: Douglass children watch their parents' killer die. *Washington Post,* p. A3.

Rose, M. R. (1999). The peremptory challenge accused of race or gender discrimination? Some data from one county. *Law and Human Behavior, 23,* 695–702.

Rosen, G. M. (1995). The Aleutian Enterprise sinking and posttraumatic stress disorder: Misdiagnosis in clinical and forensic settings. *Professional Psychology: Research and Practice, 26,* 82–87.

Rosen, J. (1996, December 9). The Bloods and the Crips. *New Republic,* pp. 27–42.

Rosenbaum, A., & Gearan, P. J. (1999). Relationship aggression between partners. In V. B. Van Hasselt & M. Hersen (Eds.), *Handbook of psychological approaches with violent offend-*

ers: *Contemporary strategies and issues* (pp. 357–372). New York: Kluwer Academic/Plenum.

Rosenbaum, R. (1990, May). Travels with Dr. Death. *Vanity Fair,* pp. 140–147, 166–174.

Rosenhan, D. L. (1973). On being sane in insane places. *Science, 179,* 250–258.

Rosenthal, R. (1991). *Meta-analytic procedures for social research.* Newbury Park, CA: Sage.

Rosner, S. (1992, May). Professionalism and money. *American Bar Association Journal, 78,* 69.

*Ross v. Moffitt,* 417 U.S. 600 (1974).

*Ross v. Oklahoma,* 108 S.Ct. 2273 (1988).

Rotgers, F., & Barrett, D. (1996). *Daubert v. Merrell Dow* and expert testimony by clinical psychologists: Implications and recommendations for practice. *Professional Psychology: Research and Practice, 27,* 467–474.

Rothenberg, P. S. (1995). *Race, class, and gender in the United States* (3rd ed.). New York: St. Martin's.

Rothfeld, C. (1991, April 26). Overcoming jury ban on the blind and deaf. *New York Times,* p. B9.

Rotter, J. B. (1966). Generalized expectancies for internal versus external control of reinforcement. *Psychological Monographs, 80*(1, Whole No. 609).

*Rouse v. Cameron,* 373 F.2d 451 (1966).

Rovella, D. (1999, Jan. 18). Man with a mission. *National Law Journal,* p. A1.

Rovella, D.E. (2000a, January 31). The best defense . . . : Rebuilding clients' lives to keep them from coming back. *National Law Journal,* p. A1.

Rovella, D. (2000b, January 10). Unclogging Gideon's trumpet. *National Law Journal,* p.1.

Rowan, C. (1993). *Dream makers and dream breakers.* Boston: Little, Brown.

Rowland, J. (1985). *The ultimate violation.* New York: Doubleday.

Royko, M. (1989, May 26). Should granny be in slammer? *Kansas City Times,* p. A17.

Ruben, D. (1995, March). Women of the jury. *Self,* pp. 186–189, 196.

Rubin, Z., & Peplau, L. A. (1975). Who believes in a just world? *Journal of Social Issues, 31*(3), 65–90.

Rubinstein, M. L., Clarke, S. H., & White, T. J. (1980). *Alaska bans plea bargaining.* Washington, D.C.: National Institute of Justice, U.S. Department of Justice.

Ruby, C. L., & Brigham, J. C. (1996). A criminal schema: The role of chronicity, race, and socioeconomic status in law enforcement officials' perceptions of others. *Journal of Applied Social Psychology, 26,* 95–111.

*Ruffin v. Commonwealth,* 62 Va. (21 Gratt) 790 (1871).

Runda, J. (1991). *Personal affidavit filed with authors.* Lexington: University of Kentucky Press.

Rusbult, C. E., Lowery, D., Hubbard, M. L., Maravankin, O. J., & Neises, M. (1988). Impact of employee mobility and employee performance on the allocation of rewards under conditions of constraint. *Journal of Personality and Social Psychology, 54,* 605–615.

Rush, C., & Robertson, J. (1987). Presentence reports: The utility of information to the sentencing decision. *Law and Human Behavior, 11,* 147–155.

Russell, D. E. H. (1984). *Sexual exploitation: Rape, child sexual abuse, and workplace harassment.* Newbury Park, CA: Sage.

*Rust v. Sullivan,* 111 S.Ct. 1759 (1991).

Ryan, W. (1970). *Blaming the victim.* New York: Vintage.

Ryerson, E. (1978). *The best-laid plans: America's juvenile court experiment.* New York: Hill & Wang.

Sachs, A. (1989, September 11). Doing the crime, not the time. *Time,* p. 81.

Sacks, A. M. (1984). Legal education and the changing role of lawyers in dispute resolution. *Journal of Legal Education, 34,* 237–244.

Saks, M. (1987). Social scientists can't rig juries. In L. Wrightsman, & S. Kassin, (Eds.), *In the jury box: Controversies in the courtroom* (pp. 48–61). Newbury Park, CA: Sage.

Saks, M. J. (1976). The limits of scientific jury selection. *Jurimetrics Journal, 17,* 3–22.

Saks, M. J., & Kidd, R. F. (1986). Human information processing and adjudication: Trial by heuristics. In H. R. Arkes & K. P. Hammond (Eds.), *Judgment and decision making: An interdisciplinary reader* (pp. 213–242). Cambridge: Cambridge University Press.

Sales, B. D., & Hafemeister, T. (1984). Empiricism and legal policy on the insanity defense. In L. A. Teplin (Ed.), *Mental health and criminal justice* (pp. 253–278). Newbury Park, CA: Sage.

Sales, B.D., & Shuman, D.W. (1993). Reclaiming the integrity of science in expert witnessing. *Ethics and Behavior, 3,* 223–229.

Salfati, C .G., & Canter, D. V. (1999). Differentiating stranger murders: Profiling offender characteristics from behavioral styles. *Behavioral Sciences and the Law, 17,* 391–406.

Samenow, S. E. (1984). *Inside the criminal mind.* New York: Times Books.

Sampson, E. E. (1975). On justice as equality. *Journal of Social Issues, 31*(3), 45–64.

Sanday, P. R. (1997) The socio-cultural context of rape: A cross-cultural study. In L. O'Toole, J. R. Schiffman, et al. (Eds.)., *Gender violence: Interdisciplinary perspectives* (pp. 52–66). New York: New York University Press.

Sandburg, C. (1926). *Abraham Lincoln* (Vol. II). New York: Harcourt Brace.

Sanders, J. (1993). The jury decision in a complex case: *Havener v. Merrell Dow Pharmaceuticals. Justice System Journal, 16,* 45.

*Santobello v. New York,* 404 U.S. 257 (1971).

*Sawyer v. Whitley,* 505 U.S. 333 (1992).

Saxe, L. (1991). Lying: Thoughts of an applied social psychologist. *American Psychologist, 46,* 409–415.

Saxe, L., & Ben-Shakhar, G. (1999). Admissibility of polygraph tests: The application of scientific standards post-*Daubert. Psychology, Public Policy, and Law, 5,* 203–223.

Saxe, L., Dougherty, D., & Cross, T. (1985). The validity of polygraph testing: Scientific analysis and public controversy. *American Psychologist, 40,* 355–366.

Saxe, L., & Fine, M. (1981). *Social experiments: Methods for design and evaluation.* Newbury Park, CA: Sage.

Saywitz, K. & Lyon, T. (1998). *Maltreated children's competence to take the oath.* Paper presented at the International Congress of Applied Psychology, San Francisco.

Saywitz, K., & Nathanson, R. (1993). Children's testimony and their perceptions of stress in and out of the courtroom. *Child Abuse and Neglect, 17,* 613–622.

Scheflin, A. (1972). Jury nullification: The right to say no. *Southern California Law Review, 45,* 168–226.

Scheflin, A. W., & Shapiro, J. L. (1989). *Trance on trial.* New York: Guilford.

*Schenck v. Pro Choice Network of Western New York,* 519 U.S. 357 (1997).

Schlossberg, H., & Freeman, L. (1974). *Psychologists with a gun.* New York: Coward, McCann, & Geoghegan.

Schneider, B. E. (1987). Graduate women, sexual harassment, and university policy. *Journal of Higher Education, 58*(1), 46–65.

Schopp, R. F., Scalora, M. J., & Pearce, M. (1999). Expert testimony and professional judgment: Psychological expertise and commitment as a sexual predator after *Hendricks. Psychology, Public Policy and Law, 5,* 120–174.

Schretlen, D., Wilkins, S. S., Van Gorp, W. G., & Bobholz, J. H. (1992). Cross-validation of a psychological test battery to detect faked insanity. *Psychological Assessment, 4,* 77–83.

Schul, Y. (1993). When warning succeeds: The effect of warning on success in ignoring invalid information. *Journal of Experimental Social Psychology, 29,* 42–62.

Schuller, R. (1995). Expert evidence and hearsay: The influence of "secondhand" information on jurors' decisions. *Law and Human Behavior, 19,* 345–362.

Schuller, R. A. (1994). Application of battered woman syndrome evidence in the courtroom. In M. Costanzo & S. Oskamp (Eds.), *Violence and the law* (pp. 113–134). Thousand Oaks, Ca: Sage.

Schuller, R. A., & Vidmar, N. (1992). Battered woman syndrome evidence in the courtroom: A review of the literature. *Law and Human Behavior, 16,* 273–291.

Schulman, J., Shaver, P., Colman, R., Emrich, B., & Christie, R. (1973, May). Recipe for a jury. *Psychology Today,* pp. 37–44, 77–84.

Schuman, D., & Champagne, A. (1997). Removing the people from the legal process: The rhetoric and research on judicial selection and juries. *Psychology, Public Policy, and Law, 3,* 242–258.

Schwartz, H. (Ed.). (1988). *The Burger years: Rights and wrongs in the Supreme Court 1969–1986.* New York: Viking.

Schwartz I., Weiner, N. & Enosh, G. (1998). Nine lives and then some: Why the juvenile court does not roll over and die. *Wake Forest Law Review, 33,* 533–552.

Schwartz-Kenney, B. M., & Goodman, G. S. (1999). Children's memory of a naturalistic event following misin-

formation. *Applied Developmental Science, 3,* 34–46.

Schwitzgebel, R. L., & Schwitzgebel, R. K. (1980). *Law and psychological practice.* New York: Wiley.

*Scott v. Commonwealth,* 197 S.W.2d 774 (Ky. 1946).

Scott, E., & Grisso, T. (1997). The evolution of adolescence: A developmental perspective on juvenile justice reform. *Journal of Criminal Law and Criminology, 88,* 137–189.

Scroggs, J. R. (1976). Penalties for rape as a function of victim provocativeness, damage, and resistance. *Journal of Applied Social Psychology, 6,* 360–368.

Sedlak, A., & Broadhurst, D. (1996). *Executive summary of the Third National Incidence Study of Child Abuse and Neglect.* Washington, D.C.: U.S. Department of Health and Human Services.

Seedman, A. A., & Hellman, P. (1974). *Chief!* New York: Fields.

Seelau, S. M., & Wells, G. L. (1995). Applied eyewitness research: The other mission. *Law and Human Behavior, 19,* 319–324.

Segell, M. (1997, February). Homophobia doesn't lie. *Esquire,* p. 35.

Sellin, T. (1968). *Capital punishment.* New York: United Nations Publications.

Shaffer, D. R. (1985). The defendant's testimony. In S. Kassin & L. Wrightsman (Eds.), *The psychology of evidence and trial procedure* (pp. 124–149). Beverly Hills, CA: Sage.

*Shannon v. United States,* 114 S.Ct. 2419 (1994).

Shapiro, J.P. (1998, November 9). The wrong men on death row. *U.S. News & World Report,* pp. 22–26.

Shaw, J. S. (1996). Increases in eyewitness confidence resulting from postevent questioning. *Journal of Experimental Psychology: Applied, 12,* 126–146.

Shaw, J. S., Garven, S., & Wood, J. M. (1997). Co-witness information can have immediate effects on eyewitness memory reports. *Law and Human Behavior, 21,* 503–523.

Sheetz, M. (2000). Cyberpredators: Police internet investigations under Florida Statue 847.0135. *University of Miami Law Review, 54,* 405–449.

Sheldon, S. (1994). The role of state bar associations in judicial selection. *Judicature, 77,* 300–305.

Sheldon, W. H. (1942). *The varieties of temperament: A psychology of constitutional differences.* New York: Harper & Row.

Sheldon, W. H. (1949). *Varieties of delinquent youth: An introduction to constitutional psychiatry.* New York: Harper & Row.

Sheley, J. F. (1985). *America's "crime problem": An introduction to criminology.* Belmont, CA: Wadsworth.

*Sheppard v. Maxwell,* 384 U.S. 333 (1966).

Sheppard, B. H., & Vidmar, N. (1980). Adversary pretrial procedures and testimonial evidence: Effects of lawyer's role and Machiavellianism. *Journal of Personality and Social Psychology, 39,* 320–332.

Sheppard, B. H., & Vidmar, N. (1983, June). *Is it fair to worry about fairness?* Paper presented at the meeting of the Law and Society Association, Denver, CO.

*Sherman v. United States,* 356 U.S. 369 (1958).

Sherman, L. W., & Berk, R. A. (1984). *The Minneapolis domestic violence experiment.* Washington, D.C.: Police Foundation.

Shuman, D. W., & Champagne, A. (1997). Removing the people from the legal process: The rhetoric and research on judicial selection and juries. *Psychology, Public Policy, and Law, 3,* 242–258.

Shuman, D. W., & Sales, B. D. (1999). The impact of *Daubert* and its progeny on the admissibility of behavioral and social science evidence. *Psychology, Public Policy, and Law, 5,* 3–15.

Sickmund, M. (1996). Minimum transfer age specified in statute [On-line]. Available: http://ojjdp.ncjrs.org. Office of Juvenile Justice and Delinquency Prevention.

Siegel, A. M., & Elwork, A. (1990). Treating incompetence to stand trial. *Law and Human Behavior, 14,* 57–65.

Sifton, C. P. (1997, November 14). The chief judge likes sentencing guidelines. *National Law Journal,* p. A24.

Silberman, C. E. (1978). *Criminal justice, criminal violence.* New York: Random House.

Silver, E. (1995). Punishment or treatment? Comparing the lengths of confinement of successful and unsuccessful insanity defendants. *Law and Human Behavior, 19,* 375–388.

Silver, E., Cirincione, C., & Steadman, H. J. (1994). Demythologizing inaccurate perceptions of the insanity defense. *Law and Human Behavior, 18,* 63–70.

Simon, R. J. (1966). Murders, juries, and the press: Does sensational reporting lead to verdicts of guilty? *Trans/ Action, 3,* 40–42.

Simon, R. J. (1967). *The jury and the defense of insanity.* Boston: Little, Brown.

Singleton, J. V., & Kass, M. (1986). Helping the jury understand complex cases. *Litigation, 12,* 11–13, 59.

Skeem, J. L., Golding, S. L., Cohn, N. B., & Berge, G. (1998). Logic and reliability of evaluations of competence to stand trial. *Law and Human Behavior, 22,* 519–548.

Skolnick, J. H. (1975). *Justice without trial: Law enforcement in a democratic society* (2nd ed.). New York: Wiley.

Skolnick, J. H., & Bayley, D. H. (1986). *The new blue line: Police innovation in six American cities.* New York: Free Press.

Slade, M. (1994, February 25). Law firms begin reining in sex-harassing partners. *New York Times,* p. B12.

Slater, D., & Hans, V. P. (1984). Public opinion of forensic psychiatry following the Hinckley verdict. *American Journal of Psychiatry, 141,* 675–679.

Sleek, S. (1998a). Better parenting may not be enough for some children. *American Psychological Association Monitor, 29* [On-line]. Available: www.apa.org/monitor/nov98/parent.htm.

Sleek, S. (1998b). Is psychologists' testimony going unheard? *American Psychological Association Monitor, 29* [On-line]. Available: www.apa.org/monitor/feb98/test.html.

Slobogin, C. (1984). Dangerousness and expertise. *University of Pennsylvania Law Review, 133,* 97–117.

Slobogin, C., Melton, G., & Showalter, S.R. (1984). The feasibility of a brief evaluation of mental state at the time of the offense. *Law and Human Behavior, 8,* 305–321.

Slobogin, C., & Schumacher, J. E. (1993). Rating the intrusiveness of law enforcement searches and seizures. *Law and Human Behavior, 17,* 183–200.

Slutske, W., Heath, A., Dinwiddie, S., Madden, P., Bucholz, K., Duhne, M., Statham, D., & Martin, N. (1998). Common genetic risk factors for conduct disorder and alcohol dependence. *Journal of Abnormal Psychology, 107,* 363–374.

Small, M. A. (1997). Introduction to Juvenile Justice: Comments and trends. *Behavioral Science and the Law, 15,* 119–124.

Smith, L., & Malandro, L. (1986). *Courtroom communication strategies.* New York: Kluwer.

Smith, M. C. (1983). Hypnotic memory enhancement of witnesses: Does it work? *Psychological Bulletin, 94,* 387–407.

*Smith v. State,* 686 N.E.2d 1264 (1997).

Smith, S. (1989). Mental health expert witnesses: Of science and crystal balls. *Behavioral Sciences and the Law, 7,* 145–180.

Smith, V. L. (1991). Impact of pretrial instruction on jurors' information processing and decision making. *Journal of Applied Psychology, 76,* 220–228.

Smolowe, J. (1994, February 7). Throw away the key. *Time,* p. 55.

Snarey, J. R. (1985). Cross-cultural universality of social-moral development: A critical review of Kohlbergian research. *Psychological Bulletin, 97,* 202–232.

Snibbe, J., Peterson, P., & Sosner, B. (1980). Study of psychological characteristics of a workers' compensation sample using the MMPI and Millon Clinical Multiaxial Inventory. *Psychological Reports, 47,* 959–966.

Snyder, H. (1998). *Estimated number of juvenile arrests, 1997.* [On-line] Washington, D.C.: Office of Juvenile Justice and Delinquency Prevention. Available: http://jjdp.ncjrs.org/ojstabb/qa001.html.

Solomon, R. C. (1990). *A passion for justice.* Reading, MA: Addison-Wesley.

Solomon, R. M., & Horn, J. M. (1986). Post-shooting traumatic reactions: A pilot study. In J. T. Reese & H. A. Goldstein (Eds.), *Psychological services for law enforcement* (pp. 383–394). Washington, D.C.: U.S. Government Printing Office.

Sontag, S. (1978). *Illness as metaphor.* New York: Farrar, Straus & Giroux.

*Sony Corp. of America v. Universal City Studios,* 78 L.Ed.2d 574 (1984).

Sorenson, S. B., & White, J. W. (1992). Adult sexual assault: Overview of research. *Journal of Social Issues, 48*(1), 1–8.

Soskis, D. A., & Van Zandt, C. R. (1986). Hostage negotiation: Law enforcement's most effective nonlethal weapon. *Behavioral Sciences and the Law, 4*, 423–436.

*South Dakota v. Neville,* 459 U.S. 553 (1983).

Spangenberg Group, The. (2000). Web site: www.criminal justice.org.

Spanos, N. P. (1994). Multiple identity enactments and multiple personality disorder: A sociocognitive perspective. *Psychological Bulletin, 116,* 143–165.

Spanos, N. P., Burgess, C. A., Burgess, M. F., Samuels, C., & Blois, W. O. (1999). Creating false memories of infancy with hypnotic and non-hypnotic procedures. *Applied Cognitive Psychology, 13,* 201–218.

Spanos, N. P., Gwynn, M. I., Comer, S. L., Baltruweit, W. J., & de Groh, M. (1989). Are hypnotically induced pseudo-memories resistant to cross-examination? *Law and Human Behavior, 13*(3), 271–289.

Spanos, N. P., Quigley, C. A., Gwynn, M. I., Glatt, R. L., & Perlini, A. H. (1991). Hypnotic interrogation, pretrial preparation, and witness testimony during direct and cross-examination. *Law and Human Behavior, 15*(6), 639–653.

*Sparf and Hansen v. United States,* 156 U.S. 51 (1895).

Sparr, L. (1995). Post-traumatic stress disorder. *Neurologic Clinics, 13,* 413–429.

Spaulding, W. J. (1990). A look at the AMA Guidelines to the evaluation of permanent impairment: Problems in workers' compensation claims involving mental disability. *Behavioral Sciences and the Law, 8,* 361–373.

Spielberger, C. D. (Ed.). (1979). *Police selection and evaluation: Issues and techniques.* Washington, D.C.: Hemisphere.

Spielberger, C. D., Spaulding, H. C., & Ward, J. C. (1978). *Selecting effective law enforcement officers: The Florida police standards research project.* Tampa, FL: Human Resources Institute.

Spielberger, C. D., Westberry, L. G., Grier, K. S., & Greenfield, G. (1980). *The police stress survey: Sources of stress in law enforcement.* Tampa, FL: Human Resources Institute.

Sporer, S., Penrod, S., Read, D., & Cutler, B. L. (1995). Choosing, confidence, and accuracy: A meta-analysis of the confidence-accuracy relation in eyewitness identification studies. *Psychological Bulletin, 118,* 315–327.

Standish, F. (1984, January 31). Child abuser sentenced to treatment. *Lawrence (KS) Journal-World,* p. 8.

*Stanford v. Kentucky,* 492 U.S. 361 (1989).

*State v. Collins,* 464 A.2d 1028 (Md. App. 1983).

*State v. Damms,* 9 Wisc.2d 183, 100 N.W.2d 592 (1960).

*State v. Dorsey,* 539 P.2d 204 (N.M. 1975).

*State v. Gardner,* 947 P.2d 630 (Ut. 1997).

*State v. Hayes,* 389 A.2d 1379 (1978).

*State v. Johnson,* 133 Wisc.2d 307, 395 N.W.2d 176 (1986).

*State v. Johnston,* 979 S.W.2d 461 (Mo. App. 1998).

*State of Kansas v. Brown,* 430 P.2d 499 (1982).

*State of Kansas v. Warren,* 635 P.2d 1236 (1981).

*State v. Lozano,* 616 So.2d 73 (Fla. App. 1993).

*State v. Massey,* 803 P.2d 340 (Wash. 1990).

*State v. Michaels,* 136 N.J. 299, 642 A.2d 1372 (N.J., 1994).

*State of Minnesota v. Mack,* 292 N.W.2d 764 (Minn. 1980).

*State of New Jersey v. Hurd,* 432 A.2d 86 (N.J. 1981).

*State v. Reeves,* 448 S.E.2d 802 (N.C. 1994).

*State v. Wilson,* 685 So.2d 1063 (La. 1996).

Steadman, H. J. (1979). *Beating a rap? Defendants found incompetent to stand trial.* Chicago: University of Chicago Press.

Steadman, H. J., & Braff, J. (1983). Defendants not guilty by reason of insanity. In J. Monahan & H. J. Steadman (Eds.), *Mentally disordered offenders: Perspectives from law and social science.* New York: Plenum.

Steadman, H. J., Cocozza, J. J., & Veysey, B. M. (1999). Comparing outcomes for diverted and nondiverted jail detainees with mental illness. *Law and Human Behavior, 23,* 615–628.

Steadman, H. J., Keitner, L., Braff, J., & Arvanites, T. M. (1983). Factors associated with a successful insanity plea. *American Journal of Psychiatry, 140,* 401–405.

Steadman, H. J., Monahan, J., Hartstone, E., Davis, S. K., & Robbins, P. C. (1982). Mentally disordered offenders: A national survey of patients and facilities. *Law and Human Behavior, 6,* 31–38.

Steadman, H. J., Rosenstein, M. J., MacAskill, R. L., & Manderscheid, R. W. (1988). A profile of mentally disordered offenders admitted to inpatient psychiatric services in the United States. *Law and Human Behavior, 12,* 91–99.

Steblay, N. (1997). Social influence in eyewitness recall: A meta-analytic review of lineup instruction effects. *Law and Human Behavior, 21,* 283–298.

Steblay, N., Besirevic, J., Fulero, S., & Jiminez-Lorente, B. (1999). The effects of pretrial publicity on jury verdicts: A meta-analytic review. *Law and Human Behavior, 23,* 219–235.

Steblay, N. M., & Bothwell, R. K. (1994). Evidence for hypnotically refreshed testimony: The view from the laboratory. *Law and Human Behavior, 18,* 635–652.

Steele, W. W., & Thornburg, E. G. (1988). Jury instructions: A persistent failure to communicate. *North Carolina Law Review, 67,* 77–119.

Steffen, L. (Ed.). (1996). *Abortion : A reader.* Cleveland, OH: Pilgrim.

Steinmetz, S. K., & Straus, M. (1974). *Violence in the family.* New York: Harper & Row.

Stevens, R. (1973). Law schools and law students. *Virginia Law Review, 59,* 551–707.

Stevens, R. (1983). *Law school: Legal education in America from the 1850s to the 1980s.* Chapel Hill: University of North Carolina Press.

Stinson, V., Devenport, J. L., Cutler, B. L., & Kravitz, D. A. (1996). How effective is the presence-of-counsel safeguard? Attorney perceptions of suggestiveness, fairness, and correctability of biased lineup procedures. *Journal of Applied Psychology, 81,* 64–75.

Stith, K., & Cabranes, J. A. (1998). *Fear of judging: Sentencing guidelines in the federal courts.* Chicago: University of Chicago Press.

Stolzenberg, L., & D'Alessio, S. J. (1997). "Three strikes and you're out": The impact of California's new mandatory sentencing law on serious crime rates. *Crime and Delinquency, 43,* 457–469.

*Stone v. Powell,* 428 U.S. 465 (1976).

Stormo, K. J., Lang, A. R., & Stritzke, W. G. K. (1997). Attributions about acquaintance rape: The role of alcohol and individual differences. *Journal of Applied Social Psychology, 27,* 279–305.

Strasser, F. (1989, June 26). Look-alikes win in court. *National Law Journal,* p. 63.

*Strauder v. West Virginia,* 100 U.S. 303 (1880).

Straus, M. A., & Gelles, R. J. (1988). How violent are American families? Estimates from the National Family Violence Resurvey and other studies. In G. T. Hotaling, D. Finkelhor, J. T. Kirkpatrick, & M. A. Straus (Eds.), *Family abuse and its consequences* (pp. 14–36). Thousand Oaks, CA: Sage.

Streib V. (1983). Death penalty for children: The American experience with capital punishment for crimes committed while under age eighteen. *Oklahoma Law Review, 36,* 613–641.

*Strickland v. Washington,* 466 U.S. 668 (1984).

Strier, F. (1996). *Reconstructing justice: An agenda for trial reform.* Westport, CT: Quorum.

Strier, F. (1999). Whither trial consulting? Issues and projections. *Law and Human Behavior, 23,* 93–115.

Strodtbeck, F., James, R., & Hawkins, C. (1957). Social status in jury deliberations. *American Sociological Review, 22,* 713–718.

Strodtbeck, F., & Lipinski, R. M. (1985). Becoming first among equals: Moral considerations in jury foreman selection. *Journal of Personality and Social Psychology, 49,* 927–936.

Strong, J. W. (1999). *McCormick on evidence.* St. Paul: West.

Studebaker, C. A. & Penrod, S. D. (1997). Pretrial publicity: The media, the law and common sense. *Psychology, Public Policy, and Law, 2/3,* 428–460.

Sullivan, C. M., & Bybee, D. I. (1999). Reducing violence using community-based advocacy for women with abusive partners. *Journal of Consulting and Clinical Psychology, 67,* 43–53.

Sullivan, R. (1991, September 26). The bar's battlers for bail: Advocacy, 24 hours a day. *New York Times,* p. A16.

Super, J. T. (1997). Selected legal and ethical aspects of fitness for duty evaluations. *Journal of Criminal Justice, 25,* 223–229.

Surgeon General's Scientific Advisory Committee on Television and Social Behavior. (1972). *Television and growing up: The impact of televised*

*violence.* Washington, D.C.: U.S. Government Printing Office.

Susman, D. (1992). *Effects of three different legal standards on psychologists' determinations of competency for execution.* Unpublished doctoral dissertation, University of Kentucky, Lexington.

Sutherland, E. H. (1947). *Principles of criminology* (4th ed.). Philadelphia: Lippincott.

Sutherland, E. H., & Cressey, D. R. (1974). *Principles of criminology* (9th ed.). New York: Lippincott.

Sutker, P., Davis, J. M., Uddo, M., & Ditta, S. (1995). War zone stresses, personal resources, and PTSD in Persian Gulf returnees. *Journal of Abnormal Psychology, 104,* 444–452.

*Swain v. Alabama,* 380 U.S. 202 (1965).

Swartz, J. D. (1985). Review of Inwald Personality Inventory. In J. V. Mitchell (Ed.), *The ninth mental measurements yearbook* (pp. 711–713). Lincoln: Buros Institute of Mental Measurements, University of Nebraska.

*Sweatt v. Painter,* 210 S.W. 2d 442 (1947), 339 U.S. 629 (1950).

Swenson, L. C. (1993). *Psychology and law for the helping professions.* Pacific Grove, CA: Brooks/Cole.

Swim, J. K., & Sanna, L. J. (1996). He's skilled, she's lucky: A meta-analysis of observers' attributions for women's and men's successes and failures. *Personality and Social Psychology Bulletin, 22,* 507–519.

Sydeman, S. J., Cascardi, M., Poythress, N. G., & Ritterband, L. M. (1997). Procedural justice in the context of civil commitment: A critique of Tyler's analysis. *Psychology, Public Policy, and Law, 3,* 207–221.

Taber, J. (1988). Gender, legal education, and the legal profession: An empirical study of Stanford law students and graduates. *Stanford Law Review, 40,* 1209–1297.

Tanford, J. A. (1990). The law and psychology of jury instructions. *Nebraska Law Review, 69,* 71–111.

Tanford, J. A. (1991). Law reforms by courts, legislatures, and commissions following empirical research on jury instructions. *Law and Society Review, 25,* 155–175.

Tapp, J. L., & Levine, F. J. (1970). Persuasion to virtue: A preliminary statement. *Law and Society Review, 4,* 565–582.

Tapp, J. L., & Levine, F. J. (1974). Legal socialization: Strategies for an ethi-

cal legality. *Stanford Law Review, 24,* 1–72.

*Tarasoff v. Regents of the University of California,* 17 Cal.3d 425, 551 P.2d 334, 131 Cal.Rptr. 14 (1976).

Taubman, B. (1988). *The preppy murder trial.* New York: St. Martin's.

*Taylor v. Louisiana,* 419 U.S. 522 (1975).

Taylor, G. (1992, March 2). Justice overlooked. *National Law Journal,* p. 43.

Taylor, G. (1993, February 1). Three grand juries hear case. *National Law Journal,* pp. 3, 35.

Taylor, S., Jr. (1986, May 6). Justices reject broad challenge in capital cases. *New York Times,* pp. 1, 12.

Taylor, S., Jr. (1987a, May 27). Court backs law letting U.S. widen pretrial jailing. *New York Times,* pp. 1, 89.

Taylor, S., Jr. (1987b, June 16). Justices, 5–4, bar impact evidence in death hearings. *New York Times,* pp. 1, 5.

Taylor, S., Jr. (1987c, June 23). Some hypnosis-enhanced testimony is upheld. *New York Times,* p. 12.

Taylor, S., Jr. (1988a, June 16). Court reaffirms limits in questioning of suspects. *New York Times,* p. 9.

Taylor, S., Jr. (1988b, June 23). Rulings curb protection in white-collar crimes. *New York Times,* p. 11.

Taylor, S. E., & Crocker, J. (1981). Schematic bases of social information processing. In E. T. Higgins, C. P. Herman, & M. P. Zanna (Eds.), *Social cognition: The Ontario symposium* (Vol. 1). Hillsdale, NJ: Erlbaum.

Taylor, S. E., Klein, L. C., Lewis, B. P., Gruenewald, T. L., Gurung, R. A.R., & Updegraff, J. A. (2000). Biobehavioral responses to stress in females: Tend-and-befriend, not fight-or-flight. *Psychological Review, 107,* 411–429.

*Teague v. Lane,* 489 U.S. 288 (1989).

Teahan, J. E. (1975a). A longitudinal study of attitude shifts among black and white police officers. *Journal of Social Issues, 31*(1), 47–56.

Teahan, J. E. (1975b). Role playing and group experience to facilitate attitude and value changes among black and white police officers. *Journal of Social Issues, 31*(1), 35–46.

Teitelbaum, L. (1991). Gender, legal education, and legal careers. *Journal of Legal Education, 41,* 443–480.

*Tennessee v. Garner,* 105 S.Ct. 1694 (1985).

Teplin, L. A. (1984). The criminalization of the mentally ill: Speculation in search of data. In L. A. Teplin (Ed.),

*Mental health and criminal justice* (pp. 63–85). Newbury Park, CA: Sage.

Teplin, L. A. (1994). Psychiatric and substance abuse disorders among male urban jail detainees. *American Journal of Public Health, 84,* 290–293.

Teplin, L. A., Abram, K. M., & McClelland, G. M. (1996). The prevalence of psychiatric disorder among incarcerated women. I: Pre-trial detainees. *Archives of General Psychiatry, 53,* 505–512.

Terman, L. M. (1917). A trial of mental and pedagogical tests in a civil service examination for policemen and firemen. *Journal of Applied Psychology, 1,* 17–29.

Terpstra, D. E., & Baker, D. D. (1987). A hierarchy of sexual harassment. *Journal of Psychology, 121,* 599–605.

Terpstra, D. E., & Baker, D. D. (1988). Outcomes of sexual harassment charges. *Academy of Management Journal, 31,* 185–194.

Terpstra, D. E., & Baker, D. D. (1992). Outcomes of federal court decisions on sexual harassment. *Academy of Management Journal, 35,* 181–190.

*Terry v. Ohio,* 391 U.S. 1 (1968).

Thibaut, J., & Walker, L. (1975). *Procedural justice: A psychological analysis.* Hillsdale, NJ: Erlbaum.

Thibaut, J., Walker, L., & Lind, E. A. (1972). Adversary presentation and bias in legal decision making. *Harvard Law Review, 86,* 386–401.

Thomas, E. (1991). *The man to see.* New York: Simon & Schuster.

*Thompson v. Oklahoma,* 487 U.S. 815 (1988).

Thompson, M. (1989, April 3). Misprint. *New Republic,* pp. 14–15.

Thompson, W. C. (1989). Death qualification after *Wainwright v. Witt* and *Lockhart v. McCree. Law and Human Behavior, 13,* 185–215.

Thompson, W. C., Cowan, C. L., Ellsworth, P. C., & Harrington, J. C. (1984). Death penalty attitudes and conviction proneness: The translation of attitudes into verdicts. *Law and Human Behavior, 8,* 95–113.

Thompson, W. C., Fong, G. T., & Rosenhan, D. L. (1981). Inadmissible evidence and juror verdicts. *Journal of Personality and Social Psychology, 40,* 453–463.

Thompson, W. C., & Ford, S. (1989). DNA typing: Acceptance and weight of the new genetic identification tests. *Virginia Law Review, 75,* 45–108.

Thornton, H. (1995). *Hung jury: The diary of a Menendez juror.* Philadelphia: Temple University Press.

Tierney, K. (1979). *Darrow: A biography.* New York: Crowell.

Tigar, M. E. (1996, July 29). At trial, grab the chance for a grand opening. *National Law Journal,* p. A19.

*Tippins v. Walker,* 889 F. Supp. 91 (S.D.N.Y. 1995).

*Tison v. Arizona,* 481 U.S. 137 (1987).

Tobey, A. E., & Goodman, G. S. (1992). Children's eyewitness memory: Effects of participation and forensic context. *Child Abuse and Neglect, 16,* 779–796.

Tomkins, A. J. (1988, October). Using social science evidence to prove discrimination. *APA Monitor,* p. 40.

Tonry, M. (1996). *Sentencing matters.* New York: Oxford University Press.

Toobin, J. (1996a, December 9). Asking for it. *New Yorker,* pp. 55–60.

Toobin, J. (1996b, September 9). The Marcia Clark verdict. *New Yorker,* pp. 58–71.

Tooley, V., Brigham, J. C., Maass, A., & Bothwell, R. K. (1987). Facial recognition: Weapon effect and attentional focus. *Journal of Applied Social Psychology, 17,* 845–859.

Toplikar, D. (1984, December 9). Court ruling won't alter local procedure on drunken drivers. *Lawrence (KS) Journal-World,* p. 6A.

Torry, S., & Lawrence, B. H. (1989, March 13–19). Free agents in the legal big leagues. *Washington Post National Weekly Edition,* p. 11.

Touhy, A. P., Wrennall, M. J., McQueen, R. A., & Stradling, S. G. (1993). Effect of socialization factors on decisions to prosecute: The organizational adaptation of Scottish police recruits. *Law and Human Behavior, 17,* 167–182.

Toulmin, S. (1990). *Cosmopolis: The hidden agenda of modernity.* New York: Free Press.

*Townsend v. Swain,* 372 U.S. 293 (1963).

Tsushima, W. T., Foote, R., Merrill, T. S., & Lehrke, S. A. (1996). How independent are independent psychological examinations: A workers' compensation dilemma. *Professional Psychology: Research and Practice, 27,* 626–628.

Tubb, V., Kassin, S., Memon, A., & Hosch, H. (2000). *Experts' views of research on eyewitness testimony after Daubert: Kassin et al. (1989) revisited.* Paper presented at American Psychology-Law Society, New Orleans.

Turkheimer, E., & Parry, C. D. H. (1992). Why the gap? Practice and policy in civil commitment hearings. *American Psychologist, 47,* 646–655.

Turkington, C. (1985, April). Psychiatric help ruled to be defendant right. *APA Monitor,* p. 2.

*Turner v. Safley,* 482 U.S. 78 (1987).

Tyler, T. R. (1990). *Why people obey the law: Procedural justice, legitimacy, and compliance.* New Haven, CT: Yale University Press.

Tyler, T. R., & Belliveau, M. A. (1995). Tradeoffs in justice principles: Definitions of fairness. In B. Bunker, J. Z. Rubin, and Associates (Eds.), *Conflict, cooperation, and justice* (pp. 291–314). San Francisco: Jossey-Bass.

Tyler, T. R., & Caine, A. (1981). The influence of outcomes and procedures on satisfaction with formal leaders. *Journal of Personality and Social Psychology, 41,* 642–655.

Tyler, T. R., Rasinski, K. A., & McGraw, K. (1985). The influence of perceived injustice on the endorsement of political leaders. *Journal of Applied Social Psychology, 15,* 700–725.

*Unauthorized Practice of Law Committee v. Parsons Technology,* 179 F.3d 956 (5th Cir. 1999).

*Unauthorized Practice of Law Committee v. Quicken Family Lawyer,* 1999 WL 47235 (C.D. Tex. 1999).

Underwager, R., & Wakefield, H. (1992). Poor psychology produces poor law. *Law and Human Behavior, 16,* 233–243.

Underwood, R. H., & Fortune, W. H. (1988). *Trial ethics.* Boston: Little, Brown.

*United States v. Armstrong,* 116 St.C. 1480 (1996).

*United States v. Barrett,* 8 F.3d 1296 (8th Cir. 1993).

*United States v. Burgess,* 175 F.3d 1261 (11th Cir. 1999).

*United States v. Burr,* 24 F.Cas. 49 (D.Va. 1807).

*United States v. Dellinger,* 475 F.2d 340, 368 (7th Cir. 1972).

*United States v. Dougherty,* 473 F.2d 1113, 1130–1137 (D.C. Cir. 1972).

*United States v. Galbreth,* 908 F. Supp. 877 (D.N.M. 1995).

*United States v. Goff,* 6 F.3d 363 (6th Cir. 1993).

*United States v. Jordan,* 924 F.Supp. 443 (W.D.N.Y. 1996).

*United States v. Leon,* 468 U.S. 897 (1984).

*United States v. Masthers,* 549 F.2d 721 (D.C. Cir. 1976).

*United States v. McVeigh,* 918 F. Supp. 1467 (W.D. Okla. 1996).

*United States v. Miller,* 425 U.S. 431 (1976).

*United States v. Montoya de Hernandez,* 105 S.Ct. 3304 (1985).

*United States v. Ovalle,* 136 F. 3d 1092 (6th Cir. 1998).

*United States v. Payner,* 447 U.S. 727 (1980).

*United States v. Robinson,* 414 U.S. 218 (1973).

*United States v. Ross,* 456 U.S. 798 (1982).

*United States v. Salerno,* 481 U.S. 739 (1987).

*United States v. Santiago-Martinez,* 94-10350, 9th U.S. Court of Appeals (1995).

*United States v. Scheffer,* 118 S.Ct. 1261 (1998).

*United States v. Telfaire,* 469 F.2d 552 (D.C. Cir. 1972).

*United States v. Twigg,* 588 F.2d 373 (3d Cir. 1978).

*United States v. Wade,* 388 U.S. 218 (1967).

U.S. Congress, Office of Technology Assessment. (1990). *The use of integrity tests for pre-employment screening* (OTA-SET-442). Washington, D.C.: U.S. Government Printing Office.

U.S. Department of Health and Human Services, National Center on Child Abuse and Neglect. (1996). *Child maltreatment 1994: Reports from the states to the National Center on Child Abuse and Neglect.* Washington, D.C.: U.S. Government Printing Office.

U.S. Department of Health and Human Services, National Center on Child Abuse and Neglect. (1997). *Child maltreatment 1995: Reports from the states to the National Center on Child Abuse and Neglect.* Washington, D.C.: U.S. Government Printing Office.

U.S. Department of Justice. (1998). *Prison and jail inmates at midyear 1998* (NCJ173414). Washington, D.C.: U.S. Department of Justice.

U.S. Department of Justice. (1999). *Eyewitness evidence: A guide for law enforcement.* Washington, D.C.: Author.

U.S. Equal Employment Opportunity Commission. (1980, November 10). Final amendment to guidelines on discrimination because of sex under Title VII of the Civil Rights Act of 1964 as amended. 19 CFR Part 1604. *Federal Register, 45,* 74675-74677.

U.S. General Accounting Office. (1990). *Death penalty sentencing.* Washington, D.C.: U.S. Government Printing Office.

Ustad, K. L., Rogers, R., Sewell, K. W., & Guarnaccia, C. A. (1996). Restoration of competency to stand trial: Assessment with the Georgia Court Competency Test and the Competency Screening Test. *Law and Human Behavior, 20,* 131–146.

Uviller, H. R. (1988). *Tempered zeal: A Columbia law professor's year on the streets with the New York City police.* New York: Contemporary Books.

*Vacco v. Quill,* 117 S. Ct. 2293 (1997).

VanDuyn, A.L. (1999). The scarlet letter branding: A constitutional analysis of community notification provisions in sex offender statues. *Drake Law Review, 47,* 635–59.

Van Dyke, J. (1977). *Jury selection procedures.* Cambridge, MA: Ballinger.

Varela, J. G., Scogin, F. R., & Vipperman, R. K. (1999). Development and preliminary validation of a semi-structured interview for the screening of law enforcement candidates. *Behavioral Sciences and the Law, 17,* 467–481.

Verlinden, S., Hersen, M., & Thomas, J. (2000). Risk factors in school shootings. *Clinical Psychology Review, 20,* 3–56.

*Vernonia School District v. Acton,* 115 S.Ct. 2386 (1995).

Vidmar, N. (1994). Making inferences about jury behavior from jury verdict statistics: Caution about Lorelei's lied. *Law and Human Behavior, 18,* 599–618.

Vidmar, N. (1995). *Medical malpractice and the American jury.* Ann Arbor: University of Michigan Press.

Vidmar, N. (1997). Generic prejudice and the presumption of guilt in sex abuse trials. *Law and Human Behavior, 21,* 5–25.

Vidmar, N. (1998). The performance of the American civil jury: An empirical perspective. *Arizona Law Review, 40,* 849–899.

Vidmar, N. (1999). Juries don't make legal decisions! And other problems: A critique of Hastie et al. on punitive damages. *Law and Human Behavior, 23,* 705–714.

Vidmar, N., & Rice, J. J. (1993). Assessments of noneconomic damage awards in medical negligence: A comparison of jurors with legal professionals. *Iowa Law Review, 78,* 883–911.

Vinacke, W. E. (1959). Sex roles in a three-person game. *Sociometry, 22,* 343–360.

Vinson, D. E., & Anthony, P. K. (1985). *Social science research methods for litigation.* Charlottesville, VA: Michie.

Vise, D. A. (1989, August 713). Using a Mafia law to bust high-flying stockbrokers. *Washington Post National Weekly Edition,* p. 20.

Visher, C. A. (1987). Juror decision making: The importance of evidence. *Law and Human Behavior, 11,* 1–18.

Wadden, T. A., & Anderton, C. H. (1982). The clinical use of hypnosis. *Psychological Bulletin, 91,* 215–243.

*Wade v. United States,* 504 U.S. 181 (1992).

*Wainwright v. Sykes,* 428 U.S. 465 (1977).

*Wainwright v. Witt,* 53 L.W. 4108 (1985).

Wakefield, H., & Underwager, R. (1992). Recovered memories of alleged sexual abuse: Lawsuits against parents. *Behavioral Sciences and the Law, 10,* 483–507.

Waldo, C. R., Berdahl, J. L., & Fitzgerald, L. F. (1998). Are men sexually harassed? If so, by whom? *Law and Human Behavior, 22,* 59–80.

Walker, L. (1979). *The battered woman.* New York: Harper & Row.

Walker, L. (1984a). *The battered woman syndrome.* New York: Springer.

Walker, L. (1984b). Sex differences in the development of moral reasoning: A critical review. *Child Development, 55,* 677–691.

Walker, L. E. (1992). Battered woman syndrome and self-defense. *Notre Dame Journal of Law, Ethics, and Public Policy, 6,* 321–334.

Walker, L. E. (1993). Battered women as defendants. In N. Z. Hilton (Ed.), *Legal responses to wife assault: Current trends and evaluation* (pp. 233–257). Newbury Park, CA: Sage.

Walker, L., La Tour, S., Lind, E. A., & Thibaut, J. (1974). Reactions of participants and observers to modes of adjudication. *Journal of Applied Social Psychology, 4,* 295–310.

Walker, S. (1982, October). What have civil liberties ever done for crime victims? Plenty! *ACJS Academy of Criminal Justice Sciences Today,* pp. 4–5.

Walker, W. (1989, February 19). In cold DNA. *New York Times Book Review,* p. 11.

Walster, E. (1966). Assignment of responsibility for an accident. *Journal of Personality and Social Psychology,* 3, 73–79.

Walster, E., Walster, G. W., & Berscheid, E. (1978). *Equity: Theory and research.* Boston: Allyn & Bacon.

Wambaugh, J. (1989). *The blooding.* New York: Morrow.

Ward, J. (1998, May 18). Boalt boosts minority enrollment by downplaying grades, scores. *National Law Journal,* p. A16.

Warner-Rogers, J. E., Hansen, D. J., & Hecht, D. B. (1999). Child physical abuse and neglect. In V. Van Hasselt & M. Hersen (Eds.), *Handbook of psychological approaches with violent offenders* (pp. 329–356). New York: Kluwer Academic/Plenum.

Warren, A. R., Woodall, C. E., Hunt, J. S., & Perry, N. W. (1996). "It sounds good in theory, but . . .": Do investigative interviewers follow guidelines based on memory research? *Child Maltreatment,* 1, 231–245.

Warren, E. (1977). *The memoirs of Earl Warren.* Garden City, NY: Doubleday.

Warshaw, R. (1988). *I never called it rape.* New York: Harper & Row.

Wasby, S. L., & Brody, D.C. (1997). Studies of repressed memory and the issue of legal validity. *Law and Human Behavior,* 21, 687–691.

*Washington v. Glucksberg,* 117 S. Ct. 2258 (1997).

*Washington v. Harper,* 494 U.S. 210 (1990).

Watson, P. (1996). The search for justice-A case for reform in the civil justice system in Britain. *ILSA Journal of International and Comparative Law,* 2, 453.

Watts, B. L., Messe, L. A., & Vallacher, R. R. (1982). Toward understanding sex differences in reward allocation: Agency, communion and reward distribution behavior. *Sex Roles,* 8, 1175–1187..

*Wayte v. United States,* 105 S.Ct. 1524 (1985).

*Webster v. Reproductive Health Services,* 109 S.Ct. 3040 (1989).

Webster, C. D. (1998). Comment on Thomas Mathiesen's *Selective Incapacitation Revisited. Law and Human Behavior,* 22, 471–476.

Webster, C. D., Douglas, K. S., Eaves, D., & Hart, S. D. (1997). *HCR-20: Assessing risk for violence (Version 2).* Burnaby, Canada, Mental Health, Law, and Policy Institute, Simon Fraser University.

Webster, C. D., Harris, G.T., Rice, M. E., Cormier, C., & Quinsey, V.L. (1994). *The violence prediction scheme: Assessing dangerousness in high risk men.* Toronto: University of Toronto, Centre of Criminology.

*Weeks v. Angelone,* 120 S.Ct. 1290 (2000).

Wegner, D. M. (1989). *White bears and other unwanted thoughts: Suppression, obsession, and the psychology of mental control.* New York: Viking.

Wegner, D. M. (1994). Ironic processes of mental control. *Psychological Review,* 101, 34–52.

Wegner, D. M., & Erber, R. (1992). The hyperaccessibility of suppressed thoughts. *Journal of Personality and Social Psychology,* 63, 903–912.

Wegner, D. M., Schneider, D. J., Carter, S., III, & White, T. (1987). Paradoxical effects of thought suppression. *Journal of Personality and Social Psychology,* 53, 5–13.

Weir, J. A., Willis, C. E., & Wrightsman, L. S. (1989). *Reactions of jurors to rape victims on the witness stand.* Paper presented at the meeting of the American Psychological Association, New Orleans.

Weir, J. A., & Wrightsman, L. S. (1990). The determinants of mock jurors' verdicts in a rape case. *Journal of Applied Social Psychology,* 20, 901–919.

Weissman, H. N. (1985). Psycholegal standards and the role of psychological assessment in personal injury litigation. *Behavioral Sciences and the Law,* 3, 135–148.

Weissman, H. N. (1991). Child custody evaluations: Fair and unfair professional practices. *Behavioral Sciences and the Law,* 9, 469–476.

Weitzer, R., & Tuch, S. A. (1999). Race, class, and perceptions of discrimination by the police. *Crime and Delinquency,* 45, 494–507.

Wells, G. L. (1980). Asymmetric attributions for compliance: Reward versus punishment. *Journal of Experimental Social Psychology,* 16, 47–60.

Wells, G. L. (1992). Naked statistical evidence of liability: Is subjective probability enough? *Journal of Personality and Social Psychology,* 62, 739–752.

Wells, G. L. (1993). What do we know about eyewitness identification? *American Psychologist,* 48, 553–571.

Wells, G. L. & Bradfield, A. L. (1998). "Good, you identified the suspect": Feedback to eyewitnesses distorts their reports of the witnessing experience. *Journal of Applied Psychology,* 83, 360–376.

Wells, G. L., & Bradfield, A. L. (1999). Distortions in eyewitnesses' recollections: Can the postidentification-feedback effect be moderated? *Psychological Science,* 10, 138–144.

Wells, G. L., & Lindsay, R. C. L. (1980). On estimating the diagnosticity of eyewitness nonidentifications. *Psychological Bulletin,* 88, 776–784.

Wells, G. L., Lindsay, R. C. L., & Ferguson, T. J. (1979). Accuracy, confidence, and juror perceptions in eyewitness identification. *Journal of Applied Psychology,* 64, 440–448.

Wells, G. L., & Loftus, E. F. (1984). Eyewitness research: Then and now. In G. L. Wells & E. F. Loftus (Eds.), *Eyewitness testimony: Psychological perspectives* (pp. 1–11). New York: Cambridge University Press.

Wells, G. L., Miene, P. K., & Wrightsman, L. S. (1985). The timing of the defense opening statement: Don't wait until the evidence is in. *Journal of Applied Social Psychology,* 15, 758–772.

Wells, G. L., & Murray, D. M. (1983). What can psychology say about the *Neil v. Biggers* criteria for judging eyewitness accuracy? *Journal of Applied Psychology,* 68, 347–362.

Wells, G. L., Small, M., Penrod, S., Malpass, R.S., Fulero, S. M., & Brimacombe, C. A. E. (1998). Eyewitness identification procedures: Recommendations for lineups and photospreads. *Law and Human Behavior,* 22, 603–647.

Wells, G .L., Wright, E. F., & Bradfield, A. L. (1999). Witnesses to crime: Social and cognitive factors governing the validity of people's reports. In R. Roesch, S. D. Hart, & J. Ogloff, (Eds.), *Psychology and law: The state of the discipline* (pp. 53–87). New York: Kluwer Academic/Plenum.

Westbrook, T. (1998). At least treat us like criminals: South Carolina responds to victims' pleas for equal rights. *South Carolina Law Review,* 49, 575–576.

Westley, W. A. (1970). *Violence and the police: A sociological study of law, custom, and morality.* Cambridge, MA: MIT Press.

Wetter, M., Baer, R., Berry, D., Smith, G., & Larsen, L. (1992). Sensitivity of MMPI-2 validity scales to random responding and malingering. *Psychological Assessment,* 4, 369–374.

Wexler, D. B. (1992). Putting mental health into mental health law: Therapeutic jurisprudence. *Law and Human Behavior, 16,* 27–38.

*Whalen v. United States,* 346 F.2d 812 (1965).

Whipple, S. B. (1937). *The trial of Bruno Richard Hauptmann.* New York: Doubleday.

White, J. W., Lawrence, S., Biggerstaff, C., & Grubb, T. D. (1985). Factors of stress among police officers. *Criminal Justice and Behavior, 12,* 111–128.

White, J. W., & Sorenson, S. B. (1992). A sociocultural view of sexual assault: From discrepancy to diversity. *Journal of Social Issues,* 48(1), 187–195.

Whittemore, K. E., & Ogloff, J. R. P. (1995). Factors that influence jury decision making: Disposition instructions and mental state at the time of the trial. *Law and Human Behavior, 19,* 283–303.

*Whren et al. v. United States,* 517 U.S. 806 (1996).

Wicker, T. (1985, June 28). Gnawing doubt—if those who are executed may prove to be innocent. *Lawrence (KS) Journal-World,* p. 4.

Widom, C. S. (1989). Child abuse, neglect, and adult behavior: Research design and findings on criminality, violence, and child abuse. *American Journal of Orthopsychiatry, 59,* 355–367.

Widom, C. S. (1992). *The cycle of violence: National Institute of Justice research in brief.* Washington, D.C.: U.S. Department of Justice.

Wiener, R. L., & Gutek, B. A. (1999). Advances in sexual harassment research, theory, and policy. *Psychology, Public Policy, and Law, 5,* 507–518.

Wiener, R. L., & Hurt, L. E. (1999). An interdisciplinary approach to understanding social sexual conduct at work. *Psychology, Public Policy, and Law, 5,* 556–595.

Wiener, R. L., Hurt, L., Russell, B., Mannen, K., & Gasper, C. (1997). Perceptions of sexual harassment: The effects of gender, legal standard, and ambivalent sexism. *Law and Human Behavior, 21,* 71–94.

Wiener, R. L., Wiener, A. T. F., & Grisso, T. (1989). Empathy and biased assimilation of testimonies in cases of alleged rape. *Law and Human Behavior, 13,* 343–356.

Wigmore, J. H. (1970). *Evidence* (Vol. 3). (Revised by J. H. Chadbourn).

Boston: Little, Brown. (Original work published 1940)

Wildman, R. W., II, Batchelor, E. S., Thompson, L., Nelson, F. R., Moore, J. T., Patterson, M. E., & de Laosa, M. (1978). *The Georgia Court Competency Test: An attempt to develop a rapid, quantitative measure of fitness for trial.* Unpublished manuscript, Forensic Services Division, Central State Hospital, Milledgeville, GA.

Wilkes, J. (1987, June). Murder in mind. *Psychology Today,* pp. 26–32.

*Wilkins v. Missouri,* 492 U.S. 361 (1989).

Will, G. (1984, January 22). Fitting laws to dynamic society likened to trousers on 10-year-old. *Lawrence (KS) Journal-World,* p. 6.

Will, G. (1987, June 21). Narrowing truths provided by victim-impact statement. *Lawrence (KS) Journal-World,* p. 5A.

*Willett v. State,* 993 S.W.2d 929 (Ark. 1999).

*Williams v. Florida,* 399 U.S. 78 (1970).

Williams, C. W., Lees-Haley, P. R., & Djanogly, S. E. (1999). Clinical scrutiny of litigants' self-reports. *Professional Psychology: Research and Practice, 30,* 361–367.

Williams, L. M. (1994). Recall of childhood trauma: A prospective study of women's memories of child sexual abuse. *Journal of Consulting and Clinical Psychology, 62,* 1167–1176.

Williams, W., & Miller, K. S. (1981). The processing and disposition of incompetent mentally ill offenders. *Law and Human Behavior, 5,* 245–261.

*Wilson v. Arkansas,* 115 S.Ct. 1914 (1995).

*Wilson v. United States,* 391 F.2d 460 (1968).

Wilson, A. E., Calhoun, K. S., & Bernat, J. A. (1999). Risk recognition and trauma-related symptoms among sexually revictimized women. *Journal of Consulting and Clinical Psychology, 67,* 705–710.

Wilson, F. L. (1995). The effects of age, gender, and ethnic/cultural background on moral reasoning. *Journal of Social Behavior and Personality, 10,* 67–78.

Wilson, J. Q. (1975). *Thinking about crime.* New York: Basic Books.

Wilson, J. Q. (1978). *Varieties of police behavior* (2nd ed.). Cambridge, MA: Harvard University Press.

Wilson, J. Q., & Herrnstein, R. (1985). *Crime and human nature.* New York: Simon & Schuster.

Wilson, J. Q., & Kelling, G. L. (1989, April 24). Beating criminals to the punch. *New York Times,* p. 23.

Wilson, J. R., & Bornstein, B. H. (1998). Methodological considerations in pretrial publicity research: Is the medium the message? *Law and Human Behavior, 22,* 585–597.

Wilson, L., Greene, E., & Loftus, E. F. (1986). Beliefs about forensic hypnosis. *International Journal of Clinical and Experimental Hypnosis, 34,* 110–121.

Wilt, G., Bannon, J., Breedlove, R., Sandker, D., & Michaelson, S. (1977). *Domestic violence and the police—Studies in Detroit and Kansas City.* Washington, D.C.: Police Foundation.

Winick, B. (1985). Restructuring competency to stand trial. *UCLA Law Review, 32,* 921–985.

Winick, B. (1996). Incompetency to proceed in the criminal process: Past, present, and future. In B. D. Sales & D. W. Shulman (Eds.), *Law, mental health, and mental disorder* (pp. 310–340). Pacific Grove, CA: Brooks/Cole.

Winick, B. (1998). Sex offender law in the 1990s: A therapeutic jurisprudence analysis. *Psychology, Public Policy, and Law, 4,* 505–570.

Winslade, W. J., & Ross, J. W. (1983). *The insanity plea.* New York: Scribner's.

Wishman, S. (1981a). *Confessions of a criminal lawyer.* New York: Times Books.

Wishman, S. (1981b, November 9). A lawyer's guilty secrets. *Newsweek,* p. 25.

Wissler, R. L., Kuehn, P., & Saks, M. J. (in press). Instructing jurors on general damages in personal injury cases: Problems and possibilities. *Psychology, Public Policy, and Law.*

Wissler, R., & Saks, M. (1985). On the inefficacy of limiting instructions. *Law and Human Behavior, 9,* 37–48.

*Witherspoon v. Illinois,* 391 U.S. 510, 88 S.Ct. 1770, 20 L.Ed.2d 776 (1968).

*Wolff v. McDonnell,* 418 U.S. 539 (1974).

Wolfgang, M. (1958). *Patterns in criminal homicide.* New York: Wiley.

Wolfram, C. (2000, March 6). In house MDPs? *National Law Journal,* p. B6.

Wolgast, E. (1987). *A grammar of justice.* Ithaca, NY: Cornell University Press.

Woocher, F. D. (1986). Legal principles governing expert testimony by experimental psychologists. *Law and Human Behavior, 10,* 47–61.

Wood, J., Schreiber, N., Martinez, Y., McLaurin, K., Strok, R., Velarde, L., Garven, S., & Malpass, R. (1998). *Child interviewing techniques in the McMartin Preschool and Kelly Michaels cases: A quantitative comparison.* Paper presented at the 1998 American Psychology-Law Society, Redondo Beach, CA.

Woodrell, D. (1996). *Give us a kiss.* New York: Holt.

Work, C. P. (1985, January 21). The good times roll for "expert witnesses." *U.S. News & World Report,* pp. 65–66.

Wortley, R. K., & Homel, R. J. (1995). Police prejudice as a function of training and outgroup contact: A longitudinal investigation. *Law and Human Behavior, 19,* 305–318.

Wright, L. (1994). *Remembering Satan.* New York: Knopf.

Wrightsman, L. S. (1989, May). *Application of the expert-novice distinction to decision making by judges versus juries.* Paper presented at meeting of the Midwestern Psychological Association, Chicago.

Wrightsman, L. S., & Kassin, S. M. (1993). *Confessions in the courtroom.* Thousand Oaks, CA: Sage.

Wrightsman, L. S., Nario, M., Posey, A., & Bothwell, R. (1993, August). *Beliefs in a Just World Scale: Its factor structure.* Paper presented at the meeting of the American Psychological Association, Toronto.

Wyatt, G. E., Guthrie, D., & Notgrass, C. M. (1992). Differential effects of women's child sexual abuse and subsequent sexual revictimization. *Journal of Consulting and Clinical Psychology, 60,* 167–173.

Wygant, S. A., & Williams, R. N. (1995). Perceptions of a principled personality: An interpretive examination of the Defining Issues Test. *Journal of Social Behavior and Personality, 10,* 53–66.

Yegidis, B. L. (1986). Date rape and other forced sexual encounters among college students. *Journal of Sex Education and Therapy, 12,* 51–54.

Yochelson, S., & Samenow, S. E. (1976). *The criminal personality: Vol. 1. A profile for change.* New York: Aronson.

Zajonc, R. B., & McIntosh, D. N. (1992). Emotions research: Some promising questions and some questionable promises. *Psychological Science, 3,* 70–74.

Zapf, P. A., & Roesch, R. (1997). Assessing fitness to stand trial: Institution-based evaluations and brief screening interview. *Canadian Journal of Community Mental Health, 16,* 53–66.

Zaragoza, M. S., Graham, J. R., Hall, G., Hirschman, R., & Ben-Porath, Y. (Eds.). (1995). *Memory and testimony in the child witness.* Thousand Oaks, CA: Sage.

Zebrowitz, L. A., & McDonald, S. M. (1991). The impact of litigants' babyfacedness and attractiveness on adjudications in small claims courts. *Law and Human Behavior, 15,* 603–624.

*Zecevic v. United States Parole Commission,* 163 F.3d 731 (1998).

Zeisel, H. (1976). The deterrent effect of the death penalty: Facts and faiths. *Supreme Court Review,* 317–343.

Zeisel, H., & Diamond, S. S. (1978). The effect of peremptory challenges on jury and verdict: An experiment in a federal district court. *Stanford Law Review, 30,* 491–529.

Zelig, M., & Beidleman, W. B. (1981). The investigative use of hypnosis: A word of caution. *International Journal of Clinical and Experimental Hypnosis, 29,* 401–412.

Zeno, S., Ivens, S., Millard, R., & Duvvuri, R. (1995). *The educator's word frequency guide.* New York: Touchstone Applied Science Associates.

Zhao, J., & Lovrich, N. (1998). Determinants of minority employment in American municipal agencies: The representation of African American officers. *Journal of Criminal Justice, 26,* 267–277.

Zickafoose, D. J., & Bornstein, B. H. (1999). Double discounting: The effects of comparative negligence on mock juror decision making. *Law and Human Behavior, 23,* 577–596.

Zigler, E., & Styfco, S. J. (1994). Head Start: Criticisms in a constructive context. *American Psychologist, 49,* 127–132.

Zimring, F. (1998). The youth violence epidemic: myth or reality? *Wake Forest Law Review, 33,* 727–743.

Zimring, F. E. (1982). *The changing legal world of adolescence.* New York: Free Press.

Ziskin, J., & Faust, D. (1988). *Coping with psychiatric and psychological testimony* (4th ed., Vols. 1–3). Marina del Rey, CA: Law & Psychology Press.

# Name Index

# Subject Index

# Credits

## PHOTOS

**Chapter 1: 2,** © Reuters NewMedia, Inc./CORBIS; **5,** © Ted Streshinsky/CORBIS; **14,** © Brian Corn/The Wichita Eagle; **18,** AP/Wide World Photos; **20,** © Reuters NewMedia, Inc./CORBIS. **Chapter 2: 34,** CORBIS; **40,** Gamma-Liaison. **Chapter 3: 51,** AP/Wide World Photos; **53,** © Photo B.D.V./CORBIS; **64,** © Johnathon Drake/Reuters/CORBIS. **Chapter 4: 96,** left, © Clark Jones/Impact Visuals; right, © UPI/CORBIS. **Chapter 5: 105,** AP/Wide World Photos; **108,** © Reuters/CORBIS; **124,** © UPI/CORBIS. **Chapter 6: 140,** © AFP/CORBIS; **152,** © Reuters/CORBIS; **160,** © AFP/CORBIS; **164,** © Kolvoord/The Image Works. **Chapter 7: 170,** © Jon Levy & Bob Strong/AFP/CORBIS; **172,** © Davis Designs. **Chapter 8: 213,** © Richard T. Nowitz/CORBIS; **223,** Scott Troy Anos/TimePix. **Chapter 9: 242,** AP/Wide World Photos; **244,** © UPI/CORBIS; **255,** AP/Wide World Photos; **256,** © Arturo Mari/Catholic News Service. **Chapter 11: 292,** © Steve Falk/Philadelphia Daily News/Gamma-Liaison; **299,** both, AP/Wide World Photos; **305,** AP/Wide World Photos; **319,** © UPI/CORBIS. **Chapter 12: 336,** © Joanne Haskin/UPI/CORBIS; **346,** © Gamma-Liaison; **348,** Chris Usher/TimePix. **Chapter 13: 360,** © UPI/CORBIS; **375,** © AFP/CORBIS; **376,** both, AP/Wide World Photos. **Chapter 14: 388,** © John Barr/Gamma-Liaison; **398,** © UPI/CORBIS. **Chapter 15: 412,** AP/Wide World Photos; **415,** © Steve Chenn/CORBIS; **424,** AP/Wide World Photos; **432,** © AFP/CORBIS; **435,** © Douglas Woods Photography. **Chapter 16: 446,** both, AP/Wide World Photos; **449,** AP/Wide World Photos; **454,** AP/Wide World Photos. **Chapter 17: 493,** © AFP/CORBIS; **495,** AP/Wide World Photos; **505,** Courtesy California Department of Corrections.

## TEXT

**Chapter 4: Box 4-5, 91,** from *Janet Reno: Doing the Right Thing* by P. Anderson, © 1994. Reprinted by permission of John Wiley & Sons, Inc. **Chapter 5: Table 5.2, 119,** adapted from Miller (1958), from "Genetic Factors in the Etiology of Criminal Behavior," by S. A. Mednick, W. F. Gabrielli, Jr., and B. Hutchings, in *The Causes of Crime* by S. A. Mednick, T. E. Moffitt, and S. A. Stack. Copyright © 1984. Reprinted by permission of Cambridge University Press. **Chapter 7: Table 7.1, 174,** from "What Do We Know from Eyewitness Identification?" by G. Wells, *American Psychologist, 48,* 553–571. **Chapter 10: Table 10.1, 271,** from "Decision Making and Information Integration in the Courts," by E. B. Ebbesen and V. J. Konecni, *Journal of Personality and Social Psychology, 32,* 805–821. Copyright © 1975 by the American Psychological Association. Reprinted by permission. **Chapter 11: Box 11-2, 300,** from "Competency for Trial: A Screening Instrument," by P. D. Lipsitt, D. Lelos, and A. L. McGarry, *American Journal of Psychiatry, 128,* 105–109. Copyright © 1971 by the American Psychiatric Association. Reprinted by permission. **Box 11-3, 302,** from *Competency to Stand Trial and Mental Illness,* by the Laboratory for Community Psychiatry. Copyright © 1974 by Jason Aronson. Reprinted by permission. **Figure 11.2, 322,** from "Identifying Insanity Acquittals: Is It Any Easier?" by C. Cirincione and C. Jacobs, *Law and Human Behavior, 23,* 494. Copyright © 1999. Reprinted by permission of Kluwer Academic/Plenum Publishers. **Chapter 12: Table 12.1, 349,** from "Child Custody Evaluation Practices: A Survey of Experienced Professionals," by W. G. Keilin and L. J. Bloom, *Professional Psychology: Research and Practice, 17,* 338–346. Copyright © 1986 by the American Psychological Association. Reprinted by permission of the author. **Chapter 13: Figure 13.1, 379,** from "The Impact of Judicial Instructions, Arguments, and Challenges on Jury Decision Making," by Irwin A. Horowitz, *Law and Human Behavior, 12,* 439–453. Copyright © 1988. Reprinted by permission of Kluwer Academic/Plenum Publishers and the author.